TOMORROW'S AGRICULTURE: INCENTIVES, INSTITUTIONS, INFRASTRUCTURE AND INNOVATIONS

TOMORROW'S AGRICULTURE: INCENTIVES, INSTITUTIONS, INFRASTRUCTURE AND INNOVATIONS

PROCEEDINGS
OF THE
TWENTY-FOURTH
INTERNATIONAL CONFERENCE
OF AGRICULTURAL ECONOMISTS

Held at Berlin, Germany
13–18 August 2000

Edited by
G.H. Peters, International Development Centre,
Queen Elizabeth House, University of Oxford, England
and
Prabhu Pingali, International Wheat and Maize Improvement Centre,
Mexico City, Mexico

INTERNATIONAL ASSOCIATION OF
AGRICULTURAL ECONOMISTS
QUEEN ELIZABETH HOUSE
UNIVERSITY OF OXFORD

2001

Ashgate

Published by
Ashgate Publishing Limited
Gower House
Croft Road
Aldershot
Hants GU11 3HR
England

Ashgate Publishing Company
131 Main Road
Burlington, VT 05401-5600 USA

Ashgate website: http://www.ashgate.com

British Library Cataloguing in Publication Data
Tomorrow's agriculture : incentives, institutions, infrastructure and
    innovations ; proceedings of the twenty-fourth
    International Conference of Agricultural Economists held at
    Berlin, Germany 13–18 August 2000. – (International
    Association of Agricultural Economists)
    1. Agriculture – Economic aspects – Congresses 2. Food supply
    – Congresses
    I. Peters, G. H. (George Henry), 1934– II. Pingali, Prabhu,
    1955– III. International Association of Agricultural
    Economists IV. International Conference of Agricultural
    Economists (24th : 2000 : Berlin, Germany)
    338.1

Library of Congress Cataloging-in-Publication Data
Tomorrow's agriculture : incentives, institutions, infrastructure and innovations ;
proceedings of the Twenty-fourth International Conference of Agricultural Economists,
held at Berlin, Germany, 13–18 August 2000 / edited by G.H. Peters and Prabhu Pingali.
        p. cm.
    "International Association of Agricultural Economists, Queen Elizabeth House,
University of Oxford".
    Includes bibliographical references.
    ISBN 0-7546-2167-7
    1. Agriculture—Economic aspects—Forecasting—Congresses. I. Peters, G. H. (George
Henry), 1934– II. Pingali, Prabhu L., 1955– III. International Conference of Agricultural
Economists (Association) (24th : 2000 : Berlin, Germany)

HD1405.T66 2001
338.1—dc21

                                                                            2001022830

ISBN 0 7546 2167 7

Typeset by Manton Typesetters, Louth, Lincolnshire, UK.
Printed and bound in Great Britain by MPG Books Ltd, Bodmin, Cornwall.

CONTENTS

Tribute to George Peters   ix
John McInerney and Joachim von Braun
Preface   xiii
Douglas D. Hedley
Introduction: The 24th Conference and the Association   xvi
George H. Peters and Prabhu Pingali

OPENING SESSION

Presidential Address: Considerations on the making of public policy
     for agriculture   3
Douglas D. Hedley

Elmhirst Memorial Lecture: The transformation of agriculture and
     the world economy: challenges for the governance of agriculture
     and for the profession   12
James T. Bonnen

SECTION I – GLOBALIZATION OF THE FOOD AND
AGRICULTURAL ECONOMY

Globalizing germ plasm: barriers, benefits and boundaries   41
Walter P. Falcon

GMOs, food safety and the environment: what role for trade policy
     and the WTO?   61
Kym Anderson and Chantal Pohl Nielsen

The 'political economy' of agricultural biotechnology for the
     developing world   86
Klaus M. Leisinger

Tomorrow's agriculture   113
Gerhard Prante

SECTION II – IMPROVED MARKET INCENTIVES IN
TRANSITION ECONOMIES

Sequencing and the success of gradualism: empirical evidence from
     China's agricultural reform   123
Alan de Brauw, Jikun Huang and Scott Rozelle

Agrarian transitions and productivity patterns: synthesis of
    experiences in Eastern Europe, the Former Soviet Union and
    East Asia   147
Karen Macours and Johan F.M. Swinnen

Land reforms and emerging agri-food markets: the Russian
    experience   163
Eugenia Serova

Market reforms in South Asian agriculture: will they deliver?   178
Ashok Gulati

SECTION III – AGRICULTURAL RESEARCH, TECHNOLOGY
DEVELOPMENT AND INSTITUTIONS

Agricultural research, technology and world food markets   193
Mark W. Rosegrant, Claudia Ringler and Michael S. Paisner

Human capital, education and agriculture   207
Wallace E. Huffman

Reassessing research returns: attribution and related problems   223
Julian M. Alston and Philip G. Pardey

The role of institutions in policy formation and delivery   243
Robin W. Johnson

SECTION IV – MAKING AGRICULTURE ENVIRONMENTALLY
SAFE

Precision agriculture: global prospects and environmental
    implications   269
George W. Norton and Scott M. Swinton

Economic incentives for conserving crop genetic diversity on farms:
    issues and evidence   287
Melinda Smale

Population pressure, land tenure and natural resource management   306
Keijiro Otsuka

Agricultural trade barriers, trade negotiations and the interests of
    developing countries   319
Hans Binswanger and Ernst Lutz

CONTRIBUTED PAPERS – DEVELOPMENT AND RESEARCH

A new approach to the evolution of primary commodity terms of
    trade and the implications for developing countries   343
George P. Zanias

Short-run and long-run elasticities for ASEAN agricultural exports
    to the European Union: an error-correction mechanism approach   353
Jyrki Niemi

International transfers and food security   368
Christian Friis Bach and Alan Matthews

Agricultural productivity growth in Asian countries   376
Kecuk Suhariyanto

Land reform initiatives in China   383
John Davis, Liming Wang and Fu Chen

Economic liberalization and rural poverty alleviation: the Indian
    experience   399
K.N. Ninan

Use of an indigenous board game, 'bao', for assessing farmers'
    preferences among alternative agricultural technologies   416
Steven Franzel

Making better sense of the numbers on developing country
    agriculture   425
Ellen Hanak Freud

Policies for private agricultural research in Asian developing
    countries   433
Carl E. Pray and Keith Fuglie

Competitive funds for agricultural research: are they achieving what
    we want?   442
Ruben G. Echeverría and Howard Elliott

CONTRIBUTED PAPERS – TRADE, EUROPEAN UNION AND METHODOLOGY

The definition of export subsidies and the Agreement on
    Agriculture   469
Isabelle Schluep and Harry De Gorter

The Agenda 2000 CAP reform in the WTO context: distortion
    effects of compensatory payments and area set-aside requirements   479
Alexandre Gohin and Hervé Guyomard

Eastern enlargement of the European Union: general and partial
    equilibrium analysis   488
Martin Banse, Wolfgang Münch and Stefan Tangermann

The CAP's impact on agriculture and food demand in Central
    European countries after EU accession: who will lose and who
    will gain?   498
Gerald Weber

A game theoretic analysis of Turkey's integration into the European
    Union   506
Cemal Atici and P. Lynn Kennedy

Land use in the European Union by 2020   516
Antonio M.D. Nucifora

Challenges and constraints for cooperative conflict management
    among land use stakeholders   527
Andrea Knierim and Uwe Jens Nagel

Targeting farm income and nutrient runoffs through
    agrienvironmental policy mixes: experience from Finland   538
Jussi Lankoski and Markku Ollikainen

Employment and efficiency of farms in transition: an empirical
    analysis for Brandenburg   553
Alfons Balmann, Britta Czasch and Martin Odening

Academic rigour or policy relevance: towards a reconciliation   565
David R. Harvey

PANEL DISCUSSION REPORTS   585

DISCUSSION GROUP AND MINI-SYMPOSIUM REPORTS   635

POSTER PAPER ABSTRACTS   715

CLOSING SESSION
    A synoptic view of the IAAE Conference, Berlin 2000   815
Joachim von Braun

NAME INDEX   825

SUBJECT INDEX   839

TRIBUTE TO GEORGE PETERS

To those outside our profession agricultural economics may seem a rather narrow, unexciting and not particularly substantial field of academic specialism. We all know it was anything but that when George Peters wrote and talked about it. He demonstrated that our subject was an area where, more than most others, the concepts and intellectual structures of economics really made sense and had something powerful to say, and where the issues relating to farming, food supply, food consumption, and rural resource use played a particular role in the workings of the overall economy. He became the senior figure active among UK academic agricultural economists, and his death on 4 November 2001 after a relatively brief battle with cancer is a great loss to us all.

He was born in Flintshire in 1934 and claimed he got the feeling for practical farming on his grandfather's farm. He gained a First Class Honours Degree in Economics at the University College of Wales, Aberystwyth, in 1955 followed by postgraduate work at Cambridge working on national income accounting, which gave him an enduring interest in and capacity for dealing with statistics. He was then commissioned as an officer during National Service in the RAF – an experience he often reflected on with typical self-deprecating humour. In 1959 George took the step which effectively led to his whole subsequent career when he went to work with Colin Clark at the Agricultural Economics Research Institute at Oxford. Clark was a monumental figure in every respect and, in working with him on the revision of his monumental *Conditions of Economic Progress*, George learned first hand the fundamental elements of the academic researcher's handbook – intellectual precision, objectivity, constant questioning of the data, meticulous attention to detail, thoroughness, and the necessity for a strong and defensible underpinning in theory. These he consistently demonstrated throughout his professional career and countless agricultural economists now in practice, both here and overseas, learned these lessons from him.

In 1967 George Peters moved to Liverpool University and three years later, still aged only 36, was appointed to the Brunner Chair of Economic Science. Here he led the Department of Economics and Commerce, a department of very applied academic endeavour which reinforced in his mind the absolute necessity for economics to relate to policy and practice rather than mere postulation. Liverpool was geographically close to George's cultural heartland of North Wales, but his intellectual home was really Oxford to where he returned in 1980 to take over the position his mentor, Colin Clark, once held as Director of the Agricultural Economics Research Institute. Much to his dismay Oxford was soon in the process of dismantling the institute, failing to see (as have some other universities also) the enduring importance of this study area to both developed and developing economies. However, along with his institute colleagues he forged a very productive working relationship in the International Development Centre at Queen Elizabeth House, where he became Deputy Director and Research Professor in Agricultural Economics.

Because he was first and foremost a first class economist, George Peters could think and talk sensibly about any of the areas in our diverse field of applied economics – and he did so, volubly and with great style. International commodity trade, agricultural policy, rural economic history, farm business management, agricultural statistics, land pricing, environmental economics, the food industries and rural economic development were all topics on which he taught, wrote and commented, as well as on the wider context of agriculture in the overall economy. His early research on agriculture and the balance of payments was highly influential in the 1960s when this was a major policy issue, and his writings on exchange rates have always been full of insight and common sense. He wrote on numerous other subjects in economics also, such as cost benefit analysis and public finance. But it was his determination and ability to keep tying agricultural economic analysis back to an intellectual base in economics (when the issues are inclined otherwise to get confused with popular social and political concerns about farming, farmers and their incomes) that was the distinctive and consistent thread through all his academic efforts. His 1991 Presidential Address to the UK Agricultural Economics Society, *Agriculture and the Macro Economy*, is still the best summary exposition on the overall scene and provides a valuable backdrop for those who wish to understand the current national and international developments in agricultural policies and markets.

George Peters had the typically impressive publication record that befits someone of his stature. However, in the last ten or more years, he turned his attentions increasingly towards the synthesis, presentation and dissemination of good research, and particularly taking a major role in the International Association of Agricultural Economists. He was an ever-present member of the Executive Committee, travelling to many countries to help organize and support conferences and symposia, and – crucially – was the Association's Editor of all the conference proceedings volumes since 1988. In doing this he exercised the maxim he always applied to his own work, that to write clearly one had to think clearly. As a result of his efforts, many an international author will have been remarkably proud and impressed at his or her own work as it appeared in the published conference proceedings after George had straightened, clarified, often corrected and sometimes effectively rewritten what the author had been trying to say! In these endeavours George was assisted hugely by his wife Judy, who herself has done an appreciable amount of editing in the current volume, and who was a very welcome civilizing presence at IAAE conferences. To her we give our sincere thanks and express our profound condolences. With the editing of the tri-annual 'Blue Books' of the IAAE conference proceedings George has provided the most important syntheses of agricultural economic thought at the end of the twentieth century. He completed this volume shortly before he died, and it serves as a fitting memorial to his longstanding intellectual and practical commitment to the work of the Association.

As well as an outstanding economist of diverse skills and interests, George Peters was universally regarded simply as one of the great guys to be around with. He had a consuming interest in sport, appreciated cricket in the same way he appreciated literature, and held to an unshakeable conviction that the Welsh rugby team could always beat the rest (one of the few instances when he ignored the data in drawing his conclusions!). He was a man of wit and ready humour, a splendid raconteur, not the least bit self-important, regularly bought his round at the bar, and was always entertaining both professionally and socially. In a way that few can claim, he was a genuine scholar as well as an effective academic. He was undoubtedly the only one amongst us who could validly claim to have known personally such luminaries as Joan Robinson, Hicks, Cairncross, Meade (and probably, in another life, Marshall, Jevons, Ricardo and Adam Smith as well, given how familiar he was with their writings!). He was a great conference attender, and could always be relied on to stand up halfway through the discussion on a paper and say 'Look, I'm sorry, you simply can't say such-and-such because …' and then proceed to dissect wishy-washy arguments with incisive logic, gentle ridicule, scholarly references to history, anecdotes about eminent economists, and then set out what the presenter or the other discussants really should have considered. All this was done with a distinctive cadence and great eloquence, but with a characteristically repetitive style of expression as he was constructing in his mind what he was about to say. (He delighted in telling the story of his first formal teaching evaluation. 'All the students told me, er, the students told me, that every time I say something, er, I say something, I don't say it once but twice, er, I say it twice'!) His ability to think quickly and speak entertainingly were memorably put to the test at the IAAE conference in Berlin last year. In the final plenary session of a long week, after the three contenders for best contributed paper had each presented their piece, George was asked at short notice to hold the floor – for anything from three to thirty minutes – while the judges went off to make their decision. Theatrically taking off his jacket and hanging it over the back of the chair, he surveyed the assembled company and declared 'I have absolutely no idea what I'm going to say' – although of course he did, even if it was only forming as he spoke. He then went on to explain the essential role of a proceedings editor – being to eliminate all unnecessary words – and demonstrated it with the help of the advertising slogan from outside a fish shop: 'fresh fish on sale here today'. With careful, convincing and amusing logic he showed progressively how the words 'today', 'here', 'on sale' and 'fresh' were all entirely superfluous, and was heavily into eliminating 'fish' when the judges came back in with their decision.

George often stressed that it is very important that IAAE should remain an association of individual members, not an association of associations. He was certainly one of our most important individual members. His achievements and contribution have been huge, long lasting and complex. Those of us remaining to carry on from where George Peters left us will miss the presence of someone we held in great affection, respected, gained intellectual stimulus from, enjoyed arguing with, and always appreciated. The subject of agricultural economics will be the poorer for his untimely death.

JOHN MCINERNEY
IAAE – Country Representative, United Kingdom

JOACHIM VON BRAUN
IAAE – President

November 2001

PREFACE

This volume represents some of the Proceedings of the 24th Conference of the International Association of Agricultural Economists held in Berlin, Germany, in August 2000. The Conference was the second IAAE meeting to be held in Germany, with the first at Bad Eilsen in 1934. Almost 1000 participants attended the gathering, along with many accompanying persons, drawn by the high quality programme prepared by our Vice-President, Prabhu Pingali, and the opportunity to see and enjoy the wonderful sights in the very dynamic and rapidly growing city of Berlin.

The papers in this volume include the President's Address, the Elmhirst Lecture by Professor James Bonnen and twenty contributed papers selected by the editors, as well as the Panel Discussion Reports, reports on the Discussion Groups and Mini-Symposia, Poster Paper Abstracts and the Synoptic View presented at the close of the Conference by the new President of the IAAE, Joachim von Braun. An additional large batch of papers were selected from those presented in Berlin for publication in *Agricultural Economics*, the journal of the IAAE. One of the important innovations at the Berlin Conference was the selection of the best contributed paper and the best poster presentations.

The theme of the 24th Conference was 'Tomorrow's Agriculture: Incentives, Institutions, Infrastructure and Innovations'. This emphasis was particularly timely given the rapid advances being made in the application of biotechnology in both the developed and developing worlds. Along with the advances, of course, come the attendant problems in science and ethics. Of equal concern were issues surrounding 'private' and 'public' goods, and the struggle for policy makers to keep up with advances in science and equitable law and regulation, both domestically and internationally. The papers in this volume and in the special issue of *Agricultural Economics* offer a rich variety of research and reports of value to researchers, teachers and scholars in universities, government and international organizations, as well as in the private sector.

The IAAE is particularly indebted to the Government of Germany, the State of Brandenburg and Humboldt University, for their efforts and monetary support for the conference, the excellent facilities provided and the tours arranged during and after the conference. The very warm welcoming comments from the German Minister of Agriculture and a number of senior officials from the City of Berlin and Humboldt University provided an excellent beginning for the conference. The venue attracted a near record number of participants and accompanying persons.

The contributed papers for the conference were organized and reviewed by a team set up under the very capable leadership of David Colman of Manchester

University (United Kingdom). David and his wife, Sue Colman, arranged for collection and review of all submissions, an editorial conference in the UK to finalize the selection of papers and, with Jock Anderson, identification of the group of papers from which the best contributed paper was selected. Three papers were chosen for presentation in a plenary session at the conference, with the final selection of the best contributed paper being based on the contents as well as the quality of the presentation. Similarly, Monika Hartmann of Halle University (Germany) took the lead in arranging the poster/computer sessions, and the process for selecting the best presentations. The efforts of David and Sue Colman and Monika Hartmann were very significant in bringing the Berlin Conference to a new high in quality and interest in IAAE members.

Special thanks are due to Harald von Witzke, Chair of the Local Organizing Committee, and his wife, Elizabeth Bermingham, for their leadership, and to the team they assembled and led for handling the local arrangements. From the opening reception, through the Wednesday afternoon tours and evening barbecue, to the closing dinner for the conference, the participants enjoyed a seamless feast of intellectual rigour and entertainment.

For this conference, Richard Meyer of the USA took the lead in organizing and editing the *Cowbell* for each day of the conference. The *Cowbell*, a longstanding tradition at our events, was filled with information about the association, local traditions and opportunities for sightseeing, information on the members of the IAAE Executive, the progress of the Council and nominees for future positions on the Executive. It has become one of the richest sources of information about each of the conferences and the history of our organization. We are also indebted to the work of the Local Organizing Committee for their efforts in assuring the timeliness, text preparation, printing and distribution of the *Cowbell* each day.

A number of members arranged one-day pre-conference sessions on topics of particular interest to our members. One of the noteworthy sessions was in honour of Carl Eicher and his work over many years in fostering the development and progression of scholars in Africa, particularly in Zimbabwe. Carl's contributions to the agricultural economics literature, to African agriculture generally and to encouraging an extensive group of students and friends throughout the region are a powerful testament to his life-long commitment, courage and scholarship.

The IAAE continues to owe a very great deal to George Peters of Oxford University for his work in editing this Proceedings volume. He has sustained these efforts on behalf of the IAAE for four conferences, beginning at Tokyo in 1991, through our meetings in Harare, Zimbabwe and Sacramento, USA, to the proceedings from Berlin. His persistence in, and dedication to, turning out a high-quality volume from the material presented is deeply appreciated and respected throughout the Association.

Thanks are also due to Tony Waterman who meticulously copy-edited this volume.

Finally, I wish to thank the members of our IAAE Executive, Bob Thompson (Past President), Joachim von Braun (President Elect), Prabhu Pingali (Vice

President Programme), Eugenia Muchnik de Rubinstein and Chris Ackello-Ogutu (Members-at-Large), Walt Armbruster (Secretary–Treasurer), Stan Johnson (Editor, *Agricultural Economics*) and George Peters (Editor, *Proceedings*), for their immense efforts and contributions during the past three years. Their friendship, encouragment and support to me in continuing to transform the IAAE and its services in the rapidly changing information age were most sincerely appreciated. As well, I want to thank former presidents, Glenn Johnson, Theodor Dams, Csaba Csaki and Michel Petit, on whom I called for advice and counsel from time to time, and who supported and encouraged me throughout my efforts on behalf of the IAAE.

DOUGLAS D. HEDLEY
Immediate Past President, IAAE

GEORGE H. PETERS AND PRABHU PINGALI*

Introduction: The 24th Conference and the Association

INTRODUCTION

The 24th International Conference of the International Association of Agricultural Economists was held in Berlin, Germany between Sunday 13 August and Friday 18 August 2000 at the 'Haus Am Köllnischen Park'. The theme was 'Tomorrow's Agriculture: Incentives, Institutions, Infrastructure and Innovations'. The Conference format will have been familiar to anyone who attended the Sacramento meeting in 1997, though a number of evolutionary changes were made in response to member suggestions. Some affected the length of the Conference, others the programme organization. Before turning to those, however, it is worth noting that the meeting was described as being 'by common consent an outstanding event; academically stimulating, professionally rewarding, institutionally fascinating and socially enjoyable'.[1] Further, 'it was truly the unique kind of international gathering that only the IAAE can offer, with 951 people attending from 83 different countries'. It will be understood that the programme is always shaped by the international community of agricultural economists, with the site organization being in the hands of a local committee.[2] It is their symbiotic relationship which provides each successive triennial event with a distinctive flavour.

ORGANIZING THE PROGRAMME

Basic outline

The familiar elements of programming, as arranged by Vice President Pingali, were very much in evidence. The 'Cowbell' was rung energetically by Past President Robert Thompson, who took the chair for an opening session consisting of speeches of welcome, followed by the Elmhirst Memorial Lecture (James Bonnen) and the Presidential Address (Douglas Hedley). Each of the following five days was structured around a plenary session, four of them

*George Peters, Research Professor in Agricultural Economics, University of Oxford, International Development Centre, Queen Elizabeth House, and Wolfson College, is Editor of Proceedings of the IAAE. Prabhu Pingali (India), IAAE Vice President, Programme is with the International Wheat and Maize Improvement Centre (CIMMYT), Mexico City, Mexico.

centred on a daily sub-theme. The details need not be repeated since they can be read from the contents page. There were then numerous 'contributed paper' sessions, invited panel discussions, poster and computer sessions, and discussion groups and mini-symposia. On the afternoon of the final day the highlight of the traditional plenary session was the 'synoptic view' of the meeting by the President Elect (Joachim von Braun), who then assumed the office of President for the next three years. A large amount of this material has a place in this volume and again can be picked up from the content pages.

One traditional feature was also maintained, namely the 'national agriculture' session, which became an exceptionally informative occasion organized and chaired by Stefan Tangermann (University of Göttingen, Germany). It hardly needs saying that one of the attractions of Berlin as a location was its position 'between east and west' which gave unique advantages in viewing the developments in the transition economies, on one side, and the European Union, on the other. Though it was a tall order to cram so much into two and a half hours, the complexity of the German agricultural scene was fully reflected in a stimulating session.[3]

Programme developments

There were two sets of programme changes. Firstly, there has been a wish among the membership to shorten the *formal* proceedings, though in the case of the Berlin meeting this involved only half a day: the Conference began on Sunday afternoon, as before, but ended on the following Friday evening. This allowed for a day of sightseeing before the post-conference tours began on Sunday 20 August. Importantly for colleagues burdened by ever-increasing pressures of work, it allowed a slightly speedier return to the desk. The two-week meetings of a generation ago are truly a thing of the past. At the same time, however, there has been a widespread member view that the Association ought to do more to foster the development of the subject, especially among the younger age group. To this end the Saturday prior to the Conference was allocated to two 'Learning Workshops'. The first dealt with 'Spatial Data Analysis' and was organized and chaired by Gerald C. Nelson, University of Illinois, Urbana-Champaign, USA. He was helped by Kenneth Chomitz (World Bank), Raymond Florax (Free University, Amsterdam) and Kathleen Bell (University of Illinois). The other tackled 'Economic Analysis of Food Security Policy', where the lead was taken by Daniel A. Sumner, University of California at Berkeley, USA. In that case the extra input came from D. Gale Johnson (University of Chicago, and now a Life Member of IAAE), Julian Alston (University of California, Davis) and Richard Barichello (University of British Columbia, Canada). Both workshops included lectures, discussion and many real-world examples as well as using problems and study questions to help participants reinforce their understanding. Background reading was provided in advance using e-mail, and lists of references were supplied. Though it was the first occasion on which a day was allowed for instruction it is worth noting that a 'training element' had been included previously in the form of 'Computer Demonstrations'. They continued in three valuable sessions organized by

Martin Banse (Germany), Krijn Poppe (Netherlands) and Peter Weingarten (Germany). Reports will be found in the poster paper section.

The second set of changes was effectively *within* the programme. To get matters moving quickly in what can be the barren space of registration on the first morning, Per Pinstrup-Andersen (International Food Policy Research Institute, Washington, DC) agreed to chair a special panel to discuss 'Globalization and Biotechnology: Risks and Opportunities for Farmers and Consumers'. A further five distinguished colleagues agreed to participate in what proved to be an extremely popular 90-minute event.[4] There were also changes which affected the Contributed Papers. One of the five morning plenary sessions was devoted to the presentation of the three submitted papers which had most impressed a small judging panel, with one (by Rinku Murgai) then emerging as the overall 'best paper'. More details will be found at a later point in this introduction.[5]

Managing the Conference programme

It is widely understood, though it cannot be stressed too often, that the management of the Conference requires enormous effort both in planning and execution. That will become increasingly apparent in what follows.

In Berlin, the four key plenary sessions were chaired by Hartwig de Haen (Germany), Johann van Zyl (South Africa), Justin Lin (China) and John McInerney (United Kingdom). The discussion openers were Michael Morris (USA/CIMMYT), Dieter Kirschke (Germany), Ruben Echeverría (Uruguay) and Mahabub Hossain (Bangladesh). The mammoth task of organizing Contributed Papers was a British effort overseen by David Colman (University of Manchester), with administrative help from Sue Colman, and input from a panel consisting of John McInerney, David Harvey, George Peters, Kenneth Thomson and Colin Thirtle, augmented by Jock Anderson (Australia). The combined group acted as a sieve for the 'referee reports' obtained on each paper from two members of the traditional international panel. Total submissions were 419, of which 131 were selected for floor presentation in contributed paper sessions and 200 were passed on for consideration as 'poster papers'. An effort was also made to isolate about 50 papers which were likely to form the batch for publication.

That was not the end of the process. Jock Anderson took on the task of selecting three contributed papers for presentation in the special plenary session.[6] This provided pyrotechnic displays of analytic and presentational skills from Rinku Murgai, Manitra Rakotoarisa (who presented a paper written jointly with Shala Shapouri) and Tancrede Voituriez. Praise for their efforts, however, should not diminish the input of the other speakers. Fitting the programme together involved finding space for 35 scheduled contributed paper sessions (five slots with seven concurrent groups, having up to four papers), in which sheer excellence was frequently on display. The patience required by the main organizers in handling all of the complexities is clearly enormous, but there is also a widespread belief among the membership that openness in submission and the intensive peer review which is undertaken at various stages pay handsome dividends in the quality and diversity of Conference material.

The other elements of the programme are familiar. Panel discussions, headed by leaders within the profession, were introduced with great success in Sacramento in 1997 and were repeated in Berlin. Discussion groups and mini-symposia are of even longer standing. The organizer was Herbert Stoevener (Virginia Polytechnic Institute and State University, USA), making his debut in that important role. Another debutante was Monika Hartmann (Institute of Agricultural Development in Central and Eastern Europe, Halle, Germany), who organized the three highly successful poster paper sessions, including the innovative 'best poster' competition.[7] All of those elements have separate reports in this volume.

A Conference would not be complete (indeed, noting the rise in importance of one particular branch of economics, it would founder for lack of *information*) without *Cowbell*, the daily 'newspaper'. The lead was taken by Richard Meyer (Ohio State University), also making a debut, but carrying off the task with great aplomb. Particular mention also has to be made of the 'Fund for the International Conference of Agricultural Economists', which quietly raises money from many donors to foster attendance by participants, particularly those from poorer areas of the world who are unable to cover their own costs. Richard Meyer has also assumed the role of president of the Fund, with Max Langham (University of Florida) as his deputy.[8]

ORGANIZING THE LOCATION

The mounting of a conference always requires effort at national and local level. For the former the German Organizing Committee was chaired by Ulrich Koester (University of Kiel) with Volker Appel, Günther Fratzscher, Klaus Frohberg, P. Michael Schmitz, Wilhelm Schopen, Stefan Tangermann, Joachim von Braun and Winfried von Urff as members. They were enormously successful in smoothing the path for the local organizers and, not least, in attracting sponsorships.[9] In Berlin, the effort was centred on Humboldt University, the lead being taken by Harald von Witzke backed by Konrad Hagedorn, Karl Jaster, Dieter Kirschke, Uwe Jens Nagel and Iris Paulus, with Ulrike Marschinke as an administrative driving force.

What might be termed the 'local events' were highly successful, from the welcoming addresses,[10] through the opening reception at Humboldt University, the Wednesday tours which finished at the Schmachtenhagen country park, to the final dinner at the Intercontinental Hotel on the western side of the city. Numerous local tours were organized through the historic heart of Berlin and visits to Potsdam were available. Some were able to take advantage of end of conference visits to Dresden and Prague, or to Poznan and other areas of Poland. Help with all of that came from Christina Fritzsching, Laura Bipes, Barbara Pohl, Markus Brem and Thomas Roth. Steffan Noleppa, Elizabeth Bermingham and Heike Höffler also assisted in numerous ways, notably with *Cowbell*.

ORGANIZATION OF PUBLICATIONS

It should now be widely understood that our publication pattern changed with effect from the Sacramento Conference of 1997.[11] There are now two vehicles which include Conference material: the Proceedings (or Blue Book) and a special issue of the Association journal, *Agricultural Economics*. The latter (to be guest edited by David Colman) includes a selection of contributed papers (identified in the Appendix), with a further group appearing in this volume. The pattern of the Proceedings content closely follows that for Sacramento 1997. The title follows the theme underlying the plenary sessions (it was the '4i' meeting!); thereafter the submission and discussion of material in Berlin was eclectic. There are so many issues which need to be aired that a whole conference cannot easily be constricted to any theme and there is never a wish to do so. But, to provide a minimal guide to classification, two 'contributed paper' sections are used to cover 'development and research'[12] and 'trade, European Union and methodology'. Use of the first will cause no surprise; the second is partly a reflection of the conference location and, in turn, of the fact that EU issues impinge on the world through trade regulation, through its internal policy stance and through enlargement. Inclusion of a paper on methodology stems from it being a further contribution to a debate which emerged in the Presidential Address, the Elmhirst Lecture and the Synoptic View.

Reporting of 'Discussion groups and mini-symposia', prepared by Herbert Stoevener, was able to follow the main plenary session topics, but it was again 'geography' which provided the basis for the arrangement of Monika Hartmann's assembly of 'Poster papers'. She was ably assisted by Guenter Peter.

There is more which *could* have been included. Eagle-eyed readers may note that the discussion opener remarks on plenary session papers have been omitted. The reason stems from the modern speed of communication – many of the authors took comments on board and rapidly amended their papers in the light of what had been said. It would have been useful to include abstracts of the contributed papers which, though they could not be selected for publication, added so much to academic debate and to the spirit of the Conference. Pressure on space is an important reason. All that is done is to list the names of authors in the appendix containing the full programme of contributed paper sessions. That also includes the names of chairpersons who often lead discussion and also did so much to keep a complex set of meetings on track.

Assistance with preparation came from many quarters. We are grateful to the Editor of *Agricultural Economics*, Stephan von Cramon Taubadel (Göttingen University, Germany) and to Sorrell Brown, the administrative controller at Iowa State, for various aspects of 'contributed paper' selection, and obviously to David and Sue Colman for organizing a huge mass of material. Judith Peters, who has experience in such matters, read a great deal of script in order to sharpen the style. At Queen Elizabeth House, Oxford, Sheila Allcock, Gill Short, Dawn Young and Rebecca Wilson maintain the library and information centre with such skill that any reference can be speedily checked, while Roger Crawford, Denise Watt and Sarah Abbott were on hand to deal with computing problems. Professional colleagues Rosemary Fennell and J. Owen Jones were ready with encouragement and advice. John Irwin and Sonia Hubbard, at Ashgate, once again provided the type of help of which only the most skilled of publishers are capable. Tony Waterman was a splendid copy editor.

ASSOCIATION BUSINESS

The Association is now preparing for its next triennial conference which, after Council resolution, is scheduled for Durban (RSA) in 2003. A new Executive Committee is in place and is actively at work on that and on a series of other initiatives. A vast transformation is taking place in the Association's style of operation, flowing from the expansion of the Internet. This was apparent in Sacramento in 1997, but it has recently grown apace with the further refinement of our site (*<www.iaae-agecon.org>*), masterminded by Sorrell Brown of Iowa State University (USA). Access to details of the costs and benefits of membership is readily available and the site includes much current information about our activities and those of related organizations.

Four new Life Members of the Association, elected in Berlin, are congratulated:

D. Gale Johnson (University of Chicago, USA), long-standing member and Conference contributor, Elmhirst Memorial Lecturer in Harare in 1994, widely honoured and the subject of a recent two-volume tribute.[13]

John Longworth (University of Queensland, Australia), organizer of an IAAE symposium in Beijing in 1987, President at the time of the 1991 Tokyo Conference, expert on the agricultural situation in China and Japan.

W.L. (Lieb) Nieuwoudt (University of Natal, South Africa), a long-standing member familiar in numerous Conference roles for many years and an important figure in his own country and in organizing the journal *Agrekon*.

Alberto Valdés (Chile, latterly World Bank and International Food Policy Research Institute), Vice President Programme for the 1988 Buenos Aires Conference, speaker at plenary and other sessions on a number of occasions and author of many publications.

CONCLUSION

Our formal statements, important to the Council, Executive Committee and the membership at large, must be repeated. Any of the views expressed in this book are not necessarily those of the IAAE or of any of the institutions to which members belong; all members or visiting speakers act strictly in their private capacity. In short, the IAAE is an organization of 'individuals' and not of 'delegates'. As such it is without any form of political affiliation and any use of geographical description is simply a matter of convenience. Debts of gratitude for vital support (either financial or 'in-kind') are, of course, owed to academic and other institutions, firms, governments and international organizations, for which we are most grateful, but our aim is to foster impartial debate and not to adopt formal positions on contemporary issues.

NOTES

[1] This came from John McInerney (Exeter University), the United Kingdom country representative, in a letter to British members written after the Conference.

[2] In effect the Vice President Programme takes the lead in the key task of forming a theme and four sub-themes for plenary sessions, but invites colleagues to organize other sections. The main theme, however, is arrived at after wide consultation with association members at large.

[3] The subjects and speakers were: 'Evolution and Perspectives of German Agricultural Policy', *Martin Wille* (Secretary of State, Federal Ministry of Food, Agriculture and Forestry); 'Transformation of Agriculture in East Germany', *Bernhard Forstner and Folkhard Isermeyer* (Institute of Farm Economics and Rural Studies, Federal Agricultural Research Centre (FAL), Braunschweig); 'Institutional Characteristics of German Agriculture', *Werner Großkopf* (Institute of Agricultural Policy and Market Research, University of Hohenheim-Stuttgart); 'The Role of Germany in the Common Agricultural Policy', *Ulrich Koester* (Institute of Agricultural Economics, University of Kiel) and 'The Value-added Chain in the German Food Sector', *Hannes Weindlmaier* (Dairy and Food Research Centre, Weihenstephan, Technical University of Munich).

[4] The five were Justin Yifu Lin (Peking University, China), Susan Offutt (USDA/ERS, USA), Wilfred Mwangi (Deputy Permanent Secretary and Director of Agriculture and Livestock Production, Government of Kenya), Eugenia Muchnik de Rubinstein (Fundación Chile, Chile) and Matin Qaim (Centre for Development Research, Bonn, Germany).

[5] While the judging panel was reaching a decision, George Peters spoke briefly about the history of the Association, drawing partly on material in the Proceedings volume for the previous meeting in Germany in 1934 (at Bad Eilsen). He also drew attention (again) to J.R. Rawburn and J.O. Jones (1990), *A History of the International Association of Agricultural Economists; Towards Rural Welfare Worldwide* (Aldershot: Dartmouth) and stressed the importance for our image of frequent citing of our publications!

[6] Full details are given in an Appendix.

[7] The judging group was chaired by Alan Matthews (Trinity College, Dublin). Three posters were regarded as outstanding, though of such equal standard that choosing one above others was deemed impossible. The three joint winners were written by Bernhard Stockmeyer (Germany), by Consuelo de Varela-Ortega, Mario Blanco and José Sumpsi (Spain) and by Thomas Randolph and Leah Ndung'u (Kenya).

[8] The other members are Walter Armbruster (USA), F. Parry Dixon (USA), Franz Heidhues (Germany), Alex McCalla (USA) and B.F. Stanton (USA – who saw long service as President).

[9] Financial support by the following individuals and organizations is gratefully acknowledged: Federal Ministry of Food, Agriculture and Forestry, Bonn, Germany; Humboldt University of Berlin, Germany; Gesellschaft für Technische Zusammenarbeit mbH (GTZ), Eschborn, Germany; International Wheat and Maize Improvement Centre (CIMMYT), Mexico City, Mexico; Japanese Branch, IAAE; Landwirtschaftliche Rentenbank, Frankfurt/M., Germany; Ministère des Affaires Étrangères, Paris, France; Ministerium für Landwirtschaft, Umweltschutz und Raumordnung, Potsdam, Germany; Rockefeller Foundation, USA; Aventis CropScience, Frankfurt/M., Germany and Lyons, France; Deutsche Landwirtschaftsgesellschaft mbH (DLG), Frankfurt/M., Germany; International Food Policy Research Institute (IFPRI), Washington, USA; Industrieverband Agrar, Frankfurt/M., Germany; R & V Allgemeine Versicherung, Wiesbaden, Germany; Schultheiss-Brauerei, Berlin, Germany; The US Agency for International Development (USAID), USA; Verein der Zuckerindustrie, Bonn, Germany; AGRA-Europe, Bonn, Germany; Allgemeiner Deutscher Automobilclub (ADAC), Berlin, Germany; BLV Verlagsgesellschaft mbH, Munich, Germany; CABI Publishing, Wallingford, UK; Gesellschaft für Agrarprojekte, Hamburg, Germany; NOMOS Verlagsges mbH, Baden-Baden, Germany; 'Partner für Berlin', Berlin,

Germany; Statistisches Bundesamt, Wiesbaden, Germany; Verlag Eugen Ulmer, Stuttgart, Germany; Zentrale Markt-und Preisberichtstelle, Berlin, Germany.

[10]The speakers were Harald von Witzke (Chair, Local Organizing Committee), Karl-Heinz Funke (then Minister of Food, Agriculture and Forestry, Federal Republic of Germany), Eberhard Diepgen (Governor of Berlin), Christoph Stölzl (Senator for Science, Research and Culture, Senate of Berlin) and Dieter Kirschke (representing Jürgen Mlynek (President, Humboldt University of Berlin).

[11]The details are in the introduction to the Sacramento Proceedings, published as G.H. Peters and J. von Braun (eds) (1999), *Food Security, Diversification and Resource Management: Refocusing the Role of Agriculture?* (Aldershot: Ashgate).

[12]To be strictly true to the record, the last paper, by Ruben Echeverría and Howard Elliott, was not submitted to the contributed paper competition. But it was aired in other Conference sessions and the first author was a plenary discussion opener. Given its salience – and its availability – it was included.

[13]J.M. Antle and D.A. Sumner (eds) (1996), *The Economics of Agriculture; Volume 1 Collected Papers of D. Gale Johnson, Volume 2 Papers in Honor of D. Gale Johnson*, Chicago and London: University of Chicago Press.

APPENDIX: THE CONTRIBUTED PAPER PROGRAMME

The full programme for the contributed paper sessions, as published in Berlin, is printed below. Symbols in the margin indicate papers which appear in this Proceedings volume (P), or in the Special Issue of *Agricultural Economics* (S) for September 2001 (volume 25, numbers 1 and 2). The listing excludes the three contributed papers which were presented in a plenary session. These were:

The Green Revolution and the Productivity Paradox: Ev'dence from the Indian Punjab
Rinku Margai (USA)

Market Power and Pricing of Commodities from Developing Countries: The Case of US Vanilla Bean Imports
Manitra Rakotoarisa (USA) and Shala Shapouri (USA)

What Explains Price Volatility Changes in Commodity Markets? Answers from the World Palm Oil Market
Tancrede Voituriez (France)

Contributed Papers 1

1:1   Estimating Frontier Production Functions: Efficiency, Productivity and Cost
Chairperson: Klaus Frohberg

> Parametric decomposition of agricultural output growth: a stochastic input distance function approach
> G. Karagiannis (Greece), P. Midmore (UK) and V. Tzouvelekas (Greece)

> A cross-sectional maximum entropy estimation of cost functions for regional programming models
> Thomas Heckelei and Wolfgang Britz (Germany)

> Technical efficiency of wheat producers in Asasa District of southeastern Ethiopia
> Mohammed Hassena, Wilfred Mwangi and Farah Hassen (Ethiopia)

S   Alternative methods for environmental by sensitive productivity analysis
      Terrence Veeman and Atakelty Hailu (Canada)

1:2   The Economics of Food Quality
Chairperson: Juan Leos-Rodriguez

> The economics of eco-labelling
> Arnab K. Basu, Nancy H. Chau and Ulrike Grote (Germany)

S   The impact of food scares on price adjustment in the UK beef market
      Tim Lloyd, C.W. Morgan, S. McCorriston and T. Rayner (UK)

The effect of incorporating nutrients in meat demand analysis using household budget data
A.M. Angulo and J.M. Gil (Spain)

Label power: new wine in old bottles?
Bodo Steiner (Germany)

1:3 Spatial Economics
Chairperson: Ulrich Koester

P   Agent-based spatial models applied to agriculture, a simulation tool for land use changes, natural resource management and policy analysis
Thomas Berger (Germany)

Spatial price transmission and asymmetric adjustment in the Ghanaian maize market
Awudu Abdulai (Switzerland)

Spatial aspects of producer milk price formation in Kenya: a joint household–GIS approach
S.J. Staal, Christopher Delgado, I. Baltenweck (France) and R. Kruska (USA)

1:4 Public and Private Sector Roles in Research and Development
Chairperson: Douglas Gollin

S   Private R&D investment in agriculture: the role of incentives and institutions
Oscar Alfranca (Spain) and Wallace E. Huffman (USA)

Private sector as an emerging institution for accelerating growth in Bangladesh agriculture
M.A. Sattar Mandal (Bangladesh)

Intellectual property rights and the NAROs in developing countries
David Bigman and Gerdien Meijerink (Netherlands)

P   Policies for private agricultural research in Asian LDCs
Carl Pray and Keith Fuglie (USA)

1:5 The CAP
Chairperson: Ewa Rabinowicz

P   The Agenda 2000 CAP reform in the WTO context: distortion effects of compensatory payments
Alexandre Gohin and Hervé Guyomard (France)

P   Short-run and long-run elasticities for ASEAN agricultural exports to the EU: an error correction mechanism approach
Jyrki Niemi (Finland)

S   The economic cost of the CAP revisited
      G. Philippidis and Lionel Hubbard (UK)

P   A game theoretic analysis of Turkish integration into the European Union
      P. Lynn Kennedy (USA) and Cemal Atici (Turkey)

1:6   Chinese Land Policy: Household Modelling
Chairperson: Nick Vink

      Labour supply, hired labour and off-farm income in the Tigray Region,
      Ethiopia: implications for an employment policy and farm/non-farm in-
      come linkages
      Tassew Woldehanna (Netherlands)

      Agricultural commercialization, women's time allocation and childrens'
      health and nutritional status in rural Nepal: an application of a household
      production model
      Khem R. Sharma (USA)

P   An overview of recent land reform initiatives in China
      John Davis, L. Wang (UK) and Fu Chen (China)

      Village land policy and intersectoral labour movements in China
      Bryan Lohmar (USA)

1:7   Poverty Alleviation in India and Africa
Chairperson: Timothy Olalekan Williams

      Housing quality and housing development in rural Ghana
      Jack Houston (USA)

      On the targeting and cost-effectiveness of anti-poverty programmes in
      rural India
      Raghav Gaiha and P.D. Kaushik (India) and Katsushi Imai (UK)

      Factors affecting food self-sufficiency among farm households in south-
      ern Ethiopia
      Stein Holden (Norway)

P   Economic liberalization and rural poverty alleviation: the Indian experi-
      ence
      K.N. Ninan (India)

Contributed Papers 2

2:1   Agrochemicals and the Environment
Chairperson: Konrad Hagedorn

      Nitrogen efficiency of Dutch dairy farms: a shadow cost system ap-
      proach
      Stijn Reinhard and Geert Thijssen (Netherlands)

S   An economic evaluation of the environmental benefits from pesticide
     reduction
     Alfons Weersink and Cher Brethour (Canada)

     Endogenous technology switches in Dutch dairy farming when environ-
     mental and agricultural policies are restrictive
     Marinus Komen and Jack H.M. Peerlings (Netherlands)

2:2   EU Enlargement and the CAP
Chairperson: Csaba Csaki

P   The CAP's impacts on agriculture and food demand in Central European
     countries after EU accession: who will lose, who will gain?
     Gerald Weber (Germany)

     Slovenian agricultural policy options in view of future accession to the
     EU
     Emil Erjavec, S. Kavcic (Slovenia) and G. Mergos, C. Stoforos (Greece)

P   Eastern enlargement of the European Union: a general and partial equi-
     librium analysis
     Martin Banse, Wolfgang Münch and Stefan Tangermann (Germany)

2:3   Market Linkages
Chairperson: Thomas Hertel

     Cash transfer programmes with income multipliers: PROCAMPO in
     Mexico
     Benjamin Davis (USA), Elisabeth Sadoulet and Alain de Janvry (France)

     Marketing strategies under different policy scenarios
     Klaus Drescher and Claus-Henning Hanf (Germany)

     Can rural areas benefit from the changing skills of labour used in US
     food processing trade?
     Gerald Schlüter and Chinkook Lee (USA)

2:4   Impacts of Biotechnology
Chairperson: Mahabub Hossain

     Biotechnology in agriculture: implications for farm-level risk manage-
     ment
     Shiva Makki, Agapi Somwaru and Joy Harwood (USA)

S   A prospective evaluation of biotechnology in semi-subsistence agricul-
     ture
     Matin Qaim (Germany)

     Market structure and innovation intensity in agricultural biotechnology
     David E. Schimmelpfenig, Carl E. Pray and Margaret Brennan (USA)

2:5   Trade Barrier Issues
Chairperson: Roland Herrmann

Effects of European Union tariffs on the South African fresh orange industry: a trade simulation
Stephan Hubertus Gay (Germany) and W. Lieb Nieuwoudt (South Africa)

Turkish vegetable oil import demand following tariff liberalization
Ali Koc, Safak Akso, Ahmet Bayaner, Turker Dolekoglu, Ayut Sener (Turkey) and Frank Fuller (USA)

Impacts of regional trade agreements: the case of US textiles and apparel
William Amponsah and Xiang Dong Qin (USA)

2:6   Agricultural Productivity and Efficiency
Chairperson: Brian Revell

Resource quality and agricultural productivity in sub-Saharan Africa: a multi-country comparison
Keith Wiebe, Meredith Soule, Clare Narrod and Vince Breneman (USA)

P   Agricultural productivity growth in Asian countries
Kecuk Suhariyanto (Indonesia)

Pesticides and the environment: do farmers know? A study of their awareness and behaviour in India
Vasant Gandhi and N.T. Patel (India)

2:7   Adjusting Farm Structure in Transitional Economies
Chairperson: Stefan Bojnec

P   Employment and efficiency of farms in transition: an empirical analysis for Brandenburg
Alfons Balmann, Britta Czasch and Martin Odening (Germany)

Income uncertainty and subsidiary farming
Lyubov A. Kurkalova and Helen H. Jensen (USA)

Restructuring large-scale farms and the exit problem
Markus Brem (Germany) and Douglas W. Allen (Canada)

Stochastic frontier models of farm-level efficiency during the early transition in Hungary
Jenifer Piesse and Xavier Irz (UK)

Contributed Papers 3

3:1   Measuring Productivity and Efficiency on Farms
Chairperson: Adam Ozanne

S   Technical efficiency in developing country agriculture: a meta-analysis
       Boris Bravo-Ureta, Abdourahmane Thiam and Teodoro E. Rivas (USA)

       Technical efficiency and policy options in small-scale food crop produc-
       tion in Nigeria: an application of the stochastic frontier production function
       Igbekele Ajibefun (Nigeria)

       Total factor productivity measurement in Bangladesh crop agriculture
       using the stochastic frontier approach, 1960/61–1991/2
       Sanzidur Rahman (Bangladesh) and Tim Coelli (Australia)

       Efficiency and technical change in the Philippine rice sector: a Malmquist
       total factor productivity analysis
       Chieko Umetsu (Japan), Thamana Lekprichakul and Ujjayant Chakravorty
       (USA)

3:2   Theory: Trade and Institutional Change
Chairperson: Daniel Sumner

       South Korean wheat and flour market comparisons: a stated preference
       analysis
       Renee Kim, Michele Veeman and J. Unterschultz (Canada)

       Institutional structure and policy formation: the case of Norwegian agri-
       culture
       Klaus Mittenzwei (Norway)

       Rent seeking with politically contestable rights to agricultural import quotas
       Harry De Gorter and Jana Hranaiova (USA)

       The contribution of the theories of institutional change to the explanation
       of property rights reform process in agriculture in a transition economy
       Achim Schlüter (Germany)

3:3   Land Use in European Countries
Chairperson: Ken Thomson

       The magic growth barrier for Swiss farms
       Priska T. Baur (Switzerland)

       Land allocation under arable area payment schemes: a farm-level study
       Pavel Vavra and David Colman (UK)

P   The environmental effectiveness of alternative agri-environmental policy
       reforms with least distortions on trade: theoretical and empirical analysis
       Jussi Lankoski and Markku Ollikainen (Finland)

P   Land use in the European Union by 2020
     Antonio Nucifora (Italy)

3:4   Demand Analysis
Chairperson: Kyrre Rickertsen

     A new look at the fundamental laws of consumer economics: a case
     study for eastern Russia
     H.L. Goodwin, Rodney Holcomb and Rimma Shiptsova (USA)

     Consumption demand for market goods and environmental quality: ex-
     perience from Taiwan during 1977–96
     Pei-Ing Wu (Taiwan)

S   A fresh meat almost ideal demand system incorporating TV coverage
     and advertising impact
     Wim Verbeke and Jacques Viaene (Belgium) and Ronald W. Ward (USA)

     A new framework to estimate and identify cointegrated demand systems:
     an application to Tunisian meat consumption
     José M. Gil, M. Ben Kaabia and B. Dhehibi (Spain)

3:5   Managing Volatility and Uncertainty
Chairperson: Ismail Shariff

     Can markets support trade? The case of sugar
     Jean-Marc Boussard and Marie-Gabrielle Piketty (France)

S   Optimal hedging decisions for Taiwanese corn traders on the way to
     liberalization
     Li-Fen Lei, Jerome Geaun and Kang Liu (Taiwan)

     Effects of external shocks on small farmers: a village general equilib-
     rium approach applied to Mexico
     Antonio Yúnez-Naude (Mexico) and J. Edward Taylor (USA)

S   Challenges and constraints for cooperative conflict management among
     land use stakeholders
     Uwe Jens Nagel and Andrea Knierim (Germany)

3:6   Food Security
Chairperson: Alberto Valdés

     Safety net policy in a global context: low-income food-importing coun-
     tries
     Michael A. Trueblood and Shahla Shapouri (USA)

S   Balancing government intervention and private competition in foodgrain
     systems: a magic bullet for India's food security?
     Dina Umali-Deininger (USA) and Klaus Deininger (Germany)

Food self-sufficiency, comparative advantage and agricultural trade: a policy analysis matrix for Chinese agriculture
John Beghin and Cheng Fang (USA)

S   Averting a food crisis: private imports and public targeted distribution in Bangladesh after the 1998 flood
Paul Dorosh and Carlo del Ninno (USA)

3:7   Markets for Water
Chairperson: Consuelo de Varela Ortega

Incentives for tradeable water rights: two case studies in South Africa
W.L. Nieuwoudt, R.M. Armitage and G.R. Backeberg (South Africa)

Willingness to pay for water in the Sahara: a proposed prediction method
Peter Calkins, Marc Vezina and Bruno Larue (Canada)

Local water markets for irrigation in southern Spain: a multi-criteria approach
Manuel Arriaza and José A. Gomez-Limon (Spain)

S   Tank irrigation management as a local common property: the case of Tamil Nadu, India
Takeshi Sakurai (Côte d'Ivoire) and K. Palansami (India)

Contributed Papers 4

4:1   Sustainable Development, Bio-Economic Models and Innovation
Chairperson: Daniel Bromley

Analysis of policy issues in the Atlantic Zone of Costa Rica using integrated bio-economic land use models
Hans G.P. Jansen, Robert A. Schipper, Huib Hengsdijk (Netherlands) and Bas A.M. Bouman, Fernando Saenz (Costa Rica) and Andre Nieuwenhuye (Bolivia)

Innovation in agriculture: innovators, early adopters and laggards
Hans Van Meijl, Paul Diederen and Arjan Wolters (Netherlands)

Innovation systems and technology policy: zero tillage in MERCOSUR
Javier Ekboir (Argentina)

Low external input agricultural systems: economics and sustainability
David Lee and Ruerd Ruben (USA)

4:2   Reform in Transitional Countries
Chairperson: George Mergos

A rent seeking model for analysing a failed agricultural reform: the Bulgarian case
Markus Hanisch and Ferdinand Pavel (Germany)

The impact of the official development assistance on economic growth in transition economies: an empirical study
Azeta Cungu (Belgium)

WTO commitments and EU accession from the candidate countries' point of view
Andrea Elekes and Peter Halmai (Hungary)

4:3   Exchange Rate Adjustment Effects
Chairperson: Alan Matthews

Devaluation under decreasing marketing margins through infrastructure investment
Peter Wobst (USA)

Welfare effects of the Franc CFA devaluation in Bénin
Jean Senahoun (Germany), Daniel Deybe (France) and Franz Heidhues (Germany)

The effect of nominal exchange rate misalignment on agricultural trade
Ian M. Sheldon, Guedae Cho (USA) and Steve McCorriston (UK)

4:4   Technological Change
Chairperson: Wallace Huffman

Cyclical concentration and biotech R&D activity: a neo-Schumpeterian model
James Oehmke, Christopher Wolf, Dave Weatherspoon, Anwar Naseem, Mywish Maredia, Kellier Raper and Amie Hightower (USA)

Technology, policies and the global poultry revolution
Clare Narrod and Carl Pray (USA)

Winter wheat in England and Wales, 1923–1995: what do indices of genetic diversity reveal?
C.S. Srinivasan (India)

P   Use of an indigenous board game, 'bao', for assessing farmers' preferences among alternative technologies
Steven Franzel (Kenya)

4:5   Climate and Development
Chairperson: Mark Rosegrant

Accelerating agricultural intensification in the riskier environments of sub-Saharan Africa
Valerie Kelly and Mbaye Yade (USA), Kako Nubukpo and Marcel Galiba (Mali)

The tropics ARE different: climate and economic growth
William Masters and Margaret McMillan (USA)

Evaluation of drought management in irrigated areas
Eva Iglesias, Alberto Garrido and Almudena Gomez-Ramos (Spain)

The implications of El Niño/southern oscillation events on world rice production and trade
Ching-Cheng Chang and Chi-Chung Chen (Taiwan)

4:6   Efficiency in African Markets
Chairperson: Tom Fenyes

How transaction costs influence cattle marketing decisions in the northern communal areas of Namibia
N. Vink, P. de Bruyn, J.N. de Bruyn and J.F. Kirsten (South Africa)

Integration of Zambian maize markets
Jens-Peter Loy and Rainer Wichern (Germany)

S   The role of intermediaries in enhancing market efficiency in the Ethiopian grain market
Eleni Gabre-Madhin (Ethiopia)

Analysis of agricultural market institutions and their impact in the southern African development community
Firmino G. Mucavele (Mozambique)

4:7   Controlling Pests and Pathogens
Chairperson: Simeon Ehui

Evaluating the economic effectiveness of pathogen reduction technology in beef slaughter plants
Scott Malcolm, Clare Narrod, Michael Ollinger and Tanya Roberts (USA)

S   Economic analysis of environmental benefits of integrated pest management: a Philippine case study
Leah C.M. Cuyno (Philippines) and George W. Norton (USA)

Hot spots in animal agriculture, emerging federal environment policies and the potential to efficiency and innovation offsets
Frank M. Wefering and Ada Wossink (USA)

Contributed Papers 5

5:1   Insurance and Uncertainty
Chairperson: Claus-Hennig Hanf

The production effects of direct payments and tax reductions on farm profits under uncertainty
Renan-Ulrich Goetz, Joan Ribas-ur (Spain) and Alois Keusch (Switzerland)

Conceptual considerations in developing an income insurance for European farmers
Miranda Meuwissen and R.B.M. Huirne (Netherlands), J.B. Hardaker (Australia), J.R. Skees and J.R. Black (USA)

Market-based commodity price insurance for developing countries: towards a new approach
Alexander Sarris (Greece)

5:2   Economics of Trade
Chairperson: Tibor Ferenczi

A simple test of discriminatory trade in a source and quality-differentiated import market
Kevin Z. Chen (Canada)

P   A new approach to the evolution of primary commodity terms of trade and implications for developing countries
George P. Zanias (Greece)

P   The definition of export subsidies and the Agreement on Agriculture
Isabelle Schluep and Harry de Gorter (USA)

5:3   Market Power and Change
Chairperson: Lars Brink

Market power in the dairy sector and structural effects of government intervention: Swedish dairy cooperatives
Anna Hedberg (Sweden)

Globalization and profitability adjustment in international food industries
Yvonne Acheampong, James E. Epperson, Timothy A. Park and Lewell F. Gunter (USA)

Free market prices and reform in the Chinese grain marketing system
Ziping Wu and Seamus McErlean (UK)

5:4   Effectiveness of Livestock Research
Chairperson: Paul Webster

S   An ex ante economic and policy analysis of biotechnology on livestock disease resistance: trypanosmosis in Africa
Cesar Augusto Falconi (Netherlands), Steven Were Omamo (Kenya) and Guy d'Ieteren (Belgium)

Impact of livestock research on poverty alleviation in sub-Saharan Africa: a global, general equilibrium analysis
Simeon Ehui (Ethiopia) and Marinos Tsigas (USA)

S   Is livestock research unproductive? Separating health maintenance from improvements
      R.F. Townsend (Zimbabwe) and Colin Thirtle (UK)

5:5   Selected Issues
Chairperson: Michelle Veeman

P   International transfers and food security
      Alan Matthews (Ireland) and Christian Friis Bach (Denmark)

P   Academic rigour or policy relevance: a reconciliation?
      David R. Harvey (UK)

P   Making better sense of the numbers on developing economy agriculture
      Ellen Hanak-Freud (France)

5:6   Microfinance and Credit
Chairperson: Peter Hazell

      The material conditions for microfinance in rural Argentina
      Mark Schreiner (USA)

      Risk, credit constraints and agricultural employment in India's SAT
      Marrit van den Berg (Netherlands)

      The theory and practice of innovations in rural microfinance
      Frederic Martin, Sylvain Larivière and Peter Calkins (Canada)

S   Infrastructure and rural development: insights from a Grameen village telephone initiative in Bangladesh
      Abdul Bayes (Bangladesh)

5:7   Economics of Forest Management
Chairperson: George Norton

      Comparative dynamics of forest resource extraction by local communities
      Ujjayant Chakravorty (USA) and Herath M. Gunatilake (Sri Lanka)

      Community resource management: the case of woodlots in Tigray, N. Ethiopia
      Berhanu Gebremedhin (Ethiopia), John Pender (USA) and Girmay Tesfaye (Ethiopia)

      Determinants of deforestation and the economics of protection: an application to Mexico
      Klaus Deininger (USA) and Bart Minten (Belgium)

OPENING SESSION

PRESIDENTIAL ADDRESS

DOUGLAS D. HEDLEY*

Considerations on the Making of Public Policy for Agriculture

INTRODUCTION

In this 24th Presidential Address of the International Association of Agricultural Economists, I want to explore the changing nature of policy formulation and application for agriculture and the agri-food systems. The systems have been under significant strain in recent years owing to increased economic globalization, changing political and economic forces, technological advances, environmental and food safety concerns, and numerous other pressures. Hence policy formulation and its application have been changing dramatically over the past decade, with more and faster changes facing all of us in the future. Policy systems around the world are the clients of our profession, and many of our members are involved both in the continuing research and analysis to support them, and in policy formulation and application itself.

Previous Presidential Addresses to the IAAE have expanded explicitly or implicitly the scope of policy formulation and application within the horizon of agricultural economics. Glenn Johnson in 1985 at Malaga, Spain, explored the increasing scope of the agricultural economics profession. To him, our profession was not defined centrally by disciplinary research in economics applied to agriculture, but by the synthesis of disciplinary and applied normative work in economics as well as the products of related disciplines such as history, law, sociology, psychology and political science for problem solving.

Robert Thompson, in his Presidential Address at our last Conference, in Sacramento, reviewed the critical issues and dilemmas of each region of the world and related these to the policy formulation and application decisions faced increasingly by governments and international institutions. The implicit message was that policy formulation and application at all levels played a key role in the well-being of agricultural and rural citizens around the world. Keith Campbell, in the 1982 Elmhirst Lecture, pushed out the frontiers of our profession to include the environmental disciplines and their application to agriculture. John Longworth, as President for the 1991 Tokyo meeting, explored the

---

*Douglas Hedley, Assistant Deputy Minister, Farm Financial Programmes Branch, Agriculture and Agri-food Canada, Ottawa, Canada. The views expressed are not necessarily those of Agriculture and Agri-food Canada.

perimeters of our profession in dealing with the emerging life sciences revolution and its potential contributions to improving the lot of mankind on a global basis.

With the changing nature of policy formulation, I argue that the scope of our profession continues to widen to include and interface with new and emerging disciplines which contribute to problem solving throughout the entire food chain, and for governments. I will present these arguments within four areas, horizontality, complexity, globalization and institutions, and citizen engagement.[1]

HORIZONTALITY

For at least four decades after the Second World War, policy formulation for the agri-food chain remained largely independent of policies and programmes carried out for the rest of the national economies (Hedley, 2000). Agricultural policy was established largely within countries, with little consideration given to programmes in other countries. International implications of policy decisions were largely residual to domestic policy-choices (Bonnen and Schweikhardt, 1998). In addition, agricultural policy was synonymous with rural policy in most countries. Agricultural policy, virtually alone, bore the responsibility for rural development, without any wider consideration of instruments needed for effective rural development. I cannot argue that writers in agricultural economics did not study or understand the sectoral linkages between farming and the rest of the economy. I can argue that policies for agriculture were largely established by governments and other institutions substantially independently of those set for other economic sectors and other countries, and equally independently of most social policies of the period, including those focused on or affecting rural areas.

Several events have combined to sharply erode the independence of domestic agricultural policy formulation and application. For example, the start of the Uruguay Round of trade negotiations in 1986, and its eventual results in 1994, linked domestic agricultural policy to trade policy for the sector for the first time. This connection, for both developed and developing countries, is now so concrete that the two strands cannot be separated. Environmental concerns about water, air and soils are influencing current and emerging farming practices and forcing policy attention to pesticide use, tillage and fertilizer application. Climate change is also calling into question many aspects of today's farming practices. Even though overall food safety for consumers appears to be improving, increased media attention to outbreaks, and some significant incidents in recent years, have meant that food safety concerns continue to rise, questioning both foodstuffs themselves and the inputs and processes used in their production.

These issues are not new to agricultural economists. However, the participants involved in forging policy for agriculture and food have dramatically widened over the past several years to include governmental and institutional mandates as well as interest groups far beyond agriculture. Nonetheless, the traditional organizational structure within governments and institutions has had agriculture departments or ministries as the basic unit for leadership in agricultural policies. Furthermore, administrative structures within governments, including Cabinet appointments and their related responsibilities, have resulted in the expectation that agricultural departments and ministries provide the leadership in policy formulation and decision making. Increasingly, these traditional policy decision mechanisms have declining legitimacy in providing policies for agriculture, and are seen as too narrowly based in their competency for the formulation of policies which affect so heavily other crucial areas of government. As a result, many governments are experimenting with horizontal decision mechanisms for policy in responding to issues that cut across the current, traditional organizations for policy decisions. Several committees and joint committees of the United States Congress, for example, now regularly address issues central to agricultural policy. In Canada, new horizontal structures, overlaid on traditional vertical organizations, are dealing with rural policy, biotechnology, climate change, clean air and water, and aboriginal affairs.

The traditional interest groups in agriculture are being joined by new and different interest groups that are demanding that their views be heard on agricultural policy. As a consequence of globalization, international interest groups are joining the regional and national interest groups in policy debate, both nationally and internationally.

For many decades, agricultural policy has been the cornerstone for the delivery of rural policies in developed and developing countries. Price and income supports, input subsidies and infrastructure for farming were the common instruments of rural policy. This policy model treated several other instruments of rural policy as independent of agricultural and rural policies. These include rural health services, education, access to non-farm business services and infrastructure, for example. Increasingly in the last decade or so, we have found that, from a policy perspective, agricultural policy as a platform for rural development cannot provide the range of tools to develop rural areas fully.

As negotiations in the World Trade Organization (WTO) increasingly restrict the levels of support that can be legitimately offered to farming through price and income support, newer, more horizontal approaches will need to be found to develop rural areas, and offer equivalent business opportunity and quality of life to that found in urban areas. Ministries of health, education, public works, industry and commerce, as well as agriculture, will need to work together to design balanced policies for rural areas. Rural development policy cannot remain the exclusive domain of agriculture. Without this wider approach to rural policies, we can expect to see novel and creative ways to support incomes in agriculture in the belief that such instruments are the only means of assuring a growing and prosperous agrarian/rural landscape. Multifunctionality has dominated much of the discussion of rural development in the past several years. However, so long as the implementation of the concept uses agricultural policy as its principal springboard, the full development of rural areas across all of its integral policy components remains suspect.

Indeed, progress in the WTO in limiting domestic support is unlikely to proceed rapidly unless, at the same time, separable rural policies can be addressed directly.

Horizontality in policy formulation and application is to be found in at least three dimensions: across mandates within governments and institutions, across countries and international institutions themselves, and across interest groups both national and international. Governments and their domestic and international institutions are increasingly looking for new and different ways to deal with the horizontal imperative for policy decisions. To a considerable degree, the continuing organizational integrity and legitimacy of agricultural ministries themselves as central policy players will need to be addressed. For international institutions, agriculture may not be necessarily the central organizational construct for addressing and resolving the array of policy issues in the future.

COMPLEXITY

The expanding universe of issues and players in policy formulation for agriculture and food is sharply increasing the complexity of policy making. But many other events and processes are also adding further problems.

The WTO Agreement of 1994, yielding a slow but sure integration of agriculture into disciplined trading relationships among countries, has dramatically added to the complexity in policy making. Combining the provisions for market access, domestic support and export subsidies with non-tariff trade barriers (NTBs) and sanitary and phytosanitary (SPS) regulations, along with the general provisions of the WTO, the opportunity set for policy choice has far more restraints and activities to consider than ever before. Jones and Bureau (2000) have argued that, throughout the Uruguay Round negotiations, there was wide acceptance of, and support for, the intellectually comfortable notion that reducing trade barriers yielded increases in economic welfare for all parties. However, this conclusion, they argue, can no longer hold as widely as before, and more careful consideration on a case-by-case basis, particularly with respect to food safety and quality, is needed before determining whether trade liberalization uniformly results in increased welfare. This view suggests that substantially more work will be needed in greater detail than ever before to inform policy processes and decisions to ensure that continuing progress in trade negotiations can take place. Our many standard tools of analysis on trade issues, which served so well throughout the last trade round, do not seem to have the technical capacity to incorporate the immense detail of the issues emerging in this round of negotiations.

As domestic policy solutions are found within this more complex opportunity set, there is also a growing requirement for documentation by every member nation to meet its obligations under the WTO. Domestic and international interest groups are demanding far more detailed information and analyses than ever before. This growth in complexity in policy formulation and presentation holds significant consequences for nations and for our profession. The human capital requirements within governments and nations to meet domestic and international obligations are such that the capacity of developed nations and the larger developing nations is substantially stretched. It is increasingly difficult to reach common understanding in interpretation and application of regulations associated with economic integration. For the smaller nations in the developing world this complexity can often outstrip their ability to cope, let alone fully exploit the opportunities that appear within domestic and international arrangements.

As the complexity of regulations and agreements affecting agriculture deepens we must give increasing attention to the development of human capital within nations, as well as the provisioning of this capacity within international institutions themselves. Greater complexity can so obscure the fairness or transparency sought in policy arrangements that the agreements, as well as the relevant institutions, can be called into question. Without the promotion of understanding through capacity building there is great risk to the institutions and to the acceptance of continuing the economic integration in agriculture and food systems around the world.

GLOBALIZATION AND INSTITUTIONS

The General Agreement of Tariffs and Trade (GATT), and its evolution into the WTO, have been premised on the notion that lowering transaction costs in trade can lead to an improvement in economic well-being for all concerned. While agriculture came late in joining other sectors in lowering trade barriers, substantial progress has been made, with there being expectations of further reducing traditional barriers in the current round. Tariffs and quantitative restrictions on trade were seen as the largest transaction costs limiting trade, and hence were the primary focus for nearly all efforts in the previous rounds. With notable exceptions, the transaction costs in trade represented by tariffs are a small component today. Several transaction costs remain, including currency risk, legal limitations on cross-border contracts, transportation arrangements and costs. Even here, groups of nations are tackling some or all of these and related issues.

These arrangements allow firms increasingly to optimize their operations across a number of countries, rather than concentrating only on national markets. In the process a much wider array of public policy issues is being brought to bear on domestic policy. Environmental policies, labour standards, biodiversity, human rights, climate change, food safety and quality, and other issues are now being thrust into the debate on trade liberalization and economic integration. In addition to the Bretton Woods institutions, many others have grown up around the relations between nations which can affect trade. There is a cacophony of acronyms signifying organizations claiming a role in trade relations and policy among nations, each of which can have quite different objectives. This adds complexity and increases the necessity for horizontal competency in policy making in an almost geometrical proportion. The declining coherence in objectives puts institutions at risk. Unfortunately, it has to be stressed that agricultural and rural interests are not necessarily central components in the debate. I think there is considerable opportunity for agricultural interests and our profession to help bring coherence to diverging objectives.

As the traditional trade barriers of tariffs and quantitative restrictions on product trade in agriculture come down, and firms optimize across nations as if they were in a single market, the direct transaction costs of trade have less and less bearing on the growth of trade. The comparative investment climate between countries will have far more to do with economic growth and expansion than the transaction costs in trade. These investment climates include corporate and personal income tax levels, social programmes ranging from health care to personal security, justice and jurisprudence in contract law, and public infrastructure investment. Production of raw agricultural products, tied to an immobile land resource, will continue where the land exists. However, the industry based on transformation of raw materials into consumer-ready products is increasingly footloose and responds rapidly, at the margin, to changing investment climates.

For economies with both a large agricultural base and a large consumer market, the USA and the European Union for example, concern for the investment climate is probably substantially lower than it is for smaller nations with a significant farm base and a small domestic market. There are very few studies which explore these issues for agriculture in either the developed or developing country literature. One does find a steadily growing literature on the investment climate for an economy as a whole, although there is little tailoring of these studies to the agricultural industries. For example, elasticities of investment in relation to taxes paid have been estimated for an entire country, but not for agricultural industries. Some are surprisingly large (Wasylenko, 1997; Bartik, 1994). A further difficulty in measuring the investment climate is that there is a very wide range of variables involved, with no clear relationships among them. They remain non-additive and non-relative.

Firms make decisions on investment location every day, though governments are not yet at the point in policy formulation of explicitly balancing all of the variables shaping the domestic investment climate. Again, I think there is great opportunity for our profession to explore the variety of forces influencing the investment climate in agricultural processing industries for developed and developing nations, with a substantial pay-off in the acceptance and legitimacy of continued progress in trade liberalization and economic integration.

CITIZEN ENGAGEMENT

In the early 2000 Newsletter of the IAAE, I tried to capture an overview of the complex processes of citizen engagement now demanded in policy formation and implementation:

> The WTO Summit in Seattle epitomizes one of the great sea changes in policy formulation and institutional process of the past decade. The Summit, including the emotion, and public interest group reactions surrounding it, reflect a decade or more of change in the way in which policy, institutions, and process work together in today's world. Civil society is demanding, indeed insisting on, a seat at the table

in the debates and ultimately the decisions about the economic, social and institutional issues that affect their lives.

This process of change is certainly not complete. While civil society increasingly wants to be part of debate and decision, it is well-organized interest groups, local, national and international, who have taken on most of this task so far. Yet the interest groups themselves are transforming and multiplying, from group coherence based on a long-standing specific interest, to new and different groups which spring up around emerging views from society itself. The puzzle for governments and international institutions, which are themselves representatives of civil society and regularly are required to test their acceptability to represent civil society, is how to create inclusive structures for policy formulation. The potential solutions are all the more complex because the coherence and resonance within the interest groups are constantly changing, and rarely conform to the representational and democratic norms required of governments.

The implications for the agricultural economics profession around the world continue to change in response to this greater involvement of civil society. No longer can analysis be carried out with scholarly product as the only result. Analysis must also be prepared for civil society and with that, the task of communicating results from research and analysis on exceedingly complex topics must be undertaken. To fail in communicating with civil society, about the implications drawn from scholarly work in agricultural economics, our profession risks having decisions and directions based on incomplete information, not only by governments and international institutions, but also by the multitude of groups spawned by specific interests in society. The lack of coherent and balanced views within society is in itself a source for creating more interest groups.

Another implication is the continuing recognition that horizontal work across disciplines and professions is needed. Few decisions on behalf of society rely exclusively on economics or agricultural economics. Merging and gap filling between agricultural economics and other professions are a critical area for all of us.

In maintaining relevance within the profession, the responsibility goes far beyond that of informing each other. We must inform and be informed by a wide spectrum of sources, including other professions and disciplines, but also civil society itself.

Since Seattle we have had a number of other examples of the same phenomenon: in Montreal at the meeting on the Biodiversity Protocol, in Okinawa for the G-8 Summit, in Windsor, Canada, for the Organization of American States, in Calgary, Canada, at the Oil Summit. Democracies are struggling to balance the democratic norms of civil representation with the demands of a multiplicity of special and single interest groups. None of these groups bears the responsibility for representing all of societal beliefs and values as do elected governments. Similarly, none bears the responsibility for decisions ultimately taken. In addition, many groups rely on preventing decisions, rather than fostering a climate for decision. Finally, few, if any, represent the groups within society least favoured economically, or least inclined to political action, leaving many, possibly a majority, unheard either by democratic governments or through reporting in the media.

The essence of democracy requires that these voices be heard and included in policy decision processes, but inclusion can be particularly frustrating in policy processes and implementation. Governments are slowly coming to realize that a passive approach to engaging citizens through interest groups is not sufficient. 'Representation by media volume' alone does not serve either social or democratic purpose. More active approaches to reaching out to citizens are increasingly necessary for progress in policy decision making. Our profession has the capacity and opportunity to serve society by providing information and analysis for governments as well as people generally.

CONCLUSIONS

In summary, policy formation is increasingly complex and more horizontal in the range of mandates and competencies required than ever before. The complexity of decision processes established within governments and in the international arena is overpowering the human capacity of many nations, calling into question the viability and continued acceptability of the arrangements made. When only larger developed countries have the resources to participate fully in international organizations it is increasingly difficult to convince other nations that the benefits for everyone are being considered, let alone enhanced. Our institutions require more rapid evolution, not only to bring coherence to the widening set of related policy dilemmas, but also to demonstrate their fairness and transparency for all nations. Agricultural economists have a greater opportunity than ever before to serve the needs of governments, organizations and the general public in framing the debate on institutions and policies for agriculture and agri-food. This means a considerable shift in the output from our profession, from primarily academic literature to a wider, more accessible, set of materials available to the public. Making this shift is a critical element in the continuity and stability of institutions as well as for our specialism.

NOTES

[1]Professor Bonnen, our Elmhirst Lecturer at these meetings, and I have struggled with these concepts individually, together and with other colleagues for a number of years. See Bonnen *et al.* (1997), Hedley (1998), Hedley (2000). From my perspective, I am no longer a researcher, but have been involved in policy processes for agriculture for many years, while Professor Bonnen continues to be a valued mentor and coach as well as a participant in these same policy processes during his career. I have approached the topics from the basis of experience in, and with, a number of policy institutions over several years. Professor Bonnen, also drawing on his experience in several institutions, has taken a more research-oriented approach than mine. Nonetheless, we draw similar conclusions, most often from quite different starting points. His reference to, and application of, Rodrik's trilemma, for example, neatly captures the continuing practical balancing act that policy processes face daily, more cogently than I have been able to express. Also our language differs in defining many of these difficult concepts. Professor Bonnen's reference to fragmentation of the structures of governance is his representation of the horizontality and complexity arguments I am making. Similarly, 'citizen engagement', a term used in the Canadian government and some Canadian academic circles, in this paper represents the continuing and changing interface between citizens and their governments and international institutions.

Professor Bonnen makes reference to the 'participatory politics' and the nature of debate about such issues as biotechnology.

BIBLIOGRAPHY

Bartik, T.J. (1994), 'Jobs, Productivity and Local Economic Development: What Implications Does Economic Research Have for the Role of Government?', *National Tax Journal*, **47**, 847–62.

Bonnen, J.T. and Schweikhardt, D.B. (1998), 'The Future of U.S. Agricultural Policy: Reflections on the Disappearance of the "Farm Problem"', *Review of Agricultural Economics*, **20**, 2–36.

Bonnen, J.T., Hedley, D.D. and Schweikhardt, D.B. (1997), 'Agriculture and the Changing Nation-State: Implications for Policy and Political Economy', *American Journal of Agricultural Economics*, **79**, 1419–29.

Campbell, K.O. (1983), 'Agricultural Economists and World Conservation Strategy', in A.H. Maunder and K. Ohkawa (eds), *Growth and Equity in Agricultural Development*, Aldershot: Gower, pp.9–19.

Hedley, D.D. (1998), 'Global Challenges: Local Issues', The Simon Brandt Memorial Lecture, Swakopmund, Namibia, South African Association of Agricultural Economists, *AGRIFUTURA, Quarterly Newsletter* no. 10, December.

Hedley, D.D. (2000), 'Values, Institutions and Governance: Global, National and Local', *Canadian Journal of Agricultural Economics*, **47**, 487–92.

Johnson, Glenn L. (1986), 'Scope of Agricultural Economics', in A.H. Maunder and U. Renborg (eds), *Agriculture in a Turbulent World*, Aldershot: Gower.

Jones, W. and Bureau, J.-C. (2000), 'Issues in Demand for Quality and Trade', paper presented at the IATRC Symposium on Consumer Demand for Quality and Global Agricultural Trade, Montreal, Canada, 26–7 June.

Longworth, J. (1992), 'Human Capital Formation for Sustainable Agricultural Development', in G.H. Peters and Stanton, B. (eds), *Sustainable Agricultural Development: The Role of International Cooperation*, Aldershot: Dartmouth.

Rodrik, D. (2000), 'How Far Will International Integration Go?', *Journal of Economic Perspectives*, **14**, 177–86.

Thompson, R.L. (1999), 'Technology, Policy and Trade: The Keys to Food Security and Environmental Protection', in G.H. Peters and J. von Braun (eds), *Food Security, Diversification and Resource Management: Refocusing the Role of Agriculture?*, Aldershot: Ashgate.

Wasylenko, M. (1997), 'Taxation and Economic Development: The State of the Economic Literature', *New England Economic Review*, March/April, 37–52.

ELMHIRST MEMORIAL LECTURE

JAMES T. BONNEN*

The Transformation of Agriculture and the World Economy: Challenges for the Governance of Agriculture and for the Profession

It is a great honour to deliver the ninth Elmhirst Lecture. Indeed, to stand where once stood eight outstanding economists, three of them Nobel laureates, is quite intimidating. I dedicate my comments to the memory of the first Elmhirst Lecturer, Theodore W. Schultz, who passed away last year. He was a professional friend, a role model and a mentor to many in my generation of agricultural economists.

I hope you will pardon a very personal story about Ted. Professor Schultz was not one who endured fools or errors in economic reasoning quietly. My peers greatly admired him for this, but he left more than a few bruised egos among his own and a prior generation of economists. During a social occasion in 1963, Ted recalled for me his first course in economics, a farm management course taken in 1926. I learned to my amazement that his instructor had been my father. I later confronted my father with this information. A quiet-spoken person with a dry sense of humour, my father said very slowly, 'Yes, that is true. But I take none of the credit and none of the blame.' When I repeated this for Ted, he broke into laughter and observed that my father's sense of humour still had the nice edge to it that he remembered. I failed to recount my father's other observation. 'Schultz,' he said, 'was a challenging student.'[1] Indeed he was, and the characteristics that made him a challenging student would later make him a demanding professional – demanding of himself and of others. Ted's life was informed by integrity, great intellectual curiosity, scientific imagination and courage. He was committed to truth and to those without voice in agriculture.

These characteristics were evident in the first Elmhirst Lecture, where Ted Schultz argued that over all stages of the development of agriculture much of what governments had done was often badly flawed. He added that 'The hard

*Michigan State University. Any effort of this scope has benefited from the critical reviews of more than a few colleagues. I am especially indebted to David Schweikhardt for his acuity and endless patience in critiquing multiple drafts and to both David Schweikhardt and Carl Eicher for their many useful ideas and for identifying additional resources. Under great constraint of time, Sandra Batie, Clarence Bonnen, Derek Byerlee, Ralph Christy, Richard Horan, Glenn Johnson, Jim Oehmke, Al Schmid and Luther Tweeten critiqued a late draft that improved the completeness and clarity of this lecture.

realities of the costs of producing goods and services are not abolished by either national or international politics. Herein lies not only the hope but the necessity of economics' (Schultz, 1977, pp.15, 16).

Despite mistakes, some governments have done enough things well for consumers in developed nations today to have the cheapest food in history. Many nations have moved from lower to higher levels of development. Nevertheless, the difficulties facing world agriculture today are as daunting, or more so, as when Professor Schultz spoke to this body 24 years ago in Nairobi. As a profession we must call on the professional characteristics exemplified by Theodore W. Schultz, if we are to deal successfully with the problems we face.

President Hedley has asked that I examine the implications of the evolving global political economy and its transforming technologies for the governance of agriculture and for the profession. This involves a large, complex and interactive set of forces. For clarity I have limited my focus to three major forces of change, set within the parameters of a simplifying framework.

Many of the challenges confronting us arise out of a new era in the continuing transformation of the agricultural sector. The previous transformations of agriculture are well understood by this audience. Early in the process of development, the economic and political characteristics of the agricultural sector provoke governments to discriminate against their relatively large, primarily subsistence, agrarian sectors (Anderson and Hayami, 1986).[2] Later, as development transforms the productivity and the economic and political characteristics of agriculture, governments of developed countries begin to protect and subsidize agriculture. In both cases, these policies are the product of the economic characteristics of the sector and the national economy and thus of the economic and political opportunities and constraints, or the opportunity set, faced by policy makers at different levels of development (Bonnen and Schweikhardt, 1998).

We have learned that, in a low income country with a large portion of its human and other resources embedded in agriculture, economic development will eventually fail, if development of the agrarian sector does not accompany that of the rest of the economy. Except for the small number of well organized farmers in the commercial export sector of some developing countries, farmers have little or no political voice. This is the opportunity set faced by policy makers in low-income, developing countries (Anderson, 1987; Anderson and Hayami, 1986).

Later in the development process entirely new opportunities and constraints emerge as the economic characteristics of agriculture change. Chronic excess capacity and low returns, plus great price and income instability and growing vulnerability to macroeconomic events, occur as the commercial sector of agriculture becomes a highly productive, integrated part of the national economy and of trade. By this time a large number of highly capitalized commercial farms are organized and have a political voice. Problems of agricultural externalities arise in such areas as environmental quality, health, food safety and resource use and in rural development. An entirely new set of constraints and capacities evolve to define the new opportunity set faced by policy makers (Bonnen and Schweikhardt, 1998).

Today we are entering another era in which the economic characteristics of the economy and its agricultural sector are changing, again creating a new pattern of economic and political opportunities and constraints. Most of the earlier economic characteristics of a developed economy continue, including chronic excess capacity with both unstable returns and prices. Externalities continue to grow, as does vulnerability to macroeconomic events. With globalization these also become the characteristics of international markets. Nations at all levels of development are affected. One of the challenges we face in this world of global markets is the necessity to recognize and integrate into national and international policy the needs of widely differing levels of development.

The continuing integration of world markets and national economies, combined with new technologies, especially in information and communication and in biotechnology, is leading to a higher level of international interdependence driven by major new reductions in the cost of time and space. As a consequence, poverty in low-income nations has become, not just an obstacle to the development of those nations, but a clear drag on the growth potential of highly developed nations. We are entering a new era of increasing international economic integration of agriculture.

THREE FORCES OF CHANGE

Important forces of change are currently shaping major economic policy issues and are modifying the conditions of governance. Information and communication technologies and institutions are creating changes in economic capacity, and in the structure and performance of the economy, worldwide. Secondly, new biological technologies have the potential for a similar impact on agriculture, health and medicine. Thirdly, the institutions that structure and order markets are being modified, not only by information and communication technologies, but by international treaties and by private sector innovations in the institutions of capital and commodity markets. This is leading the world towards globalization of markets or international economic integration, as economists understand this ill-defined and much abused term. Other forces contribute to these changes, but are not addressed here.

The different forces of change are interactive. The new information technologies and the economic integration of the world's markets are complements with reinforcing effects on each other. For international agricultural markets, the biotech revolution adds even greater potential, but many uncertainties still attend its commercial applications and acceptance in different societies.

Technology is important, but equally important and frequently overlooked are the changes in the physical capital, human skills, institutions and values. These are often more important because, as scholarship on the history of technology clearly shows, human capital, value beliefs and institutions will shape the ultimate uses and consequences of technology, not just the other way around – as is commonly assumed. Change in any one of the forces can induce change in another. All of these forces of change are essential complements

(G.L. Johnson, 1997). They all have the potential to increase the capacity of society to achieve its goals. To what extent and how, whether for good or bad, is determined by the choices we make as individuals and as a society.

These forces are leading to a transformation of the fundamental nature and capacity for governance, not only of nation states, but governance of most major economic sectors such as agriculture. We are in the middle of creating a very different and more complex world compared with that of the past century, about which there is a voluminous and growing literature.[3] We face an agenda of problems and policy issues, some of which are entirely new and many of which will challenge our profession over the next generation. Our responses to these challenges will often involve choices between conflicting prescriptive beliefs and ideologies.[4] Consequently, our participation in addressing such problems will be plagued by uncertainty and by personal and professional risk.

Turning back toward protectionism at this point would involve great loss of economic welfare worldwide. But moving ahead will not be costless. Inequality of income and wealth in the developed world is increasing. Poverty and its ills are the largest challenge faced in the development of low-income nations. Any increase in the economic welfare of nations, developed and especially developing, now depends on a nation's fabric of institutions, on the rules for trade and finance and the resulting gains from specialization. As dramatic as the impact of the emerging new economy has been, we are only in the early stages of this economic and political transformation.

Since the Second World War, the world economy has slowly become one of more integrated global service, commodity and capital markets. As a consequence, despite many problems, we are experiencing growing worldwide economic interdependence of national economies and their major economic sectors – including agriculture. We are still a long way from the 'deep integration' that would permit global markets to operate across economic sectors and national borders without significant discrimination or costly restraint. Deeper integration would require still greater international coordination of market grades and standards, of property right laws and of the institutions and rules for commodity, service and financial markets. In this process international governance grows more complex and problematic.

ANALYSING THE FORCES OF CHANGE IN A GLOBAL SETTING

In examining the new opportunities and constraints affecting the agricultural sector, I will draw upon some well-developed principles of policy analysis that have recently been recast in a form applicable to the problems facing agriculture. Nearly a half-century ago, in examining the multiple macroeconomic objectives confronting policy makers, Jan Tinbergen demonstrated that, for policy makers to achieve all of their objectives, the number of *independent* policy instruments (or tools) must at least equal or exceed the number of policy objectives. If the number of available instruments is less than the number of policy objectives, or if they are not fully independent of each other, policy makers face an unavoidable choice of which objective will go unfulfilled. The relative independence and thus the ability of each instrument to achieve each objective – or its 'efficiency' of achieving each objective – is determined by the economic characteristics that define the policy problem (Tinbergen, 1956; Fox and Thorbecke, 1965; Obstfeld and Taylor, 1998).[5]

Tinbergen's work demonstrated what is widely known as the classic national problem of macroeconomic policy: the simultaneous effort to maintain (a) fixed exchange rates, (b) open capital markets and (c) national autonomy of monetary policy (Figure 1). As Tinbergen defined this problem, policy makers have a choice of achieving any two, but never all three, of these policy objectives. This choice of the combination of instruments and targets represents the opportunity set that macroeconomic policy makers must confront in making their decisions.

Dani Rodrik (2000) has recast Tinbergen's original model of macroeconomic policy making into a much broader model of policy making and political economy within an integrated world economy (Figure 1). Rodrik's 'trilemma' involves three targets: the international integration of national economies, the sovereignty of policy making by the nation state and the practice of 'mass politics' in which a fully participating polity expresses its political preferences in a democratic state.

There is a prior condition that is crucial to understanding this dilemma. Today, if you opt for a policy of attaining above-average, or high rather than lower, rates of growth, you find you are dependent for investment on what is now a single, immense, worldwide capital market. This capital market is driven by thousands of anonymous stock and bond traders all over the world who, with the click of a 'mouse', can instantaneously move large amounts of money

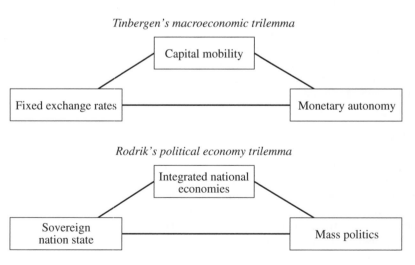

Source: Adapted from Rodrik (2000).

FIGURE 1   *The trilemmas of Tinbergen and Rodrik*

over the Internet from one investment category to another, *or from one country to another*. A nation can have access to far more capital than in the past, but it must live by open, free market rules to maintain its credit rating. Lose a high rating and you lose market access and can suffer a crisis of capital flight. The power to set one's own policy rules is compromised before any policy goal has been set. This global capital market is replacing governments as the source of capital for both corporations and governments.

It is almost impossible to run an open economy without a reasonably open or democratic society. This raises the question of 'mass politics', which needs to be defined clearly. Rodrik's mass, or participatory, politics exists where the franchise is expanded well beyond the right to vote, to include the lobbying efforts of all organized interests. Thus, if the political franchise is unrestricted, any social or economic interest may have a voice in the policy decision process along with government policy makers. In addition, a high degree of political mobilization must exist; that is, all significant social and economic interests are organized and politically active. While all interests may have the same right of access, in reality different interests will have quite different capacities to make their voices heard. Finally, political institutions are responsive to mobilized interests; that is, policy makers cannot ignore opposing interests, but must deal with the opposition, presumably at some political cost. Thus, if mass politics prevails, the policy maker in Rodrik's trilemma is forced to choose between international economic integration and state sovereignty. One goal must be abandoned (Rodrik, 2000).

Participatory or mass politics is in some degree a product of development itself. As development proceeds, specialization breaks large, older markets into many new markets. As income rises, consumer preferences extend beyond food, shelter and security to new values and to new value-added products. The previous structure of products and markets fragments and the number of economic interests proliferates. Inevitably, there are externalities to these changes that induce new interests to organize in opposition to some element of that change. Thus development produces a far more complex set of markets and interests and often a countervailing set of economic and social critics. These unavoidable economic characteristics of development produce a significant level of interdependence between the policy tools needed to address the three policy goals in Rodrik's trilemma.

Thus the policy maker in Rodrik's framework is faced with an unavoidable choice among policy targets. If policy makers choose to maintain the sovereignty of the nation state and *also must respond* to the participation in national politics by *all organized interests*, including those who oppose international economic integration, they cannot achieve *full integration* into international markets. Alternatively, if they attempt to achieve full international integration and also practise mass or full participatory politics, then the nation state must yield some of its sovereign power to those international institutions to which the polity must express its preferences for a framework of international integration. Finally, if the nation state is to maintain its sovereignty and simultaneously achieve integration with international markets, the range of political options available to the polity – or the responsiveness of the nation state to the demands of a broad range of domestic interests – must be reduced. The number of private sector institutions and their role in governance grow while those of a nation's public sector shrink.[6] Rodrik's model provides a framework within which to examine the continuing international transformation of the agricultural sector.

THE INFORMATION ECONOMY AND GLOBAL MARKETS

An important force in the current transformation of the world economy is a significant reduction in economic transaction costs driven by the new information, communication and computation technologies and their implementing institutions and human capital. In global markets, intermediate stages in the production of commodities and especially services are being unbundled and scattered to lowest-cost sites across the globe, making government regulation and taxation difficult to design or enforce. Electronic commerce is even more difficult to regulate or tax.

Economic characteristics of knowledge and information

Lowering transaction costs reduces organizing and operating costs and is leading to great increases in financial wealth and to changes in economic and political organization. Lowering economic transaction costs also lowers the barriers to entry, especially in knowledge and communication-intensive sectors. The potential for smaller scale, private sector entrepreneurial and political initiatives increases.[7]

Financial, commodity and service markets become so interdependent, country of origin so confused, and transactions so elusive that governments lose much of the ability to identify domestic production or to regulate and tax it. A primary signature of sovereignty is identifiable geographic boundaries and the power to tax and regulate within and at those boundaries (Krasner, 1999).

High costs of the first copy of information and information technologies often lead to market price and product differentiation. This frequently becomes a strategy of customer differentiation aimed at capturing the subset of the market that generates the highest profits. The cost of producing (or copying) additional units is so small that defending property rights is costly. Because of this cost structure the marginal cost-based pricing strategies of 'Economics 101' (the course which we have all taken!) are not a viable choice for firms in information markets. This leads to aggressive strategies focused on gaining a dominant market share early on so that your firm's information technology becomes the national and international industry standard. If successful, this assures your market, since information technologies exist as systems of interconnected technologies that are complements in production. If your technology becomes an industry standard and you have a dominant market share, your customers get 'locked in'. This was Microsoft's strategy. Over the long run, a high rate of innovation in information technologies can make obsolete the technological base of your market position. Thus continuous innovation in technology and smart marketing are often necessary for long-term survival of even the largest, best financed firms. This means that many information products and technologies may have limited proprietary lives (Shapiro and Varian, 1999).

We are still in the early stages in the development of computer-based internal and interorganizational networks. Distributive computing is a new frontier in information technology. Business and most service organizations are moving towards real-time decisions, which requires real-time information and increases the vulnerability of such systems to power outages, security breaches and privacy problems. The stupendous power of the Internet and other interorganizational networks to force change on the organization of business and services is yet to be fully appreciated. Not only are transaction costs of operations falling, but inventories and capital requirements are declining. The survivors will be very customer-oriented. At the macroeconomic level, lower inventory and capital requirements should dampen the business cycle. The norms for policy action based on measures of unemployment, inflation and productivity in the new information-intensive economy appear to be changing.

Information products and products that have become more information-intensive will often have lower exclusion costs, which can transform the margin between what have been publicly or privately provided goods. Lower exclusion costs permit privatization of some formerly publicly provided goods and raise policy issues over others as to who should provide, or pay for, a specific product or service. On the other hand, high first copy costs *plus diffuse benefits* will limit other information products to public provision.

New opportunities, constraints and choices

The major constraints to be faced in exploiting the opportunities in the economics of information-intensive products, the new communication technologies and global markets are (a) an erosion of a nation's capacity to regulate or tax commerce in domestic and international markets, (b) increasing loss of control over financial flows, over a nation's monetary policy, and thus exposure to events such as the recent Asian financial crisis, (c) growing private economic power, much of it beyond national accountability in mergers and concentration in domestic and international markets, and (d) the high incidence of poverty and its associated ills in many of the low-income nations which deprives these countries of the capacity necessary to access the information and communication technologies, institutions and skills needed for successful development.

An additional constraint is inherent in information management itself. Three decades ago, Herbert Simon (1971) pointed out that the social cost of information includes the cost to the user of the effort needed to retrieve information for any specific decision. Thus, in an information-rich environment, as the amount of information increases, the amount of attention a user can devote to any specific bit of information declines. In the current explosion of information and its ease of access, one faces far more difficulty in identifying, organizing and integrating relevant information for any specific decision. This has serious implications for governance since the difficulty increases as one goes from lower to higher levels of decision. Thus the problem of getting the right information to the right decision nexus is most complex and costly at the international level – something that must be considered in designing the institutions of governance.

Rodrik's trilemma

Exploiting these information and global market opportunities leads towards one side of Rodrik's triangle of choice, towards international integration of national economies, international regulation of markets and ultimately towards an international system of governance. One is left with a choice between sovereignty of policy making by nation states or mass politics at all levels of governance, but not both. At present, many developed nations seem to be embracing mass or participatory politics, with a loss of national sovereignty. A reaction in developed nations has begun to mobilize the forces of nationalism and of political extremism.

The growth of concentrated economic power combined with high levels of wealth in some nations and great poverty and political disorder in others induces large human migrations. Depending on the political and economic context, large migrations have in the past led to significant economic growth or contributed to social instability, or both. In reaction to migrations today, populist and nativist political movements are developing in wealthy receiving nations. Most highly developed nations now also face a future of rapidly aging populations with a declining size of workforce. Thus, if they are to maintain their economic capacity over the next several decades, these nations need an influx of younger but reasonably well trained migrants. Many migrants today, however, lack the needed education or skills. That will continue to be the case unless the developing nations are able to create the human and institutional capacity needed to gain access to the technologies, institutions, human capital and financial markets of the developed world.

There will be political and economic costs, whether the world moves towards greater international economic integration or retreats to protectionism, xenophobia and a search for national sovereignty. We should remember that the same political forces helped destroy the global markets of the nineteenth century. Then the First World War and the Great Depression finished the job. Serious critics cannot be ignored or shouted down. The outcome remains at issue.

AGRICULTURAL BIOTECHNOLOGY AND GLOBAL MARKETS

Another primary force in the transformation of the economy is that of biotechnology. The introduction of agricultural biotechnology has been badly managed and politicized. Most biotech innovations are little more than extensions of traditional plant and animal breeding techniques that have been going on for thousands of years, the risks of which are limited and well understood today. The still emerging field of molecular knowledge in plant and animal genetics (genomics) enables far more precise and efficient breeding without recourse to transgenics (often called 'genetically modified organisms' or GMOs). Transgenic modifications are another matter, since they involve the transfer of genetic material between different genotypes. But transgenic research is as yet a relatively small proportion of total biotech R&D (Byerlee, 2000; Horstkotte-Wesseler and Byerlee, 1999). Here there are highly uncertain benefits and risks that must be explored. So far demagogues and poorly informed participants have confused the debate by treating all biotech as if it were transgenic. We need to be working with biological scientists on biotech risk assessment and on the larger market and equity issues. Agriculture must take far more care in informing society's understanding of these risks and benefits. Food is psychologically sensitive and consumers will have the last word on what risks are socially acceptable.

Public discussion often assumes that absolute certainty and zero risk are reasonable goals of food safety. Especially at the individual consumer level, there can be no absolute certainty or zero risk in the interaction among production inputs, foods consumed and the diversity of human biological characteristics. Individual variation in biological organisms is just too great. With all of its limitations, the role of risk analysis and its integration in policy assessment are important. Two very different questions arise: what is the level of risk, and is that risk socially acceptable? While both are subject to various levels of uncertainty, the first is largely a question of science. The second is primarily a question of politics involving social values. The socially acceptable level of risk relative to benefits will differ between the rich and the poor, and will be different in different cultures.

The potential impact of biotech on productivity may eventually exceed that of information and communication technologies. Some economists question whether the productivity gains created by the 'information revolution' will spread beyond the information industry into other sectors as far as did the chemical, electrical and mechanical technologies of the industrial revolution of the nineteenth century (Gordon, 1999; Jorgenson and Stiroh, 1999). Intuitively, it would seem that biotechnology innovations in agriculture, health and medicine have a potential to spill over into many other sectors of human activity, perhaps adding more to total productivity than the information revolution, the gains of which so far appear to be limited to the information industry and its customers (Gordon, 1999).

Economic characteristics of biotechnology

The investments countries make in agricultural research, especially basic research, often lead to significant spillovers of benefits to other nations. Left unattended, this results in a cumulative underinvestment in agricultural research, both in the investing nations and worldwide (Schweikhardt and Bonnen, 1992). Major differences in national property rights laws and their enforcement can constrain the economic value of biotech products in global markets. The development of agricultural biotechnology has the potential of compounding the problem of the growing gap between the economic performance of developed and developing nations. This is a complex set of problems, but evidence for chronic public underinvestment in research for agriculture, at both national and international levels, continues to grow. Improved international institutions and public support for financing, producing and disseminating public agricultural research for low-income nations are a clear need and a necessary complement to private investments in agriculture.

Many biotech products to date have high fixed costs and very low marginal costs, much as in pharmaceuticals and the information industry (Rausser, 1999). How costly it will be to protect property rights in biotechnology remains to be seen. The outcome will affect research strategies and their public–private mix. The structure of the biotech industry will certainly be concentrated initially. The developed countries are experiencing a complex series of mergers of seed companies with a small number of large international chemical and pharmaceutical firms. This strategy is focused on the potential of biotechnology and could end with only a few vertically integrated firms exercising monopoly power over the supply of high-productivity germ plasm in large regions of the world. They would control the farm input market from germ plasm to the provision of seeds bundled with pesticides and herbicides. Wally Falcon explores these issues in detail in his fine paper 'Globalizing Germ Plasm: Barriers, Benefits and Boundaries', found later in this volume. With high rates of biotech innovation, the potential for concentration may eventually decline.

The income elasticity of demand for the multiple dimensions of food safety rises across the process of development. It exceeds the declining income elasticity of demand for food in most highly developed nations. Similarly, the income elasticity of demand for protection of the ecosystem and the environment rises with income over the development process. It too appears to exceed the declining income elasticity of demand for food in highly developed nations. This assures serious consideration of regulation to achieve environmental and food safety policy goals in agriculture.

The political characteristics that have followed the introduction of biotechnologies involve the mobilization of food safety, ecosystem and environmental advocacy and anti-biotech interest groups (NGOs) at all levels of governance from subnational to international. Some groups now participate with and add strength to the anti-globalization movement.

The battle over agricultural biotechnology has thus far been primarily between factions in developed industrial nations. Our profession should be working to improve the capacity of developing nations to participate in and shape biotech research and policy agendas. The stake of the developing nations in biotech must be kept a central part of the debate. I expect biotech products will eventually become a major dimension of agricultural productivity. They clearly have the greatest potential value in the developing world, especially in resource-constrained environments such as arid regions, high altitudes and parts of the tropics. If market rules permit a private-sector, developed-nation monopoly of biotech products, the gap between rich and poor nations will grow even larger. National security and economic interests of both the developed and the developing world are endangered by a growing chasm between rich and poor. This cannot be allowed to continue, if a stable, food-secure world is ever to be attained (Runge and Senauer, 2000). Interdependence now leaves all nations too vulnerable.

Biological innovations, especially biotech, must be available as a publicly provided good in the developing world (Harl, 1999; Stiglitz, 1999). How to finance this on a scale needed for success has not, to my knowledge, been seriously addressed. Both governments and private sector leadership in highly developed nations have a major responsibility to help organize and finance biotech capacities in those developing nations willing to make a serious commitment themselves. Those who today argue that markets alone can deal with this problem are wrong. They are ignoring the challenge in agricultural development faced by the poorest nations and by smaller-scale farms in a capital-intensive industry. Also 'minor crops' important in developing nations present a classic problem where the returns on private research investment in such small markets are limited relative to the investment costs and associated risk. The public sector also faces serious limitations in dealing with this challenge. One potential solution can be found today in various kinds of public–private partnerships now under way in a few low-income, developing countries. Several donor nations are committed to this initiative (Horstkotte-Wesseler and Byerlee, 1999; Lewis, 2000). Partnerships are highly varied combinations of national agricultural research systems, universities, donors and private firms. For the long term it is especially important to develop capacity for biotech collaboration between universities and national research systems in low-income, developing nations.

Eventually, the rate of innovation in biotech should be very high, since the developing knowledge base is so fundamental to the entire plant and animal kingdoms. If this occurs, many genetic inventions may have limited lives of proprietary value. The rate of biotech invention will certainly proceed far faster than has that of traditional breeding. If the commercial value of many plant biotech products erodes within a few years, it may then be possible to provide them as public or low-priced goods in low-income, developing nations.

The growing practice of patenting genes, not only by private but by public sector organizations, raises questions about the ability to maintain biotech products as broadly accessible, low-cost products. Public research organizations face a dilemma. If they fail to patent their biological innovations, private sector firms may expropriate public innovations in their private patents. This behaviour by firms could endanger the long, highly productive, tradition of public support for agricultural research. Even when public research organizations patent their discoveries, there is still a complex problem of market development and distribution for which the public sector has limited capacity. This dilemma has caused the International Wheat and Maize Improvement Centre in Mexico to begin patenting their genetic innovations as a defensive strategy to protect their broader availability to poor farmers (*New York Times*, 2000). How well this will work is uncertain, since implementation clearly requires new protocols and institutions including expansion of public–private collaboration. This is a major institutional challenge.

In the USA, many public universities are systematically patenting all research results with commercial potential, not to protect a public good, but simply for the income generated. This practice threatens to subvert the intellectual independence, integrity, incentive structure, culture and purpose of public universities. Involved is a complex issue including long-term decline in public funding and competition with private universities.

Assuring a substantial flow of publicly provided germ plasm and biotech innovations into the market would help restrain market power. If this is to be achieved, publicly financed national agricultural research and development must resist the trend towards privatization. Biotech R&D began as a public sector investment, but is now predominantly a private sector enterprise. The financing of national R&D and that of the CGIAR system of international research centres urgently needs to be greatly expanded and efforts better coordinated in providing some of the global public goods needed in agricultural development. CGIAR investment in biotech is less than 10 per cent of its current budget (Serageldin, 2000). Without improved agricultural productivity, national economic development eventually stalls in a low-income, developing nation (Anderson, 1987; D.G. Johnson, 2000).

New opportunities, constraints and choices

Thus there are a number of constraints to be faced in exploiting the opportunities that arise out of the characteristics of agricultural biotechnology in global markets. First is the uncertainty over whether some biotech food products pose high risks to consumer health and endanger the ecosystem and the environment when the public does not understand the difference between transgenic and non-transgenic biotech. Second, rising income elasticity of the demand for food safety and environmental quality ensures that the demand for these characteristics will grow faster than the demand for food, especially in developed countries. Third, the new information technologies reduce transaction costs and thus the cost of creating and operating an organization. This now permits many more interests to organize an effective political voice in decisions on biotech. Fourth, the cost structure of the biotech industry will concentrate market power in an industry that is dominated by developed nations. This threatens to widen the gap between rich and poor nations, if developing nations are denied access to biotech products by high proprietary prices and the developed nations fail to invest in public-good biotech products for the location-specific needs of developing nations. Fifth, in many low-income nations, there is also a lack of capacity to gain access to biotechnology and its supporting scientific institutions and skills. Without the access to biotech, most of these nations have little chance of escaping a permanent state of low productivity and human welfare – falling even further behind the developed nations. Sixth, chronic underinvestment in public agricultural research persists because of the high spillover of benefits from national R&D programmes and of donor fatigue and other problems now plaguing the CGIAR research system. Finally, the large volume and political sensitivity of global trade in food and farm inputs make biotech constraints not just national, but international, issues.

It is uncertain whether, and in what form, these constraints on biotech can be overcome to realize the potential benefits. My guess is that, in the short run, biotech will slow, but ultimately add to, the movement towards international economic integration. The outcome depends on the strength of leadership and the conclusion about biotech risks. In the long run, if benefits relative to risks are within a socially acceptable range for many countries, the rest of the world is likely to be forced to join in biotech product use – or fall behind in development.

Biotech has the greatest value in the developing world. Agricultural economists must keep the developing world's stake in biotech a central part of the debate. If we fail, the gap between the rich and poor nations will grow. In an increasingly interdependent world, the political and economic security of both the developing and developed nations will be endangered.

Clearly, biotech funding and scientific capacity must be increased in developing nations and biotech R&D must be a publicly provided good, or nearly so. Biotech products must be available at prices well below developed nation proprietary prices. The market alone will not solve this problem. We need complex public–private partnerships involving national research systems, donors, universities and private firms. Some pioneering efforts are under way.

The opportunities and constraints in crop production are generally location-specific. Most plant biotech products created for use in developed nations will not be immediately useful in many low-income nations. The adaptation of basic biotech knowledge for use in low-income nations is a logical role for the CGIAR research centres, and for donor nation development projects, especially working in public–private partnerships in individual countries. There is a complex property right, patenting puzzle here that we need to work on.

Rodrik's trilemma

While it is too early in the development of biotechnology to foresee its full implications and pervasiveness, clearly its safe and effective implementation will require international standards and regulation. Thus exploiting the opportunities in biotechnology and global markets pushes one towards international integration of national economies, international regulation of markets and, ultimately, towards an international system of governance. In this situation, one will be forced, step by step, to relinquish more of the nation's control of policy and to deal with a broader array of participants and conflict in policy making. Here again, this must be managed well politically, or one faces the risk of a backlash of nationalistic and extremist movements, including populist and nativist political forces that could stall or derail the movement towards international integration of national economies and markets.

THE GOVERNANCE OF AGRICULTURE[8]

Governance grows more complex

The problem of governance at all levels has grown more complex, politically and technically. International economic integration and the revolution in information technologies are making national governments more dependent on international agreements. At the same time, governments are having greater difficulty reaching agreement and enforcing resulting policy rules. The transaction costs of governance are increasing.[9] It is at the international level that transaction costs present the greatest challenge to the design and maintenance of governance institutions.

International treaties are no longer just the product of negotiations between sovereign nations. A heterogeneous and growing number of national and multinational economic and civil society political interests have organized. They now intervene in national policy making, in international treaty making and with various international governance structures, such as the IMF, World Bank, the WTO and even the CGIAR. These range from commercial market interest groups, animal welfare groups, labour organizations, human rights and anti-poverty advocates, environmental groups and multinational corporations to anti-globalization advocates, anarchists and others – all competing to create, shape or destroy the international institutions of governance necessary for an orderly world. Within open, fully enfranchised democratic societies this is a legitimate form of public voice, but if policy makers are unable to ignore the pressure of interests that conflict directly with the state's clearly committed policies, the state is less than sovereign in its powers.[10]

Political transaction costs of governance

The new information technologies have reduced the costs of economic transactions. Lower economic transaction costs, in turn, make it easier and less costly to create and manage political action groups. This increases the potential number of policy participants and gives individuals and groups greater political access and policy voice, locally, nationally and internationally. The resulting proliferation in the number and reach of privately organized political voices raises the political transaction costs of negotiating and implementing policy decisions. It fragments, disorders and flattens the traditional hierarchical structure of political institutions within which public policy has been made in the past.

Some organized interests make major contributions to the balance and stability of international agreements, and to their enforcement, especially when nations fail to address international externalities or problems of the 'commons'. Some others are uninformed or destructive.

As nations move towards more open and democratic political institutions that are accessible to all organized political interests, politicians and political institutions face the necessity of managing ever-larger political transaction costs (Olson, 1965; Buchanan and Tullock, 1962). Political transaction costs can increase to the point that some important issues cannot be addressed at all. Others, if considered, lead to highly conflicted, poorly informed decisions. We have already reached this point in many developed nations. At the national level this leads well-organized interests to bypass the legislative and executive institutions of policy formation. With increasing frequency, such interests find it most effective and cost-efficient to pursue their policy goals in the courts, and through campaigns to rally public opinion in highly visible public confron- tations (or threats of such) with the regulatory agencies or private firms whose behaviour they wish to modify. Policy making and politics that bypass tradi- tional political institutions leave policy formation and democratic accountability problematic and uncertain.

Today, we face new issues and economic characteristics as we enter a new era of even greater international interdependence of markets and national econo- mies. Rising income levels cause developed nations' consumer food preferences to grow ever more diverse. The food industry responds by designing new food products for specific preferences. Non-food uses for farm products grow. The potential export market for developing nations expands. Biotechnology now has the ability to create products 'designed' to fit new preferences. In the process, the homogeneous bulk product markets of agriculture fragment. Mar- ket fragmentation eventually leads to such a diversity of interests and such a high level of political transaction costs that it becomes impossible to negotiate, or even conceive of, a single, well-integrated legislative vehicle for national agricultural policy. Eventually, we are likely to be left with such diverse characteristics that both domestic and international agricultural policies, and the agricultural policy process itself, will break into many different pieces.

The structure of institutions for the international governance of agriculture are almost certain to become much more segmented, if not fragmented. Re- source-limited developing nations will face even greater difficulty than they do now in dealing with the international institutions of governance (Bonnen and Schweikhardt, 1998).[11]

The changing politics of multinational negotiations

A different political chemistry and balance is evolving in multinational nego- tiations. Developing countries are no longer willing to accept multilateral rules imposed by developed countries to achieve developed-country goals. This is especially clear in trade negotiations. The great increase in GATT–WTO par- ticipants, not only of governments but of advocacy and interest groups, does not bode well for the transaction costs of the current round of negotiations. Over 130 nations now participate in the WTO, not the 20 of the first round, or the 85 at the beginning of the previous, Uruguay Round. Most of the new participants are low-income, developing nations whose future depends signifi- cantly on what happens in agricultural trade and finance. A rapidly evolving East Asian bloc of nations may add a strong voice as a third force. If recent Asian country regional negotiations are any indication, financial market inte- gration may now be more important to developing nations than trade. Indeed, problems of phytosanitary rules, e-commerce rules, human rights and rules for labour and employment conditions have become more important issues facing multinational negotiations than tariff barriers. Past trade negotiations have been dominated by US versus European issues. In three-way negotiations, the dynamics and outcomes of multinational negotiations are sure to differ from the past, especially if current GATT–WTO decision rules remain in force.

The poverty of developing nations as a drag on developed nation growth

Today, we shall either develop together in an integrated market regime or fall well short of our potential economic capacities. Indeed, some argue that the primary justification for pursuing global market development is to reduce poverty and close the growing gap in human welfare within countries and between developed and developing countries.

In developed countries, economists must help their leadership, in both public and private sectors, to recognize their dependence for political stability and growth on the achievement of higher incomes and reduction of poverty in the developing world. Developing country economists must help their leadership to understand that corruption, disorder, direct government control of markets and the lack of market standards (rules) and enforceable property rights limit development and undermine the potential for growth and the collaboration that both developed and developing countries need. Developed nations still face a few of these problems, including maintaining discriminatory barriers to trade in agricultural markets. Compromise must still be reached on differences in national interest, but the glittering corpse of mercantilism still leads some to view international trade and finance rules as a zero-sum game – which they cannot be, if we are to achieve the potential in growth we all desire, in both developed and developing nations.

Concentration of market power

A rapidly developing problem of concentrated market power in world agriculture can undermine rural economies and discriminate against price-taking farmers. Despite complaints of a lack of access to capital, the industrialization of the food system continues apace. The structure of the food system is changing. A worldwide merger movement, taking advantage of new technologies and growing global markets, is restructuring and concentrating both farm input and farm product markets. In most industrial countries national and multinational retail food firms are, through vertical integration or contractual coordination, reaching back from the retail to the farm level to control product specifications, contractual conditions, risk and timing. In commodities where vertical coordination via contracting is prevalent, farms producing, for example, poultry, hogs or specialized niche market crops will often face only one effective buyer within their marketing reach. Commercial farm input sectors have long been concentrated. Many international markets are dominated by large developed nation firms. As in the past, concentration raises issues about the regulation of market structure and behaviour or governance of the sector – issues that now urgently need research attention and intelligent policy advice.

When independent farmers, who are competitive price takers, face monopoly power, farmers lose. Farm prices and costs squeeze the farmer, and farm asset values decline. This is both an economic and a political problem. The traditional response has been farmer cooperative organizations or national anti-monopoly legislation. But these are world markets, not just national ones, that are becoming concentrated. National cooperatives have not usually offset monopoly power. Multinational, farmer-controlled cooperatives, if comprehensive and well run, might have an impact. Maintaining reasonably competitive world markets is necessary for efficient use of resources, but it is equally necessary for fairness to consumers and farmers who have little organized market power. This problem may give rise to pressures for international regulation. The current growth of market power in farm inputs is primarily based on control of innovations in agricultural research and development, especially in germ plasm and biotech applications.

Globalization of externalities

Externalities become globalized along with the markets in which they occur. Environmental and ecosystem effects of private and public economic activity constitute perhaps the most pervasive negative externality creating policy conflicts today. Earlier we described the problem of chronic underinvestment in agricultural research caused by the spillover of benefits from national research investments. Significant third-party losses can arise in agricultural markets from domestic production subsidies and from bilateral and regional trade agreements. Domestic subsidies for one sector almost always create a tax on the exports of other sectors.

The simultaneous growth of economic inequality within and between countries, great poverty in low-income developing nations and the increased mobility of people and their knowledge of economic disparities has led, along with civil disorder and war, to large human migrations from disadvantaged and disturbed regions to prosperous and advantaged areas and nations. Rural areas and agricultural and natural resource industries are often profoundly affected at both ends of a migration. Understanding and managing the complex economic and political consequences of widening inequality and migration present a serious challenge in many regions of the world.

Many other international externalities exist. If these become significant problems, the only solution involves internationally negotiated agreements, which again push one towards international economic integration of national economies, with a residual choice between national sovereignty and mass politics.

What of the future of global economic integration?

Our era is not the first time the world has experienced global integration of commodity and financial markets. World trade and financial markets were far more open during the latter part of the nineteenth century until the cataclysm of the First World War and Great Depression (O'Rourke and Williamson, 1998). This could happen again, with even more destructive results, if strong and informed leadership is not forthcoming (Gilpin, 2000).

International economic integration is not inevitable. The Seattle WTO disaster and the recent World Bank–IMF meeting disturbances should warn everyone of that. Seattle may have been a civil disaster in the streets, but the WTO meeting itself was a fiasco. Without access to global finance, commodity and service markets, much of the developing world is likely to be condemned to slow growth at best and stagnation in those cases where there is poor leadership or a grossly inadequate base of human and natural resources.

Negative reactions to global markets and to the new information and biological technologies should not have been a surprise. Historically, revolutionary change has been followed by counter-revolutions to overturn the original revolution or modify and reshape its perceived excesses. Nineteenth-century global markets started to unravel in a political backlash to the distributional effects of globalization well before the First World War and the Great Depression. Today, a backlash is growing and critics cannot be ignored or shouted down. This profession has a responsibility to address the substantive market and non-market distributional issues in agriculture.

Some economic and political interests argue today that, because of international competition, a nation cannot afford the cost of a significant social safety net for those who are left behind in international economic integration, whether owing to job displacement, inadequate education and skills or even major loss of political influence. They are quite wrong. First, historically we know that failure to provide an adequate social safety net for those who are losers in international integration of national economies has led eventually to a political reaction that can undermine the institutions of international economic integration (Williamson, 1998; Gilpin, 2000). Second, empirical evidence shows that the nations with the greatest exposure to international markets are now also the nations with the largest percentage of the national budget spent on a social safety net (Rodrik, 1997). If international integration of national economies continues to be a common goal, we must pay close attention to the social investments necessary to maintain the welfare of those groups which see themselves injured by technological change and international economic integration.[12]

Markets and government constitute an unavoidable nexus. The issue is not a question of one versus the other. It is one of achieving an appropriate combination and the complementarity of their different roles within the economics, culture and historical experience of a specific country. Ideology aside, what now complicates any decision on the appropriate balance between public and private regulation of markets is the large reduction of economic transaction costs and the growing importance of information as an economic good in the new information and service-based sectors. The markets for and the economics of information, as we know, differ greatly from those of homogeneous physical commodities. As a consequence, once again we are struggling to determine which activities should now be a private function, a public function, or some complementary mix. This is both an economic and a political question.

Rodrik's trilemma and governance

On balance, at this point, I believe the constraints and pressures on governance will continue pushing us towards international integration of national economies and towards participatory politics internationally, and thus away from the sovereignty of nations. The continuing decline in the costs of time and space push us in this direction. We have reviewed the many pressures on governance that require international cooperation, regulation and institutions of implementation. These interact with the new information and communication technologies that empower many new internationally active social and economic advocates and interests. If you wish for internationally integrated national economies with an unrestricted domain of politics, then you must cede some of the sovereign authority of the nation state to institutions of international governance – ultimately, perhaps, a federation in form.

The European Union now faces this dilemma. We may all face it eventually. It appears to have led German Foreign Minister Joschka Fischer to suggest that the EU explore the issues of federation. Federation implies unified executive, legislative and judicial functions. Today's European nations would then become subnational units of a federal government, just as the original, newly independent, American colonies did after ratifying the US Constitution. Achieving a highly integrated world economy will come at a high price to existing institutions of governance. Success in getting there will involve decades of effort. This process is obviously problematic, with significant economic and political consequences that must be considered carefully. One can envision politically unstable outcomes and failure. In any case, absolute sovereignty is an illusion in a world that grows steadily more interdependent as a result of technological change alone.

If international economic integration begins to unravel, we will pay a high immediate price in lost economic welfare and in long-run economic growth. In addition, it is difficult to see how one can ever get the social and economic interests now operating at many national levels and at international levels back into the bottle of national sovereignty.

It has to be remembered that politics is not invariably subject to the rule of reasoned interest. Emotion without the anchor of pragmatic and informed reason can drive contentious issues. In addition, history is filled with sudden disruptive events that re-order economic incentive, national interest and balances of power. Thus great care in political management and strong, informed political leadership are still required. We must contribute to this effort.

CONCLUSION: MAJOR CHALLENGES FOR THE PROFESSION

We are entering a period of fundamental disruption and transformation of the world economy and society on a scale approaching that of the industrial revolution of the 19th and early 20th centuries. For our profession this is a research, teaching and policy challenge perhaps unmatched since Ted Schultz and others of the pioneering generation of agricultural economists struggled with the transformation of the world around them in the early decades of the 20th century. They worked to understand and adapt the forces of the industrial revolution to the needs of human beings in agriculture and society at large. The existence of our profession and, indeed, of this association is a monument to their success. I believe we face a challenge of similar scale today.

Although this profession has significant and growing international capabilities, our problems are becoming even more intensely global. It follows that agricultural economists should greatly increase their international collaboration in teaching and research and in extending their research and policy analysis. Building on existing efforts, I believe this Association could make a great contribution working with its affiliated national organizations to expand the profession's international capability. Greater interactive linkages with cooperative institutions, including government ministries, foundations, other social and natural sciences, and even some social and economic interest organizations are needed to extend our capacity to help deal with global and regional challenges. The form of such cooperative institutions will depend on the nature of the problems they address.

Our profession has long had a critical role informing the decisions that adapt new technologies to human use. In agriculture, food, natural resource use and the environment today, agricultural economists are responsible for providing an understanding of the economic problems faced, the choices available and their consequences. We have a theoretical framework capable of helping to inform choices, including those that involve conflicting human values and institutions. We should focus much of our economic and policy analysis on the most important forces of change. This begins with the impact of information technologies and biotechnology, but extends to many other complementary emerging technological changes, institutions and human and physical capital, the importance of which will vary by region and country. Even the worldwide impact of global markets will vary by country. We must put our policy analyses and advice within the specific contexts in which policy makers work and in a form they can understand and respect, if we are to have any real impact on the future. More of us have to become involved in combat over policy and institution building.

A growing international need now exists for publicly provided information, products and services and for the creation of new institutions and new human capital. This may be the single most urgent, long-term problem for agriculture, the food system, food safety and the environment. What new institutions and human capacities are needed, and for what purpose? How should they function? How should authority be distributed? How should they relate to the private and public sectors? How and to whom should they be accountable? These are both disciplinary and applied subject matter questions that fall within the domain of the social sciences. In agriculture, they are a challenge for our profession (Ruttan, 1984). It is important that we do our work and introduce the results well ahead of the political debate so that our analysis is absorbed and seen as useful, non-partisan information and is not instantly politicized by policy conflict.

When the world economy and agriculture begin to change as fundamentally as at present, our current professional capacity grows obsolescent. That is, the concepts, databases and analytical modes by which we comprehend the world begin to lose relevance. New problems arise that require more data and analysis – and integration with other databases and analytical modes. We now face a growing need to rebuild and extend the information base for research and policy decision. Without this intellectual investment we shall slowly lose professional capacity and social relevance. Trade, development, environmental and other economists have been struggling with this problem for several decades in agriculture. But the problem is rapidly getting worse. The international integration of relevant databases and the development of international statistical standards are needed now, if we are to deal with the policy conflicts that lie ahead. In this arena international collaboration is absolutely necessary, if the data for policy purposes are to be assembled from both public and private sources.

Governance issues and choices involve choosing who wins and who loses rights. This is always risky terrain. But we must plunge in, if we wish to have any impact on the choices made. This involves redistribution, which is a political and moral, not just an economic, decision. Redistribution, in turn, involves interpersonal comparisons, which we as economists are typically trained to avoid, since such political judgments can endanger the objectivity of economics. Nevertheless, some of our leadership must participate in these decisions, if the profession's knowledge base is effectively to inform policy for agriculture.

The profession's experience in development has demonstrated time after time that investment in non-market redistributions is necessary before the market can work to capacity. This is especially clear in the early stages of development and in the midst of revolutionary change. It will be the case for any successful introduction of biotech or information technologies in developing nations. The market alone is not able to extract the full potential of a developmental innovation without non-market redistributive investments in some set of initial complements, whether in technology, human capital, institutions or biophysical capital. Some of these will be non-market redistributions, since the return to whoever pays for the needed complement will be less than their 'donation'. Returns to those who subsidize non-market redistributions, if any, are secondary, diffuse and long-run.

We must recognize that some of the greatest advances in human welfare over the past century have been the product of redistributions of rights: for example, anti-slavery laws, emancipation of women and universal suffrage. Many nations have adopted universal primary and secondary education, national public health systems and public higher education. One large, predominantly non-market, redistribution challenge lies directly in our path: world poverty and its ills.

More of the profession's leadership must participate directly in these policy debates at national and international levels, whether redistributive or not. We must as a profession be prepared, as Ted Schultz was, to speak for those without voice in agriculture as well as to puncture the rhetoric of economic nonsense. Our role is to inform policy makers and policy decisions, by defining problems clearly and more completely, and by developing policy and other institutional alternatives. Some of us must play an advocate's role for stakeholders and for relevant ideas that lack a voice in the policy process, much as did some of the pioneering generation when they too faced a fundamental transformation of agriculture and its environment.

NOTES

[1]Also see the oral history interview of C.A. Bonnen in Hopkin and Durden (1985), Appendix D.

[2]These economic characteristics include the price elasticity of aggregate demand for farm products; the income elasticity of the demand for farm products; the market structure of the farm sector with farmers acting as price takers; the price elasticity of the supply of farm output; the rate of technological change in the farm sector; the degree of asset fixity – or asset specificity – that may affect the ability of the agricultural sector to adjust its output in response to changing prices; the share of total population engaged in agricultural production; the share of consumers' income spent on food; and the population growth rate (Anderson, 1987; Anderson and Hayami, 1986; Bonnen and Schweikhardt, 1998; Schweikhardt, 2000).

[3]In addition to the references cited elsewhere in this paper, a sense of the nature and complexity of the evolving political economy can also be usefully explored in a number of additional sources: Bonnen *et al.* (1997); Cable (1999); Cohen (1998); Creveld (1999); Guéhenno (1995); Hammond (1998); Held *et al.* (1999); Helliwell (1998); Joffe (1999); Kahn (1996); Keohane and Nye (1998); Mathews (1997); Ohmae (1995); Strange (1996); Weiss (1998).

[4]One needs to be clear about several terms used here. An ideologue is to be distinguished from an ideology. Ideology refers to any system of beliefs. Belief systems and all policy decisions involve value judgments and arise out of prescriptive (or proscriptive) conclusions about the right (or wrong) action to take. Any prescription (proscription) to act combines factual beliefs (about what is true or false) with value beliefs (about what is good or bad), which are then constrained and legitimized by the rules, laws and customs of society. There are rational belief systems and less than rational (or non-rational) belief systems. Those who are rational will submit their beliefs to (and accept the results of) such tests as those of (a) correspondence with observed reality, (b) logical coherence as a system of beliefs and (c) sufficient clarity (lack of ambiguity) to make tests of correspondence and coherence possible. Those who persist in adherence to belief systems despite substantial, if not overwhelming, evidence that their beliefs fail these tests are 'true believers' or ideologues. The belief system of an ideologue is impervious, not only to tests of factual validity, but to the relevance of any other system of belief. These, of course, are the extreme ends of a distribution with a confounded middle ground dominated by incomplete information and uncertainty.

[5]Tinbergen's work is widely recognized for its application to macroeconomic policy, but he applied these same principles to a wide range of policy issues, including the choice of targets and instruments in agricultural policy. Tinbergen examined the necessity of making a simultaneous choice of domestic price policies and border policies in agriculture and the simultaneous choice of income stabilization and production regulation in agriculture. The characteristics that Tinbergen identified as affecting the efficiency of any policy instrument in agriculture are nearly identical to the fundamental characteristics of the agricultural sector defined in note 2.

[6]Thomas Friedman has referred to the inevitable tensions between integration, national sovereignty, and mass politics as the 'Golden Straitjacket' that limits the discretion of government. 'As your country puts on the Golden Straitjacket, two things tend to happen: Your economy grows and your politics shrinks ... [The] Golden Straitjacket narrows the political and economic policy choices of those in power to relatively tight parameters. That is why it is increasingly difficult these days to find any real differences between ruling and opposition parties in those countries that have put on the Golden Straitjacket' (Friedman, 1999, p.87). In reality, some dimensions of the power of decision are always constrained. Despite supernationalists, sovereignty is never absolute and declines as the world becomes smaller in cost of time and space, and thus more interdependent (Krasner, 1999).

[7]Transaction costs include the ex ante and ex post costs of analysing, negotiating and implementing decisions (Williamson, 1985, p.21). At this point the single, most accessible, overview of the economics of information from an applied policy point of view can be found in Shapiro and Varian (1999). It will not provide the rigour a theorist needs but its breadth and many case examples make it an excellent introduction for policy. See Lamberton (1996) for a volume of readings that lead to many of the contributions to the theory and application of the economics of information, communication and computation. Lamberton's introduction provides a brief overview of the conceptual evolution of the theory base. On the economics of information in a global public good context, see Stiglitz (1999) and also Kaul *et al.* (1999).

[8]A system of governance consists of the institutions, including laws, standards and customs, through which authority is exercised to control, direct or order the conduct of a sector or the totality of a society. Robin Johnson's excellent analysis of 'The Role of Institutions in Policy Formation and Delivery' in this volume is a comprehensive treatment of the concept and role of institutions.

[9]The role of transaction costs in the design and maintenance of the institutions of governance has been explored by Williamson (1996). In his Munich lectures, Dixit (1998) examines the role of political transaction costs in economic policy making.

[10]Chapter 10, 'Globalization and its Discontents' of Gilpin (2000) provides a brief description and a thoughtful assessment of the different pro-globalization and anti-globalization positions.

[11]President Hedley and I have focused on changes in governance at very different levels, but we have come to similar, if not completely parallel, conclusions. His 'horizontality' and increased 'complexity' are, I believe, different descriptors for what I have described as the fragmentation of the structures of governance caused by the prior fragmentation of economic and social interests and the growth of political transaction costs over the process of development. Hedley is surely correct that this leads to a 'declining coherence in objectives that puts institutions at risk'. In 'citizen engagement' he describes, as I do, the current proliferation and fragmentation of interests, but he goes on to identify its dangers and disturbing consequences as civil society's conflicting interests intervene directly in the policy decision process.

[12]Williamson (1998) examined this question from an historical perspective for the major Atlantic nations during the industrial revolution of the 19th and early 20th centuries. Rodrik (1997, 2000) approaches it with an empirical (statistical) analysis of a cross-section of 21 developed nations in 1980. Little of this is news to economic historians. There are many parallels between today's revolutionary changes and those of the early British industrial revolution. Some of these can be seen in T.H. Ashton's 1948 classic, *The Industrial Revolution* (see especially pp.88–9, 104–9, 138–41). Other examples can be found in Sir Arthur Lewis's 1978 lectures, *The Evolution of the International Economic Order*, which explore the question why some nations developed and others lagged behind in 19th and 20th century industrial development.

REFERENCES

Anderson, K. (1987), 'On Why Agriculture Declines With Economic Growth', *Agricultural Economics*, **1**, 195–207.

Anderson, K. and Hayami, Y. (1986), *The Political Economy of Agricultural Protection: East Asia in International Perspective*, Sydney: Allen and Unwin.

Ashton, T.H. (1948), *The Industrial Revolution: 1760–1830*, London: Oxford University Press.

Bonnen, J.T. and Schweikhardt, D.B. (1998), 'The Future of U.S. Agriculture Policy: Reflections on the Disappearance of the "Farm Problem"', *Review of Agricultural Economics*, **20**, 2–36.

Bonnen, J.T., Hedley, D.D. and Schweikhardt, D.B. (1997), 'Agriculture and the Changing Nation-state: Implications for Policy and Political Economy', *American Journal of Agricultural Economics*, **78**, 1419–28.

Buchanan, J.M. and Tullock, G. (1962), *The Calculus of Consent*, Ann Arbor, MI: University of Michigan Press.

Byerlee, D. (2000), personal communication.

Cable, V. (1999), *Globalization and Global Governance*, London: Royal Institute of International Affairs.

Cohen, D. (1998), *The Wealth of the World and the Poverty of Nations*, Cambridge, MA: MIT Press.

Creveld, M.V. (1999), *The Rise and Decline of the State*, Cambridge: Cambridge University Press.

Dixit, A.K. (1998), *The Making of Economic Policy: A Transaction-cost Politics Perspective*, Cambridge, MA: MIT Press.

Fox, K.A. and Thorbecke, E. (1965), 'Specification and Data Requirements in Policy Models', in B.G. Hickman (ed.), *Quantitative Planning of Economic Policy*, Washington, DC: Brookings Institution, pp.43–86.

Friedman, T.L. (1999), *The Lexus and the Olive Tree: Understanding Globalization*, New York: Farrar, Straus and Giroux.

Gilpin, R. (2000), *The Challenge of Global Capitalism: The World Economy in the 21st Century*, Princeton, NJ: Princeton University Press.

Gordon, R.J. (1999), 'U.S. Economic Growth Since 1860: One Big Wave?', *American Economic Review*, **89**,123–8.

Guéhenno, J.M. (1995), *The End of the Nation-state*, Minneapolis: University of Minnesota Press.

Hammond A. (1998), *Which World?: Scenarios for the 21st Century*, Washington, DC: Island Press.

Harl, N.E. (1999), 'The Age of Contract Agriculture: Consequences of Concentration in Input Supply', paper presented at the National Symposium on the Future of American Agriculture, University of Georgia, Athens, 25–7 August.

Held, D., McGrew A., Goldblatt, D. and Perriton, J. (1999), *Global Transformations: Politics, Economics and Culture*, Stanford, CA: Stanford University Press.

Helliwell, J.F. (1998), How *Much Do National Borders Matter?*, Washington, DC: Brookings Institution Press.

Hopkin, J.A. and Durden, K.S. (1985), *Agricultural Economics, Its History and Development at Texas A&M University Through 1983*, College Station, Texas: Department of Agricultural Economics.

. Horstkotte-Wesseler, G. and Byerlee, D. (1999), 'Agricultural Biotechnology and the Poor: The Role of Development Assistance Agencies', paper presented at the Conference on Agricultural Technology in Developing Countries: Towards Optimizing the Benefits for the Poor, University of Bonn, Germany, 15–16 November.

Joffe, J. (1999), 'Rethinking the Nation-state: The Many Meanings of Sovereignty', *Foreign Affairs*, **78**,122–7.

Johnson, D.G. (2000), 'Population, Food and Knowledge', *American Economic Review*, **90**, 1–14.

Johnson, G.L. (1997), 'Doing Policy Work', in A.A. Schmid, (ed.), *Beyond Agriculture and Economics*, East Lansing, MI: Michigan State University, pp.157–68.

Jorgenson, D.W. and Stiroh, K.J. (1999), 'Information Technology and Growth', *American Economic Review*, **89**, 109–15.

Kahn, L.A. (1996), *The Extinction of Nation-states: A World Without Borders*, The Hague: Kluwer Law International.

Kaul, I., Grunberg, I. and Stern, M.A. (1999), 'Defining Global Public Goods', in I. Kaul, I. Grunberg and M.A. Stern (eds), *Global Public Goods*, New York: Oxford University Press.

Keohane, R.O. and Nye, Jr, J.S. (1998), 'Power and Interdependence in the Information Age', *Foreign Affairs*, **77**, 83–94.

Krasner, S.D. (1999), *Sovereignty: Organized Hypocrisy*, Princeton: Princeton University Press.

Lamberton, D.N. (ed.) (1996), *The Economics of Communication and Information*, Cheltenham, UK and Brookfield, US: Edward Elgar.

Lewis, J. (2000), 'Leveraging Partnerships Between the Public and Private Sector: Experience of USAID's Agricultural Biotechnology Programs', in G.J. Persely and M.M. Lantin (eds), *Agricultural Biotechnology and the Poor: An International Conference on Biotechnology*, Washington, DC: Consultative Group on International Agricultural Research.

Lewis, W.A. (1978), *The Evolution of the International Economic Order*, Princeton: Princeton University Press.

Mathews, J.T. (1997), 'Power Shift', *Foreign Affairs*, **76**, 50–66.

New York Times (2000), 'The Slippery Slope of Patenting Farmers Crops', Wednesday, 24 May, p.A-4.

Obstfeld, M. and Taylor, A.M. (1998), 'The Great Depression as a Watershed: International Capital Mobility over the Long Run', in M.D. Bordo, C. Goldin and E.N. White (eds), *The Defining Moment: The Great Depression and the American Economy in the Twentieth Century*, Chicago: University of Chicago Press.

Ohmae, M. (1995), *The End of the Nation-state: The Rise of Regional Economies*, New York: Free Press.

Olson, M. (1965), *The Logic of Collective Action*, Cambridge, MA: Harvard University Press.

O'Rourke. K.H., and Williamson, J.G. (1998), *Globalization and History: The Evolution of the 19th Century Atlantic Economy*, Cambridge, MA: MIT Press.

Rausser, G.C. (1999), 'Public/Private Research: Knowledge Assets and Future Scenarios', *American Journal of Agricultural Economics*, **81**, 1011–27.

Rodrik, D. (1997), 'Sense and Nonsense in the Globalization Debate', *Foreign Policy*, **76**, 19–37.

Rodrik, D. (2000), 'How Far Will International Economic Integration Go?', *Journal of Economic Perspectives*, **14**, 177–86.

Runge, C.F. and Senauer, B. (2000), 'A Removable Feast', *Foreign Affairs*, **79**,39–51.

Ruttan. V.W. (1984), 'Social Science Knowledge and Institutional Change', *American Journal of Agricultural Economics*, **66**, 549–59.

Schultz, T.W. (1977), 'On Economics, Agriculture and the Political Economy', in T. Dams and K.E. Hunt (eds), *Decision-Making and Agriculture* (Proceedings of the Sixteenth International Conference of Agricultural Economists), Lincoln, Nebraska: University of Nebraska Press.

Schweikhardt, D.B. (2000), 'Reconsidering the Farm Problem Under an Industrializing Agricultural Sector', *Canadian Journal of Agricultural Economics*, Proceedings Issue, December.

Schweikhardt, D.B. and Bonnen, J.T. (1992), 'Financing Agricultural Research in the Presence of International Benefit Spillovers: The Need for Institutional Coordination and Innovation', in G.H. Peters and B.F. Stanton (eds), *Sustainable Agricultural Development: The Role of International Cooperation* (Proceedings of the Twenty-first Conference of Agricultural Economists), Aldershot, UK: Dartmouth.

Serageldin, J. (2000), 'The Challenge of Poverty in the 21st Century: The Role of Science', in G.J. Persley and M.M. Lantin (eds), *Agricultural Biotechnology and the Poor: An International Conference on Biotechnology*, Washington DC: Consultative Group on International Agricultural Research.

Shapiro, C. and Varian, H.R. (1999), *Information Rules: A Strategic Guide to the Network Economy*, Boston, MA: Harvard Business School Press.

Simon, H. (1971), 'Designing Organizations for an Information-Rich World', in M. Greenberger (ed.), *Computers, Communications and the Public Interest*, Baltimore, MD: Johns Hopkins University Press.

Stiglitz, J.E. (1999), 'Knowledge as a Global Public Good', in I. Kaul, I. Grunberg and M.A. Stern (eds), *Global Public Goods*, New York: Oxford University Press, pp.308–25.

Strange, S. (1996), *The Retreat of the State: The Diffusion of Power in the World Economy*, Cambridge: Cambridge University Press.

Tinbergen, J. (1956), *Economic Policy: Principles and Design*, Amsterdam: North-Holland Publishing.

Weiss, L. (1998), *The Myth of the Powerless State*, Ithaca, NY: Cornell University Press.

Williamson, J.G. (1998), 'Globalization, Labor Markets and Policy Backlash in the Past', *Journal of Economic Perspectives*, **12**, 51–72.

Williamson, O.E. (1985), *The Economic Institutions of Capitalism*, New York: The Free Press.

Williamson, O.E. (1996), *The Mechanisms of Governance*, New York: Oxford University Press.

SECTION I

Globalization of the Food and Agricultural Economy

WALTER P. FALCON*

Globalizing Germ Plasm: Barriers, Benefits and Boundaries

INTRODUCTION

Globalization and liberalization were rallying cries of the 1990s and, as a consequence, the world economic system at the turn of the 21st century is much more open than it was only a decade ago. Yet world agriculture, in many ways, has been a rather stubborn holdout. One particular subsector of agriculture – plant germ plasm – provides a particularly arresting counter-example to globalization. Herdt (1999) has described the consequences of privatization and nationalization of plant genetic materials as the closing of another 'commons', comparable in importance to the closing of the land commons in England between the 15th and 19th centuries.

In this paper, I seek to shed light on the causes and potential consequences of restricted germ plasm flows among nations. My objective is to provide a synthesis of existing literature and an account of several events in which I took part, with a focus on food security in poor countries. My discomforting conclusions are that the mechanisms restricting flows are complicated, the data on the size and direction of flows meagre, the outcomes uncertain and the policy mechanisms for alleviating the problems largely untested. Yet, if the recent institutional innovations highlighted in the final section of this paper can be replicated on a sizeable scale, cautious optimism still seems warranted about the future spread of improved germ plasm.

Following a short historical introduction, I identify four separate forces that are now interacting in ways which should worry everyone concerned with the transfer of technology, particularly improved crop varieties, to scores of the world's poorest nations. These elements are new provisions on intellectual property, especially patenting in the United States; an increased concentration of new enabling technologies into a few large multinational companies; heightened anxieties over transgenic foods, especially in Europe; and new problems arising from old ambiguities in the Convention on Biodiversity. Individually, these components are reasonably well described in the literature. Collectively, however, they are poorly understood and their combined impacts on the poorer countries of the world are very troublesome.

*Stanford University, Stanford, California, USA and International Wheat and Maize Improvement Centre (CIMMYT), Mexico Federal District, Mexico. I am grateful for the helpful comments of Rosamond Naylor, John Barton, Cary Fowler, Timothy Josling, Donald Kennedy, Michael Morris, Anne Peck, Timothy Reeves, Daniel Rochberg and Nikolas Wada.

HISTORICAL CONTEXT

Need for domestic agricultural development

This paper takes as given the projected food security problems of about 70 of the world's poorest countries, many of which are in sub-Saharan Africa (USDA, 1997).[1] These projections also suggest that world cereal demand will rise by about 40 per cent over the next 20 years. Providing enough grain to meet this target will be no simple feat, since this increase will need to be accomplished with less irrigation water and perhaps with less arable land as well (Smil, 2000; Pinstrup-Andersen *et al.*, 1999). Increasing yields by 2 per cent annually is not unprecedented, but it will certainly stretch the human, financial and natural resources of the world, especially if the environment is not to be destroyed in the process.

Increasing 'the global pile of grain' is a daunting necessary condition. But it is by no means sufficient to assure food security among the poor. If developing countries with a large percentage of undernourished people are to solve employment, income and food access problems, most of the increased agricultural output must be grown within the borders of these nations. The first Green Revolution was initially most successful at improving yields in irrigated areas and in regions of favourable rainfall. Some technology remains to be transferred to these areas, but the more serious problems are in regions still subject to drought and flooding, and in countries with little physical and human capital, inadequate policies and a high percentage of the workforce in rural areas. For this set of nations, access to improved germ plasm is one vital component for a successful attack on poverty and hunger.

There are some who argue that increased yields are unimportant for such countries, since the *world* already has 'enough' grain. This argument misses the key linkages at the regional and household levels among increases in food production, growth in per capita incomes and increases in food consumption. Both external technology for and internal knowledge about these agricultural systems will surely be needed. Increasing productivity *and* alleviating poverty are both crucial and very much related. To frame either of the foregoing propositions as 'or' rather than as 'and' questions does not usefully serve those developing countries plagued by serious food security problems.[2]

Changed institutional circumstances

Men and women have been improving plant genetic materials for 10 000 years (Smith, 1998). Both the origins of various crops and appropriate methods for their improvement continue to be sources of controversy. The central issue for this discussion, however, is whether recent developments represent only minor variations in plant improvement processes or rather a fundamental watershed in the scope and methods of plant breeding, especially as they affect poor countries of the world.

Prior to the Second World War, much of the basic and applied seed technology for agriculture, especially for cereals, originated as public goods from the nonproprietary sector. In the USA, for example, land grant universities played key roles in developing germ plasm and then in ensuring that the resulting genetic materials flowed with few restrictions across state and national boundaries.

Hybrid maize was a partial exception to this pattern of public provision of germ plasm: companies typically drew on basic research from the public sector when developing hybrid maize, but they then privatized inbred lines, mostly through the use of trade-secret mechanisms. In 1970, more formal protection was given to the private sector in the USA via the Plant Variety Protection Act. This legislation gave developers of 'distinct, uniform and stable' seeds patent-like protection for 17 years, including the right to set conditions on the sale and resale of seed.[3]

Two mutually reinforcing events occurred during the last quarter of the 20th century that greatly altered the norms of germ plasm development. The first event – really a process – was the development of modern biotechnology, including computational and other laboratory methods for discovering, cloning and transferring separate genes. When these specific methods were combined with the second component – a series of new legal rulings on patenting – the plant genetic environment was radically transformed. In addition, the new biology gave entrepreneurs the scientific methods, such as plant fingerprinting, to detect and enforce patent infringements. New interactions among law, biology and information technology were thus the primary forces that brought about a new institutional setting for germ plasm development and transfer.

PRINCIPAL ELEMENTS OF CHANGE

Moves towards protection and patenting

The protection of intellectual property is long-standing and such protection embraces much more than just patenting. Yet it is patenting (rather than trade secrets, trademarks, plant variety protection or copyrights) in the USA that has caused the most confusion in the plant genetics world during the past two decades. Other countries obviously also have patent offices; however, the scale of the biotechnology industry in the USA, coupled with the large US share of internationally traded agricultural goods, has made the USA the forerunner on intellectual property issues.

The US Patent and Trademark Office (USPTO) works on the principle of 'prior knowledge' in determining whether or not a discovery is 'novel' and 'non-obvious'. When scientific history is long and discoveries are gradual, USPTO is generally regarded as being competent and consistent, although the Office is sometimes accused of having a bias towards new patent applicants (Barton, 2000). When there is a sharp break with past scientific methods, however, USPTO has little prior knowledge on which to build, and questionable decisions occur. Such was the situation following *Diamond* v. *Chakrabarty* (1980), when, on appeal, the US Supreme Court ruled in a five to four vote that a live micro-organism, constructed by gene-transfer technology, was patentable.[4]

Great uncertainties arose with *Chakrabarty* and later decisions as to what was patentable and also how broad or narrow the patent coverage could be. Given this uncertainty, there were understandable pressures for firms to maximize the number of biotechnology patents, and to do so as rapidly as possible – reminding one of speculative land grabs in an earlier era. Initially, the bar on gene claims was perceived to be low, and the number of patent applications exploded during the 1990s (Enserink, 2000).[5] With little prior history, USPTO had great difficulties in implementing the 'utility' aspect of applications; that is, in determining whether or not a new proposal had merit. Although there was widespread scientific agreement that short sections of DNA – sometimes called Expressed Sequence Tags – were too narrow as a basis for patenting, more than a million such claims were filed with USPTO (ibid.).[6] There were equal concerns that patent claims might be unreasonably broad. In a case especially notorious and worrisome to developing nations, the USPTO issued broad protective rights in the USA for a type of yellow bean (*Phaseolus vulgaris*) grown commonly throughout Mexico (Friedland, 2000). The yellow-bean patent also raised the ugly spectre of bio-piracy and the misappropriation of the research products of others.

The USPTO is apparently now in the process of raising the claims bar with respect to 'utility' (Enserink, 2000). Nevertheless, two lasting problems arise from the new patent processes as they affect poor countries. First, thousands of relevant patents have already been issued that affect the 'creation' of modern agricultural germ plasm appropriate for developing countries. Intellectual property coverage includes genes, traits, molecular constructs and transformation procedures – so-called 'enabling technologies'. For important genetic modifications like the new vitamin A-enhanced rice, dozens of patents can be involved in a single transformation (Guerinot, 2000). As discussed below, the multiple-patent problem already affects the industrial structure in the private sector. Multiple patents also effectively force the public sector to use alternative research methods if crucial patents are unavailable for use on products important for poor countries. Second, the fear that 'outsiders' will patent existing products, such as yellow beans, has left national agricultural research systems and the international agricultural research centres in a quandary as to whether or not to employ patenting as a defensive strategy against bio-piracy.

Privatization of research and industrial concentration in the seed industry

The patenting of genes and traits has had a profound effect on both the structure of germ plasm science and on industrial concentration in the seed industry. Leaders of several large firms such as Monsanto and Novartis arguably saw agricultural biotechnology as a mechanism for generating dominant commercial strategies for their companies. Although consumer and stockholder reactions eventually interceded to limit the strategies and to decrease genetically modified organism (GMO) budgets within these companies, there were two early waves of investment activity that reshaped the plant genetics industry.

The first of these waves featured the acquisition of smaller biotech start-ups by large multinational firms that were predominantly focused on agricultural chemicals (Brennan *et al.*, 1999; RAFI, 1998). These mergers and acquisitions were driven primarily by 'freedom to operate' considerations. Companies and many public agencies simply found themselves unable to cope with the economies of scale inherent in certain types of molecular-based research and with their inability to acquire both the expertise and patents needed for cutting-edge research (Brennan *et al.*, 1999).

The second wave involved the acquisition of seed companies, also by the large chemical and pharmaceutical firms. When the latter realized that revenue generation would be difficult if based strictly on technology licences to seed companies, they began acquiring seed firms at a pace so rapid that the name, number and scope of the resulting conglomerates changed almost on a monthly basis. It sometimes appeared as if virtually all firms were simultaneously trying to buy, sell and sue one another! Many of the mergers seemed complete by 1999, only to be followed by another round of reorganization. Under shareholder pressures, several of the mega-firms began to spin off or combine their genetic material and seed units.

Much more could be written about the personalities and purposes behind the various mergers and realignments, and about the several public relations disasters that befell them. However, five important implications derive from the new industrial structure summarized in Table 1. First and foremost, the plant genetics industry is now heavily concentrated in a half-dozen major firms, which also hold substantial numbers of key patents on germ plasm and related enabling technologies such as gene guns (physical devices for injecting DNA through cell walls) and agro-bacterium (*Bacillus thuringiensis* or *Bt*) transformation systems. Second, any research institution, public or private, wishing to use either the seeds or the enabling technology must, as a practical matter, have commercial relationships or alliances with these firms. Third, the control of patents and seed distribution exercised by these companies has substantially increased the barriers to entry for new firms in the field of germ plasm development. The scale of these operations is now enormous: for example, Dupont paid $9.4 billion for just one company, Pioneer, to underpin its seed operation. Fourth, given the profitability needs of these companies, much of their research has been aimed at innovations that can generate linked sales of seeds and chemicals. It was no accident, for example, that two of Monsanto's early seed products, Roundup Ready™ corn and soybeans, were linked to the company's major herbicide. Lastly, the need for private profitability has created many 'orphan' crops and countries; that is, commodities and nations that are simply unprofitable for the private sector to pursue.[7]

Together, these circumstances pose serious difficulties for the poorest countries of the world. Most of these nations have small gross domestic products (GDPs) and rely importantly on non-hybrid or tropical food crops not of principal concern to major plant biotechnology companies. Furthermore, they typically lack the trained scientists needed to gain access to or develop the new technology.

As a consequence, international agencies supplying research products that are public goods face the deepest kinds of questions. What kinds of alliances should the not-for-profit-sector form with the private sector to move key aspects

TABLE 1 *Changing structure of the 'plant genetics' industry (circa June 2000)*

Company	Agricultural Chemicals	Biotech	Seeds
		Purchases	
Monsanto (merged in April 2000 with Pharmacia & Upjohn to create Pharmacia Corp.)		Agracetus Calgene Ecogen (13%) Millennium Pharmaceutical (joint venture for crops genes)	DeKalb Asgrow (corn and soybeans) Holden's Foundation Seeds Delta and Pine Land (deal cancelled by Monsanto) Cargill Int'l Seeds Plant Breeding Int'l
AgrEvo (merged in December 1999 with Rhône-Poulenc to form Aventis)	Hoechst & Schering	Plant Genetic Systems PlantTec	Nunherns Vanderhave Plant Genetic Systems Pioneer Vegetable Genetics Sunseeds Cargill U.S. Seeds
Rhône-Poulenc (merged in December 1999 with AgrEvo to form Aventis)			Alliance with Limagrain which owns Nickersons, Vilmorin, Ferry Morse and others
Novartis (announced in December 1999 plans to spin off Novartis	Ciba-Geigy and Sandoz, merger Merck bought pesticide business		Merger brought together Northrup-King, S&G Seeds, Hilleshog, Ciba Seeds, Rogers Seeds Co.

46

Crop Protection and Seeds to merge with Zeneca Agrochemicals, forming Syngenta)			
AstraZeneca (announced in December 1999 plans to spin off Zeneca Agrochemicals to merge with Novartis Crop Protection and Seeds, forming Syngenta)		Mogen International N.V. Alliance with Japan Tobacco on rice	Advanta (merger of Zeneca seed and Vanderhave)
Dow Chemicals	Dow purchased Eli Lilly's 40% share of Dow Elanco	Mycogen Ribozyme Pharmaceuticals, Inc.	Mycogen bought Agrinetics United AgriSeeds became part of Mycogen
DuPont		Alliances with Human Genome Sciences Curagen	Pioneer Hybrinova
Seminis/Empresas La Moderna		DNA plant technology	Asgrow (sold corn and soybeans to Monsanto) Petoseed Royal Sluis Seminis

47

Source: Modified from RAFI (1998), Brennan *et al.* (1999) and supplemented by numerous stories from the *Wall Street Journal.*

of the technology into crops and countries that otherwise would be left behind? How much financial and human capital should be spent on 'inventing around' patents not easily obtained under favourable licensing terms from the private sector? And should CG centres and other similar agencies simply disregard the ownership of intellectual property if the products or processes are not patented or registered in a particular country?[8]

Transgenic (GMO) controversies

Industrial structure and patents present a formidable set of technology access problems for poor countries. In a less direct, but no less important manner, these nations have been partial victims of transgenic organism battles. Volumes have been written about the controversy surrounding GMOs as they affect Europe and the USA.[9] However, few analyses have been made of the effects of this debate on poor countries.[10]

Most observers recognize that the use of transgenics carries both costs and benefits. There are potential problems, for example, with respect to allergens and also potential negative effects on ecosystems and the goods and services they provide to humans. There are potential benefits as well, such as increased plant resistance to biotic and abiotic stresses (Nelson *et al.*, 1999). Honourable men and women can assess risk–return profiles quite differently across nations and economic classes and, not surprisingly, there have been vigorous debates on the nature of those profiles.

The GMO debate has also featured several other themes. For example, consumer confidence in regulatory agencies appears to be substantially lower in Europe than in the USA, in part because of the European experience with mad cow disease. European consumers seem also to have a keener interest in labelling and in consumers' rights to know than do their US counterparts (Gaskell *et al.*, 1999). Opinions have differed on the regulation process, specifically as to whether it is the research process (for example, transgenic versus classical breeding) or the final agricultural product that should be regulated.[11] More strident parts of the debate have entailed charges and counter-charges over whether GMOs have been used as an excuse to advance protectionism (Nelson *et al.*, 1999).

This paper does not assess the merits of various positions in the GMO debate; rather it emphasizes the effects of that debate on developing country interests. Developing countries are concerned that their interests are being neither sought nor heard in many of the arguments over transgenics.[12] In discussions at CIMMYT, numerous leaders from developing countries have said that they resent having either Americans or Europeans speak for them in arguments over the risk–benefit ratios of transgenics. They also express concern that key research initiatives with biotechnology will not be pursued because of what they perceive to be the private sector's focus on the wrong products, for the wrong reasons, at the wrong time.

Representatives from developing countries have instead pointed out that the development of apomixis – a reproductive trait that would permit the seed of a hybrid plant to be replanted and to retain characteristics identical to those of the mother plant – would be invaluable to them for regions not well served by the commercial seed industry. They also argue that the potential for nutritional enhancements, such as vitamin A, could have enormous benefits for poor consumers. Similarly, they assert that drought and pest resistance or striga control for maize in Africa might be the difference between life and death for millions of people on that continent, yet might only add to maize surpluses in the USA.[13] In short, most groups in most developing nations believe that each nation should make its own decision on transgenics. They fear particularly that the transgenic products first introduced by the private sector have needlessly fuelled the GMO debate (Conway, 1999). If that debate, in turn, kills some or all of the incentives for firms to develop the new technology, policy makers from developing countries fear that the technology's potential will not be mobilized for food security improvements – over which there otherwise would be little controversy. They also fear that any involvement on their part with GMOs may jeopardize aid funds from a number of donors.

Ironically, some of these same spokespersons feel that, even if biotechnology does go forward, it will not be accessible or usable by them. As one example, poor countries feel very much caught up in a trade war not of their own making. They are concerned that regulations developed under the biosafety convention using 'precautionary principles' will cause GMOs to be barred from entry into Europe and perhaps elsewhere. They worry that these rules could then preclude developing nations from the possibility of using transgenic technologies to expand their agricultural trade.

Convention on Biological Diversity and other international initiatives

Private sector issues have featured prominently in the foregoing discussions of patenting, industrial concentration and GMOs. Unresolved issues from the Convention on Biological Diversity also threaten to impede germ plasm flows from public and non-profit agencies.[14]

The current flow of germ plasm is impressively large. Indeed, the potential slowdown of this flow is the major concern of this paper. For the most part, these flows originate from 1320 ex situ genebanks (FAO, 1998). These banks contain a total of over 6 million accessions (varieties or landraces) for all crops and an estimated 95 per cent of all landraces for the cereals (Smale, 1996). Among these banks and accessions, none are more important for developing countries than those maintained by the 16 Centres of the Consultative Group for International Agricultural Research (CGIAR). Collectively, the centres' genebanks hold about 600 000 accessions. This sum is only 10 per cent of the total in all genebanks, but there are many duplicate samples throughout the world. Fowler (2000) estimates that the CG collections, which also contain a much higher percentage of the associated landraces than do typical national collections, contain almost half of the genetic diversity for the foodcrops.

A breeder seeking a particular variety or a specific trait would therefore most likely be in touch with the specific CG Centre focused on that commodity. Centres hold virtually all of these genetic materials in trust for the world and they make available research quantities of seeds to all legitimate breeders regardless of nationality or affiliation. Moreover, under a supplemental FAO (Food and Agriculture Organization) agreement, none of the varieties in trust can be patented by either the public or private sector, a proviso 'enforced' by the material transfer agreements under which the seeds change hands.

At a superficial level, there appear to be few problems with public germ plasm flows to and from poor countries. Unfortunately, deeper analysis reveals two quite troublesome issues, both of which revolve around definitions within the context of international treaties. New accessions to the genebanks constitute one of the hurdles. The 1992 Convention on Biological Diversity (CBD) reaffirmed state sovereignty over genetic resources and provided them with authority to control access. The devil of that provision is in its details. Article 2 of the CBD states that the country of origin of genetic resources means 'the country which possesses those genetic resources in *in-situ* conditions ... surroundings in which they have developed their distinctive properties'. Even the genebanks with the best historical data on accessions are able only to pinpoint the country from which the variety was *collected*. No genebank can identify the 'origin' of a variety, much less of individual alleles, in part because a workable definition of 'distinctive properties' is lacking. Most of a variety's 'old' properties were defined in Neolithic times, or even before. New properties have evolved or co-evolved through mutation or crosses, either intended or accidental, but often the country of origin even of the 'new' properties would not be known with certainty. Moreover, if a 'distinctive property' were discovered and its origin confirmed, how would compensation be determined? For example, one of the most popular wheat varieties in the world, the VEERY line, is the product of 3170 crosses involving 51 parents from 26 countries! It thus seems quite clear that the CBD approach to access and benefit sharing is unworkable in both scientific and practical terms.[15] However, if most of the varieties and traits of economic or ecological interest for a species have already been collected, the direct consequences of the CBD may be minor.

Unfortunately, an indirect consequence of the CBD debate is more serious. Decision makers in numerous agricultural ministries have now started to believe that they are sitting on genetic fortunes and that they must therefore restrict the movement of germ plasm from their countries to capitalize on these 'goldmines'. These restrictions can take the form of rejecting requests by prospecting missions for new varieties or landraces and, more importantly, of being unwilling to exchange plant genetic materials for research and field trials with neighbouring countries and research groups. Such an approach is shortsighted, because the basic financial assumption on which it is based is wrong. Smaller, poorer countries are those most likely to gain from cooperative breeding efforts and the exchange of plant materials. Preliminary evidence from 1992, for example, indicates that developing countries received approximately 100 times more seed samples than they sent (Fowler and Smale, 2000). Although it is often said that developing countries are 'gene rich', while the developed countries are 'gene poor', this statement masks the reality that many of the poorest countries, for example the Sahelian countries and many island states, have relatively few genes to trade or sell. A restricted access regime would thus be particularly harmful to them.

A second definitional problem also plagues the international flow of germ plasm and particularly the CG Centres. As noted previously, most accessions in the Centres' genebanks are held in trust, and cannot themselves be patented. But at what point does an accession cease to be an accession and become a product or derivative that *could* be protected? Does a new research product exist after one cross of two accessions? After ten crosses? At what point do derivatives become patentable? And, if they are patentable, are countries of origin (defined how?) entitled to compensation for the patent and, if so, on what basis is compensation to be made? These are more than rhetorical questions, for they go to the heart of the way in which the public and not-for-profit sectors organize themselves in the new world of biotechnology and intellectual property.

The problem, in fact, is even more complicated than the one suggested above. A breeder working on wheat, for example, in a particular country would likely contact CIMMYT, the relevant CG Centre, but not to ask for an *accession*. He or she would be much more likely to request particular lines that CIMMYT breeders had already refined with respect to certain traits or characteristics. In breeding for disease resistance, for example, CIMMYT may have found a gene or set of genes that it uses in crosses for elite (advanced) breeding lines. On the other hand, CIMMYT, a not-for-profit institution committed to helping resource-poor farmers, is unlikely to have sequenced or cloned that gene, which are steps now deemed necessary prior to securing a patent.

But what if a private firm, public agency or individual were to request seed samples, do the sequencing and cloning, and then obtain the patent? In order to continue using the gene, the Centre, and indirectly the poor countries as well, might need to obtain a licence from the patent holder. Under certain plausible circumstances, the Centre might even be excluded altogether from using what was essentially its own research. Under these circumstances, should not the Centre producing these public goods protect, through patenting, its ability to deliver these goods to the poor?

A final issue hinges on the use of intellectual property for research versus commercial purposes. There is still a widespread tradition in both the public and private sectors to trade research material and genetic constructs *for research purposes*. But problems arise when Centres or national systems develop varieties for release to farmers based on techniques or constructs that were made available on a research-only basis. Holders of the original intellectual property are then in powerful bargaining positions to extract rents from those who have used the property – innocently or otherwise – in the development of the new variety.

In summary, the flow of germ plasm for agriculture has changed from a relatively open system of public sector development of germ plasm to a much more confidential, rights-oriented system of seed development and diffusion. Obviously, the new system has produced significant new products that have benefited numerous companies and many farmers. However, issues of patenting, industrial concentration, transgenics and international initiatives are now interacting in ways that are limiting germ plasm flows to poorer countries. Without wise decisions at this time, there is every reason to believe that these constraints will become more binding in the future. Two relevant questions thus remain. Are these constraints important, or are they merely interesting? And, if important, what kinds of institutional innovations are now required to reverse these trends before they further impede the attainment of food security in poor nations?

THE GREEN REVOLUTION REVISITED

Running history backwards is always a delicate analytical procedure, yet it is sometimes revealing. In the paragraphs that follow, I address the important question of whether the initial Green Revolution would have been possible if the current 'rules' on germ plasm had been in force from 1950 to 2000. I believe that the answer is 'no'.

A key feature of the Green Revolution was the strategic use of dwarfing genes in rice and wheat plants to prevent lodging under the growth made possible by high-fertilizer regimes. As Evans (1998, p.137) states, 'The greatest impact on world food production as the population grew towards 4 billion came from the deployment of dwarfing genes in wheat and rice in the 1960s.' The wheat story is particularly interesting. Ironically, the wheat dwarf gene. Norin 10, probably came from Korea via Japan (Evans, 1998). It was brought to the USA in the late 1940s, manipulated by several breeders, and sent in a series of crosses to Norman Borlaug in Mexico in 1954. This dwarfing trait, when combined by Borlaug with other desirable genetic and agronomic characteristics, launched the Green Revolution, and there ensued four decades of extraordinary growth in wheat yields. Some 40 years later, slightly more than 80 per cent of all of the wheat grown in developing countries is planted to semi-dwarf varieties (Pingali, 1999) (see Table 2). A phenomenal 75 per cent of the semi-dwarf area in wheat is planted to CIMMYT lines (or lines with CIMMYT ancestors), virtually all of which include the Norin 10 gene.

Could a comparable sequence of events have taken place under current institutional circumstances? In my view, the probability is low. The key assumption in this thought experiment is whether or not the dwarfing gene would be patented or kept in the public domain. If patented, how hard would the patent holder have worked to promote this characteristic in a crop that is self-pollinated, not easily subject to hybridization and, therefore, not a great generator of seed sales? Perhaps an entire new line of hybrid wheat would have been developed, but would it have reached 80 per cent of the areas of less developed countries? Unlikely. Would CIMMYT or some other agency have been in a position to send out seed samples, which in 1994 alone totalled 1.2 million packets, three-quarters to developing countries and almost all carrying the dwarfing gene (Fowler and Smale, 2000)? Probably not. Would global yields of wheat have been lower, more mountain and forest land lost to crop production, and more people left food-insecure? Probably so. Protection of the dwarfing gene would almost surely have been successful in OECD countries and from a private profitability perspective. However, the social costs in terms of benefits forgone – at least on the basis of this retrospective analysis – would have been extremely high.

TABLE 2 Area (million hectares) grown to different wheat types in 1997, classified by the origin of the germ plasm

	Spring bread wheat	Spring durum wheat	Winter/facultative bread wheat	Winter/facultative durum wheat	All wheat types
CIMMYT cross	17.8	3.4	0.6	0	**21.8**
CIMMYT parent	22.4	1.2	1.9	0	**25.5**
CIMMYT ancestor	12.6	0.02	4.2	0	**16.8**
Other semi-dwarf	7.7	0.11	11.6	0.1	**19.5**
Tall	5.2	0.3	2.2	1.0	**8.7**
Landraces	1.4	1.5	4.1	0.1	**7.0**
Unknown cultivars	1.0	0.1	2.6	0	**3.8**
All	**68.1**	**6.7**	**27.2**	**1.2**	**103.2**

National Research System Cross { CIMMYT parent, CIMMYT ancestor, Other semi-dwarf, Tall }

Source: Pingali (1999).

53

Other scenarios could be written about the dwarfing gene; however, the analysis just presented seems sufficiently plausible to persuade one that the issues of germ plasm flow are important as well as interesting. The dwarfing example also suggests some of the future institutional modifications that should be made in the interests of global food security.

MOVING FORWARD

Changed attitudes

A great many agriculturists wish that the rulings that permit the patenting of living organisms had never been made. Nevertheless, many of them will also concede the benefits of patent protection to the pharmaceutical industry, because of that industry's long lead times with product development and the high cost of human trials. They understand further that many of the key decisions affecting agriculture, in fact, have their origins in the life sciences.[16] While they typically see no similarly compelling logic with respect to agricultural products, they also see no way of turning back the clock. Providing germ plasm to poor countries thus requires altered attitudes, procedures and institutions.

Changes in biology, information technology and law now dictate altered procedures for both the private and the public sectors. There has been a role reversal, and now the proprietary sector rather than the public sector is the dominant force in germ plasm development. Inevitably, the public sector will become less open as circumstances dictate the development of intellectual property, or at least the use of such property controlled by others. Confidentiality agreements have (or will) become the norm for not-for-profit institutions, rather than the exception. The private sector, in turn, will need to become more sensitive to consumer desires and to the problems of orphan countries and crops.[17] Much of the solution will be in the form of new public–private partnerships more in the private tradition, and part will be in altered strategies that keep substantial portions of the new science as public goods.

Continued use of the public domain

One obvious way to assist poor countries is via disclosure processes that preclude patenting by others. Such processes keep germ plasm and genetic technologies in the public domain, thereby providing the freedom to operate for agencies producing public goods. This approach has long been a hallmark of the public sector; interestingly, it is also becoming a feature of some firms within the private sector.[18] Monsanto's recent willingness to share genomic information on rice is one important example (Gillis, 2000). There has been much speculation about this decision, but it has set an important precedent for the private sector. Similarly, the announced intention to publish (disclose) electronically the full genome for *Arabidopsis thaliana*, a member of the mustard family, is another important example (Somerville and Somerville, 1999). A comparison of these two genomes will be especially revealing, because there is strong homology suspected between the genomes of rice, *Arabidopsis*, and 250 000 other plant species. But there is also a potential downside to disclosure. Protection is afforded only to that which has been disclosed, and not to the 'surrounding' data or constructs. Moreover, partial disclosure may give others clues that result in their patenting the rest of the genetic mechanism in question, an action that the initial disclosure was specifically trying to prevent. Therefore, in spite of the widespread progress with genomics, the specific technologies that govern function, use and manipulation of these recorded genes, or sets of genes, are increasingly likely to be held under some form of intellectual property protection. Such protection provides, in turn, both the opportunity and the forcing mechanism for new partnerships and alliances within and between the public and private sectors.

Limited use of defensive patenting by the public sector

Most public sector agencies are not well set up to deal with the protection of intellectual property. The culture and mission of these agencies, the outlook of their staffs, their historic openness with scientific findings and their general lack of legal talent all militate against the use of protective devices. If these agencies wish to remain at the forefront of future agricultural research, many of them will find it essential to use patents or other forms of protection. Revenue generation may be one motive, especially given the global decline in support for agricultural research. Much more important than revenues, however, will be the need for first-class research organizations to maintain operating freedom. Alliances with private sector firms may require that the public sector hold patents for bargaining purposes. At a minimum, the capacity to use protected methods and materials from the private sector will require having confidentiality agreements in place, even if patenting is not pursued directly by the public agency. Tapping the private sector's capacity and experience in scaling up from the test tube through product distribution is also likely to be invaluable. Finally, bio-piracy of public sector findings will likely become more commonplace unless the intellectual property dimensions of those findings are considered on a systematic basis.

Clearly, not all research findings need to be protected; indeed, as a practical matter, very few of them do. There are also a variety of methods, including outsourcing, which can be effective in managing intellectual property at reasonable cost. However, for public and non-profit agencies to disregard recent trends in the protection of intellectual property is to put both them and the countries they serve in jeopardy. Unfortunately, a great many of these agencies are seemingly still at the denial stage on this issue.

Renewed efforts at capacity building in poor countries

If poor countries are to reap the benefits of 21st-century research, they will need help. Part of this assistance can come from intermediary agencies who can help transform, adapt and develop new forms of technology for orphan crops and lagging regions. But there are severe limits to what outsiders can do, just as there are severe limits to what technology alone can do to solve problems of food security. Inadequate investments in human resources within these countries is a major part of the problem, and recent educational and R&D investments are not sums that should make either developed or developing countries very proud. While it is true that the number of trained personnel in sub-Saharan Africa was greater in 1991 than in 1961, as Pardey *et al.* (1997) show in their important study, it is also true that sub-Saharan numbers are still pitifully small. The total number of agricultural research workers in 21 countries of sub-Saharan Africa in 1991 was less than 7000, and total expenditures in 1991 (in 1985 dollars) for agricultural research were less than $700 million.[19] In a global review of agricultural research systems, Traxler and Pingali (1999) have classified some 40 national research systems with respect to their ability to provide significant amounts of parent materials for their crossing programmes (so-called Stage 3 capacity), their ability to undertake crossing programmes and to produce the occasional variety (Stage 2 capacity), and all others (Stage 1 capacity). They concluded that only seven national research systems for wheat and 13 for rice belonged in either Stage 2 or Stage 3. Since the poorest countries are precisely the places which private sector firms are least likely to serve, a rapid upgrading of national research capabilities is vital for *all* forms of technology development and transfer. Unfortunately, this sobering conclusion far overshadows this paper's more specialized discussion of improving germ plasm flows.

Expanded use of market sharing and licensing agreements

More than anything else, the successful transfer of plant genetic materials to poorest countries during the next 25 years will require new types of partnerships, alliances and market sharing (Serageldin, 2000). Neither the public nor the private sector institutions will be completely comfortable with these arrangements, but the limited experience to date suggests that several forms are indeed workable. Wright (2000) has developed a useful taxonomy of formal and informal arrangements that could be used to bring biotechnology to the poor. These mechanisms include licensing under varying cost and technology-sharing arrangements, market segmentation, technology grants, joint ventures, alliances and various kinds of direct research support. There is a high probability that almost any of these forms of cooperation can be made to work, provided that the partners know specifically what they wish to achieve, each party has something to offer others in the partnership, and everyone is willing to spend sufficient time to understand each other's positions and to build trust.[20]

Institutional arrangements designed to use biotechnology specifically in support of poor countries are in their infancy, but progress is being made. For example, Novartis presented the International Rice Research Institute (IRRI) with the *Bt* gene construct for rice as a gift in 1993. CIMMYT began a strategic alliance in 1998 with Institut de Recherche pour le Développement (IRD) and three private companies (Novartis, Limagrain and Pioneer) for the development of apomixis in maize. CIMMYT has also begun a very specific collaborative arrangement with Monsanto on the development of hybrid wheat, and the International Livestock Research Institute (ILRI) has joined with The Institute for Genomic Research (TIGR) on sequencing research related to the parasite *Theileria parva* that causes East Coast Fever in cattle. These are only examples, but they are important examples because they demonstrate the diversity of arrangements now being undertaken.

Five preliminary but important conclusions can be drawn from the early experience of the CGIAR Centres. First, it *is* possible to negotiate effective public–private arrangements, even those involving several private companies in non-exclusive relationships; however, the negotiations tend to be neither quick nor easy. (Negotiating time appears to go up by the square of the number of parties involved!) Second, it has also proved feasible to provide preferential access to research findings for particular national agricultural programmes. Mexico, in the case of CIMMYT's apomixis project, is an especially noteworthy case, in that this nation is a centre of origin for maize.

Third, market sharing has been a key element in most of the early agreements. The private partner typically retains the rights to distribute, sell or license products in the developed countries, whereas the public agency retains rights for the developing world. Many countries fall neatly into one category or another: however, countries such as China and India are typically a source of contention among public and private parties concerning whose rules should prevail in the market-segmentation agreements. Although relatively poor in per capita income terms, both countries are large in terms of aggregate GDPs, and both also have strong agricultural research systems. But the problems regarding how the market is to be segmented, how poor regions within richer countries are to be dealt with, how the trade flows of products are to be regulated between the two sets of countries and how the technology differential is to be implemented (gifts, licensing at zero cost and so on) help explain why negotiations between the public and private sectors are rarely easy or short. Indeed, principles of market segmentation and the development of prototype agreements appear to be important areas for further research.

Fourth, public sector negotiations with the private sector have been complicated substantially by the changing structure of the biotechnology industry. The many changes within and among various mega-firms have been disruptive in the formation of partnerships to serve poor countries. Perhaps the seed and biotechnology industries have now reached quasi-stability and, if so, negotiations may be much easier in the years ahead.

Finally, there is the generosity factor. Much has been written about the short-run profit imperative for private firms, a point that at one level is obviously correct. However, the early negotiating experience of the CGIAR Centres indicates, on balance, that companies in the private sector have a gratifying concern with poverty issues and have been remarkably generous with respect to legitimate use of their technologies in support of poor countries. It has indeed been possible, if not easy, to find 'win–win' solutions that embrace both the public and the private sectors. These new kinds of partnerships represent the greatest hope for improving germ plasm flows into poor countries during the 21st century.

NOTES

[1]The number 70 is clearly arbitrary. The USDA analysis (1997) uses a series of food gap, income growth and income inequality variables to identify 66 countries with moderate or severe food security problems. However, the two largest developing countries, China and India, have very strong national agricultural research systems. Correlations between per capita GDP and 'agricultural research vulnerability' are thus far from perfect – a point of some importance for the final section of the paper.

[2]Lipton (1999) provides a useful statement on various positions on these topics. Various viewpoints are also highlighted in a series of articles under the heading, 'Can Biotechnology End Hunger?' in the Summer 2000 issue of *Foreign Policy*.

[3]Plants that reproduce asexually had long been covered in the United States by the 1930 Plant Patent Act; however, that act excluded bacteria from protection. See also note 4.

[4]In a series of lower-court decisions, cells, organelles, genes, molecular constructs and lines were also held to be patentable.

[5]Many of these fragments were of interest because of potential human health products rather than for their importance to agricultural crops.

[6]A few of the early applications received patents; however, ESTs were given new, more stringent guidelines for patenting in March 2000.

[7]Sachs (2000) has written perceptively about technologically excluded countries in the process of development.

[8]Ingo Potrykus, the chief architect of vitamin A-enhanced rice is quoted as saying, 'So many fields of research are blocked by corporate patents. I had to ignore them or I couldn't move at all' (*www.gene.ch/infor4action/2000/Mar/mag00002.html*).

[9]The terms 'transgenic' and 'GMO' are used interchangeably in this paper to refer to an organism that has had a gene or genes from another species inserted into it. These concepts differ from genomics, which is the study of structure and function of very large numbers of genes within an organism.

[10]Gaskell *et al.* (1999) provides a useful summary of European versus US attitudes. One of the most complete discussions of biotechnology in developing countries is that of Persley and Lantin (2000).

[11]In April 2000, a committee of the US National Academy of Sciences concluded that regulation of 'genetically modified pest protected plants' should be product- rather than technique-based (National Research Council, 2000). Although most US scientific opinion has supported this position, it has fared less well politically.

[12]Persley and Lantin (2000) as well as Gisselquist and Srivastava (1997) provide case studies on biotechnology in developing countries.

[13]The 'Insect Resistant Maize for Africa Project' provides a very illuminating example from Kenya of African attitudes and approaches (KARI, 1999; Mgendi, 1999).

[14]Much of this section draws on conversations with, and research by, Fowler (2000).

[15]When the Convention on Biological Diversity was adopted, it was recognized that certain issues, including the status of genebank collections assembled prior to the coming into force of the Convention, were still unresolved. Since 1994, FAO has been hosting formal, intergovernmental negotiations on the status of plant genetic resources for food and agriculture, with the aim of bringing an earlier agreement, the 'International Undertaking', into harmony with the Convention. If successful, the outcome would produce a multilateral system for access and benefit sharing of genetic resources at least for the 25–35 crops most important to world food security. It is likely, however, that minor crops, including many of importance to subsistence farmers and poor in developing countries, would be 'orphaned' by this approach.

[16]Barton (1997) has written more generally about some of the fundamental differences between the agricultural and pharmaceutical sectors.

[17]That some firms in the private sector needed reminders about consumer interests is ironic and speaks volumes about the public relations débâcle that surrounded terminator technology and several other GMO initiatives. Good science was simply not enough (Conway, 1999).

[18]It may well be that publishing the human genome will also help to establish procedures and precedents for a more open system for plant agriculture.

[19]By way of ludicrous comparison, Stanford University alone had a consolidated budget of $875 million in 1991, also measured in 1985 dollars.

[20]Leisinger (2000) offers insights on the practical and tactical aspects of building partnerships and alliances. A very useful statement of principles on public sector–private sector alliances for assisting poor countries can be found in the Tlaxcala Statement (CIMMYT, 2000).

REFERENCES

Barton, J.H. (1997), 'The Biodiversity Convention and the Flow of Scientific Information', in K.E. Hoagland and A.Y. Rossman (eds), *Global Genetics Resources*, Washington, DC: Association of Systematics Collections, pp.57–62.

Barton, J.H. (2000), 'Reforming the Patent System', *Science*, **287**, 1933–4.

Brennan, M.F., Pray, C.E. and Courtmanche, A. (1999), *Impact of Industry Concentration on Innovation in the U.S. Plant Biotech Industry* (working paper), Rutgers University.

CIMMYT (2000), *Tlaxcala Statement on Public/Private Sector Alliances in Agricultural Research* (occasional paper), Mexico: CIMMYT.

Conway, G. (1999), *The Rockefeller Foundation and Plant Biotechnology* (occasional paper), New York City: The Rockefeller Foundation.

Enserink, M. (2000), 'Patent Office May Raise The Bar on Gene Claims', *Science*, **287**, 1196–7.

Evans, L.T. (1998), *Feeding the Ten Billion: Plants and Population Growth*, Cambridge: Cambridge University Press.

FAO (1998), *The State of the World Plant Genetic Resources for Food and Agriculture*, Rome: FAO.

Fowler, C. (2000), *Implementing Access and Benefit-sharing Procedures Under the Convention on Biological Diversity: The Dilemma of Crop Genetic Resources and Their Origins* (Dresden Conference Report), Aas: Agriculture University of Norway.

Fowler, C. and Smale, M. (2000), *Germplasm Flows Between Developing Countries and the CGIAR: An Initial Assessment* (working paper), Mexico: CIMMYT.

Friedland, J. (2000), 'As Two Men Vie To Sell Yellow Beans, Litigation Sprouts', *The Wall Street Journal*, 23 May, p.A1.

Gaskell, G. *et al.* (1999), 'Worlds Apart? The Reception of Genetically Modified Foods in Europe and the U.S.', *Science*, **285**, 384–7.

Gillis, J. (2000), 'Monsanto Assembles Genetic Map of Rice', *Washington Post*, 5 April, p.E1.

Gisselquist, D. and Srivastava, J. (1997), *Easing Barriers to Movements of Plant Varieties for Agricultural Development* (discussion paper), Washington, DC: World Bank.

Guerinot, M.L. (2000), 'The Green Revolution Strikes Gold', *Science*, **287**, 241–3.

Herdt, R.W. (1999), *Enclosing the Global Plant Genetic Commons* (occasional paper), New York: The Rockefeller Foundation.

KARI (1999), *Insect Resistant Maize for Africa (IRMA) Project* (occasional paper), Nairobi: Kenya Agricultural Research Institute.

Leisinger, K.M. (2000), *The 'Political Economy' of Agricultural Biotechnology for the Developing World* (IAAE Berlin Conference Report), Basle: Novartis Foundation for Sustainable Development.

Lipton, M. (1999), *Reviving Global Poverty Reduction: What Role for Genetically Modified Plants?*, Washington, DC: The CGIAR Secretariat.

Mgendi, C. (1999), 'Local Scientists Snub the West in Biotech War', Nairobi, *Daily Nation*, 21 October.

National Research Council (2000), *Genetically Modified Pest-Protected Plants: Science and Regulation*, Washington, DC: National Academy Press.

Nelson, G.C. *et al.* (1999), *The Economics And Politics Of Genetically Modified Organisms In Agriculture: Implications for WTO 2000*, Urbana-Champaign: University of Illinois.

Pardey, P., Roseboom, J. and Beintema, N. (1997), 'Investments in African Agricultural Research', *World Development*, **25**, 409–23.

Persley, G.J. and Lantin, M.M. (2000), *Agricultural Biotechnology and the Poor*, Washington, DC: Consultative Group on International Agricultural Research.

Pingali, P.L. (1999), *CIMMYT 1998–99 World Wheat Facts and Trends. Global Wheat Research in a Changing World: Challenges and Achievements*, Mexico: CIMMYT.

Pinstrup-Andersen, P., Pandya-Lorch, R. and Rosegrant, M.W. (1999), *World Food Prospects: Critical Issues for the Early Twenty-first Century*, Washington, DC: International Food Policy Research Institute.

RAFI (1998), *Seed Industry Consolidation: Who Owns Whom?* (occasional report), Winnipeg: Rural Advancement Foundation International.

Sachs, J. (2000), 'A New Map of the World', *The Economist*, 24 June, pp.95–7.

Serageldin, I. (2000), *International Cooperation for the Public Good: Agricultural Research in the New Century* (Dresden Conference Report), Washington, DC: World Bank.

Smale. M. (1996), *Understanding Global Trends in the Use of Wheat Diversity and International Flows of Wheat Genetic Resources* (working paper), Mexico: CIMMYT.

Smil, V. (2000), *Feeding the World: A Challenge for the 21st Century*, Cambridge: MIT Press.

Smith, B.D. (1998), *The Emergence of Agriculture*, Scientific American Library Paperback, New York: Scientific American Library.

Somerville, C. and Somerville, S. (1999), 'Plant Functional Genomics', *Science*, **285**, 380–83.

Traxler, G. and Pingali, P. (1999), *International Collaboration in Crop Improvement Research* (working paper), Mexico: CIMMYT.

USDA (1997), *Food Security Assessment*, Washington, DC: United States Department of Agriculture.

Wright, B.D. (2000), *IPR Challenges and International Research Collaborations in Agricultural Biotechnology* (Bonn Conference Report), Berkeley: University of California, Berkeley.

KYM ANDERSON AND CHANTAL POHL NIELSEN*

GMOs, Food Safety and the Environment:
What Role for Trade Policy and the WTO?

INTRODUCTION

The use of modern biotechnology to create genetically modified organisms (GMOs) through agricultural research has generated exuberance in those looking forward to a new 'Green Revolution'. But GMOs have also attracted strong criticism. The opposition is coming from groups concerned about the safety of consuming genetically modified foods, the environmental impact of growing genetically engineered plants, and the ethics related to using that technology per se. Scepticism towards genetic engineering has been particularly rife in Western Europe, which has stunted that region's contribution to the development and use of genetically engineered crop seeds. In contrast, farmers in North American and several large developing countries (notably Argentina and China) have actively developed and adopted GM crops, and citizens there have generally (perhaps unwittingly) accepted that development.

In Western Europe, where food supplies are abundant and incomes are high, people can afford to be critical of the introduction of new agricultural biotechnologies and production processes about which they are unsure. In developing economies, by contrast, the benefit–cost ratio is very different. Many food-insecure people in developing countries live in rural areas, earn a significant share of their income from agriculture, and meet a substantial share of their food needs from their own production. For them, increasing agricultural productivity and thereby real income is a high priority. And, for the urban poor in those countries, anything that lowers the effective price of basic foods and/or boosts the nutritional value of those foods is highly desirable. Given the large value shares of agriculture and textiles in production and food in consumption in developing economies, GMO technologies for such crops as rice and cotton have the potential to generate significant economy-wide benefits that may well dwarf any costs as perceived in those countries in terms of environmental and food safety risks. The same is true for GM maize and soybean from which,

*Kym Anderson, Centre for International Economic Studies, University of Adelaide, Australia; Chantal Pohl Nielsen, Danish Institute of Agricultural and Fisheries Economics, and University of Copenhagen, Denmark. The authors are grateful to the World Bank and Australia's Rural Industries Research and Development Corporation for seed funding this research, and to the International Food Policy Research Institute for providing Nielsen with a visiting fellowship in 2000.

along with *Bt* cotton, rich-country adopters (most notably the United States) appear to be already benefiting, judging by the rapid rate of adoption.

Environmental, food safety and ethical concerns with the production and use of GM crops have been voiced so effectively as to lead to the recent negotiation of a Biosafety Protocol (UNEP, 2000) with its endorsement of the use of the precautionary principle. However, if that Protocol were to encourage discriminatory trade barriers or import bans, or even just long delays in approving the use of imported GM seeds, it might be at odds with countries' obligations under the World Trade Organization (WTO). The first part of this paper provides a brief overview of the trade policy issues at stake here. It concludes that these issues have the potential to lead to complex and wasteful trade disputes. The extent to which that potential is realized depends on the economic stakes involved. They can only be determined by quantitative economic modelling, using – pending more reliable knowledge – assumptions about the sizes of any shifts in the crop supply (or demand) curves. The second part of the paper illustrates one way in which this can be done. We use a well-received empirical model of the global economy (GTAP) to quantify the effects on production, prices, trade patterns and national economic welfare of certain countries' farmers adopting GM maize and soybean crops without and then with trade policy or consumer responses in Western Europe (where opposition to GMOs is most vocal). The results suggest that such policy or consumer responses can alter significantly the potential size of the global GMO dividend and its distribution.

GMOS, AGRICULTURAL TRADE POLICIES AND THE WTO

National policy reactions to GMOs

While traditional biotechnology improves the quality and yields of plants and animals through, for example, selective breeding, genetic engineering[1] is a new biotechnology that enables direct manipulation of genetic material (inserting, removing or altering genes). In this way the new technology accelerates the development process, shaving years off R&D programmes. Protagonists argue that genetic engineering entails a more controlled transfer of genes because the transfer is limited to a single gene, or just a few selected genes, whereas traditional breeding risks transferring unwanted genes together with the desired ones. Against that advantage, antagonists argue that the side-effects in terms of potentially adverse impacts on the environment and human health are unknown.

Genetic engineering techniques and their applications have developed very rapidly since the introduction of the first genetically modified plants in the 1980s. Transgenic crops currently occupy about 4 per cent of the world's total agricultural area (compared with less than 0.5 per cent as recently as 1996). Cultivation so far has been most widespread in the production of GM soybeans and maize, accounting for 54 per cent and 28 per cent of total transgenic crop production in 1999, respectively, with the USA accounting for almost three-quarters of the total GM crops area. Other major GM crop producers are

Argentina, Canada, China, Mexico and South Africa, but India and several Eastern European countries also have a number of transgenic crops in the pipeline for commercialization (James, 1997, 1998, 1999; European Commission, 2000).

Meanwhile, the resistance to GMO production and use in numerous countries, especially by well organized activists in Western Europe, triggered the imposition in October 1998 of a *de facto* moratorium on the authorization of new releases of GMOs.[2] This could be a prelude to a future EU ban on the cultivation of GM crops and on imports of food containing GMOs (following the EU ban on imports of beef produced with the help of growth hormones). Before the imposition of the moratorium, releases of GMOs were reviewed on a case-by-case basis and had to be approved at every step from laboratory testing through field testing to final marketing. By contrast, the permit procedure is far simpler and faster in the USA.

There are also marked differences in national labelling requirements. The US Food and Drug Administration does not require labelling of GM foods per se, demanding it only if the transgenic food is substantially different from its conventional counterpart. The EU, by contrast, requires labelling of all foodstuffs, additives and flavours containing 1 per cent or more genetically modified material (Regulations 1139/98 and 49/2000). Individual countries within the EU have added further requirements (OECD, 2000). In Denmark, for example, suppliers must label their products not only if GMO presence is verifiable but also if there is a possibility that they could contain GMOs. Numerous non-European countries, including some developing countries, have also enacted GMO consumer legislation. Australia and New Zealand are to introduce mandatory labelling for all foods containing GMOs (that is, a zero threshold), following a poll showing that more than 90 per cent approved such a move. Brazil has introduced restrictive conditions on imports of GM products in 2000. And Sri Lanka has taken the extreme step of banning the import of GMOs, pending further clarification as to their environmental and food safety impacts.

Needless to say, identity preservation systems to enable reliable labelling of food can be costly, and more so the more stages of processing or intermediate input use a crop product goes through before final consumption. A recent European survey suggests full traceability could add 6–17 per cent to the farmgate cost of different crops.[3] Who bears those costs, and are the benefits sufficient to warrant them? Products containing GMOs that are not verifiably different from their GM-free counterparts are not going to attract a price premium, so their producers would not volunteer to label them as containing GMOs, given (a) the cost of identity preservation throughout the food chain and (b) the negative publicity about GMOs which is likely to lower the price of goods so labelled. Coercion would therefore be required.

A non-regulatory alternative to positive labelling regulations is to encourage the voluntary use of negative labels such as 'this product contains no GMOs' (Runge and Jackson, 1999). With perhaps the majority of processed foods now containing some GMOs, this market alternative would require labels on a much smaller and presumably declining proportion of products. And that subset, like organic food, could attract a price premium sufficient to cover the cost of identity preservation and labelling. This still requires the separation of GM-free products from GM-inclusive ones, however. Furthermore, it begs the question as to what is the threshold below which 'this product contains no GMOs' should apply. For the label to be meaningful abroad for exported GM-free products, multilateral agreement on that threshold would be needed.

The Cartagena Protocol on Biosafety

Given the different attitudes and national approaches to regulation of genetically modified products, future trade disputes are a distinct possibility. With the objective of ensuring safe transboundary movement of living modified organisms resulting from modern biotechnology, the Cartagena Protocol on Biosafety (finalized in Montreal on 29 January 2000) may have added to that likelihood. The Biosafety Protocol, if ratified by the parliaments of 50 signatories, not only reconfirms the rights of signatory countries to set their own domestic regulations but also ostensibly allows each country to decide whether and under what conditions it will accept imports of GM products for release into the environment (for example, as planted seeds). This condoning of import restrictions appears also to apply to GMOs intended as food, feed or for processing.[4] This was sought not only by rich countries; some in developing countries also support it, fearing that their regions might be used as testing grounds for GM food production. Importantly, the Protocol stipulates that lack of scientific evidence regarding potential adverse effects of GMOs on biodiversity, taking into account also the risks to human health, need not prevent a signatory from taking action to restrict the import of such organisms in order to reduce perceived risks (UNEP, 2000). In essence, this reflects an acceptance of the guiding influence of the precautionary principle, 'better safe than sorry'.[5] The Protocol requires that GMOs intended for intentional introduction into the environment or for contained use must be clearly identified as living modified organisms; but modified organisms intended for direct use as food or feed, or for further processing, just require a label stating that the produce 'may contain' such organisms. No labelling requirements for processed foods such as cooking oil or meal were established. Hence the Protocol does not address growing demands by hard critics of biotech who call for labelling of products if genetic engineering techniques have been used at any stage in their production process, regardless of whether or not this can be verified in the final product through testing – but it goes well beyond the minimalist stance that some GM-exporting countries might have preferred.

WTO agreements and GMOs

An important aspect of the Biosafety Protocol that is unclear and hence open to various interpretations concerns its relationship with the WTO agreements. The text states that the 'Protocol shall not be interpreted as implying a change in the rights and obligations of a Party under any existing international agreements', but at the same time the Protocol claims that this statement is 'not intended to subordinate [the] Protocol to other international agreements' (UNEP, 2000, p.1). Certainly, the Protocol's objective of protecting and ensuring sustainable use of biological diversity while also taking into account risks to human health is not inconsistent with WTO agreements. The WTO acknowledges the need of member states to apply and enforce trade-restricting measures in order to protect human, animal or plant health and life as well as public morals. That right for a country to set its own environmental and food safety regulations at the national level is provided for in Article XX of the GATT. But the key goal of the WTO is to achieve effective use of the world's resources by reducing barriers to international trade. For that reason WTO members have also agreed not to use unduly trade-restrictive measures to achieve environmental or food safety goals. More than that, such measures must be consistent with the key principles of the WTO: non-discrimination among member states, 'national treatment' of imports once having entered the domestic market, and transparent customs procedures. Whether the current WTO agreements prove to be in conflict with the rights to restrict trade in living modified organisms apparently provided for in the Biosafety Protocol only time – and possibly legal proceedings via the WTO's Dispute Settlement Body – can tell.

Members of the WTO also have trade obligations under other WTO agreements that restrict the extent to which trade measures can be used against GMOs. More specifically related to food safety and animal and plant health are the Agreement on Sanitary and Phytosanitary Measures (SPS) and the Agreement on Technical Barriers to Trade (TBT). These agreements allow member states to impose certain restrictions on trade if the purpose of the measure is to protect human, animal or plant life and health. The TBT agreement also covers technical measures aimed at protecting the environment and other objectives. At the same time the agreements aim at ensuring that applied measures and technical regulations are no more trade-restrictive than necessary to fulfil the stated objectives (WTO, 1995, 1998a, 1998b).

Both the SPS and TBT agreements encourage the use of international standards, guidelines and recommendations where they exist, such as in the realms of Codex Alimentarius (the FAO's international food standards body). Currently there are no international standards for genetically modified products,[6] although the Biosafety Protocol explicitly notes that signatories 'shall consider the need for and modalities of developing standards with regard to the identification, handling, packaging and transport practices, in consultation with other relevant international bodies' (UNEP, 2000, p.10, Art. 18.3). International harmonization of regulatory approval procedures for genetically modified products is currently under discussion in several forums, including the FAO and OECD. The establishment of international standards for the production, regulation and labelling of these products may be helpful as a way of reducing future trade disputes among developed countries, but could impose onerous compliance costs on poorer GM-exporting countries.

Under the SPS agreement a country may apply higher than international standards *only* if these can be justified by appropriate scientific risk assessments. In other words, while the SPS agreement explicitly allows member states to set their own standards for food safety and animal and plant health, it requires that measures be based on scientific risk assessments in a consistent way across commodities. The TBT agreement is more flexible because member states can decide that international standards are inappropriate for a number of other reasons, such as national security interests (GATT Article XXI). Hence determining which WTO agreement a given trade measure is covered by is of key importance. The SPS agreement covers food safety measures and animal and plant health standards regardless of whether or not these are technical requirements. The TBT agreement, on the other hand, covers all technical regulations, voluntary standards and compliance procedures, except when these are sanitary and phytosanitary measures as defined in the SPS agreement (WTO, 1998a).

The SPS agreement's scientific requirement is important because it is more objective than the TBT agreement's criteria for determining what is a justifiable trade restriction and what is hidden protectionism. On the other hand, the SPS agreement may be inadequate for legally justifying restrictions introduced on the basis of some vocal groups' opposition to GM foods. Official disputes about trade in genetically modified products have not yet materialized, but experience from earlier WTO dispute settlement cases that are comparable to the GMO debate give an indication as to how the existing rules may be applied. The SPS agreement was used in the beef hormone dispute between the USA and the EU, for example (WTO, 1998c). In short, the EU import ban on meat and meat products from hormone-fed livestock was found to be in conflict with the EU's WTO obligations, the main argument being that the EU could not present documented scientific risk assessment of the alleged health risk to justify the ban.

Scientific evidence is not always sufficient for governments to make policy decisions, or it may simply be unavailable. In such cases, Article 5.7 of the SPS agreement allows WTO member states to take precautionary measures based on available pertinent information. At the same time, members are obliged to seek additional information so that a more objective evaluation of the risks related to the relevant product or process can be made within a reasonable period of time. The precautionary principle is an understandable approach to uncertainties about genetically modified products, but there is a risk that, when used in connection with internationally traded products, it can be captured by import-competing groups seeking protection against any new technology-driven competition from abroad. It may thus be extremely difficult to assess whether a measure is there for precautionary reasons or simply as a form of hidden protectionism. For this reason, attention will focus on how the provisions of the Biosafety Protocol – the most explicit acceptance of the use of the precautionary principle in an international trade agreement relating to food products to date – are interpreted given current WTO commitments.

The existing trade agreements deal with regulations and standards concerning not just products but also production processes and methods *if but only if they affect the characteristics or safety of the product itself*: standards for production processes that do *not* affect the final product are not covered by the existing agreements. In relation to genetically engineered products, if the process itself were to alter the final product in such a way that there are adverse environmental or health effects associated with consumption, use or disposal of the product, restricting trade in this product need not violate existing WTO rules, ceteris paribus. However, if genetic engineering only concerns the production process and not the final characteristics of a transgenic product, domestic regulations that restrict the use of this method of production cannot be used to restrict imports or products produced by this method simply because the importing country finds it unacceptable by its own environmental, ethical or other norms.[7]

This discussion leads back to the role of scientific evidence. Some would argue that genetically modified products are different from conventional products *regardless* of whether or not this can be verified scientifically in the final product. One of the priorities of the European Commission in the next WTO round of multilateral trade negotiations is to obtain a clarification of the role of non-product-related processes and production methods within the WTO (European Commission, 1999). If trade restrictions based on production methods are allowed, this could lead to the inclusion of a long list of non-tariff barriers, and not only in relation to biotechnology products.

Labelling of foods in relation to international trade is normally covered by the TBT agreement unless the label relates directly to food safety, in which case it is covered by the SPS agreement. Only labelling programmes that concern production processes affecting the final product would be covered by the existing TBT agreement. Determining whether or not a genetic modification affects the final product will probably have to be done on a case-by-case basis. Where labelling programmes are not encompassed by the TBT agreement, which potentially may be the case for many transgenic products, the other agreements of the WTO will be applicable without exceptions (Tietje, 1997). GATT Article III concerning non-discrimination, for example, stipulates that member states may not discriminate between otherwise like goods on the basis of their country of origin. A key issue using this article will be the interpretation of the concept of 'like goods' and whether the presence of genetically modified material is 'sufficient' to differentiate products. Article III seeks to avoid measures that are based on a false differentiation of products.

In short, the emergence of GMOs in agricultural and food production introduces several new and contentious issues to be dealt with by the WTO membership and ultimately its dispute settlement body (DSB). The DSB has not yet been able to resolve the dispute over the EU's ban on imports of beef produced with growth hormones (WTO, 1998c), so it is difficult to see how it will be able to do any better with the far more complex issue of GM products should the EU choose to ban their importation too – particularly now that there is a Biosafety Protocol on the table condoning the use of the precautionary principle and suggesting that scientific evidence need not prevent importing countries from restricting GM trade.

To get a sense of the risk of trade disputes erupting over GMOs, it is necessary to assess the economic stakes involved. That is, how large are the potential gains from GMO crop technologies, to what extent will various countries benefit (or lose) from their adoption, and how would trade policy responses or adverse consumer reactions affect those projected outcomes? It is to these questions that we now turn.

AN EMPIRICAL ILLUSTRATION

Theory alone is incapable of determining even the likely direction, let alone the magnitude, of some of the effects of subsets of farmers adopting GM-inclusive seeds. Hence an empirical modelling approach is called for. To illustrate its usefulness in informing GMO debates, this section summarizes one recent quantitative effort by the authors. It makes use of a well-received empirical model of the global economy (the GTAP model) to examine what the effects of some (non-European) countries adopting the new GMO technology might be (Nielsen and Anderson, 2000b). Specifically, the effects of an assumed degree of GM-induced productivity growth in selected countries are explored for maize and soybean.[8] Those results are compared with what they would be if (a) Western Europe chose to ban consumption and hence imports of those products from countries adopting GM technology or (b) some Western European consumers responded by boycotting imported GM foods.

Being a general equilibrium model, GTAP (Global Trade Analysis Project) describes both the vertical and horizontal linkages between all product markets both within the model's individual countries and regions and between countries and regions via their bilateral trade flows. The database used for these applications reflects the global economic structures and trade flows of 1995, and has been aggregated to 16 regions to highlight the main participants in the GMO debate and other key interest groups, and 17 sectors with focus placed on the primary agricultural sectors affected by the GMO debate and their related processing industries.[9]

The scenarios analysed here assume that GM-driven productivity growth occurs only in the following GTAP sectors and for a subset of countries: coarse grain other than wheat and rice (primarily maize in the countries considered) and oilseeds (primarily soybean in the countries considered). Detailed empirical information about the impact of GMO technology in terms of reduced chemical use, higher yields and other agronomic improvements is at this stage quite limited (see, for example, OECD, 1999, Nelson *et al.*, 1999). Available empirical evidence (for example, USDA, 1999; James, 1997, 1998) does, however, suggest that cultivating GM crops has general cost-reducing effects.[10] The following scenarios are therefore based on a simplifying assumption that the effect of adopting GM crops can be captured by a Hicks-neutral technology shift; that is, a uniform reduction in all primary factors and intermediate inputs to obtain the same level of production. For present purposes the GM-adopting sectors are assumed to experience a one-off increase in total factor productivity of 5 per cent, thus lowering the supply price of the GM crop to that extent.[11] Assuming sufficiently elastic demand conditions, the cost-reducing technology will lead to increased production and higher returns to the factors of production employed in the GM-adopting sector. Consequently, labour, capital and land will be drawn into the affected sector. As suppliers of inputs and buyers of agricultural products, other sectors will also be affected by the use of genetic engineering in GM-potential sectors through vertical linkages. Input suppliers will initially experience lower demand because the production process in the GM sector has become more efficient. To the extent that the production of GM crops increases, however, the demand for inputs by producers of those crops may actually rise despite the input-reducing technology. Demanders of primary agricultural products such as grains and soybean meal for livestock feed will benefit from lower input prices, which in turn will affect the market competitiveness of livestock products.

The widespread adoption of GM varieties in certain regions will affect international trade flows, depending on how traded the crop in question is and whether or not this trade is restricted specifically because of the GMOs involved. To the extent that trade is not further restricted and not currently subject to binding quantitative restrictions, world market prices for these products will have a tendency to decline and thus benefit regions that are net importers of these products. For exporters, the lower price may or may not boost their trade volume, depending on price elasticities in foreign markets. Welfare in the exporting countries would go down for non-adopters but could also go down for some adopters if the adverse terms of trade change were to be sufficiently strong. Hence the need for empirical analysis.

In order to appreciate the relative importance of these primary agricultural sectors and their related processing sectors to the economies of different regions, note that coarse grains (particularly maize) and oilseeds (particularly soybean) are of equal or greater importance to North American and Western European agriculture than they are to the farm sectors of most developing country regions. It is also important to understand the various regions' net trading situations in raw and processed forms, and the export dependence of these products. (Details are provided in Anderson *et al.*, 2000, Tables 2–4.)

Scenario 1: selected regions adopt GM maize and soybean

Three maize/soybean scenarios are considered. The first of them (scenario 1) is a base case with no policy or consumer reactions to GMOs. GM-driven productivity growth of 5 per cent is applied to North America, Mexico, the Southern Cone region of Latin America, India, China, Rest of East Asia (excluding Japan and the East Asian NICs) and South Africa. The countries of Western Europe, Japan, other sub-Saharan Africa and elsewhere are assumed to refrain from using or to be unable at this stage to adopt GM crops in their production systems. The other two scenarios impose on this base case a policy or consumer response in Western Europe. In scenario 2, Western Europe not only refrains from using GM crops in its own domestic production systems, but the region is also assumed to reject imports of maize and soybean products from GM-adopting regions. Scenario 3 considers the case in which consumers express their preferences through market mechanisms rather than through government regulation.

Table 1 reports the results for scenario 1. A 5 per cent reduction in overall production costs in these sectors leads to increases in coarse grain production of between 0.4 per cent and 2.1 per cent, and increases in oilseed production of between 1.1 per cent and 4.6 per cent, in the GM-adopting regions. The production responses are generally larger for oilseeds than for coarse grain.

TABLE 1 Scenario 1: effects of selected regions[a] adopting GM maize and soybean
(a) Effects on production, domestic prices and trade (percentage changes)

	North America	Southern Cone	China	India	Western Europe	Sub-Saharan Africa
Production						
Coarse grain	2.1	1.6	1.0	0.4	-4.5	-2.3
Oilseeds	3.6	4.6	1.8	1.1	-11.2	-1.3
Livestock	0.8	-0.0	0.1	0.4	-0.2	-0.1
Meat & dairy	0.5	0.0	0.1	1.3	-0.1	-0.1
Veg. oils, fats	1.1	4.5	1.4	0.0	-0.9	-1.2
Other foods	0.2	0.1	0.4	1.5	-0.1	0.0
Market prices						
Coarse grain	-5.5	-5.5	-5.6	-6.7	-0.5	-0.4
Oilseeds	-5.5	-5.3	-5.6	-6.5	-1.2	-0.3
Livestock	-1.8	-0.3	-0.4	-1.4	-0.3	-0.3
Meat & dairy	-1.0	-0.2	-0.3	-1.0	-0.2	-0.2
Veg. oils, fats	-2.4	-3.1	-2.6	-1.0	-0.5	-0.2
Other foods	-0.3	-0.2	-0.5	-1.0	-0.1	-0.2
Exports[b]						
Coarse grain	8.5	13.3	16.8	37.3	-11.5	-20.0
Oilseeds	8.5	10.5	8.2	21.5	-20.5	-26.5
Livestock	8.9	-2.0	-3.3	9.4	-1.1	-1.5
Meat & dairy	4.8	-0.9	-0.9	5.8	-0.5	-0.2
Veg. oils, fats	5.8	14.3	5.6	-3.8	-4.9	-5.3
Other foods	0.2	0.1	1.6	7.6	-0.6	0.1

Imports[b]

Coarse grain	-1.6	-4.2	-20.5	0.1	11.3
Oilseeds	-2.6	-1.6	-8.6	2.5	16.5
Livestock	-2.1	0.9	-5.2	0.2	0.5
Meat & dairy	-1.9	0.8	-1.7	-0.0	0.1
Veg. oils, fats	-3.7	-1.7	3.1	1.3	3.4
Other foods	0	-0.6	-3.1	0.1	-0.1

(b) Effects on regional economic welfare

	Equivalent variation (EV) US$ mn p.a.	Decomposition of welfare results, contribution of (US$ mn)		
		Allocative efficiency effects	Terms of trade effects	Technical change
North America	2 624	-137	-1 008	3 746
Southern Cone	826	120	-223	923
China	839	113	66	672
India	1 265	182	-9	1 094
Western Europe	2 010	1 755	253	0
Sub-Saharan Africa	-9	-2	-9	0
Other high-income[c]	1 186	554	641	0
Other developing and transition economies	1 120	171	289	673
WORLD	9 859	2 756	0	7 108

Notes: [a]North America, Mexico, Southern Cone, China, Rest of East Asia, India and South Africa. For space reasons, results for numerous regions are omitted from this table.
[b]Includes intra-regional trade.
[c]Japan, newly industrialized Asia, Australia and New Zealand.

Source: Nielsen and Anderson's (2000b) GTAP model results.

This is because a larger share of oilseed production as compared with coarse grain production is destined for export markets in all the reported regions, and hence oilseed production is not limited to the same extent by domestic demand, which is less price-elastic. Increased oilseed production leads to lower market prices and hence cheaper costs of production in the vegetable oils and fats sectors, expanding output there. This expansion is particularly marked in the Southern Cone region of South America where no less than one-quarter of this production is sold on foreign markets. In North America, maize and soybean meal are used as livestock feed, and hence the lower feed prices lead to an expansion of the livestock and meat processing sectors there.

Because of the very large world market shares of oilseeds from North and South America and coarse grain from North America, the increased supply from these regions causes world prices for coarse grain and oilseeds to decline by 4.0 per cent and 4.5 per cent, respectively. As a consequence of the more intense competition from abroad, production of coarse grain and oilseeds declines in the non-adopting regions. This is particularly so in Western Europe, a major net importer of oilseeds, of which about half comes from North America. Coarse grain imports into Western Europe increase only slightly (0.1 per cent), but the increased competition and lower price are enough to entail a 4.5 per cent decline in Western European production. In the developing countries, too, production of coarse grain and oilseeds is reduced slightly. The changes in India, however, are relatively small compared with, for example, China and the Southern Cone region. This is explained by the domestic market orientation of these sales. That means India's relatively small production increase causes rather substantial declines in domestic prices for these products, which in turn benefits the other agricultural sectors. For example, 67 per cent of intermediate demand for coarse grain and 37 per cent of intermediate demand for oilseeds in India stems from the livestock sector, according to the GTAP database.

Global economic welfare (as traditionally measured in terms of equivalent variations of income, ignoring any externalities) is boosted in this first scenario by US$9.9 billion per year, two-thirds of which is enjoyed by the adopting regions (Table 1b). It is noteworthy that all regions (both adopting and non-adopting) gain in terms of economic welfare, except sub-Saharan Africa which loses slightly because of a small change in terms of trade. Most of this gain stems directly from the technology boost. The net-exporting GM-adopters experience worsened terms of trade due to increased competition on world markets, but this adverse welfare effect is outweighed by the positive effect of the technological boost. Western Europe gains from the productivity increase in the other regions only in part because of cheaper imports; mostly it gains because increased competition from abroad shifts domestic resources out of relatively highly assisted segments of EU agriculture. The group of other high-income countries, among which are East Asian nations that are relatively large net importers of the GM-potential crops, benefits equally from lower import prices and more efficient use of resources in domestic farm production.

Scenario 2: selected regions adopt GM maize and soybean; Western Europe bans imports of those products from GM-adopting regions

In this scenario, Western Europe not only refrains from using GM crops in its own domestic production systems, but the region is also assumed to reject imports of genetically modified oilseeds and coarse grain from GM-adopting regions. This assumes that the labelling enables Western European importers to identify such shipments and that all oilseed and coarse grain exports from GM-adopting regions will be labelled 'may contain GMOs'. Under these conditions the distinction between GM-inclusive and GM-free products is simplified to one that relates directly to the country of origin, and labelling costs are ignored. This import ban scenario reflects the most extreme application of the precautionary principle within the framework of the Biosafety Protocol.

A Western European ban on the imports of genetically modified coarse grain and oilseeds changes the situation in scenario 1 rather dramatically, especially for the oilseed sector in North America, which has been highly dependent on the EU market. The result of the European ban is not only a decline in total North American oilseed exports by almost 30 per cent, but also a production decline of 10 per cent, pulling resources such as land out of this sector (Table 2). For coarse grain, by contrast, only 18 per cent of North American production is exported and just 8 per cent of those exports is destined for Western Europe. Therefore the ban does not affect North American production and exports of maize to the same extent as for soybean, although the downward pressure on the international price of maize dampens significantly the production-enhancing effect of the technological boost. Similar effects are evident in the other GM-adopting regions, except again for India.

For sub-Saharan Africa, which by assumption is unable to adopt the new GM technology, access to the Western European markets when other competitors are excluded expands. Oilseed exports from this region rise dramatically, by enough to increase domestic production by 4 per cent. Western Europe increases its own production of oilseeds, however, so the aggregate increase in oilseed imports amounts to less than 1 per cent. Its production of coarse grain also increases, but not by as much because of an initial high degree of self-sufficiency. Europe's shift from imported oilseeds and coarse grain to domestically produced products has implications further downstream. Given an imperfect degree of substitution in production between domestic and imported intermediate inputs, the higher prices of domestically produced maize and soybean mean that livestock feed is slightly more expensive. (Half of intermediate demand for coarse grain in Western Europe stems from the livestock sector.) Inputs to other food processing industries, particularly the vegetable oils and fats sector, also more expensive. As a consequence, production in these downstream sectors decline and competing imports increase.

Aggregate welfare implications of this scenario are substantially different from those of scenario 1. Western Europe now experiences a decline in aggregate economic welfare of US$4.3 billion per year instead of a boost of $2 billion (compare Tables 2(a) and 1(b)). Taking a closer look at the decomposition

TABLE 2 *Scenario 2: effects of selected regions[a] adopting GM maize and soybean, plus Western Europe ban on imports of those products from GM-adopting regions*

(a) Effects on production, domestic prices and trade (percentage changes)

	North America	Southern Cone	China	India	Western Europe	Sub-Saharan Africa
Production						
Cereal grain	0.9	0.0	0.8	0.4	5.3	-2.2
Oilseeds	-10.2	-3.6	-0.8	0.8	66.4	4.4
Livestock	1.2	0.3	0.2	0.4	-0.8	0.0
Meat & dairy	0.8	0.3	0.2	1.4	-0.5	-0.0
Veg. oils, fats	2.4	8.1	1.6	0.1	-3.4	0.0
Other foods	0.3	0.4	0.5	1.6	-0.5	-0.1
Market prices						
Cereal grain	-6.2	-6.0	-5.6	-6.7	0.8	-0.0
Oilseeds	-7.4	-6.8	-6.0	-6.5	5.8	0.4
Livestock	-2.2	-0.7	-0.4	-1.4	0.5	0.1
Meat & dairy	-1.3	-0.4	-0.3	-1.0	0.3	0.1
Veg. oils, fats	-3.3	-4.0	-2.7	-1.0	2.0	0.0
Other foods	-0.4	-0.3	-0.5	-1.0	0.1	0.0
Exports[b]						
Cereal grain	0.3	-2.9	5.0	23.4	15.9	-13.1
Oilseeds	-28.8	-69.2	-18.4	-8.7	167.2	105.0
Livestock	13.7	4.0	-1.4	12.6	-3.8	-1.8
Meat & dairy	7.5	2.1	0.1	7.1	-1.4	0.3
Veg. oils, fats	14.4	26.2	7.0	1.3	-15.0	5.8
Other foods	1.5	1.9	2.0	8.0	-1.4	-0.6

74

Imports[b]

Cereal grain	-1.9	-5.3	-2.8	-20.0	3.3	13.4
Oilseeds	-5.6	-21.9	3.0	-3.7	0.6	22.5
Livestock	-3.2	0.1	0.1	-5.9	0.9	0.5
Meat & dairy	-2.8	-0.5	0.8	-1.8	-0.2	-0.0
Veg. oils, fats	-7.7	-5.5	-1.7	4.0	5.5	2.4
Other foods	-0.6	-0.6	-0.8	-2.8	0.1	0.2

(b) Effects on regional economic welfare

	Equivalent variation (EV) US$ mn p.a.	Decomposition of welfare results (US$ mn p.a.)		
		Allocative efficiency effects	Terms of trade effects	Technical change
North America	2 299	27	-1 372	3 641
Southern Cone	663	71	-303	893
China	804	74	70	669
India	1 277	190	-3	1 092
Western Europe	-4 334	-4 601	257	0
Sub-Saharan Africa	42	5	38	0
Other high-income[c]	1 371	592	782	0
Other developing and transition economies	1 296	101	531	672
WORLD	3419	-3 541	0	6 966

Notes: [a]North America, Mexico, Southern Cone, China, Rest of East Asia, India and South Africa. For space reasons, results for numerous regions are omitted from this table.
[b]Includes intra-regional trade.
[c]Japan, newly industrialized Asia, Australia and New Zealand.

Source: Nielsen and Anderson's (2000b) GTAP model results.

75

of the welfare changes reveals that adverse allocative efficiency effects explain the decline. Most significantly, EU resources are forced into producing oilseeds, of which a substantial amount was previously imported. Consumer welfare in Western Europe is reduced in this scenario because, given that those consumers are assumed to be indifferent between GM-inclusive and GM-free products, the import ban restricts them from benefiting from lower international prices. Bear in mind, though, that in this as in the previous scenarios it is assumed citizens are indifferent to GMOs. To the extent that some Western Europeans in fact value a ban on GM products in their domestic markets, that would more or less offset the above loss in economic welfare.

The key exporters of the GM products, North America, Southern Cone and China, all show a smaller gain in welfare in this as compared with the scenario in which there is no European policy response. Net importers of maize and soybean (for example, 'Other high-income', which is mostly East Asia), by contrast, are slightly better off in this scenario than in scenario 1. Meanwhile, the countries in sub-Saharan Africa are affected in a slightly positive instead of slightly negative way, gaining from better terms of trade. In particular, a higher price is obtained for their oilseed exports to Western European markets in this scenario as compared with scenario 1.

Two thirds of the global gain from the new GM technology as measured in scenario 1 would be eroded by an import ban imposed by Western Europe: it falls from \$9.9 billion per year to just \$3.4 billion, with almost the entire erosion in economic welfare borne in Western Europe (assuming as before that consumers are indifferent between GM-free and GM-inclusive foods). The rest is borne by the net-exporting adopters (mainly North America and the Southern Cone region). Since the non-adopting regions generally purchase most of their imported coarse grain and oilseeds from the North American region, they benefit even more than in scenario 1 from lower import prices: their welfare is estimated to be greater by almost one-fifth in the case of a Western European import ban as compared with no European reaction.

Scenario 3: selected regions adopt GM maize and soybean; some Western Europeans' preferences shift against GM maize and soybean

As an alternative to a policy response, this scenario analyses the impact of a partial shift in Western European preferences away from imported coarse grain and oilseeds and in favour of domestically produced crops.[12] The scenario is implemented as an exogenous 25 per cent reduction in final consumer and intermediate demand for *all* imported oilseeds and coarse grain (that is, not only those which can be identified as coming from GM-adopting regions).[13] This can be interpreted as an illustration of incomplete information being provided about imported products (still assuming that GM crops are not cultivated in Western Europe), if a label only states that the product 'may contain GMOs'. Such a label does not resolve the information problem facing the most critical Western European consumers who want to be able to distinguish between GMO-inclusive and GMO-free products. Thus some European consumers and firms are assumed to choose to completely avoid products that are produced outside Western Europe. That import demand is shifted in favour of domestically produced goods. Western European producers and suppliers are assumed to be able to signal – at no additional cost – that their products are GM-free, for example by labelling their products by country of origin. This is possible because it is assumed that no producers in Western Europe adopt GM crops (perhaps owing to government regulation) and hence such a label would be perceived as a sufficient guarantee of the absence of GMOs.

As the results of Table 3 reveal, having consumers express their preferences through market mechanisms rather than through a government-implemented import ban has a much less damaging effect on production in the GM-adopting countries. In particular, instead of declines in oilseed production as in scenario 2 there are slight increases in this scenario, and production responses in coarse grain are slightly larger. Once again the changes are less marked for India and in part also for China, which are less affected by international market changes for these products. As expected, domestic oilseed production in Western Europe must increase somewhat to accommodate the shift in preferences, but not nearly to the same extent as in the previous scenario. Furthermore, there are in fact minor price reductions for agri-food products in Western Europe in part because (by assumption) the shift in preferences is only partial, and so some consumers and firms do benefit from lower import prices. In other words, in contrast to the previous scenario, a certain link between EU prices and world prices is retained here because we are dealing with only a partial reduction in import demand. The output growth in sub-Saharan Africa in scenario 2, by taking the opportunity of serving European consumers and firms while other suppliers were excluded, is replaced in this scenario by declines: sub-Saharan Africa loses export share to the GM-adopting regions.

The numerical welfare results in this scenario are comparable with those of scenario 1 (the scenario without the import ban or the partial preference shift) for all regions except, of course, Western Europe. Furthermore, the estimated decline in economic welfare that Western Europe would experience if it banned maize and soybean imports is changed to a slight gain in this scenario. The dramatic worsening of resource allocative efficiency in the previous scenario is changed to a slight improvement in this one. This is because production in the lightly assisted oilseeds sector increases at the expense of production in all other (more heavily distorted) agri-food sectors in Western Europe.

The welfare gains for North America are more similar in this scenario than in the previous one to those of scenario 1. But even in scenario 2 its gains are large, suggesting considerable flexibility in both domestic and foreign markets to respond to policy and consumer preference changes, plus the dominance of the benefits of the new technology for adopting countries. Since the preference shift in scenario 3 is based on the assumption that non-adopters outside Western Europe cannot guarantee that their exports to this region are GMO-free, sub-Saharan Africa cannot benefit from the same kind of 'preferential' access the region obtained in the previous scenario, where coarse grain and oilseeds from just identifiable GMO-adopting regions were banned completely. Hence sub-Saharan Africa slips back to a slight loss due to a net worsening of its terms of trade and the absence of productivity gains from genetic engineering

TABLE 3 *Scenario 3: effects of selected regions[a] adopting GM maize and soybean, plus partial shift of Western European preferences away from imports of GM products*
(a) Effects on production, domestic prices and trade (percentage changes)

	North America	Southern Cone	China	India	Western Europe	Sub-Saharan Africa
Production						
Coarse grain	1.8	1.3	1.0	0.4	-2.0	-2.6
Oilseeds	1.0	2.8	1.1	1.0	8.7	-1.6
Livestock	0.9	0.0	0.2	0.4	-0.4	-0.1
Meat & dairy	0.6	0.1	0.1	1.3	-0.2	-0.0
Veg. oils, fats	1.2	5.0	1.4	-0.0	-1.1	-1.2
Other foods	0.2	0.2	0.4	1.5	-0.2	0.1
Market prices						
Coarse grain	-5.7	-5.6	-5.6	-6.7	-0.2	-0.4
Oilseeds	-5.9	-5.6	-5.7	-6.5	0.1	-0.3
Livestock	-1.9	-0.4	-0.4	-1.4	-0.1	-0.3
Meat & dairy	-1.1	-0.2	-0.3	-1.0	-0.1	-0.2
Veg. oils, fats	-2.6	-3.3	-2.6	-1.0	-0.4	-0.2
Other foods	-0.3	-0.2	-0.5	-1.0	-0.1	-0.2
Exports[b]						
Coarse grain	6.6	9.7	13.9	34.1	-29.7	-24.1
Oilseeds	1.4	-4.5	2.1	14.1	-41.5	-32.4
Livestock	9.8	-0.9	-3.0	10.0	-1.8	-1.2
Meat & dairy	5.3	-0.4	-0.8	6.0	-0.7	0.1
Veg. oils, fats	6.7	15.8	5.5	-4.0	-5.8	-4.9
Other foods	0.4	0.4	1.7	7.6	-0.7	0.1

Imports[b]

Coarse grain	-1.7	-4.8	-3.9	-20.4	-23.6	11.5
Oilseeds	-2.9	-9.6	-0.7	-7.4	-17.7	17.3
Livestock	-2.3	1.1	0.8	-5.3	0.4	0.2
Meat & dairy	-2.1	0.1	0.8	-1.7	-0.1	-0.0
Veg. oils, fats	-4.2	-3.8	-1.5	3.4	1.5	3.4
Other foods	-0.1	-0.2	-0.6	-3.0	0.1	-0.1

(b) Effects on regional economic welfare

	Equivalent variation (EV) US$ mn p.a.	Decomposition of welfare results, contribution of (US$ mn)		
		Allocative efficiency effects	Terms of trade effects	Technical change
North America	2 554	-100	-1 092	3 726
Southern Cone	785	109	-246	917
China	834	106	69	672
India	1 267	184	-9	1 093
Western Europe	715	393	319	0
Sub-Saharan Africa	-5	0	-7	0
Other high-income[c]	1 233	567	674	0
Other developing and transition economies	1 120	168	293	673
WORLD	8 503	1 428	0	7 081

Notes: [a]North America, Mexico, Southern Cone, China, Rest of East Asia, India and South Africa. For space reasons, results for numerous regions are omitted from this table.
[b]Includes intra-regional trade.
[c]Japan, newly industrialized Asia, Australia and New Zealand.

Source: Nielsen and Anderson's (2000b) GTAP model results.

79

techniques. Globally, welfare in this case is only a little below that when there is no preference shift: a gain of $8.5 billion per year compared with $9.9 billion in scenario 1, with Western Europe clearly bearing the bulk of this difference.

CONCLUSIONS

Lessons

What have we learned? First, the potential economic welfare gains from adopting GMO technology in even just a subset of producing countries for these crops is non-trivial. In the case considered in the first scenario it amounts to around $10 billion per year for coarse grain and oilseeds (gross of the cost of the R&D that generated GM technology). Moreover, developing countries would receive a sizeable share of those gains, and more so the more of them that are capable of introducing the new GM technology. These gains, especially for developing countries, are sufficiently large for policy makers not to ignore them when considering policy responses to appease opponents of GMOs.

Second, the illustrative scenarios show that the most extreme use of trade provisions, such as an import ban on GM crops by Western Europe, would be very costly in terms of economic welfare for the region itself – a cost which governments in the region should weigh against the perceived benefits to voters of adopting the precautionary principle in that way. Imposing a ban prevents European consumers and intermediate demanders from gaining from lower import prices. It also means domestic production of corn and soybean would be forced to rise at the expense of other farm production, and hence overall resource allocative efficiency in the region would be worsened. In the case modelled, the GM-adopting regions still enjoy welfare gains due to the dominating positive effect of the assumed productivity boost embodied in the GM crops, but those gains are reduced by the import ban as compared with the scenario in which GM crops are traded freely. To the extent that some developing and other countries do not adopt GM crops (by choice or otherwise) and they can verify this at the Western European borders, our results suggest it is possible they could gain slightly in gross terms from retaining access to the GMO-free markets when others are excluded. Whether they gain in net terms would depend on the cost of compliance with European regulations (a cost not included in the above analysis).[14]

Third, even if many consumers in Western Europe are concerned about GMOs, the results of the market-based partial preference shift experiment (scenario 3) suggest that letting consumers express that preference through the market reduces the welfare gains from the new technology much less for both Europe and the GM adopters than if (as in scenario 2) a GMO import ban is imposed in Europe. The results also suggest, however, that developing countries that do not gain access to GM technology may be slightly worse off in terms of economic welfare if they cannot guarantee that their exports entering the Western European markets are GMO-free. A complete segregation of GMO-inclusive and GMO-free markets, or a decision not to produce GM crops at all, may be ways in which these developing countries could reap benefits from selling 'conventional' products to GM-critical consumers in industrialized countries. Whether that is profitable will depend on the premium those consumers are willing to pay to avoid GMOs and thus the aggregate degree of substitutability between the GM-free and GM-inclusive variant of each product.[15]

And fourth, large though the estimated welfare gains from the adoption of GM technology are, they are dwarfed by the welfare gains that could result from liberalizing global markets for farm products and textiles and clothing. Those gains were recently estimated at around $180 billion per year *even after* the Uruguay Round is fully implemented in 2005, almost one-third of which would accrue to developing countries (Anderson, Francois *et al.*, 2000). Should opposition to GMOs lead to the erection of further barriers to farm trade, that would simply add to the welfare cost of restrictive trade policies. Western Europe may consider that cost small (the difference in their welfare as between scenarios 2 and 3 is only $13 per capita per year), but four caveats need to be kept in mind: that estimate refers to only two of many products that the new biotechnology may affect; the next generation of GM foods may be quality-enhanced as well; a ban on imports will dampen investment and so reduce future growth in GDP; and developing countries in particular would enjoy less technological spillovers as a result, and for the poor in those countries especially the welfare forgone would be a far higher percentage of their income than is the case in Europe.

What role for trade policy and WTO?

We know from trade theory that trade policy measures are almost never first-best ways to achieve domestic objectives, and food safety is no exception (see Corden, 1997). Voluntary verifiable labelling of products free of GMOs, together with credible identity preserved production and marketing (IPPM) systems, should be able to satisfy most people's food safety concerns. IPPMs for GM-free products need not be prohibitively expensive, as markets for organic food and for grains with other special quality attributes testify.

The above facts may well not prevent some countries from imposing import restrictions on GM products, however, for at least three reasons. First, the Biosafety Protocol might be interpreted by them as absolving them of their WTO obligations not to raise import barriers. Second, if domestic production of GM crops is banned, farmers there would join with GMO protesters in calling for a raising of import barriers so as to keep out lower-cost 'unfair' competition. And third, the current lowering of import barriers, following the Uruguay Round Agreement on Agriculture and the information revolution's impact in reducing costs of trading internationally, would pressure import-competing farmers to look for other ways of curtailing imports.[16]

Given these political economy forces, is there a way for WTO to accommodate them without having to alter WTO rules? Bagwell and Staiger (1999) address this question in a more general setting and offer a suggestion. It is that, when a country is confronted by greater import competition because of the adoption of a new domestic standard that is tougher than applies aboard, it should be allowed to raise its bound tariff by as much as is necessary to curtail that import surge. One can immediately think of problems with this suggestion, such as how to determine what imports would have been without that new standard, but options of this sort may nonetheless have to be contemplated if the alternative is to add to the EU beef hormone case a series of dispute settlement cases at the WTO that are even more difficult to resolve.

NOTES

[1]Definitions of genetic engineering vary across countries and regulatory agencies. For the purpose of this paper, a broad definition is used, in which a genetically modified organism is one that has been modified through the use of modern biotechnology, such as recombinant DNA techniques. In the following, the terms 'genetically engineered', 'genetically modified' and 'transgenic' will be used synonymously.

[2]Even stricter standards are mooted in the revised Directive 90/220, according to the August 2000 issue of *Agra Focus*.

[3]European Commission (2000). This cost estimate may be excessive, at least after the initial set-up costs of segmentation are sunk. After all, one of the consequences of the information revolution and globalization is that product differentiation and quality upgrading are increasing rapidly in all product areas including foods and drinks. Spring water, for example, now sells in many locations for more than soft drinks and even beer and non-premium wine. Many consumers are willing to pay extra for superior quality, allowing economies of scale to lower the premium required.

[4]Details concerning the latter products are still to be decided, however, pending the findings of the FAO/WHO Codex Alimentarius Commission's Ad Hoc Intergovernmental Task Force on Foods Derived from Biotechnology. The Task Force is due to report within four years of its creation in June 1999.

[5]The precautionary principle implies that considerations of human health and the environment rank higher than possible economic benefits in circumstances where there is uncertainty about the outcome. This principle is already used in certain international agreements concerning chemicals. See O'Riorden *et al.* (2000) for current perspectives on this issue in various OECD countries.

[6]However, the Codex Committee on Food Labelling is currently considering the adoption of an international standard on GMO labelling.

[7]This product/process distinction came to a head at the WTO in the famous tuna-dolphin case in the early 1990s. The general issue continues to be hotly debated. See, for example, the recent paper by Howse and Regan (2000).

[8]These two crops are perhaps the most controversial because they are grown extensively in rich countries and are consumed by people there both directly and via animal products. Much less controversial are cotton (because it is not a food) and rice (because it is mostly consumed in developing countries). For a parallel quantitative assessment of the latter two products, see Nielsen and Anderson (2000c).

[9]The GTAP model is a multiregional, static, applied general equilibrium model based on neoclassical microeconomic theory with international trade described by an Armington (1969) specification (which means that products are differentiated by country of origin). See Hertel (1997) for comprehensive model documentation and McDougall *et al.* (1998) for the latest GTAP database.

[10]Nelson *et al.* (1999), for example, suggest that glyphosate-resistant soybeans may generate a total production cost reduction of 5 per cent, and their scenarios have *Bt* corn increasing yields by between 1.8 per cent and 8.1 per cent.

[11]Owing to the absence of sufficiently detailed empirical data on the agronomic and hence economic impact of cultivating GM crops, the 5 per cent productivity shock applied here represents an average shock (over all specified commodities and regions). Changing this shock (for example doubling it to 10 per cent) generates near-linear changes (that is, roughly a doubling) in

the effects on prices and quantities. This lowering of the supply price of GM crops is net of the technology fee paid to the seed supplier (which is assumed to be a payment for past sunk costs of research) and of any mandatory 'may contain GMOs' labelling and identity preservation costs. The latter are ignored in the CGE analysis to follow, but further research might explicitly include them and, to fine-tune the welfare calculations, even keep track of which country is the home of the (typically multinational) firm receiving the technology fee. The mergers and acquisitions among life science firms in recent years, induced in part by reforms to intellectual property rights (Maskus, 2000; Santaniello *et al.* 2000), has concentrated ownership of biotechnology patents in the hands of a small number of US and EU conglomerates (see Falcon, present volume).

[12]See the technical appendix of Nielsen and Anderson (2000a), which describes how the exogenous preference shift is introduced into the GTAP model, a method adopted from Nielsen (1999).

[13]The size of this preference shift is arbitrary, and is simply used to illustrate the possible direction of effects of this type of preference shift as compared with the import ban scenario.

[14]For more on the impact of agricultural biotechnology on developing countries, see Persley and Lantin (2000) and, as it affects trade agreements, Zarrilli (2000).

[15]A first attempt to model such segregation of maize and soybean markets globally is reported in Anderson, Nielsen and Robinson (2000).

[16]The emergence of the concept of agriculture's so-called 'multifunctionality', and the call for trade policy and the WTO to deal with environmental and labour standards issues, can be viewed in a similar light (Anderson, 1998, 2000).

BIBLIOGRAPHY

Anderson, K. (1998), 'Environmental and Labor Standards; What Role for the WTO?', in A.O. Krueger (ed.), *The WTO as an International Organization*, Chicago: University of Chicago Press.

Anderson, K. (2000), 'Agriculture's "Multifunctionality" and the WTO', *Australian Journal of Agricultural and Resource Economics*, **44**, 475–94.

Anderson, K., Francois, J., Hertel, T., Hoekman, B. and Martin, W. (2000), 'Potential Gains from Trade Reform in the New Millennium', paper presented at the 3rd Annual Conference on Global Economic Analysis, Monash University, Mt Eliza, 28–30 June.

Anderson, Kym, Nielsen, C.P. and Robinson, S. (2000), 'Estimating the Economic Effects of GMOs: the Importance of Policy Choices and Preferences', plenary paper presented at the 4th International Conference on the Economics of Agricultural Biotechnology, Ravello, Italy, 24–8 August.

Armington, P.A. (1969), 'A Theory of Demand for Products Distinguished by Place of Production', *IMF Staff Papers*, **16**, 159–78.

Bagwell, K. and Staiger, R.W. (1999), 'Domestic Policies, National Sovereignty and International Economic Institutions', *NBER Working Paper 7293*, Cambridge, MA, August.

Corden, W.M. (1997), *Trade Policy and Economic Welfare*, 2nd edn, Oxford: Clarendon Press.

European Commission (1999), *The EU Approach to the Millennium Round: Communication from the Commission to the Council and to the European Parliament*, Note for the 133 Committee, MD: 400/99, Brussels: European Commission.

European Commission (2000), *Economic Impacts of Genetically Modified Crops on the Agri-Food Sector: A Synthesis* (working document), DG-Agriculture, Brussels: European Commission.

Falck-Zepeda, J.B., Traxler, G. and Nelson, R.G. (2000), 'Surplus Distribution from the Introduction of a Biotechnology Innovation', *American Journal of Agricultural Economics*, **82**, 360–69.

Hertel, T.W. (ed.) (1997), *Global Trade Analysis: Modeling and Applications*, Cambridge and New York: Cambridge University Press.

Howse, R. and Regan, D. (2000), 'The Product/Process Distinction – An Illusory Basis for Disciplining Unilateralism in Trade Policy', mimeo, University of Michigan Law School, Ann Arbor.

James, C. (1997), 'Global Status of Transgenic Crops in 1997', *ISAAA BRIEFS No. 5*, Ithaca, NY: International Service for the Acquisition of Agri-biotech Applications.

James, C. (1998), 'Global Review of Commercialized Transgenic Crops: 1998', *ISAAA BRIEFS No. 8*, Ithaca, NY: International Service for the Acquisition of Agri-biotech Applications.

James, C. (1999), 'Global Status of Commercialized Transgenic Crops: 1999', *ISAAA BRIEFS No. 12*, Ithaca, NY: International Service for the Acquisition of Agri-biotech Applications.

McDougall, R.A., Elbehri, A. and Truong, T.P. (eds) (1998), *Global Trade, Assistance and Protection: The GTAP 4 Data Base*, West Lafayette: Centre for Global Trade Analysis, Purdue University.

Maskus, K.E. (2000), *Intellectual Property Rights in the Global Economy*, Washington, DC: Institute for International Economics.

Nelson, G.C., Josling, T., Bullock, D., Unnevehr, L., Rosegrant, M. and Hill, L. (1999), '*The Economics and Politics of Genetically Modified Organisms: Implications for WTO 2000*', Bulletin 809, College of Agricultural, Consumer and Environmental Sciences, University of Illinois at Urbana-Champaign.

Nielsen, C.P. (1999), '*Økonomiske virkninger af landbrugets anvendelse af genteknologi: Produktion, forbrug og international handel*' (Economic effects of applying genetic engineering in agriculture: Production, consumption and international trade), with an English summary, report no. 110, Danish Institute of Agricultural and Fisheries Economics (SJFI), Copenhagen.

Nielsen, C.P. and Anderson, K. (2000a), 'GMOs, Trade Policy and Welfare in Rich and Poor Countries', paper presented at the World Bank Workshop on Standards, Regulation and Trade, Washington, DC in condensed form in K. Maskus and J. Wilson (eds), *Standards, Regulation and Trade*, Ann Arbor: University of Michigan Press.

Nielsen, C.P. and Anderson, K. (2000b), 'Global Market Effects of Alternative European Responses to GMOs', *CIES Discussion Paper 0032*, Adelaide: Centre for International Economic Studies, University of Adelaide.

Nielsen, C.P. and Anderson, K. (2000c), 'Global Market Effects of Adopting Transgenic Rice and Cotton', mimeo, Centre for International Economic Studies, University of Adelaide.

O'Riorden, T., Cameron, J. and Jordan, A. (eds) (2000), *Reinterpreting the Precautionary Principle*, London: Cameron May.

OECD (1999), *Modern Biotechnology and Agricultural Markets: A Discussion of Selected Issues and the Impact on Supply and Markets*, Directorate for Food, Agriculture and Fisheries, Committee for Agriculture, AGR/CA/APM/CFS/MD(2000)2, Paris: OECD.

OECD (2000), *Report of the Task Force for the Safety of Novel Foods and Feeds*, C(2000)86/ADD1, Paris: OECD.

Persley, G.J. and Lantin, M.M. (2000), *Agricultural Biotechnology and the Poor*, Washington, D.C.: CGIAR Secretariat and US National Academy of Sciences (chapters available at *www.cgiar.org/biotech/rep0100/contents.htm*).

Runge, C.F. and Jackson, L.A. (1999), 'Labeling, Trade and Genetically Modified Organisms (GMOs): A Proposed Solution', (*Working Paper WP99–4*), University of Minnesota, Centre for International Food and Agricultural Policy, November.

Santaniello, V., Evenson, R.E., Zilberman, D. and Carson, G.A. (eds) (2000), *Agriculture and Intellectual Property Rights: Economic, Institutional and Implementation Issues in Biotechnology*, Oxford and New York: CABI Publishing.

Thorson, N.W. (2000), 'International Trade in Genetically Modified Food: Reconciling the Biosafety Protocol with the WTO Agreements', paper presented at the 4th International Conference on the Economics of Agricultural Biotechnology, Ravello, Italy, 24–8 August.

Tietje, C. (1997), 'Voluntary Eco-Labelling Programmes and Questions of State Responsibility in the WTO/GATT Legal System', *Journal of World Trade*, **31**, 123–58.

UNEP (2000), *Cartagena Protocol on Biosafety to the Convention on Biological Diversity* (*http://www.biodiv.org/biosafe/biosafety-protocol.htm*).

USDA (1999), *Impact of Adopting Genetically Engineered Crops in the U.S. – Preliminary Results*, Washington, DC: Economic Research Service, USDA.

WTO (1995), *The Results of the Uruguay Round of Multilateral Trade Negotiations: The Legal Texts*, Geneva: World Trade Organization.

WTO (1998a), *Understanding the WTO Agreement on Sanitary and Phytosanitary (SPS) Measures*, Geneva: World Trade Organization.

WTO (1998b), 'Goods: Rules on NTMs', in *WTO: A Training Package*, module 3, Geneva: World Trade Organization.

WTO (1998c), *EC – Measures Concerning Meat and Meat Products (Hormones), Report of the Appellate Body*, 13 February, WT/DS26/AB/R. WT/DS48/AB/R AB-1997–4, Geneva: World Trade Organization.

Zarrilli, S. (2000), 'Genetically Modified Organisms and Multilateral Negotiations: A New Dilemma for Developing Countries', mimeo, UNCTAD, Geneva, 26 June.

KLAUS M. LEISINGER*

*The 'Political Economy' of Agricultural Biotechnology
for the Developing World*

INTRODUCTION

At the beginning of the new millennium, the 150-year-old conceptual skeleton of 'political economy' is rattling loudly in the closet. Early in his work Marx (1859) argued that there is a close and circular relationship between the social conditions of a nation and its conditions of production, the latter determining its level of economic development. In this context institutional structures and social values, as well as ways of thinking and attitudes of members of civil society, are very important. In the current discussion of agricultural biotechnology for developing countries this part of Marxian analysis is highly relevant, particularly for urban impoverished groups as well as resource-poor farmers and their families. This paper looks at the impact current politicized discussion in Europe is having on public research for the developing world and proposes a way of building a bridge over the troubled waters currently dividing proponents and opponents of agricultural biotechnology.

THE FUTURE OF FOOD SECURITY

The United Nations observed 12 October 1999 as the Day of Six Billion – the world's population had doubled since 1960. In some parts of the developing world, the population grew even faster; in sub-Saharan Africa, for example, it tripled. The number of people in Asia grew most in absolute terms, by nearly 2 billion. Most population experts expect that world population will grow by another 50 per cent, which means at least 3 billion more people by 2050. Table 1 shows that almost all this growth will occur in less developed regions (UN, 1999; Population Reference Bureau, 2000).

In the developing world today, an estimated 800 million people already do not have enough to eat. Countless children die from nutritional deficiencies or grow up with reduced physical or intellectual abilities, and will later suffer from lower productivity (FAO, 1999a; Smith and Haddad, 2000). In addition to the absolute increase in the number of people to be fed, structural changes will

*Klaus M. Leisinger, Novartis Foundation for Sustainable Development and University of Basle (Switzerland).

TABLE 1   *Current and projected population, by region, 2000–2050 (millions)*

Region	Population		
	2000	2025	2050
World	6 070	7 909	9 243
More developed	1 184	1 232	1 222
Less developed	4 886	6 677	8 021
of which in			
Africa	800	1 258	1 804
Asia	3 566	4 707	5 379
Latin America	520	712	838

Source: Population Reference Bureau, Washington, DC, personal communication, May 2000.

have an impact on the quantities needed. Urbanization will soar, for example. The global urban population is expected to nearly double from 2.6 billion people in 1995 to 5.1 billion in 2030. By then, 57 per cent of the population of developing countries will live in cities (UN, 1998). A high rate of urbanization will not only confront inhabitants with social, environmental and probably political problems of unprecedented magnitude, but will also have notable consequences for food security.

Whatever the hopes for urban gardens and nearby farms, people living in cities are unable to feed themselves through subsistence food production in the same way as rural dwellers. This necessitates a significant increase in marketed food supplies. Since the eating patterns of urban populations differ substantially from those of rural folk, different food will have to be produced. The amounts of high-value, transportable and storable grain (such as rice and wheat), animal protein (both meat and milk) and vegetables are higher in urban diets, while the proportion of traditional foodstuffs in the diet decreases. This means that there will be a diversion of cereals from food to animal feed.

If incomes continue to rise for urban professional groups as they have in the past ten years, the number of people who move up the food chain and eat more livestock products will continue to grow rapidly. This again means that grain demand will probably grow even faster. For political, cultural, economic and logistical reasons, this increased demand should be met as little as possible by imports from North America, Europe or Australia, so there is a need to increase production in developing countries.

If increased production is done in a sustainable way and with increased productivity, additional benefits will be achieved in poverty alleviation and improved livelihoods. Nearly three-quarters of the poor live in rural areas. As long as the number of rural poor is high, and indeed rising as in sub-Saharan Africa, food security as a general political goal cannot be achieved. Higher productivity for those who depend on agriculture and on common property resources is a precondition for poverty alleviation. For the quality of life of poor people in cities, who depend on the market for nearly 90 per cent of their food supply, a low and stable price for food is the most important variable (McCalla, 2000).

Higher productivity is also of ecological value. If average annual per hectare productivity increases by just 1 per cent, the world will have to bring more than 300 million hectares of new land into agriculture by 2050 to meet expected demand. But a productivity increase of 1.5 per cent could double output without using any additional cropland (Goklany, 1999). To increase local output through larger production volumes or higher productivity will be very difficult, however. A world of 9 billion by 2050 will meet significant constraints.

Water scarcity

Water, the source of all life, is going to become increasingly scarce. More than a quarter of the world, and a third of the population in developing countries, lives in regions that will experience severe scarcity (IWMI, 1999). The deforestation of the planet continues unabated, reducing the capacity of soils and vegetation to absorb and store water (FAO, 1999b). Water demand continues to rise much faster than supply, and the distributional battles between industry and urban households and agricultural irrigation are not likely to be won by agriculture. Today the irrigated sector accounts for close to 60 per cent of the food grown in all developing countries. The Consultative Group for International Agricultural Research estimates that, taking into account constraints on rainfed agriculture, the irrigated sector will have to meet 80 per cent of increased food demand in developing countries, which will be home to 2 billion more people in 2025 (CGIAR, 2000a). If, however, the availability of irrigation water stagnates or (what is more likely) decreases, average yields are likely to fall. Water supply for agriculture has already started to decrease in India, for example, as a result of overpumping in highly productive agricultural areas, and in China because of reallocation for industrial purposes or higher urban demand (Postel, 1999).

Pressure on land

There is growing concern that the developing world is facing a decline in long-term soil productivity. Wide areas of land are already heavily degraded, and this process, including salinization and waterlogging of irrigated land, has adverse effects on rural food consumption, on agricultural markets and hence on rural incomes (Scherr, 1999). Low and declining soil fertility is a serious problem in Africa, where about 86 per cent of the countries show losses of nutrients greater than 30 kilograms of fertilizer (NPC) per hectare per year (Pinstrup-Andersen *et al.*, 1999).

In 1960, the world still had 0.44 hectares of arable land per person; today the figure is about 0.22 hectares, and by 2050 it is expected to drop to 0.15

hectares (WRI, 1998). Since the reserves of unused arable land are dwindling, the expansion of cultivated areas will contribute a mere 20 per cent to the increase of food production (mainly cereals) (Pinstrup-Andersen *et al.*, 1999). Thus higher food quantities to meet the needs of a growing world population will have to come from higher yields, which is more easily said than done.

Reduction in the rates of increase in basic grain yields

There is considerable debate about the outlook for agricultural productivity. The Green Revolution increases in yields of cereals from conventional breeding have reached a plateau and are beginning to decline. Even the gap between yields obtained on experimental stations (maximum potential) and those obtained by the best farmers in the best production regions is narrowing (Pingali and Heisey, 1996). The question for agriculturists has therefore been, and remains, how to attain and sustain higher yields.

Scientific agriculture is one of the most important answers, not only to achieve desired production goals, but also to improve resistance to both biotic and abiotic stress. Reducing total costs of production by reducing chemical inputs through genetic research has implications both for production and for the environment. Moreover, research to reduce high post-harvest losses of crops can result in significant increases in the amount of usable agricultural production. This research ought to be publicly financed in order to reach those who do not have the purchasing power to buy research results on market terms.

Unforeseeable changes in climate

Although difficult to predict, climatic change might create additional problems for countries whose economies are heavily dependent on agriculture. Climate change is expected to have dramatically adverse effects on food security in the low and middle latitude areas of low-income countries. In addition, the warming of the Earth is expected to bring extreme climate events, such as Hurricane Mitch (Brown, 1999; Worldwatch, annual).

FOOD SECURITY AND GOOD GOVERNANCE

Summing up, population growth, urbanization and rising incomes will increase food demand, which will necessitate increases in food production. As water and land for agricultural use become increasingly scarce, more food will have to be produced through higher yields per unit of water and land. But, to avoid any misinterpretation, let me stress that more food production is not the only issue that matters for the welfare of poor people; what they need is more food security.

The Food and Agriculture Organization of the United Nations (FAO, 1996) defines food security as a situation in which all people at all times have access to safe and nutritious food to maintain a healthy and productive life. Food security has at least three characteristics: first, producing or importing safe, nutritious food in sufficient quantities; second, giving economic and physical access to rich and poor, male and female, old and young, on a continuous basis. The third characteristic has to do with the use and preparation of available food. This depends on the knowledge, skills and care of mothers as well as the health of those who eat. Since parasitic and other diseases substantially hamper metabolism and assimilation, health conditions figure significantly in the food security equation.

Shortfalls in food security can and do result from various interlinked adverse conditions in a country's socioeconomic and political system (Sen, 1981). Most of what is politically right or wrong for food security is known; also known are the emerging issues and the unfinished business (Pinstrup-Andersen, 2000). In the end, the only reliable pathway to food security is sustainable human development.

We know what needs to be done. The 'wheel' of sustainable development does not have to be reinvented. 'Good governance', with transparency of political decision making, accountability for politicians and state employees, institutional pluralism and the rule of law, is the most important prerequisite. Lack of sufficient allocations in national development planning in the socio-economic areas of health, education and food security are often the result of denial of civil and political rights, such as the right of democratic elections, free speech and information dissemination. Authoritarian governments that deny freedom of speech and the right to vote do not provide adequate information on the causes of famine and lack of food security, or on the low levels of literacy and health.

The best of present thinking indicates that a human-centred and market-friendly approach with an emphasis on good governance is the most effective way to break the vicious circle of continuing poverty, environmental deterioration and acute institutional deficiencies. There may be a need for adaptations to different sociopolitical and national circumstances, but, in comparison to the available knowledge with regard to the political, economic, social and ecological essentials of sustainable development, adaptation is a relatively minor issue. Good governance alone, however, will not be sufficient for food security; something has to happen on the supply side as well.

More local food production, not more imports

In order to supply enough food to the growing populations of Asia, Africa and Latin America without increasing dependence on international markets or food aid, more food has to be produced where people live. This will be predominantly in the tropical and subtropical, low-yielding farming systems (McCalla, 2000). Imports may be appropriate to bridge short-term gaps or in cases of emergency, but, for most developing countries, imports cannot substitute for local production. The argument that global food production is sufficient and that food security problems can be solved by redistribution is inadequate, for a number of reasons.

First and foremost, agriculture in developing countries is far more than just a producer of food. In most cases it still provides 60–80 per cent of all gainful employment. Agriculture is a source of income not only for rural farm workers but also for those employed in related trades and small industries, be they landless labourers, small traders or those working in cottage industries. Whatever productivity increase can be achieved, the income effects will be even higher. A dynamic agriculture is not only the best remedy against rural poverty: the sustained growth of industry and services has rarely been possible without the basis of growth fuelled by a flourishing agriculture.

Second, appropriate agriculture always means sustaining ecological intactness and caring about the environment. Third, as the word implies, agri-'culture' is a constituent of the many-faceted cultural patrimony of developing countries. And last but not least, the idea of feeding the African or Asian poor with surplus grains from the United States, Europe, Australia or Argentina implies the heroic assumption that immense logistical problems could be solved in a sustainable way.

BIOTECHNOLOGY AND GENETIC ENGINEERING

While good governance and appropriate rural and agricultural development endeavours remain necessary conditions, they are far from sufficient. There is a need for technologies that raise agricultural productivity and hence rural welfare. Considering the continuing absolute population growth, threats of water scarcity and the shrinking of arable land, and bearing in mind that the yield increases from conventional breeding for at least some crops are moving in the wrong direction, whatever has to happen on the production side will have to happen with new varieties. Hence something has to happen on the technology side. Biotechnology and genetic engineering – used wisely within a pluralistic technological portfolio – can play a crucial role in the development of the modern varieties that will be needed.

The term 'biotechnology' describes the integrated application of biochemistry, microbiology and process technology with the objective of turning to technical use the potential of microorganisms and cell and tissue cultures (including parts thereof). The key components of modern biotechnology include the following:

- genomics – the molecular characterization of all species;
- bioinformatics – the assembly of data from genomic analysis into accessible forms ('genetic fingerprinting');
- tissue culture;
- transformation – the introduction of single genes conferring potentially useful traits into plants, livestock, fish and tree species;
- molecular breeding – increased efficiency of selection for desirable traits in breeding programmes using molecular marker-assisted selection; and
- diagnostics – the use of molecular characterization to provide more accurate and quicker identification of pathogens.

In addition, there is hope for new health technologies such as vaccine technology, which uses modern immunology to develop recombinant DNA vaccines for improving control of lethal diseases. In view of the vastly increased capacity to accumulate knowledge that is made possible by molecular techniques, the goal of a 'knowledge-driven' agriculture, in particular plant breeding, is now entirely realistic.

Technologies such as molecular breeding or diagnostics are relatively non-controversial. This is not the case, however, with genetic engineering: the precise modification of hereditary genetic material in living organisms by the addition, removal or exchange of one or more genes, resulting in altered genetic information being passed on to descendants. One of the key differences between conventional breeding and genetic engineering is that with the latter it becomes possible to overcome natural cross-breeding barriers – in other words, to insert genes from one species into another unrelated species to produce 'transgenic varieties'.

This part of biotechnology has triggered enormous controversy in some European countries, raising similar concerns all over the world. In Germany, the United Kingdom or Switzerland, the broader public perceives genetic engineering as structurally different from other new technologies. Public opinion regarding the use of biotechnology in agriculture is predominantly sceptical or negative (Environmental Monitor, 1998).

In order to assess the value of biotechnology and genetic engineering for a growing population in the developing world, we must look at what has been achieved so far and what is likely to be achieved, consider the risks, and then weigh risks and benefits in a fair way.

Expectations and objectives of agricultural biotechnology

The main objectives of biotechnological research and development for food security are basically similar to those of conventional breeding: (a) to secure the given yield potential, (b) to increase the yield potential, and (c) to raise productivity. Efforts to achieve this include research for varietal qualities such as resistance to or tolerance of plant diseases (fungi, bacteria, viruses) and animal pests (insects, mites, nematodes) as well as to stress factors such as climatic variation or aridity, poor soil quality and crop rotation practices. Ideally, crop varieties that result from such research endeavours should lead to the cultivation of plants that fall into the category of 'sustainable agriculture': that is, they should not abet erosion or leaching of the soil. To complete the packet of desired characteristics, seed of improved varieties should be affordable to resource-poor farmers and have better product quality traits (more protein, minerals or vitamins).

Conventional crop-breeding programmes will remain important for the foreseeable future. They have a competitive disadvantage, however, in that they have to proceed in small steps toward single targets and are thus time-consuming; in addition, conventional breeding is more limited in scope as it cannot overcome natural cross-breeding barriers. If, in contrast, selection systems are developed that can be implemented in the test tube – through characterization of genetic markers for certain properties, for example – then research can be carried out with much greater efficiency. With the help of biotechnology, it seems likely that apomixis (asexual type of reproduction) for hybrids will be achieved, providing a potential breakthrough for small and big farmers alike. In the long term, plants may also be developed that can produce cheap, edible vaccines for humans from locally grown crops (Staubl, 2000; McGloughlin, 1999).

Case studies show that over the past few years biotechnology, with a lesser contribution from genetic engineering, has helped make progress towards food security, whether through resistance to fungal and viral diseases in major food crops or through improved plant properties (Potrykus, 1996; Krattiger and Rosemarin, 1994). The implementation of these research results is theoretically scale-neutral, though it is worth noting that the small farmer does not have to learn a sophisticated new agricultural system, since he or she has only to plant the new seeds embodying the research results. But research and science are only able to solve problems that are allowed to be solved by political leaders and the social setting. What is needed to put the theory into practice is well known by anyone who looks for the answer.

Hopes continue to be high. A World Bank panel predicts, for example, that efforts to improve rice yields in Asia through biotechnology will result in a production increase of 10–20 per cent over the next ten years (Kendall *et al.*, 1997). A German poll of scientists found that they expect that genetically engineered drought and salt tolerance will be achieved by 2012 and nitrogen fixation by 2017 – within the next generation, and before world population reaches 9 billion (ISI, 1998).

Achievements so far

First of all, by using non-renewable resources more efficiently, germ plasm enhancement has in most instances the same effects on preserving natural resources and improving the environment as germ plasm enhancement through conventional methods. To quote an example used by Norman Borlaug, in 1999 India produced about 220 million tonnes of grain, with an average yield of 2.2 tonnes per hectare. In 1961–3, the yield figure stood at 0.95 tonnes per hectare. If India had continued using the agrarian technology of the 1960s – that is, if the yield per hectare had not more than doubled – India would need more than twice the amount of arable land to produce today's food quantity. That land is simply not available; creating some of it would have involved conversions at high ecological cost.

Much has been achieved during the past ten years (Persley and Lantin, 2000; Hohn and Leisinger, 1999). Genome mapping and biotechnology research offer powerful tools for crop improvement, for example, in China, where transgenic varieties are now routinely produced in crops such as rice, corn, wheat, cotton, tomato, potato, soybean and rapeseed. The objectives of this research and development are crops that are disease-resistant, tolerate abiotic stress and have improved product quality and increased yield potential (Zhang, 2000). According to Gordon Conway, president of the Rockefeller Foundation,

China is doing 'spectacularly well' with *Bt* cotton, increasing yields and reducing the number of pesticides sprayings from about 12 to three per season (Conway, 2000).

Achievements in India include tissue culture regeneration, stress biology and market-assisted breeding, as well as new types of biofertilizer and biopesticide formulations. Research to develop genetically improved (transgenic) plants for brassicas, mung bean, cotton and potato is well advanced (Sharma, 2000). Programmes adapted to local needs and priorities are under way in the Philippines, Thailand, Brazil, Costa Rica, Mexico, Egypt, Iran, Jordan, Kenya, South Africa and Zimbabwe (Wambugu, 1999). Of particular interest for Africa are the research results on the transgenic sweet potato resistant to feathery mottle virus in Kenya and on South African types which contain up to five times the normal protein levels. Early laboratory results of research for nematode resistance in potatoes of indigenous Bolivian small farmers give rise to great hopes for a resource-poor population.

In many countries tissue culture has produced plants that increase yields by providing farmers with healthier planting material. In addition, marker-assisted selection and DNA fingerprinting allow a faster and more focused development of improved genotypes for important agricultural species. Moreover, as FAO points out, these technologies make available new research methods 'which can assist in the conservation and characterization of biodiversity. The new techniques will enable scientists to recognize and target quantitative trait loci and thus increase the efficiency of breeding for some traditionally intractable agronomic problems such as drought resistance and improved root systems' (FAO, 2000).

Among the many achievements one is of particular value. It has become possible to genetically modify rice so that it contains increased levels of vitamin A. It will soon be possible to achieve a similar result with regard to iron. This could be of immense benefit to about 250 million poor, malnourished people who are forced to subsist on rice. The consequences of this restricted diet are well known: 180 million people are vitamin A-deficient. Each year 2 million of them die, hundreds of thousands of children turn blind, and millions of women suffer from anaemia, one of the main killers of women of child-bearing age (WHO, 1999; UN, 2000).

Another achievement could turn out to be a major breakthrough. Researchers from Washington State University were able to transfer a maize gene into rice. The new strain of genetically modified rice, unveiled in late March 2000 in the Philippines at an international conference, boosts yields by a massive 35 per cent. As an added benefit, the genetically modified (GM) rice, which has been tested in China, South Korea and Chile, extracts as much as 30 per cent more carbon dioxide from the atmosphere than controls, offering a way of curbing climate change.

Since I will later deplore the fact that some of the louder critics seem to see risks, only to overemphasize them and fail to put them into context, I want to put these benefits in perspective. Agricultural biotechnology is no *deus ex machina*. No technology is of intrinsic value. Humanity has always used and will continue to use technologies as a means to an end – to facilitate living or to achieve other desirable goals. In their decision processes, societies and individuals have always weighed benefits and risks to arrive at a benefit–risk assessment they can tolerate. Advocating the use of biotechnology and genetic engineering to help improve food security in developing countries is not meant to support these technologies for their own sake or out of context. Using them is desirable only if and where, on a case-by-case basis, they have a comparative advantage in solving constraints related to agricultural objectives: that is, if they prove superior to other technologies with regard to cost-effectiveness.

Potential risks

Of course there are potential dangers associated with this technology, since every action has implicit and explicit risks. No technology in and of itself is good or bad, safe or unsafe, although some are inherently riskier than others, such as live vaccines versus new crop varieties. What makes a technology safe or unsafe is the way it is applied and the outcome of that application. The quantification of perceived risk can be described as a function of four interrelated variables (Daniell, 2000):

(1)   the scale of the potential harm, adjusted by
(2)   the likelihood of that harm occurring net of
(3)   the ability of an effective response to be put in place, adjusted by
(4)   the likelihood of that response mechanism being deployed effectively.

To a significant extent in today's debate in Europe, risk analysis is not done that way: risks are too often isolated from benefits and blown out of proportion, immensely small probabilities are not revealed in public discussion, and available effective responses are ignored or denied. Countless websites and publications tell horror stories about the perceived risks of biotechnology;[1] few discuss the weight and management of risks in a scientific manner (Rifkin, 1999).

For a variety of good reasons, perceived risks must be divided into those that are technology-transcending and those that are inherent to a technology (Leisinger, 1999). Fairness of discussion would also demand division of risks into hypothetical and speculative. Hypothetical risks are ones scientists know can occur, and they know how they occur, in the given technological or biological context. Speculative risks are those related to potential (hitherto) unknown interactions, with risk assessments commonly being brought forward in a dramatic scenario of assumptions that can neither be scientifically proven nor refuted. As there is scientific consensus that 'the same physical and biological laws govern the response of organisms modified by modern molecular and cellular methods and those produced by classical methods' (US National Research Council (1989)), and as 'no conceptual distinction exists', the introduction of speculative risks into the debate on transgenic crops is a deliberate attempt to stir up controversy.

Technology-inherent risks

As far as technology-inherent risks (such as allergic reactions or the unwanted flow of genes into wild species or landraces) are concerned, the best of present judgment indicates that genetically modified organisms (GMOs) pose no substantial unmanageable long-term health hazards for humans or animals (Cohen, 1999; Qaim and Virchow, 1999). Many unsubstantiated claims continue to circulate, but let the record show the following:

- The sensational report that potatoes transformed with a lectin protein could end up as being poisonous to human health has been rejected by the vast majority of reviewing scientists either because the methodology was flawed or on the grounds that the data do not support the conclusions.
- The old L-Tryptophane scare story (EMS syndrome due to the use of a genetically altered Bacillus amyloliquefaciens) has been proved wrong.
- Even the much-quoted Monarch butterfly laboratory study has been put into empirical perspective. Follow-up studies at Iowa State University and the University of Guelph have indicated that harm to Monarchs under field conditions are minimal. According to Mark K. Sears, chair of the Department of Environmental Biology at the University of Guelph, reports that *Bt* maize kills monarch butterflies are overly alarmist. After a six-month study of how pollen from GM maize affects butterfly larvae under field conditions, the preliminary findings indicate that 90 per cent of pollen fell within 5 metres of the cornfield. Pollen counts on milkweed leaves were lower than those demonstrated to be toxic to neonates, hence posing little risk to larvae (Sears *et al.*, 2000). In addition, there is increasing evidence that the time overlap of the pollen flight and the vulnerable development of the larvae is very small.
- The risk of allergy to genetically modified foods seems to be controllable and therefore minimal.
- In 1999, nearly 100 million acres around the world were planted with transgenic crops. No serious issues – forget about uncontrollable risks – came up.

To date, most empirical evidence supports the conclusion of the US National Academy of Sciences (1987): the safety assessment of a recombinant DNA-modified organism should be based on the nature of the organism and the environment into which it will be introduced, not on the method by which it was modified. The same view is contained in the declaration signed by more than 1500 scientists worldwide (including several Nobel laureates) in support of agricultural biotechnology.[2] If and where unresolved questions arise concerning risks of genetically modified food, science-based evaluations should be used on a case-by-case approach to answer them.

Technology-transcending risks

As far as social and political risks are concerned, today's criticism of genetic engineering and biotechnology is structurally similar to discussions about the Green Revolution in the 1970s. The improved plant varieties that appeared in the 1950s and 1960s were developed through systematic selection and crossing (hybridization), with the objective of increasing production and averting famines, particularly in Asia. Despite undisputed success in achieving significantly higher food production and an overall positive employment effect, there was (and still is) substantial criticism of the Green Revolution as being responsible for growing disparities in poor societies and for the loss of biological diversity. These developments, however, were not a consequence of the technology itself but of its use in a particular social setting. Risks of such type are neither caused by nor able to prevent the technology as such. Consequently, the successful management of such risks depends on an appropriate national framework for socially and ecologically sustainable agriculture.

The Green Revolution has certainly created some environmental problems, but it has reduced others, for example by allowing farmers to concentrate production on the best cropland and hence preventing the destruction of vulnerable biotopes or protected areas. As far as social problems are concerned, the overall effects are also good for small farmers. Owing to a social setting that was described by Gunnar Myrdal in 1968, the rich got richer. But the poor also got less poor (Hazell and Ramasamy, 1991).

A new category: risks of not acting proactively

Normally not part of technological risk assessments are the social, economic and political risks of not using genetic engineering for developing country agriculture. In view of expected population and natural resource developments over the next 50 years, an approach that tends to overemphasize present perceptions and underestimate the vulnerabilities of future generations presents a great risk to humankind and those future generations.

In this context there is an accountability issue. Who stands accountable for the anti-GMO activism that results in denying poorer nations access to a technology that could help them produce more and better food? Who stands accountable for scientific results not available in 10–15 years owing to political resistance today – results that might make the difference between food shortages and normal supply in resource-poor countries? There is no 'polluter pays principle' for pressure groups that poison today's discussions and are proud to go on record that they, as self-appointed attorneys for poor people in the South, can prevent agricultural biotechnology for the developing world.

The dominance of private sector research

If society approves of better access to improved technologies by food-insecure countries in the South, then public research has to be supported. Today, two-thirds to four-fifths of R&D in agricultural biotechnology is carried out in the private sector. On the one hand, this is desirable, as the public sector should cease supporting activities wherever the private sector can do things better or more cost-effectively. On the other hand, this dominance is a cause for concern to some who favour and most who oppose agricultural biotechnology (Lappé and Bailey, 1998).

Because the life sciences corporations must compete to appear attractive to the international financial community, their research priorities are determined by the financial returns on investment, and hence the needs of those who wield purchasing power in the relevant markets. To put this another way, it is not very likely that these corporations will be willing to fund research for drought tolerance, tolerance to soil and mineral toxicity, or other characteristics of relevance to the typical resource-poor farmer family in poor countries. Even if they were to make progress in these areas, the costs of developing useful products would be high and hence the products would remain out of reach for those who need them most. Part of the explanation for this is intellectual property rights: the knowledge and technologies, including DNA sequences, research tools and output traits are now largely proprietary. This, according to the CGIAR, has partly impeded secondary innovation and led to conflicting proprietary claims and high transaction costs (CGIAR, 2000b).

For private industry, a focus on profitable markets is necessary for survival. Some people may regret this reality, but then they should look for alternatives. The alternative to private sector research is public research. There the emphasis can be given to plant species that are most relevant to poverty reduction and income generation of specific ecological regions, and research can focus on losses caused by biotic and abiotic factors and on stabilizing yields on poor soils. The fruits of public research can be passed on to small farmers at cost or, via subsidized channels, even free of charge. As in the past, the CGIAR, with its focus on the needs of developing countries, will have to play a conspicuous role in such efforts in close cooperation with the different national agricultural research systems. The record shows how much has been achieved in the past 30 years through CGIAR and local partners (CGIAR, 1998; Anderson and Dalrymple, 1999; Shah and Strong, 1999).

Public agricultural research systems, however, depend heavily on public funding, which depends on political goodwill. That, in turn, depends to a large extent on judgments made by civil society about the objectives of the research. If these are seen as contributing to solutions, it will be feasible to raise funds. If they are seen to be adding to the problems, it will become impossible, especially in the long run. In order to make cutting-edge biotechnology available to small farmers, more public research has to be financed and more public –private partnerships (as when the private sector provides access to cutting-edge technology and gives permission to use it for the benefit of resource-poor farmers) need to be established. Successful cooperation for the poor will do a lot to improve the perception of a complex technology. The Insect Resistant Maize for Africa Project, which involves the Kenya Agricultural Research Institute, the International Maize and Wheat Improvement Centre (CIMMYT) and the Novartis Foundation for Sustainable Development, could serve as a pilot for more projects with different constituencies. But a politicized discussion in some northern countries about biotechnology is likely to prevent wider use of these options.

The tenor of the current public debate

Over the past several years we have witnessed an intense and highly controversial discussion of biotechnology and, especially, genetic engineering. Protests against food containing GMOs cross all social barriers, and opponents range from members of the English royal family to Indian trade union leaders. The degree of polarization is very high, as are the passions. While technological innovations are always associated with some anxiety and fears (remember the early story of the railway, penicillin and vaccination), the degree of scaremongering and the heat of the current discussion cannot be explained in terms of natural science, or at least not in these terms alone.

Genetic engineering is not very different from other types of activities that are carried out with the objective of creating organisms with desirable characteristics. Conventional plant breeding also involves gene transfer. Genetic engineering differs from conventional breeding inasmuch as it allows that to be done more easily across taxonomic boundaries, but this difference in technology cannot account for the difference in public perception. Clearly, there are more complex elements at work here. Analysing the current debate, it seems that highly sophisticated anti-biotech activists are easily able to mislead a scientifically uneducated public about issues of high scientific complexity.

'Hate sites'

One of the most important constraints on the social acceptance of biotechnology and genetic engineering is an unusually negative social marketing. There are biotech-related websites that read like 'hate sites'. Far away from any scientific evidence and often in contrast to the truth, biotechnology is associated with the worst disasters of modern history.

On several websites, risks of field trials with GMOs are compared with the impact of a nuclear disaster such as Chernobyl. This is not only far from a scientific risk assessment, it ridicules and derides innocent victims of Chernobyl. Food containing GMOs is referred to as 'Frankenfood' and food from genetically modified crops is labelled 'contaminated'. Opponents even criticize food aid to drought-stricken countries in sub-Saharan Africa as a conspiracy between the US government and the World Food Programme, 'dumping unsafe, American genetically modified crops into the one remaining unquestioning market-emergency: aid for the world's starving' (Walsh, 2000). This is an enormously cynical view to dump on the backs of starving people. Several websites use sophisticated Machiavellism instead of reason: on the one hand, they warn about unknown risks in the context of the environmental impact of a release of GMOs, and they ask for more studies; on the other hand, they call for vandalism and destruction of trials that have been set up to answer unresolved questions. Where more research is needed to create more data for the assessment of the likelihood and seriousness of risks, such research ought not to be prevented. Obviously, those who oppose the research have no interest in the results – at least in terms of the traditional concept of rationality that is based on plausibility and comprehensibility. Still worse, masters of political social marketing blow up risks with an extremely low likelihood through worst-case scenarios (for example, 'genetically altered food could trigger rare but deadly allergies').

Regulation as a political process

As a result of the negative tenor of the discussion, even politically neutral regulators want to be on the safe side. Thus food from genetically modified crops is 'held to standards that are irrational, far beyond those that any other product can or should meet, and that prevent their competing successfully' (Miller, 2000). Instead of applying the scientific consensus for a risk analysis – that the risk-based characteristics of a new product should be the focus of attention, regardless of the production techniques used – the method by which a product was created becomes the bone of contention.

The current work of a task force of the Codex Alimentarius is 'en route to codifying various procedures and requirements more appropriate to potentially dangerous prescription drugs or pesticides than to GM tomatoes, potatoes and strawberries. They include long-term monitoring for adverse health effects and batteries of tests for genetic stability, toxins, allergenicity, and so on' (ibid.). In industrial countries, food production has a low profit margin, and in developing countries regulatory absorptive capacity is low, so such over-regulation is likely to achieve the political goal of preventing GM food from reaching markets. Regulation of this degree violates a fundamental principle of regulation: that the degree of scrutiny should be commensurate with the risk.

Labelling should also be commensurate with the issues at stake. Would it serve the purpose of warning consumers of food risks if all organically produced food were labelled 'May contain bacteria and aflatoxin'? Would the consumer be wiser or better off if all meat from the European Community carried the label, 'May contain BSE'? And if not, what difference in substance makes the labelling of GM food mandatory? It is a fact that not all regulators are politically neutral, and it is my perception that at the moment there is no political downside to being against biotechnology and genetic engineering. While those promoting the technology are kept busy producing assessment after assessment, those opposing it get away with their self-made image of saving the world from disaster. The outcomes of publicly funded symposia may be manipulated by organizers inviting predominantly opponents while rejecting offers of lecturers with positive case studies on GM crops. The results of such conferences can then be used as 'evidence' by politicians and regulators who had made their mind up against the technology long before, but needed 'events' to go public with their negative preoccupations. In other words, tell me on what political grounds you want to decide and I tell you which institute or 'expert' should be given the job to write the report you need as 'scientific evidence' for your decision. Is it any surprise that the public has developed a considerable amount of distrust of 'experts'?[3]

Whereas, in a perfect world, regulation should rest on independent and unbiased expert knowledge, the real world has different parameters. In most states there is a close relationship between regulators and politicians. While scientists can assess the structure and extent of a risk, the decision on what exactly represents an 'acceptable' risk is a purely political one. As politicians decide on the key personnel of regulatory authorities, it should be no surprise that this has consequences for the direction of decisions. This political judgment is today different – in my view, biased in a negative way – in Europe than in the rest of the world. While this bias will not make a difference to the food security of Germany, Switzerland, the United Kingdom or the United States, it may affect resource-poor farmers in the developing world significantly and in a negative way.

Consequences for public agricultural research funding

As noted earlier, public agricultural research is of great importance for a sustained growth of food production in the developing world. But despite the known facts about population growth and environmental pressures, funding for this research for developing countries has declined. For example, the CGIAR – despite high praise for its work, which sparked an agricultural revolution in Asia and Latin America, with dramatic increases in food production and reduced food costs – has experienced a significant downturn in funding over the past few years. In most developing countries, where drastic reductions in public support for agricultural research have taken place, there are no compensating increases in private sector support. Unfortunately, the outlook for a substantial increase in funding is bleak.

Over the past ten years, most of the world went through dramatic changes in terms of geostrategic interests, political concepts, understanding of 'good governance', the role and understanding of technology, and other determinants of life. Partly as a result of this, the concept of the state's role in sustainable development and development assistance changed. Different ideas about what the state is best able to do led to critical choices about what to do and what not to do, and this had practical consequences. In addition, the value of macroeconomic stability and fiscal discipline for economic development is today better understood, which has led to consistent efforts to close budget deficits.

During this time, donor countries' official development assistance (ODA) dropped significantly, reversing a long-term trend, while private flows rose appreciably (albeit concentrating mostly on a limited number of emerging countries). This necessitated cuts within ODA budgets. In one area, mainly owing to a negative public perception of agricultural research in the context of the Green Revolution and genetic engineering, politicians obviously did not have to be afraid of incurring the wrath of the electorate, and that was support for research in favour of resource-poor farmers. Very personal convictions of individual critics and pressure groups about right and wrong, along with very different living conditions and natural resource bases, form the basis of protests that will have a harmful effect on people in sub-Saharan Africa and Asia. The fact that farmers in developing countries who are short of resources are thereby deprived of options for the future is either not apparent or not considered important.

Reviving dialogue and consensus-driven action

To a certain extent, pluralism of opinion is normal in modern societies, which are immensely pluralistic in their values, interests and beliefs. And the knowledge and experience that inform these societies also show an extremely diverse range of content and form. Modern, open societies are thus much more sophisticated social organizations than closed authoritarian societies – at a price that is worth paying. The assessment of new technologies occurs within this pluralistic structure; simple answers and undisputed processes for consensus are therefore not at hand.

The strength of the negative overtones that currently dominate the debate about agricultural biotechnology and affect the views of the public and, as a consequence, of many politicians does not give cause for optimism. Fair discussion on the Internet and elsewhere remains the exception to the rule.[4] My concern is that, in the next two to three years, little can be done to turn around the public perception. Recent public opinion polls indicate substantial scepticism about scientists working for the chemical industry and about regulatory authorities. Environmental pressure groups arguing against GMOs are seen in a much more favourable light. According to one recent poll, 63 per cent of British citizens tend to oppose or strongly oppose GM crop testing in their local area, being at least somewhat afraid of a potential negative impact.

It seems that things will have to get worse in order for them to get better. More visible consequences of the low productivity of resource-poor agriculture will have to occur. Issues like increasing poverty-driven migration, political upheavals, humanitarian disasters in these contexts and environmental destruction will be needed to bring the message home to the broader public: research that can raise the productivity and hence the income and the quality of life in poor countries is in the enlightened self-interest of all. It is preferable from a human dignity point of view and also more cost-effective than the political management of poverty-driven mass migration.

Thus, while doing whatever can be done technically, legally, in the media, and otherwise to improve the situation in the short term, we must focus on the medium and longer term. The current impasse is only to a small degree due to lack of information. It is much more a matter of attitudinal rejection. There is already a wealth of information on all important aspects of agricultural biotechnology, and there is excellent advice for all parties on how to deal with this information.[5] But more information alone is not the answer. Rather, those of us who are convinced of the potential benefits of biotechnology and genetic engineering must engage in spreading the 'gospel' through dialogue and cooperation.

To turn the situation around, we need a number of changes. First and foremost, research in agricultural biotechnology must come up with results that are more tangible and more easily understood by a wider public. Empirical social science suggests that lay people strongly believe that some scientific developments are beneficial and others are not. Their opinions are mainly coloured by whether people will benefit from the development and whether the application will be safe to use. While characteristics such as insect or herbicide resistance might warm the hearts of some researchers or farmers, most consumers will neither understand nor appreciate the blessings of this technology. Those must be brought home to a wider public by success stories such as the vitamin A rice or 'iron-rice' or by other improvements of the nutritional profile that are easier understood – and by putting potential risks into perspective. If they perceive the technology as beneficial, people are prepared to overlook benefit–risk trade-off objections. If the expected benefits are of questionable value (such as extended shelf life for tomatoes in countries with ample refrigeration facilities), there may be little justification for accepting any appreciable amount of risk. But if the expected benefits are clearly enormous (such as vitamin-A-enriched rice), it may make sense to accept a limited degree of risk.

Advantages for the consumer (better nutritional value, reduction of toxins) as well as advantages for farmers (less costly inputs) and the environment (fewer chemicals) must be empirically substantiated and properly explained. It should be possible to explain to a broader public the benefits of insect-resistant cotton – achieved by genetic modification with *Bt* – that cuts the use of cotton insecticides by nearly 40 per cent.[6]

DIALOGUE AND COOPERATION: FROM RITUALISTIC FIGHTS TO ISSUE-ORIENTED DISCOURSE

In addition to positive case studies for the improvement of human quality of life, consistent and coherent dialogue as well as practical cooperation are necessary to bring about a change in public perception of agricultural biotechnology. Dialogues are able to improve mutual understanding by providing and exchanging information, learning about other people's concerns and reducing prejudice. In addition, cooperation between different members of civil society can build up and strengthen mutual trust.

As people do not trust what they do not understand, communication becomes crucial. What cannot be communicated cannot be done. Experience from other social or political conflicts suggests that the vast majority of those involved in discussions want to be taken seriously and hence given competent and reliable information (European Federation of Biotechnology, 2000). Most people look to minimize possible risks through fair controls and want to participate in the decision process about values and objectives. This is possible, but quick results are unlikely. The fight for public acceptance will be a lengthy uphill battle and will have to involve many different constituencies.

Dialogue

All institutions, whether business enterprises, research centres, government agencies or non-governmental organizations, tend to be self-referring: that is, every organization has a more or less self-contained system of values and interests that it takes for the full version of reality. If people proceed on the assumption that their convictions are the sole correct ones, their ideas the best, their proposals the most telling, then – like all narcissists – they court danger: unable to size up chances and risks dispassionately, they commit errors that could have been avoided.

Dialogues, as search processes for better solutions, are not easy. In a perfect world, all parties can listen, evaluate, learn and, if necessary, change their opinion. The fact that people get into arguments over their positions only shows that they are concerned about the same things. A plurality of opinions and a competition of ideas are the expression of a dynamic intellectual climate. A plurality of interests in a society gives rise not only to conflicts but to significant opportunities as well. Why not make the most of this pluralistic situation when it comes to working out a path to consent on a politically sensitive issue such as agricultural biotechnology? To be sustainable, solutions to problems must reflect more than the narrow horizon of a single party. They also need to include other varieties of experience and interests. In view of the urgency and complexity of the many problems besetting our time, including the need to achieve world food security, a narrow-minded approach to problem analysis and solutions is just as hazardous as thinking in simplistic 'left/right' terms.

Dialogue does not do away with conflicts, of course, but it does help to resolve them constructively. The four prerequisites of dealing rationally with conflicts posited by Ralf Dahrendorf are central here (Dahrendorf, 1981).

(1) Conflicts must be looked upon as right and meaningful, for they can inaugurate or speed up significant social change.
(2) Intervention in conflicts must be limited to agreeing ground rules on the forms it should take.
(3) Conflicts must be organized and channelled, for example in political parties, trade unions, employers' associations, and so on.
(4) There must be agreement on the 'rules of the game' governing how a conflict is resolved.

Yet, even with these stipulations, dialogue is an open-ended process. The course dialogues take cannot be planned beforehand, and their outcomes are comprehensible only to a limited extent.

Dialogue participants

The question of who should be represented in a dialogue is difficult to answer. On the one hand, the full spectrum of opinion should be represented. On the other hand, at least in my experience, there is little sense in including fundamentalist advocates of particular interests. Organizations that explicitly state a preferred strategy of confrontation choose not to be involved in genuine dialogue. They seem to be so bent on confirming the 'truth' of their opinions about the way the world works and so preoccupied with the public splash this makes that they would feel themselves completely invalidated by any kind of compromise.

So-called 'issue champions' often seem unable to permit themselves the luxury of objectivity. They have moulded themselves to the opinion profile that works for their public, and the slightest compromise could mean a loss of face or lead to an identity crisis. So the role assignment that defines their persona takes on the function of a hypothesis corroborated by every act that does not conclusively refute it. Ideological reasoning adopts a given thesis as the un-questionable truth – also known as dogma.

Very often, even qualified experts, depending on whether they are on the supporting or the opposing side of a controversial issue, will evaluate one and the same set of facts quite differently. 'Schools of thought' tend to exert on their adherents a certain pressure to conform. Diverging opinions, being insti-tutionally unacceptable or upsetting, are brushed aside. Yet many of the positions on technical and political issues espoused 10–15 years ago by outsider minor-ity groups enjoy broad acceptance today.

In order to reach a consensus, both sides must be willing to join in learning together and in this way, perhaps, to arrive at a new, shared platform of certainty. This calls not only for scientific understanding but also for methodi-cal efforts to keep dialogues between different participants with different interests and values results-oriented. One path to this state of affairs, already mapped out in antiquity, is still useful today. First, find out what everyone can agree on. Second, discuss the remaining areas of disagreement in a spirit of aiming to reconcile them. Third, ascertain the consensus reached at this point in the discussion. Fourth, identify the areas of disagreement still remaining. (These usually have to do with different priorities in considering pros and cons or differing expectations where decisions attended with uncertainty are concerned.) Finally, strive for a fair compromise.

By fair compromise I do not mean the arithmetical mean between two standpoints. If that were the definition of a fair compromise, all the partici-pants would simply demand twice as much as what they actually hope to get. A fair compromise consists of a reasonable joint framework of action elicited through forthright argumentation and based on the participants' elementary interest in coexisting in concord.

Essential ingredients of productive dialogue

The ingredients of a constructive and productive dialogue are known: bring together all relevant factual knowledge; clarify the value questions that divide the participants; honour the right of self-determination of individuals and groups as indispensable in a democratic society. For a discussion to lead to better understanding and more consensus, it can be neither a playground for politics nor a stage for boosting NGO portfolios or making exaggerated prom-ises by life sciences corporations or research institutes. All must lower the rhetoric and deal honestly with the issues. More subtlety must allow more differentiation. All opportunities for dialogue must be used and include as many people of good will as possible. New coalitions must be formed to find constructive ways out of the impasse. The interests of the participants should be made explicit, along with the responsibilities, rights and duties.

Criticism and opposing views, whether based on science or emotions, have to be taken seriously. Euphemistic or horror language has to be avoided. Once mutual understanding and respect for each other's intellectual integrity has been established, open issues can be solved in a scientific manner rather than discrediting the personalities voicing the opposing view.

Credible dialogue will never focus on benefits only. As all human actions (or non-actions) have risks, these too must be part of the communication. If risks can be anticipated, they must be named and discussed proactively; there is nothing more destructive for the credibility of science or industry than pretending that there are no risks, only to be forced later by circumstances to admit their existence. Such behaviour is also incompatible with high professional competence and integrity.

Dominance-free communication

When masters and underlings talk to or about one another, the conversational tone is not the same as between those who are free and equal. Dominance-free communication denotes an ideal situation in which the rulers do not try to impose their claims to the truth on the ruled, but in which all participants have the same chance to speak their piece. In this model situation, the interlocutors must not deceive themselves or others as to their intentions, and there is no place for privileges in the sense of 'rules of order' binding on one side only.

A further part of dominance-free communication is the timely imparting of information, ensuring that everyone is equally informed. Whatever information is available and needed for the dialogue must be made freely available before discussions start. Tactically produced knowledge deficits are neither helpful nor necessary. Publications such as the one by Feldman *et al.* (2000) are a good start, especially for information disseminators such as science journalists, political advisors and public servants of national and international institutions. The information provided must be honest, complete, comprehensive and factually accurate. Unsupported claims or accusations are a waste of time and counterproductive to reaching informed consent. Appropriate information emanating from a joint venture of different constituencies could help an interested lay public to digest conflicting or controversial information and deal with the pressure of activist groups.

To expect that science will provide final proof at any time and in any event as a condition of taking action would be to paralyse our very ability to act. To put the 'precautionary principle' into perspective, every act, not excluding an act rooted in scientific theory, is 'tainted with provisionality'. But perhaps that is not our real problem, for no matter how narrow the margin of uncertainty in scientific pronouncements may become, people will bet on it when theory appears inadmissible and unbearable in practice.

Relinquishing animosities and 'searchlights'

Time and again we can see how people take up a hostile stance the moment their opinions encounter opposition. From that point on the mind is no longer open to impulses or ideas emanating from other directions; it only takes in the arguments that come from a 'friendly' quarter and therefore jibe with its own set convictions. Under such circumstances, it is not the facts that determine whether an argument is accepted or rejected but rather two mirror-image hypotheses: the 'presumed friend hypothesis', which lets people place their trust in what they have direct knowledge of and are able to understand; and the 'presumed enemy hypothesis', with the help of which everything that is unfamiliar or incomprehensible is seen as a potential enemy that must be foiled. Who turns out to be friend and who an enemy depends, of course, on personal experience and interests and on socially conditioned preconceptions.

With his 'searchlight' theory of science, Karl Popper drew attention to the fact that lay people are not alone in being susceptible to prejudices. Every scientific description of facts is also selective and dependent on hypotheses. The situation, said Popper, can best be described by comparison with a searchlight. What the searchlight makes visible will depend on its position, our way of directing it, and its intensity, colour and so on. It will, of course, also depend very largely on the things illuminated by it. Similarly, a scientific description will depend largely on our point of view and our interests, which as a rule are connected with the theory or hypothesis we wish to test. It will also depend on the facts described. No theory is final, and every theory helps us to select and order facts (Popper, 1980). As we all have our intuitions and assumptions, preconceived opinions, fiercely held beliefs and other searchlights, and as we all have tendencies to avert loss and a preference for the status quo, we all should do our best to be aware that it is not only our opponents who have limits. So do we.

The practical limits to dialogue

In practice, a dialogue cannot go on being prolonged until every last potentially or actually involved party is convinced. So it is necessary to agree on guidelines governing the technical aspects (beginning, end, breaks, sufficient familiarity with the subject) and the content (a demarcation of what is to be discussed). And there must be rules defining what constitutes a majority. Less than absolute majorities have to suffice for a decision, otherwise action will be stymied. The right of the majority does not rest on the erroneous assumption that it is always right. Nor does it rest on the assumption that one group has a natural authority over the other just because it is more numerous. Rather it rests on the absence of something like a higher authorization.

And there is another obstacle. Years of experience in stakeholder dialogue show that those who are normally delegated by companies or regulatory authorities to take part are not usually those who are able to implement what has been achieved as a compromise through consensus. Although the top management of companies and regulatory authorities – at least among the enlightened institutions – have no problem delegating representatives to such talks, the persons doing the delegating do not go through the all-important learning processes that the delegates experience. This gives rise to divergent perceptions and realities of the task ahead.

In the end, it is the benefit–risk analyses that should convince not only the scientists and experts but also a broader public. Democracy, not oligarchy, also has to work here. This also means that scientists will have to learn to explain their work in a manner that is understandable at least by an interested lay public. Myths have their own life and will only slowly fade away through continual communication and a consistent and coherent 'walk-as-you-talk' attitude by all parties involved in agricultural biotechnology.

Cooperation

Dialogues will not suffice. There must also be 'dialogue through cooperation'. Common research can lead to positive case studies of societal learning for different constituencies, including scientific committees, science journalists and other interested stakeholders. When people join together to work on a concrete project to achieve goals that are judged to be important to everyone, prejudices eventually disappear and labels that have been acquired lose their importance. The cooperation in the laboratories and fields allows differentiation between justifiable hopes and worries and unjustifiable ones. The opportunities, mechanisms and limits of such cooperation are made clear in the Tlaxcala Statement on Public/Private Sector Alliances in Agricultural Research initiated by CIMMYT.[7]

Different stakeholders can contribute diverse knowledge, on an equal footing and without any differences in social class, for the benefit of all. Controversies are dealt with on a case-by-case basis and as a side effect of the concrete work at hand. The process of moving from ignorance through arrogance and then to tolerance of different views of the world cannot be delegated. It has to be lived. It is a unique opportunity to discover parallel perceptions of reality, to cope with them and to combine them to form a larger whole. The ability to engage in constructive teamwork will separate the chaff from the wheat: anyone who is not capable of breaking free from the kind of friend/ enemy thinking anchored in dogma and of working towards coalition, who prefers demarcation to teamwork for political reasons, will have to put up with the slur of being a fundamentalist.

Those who have broader shoulders must exercise visible solidarity in a consistent way. First and foremost, in view of today's limitations, capacity and institution building for biotechnology must be supported and funded by development assistance resources. Only if there is a national absorptive capacity to understand the technology and deal with it safely can the benefits of technology transfer be maximized and its risks minimized. This support can range from consulting for state-of-the-art bio-safety regulation, best practices of capacity building, and clearing house advice to genetic material and laboratory equipment. Support from the private sector can also make a major contribution to putting constructive partnerships into practice in developing countries.

CONCLUSIONS

Public acceptance of agricultural biotechnology is at a critical juncture. The next two to three years will be decisive for its long-term viability. The discussion today in Europe is a predominantly political one, and has, in the old Marxian sense, a direct influence on society and the economy. In addition, it does harm to the public acceptance of technologies outside Europe and to the support for public research for resource-poor farmers.

The political economy of agricultural biotechnology could well turn into a missed opportunity to provide the developing world with effective means to facilitate food security for a growing population with shrinking natural resources. Given the complexity of socioeconomic, political and ecological problems behind deficits in food security, agricultural biotechnology cannot be a silver bullet or a miracle cure for all problems in all countries. A successful battle for food security in the developing world requires battles on many different fronts: economy, social policy, gender policy, ecology, water and soil management, agronomy, breeding programmes, agricultural extension, farm management, pest management, and others. New technologies, however, are part and parcel of a successful package. If agricultural biotechnology is used wisely in conjunction with conventional breeding, improved agricultural methods and better agricultural policies, it can become a powerful tool in the fight for higher productivity in the small farmer's field.

More than 100 years ago, it took the scientific world a whole generation to understand the significance of Gregor Mendel's findings. I hope that it will take much less time to grasp the importance of genetic engineering for a world that will have to feed nearly 9 billion inhabitants in 2050.

NOTES

[1] For the horror stories, see <*biotech_activists@iatp.org*>; for a scientific discussion of risks, see <*www.agbioworld.com*> or <*www.cropgene.com*> and <*kamman@sgi.unibe.ch*>. Another (<*www.gene.ch/pmhp/gs/media.htm*>) is a guide to media exploitation.

[2] The scientific declaration (found in <*www.agbioworld.com*>) states: 'No food products, whether produced with recombinant DNA techniques or with more traditional methods, are totally without risk. The risks posed by foods are a function of the biological characteristics of those foods and the specific genes that have been used, not of the processes employed in their development.'

[3] There is some evidence of obvious conflicts of interest. For an interesting example relating to the U.S. National Academy of Sciences, refer to Henry Miller, Senior Research Fellow at Stanford University's Hoover Institution on 'Nescience, not Science, from the Academy' (at <*miller@hoover.standforf.edu*>).

[4] More balance is to be found in the excellent work by C.S. Prakash of the Centre for Plant Biotechnology Research at Tuskegee University, Alabama (<*prakash@tusk.edu*>), and Klaus Ammann, director of the Botanical Garden of the University of Berne, Switzerland (<*kammann@sgi.unibe.ch*>) as well as of all those who contribute to <*AgBioView@listbot.com*>.

[5] For the basic information, see Nuffield Council on Bioethics (1999) and Dag Hammarskjöld Foundation (2000). For how to deal with the information, see <*www.ificinfo.org/resource/guidelines.htm*>.

[6] Described by Traxler *et al.* (2000). Such a substantial reduction has not been achieved in all years and in all areas where *Bt* technology is applied, as shown by the Economic Research

Service (1999). The easily understandable reasons for this are explained in Gianessi and Carpenter (1999).

[7]See <*www.cimmyt.cgiar.org*>.

REFERENCES

Anderson, J.R. and Dalrymple, D.G. (1999), *The World Bank, The Grant Program and the CGIAR: A Retrospective Review*, Washington, DC: World Bank Operations Evaluation Department.

Brown, L.R. (1999), *State of the World 1999*, New York: W.W. Norton.

CGIAR (1998), *The Impact of Knowledge* (Annual Report 1998), Washington, DC: CGIAR.

CGIAR (2000b), *Synergies in Science: Intercenter Collaboration to Eradicate Hunger and Poverty*, Washington, DC: CGIAR.

Cohen, J.J. (ed.) (1999), *Managing Agricultural Biotechnology – Addressing Research Programme Needs and Policy Implications*, London: CAB International.

Consultative Group on International Agricultural Research (CGIAR) (2000a), *A Food Secure World For All: Towards a New Vision and Strategy for the CGIAR in 2010*, Rome: CGIAR.

Conway, G. (2000), 'The Voice of Reason in the Global Food Fight', interview by David Stipp, *Fortune*, 21 February.

Dag Hammarskjöld Foundation (2000), *Seeding Solutions: Policy Options for Genetic Resources – Crucible II Report: People, Plants and Patents Revisited*, Stockholm: Hammarskjöld Foundation.

Dahrendorf, R. (1981), *Gesellschaft und Freiheit*, Munich: Piper.

Daniell, M.H. (2000), *World of Risks: Next Generation Strategy for a Volatile Era*, Singapore: John Wiley.

Economic Research Service (1999), *Genetically Engineered Crops for Pest Management*, Washington, DC: U.S. Department of Agriculture.

Environmental Monitor (1998), *Global Public Opinion on the Environment: 1998 International Report*, Washington, DC: Environmental Monitor.

European Federation of Biotechnology (2000), *Task Force on Public Perceptions of Biotechnology: Biotechnology for Non-specialists. A handbook of information sources*, Delft and London: European Federation of Biotechnology.

Feldman, M.P., Morris, M.P. and Hoisington, D. (2000), 'Genetically Modified Organisms: Why All The Controversies?', *Choices, The AAEA Magazine of Food, Farm, and Resource Issues*, first quarter, 8–12.

Food and Agriculture Organization (1996), *Food Security Assessment*, Document WFS 96/Tech/7, Rome: FAO.

Food and Agriculture Organization (1999a), *The State of Food Insecurity in the World 1999*, Rome: FAO.

Food and Agriculture Organization (1999b), *The State of the World's Forests 1999*, Rome: FAO.

Food and Agriculture Organization (2000), *Statement on Biotechnology*, Rome: FAO.

Gianessi, L.P. and Carpenter, J.E. (1999), *Agricultural Biotechnology: Insect Control Benefits*, Washington, DC: National Center for Food and Agricultural Policy.

Goklany, I.M. (1999), 'Meeting Global Food Needs: The Environmental Trade-offs between Increasing Land Conversion and Land Productivity', *Technology*, **6**, 107–30.

Hazell, P.B. and Ramasamy, C. (1991), *The Green Revolution Reconsidered*, Baltimore: Johns Hopkins University Press.

Hohn, T. and Leisinger, K.M. (eds) (1999), *Biotechnology of Food Crops in Developing Countries*, New York: Springer.

International Water Management Institute (1999), *Water Scarcity in the Twenty-First Century*, Colombo, Sri Lanka: IWMI.

ISI/Fraunhofer Institut für Systemtechnik und Innovationsforschung (1998), *Studie zur Globalen Entwicklung von Wissenschaft und Technik*, Karlsruhe: ISI.

Kendall, H.W. *et al.* (1997), *Bioengineering of Crops: Report of the World Bank Panel on Transgenic Crops*, Washington, DC: World Bank.

Krattiger, A.F. and Rosemarin, A. (eds) (1994), *Biosafety for Sustainable Agriculture*, Stockholm: Stockholm Environment Institute.

Lappé, M. and Bailey, B. (1998), *Against the Grain: Biotechnology and the Corporate Takeover of Your Food*, London: Earthscan.

Leisinger, K.M. (1999), 'Disentangling Risk Issues', in G.J. Persley (ed.), *2020 Vision Focus 2*, Washington, DC: IFPRI.

McCalla, A.F. (2000), *Agriculture in the 21st Century* (Economics Programme, Fourth Distinguished Economist Lecture), El Batan: CIMMYT.

McGloughlin, M. (1999), 'Ten Reasons Why Biotechnology Will Be Important to the Developing World', in University of Missouri (ed.), *The Economics of Biotechnology in Developing Countries* (at <*www.agbioforum.org*>).

Marx, K. (1859), 'Zur Kritik der Politischen Ökonomie', Preface to K. Marx and F. Engels, *Werke*, Bd. 13, 1985 edn, Berlin: Dietz Verlag.

Miller, H. (2000), 'Anti-Biotech Sentiment Has Its Own Risks', *Financial Times*, 22 March.

Myrdal, G. (1968), *Asian Drama*, 3 vols, Harmondsworth, UK: Methuen.

National Academy of Sciences (1987), *Introduction of Recombinant DNA-Engineered Organisms into the Environment: Key Issues*, Washington, DC: National Academy Press.

National Research Council (1989), *Field Testing Genetically Modified Organisms – Framework for Decision*, Washington, DC: National Academy Press.

Nuffield Council on Bioethics (1999), *Genetically Modified Crops: The Ethical and Social Issues*, London: Nuffield Council.

Persley, G.J. and Lantin, M.M. (eds) (2000), *Agricultural Biotechnology and the Poor*, Washington, DC: CGIAR/National Academy of Science.

Pingali, P. and Heisey, P. (1996), 'Cereal Crop Productivity in Developing Countries: Past Trends and Future Prospects', Conference Proceedings: Global Agricultural Science Policy for the Twenty-First Century, Melbourne, Australia.

Pinstrup-Andersen, P. (2000), 'Food Policy Research for Developing Countries: Emerging Issues and Unfinished Business', *Food Policy*, **25**, 125–41.

Pinstrup-Andersen, P., Pandya-Lorch, R. and Rosegrant, M.W. (1999), *World Food Prospects: Critical Issues for the Early Twenty-First Century*, Washington, DC: IFPRI.

Popper, K. (1980), *Die offene Gesellschaft und ihre Feinde*, Tübingen: Francke.

Population Reference Bureau (2000), *World Population Data Sheet 2000*, Washington, DC: Population Reference Bureau (or at <*www.prb.org*>).

Postel, S. (1999), *Pillar of Sand: Can the Irrigation Miracle Last?*, New York: W.W. Norton.

Potrykus, I. (ed.) (1996), *New Horizons in Swiss Plant Biotechnology – from the Laboratory to the Field*, Proceedings of a Symposium organized at the ETH Zurich on the occasion of the 125th anniversary of the Department of Agronomy and Food Sciences.

Qaim, M. and Virchow, D. (1999), *Macht die Grüne Gentechnik die Welt satt? Herausforderungen für Forschung, Politik und Gesellschaft*, Bonn: Friedrich-Ebert-Stiftung.

Rifkin, J. (1999), *The Biotech Century: Harnessing the Gene and Remaking the World*, New York: Penguin Putnam.

Sears, M.K., Stanlex-Horn, D.E. and Mattila, H.R. (2000), *Preliminary Report on the Ecological Impact of* Bt *Corn Pollen on the Monarch Butterfly in Ontario*, Guelph: University of Guelph.

Sen, A. (1981), *Poverty and Famine: An Essay on Entitlements and Deprivation*, New York: Oxford University Press.

Scherr, S.J. (1999), *Soil Degradation: A Threat to Developing-Country Food Security by 2020?*, Washington, DC: IFPRI.

Shah, M. and Strong, M. (1999), *Food in the 21st Century: From Science to Sustainable Agriculture, Highlights of the System Review 1998/99*, Washington, DC: CGIAR.

Sharma, M. (2000), 'India: Biotechnology Research and Development', in G.J. Persley and M.M. Lantin (eds), *Agricultural Biotechnology and the Poor*, Washington, DC: CGIAR/National Academy of Science.

Smith, L.C. and Haddad, L. (2000), *Overcoming Child Malnutrition in Developing Countries. Past Achievements and Future Choices*, Washington, DC: IFPRI.

Staubl, J.M. (2000), 'High-Yield Production of a Human Therapeutic Protein in Tobacco Chloroplasts', *Nature Biotechnology*, **March**, 333–8.

Traxler, G., Falk-Zepeda, J.B. and Sain, G. (2000), 'Genes, Germplasm and Developing Country

Access to Genetically Modified Crop Varieties', contribution to ICABR conference, The Shape of the Coming Agricultural Biotechnology Transformation, Rome.

UN Sub-Committee on Nutrition (2000), *The 4th Report on The World Nutrition Situation*, New York: United Nations.

United Nations Population Division (1998), *World Urbanization Prospects: The 1996 Revision*, New York: United Nations.

United Nations Population Fund (1999), *The State of World Population 1999*, New York: Oxford University Press.

Walsh, D. (2000), 'America Finds Ready Market for GM Food – The Hungry', *The Independent*, 30 March.

Wambugu, F. (1999), 'Why Africa Needs Agricultural Biotech', *Nature*, **400**, 15–16.

World Health Organization (1999), *Nutrition for Health and Development: Progress and Prospects on the Eve of the 21st Century*, Geneva: WHO.

World Resources Institute (annual), *World Resources 1998–99*, New York: Oxford University Press.

Worldwatch Institute (annual), *Vital Signs*, New York: W.W. Norton.

Zhang, Q. (2000), 'China: Agricultural Biotechnology Opportunities to Meet the Challenges of Food Production', in G.J. Persley and M.M. Lantin (eds), *Agricultural Biotechnology and the Poor*, Washington, DC: CGIAR/National Academy of Science.

GERHARD PRANTE*

Tomorrow's Agriculture

INTRODUCTION

Agriculture may never have faced as many challenges as it does at the beginning of the 21st century. Food and feed production needs to approximately double until 2025 owing to (a) population growth, with 73 million being expected to be added to the world population annually, which is an increase of about 32 per cent between 1995 and 2020 to give a total of 7.5 billion, (b) increased food calories consumed and (c) higher-quality food being demanded, particularly as regards meat.

Secondly, in the developing countries urbanization is gaining momentum, bringing additional food demand. By 2020, more than half of the population in developing countries will live in urban areas. The global village is becoming a global city. Thirdly, the land area available for food and feed production cannot be increased substantially: most fertile land is in use. Finally, water will increasingly become a scarce resource.

ASPECTS OF CHANGE

There will also be changes in the agricultural global business environment. These will involve continued decline in farm subsidies, commodity prices will remain flat and the agricultural economy will become increasingly 'market-driven'. At the farm level, contract production will become more attractive and there will be continuous consolidation at industry and grower level. In general terms, if agriculture is to meet the demand for food, feed and fibres, as well as new demand for renewable resources, the world's agricultural production and trading systems will have to go through substantial changes in order to be able to capture the production potential of innovations driven by advances in biological sciences.

The globalization of economic activities is a development which also affects agriculture. It will support the needed efficiency improvements of natural resources, if financial support systems do not undermine the process. It is to be expected that WTO negotiations will continue to lead to more common standards and guidelines for financial support where it is needed. The food industry

*Aventis Crop Science, Frankfurt-am-Main, Germany.

will increasingly develop international standards for the production of raw materials, hence the food industry will increasingly influence the way agricultural commodities are produced. Contract growing is important in that context.

Advances in biotechnology and genetic engineering will profoundly influence farm productivity and agriculture's ability to meet the sustainability challenge in coming decades. These advances will in most cases come to the market through new seed varieties. Therefore the importance of seeds as the carrier of technology and of value improvement will increase in importance at the farm level, as well as being a value driver of the food chain beyond the farm gate. Biotechnology is already a catalyst for changes of the farm input value chain. Tomorrow it will be a catalyst for change of the food value chain.

Most fertile land is in use already and low cost irrigation cannot be added. Likewise, the increase in agricultural production has been declining since the days of the Green Revolution. But the world's farmers will have to produce 40 per cent more grain in 2020 compared with today. In spite of the fact that food production is increasing much faster in the developing world than in the developed world, it seems likely that cereal production in developing areas will not meet the growing demand. Globally, 2 per cent growth in agricultural output is needed to meet the expected demand. This is about the rate of recent decades, but it is rather slower than the 3 per cent per year of the 1960s and below the 2.3 per cent of the 1970s. Pessimists would argue that the target cannot be met and that the growth rate will have dropped further, to about 1.8 per cent, by 2010.

Some of the changes which have occurred have been remarkable. For example, the increased yield of grains between 1950 and 1995 meant that the per capita area needed for grain could virtually be halved. The fall was from about 2.200 to 1.100 m^2/capita (Figure 1). Selected illustrative material for various crops by country appears in Figure 2. All show very large increases, though some areas cannot match others for the same crop (for example, Indonesian rice against China's or South African corn against that of the United States).

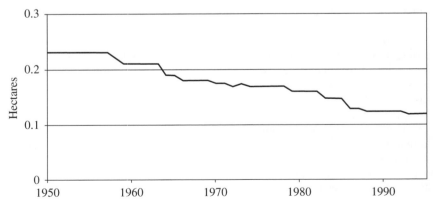

FIGURE 1   *World grain harvested area per person, 1950–95*

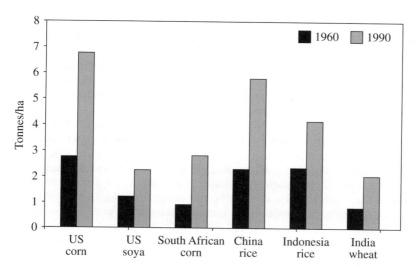

FIGURE 2   *Gain in crop yields, 1950s–1990s*

Without the contribution to agricultural supply millions of hectares of very valuable natural habitats would have had to be destroyed for food production. This very substantial contribution of high-yielding agriculture, with today's farming practices, to the environment and to biodiversity is not sufficiently appreciated. In the coming decades, agriculture must be able to make the same contribution. This can be regarded as a *sustainability challenge* which will have to be met by providing farmers globally with the technology and the incentives to repeat their previous successes.

It has to be stressed that increased agricultural output must come primarily from the productivity impact of higher yields. The easier path of reliance on increasing use of available natural resources of land and water is closed. But increasing yields is most likely be a greater challenge than during the past 50 years since it needs to be coupled with a sustainable, more efficient, use of natural resources which will require new technologies and improved management techniques to be employed on farms of all sizes.

SUSTAINABILITY

The United Nations Conference on Environment and Development in Rio de Janeiro in 1992 established important basic principles for environmental policy, to which more than 170 countries gave their consent. Governments, non-governmental organizations, industry and academic and civil society are struggling to find a new vision that will meet the sustainability challenge. Sustainability needs to become the organizing principle for attaining growth, with environmental protection recognized as an integral part of technology and management development. Effective dialogue at all levels must reduce misinformation in order to establish effective cooperation between business, governments and society. We need together to find ways to overcome such controversies as exist today regarding genetically modified (improved) organisms (GMOs). We must be able to make this technology available to the farming community globally in a responsible way in order to achieve the needed productivity improvement and the more efficient use of natural resources.

To be sustainable, food production must satisfy important criteria. It should use locally adapted technology and crop management systems which are compatible with the prevailing environmental conditions. Additionally, it should have economic benefits for all involved in the food production chain and thus provide net benefits to society. In order to achieve all of this, more effective ways to share information need to be promoted, in order to promote mutual learning to bridge and reduce the growing knowledge gap. The information and communication technologies of today, with their expected further development, are a tremendous opportunity, particularly for the rural areas, if they are used for training and education.

NEW TECHNOLOGY AND OTHER CHANGES IN AGRICULTURE

Compared with the past, the globalization of the food business and technological developments (information and communication technology as well as biotechnology) will be key drivers for change. As noted above, biotechnology is already a catalyst for the integration of an important part of the farm input value chain, from seeds to crop protection. In the future it will also be a catalyst for change in the food chain beyond the farm gate as the relationship of the participants becomes redefined. All participants in the agricultural value chain are facing substantial pressure to consolidate, though for different reasons. These include the general search for efficiency improvement, the need to make substantial investment in information technology and the need to spend increasing amounts on R&D.

While there are still 3 million farmers in Europe, about 70 per cent of crop protection business is done with about 700 000 farmers. In North America, 70 per cent of that business is done with only 500 000 farmers. There is an even smaller number in Latin America: only 150 000 farmers are involved in accounting for the same share of business. In all these regions, and eventually elsewhere, the trend will continue. Particularly in North America and Europe, the management of farms and the ownership of the land will be decoupled, leading to more specialization and professionalism. Higher professionalism is supported by the development of information and communication technology. The use of the information available through the Internet in the decision-making process of farm managers will probably increase faster than expected even one or two years ago. The same applies to develop merit of precision farming, using global positioning technology, to adapt inputs to the detailed needs of small areas of land as revealed by soil and yield mapping. There is also likely to be improved environmental compatibility in production systems.

The other key influence in agriculture will be biotechnology. The innovations for sustainable improvements in crop productivity will be driven by scientific advances derived from the rapidly accumulating knowledge about the biology of the plants. More than 25 000 GMO field trials with many different crop species have been done in some 45 countries, including most of the 15 European Union states. In the past five years the technology has been adopted particularly quickly in North America, Argentina and China. GMO crops available today are typically altered to resist insects or virus disease, or some specific herbicides. The inbuilt crop protection offers the farmer another option to cope with insects, disease or weeds, which still destroy some 30 per cent of the annual potential harvest in global agriculture. When the respective genes are bred into elite germ plasm, this new option improves the utilization of natural resources and improves the yielding capacity of a crop. As shown in many trials, food obtained by using commodities from GMO crops are equally nutritious and equally safe as any others. More obvious benefits to the consumer than improved environmental compatibility of agricultural production systems are also visible already. One example is β-Carotene GMO rice, which could help the 250 million people in the world who have vitamin-A deficiency.

The opportunities are now broadening from crop protection to crop production. In the foreseeable future, biotechnology will offer more to the farmer than improved agronomic characteristics like inbuilt crop protection, improved yielding capacity, more efficient use of water or fertilizer and improved stress tolerance. Plant varieties will become available which produce vegetable oil according to customer specifications, or modified starches and proteins. Within the next two decades, agriculture will have the ability to go beyond food and feed production. On the basis of specific genetics, the plant will be used to yield specific products for different industries and value chains. And the plant will be a very efficient production unit since it uses sunlight as its energy source and, by its very nature, is biodegradable. Indeed, plant biotechnology is a key tool for meeting many of the environmental goals defined in 1992 at Rio de Janeiro.

Soybean, corn, canola and cotton are the crops in which biotechnology has been most widely adopted. But there is a long list of other items (pumpkins, potatoes, chicory, tomatoes, tobacco, papaya and cloves) which go towards making up the list of over 70 transgenic plant varieties which have registrations in some part of the world. In spite of the continued controversial discussion, particularly in Europe, the GMO cotton and soybean acreage has continued to increase in the USA, though the GMO corn acreage has recently declined slightly. With very low commodity prices, farmers need to lower their input costs wherever possible, and GMO varieties offer such an option.

The secret, of course, lies in the science. Since the beginning of systematic crop cultivation, and particularly over the past 150 years, the methods of 'selecting – breeding – selecting' have been continuously refined and improved. However, the actual steering mechanisms within the plant at cellular and molecular level remained a mystery. Plant breeding is moving from trial and error to a more focused scientific activity. The resulting opportunities (not only feeding a growing population but also producing renewable resources for other value chains and thereby improving the efficiency of the natural resources) are breathtaking. But we certainly also have to address potential adverse consequences in a responsible way as well as addressing risk and ethical issues. We have to weigh the opportunities and risks in a science and fact-based, frank, open and transparent dialogue against the background of the huge demand and sustainability challenge of the coming decades.

Figure 3 outlines the main hurdles to the acceptance of GMOs. The food industry sector is surrounded by a political/regulatory machinery, by a suspicious public and a media which can be critical, and by numerous non-governmental organizations (NGOs) which represent a range of special interests. The latter include consumers, with obvious interests in food safety, and environmental pressure groups. Advocacy of the 'precautionary principle' is common.

Hurdles to Technology Acceptance: GMO Concerns

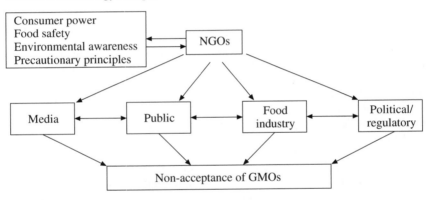

FIGURE 3   *Biotechnology: a catalyst for change (1)*

Because there are so many hurdles to their easy acceptance, biotechnology products need to be properly regulated and cautiously adopted. Such regulations should be harmonized internationally as much as possible in order not the hinder the global movement of agricultural commodities. Much is at stake in this regard if proper regulatory requirements are not established quickly. These uncertainties support activities of consumer and environmental groups, keep the technology off the market and hinder consumer choice. Nor will the biotechnology products be able to support the goal of sustainable development. Figure 4 provides an outline of the mechanisms and objectives of government, the food industry and the general public. While the principles lying behind the messages are largely self-evident, it needs to be emphasized that some mechanisms, notably those relating to labelling and possible segregation, will not be easy to design.

Hurdles to Technology Acceptance: GMO Concerns

Target area ⟶	*Mechanisms to adopt* ⟶	*Objective*
Government	Improve regulatory controls Global trade agreements	Public confidence Economic stability
Food industry	Improve regulatory controls Segregation Labelling	Public confidence Market opportunity Consumer choice
Public	Improve regulatory controls Labelling Independent science	Public confidence Consumer choice Public confidence

FIGURE 4   *Biotechnology: a catalyst for change (2)*

CONSOLIDATION

All participants in the agricultural value chain are facing substantial consolidation pressure. The crop protection and seed industries are no exception to this; rather, they are standing in the forefront, particularly in the case of crop protection. The top eight companies share 90 per cent of the global crop protection market, whereas the seed industry is more fragmented, with the top nine companies sharing 44 per cent of the global market (see Figure 5).

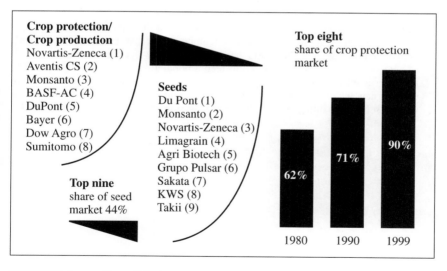

Crop protection/
Crop production
Novartis-Zeneca (1)
Aventis CS (2)
Monsanto (3)
BASF-AC (4)
DuPont (5)
Bayer (6)
Dow Agro (7)
Sumitomo (8)

Seeds
Du Pont (1)
Monsanto (2)
Novartis-Zeneca (3)
Limagrain (4)
Agri Biotech (5)
Grupo Pulsar (6)
Sakata (7)
KWS (8)
Takii (9)

Top nine
share of seed
market 44%

Top eight
share of crop protection
market

62%   71%   90%

1980   1990   1999

FIGURE 5   *Consolidation: crop protection/crop production and seed companies*

High R&D costs, high regulatory costs to keep products on the market and the need for attractive returns to shareholders require global market access and a degree of size. The substantial R&D investment in biotechnology also requires germ plasm access and breeding competencies. Consequently, we are now witnessing not only a continued consolidation process in the crop protection industry, but also a consolidation process across the crop production and seed sectors. So far as trends are concerned, the value of the crop protection market in 1999 was 28.5 billion Euro and does not offer much growth in the years to come. The 18 billion Euro seed market will see more value growth due to the potential of biotechnology. The new options for inbuilt protection offered with biotechnology products, through seeds like those which convey *Bt* insect resistance in corn or cotton, will shift the generation of revenues from the sale of crop protection products to the collection of technology fees based on planted acreage of GMO-based seeds.

The major changes will be technology-driven. Seeds will become increasingly the major value driver for the farmer as well as for the food chain, since so much technology will be residing in the seed base. This development will take market share away from the conventional crop protection and conventional seeds markets. Both markets will become increasingly cost and efficiency-driven, leading to more consolidation. This development may be witnessed already for some crops in the USA, Canada, Argentine and Australia. It will gain speed with the acceptance and adoption of biotechnology products. Those products will be needed if agriculture is to meet the demand and sustainability challenge, first of the next two decades and then of the more distant future. But, since the controversial debate is still going on, I would like to finish by citing Norman E. Borlaug, the passionate and very successful plant breeder:

> Twenty seven years ago, in my acceptance speech for the Nobel Peace Prize, I said that the Green Revolution had won a temporary success in man's war against hunger. I now say that the world has the technology – either available or well advanced in the research pipeline – to feed a population of 10 billion people. The more pertinent question today is whether farmers and ranchers will be permitted to use this new technology. Extremists in the environmental movement from the rich nations seem to be doing everything they can to stop scientific progress in its tracks.

SECTION II

Improved Market Incentives in Transition Economies

ALAN DE BRAUW, JIKUN HUANG AND SCOTT ROZELLE*

Sequencing and the Success of Gradualism:
Empirical Evidence from China's Agricultural Reform

INTRODUCTION

At its most basic level the Big Bang versus gradualism debate can be characterized by two questions. Should reforming nations lead with radical market liberalization policies? Or should institutions that offer strong incentives to those involved with economic activity be fostered and be allowed to evolve before central planning is dismantled and markets are unleashed?

While the debate has raged for more than ten years, there has been little progress in understanding exactly what has accounted for the success of countries adopting gradualism and why most countries beginning their reforms with market liberalization have not enjoyed rapid growth. Most explanations of the success of gradualism relative to rapid reform have considered the comparative growth record of countries in East Asia which were normally gradual reformers, or those in Europe which began with radical liberalization policies (Roland and Verdier, 1999). According to almost any performance criteria, East Asian gradualism is the clear winner (see Macours and Swinnen in the present volume). In response, researchers who still believe in the necessity of Big Bang reforms argue that the comparison of East Asia and Europe is not valid because of structural differences in the economies (Sachs and Woo, 1994).

Despite great interest among academics and policy makers, progress in settling the debate has stalled, almost certainly because few researchers have been able to isolate the factors contributing to the performance of the different transition economies. So, in a sense, the aim is to respond to this lack of evidence; our paper seeks to show empirically that the sequencing of policies in transitional economies matters. Though our study is limited to the case of China's agricultural sector and its reforms, we argue that our findings help to explain why gradualism works. To meet our goal, we pursue three objectives. First, we briefly delineate the various gains that countries can expect from incentive changes (that is, decollectivization), on one hand, and market liberalization, on the other. Second, we lay out a framework for measuring the

*A. de Brauw and S. Rozelle, University of California, Davis, USA; Jikun Huang, Centre for Chinese Agricultural Policy, Chinese Academy of Agricultural Sciences, Beijing, PR China. The financial support from the Ford Foundation, Rockefeller Foundation and China National Outstanding Youth Science Foundation is gratefully acknowledged. Authors share senior authorship.

123

source of, and returns to, incentive reforms (studied in the past by, for example, McMillan *et al.*, 1989; Lin, 1992) and market liberalization initiatives (our main methodological contribution). Finally, we offer initial estimates of the timing and magnitudes of returns to incentive and market reforms.

INCENTIVES, MARKETS AND BEHAVIOUR

The literature has carefully documented the returns to increased incentives in China's early stages of reform. Decollectivization, commonly called the Household Responsibility System (HRS), made the household the residual claimant and left production decisions to those with the best information (Putterman, 1992). Although McMillan *et al.* (1989), Fan (1991), Lin (1992) and Huang and Rozelle (1996) used different data sets, examined different subsectors of the economy and applied different methods, they all concluded that HRS led to sharp increases in output and greater efficiency. The HRS variable is assumed to proxy for the added incentives that decollectivization provided for producers in the early 1980s. In the rest of this study, we assume that the incentive effects are synonymous with the reforms embodied in HRS.[1]

Unlike what happened in the transition economies in Europe, leaders in China did not move to dismantle the planned economy in the initial stages of reform in favour of liberalized markets. Policy makers only began to shift their focus to market liberalization in 1985, after decollectivization was complete. Even then, liberalization was 'stop and start' (Sicular, 1995). For example, in the case of fertilizer, Ye and Rozelle (1994) show that, after an early attempt at market liberalization in 1986 and 1987, perceived instability in the rural economy in 1988 led to sharp retrenchments. Agricultural officials only took controls back off fertilizer marketing and began encouraging private trade in the early 1990s. Lin *et al.* (1996) offer a detailed analysis of reform policy. They argue that leaders were mainly afraid of the disruption that would occur if the institutions through which leaders controlled the main goods in the food economy (such as grain, fertilizer and meat products) were eliminated without first having the institutions in place which work to support more efficient market exchange.

Rozelle (1996) shows that the sequencing of agricultural reform policies followed the gradualism strategy of China's more general, economy-wide reforms described by McMillan and Naughton (1991). In the initial stages of reform, leaders consciously restricted the promotion of market-based economic activity, allowing exchanges only of less important products (for example, minor fruits and vegetables) in sharply circumscribed regions. Not until 1985, after the completion of HRS, did policy makers begin to encourage market activity for more important commodities (such as grain), although initially market activity only occurred within the framework of China's renowned two-tier price system (Sicular, 1988). There was no commitment to more complete market liberalization until the early 1990s, more than a decade after the initiation of HRS. From this description, it is clear that China's reforms fall into two distinct stages: the incentive reforms that dominate the period from 1978 to

1984, and a period of gradual market liberalization that begins in 1985 and extends through the 1990s.

The record of market liberalization

Attempts to quantify the gains from market liberalization, unfortunately, have been largely unsuccessful. Part of the problem may be the period of analysis and the inability of the various research approaches to separate efficiency gains of market reform from overall gains in the reforming economy. For example, Wen (1993) found total factor productivity (TFP) growth had stopped in the post-1985 period, a trend he blames on the failure of the second stage of reform. Holding constant the effect of technology, Huang and Rozelle (1996) find that TFP growth restarts in the 1990s and is in at least a small way linked to increased liberalization of the economy. Fan (1999) uses frontier methods to decompose the efficiency gains of Jiangsu provincial farm producers in the late reform era. He concludes that there have been only limited gains from market liberalization. If one were to take the findings of this admittedly scant literature seriously, it would appear as if there is at most only a relatively small measured gain from market reforms in China. We believe there are three possible explanations for the findings, though only one is plausible. First, if market liberalization actually contributes little or nothing to growth, output or incomes, this would, of course, in part explain why economies that lead reform with market liberalization do not experience significant gains. Theory and the experiences of other economies in other settings, however, would argue against such an interpretation. Second, it could be that China's agricultural market liberalization has just proceeded so slowly that it is still too early for output to have been positively affected. But, as seen above, the record on market expansion and the observations of many researchers would not support this view.

If the first two arguments are faulty, we are left with just one explanation. It may be that the methods previously used to measure the return to markets have not fully captured the effect of market liberalization. In fact, almost all of the previous literature on this subject (with the exception of Fan, 1999) has tried to capture the liberalization effect by examining the residual growth of output after other sources of growth have been accounted for. It may be that the part of the efficiency gains coming from markets is missed because of the presence of measurement error or other factors.

RETURNS TO MARKETS

Absent or poorly functioning markets impose two constraints on producers. First, when markets are not well developed, or when policies or institutional constraints raise transaction costs and limit market-based exchange, producers lack the *flexibility* to change the allocation of their productive assets and choice of enterprises. Second, as prices and other factors in the economy change, producers are less *responsive* when shifting their variable inputs. This section will explain the effects of market liberalization on flexibility and responsiveness in more detail.

Flexibility

To understand more precisely what is meant by flexibility, we refer to Figure 1. Suppose a country's aggregate agricultural production function is F_A in a pre-liberalization period in panel A and F_B in a post-liberalization period in panel B. A profit-maximizing farmer who in year $t-1$ faces an output price p_{t-1}, chooses to produce at point A, and uses a quantity of the quasi-fixed input, X_{AA}. The first subscript refers to the point on the figure, and the second refers to the panel. In year t, the price changes to p_t. A farmer who is unconstrained would

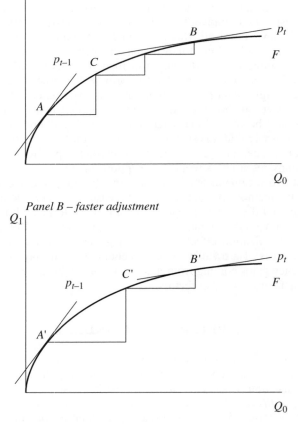

FIGURE 1   *Flexibility in adjustment*

move to the point of optimal production by increasing the use of the input to X_{BA} (by moving from point A to point B).

However, if there are frictions in the economy, the producer will not be able to perfectly adjust the quantity of the quasi-fixed input, X, in response to the price change within one year. Instead, the producer is only able to increase the quasi-fixed input to X_{CA}, and can only produce at point C in year t. While profits increase, they do not rise as much as they would have had the producer increased inputs to X_{BA}. The lost profit from producing at C rather than B is a measure of the inefficiency due to inflexibility.

Market liberalization can reduce the amount of inefficiency as follows. In panel B, although the producer is not able to adjust perfectly, market liberalization policies have facilitated exchange. In response to the price change, from p_{t-1} to p_t, the producer can increase the use of the quasi-fixed input to $X_{C'B}$ and move further, to point C'. The more rapid adjustment can be most easily seen by comparing the number of years that it takes to make the full adjustment from the original point (A) to the point of long-run optimality. In Figure 1, it is three years before the producer reaches point B before market liberalization, and only two years after.

Certainly, there is reason to believe that China's producers have begun operating in more flexible environments in the late reform period, especially with regard to their choices of sown area and labour. In the late reform period, as quotas have fallen (Wang, 2000) and labour markets developed (Parish *et al.*, 1995), the scope for farmer decision making has expanded greatly. In particular, the rise of rural industry and increased opportunities to work off the farm in areas near the farmer's home village conceivably have had a large effect on the flexibility of labour use.

Responsiveness

The lack of well-functioning markets may also limit the *responsiveness* of farmer supply and associated derived demand decisions. According to one of Marshall's fundamental principles, the more variable factors of production there are, the more responsive producer choices are to changes in price and other fixed factors. If newly emerging markets allow farmers to choose more of their inputs, the increased scope for substitution among inputs will make farmers at least as responsive, ceteris paribus.

To examine responsiveness in terms of Figure 1, suppose the production function, F_A, illustrates the relationship between X and Y, holding Z constant. Z is a set of other production factors needed to produce Y (panel A), and is composed of two subsets: Z_1, a set of n variable factors of production that can be bought and sold in a market, and Z_2, a set of m fixed factors. The rate at which Y increases in response to an increase in the price, p, is, among other things, a function of the curvature of the production surface. If in time period 2, where the relationship between X and Y is shown in panel B as F_B, the rate at which Y increases for the same increase in price, p, could change if Y were more responsive. Market liberalization could cause Y to become more responsive, because in essence the technology could change. The relationship between

X and Y after market liberalization might, for example, be conditioned on $n+1$ variable factors of production (Z'_1) and $m-1$ fixed factors (Z'_2). If so, for a given increase in Y, profits realized from moving from A' to B' in panel B would be greater than the profits from moving from A to B in panel A, since the producer is able to produce more of Y as its price rises. The difference in profits would measure the magnitude of the gain to efficiency caused by greater responsiveness due to market liberalization.

Incentive reforms and market liberalization

While we are trying to isolate the behavioural effects of the incentive reforms from those of market liberalization, in reality it is likely the two are interrelated. For example, Lin (1991) and Huang and Rozelle (1996) have shown that China's agricultural sector has experienced both positive and negative interactions between market improvements and increased incentives.[2] Since we are trying to identify the impact of market liberalization in the late reform period, quantitative measures of the liberalization effects should not be affected if the incentive reforms were already implemented (and fully effective) by the mid-1980s. When considering issues of policy sequencing, however, to the extent that increased responsiveness is conditional on having good incentives, the true returns to liberalization policies will be overstated if all of the efficiency gains in the late reform period are attributed to them.

MEASURING BEHAVIOURAL EFFECTS OF LIBERALIZATION

Flexibility

As discussed above, the increase in the speed by which quasi-fixed factors adjust corresponds to increased *flexibility*. To estimate the adjustment speed of quasi-fixed factors while considering the main sources of production growth, a theoretical/empirical framework is needed. It must explicitly account for the elements that facilitate or constrain producers from adjusting inputs and outputs to their optimal levels in response to exogenous shocks. Such approaches exist. They include the agricultural treadmill approach (Cochrane, 1965), fixed asset theory (Johnson, 1956; Hathaway, 1963) and adjustment cost models (Lucas, 1967; Johnson and Quance, 1972).

The adjustment cost approach is particularly appropriate for modelling the production behaviour of China's farmers in a reform economy because it allows us to measure the rate of adjustment of resources in response to exogenous changes. Factors that are slow to adjust are called quasi-fixed inputs, and are endogenous variables; their levels and rates of change are in part chosen by the producer in response to changes in exogenous factors. Quasi-fixed inputs affect production in both the short and long run. A theoretical framework is described in Appendix A as well as in Warjiyo (1991) and de Brauw *et al.* (2000).

Empirical model for measuring flexibility

To estimate the dynamic supply response system that is defined by equations (A3)–(A5) in Appendix A, and measure quasi-fixed factor flexibility, we use a normalized quadratic value function, developed by Epstein (1981), which is a specification that has been used frequently in empirical work and is expressed as follows:

$$V(p,w,q,K,Z) = a_0 + [a_1 a_2 a_3 a_4][pwqK]' +$$

$$\frac{1}{2}[pwqK] \begin{bmatrix} AF'G'H' \\ FBL'N' \\ GLC(R^{-1})' \\ HNR^{-1}D \end{bmatrix} [pwqK]' + \tag{1}$$

$$[a_5 pwqK][T_0 T_1 T_2 T_3 T_4]'Z$$

where V, p, w, q, K and Z are as defined in Appendix A and $a_0,\ldots, a_5, A, F, G, H, B, L, N, C, R, D, T_0, \ldots, T_4$ are parameter matrices with the appropriate dimensions. Following the steps outlined in Appendix A, the empirical formulation of the complete system of input demand and output supply equations has the following form:

$$\Delta K_{(t)} = B_{12} + (rU + R)K_{(t-1)} + rRGp_{(t-1)} + rRLw_{(t)} \\ + rRCq_{(t)} + T_{12}Z_{(t)} + e_{12(t)} \tag{2}$$

$$L_{(t)} = B_{03} - rFp_{(t-1)} - rBw_{(t)} - rL'q_{(t)} - N'K^*_{(t)} - T_3 Z_{(t)} + e_{3(t)} \tag{3}$$

$$Y_{12(t)} = B_{45} + rAp_{(t-1)} + rF'w_{(t)} + rG'q(t) + H'K^*_{(t)} + T_{45}Z(t) + e_{45(t)} \tag{4}$$

$$Y_{3(t)} = B_{06} + ra_4 K^*_{(t)} - 0.5rp'_{(t-1)}Ap_{(t-1)} - 0.5rw'_{(t)}Bw_{(t)} - 0.5rq'_{(t)}Cq_{(t)} \tag{5}$$

$$- rp'_{(t-1)}F'w_{(t)} - rp'_{(t-1)}G'q_{(t)} - rw'_{(t)}L'q_{(t)} + 0.5rK'_{(t-1)}DK_{(t-1)}$$

$$- K_{(t)}DK_{(t-1)} + ra_5 T_{60}Z_{(t)} + Z'_{(t)}T_{61}K^*_{(t)} + e_{6(t)}$$

where $B_{12} = rRa_3$, $B_{03} = -ra_2$, $B_{45} = ra_1$, $B_{06} = ra_0$, $K^* = rK_{(t-1)} - \Delta K_{(t)}$, $T_{12} = rR^{-1}T_3$, $T_3 = -rT_2$, $T_{45} = rT_1$, and U is an identity matrix. Conditions for consistent aggregation requires $V_{KK} = D = 0$ (Epstein and Denny, 1983), which is imposed in estimation.

The adjustment cost model generates two useful sets of relationships between the choice variables (that is, variable and quasi-fixed inputs and outputs) and exogenous factors. The first, defined as short run elasticities, measure the one-period response of choice variables to shifts in prices and policy variables, including *direct and indirect changes* of variable inputs and outputs. *Indirect changes* occur through the *partial* quasi-fixed factor response of the producer.

As quasi-fixed factors do not fully adjust in one time period, the indirect change in the variable input or output amount reflects the speed of adjustment of quasi-fixed inputs. Therefore, the slower the adjustment process, the smaller the elasticities are, in an absolute value sense. Long-run elasticities, on the other hand, account for the full adjustment of quasi-fixed inputs, and measure the optimal *direct and indirect* response of producers to price changes. The indirect portion of the elasticity accounts for the *full* shift in quasi-fixed inputs to their optimal amounts after the price change occurs. Warjiyo (1991, p. 78) includes detailed calculations for deriving the short- and long-run elasticities from the estimated parameter matrices in equations (2) to (5). We will take advantage of the differences between these two relationships, since one measure, the long-run elasticity, lets us measure the full response to a change in price. The other measure, the short-run elasticity, captures the extent of the inefficiency since, ceteris paribus, the smaller the response, the greater the inefficiency.

Our empirical model includes three crops; Y_{12} is a two-element output vector for wheat and maize, and Y_3 is cash crop output. Prices for wheat and maize, the variable input (fertilizer), and the two quasi-fixed inputs (labour and sown area) are normalized by the cash crop price to satisfy homogeneity. The Z vector is made up of three shifter variables:[3] national research stock, irrigation capacity and a variable reflecting the effect of institutional incentive reform.[4] Provincial dummy variables account for fixed, province-specific effects.

We consider sown area and labour to be quasi-fixed inputs. The R matrix in equations (1) and (2) is the adjustment matrix, and the coefficients on the diagonals of R are called 'adjustment cost parameters'. The parameters are estimates of the average, one-period proportional adjustment of a quasi-fixed factor to its long-run optimal level that is made in response to a change in an exogenous variable. The adjustment cost model, then, gives us explicit measures of the flexibility of quasi-fixed factors. The diagonals of the R matrix, in some sense, are exactly what we are interested in: a measure of how well markets allow factors to adjust. Appropriately, some researchers call these estimated parameters 'flexible acceleration coefficients'.

To measure the *change of flexibility*, we interact a dummy variable (that is, zero for the early reform period, 1975–84, and one for the late reform period, 1985–95) with all of the variables in equation (1) and (2) associated with the adjustment parameters (called R11 and R22). The parameters associated with the interaction term (denoted R11D and R22D) measure how much more or less flexible quasi-fixed factors become in the market liberalization period.

Responsiveness

Since our model includes quasi-fixed factors and variable inputs, we can estimate responsiveness by using the parameters of the model to calculate measures such as input price elasticities. Ideally, we should measure the *change* in responsiveness between the early and late periods by separately estimating equations (2) to (5) for the early and for the late periods and comparing the results. In the period after market liberalization has begun, we would expect to find higher absolute values of the elasticities. Such a finding would intuitively show that producers were becoming more responsive as markets emerged. And a more responsive producer will see higher profits than a less responsive one.

Unfortunately, the lack of data makes the estimation of two separate models impossible.[5] As a compromise, we re-estimate our original model for the full period with a more 'flexible specification' by interacting the parameters associated with the own-price responses with the subperiod dummy variable.[6] We use the parameters from this estimation to generate short-run elasticities for early and late periods to examine how the responsiveness of China's producers changes as markets emerge.

EFFICIENCY GAINS, RESPONSIVENESS AND FLEXIBILITY

Creating the measure of increased efficiency due to market liberalization

The first step in arriving at an estimate of the gains to market liberalization is to calculate the inefficiency *in any given economy* (or any given period, *P*) that arises from imperfect adjustment. The difference in lost profits between the full adjustment and the partial adjustment is a measure of the inefficiency due to partial adjustment, and is defined as:

$$\Omega_t = \Delta\Pi_{t,\,full} - \Delta\Pi_{t,\,partial} \tag{6}$$

where $\Delta\Pi_{t,\,full}$ is the amount of additional profits that the farmer will earn from a price increase (from p_{t-1} to p_t) if there are no adjustment costs from year $t-1$ to t (or if full adjustment occurs in one year); and $\Delta\Pi_{partial}$ is the additional profits realized if the farmer only partially adjusts.

To create a measure of the change in inefficiency between two periods, we first label the early reform period when producers are less responsive as 'slow', and the late reform period when partial adjustment is faster as 'fast'. Then we can simply calculate equation (6) for the late reform period as:

$$\Omega_{t,\,fast} = \Delta\Pi_{t,\,full,\,fast} - \Delta\Pi_{t,\,partial,\,fast} \tag{7}$$

We do the same calculation using the parameters from the slower adjusting, pre-liberalization period:

$$\Omega_{t,\,slow} = \Delta\Pi_{t,\,full,slow} - \Delta\Pi_{t,\,partial,slow} \tag{8}$$

The overall gain in year *t*, G_t, to increased flexibility and responsiveness from a one year change in an exogenous variable can be calculated by subtracting equation (7) from equation (8):

$$G_t = \Omega_{t,\,slow} - \Omega_{t,\,fast} \tag{9}$$

To compute measures of efficiency, Ω and G, we need to start with a measure of profits. Since almost no land is rented in China and almost no labour is hired for farming, we define profits as returns to land and labour, and can write this as:

$$\Pi_t = \sum_i p_{it} q_{it} \tag{10}$$

where p represents all output and variable input prices, q represents output and variable input quantities, and i indexes them (i = wheat, maize, cash crop and fertilizer). Variable inputs (in our case, fertilizer) are taken to be negative quantities. Following this notation, the change in profits, $\Delta\Pi_t$, from year t−1, Π_{t-1}, to year t, Π_t, can be expressed as:

$$\Delta\Pi_t = \Pi_t - \Pi_{t-1} = \sum_i (p_{it}\Delta q_{it} + q_{it-1}\Delta p_{it}) \tag{11}$$

where Δq_{it} is the change in output or input quantities between t−1 and t, and Δp_{it} is the corresponding price change. The term Δq_{it} is estimated by equation (12):

$$\Delta q_{it} = q_{it} \sum_j (\Delta\rho_{jt} / \rho_{jt})\varepsilon_{jt} \tag{12}$$

where ρ represents all prices and government policy variables, j indexes them (j = wheat, maize, cash crop, fertilizer, research and irrigation), and ε represents all elasticities.

Equation (12) can be calculated using either the long- or short-run elasticities. When it is calculated with long-run elasticities, the quantity responses reflect the fact that quasi-fixed factors *fully* adjust and the producer is at a point of optimal profits. When it is calculated with short-run elasticities, quasi-fixed factors only *partially* adjust, the indirect responses are ignored and profits have not been maximized.

After plugging long-run elasticities into equation (12) and getting the profit-maximizing output responses to a given change in an exogenous variable, we can then find the predicted change in profits by plugging the predicted Δq_{jt} into equation (11). In fact, if our change in an exogenous variable is a change in price from year t−1 to t (which we can call Δp_{jt}), then our resulting change of profits, $\Delta\Pi_{full}$, is exactly what we need to calculate inefficiency. If we are using long-run elasticities from the pre-liberalization era and changes in the exogenous variables from the second period, then the change in profits is $\Delta\Pi_{full, slow}$. The short-run quantity response to a change in exogenous variables is called $\Delta\Pi_{partial, slow}$, is different, as quasi-fixed factors do not fully adjust, and reflects the fact that short-run elasticities from the early reform period are used. The difference between early reform profits, calculated with long-run and short-run elasticities in year t given the change in the exogenous variables in year t−1 (from the second reform period), is our measure of the inefficiency (Ω_{slow}) due to market imperfections. In essence, Ω_{slow} is derived from a conceptual experiment; if flexibility and responsiveness remained the same during the incentive reform period and during the market liberalization period, the level of inefficiency would be Ω_{slow}.

To compute our measure of the change in efficiency due to market liberalization, we need to measure the actual inefficiencies in the post-liberalization period, Ω_{fast}. These calculations are exactly the same as for Ω_{slow}, except that the long- and short-run elasticities from the second period are used. Once calculated, the estimates of Ω_{fast} and Ω_{slow} can be substituted into equation (9) to get a measure of the overall gain in efficiency in year t from market liberalization, G_t.

Decomposing the measure of the gain to efficiency from market liberalization

We actually break down the total efficiency gains, G_t, even further, into one part that comes from increased flexibility and one that is due to increased responsiveness. By substituting equations (7) and (8) into (9) and rearranging, we find that we can write G_t as

$$G_t = -((\Delta\Pi_{partial,fast} - \Delta\Pi_{partial,slow}) + (\Delta\Pi_{full,fast} - \Delta\Pi_{full,slow})) \qquad (13)$$

Written this way, the two terms in equation (13) have intuitive interpretations that correspond to the two components of market liberalization. The first term is just the loss of profits that would have resulted had the speed of adjustment been the same in the second period as in the first. This is just a measure of the change in efficiency due to flexibility (F_t). The second term is just the profit lost if market liberalization had not led to larger long-run elasticities, which is just responsiveness (R_t). Hence we can write G_t as $G_t = F_t + R_{gt}$.

Measuring the gain to better incentives

To meet our ultimate goal of comparing the gains from market liberalization with the gains from the incentive reforms, we will use our estimated empirical model to simulate profits in the early reform period (1978–84), both including and excluding the effect of the incentive reform. The difference between the simulated profits with (Π_t^*) and without ($\Pi_t^{*\prime}$) the incentive reform measures the gains in efficiency. Normalizing by Π_t^*, we have a measure of the gain to incentive reforms, I_t, which is the proportion of increased profits due to those reforms:

$$I_t = (\Pi_t^* - \Pi_t^{*\prime})/\Pi_t^* \qquad (14)$$

DATA

Provincial-level cross-section, time-series data for 1975–95 are used in the analysis.[7] Output for wheat, maize and other grains, and cash crops (cotton, sugar cane, peanuts and rapeseed) are measured in kilograms and after 1980 are from published statistical compendia (ZGTJNJ, 1980, 1986–93; ZGNYNJ, 1981–93). Prior to 1980, data for these variables come from provincial yearbooks. Data on total sown area in each province are from the same source.

Cash crop output is an aggregated variable; output values for each individual crop are summed, then divided by a Stone price index.

Prices for grain, cash crops and fertilizer are obtained from China's national 'Cost of Production Survey'.[8] This information comes from a data-collection programme run by the State Price Bureau since the mid-1970s (SPB, 1988–95). Based on annual household surveys conducted by county level Price Bureau personnel, detailed information is available by crop and by variety for over 50 variables, including both revenue and expenditure (in value terms) and quantity data.[9] Prices are generated by dividing total revenues or expenditures by the quantity.[10] The price for land is calculated as net return to cultivated land (total revenue per unit of cultivated land for each commodity less per land unit expenditures on labour, fertilizer and other variable inputs). The wage is derived from per capita labour income in rural areas. The data are from each province before 1984 and ZGTJNJ thereafter.

The irrigation stock, research stock and incentive reform variables were created using data from the following sources. Irrigation expenditures are from each province, and are documented in a statistical compendium published by the Ministry of Water Resources and Electrical Power (MWREP, 1988–96). They include all sources of investment in water control that pass through the financial system to regional water conservancy bureaus. National grain research expenditures are assumed to have the same effect on production in each province, implicitly implying that breakthroughs spill over into all provinces. Because irrigation and research stocks, rather than expenditures, affect input demands and output supply, irrigation and research expenditures are transformed into stock variables (see de Brauw *et al.*, 2000). The incentive reform variable measures the cumulative proportion of households in China each year implementing decollectivization policies.

ECONOMETRIC RESULTS

Grain and cash crop production in North China's reforming economy

To estimate the relationship among the two quasi-fixed inputs (equation 2), three outputs (equations 4 and 5) and one variable input (equation 3), a non-linear, three stage least squares estimator is used (Gallant, 1977). The estimator accounts for contemporaneously correlated error terms. The equation system for North China contains 46 exogenous variables and 135 parameters.

The entire set of estimated coefficients for equations (2) to (5) is reported in Appendix B. Many of the coefficients have relatively high *t*-ratios and the signs and magnitudes of most of them are as expected. The important results also appear to be robust to the choice of estimator. In particular, the flexible accelerator parameters, R11 and R22, are negative and significant (Table 1). Because the model is written in terms of first differences, the eigenvalues of the adjustment matrix R provide a check on the stability of the adjustment process of land and labour. Since the absolute values of the estimated eigenvalues for R are less than unity, the quasi-fixed demand system is stable.

TABLE 1 *Adjustment parameter estimates from non-linear, three-stage least squares estimators for Northern China*

Parameter	Estimate
R11	−0.16
	(3.65)
R22	−0.35
	(8.38)
R11D	−0.04
	(2.98)
R22D	−0.25
	(5.49)

Notes: t-ratios in parentheses; the full set of parameter estimates is reported in Appendix B.

The properties of the value functions also are mostly satisfied. The estimated value function is non-declining in p (wheat and maize), K_1 (sown area) and Z (agricultural research and irrigation investment) and is non-increasing in w (wage) and q (the price of labour and value of land). The only violation of monotonicity is found in K_2 (labour), a result commonly found in other studies (see the survey by Warjiyo, 1991). When considering parameters significant at the 10 per cent level, convexity is satisfied for the sets of equations; the own-price response matrices (A, B and C) are all positive semi-definite.

Estimates of government policy variables also have the expected impacts on agricultural production. For example, positive signs on the IRR4 and IRR6 parameters (Appendix B) indicate that irrigation investment boosts wheat and cash crop production. The estimated coefficient for maize, IRR5, is negative and insignificant, which reflects the fact that Chinese farmers tend to grow maize on more marginal, hilly land. Irrigation also seems to save labour (IRR2). Agricultural research boosts both wheat and maize output (RES4 and RES5), but has an insignificant effect on cash crop production (RES6). This result reflects the observation of Fan and Pardey (1992) that the agricultural research system has been focused on grain. The positive and significant coefficients on the variable associated with the effect of research on labour (RES2) indicates that agricultural research has intensified labour use.

The signs of the coefficients associated with the variables measuring incentive reform (HRS), imply that it had a positive impact on the production of all crops except for maize in North China, which coincides with the result found by other studies (Lin, 1992; McMillan *et al.*, 1989; Fan, 1991; Huang and Rozelle, 1996). This decollectivization-led increase in output, however, did not come about by increased labour use. Consistent with the labour use pattern since the late 1970s, incentive reforms led to substantially lower labour use.[11] Farmers in the post-reform period use chemical fertilizers to substitute for labour, an insight described by Ye and Rozelle (1994) in their study of Jiangsu rice farmers in the late 1980s.

INCREASING FLEXIBILITY DURING CHINA'S REFORMS

Adjustment in the early reform period

The model allows us to test a series of hypotheses relating to the initial assumption that changes in the use of labour and land require significant adjustment costs, and the hypothesis that the speed of adjustment increases after the HRS reform is complete. The results of two sets of hypothesis tests are reported in Table 2. Since we have interacted the variables associated with the speed of adjustment parameters with a period dummy variable, the interpretations of R11 and R22 relate to the early reform period.

TABLE 2   *Hypotheses testing for the presence of adjustment costs, quasi-fixity of inputs and increase in speed of adjustment*

Hypotheses	Lagrange multiplier statistic
No adjustment cost or no quasi-fixity	
(1) Crop area	
$(R_{11} = -1 \ \& \ R_{12} = 0)$	383.82*
(2) Agricultural labour	
$(R_{22} = -1 \ \& \ R_{21} = 0)$	271.69*
(3) Both crop area and agricultural labour	
$(R_{11} = R_{22} = -1 \ \& \ R_{12} = R_{21} = 0)$	663.31*
Independent adjustment	
(4) Crop area v. agricultural labour	
$(R_{12} = R_{21} = 0)$	9.97*
No adjustment cost during market liberalization	
(5) Crop area	
$(R_{11} + R_{11d} = -1)$	519.32*
(6) Agricultural labour	
$(R_{22} + R_{22d} = -1)$	28.71*
No increase in speed of adjustment post-HRS reform	
(7) Both crop area and	
agricultural labour $(R_{11d} = R_{22d} = 0)$	25.50*

Notes: The * indicates statistical significance at the 1% level. All test statistics are calculated from the non-linear three-stage least squares estimates of the entire system of equations. The null hypotheses for the tests are in parentheses.

The high test statistics in the analysis of quasi-fixity of sown area by itself (row 1) and labour by itself (row 2), and the joint test of the two quasi-fixed inputs (row 3), highlight the importance of accounting for dynamic adjustment costs in the analysis of China's agricultural crop area and farm labour decisions during the incentive reform period. Tests of quasi-fixity for adjustment coefficients in the market liberalization period also indicate that sown area and labour do not fully adjust (rows 4 and 5). Given that there are adjustment costs, the next test in this set (row 6) indicates that the adjustment paths are not independent. In other words, if an exogenous shock occurs, making the previous allocations of sown area and labour less than optimal, the movement of sown area towards its new, long-run equilibrium point (that is, the profit-maximization point) is affected by the adjustment process of labour (and vice versa).

To estimate the time of adjustment in the early reform period, we invert the R matrix and find that, in the early reform period, land adjusts in about six years and labour in three years. These figures are consistent with the findings of Huang *et al.* (1995), who found adjustment times of five years for land and four years for labour for the agricultural economy as a whole during the entire post-1978 era. Hence our results can be interpreted as indicating that frictions in the economy kept producers from fully adjusting their labour or sown area during the incentive reform period.

Interestingly, even though adjustment is not instantaneous, China's rural economy is not particularly rigid in a comparative sense. Natural, behavioural and policy-created barriers exist everywhere. In fact, when the results are compared with those of similar adjustment cost analyses, it could be argued that China's crop sector adjusted rather quickly. With the exception of Vasavada and Chambers, who found land in the USA being adjusted to a new optimum after two years, land adjustment in Canada can take up to 15 years to equilibrate after exogenous shocks, whereas labour adjustment requires six to 19 years (Warjiyo, 1991; Luh and Stefanou, 1991; Vasavada and Chambers, 1986). Despite the existence of policy-created barriers in China, adjustment may occur faster than in North America because the relatively labour-intensive farming systems and more responsive, small-scale rural-based industrial sector ultimately make resource reallocation among sectors less costly. Apparently, even though formal markets are not complete, informal institutional arrangements may have allowed China's farmers to engage in exchange even in the early reform period.

Changes in flexibility in the late reform period

So have the market liberalization reforms increased the flexibility of China's agriculture? The negative and statistically significant coefficients on the interaction terms in Table 1 (R11D and R22D) demonstrate that quasi-fixed factors have begun to adjust even faster in the late reform period. The negative coefficients are to be interpreted as the degree by which flexibility increases in the market liberalization period.

The results demonstrate that flexibility increased significantly in the second period. The flexible acceleration parameters for labour and sown area are

–0.60 (–0.35–0.25) and –0.20 (–0.16–0.04). In terms of the time to fully adjust, the speed becomes faster at five years for land and one year eight months for labour after market reform begins. If faster adjustments by producers are made possible by better markets and fewer restrictions on producers, the liberalization reforms have increased efficiency in China's late reform economy. In the last section of the paper, we examine the magnitude of these efficiency gains.

Changes in responsiveness

We have also produced evidence that responsiveness increased in the market liberalization period. To show this, we estimate elasticities that are based on the parameters from the more flexible model (that is, the additive parameters from the 'period dummy – own-price variable' interaction terms). The interaction terms are all significant at the 10 per cent level, which indicates that own-price responses change after market liberalization begins (see de Brauw *et al.*, 2000, for parameter estimates). Table 3 summarizes the changes in responsiveness of quasi-fixed and variable inputs to own prices (own-price elasticity changes based on estimating changes in parameters across periods). Among all inputs, responsiveness of labour appears to rise most significantly (row 2). The elasticity of sown area does not change (row 1). Somewhat unexpectedly, the own-price elasticity for fertilizer seems to show less price responsiveness in the second period (row 3).

To explain the somewhat counter-intuitive results for fertilizer, we return to our earlier discussion of the 'start and stop' nature of the fertilizer market liberalization. Since that did not become permanent until the 1990s, it is possible that we should not expect to see producers change their behaviour during the entire post-1985 period; increased responsiveness should not be expected to begin until 1990. To test whether the fertilizer own-price elasticity becomes more responsive for the second half of the late reform period, we re-

TABLE 3   *Changes in responsiveness of quasi-fixed and variable inputs: own-price elasticity changes based on estimating changes in parameters across periods*

Own price elasticity of:	1975–84	1985–95
Sown area	–0.001	–0.001
Labour	–0.013	–0.082
Fertilizer	–0.867	–0.467
Own price elasticity of:	1975–89	1990–95
Fertilizer	–0.229	–0.446

Notes: Elasticities are calculated using a modification of the model that allows for the own-price response of each output or input to change for the later period (1985–95 or 1990–95). See de Brauw *et al.* (2000) for the parameter estimates that were used to calculate these elasticities.

estimate the model with own-price responses again, this time interacting them with a dummy variable that is 0 for all years before 1990 and 1 thereafter. Our new results show increased responsiveness in the use of fertilizer in the second reform period. The own-price fertilizer elasticities calculated with these parameters are in Table 3, row 5. Our findings suggest that, after 1990, fertilizer becomes more own-price responsive (–0.229 before, –0.446 after). With the exception of sown area, the results are consistent with the interpretation that the late-period liberalization policies have made producers more sensitive to input price changes.

EFFICIENCY, RESPONSIVENESS AND FLEXIBILITY

Efficiency measurements for comparing returns to the incentive reforms in the early reform period with the returns to market liberalization in the late reform period are presented in Table 4. Gains to incentive reform are only calculated for the years 1978 to 1984 in order to highlight the fact the HRS significantly boosted farm incomes in the early reform era. In fact, the gains in profits from HRS continue indefinitely, since there would likely be a fall in income after 1985 if the HRS policy were reversed and the incentives that HRS brought to farmers were weakened. By contrast, the gains to market liberalization are only calculated over the late reform period (1985–95) on the assumption that policy officials implemented few policies beyond HRS prior to 1985 that led to a richer environment for exchange.

Our results clearly show the large contribution of HRS to farm incomes during the early reform period. The gains from the incentive reform increased throughout the period, rising as HRS spread through the economy. In 1984, the peak year, farm profits rose by more than 7 per cent. While this percentage is less than the additions to production output and production growth measured by McMillan *et al.* (1989) and Lin (1992), they are not inconsistent. To obtain the large increases in output, many of the factors that we deduct from our measure are included. Moreover, since farm income during the reform period was such a large part of total rural household income, this does represent a significant increase in the wealth of rural areas. Moreover, this is an average figure; some regions gained more and others gained less. Aggregating the total increase in profits from just farm production across more than 200 million rural households still represents an immense gain of wealth.

The results of this exercise show that, on a year-to-year basis, the overall gains from market liberalization have increased efficiency overall, between 0.12 and 1.73 per cent (Table 4, column 2). G_t was lower when prices declined, and higher in years when the price level increased sharply. At the extremes, in 1990, when the real price of wheat declined by 4 per cent and that for maize fell by 8 per cent, G_t was the smallest. On the other hand, as real prices rose steadily through the mid-1990s, G_t reached its highest annual growth in 1994/5.

Relative to the gains in the incentive reforms, those from market liberalization not only start later (by policy choice), they are much smaller (Table 4,

TABLE 4   *Estimated efficiency gains to HRS, increased responsiveness and faster adjustment in the reform and post-reform periods*

	Incentive Reform Period	Market Liberalization Reform Period		
Year	Cumulative percentage return to incentive reform (I_t)	Total percentage change in returns due to market reforms (G_t)	Percentage change in returns due to increased flexibility (F_t)	Percentage change in returns due to increased responsiveness (R_t)
1978	0.00	–	–	–
1979	0.07	–	–	–
1980	1.16	–	–	–
1981	3.25	–	–	–
1982	5.24	–	–	–
1983	6.51	–	–	–
1984	7.55	–	–	–
1985	–	0.38	–0.01	0.39
1986	–	0.63	0.21	0.43
1987	–	0.21	–0.20	0.41
1988	–	0.79	0.14	0.66
1989	–	1.01	0.30	0.70
1990	–	0.12	–0.42	0.54
1991	–	0.69	–0.25	0.94
1992	–	0.79	0.23	0.56
1993	–	0.58	0.05	0.53
1994	–	1.73	0.86	0.87
1995	–	1.11	0.48	0.63

Note: Percentages are calculated by taking estimated total year-to-year gains and dividing by total estimated returns to land and labour.

column 2). The average annual gain to liberalization over the entire period is 0.73 per cent, which means it is roughly 10 times smaller than the annual rise in profits from the gains to incentive reforms at the end of that period (7.55 per cent). Even at the peak, in 1994, aggregate gains to market liberalization are less than four times the size of the gains to incentive reform. These findings suggest that reforming incentives have much higher returns than reforming markets. This conclusion is reinforced when we consider the fact that our returns to market liberalization may be overstated since, in some sense, the returns are conditioned on the earlier reform of incentives.

Decomposing the returns to market liberalization, we see that most of the change has come from increased responsiveness (Table 4, column 4). On a year-to-year basis, the returns to producers being more responsive to exogenous changes to prices and other factors average more than 0.50 per cent per year. The responsiveness gains have also been fairly constant over time, ranging from 0.39 to 0.94 per cent. Moreover, since producers became more responsive between the periods and the level of most of the exogenous variables, such as prices and the research and capital stock, rose, the returns to responsiveness were never negative.

In contrast to the returns from increased responsiveness, the benefits of increased flexibility are smaller, more variable, and are even negative in some years (Table 4, column 3). In part, the cause of the small gain is simply that the increase in speed of adjustment, especially for sown area, is relatively small. The variability of the returns and the appearance of negative values demonstrate that increased adjustment speed is not always a virtue, especially in an economy like China's that is experiencing year-to-year fluctuations in important factors that affect production, such as the output price. If prices soar in one period and then fall in the next, it is easy to see why slower adjustment could be beneficial. While there are lost profits in the first year when adjustment is slower, the second-period adjustment made in an attempt to catch up to the rising price in the first year might be exactly the right allocation (by accident) when prices in the second year fall. The more flexible producer is able to catch up more quickly, but the new flexibility could make him chase the prices back down in the second year (as opposed to being correct, as in the case of the producer who adjusts more slowly).

CONCLUSIONS

In this paper we have tried to develop a framework to estimate the return to incentive and market liberalization reforms. Building on the adjustment cost literature, which provides us with ways to assess whether or not producers have become more flexible or responsive over time, we have developed a measure of the changes in efficiency that arise during periods of market liberalization. The measure can be broken down into two components, the returns to responsiveness and to flexibility.

We find that the behaviour of producers in China has been affected by the liberalization reforms, but that the gains have been relatively small. Farmers have increased their speed of adjustment between the early and late reform period for both labour and sown area. According to our estimates of own-price elasticities for labour and fertilizer, producers are also becoming more responsive. The magnitude of the gains in efficiency from increased responsiveness and flexibility in the late reform period, however, is substantially less in percentage terms (less than 1 per cent per year) than that from the incentive reforms in the early reform period (up to 7 per cent). Given these results, we argue that gradualism has succeeded where Big Bang has not.

In its most simple version, our story is as follows. Although we find that market liberalization policies in China's agriculture have increased producer responsiveness and flexibility, the returns to the incentive reforms were much larger in terms of their impacts on farm profits, and household income, than market liberalization. Since the incentive reforms came first, and occurred without the disruption that almost invariably accompanies market transition in a reform setting, the large rise in wealth that was generated by the incentive reforms almost certainly gave the economy its initial positive boost. This may also have helped to trigger a series of positive downstream actions. While this is speculative, we believe that the initial surge of productivity helped raise the ability of households to make further investment, increase the demand for goods and services across the economy, and provide regional and national governments with a larger pool of resources from which they were able to draw taxes needed to finance transition. According to our estimates, at most only a fraction of these resources would have been generated if leaders started reforms by liberalizing markets. In fact, it is possible that liberalizing markets before agents face the right incentives and have the support of certain institutions and infrastructure leads to greater disruption and even smaller (or negative) returns that would have limited, not triggered, subsequent economic activity.

On the basis of our findings, we believe that leaders in transitional countries should first work hard to increase incentives and build the institutions that agents need to operate efficiently before moving to 'free up' markets radically. Our results need to be interpreted carefully, however. The study was limited to agriculture. In more complex sectors, reforming incentives may not lead to greater efficiency if markets are not already in place, given the need for greater coordination. We are also estimating the changes in parameters between periods with relatively few observations. It would be worth trying to replicate these results on other sectors with larger time series.

NOTES

[1]Other institutional changes have had a number of important incentive effects associated with them, such as land tenure. We are ignoring them here, or claiming that the incentives for investing in land were sufficiently strong in the HRS reforms for the residual rights to farm output and the claim to the increase in land value to be indistinguishable. As argued below, we believe the rise of markets, although affecting incentives, should not be confused with incentives (see Lin, 1991; Huang and Rozelle, 1996). Rather, markets allow participants more scope for efficiently using resources. In this respect, we interpret market liberalization narrowly.

[2]In both Lin (1991) and Huang and Rozelle (1996), own-price output elasticities of farm producers rise after HRS, but the total output shows a secular drop due to the demise of some centrally planned functions that free market agents do not take over.

[3]The two quasi-input equations only contain a three-element vector as the three environmental variables are hypothesized to affect only the three output commodities.

[4]When explaining aggregate grain yields in China's provinces, Huang and Rozelle (1993) found four factors to have an important and robust effect: erosion, damage due to the deterioration of the local environment, salinization and soil fertility exhaustion from over-intense land use. The first two of these variables are included in the three output equations in this analysis.

[5]We currently have only 260 observations for the whole study period and there are 135 parameters to be estimated. If we were to divide the sample into two subperiods, we would have negative degrees of freedom for estimating the model for the first period and only 24 for the second period.

[6]We interact a dummy with all own-price responses except for wheat. The parameter for wheat is not precisely estimated in the original specification; it has a t-ratio of 0.26, and varies

widely when the model is specified differently. Other own-price response parameters are well-behaved when interacted with a dummy and are robust to different econometric specifications.

[7]Data were available for 13 provinces in North China (all provinces except for Inner Mongolia and Qinghai).

[8]The prices for creating the cash crop output variable come from the Cost of Production Data. The price used as an explanatory variable for equations 2–5 is from a national cash crop price index.

[9]Some people have questioned the reliability of the data since they are based on a relatively small sample size. A closer examination would indicate otherwise. In the 1990 enumeration, over 15 000 households living in 2245 counties were questioned about their costs of production for the six major grain crops. Price Bureau officials claim that they have maintained a random selection process. Consistency in the data is maintained by carrying over respondents for an average period of three to four years. Data are recorded by the households.

[10]Lin (1992) shows theoretically that, if the producer's marketing quota is output-dependent, production decisions depend on both the quota and market price. The best specification would include both prices. Unfortunately, these data are unavailable and the 'mixed' price is used as a proxy. The construction of these average prices implicitly assumes that producers are responding to an average price, constructed of quantity-weighted state and market (or 'negotiated') prices.

[11]The signs of the environmental variables are consistent with those found by Huang and Rozelle (1995). The erosion and deterioration of the local environment effects are particularly harmful to other grains, the crop grown in the most environmentally fragile regions. Salinity has the most significant impact on cash crops, especially in the North China Plain, China's cotton and peanut belt.

REFERENCES

de Brauw, A., Huang, J. and Rozelle, S. (2000), 'Increased Flexibility, Responsiveness and Efficiency from Market Liberalization Reforms in China's Agricultural Sector', working paper, Department of Agricultural and Resource Economics, University of California, Davis.

Cochrane, W.W. (1965), *The City Man's Guide to the Farm Problem*, Minneapolis: University of Minnesota Press.

Epstein, L. (1981), 'Duality Theory and Functional Forms for Dynamic Factor Demands', *Review of Economic Studies*, **48**, 81–95.

Epstein, L. and Denny, M. (1983), 'The Multivariate Flexible Accelerator Model: Empirical Restrictions and Application to U.S. Manufacturing', *Econometrica*, **51**, 647–74.

Fan, S. (1991), 'Effects of Technological Change and Institutional Reform on Production Growth in Chinese Agriculture', *American Journal of Agricultural Economics*, **73**, 266–75.

Fan, S. (1999), *Technological Change, Technical and Allocative Efficiency in Chinese Agriculture: The Case of Rice Production in China*, EPTD discussion paper, January, Washington DC: International Food Policy Research Institute.

Fan, S. and Pardey, P.G. (1992), *Agricultural Research in China: Its Institutional Development and Impact*, The Hague: International Service for National Agricultural Research.

Gallant, A. (1977), 'Three-Stage Least Squares Estimation for a System of Simultaneous, Nonlinear, Implicit Equations', *Journal of Econometrics*, **5**, 71–88.

Hathaway, D.E. (1963), *Government and Agriculture: Public Policy in a Democratic Society*, New York: Macmillan.

Huang, J. and Rozelle, S. (1993), 'Environmental Stress and Grain Yields in China', *American Journal of Agricultural Economics*, **77**, 853–64.

Huang, J. and Rozelle, S. (1996), 'Technological Change: Rediscovering the Engine of Productivity Growth in China's Rural Economy', *Journal of Development Economics*, **49**, 337–69.

Huang, L., Rosegrant, M. and Rozelle, S. (1995), 'Public Investment, Technological Change, and Reform: A Comprehensive Accounting of Chinese Agricultural Growth', working paper, Food Research Institute, Stanford University.

Johnson, G.L. (1956), 'Supply Functions: Some Facts and Notions' in E.O. Heady (ed.), *Agricultural Adjustment Problems in a Growing Economy*, Ames: Iowa State University Press.

Johnson, G.L. and Quance, L. (1972), *The Overproduction Trap in U.S. Agriculture*, Baltimore: Johns Hopkins University Press.

Lin, J.Y. (1991), 'Prohibitions of Factor Market Exchanges and Technological Choice in Chinese Agriculture', *Journal of Development Studies*, **27**, 1–15.

Lin, J.Y. (1992), 'Rural Reforms and Agricultural Growth in China', *American Economic Review*, **82**, 34–51.

Lin, J.Y., Cai, Fang and Li, Zhou (1996), *The China Miracle: Development Strategy and Economic Reform*, Hong Kong: Chinese University Press.

Lucas, R.E., Jr (1967), 'Adjustment Costs and Theory of Supply', *Journal of Political Economy*, **75**, 321–34.

Luh, Y-H. and Stefanou, S.E. (1991), 'Productivity Growth in U.S. Agriculture Under Dynamic Adjustment', *American Journal of Agricultural Economics*, **73**, 1116–25.

McMillan, J., Whalley, J. and Zhu, L. (1989), 'The Impact of China's Economic Reforms on Agricultural Productivity Growth', *Journal of Political Economy*, **97**, 781–807.

McMillan, John and Naughton, Barry (1991), 'How to Reform a Planned Economy: Lessons from China', *Oxford Review of Economic Policy*, **8**, 130–44.

MWREP (Ministry of Water Resources and Electric Power) (1988–96), *Compiled Statistics on the Development of China's Water Conservancy System*, Beijing: Ministry of Water Resources and Electric Power.

Parish, W., Zhe, Xiaoye and Li, Fang (1995), 'Nonfarm Work and Marketization of the Chinese Countryside', *China Quarterly*, **143**, 697–730.

Putterman, L. (1992), *Continuity and Change in China's Rural Development*, New York: Oxford University Press.

Roland, G. and Verdier, T. (1999), 'Transition and Output Fall', *Economics of Transition*, **7**, 1–28.

Rozelle, S. (1996), 'Gradual Reform and Institutional Development: The Keys to Success of China's Rural Reforms', in B. Naughton (ed.), *Economic Reform in China: Lessons for Economics in Transition*, Ann Arbor: University of Michigan Press.

Sachs, J. and Woo, Wing Tai (1994), 'Structural Factors in the Economic Reforms of China, Eastern Europe and the Former Soviet Union', *Economic Policy*, **18**, 101–45.

Sicular, T. (1988), 'Plan and Market in China's Agricultural Commerce', *Journal of Political Economy*, **96**, 283–307.

Sicular, T. (1995), 'Redefining State, Plan, and Market: China's Reforms in Agricultural Commerce', *China Quarterly*, **144**, 1020–46.

SPB (State Price Bureau) (1988–95), *Quanguo Nongchanpin Chengben Shouyi Ziliao Huibian* (National Agricultural Production Cost and Revenue Information Summary), Beijing: China Price Bureau Press.

SSB (State Statistical Bureau) (1993), *Nongye Kexue Jishu Tongji Huibian* (A Compendium of Statistical Material on Agricultural Science and Technology), Beijing: State Statistical Bureau.

Vasavada, U. and Chambers, R.G. (1986), 'Investment in U.S. Agriculture', *American Journal of Agricultural Economics*, **68**, 950–60.

Wang, D. (2000), 'The Determinants of Quotas and Impact on Grain Supply and Sown Area', unpublished PhD dissertation, Nanjing Agricultural University, Department of Agricultural Economics, Nanjing, China.

Warjiyo, P. (1991), 'Resource Adjustment, Dynamic Price Responses and Research Impacts in the United States Agriculture, 1950–1982', unpublished PhD dissertation, Department of Agricultural Economics, Iowa State University, Ames, Iowa.

Wen, J.G. (1993), 'Total Factor Productivity Change in China's Farming Sector: 1952–1989', *Economic Development and Cultural Change*, **4**, 1–42.

Ye, Q. and Rozelle, S. (1994), 'Fertilizer Policy in China's Reforming Economy', *Canadian Journal of Agricultural Economics*, **42**, 191–208.

ZGNYNJ (1981–93), *Zhongguo Nongye Nianjian* (China Agricultural Yearbook), Beijing: China Agricultural Press.

ZGTJNJ (1980, 1986–93), *Zhongguo Tongji Nianjian* (China Statistical Yearbook), Beijing: China Statistical Press.

APPENDIX A: THEORETICAL MODEL

Facing adjustment problems with a set of their quasi-fixed inputs (K), farmers are assumed to select optimal levels of variable inputs (L), investment rate (I), and K, given the prices of output (p), variable input (w) and quasi-fixed inputs (q), and the level of external constraints. This maximization problem can be written as

$$V(p,w,q,K,Z) = \underset{Y,L,I}{Max} \int_0^\infty e^{-rt}(pY - wL - qK)dt \qquad (A1)$$

subject to: $\dot{K} = I - \delta K$, $K(0) = K_0 > 0$, and $Y = f(K, L, I, Z)$, where r is the discount rate, K is the net investment in quasi-fixed inputs, $K(0) = K_0$ is the stock of investment at the base year, and δ is a diagonal matrix with positive depreciation rates on the diagonal. The function, $f(\cdot)$, is a multi-product pro-duction function. Given the regularity conditions on $f(\cdot)$ and static price expectations, the value function in equation A1 satisfies the following Hamil-ton–Jacobi equation:

$$rV(p,w,q,K,I,Z) = Max[\pi^*(p,w,q,K,I,Z) - q'K$$
$$+ V_K'(p,w,q,K,Z)(I - \delta K)] \qquad (A2)$$

where π^* is variable profit, V_K is derivative of V with respect to K. Epstein (1981) has shown that by applying duality and the envelope theorem to (A2), the following investment (K^*), variable input derived demand (L^*) and output supply (Y^*) equations can be obtained:

$$\Delta K^* = V_{Kq}^{-1}(rVq + K) \qquad (A3)$$

$$L^* = -rV_w + V_{Kw}'K \qquad (A4)$$

$$Y^* = rV_p - V_{Kp}'K \qquad (A5)$$

where the lower-case subscripts are used to designate derivatives.

APPENDIX B: PARAMETER ESTIMATES

TABLE B1   *Parameter estimates of dynamic supply response system using non-linear three stage least squares estimator, Northern China*

Parameter	Estimate	T-ratio	Parameter	Estimate	T-ratio
B01	−45.25	0.73	H22	−0.37	0.57
B02	−148.27	2.54	IRR1	0.0024	0.69
B03	−494.11	1.41	IRR2	−0.0069	2.16
B04	−1799.31	2.16	IRR3	−0.038	2.23
B05	−2412.72	3.29	IRR4	0.054	1.64
B06	9.98	0.05	IRR5	−0.0033	0.12
A11	11574.59	0.26	IRR60	0.81	3.87
A12	71334.97	1.79	IRR61	5.70e-06	0.36
A22	73741.03	1.33	IRR62	1.64e-05	0.48
A41	−2.87	1.64	RES1	0.36	1.78
A42	−0.92	0.36	RES2	0.95	5.00
R11	−0.16	3.65	RES3	0.40	0.33
R12	−0.21	4.22	RES4	6.76	3.10
R21	0.12	1.64	RES5	17.30	8.93
R22	−0.35	8.38	RES60	−21.69	1.25
R11D	−0.04	2.98	RES61	0.0059	1.74
R22D	−0.25	5.49	RES62	0.00095	0.22
G11	0.14	0.03	HRS 1	−31.59	0.80
G12	6.41	1.37	HRS2	−140.71	3.84
G21	−3257.79	1.30	HRS3	564.06	2.50
G22	−12412.82	4.69	HRS4	927.59	2.31
L1	−8.60	3.14	HRS5	−684.74	1.92
L2	2575.69	1.80	HRS6	145.73	1.42
C11	−0.0010	0.73	DIS1	−2470.11	2.38
C12	0.54	0.93	DIS2	−3141.24	3.51
C22	879.83	2.32	DIS3	−225.27	0.94
F1	−31364.86	2.27	EROI	−660.72	1.71
F2	−39668.19	2.52	ER02	−1247.29	3.74
B	52181.49	4.79	ER03	−74.67	0.81
N1	−0.033	0.09			
N2	−0.067	0.16	Objective function *N = 757.3		
H11	4.02	5.97	Provincial dummies: not reported		
H12	0.68	1.18	Number of parameters: 135		
H21	−2.19	2.89	Number of equations: 6		

KAREN MACOURS AND JOHAN F.M. SWINNEN*

Agrarian Transitions and Productivity Patterns: Synthesis of Experiences in Eastern Europe, the Former Soviet Union and East Asia

INTRODUCTION

Economic reforms have induced important output and productivity changes in the agricultural sectors of transition countries (TCs), but with large differences between the countries. In general, agricultural output increased considerably in the East Asian TCs, while declining strongly in most Central and East European countries (CEECs) and the former Soviet Union (FSU).[1] However, productivity increased in some Central European countries, as in East Asia. In other regions there was a considerable decline in productivity. Furthermore, important differences exist within regions.

There are three 'extreme' patterns in agricultural transition, summarized in Figures 1 and 2 for the first nine years of transition.

- *Pattern I ('Central Europe)*: a strong decline in gross agricultural output (GAO) coincides with a sharp increase in output per worker because of a marked outflow of labour from agriculture. This is the pattern followed by the Czech Republic, Slovakia and Hungary: GAO declines by around 30 per cent during the first years of transition, but stabilizes after four years. At the same time, agricultural labour productivity (ALP) increases rapidly: on average around 10 per cent annually during the first nine years of transition.
- *Pattern II ('Russia')*: a strong decline in GAO coincides with an appreciable decline in ALP. Russia, Ukraine and Belarus are typical examples of this pattern, as are several other newly independent states (NIS). On average, output fell by almost 50 per cent in these countries and labour productivity by around 30 per cent.

*Karen Macours, Department of Agricultural and Resource Economics, University of California at Berkeley and Department of Agricultural and Environmental Economics, Katholieke Universiteit, Louvain, Belgium. J. Swinnen, European Commission, DG-II (Economic and Financial Affairs) and Department of Agricultural and Environmental Economics, Katholieke Universiteit, Louvain, Belgium. We thank Zvi Lerman, Azeta Cungu, Jikun Huang, Nguyen Tri Khiem, Stefan Bojnec, Olga Liefert, Aleksander Kaliberda, Irina S. Plakhotnik, Don Van Atta, Gennaro Volpe, Tomas Doucha, Gezja Blaas and Tibor Ferenczi for much-appreciated assistance with the data collection. This research project was financially supported by FWO (project G.0288.99). The authors are solely responsible for the views expressed, which do not necessarily reflect those of the European Commission.

147

• *Pattern III ('China')*: a strong increase in GAO coincides with an increase, albeit slower, in ALP. Examples are China, Vietnam and, in Europe, also Albania. On average, output increased by more than 50 per cent in China and Vietnam, while labour productivity increased by 25 per cent.

The causes of these differences in post-reform economic performance include the choice of the reform policies, initial conditions, disruption of exchange relationships, regional tensions and conflict. While there is general agreement that these factors have affected transition performance, 'here is less agreement on their relative importance. The most intense debate has been over the Chinese reforms, and on what they imply for reforms elsewhere. Chinese reforms have resulted in extraordinary growth and are argued to have been successful because they were 'gradual', in contrast with those of the CEEC and FSU (Roland and Verdier, 1999). However, others have argued that the difference in structural characteristics of the Chinese economy at the outset of transition made the situation unique, with very few policy lessons for other transition countries (Sachs and Woo, 1994).

This paper analyses the causes of the differences in transition performance in agriculture. It draws on three empirical studies in which we estimated the

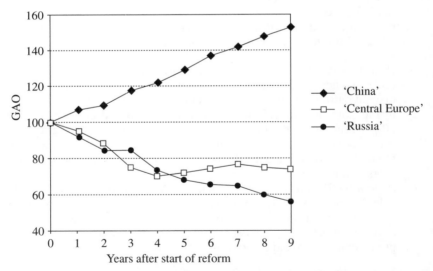

Note: 'China' is the average for China and Vietnam; 'Central Europe' is the average for Czech Republic, Slovakia and Hungary; 'Russia' is the average for Russia, Ukraine and Belarus.

Source: Own calculations based on data from OECD (2000) and FAO (1999).

FIGURE 1   *Changes in gross agricultural output (GAO) during first nine years of transition*

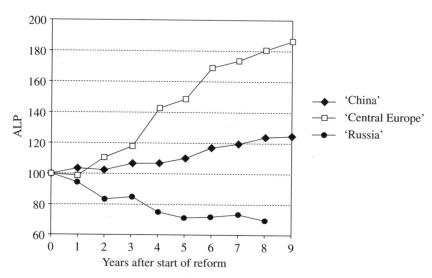

Note: 'China' is the average for China and Vietnam; 'Central Europe' is the average for Czech Republic, Slovakia and Hungary; 'Russia' is the average for Russia, Ukraine and Belarus.

Source: Own calculations based on data from OECD (2000), FAO (1999), ADB (1997) and national statistics.

FIGURE 2 *Changes in agricultural labour productivity (ALP) during first nine years of transition*

impact of reform policies and initial conditions, and their 'intermediate results' (that is, changes in relative prices, farm restructuring, changes in property rights and overall economic liberalization) on performance. The latter was indicated by agricultural productivity and output. Two studies (Macours and Swinnen, 1999, 2000b) used aggregate data for 15 transition countries (as presented in Figure 3); the third (Macours and Swinnen, 2000a) used annual crop output data for eight CEECs. The presentation here is organized mostly around the three patterns identified above; our three empirical studies provide for more detail on the other transition countries.

Initial conditions vary substantially among the countries (see Table 1).[2] At the outset of transition, China and Vietnam had the lowest GNP per capita. Since it is related to the level of development the share of agriculture in employment was considerably higher in China (around 70 per cent) than in Russia (less than 20 per cent). It was lowest in Central Europe (13 per cent). China and Vietnam had a very labour-intensive agriculture. The man/land ratio was higher than unity, compared with less than 0.15 in Central Europe and Russia. Pre-transition agriculture in all countries in Table 1 was characterized by the dominance of large-scale farms.[3] In China, the collective farms had

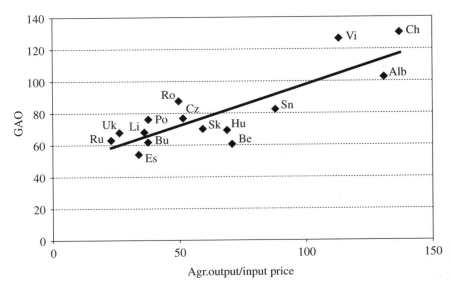

Source: Macours and Swinnen (1999).

FIGURE 3   *Output and price changes after five years of reform in 15 transition countries*

legal and effective property rights while land in Vietnam was state-owned, though the effective property rights were controlled by the collective farms. In Russia and other FSU countries, land was nationalized during communism, while in Central Europe most collective farm land was still legally owned by individuals, but effective property rights were controlled by the state or the collective farms. The collectivization of agriculture and introduction of central planning occurred after the Second World War in Central Europe and East Asia, while in Russia it was done earlier in the Communist period. When transition began, experience with private and individual farming was therefore more likely to be present in the rural households in the first group.

In China and Vietnam, agriculture was heavily taxed, while in most of the CEECs and the FSU, agriculture was generally supported by heavy subsidies. Also, pre-reform, China and Vietnam traded mainly with non-CMEA (Council for Mutual Economic Assistance) countries, while the NIS countries were fully integrated into the CMEA system, trading mainly with other communist countries. The Central European countries were somewhat less integrated, but a large part of their trade still went through the CMEA system.

TABLE 1   *Initial conditions and policies in transition patterns[1]*

	Patterns		
	Central Europe	Russia	China
Initial conditions (IC)			
GNP/capita PPP	7 670	6 803	950
Share of agr. in employment	13	17	70
Agric. labour intensity	0.13	0.09	1.49
Legal land ownership	individuals[2]	state	state
Pre-reform agr. price policy	subsidized	subsidized	taxed
Years under central planning	42	73	32
Reform policies (RP)			
Land reform procedure	restitution[2]	share distrib.	phys. distrib.
Property rights reform	fast	slow	fast
Policy outcomes (PO)[3]			
Relative price change	–41	–60	+24
Use rights	strong	weak	strong
Agr. land in individual farms (%)	16	11	99
Overall liberalization index	0.86	0.60	0.15

Notes: [1] The values are the averages of the representative countries from each
pattern (Czech Republic, Slovakia and Hungary for 'Central Europe';
Russia, Ukraine and Belarus for 'Russia'; China and Vietnam for 'China'.
[2] Part of the land in Hungary was owned by collective farms and (therefore) only one-third of Hungarian land was restituted; the rest was
privatized through compensation bonds and physical distribution.
[3] Five years after start of the reforms.

Source: Macours and Swinnen (1999).

REFORM POLICIES

Price and trade liberalization

All transition countries adopted some form of price reform. In Central Europe
agricultural prices were liberalized in 1989–91. In Russia and Ukraine, price
reforms occurred later, while in countries like Belarus prices remained heavily
controlled. While the Chinese reforms are usually described as 'gradual', the
changes in administered prices that were introduced had a significant impact.
In both China and Vietnam, reforms coincided with strong agricultural price
increases and a switch from compulsory deliveries to a contract system. In
Central Europe, Russia and Ukraine, trade liberalization followed the collapse
of the CMEA trading system. There were major effects on relative prices. The

impact of the disruption of former CMEA trade flows was more important for smaller countries and those more integrated in the system.

Privatization and land reform

There are three main land reform processes. *Restitution* of farm land to former owners is most important in Central Europe, although a significant part of Hungarian land was allocated through vouchers and distribution to farm workers (Swinnen, 1999). Typically, the reform laws specified that land be restituted to former owners in historical boundaries, if possible. Otherwise they receive property rights to a plot of land of comparable size and quality. Russia and Ukraine *distributed* most of the collective and state farm land equally per capita among collective farm members or state farm employees *in the form of paper shares or certificates*. In Belarus, however, private ownership of household plots was all that was allowed (Lerman, 1997). *Physical distribution* of farm land on an equal per capita basis to farm workers or rural households occurred in China and Vietnam, although only *use rights* were transferred to farmers.

In many cases, non-land assets were privatized using vouchers, which were distributed among cooperative members who had contributed land, labour or other assets.

Farm restructuring

Farm restructuring includes a reallocation of production factors (land, labour and capital) as well as an organizational reform, from cooperatives to family farms, for example. However, most TCs have a mix of various farm organizations, including private cooperative farms, joint-stock companies, family farms and part-time farms. The most radical form of restructuring was the break-up of the collective or state farms into individual holdings. This 'farm individualization' process was strongest in East Asia, where there was a complete break-up of the collective farms. In contrast, the share of land used by individual farms was less than 20 per cent five years after the start of the reforms in Russia, Ukraine and Belarus, and also in Central Europe.

The process of farm restructuring has been determined by a combination of reform policies, initial conditions and economic developments (Mathijs and Swinnen, 1998). First, the break-up of the collective farms was substantially higher when an important share of the land was distributed to farm workers instead of being returned to former owners. Distribution of farmland to workers reduced the transaction costs of renting or buying land and other assets for individuals wanting to leave the collective farms. Second, government policies differed significantly in the incentives or hurdles created for individual farming. Third, there is an inverse correlation between the break-up of collective farms into family farms and the pre-reform average productivity and capital intensity of the collective farms. Individuals were more reluctant to leave the large-scale farms where those farms were more productive and had fewer incentive problems.

Countries characterized by a strong shift to individual farms have typically distributed land ownership or use rights in physical terms to farm workers, have transformation regulations that do not increase the cost of leaving the collective farm, had low labour productivity and high labour intensity in collective farms and had a tradition of family farms prior to 1939–45. For example, in countries such as China and Vietnam (but also Albania and, to a lesser extent, Romania) characterized by these conditions, the larger share of land was managed by individual farms five years after the start of the reforms.

Overall liberalization

The liberalization index in Table 1 is from de Melo *et al.* (1996) and measures the average liberalization level in the whole economy five years after the start of the reforms. The index combines the extent of liberalization of internal markets (domestic prices and state trading monopolies), external markets (foreign trade regime and current account convertibility) and private sector entry (privatization of small-scale and large-scale enterprises and banking reform). The overall liberalization had progressed considerably further in Central Europe than in the NIS after five years.

IMPACT ON OUTPUT AND PRODUCTIVITY

First, the relative price changes following *price and trade liberalization* have had important effects on post-reform output developments. For example, Figure 3 shows a positive relationship between the relative price changes and the output changes after the first five years of reform. Importantly, the only TCs where GAO has increased during transition are the countries where relative prices have increased. Macours and Swinnen (2000a) estimate that terms of trade effects caused 40–50 per cent of the fall in average crop output in eight CEECs during transition (see Table 2).

Second, the *shift from collective farming* to individual (family) farming had a favourable impact on agricultural output. Owing to monitoring problems, the incentive to work in a cooperative is lower than in an individual farm. After the change from collectives to individual enterprise the income of the farmer is directly related to immediate performance, and therefore individual farming increases incentives for labour effort. This has caused an increase in the productivity of labour as well as in the intensity with which the other inputs are used. A similar effect has been found in studies of China (Lin, 1992) and Vietnam (Pingali and Xuan, 1992).

Interestingly, the shift to individual farms had an adverse impact on average labour productivity in agriculture, since the positive effect on labour productivity of improved effort and lower monitoring costs was more than offset by other features. First, the fragmentation of assets induced by the break-up of collective farms did not help. Second, replacement of other inputs by labour contributed to the negative relationship with *average* labour productivity. Substitution can be caused both by the increase in the marginal productivity of labour, ceteris paribus, with the shift to individual farms and by a change in the relative price of labour vis-à-vis the cost of other inputs. The latter is reinforced by capital constraints and credit market imperfections, which are widespread during agricultural transition. Finally, in food insecure circumstances worker owners will prefer individual farming rather than face the alternative of leaving agriculture.

Third, *privatization* affected performance differently depending (a) on how it affected property rights and (b) on the economic environment. Regarding property rights one can distinguish between those of transfer and those of use. Transfer rights have been established in CEECs, and since 1994 also in Russia. Although land transfers have occurred on some occasions in China, there is no legal framework guaranteeing the right to transfer. However, even in the TCs where land transfer rights are legal, sales are de facto largely absent during the period analysed.

The restitution process, as in Central Europe, and the land distribution process in China, created stronger individual use rights than the share distribution process in Russia and Ukraine. Despite the allocation of land shares to members, the land remains in joint cultivation pending a further restructuring decision by the 'shareowners' (Lerman, 1997). Important transaction costs limit the effective use rights of the individual owners. These differences are important since the transfer of effective use rights to individuals generally induced a decline in output and an increase in productivity. The creation of effective use rights caused profit-maximizing behaviour with hard budget constraints. This resulted in a reduction of surplus input use and therefore a decline of output. At the same time it improved the allocation and efficiency of input use, causing an increase in productivity.

Fourth, the impact of privatization on productivity is conditional upon *liberalization in the rest of the economy*. In particular, slow liberalization resulted in significant rigidities in the capital and labour markets, reducing the inflow of capital both for working purposes and for investment, as well as slowing the outflow of surplus labour. Macours and Swinnen (2000a) conclude that, because of market imperfections, the direct efficiency impact of privatization in countries such as Romania and Bulgaria was negative, but positive in the Central European countries, such as Hungary and the Czech Republic, where liberalization removed factor market imperfections to a greater extent. In countries such as Romania and Albania, productivity gains from privatization arrived primarily indirectly through the shift to individual farming (Table 2).

Furthermore, in Central Europe strong productivity gains occurred despite a relatively limited shift to individual farming. Compared with Russia and Ukraine, where large-scale farms continued to dominate as well, farms in Central Europe generally have undergone more effective restructuring, including both management reform and operation adjustments. In contrast, Lerman and Csaki (1997) report that, despite some 'downsizing' in restructured farms, internal reorganization has not produced major results in Russia and Ukraine and the collective framework has preserved most of its traditional function. As a result of this lack of restructuring, Sedik *et al.* (1999) detect a decline in farm efficiency during transition in Russia.

TABLE 2   *Contribution of different causal factors to crop output changes in eight CEECs between 1989 and 1995*

Explanatory variable	% of total change	% of explained change
Relative prices	−46	−52
Weather	−10	−11
Farm restructuring	+18	+20
Shift to individual farms	+68	+77
Disruption	−50	−57
Land privatization	−39	−44
Czech, Slovakia, Hungary	−24	−27
Other CEECs*	−51	−58
Uncertainty	−12	−13
Residual	−12	
Total output change	−100	−100

Note: * Primarily Albania, Romania and Bulgaria, since in Poland and Slovenia land privatization was less important.

Source: Macours and Swinnen (2000a).

Finally, organizational and contractual disruptions caused a decline in output and productivity during transition. *External* disruptions resulted from the collapse of the CMEA trading system. *Internal* effects arose from the break-up of the strong integrated system within supply chains, with central planning as the enforcement mechanism. The break-up of this contracting system with privatization, restructuring and liberalization, in the absence of alternative contract enforcement mechanisms and information distribution systems, caused dislocation in output and investment (McMillan, 1997). Several explanations of this result focus on the disruptions of relation-specific investments, due to information problems, search frictions and absence of contract enforcement mechanisms.

Roland and Verdier (1999) argue that the Chinese dual-track liberalization allowed enterprises to reap the informational benefits from price liberalization while avoiding the disruption associated with the breakdown of the planning system. Despite the inefficiencies of only liberalizing some of the prices, partial continuation of state control at the beginning of transition may avoid the output disruption and temporary fall in investment generated by a 'Big Bang' policy. Rozelle (1996) explains how the initial and abrupt liberalization of the fertilizer market in China in 1985 caused major disruptions in fertilizer supplies, leading the government to take back control of sales in 1987. Five years later, by which time China's domestic marketing capacity had developed, new fertilizer liberalization resulted in no disruption.

Macours and Swinnen (2000a) estimate that between 30 per cent and 60 per cent of average crop output decline in CEECs was due to institutional disruptions. On the basis of a case study of the Slovakian sugar sector, Gow and Swinnen (1998) show that output and yields increased dramatically, both at the processing and at the farm level, after new contract enforcement mechanisms and solutions to input contracting were implemented. The solution to contract hold-ups in this case – as in other transition countries (McMillan, 1997) – came from private rather than public enforcement. Foreign direct investment was of major importance in the change.

INITIAL CONDITIONS, REFORM POLICIES AND PERFORMANCE

To separate the impact of initial conditions on performance from those of reform policies, we used a combination of a principal component analysis and regression analysis in Macours and Swinnen (2000b). We show that six indicators of initial conditions (see Table 1) can be captured by two principal components. PC1 has high negative weight for income level, and high positive weights for labour intensity and the importance of agriculture in the economy, and can therefore be interpreted as an *index of the level of development* at the beginning of transition. PC2 has high positive weights for years under central planning and integration in the CMEA, and a high negative weight for land in private ownership pre-reform, and can be interpreted as an *index of the level of distortions* at the beginning of transition.

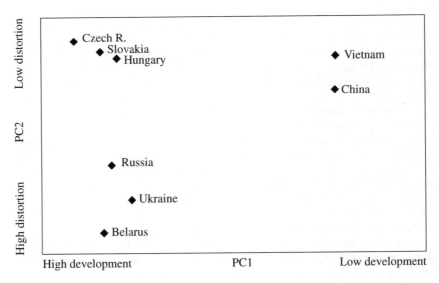

Source: Macours and Swinnen (2000b).

FIGURE 4   *Classification by principal components of initial conditions: index of pre-reform development (PC1) and index of pre-reform distortions (PC2)*

Figure 4 plots all the countries according to these indices of development (PC1) and distortion (PC2). The three patterns of transition, based on performance, can be clearly distinguished within this classification of initial conditions. The Central European group had a higher level of development (PC1) and lower pre-reform distortion (PC2). Russia, Ukraine and Belarus differed mostly from this first group by higher pre-reform distortion. China and Vietnam had a much lower level of development than the other groups, and moderate levels of distortion.

Our regressions show that, during the first five years of transition, the development of agricultural output was, to an important extent, determined by initial conditions, both directly and indirectly, through their effect on policy outcomes. We concluded that *initial conditions explain the main differences between countries in output changes during the first five years after the reforms*. However, the estimation results also suggest that (exogenous) *reform policy choices played an important role in determining labour productivity developments* during the first years of transition. After correcting for the endogenous part of the different policy outcomes, the establishment of strong use rights and the overall liberalization of the economy had a significant positive effect on agricultural labour productivity.

PATTERNS OF TRANSITION

Table 1 summarizes the relationship between the differences in economic performance and the initial conditions, the key reform policies and the policy outcomes. Both Russia and Central Europe were characterized by pre-reform subsidization of agriculture, relatively low labour intensity of farms and a small share of agriculture in the economy, but differed in the pre-reform land ownership and the period under central planning. In Russia and Central Europe, terms of trade declined in agriculture following price and trade liberalization due to pre-reform taxation of agriculture, but the choice and implementation of privatization, land reform and overall liberalization policies differed substantially.

In Central Europe, land reform through restitution and physical distribution led to stronger individual property rights. Further, the more extensive and more radical liberalization of the general economy in Central Europe reduced obstacles for intersectoral labour mobility. In contrast, in Russia land ownership rights were allocated in the form of shares in the former collective and state farms, causing weak individual property rights and limited incentives for resource allocation improvements. Also the dependence of individuals on farms for food security and social benefits, such as housing, further reduced mobility and the outflow of labour from agriculture. In combination with low overall liberalization and the lack of individual farming skills after several generations of communist rule, labour mobility from farms and to other sectors has been constrained. Hence surplus labour has not left agriculture and is trapped in large-scale farms that continue to be dominated by old management. The consequence is that, with decreasing terms of trade, while agricultural output has declined to a similar extent to that in Central Europe, labour productivity has fallen with output in Russia, while it increased strongly in Central Europe.

A third pattern, followed by China and Vietnam, is characterized by growth in both output and productivity during transition. These countries started from a very labour-intensive agriculture, which was taxed. Price and trade liberalization caused an improvement in the terms of trade. Institutional reforms included the distribution of clear and strong land use rights to farm workers and rural households, and a complete break-up of the collective and/or state farms into individual holdings. Because of the high labour intensity (and low labour productivity) on the collective farms the shift to individual farming implied important benefits because of improved labour incentives and profit maximization, and low costs from fragmentation. The strong shift to individual farming was also stimulated by the low level of income in countries where food security concerns played an important role: in China and Vietnam cases of radical and widespread decollectivization emerged to some extent spontaneously as a reaction to a major crisis.

In combination, these factors contributed to increases in output and productivity. However, the food security worries, as well as the link between social benefits (such as housing) and economic sectors, increased intersectoral (and rural–urban) mobility costs, contributing to the slower growth of labour productivity than output. Institutional and organizational disruptions contributed to investment and output declines. They are argued to have been more important in Central Europe and Russia than in China, with its more 'gradual approach' to market liberalization. Several analyses show that these disruptions have caused important declines in output.

However, our analysis suggests that key determinants of output growth in China are (a) the terms of trade effect, which was importantly determined by the pre-reform taxation of agriculture, and (b) radical reforms in the allocation of land property rights and in the reorganization of agricultural production. In fact, Albania, the only European country with structural characteristics similar to those of China (and Vietnam), introduced radical market liberalization, causing strong disruptions in exchange relationships. This has not prevented it from recording high growth rates in GAO as in China (and Vietnam) – in fact, since the start of the reform in 1991, and despite the chaos following the 1997 political upheaval, average output growth in Albania has been almost 10 per cent annually (Cungu and Swinnen, 1999).

All this suggests that key determinants of agricultural growth during the first years of transition in China have also been initial conditions, (radical) land reform and farm restructuring. Hence one should be careful in using the 'Chinese miracle' as an example for advocating gradual reforms in other transition countries.

TRANSITION DYNAMICS

During the first years of transition, output changes have been greatly affected by initial conditions. However reform policies, relative to initial conditions, increased in importance as the transition progressed. Figure 1 shows that, while output continued to drop in Russia, this trend was reversed in Central Europe where, after the initial decline, output started recovering.

We observe in several Central European agricultural markets (more so in the crop sector than in livestock production) that output development is U-shaped, with three phases: an initial decline caused primarily by deteriorating terms of trade and contract disruptions, a bottoming out when the terms of trade stabilize and their effect phases out, then a later increase in output caused by increases in productivity. The latter phase is crucially affected by reform policies, rather than by initial conditions.

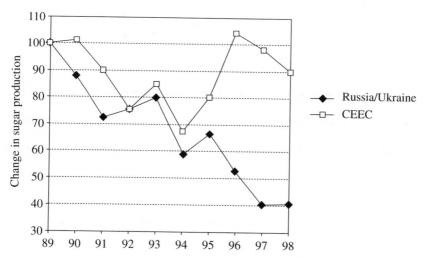

Note: CEECs: average for Poland, Hungary, Czech Republic and Slovakia.

Source: Swinnen *et al.* (2000).

FIGURE 5   *Evolution of sugar production (based on domestic sugar beet)*

Figure 5 illustrates this effect for the case of sugar. In Central Europe, Russia and Ukraine sugar output initially declined, then recovered significantly in Central Europe after growth resumed with an inflow of foreign direct investment and improved farm management following the necessary reforms (Swinnen *et al.*, 2000). Figure 6 shows that, while the initial fall in output coincided with the relative price decline, the recovery of output has been due to increases in yields resulting from the reforms. In contrast, in Russia and Ukraine no such recovery occurred.

The conclusion from these comparisons is consistent with our previous argument: transition output falls have been determined largely by initial conditions, but productivity changes and growth resumption are much more affected

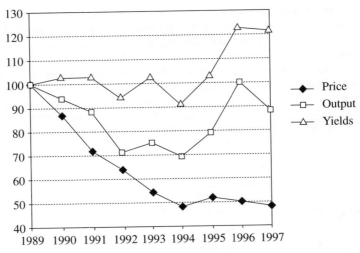

Note: CEECs: average for Poland, Hungary, Czech Republic and Slovakia.

Source: Swinnen *et al.* (2000).

FIGURE 6 *Evolution of output, relative prices and yields of sugar beet in CEECs*

by reform policies. The impact of the policies becomes dominant as transition progresses.

CONCLUSIONS

Both initial conditions and reform policies have affected the performances of transition countries. Agricultural output has been strongly affected by initial conditions, while productivity was influenced more by reform policies. Furthermore, it has been mainly the initial output changes which have been dependent on initial conditions, while later changes have been more affected by reform policies. More specific conclusions are the following.

First, relative price developments resulting from the price and trade llberalizations are a key factor in explaining the differences in agricultural performance between transition countries. Second, a key condition for productivity improvement is the allocation of (at least) strong use rights on agricultural production factors, including land, to individuals. The allocation of strong use rights induces an effective restructuring of production organizations. Third, the extent to which management differs in efficiency from pre-reform management, rather than the shift to individual farming in itself, is a key factor in improving productivity in agriculture.

Fourth, the overall liberalization of the economy, along with assured food supply and social security, affect the opportunity and mobility costs for labour employed in agriculture and therefore the labour productivity changes during transition. Finally, liberalization and the restoration of secure tenure rights stimulate factor market developments, which improve access to capital and land and enhance productivity.

NOTES

[1]In this paper East Asian transition countries include China, Vietnam, Laos and Myanmar; CEECs are the Balkan TCs (Albania, Bulgaria, Romania and Slovenia) and the Visegrad TCs (Czech Republic, Hungary, Poland, Slovakia); FSU refers to the 15 republics of the former Soviet Union, NIS (newly independent states) refers to the FSU without the Baltics (Estonia, Latvia and Lithuania).

[2]Table 1 summarizes the initial conditions and reform policies for the three 'extreme' transition patterns. Details on initial conditions and reform policies for all transition countries are in Macours and Swinnen (1999).

[3]Only in former Yugoslavia, Poland, Laos and Myanmar was most agricultural land managed by individual (family) farms.

REFERENCES

ADB (1997), *Statistical Data of DMCs*, on line (*http://internotes.asiandevbank.org/*).

Cungu, A. and Swinnen, J.F.M. (1999), 'Albania's Radical Agrarian Reform', *Economic Development and Cultural Change*, **47**, 605–19.

FAO (1999), *FAOSTAT Agricultural Data*, on line (*http://apps.fao.org*).

Gow, H.R. and Swinnen, J.F.M. (1998), 'Agribusiness Restructuring, Foreign Direct Investment, and Hold-Up Problems in Agricultural Transition', *European Review of Agricultural Economics*, **25**, 331–50.

Lerman, Z. (1997), 'Experience with Land Reform and Farm Restructuring in the Former Soviet Union', in J.F.M. Swinnen, A. Buckwell and E. Mathijs (eds), *Agricultural Privatization, Land Reform and Farm Restructuring in Central and Eastern Europe*, Aldershot: Ashgate.

Lerman, Z. and Csaki, C. (1997), 'Land Reform in Ukraine: The First Five Years', *World Bank Discussion Paper 371*, Washington DC: World Bank.

Lin, J.Y. (1992), 'Rural Reforms and Agricultural Growth in China', *American Economic Review*, **82**, 34–51.

McMillan, J. (1997), 'Markets in Transition', in D. Kreps and K.F. Wallis (eds), *Advances in Economics and Econometrics: Theory and Applications*, vol. 2, Cambridge: Cambridge University Press.

Macours, K. and Swinnen, J.F.M. (1999), 'Patterns of Agrarian Transition: A Comparison of Output and Labour Productivity Changes in Central and Eastern Europe, the Former Soviet Union and East Asia', *Policy Research Group Working Paper-19*, Louvain: Department of Agricultural and Environmental Economics, Katholieke Universiteit.

Macours, K. and Swinnen, J.F.M. (2000a), 'Causes of Output Decline in Economic Transition: The Case of Central and Eastern European Agriculture', *Journal of Comparative Economics*, **28**, 172–206.

Macours, K. and Swinnen, J.F.M. (2000b), 'Impact of Reforms and Initial Conditions on Agricultural Output and Productivity Changes in Central and Eastern Europe, the Former Soviet Union and East Asia', *American Journal of Agricultural Economics*, **82**, 1149–55.

Mathijs, E. and Swinnen, J.F.M. (1998), 'The Economics of Agricultural Decollectivization in East Central Europe and the Former Soviet Union', *Economic Development and Cultural Change*, **47**, 1–26.

de Melo, M., Denizer, C. and Gelb, A. (1996), 'From Plan to Market: Patterns of Transition', *The World Bank Economic Review*, **10**, 397–424.

OECD (2000), *Agricultural Policies in Emerging and Transition Economies: Indicators*, on line (*http://www.oecd.org/agr/apnme/*).

Pingali, P.L. and Xuan, V.-T. (1992), 'Vietnam: Decollectivization and Rice Productivity Growth', *Economic Development and Cultural Change*, **40**, 697–718.

Roland, G. and Verdier, T. (1999), 'Transition and the Output Fall', *Economics of Transition*, **7**, 1–28.

Rozelle, S., (1996), 'Gradual Reform and Institutional Development: The Keys to Success of China's Agricultural Reforms', in J. McMillan and B. Naughton (eds), *Reforming Asian Socialism. The Growth of Market Institutions*, Ann Arbor: University of Michigan Press.

Sachs, J. and Woo, W.T. (1994), 'Structural Factors in the Economic Reforms of China, Eastern Europe and the Former Soviet Union', *Economic Policy*, **18**, 101–45.

Sedik, D.J., Trueblood, M.A. and Arnade, C. (1999), 'Corporate Farm Performance in Russia, 1991–1995', *Journal of Comparative Economics*, **27**, 514–33.

Swinnen, J.F.M. (1999), 'Political Economy of Land Reform Choices in Central and Eastern Europe', *Economics of Transition*, **7**, 637–64.

Swinnen, J.F.M., Gow, H. and Maviglia, I. (2000), 'Modest Changes in the West, Radical Reforms in the East, and Government Intervention Everywhere: European Sugar Markets at the Outset of the 21st Century', in A. Schmitz, T. Spreen and W. Messina (eds), *Sweetener Markets in the 21st Century*, Amsterdam: Kluwer Academic Publishers.

EUGENIA SEROVA*

Land Reforms and Emerging Agri-food Markets: the Russian Experience

INTRODUCTION: LAND REFORM, FARM RESTRUCTURING AND EMERGING MARKETS

Agrarian reforms were an important constituent element of general economic reforms in all the post-socialist countries. The major objective of agrarian change was the creation of a market-oriented sector. In the USSR and most Central and East European countries there was an additional wish to reduce the burden of state subsidies to the agri-food sector. In the process of reform, countries in transition have to undertake three tasks: to implement institutional changes in agriculture, to promote the emergence of market institutions and infrastructure, and to frame new agri-food policies to match those of a more pervasive market economy. The issues of land reform and farm restructuring can be taken first, with discussion of emerging markets following at a later stage.

The processes of reform have been strongly dependent on whether the economic structure was predominantly agrarian or industrial (Wedekin, 1991; Zhou, 1996). Agrarian countries are characterized by a high share of agriculture in gross domestic product (GDP) and of rural population in total population, low levels of technology in agriculture, relatively low per capita food consumption and a correspondingly high share of food spending in the total incomes of households. Table 1 illustrates some of these features. The high level of taxation of agriculture in favour of industrialization has also been an important feature of the transition economies. In our sample, Albania, Romania and China represent the 'agrarian' economies, though there are others in transition within the broad group (including Vietnam) for whom comparable information is not available.

Within the agrarian countries simple land distribution to households provided rapid growth both in output and in per capita consumption (for output growth, see Table 2). Indeed, low-level technologies in the collectivized farms did not allow much gain to be made from scale economies, but did create losses from weak labour motivation. Distribution of land to households normally did not harm technology, but markedly increased work incentives, leading to growth in output fairly soon after land distribution. China had growing gross

* Analytical Centre AFE (IET) and Higher School of Economics, Moscow; Gazetny 5, Moscow 103918, Russia.

TABLE 1   *Features of agrarian and predominantly industrial socialist countries before reforms*

	Year	GDP	Share of agriculture (%) in Total employment	Share of food expenditures (%) in total household spending
Bulgaria	1989	11.0	18.1	29.5
Hungary	1989	15.6	17.9	25.4
Latvia	1989	10.2	14.6	30.3
Lithuania	1989	26.5	17.6	34.9
Russia	1990	15.3	12.9	36.1
Slovak Rep	1989	9.4	12.2	35.4*
Czech Rep	1989	6.3	9.9	32.9*
Estonia	1989	17.8	12.0	28.2
Albania	1989	32.0	49.0	56.5
Romania	1989	27.0	60.0	55.7
China	1990	13.7	28.2	48.0

Note: *Includes beverages and tobacco.

Source: *Agricultural Policies, Markets and Trade in Transition Economies/ Monitoring and Evaluation*, Paris: OECD, 1996.

agricultural output (GAO) over the 1980s, which continued, while the pause in Albania and Romania was short-lived. It is worth noting that land distribution was implemented as privatization for households, as in Albania and Romania, or as a distribution of use rights, as in China. The results were similar.

In agrarian economies the majority of people live in rural areas and the biggest part of agri-food trade is maintained on local markets. Hence any growth in GAO leads rapidly to increased per capita food consumption, effectively through the nation as a whole. Abolishing implicit taxation of agriculture as part of the reform can provide an additional stimulus to a quick increase in sector efficiency, to reinforce the effect of land distribution. Later, agrarian economies will inevitably face the need to facilitate legal land ownership and transfer, as well as fostering more general market development. However, they have usually enjoyed visible growth in GAO in the first stage of transition.

For predominantly industrial countries it was not sufficient just to undertake land reform, because even at the first stage of transition they faced serious problems which resulted in declining production and deteriorating consumption. Splitting large-scale farms into households or small partnerships aids labour incentives, but loses economies of scale when agricultural technologies are already more or less modernized. The trade-off among motivation benefits and technological losses is uncertain and not necessarily in favour of incentives. Technological adjustment in agriculture, during any radical change in

TABLE 2   *Indices of change in GAO in the selected transition economies*

	1989	1990	1991	1992	1993	1994	1995	1996	1997	1998
Bulgaria	0.8	−6.6	4.5	−12.9	−18.3	6.8	15.4	−13.1	30.2	−6.2
Croatia	4.0	−3.0	−5.0	−5.0	−5.0	−3.0	0.7	1.2	2.1	−1.4
Czech Rep	2.3	−2.3	−8.9	−12.1	−2.3	−6.0	5.3	−0.9	−5.9	5.8
Estonia	7.5	−13.1	−5.8	−19.5	−12.2	−12.9	−0.9	−6.3	−1.5	−0.5
Hungary	−1.8	−4.7	−6.2	−20.0	−9.7	3.2	2.6	4.9	−0.6	−0.3
Latvia	3.9	−10.2	−3.9	−15.6	−22.4	−20.6	−6.0	−7.4	−2.4	−4.0
Lithuania	1.5	−4.4	−5.8	−23.5	−5.4	−20.2	6.0	10.3	6.5	−3.3
Poland	1.8	−5.5	−1.6	−10.7	8.0	−10.8	16.3	−8.9	−0.7	3.8
Russia	1.7	−4.6	−4.5	−9.4	−4.6	−12.0	−8.0	−7.0	1.4	−12.0
Slovak Rep	0.6	−7.1	−7.0	−12.8	−7.2	9.3	2.1	4.1	−0.8	−3.1
Slovenia	−0.7	3.5	0.4	−5.5	−1.0	9.1	1.3	1.1	−2.6	2.1
Albania	65	−2.0	−17.4	17.1	18.6	8.3	13.2	3.3	1.0	6.0
China	n.a.	7.7	3.8	5.0	9.1	6.2	6.8	5.3	6.4	−0.4
Romania	−5.1	−2.9	0.8	−13.3	10.2	0.2	4.5	1.8	1.6	−6.2

Source: OECD data.

structure from large-scale production towards a smaller scale, requires time. The majority of people are also city dwellers and therefore continued food supply depends on the maintenance or the redevelopment of market institutions and infrastructure. During central planning, the state organized distribution and there was no true 'market provision'. The shift from one system to the other cannot be accomplished overnight. Any growth in agricultural output, therefore, does not necessarily expand food consumption. In addition, the earliest reforms throughout the region were accompanied by abolition, or severe reduction, of subsidies to the agri-food sector, which greatly aggravated the situation. Hence, at the beginning of their agrarian reforms, the predominantly industrial economies were challenged by a sharp drop in agricultural output, from which there was frequently either a slow recovery or, at worst, little sign of recovery at all (Table 2).

The results were not greatly affected by differences in the *outcome* of land reform. There were similar experiences in the Slovak Republic, dominated by large-scale farms in the post-reform period, or for Latvia, where a small-scale farm structure emerged. The consequences were also similar as between countries where the *method* or reform differed. The primary method in the Czech Republic was 'restitution' to former owners who could prove their claim as of 1948, though there was also some privatization (especially of former state farms) through the local concept of a 'joint stock company'. In Russia, farmland was allocated to the working and retired personnel of collective and state farms in the form of conditional shares. The shares were transferable, withdrawable as a land area for individual farming, or could be held as shareholdings in large-scale enterprises. In Hungary, shares were 'compensation' for previous losses under communism, while in the case of Poland much of the old private

structure of farming had been retained throughout the post-1945 period and
major change was unnecessary.

Land reforms have been a complex process because of variation in local
conditions. In many of the countries in transition the commune period in
agriculture was not coupled with explicit land nationalization and lasted for
little more than the lifetime of one generation. As a result, farm people could
remember their plots and experience of family farming was still alive. Under
communism a system of land transactions had also sometimes been maintained, and that helped to maintain a consciousness of family farming. Land
cadastres, also, were often preserved. Therefore it was sometimes possible to
launch the restitution process in agriculture or to provide a means for compensation. Other countries, like most former Soviet Republics, with less basis for
restitution or compensation, had to introduce sharing procedures and often
faced severe public protest against farmland transactions.

In spite of the different approaches to redistribution, the land use structure
formed during the reform period resulted either in domination by large-scale
farms, or by a preponderance of small-scale, mostly family, holdings. It is

TABLE 3   *Family farms in the agriculture of selected post-socialist
countries, 1994–5*

	Land distribution by farm size (%)		
	below 5 hectares	5–100 hectares	over 100 hectares
Bulgaria	30	6	64
Czech	2	5	93
Estonia	25[a]	15[a]	60
Hungary	22	20	58
Latvia	23	58	19
Lithuania	33[a]	32[a]	35
Russia	4	5	91
Slovak	2	2	96
Albania	~95	~2	3
China[b]	95[c]	—	5
Romania	~45	~10	~45

Notes: [a]Below 3 hectares and 3–100 hectares.
              [b]1997.
              [c]Below 0.5 hectares.

Source: *Agricultural Polices, Markets and Trade in Transition Economies/
              Monitoring and Evaluation*, Paris: OECD, 1996. It is pertinent to note
              that the data relate to 1994–5. Since then the situation has changed and
              the share of individual farming has increased in the majority of CEECs.
              However, individual farming is still not the prevailing sector in land area.

worth noticing that the different approaches are not correlated with the outcome in terms of farm structure, as Table 3 shows. Figure 1 indicates how the
'type' of national economy affects transformation. On the horizontal axis, the
share of land occupied by small-scale farms (below 100 hectares) in total
farmland is shown. The vertical axis indicates the average annual rate of
growth in output (GAO) from 1989 to 1998. Data from 11 selected countries in
transition are shown. There are two evident clusters for countries with 'agrarian' and with 'industrial' economies. For the agrarian group, growth positively
correlates with the share of small-scale farms; for the industrial group, the
correlation is inverse. From these simple calculations it can hardly be concluded that fragmentation in agriculture in agrarian countries facilitates the
long-period growth of the sector, with the opposite applying in industrial
countries. However, over the first stage of agrarian reforms the relationship has
some credence. This result also suggests that, for predominantly industrial
countries, agricultural transition requires the development of an adequate market infrastructure. Land reform does not provide much effect at the start of
reform; if it is to have an impact, market institutions in the agri-food sector
have to emerge in order for recovery and growth to begin.

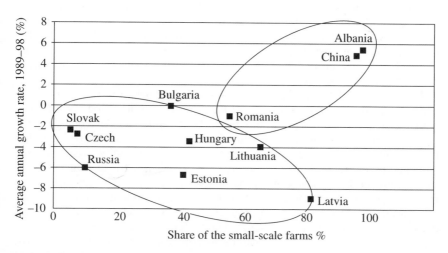

FIGURE 1   *Correlation between type of economy, rate of growth in GAO
and type of agrarian structure in selected transition countries*

EMERGENCE OF MARKET INFRASTRUCTURE: THE RUSSIAN EXPERIENCE

Agricultural markets

In the reform years, Russian agricultural marketing has undergone noticeable changes. Our survey in 1994–5 had shown a considerable diversification of marketing channels and growth in deals through what, for the Soviet economy, were non-conventional means, including trade through private intermediaries. Farms experienced competition among buyers, with most products potentially being sold through four or five possible marketing alternatives. It is true that conventional outlets remained as the most significant buyers; nevertheless, they did not retain monopsonistic dominance.

Later, as shown by our survey in 1997, there was a definite reduction in the number of marketing channels used, indicating that there was some concentration within the food chain. But at the same time other developments were occurring. Barter trade, deliveries to local outlets rather than wider-scale distribution, and payments in kind to workers all grew sharply. The cause was an acute shortage of working capital in agriculture. Grain trading provides a notable example, since grain is a universal money substitute in the current climate within Russia's agriculture. Survey work has shown that one-quarter of grain sales involve deliveries being made as payments for physical inputs, services and even taxes (Gaidaer, 1998). The same tendency occurs for milk, although, since more and more is sold on urban markets, cash transactions cannot be so easily supplanted.

The growth in deliveries to the agencies acting on behalf of regional administrations is also notable. This covers the various regional food corporations which can accumulate agricultural products. Despite the development of a market environment, the share of deliveries to regional funds is growing rather than being reduced. The original trigger was a commodity credit scheme launched by the federal government in 1995. That was abolished in 1997, but the regional authorities prolonged the programmes at rather heavy cost to the regional budget funds. The major drawback of the commodity credit schemes is a requirement to deliver farm products to the agencies in return for input deliveries. In effect, this provides an incentive for reliance on barter. Since they frequently do not have working capital to purchase seasonal resource needs, farms are compelled to engage in barter exchange. Another result has been that the implicit 'prices' received for a considerable proportion of output are extremely unprofitable for agriculture and the ratios of input to output prices are higher than those in market transactions.

The growth in wheat deliveries to the regional funds is especially marked, while meat and dairy products are rarely involved. This points to a clear inference about the purpose underlying use of the regional funds. It is usually declared that the aim is to maintain a continuous supply of staple foodstuffs for local populations. However, meat and milk are key products in Russia as well as bread, so it appears that the priority purchase of grain is not absolutely justified from a food security point of view. Since grain is a major money substitute, its accumulation in the hands of regional administrations, purchased at low price, is simply as a source of financial revenues.

Major first-hand buyers of agricultural products are now traders, wholesalers and processing firms. The main changes in this aspect of the food chain have taken place in grains. In the first years of the reforms there was a considerable number of private wholesalers, especially in the main grain-producing regions. These companies, as a rule, conducted speculative operations, buying grain and bearing all the risks of its further resale. Any sudden price variation on Russian markets could obviously affect the profitability of wholesalers. There were few commission dealers. In time there has been some concentration among the active dealers in grain-producing regions which has prompted an ever sharper decrease of numbers of intermediaries in net importing regions. It has already been stressed that barter is important and that regional agencies operate in the grain market. There has also been a rather noticeable development of small-size private intermediaries in the meat and dairy primary markets. These are mainly self-financed individuals working on their own account, often using their own vehicles. Usually, they collect products from farms, or from households which engage in animal husbandry, and deliver to urban markets. Naturally, all payments are conducted for cash. These individuals also make some deliveries to processing firms. Marketing cooperatives serving small-size farms have not achieved any significant growth.

By the end of the 1990s, processing firms as the buyers on the agricultural markets have changed purchasing tactics. Owing to increasing shortages of basic materials, especially in cattle farming, they are compelled to collect meat animals and milk from small household producers, from farms and from individual dealers. Processors bear large transaction costs, collecting supplies over wide areas and from numerous small-scale suppliers.

Strong incentives for vertical integration in agricultural markets have appeared. Shortage of raw materials, weak contract enforcement, lack of working capital and regional trade barriers force the operators within the food chain towards integration. Sometimes vertical links are of an informal nature; some involve long-term contracts; sometimes there is vertical integration through joint ownership of property or merger. The most widespread form of integration, however, is the development of retail networks by large farms, while processors also quite frequently forge vertically integrated linkages with farms. Shortages provided the incentive for processors to seek supplies in other regions and, notably in the case of meat, from abroad. This was becoming common until the financial crisis of 1998, with the accompanying devaluation of the rouble in August 1998, made importing expensive.

Forms of contract

Apart from changes in marketing channels the forms of contract used in agricultural markets have also altered. Early in the reform period, against a background of galloping inflation, it was impossible to use forward contracts of any sort. Later, annual contracting of deliveries became more common (Table 4) in the markets for wheat, milk and cattle. But in 1997, forward

TABLE 4   *Use of forward contracts in agricultural markets**

	Wheat		Milk		Cattle	
Marketing channels	1995	1997	1995	1997	1995	1997
Processors	X	0	X	X	X	0
Conventional purchasers	X	0	X	0	X	0
Agents of regional administration	X	0	0	0	0	0
Large intermediates	X	0	0	0	X	0
Direct deliveries to purchasing institutions	X	0	0	0	0	0

Notes: X, forward contracts were used; 0, they were not used.
*Results of survey in 1995 and 1997 of farms in Oryol, Pskov and Rostov regions, implemented by Centre AFE and ZEF of University of Bonn.

contracting almost disappeared. It was retained only for milk deliveries to dairy processing plants, where the need for regular supplies is of obvious importance.

The reasons for the change are unclear. It is well known that forward contracting at a fixed price insures the buyer against uncertainty of supply and the seller against uncertainty of demand. The situation in 1997 could be formally explained either by a change of risk aversion behaviour of market participants, or by reduction of uncertainty in supply and demand. We do not have any basis for favouring either explanation. It seems more plausible to argue that the contracting which was developing was somewhat ineffective owing to the frequent opportunism of participants, strong impacts of external events on the fulfilment of contracts, weak legal contract enforcement and the spreading of criminal forms of enforcement. The extreme narrowness of the market could also have been a factor: in particular, when a narrow spot market leads to increased risks on forward markets and to growth in the attractiveness of vertical integration. Such developments in Russian agricultural markets have already been discussed.

Forms of payment

The extremely difficult financial situation in agriculture and the food trade has given rise to perverse forms of payment. In the survey which was conducted, only 9–18 per cent of total sales passed through the bank accounts of farms (Table 5). The remaining deals were settled in cash, conducted by barter, or involved 'clearing' or 'talling'.

Cash payments were usually made at lower prices than other types of settlement. Indeed, the prices recorded for accountancy purposes did not always mirror the actual dealing prices, with the difference often being divided be-

TABLE 5   *Means of payment for agricultural products by buyers, 1997, in percentages of total sales measured in physical terms**

Method of payment	Wheat	Milk	Cattle
Cash	36	53	36
Cash in 1995	45	39	28
Through bank account	9	18	14
Barter	27	12	29
Promissory note	5	0	0
Clearing	18	17	14
Talling	5	0	7

Note: *Results of survey in 1995 and 1997 of farms in Oryol, Pskov and Rostov regions, implemented by Centre AFE and ZEF of University of Bonn.

tween a farm manager and the representative of a buyer. The barter proportions were also often fixed in terms unfavourable to agriculture, especially under commodity credit arrangements.

Clearing is a widespread form of payment in Russia, with agricultural markets being no exception. The method was used in 14–18 per cent of transactions in the survey. Clearing is a specific form of payment in which a firm covers debts for inputs or services with part of its product. The clearing chain can consist of several firms. Very often the regional budgets are also involved in clearing networks. It is a somewhat complex mechanism in which the payment of farm debts for inputs can be offset by deliveries to official agencies so that regional budget subsidies are effectively 'paid' to agriculture without the use of what could be termed 'live money'. The only particular feature of agriculture in that respect is that it is one of the most heavily subsidized sectors of the economy.

In the Soviet economy, a 'talling' arrangements scheme was mostly used in the case of sugar beet, but then spread to cover many more products. Talling is the operation whereby farmers make use of processing facilities and pay for the service with part of the processed output (which can be as much as 20–40 per cent). Farm producers retain all ownership rights on primary and processed product except for the 'in kind' payment. The scheme has the effect of avoiding transactions through farm bank accounts and also provides better marketing opportunities for farms. Markets for processed goods are much broader than for raw material and they are easier to market. An incidental advantage is that it is much easier to pay workers in foodstuffs than in many agricultural kinds of raw products. In addition, sale of finished products provides, as a rule, a higher return per unit of primary product than direct sales of the product. In a 1995 case study of two farms in the Oryol region, wheat sales by different channels were observed: directly to local mills, to the mills but on talling terms, with barter, and as 'in kind' wages to workers. The profit per unit of wheat from sales of flour obtained through the talling scheme was more than three times higher than profit from direct sales to mills.

Such divergence of returns per unit of primary product undoubtedly testifies to the ineffectiveness and imperfection of agri-food markets. It provides a stimulus for talling as one way of overcoming the problems of marketing as well as promoting the development of on-farm processing and vertical integration.

The food markets

Development of an intermediary sector has become a basic feature of change in food marketing. At the start of reform, elimination of the conventional Soviet wholesale sector was undertaken and the old, large, wholesale institutions have now virtually ceased to operate. After privatization in the downstream sector, major facilities were rented out to new private intermediaries, usually specializing in one to two products. As a rule they work with several large suppliers, both inside and outside their region. All work basically in cash. The movement of products from suppliers to retailers, and any processing involved, is now a market activity seldom regulated by local authorities. The food sector is characterized by vertical integration.

The markets for inputs

With the sharp reduction of working capital on farms in 1992, the inputs market was also sharply narrowed. The gross output of the main items of machinery was reduced much more than in any other industry (Table 6). In spite of the fact that the Soviet system of input distribution has been eliminated, it is too early to speak about the full liberalization of Russia's input markets, either for heavy items or for current requirements. The majority of inputs obtained by farms are obtained through the commodity credit scheme or the state leasing system. Machinery is mostly delivered to farms within the framework of the state programme of leasing, which began in 1994. The

TABLE 6   *Gross output of main types of machinery, thousands*

	1991	1998
Tractors	178.0	9.8
Grain harvesters	55.4	1.0
Fodder harvesters	7.4	0.2
Flax harvesters	2.7	0.2
Tractor ploughs	81.2	1.1
Tractor seeders	41.0	1.3
Tractor cultivators	72.0	3.3
Mowers and threshers	20.4	6.5
Milking equipment	17.7	0.4

Source: Data of National Statistics Office.

scheme is effectively one for centralized supply, with a unified supplier, linked to recipients in an administrative way. State commodity credit was launched in 1995 and since then has been reinforced by similar regional level arrangements. Since they have little working capital for the inputs needed from season to season, notably fuel oils and fertilizers, farms are compelled to agree on commodity crediting, which is usually unprofitable for them. In addition, input manufacturers and dealers are usually appointed to be responsible for each territory, creating monopoly power for them.

The land market

The land market is only just beginning to emerge in Russia. Land sales, where permitted, affect less than 0.5 per cent of total area and there is only 1.4 per cent which is leased. Most land transactions, however, occur in cities, and farmland is hardly affected. Due to the decline in gross agricultural output, demand for land is tiny and, although the federal land legislation is quite liberal, development of the land market is very slow.

TABLE 7   *Land deals, 1996–8*

	1996		1998	
	Number of deals	Area (hectares)	Number of deals	Area (hectares)
Sales by local administrations	43 907	8 990	11 467	7 483
Sales–purchases by citizens and legal entities	218 759	33 622	234 590	40 945
Donations	34 094	8 270	26 452	6 610
Inheritance	132 171	128 448	158 512	144 735
Mortgage	760	2 982	2 789	3 693

Source: The 'State Report on Status and Use of Land in the Russian Federation'.

The area per deal in all of the cases shown in Table 7 is very small; the information picks up all types of land transaction. In Table 8, the material is specific to farmland, referring to sales or leasing. The areas involved in the former are minute, while the leases are basically for nothing more than tiny plots. The pattern is repeated in Table 9, dealing with the district funds for land reallocation. During the period when land shares were being allocated, federal legislation allowed regions to accumulate some land in local reserves, the aim being to distribute land, without payment though with some limitations on the individual areas involved, for anyone willing to run a farm and who made an application. In effect, the (quite considerable) area held has been expanding, since willingness to participate is limited.

Nevertheless, the method of reorganization of collective and state farms based on the principle of land shares has resulted in the appearance of a quasi-market in shares. This does create a tendency for land to be concentrated in the hands of the most effective producers. Leasing, rather than outright sale, is the most widespread contractual form, taking up more than half of the transactions in the main agricultural producing areas of the country.

The capital market

Agriculture does not attract capital easily. The main reasons have been uncertainty about property rights and relative overproduction. Nevertheless, the sector has some potential advantages in the rather quick turn-round of working capital and the relatively small scale of the sums required for investment. Since the crisis and devaluation of 1998, when agri-food imports were sharply reduced, investors have begun to demonstrate an interest in farming (Serova *et al.*, 1999). However, the investors involved are rather specific; they tend to be vertically integrated firms interested in steady supplies of raw materials. The integrators prefer to lease land, set up co-production on the land of an agricultural partner, or to invest in farms through some other type of production agreement such as leasing machinery, supplying technology or financing the purchase of cattle.

TABLE 8   *Sale and leasing of farmland by local administrations to large-scale farms and individual farmers*

	1995		1996		1997	
	Number of deals	Area (ha.)	Number of deals	Area (ha.)	Number of deals	Area (ha.)
Sales	173	6.7	522	1.4	206	2.6
Lease	210 036	13 053	77 111	14 374	60 365	17 777

Source: The 'State Report on Status and Use of Land in the Russian Federation'.

TABLE 9   *District funds for reallocating land*

	Thousand ha.
1.2.1992	9 490
1.3.1993	6 636
1.3.1994	13 095
1.1.1995	13 758
1.1.1996	14 621

Source: Data of the Agrarian Institute.

The situation is different in the food-processing industry, which in all the years of reforms has been one of the most attractive investment sectors for investment, after oil and gas production. Foreign direct investment has been common. Since the crisis, investment has increased. There is now some evidence that investments in the food industry accompanied by a drop in imports of raw products will lead to some influx of capital directly to agriculture. Nevertheless, there is still a lack of transparency in the agri-food sector. Investment occurs within the framework of vertical coordination and integration and there is an insufficient flow of direct bank investment.

The labour market in agriculture

In the Soviet era the rural population was employed predominantly in agriculture. Reduction of food demand, growth of agri-food imports and corresponding decreases in agricultural output led to a considerable reduction in the real need for workers. According to the farm managers' estimates, this reduction could be up to 75 per cent. Nevertheless, employment in agriculture is virtually unchanged. The lack of alternative, non-agricultural, jobs in rural areas is the main cause. Dismissal of workers without there being any prospects for them to find other sources of income would be degrading and, since social security is lacking, it could lead to violence and theft of agricultural products from farms. Generally managers prefer to retain staff, though at very low levels of earnings – the lowest among all sectors of the Russian economy. Hidden unemployment is a signal that restructuring will eventually become necessary.

THE IMPACT OF THE 1998 CRISIS ON THE AGRI-FOOD SECTOR IN RUSSIA

The agri-food sector of Russia is now influenced by the effects of the 1998 crisis and relatively favourable weather conditions of 1999. The devaluation of the rouble has made food imports notably less expedient, while exports of Russian agricultural raw products are favoured. It has improved the prospects for domestic producers through the possibilities of import substitution and export expansion. On the other hand, the dip in real incomes has limited demand by the population on income-elastic items, notably for livestock products. Reductions in the prospects for gambling in financial markets and limitations on capital flight have also boosted the advantages of investing in activities with short reinvestment cycles, notably the food industries.

As a result of these trends a rather strong process of import substitution in the food distribution and processing industries began in the second half of 1998, which was then transmitted directly into agriculture. There were no other causes for this growth, such as noticeable changes in agrarian policy or increased budget support. The year 1999 simply confirms the hypothesis that the main constraining factor in the agri-food sector has been lack of effective demand. The gross product in agriculture grew by 2.4 per cent, the rise in crop output of 9.0 per cent being somewhat offset by a reduction in livestock output by 3.7 per cent. The food-processing industry has grown by 7.5 per cent. The trends appear to be accelerating in 2000. The changes do not appear to be solely due to the weather.

In agriculture there were signs of major change. The financial position of producers has improved and they have been quick to increase demand for fertilizers and other inputs. Tendencies towards decapitalization may have been arrested. There has also been growth of productivity, especially in milk yields, in the number of eggs per layer and in the health of animals. Barter trade, so disadvantageous to farmers, seems to have reduced. With greater incentives another problem is lessening in importance, namely that of lack of infrastructure. At the beginning of the reforms that shortage was responsible for a situation in which there was 'overproduction' at the farm level without satisfaction of consumer needs (or their being met by imports). In 1998–9, the situation radically changed. Though infrastructure has still not fully developed, a great deal has been done and there are indications that advantage will be taken of the opportunities created by rouble devaluation.

CONCLUSIONS

In predominantly industrial economies in transition, the agrarian reforms could not be limited to the transformation in land holding arrangements; market infrastructure and mechanisms needed to emerge. Institutional changes in agriculture, namely land reform and farm restructuring, are necessary but not sufficient tasks of the reforms in agriculture and the real recovery of the sector can start only after establishment of new market institutions.

In Russia's agri-food sector, the basic elements needed for market provision have emerged (von Braun *et al.*, 1996). The product markets are more developed institutionally than capital, land or labour markets. However, even the product markets have numerous drawbacks caused by the way in which they have been formed and by general economic instability. These drawbacks include the extreme vertical integration of the food chain, prompted by the initial underdevelopment of markets, which prevents transparency, hinders interregional arbitrage and suppresses competition. Perverse forms of payments in the agri-food chain still hamper recovery and worsen the financial state of farmers. Eliminating these features will be very complicated, since they have become rooted in the economy.

Sound agri-food policy should promote development of the new market institutions and do nothing to provide substitutes for them. Arrangements set up by the state tend to monopolize activities and prevent emergence of real market entities. Thus the state leasing programmes in Russia hamper the land and capital markets, while state purchases limit the development of agri-food markets based on private enterprise. This has not prevented some recovery from taking place, which is seen in the end of the deep drop in agri-food production and more satisfactory supply to consumers. The creation of infrastructure and institutions is, however, a rather slow process. It will certainly be one which will be faced by the 'rural economies' as they attempt to move beyond the positive results already achieved through their initial land transformations.

REFERENCES

Gaidaer, E. (ed.) (1998), *Economics of the Transitional Period*, especially Chapter 15, 'Institutional Reforms in Russia's Agriculture' (in Russian), Moscow: Institute of Economies in Transition.

Serova, E., von Braun, J. and Wehrheim, P. (1999), 'The impact of financial crisis on Russia's agro-food economy', *European Review of Agricultural Economics*, **26**, 349–70.

Von Braun, J., Serova, E., tho Seeth, H. and Melukhina, O. (1996), *Russia's Food Economy in Transition: Current Policy Issues and the Long-Term Outlook*, Washington, DC: International Food Policy Research Institute.

Wedekin, K.-E. (1991), 'Land Reform in the Soviet Union', paper presented at the FAO Moscow conference.

Zhou, Q. (1996), *Agricultural Reform: Property Rights and New Organization: Comparing the Case of China and Russia*, Beijing: Beijing University Press.

ASHOK GULATI*

Market Reforms in South Asian Agriculture: Will they deliver?

INTRODUCTION

With a population of about 1.3 billion and an overall growth rate of GDP hovering around 5 to 6 per cent per annum, South Asia is finally attracting the attention of global business. If ethnic strife remains under control, it will not be a surprise if this region soon witnesses the landing of 'flying geese' of development. South Asia also attracts the attention of development and agricultural economists for other reasons. It is a region with the largest concentration of workers engaged in agriculture and there is associated poverty. About 400 million people in this region still survive on an income level of a dollar a day, and their main occupation remains agriculture. Thus, unless agriculture prospers, the chances of faster alleviation of poverty seem rather bleak. Further, outside the socialist block, South Asia has been a region that insulated its economy most from the world markets by according high protection to industry, which had ramifications for agriculture.

During the 1970s and 1980s, there was a definite and significant dent in poverty levels in the region, triggered primarily by the onset of the 'Green Revolution'. That was a marvel of agricultural technology, heavily supported by positive incentives to cultivators and improved input delivery mechanisms. Dramatic increases in yields of wheat and rice led to widespread adoption of new seeds, resulting in perceptible gains in foodgrain production. The real prices of wheat and rice declined and poverty levels fell. But this process of growth in foodgrains slowed down during the 1990s, raising doubts about whether the Green Revolution had begun to falter. The pace of poverty reduction also appears to have diminished. This necessitates a deeper study of what has happened to South Asian agriculture during the recent past, and what is likely to happen during the next two decades or so. This has to be analysed against the backdrop of a fundamental change that is under way in much of South Asia, namely a distinct move towards liberalization and globalization. Almost all the countries in the region are going through this phase of liberalization in varying degrees, under structural adjustment programmes or through the locking in of reforms stemming from the Uruguay Round Agreement.

This paper is an attempt to decipher the changes taking place in South Asian agriculture, the reforms that are under way and how they are likely to

* Institute of Economic Growth, University of Delhi, India.

affect the future. Accordingly, the next section provides a background to South Asian agriculture, across major countries of the region as well as against the global economy. That is followed by a description of the nature and dimensions of reforms under way in different South Asian countries. Evidence on what is likely to be the result of such reforms on agriculture is then presented.

SOUTH ASIA IN A GLOBAL CONTEXT

South Asia, comprising Bangladesh, Bhutan, India, the Maldives, Nepal, Pakistan and Sri Lanka, accounts for about 22 per cent of the world population but less than 2 per cent of world GNP and only about 1.2 per cent of world trade. In 1997, the GNP per capita in this region was just US$387 per annum, only a notch higher than that of the low-income countries at US$350. On a purchasing power parity (PPP) basis, however, the per capita GNP of South Asia turns out to be US$1600 per annum (Athukorala, 1999). Measured in PPP, the World Development Indicators suggest that the absolute size of the Indian economy makes it the fourth largest in the world after the USA, China and Japan.

In geographical dimensions, South Asia has only 3.3 per cent of the world's surface area. As against an average of 11 per cent of surface area being arable and under permanent crops in the world as a whole, South Asia has almost half of its area utilized in that way. That is an indicator of high population pressure on land as well as the availability of large amounts of cultivable land.

The structure of South Asian economies is typified by high employment of the workforce in agriculture (a little higher than 60 per cent) but a much lower share of agriculture in GDP (about 25 per cent). Together with low to moderate yield levels, South Asian agriculture also exhibits much lower levels of labour productivity compared with the rest of the world.

India is by far the largest economy in the region, accounting for almost three-quarters (74 per cent) of regional GDP, followed by Pakistan (13 per cent), Bangladesh (9 per cent), Sri Lanka (3 per cent) and Nepal (1 per cent). On a per capita PPP basis for the five major countries in the region, Sri Lanka is most developed, followed by India, Pakistan, Bangladesh and Nepal. Agriculture contributes only 22 per cent to GDP in Sri Lanka, as against 41 per cent in Nepal and 25 per cent in India. More than 90 per cent of the workforce in Nepal is employed in agriculture, as against only one-third in Sri Lanka and about 64 per cent in India. Given such overwhelming weight of the Indian economy in the South Asia region, it is obvious that what happens in India has a strong influence on the whole region. Accordingly, this paper gives proportionately a higher weight to India in its analysis.

South Asia accounts for about 30 per cent of world rice production, 30 per cent also for pulses and 15 per cent for world wheat. In coarse grains, however, its share is much lower: less than 4 per cent of world production. For horticulture (fruits and vegetables), South Asia accounts for about 12 per cent. Edible oil crops account for about 11 per cent and sugar cane about 26 per cent of world production. India is the largest producer of milk in the world, taking

South Asia's world share to about 16 per cent. In fisheries the share is lower at about 6 per cent.

The overall growth in the region during the 1980s and 1990s has hovered between 5 and 6 per cent per annum. There was a peak during 1994–7, when it touched 6.4 per cent, and in India even 7 per cent. This compares very well with many south-east Asian economies during the take-off stage. The growth in agriculture, however, has been much lower, averaging around 2.5 to 3 per cent per annum during the 1980s and the 1990s. But the growth pattern in agriculture has shown wide fluctuations, especially in India (RIS, 1999). This is primarily due to the dependence of Indian agriculture on the monsoon. About 60 per cent of the gross cropped area still remains without any assured irrigation, and only 30 per cent of the area is double cropped. This is one of the major reasons behind low and fluctuating yields in India. It also applies in South Asia generally. The other reason behind relatively low growth in agriculture, perhaps, lies in the policy environment adopted in the past. Most of the countries in the region, like many other developing countries around the world, followed a policy of high protection for manufacturing, which discriminated against agriculture (see Schiff and Valdés, 1992, for Pakistan and Sri Lanka, and Pursell and Gulati, 1995, for India).

An interesting feature of the agricultural growth pattern is that the poultry, fishery and dairy sectors have advanced more quickly than the crop sector. And among the crops horticulture, and other cash crops, exhibit higher growth than foodgrains where, typically, growth has been only marginally higher than the growth rate of population. Cereals, for example, grew at an annual compound rate of 2.8 per cent during 1986–96, pulses by 1.6 per cent, sugarcane by 4 per cent, edible oil crops by 5 per cent, fruits by 4.5 per cent, milk by 3.4 per cent, eggs by 5.4 per cent and fish by 5.2 per cent.

One plausible reason behind the growth pattern within agriculture is the changing pattern in diets. The consumption basket is changing fast in favour of non-grain items, creating a 'market pull' for the development of this segment of agriculture. The expenditure elasticities based on the Food Characteristic Demand System (FCDS) are revealed as extremely low for major grains (rice and wheat) and relatively very high for fruits and vegetables, milk, eggs, meat and fish (Paroda and Kumar, 2000).[1] These are the emerging segments of agriculture, where government intervention has been least. Market incentives have been the major drivers. But in the case of foodgrains, perpetual deficits in the pre-Green Revolution days led the governments of South Asian countries to intervene heavily in the markets. Many of the control mechanisms remain in place despite the situation on the foodgrain front having dramatically changed. There is a high degree of self-sufficiency, with only marginal imports now and then. In fact, in India, as of June 2000, the government was holding foodgrain stocks of more than 40 million tonnes. This is at least 60 per cent more than the government would like to keep to service its public distribution system and to take care of food security in the event of crop failure. But the laws governing foodgrain marketing, including external trade, remain quite restrictive. They discourage the entry of major grain companies and minimize the influence of market forces on farmer's production decisions. The underlying fear stems from uncertainty regarding the distant future.

Will South Asia remain as comfortable in grains in the medium to long run as it is now? On that experts differ. One view (Rosegrant *et al.*, 1995) is that South Asia will be in deficit in cereals by around 22 million tonnes by 2020 (under the baseline scenario). Similar views are expressed about India by Bhalla *et al.*, (1999). They suggest that, by 2020, under the assumption of reasonable increases in fertilizer and irrigation, with per capita income growth of 3.7 per cent per annum, India would be falling short of cereal demand by as much as 64 million tonnes, which is almost three times the deficit forecast by Rosegrant *et al.* for South Asia as a whole. The proponents of this view cite emerging signs of deceleration in yield levels during the 1990s and, in a well-fed India (with high income growth), supplies could fail to match the surging demand. As a result, India may emerge as a major net importer of grain, making South Asia in deficit by 2020.

These estimates have been contested, especially on the demand side. The alternative view on the likely demand for foodgrains in the countries of South Asia reveals no alarming picture even by 2030. Paroda and Kumar (2000), for example, by using FCDS to derive expenditure elasticities, show that the demand for foodgrains in South Asia is likely to increase by only 1.2 per cent per annum during 1995–2030. To meet the demand for cereals, South Asia needs to raise its yield levels (of cereals as a group) from 1.74 tonnes in 1994–6 to 2.67 tonnes by 2029–30. This is certainly within the potential reach of South Asia, despite increasing pressures on land and water, provided some priority is given to investments in agriculture and to raising the level of incentives. The record of the past three decades, and the fact that full potential of the Green Revolution is not yet exhausted in the region, make it probable that South Asia will remain more or less self-sufficient in grains during the next two to three decades. By that time, newer technologies could come on to the horizon to shift the production frontier outwards.

In the case of India, in the forseeable future (say by 2010), the probability is that marginal surpluses of grains will emerge (see Gulati and Dev, 1996). The preliminary indications are already there in terms of bulging foodgrain stocks. If their grain exports were not subsidized by the EU and the USA, India would already be exporting marginal quantities (say at least 3 to 5 million tonnes of grains annually).

TOWARDS REFORMS AND IMPROVED MARKET INCENTIVES

Most of South Asia is undergoing a process of economic reforms. Sri Lanka has been a forerunner, having initiated reforms in 1977; Pakistan and Bangladesh followed in the late 1980s, and India and Nepal began in the early 1990s. The political consensus favouring reforms in South Asia was formed in three distinct phases: first, the emergence of circumstances that called for reforms; second, a broad agreement among political parties to initiate reforms; and third, agreement on the basic content of the reform package (Shand, 1999).

Although reforms in South Asia were occurring before 1991, the really wide-ranging process was initiated only then, when India became engaged (Williamson, 1999). Political instability can affect the reform process at any stage, especially when reforms are still in a nascent state. And South Asia has been under constant flux as far as political stability is concerned, be it the case of India, Pakistan, Bangladesh or Nepal.

In most cases, reforms have been triggered by worsening fiscal situations spilling over to inflation and balance of payments problems. The reform package adopted by all these countries is also similar: contain fiscal deficits, ease exchange rates, at least on current account, free external trade from restrictions, and bring down tariff levels gradually over time. This is more or less in line with the standard reform package often suggested by the IMF/World Bank.

Interestingly, despite these reforms, the fiscal deficits in most countries remain high, although there have been significant changes in exchange rate regimes and trade policies. For example, during the 1991–7 period, on average, the central government budget deficit was in the range of –6 to –7 per cent of GDP for South Asia as a whole (Bangladesh –4.1 per cent, India –6.6 per cent, Nepal –6.4 per cent, Pakistan –6.9 per cent, and Sri Lanka –8.7 per cent) (RIS, 1999, p. 39). This resulted in high rates of inflation of around 10 per cent (based on consumer prices) during 1991–7, except in Bangladesh, where it was contained at about 4 per cent. In India, too, inflation was brought down in subsequent years. Although higher inflation rates put pressure on exchange rates, forcing depreciation of domestic currencies, South Asia has survived the East Asian-type crisis in exchange rates. The credit for this, perhaps, goes to the gradualist approach adopted by South Asian countries, especially India, with respect to their foreign exchange regimes. India, for example, allowed convertibility of domestic currency on current account but not on capital account. As a result, the depreciation of domestic currencies has been gradual and has been absorbed into the system without any major shocks.

Over the years, the reform package has expanded in size and depth. It has encompassed several elements, ranging from privatization of public sector enterprises to cutting down of subsidies with a view to reining in fiscal deficits. The role of the private sector in infrastructure development has increased. Trade and exchange rate policy regimes have been liberalized. In agriculture, the first attempt has been to contain subsidies, especially on fertilizers.

In India, for example, in the first year of reform (1991–2), urea prices were raised by 30 per cent. In the following year, on the recommendations of a Joint Parliamentary Committee, phosphate (P) and potassium (K) fertilizers were freed from controls and urea prices were reduced by 10 per cent. Prices of P and K went up by more than 100 per cent, creating a major imbalance in the use of nitrogen N, P and K. To contain the rising prices of P and K fertilizers, imports of DAP were opened to the private sector with a flat rate subsidy of Rs1000/tonne announced on P and K in September 1991. However, since the price of imported DAP was lower than the cost of domestic fertilizers, imports hit the existing production plants adversely. About eight out of 11 plants came to a grinding halt. To revive them, higher flat rate subsidies were announced on

P in 1994, more on domestically produced DAP (Rs3000/tonne) than on imported DAP (Rs1500/tonne). The administered price of urea was, however, raised by 20 per cent in June 1994, and then again by 10 per cent in February 1997. Between 1994 and 1997, there was a lull of urea prices, presumably owing to political instability. In the year 2000, urea prices were further raised by 15 per cent, but urea production remains under the so-called retention price scheme in which each plant receives a different price from the government, based on its cost of production, subject to some norms of efficiency. India today produces about 20 million tonnes of urea, the marginal cost of which is about Rs11 000 to 12 000/tonne while the import parity price falls between Rs5000 and 6000/tonne. It is a matter of intense debate whether the fertilizer subsidy is a subsidy to agriculture or to the high-cost fertilizer industry (Gulati and Narayanan, 2000). The reforms in the subsidy, therefore, are closely linked with the reforms in the industry, and India has still to go a long way in that direction. In the meantime, the fertilizer subsidy touched a figure of about US$3 billion in the year 1999–2000. Containing it has been a politically hard nut to crack.

The more interesting changes in agriculture that have swept South Asia have come from the trade policy side. In fact the reforms in trade policies for agriculture, as for non-agricultural commodities, have begun to lock in as a result of the commitments made under the Uruguay Round Agreement (URA). It is interesting to see how different South Asian countries have committed themselves in the URA to carry out agricultural trade policy reforms, what progress they have made between Marrakesh and Seattle, and what impact reforms are likely to have on the future of agriculture in the region.

Sri Lanka, perhaps, has been more liberal than any other country in South Asia in terms of binding agricultural tariffs under the URA. It followed a simple rule and bound its agricultural commodities at a flat 50 per cent duty. Pakistan bound them in the range of 100 to 150 per cent, while Bangladesh bound most agricultural tariff lines at 200 per cent (except 13 six-digit HSC items, at 50 per cent) (Athukorala, 1999). India, however, appears to have been most protectionist in the region in terms of URA bindings, most of which fell in the range of 100, 150 and 300 per cent. There were some agricultural commodities which were committed at zero (such as rice and skimmed milk powder) or very low tariff rates in the pre-Uruguay Round of GATT. Nepal, Bhutan and the Maldives are not yet members of World Trade Organization (WTO), but they have already adopted a policy of almost free trade at low tariff levels. In Nepal, for example, most of the goods are freely importable. Items attracting high duties are basically passenger vehicles, firearms, liquor and tobacco (Pigato *et al.*, 1997). Thus, overall, the bound tariffs of India, Bangladesh and Pakistan, which form the bulk of South Asia, seem to be some of the highest in the world. India also invoked the balance of payments clause to retain quantitative restrictions on imports.[2]

Does that mean that South Asian agriculture is the most protected in the world? Not necessarily so. To understand this better, one needs to look at the actual tariffs vis-à-vis the bound tariffs. Take the case of India, which appears to be the most protectionist economy in South Asia, and presumably in the world. In the early years of the reform process in India, the government set up a Tax Reform Committee with a view to overhauling the tax structure, including import duties. This committee (GOI, 1993) had recommended that agricultural commodities should basically attract three rates of import duties. First, essential agricultural commodities like wheat and rice should be imported at zero duty; second, commodities like oilseeds and pulses should attract 10 per cent duty; and third, non-essential agricultural products like almonds and cashew nuts should be imported at 50 per cent duty. This tariff structure, recommended by such a very important committee even before the URA was signed, is widely at variance with the duty rates that India bound itself to in the URA. Does that imply a U-turn in the thinking of the government, or was there something more than that?

Our reading of what has happened in India over agricultural tariffs is that the government wanted to play safe, given its overriding concerns for food security. It had gone in for very high tariff bindings just to give it enough space for manoeuvring negotiations in the years to come. This was presumably also necessitated by the fact that there was huge subsidization of agriculture in several developed nations, especially the exporting countries. Large export subsidies, or even domestic support through 'decoupled' income payments, in those countries were severely distorting world markets. It was thought, therefore, that a sufficient buffer was needed to counter the potential deluge of subsidized imports of agricultural commodities that might undermine the livelihood of millions of small and marginal farmers in India. It is, perhaps, this interpretation of the world agricultural situation that prompted India to bind high tariffs on farm commodities.

In fact the actual rates of import duties have been much lower. In 1999, for example, out of the 673 agricultural tariff lines bound at the 6-digit level of the Harmonized System of Classification, the actual rates for 401 lines were lower than their bound rates by as much as 75 percentage points or more. For another 155 tariff lines, the actual rates were below the bound rates by 50 to 75 percentage points, and so on (Gulati et al., 1999). Major commodities like wheat were being imported in 1998–9 at zero import duty despite the bound rate at 100 per cent. Similarly, sugar imports were attracting zero duty, though the bound rate was 150 per cent, and edible oils were being imported at 15 per cent duty as against their binding of 300 per cent. There have been some increases in these duty rates since world prices touched rock bottom in 1999–2000, but it is precisely to safeguard against such wide fluctuations in world prices that India seems to have bargained for higher bound duties. The situation in other South Asian countries is not very different. The applied tariffs are much below their bindings.

On the export front, the opening up of agriculture has been slow, and full of stops and starts, especially in India. When India's reforms began in 1991, major agricultural commodities like rice, wheat, coarse cereals, oilseeds/edible oils, cotton and sugar were subjected to stringent export controls, including minimum export prices, export quotas or even complete export bans. Even within the domestic economy, they were subjected to several marketing controls such as levies, movement controls from one state to another (sometimes even from one district to another within the same state), stocking limits on traders, denials of institutional credit to traders for stocking of agricultural produce, more or less a general ban on futures trading, and so on. Rice millers had to pay a levy to the government to the tune of 75 per cent: in effect, that percentage of the rice milled had to be given to the government compulsorily at government-determined prices. The arrangement still exists in Punjab, Haryana and some other states of India in varying degrees. On sugar mills the levy was high, at 40 per cent, and molasses were almost completely controlled.

Exports of common rice were begun in the year 1995–6. Almost from nowhere, India emerged as the world's second largest exporter, supplying 5.1 million tonnes in that year. Although that high level could not be maintained, on average, rice exports have remained at around 3 million tonnes. Exports of wheat were begun in 1996, but led to spiralling of domestic prices, which prompted the Indian government to ban exports of wheat and wheat products, and simultaneously to allow imports of wheat at zero import duty. A similar thing happened in the case of onions, where exports led to high prices, forcing the government to ban shipments. All these disturbances in policy making suggest one basic thing: that in countries ridden with a large mass of poverty, it is a challenge for any policy maker to improve incentives of producers by removing all controls on exports and domestic marketing of agricultural commodities and also to care for poorer consumers.

LIKELY IMPACTS OF REFORM ON SOUTH ASIAN AGRICULTURE

Exchange rate liberalization alone has made transparent the relative incentive structure across different sectors within the economy. In much of South Asia, overvalued exchange rates and much higher protection to the manufacturing sector than to agriculture had meant 'implicit taxation' of agriculture. Under administered exchange rates, this remained largely hidden. But now, with exchange rate liberalization, and consequent depreciation of domestic currencies, the degree of the implicit tax is glaring. In India, for example, in 1991–2, grain production fell short of effective demand, necessitating import of about 3 million tonnes of wheat. The import parity price of wheat was Rs5000/tonne as against the domestic support price of Rs2250. This led the Indian government to raise the wheat support price to Rs2750 in 1992–3 and then to Rs3300/tonne in 1993–4, an increase of almost 50 per cent in two years. Similar jumps occurred in wheat support prices in 1997–8, when there was scarcity of wheat at home and the import price was higher than the domestic support price. Rice support prices also followed a similar pattern, though to a smaller extent. Although this correction in the support prices of rice and wheat led to a fierce debate in the country, since there were fears for the impact on the poor, it did help to transfer incomes to surplus farmers. That appears to have resulted in positive private sector investments in agriculture and contributed to maintaining the rates of growth in agriculture.

The other impact on agriculture is likely to come from the reduction in the tariff walls for manufacturing. Pursell and Gulati's (1995) work on India and that of Schiff and Valdés (1992) on Sri Lanka and Pakistan clearly reveal that protection accorded to manufacturing sectors has been much higher than for agriculture. In fact, agriculture has been 'disprotected' through trade policy. Reduction in manufacturing protection and elimination of 'disprotection' of agriculture, either by freeing exports of agricultural commodities or raising their support prices to at least export parity levels, should logically improve the agricultural terms of trade. In theory, this improvement in incentives in favour of agriculture should invite the attention of private investors, including processors, and thereby lead to higher growth of South Asian agriculture.

The trade policy reforms, both of industry and of agriculture, seem to have set in motion this process of improvement in relative incentives for agriculture, but the ultimate results of higher growth and widespread prosperity in rural areas is yet to be seen. There are a number of reasons underlying this delay. First, the world markets for many agricultural commodities remain highly distorted by the huge subsidization practised by some exporting countries. The slump in world prices during 1997–2000 has shaken the faith of many South Asian economies in import liberalization of agriculture. The prices of edible oils, which were hovering around $700/tonne in late 1996, tumbled to about $350/tonne by early 2000. India was flooded with imports in excess of 4 million tonnes, almost half of her annual consumption requirement. This led to widespread opposition to imports at low import duty (15 per cent) by the domestic oilseeds-processing industry, forcing the government to raise duty to 25 per cent on refined oils. Similarly, wheat prices in world markets tumbled from about $200/tonne to about $100 over the same period. When wheat imports started appearing in large quantities at zero import duty, despite bumper harvests at home, there was a kneejerk reaction and the government clamped on a 50 per cent duty. The problem is compounded when exporting countries first give high domestic support to their agriculture, which generates surpluses, and then those surpluses are 'dumped' in the world markets with export subsidies. So unless distortions by major players, namely the USA and EU, in world agricultural trade are contained, faith in liberalization of agriculture will remain very fragile.

The unfortunate situation is emphasized by attempts that have been made to see how South Asian agriculture would fair as the bindings under URA become operative around the world. Sharma *et al.* (1999), for example, show that the impact of agricultural reforms alone would be in the range of US$1.2 billion to US $3.3 billion under the baseline scenario, which is about 0.4 per cent to 1 per cent of the GDP. These are the highest percentage gains of any other region of the world, with the exception of East Asia. But, as Schiff and Valdés (1992) have shown that the greater impact on agriculture in developing countries is likely to come from the correction of tariff protection in manufacturing, one should expect even bigger gains to South Asian agriculture.

For important commodities, Sharma *et al.* (1999) show that South Asia could reduce its deficits of wheat, which would be limited to Pakistan and Bangladesh. India would wipe out her wheat deficit by 2000. In the case of rice, South Asia would remain a net exporter, with Bangladesh and India increasing their exports by about 500 000 tonnes compared with the baseline scenario. It is interesting to see that the rice-exporting potential of India has probably been underestimated in this study. India has already emerged as an important rice exporter, with an average of about 2.5 to 3 million tonnes per annum during 1995–2000. For edible oils, South Asia's imports are likely to increase. In fact, this region is going to be the largest importer of edible oils for human consumption.

Gulati and Kelley (1999) also provide some estimates for India. There is a possibility of India emerging as a net exporter of grains (about 3 to 5 million tonnes) in the medium term under a unilateral agricultural trade liberalization scenario. India would remain a net importer of edible oils under trade liberalization (zero tariffs). In other commodities, cotton producers could be major gainers through exports.

It is worth stressing that the existing empirical analysis of the probable impact of liberalization on South Asian agriculture reveals that incentives for cultivators in the region are likely to improve. This is conditional on distortions in world markets being contained and, in fact, reduced over time. For this to happen, South Asia will have to engage itself more in multilateral negotiations and perhaps align itself with the Cairns Groups to ensure that export subsidies are eliminated in America and Europe as soon as possible, and also that domestic support for agriculture in these areas is reduced over time. Unless this is ensured, the potential for gaining markets will remain a distant dream.

It would also be useful if the regime of tariff quotas adopted by some South Asian countries could be replaced by transparent tariffs on an *ad valorem* basis. It would be good for South Asian countries to follow Sri Lanka and have a tariff binding of all agricultural products at 50 per cent. And this is what should be demanded in multilateral negotiations as the peak tariff at 10-digit HSC level for any agricultural commodity in any country. It would open up attractive markets for many South Asian agro-products, including rice in East Asian economies, improving incentives for the farmers of South Asia.

Even when the incentives for agriculture improve, in South Asian agriculture large investments are still required, both in the public and private sectors, to ensure an appropriate supply response. This calls for major institutional changes in the way water (irrigation) and power supplies are managed, while roads and infrastructure for rural markets are also matters of concern. Experiments involving user participation in the management of these facilities would be a step in the right direction.

Domestic reform of markets must precede, or at least go hand in hand, with external action to ensure that the benefits of international trade liberalization percolate down to the culativators. This calls for abolition of all restrictive marketing practices in agriculture, whether restrictions on the movement of agricultural commodities across the country, stocking limits on traders or bans on futures, and so on. It is a big agenda for the policy makers of South Asia since it involves significant changes in the existing institutional framework, including the operation of many parastatals.

Finally, given the mass of poverty in Asia, trade liberalization in agriculture will require a very fine calibration between the opening of exports and protection of the poor. The job would be made easier if an appropriate income policy (safety net) could be devised for the poor and needy. Hitherto, many of the

South Asian countries have been following price policy to achieve equity ends, which has led to pervasive inefficiency in the system and reduced supply response. This has to alter if regional agriculture is to emerge as an efficient system within the global context. Use of price (trade) policy to achieve efficiency and income policy to pursue equity objectives requires a major restructuring of existing policies. That will remain a challenge to South Asian policy makers for many years to come.

NOTES

[1]In India, for example, the authors' estimates reveal that the expenditure elasticity for rice is −0.016, for wheat −0.109, for coarse grains −0.147, for vegetables 0.673, for fruit 0.702, for milk 0.589, for meat, fish and eggs 0.892. A similar pattern is common to all South Asian countries (Paroda and Kumar, 2000).

[2]India's stand on quantitative restrictions (QRs) was challenged by the USA, EU, Canada, Australia, New Zealand and Switzerland (and Japan as third party) through a dispute settlement process. India reached mutual agreements with all but the USA on the schedule for removing QRs. The USA filed the dispute and a panel was constituted in November 1997 to examine the allegation that India's continued QR regime was not consistent with obligations under the WTO agreement. In August 1999, the Appellate Body of WTO announced that India should announce a time schedule for removal of QRs in consultation with the USA. In December, 1999, India reached an agreement to remove QRs within two years. Half of them were removed in 2000 and the other half should go by April 2001.

REFERENCES

Athukorala, P.-C. (1999), 'Agriculture and the New Trade Agenda in the WTO 2000 Negotiations: Interests and Policy Options for South Asia' (mimeo), paper for the conference on Agriculture and the New Trade Agenda from a Development Perspective: Interests and Options in the Next WTO Negotiations, Geneva, 1–2 October.
Bhalla, G.S., Hazell, P.B.R. and Kerr, J. (1999), *Prospects for India's Cereal Supply and Demand to 2020*, Washington, DC: International Food Policy Research Institute (2020 Vision).
Government of India (1993), *Tax Reform Committee* (chairman: Raja J. Chelliah) part II, New Delhi: Ministry of Finance.
Gulati, A. and Dev, M. (1996), 'India's Integration into the Global Economy: Medium and Long Term Implications for Indian Agriculture and Linkage to OECD Countries' (mimeo), unpublished consultancy paper written for OECD.
Gulati, A. and Kelley, T. (1999), *Trade Liberalization and Indian Agriculture*, New Delhi: Oxford University Press.
Gulati, A. and Narayanan, S. (2000), 'Demystifying Power and Fertiliser Subsidies in Indian Agriculture', *Economic and Political Weekly*, 4–10 March, Mumbai, India.
Gulati, A., Mehta, R. and Narayanan, S. (1999), 'From Marrakesh to Seattle: Indian Agriculture in a Globalising World', *Economic and Political Weekly*, 9–15 October, Mumbai, India.
Paroda, R.S. and Kumar, P. (2000), 'Food Production and Demand Projections in South Asian Countries: Policy Implications for Indian Agriculture', paper presented in the seminar on Agricultural Incentives and Sustainable Development: Past Trends and Future Scenarios, organized by the Centre de Sciences Humaines along with India International Centre, New Delhi, 3–4 April.
Pigato, M., Farah, C., Itakura, K., Jun, K., Martin, W., Murrell, K. and Srinivasan, T.G. (1997), *South Asia's Integration into the World Economy*, Washington, DC: World Bank.
Pursell, G. and Gulati, A. (1995), 'Liberalizing Indian Agriculture: An Agenda for Reform', in R.

Cassen and V. Joshi (eds), *India: The Future of Economic Reforms*, Delhi: Oxford University Press.

RIS (1999), *SAARC Survey of Development and Cooperation, 1998/99*, New Delhi: Research and Information Systems for the Non-Aligned and other Developing Countries.

Rosegrant, M.W., Agcaoili-Sombilla, M. and Perez, N.D. (1995), *Global Food Projections to 2020: Implications for Investment*, Washington, DC: International Food Policy Research Institute (2020 Vision).

Schiff, M. and Valdés, A. (1992), *The Political Economy of Agricultural Pricing Policy*, vol. 4, *A Synthesis of the Economics in Developing Countries, A World Bank Comparative Study*, Baltimore and London: Johns Hopkins University Press.

Shand, R. (1999), 'Introduction', in *Economic Liberalisation In South Asia*, New Delhi: Macmillan India Limited.

Sharma, R., Konandreas, P. and Greenfield, J. (1999), 'A Synthesis of Assessments of the Impact of the Uruguay Round on Global and South Asian Agriculture', in B. Blarel, G. Pursell and A. Valdés (eds), *Implications of the Uruguay Round Agreement for South Asia: The Case of Agriculture*, Washington, DC: World Bank.

Williamson, J. (1999), *Economic Reform: Content, Progress, Prospects*, New Delhi: Indian Council for Research on International Economic Relations and The Maharaja Sayajirao University of Baroda, India.

SECTION III

Agricultural Research, Technology Development and Institutions

MARK W. ROSEGRANT, CLAUDIA RINGLER AND
MICHAEL S. PAISNER*

Agricultural Research, Technology and World Food Markets

INTRODUCTION

Between 1970 and 1995, global cereal production increased by 58 per cent (625 million mt) at a time when population increased by 53 per cent and world food prices rapidly declined. Moreover, malnutrition among children under five in developing countries declined from an aggregate rate of over 45 per cent to 31 per cent during this period. Agricultural research has played a fundamental role in bringing about the tremendous improvements in per capita cereal availability of the last several decades. Serious questions remain, however, about the ability of world agriculture to continue to realize significant increases in developing-country food availability into the 21st century. With suitable arable area throughout much of the world already under crop production, agricultural research and development will be an increasingly crucial variable affecting future cereal production increases, and contributing to improved food security.

According to new baseline results from IFPRI's IMPACT model, global cereal production is projected to increase by 39 per cent over 25 years, from 1776 million mt in 1995 to 2466 million mt in 2020, to meet effective food demand. Global meat production will grow at a more rapid 58 per cent, from 198 million mt in 1995 to 313 million mt in 2020. Developing countries will account for an increasing share in global cereal demand: 59 per cent in 2020, up from 54 per cent in 1995. The role of developing countries in global meat demand will also increase rapidly: from 50 per cent in 1995 to 61 per cent by 2020. Imports from developed countries will be required to meet a growing share of increased cereal and meat demand in developing countries. Under the IMPACT baseline, the developing world will import a projected 195 million mt of cereals in 2020, an increase of 83 per cent (88 million mt) on cereal imports in 1995. Increased cereal imports from the developed world will thus represent 15 per cent of the additional 583 million mt of cereals that the developing world will utilize in 2020. The figures for meat imports are even more dramatic, with imports into the developing world increasing by 714 per cent (6 million mt) from barely one million mt in 1995, representing 7 per cent of the rise in meat demand in the developing world. Real world prices of cereals are

* International Food Policy Research Institute, Washington, DC, USA.

projected to decline only slowly, indicating a much stronger market for these commodities than in the past few decades, when real prices declined rapidly. Despite declining real food prices and expanding world trade, there will be little improvement in food security for the poor in many regions, as shown by slow projected reductions in the number of malnourished children.

These baseline results represent the outcomes under our best estimates of a huge number of underlying drivers of world food markets. These drivers, in turn, are influenced by the complex interaction of technology, policy, investments, environment and human behaviour. In order to understand the future of food supply and demand and food security, it is essential to focus on the long-term, fundamental drivers such as income and population growth, and technological change in agriculture as influenced by investments in agricultural research, irrigation and other factors. In the remainder of this paper we take a new look into the future role of agricultural research and technology development in world food markets based on alternative scenario simulations with IFPRI's IMPACT model. The paper starts out by very briefly describing the model, and then presents and discusses alternative scenarios with a focus on the role of technological change.

THE IMPACT GLOBAL FOOD MODEL

The International Model for Policy Analysis of Agricultural Commodities and Trade (IMPACT) covers 36 countries and 16 commodities, including all cereals, roots and tubers, meats and milk, soybean, meals and oils. IMPACT is a non-spatial partial equilibrium model focusing on the agriculture sector. Despite its focus on agricultural commodities, however, relationships linking income growth in the agriculture and non-agricultural sectors are incorporated into the model. The model represents a competitive agricultural market for crops and livestock. Country and regional submodels are linked through trade, solving simultaneously for annual supply, demand, trade and world prices. In order to explore food security effects, IMPACT projects the percentage and number of malnourished pre-school children (0 to 5 years old) in developing countries as a function of average per capita calorie availability, the share of females with secondary schooling out of the corresponding female school-age population, the status of females relative to men as captured by the ratio of female to male life expectancy at birth, and the percentage of the population with access to treated surface water or untreated but uncontaminated water from another source (see also Smith and Haddad, 2000).

Crop yield trends are influenced by technological change, investments and output and input prices. The non-price component of yield projections is broken down into public research components, including management research, conventional plant breeding, wide-crossing/hybridization breeding and biotechnology (transgenic) breeding; private sector agricultural research and development; agricultural extension; markets; infrastructure; and irrigation. To generate the projected time path of yield growth, use has been made of 'before-the-fact' and 'after-the-fact' studies of agricultural research, priority setting, sources of agricultural productivity growth and 'expert opinion'. Projections are also made for harvested crop area. Estimation of non-price area growth rates depend on the availability of cultivable land, irrigation, infrastructure investment and productivity gains, as well as on prices (for additional details, see Rosegrant *et al.* 2000).

CHOOSING ALTERNATIVE SCENARIOS

A vast range of policy-relevant alternative scenarios could be simulated. Beyond the general vagaries of world economic trends and shocks, controversy swirls today in international and national arenas about the future contributions of biotechnology, and agricultural research more generally, to food production growth. Possible regional scenarios have also entered the public debate as having potential reverberations worldwide – agricultural slowdown in China, for example, or worsening productivity in sub-Saharan Africa. Under these situations, could enough food be produced and sold at reasonable prices to take care of those most in need? Establishing a range of outcomes around the baseline projections in accordance with such broad alternate views of the future serves a dual purpose. First, it shows whether, and how, the model's most important results depend on assumptions about likely trends for the underlying drivers of the world food situation. More fundamentally, the range of outcomes can be seen, not as modifications in the parameters of a projections model, but as possible realities influenced significantly by policy decisions at the national and international levels. From the wide range of possible scenarios, we present global scenarios assessing the impact of alternative rates of growth in crop and livestock yields and two sets of regional scenarios that explore the effect of technological change alone, and in combination with other important drivers.

CEREAL YIELDS: A DETERMINING FACTOR IN WORLD FOOD PRODUCTION

Trends and projections of cereal yields

The role of agricultural research in driving worldwide expansion in food production has risen in importance as area expansion has slowed in the face of a shrinking supply of unexploited agricultural land. Globally, with cereal area actually declining after 1982, the contribution of cereal yield growth to cereal production growth has increased from 85 per cent during the peak 'Green Revolution' period between 1967 and 1982, to 112 per cent between 1982 and 1995. Moreover, the role of cereal yields increased at an accelerating pace during the latter period, with the share of yield growth in overall production growth increasing from 111 per cent between 1982 and 1989 to 114 per cent between 1989 and 1995 (Table 1). In developing countries, the contribution of yields to overall cereal production growth actually declined from 85 per cent to

TABLE 1   *Contribution of area and yield growth to growth in cereal production (per cent per year)*

	Developing countries		Developed countries		All countries	
	Area	Yield	Area	Yield	Area	Yield
1967–82	0.50	2.89	0.24	1.73	0.39	2.21
1982–95	0.59	1.89	−1.29	1.48	−0.17	1.50
1982–89	0.69	1.94	−1.42	1.95	−0.18	1.71
1989–95	0.46	1.83	−1.15	0.93	−0.16	1.25
1967–95	0.54	2.42	−0.48	1.61	0.13	1.88

76 per cent following the peak Green Revolution period, but picked up during the early 1990s to reach 79 per cent.

Yield growth is projected to continue to provide the major impetus behind global increases in cereal production. Figure 1 presents the projected relative contribution of area expansion and yield growth to overall cereal production growth between 1995 and 2020. Only in sub-Saharan Africa (SSA), where the area under cereal production will expand by 35 per cent (25 million ha.), is area expansion expected still to account for a sizeable amount of future cereal production increases, at 33 per cent. On average, area expansion will contribute only 14 per cent of future growth in cereal production in developing countries, with Asia, in particular, possessing little additional arable land. The area under cereal cultivation in the developed world will expand by only a marginal

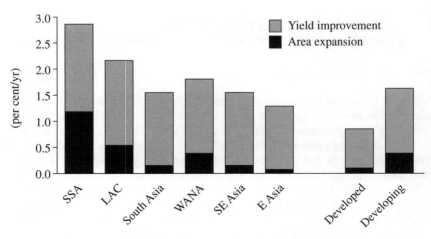

FIGURE 1   *Sources of growth in cereal production, 1995–2020*

amount, and contribute very little to cereal production increases between 1995 and 2020.

However, cereal yield growth rates are also projected to continue to slow down over the next 20 years. As Figure 2 shows, cereal yield growth rates in developing countries averaged 1.9 per cent per year between 1982 and 1995, but are expected to decline to 1.3 per cent annually between 1995 and 2020. In developed countries, cereal yield growth is also expected to slow down, from 1.5 per cent annually to 0.8 per cent annually over the same period. Annual growth in yield is expected to decrease during the projection period from rates achieved between 1982 and 1995 in all regions, with the notable exception of sub-Saharan Africa, where yield is expected to recover to a rate of growth of 1.7 per cent per year between 1995 and 2020. The slowdown in annual yield growth is projected to be particularly great in South and East Asia. Several factors are responsible for such sharp declines in Asian yield growth rates: slowly declining commodity prices (see below) provide disincentives for investments in yield-enhancing technologies at the farm level for some crops and areas; for others, input use levels are already very high and marginal returns to additional inputs are quite low. Moreover, most irrigation potential in the region has already been exploited, and further investments in irrigation expansion or rehabilitation have become unpopular internationally and among many domestic interest groups. Finally, the advances and exploitation of crop yield potential brought about by the Green Revolution have essentially run their course in much of the region.

However, future crop yield trends are highly uncertain. The potential for future crop science developments is particularly difficult to project. Worse than expected future performance in the areas of agricultural research and develop-

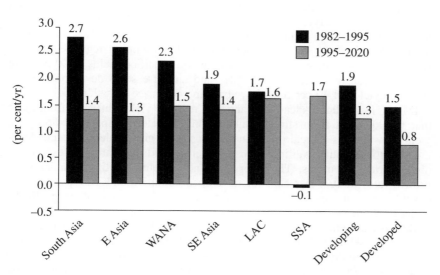

FIGURE 2   *Annual growth in cereal yield, 1982–95, 1995–2020*

ment, irrigation infrastructure and trade liberalization, among other things, could cause even greater drops in yield growth than projected under the baseline. Alternatively, it is possible that potential threats to world agricultural production and changes in incentives will galvanize governments, multilateral institutions and private firms into increasing their investments in agricultural research and irrigation, thus leading to significant yield increases and expansion of irrigation infrastructure. This range of alternatives is examined in the next section.

Cereal yields under alternative scenarios

In order to assess the sensitivity of cereal prices to future yield growth rates, four alternative yield scenarios are explored. One possible general trend over the next 25 years involves significant further declines in the resources available for agricultural research and irrigation development than projected under the baseline. This low-yield (Lyld) growth alternative is implemented in two separate scenarios, both of which assume no growth in irrigated area during the projections period (growth in irrigated area would affect yield improvements through a yield differential between rainfed and irrigated rice). Additionally, Lyld1 assumes a decline in specified yield growth rates for all crop and livestock products in the developed world of 40 per cent from the baseline level, and a decline in specified yield growth rates for all crop and livestock products of 20 per cent from the baseline in all developing regions. Lyld2 assumes a decline in specified yield growth rates of 50 per cent from baseline assumptions in the developed world and of 40 per cent in the developing world.

The rapid yield (Hyld) growth scenarios explored incorporate an increase in the expansion of irrigated area of 2 per cent per year above the baseline growth rate. Additionally, Hyld1 assumes an increase in specified yield growth rates for all livestock, milk and crops of 10 per cent above baseline assumptions in the developed world and of 20 per cent in all developing regions. Scenario Hyld2 assumes an increase in developed world specified yields of 20 per cent above baseline non-price growth rates and an increase in developing world specified yields of 40 per cent above baseline non-price growth rates.

IMPACT simulations lead to changes in realized yields different from those that would result from straight calculations made from specified non-price yield growth rates. Cereal prices increase as yield growth declines, thus leading to partially countervailing increases in crop yields (and area) in response to higher price incentives. Thus, for example, baseline realized annual yield growth rates of 0.77 per cent for developed countries and 1.27 per cent for developing countries are still 0.58 per cent and 0.84 per cent, respectively, under the Lyld2 scenario.

Realized developing country cereal yields in 2020 decline from 3.1mt per ha. under the baseline to 2.9mt per ha. under Lyld1 and 2.7 mt per ha. under Lyld2. Developed country cereal yields in 2020 drop from 3.9mt per ha. under the baseline to 3.7mt per ha. under both alternative scenarios. Declines under Lyld2 are modest, since high cereal prices bid up growth in both realized crop area and

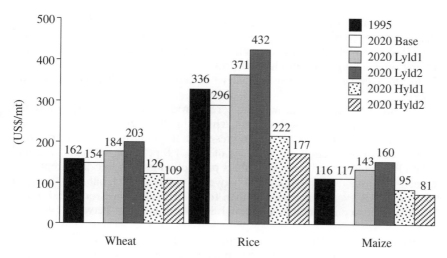

FIGURE 3   *International prices for selected cereals under alternative yield growth scenarios, 1995 and projected 2020*

realized yields (see Figure 3). The positive yield growth scenarios translate into achieved cereal yields in developing countries of 3.3mt per ha. in 2020 under Hyld1 and 3.5mt per ha. in 2020 under Hyld2. In the higher yield scenarios, the large drop in international cereal prices caused by higher food production in developing countries dampens production in developed countries.

Rice prices are particularly sensitive to change in yield growth rates, with a price jump of 25 per cent under Lyld1 and of 45 per cent under Lyld2 in 2020 compared to the baseline international price. On the other hand, prices drop by 25 and 40 per cent under the accelerated yield growth scenarios (Figure 3). The rates of growth in crop and livestock yields achieved in the next decades – and therefore the rates of growth in investment in agricultural research – will fundamentally determine the price of food for the poor.

ALTERNATIVE PRODUCTION GROWTH SCENARIOS IN SUB-SAHARAN AFRICA

The baseline scenario projects burdensome, yet manageable, agricultural import needs for sub-Saharan Africa. The region's US$4.4 billion worth of projected agricultural net imports of IMPACT commodities in 2020 represent 1.3 per cent of projected regional GDP, a decline from an agricultural import burden of 2.2 per cent of GDP in 1995. Agricultural net imports as a percentage of agricultural production are expected also to decline between 1995 and 2020, from 9.2 per cent to 7.1 per cent.

However, these projections rest on a fairly optimistic set of assumptions, given the recent agricultural performance of the region. Under the baseline scenario, annual cereal production growth is projected at 2.8 per cent for maize, 2.9 per cent for other grains, 3.1 per cent for wheat and 3.2 per cent for rice. Roots and tubers production is more important to sub-Saharan Africa than to any other region, and production growth rates of these crops are also projected to average a relatively high 2.4 per cent annually between 1995 and 2020.

The projected rates of growth for cereal production are slightly below the annual rate of increase of 4.0 per cent achieved in the region between 1982 and 1995. This rapid rate of growth represented the continent's recovery from dismal cereal production growth rates of only 1.8 per cent between 1962 and 1982. Projected annual roots and tubers production growth rates also represent a decline from a rate of 4.5 per cent between 1982 and 1995, but here the trend of recovery is even more extreme than for the cereals, since roots and tubers production also only grew at a rate of 1.8 per cent per year between 1967 and 1982.

Given the uncertainties facing agricultural technology and productivity growth in sub-Saharan Africa, a more pessimistic scenario may represent a more plausible future for the region. More generally, much of sub-Saharan Africa lacks the research capacity to produce technological advances suited to the specific challenges of the continent: low population densities, highly variable water availability and low input application. Furthermore, with the decline of public funding for international agricultural research, the private sector has become increasingly responsible for technological advances, and the great majority of these advances are unsuited to the agroclimatic environment of sub-Saharan Africa.

Additionally, it is increasingly clear that the potential for irrigation expansion is limited, and evidence is mounting regarding the toll that land degradation and soil erosion have taken on the sustainability of many production systems currently in operation (see, for example, Rosegrant and Perez, 1997). Given the importance of agricultural production to sub-Saharan Africa, the estimated GDP growth rate in the region under the baseline is probably optimistic at a rate of 3.4 per cent per year, with per capita GDP increasing at a rate of 1.0 per cent per year.

The pessimistic scenario posits that agricultural production growth will be impeded by a variety of factors, including accelerating land degradation, limited irrigation, extension and crop research investment, and continued political instability. These effects are quantified in IMPACT by a reduction in crop area and yield growth of 50 per cent and a 30 per cent reduction in livestock, milk and egg numbers growth. Because of the importance of agricultural production to African economies, GDP growth rate assumptions are cut by 50 per cent. With population growth projected at the UN medium variant levels (UN, 1998), regional per capita GDP under the negative scenario declines from US$280 in 1995 to US$231 in 2020.

The pessimistic outlook in sub-Saharan Africa will adversely affect overall agricultural production, reducing cereal output in 2020 to 96 million mt, or 29 per cent below the baseline level. The total agricultural production value of all IMPACT commodities, estimated under the baseline scenario to increase by 79 per cent above 1995 values to US$63 billion in 2020, will plunge to US$57 billion under these less optimistic assumptions.

On the trade side, sub-Saharan Africa's high but relatively manageable net cereal imports of US$3.0 billion (14 million mt) under the baseline scenario will rise to US$5.4 billion (32 million mt) under the alternative scenario, reaching a level that may not be sustainable over any extended period. The overall trade balance of IMPACT commodities will decline precipitously, to US$6.7 billion of net agricultural imports, in 2020 under the alternative scenario, representing 3 per cent of GDP and 12 per cent of total agricultural production in that year.

The negative scenario would significantly increase malnutrition in sub-Saharan Africa. Per capita calorie availability would decline from 2135 kilocalories in 1995 to 2055 kilocalories in 2020, reversing the slight improvement of 142 kilocalories achieved between 1995 and 2020 under the baseline scenario. The region's number of malnourished children would also increase, from 31 million children in 1995 to 44 million children in 2020, 4 million more children than projected under the baseline scenario.

A high level of food insecurity and heavy dependence on food aid characterizes sub-Saharan Africa in the present day. The region can ill afford further declines in per capita income, and does not possess the necessary foreign exchange to satisfy its food needs through imports in the absence of significant expansion of domestic production. While the negative scenario assumptions do result in a substantial increase in net imports of agricultural commodities, especially cereals, to help mitigate the projected production gap, the region still experiences a significant decline in per capita calorie availability and a significant increase in child malnourishment even at these high and potentially economically unsustainable import levels. A failure to finance the increased imports would further worsen food security.

Sustained growth: a future for Africa's children

While IMPACT results indicate an increase in the number of malnourished children in sub-Saharan Africa, from 31 million children in 1995 to 40 million children by 2020 under the baseline scenario, the developing world excluding sub-Saharan Africa is expected to achieve a decline in the absolute number of malnourished children by 27 per cent, from 129 million children in 1995 to 95 million children in 2020. What kind of transformations, in terms of economic and agricultural growth, education and health, will be necessary for sub-Saharan Africa to battle against childhood malnutrition as effectively as the rest of the developing world? Is it feasible to hope that even a major economic and agricultural transformation on the continent could lead to real inroads against childhood malnutrition?

In order to provide a sense of the magnitude of the challenges facing sub-Saharan Africa and the necessity of concerted attention by national governments and international organizations to these challenges, an alternative scenario is explored in IMPACT to describe one possible path to achieve a 28 per cent reduction in the number of malnourished children, from 31 million in 1995 to

22 million children by 2020. Such a decline would bring trends in malnutrition in sub-Saharan Africa in line with those occurring elsewhere in the developing world.

To achieve such a dramatic improvement in childhood malnutrition would require increases in income, food production and social investments to improve the status and education of women and the access of the population to clean water. Any given level of improvement in malnutrition could be achieved through alternative combinations of these factors. In the scenario presented here, we first assume large increases in social investments and then assess the combination of additional income and production required to generate a 28 per cent decline in the number of malnourished children. The social parameters that contribute to the estimation of child malnutrition in 2020 – the ratio of female to male life expectancy, females attending secondary school as a share of the female school-age population, and the share of the population with access to clean water – are increased by equal proportions (by 0.10, 20 percentage points, and 10 percentage points, respectively) across the five IMPACT subregions in sub-Saharan Africa (Nigeria, Northern, Central and Western, Eastern, and Southern sub-Saharan Africa) under the alternative scenario. Thus the female/male life expectancy ratio for Nigeria in 2020 increases from the baseline projection of 1.029 to 1.039, the share of female secondary schooling in the female school-age population increases from the baseline projection of 39 per cent to 59 per cent, and the share of the population with access to clean water increases from 69 per cent to 79 per cent. Achievement of this impressive advancement in quality of life would require a tremendous level of commitment and investment at all levels, and a major effort to focus on the status, education and health of women.

With this improvement in social investments, GDP growth in the five sub-Saharan Africa sub-regions would have to increase from the baseline range of 3.2–3.6 per cent per year between 1995 and 2020 to an annualized rate of growth of 8 per cent. In order to generate this GDP growth, cereal crop yield growth would need to rise from between 1.6 and 1.9 per cent per year under the baseline to an annualized rate of 3.1–3.9 per cent between 1995 and 2020, depending on the crop, based on the share of agriculture in GDP. Yield growth rates of this level would satisfy rising cereal demand on the continent without increasing the level of net imports. Livestock production would need to rise by similar proportions.

What this highly optimistic, possibly unfeasible, scenario shows is that poverty alleviation in sub-Saharan Africa is an immense task that will require an equally immense level of commitment. Parts of East and Southeast Asia have realized impressive gains over the last three decades in generating economic growth and reducing malnutrition, and a similarly remarkable transformation will be necessary for equivalent improvements in childhood malnutrition to take place in sub-Saharan Africa. Eight per cent per year GDP growth is perhaps not an impossible dream for the region, but peace and good economic policies will be required in far more abundance than in the present day if such a goal is to be achieved.

INDIA AND CHINA: AGRICULTURAL GROWTH SLOWDOWN

The two most populous regions in the world, China and India, have both realized rather remarkable developments in agricultural production growth over the last several decades. Nonetheless, while India can claim the achievement of virtual cereal self-sufficiency, levels of per capita food availability are still quite low on the sub-continent at 2405 kilocalories per day, and 53 per cent of pre-school children are malnourished, a proportion far higher than sub-Saharan Africa's corresponding figure of 33 per cent. China's record on child malnutrition is far better, but the rapid migration of Chinese peasants out of rural farming and into urban areas may increasingly strain the capacity of Chinese agriculture to feed the nation. Continued agricultural growth in China and India is thus crucially important to future poverty alleviation in both regions. The importance of these two countries to global cereal production – together they accounted for 30 per cent of world wheat production and 56 per cent of world rice production in 1995 – also raises important questions with respect to the ability of global markets to absorb significant downward shocks to production in these countries.

Continued agricultural growth in China and India is dependent on a number of assumptions regarding the possibility for continued yield increases, moderate but not overly burdensome levels of land degradation and a continued national ability to manage pressures from growing competition between the agricultural, urban and industrial sectors over land and water resources. Many observers believe that these assumptions are optimistic, and that both nations will face severe impediments to the expansion of agricultural production in the form of growing and increasingly urbanized populations, high levels of land degradation, declining investments in the agricultural sector, and other pressures impinging on both land quality and yields. In order to model a reasonable worst-case scenario, a decline of 50 per cent in the crop area and yield growth rates in China and India between 1995 and 2020 is assumed. For crops in which the area actually declined during the projections period, a doubling of this decline is assumed.

As in the case for the global yield scenarios, a change in yield (and area) growth rate assumptions translates through the IMPACT model into somewhat different actual declines in the output value of these variables, because the price increases caused by the low growth assumptions induce a partial recovery of yield growth.

As expected, declining yield and area growth rates have a severe effect on total crop production in India and China. Indian cereal production declines by 10 per cent, from 254 million mt in 2020 under the baseline scenario to 228 million mt. As a result, India shifts from near self-sufficiency in cereals under the baseline scenario to net cereal imports of 23 million mt (at a cost of US$5 billion at projected international prices) in 2020. Meanwhile, production in China declines by 12 per cent, from 497 million mt to 435 million mt under the alternative scenario. As a result, China's cereal trade deficit doubles from 51 million mt under the baseline scenario to 102 million mt or US$17 billion under the alternative scenario in 2020. Moving beyond a narrow focus on cereals, India's overall agricultural trade balance for IMPACT commodities will shift from a 1995 surplus of US$1.7 billion to a deficit of US$9.9 billion in 2020, while China's overall trade deficit will grow from net imports of US$5.9 billion in 1995 to net imports worth US$37.9 billion in 2020. In relative value terms, India's trade deficit in 2020 will represent 0.8 per cent of projected GDP and 7.5 per cent of the value of agricultural production of IMPACT commodities, while China's trade deficit in 2020 will represent 1.3 per cent of projected GDP and 13.8 per cent of the value of agricultural production.

Area and yield slowdowns in India and China affect world cereal prices in a significant but not disastrous way. As can be seen in Figure 4, under the low growth scenario, wheat prices increase by 11 per cent (US$17 per mt) from the baseline 2020 value to US$171 per mt; maize prices increase by 15 per cent (US$18 per mt); other grains prices increase by 13 per cent or US$13 per mt; and rice prices rise by 21 per cent (US$62 per mt).

Moreover, food availability in India declines from 2719 kilocalories per capita under the baseline to 2655 kilocalories per capita in 2020 under the low area and yield growth scenario, and in China from 3117 kilocalories per capita to 3059 kilocalories per capita. While these changes seem moderate, it should be kept in mind that they are highly dependent on the ability of China and India to finance massive agricultural imports. Political pressures may render such high levels of net imports unacceptable. Measures to lower agricultural import dependency, such as high import tariffs and subsidies to domestic production, would considerably worsen the food availability under the alternative scenario.

The results show that a slowdown in technological change in agriculture in China and India primarily affects the countries themselves. The effect on projected world prices is significant, but not devastating. The results also

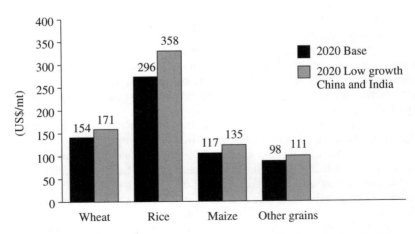

FIGURE 4   *International prices for cereals under baseline and China and India low growth scenarios, projected 2020*

indicate that world markets are in fact quite resilient and can absorb large increases in Chinese net imports without huge price consequences. Although China is already a significant player in world food markets, and its importance is likely to increase substantially, the country does not represent a major threat to the long-term stability in these markets. Considerable price flexibility in global supply response still exists.

CONCLUSIONS

This paper has briefly summarized the IMPACT baseline outcomes under our best estimates of a huge number of underlying drivers of world food markets. These drivers, in turn, are influenced by the complex interaction of technology, policy, investments, environment and human behaviour. Our best estimates indicate that effective food demand can be met in the future with very slowly declining international food prices if adequate investments in research, development and irrigation are undertaken by national, international, private and public organizations.

However, only time will show if plant breeding and other yield-improving technologies, including irrigation, will actually bring about adequate increases in yield growth, even in marginal areas, or if environmental degradation, lack of investment in developing country-suited research and development, unfavourable policy environments and other factors will slow down improvements in yields.

Alternative scenarios demonstrated that plausible changes in these drivers could have dramatic impacts on the outcomes for food supply, demand, prices, trade and malnutrition. The alternative global productivity scenarios demonstrate the importance of crop yield growth as a determinant of world food prices. The fragility of food security in sub-Saharan Africa is sharply drawn through an exploration of alternative growth paths for this region, with slowdowns in agricultural yield growth and income leading to a significant worsening of the already severe malnutrition problem. The alternative scenario for China and India shows that significant declines in area and yield growth over the next 25 years would lead to reductions in food consumption in these countries and moderate increases in international prices for agricultural commodities. Net imports by the two countries would increase dramatically, with the possibility of triggering protectionist trade policies in these countries.

The contrast between the baseline and alternative scenarios shows that the future of agricultural yield growth, both in isolation and in conjunction with changes in income growth and social investments, significantly influences global food markets and, more dramatically, the food security and trade outcomes for specific countries and regions. The sensitivity of global and regional food markets to changes in agricultural productivity growth that can be directly influenced by national and international policy and investment decisions offers both hope and concern, during a period of uncertainty, regarding future directions and the magnitude of agricultural investments.

REFERENCES

Rosegrant, M.W. and Perez, N.D. (1997), *Water resources development in Africa: A review and synthesis of issues, potentials, and strategies for the future*, EPTD Discussion Paper, Washington, DC: IFPRI.

Rosegrant, M.W., Paisner, M. and Witcover, J. (2000), *Global food projections to 2020: Emerging trends and alternative futures*, IFPRI 2020 Vision Discussion Paper, Washington, DC: IFPRI.

Smith, L.C. and Haddad, L. (2000), *Exploring child malnutrition in developing countries: A cross-country analysis*, IFPRI Research Report no. 111, Washington, DC: IFPRI.

United Nations (1998), *World population prospects: the 1998 revision*, New York: United Nations.

WALLACE E. HUFFMAN*

Human Capital, Education and Agriculture

INTRODUCTION

Education is widely considered to be the most important form of human capital, with human health as the second most important form (Schultz, 1999). Formal education or general intellectual achievement is obtained primarily in elementary and secondary schools and in colleges and universities. Although the creation of useful skills for work has frequently focused only on formal schooling, there is growing recognition that useful skill creation starts early, before an individual's formal schooling, and continues after formal schooling ends: lifelong learning, especially in developed countries (Heckman, 1999). Early childhood activities and experiences that are shaped by a child's family and community are very important to the formation of early ability, motivation and social adaptability. Ability and learning seem to be dynamic complementary processes over time for children (ibid.). Post-schooling forms of learning occur in learning-by-doing (for example, apprenticeships, on-the-job training) and informal settings. Although some of this learning is difficult to measure, it has the potential to grow in importance over the next two decades with the rapid advances in communication and information technologies, the dramatic fall in the real cost of services from these technologies and the prospects for rapid global adoption (World Bank, 1999).

The most recent international empirical evidence shows that the return to schooling, both social and private, remains attractive (Psacharopoulos, 1994). In low-income countries, the social rate of return to investments in primary schooling is very high (about 23 per cent), for secondary schooling it is lower but attractive, with higher education being lowest (11 per cent). In lower- and upper-middle-income countries, the social rates of return to primary and secondary schooling are less than for low-income countries, but the ordering of rates of return across schooling completion levels remains the same (ibid., p. 1331).

The objective of this paper is to provide a review of the broad effects of education in agriculture and examine some of the prospects and potential for the future. Worldwide, about one-half of the labour force continues to be

*Iowa State University, Ames, IA, USA. Helpful comments were obtained from Peter Orazem, Bruce Gardner, Robert Emerson and Derek Byerlee. Journal Paper No. J-19037 of the Iowa Agriculture and Home Economics Experiment Station, Ames, IA.

employed in agriculture. In the low-income countries, which account for about 55 per cent of the world's population, the share of the labour force in agriculture exceeds 65 per cent, but in developed countries, which account for about 15 per cent of the world's population, the share drops to only 5 per cent (World Bank, 2000). In what are now the developed countries, the long-term increase in agricultural productivity associated with advances in knowledge has been a major factor in the long-term transformation from an agrarian to an urban-based, service-oriented society (Johnson, 2000). The paper will be organized as follows: a conceptual framework, a summary of empirical evidence, and a discussion of rapid changes which are on the horizon.

A CONCEPTUAL FRAMEWORK

Growth in knowledge is a major factor causing the long-term rise in labour productivity, real wage rates and per capita incomes in market economies. First, as the stock of knowledge grows, the opportunities for individuals to invest in specialized knowledge (for example, schooling, training) that raises their productivity occurs (Becker and Murphy, 1993; Jones, 1998, pp. 71–87). The returns to labour's specialization arise through workers taking on narrower and more specialized tasks. To produce output, this means that workers who have different skills must frequently cooperate. 'Team production' within or across firms, however, raises special incentive problems (Becker and Murphy, 1993; Gibbons, 1998). As the degrees of specialization rises, the number of different tasks and specialists to be coordinated increases. If growth through knowledge creation and transmission is to continue, markets must organize in a way to coordinate team labour efficiently. Economies that have high coordination/transaction costs because of weak institutions (that is, absence of private property, weak contracts, suppressed prices and markets) makes it very difficult for workers and firms to specialize, given any stock of knowledge, and reduce labour productivity and per capita incomes (Williamson, 1985). Second, as the stock of knowledge grows, the opportunities occur to produce new technologies that become embodied in new capital goods (see, for example, Romer, 1990) and intermediate goods (see Jones, 1998, pp. 88–107; Huffman and Evenson, 1993).

Agricultural production has a large biological component where differences exist between crops and livestock. The seasonal and spatial nature of crop production places severe constraints on large-scale or specialized units and mechanized production. With plant biological processes sequenced by day length and temperature, little opportunity exists to use mechanization to speed up the production processes, even on large farms. Because planting and harvesting for any given crop must occur within a narrow time window at any location, a major limit to size of specialized enterprises occurs. In temperate climate regions, crop rotation, or non-specialized production, has historically been one important method of controlling pest and disease problems in crops and balancing soil nutrient availability with plant nutrient needs. Chemical and biological control of pests and chemical fertilizer applications are relatively new technological alternatives to crop rotation, and they have facilitated crop specialization. Livestock production, however, is relatively free of constraints owing to seasonal and spatial attributes. It is economically feasible to speed up or slow the rate of production by changing the diet and activity level of animals and poultry during the growing and finishing phases.

When firms are heterogeneous within a sector because of specialized resources, including land, climate and knowledge, the potential impact of new technologies will differ across them. It is costly for entrepreneurs to acquire information, evaluate available technologies and adopt only the new ones that are expected to benefit them. Considerable evidence exists that schooling of entrepreneurs is a valuable skill when the technology is changing: for example, when agriculture undergoes a transition from traditional to modernizing methods (Schultz, 1975; Becker, 1993; Huffman, 1998).

The multi-period agricultural household model

The decisions of agricultural households have been modelled from different perspectives depending on the central issue researchers are emphasizing. When human capital investment decisions (for example, how much schooling, informal training and information to obtain, or whether to adopt a new technology) are the central focus, models of multi-period household utility maximization with human capital production or innovation provide a useful guide to empirical models. When household members have obtained their human capital (for example, formal education) and the impacts of this on other outcomes (occupational choice, hours of work, purchased input use, wage rates, income and so on) are the central focus, one-period static agricultural household models provide researchers with a useful guide (Singh *et al.*, 1986). In particular, behavioural models provide one useful guide for deciding which variables should be treated as endogenous and which are exogenous or causal variables.

Consider a risk-neutral household living three periods. In each period, the farm household consumes human capital services and purchased goods that give utility. The production of human capital investment uses human capital services from the existing stock, purchased inputs and a fixed individual household-specific genetic or innate ability factor and exhibits decreasing returns to scale in production. The production of farm output uses variable inputs of human capital services of household members and purchased inputs and is conditional on technology and agroclimatic conditions. The farm production technology exhibits decreasing returns to scale in the variable inputs (see Huffman, 1999, for details).

This modelling strategy treats human capital investment as changing the quantity of human capital services available for all uses but does not change the real wage for a unit of the services. Human capital depreciates at some constant rate, and available human capital services in each time period are allocated among leisure, human capital production, farm production and wage work. The household faces a multi-period discounted cash income constraint in maximizing its intertemporal utility function.

The following important results follow from this model. First, it provides the optimal size of the human capital investment in each period, the quantity or rate where the present value of the marginal return from a unit equals the present value of the marginal cost. Second, insights about the tendency for investing in skill to weaken or strengthen ties to farming are obtained by examining the present value of the marginal return to investment in human capital. There are two effects: the change in the present value of the additional farm production that results from allocating part of an incremental unit of human capital services to this activity, and the change in the present value of the additional labour market earnings that results from allocating the remaining part of an increment of human capital services to non-farm wage work.

The allocation of an increment of human capital services between farm production and off-farm work is quite sensitive to the relative impact of human capital on the marginal product of labour in farm and non-farm work or to the elasticity of demand faced by the individual for human capital services. If the marginal product of human capital services is low in farm production but relatively high in non-farm wage work, and it is optimal to invest in human capital, then an agricultural household will increase the share of employed human capital services allocated to non-farm wage work.

Third, given the three-period lifetime, a comparison of the present value of the marginal return to an investment in period t and $t+1$, shows that delaying the investment from t to $t+1$ significantly reduces the present value of the marginal return. Hence it is optimal for agricultural households to make large

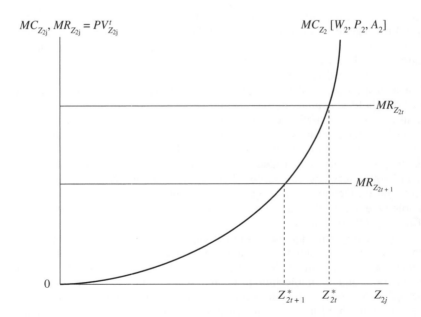

FIGURE 1   *Optimal production of human capital*

human capital investments early in an individual's life, rather than later. Furthermore, it is never optimal in this model for a household to invest any resources in human capital production in the final period ($t+2$), because there is cost but no return (see Figure 1).

Fourth, because the marginal cost of human capital production is increasing, it will frequently be optimal for an agricultural household to spread its human capital investment in an individual over more than one period, even with finite life and associated reduction in the present value of the marginal return. Spreading the investment over time is a good decision when the cost saving exceeds the reduction in returns due to delaying (see Figure 1). Fifth, if the length of life were to be extended to four periods (for example, owing to better public health measures), this would increase the demand for human capital investment and, other things being equal, increase lifetime human capital (for example, schooling) investment per individual (see also Huffman, 1999).

Some implications

Schooling and learning-by-doing may be productive or unproductive in agriculture, depending on economic conditions, but in economies with freely mobile resources, agriculture must compete with other sectors for skilled (and unskilled) labour. The wage for similarly skilled labour need not be equal across sectors, but in equilibrium the marginal compensation, including monetary value of non-monetary attributes of the farm and non-farm work, will be equal. Recently, the US farm–non-farm compensating differential has been small (Huffman, 1996). Although technical change in agriculture is frequently at least as large as in the non-farm sector of countries, the opportunities for raising labour productivity in agriculture through task specialization and coordination may be modest compared with the non-farm sector. On a farm, the skilled individual may face a more inelastic demand for his/her services than in a large non-farm business. Also, because of poor infrastructure and institutions, the agricultural sector may in some cases face small market size and high coordination costs that put it at a disadvantage.

In some agricultural environments, informal learning rather than schooling may be a more important form of human capital, while in other environments schooling may be a better public investment (Schultz, 1964; Huffman, 1985, 1991; Becker, 1993, pp. 1–13; Johnson, 2000). For example, in the traditional environment which exists in some low-income countries, accumulated experience is a better investment than schooling. Information accumulated informally does not depreciate when the decision-making environment is static. However, when the political and economic environments are changing in a market economy, or new technologies are regularly becoming available, skills obtained from formal schooling prove an important foundation for informal post-school learning. Most new agricultural technologies are geoclimatic and/ or land-specific, and changing technologies cause rapid depreciation in land-specific human capital. Being able to make good decisions on information acquisition and technology adoption is a valuable skill. Hence a changing agricultural environment increases the expected return to formal schooling through allocative efficiency effects, which seem likely to be more important than technical efficiency effects.

SUMMARY OF EMPIRICAL EVIDENCE

The following material summarizes a careful review of the literature, but the details are reported in Huffman (1999).

Choice about where to work

Worldwide, about one-half of the labour force works in agriculture (World Bank, 2000). A large majority are unpaid farm workers – the farmers who make decisions and work, and other farm family members who work generally without direct compensation – and a majority are hired (non-farm family) workers. Hired workers are generally of two types: regular full-time and seasonal. Seasonal labour demand variation arises largely from the definite seasonal pattern to biological events in plants, which creates unusually large labour demand at planting, weeding and/or harvest time. The supply of seasonal agricultural labour frequently has a local component and a migratory component.

Over the long term, the share of the labour force employed in agriculture has declined dramatically in what are now developed countries, but slowly or not at all in low-income or developing countries (OECD, 1995; Johnson, 2000). Decisions on schooling by families and communities are an important factor determining whether individuals work in agriculture or elsewhere. Even in developed countries where farmers are relatively well educated, hired farm workers generally have significantly less education.

Choosing agriculture   Whether to work in agriculture or in another industry is an important decision worldwide. In non-centrally planned countries, individuals make a choice of an occupation/industry for work. Schooling decisions affect later occupational choice decisions.

Migration   As economic conditions change in interconnected labour markets, workers in free societies invest in migration to improve their future economic welfare (see the three-period model in the previous section), which tends to reduce or eliminate inter-market wage differences. This complicates the problem of explaining migration, because individuals are acting on anticipated wage rate differences rather than the ex post values. Schooling plays a significant role in these adjustments or reallocations because of its effect on the costs and returns to migration.

Off-farm work   Although farmers tend to be tied to the land and to be geographically immobile, off-farm work of farmers is a relatively common international phenomenon. Since the 1950s and 1960s, aggregate demand for operator and family farm labour in all of the developed countries has declined (see OECD, 1995), the demand for housework in farm households has generally declined as family sizes have declined and labour-saving household technologies have been adopted, and the real non-farm wage has generally increased. Faced with needing to make adjustments in labour allocation, farm households in developed countries have frequently chosen to continue in farming but also to supply labour of some of its members to the non-farm sector (for example, OECD, 1994).

Summary   Overall, the review of the literature (Huffman, 1999) shows that the quantity and quality of individuals' schooling affects their choice of where to work. In the United States, completing secondary schooling reduces the likelihood of an individual choosing an occupation in agriculture. Among US hired farm workers, schooling completion levels are low and have not risen, as immigrant workers having less then eight years of schooling have become an increasing share of the workforce. US domestic and undocumented migratory farm workers seem to function relatively well with low levels of schooling. For individuals in developed countries who are farmers and continue farming, additional schooling increases the likelihood that they will participate in off-farm wage work, but this is not necessarily the case for those in 'Green Revolution' areas of developing countries. Higher schooling levels are in general associated with a population that is more geographically mobile.

Technology adoption and information acquisition

The decision to adopt new technologies is an investment decision, because significant costs are incurred in obtaining information and learning about the performance characteristics of one or more new methods, while the benefits are distributed over time. Furthermore, for any given farmer only a small share of the new technologies that become available will be profitable to adopt. This means that there is a large amount of uncertainty facing farmers, and additional schooling may help them make better adoption decisions and increase farm profitability. Because additional schooling affects the amount of knowledge that a farmer has about the way technologies might work and his or her information evaluation skills, additional schooling may affect his or her choice of the type and amount of information to acquire. Hence the three-period model of the previous section provides a useful guide.

When technology is new and widely profitable, farmers' schooling has been shown to be positively related to the probability of adoption. When a technology has been available for an extended period (for example, several years) or it is not widely profitable, farmers' schooling is generally unrelated to its adoption or use. Schooling has been shown to affect choice of information channels about technological advances.

Although successful adoption of innovations clearly requires information, few studies have considered the important joint decisions on information acquisition and new technology adoption. This seems to be a fruitful area for new research. When several information sources exist, early adopters might prefer sources that facilitate faster learning about the innovation. The information channels for early adopters might also be different from those for late adopters. Wozniak (1993) is an exception, in that he examined farmers' joint decisions on information acquisition and technology adoption. He considered the adoption of two technologies – one new and one mature – and four channels of information – one active and one for both extension and private sector information providers. In the study, he found that farmers' education significantly increased the probability of adopting new and mature technologies and acquiring information from extension by talking with extension personnel (passive) and attending demonstrations or meetings (active) about the use of new products or procedures sponsored by extension. Education did not have a statistically significant effect on acquiring information by talking with private industry personnel or attending demonstrations or meetings on the use of new products or procedures sponsored by private companies. Farmers were more likely to be early adopters if they acquired information actively or passively from private industry than if they obtained it from extension. For both new and mature innovations, positive and significant interaction effects existed between gathering information from public and private sources; that is, the sources appear to be complementary.

Summary   Overall, the review of the literature (Huffman, 1999) shows that additional schooling of farmers increases the rate of early adoption of useful agricultural technologies in developed and developing countries. A surprisingly small amount of research, however, has examined farmers' joint decisions on information acquisition and technology adoption, and this is an area for much-needed new research.

Agricultural production

Education of farmers and other farm labour has the potential for contributing to agricultural production, as reflected in gross output/transformation functions, and in value-added or profit functions. These influences are frequently referred to as affecting technical efficiency, allocative efficiency or economic efficiency. When the effects of schooling on production are considered in a gross output-complete input specification, the marginal product of education, a measure of technical efficiency, is limited by the other things that are held constant. A value-added or profit function representation accommodates a much broader set of effects of farmers' education associated with allocative efficiency: the adoption of new inputs in a profitable manner, the allocation of land (and other quasi-fixed inputs) efficiently among alternative uses, the allocation of variable inputs efficiently, and the efficient choice of an output mix. The empirical evidence has shown that the productivity of farmers' education is enhanced by a wider range of choices, and Welch (1970) is generally given credit for delineating these substantive differences.

Summary   Overall, in developing, transition and developed countries, the review of the literature (Huffman, 1999) shows that farmers' schooling has generally greater value through allocative than through technical efficiency effects, though there have been suggestions that in Green Revolution Asia the technical and allocative effects are about equal in importance (Hussain and Byerlee, 1995). The positive allocative effects are, however, closely associated with a farming environment where technologies are changing and relative prices alter. Farmers' schooling has infrequently been shown to increase crop yields or gross farm output, because technical efficiency gains from skills provided by farmers' schooling seem generally to be small. Farmers' schooling has also been shown to change the optimal mix or composition of farm inputs and outputs where production is multi-input and multi-output.

Total factor productivity decomposition

Productivity statistics, measuring output per unit of input, started in the 1950s, showing seemingly costless increases in output. Three main classes of methods have been applied in source of productivity analysis: (a) imputation-accounting methods, (b) statistical meta-production function methods, and (c) statistical productivity decomposition methods (Evenson, 1999). In all of the methods, there is considerable investment in data construction, especially trying to account accurately for quality and quantity of inputs and outputs. Schooling enters primarily at two places: schooling of agricultural labour can reasonably be expected to enhance labour quality or the effective units of labour, and schooling of the farmer or decision maker may more generally increase productivity by enhancing economic efficiency in agriculture.

Summary   In agricultural productivity data sets, the incorporation of labour quality adjustments has not been uniform. One strand of the literature, started by Griliches (1963) and continued by Ball *et al.* (1997) at the United States Department of Agriculture, emphasizes effective units of labour, which is the product of agricultural labour quantity (days or hours) and an index of labour quality. This approach can lead to overadjusting for quality effects. Another strand of the literature places labour quality effects in the productivity index (residual) and uses an education index, generally for farm operators, to explain total factor productivity levels. When the latter approach has been followed, farmers' schooling has generally had a positive and significant effect on agricultural productivity. In cross-country studies of agricultural labour productivity, it has been difficult to obtain a satisfactory empirical measure of schooling. Consequently, the weak effects of education in cross-country studies seem more likely to be due to data problems than to absence of real effects. Although the progress may be slow, this is an area where progress can be made.

Knowledge creation and transfer

Knowledge creation can occur informally (for example, through accumulated experiences of farmers, mechanical innovations by farmers and blacksmith shops) and in formal institutions specializing in the development and transmission of knowledge (universities and research institutes). Informal research can occur with little or no education, but the rate of knowledge accumulation is very slow (Johnson, 2000). Successful institutionalized research requires scientists whose considerable ability has been polished by intensive higher education and training (Huffman and Evenson, 1993). Institutionalized research has been the source of rapid knowledge creation leading to new agricultural technologies (for example, chemicals, pharmaceuticals, plant varieties) and increases in agricultural productivity.

Research produces discoveries that are pure public goods, being non-rival and non-excludable, and discoveries and innovations that are impure public goods because they are partially excludable, for example owing to spatial limits associated with heterogeneous geoclimate conditions, species limits or intellectual property rights (Huffman and Just, 1999; Kanbur and Sandler, 1999). With knowledge that is a pure public good, the social opportunity cost of additional users is zero. Hence knowledge acquisition can frequently occur through transfers or spillovers, but using this knowledge generally requires further research to adapt the discovery to local geoclimatic conditions. Adaptive research, however, requires less highly trained scientists.

Summary   Knowledge creation, acquisition and adaptation, which are part of the services sector, are important channels through which higher education affects agriculture. The productivity of agricultural research centres differs worldwide, but, for developing countries, borrowing discoveries made by others and adapting them to local agroclimatic conditions will be generally more efficient than creating basic advances in knowledge.

Household income

The emphasis is on impacts of education on incomes of agricultural workers and farm households. The influence of schooling on incomes of hired agricultural labour seems small in developed countries and insignificant in others. In a study of Florida farm workers, Emerson (1989) found a very small positive and significant effect of workers' schooling on earnings (1.4 per cent per year for migrants and 1.6 per cent per year for non-migrants, holding weeks worked per year constant). The coefficients for experience were about 50 per cent larger for migrants than for non-migrants. Furthermore, domestic farm workers sorted or selected themselves into migratory and non-migratory groups in a manner that was consistent with the theory of comparative advantage: that is, migrants earned more as migrants than they would as non-migrants, and non-migrants earned more as non-migrants than they would as migrants.

In developing countries, transport and communication are relatively expensive, average schooling completed is low, and housing in a new location may be difficult to find. Hence workers tend to be less geographically mobile than in the USA, and rural labour markets are less integrated.

For farm or landed households, the effects of schooling on income arise primarily from impacts on farm profit or value-added and off-farm earnings. Farmers' schooling increases profit in an environment where technology and relative prices are changing, but in other agricultural environments, where technology and prices are not changing or where farmers' schooling is below the permanent literacy level, there is unlikely to be much impact on farm profit, value-added or household income (Huffman, 1999). Furthermore, in an agricultural environment where farmers have a large number of opportunities to make good or bad decisions and schooling completion levels differ significantly across farmers, additional schooling of full-time farmers can be expected to increase net farm income, controlling for their age. When price and technology policies greatly limit farmers' decision-making opportunities, farmers vary in their extent of farm/off-farm work, or little variation exists in farmers' schooling, weak or negative schooling and net farm income relationships may exist.

Summary Overall, the review of the literature (Huffman, 1999) shows that the effects of education on incomes of hired farm workers are mixed. If hired farm workers work piece-rate, schooling does not affect their wage, but experience may be important if they can acquire skills by specializing in an activity. If they are time-pay wage workers, added schooling may have a small positive impact on their wage. For farm household members in developed and developing countries, the impact of schooling on farm profit or value-added is positive when technology is changing rapidly. In developed countries, schooling usually has a favourable impact on the off-farm wage and off-farm earnings, but in developing countries the results are mixed: for example, negative in the Indian Green Revolution areas and positive in China. In developed countries, schooling of husbands and wives has a positive effect on farm household (net) income and, in developing countries, the impact is probably positive. Empirical studies, however, have infrequently focused on the effects of education on households or family income.

Non-market returns

Non-market work associated with caring for a family is an important activity of married women. For married and educated women living in rural areas, non-farm employment opportunities are more limited than in urban areas. The education of married women has been shown to be productive in home production. Mothers' education improves child health as measured by birth weight, nutrition status and survival rate (Schultz, 1993, 1997). The primary reason is that the most important deliverer of health care to a child is the mother. Schooling equips her with general and specific knowledge and the means and confidence to seek new ideas. The impact of mothers' schooling on child health is largest in unsanitary environments and in areas that are farther from health care facilities, for example, larger in rural than in urban areas.

Married women with education also have fewer children, especially holding husbands' education and wage constant (Schultz, 1993). This reduction is associated with smaller desired family size and more efficient use of contraceptive information. With a smaller family size, larger investments per child in health and schooling are possible, and this improves the adult standard of living prospects of a family's children.

Summary   Schooling for married women in rural areas has been shown to increase their productivity at home and to increase their participation in off-farm work in areas that offer employment opportunities for women having education. Hence the return to women's schooling is positive, and it is frequently greater than for investments in men's schooling.

RAPID CHANGES ON THE HORIZON

Agriculture worldwide can expect to undergo some dramatic changes in the early 21st century, and investments in education will be important.

Communication and information technologies

The stock of knowledge about technologies and attributes of goods is growing rapidly, creating knowledge gaps. The potential for communicating knowledge is growing rapidly, with a coming together or integration of new technologies associated with computers and telephony into a large global network of interconnected communication and information systems (World Bank, 1999). This includes the use of satellites, fibre optics and wireless technologies. Wireless communication technologies have great potential for low fixed-cost infrastructure in sparsely populated, difficult terrains and harsh climates, which frequently categorize rural areas. The technologies have been advancing rapidly, and the cost has been falling.

The new technologies have potential for agriculture. New markets for agricultural inputs, outputs and consumer goods can be, and are being, created. Farmers and other household members can get direct access at low cost to price information for distant markets and make contracts within them. This has the potential dramatically to improve the general efficiency with which markets operate, reducing spatial price differentials and opportunities for intermediaries/traders, which can be large in 'spatially thin markets for goods' and sparsely populated areas. The potential is great in developing countries. However, since buyers and sellers often do not know one another and lack direct contact, participants must develop new skills to judge the quality of products and the reputation of individuals, and new institutions may be needed to guarantee product quality, enforce contracts and police fraud (World Bank, 1999).

This new technology provides a potentially new source of knowledge/information for farm household members. A large amount of information is becoming available in virtual libraries containing information that can be used for decision making on production and management practices for farm businesses and consumer information for households. A new type of extension or dissemination of information is emerging, because the real cost of storing and disseminating information, once created, is falling rapidly. New information clubs to reduce the cost of specialized information seem likely to emerge (Kanbur and Sandler, 1999).

New types of education programmes are becoming available using these new information technologies, and the market is expected to grow in the future. This includes long-distance access to formal degree programmes, such as a Harvard undergraduate degree by someone living in rural India, long-distance access to web-libraries, journals, books, bulletins and other published materials. The potential exists for the information to be used in informal learning, post-school and pre-school. It frequently has a flexibility dimension that enables self-pacing of effort and progress and picking the most relevant information. It has some disadvantages of low interpersonal interaction with teachers/instructors/professors and other students, but e-mail interactions are possible.

New institutions are needed that specialize in verifying information, including scientific discoveries and quality dimensions of commercially available goods and services. The necessary information is costly to create but is a public good once provided, so private incentives lead to major underprovision (Cornes and Sandler, 1996; Kanbur and Sandler, 1999). Problems with highly variable quality, unverifiable quality, customer service and general information problems can prevent large social gains from these new information technologies (Molho, 1997; World Bank, 1999).

Restructuring of agriculture

During the coming quarter-century, a major restructuring of agriculture in many countries and regions seems likely, building on new agricultural and communication technologies, innovations in organizational structures, greater openness to world trade in goods and services and transfers of technologies, including intellectual property, and integration of rural economies into the larger economy (Thompson, 1999). In general, there will be widespread economic pressures for successful farms to become larger, more specialized, but less labour-intensive. This will mean a decline in the share of the labour force in agriculture in most countries. A major public issue will become what to do with excess adult labour in agriculture or displaced labour from agriculture.

Public retraining programmes for unskilled and narrowly skilled displaced adult workers is one possibility, but much evidence now exists that public training programmes of this type have very low social rates of return in Western developed countries and sometimes yield negative rates of return (Heckman *et al.*, 1999). Training programmes for young people have a better record, and solid evidence exists that investing in social and cognitive skills of pre-school children has a good social pay-off. Early motivation for work is important, and it comes from a child's family and community and can be reinforced in older children by tying schooling and working together. In fact, the agricultural sector has provided many opportunities for young children to work with their parents or for others while they are growing up, but this opportunity for useful work at a younger age is lost in urban societies. Hence motivating the young for work is a greater social problem in urban than in agrarian societies, and this problem is expected to get worse. Furthermore, a move to year-round full-time schooling for children with no time for working, which has been proposed in some Western developed countries, would be the wrong direction for new schooling policy. The practice of teenagers and young adults working in the private sector in apprenticeship and internship programmes has been shown to be a good investment (Heckman, 1999).

Early experiences and learning before school age appear to be important to the development of an individual's long-term learning potential. Strong primary education provides much of the needed foundation for later learning that tends to be highly correlated with ability at age eight, and measured ability in children is well set by age 14. An early foundation for lifelong learning has large social pay-offs, and later investments are a poor substitute (Heckman, 1999). Lifelong learning has become the description of education for a large share of the world's population during the early 21st century and the main human tool for absorbing and productively using the rapidly growing knowledge base that is being made available globally at low cost through modern communication and information systems. This is the future route to useful knowledge gap reductions.

CONCLUSIONS

Countries face important decisions on how to allocate public resources. The choice and adaptation of institutional structures seem likely to be as important as decisions on schooling, health and technology policies. Weak and inefficient institutions lower the expected private return to all forms of non-political investments and increase the uncertainty about these returns. Hence weak institutions can undermine future economic growth and development.

Schooling cannot be viewed as unconditionally productive in agriculture. It requires a price and technology environment that is dynamic and the option for off-farm work and migration out of rural areas. In a modernizing economy, investments in schooling of children in rural areas will increase their long-term income or standard of living prospects. Some of them will, however, work in agriculture, some in non-agricultural employment and some at non-market activities. Where openness and economic incentives exist, schooling will facilitate migration to reduce regional and occupational compensation differentials, and young and more educated adults will be the most responsive to these incentives.

With the rapid advances in communication and information technologies that are occurring and increased availability at low cost, farm people of the future will need strong basic education in order to participate in this new global information system. We expect to see dramatic new options for learning from distant sources (for example, degree programmes, short causes), obtaining information about new technologies (new types of extension using web-sites and e-mail), rapid access to price information on agricultural outputs and inputs in widely dispersed markets, and contracting in new types of virtual markets. In the future, the new technologies seem likely to place new demands on the skills of farm people to use information and to speed structural change in agriculture globally. A new set of adjustments for farm families can be expected.

Public retraining programmes for unskilled and narrowly skilled displaced adult workers have a poor return in Western developed countries. Prospects are no better for low- and middle-income countries. Broadening and strengthening the training of young boys and girls seems a better social investment. Long-term positive effects exist from pre-school social and cognitive skill development. Motivating the young to work has generally not been a problem in farm families or low-income countries, but it has only recently been redis-covered that this has important pay-offs in non-agrarian societies. The rate of return will be very high to investments in primary schooling in low-income countries and, in other countries, strong primary schooling will be needed to provide the foundation for later formal and informal learning. With the ad-vances in communication and information systems and their dispersion globally, lifetime learning will become important to a large share of the population in the future.

It remains somewhat puzzling why schooling in agriculture does not have broader direct effects and is not unconditionally productive. One hypothesis is that the domination of agriculture by biological processes, which are control-led largely by climate and its land surface area-intensive nature, greatly limits the potential for raising labour productivity through skill specialization and cooperation. The big pay-off to agriculture from highly skilled labour comes from knowledge creation through institutionalized research and development.

REFERENCES

Ball, V.E., Bureau, J.-C., Nehring, R. and Somwaru, S. (1997), 'Agricultural productivity revis-ited', *American Journal of Agricultural Economics*, **79**, 1045–63.

Becker, G.S. (1993), *Human capital*, vol. 3, Chicago: University of Chicago Press.

Becker, G.S. and Murphy, K.M. (1993), 'The division of labour, coordination costs, and knowl-edge', in G.S. Becker (ed.), *Human capital*, vol. 3, Chicago: University of Chicago Press.

Cornes, R. and Sandler, T. (1996), *The theory of externalities, public goods and club goods*, New York: Cambridge University Press.

Emerson, R. (1989), 'Migratory labor and agriculture', *American Journal of Agricultural Eco-nomics*, **7**, 617–29.

Evenson, R.E. (1999), 'Economic impacts of agricultural research and extension', in B.L. Gardner and G.C. Rausser (eds), *Handbook of Agricultural Economics*, Amsterdam: Elsevier Science.

Gibbons, R. (1998), 'Incentives in organizations', *Journal of Economic Perspectives*, **12**, 115–32.

Griliches, Z. (1963), 'The source of measured productivity growth: United States agriculture, 1940–1960', *Journal of Political Economy*, **71**, 331–46.

Heckmann, J.J. (1999), 'Policies to foster human capital', Department of Economics, University of Chicago.

Heckman, J.J., La Londe, R.J. and Smith, J.A. (1999), 'The economics and econometrics of active labour market programs', in O. Ashenfelter and D. Card (eds), *Handbook of Labour Economics, Vol. III*, Amsterdam: Elsevier Science.

Huffman, W.E. (1985), 'Human capital, adaptive ability, and the distributional implications of agricultural policy', *American Journal of Agricultural Economics*, **67**, 429–34.

Huffman, W.E. (1991), 'Human capital for future economic growth', in Glenn L. Johnson and J.T. Bonnen (eds), *Social Science Agricultural Agendas and Strategies. Part III*, East Lansing: Michigan State University Press.

Huffman, W.E. (1996), 'Labour markets, human capital, and the human agent's share of produc-tion', in J.M. Antle and D.A. Sumner (eds), *The Economics of Agriculture, Vol. 2 (Papers in honor of D. Gale Johnson)*, Chicago: University of Chicago Press.

Huffman, W.E. (1998), 'Modernizing agriculture: a continuing process', *Daedalus*, **127**, 159–86.

Huffman, W.E. (1999), 'Human capital: education and agriculture', in B.L. Gardner and G.C. Rausser (eds), *Handbook of Agricultural Economics*, Amsterdam: Elsevier Science.

Huffman, W.E. and Evenson, R. (1993), *Science for Agriculture*, Ames: Iowa State Press.

Huffman, W.E. and Just, R.E. (1999), 'The organization of agricultural research in western developed countries', *Agricultural Economics*, **21**, 1–18.

Hussain, S.S. and Byerlee, D. (1995), 'Education and farm productivity in post- "green revolution" agriculture in Asia', invited paper, XXII International Conference of Agricultural Economists, Harare, Zimbabwe, in G.H. Peters and D.D. Hedley (eds), *Agricultural Competitiveness: Market Forces and Policy Choice*, Aldershot: Dartmouth.

Johnson, D. Gale (2000), 'Population, food, and knowledge', *American Economic Review*, **90**, 1–14.

Jones, C.I. (1998), *Introduction to economic growth*, New York: W.W. Norton & Co.

Kanbur, R. and Sandler, T. (1999), *The future of development assistance: common pools and international public goods*, Policy Essay No. 25, Overseas Development Council, Baltimore, MD: Johns Hopkins University Press.

Molho, I. (1997), *The economics of information*, Malden, MA: Blackwell.

OECD (1994), *Farm employment and economic adjustment in the OECD*, Paris: OECD.

OECD (1995), *Technological change and structural change in OECD agriculture*, Paris: OECD.

Psacharopoulos, G. (1994), 'Returns to investments in education: a global update', *World Development*, **22**, 1325–43.

Romer, P. (1990), 'Endogenous technological change', *Journal of Political Economy*, **98**, S71–S102.

Schultz, T.P. (1993), 'Returns to women's education', in E.M. King and M.A. Hill (eds), *Women's education in developing countries*, Baltimore, MD: Johns Hopkins University Press.

Schultz, T.P. (1997), 'Demand for children in low income countries', in M.R. Rosenzweig and O. Stark (eds), *Handbook of population and family economics*, Vol. 1B, New York: Elsevier Science.

Schultz, T.P. (1999), 'Productive benefits of improving health: evidence from low-income countries', Economic Growth Center, Yale University.

Schultz, T.W. (1964), *Transforming traditional agriculture*, New Haven: Yale University Press (reprint edition, New York: Arno Press, 1976).

Schultz, T.W. (1975), 'The value of the ability to deal with disequilibria', *Journal of Economic Literature*, **13**, 827–46.

Singh, I., Squire, L. and Strauss, J. (eds) (1986), *Agricultural household models*, Baltimore, MD: Johns Hopkins University Press.

Thompson, R.L. (1999), 'Technology, policy and trade: the keys to food security and environmental protection', in G.H. Peters and J. von Braun (eds), *Food security, diversification and resource management: refocusing the role of agriculture?* Aldershot: Ashgate.

Welch, F. (1970), 'Education in production', *Journal of Political Economy*, **78**, 35–59.

Williamson, O. (1985), *The economic institution of capitalism*, New York: The Free Press.

World Bank (1999), *Knowledge for development. World Development Report 1998/1999*, New York: Oxford University Press.

World Bank (2000), *Entering the 21st century. World Development Report 1999/2000*, New York: Oxford University Press.

Wozniak, G. (1993), 'Joint information acquisition and new technology adoption: later versus early adoption', *Review of Economics and Statistics*, **75**, 438–45.

JULIAN M. ALSTON AND PHILIP G. PARDEY*

Reassessing Research Returns: Attribution and Related Problems

INTRODUCTION

It appears to be widely believed that, in general, public sector agricultural R&D has paid handsome dividends for society as a whole, but even those who hold that view may be sceptical about some of the very high reported estimates of rates of return to research.[1] An interest in the outcome might lead to biased estimates in some cases since rate-of-return estimates are often intended to be used to justify past investments and shore up support for future investments. Both implausibly high and unfavourable results are less likely to be acceptable for this purpose. Rates of return are also likely to involve errors even when the analyst is disinterested because it is inherently difficult to identify which research investment was responsible for a particular productivity improvement (or, conversely, which parts of the productivity benefits are attributable to a particular research investment).

Consider an ex post analysis of the contribution of agricultural R&D by the California Agricultural Experiment Station (CAES) to current productivity in California. For such an analysis we want to be able meaningfully to measure productivity growth and then attribute it among those investments by the CAES, other public R&D investments by the California state government and by other states and the United States Department of Agriculture (USDA), international R&D and private R&D investments. Moreover, we have to attribute the productivity growth not just between the CAES research and the other elements at a point in time, but among these elements over time, including the distant as well as the recent past. We want to be able to say which research, conducted (or paid for) by whom, and, in particular, when, was responsible for a particular productivity improvement. This *attribution* problem is difficult; it relates to the *appropriability* problem that underpins the in-principle argument for government involvement in research. Spillover effects of research, where research conducted by one firm (or state or country) yields benefits for free-riders, account for private sector underinvestment and the possibility of high social

*Julian Alston, Department of Agricultural and Resource Economics, University of California at Davis, and a member of the Giannini Foundation of Agricultural Economics. Philip Pardey, International Food Policy Research Institute, Washington, DC, USA and Department of Applied Economics at the University of Minnesota. The authors thank Connie Chan-Kang, for valuable research assistance, and Ruben Echeverría, Will Masters and Michel Petit, for comments on an earlier version of the work.

rates of return. If it were easy to attribute benefits to particular investments, it should be possible to devise institutions to make the benefits appropriable. Thus the characteristics of research that gives rise to the potential for high rates of return also give rise to measurement problems.

In this paper we reassess the evidence on rates of return to research with an emphasis on the nature of the attribution problem and the likely implications of conventional evaluation methods. We suggest that the effects of attribution problems have not been neutral; on the whole, the rate-of-return estimates are likely to have been biased upwards.

OVERVIEW OF THE LITERATURE

Alston, Marra *et al.* (2000) and Alston, Chan-Kang *et al.* (2000) provide a comprehensive compilation, synthesis and quantitative meta-analysis of rate-of-return estimates that reveals interesting and useful patterns. A total of 292 benefit–cost studies of agricultural R&D (including extension) were compiled and these studies provide 1886 separate estimates of rates of return.[2] The estimates of rates of return to agricultural R&D range from small negative numbers to more than 700 000 per cent per annum. This large range reflects variation *within* groups (such as applied versus basic research, or research on natural resources versus commodities) more than *among* groups, and such large within-group variation makes it difficult to discern differences among groups. The estimated annual rates of return averaged 99.6 per cent for research only, 47.6 per cent for research and extension combined, and 84.6 per cent for extension only (Figure 1). Moreover, the distributions are generally positively skewed, with a significant number of exceptionally high rates of return.

Table 1 shows the ranges of rates of return and the mean, standard deviation, mode and median rates of return according to the nature and commodity orientation of the research and the geographic location of the research performer. The preponderance of studies reported the returns to *all research* (mainly returns to aggregate investments in agricultural R&D), while just over half the observations pertained to *field crops* research and research performed in *developed countries*.

The estimates in Figure 1 and Table 1 predominantly refer to real (that is inflation-adjusted), marginal (that is, for incremental research expenditures), ex post (that is, for past investments), internal rates of return (IRRs). The implication when reporting an IRR is that the benefits from the research are being evaluated as though they can be reinvested, along with the original investment, at the same rate of return. Since the benefits are often accruing to farmers and consumers who typically do not have opportunities to invest at such high rates, it is worth dwelling briefly on what is implied by very high IRRs. A rate of return of 700 000 per cent is obviously implausible but more clearly so when we conduct a simple calculation; investing $1 at an internal rate of return of 700 000 per cent per annum would generate $7000 after one year, $49 million after two years, $343 billion after three years and

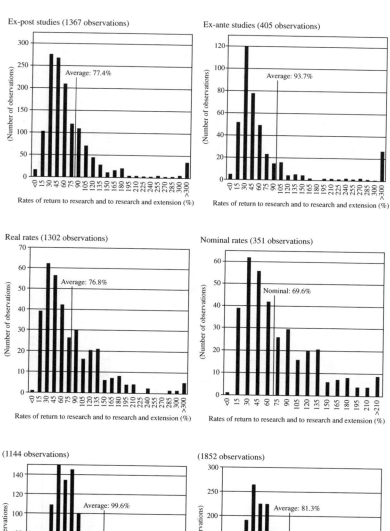

Ex-post studies (1367 observations)

Average: 77.4%

Rates of return to research and to research and extension (%)

Ex-ante studies (405 observations)

Average: 93.7%

Rates of return to research and to research and extension (%)

Real rates (1302 observations)

Average: 76.8%

Rates of return to research and to research and extension (%)

Nominal rates (351 observations)

Nominal: 69.6%

Rates of return to research and to research and extension (%)

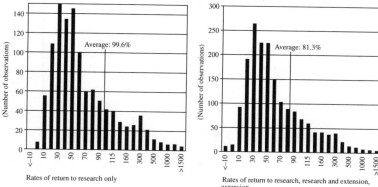

(1144 observations)

Average: 99.6%

Rates of return to research only

(1852 observations)

Average: 81.3%

Rates of return to research, research and extension, extension

Source: Alston *et al.* (2000).

FIGURE 1   *Histogram of rates of return*

TABLE 1 *Rates of return*

	Number of estimates (count)	Rates of return (per cent per year)						
		Mean	Standard deviation	Mode	Median	Minimum	Maximum
Nature of research							
Basic	30	79.2	88.7	75	61.3	−1.3	457
Applied	192	163.5	557.0	38	46.0	6.0	5 645
All research	904	88.4	148.6	46	49.0	−7.4	1 720
Research & extension	643	46.8	43.4	28	36.0	−100.0	430
Commodity orientation							
Multi-commodity	436	80.3	110.7	58	47.1	−1.0	1 219
Field crops	916	74.3	139.4	40	43.6	−100.0	1 720
Livestock	233	120.7	481.1	14	53	2.5	5 645
Tree crops	108	87.6	216.4	20	33.3	1.4	1 736
Natural resources	78	37.6	65.0	7	16.5	0.0	457
Geographic location							
Developed countries	990	98.2	278.1	19	46	−14.9	5 645
Developing countries	683	60.1	84.1	46	43	−100.0	1 490
Multiregional	74	58.8	98.3	32	34	−47.5	677
IARC	62	77.8	188.6	26	40	9.9	1 490
All studies	1 772	81.2	216.1	46	44	−100.0	5 645

Note: Sample excludes two extreme outliers and includes only returns to research and combined research and extension, so that the overall sample size is 1772.

Source: Adapted from Alston, Chan-Kang *et al.* (2000, Tables 15 and 17).

$2401 trillion the following year; that is, much more than the GDP of the world ($26.2 trillion in 1997). Using a similar approach, we can also review the implications of a more typical estimate. If the investment of $1.21 billion in 1980 in US public agricultural R&D had earned an internal rate of return of 48 per cent per annum, the mean for the US studies of agriculture in aggregate, the accumulated stream of benefits would be worth $3 trillion (1980 dollars) by the year 2000, 4.5 months' worth of US total GDP, and more than 20 years' worth of US agricultural GDP. This is the implied benefit from the investment in 1980 alone. Such calculations might give rise to some doubts about whether the estimates rates of return really represent *internal* rates of return, or for that matter the true returns to research.[3]

MEASUREMENT ISSUES AND PROBLEMS

Problems with data or measurement or misconceptions can result in an estimated rate of return that is higher or lower than the true value. One important problem is defining the relevant counterfactual alternative. In particular, to define what the world might be like in the absence of the particular research investment being evaluated, we have to take account of other things that might also be caused to change. Holding the right things constant is necessary to derive a stream of benefits that properly matches the stream of expenditures being evaluated.

Alston and Pardey (1996, ch. 6) suggested that the estimated rates of return to R&D in the literature have tended to be overoptimistic, relative to the corresponding true values, because the commonly used procedures understate the costs, overstate the benefits and often predetermine the research lag structure (that relates changes in productivity to past investments in research) in ways that lead to higher estimated rates of return. While some other common practices might lead to understatement of benefits, so that a particular estimated rate of return may be too high or too low, on balance we suspect that the tendency to overestimate has predominated.[4]

Productivity measurement

The ex post evaluation of public agricultural R&D investments often begins with a consideration of agricultural productivity. At a minimum, we want to avoid measurement problems associated with inappropriate aggregation or indexing procedures. Index number problems can account for some errors in measurement of productivity growth attributable to research, and aggregate productivity measures can be statistically sensitive to aggregation procedures (for example, Acquaye *et al.*, 2000).

As pointed out by Schultz (1956), growth in the use of conventional inputs does not account for much of the growth in agricultural output. A part of the attribution problem is to remove the effects of various other (non-research) factors before attempting to attribute residual productivity growth to particular research investments. Understanding the sources of the growth not attributable to conventional inputs is the first step to measuring the benefits from public R&D investments. Other factors, beyond conventional inputs, include such things as changes in input quality, output quality, improvements in infrastructure, economies of size and scale, and improvements in technology.[5]

Schultz (1956) and Griliches (1963) demonstrated the important role of changes in input quality in accounting for measured productivity growth in agriculture. Yet many subsequent studies of returns to public sector R&D have measured aggregate input quantities using index numbers that were not adjusted appropriately to account for changes in input quality. Such analysis overstates the productivity growth attributable to the public sector R&D by giving it credit for effects attributable either to schooling (from private or public investments in education unrelated to R&D) or to private R&D (in the case of embodied technological change).[6]

Craig and Pardey (1996, 2001) and Acquaye *et al.* (2000) among others have shown that correcting for changes in input quality can have major implications for understanding changes in input use and productivity in US agriculture. Adjusting for input quality change is likely to lead to a lower estimated rate of return to public sector R&D and a better appreciation of the different roles played by private and public sector R&D (in agriculture and elsewhere) and education.[7] Less is known about the quantitative effects of accounting for research-induced changes in output quality.

Acquaye *et al.* (2000) compared the estimates of US state-specific and national productivity growth for the 1960–90 period, as reported by Ball *et al.* (1999), and corresponding estimates based on their own calculations. In Figure 2, the annual rates of growth in these alternative indexes are plotted against

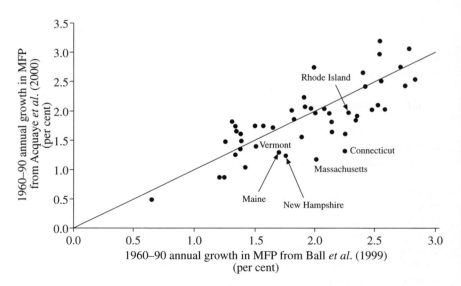

FIGURE 2   *Growth in productivity, 1960–90, Ball* et al *v.* Acquaye *et al.*

each other, state by state. The national average annual growth rates are essentially indistinguishable (1.99 versus 2.00). The state-specific annual growth rates differ quite substantially in some cases, with positive or negative differences of up to 40 per cent of the estimates from Ball *et al.*, and little in the way of systematic patterns, apart from the Northeast region, where the Ball *et al.* estimates were generally substantially greater than those of Acquaye *et al.* Comparing the state-by-state estimates, by subtracting the latter estimate from that of Ball *et al.* (1999), the mean difference was small (0.07 per cent per annum) but some of the differences were quite large (the standard deviation of the differences was 0.37 per cent per annum). The simple correlation between the estimates was 0.78.

Possible explanations for these differences include differences in the raw data, and differences in the inputs and outputs included in the definition of agriculture, as well as differences in the treatments of the data. Preliminary analysis points to the importance of differences in the approaches taken to measure capital, and in the resulting measures of the stock of capital and service flows from it, and differences in the quantity indexes of land and labour arising from different quality adjustments, even though the two studies both adjusted their series for input quality changes. The point of this comparison was not to find fault with the estimates: both sets may be valid, but for different purposes. The key point is that two careful studies produced very different measures of productivity patterns, and they would imply contrasting estimates of benefits attributable to public research rather than, say, schooling reflected in labour quality, or investment in improvements reflected in land quality.

Matching benefits and costs: attribution among groups

Multi-factor productivity is the measurable stream of output not accounted for by measured inputs. We can translate the productivity measures into measures of streams of research benefits using conventional procedures. The attribution of these benefits to particular inputs can be thought of as a two-step process. Having accounted for the contribution of factors other than R&D in the first step, a second step involves discerning the share of these residual benefits most appropriately attributed to research by a particular individual, programme, state, nation or other aggregate. This attribution problem can be thought of in terms of matching streams of research benefits to corresponding streams of costs.

Understated costs   Understatement of public sector research costs arises in a number of ways. As pointed out by Fox (1985), a common source of understatement is not allowing for the full social cost of using government revenues for R&D. General taxation involves a social cost of more than one dollar per dollar raised, an excess burden (see Findlay and Jones, 1982; Fullerton, 1991; Ballard and Fullerton, 1992). Most studies have not adjusted for the effects of the excess burden of taxation on the measures of costs, an omission that will lead to a systematic understatement of the social costs and an overstatement of the social rate of return.

Occasionally, studies of particular programmes of research fail to attribute an appropriate portion of R&D overhead (including the costs of associated basic research and institutional overheads) to the particular projects being evaluated, or they omit components of the effort involved in the development and extension phases of a project. It is not easy to estimate costs attributable to total research (let alone research on a particular set of issues), but there seems to be a tendency to understate costs of individual research programmes, and research overall, through the tendency to omit or underestimate overhead costs.

Agricultural research consists of a continuum of activities, from basic science through to field extension work, that interact with and complement one another. To measure properly the contribution of one element of the whole, it is important to control for the effects of all of the others. Many previous studies have failed to take proper account of other elements and, as a result, they have tended to overestimate the gains in productivity attributable to a particular element of total expenditures on R&D. Equivalently, many studies have underestimated the total expenditure (that includes foreign and domestic, private and public, and basic and applied work and extension) required to achieve a particular productivity gain.

Overstated benefits   Overstatement of benefits sometimes arises from not counting the effects of private-sector R&D or spillovers of technology from other places (states, countries or competing institutions) and, instead, attributing all of the gains in productivity to only a part of the total relevant R&D spending.[8] Private sector research is often omitted from the analysis, or its effects are considered but not properly taken into account. This is a problem in econometric studies, in particular, where the omission of relevant explanatory variables can lead to biased estimates of the effects of variables included in the analysis.[9] The same may also be true of synthetic (benefit–cost) approaches, where productivity gains are deduced or assumed rather than statistically estimated, depending upon how the growth in productivity attributable to public sector R&D is estimated. Similar concerns arise in relation to the treatment of extension, private or public sector research conducted elsewhere (for example, overseas or in sectors other than agriculture) that spills into agriculture, basic (or pre-technology) research that may underpin the applied research whose effects are being assessed, and development work that was necessary to allow the commercial adoption of the results.

R&D spillovers appear pervasive and confound the attribution of research benefits. Using firm-level data from the chemical industry, Mansfield (1977) reported that the returns to innovators (private rates of return) were significantly smaller than 'social' rates of return. More recently, Jaffe (1986) developed a patent-based metric of R&D 'spillover pools' to investigate firm-to-firm spillover effects. He found indirect but convincing econometric evidence of the existence of R&D spillovers, demonstrating that, on average, firms had higher returns to their own R&D (in terms of accounting profits or market value) if that research was conducted in areas where other firms do much research. Analogous firm-to-firm spillover effects are no doubt a feature of privately performed agricultural R&D.

Agricultural economists also have been giving attention to economies of size, scale and scope in agricultural R&D, and the related questions of spatial spillovers of public agricultural research benefits (and costs), especially in recent years (for example, see Johnson and Evenson, 1999; Byerlee and Traxler, 2001). Efforts to measure spatial spillovers of agricultural research results to date have tended to apply arbitrary assumptions based on geopolitical boundaries and geographic proximity rather than agroecological similarity (for example, Huffman and Evenson, 1993).[10] In our own work, still in progress, in which we have used measures of agroecological similarity to parameterize technological spillover potential, we have found very substantial spillover effects among US states. An implication is that the typical studies that do not allow for interstate or international spillovers, or that capture them crudely using arbitrary assumptions, will tend to overstate the own-state research responsibility for state-level productivity growth, and understate the benefits from technological spilling from other states or elsewhere. A tendency to overstate own-state responsibility for productivity growth means that state-specific rates of return to research will tend to be overstated.

Ambiguous effects   Some other choices in an analysis may have important implications for the estimated rate of return, but often we cannot generalize about the size and direction of the bias. For instance, most studies have not attempted to correct for the commodity programmes or other distortions, an omission which Alston *et al.* (1988) showed might lead to over- or understatement of the benefits and the rate of return.[11] Similarly, selection bias can be a problem – projects may have been selected for analysis because they are known to be winners, without regard for the higher proportion of unsuccessful projects, which could be regarded as contributing to an overhead cost to be borne by the successful projects. On the other hand, this should not be a problem with studies based on analyses of aggregate data, and more aggregative studies do report lower rates of return (Alston, Chan-Kang *et al.*, 2000; Alston, Marra *et al.*, 2000).

Research and adoption lags: attribution over time

Investing in research is like investing in physical capital in some respects: current productivity depends on the flow from the *stock* of usable knowledge, derived from the history of past investments, not simply the current rate of investment. Hence investment decisions taken in one period have consequences that last into the future. Indeed, the lags and dynamics in agricultural R&D are, perhaps, of greater duration and importance than those for most other types of capital investments. There are lags of several years, typically, between when an expenditure is made on research and when the resulting innovation or increment to knowledge begins to be adopted and to affect production and productivity.

The effects of a particular investment today can persist over many future production periods, perhaps forever. The effects of other R&D investments may be short-lived or non-existent. Estimating the parameters that characterize this overall dynamic research–development–adoption–'disadoption' process is the most challenging empirical problem in evaluating R&D. In the evaluation of individual process innovations (for example, Griliches, 1957; Schmitz and Seckler, 1970) it is sometimes possible to obtain good information on the timing of events. More often, however, and inevitably in the case of aggregative analysis across programmes and commodities, the information is not directly accessible and must be either estimated as a part of the analysis, or imposed on it.

Even the more data-rich studies of aggregate national research systems typically use only 40 or 50 years of annual observations on research (and, perhaps, extension) expenditures to attempt to explain 20 or 30 years of variation in production or productivity. Such data are not sufficient to estimate the research lag profile accurately. Indeed, to obtain estimates at all, it has been found necessary to impose a lot of structure on the lag relationship – including presumptions about its length, smoothness and general shape – and these generally untested (or inadequately tested) restrictions have affected the answers obtained. These presumptions may have been devised arbitrarily, with a view to convenience of estimation as much as anything, rather than empirically. For example, studies have typically imposed a finite lag structure linking R&D spending to changes in productivity over less than 20 years. But some types of research have effects that persist indefinitely (for example, we still use electricity), while others have effects that are finite, as the innovation loses effect (for example, pest resistance is eroded) or is replaced by other innovations and becomes obsolete (for example, new and better agricultural chemicals or plant varieties supersede the old); some are very short-lived (for example, specific computer chips). Hence a flexible, infinite lag with some allowance for research obsolescence may be appropriate for econometric work, especially work that aims to estimate the returns to aggregate R&D.

In principle, given sufficient data, a flexible infinite lag model could be implemented using modern time-series econometric approaches. In practice, given data (and other) constraints, the infinite lag structure might be better approximated by the use of a longer finite lag structure than most studies have used (although the potential for bias might still arise). The few studies that have attempted to estimate econometrically lag lengths for aggregate agricultural R&D in the United States and the United Kingdom have found that lag lengths of *at least* 30 years may be necessary (for example, Pardey and Craig, 1989; Chavas and Cox, 1992; Huffman and Evenson, 1992, 1993; Schimmelpfennig and Thirtle, 1994; Alston *et al.* 1998). This suggests that the typical study has used a truncated lag structure that is too short.

In a synthetic study, where the research-induced shifts are given, the truncation of the lag amounts to leaving out benefits, which would, holding other things constant, bias the rate of return downwards. In an econometric study, however, truncation of the lag amounts to omitting relevant explanatory variables, which will lead to biased parameter estimates, with too much econometric weight (yielding larger values for the parameters) on the more recent lags. By itself, the omission of long lags here, as with the synthetic approach, amounts to understating total benefits, but, unlike the synthetic studies, the present value of the benefits associated with the shorter lags is now greater. In a discounting context, given the typically high rates of return, the latter effect is likely to dominate (since the benefits associated with the long-past research expenditures are heavily discounted), so that truncation of the lag has biased rates of return upwards. This view is supported by the meta-analysis of Alston, Chan-Kang *et al.* (2000) and Alston, Marra *et al.* (2000), and by the econometric analysis of Alston *et al.* (1998).

ILLUSTRATIVE EXAMPLES OF ATTRIBUTION PROBLEMS

To illustrate the nature and importance of the attribution problems underlying estimates of rates of return to research, two examples are used. First, there is an assessment of the US benefits from wheat variety improvement R&D conducted by the Consultative Group on International Agricultural Research (CGIAR). Second, evidence on the effects of different treatments of the research lag structure on the evaluation of rates of return to agricultural R&D is considered.

Attribution among investors: US benefits from the CGIAR

Pardey *et al.* (1996) investigated the impacts in the USA of varietal improvement research performed at the international agricultural research centres funded by the CGIAR. This investigation focused on two cases: the wheat-breeding work carried out at the International Wheat and Maize Improvement Centre (CIMMYT) in Mexico (and its antecedent agencies) and the rice-breeding programme of the International Rice Research Institute (IRRI) in the Philippines. Both of these programmes are very well known: they have been at the centre of efforts to develop the high-yielding grain varieties whose use in developing countries has contributed to large increases in worldwide food supplies – increases commonly referred to as the 'Green Revolution'.

The contributions of these new varieties to farm technology in the USA have been important secondary outcomes of the CGIAR varietal improvement efforts. The objective of the work by Pardey *et al.* (1996) was to evaluate these contributions and compare the US benefits with the US contributions to the CIMMYT and IRRI wheat- and rice-breeding programmes. A review of that study illustrates the point that substantial attribution problems can arise even when the details of the technology and the timing of events are well documented and understood.

Consider the case of wheat. New varieties have been introduced into the USA at an increasing rate during the past few decades, and have made a substantial contribution to the maintenance and growth of per acre yields. Between 1900 and 1970, an average of five varieties were released in the USA every year; since 1970, over 21 wheat varieties per year have appeared. Even in the absence of increases in biological potential, there is a continuing demand for new varieties, so that host plant resistance can evolve to respond to the evolution of plant diseases and pests.

Pardey *et al.* (1996) obtained detailed data on experimental yields of the many wheat varieties at multiple locations in each of the different wheat-growing states. Comparison of experimental plot yields of new varieties with those in production in 1970 indicates that, in the absence of the new varieties, overall wheat yields would have been 33 per cent lower in 1993. The authors estimated that, over 1970–93, gains in yield generated economic benefits with a present value in 1993 of about $43 billion (1993 dollars); that is, approximately one-ninth of the total value of wheat production over the period is attributed to increases in yields resulting from the introduction of new varieties. These are the *gross* benefits to producers and consumers as a result of the US *adoption* of the new varieties. One important aspect of the attribution problem here involves determining who deserves the credit for these gains. In particular, what is the fraction of the total benefit that can be attributed to the work done at CIMMYT?

Pardey *et al.* (1996) had complete information on the genetic (and breeding) history of each important variety grown in the USA, for each wheat-growing state, along with an extensive data set on experimental yields by variety for multiple experimental sites (within states). Unfortunately, even such uncommonly detailed information is not enough to solve the attribution problem; genotype does not translate simply into yield gains or other phenotypic characteristics such as seed size and colour as well as protein and fibre content that translate into tangible economic value. How much of the credit for the improvement in US wheat yields associated with semi-dwarfing should go to Norman Borlaug (who led the effort at CIMMYT, and earlier at the Rockefeller Foundation-sponsored research programme in Mexico that began in 1943) compared with the breeders at Washington State University (who previously made the first US cross with the *Norin 10* variety from Japan)? How much credit for the excellence of today's variety should go to the breeder who bred it, compared with the breeders and farmers who bred or selected its parents, grandparents, and so on? It is not easy to identify the separate marginal product of any particular breeder in the chain. Consequently, economists studying this type of issue have ended up using mechanistic rules to apportion the total benefits across steps in the history of development of a new variety.

Pardey *et al.* (1996) examined the effects of using a variety of subjective rules to accommodate differing perceptions of the relative importance of earlier and later breeding steps, to compute and attribute the benefits from wheat breeding. In general, they found that the US benefits from the CIMMYT wheat-breeding programme were very large. Even using their most conservative attribution rule (giving the greatest credit to the more recent, US-based innovations, and the least credit to the earlier CIMMYT-based innovations), the additional wheat produced in the USA as a consequence of the CIMMYT programme was worth $3.6 billion dollars from 1970 to 1993. US government support of the wheat-breeding programme at CIMMYT since 1960 was about $68 million (in present value terms as of the end of 1993). Counting only the benefits from the yield gains in the USA, the benefit–cost ratio of US support was greater than 49 to 1. This is the most conservative estimate. Using alternative attribution rules, the benefit–cost ratio could have been as high as 199 to 1.

Recall that this is the benefit from US *adoption* of varieties containing CIMMYT-derived germ plasm, which is a gross rather than net measure of the benefits to the USA from CIMMYT's wheat variety improvement programme. It does not account for the costs to the USA as a net exporter, which arise when the rest of the world adopts new CIMMYT-based wheat varieties and this leads to a reduction in the demand and price for US wheat. To evaluate this effect is a much larger undertaking; it involves measuring the effect of CIMMYT's wheat-breeding programme on the entire world. This is yet another form of attribution problem, one which generally has not been recognized in previous studies of the country-specific benefits from international agricultural research (one exception is Brennan and Bantilan, 1999).

Attribution over time: specifying and estimating lag relationships

In empirical work on models of effects of research on aggregate agricultural productivity, the number of lags and the shape of the lag structure are usually chosen arbitrarily; rarely is either the lag length or the lag form tested formally. Common types of lag structures include the de Leeuw or inverted-V (for example, Evenson, 1967), polynomial (for example, Davis, 1980; Leiby and Adams, 1991; Thirtle and Bottomley, 1988) and trapezoidal (for example, Huffman and Evenson, 1989, 1992, 1993; Evenson 1996). A small number of studies have used free-form lags (for example, Ravenscraft and Scherer, 1982; Pardey and Craig, 1989; Chavas and Cox, 1992), but most have restricted the lag distribution to be represented by a small number of parameters, because the time span of the data set is usually not much longer than the assumed maximum lag length.

Until quite recently, it was common to restrict the lag length to less than 20 years. In the first studies, available time series were short and lag lengths were very short. The more recent studies have tended to use more flexible, and longer, lags. Pardey and Craig (1989) used a free-form lag structure to model the relationship between agricultural productivity and public sector agricultural research, and found 'strong evidence that the impact of research expenditures on agricultural output may persist for as long as thirty years' (p.9) and that 'long lags – at least thirty years – may be necessary to capture all of the impact of research on agricultural output' (p.18). Using a non-parametric approach, Chavas and Cox (1992, p.590) confirmed Pardey and Craig's result, finding that 'at least 30 years of lags are necessary to capture the effects of public research'. Several subsequent studies have followed this advice. However, none of these studies, including Pardey and Craig (1989) and Chavas and Cox (1992), tested how much longer than 30 years or so the lag should be. In contrast, Alston *et al.* (1998) argued for representing an infinite lag between research investments and productivity with a finite lag between research investments and *changes in* the stock of knowledge.[12]

Alston *et al.* (1998) laid out a model in which current aggregate production depends on the utilization of a stock of useful knowledge, which is itself a function of the entire history of relevant investments in R&D – potentially an infinite lag between past investments in research and the effects on production.

They noted that the stereotypical study of returns to agricultural research has used a comparatively short, finite, lag structure (typically with fewer than 30 years and often fewer than 15 years of past research investments used to explain current productivity). A short, finite lag may reasonably represent the link between investments in research and increments to the stock of useful knowledge, but it would be a significant conceptual error to use the same lag to represent the relation between investments in research and production, since production depends on flows from the entire stock of useful knowledge, not just the latest increment to it. Moreover, an inappropriate truncation of the research lag would be likely to lead to an upward bias in the estimated rate of return to research, since truncating the lags amounts to introducing an omitted-variables problem, which will bias upwards the coefficients on the remaining, shorter lags (as argued by Alston and Pardey, 1996).

Table 2 summarizes the results from past econometric studies of returns to agricultural research across countries, classified according to the length and form of the research lag, and it can be seen that the results are consistent with expectations. Most studies have used short lags (and other restrictions on the form of the lag) and shorter lags tend to coincide with larger estimated rates of return.

To illustrate their ideas and implement the arguments, Alston *et al.* (1998) assumed a linear model of agricultural productivity of the form:

$$MFP_t = \alpha + \beta K_t + \gamma Z_t + u_t$$

where MFP_t is multi-factor productivity in year t, K_t is the knowledge stock in year t, Z_t is a weather-related variable in year t, and u_t is a random residual in year t. They assumed the knowledge stock grows according to:

$$K_t = (1-\delta)K_{t-1} + I_t$$

where δ is a proportional (declining balance) knowledge depreciation rate and I_t is the increment to knowledge as a result of (recent) research. Taking innovations to be given by a finite lag (of length L_R) of past logarithms of research investments (R_{t-s}) they defined:

$$I_t = \sum_{s=0}^{L_R} b_s \ln R_{t-s}$$

Combining these elements, they obtained an empirically useful model,

$$MFP_t = \alpha\delta + \beta\sum_{s=0}^{L_R} b_s \ln R_{t-s} + \gamma(Z_t - (1-\delta)Z_{t-1}) + (1-\delta)MFP_{t-1} + v_t$$

This model nests the primary alternatives in the literature: (a) the stock of useful knowledge never depreciates ($\delta=0$), (b) the stock of useful knowledge vanishes in finite time ($\delta=1$), which is implied by the archetypal model which uses a finite lag between research investments and production, and (c)

TABLE 2 *Lag structure and estimated rates of return to research from econometric models*

Lag structure	Mean lag (years)	Number of estimates (count)	Rate of return (per cent per year)				
			Mean	Mode	Median	Minimum	Maximum
Form							
Polynomial	13.2	285	79.9	58	58	4.5	729.7
Trapezoidal	32.7	55	97.7	95	67	11.0	384.4
Free form	28.0[a]	6	26.5	6	30	6.0	45.0
Inverted 'V'	12.0	33	134.5	30	72	23.0	562.0
Other	13.3[a]	304	75.6	46	48	−1.0	1 219.0
No structure	26.6	79	45.8	54	51	0.3	185.0
No lag	0	36	48.0	46	44.4	20.9	111.0
All forms	16.3[a]	762	77.9	58	53	−1.0	1 219.0
Length							
0	0	36	48.0	46	44.4	20.9	111.0
>0 and <15	9.9	408	95.2	58	60.7	0.0	1 219.0
15 to 30	22.3	174	58.1	46	49.9	4.5	260.0
>30	38.0[a]	144	60.1	40	41.6	−1.0	384.4
Unspecified		100	60	27	41.2	8.9	337.0

Notes: The figures in this table encompass studies reporting econometrically estimated rates of return to research only, and to research & extension reported in Alston, Chan-Kang *et al.* (2000; Table 16).

[a] represents the mean length of the R&D lags for rate of return estimates based on finite lag structures. One of the 6 *free form* estimates is based on an infinite lag structure, as are 43 of the 304 *other* estimates, 44 of the 762 *all forms* estimates and 44 of the 144 >*30 years* estimates.

an intermediate case in which knowledge decays, but only gradually (that is, $0 < \delta < 1$). This structure can be used to evaluate the typical assumptions about the shape of the research lag, as well as the implicit assumptions about knowledge depreciation associated with explicit assumptions about the research lag length.

Alston *et al.* (1998) applied this type of model to data on US aggregate agricultural productivity for the period 1949–91, making use of annual data on total agricultural R&D (including extension) expenditures by the federal government and 48 state governments, for the period 1890–91. The agricultural input data were adjusted for quality change over time, which will account for certain types of private R&D expenditures and human capital improvements, and so on, but there may still be an omitted-variables bias from the exclusion of private R&D and spillover effects. The details of the data, estimation procedures and so on, can be found in Alston *et al.* (1998).

The primary conclusion was to reinforce the view that agricultural research affects productivity much longer than most previous studies have allowed, possibly forever. A model consistent with infinite lags was statistically preferred over a more conventional model with finite lags. The results also suggest that many previous studies may have unduly restricted the shape of the research lag profile – often basing the entire distribution of lag coefficients on a single estimated parameter. The implications for reported rates of return were quite dramatic. The statistically preferred model indicated a much lower real, marginal internal rate of return to public agricultural research in the USA than was implied by a more typical model, using a trapezoidal lag structure with shorter lags.

CONCLUSION

Studies of returns to agricultural research have yielded results suggesting that the investment has been enormously socially profitable. Many of the estimates are likely to have been biased upwards, however, as a result of attribution problems. The challenge is to determine what productivity growth would have been in the absence of a particular research investment. The typical approaches understate the period over which research affects productivity and, in econometric studies using time-series data, this means they overstate the shorter-term impacts, leading to overstated rates of return. Typical approaches also fail to take into account the effects of work done by others in the research–development–extension continuum, and this gives too much credit to the particular investor being evaluated. Corresponding work remains to be done to establish the empirical importance of incomplete correction for locational spillovers of research results in biasing estimated returns of return to research.

NOTES

[1]Contrary views are the exception (for example, Pasour and Johnson, 1982; Kealey, 1996).

[2]Partial periodic tabulations and narrative reviews can be found in Evenson *et al.* (1979), Echeverría (1990), Alston and Pardey (1996) and Fuglie *et al.* (1996).

[3]Of course, even though there is a unique true rate of return to any particular set of past investments, there is no such thing as *the* rate of return to agricultural research. In a typical agricultural research portfolio, some (perhaps most) investments yield no benefits whatsoever, whereas others in the same portfolio yield very high returns, sufficient to make the portfolio as a whole profitable. Even though very high rates of return are not implausible in every context, they are much less plausible for the more aggregative investments that represent extensive portfolios.

[4]In particular, the conventional estimates may exclude benefits from 'maintenance' research, benefits from disease prevention, food safety R&D, or social science research related to agriculture (some of which may not show up clearly in commodity markets and some of which are not captured in conventional productivity measures) and the spillover benefits from agricultural R&D into non-agricultural applications.

[5]In addition, conventional productivity measures do not account for the consumption of unpriced natural resource stocks in the process of production. Rate-of-return studies that use conventional productivity indexes will tend to overstate the social value of technological changes that involve a faster rate of consumption of natural resource stocks, and will understate the benefits from technologies that involve greater environmental amenities or resource stock savings (for example, see Alston, Anderson and Pardey, 1994; Perrin and Fulginiti, 1996).

[6]Some studies have included additional explanatory variables to represent the effects of factors such as 'education', 'infrastructure' or 'private R&D' in a model of productivity. Clearly, the appropriate adjustments of the dependent variable can be different, depending upon the explanatory variables other than public R&D that are to be included in the model to account for the effects of input and output quality, and so on.

[7]It is tricky to isolate the effects of schooling from the benefits of training in the context of research programmes, a benefit that should be attributed to R&D.

[8]Griliches (1992) discussed the problems of accounting for R&D spillovers. Building on Griliches (1974), Pray and Neumeyer (1990) discuss the role of private sector R&D.

[9]Private R&D expenditures (R^P) are likely to be positively correlated with public R&D expenditures (R^G) and, as a result, the omission of R^P from a productivity model would be expected to lead to an upwards bias in the coefficient on R^G. The confounding of effects extends beyond overstating the rate of return to R^G when we go beyond the consequences of statistical correlation and consider causal connections between the two types of expenditure and, perhaps, complementary or substitution interactions between R^P and R^G in affecting productivity.

[10]The pattern of geographical spillovers is largely conditioned by agroecological factors, although economic and policy factors play important roles too. For example, Pardey and Wright (2000) discuss the intellectual property protection aspects that affect the international flows of germ plasm and related biotechnologies.

[11]Exceptions include Oehmke (1988), Zachariah *et al.* (1989) and Huang and Sexton (1996).

[12]Some other recent studies, beginning from an examination of the time-series structure of the data, rather than reflection about the structural relationships, have been tending in a similar direction (for example, Akgüngör *et al.*, 1996; Makki *et al.*, 1996; Myers and Jayne, 1996). They have used time-series methods involving data transformations, such as first differences, and they have found smaller estimated rates of return as a result.

BIBLIOGRAPHY

Acquaye, A.K.A., Alston, J.M. and Pardey, P.G. (2000), 'A Disaggregated Perspective on Post-War Productivity Growth in U.S. Agriculture: Isn't that Spatial?', presented at the NC-208 conference on Agricultural Productivity: Data, Methods, and Measures, Waugh Auditorium, USDA-ERS, Washington, DC.

Akgüngör, S., Makanda, D.W., Oehmke, J.F., Myers, R.J. and Choe, Y.C. (1996), 'Dynamic Analysis of Kenyan Wheat Research and Rate of Return', contributed paper proceedings from the conference on Global Agricultural Science Policy for the Twenty-First Century, Melbourne, Australia, August.

Alston, J.M. and Pardey, P.G. (1996), *Making Science Pay: The Economics of Agricultural R&D Policy*, Washington, DC: American Enterprise Institute Press.

Alston, J.M., Anderson, J.R. and Pardey, P.G. (1995), 'Perceived Productivity, Forgone Future Farm Fruitfulness and Rural Research Resource Rationalization', in G.H. Peters and D.D. Hedley (eds), *Agricultural Competitiveness: Market Forces and Policy Choice*, proceedings of the twenty-second international conference of agricultural economists, Aldershot: Dartmouth.

Alston, J.M., Chan-Kang, C., Marra, M.C., Pardey, P.G. and Wyatt, T.J. (2000), *A Meta-Analysis of Rates of Return to Agricultural R&D: Ex Pede Herculem?*, research report no. 113, Washington, DC: International Food Policy Research Institute.

Alston, J.M., Craig, B.J. and Pardey, P.G. (1998), 'Dynamics in the Creation and Depreciation of Knowledge, and the Returns to Research', *EPTD Discussion Paper no. 35* Washington, DC: International Food Policy Research Institute.

Alston, J.M., Edwards, G.W. and Freebairn, J.W. (1988), 'Market Distortions and the Benefits from Research', *American Journal of Agricultural Economics*, **70**, 281–8.

Alston, J.M., Marra, M.C., Pardey, P.G. and Wyatt, T.J. (2000), 'Research Returns Redux: A Meta-Analysis of the Returns to Agricultural R&D', *The Australian Journal of Agricultural and Resource Economics*, **44**, 185–215.

Alston, J.M., Norton, G.W. and Pardey, P.G. (1995), *Science under Scarcity: Principles and Practice for Agricultural Research Evaluation and Priority Setting*, Ithaca: Cornell University Press (paperback edition, CAB International, 1998).

Ball, V.E., Gollop, F.M., Kelly-Hawke, A. and Swinand, G.P. (1999), 'Patterns of State Productivity Growth in the U.S. Farm Sector: Linking State and Aggregate Models', *American Journal of Agricultural Economics*, **81**, 164–79.

Ballard, C.L. and Fullerton, D. (1992), 'Distortionary Taxes and the Provision of Public Goods', *Journal of Economic Perspectives*, **6**, 117–31.

Brennan, J.P. and Bantilan, M.C.S. (1999), *Impact of ICRISAT Research on Australian Agriculture*, Economic Research Report no. 1, Australian Centre for International Agricultural Research, Wagga Wagga.

Byerlee, D. and Traxler, G. (2001), 'The Role of Technology Spillovers and Economies of Size in the Efficient Design of Agricultural Research Systems', in J.M. Alston, P.G. Pardey and M.J. Taylor (eds), *Agricultural Science Policy: Changing Global Agendas*, Baltimore, MD: Johns Hopkins University Press.

Chavas, J.-P. and Cox, T.L. (1992), 'A Nonparametric Analysis of the Effects of Research on Agricultural Productivity', *American Journal of Agricultural Economics*, **74**, 583–91.

Craig, B.J. and Pardey, P.G. (1996), 'Productivity in the Presence of Quality Change', *American Journal of Agricultural Economics*, **78**, 1349–54.

Craig, B.J. and Pardey, P.G. (2001), 'Input, Output, and Productivity Developments in U.S. Agriculture', in J.M. Alston, P.G. Pardey and M.J. Taylor (eds), *Agricultural Science Policy: Changing Global Agendas*, Baltimore, MD: Johns Hopkins University Press.

Davis, J.S. (1980), 'A Note on the Use of Alternative Lag Structures for Research Expenditure in Aggregate Production Function Models', *Canadian Journal of Agricultural Economics*, **28**, 72–6.

Echeverría, R.G. (1990), 'Assessing the Impact of Agricultural Research', in R.G. Echeverría (ed.), *Methods for Diagnosing Research System Constraints and Assessing the Impact of Agricultural Research, Vol. II, Assessing the Impact of Agricultural Research*, The Hague: International Service for National Agricultural Research.

Evenson, R.E. (1967), 'The Contribution of Agricultural Research to Production', *Journal of Farm Economics*, **49**, 1415–25.

Evenson, R.E. (1996), 'Two Blades of Grass: Research for U.S. Agriculture', in J.M. Antle and D.A. Sumner (eds), *The Economics of Agriculture Volume 2, Papers in Honor of D. Gale Johnson*, Chicago: University of Chicago Press.

Evenson, R.E., Waggoner, P.E. and Ruttan, V.W. (1979), 'Economic Benefits from Research: An Example from Agriculture', *Science*, **205**, 1101–7.

Findlay, C.C. and Jones, R.L. (1982), 'The Marginal Cost of Australian Income Taxation', *Economic Record*, **58**, 253–66.

Fox, G. (1985), 'Is the United States Really Underinvesting in Agricultural Research?', *American Journal of Agricultural Economics*, **67**, 806–12.

Fuglier, K., Ballenger, N., Day, K., Klotz, C., Ollinger, M., Reilly, J., Vasavada, U. and Yee, J., with contributions from J. Fisher and S. Payson (1996), *Agricultural Research and Develop-*

ment: Public and Private Investments Under Alternative Markets and Institutions, USDA-ERS-NRED Agricultural Economic Report 735, Washington, DC: United States Department of Agriculture.

Fullerton, D. (1991), 'Reconciling Recent Estimates of the Marginal Welfare Cost of Taxation', *American Economic Review*, **81**, 302–8.

Griliches, Z. (1957), 'Hybrid Corn: An Exploration in the Economics of Technological Change', *Econometrica*, **25**, 501–22.

Griliches, Z. (1963), 'The Sources of Measured Productivity Growth: Agriculture, 1940–1960', *Journal of Political Economy*, **71**, 331–46.

Griliches, Z. (1964), 'Research Expenditures, Education, and the Aggregate Agricultural Production Function', *American Economic Review*, **54**, 961–74.

Griliches, Z. (1974), 'Errors in Variables and other Unobservables', *Econometrica*, **42**, 971–8.

Griliches, Z. (1979), 'Issues in Assessing the Contribution of Research and Development to Productivity Growth', *Bell Journal of Economics*, **10**, 92–116.

Griliches, Z. (1992), 'The Search for R&D Spillovers', *Scandinavian Journal of Economics*, **94**, 29–47.

Griliches, Z. (2001), 'R&D and Productivity: The Unfinished Business', in J.M. Alston, P.G. Pardey and M.J. Taylor (eds), *Agricultural Science Policy: Changing Global Agendas*, Baltimore, MD: Johns Hopkins University Press.

Huang, S.-Y. and Sexton, R.J. (1996), 'Measuring Returns to Innovation in an Imperfectly Competitive Market: Application to Mechanical Harvesting of Processing Tomatoes in Taiwan', *American Journal of Agricultural Economics*, **78**, 558–71.

Huffman, W.E. and Evenson, R.E. (1989), 'Supply and Demand Functions for Multiproduct U.S. Cash Grain Farms: Biases Caused by Research and other Policies', *American Journal of Agricultural Economics*, **71**, 761–73.

Huffman, W.E. and Evenson, R.E. (1992), 'Contributions of Public and Private Science and Technology to U.S. Agricultural Productivity', *American Journal of Agricultural Economics*, **74**, 752–6.

Huffman, W.E. and Evenson, R.E. (1993), *Science for Agriculture: A Long-Term Perspective*, Ames: Iowa State University Press.

Jaffe, A.B. (1986), 'Technological Opportunity and Spillovers of R&D: Evidence from Firm's Patents, Profits, and Market Value', *American Economic Review*, **76**, 984–1001.

Johnson, D.K.N. and Evenson, R.E. (1999), 'R&D Spillovers to Agriculture: Measurement and Application', *Contemporary Economic Policy*, **14**, 432–56.

Kealey, T. (1996), *The Economic Laws of Scientific Research*, Houndmills: Macmillan Press.

Leiby, J.D. and Adams, G.D. (1991), 'The Returns to Agricultural Research in Maine: The Case of a Small Northeastern Experiment Station', *Northeastern Journal of Agricultural and Resource Economics*, **20**, 1–14.

Makki, S.S., Tweeten, L.G. and Thraen, C.S. (1996), 'Returns to Agricultural Research: Are We Assessing Right?', contributed paper, proceedings from the conference on Global Agricultural Science Policy for the Twenty-First Century, Melbourne, Australia, August.

Mansfield, E. (1977), *The Production and Application of New Industrial Technology*, New York: W.W. Norton.

Myers, R.J. and Jayne, T. (1996), 'Regime Shifts and Technology Diffusion in Crop Yield Growth Paths: An Application to Maize Yields in Zimbabwe', contributed paper, proceedings from the conference on Global Agricultural Science Policy for the Twenty-First Century, Melbourne, Australia, August.

Oehmke, J.F. (1988), 'The Calculation of Returns to Research in Distorted Markets', *Agricultural Economics*, **2**, 291–302.

Pardey, P.G. and Craig, B. (1989), 'Causal Relationships Between Public Sector Agricultural Research Expenditures and Output', *American Journal of Agricultural Economics*, **71**, 9–19.

Pardey, P.G. and Wright, B.D. (2000), 'Addressing Freedom to Operate Questions in Agricultural Biotechnology in the CGIAR', mimeo, International Food Policy Research Institute, Washington, DC.

Pardey, P.G., Alston, J.M., Christian, J.E. and Fan, S. (1996), *Hidden Harvest: U.S. Benefits from International Research Aid*, IFPRI Food Policy Report, Washington, DC: International Food Policy Research Institute.

Pasour, E.C., Jr and Johnson, M.A. (1982), 'Bureaucratic Productivity: The Case of Agricultural Research Revisited', *Public Choice*, **39**, 301–17.

Perrin, R. and Fulginiti, L. (1996), 'Productivity in the Presence of "Poorly Priced" Goods', *American Journal of Agricultural Economics*, **78**, 1355–9.

Pray, C.E. and Neumeyer, C.F. (1990), 'Problems of Omitting Private Investments in Research when Measuring the Impact of Public Research', in R.G. Echeverría (ed.), *Methods for Diagnosing Research System Constraints and Assessing the Impact of Agricultural Research, Vol. II, Assessing the Impact of Agricultural Research*, The Hague: International Service for National Agricultural Research.

Ravenscraft, D. and Scherer, F.M. (1982), 'The Lag Structure of Returns to Research and Development', *Applied Economics*, **14**, 603–20.

Schimmelpfennig, D. and Thirtle, C. (1994), 'Cointegration and Causality: Exploring the Relationship Between Agricultural R&D and Productivity', *Journal of Agricultural Economics*, **45**, 220–31.

Schmitz, A. and Seckler, D. (1970), 'Mechanized Agriculture and Social Welfare: The Case of the Tomato Harvester', *American Journal of Agricultural Economics*, **52**, 569–77.

Schultz, T.W. (1956), 'Reflections on Agricultural Production Output and Supply', *Journal of Farm Economics*, **38**, 748–62.

Thirtle, C.G. and Bottomley, P. (1988), 'Is Publicly Funded Agricultural Research Excessive?', *Journal of Agricultural Economics*, **39**, 99–111.

Zachariah, O.E.R., Fox, G. and Brinkman, G.L. (1989), 'Product Market Distortions and the Returns to Broiler Chicken Research in Canada', *Journal of Agricultural Economics*, **40**, 41–51.

ROBIN W. JOHNSON*

The Role of Institutions in Policy Formation and Delivery

INTRODUCTION

The role of institutions in agricultural policy refers to the way agricultural policy, or any economic policy for that matter, depends on the particular institutional background prevailing in a particular country. Thus, within countries, the same institutional background applies across different economic policies while, between countries, the institutional background differs and is likely to lead to different policy frameworks and different policy delivery systems for dealing with the same problem. This is apparent in the international aid arena (Johnson, 1999) and in regional groupings of independent countries like the EU with overriding needs for policy coordination (Williams, 1997).

By institutions I mean any established law, custom or practice (*Oxford English Dictionary*). In the realm of government, the set of rules and codes for governing form *recognizable policy making and forming institutions* such as parliaments, parties and bureaucracies. Governments pass legislation to regulate trade and commerce, and draw on established law and custom to implement their objectives. These include the existing rules for the sanctity of contracts and the protection of property rights where they exist. Thus the institutional environment includes government law-making bodies, the rules and conventions that surround these bodies, and the formal and informal mechanisms which govern the conduct of commerce and trade.

Institutional analysis recognizes a difference between operational and constitutional levels of decision making (Johnson, D.B., 1991). The operational level consists of decisions made within a given set of already existing and broadly accepted constitutional rules. The latter include voting procedures and means of raising the revenue. The constitutional level is where the rules of the game are established, including the rules for the application of property rights. These constitutional rule are thought to be established in an atmosphere of conceptual impartiality because the future effects on individuals cannot be foreseen (Dixit, 1996, p.13). Once established, they change only very slowly,

*Formerly Policy Director, Ministry of Agriculture, Wellington, New Zealand. Helpful suggestions have been received from J. Martin (Victoria University, New Zealand), J. Anderson (World Bank) and P. Arcus (Canada). Parts of the paper are drawn from a report prepared for the World Bank (Johnson, 1999).

but sometimes cataclysmically (the French Revolution, for example). In between such times, individuals/corporations/governments operate in a relatively
unchanging institutional environment and can make operational change in
policies, revenue collection and so on (incrementalism).[1]

Davis and North (1971) call the set of fundamental political, social and legal
ground rules that establish the basis for production, exchange and distribution
the *institutional environment*. Arrangements between economic units that govern the way these units cooperate and/or compete are identified as institutional
arrangements. These provide a structure within which members can cooperate
and also provide a mechanism that can effect a change in laws or property
rights. Buchanan (1975, p.226) makes the distinction between the constitution
that governs the whole policy process and individual instances of policy making within this constitution. Williamson (1995, p.174) refers to institutional
arrangements as the *institutions of governance* in his transaction cost analyses.
Dixit (1996, p.18), following Buchanan, refers to the constitutional framework
and policy acts. More recently, Williamson (2000) distinguishes between 'informal institutions, customs, traditions, norms and religion', formal rules of
the game, governance or playing the game and neoclassical economics and
agency theory. I will use the Davis and North language.

In a given country jurisdiction, the making of economic policy therefore
takes place mainly in the area of institutional arrangements. Certain constitutional constraints are taken for granted. Politicians and bureaucrats understand
this. Nevertheless, the making of policy is essentially a political process that
reflects the pressures that face government decision makers. In this paper, the
focus will be on the formation and implementation of economic policies mainly
referring to agriculture and the role of institutions in this process.[2]

Since this literature was developed in economies with Western democratic
institutions, it is not a universal paradigm for policy making and implementation. On the other hand, the sheer need to organize the business of government
in any country will require some rudimentary organization and command
structure. Most countries should be able to draw from Western experience to
improve their own performance. Nevertheless, it remains imperative for international advisors and country economists to adapt their policy advice to the
institutional environment as it is, and not force new structures on to economies
already in some difficulty.

This paper first discusses different theories on the political economy of
government decision making and implementation, including public choice economics, institutional economics and transaction cost economics. It then discusses
policy-forming processes, the respective role of legislators, advisors and interest groups, the new public management and differences between countries.
This is followed by an analysis of transaction costs in government and the
measures and strategies which might improve the efficiency of the policy
process.

POLITICAL ECONOMY OF GOVERNMENT DECISION MAKING[3]

For present purposes, there is a need to distinguish between the traditional view of government as altruistic and benevolent, and government as another bargaining group in the wider game of politics. The two views are represented by the public interest model of government and the individualistic (private) model (Martin, 1990).

The public interest model

In this case, the national interest is achieved by the legislature/congress agreeing to policy acts that evolve from compromise and bargaining among the elected representatives. The national interest can be broadly interpreted as the Benthamite 'greatest good of the greatest number' as seen in the eyes of the decision makers. Civil servants (bureaucrats) provide independent advice to legislators and implement the policies that result from the political decision. A career civil service based upon expertise and non-political appointments is assumed to be available. While this model may appear to be based on the British parliamentary system, it has generic value in providing an example for many other countries (World Bank, 1997, p.79).

The economic role of government in this framework is to introduce policies that increase social welfare. The welfare maximization perspective sees government as an omniscient and benevolent dictator (Swinnen and van der Zee, 1993). Governments intervene in the private economy where it fails to function properly in allocating and distributing resources ('market failure'). The nation state can produce goods, internalize social costs and benefits, regulate decreasing cost industries and redistribute income. In theory, these government actions can redistribute resources to maximize welfare.

Randall (1987) notes the philosophical lineage of this model from Rousseau, Marshall and Pigou. Its basic premises are that the true public interest will be revealed in the political process; that programmes to promote economic activity, to rectify market failure (to internalize externalities), to provide public goods and merit goods, and to promote equality of opportunity, all may be seen as enhancing the general welfare, and that continued vigilance and effort are necessary to ensure that government remains responsive to the public interest.[4]

The individualistic model

This is based on the idea that the nation state is not an organic body apart from the collection of individuals comprising it, and that the central role of economists is to analyse how efficiently government institutions enable individuals to express and realize their preferences about public goods, public services and policies (Johnson, D.B., 1991, p.11). In this view, bureaucrats have their own preferences and goals which they can achieve by enlarging the size and budgets of their agencies. Politicians can achieve their goals by being elected to office and bestowing favours. Interest groups act on behalf of individuals in getting favourable policies passed in the legislature. While this view of government institutions originated in the United States, it also expresses an alternative view of political decision making and administration (World Bank, 1997, p.81).

The model postulates that government decision making is subject to pressures from interest groups, lobbying and voting behaviour, as well as self-interest. Decisions tend to reflect the respective power bases of the participants.[5] Randall (1987) notes the lineage of this model from the writings of Wicksell and Locke, as modified by Buchanan (1987), Tulloch (1983) and others. All rights are assumed to rest with the individual and, to avoid anarchy, individuals rationally delegate some rights to a central authority. The emphasis is on voluntary exchange and freedom of choice, and on individual liberty. 'The cornerstone of liberty is a set of complete, carefully specified, secure, enforceable, and transferable property rights' (North, 1990).

The resulting decisions made by government in this environment are said to reflect the 'private interest point of view'. Outcomes are determined by the weight of the respective power bases of the participants. Interest groups can earn economic rents from their activities by influencing political decision making. Capture of politicians, agencies and civil servants is often observed. While this paper leans to a private interest view of government institutions, it is recognized that some policy decisions are more altruistic than others, and that a cross-section of policies introduced by a government may include elements of both (Martin, 1989, 1990; Johnson, 1994). In this paper, the view is taken that government is conditioned by some of the same forces as private participants in the economy.

The transaction cost model

There is a third alternative. This is the *transaction cost model*, based on an approach originally applied to the structure of firms and emphasizes the relative costs of planning, adapting and monitoring under alternative governance structures (Williamson, 1995, p.175). Decision makers see the need to minimize their aggregate costs of production *and* transaction costs like monitoring and contractual arrangements (Boston *et al.*, 1996, p.21). The literature on transaction costs indicates that some commercial relationships are better suited to market-type arrangements, while others are better suited to hierarchical or rule-driven organizations (Williamson, 1995; Bale and Dale, 1998).[6] In-house provision of services, for example, is likely to be more efficient than contracting out where there is a high risk of self-interest, conflicts of interest, substantial uncertainty, and recurrent, complex transactions.

In recent years, these organizational arguments have been applied to bureaucratic organizations (Horn, 1995; Boston *et al.*, 1996; Dixit, 1996). This has led to greater interest in contracting out services, privatization of government services, arrangements aimed at reducing monitoring costs (between central governments and their agents) and arrangements that reduce opportunism and shirking among agents (bureaucratic ineptitude and corruption[7]).

In terms of policy formation and implementation, transaction costs are emphasized in public administration models of the legislative process (Horn,

1995). Legislators are regarded as self-seeking in using legislation to increase their net political support. Their opportunities are limited by a number of specific difficulties encountered in maintaining their political base and satisfying the supporters of their policies. The legislators who are most likely to remain in power are those who are most successful in overcoming these 'transaction' problems, such as those who are best able to reassure their supporters that the benefits of legislation will not be lost to administrators in the implementation, or undone by subsequent legislatures (ibid., p.14). The primary thesis of this approach is that effective public administration requires that these specific transaction costs be minimized in determining and pursuing society's goals (Zeckhauser, 1995). In most circumstances, agreement on the resulting policies will lead to more efficient organizational forms for society (Williamson, 2000, p.7).

The models of institutional economics emphasize the results of individual and cooperative attempts to solve problems posed in a world of potentially large transaction costs. The new institutional economics is said to be firmly rooted in a second-best world where the *relative efficiency of institutional arrangements* is the concern. It acknowledges the importance of bounded rationality, complexity and costly information, combined with opportunism (Murrell, 1995). These lead to the emphasis on transaction costs and the belief that there may be a variety of institutional arrangements that reduce transaction costs successfully. If cooperative solutions can be found, the emphasis on opportunism is decreased. If satisfactory norms of behaviour can be agreed, transaction costs are also reduced, and efficiency is improved.

The literature emphasizes the innovativeness of individual and collective attempts to solve transaction cost problems.[8] Transaction cost models apply equally to private economic relationships as well as the political sphere, where cooperative efforts can result in new political constructs aimed at solving problems caused by poorly constructed property rights (ibid., p.202):

> The picture emerging is one of complexity – arrangements or institutions of enormous variety and complexity that have been developed to solve the difficult problems that arise when economic interactions are other than the simplest kind of spot transactions. This picture does not give us the simplicity and harmony of the Newtonian system that is echoed in general equilibrium economics, but instead has all the complexity of a catalogue of the earth's ecology.

GOVERNMENT STRUCTURES AND DEVELOPMENTS

Role of rules and institutions

Constitutional economics is the application of economic analysis to *the selection of efficient rules and decision making institutions* through the analysis of transaction costs (Johnson, D.B., 1991, pp.341–5). Rules and conventions essentially make commerce and government easier to conduct. Rules are a time-saving and efficient way of governing how individuals interact. Constitutional rules set the conduct of operational rules and do not need to be changed in the short term. In modern societies characterized by multiple inter-dependencies and externalities, economic growth and increases in the standard of living have become increasingly dependent upon establishing an institutional environment that provides members of society with the correct economic signals, information and incentives. These institutions of society guide everyday conduct.

The growth of trade and commerce is dependent on such rules (North, 1987, p.421). Modern societies have devised formal contracts, bonding of participants, guarantees, brand names and elaborate monitoring and enforcement systems to protect the individual, but also to create security and confidence in commerce.[9] North calls this *a well-enforced and well-specified system of property rights*. He points out that the resources devoted to transacting are large (although small per transaction) but the productivity gains from trade are even larger. Governments have a coordinating and facilitating role in providing the environment where transaction costs of trade and commerce are minimized and property rights secure and protected. In turn, governments can make international agreements that provide security of contracts and protection of property rights that thus facilitate trade.[10]

Rules can be written (as in constitutions or international agreements) or unwritten (as with common understandings between individuals) (North, 1990, pp.4–6). The conduct and performance of public policy depends on the extent to which a government can design, adapt or modify the written and unwritten rules in its environment. Constitutional rules, particularly, are difficult to change easily, but when they do change, the changes to society may be quite profound.

Rules are important in the study of political and economic institutions. They characterize the institutions surrounding political decision making. They help reduce transaction costs. They make policy formation easier and more productive. They reduce reliance on negotiating skills on a case-by-case basis in the presence of high transaction costs. They provide opportunities for increased efficiency and hence general welfare (Martin, 1989, p.5). But they may increase litigation as they can be appealed and reinterpreted through the courts.

Secondly, they reduce uncertainty and promote solidarity between various participants in the political process through the development of routines and standard procedures (Considine, 1996, p.71). When these settled sets of rules and codes for governing become fully acceptable, they form recognizable policy making and forming institutions such as parliaments, parties and bureaucracies.

From this point of view, institutions are any standardized behaviours which are regularly represented throughout the political or policy system that built up over a long time: 'institutions accumulate historical experience through learning. The results and inferences of past experience are stored in standard operating procedures, professional rules, and the elementary rules of thumb of a practical person' (ibid., pp.71–2). The importance of these means for settling and defining what has been learned cannot be overestimated. Without them any social group would be forced to keep rediscovering the simplest ways of organizing themselves and dealing with the common tasks of survival. As well as being practical devices for solving routine problems, institutions are the group's way of establishing priorities, fixing values and turning profound philosophical problems into simple routines. How long the routine will hold is as important a question as asking what function the institution itself performs.

In discussing these issues, Buchanan (1975) observes that individual policy acts have to complement and fill gaps in the constitution, and to this extent the distinction between the constitutional contract and individual policy acts is often blurred, since the policy act may provide a wide measure of interpretation of parts of the constitution. In almost no circumstances will advisors start with a clean sheet to correct some example of market failure. Given the continuing nature of government policy making, economists should consider the economic problems of government not as agents seeking to maximize economic welfare but as arbitrators, seeking to work out compromises between conflicting claims. Dixit (1996, p.71), emphasizes that constitutions are incomplete contracts, and the distinction between them and policy acts is one of degree, and not kind.

The policy process

The altruistic public interest model sees economic advisors giving independent and objective advice, and political decision makers making inspiring national interest decisions. The individualistic model sees the legislature and the bureaucracy as competing forces with separate agendas, with the emphasis on self-interest. By way of contrast, the actual relationship between the legislature and the bureaucracy is more likely to be characterized by a mixture of duties and obligations with changing emphasis on different aspects of policy making and direction as circumstances change.

In addition, the policy advice process itself is surrounded by considerable uncertainty, and a clear-cut principal–agent relationship is complicated by incomplete information in the exchange, asymmetrical information supply and uncertainty as to any outcomes (Boston *et al.*, 1996). In terms of logistics, the bureaucracy tends to have a monopoly of strategic information relevant to every political decision. While the role of advisors is to process the necessary information that decision making requires and put forward alternative courses of action that might be consistent with the stated aims of the legislature (the passive view), the role of the legislature is to be seen to be acting in the national interest *and* meeting any sectional interests they may represent. Uncertainty about the outcomes of the policy proposed means that the process itself has to be viewed as a probabilistic problem rather than a certainty one.[11]

The passive view of economists as advisors is that they only have a role in analysing the alternatives that face decision makers, and that they should not impose their own values on to the political decision-making process. Government decision making should define some objective function in terms of multiple ends or goals of economic activity (outcomes) and economists should delineate what is possible and the costs and benefits of each course of action (Blaug, 1992, p.128). This is a technocratic view of the policy advice process.

The legislature, or principal in this argument, may well have any number of well-defined and not so well-defined goals. In economic terms these are the preference functions of the legislature and these may articulate national interest concerns and/or private interest concerns. Most commentators, including Blaug, believe that the legislature does not have a well-defined preference function, but is more engaged in a constant search for new preference functions as a result of learning by doing and responding to the changing situation.

Blaug says that any legislative decision maker starts with current activities and gradually begins to define his/her objectives in the light of experience with actual policies. Political decision makers do not try to get what they want; rather they learn to want by appraising what they get. Means and end are indissolubly related, and evaluation of past decisions, or technical advice about future decisions, have to serve this purpose (Trebilcock, 1995, pp.24–9). Thus decision making is disjointed, as it is repeatedly reviewed in bits and pieces (by different people),[12] and it is incremental because it considers only a limited range of policies that differ little from existing ones.[13] *Disjointed incrementalism* does not merely adjust means to ends but explores the ends while applying the means, in effect choosing the ends and means simultaneously (Braybrookee and Lindblom, 1963).[14]

These details of the political decision process are consistent with the transaction cost model of government decision making. Legislators do have a choice of delivery institutions at the policy formation stage; they usually consult the bureaucracy, and constituents/supporters are likely to be consulted as to that decision's effects on them. Once the delivery structure is decided, responsibility passes to the delivery agent (usually the bureaucracy). The problem then becomes one of conduct rather than structure, as administrative details are unlikely to have been highly specified in the original enactment.[15] In this area, bureaucracies have their own sets of rules and conventions, which vary from country to country and institution to institution, but which will probably be the guiding force in determining the continuing delivery of the enacted policy programme. According to Sandiford and Rossmiller (1996), it is this implementation stage which will primarily determine the resulting *performance* of the policy in terms of the original aims.

This paper therefore follows the transaction cost view of the policy-making process. While it adopts features of the public and private interest models, such as self-interest and agency theory, it is quite different in its approach to economic optimization. Instead of seeking to analyse market failure and possible corrective mechanisms, transaction cost analysis diverts attention to the reduction of transaction costs and the rules of governance. The implications of this approach are now more fully debated.

Implications for policy implementation

The above paragraphs have drawn attention to the important dual role of the bureaucracy in advising the legislators of the options that are available to them as well as the carrying out of what is decided. It has been noted that the typical bureaucracy is subject to some of the same pressures as the political arm of government, viz. self-interested activities, responding to interest groups (sometimes representing them) and poor decision making. Bureaucracy also is subject to problems of its own such as developing private agendas, slow response and obfuscating the objectives handed down to them. It has been noted that bureaucratic organizations have been subject to reforms in some countries in the interests of better accountability to the nation and greater efficiency. Finally, it is noted that bureaucratic processes make use of procedural rules to simplify and decentralize tasks, as do other organizations and firms.

The response to these concerns has been to introduce new systems of management in the *public* sector in some countries (organizational changes). The aim has been to bring about better results from the bureaucracy in terms of work output, efficiency and accountability. Some of these procedures have been borrowed from the private sector.

New public management

Aucoin (1990, p.116) has noted how two separate paradigms of government and management in Western democracies have developed. Compared with public choice theory which focuses on the need to re-establish the primacy of representative government over bureaucracy, the new public management focuses on the need to re-establish the primacy of managerial principles over bureaucracy. Managerialism is a set of ideas emanating from sources external to public management per se, namely the literature on private sector or business administration. It stresses that the capacities of modern complex organizations to realize their objectives can be enhanced by management structures and practices that *reduce* bureaucratic procedures in organizational systems.

The two paradigms are likely to introduce a measure of tension, even contradiction, in their application to changes in organization (ibid., pp.125–6). Public choice sees politics as pervading management; that is, politics is present in both the formulation and the implementation of policies. Managerialism sees politics as present essentially in the determination of the basic values or missions, and thus the policies, of an organization. Thus, in one case, politicians must 'tame' the bureaucracy via a concentration of power in the elected representatives, while, on the other, bureaucracy must be freed of excessive controls, especially on line managers. In the first case, the perceived need is to eliminate the capture of the bureaucratic organs of the nation state in order that elected representatives are able to represent the public's interest in public policy; in the second, to give priority to the bureaucratic machine to carry out its designated tasks.

Hood (1991) has identified the following components of the new public management:

- professional management in the public sector;
- use of standards and measures of performance;
- an emphasis on output controls;
- a shift to disaggregation of bureaucratic units;

- an opening up to competitive services;
- the introduction of private sector management styles; and
- more stress on discipline and parsimony in resource use.[16]

These trends suggest a greater stress on management skills as opposed to professional skills, greater accountability through measures of performance, a shift from input controls to output controls, the separation of commercial from non-commercial functions, a shift to contracts and public tendering procedures, more flexibility within departments and cutting costs in the public sector.[17] The adoption of these changes varies from country to country and may often be associated with assistance packages from the IMF and the World Bank.[18]

According to Bale and Dale (1998, p.106), this approach to bureaucratic accountability has five main advantages:

- it establishes clear lines of accountability between government ministers and their departments;
- it defines performance in an unambiguous and measurable way;
- it delegates authority to chief executives;
- it establishes incentives that reward or punish results relative to the agreed outcome; and
- it enables reporting and monitoring performance to take place.

In agricultural economics, a fresh approach to policy accountability has recently been put forward (Sandiford and Rossmiller, 1996; Williams, 1997; Haebig *et al.*, 1998). These papers focus on the implementation of policy rather than on policy formation. The papers use a comparative institutional approach to the delivery of agricultural policy in different countries and originated in the Food and Agriculture Organization (FAO) of the United Nations. The emphasis is on the implementation of policy proposals as enacted in legislatures and asks whether the intent of the legislators is being met in the delivery process and whether such processes meet wider economic criteria such as the meeting of set targets (effectiveness), avoiding unwanted effects (equity and income distribution considerations) and delivering at least cost (efficiency).

The authors suggest using a structure/conduct/performance approach to individual policy programmes to bring out the contrast between the original intentions and actual management of the programme (Koch, 1980). Structure is used to identify what was originally set out in any legislation including design of policy instruments; conduct is used to identify how the legislative programme was interpreted and managed in practice; and performance is used to assess how well the policy system met the original objectives of the programme in terms of delivering the scheduled benefits to the target recipients. The authors suggest that this latter task will be made easier by examining four criteria of performance: effectiveness, efficiency, enforceability and equity (Sandiford and Rossmiller, 1996, pp.7–12; Williams, 1997, pp.7–14).

Institutional environment in different countries[19]

In an international context, the institutions of government vary widely. At the constitutional level, many countries have undergone major upheavals in their parliamentary arrangements. In former colonial territories, some countries have passed through a process of decolonization, temporary experience with a demo-cratic constitution and then various upheavals, to emerge as one-party political states. These upheavals involve major changes in the ruling elites, with conse-quent changes at the administrative level. In Europe, communist systems of government have been replaced by various versions of liberal–democratic re-gimes, again with administrative implications (Blondel, 1990, pp.29–30).

The previous discussion has been based on Western government systems, particularly the United Kingdom and its former colonies, and the United States. Within these democratic political systems, there are at least four main subtypes based on the sharing of power and political parties (Weaver and Rockman, 1993): presidential systems, party governments, multiparty coalitions and sin-gle party dominants. Outside these types, readers will recognize other possibilities in their experience, such as traditional or monarchic systems, communist systems and countries with popular but generally anti-democratic governments (Blondel, 1990).

Furthermore, there is a wide range of legal systems in use outside Western systems (Lane, 1996). Muslim and Hindu law are examples of religious legal systems, whereas Chinese law and African law represent customary systems. Even in Western countries there is a division between Romano-Germanic law and common law. Romano-Germanic law or civil law emphasizes codification, and the establishment of general principles of law. The most well-known are the five Napoleonic codes enacted between 1804 and 1811.

These distinctions are important because trade and commerce has to be conducted over international boundaries and because international policy advi-sors are continuously refreshing themselves about these entities for the countries in which they are working. The differences are important in the event of disputes over contracts, the time taken to get resolution of disputes through the courts, and the treatment of property rights. The resolution of these issues raises transaction costs as flexibility is reduced, transactions are slower, litiga-tion is slower and representation/participation is increased.

While policy formation and implementation within countries remain rela-tively straightforward in institutional terms, it becomes more and more complex when countries are compared or when advisors have frequently to move from one country to another, and when international trade issues are being negoti-ated.

Sovereignty and the institutional environment

Different countries have different constitutions and hence provide different institutional environments for policy making. I therefore see a variety of expe-riences in policy formation and implementation as sovereignty differences are observed. The first will be domestic economies of countries which may or may not have some kind of federal structure of government. The second will be regional groupings of countries with common interests (European Union, MERCOSUR, NAFTA). The third will be true multilateral agreements that require overall agreement between participants still with different national objectives (World Trade Organization, WTO). In addition, there is the specific case of multilateral aid organizations which necessarily have to embrace many different country institutional environments.

In single legislature non-federal constitutions, policy formation is determined by the single elite group with electoral or other powers. The conventions of policy making are widely accepted, hence institutional issues scarcely arise in day-to-day policy making. Changes tend to take place in the conventions in line with changes in the electoral cycle, though we should not overlook Buchanan's observation that some policy making eats away at the constitutional conventions. The situation is more complex with federal constitutions, as other semi-autonomous groups have some residual constitutional powers which they readily defend. Institutional arrangements, such as prior consultation, are usually found to achieve coordination in these circumstances. Australian and Canadian policy economists (in federal constitutions) are more aware of these constraints than New Zealand economists (in a single house majority) for example.

In regional economic treaties, more complex arrangements are required for coordination across sovereign boundaries. Williams (1997, p.7) observes that The Treaty Establishing the European Community signed in Rome in 1957, and the Treaty of European Union signed at Maastricht in 1992, and the various amending treaties together provide the constitution of the Union. This allows the Union to make individual acts of common policy (in the form of Regulations, Directives or decisions of the Council of Ministers or decisions of the European Court). Complexity arises in that member states themselves have a diversity of political constitutions, ranging from the Westminster system in the UK to different types of written constitution in other states, all of whom have constitutions with long histories and traditions surrounding them. While the treaties require national acts of legislation to be harmonized so as not to impede the establishment of the common market, the implementation of policies within member states still depends on governments and agencies that are dependent on the traditions of past policies and the national legislation of member states. Williams says of these institutional arrangements: 'There can be no doubt that in the implementation of the common dairy policy these differences have played a part' and affect country performance.[20]

The classic case for multilateral coordination to overcome international transaction costs between nations is the General Agreement on Tariffs and Trade (GATT). The Uruguay Round made great advances in setting up additional trade rules and penalty provisions. One observer (Abbott, 1997, pp. 33–4) talks about the enhanced legalization of the GATT system turning a 'soft law' to a 'hard law' system. Soft law is used by international lawyers to characterize legal norms that do not effectively compel compliance (for example, the recommendations of the Rio Conference on the Environment, 1992). Hard law refers to a system of norms to which a relatively high expectation of compliance exists (the WTO Agreement). Evidence of these trends may be found in the progressive refinement of rules from the general to the specific since the founding of GATT, and the transformation of the dispute settlement system from concensus-based to quasi-judicial in the WTO.[21] Though these advances were not continued at Seattle in 1999, past rounds of the GATT have been instrumental in obtaining quite wide agreement on trading rules for industrial and agricultural goods, and for the technical conditions under which sanitary and phytosanitary measures can be imposed. Without agreed rules in these areas, international trade would break down and severely disadvantage many developing countries. Abbott (1997, p.48) also observes that the success of the WTO rule system depends largely on its emerging relationship to competing rule systems (that is, that of the European Union) and also on changes in the balance of power in the organization (that is, the entry of China and Russia into membership of the WTO).

In terms of the international aid community, reform in former communist country governments in Eastern Europe put some stress on the privatization of property rights in the institutional approach adopted. But Frydman and Rapacynski (1993, p.13) found 'the meaning of privatisation in Eastern Europe has turned out to be complex and ambiguous. Instead of the clarification of property rights and the introduction of incentives characteristic of a captitalistic society, the privatisation process has so far often led to a maze of complicated economic and legal relations that may even impede speedy transition to a system in which the rights of capital are clearly delineated and protected' (quoted by Williamson, 1995). Williamson goes on to observe that getting the property rights right is too narrow a conception of the wider institutional problems which require addressing in these countries.

More recently, Stiglitz (1999, p.4) identified the importance of political institutions and processes in a review of the transition in the Russian economy:

> Policy advisors put forward policy prescriptions in the context of a particular society – a society with a particular history, with a certain level of social capital, with a particular set of political institutions, and with political processes affected by (if not determined by) the existence of particular political forces. Interventions do not occur in a vacuum. How those recommendations are used, or abused, is not an issue from which economists can simply walk away. And this especially so in those instances where one of the arguments for the economic reforms is either failures in the political process or their impact on the political process itself. ... The point is not to refight old battles, but to learn the lessons of the past, to help guide the future.

These comments indicate to me that there is increasing recognition of the role of institutions in making and implementing economic policy. There is a need for national and international policy advisors to understand the processes involved and apply them in their day-to-day work. The very theme of this Conference reflects an increasing awareness of the issues.

ADMINISTRATIVE MODELS: A SYNTHESIS

Transaction costs, policy formation and public administration

The difficulties that political decision makers have in securing continued electoral support are the basis of the transaction cost model of public administration. The difficulties encountered in securing that support create the transaction costs that have to be overcome to achieve lasting and worthwhile policy change. This approach deploys the rationality hypothesis and transaction costs to explain how government policy making and delivery works. It posits that effective public administration requires that these transaction costs be *minimized* in determining and pursuing society's goals (Zeckhauser, 1995). Legislators are regarded as self-seeking in their use of legislation to increase their net political support and lasting power.[22] Their opportunities are limited by the transaction costs of achieving agreement on their proposals. These are the time and effort it takes to reach agreement on legislative refinements and any time and effort that affected private interests have to devote subsequently to participating in implementation and administration; political uncertainty that the legislation will last; uncertainty that the legislation will be administered as intended; and uncertainty about the distribution of private benefits and costs (Horn, 1994, p.13).[23]

The elected/political appointees who are most likely to remain in power are those who are most successful in overcoming these transaction problems, such as those who are best able to reassure their supporters that the benefits of legislation will not be lost to administrators in the implementation, or undone by subsequent legislatures (ibid., p.14). Implementation of legislation will depend on the following agency relationships: (a) the enacting coalition and its constituents (supporters) must rely on administrative agents to implement their proposals – it must delegate to get things done; (b) these agents do not necessarily share the objectives of the enacting coalition and its constituents; and (c) it is very difficult to monitor these agents and create a system of ex post rewards and sanctions that will ensure that they act to protect the interests represented at enactment.

These problems create agency costs: that is, the costs incurred to induce administrators to implement faithfully what was intended in the legislature, and the losses legislators and constituents sustain by being unable to do so perfectly. They include the costs associated with selecting administrators and monitoring their compliance, the costs of using ex post corrective devices (rewards, sanctions and legislative direction) and the cost of any residual non-compliance that produces a difference between the policy enacted and what is implemented (ibid., p.19). There are a number of administrative mechanisms that legislators can draw on that *minimize* these costs: contracting out versus in-house delivery, tax-funded bureaux (departments), non-profit tax-financed regulatory agencies (for example, in the USA) and revenue-earning state-owned enterprises (as in the British system). Each has its advantages and disadvantages (Williamson, 1995, p.179; Horn, 1995, pp.9, 40, 170).

Private interests have a definite interest in *implementation* (Horn, 1995, p.13):

Legislators and their constituencies [Horn's term for private interests] are seen as engaged in a form of exchange. Legislators want electoral support and constituents want private benefits – or reduced private costs – in legislation. The amount of net electoral support legislators receive from promoting a piece of legislation depends on the flow of benefits and costs that private interests expect it to generate over time. The implementation features of the legislation bear on this calculus because private interests are sufficiently forward looking to anticipate how decisions on implementation will affect the flow of benefits and costs. That is why there are often heated disputes over decisions on matters like the scope of delegated authority, the form of organisation charged with implementation, and the procedures administrative agents must adopt. These factors affect 'who' ultimately 'gets what' out of the legislation.

Thus, the design of legislation reflects the interests of the different groups taking part in the political process and this reflects society's preferences for equity and efficiency considerations. Most important is what Horn calls the 'commitment' problem. The flow of benefits to legislators is often much more immediate than the flow of benefits to constituents (ibid., p.16). Constituents run the risk that the present or subsequent legislative coalitions might undermine the benefits of given legislation. This is a problem for legislators because forward-looking constituents will assess the durability of future legislative benefits and costs and reflect that assessment in the degree of electoral support they are willing to offer. Thus legislators cannot guarantee constituents durable benefits but they can make binding arrangements that might tie down future legislators. Constituents respond by seeking guarantees that these bindings will be in the implementation design, and that they will be consulted on the matters involved. Competition between different organizational forms will be vigorous enough to ensure that only the most efficient survive (ibid., p.37).

In the same way, the distribution of costs and benefits might explain legislators choosing policies that confine the benefits to marginal voters (those whose votes count) and confining the costs to inframarginal voters (those who are strongly committed to the governing party); or choosing policies that provide benefits in concentrated form and impose costs in dispersed forms; choosing policies that will secure the cooperation of the bureaucracy; choosing policy instruments that minimize real costs over time when they fall on a small group; and choosing policy instruments that bring benefits within the current electoral cycle. Such behaviour is unlikely to be the random product of mistakes, ignorance or stupidity on the part of collective decision makers, but in many cases is likely to reflect systematic incentive structures that the community has built into *political institutions* such as one man-one vote and regular cycles of elections (Trebilcock, 1995, p.27).[24]

Reducing transaction costs in government[25]

Economists and political scientists have developed several alternative working models to explain how governments reach decisions. These, in turn, determine the structure and intended conduct of specific economic policies or acts for agriculture or any other sector or interest. This paper has focused on the

transaction costs involved in the day-to-day political process. From the analysis presented, the particular attributes of the process that influence the final
shape of policy and delivery have been identified. In political economy terms,
these solutions are more likely to represent some kind of consensual optima
than a purely economic one (North, 1990, p.15).

Policy advisors, by and large, have to work within these parameters. Economists might take a technocratic view and offer an analysis of the economic
effects of different strategies under consideration. Alternatively, they may have
need to refer to the institutional parameters that might shape the outcome of
the policy act proposed. Dixit (1996, pp.149–55) argues that this is inevitable
and the advice process is not complete without it: 'the policy process should be
thought of as an evolving, dynamic game; perhaps the economists' role should
be viewed in a very similar manner'.

Policy advisors will continue to control the information base. In the case of
particular policy acts, evaluation of past policy proposals should be an established part of the activities of a responsible bureau in central government.
Evaluation (including monitoring) should include testing for the efficiency and
equity effects of a given policy programme, as well as the distribution of
benefits and costs. Evaluation of past policy and new proposals should take
account of the institutional environment along the following lines (following
Horn, 1995):

- aims of the enacting legislation (structure);
- consultation with stakeholders at the enactment phase of the legislation (design);
- choice of delivery instruments (efficiency);
- behaviour of the delivery agents (conduct);
- performance in terms of the original aims; and
- getting commitment from the respective parties.

The concentration on aims is to separate the aims of the legislators from
abstract notions of altruism or economic welfare. At some point the legislation
must be treated as a given and evaluated in its own right. In terms of consultation with stakeholders, there has been a widespread recognition that greater
public input could be made into the policy formation process. Greater transparency reduces information asymmetries and reduces some transaction costs in
the decision-making process (Dixit, 1996, p.149). The Industry Commission in
Australia (Industry Commission, 1991) (now the Productivity Commission)
and the National Center for Food and Agricultural Policy in Washington, USA
(NCFAP, 1994), are organizations which conduct public reviews of policy
issues.

There have been public review processes in Australia since 1973.[26] The
Industries Assistance Commission was established, on the recommendation of
Sir John Crawford, to advice the federal government on assistance which
should be given to, or withdrawn from, industries in Australia. Crawford
identified the following reasons for establishing the Commission (Uhrig, 1983,
p.4):

- to assist the government to develop policies for improving the allocation of resources among industries in Australia;
- to provide advice on those policies in an independent and disinterested manner; and
- to facilitate public scrutiny of these policies.

The Commission was to report back on matters referred to it but could also initiate enquiries under certain circumstances. The Commission later became the Industries Commission and then the Productivity Commission. While the focus was on the need for industry assistance, there is an implication in the aims of the legislation that the implementation of the policy and the suitability of the instruments should also be assessed.[27] In particular, the Australians were concerned with the tariff structure introduced in the 1930s and its implication across sectors (Martin, 1989).

In terms of the behaviour of delivery agents, some countries (for example, New Zealand and the UK) have introduced corporate management systems into the public arena (Aucoin, 1990; Horn, 1995). These emphasize professional management in the public sector, the use of standards and measures of performance, and outsourcing of services which were suitable for such treatment. These represent new 'institutional arrangements' for the conduct of government business and help reduce the transaction costs of implementing policy acts.

Formal proposals for evaluation and review of policy programmes have been systematically introduced in some countries. A wide range of procedures have been introduced in New Zealand[28] and Australia (see World Bank, 1997, p.82), including regulatory impact statements. While introduced in the name of increased accountability, there is also increased concern for (private) compliance costs and distributive effects of policy change. There has also been a political interest in the permanency of policy change with the introduction of a Fiscal Responsibility Act in New Zealand which partially binds future governments to current decisions, thereby reducing the costs of commitment (Horn, 1995, p.191).

Regulatory impact statements (RISs) have been introduced in both Australia and New Zealand. A statement must be prepared for all new or amended regulations that directly or indirectly affect business, or restrict competition. In Australia, each statement should be prepared early in the policy development process, and should set out (among other things), the options (regulatory and/ or non-regulatory) that may constitute viable means of achieving the desired objective(s), an assessment of the impacts (cost and benefits) on consumers, business, government and the community of each option, and a consultation statement (Productivity Commission, 1998). These directives are aimed at reducing the cost of mistakes, the cost of unacceptable outcomes and the costs of poor implementation.

The new institutional economics has changed the thrust of policy analysis away from market failure to design and delivery issues. The broad aim is to devise rules and procedures that reduce transaction costs and improve outcomes. Clarification of the appropriate methodologies will enable policy analysts and advisors to governments to design better policy programmes, as well as focus international advisors on the different institutional environments they will encounter (Williams, 1997; Johnson, 1999).

SOME CONCLUSIONS

This survey of the role of the institutional environment in policy making and implementation has focused on political economy models of government. It has assumed that elected representatives are motivated by a desire to play a part in economic design making as long as they can. This will be reflected in their attitude to economic planning and legislation by attempts to bind future legislatures to present plans, and by attempts to prevent their aims and desires from being obstructed in the implementation of policies. Incumbent legislators will also seek cooperation of powerful interest groups so that their electoral support base is more secure.

From this viewpoint, policy delivery cannot be considered separately from the legislation which provides for it. For example, the work of Williams (1997) on European milk policy demonstrates that delivery should be seen in terms of the original aims of the policy rather than abstract notions of welfare. The design of legislation in theory should anticipate the agency and durability problems likely to be encountered. At the end of the day, it is the work of the economic and legal advisors in government to see that legislators' objectives are met, within the political parameters set out.

In the international arena, agreement on institutional rules is more difficult. The present arrangements for the WTO represent an attempt to make rules more enforceable for the management of trade disputes. At the same time, the agreements continue to protect national sovereignty in economic decision making in line with each country's own constitutional arrangements.

International aid organizations also are interested in building institutions for a capable public sector (World Bank, 1997, p.79). The World Bank observes that a gap has opened up between what the state says it will do and what it does – between the formal rules of public institutions and the real ones. Efforts are required to re-establish the credibility of government policies and the rules it claims to live by, making sure they operate in practice. This includes setting hard budget limits, implementing budgets and other policies as approved, making the flow of resources predictable, instituting accountability for the use of financial resources and curbing rampant political patronage in personnel decisions (ibid., p.97).

To lay the foundations of an effective public sector, countries need to concentrate on three essential building blocks (ibid., p.80): (a) a strong central capacity for formulating and coordinating policy, (b) an efficient and effective delivery system, and (c) motivated and capable staff. The transaction cost model put forward in this paper provides a very satisfying explanation of the reasons for these policy implications.

NOTES

[1]Stiglitz (1999) uses the French Revolution and incrementalism as metaphors in a recent discussion of transition economics in Russia.

[2]I shall argue that policy implementation cannot be considered separately from policy formation.

[3]For a recent review of this material, see van der Zee (1997). He aims to integrate the motives and activities of interest groups, politicians, voters and bureaucrats involved in agricultural policy formation.

[4]Recent critiques of this literature include North (1990, pp.15–16), Dixit (1996, p.9) and Williams (1997, pp. 5–6). The introduction of transaction cost analyses has shifted the emphasis away from welfare models to cost minimization models. According to Dixit, many economists have been reluctant to follow this path.

[5]Standard welfare models posit the participants as producers, consumers and taxpayers. Political preference models show that quite a diversity of groups can be identified, down to individual lobby groups. Rausser *et al.* (1995) identify (in an East European context) producers seeking economic surpluses, the *nomenklatura* (the old ruling elite) seeking their former rents and a central reform group interested in social welfare. Zusman and Amiad (1977) identify the interest groups as kibbutz (cooperative) farms, moshav (family) farms and consumers. Beghin (1990), for Senegal, uses farmers, consumers and the marketing board/government complex.

[6]Williamson (1995, pp.171, 193) maintains that institutions are important, and they are susceptible to analysis; the action resides in the details; positive analysis (with emphasis on private ordering and de facto organization) as against normative analysis (court ordering and de jure organization) is where the new institutional economics focuses attention, and taking institutions seriously is the first step. Working out the microanalytic logic of economic organization is the second. The argument is that the institutional economics approach, especially of a bottom-up kind, helps inform these issues.

[7]For a recent discussion of political stability and malfeasance, see Johnson (1999). The OECD member countries, and five others, have adopted a Convention on Combating Bribery of Foreign Public Officials in International Business Transactions to establish bribery as a criminal offence (OECD, 1997). The Commonwealth Heads of Government meeting in Durban in 1999 apparently discussed an expert report on corruption, details of which have not been released.

[8]Williams (1997, p.9) has shown that transaction cost models are highly applicable to EU milk policy.

[9]Different countries will have different attitudes to property rights and the resolution of conflict. Civil codes arising out of the Napoleonic reforms in France tend to circumscribe commercial relationships and hence property rights in order to protect the state. Codes of this kind are resistant to reform. Effects on governance and commerce include high direct transaction costs, inflexibility, slow speed of transactions, the need to resort to the courts to resolve conflict, and a low level of effectiveness and efficiency of litigation (Sandiford-Rossmiller and Rossmiller, personal communication).

[10]For an application of this argument to third world countries, see North (1990, p.67). Transaction costs are sometimes so high that no transaction takes place.

[11]This means that policy advice to decision makers always carries a risk element, in that future outcomes cannot be predicted very accurately.

[12]Braybrookee and Lindblom (1963) see disjointedness arising out of the US political system where responsibility is divided between Congress and the President.

[13]Incrementalism is not a universal phenomenon. Hall (1986, pp.8–9) points out that officials in Britain and France can display considerable forcefulness and real innovative capacity when occasion demands.

[14]Blaug only refers to one part of the Braybrookee and Lindblom model (B&S). B&L (1963, pp.66–79) actually distinguish between incremental and large change, *and* low and high levels of understanding. The model adopted by Blaug, and used here, is the incremental change and low understanding model. Decisions with incremental change and high understanding can be dealt with by the administrators; but decisions with large change, with low or high understanding, are not easily explained by the B&S approach. Constitutional economics also makes use of the distinction between small and large changes.

[15]In US farm legislation, the struggle for power between the Congress and the executive has resulted in larger and larger farm bill texts. Farm Bills in the 1960s and 1970s ran to 200–300 pages; the 1996 FAIR Act exceeded 1600 pages as Congress sought to bind the hand of the Secretary of Agriculture (Sandiford-Rossmiller and Rossmiller, personal communication).

[16]For a comprehensive discussion of the applicability of these components to developing countries, see Bale and Dale (1998).

[17]Schwartz (1996) links these reforms to restructuring the institutional fabric of the state in order to change the behaviour of both citizens and public sector employees by changing the incentive structure these groups face. The aim is to insulate the state from rent seeking and to reduce the role of the state in economic affairs.

[18]As Aucoin (1990) points out, reforms have followed the application of business principles to the state, and from the application of organizational theory to the state. The two seem to be inextricably mixed in actual application. The delivery of agricultural services by governments has certainly been subject to reform in many countries as fiscal imperatives close in. For discussion of livestock services in Africa, see Leonard (1993) and Leonard *et al.* (1999); for contracting out in developing countries, see Hubbard (1995); for alternative policy advice see Storey (1996); for irrigation services in Bolivia and extension services in Ecuador, see Haebig *et al.* (1998).

[19]Dixit (1996, pp.107–12) notes the peculiarities of history, geography, culture, population, language and other characteristics which determine the operation and evolution of politics and institutions in a country. He suggests there is a general merging of systems towards the US system owing to the international mobility of people and ideas. Weaver and Rockman (1993) provide a detailed comparison of parliamentary systems and presidential systems.

[20]North (1990, p.1010) asks, why does a fundamental change in relative prices affect two societies differently? He answers that the bargaining power of groups in one society will clearly differ from that in another and adaptations at the margin (in reaching solutions) will reflect this. With different past histories and incomplete feedback on the consequences, the actors will have different subjective models and therefore make different policy choices.

[21]Dixit (1996, pp.124–5) points out the key political conflict in international trade is a Prisoners' Dilemma for the group countries seeking to agree to a more liberal trading system. Each country wishes to restrict its trade – sometimes because it wants to exert some national monopoly or monopsony, sometimes because it wants to pursue a strategic industrial policy that is at least in principle in its national interest, sometimes because the trade barriers are thought to counter some domestic market failure, but mostly because some interest group powerful in its domestic politics wants protection from foreign competition. If all countries give way to the pressure, all will be losers. Therefore they have an incentive to get together and exchange credible promises of retaining open trade regimes. Each retains an incentive to renege on such an agreement and then to try to prevent others from doing the same!

[22]Downs (1957) regarded government, not simply as a black box processing the preferences of citizens, but as a composite actor made up of politicians and voters, each with their own set of objectives and constraints. He observed, 'parties formulate policies in order to win elections, rather than win elections to formulate policies'.

[23]Dixit (1996) appears to have developed a similar approach to Horn (1995) without any cross-citing of references. He identifies costs involved in overcoming the asymmetric distribution of information between parties (signalling and screening costs, costs of monitoring and incentives, auditing costs and costs of misrepresentation), costs involved in managing agents (monitoring, incentives and contractual obligations), costs of agents responding to multiple principals (coordination of policies, playing off one principal against another), and costs related to asset specificity (irreversible investments and lack of durability). Dixit also makes clear that the transaction cost associated with Horn's definition of commitment is the consequent loss of flexibility.

[24]This presentation neatly sidesteps the issue of analysing political behaviour. It says that, if the political institutions in place deliver a clear mandate to one group or another (political parties), then the policy-forming processes are likely to follow the behaviours set out in this section.

[25]This section depends somewhat on the author's experience, but indicates the main issues involved.

[26]G.E. Rossmiller (personal communication) points out that the National Center for Food and Agricultural Policy (NCFAP) plays a similar role in Washington.

[27]Similar processes are carried out by the Australian National Audit Office. These are strong on administrative detail about implementation and alignment with professed objectives, but are not critical of policy per se. Since 1997, Regulatory Impact Statements have been mandatory for all Commonwealth legislation that has the potential to affect business. 'The costs and benefits of regulation are to be weighed up carefully to ensure that the putative [supposed] benefits are not outweighed by excessive economic and financial costs, including the compliance burden on business' (Prime Minister Howard, 1997).

[28]Formal review of policy is provided for by the Audit Office, Regulatory Impact Statements to Cabinet, and the Crown Company Monitoring and Advisory Unit. The Audit Office has a statutory requirement to provide reports on whether public sector organizations operate and account for their performance *in a manner consistent with Parliament's intentions*

REFERENCES

Abbott, F.M. (1997), 'The Intersection of Law and Trade in the WTO System: Economics and the Transition to a Hard Law System', *Proceedings of a Conference of the International Agricultural Trade Research Consortium*, Tucson, Arizona, December 1995.

Aucoin, P. (1990), 'Administrative Reform in Public Management: Paradigms, Principles, Paradoxes and Pendulums', *Governance*, **3**, 115–37.

Bale, M. and Dale T. (1998), 'Public Sector Reform in New Zealand and Its Relevance to Developing Countries', *The World Bank Research Observer*, **13**, 103–21.

Beghin, J.C. (1990), 'A Game-Theoretic Model of Endogenous Public Policies', *American Journal of Agricultural Economics*, **72**, 138–48.

Blaug, M. (1992), *The Methodology of Economics: How Economists Explain*, 2nd edn, Cambridge: Cambridge University Press.

Blondel, J. (1990), *Comparative Government: An Introduction*, New York: Philip Allan.

Boston, J., Martin, J., Pallot, J. and Walsh, P. (1996), *Public Management: the New Zealand Model*, Auckland: Oxford University Press.

Braybrookee, D. and Lindblom, C.E. (1963), *A Strategy of Decision: Policy Evaluation as a Social Process*, New York: Free Press.

Buchanan, J.M. (1975), 'A Contractarian Paradigm for Applying Economic Theory', *American Economic Review*, **65**, 225–30.

Buchanan, J.M. (1987), 'The Constitution of Economic Policy', *American Economic Review*, **77**, 243–50.

Considine, M. (1996), *Public Policy: A Critical Approach*, Melbourne: Macmillan.

Davis, L.E. and North, D.C. (1971), *Institutional Change and American Economic Growth*, Cambridge: Cambridge University Press.

Dixit, A.K. (1996), *The Making of Economic Policy: A Transaction-Cost Politics Perspective*, Cambridge, MA: MIT Press.

Downs, A. (1957), *An Economic Theory of Democracy*, New York: Harper & Row.

Frydman, R. and Rapacynski, A. (1993), 'Privatization in Eastern Europe', *Finance and Development*, (June), 10–13.

Haebig, M., Johnson, R., Rossmiller, E., Sandiford-Rossmiller, F., Urban, K. and Williams, R. (1998), 'The Changing Environment for Agricultural Policy Implementation', paper presented to Annual Conference of the Agricultural Economics Society, University of Reading.

Hall, P.A. (1986), *Governing the Economy: The Politics of State Intervention in Britain and France*, Cambridge: Polity Press.

Hood, C. (1991), 'A Public Management for all Seasons?', *Public Administration*, **69**, 3–19.

Horn, M. (1995), *The Political Economy of Public Administration*, New York: Cambridge University Press.

Hubbard, M. (1995), 'The "new public management" and the reform of public services to agriculture in adjusting economies: the role of contracting', *Food Policy*, **20**, 529–36.

Industry Commission (1991), *Australian Dairy Industry*, Report no. 14, Canberra: AGPS.

Johnson, D.B. (1991), *Public Choice: An Introduction to the New Political Economy*, California: Bristlecone Books.

Johnson, R.W.M. (1994), 'The National Interest, Westminster, and Public Choice', *Australian Journal of Agricultural Economics*, **38**, 1–30.

Johnson, R.W.M. (1999), *The Role of Political and Economic Institutions in Rural Strategy Formulation and Implementation*, World Bank Rural Development Division, Background Papers, Washington, DC: World Bank (*http://WBLN0018.worldbank.org*).

Koch, J.V. (1980), *Industrial Organisation and Prices*, 2nd edn, New York: Prentice-Hall.

Lane, Jan-Erik (1996), *Constitutions and Political Theory*, Manchester: Manchester University Press.

Leonard, D.K. (1993), 'Structural Reform of the Veterinary Profession in Africa and the New Institutional Economics', *Development and Change*, **24**, 227–67.

Leonard, D.K., Koma, L.M.P.K., Ly, C. and Woods, P.S.A. (1999), 'The New Institutional Economics of Privatising Veterinary Services in Africa', *Revue Scientifique et Technique, Office International Epizooties*, **18**, 544–61.

Martin, W. (1989), 'Australian Agricultural Policy: 1983–88', paper presented to 33rd Annual Conference of the Australian Agricultural Economics Society, Christchurch.

Martin, W. (1990), 'Public Choice Theory and Australian Agricultural Policy Reform', *Australian Journal of Agricultural Economics*, **34**, 189–211.

Murrell, P. (1995), 'Comment on "The Institutions and Governance of Economic Development and Reform", by O.E. Williamson', *Proceedings of the World Bank Annual Conference on Development Economics, 1994*, Washington, DC: World Bank, pp. 201–5.

National Center for Food and Agricultural Policy (NCFAP)(1994), *A Decade of Service*, Washington, DC: NCFAP.

North, D.C. (1987), 'Institutions, Transaction Costs and Economic Growth', *Economic Inquiry*, **25**, 419–28.

North, D.C. (1990), *Institutions, Institutional Change and Economic Performance*, Cambridge: Cambridge University Press.

Organisation for Economic Cooperation and Development (OECD)(1997), *Convention on Combating Bribery of Foreign Public Officials in International Business Transactions – Text*, Paris: OECD (*http:www.oecd.org//daf/nocorruption/20nov1e.htm*).

Prime Minister (1997), 'More Time for Business', statement by the Prime Minister, the Hon. John Howard MP, 24 March, AGPS, Canberra.

Productivity Commission (1998), *Regulation and its Review 1997–98*, annual report series, Canberra: AusInfo.

Randall, A. (1987), *Resource Economics*, New York: John Wiley and Son.

Rausser, G., Simon, L.K. and van't Veld, K.T. (1995), 'Political Economic Processes and Collective Decision Making', in G.H. Peters and D.D. Hedley (eds), *Agricultural Competitiveness: Market Forces and Policy Choice*, Aldershot: Dartmouth.

Sandiford, F. and Rossmiller, G. (1996), 'Many a Slip: Studying Policy Delivery Systems', paper presented to the Agricultural Economics Society Conference, University of Newcastle-upon-Tyne, 27–30 March 1996, reprinted in *FAO Economic and Social Development Paper 142*, FAO, Rome.

Schwartz, H.M. (1996), 'Public Choice Theory and Public Choices: Bureaucrats and State Reorganization in Australia, Denmark, New Zealand, and Sweden in the 1980s', Department of Government and Foreign Affairs, University of Virginia, Charlottesville (*http://darwin.clas.virginia.edu/~hms2f/pubchoic.txt*).

Stiglitz, J.E. (1999), 'Whither Reform? Ten Years of the Transition', Annual World Bank Conference on Development Economics, Washington, DC, 28–30 April (*www.worldbank.org./research/abcde/stiglitz.html*).

Storey, G.G. (1996), 'Investigation on the Implications of Government Reform in New Zealand for Obtaining Economic and Policy Analysis for the Agri-Food Sector', Department of Agricultural Economics, University of Saskatchewan, Saskatoon.

Swinnen, J. and van der Zee, F. (1993), 'The Political Economy of Agricultural Policies: A Survey', *European Review of Agricultural Economics*, **20**, 261–90.

Trebilcock, M. (1995), 'Can Government be Reinvented?', in J. Boston (ed.), *The State Under Contract*, Wellington, NZ: Bridget Williams Books.

Tulloch, G. (1983), 'Public Choice and Regulation', in *Economics of Bureaucracy and Statutory Authorities*, St Leonards, NSW, Australia: Centre for Independent Studies.

Uhrig, J. (chairman)(1983), *Review of the Industries Assistance Commission*, Volume 1, Report, Commonwealth of Australia, Canberra: Australian Government Publishing Service, 1984.

Van der Zee, F.A. (1997), *Political Economy Models and Agricultural Policy Formation: Empirical Applicability and Relevance for the CAP*, Leyden: Backhuys Publishers.

Weaver, R.K. and Rockman, B.A. (1993), *Do Institutions Matter? Government Capabilities in the United States and Abroad*, Washington, DC: Brookings Institution.

Williams, R. (1997), 'The Political Economy of the Common Market in Milk and Dairy Products in the European Union', in *FAO Economic and Social Development Paper 142*, FAO, Rome.

Williamson, O.E. (1995), 'The Institutions and Governance of Economic Development and Reform', *Proceedings of the World Bank Annual Conference on Development Economics, 1994*, Washington, DC: World Bank, 171–97.

Williamson, O.E. (2000), 'The New Institutional Economics: Taking Stock/Looking Ahead', invited paper presented to Annual Conference of the Australian Agricultural and Resource Economics Society, Sydney, 23–5 January.

World Bank (1997), *World Development Report 1997*, Washington, DC: World Bank.

Zeckhauser, R. (1995), Dust jacket: Horn, M. (1995), *The Political Economy of Public Administration*, Cambridge: Cambridge University Press.

Zusman, P. and Amiad, A. (1977), 'A Quantitative Investigation of a Political Economy – The Israeli Dairy Program', *American Journal of Agricultural Economics*, **59**, 88–98.

SECTION IV

Making Agriculture Environmentally Safe

GEORGE W. NORTON AND SCOTT M. SWINTON*

Precision Agriculture: Global Prospects and Environmental Implications

INTRODUCTION

Producers in industrialized countries have been inundated by ideas and information about precision agriculture (PA) and how new site-specific management (SSM) technologies will revolutionize their farm operations. Conjuring up 'Star Wars' imagery, farmers and their computerized machinery communicate with satellites while speeding up and down the information highway. The farm press has hailed the advent of these technologies as a win–win situation, with higher farm profits and improved environmental quality. Certainly the potential is there for greater economic returns and better environmental stewardship. But what exactly is precision agriculture, who is applying it, and where? Is the technology only relevant for developed countries and are there implications for markets? What is the likelihood that environmental benefits will be realized? This paper addresses these questions by drawing on literature, data and expert opinion.

WHAT IS PRECISION AGRICULTURE?

Before the advent of the tractor, farmers tilled small fields, making agronomic management decisions based on the special characteristics of each tiny parcel of land. When mechanization took over, it no longer made economic sense for producers to focus at the site-specific level. Uniform management over larger fields was more cost-effective, even though less precise pest, fertility and moisture control was achieved (Swinton and Lowenberg-DeBoer, 1998). The objective of precision agriculture is to allow farmers cost-effectively and more precisely to address spatial and temporal variability within large fields. A broad definition of precision agriculture based on one provided by the National Research Council (NRC, 1997) is: 'Precision agriculture is a management

*George Norton, Virginia Polytechnic Institute and State University (Virginia Tech), Blacksburg, VA, USA. Scott Swinton, Michigan State University, East Lansing, MI, USA. The global scope of the adoption assessment was made possible by help from Stan Daberkow, Jon East, Harold Reetz, John Schueller, Hermann Waibel, Paul Winters, Ada Wossink and participants in the Precision Agriculture e-mail list server maintained by the University of Minnesota (*listserv@coal.agoff.umn.edu*). We thank Jess Lowenberg-DeBoer for helpful comments on an earlier draft.

strategy that uses information technologies to provide and process data with high spatial and temporal resolution, for decision-making with respect to crop production.' By encompassing performance measures (such as yield maps), this definition is broader than many input-oriented definitions (for example, Khanna and Zilberman, 1997). What makes PA possible is not one new technology, but the convergence of a whole suite of technologies (Swinton and Lowenberg-DeBoer, 1998).

The key innovation compared with conventional management is the application of modern *information* technologies. PA technologies are most often directed at spatial variability within fields, although some focus on temporal variation as well. Precision agriculture is based on addressing the variability of soils, pests, moisture, micro-climates and other factors that are present in agricultural settings, notably cropped fields. It relies on three major components: (a) capture of data at an appropriate scale and time, (b) interpretation and analysis of that data, and (c) implementation of a management response at an appropriate scale and time (NRC, 1997). We distinguish between two categories, the site-specific (SS) and the development-specific (DS). SS technologies focus on spatial management, usually for crops. DS technologies deal with temporal management and include applications to crops, livestock and pests. Our main concern will be the SS technologies as used in the capital-intensive computer-based systems that seem to have captured the term 'precision agriculture' in the popular press.

Site-specific management (SSM) relies heavily on four component sets of computer-based technologies: geographic information systems (GIS), global positioning systems (GPS), variable rate application (VRA) input systems and sensing technologies. Geographic information systems (GIS), as used in SSM, spatially reference layers of data about field attributes to help in managing small units and in comparing different types of information at multiple locations. Global positioning systems use mobile field instruments to receive satellite signals to identify the location of a piece of equipment in the field. Variable rate technologies use a computerized controller to vary spatially inputs such as seed, fertilizer and pesticides based on the needs calculated by linking GIS information to a specific field position. The VRA system may be map-based and use a GPS and a controller that stores a plan of the desired application rate for each location in the field. Alternatively, it may use sensing technologies that signal the controller to vary application rates based on real-time analysis of soil and/or crop sensor measurements. In-field sensing technologies do not necessarily require a GPS and permit relatively low-cost data collection about field characteristics such as organic matter, cation exchange capacity, top soil depth, moisture, soil nitrates and crop spectral reflectance.[1] VRA fits into existing systems relatively easily because it may be used for one or two inputs as a stand-alone practice without changing other elements of the system.[2]

Yield monitors are the most common SS sensing technology, with data typically being stored in a GIS and statistically smoothed for printing as a yield map. Farmers may use yield maps to identify problem areas in the field, often combining the information with soil sampling on a grid basis in the field.

Yield maps are used not only for VRA but also to suggest areas that would benefit from drainage, irrigation, land levelling, fences and other investments. Mapping records the spatial distribution of yield while the crop is being harvested. Systems have been used mostly for grains, and use mass flow and moisture sensors to determine grain mass and GPS receivers to record position. Yield maps can also help farmers make decisions such as how much to bid, or whether to bid, on renting a field. Precision agriculture data generated for subfield management may have additional value when combined with similar material from other fields and farms.

Some PA technologies are development-specific, relying on computer models to predict crop growth, pasture growth, animal digestion and growth, or pest damage. They mostly take the form of decision support tools that predict crop or animal response to management actions. Examples are integrated pest management (IPM) threshold programmes that predict how crop yield and net revenues would respond to control of weeds, insects or diseases. IPM threshold programmes for insects and weeds typically simulate pest demographics, cumulative crop damage projected from rising populations and response to alternative pest control practices (Pedigo *et al.*, 1986; Cousens *et al.*, 1987). IPM thresholds for diseases typically focus on predicting disease spread based upon weather prediction and length of opportunity for disease control, since many diseases are devastating once they spread (Travis and Latin, 1991). Other DS software predict livestock weight gain under alternative feeding regimes at different life cycle stages (for example, Rotz *et al.*, 1989). Because site-specific technologies are relatively new, we will focus primarily on them rather than on the development-specific technologies.

ADOPTION: WHAT TO EXPECT

A conceptual model can assist in forecasting the settings in which adoption of PA information technologies is likely to occur. Consider the dynamic problem of choosing a stream of inputs over time that will maximize a farmer's discounted net revenue stream. In particular, the problem is to choose those capital inputs (both information technologies, k_I, and conventional technologies, k_x and the annual variable inputs (custom PA services, cs_I, and conventional inputs, x) whose costs depend in part on the level of capital investment in related technologies:

$$Max \int_{t=1}^{T} \delta^t E(\pi_t) dt$$

$$k_I, cs_I, k_x, x$$

(1)

subject to:

$$\pi = r(p, A, y[x,z]) - c(w_x, x, w_I, cs_I[K_I, CS_I]) - k_I - k_x - FC$$

$$k_j = k_j(K_{jt-1}, L_f, \int \delta^t \pi_t dt, WK(Y^{nf}, credit[K_{jt-1}, i, A]) \quad \forall j = I, x$$

(2)

$$K_{jt} = K_{jt-1} + k_{jt}$$

$$K_{I0} = 0; K_{x0} = K_0$$

In this model, $E(\cdot)$ is the expectations operator, δ is a discount factor, and π_t is net revenue in period t, with integration covering all periods up to time horizon T. In the constraint set, the time subscript is suppressed for simplicity. Annual net revenue, π_t, depends upon revenue ($r(\cdot)$), variable costs ($c(\cdot)$), and capital costs (k_j, FC). The revenue function, $r(\cdot)$, depends upon product price, p, land operated, A, and productivity, y. Productivity, in turn, depends upon conventional inputs, x (including seed, fertilizers, pesticides, hired labour) and conditioning factors, z (such as human capital, management ability and land quality). The variable cost function, $c(\cdot)$, depends on input levels and unit input prices, w_x, for conventional input x and w_I for information custom services, cs_I. The demand for custom services will depend on both the level of existing farm investment in information technologies, K_I, and the existing set of custom services available in the local economy, CS_I. The annual capital costs for information technologies (k_I) and conventional technologies (k_x) also figure in net revenue, along with other fixed costs, FC. Annual investment costs of either technology, k_j, depend upon prior capital stocks, K_{jt-1}, the availability of family labour (L_f), expected future net revenues from changes in capital level (the second term) and the availability of working capital, WK. WK, in turn, depends upon non-farm income, Y^{nf}, and credit, which is a function of current ownership of capital (K_{jt-1}), interest rate (I), and land (A). The final two constraint equations specify the dynamics of motion and initial conditions.

Creating a Hamiltonian from (1) and (2) and differentiating with respect to k_I or cs_I leads to a reduced-form input demand function that highlights the expected determinants of adoption for PA technologies:

$$k_I = k_I(p, w_I, w_x, i, K_0, Y^{nf}, CS_I, A, z)$$

(3)

Equation (3) suggests that, apart from input and output prices, SS PA technology adoption depends on the farm's access to investment capital, be it from an initial endowment, off-farm income or land. Because PA technologies can enhance land productivity, land also matters for its role in the revenue function. Embedded in the z variable are management quality elements, including human capital, suggesting that more rapid adoption of PA technologies occurs where education levels are higher. The model also points to the importance of an agribusiness infrastructure that makes available PA custom services.

This conceptual model provides a starting point for a critical assessment of PA technology adoption. If the model is extended, further attributes can enter. For example, if risk is included in the utility function of the decision maker, then the determinants of yield variability may enter the adoption function. Likewise, where governments enact policies to reduce non-point source water pollution from agricultural chemicals, policy parameters may also enter the adoption function. In such nations, adoption may be more advanced for environmental policy reasons, other things being equal.

The model suggests we might expect earliest adoption of PA technologies among farms and in countries where agricultural land and capital are abundant. After all, site-specific technologies automate management decisions for mechanized agriculture. They can be thought of as another wave of technological innovation induced by factor prices that enhance the productivity of labour in regions where it is relatively most scarce (Hayami and Ruttan, 1985). Focusing on complementary inputs per worker, Figure 1 compares existing levels of agricultural land and capital (as tractors) per worker in major agricultural regions of the world. The relative abundance of land and capital relative to labour (or conversely, the relative scarcity of labour) suggests that Canada, the United States and Australia would be prime candidates for site-specific technology adoption.

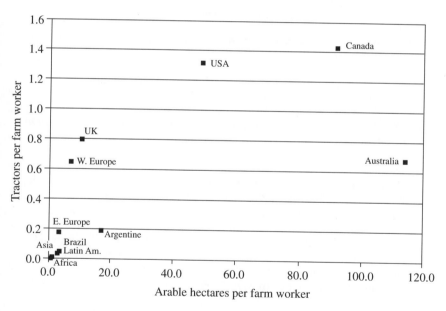

Notes: Africa = sub-saharan Africa; Asia excludes Japan and Israel; population data refer to 1990.

Source: FAOSTAT databases on land, fertilizers and economically active agricultural population (*http://apps.fao.org/lim500/agri_db.pl*).

FIGURE 1   *Tractors and arable land per farm worker: selected nations and regions, 1997*

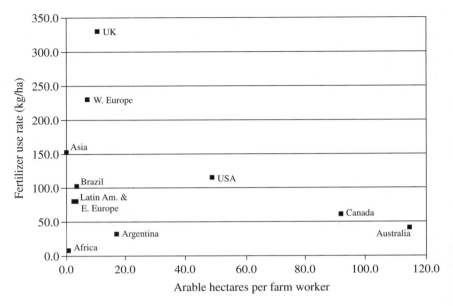

Notes: Africa = sub-Saharan Africa; Asia excludes Japan and Israel; population
             data refer to 1990.

Source: FAOSTAT databases on land, machinery and economically active
             agricultural population.

FIGURE 2   *Fertilizer rates and arable land per worker: selected nations
and regions, 1997*

To the extent that SS PA technologies offer agrochemical input cost savings,
Figure 2 suggests that a second category of PA adopter countries could be
those land-abundant nations where fertilizer use is high (especially if environmental regulations discourage non-point source water pollution from agricultural
chemicals). Figure 2 reveals that no countries combine both land abundance
and heavy fertilizer use rates. However, in Western Europe, fertilizer use is
quite high. So if input cost saving and environmental protection are major
adoption determinants, these may be areas for willing adoption of PA technologies.

ADOPTION: WHAT WE OBSERVE

Where PA adoption is occurring

At present, there exist no inter-country data with which to test formally the
hypothesis that adoption of PA technologies would occur where land and

capital are abundant compared to labour. However, fragmentary survey data bolstered by anecdotal evidence are highly supportive. Adoption of site-specific technologies appears to be highest in the USA, followed by Canada and then, probably, Australia and/or Great Britain. But farm-level adoption of site-specific technologies is still concentrated in certain crops and regions, even in these countries.[3] What data are available focus on the two practices that are easiest to measure: the use of yield monitors and VRA controllers.

In the USA, results from the 1996 national Agricultural Resource Management Survey (ARMS) indicate that approximately 9 per cent of US corn growers had adopted site-specific PA technologies, representing about 19 per cent of the corn acreage (Daberkow and McBride, 1998a, 1998b). Soil sampling, using a grid or map approach, was the most adopted practice with 15.8 per cent of corn acreage, followed by yield monitoring with 15.6 per cent. In the corn, soybean and wheat country of the Midwestern USA, where SS technology adoption is most widespread, Khanna *et al.* (1999) found that nearly 14 per cent of farmers were grid sampling their soils in 1997. Eleven per cent of the farmers used VRA for fertilizer application, 2.5 per cent used VRA for pesticide application and 2.4 per cent used it for seed application.

More than 18 per cent of US corn and soybean acreage was under yield monitors in 1998 (Table 1), according to the ARMS studies. Khanna *et al.* (1999) found similarly that in 1997 almost 10 per cent of farmers surveyed in Illinois, Iowa, Wisconsin and Indiana had adopted yield monitors for use on farms covering more than 17 per cent of the cropped acreage surveyed.

TABLE 1   *Percentage of US corn, soybean and wheat acreage under yield monitors, 1996–8*

	Corn	Soybeans	Wheat
1996	15.6	13.0	5.0
1997	17.3	12.2	6.0
1998	18.5	18.6	7.9

Source: USDA/ERS agricultural resource management surveys (ARMS).

Data on adoption of site-specific technologies are spotty elsewhere. In Canada and Australia, wheat growers have begun adopting yield monitoring, but low crop prices and yields have limited the level of investment in nutrient management technologies such as spatial soil sampling and VRA fertilizer application (East, 1999). Likewise, a recent account of PA adoption in Argentina indicates that roughly 1–2 per cent of combines are equipped with yield monitors, but that adoption of VRA for fertilizer application is slow (Lowenberg-DeBoer, 1999). Anecdotal information suggests a similar pattern among large farms in Mexico and Brazil,[4] where in the latter 50 combines were reportedly equipped with yield monitors in early 2000.[5]

Adoption in Europe has been highest in Germany and the UK, and concentrated among larger producers. A 1997 mail survey of 90 crop farmers in the UK found 15 per cent using some form of site-specific technology, including 6 per cent using cereal yield mapping, 7 per cent using VRA for fertilizer application and 12 per cent doing spatially referenced soil sampling and mapping (Fountas, 1998). Eastern Europe lags far behind. In Asia, adoption of site-specific technologies was virtually non-existent by 1998 (Srinivasan, 1998). Emerging Asian use of SS PA technologies appears principally to be applied to perennial plantation crops.[6] In sub-Saharan Africa, experimentation with yield monitors and VRA fertilizer has been reported in South Africa,[7] with anecdotal reports of use in Zimbabwe.

Why PA adoption is occurring

Expected profitability is the mostly widely touted reason for adoption of site-specific technologies. More precise information offers the promise of increasing yields (where nutrients were deficient or pests excessive) and decreasing input use (where nutrients were overabundant or pests sparse) (Lowenberg-DeBoer and Boehlje, 1996). Yield risk reduction may also result from VRA fertilization (Lowenberg-DeBoer and Aghib, 1999). Environmental benefits from the reduction of unnecessary agrochemical applications is another potential benefit that farmers could find desirable. Apart from the appeal of site-specific technologies, the feasibility of adoption is another matter, as implied in the conceptual model presented in equations (1) and (2). What is the evidence?

The results of 17 studies that assessed the profitability of SSM are presented in Lowenberg-DeBoer and Swinton (1997). Most of the studies focus on only a single PA practice, but it is clear that the profitability of SSM practices varies significantly by crop, location and year. Five studies found SSM not profitable, six had mixed or inconclusive results, and six showed potential profitability. Upon applying standard cost assumptions to the nine studies based on field (rather than simulated) data, Swinton and Lowenberg-DeBoer (1998) found that profitability correlated closely with crop value. This result supports inclusion of output price in the adoption function above (equation 3). Recent evidence suggests that site-specific management is beginning to see use on fruits, vegetables and other high-value crops (Tisseyre *et al.*, 1999; Chan *et al.*, 1999).

If crop value is so important, why has adoption of site-specific technologies been greatest to date on lower value crops such as corn, wheat and soybeans? One reason may be the ease of adapting existing machinery to the technologies such as yield monitors, and the importance of large field size. McBride *et al.* (1999) conducted a logit analysis of factors influencing corn producers' attitudes toward site-specific farming. Among other things, they found that producers with a favourable attitude farmed more corn land (80–100 acres).

But human capital also favours PA adoption, perhaps because better educated farmers are able to wring higher profit out of complicated site-specific technologies. Khanna (1999) found that education and innovativeness favoured adoption of VRA fertilizer application. Likewise, McBride *et al.* (1999) found farmers favourably inclined towards site-specific technologies were younger (by 4–6 years), had more formal education (by one year), and were more likely to use crop consultants.

This last point highlights the importance of agribusiness infrastructure. The USA has an exceptionally high number of agricultural input dealers who make PA services available to farmers. In 1999–2000, 38–45 per cent of fertilizer dealers in the USA offered soil sampling with GPS, 23–29 per cent offered yield monitoring, and 32–40 per cent offered agronomic analysis of GPS data (Whipker and Akridge, 1999, 2000). Contracting for services with dealers allows producers to test the technology without making a long-term investment. The technically simpler and less expensive technologies such as grid soil fertility testing and pest scouting are used by a larger fraction of the farmers than are the more sophisticated technologies. Interestingly, adoption of SS PA services among US input dealers is beginning to stabilize, perhaps in response to low crop commodity prices. In each case above, the smaller adoption figure in the range given refers to the year 2000, the larger to 1999.

Larger farms are more likely to adopt site-specific methods. As suggested by equations (1) and (2), this occurs because of both the revenue effect from added yield and the fixed cost effect of being able to spread capital costs over a larger output. As illustrated by Thirkawala *et al.* (1999), the profitability of VRA increases with farm size and field variability. Apart from technical economies of scale, large farms may also obtain pecuniary gains in the form of quantity discounts for consulting and custom hire services. The empirical evidence contradicts the assertion that there 'does not appear to be an unambiguous size bias in precision agriculture or similar technologies' (NRC, 1997, p.81). Khanna *et al.* (1999) found that farms adopting PA technologies were 1.6 times larger than non-adopters.

The adoption appeal of potential environmental benefits from site-specific technologies seems to be negligible. Khanna *et al.* (1999) found that only 8 per cent of the Midwestern US farmers surveyed indicated that their first or second most important reason for adopting PA would be its environmental benefits.

Global prospects for adoption of site-specific technologies

While it is not known which technologies will prove to be the most practical and standard PA practices in the long term, evidence to date suggests that PA adoption is likely to increase slowly, but will be concentrated primarily in certain regions in developed countries.

For crop production in the USA, Khanna *et al.* (1999) predict that adoption of VRA for fertilizer application and yield monitors may rise from their 1997 levels of 10–11 per cent to be adopted by about 40 per cent of Midwest farmers by 2001. PA adoption elsewhere in the USA is likely to be lower as profitability is mixed (Swinton and Lowenberg-DeBoer, 1998). The larger and more educated crop farmers in the Midwest have adopted PA quite rapidly. As the technologies are adapted to other crops (for example, yield monitors for cotton) continued spreading among larger farmers in other regions of the country can be expected.

PA adoption for livestock management is yet to begin, but remote sensing is likely to become attractive for range-fed livestock production in land- and capital-abundant areas. Remote sensing of vegetative vigour provides a low-cost means of locating good pastures. Such technologies may see adoption by ranchers not only in areas like the western prairies of North America, but also in other semi-arid regions where livestock are grazed extensively, such as Argentina, Brazil and Australia.

Despite the high rates of agrochemical input use in Western Europe (Figure 2), less land per farm worker is likely to make adoption of site-specific crop technologies less urgent. In selected countries, such as the Netherlands, environmental regulations provide an incentive to reduce fertilizer use, but it is unclear whether costly PA site-specific technologies are the best way to achieve this when fields are small. While the large fields of Eastern Europe are technically suited to site-specific technologies, a shortage of capital will likely continue to hinder adoption of these technologies.[8]

What about developing countries? First, it is likely that SS PA adoption will remain low in developing countries for the foreseeable future. A recent literature review ascribes low fertilizer adoption in sub-Saharan Africa to reliance on subsistence crops and shortages of financial, human and physical capital (Reardon *et al.*, 1999). Such barriers are infinitely more formidable for costly site-specific PA technologies. Indeed, where fields are small and operators know them intimately, PA technologies offer few advantages. The absence of a supporting agribusiness infrastructure is another major deterrent to the diffusion of site-specific technologies in those areas of Africa, Asia (Srinivasan, 1998), and Latin America dominated by peasant agriculture.

Plantation agriculture is the likely exception to the general prediction that SS PA is unlikely to be adopted in developing countries. Plantations growing perennial crops such as coffee, tea, bananas and rubber have the land and capital to take advantage of the potential variable input savings and yield benefits from precision agriculture. Indeed, incipient adoption of PA technologies for plantation crops has been reported in Latin America and Asia.[9]

In certain areas of middle-income developing countries, conditions exist that will favour the adoption of site-specific farming methods. Brazil, Argentina and Mexico include regions with very large farms, despite the fact that the average land per agricultural worker does not stand out on a national scale (Figure 1). In all three countries, farm supply dealers have recently expressed growing interest in site-specific technologies.[10] As noted above, Argentina is seeing the beginnings of yield monitor adoption (Lowenberg-DeBoer, 1999). For similar reasons, there may be spotty adoption of site-specific technologies in South Africa.

Second, the relatively slow adoption in developed countries means that aggregate cost effects and therefore effects of the technologies on world output prices are also likely to be small for the next few years. Adjustments within developed countries are likely to be significantly greater than impacts on developing countries. The relatively small price effects imply that most of the economic benefits of PA technologies are likely to accrue to producers rather than consumers.

Although private adoption of site-specific technologies is unlikely to be widespread in developing countries, there are several public uses of site-specific technologies that may see significant adoption. Remote sensing technologies have been used for 20 years for national crop inventory statistical estimates (Srinivasan, 1998) and yield estimates for early warning of famine risk (Unganai and Kogan, 1998). Remote sensing has other public natural resource management applications, such as monitoring the health of forests and public range land.

ENVIRONMENTAL IMPLICATIONS OF PRECISION AGRICULTURE

The resource conserving/environmental benefits of PA will depend on the potential of the practices to reduce environmental costs if adopted and on incentives for their adoption. Although farmers may include environmental benefits in their utility functions, it cannot necessarily be assumed that the effects of all PA practices are positive for the environment, or that farmers value those benefits enough to adopt the practices if they are only marginally or not profitable.

Part of the enthusiasm for PA off the farm is due to a belief that there will be environmental benefits from more precisely matching inputs such as fertilizers and pesticides to the needs of a crop in small areas and from applying these chemicals exactly when needed (NRC, 1997). Khanna and Zilberman (1997) argue that the root cause of agricultural pollution is not modem technology, input use, or production per se, but inefficient utilization of inputs in the production process. Agricultural pollution comes from inputs that do not reach their target. Residuals from inputs such as irrigation water, fertilizers and pesticides are a major source of mineralization and salinization of soil and chemical contamination of ground and surface water (ibid.). And controlling pollution at the source is likely to be cheaper than cleaning it up afterwards. Indeed, field-level agronomic studies indicate that PA may permit large reductions in input use without sacrificing yields.

Evidence suggests, however, that PA may result in less environmental improvement than indicated by field-level agronomic studies (NRC, 1997; Kitchen *et al.*, 1995; Redulla *et al.*, 1996). One reason is that a major source of nutrient loss from agricultural production systems arises from leaching that occurs during the part of the year when the plants are not in the field (Groffman, 1997). Nutrients lost in the autumn, winter and spring are not so much 'leftover' fertilizer from growing season applications as nutrients lost owing to a lack of a plant 'sink' when the ground is bare (Groffman, 1997; Shipley *et al.*, 1992). Therefore winter catch crops, buffer zones or reduced autumn tillage may have a greater effect than PA, at least for control of nitrogen leaching in temperate climates. Shipley *et al.* (1992) found that only about 20 per cent of total nitrogen in a field of maize in Maryland was derived from fertilizer applications. Second, field-level effects often do not scale up to ambient effects as the latter correlate most closely with factors such the location of the field where PA is being applied in relation to streams or lakes. Third, PA technologies do not always imply lower total input use *per unit of land* even though they would generally not have been applied if they did not reduce inputs *per unit of output*. More precise measurements may suggest lower input use in some parts of the field, but greater use in other parts.

The NRC study speculates that PA might also make it attractive to expand production on certain marginal and heterogeneous fields, possibly creating new environmental problems (NRC, 1997). The marginal lands factor might work the other way, if PA increases yields and total production, thereby reducing pressures to keep marginal areas in production.

The potential clearly exists for environmental improvements as a result of specific PA technologies for certain crops, regions and environmental categories (Larson *et al.*, 1997). Schmerler and Jurschik (1997) found nitrogen fertilizer savings of 5 to 15 per cent and higher yields for site-specific fertilization compared to uniform fertilization on winter wheat and spring barley in Germany. In a four-year study of site-specific weed control in Germany, Gerhards *et al.* (1999) found significant herbicide reductions on maize, sugar beets and wheat. Leiva *et al.* (1997) estimate that PA might save up to 40 per cent in herbicide costs and reduce nitrogen applications by 10 per cent on a farm producing cereals in the UK. Lu and Watkins (1997) found that conventional production was more profitable than three alternative variable-rate nitrogen practices on potatoes in Idaho, and VRA-reduced nitrogen loss only marginally. Thirkawala *et al.* (1999) found that VRA technology on corn in Ontario, Canada has the potential to reduce nitrogen leaching by 4 to 36 per cent, with the variation depending on the natural level of fertility and variability in the fields.

Many studies to date of the environmental impacts of SS management have been based on simulation as opposed to measurement of actual impacts. Hoskinson *et al.* (1999) applied an expert system to model variable rate fertilizer application to wheat and potatoes in Idaho, USA and found a 30 to 40 per cent fertilizer cost decrease on wheat, although they found a significant increase on potatoes. Weiss (1997) found precision application of phosphorus on an Illinois cornfield to be uneconomical, although it did reduce excess residual phosphorus.

Apart from nutrient management, some promising results have been reported for pesticides as well. Weisz *et al.* (1996) report reducing insecticide use by 60 to 95 per cent for control of Colorado potato beetle. Khakural, Robert and Koskinen (1995, cited in Larson *et al.*, 1997) reported reductions in concentrations of alachlor herbicide in runoff water and sediments from SS applications compared with uniform ones. Heisel *et al.* (1999) found that using site-specific weed management reduced herbicide use on winter wheat and barley in Denmark by 47 to 62 per cent compared to label recommendations.

In summary, these and other studies indicate significant *potential* for environmental gains from PA, but those gains will be far from uniform across commodities and locations. In addition, limited profitability may constrain adoption even though environmental gains might be great. Where societal benefits exceed private profitability, there may be a need for public policies to encourage adoption. As illustrated in Figure 3, if there is a negative externality associated with crop production, perhaps due to residuals from agricultural

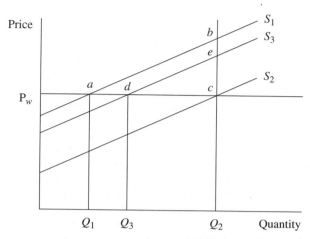

FIGURE 3   *Benefits of precision agriculture with no price effect, but a production externality*

chemicals, the marginal social cost curve S_1 may lie above the private supply curve, S_2. The optimal private quantity, Q_2 is produced rather than the quantity that is optimal from society's point of view, Q_1. The net social cost due to the externality is area *abc*. If adoption of PA technologies reduces the environmental externality, and therefore shifts the marginal social cost curve down to Q_3, the net social cost is reduced, to *dec* in our example. Of course the technology may shift the private supply curve down as well, and the net savings in marginal social cost depend on whether the distance between the old and new private and social cost curves has narrowed.

If there is potential for environmental gains and yet profitability constrains PA adoption for at least some commodities and regions, several policy options exist as discussed by Khanna and Zilberman (1997) and Casey *et al.* (1999). A few are input taxes, technology taxes or subsidies, uniform technology standards, and tax-free quotas for inputs such as nitrogen with taxes on additional input purchase. Regardless of the approach chosen, the cost effectiveness or opportunity cost of devoting resources to encouraging PA adoption as opposed to other means of improving the environment must be considered.

Input taxes, differentiated by PA versus non-PA technology, might be appropriate if there were means to observe how the inputs were being applied. However, less efficient uniform input taxes are likely to be more practical owing to prohibitive monitoring costs. Even these taxes may not be effective in influencing behaviour, however, since fertilizer and pesticide demand appears to be relatively inelastic. Water demand may be more elastic and therefore a better candidate for a tax solution.

Technology subsidy schemes can be used where it is more difficult to monitor inputs such as fertilizer, water and pesticides. Influencing the relative fixed costs of conventional versus PA technologies should influence incentives to adopt the technology, assuming the savings are passed on to farmers by the dealers who are often the ones purchasing and renting out their services to farmers. Of course, one way to get around the 'middleman' effect is to grant farmers direct payments or tax deductions. In a survey conducted by Khanna *et al.* (1999) in 1997, 61 per cent of farmers said they would be willing to adopt advanced PA technologies if a cost-share subsidy of up to 50 per cent were offered.

Uniform technology standards such as mandated equipment are less flexible than the tax or subsidy schemes. While they have worked for certain other cases such as pesticide restrictions and regulations on spraying equipment standards, they may be difficult to enforce with PA technologies.

Dubgaard (1990) advocates a policy that includes a tax-free quota of nitrogen combined with taxes on additional nitrogen purchases. PA could greatly aid such a system. Setting quota levels that differ by farm size, location and so on, however, would involve significant transactions costs and might spur unproductive rent-seeking activity, depending on rules for allocating the quotas.

Batie and Ervin (1999) propose other policy approaches. Marketable pollution permits, for example, would reward producers who could reduce their pollution to levels below permit thresholds (perhaps by using PA). Such successful containment of pollution would permit sales of surplus permits to other growers. Eco-labels represent another potential approach. Product labels that certify responsible environmental stewardship during the production process can attract consumers to pay a premium for environmental attributes in the product. Though primarily a private sector strategy, eco-labelling may require government bodies to establish or monitor certification standards (van Ravenswaay and Blend, 1999).

In the USA, farmers are encouraged to adopt practices that reduce environmental and resource problems through a programme called the Environmental Quality Incentives Programme (EQIP). Producers who enter into contracts are offered technical assistance, education, cost-sharing and incentive payments. Cost sharing and incentive payments go directly to the farmer, thereby avoiding uncertainties about whether a dealer will pass them along. The EQIP programme may be the preferred mechanism to implement a PA adoption incentives programme for that country. The programme works primarily in watersheds or areas where significant natural resource problems exist. Priority areas are identified through a locally led process. The advantage of working through the EQIP programme is that environmental benefits of PA would be judged against the benefits of spending public resources on other environmentally friendly practices.

CONCLUSION

The set of information-intensive technologies collectively known as site-specific precision agriculture have experienced significant growth over the past decade, with potentially favourable implications for the environment in regions where they can be profitably adopted. Although adoption should continue to increase in developed countries, there is likely to be little immediate impact in, or on, developing countries. One exception is the use by the public sector of remote sensing for early warning of famine dangers in parts of Africa and Asia. Environmental benefits are not well documented as yet, and they will vary with the crop, production environment and specific PA technologies. To the extent that the technologies have favourable environmental impacts, developed countries may want to consider encouraging their adoption through public policies. Whether and when policy incentives are needed to induce the adoption of PA technologies remain empirical questions. Their answers will be context-, technology- and site-specific.

NOTES

[1]Remote sensing also has the potential to contribute to PA, as the possibility of frequent acquisition of remote sensing data by satellites seems likely in the future. Several additional earth-observing satellites are scheduled for launch over the next few years, and some companies are concentrating their marketing and sales efforts on PA (NRC, 1997). Growth in the use of remote sensing for crop management will require an expanded set of people who understand the relationship between crop-soil properties and remote sensing (ibid.).

[2]Map-based VRT systems are most common for high-volume application of fertilizers and lime. However, these systems are available for farm tractor use with liquid fertilizers, anhydrous ammonia, herbicides and seeds. They are also available for water and fertilizer application through centre-pivot irrigation systems (NRC, 1997). Sensor-based VRT is employed to vary anhydrous ammonia in response to soil types, seeding rates in response to soil cation exchange capacity and topsoil depth, herbicide rates in response to organic matter, starter fertilizer in response to soil cation exchange capacity, and side-dress nitrogen fertilizer in response to soil cation exchange capacity, topsoil and soil nitrate levels (ibid.).

[3]The only exception to this generalization would be selected development-specific technologies, which have seen widespread adoption, especially in North America and Europe. Among IPM practices, the use of scouting to predict crop pest damage thresholds had spread to 78 per cent of US corn growers and 84 per cent of apple growers by 1996 (Fernandez-Cornejo and Jans, 1999).

[4]Harold Reetz, Midwest Director, Phosphate and Potash Institute, Monticello, IL, personal communication to Precision Agriculture e-mail List, 4 October 1999.

[5]José P. Molin, ESALQ/USP Piracicaba, personal communication to Agriculture e-mail list, 17 May 2000.

[6]Ancha Srinivasan, senior researcher, Regional Science Institute, Kita-ku, Sapporor, Japan, personal communication to Agriculture e-mail list, 16 May 2000.

[7]Jess M. Lowenberg-DeBoer, Purdue University, W. Lafayette, IN, USA, personal communication to Agriculture e-mail list, 15 May 2000.

[8]John K. Schueller, Department of Mechanical Engineering, University of Florida, personal communication to Precision Agriculture e-mail list, 4 October 1999.

[9]Ancha Srinivasan, Regional Science Institute, Kita-ku, Sapporo, Japan, personal communication to Precision Agriculture e-mail list, 16 May 1999.

[10]Harold Reetz, Midwest Director, Phosphate and Potash Institute, Monticello, IL, personal communication to Precision Agriculture e-mail list, 4 October 1999.

REFERENCES

Batie, S.S. and Ervin, D.E. (1999), 'Flexible Incentives for the Adoption of Environmental Technologies in Agriculture: A Typology', in C.F. Casey, A. Schmitz, S.M. Swinton and D. Zilberman (eds), *Flexible Incentives for the Adoption of Environmental Technologies in Agriculture*, Boston: Kluwer Academic Publishers.

Casey, F., Schmitz, A., Swinton, S.M. and Zilberman, D. (eds) (1999), *Flexible Incentives for the Adoption of Environmental Technologies in Agriculture*, Boston: Kluwer Academic Press.

Chan, C.W., Schueller, J.K, Miller, W.M., Whitney, J.D. and Wheaton, T.A. (1999), 'Accuracy in Spatially-Variable Crop Production and an Illustration in Citrus Yield Mapping', in J.V. Stafford (ed.), *Precision Agriculture '99*, Sheffield, UK: Academic Press.

Cousens, R., Moss, S.R., Cussans, G.W. and Wilson, B.J. (1987), 'Modeling Weed Populations in Cereals', *Reviews of Weed Science*, **3**, 93–112.

Daberkow, S.G. and McBride, W.D. (1998a), 'Adoption of Precision Agriculture Technologies by U.S. Corn Producers', P. Robert, R. Rust and W. Larson (eds), *Proceedings of the Fourth International Conference on Precision Agriculture*, Madison, WI: ASA/CSSA/SSSA.

Daberkow, S.G. and McBride, W.D. (1998b), 'Socioeconomic Profiles of Early Adopters of Precision Agriculture Technologies', *Journal of Agribusiness*, **11**, 151–68.

Dubgaard, A. (1990), 'The Need for a Common Nitrogen Policy in the EC', in R. Calvet (ed.), *Nitrates–Agriculture–Eau*, Paris: Institut National de la Recherche Agronomique.

East, J. (1999), 'Capitalising on Innovation: The Future of Precision Agriculture in Australia', Bureau of Rural Sciences, Australia (*http://www.brs.gov.au/agrifood/agsystems/painet.html*, last updated 1 September 1999).

Fernandez-Cornejo, J. and Jans, S. (1999), *Pest Management in U.S. Agriculture*, Agricultural Handbook no. 717. Resource Economics Division, Economic Research Service, Washington, DC: U.S. Department of Agriculture.

Fountas, S. (1998), 'Market Research on the Views and Perceptions of Farmers about the Role of Crop Management within Precision Farming', MSc thesis, Silsoe College, Cranfield University, UK (*http://www.silsoe.cranfield.ac.uk/cpf/papers/spyridonFountas/index.htm*).

Gerhards, R., Sokefeld, M., Timmermann, C., Reichart, S. and Kuhbauch, W. (1999), 'Results of a Four-Year Study on Site-Specific Herbicide Application', in J.V. Stafford (ed.), *Precision Agriculture '99*, Sheffield, UK: Academic Press.

Groffman, P.M. (1997), 'Ecological Constraints on the Ability of Precision Agriculture to Improve the Environmental Performance of Agricultural Production Systems', in *Precision Agriculture: Spatial and Temporal Variability of Environmental Quality*, Ciba Foundation Symposium 210, Chichester: Wiley.

Hayami, Y. and Ruttan, V.W. (1985), *Agricultural Development: An International Perspective*, 2nd edn, Baltimore, MD: Johns Hopkins University Press.

Heisel, T., Christensen, S. and Walter, A.M. (1999), 'Whole-Field Experiments With Site-Specific Weed Management', in J.V. Stafford (ed.), *Precision Agriculture '99*, Sheffield, UK: Academic Press.

Hoskinson, R.L., Hess, J. R. and Fink, R.K. (1999), 'A Decision Support System for Optimum Use of Fertilizers', in J.V. Stafford (ed.), *Precision Agriculture '99*, Sheffield, UK: Academic Press.

Khanna, M. (1999), *Sequential Adoption of Site-Specific Technologies and its Implications for Nitrogen Productivity: A Double Selectivity Model*, Working Paper Series, 17, Environmental and Resource Economics, University of Illinois at Urbana-Champaign, Urbana, IL.

Khanna, M. and Zilberman, D. (1997), 'Incentives, Precision Technology, and Environmental Incentives', *Ecological Economics*, **23**, 25–43.

Khanna, M., Epouhe, O.F. and Hornbaker, R. (1999), 'Site-Specific Crop Management: Adoption Patterns and Incentives', *Review of Agricultural Economics*, **21**, 455–72.

Kitchen, N.R., Hughes, D.F., Sudduth, K.A. and Birrell, J. (1995), 'Comparison of Variable Rate to Single Rate Nitrogen Fertilizer Application: Corn Production and Residual Soil N03–N', in P. Robert, R. Rust and W. Larson (eds), *Site Specific Management for Agricultural Systems*, Madison, WI: ASA, CSSA, SSSA.

Larson, W.E., Lamb, J.A., Khakural, B.R., Ferguson, R.B. and Rehm G.W. (1997), 'Potential of Site-Specific Management for Nonpoint Environmental Protection', in F.J. Pierce and E.J. Sadler (eds), *The State of Site-Specific Management for Agricultural Systems*, Madison, WI: ASA/CSSA/SSSA.

Leiva, F.R., Morris, J. and Blackmore, S.B. (1997), 'Precision Farming Techniques For Sustainable Agriculture', *Precision Agriculture '97*, Oxford: BIOS Scientific Publishers.

Lowenberg-DeBoer, J. (1999), 'Precision Agriculture in Argentina', *Modern Agriculture*, Spring (at *http//:www.eomonline.com/ageconomics.htm*).

Lowenberg-DeBoer, J. and Aghib. A. (1999), 'Average Returns and Risk Characteristics of Site Specific P and K Management: Eastern Corn Belt On-Farm Trial Results', *Journal of Production Agriculture*, **12**, 276–82.

Lowenberg-DeBoer, J. and Boehlje, M. (1996), 'Revolution, Evolution or Dead-End: Economic Perspectives on Precision Agriculture', in P. Robert, R. Rust and W. Larson (eds), *Site Specific Management for Agricultural Systems*, Madison, WI: ASA, CSSA, SSSA.

Lowenberg-DeBoer, J. and Swinton, S.M. (1997), 'Economics of Site-Specific Management in Agronomic Crops', in F.J. Pierce and E.J. Sadler (eds), *The State of Site-Specific Management for Agricultural Systems*, Madison, WI: ASA/CSSA/SSSA.

Lu, Y.-C, and Watkins, B. (1997), 'Economic and Environmental Evaluation of Variable Rate Nitrogen Fertilizer Applications Using a Biophysical Model', in J.V. Stafford (ed.), *Precision Agriculture '97*, Oxford:BIOS Scientific Publishers.

McBride, W.D., Daberkow, S.G. and Christensen, L.A. (1999), 'Attitudes About Precision Agriculture Innovations Among Corn Growers', in J.V. Stafford (ed.), *Precision Agriculture '99*, Sheffield, UK: Academic Press.

National Research Council, (1997), *Precision Agriculture in the 21st Century*, Washington, DC: National Academy Press.

Pedigo, L.P., Hutchins, S.H. and Higley, L.G. (1986), 'Economic Injury Levels in Theory and Practice', *Annual Review of Entomology*, **31**, 341–68.

Reardon, T., Kelly, V., Yanggen, D. and Crawford, E. (1999), *Determinants of Fertilizer Adoption by African Farmers: Policy Analysis Framework, Illustrative Evidence and Implications*, Staff Paper 99-18, Department of Agricultural Economics, Michigan State University, East Lansing, MI.

Redulla, C.A., Havlin, J.L., Kluitenberg, G.J., Zhang, N. and Schrock, M.D. (1996), 'Variable Nitrogen Management for Improving Groundwater Quality', in P. Robert, R. Rust and W. Larson (eds), *Site Specific Management for Agricultural Systems*, Madison, WI: ASA, CSSA, SSSA.

Rotz, C.A., Buckmaster, D.R., Mertens, D.R. and Black, J.R. (1989), 'DAFOSYM: A Dairy Forage System Model for Evaluating Alternatives in Forage Conservation', *Journal of Dairy Science*, **72**, 3050–63.

Schmerler, J. and Jurschik, P. (1997), 'Technological and Economic Results of Precision Farming from a 7,200 Hectare Farm in East Germany', in J.V. Stafford (ed.), *Precision Agriculture '97*, Oxford, UK: BIOS Scientific Publishers.

Shipley, P.R., Meisinger, J.J. and Decker, A.M. (1992), 'Conserving Residual Corn Fertilizer Nitrogen With Winter Cover Crops', *Agronomy Journal*, **84**, 869–76.

Srinivasan, A. (1998), 'Precision Farming in Asia: Progress and Prospects', in P. Robert, R. Rust and W. Larson (eds), *Proceedings of the Fourth International Conference on Precision Agriculture*, Madison, WI: ASA/CSSA/SSSA.

Swinton, S.M. and Lowenberg-DeBoer, J. (1998), 'Evaluating the Profitability of Site Specific Farming', *Journal of Production Agriculture*, **11**, 439–46.

Thirkawala, S., Weersink, A., Kachanoski, G. and Fox, G. (1999), 'Economic Feasibility of Variable Rate Technology for Nitrogen on Corn', *American Journal of Agricultural Economics*, **81**, 914–27.

Tisseyre, B., Ardoin, N. and Sevilla, F. (1999), 'Precision Viticulture: Precision Location and Vigour Mapping Aspects', in J.V. Stafford (ed.), *Precision Agriculture '99*, Sheffield, UK: Academic Press.

Travis, J.W. and Latin, R.X. (1991), 'Development, Implementation, and Adoption of Expert Systems in Plant Pathology', *Annual Review of Phytopathology*, **29**, 343–60.

Unganai, L.S. and Kogan, F.N. (1998), 'Drought Monitoring and Corn Yield Estimation in Southern Africa from AVHRR Data', *Remote Sensing of Environment*, **63**, 219–32.

Van Ravenswaay, E.O. and Blend, J. (1999), 'Using Ecolabeling to Encourage Adoption of Innovative Environmental Technologies in Agriculture', in F. Casey, A. Schmitz, S.M. Swinton and D. Zilberman (eds), *Flexible Incentives for the Adoption of Environmental Technologies in Agriculture*, Boston: Kluwer Academic Press.

Weiss, M.D. (1997), 'Phosphorus Fertilizer Application Under Precision Farming: A Simulation of Economic and Environmental Implications', in J.V. Stafford (ed.), *Precision Agriculture '97*, Oxford, UK: BIOS Scientific Publishers.

Weisz, R., Fleischer, S. and Smilowitz, Z. (1996), 'Site-specific Integrated Pest Management for High-value Crops: Impact on Potato Management', *Journal of Economic Entomology*, **89**, 501–9.

Whipker, L.D. and Akridge, J.T. (1999), 'The Evolution Continues', *Farm Chemicals*, June, 9–14.

Whipker, L.D. and Akridge, J.T. (2000), 'Dealers and Precision: Taking a Breather', *Farm Chemicals*, June, 20–22.

MELINDA SMALE*

Economic Incentives for Conserving Crop Genetic Diversity on Farms: Issues and Evidence

INTRODUCTION: THE DECISION TO MAKE

Scientific methods of genetic improvement, building on millennia of farmers' selection in their own fields, are the basis for changes in the supply of food on which societies depend. Whether farmer selection practices, conventional breeding methods or techniques of genetic transformation are the principal means of seed technological change, genetic improvement of crop plants depends on the exploitation of allelic diversity and genetic recombination.

Since the 1970s, when conservationists first raised public concern for the loss of plant populations believed to contain rare alleles, large numbers of landraces and wild relatives of cultivated crops have been sampled and stored in ex situ gene banks. An alternative form of conservation in situ has also received some scientific attention (Maxted *et al.*, 1997) though it raises intricate social and economic issues. For cultivated crops, conservation of genetic resources in situ refers to the continued cultivation and management by farmers of crop populations in the agroecosystems where the crop has evolved (Bellon *et al.*, 1997). Since the genetic diversity of populations evolves differently in situ and ex situ, the units conserved by these two strategies are not perfectly substitutable.

The basic economic problem for in situ conservation of cultivated plants is that crop genetic diversity on farms is an impure public good. Each choice of variety and management practices jointly produces a crop output with has private value to the farmer as well as a contribution to a public good, the genetic diversity of crop populations. Since farmers are not likely to be willing or able to consider the contributions of all other farmers to genetic diversity in their community or elsewhere, the theory of impure public goods implies that the farmers as a group will generate less genetic diversity than is socially optimal. While it is clear that public interventions are necessary to close the divergence between private and social optima, the magnitude of the divergence between them, and therefore the extent of public intervention as well as the appropriate form of the intervention, depends on the agroecology and economic system in which the farmer chooses varieties.[1]

*International Wheat and Maize Improvement Centre, Mexico, D.F. and International Plant Genetic Resources Institute, Rome, Italy.

This paper organizes evidence on the problem of in situ conservation for rice, wheat and maize around the decision-making criterion of the minimum viable reserve (Krutilla, 1967). Put simply, Krutilla argued that, while technological change can compensate for the depletion of some stocks, amenities that members of advanced economies (and developing societies) consume may be lost. Acknowledging that too little was known about the instrumental variables in this dynamic problem, he recommended the identification, based on scientific assessments, of a minimum reserve. He argued that these reservations should meet not only scientific purposes but also the demand for 'esoteric' or recreational consumer tastes, such as the enjoyment of the existence of a grand scenic wonder. Similarly, though modern biological techniques can in some instances modify the size of the crop genetic resource stock, proponents of in situ conservation of cultivated crops would argue that certain alleles may be lost as the spatial pattern of crop varieties grown by the world's farmers changes with economic development. Furthermore, some food-related amenities around which culture is now defined in local communities, as well as 'esoteric' (luxury) food attributes for which consumers in richer societies could eventually be willing to pay, may also disappear.

To implement this criterion even in simple terms, we need to be able to answer several questions. First is that of location. On the basis of past experience in breeding for crop improvement, theories of population genetics, ecosystems and geography, scientists have prior beliefs about the relative probabilities of finding rare alleles of a given crop species in different geographical areas. Though genetic analyses from samples drawn in the field are necessary to test and refine these hypotheses, these may be taken as the best available estimate of the relative ranking of expected, future, direct use benefits from on-farm conservation. Indirect future use benefits and existence values of crop infraspecific diversity are not likely to be great. Option values other than those subsumed in scientists' assessments of information value are not likely to be estimable (Brown, 1990).

Second is the question of size. Determining the minimum effective size of on farm crop genetic reserves involves some complex considerations since (a) isolating crop populations may destroy the very genetic structure that makes them potentially valuable (Louette, 1994; Henry *et al.*, 1991) and (b) identifying this underlying genetic structure and its evolutionary potential from the varieties named by farmers is a non-trivial scientific problem (Jarvis and Hodgkin, 1998; Brown, 1990; Brown, 2000). Most experts view farm conservation as a dynamic farmer-led process that cannot be constrained by artificially imposed boundaries.

A third issue concerns the nature of costs. Why should farmers choose to grow those varieties believed to be of great potential value to future crop improvement? While the costs of species preservation in protected reserves consists primarily of the opportunity costs of land use and enforcement, the cost of conserving crop genetic resources on farms is the opportunity cost to farmers who grow them – which varies according to their economic opportunities and shifts over time as economies change.

Briefly, least-cost conservation will occur in sites that are most highly ranked in terms of expected future benefits to producers and consumers and where, because farmers' private incentives for conservation are greatest, public interventions to encourage them to do so will be least. In these sites, private and social costs will be least.

The next section summarizes the evidence on the location and size of on-farm crop genetic reserves for the world's three major cereals, rice, wheat and maize. This section concludes that diversity in both systems of modern varieties and systems of mixed and/or landrace populations is relevant for the conservation of crop genetic diversity on farms and its utilization by society. Subsequent material presents hypotheses and evidence regarding the costs associated with maintaining diversity in these two systems.

EVIDENCE ON THE LOCATION AND SIZE OF RESERVES

Historical location of reserves

Our first candidates for reserves might be the areas where the crops were domesticated, based on popular notions of centres of origin and diversity (Kloppenburg and Kleinman, 1988). However, the idea that the world's most potentially valuable crop genetic resources are concentrated in delineable centres of crop origin and diversity is misleading. The latter are subjects of continuing scientific research rather than established facts. Vavilov's famous hypothesis (1926, 1951) was that the centres of origin of crop species are the areas that exhibit the greatest observed genetic variation. Harlan (1971, 1992) proposed instead that, although some crops exhibit centres of diversity, a number of ecological, natural or social factors may cause genetic variation to accumulate in secondary centres.

African rice (*Oryza glaberrima*) is one of the few examples of 'semi-endemic' variation, meaning that the crop originated in a definable centre (the upper Niger river, with two secondary centres to the southwest near the Guinean coast) with limited dispersal by humans (Harlan, 1992). Opinions remain divided (Oka, 1988; Vaughan and Chang, 1992) concerning the original point of domestication of Asian rice (*Oryza sativa*). Similarly, the origins of maize are 'diffuse' since the crop is believed to have been domesticated thousands of years ago in a limited geographical area of southern Mexico but to have changed radically as it dispersed across the continents of North and South America and throughout the Caribbean (Goodman, 1995). Wheat is an extreme example of 'diffuse' (Harlan, 1992) or 'confused' (Zohary, 1970) origins, and its centre of origin is disputed (Zohary, 1970; Zhukovsky, 1975; Harlan and Zohary, 1966; Harlan, 1971).

We might then propose areas where modern varieties are not grown, based on the assumption that they are narrower genetically than earlier plant types. Yet the timing and cause of genetic narrowing in the major cereal crops is also a matter of historical and scientific perspective (for examples, see Evenson and Gollin, 1997; Vaughan and Chang, 1992; Porceddu *et al.*, 1988; Hawkes,

1983). Modern cereal cultivars have developed through three main phases of selection: (a) subconscious selection by the earlier food growers in the process of harvesting and planting, (b) deliberate selection among variable materials by farmers living in settlements and communities, (c) purposeful selection by professional breeders using scientific methods. The last two phases are concurrent today.

The main attainment of the first phase was to make the crop more suitable for planting and harvest, threshing or shelling, and consumption. Higher germination rates, more uniform growing periods, resistance to shattering, and palatability were some of the products of this efforts. In the second phase, many farmers exerted (and continue to exert) pressure in numerous directions, resulting in variable populations adapted to local growing conditions and consumption preferences. These are broadly known as 'landraces'. During the third phase, fields of cereals have become more uniform in plant types with less spontaneous gene exchange and more planned gene migration through the worldwide exchange of germ plasm. The products of this third phase are loosely referred to as 'modern varieties'.

Wood and Cox (1999) have argued that, historically, bread wheat has always suffered from a precarious genetic base because it evolved through a natural genetic bottleneck: a rare spontaneous hybrid of emmer wheat with goatgrass. In plant breeding, the same scientific breakthrough that widens the gene pool at one point in time can lead to the widespread cultivation of a single, outstanding, variety. When many farmers choose to grow the variety, the germ plasm base of the materials grown in fields may narrow temporarily – until the next popular variety comes along. Hawkes (1983) cites the introduction of Rht1 and Rht2 genes into Western wheat breeding lines, which led to the development by Norman Borlaug of semi-dwarf wheat varieties, as an example of how diversity has been broadened by scientific breeders. These, and the rice varieties of the 'Green Revolution', have been cited elsewhere by scientists as the cause of genetic erosion.

The term 'genetic erosion' was used by Harlan (1972) to describe what he viewed as a potentially disastrous narrowing of the germ plasm base required for the improvement of food crops. Harlan was one of the first scientists to refer to the crop germ plasm base as economists refer to a natural 'resource'. Since major crop species of wheat, rice and maize are not likely to disappear in the foreseeable future, the term probably signifies a dramatic shift in population structure within a crop species that can result from a range of natural or human-led processes.

'Genetic erosion' has become synonymous with the displacement of landraces by modern varieties. Harlan asserted that the 'destruction of genetic resources is caused primarily by the very success of modern plant breeding programs' (1972, p.212). Frankel, also, was calling for urgent collection to forestall 'the loss of ancient patterns of diversity in the Vavilovian centres', since modern varieties contain 'a minimum of genetic variation' and 'in many instances ... have a narrow genetic base' (1970, p.11). We examine these hypotheses below.

Effective location and size of reserves

Have the world's rice, wheat and maize landraces been displaced by modern varieties? Recent estimates of the extent of the area planted to modern varieties and landraces are shown in Table 1. Based on CIMMYT data, roughly 80 per cent of the wheat area in the developing world was sown to semi-dwarf varieties in 1997, with the remainder split almost equally between improved tall varieties and landraces, or varieties with unknown ancestry (Heisey *et al.*, 1999). The relative importance of tall wheat varieties remains greater in the industrialized than in the developing countries, probably for reasons related to wheat growing environment and management practices.

IRRI estimates that about three-quarters of the rice area in Asia, which produces most of the world's rice, is sown to semi-dwarf varieties. These varieties dominate the irrigated rice ecosystems and cover large areas in the rainfed lowlands (M. Jackson and G. Khush, IRRI, personal communication). In sub-Saharan Africa, landraces are still planted to a greater proportion of rice area than modern varieties (T. Dalton, WARDA, personal communication; IRRI, 1995), while in Latin America they occupy a very small niche (L.R. Sanint, CIAT, personal communication). Figure 1 provides a depiction of the principal geographical locations of areas sown to rice and wheat landraces.

Data from maize surveys conducted by CIMMYT in 1992 and 1997 indicate that a much lower proportion of the maize area in the developing world is planted to modern types (see Table 1 and Figure 2). For sub-Saharan Africa and Latin America as a whole, roughly half of the maize area is planted to landraces, but they dominate in Mexico and Central America. At least some of the area listed under landraces is planted to populations that result from the genetic integration of modern varieties with landraces when farmers save seed or plant seed of different types in adjacent fields. Similarly, a substantial proportion of the maize area in sub-Saharan Africa is planted to advanced generations of improved varieties whose seed farmers could not afford to replace on a regular basis, introgressed with landrace populations brought to the continent with the slave trade several centuries ago. Though the proportion of area in maize landraces seems high in West Asia and North Africa, maize area in that region is limited and many of these materials are of unknown origin. In the industrialized world, only a trace of maize area is planted to either improved open-pollinated varieties or landraces.[2]

The data in Table 1, represented geographically in Figures 1 and 2, confirm that the effective 'size' of reserves for wheat and rice landraces is relatively small compared with the estimated share of maize area in landraces, though for maize this share includes advanced generations of modern types that visually resemble landraces. Even in regions of crop domestication, wheat landraces often persist 'as patches and islands of farming systems' (Brush, 1995, p.246) or 'micro-centres of diversity', '100 to 500km across' (Harlan, 1992, p.147). Oka (1988) has called the Jeypore Tract in India a micro-centre of diversity in Asian rice, and M. Jackson (IRRI) refers to some of the upland rice areas of Asia as 'pockets' of diversity.

TABLE 1   Percentage distribution of rice, wheat and maize area by type of germ plasm in the 1990s

Region	Wheat			Maize			Rice		
	semi-dwarf improved	tall improved	landraces/ unknown	hybrid	improved open-pollinated	landraces/ unknown	semi-dwarf improved	other improved	landraces/ unknown
Sub-Saharan Africa*	66	14	20	38	8	54	25	15	60
West Asia/North Africa	66	10	24	22	7	71	11	—	—
Asia	86	7	6	70	7	23	73	13	14
Latin America	90	9	1	43	5	52	59	36	5
All developing countries	81	9	11	53	7	40	71		
Industrialized countries	55	45	(trace)	99	1	(trace)	78		

Note: *Figures for rice in sub-Saharan Africa are West Africa only.

Sources: IRRI World Rice Statistics (1995); CIMMYT Global Maize and Wheat Impacts Surveys (1992, 1997); Heisey *et al.* (1999); Morris and Heisey (1998); Morris and López-Pereira (1999); Luis Roberto Sanint, CIAT; Timothy Dalton, WARDA; Pardey *et al.* (1996); Cabanilla *et al.* (1999).

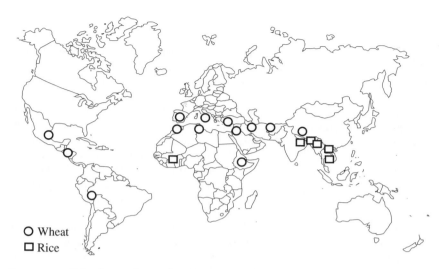

Source: Scientists at CIMMYT, IRRI, WARDA and CIAT.

FIGURE 1 *Pockets of wheat and rice landraces*

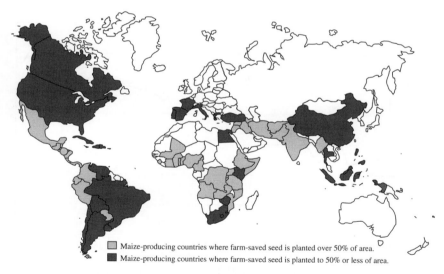

Notes: Data not available for Eastern Europe and Former Soviet Union. Definitions: developing country maize producer = more than 0.1m. mt/yr; high-income maize producer = more that 1m. mt/yr. Farm-saved seed includes landraces, farmer-bred varieties and advanced generations of modern varieties.

Source: CIMMYT data files (M. Morris).

FIGURE 2 *Areas in farm-saved maize seed*

Systems of crop genetic variation

As predicted by Harlan and Frankel, modern varieties of the major cereal crops
have largely replaced 'the ancient patterns of diversity' in the fields of farmers.
Modern and traditional patterns of variation coexist, but on vastly different
scales.

At least two aspects of these predictions are disputable. First, though it is
clear that the patterns of genetic variation in farmers' fields have changed over
time, the hypothesis that the spread of semi-dwarf varieties caused genetic
erosion cannot be tested because it 'goes beyond our knowledge of the facts of
genetic erosion' (Wood and Lenné, 1997; Smale, 1997). Second, evidence
from a number of studies does not support the pessimistic view that the genetic
base of modern varieties is restricted and tends to narrow (Witcombe, 1999).
For example, nearly 90 per cent of the modern varieties grown in 1997 (excluding those in China) are CIMMYT-related, meaning that they are CIMMYT
crosses or selections from CIMMYT crosses released as varieties, or they have
proximate or more distant CIMMYT ancestors in their pedigrees. CIMMYT-
relatedness does not imply uniformity, however, since these lines are a vast
array of germ plasm constituted by genetic recombination of different sources
of materials from throughout the wheat growing world. Genealogical analysis

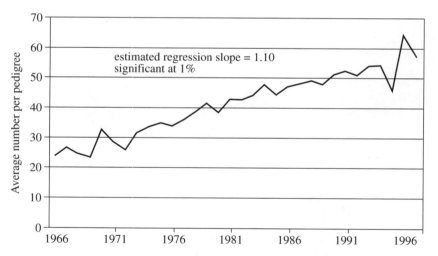

Notes: Calculations based on CIMMYT 1997 global wheat impacts survey data
            prepared by Heisey, Lantican and Dubin, and pedigree information in
            CIMMYT Wheat Pedigree Management System. Data were available for
            1162 (included here) of the 1749 spring bread wheats recorded (in the
            survey data) as released during these years. Coverage is less complete for
            China and for wheats released in the last few years.

FIGURE 3   *Landrace ancestors in spring bread wheats released by*
developing countries, 1966–97

shows (a) a significant positive trend in the number of distinct landrace ancestors in the pedigrees of over one thousand varieties of spring bread wheat
released by national agricultural research systems in the developing world
since 1966 (Figure 3) and (b) a significantly higher number of different landrace
ancestors among releases that are CIMMYT-related than those with no known
CIMMYT ancestry.

Numbers of landraces, in and of themselves, do not constitute diversity since
their genetic contribution is likely to be small. In modern breeding programmes,
landraces are typically distant ancestors. Rather, these numbers demonstrate
conclusively that germ plasm with different genetic backgrounds is continually
brought into the crossing blocks of CIMMYT and national programme col-
laborators through an international research system. Though the numbers are
smaller for rice than for wheat, Gollin and Evenson's findings (1998) demonstrate a similar breadth of genetic backgrounds.

In addition, cumulated scientific evidence (summarized in Smale *et al.*,
2001) presents a strong case that, while the molecular genetic diversity and
genealogical diversity of CIMMYT wheats has been maintained or has increased over the past 30 years, their performance with respect to yield stability,
nitrogen use efficiency, genetic resistance to disease and tolerance to heat and
drought has improved. The genetic diversity in CIMMYT lines represents a
lower bound on the diversity of the wheat germ plasm currently available in
national programmes since national breeders cross them with their own material.

These statements in no way contradict the idea that society may be willing
to pay to conserve some of the remaining on-farm variability in landraces,
provided that these sources are assessed to be of value. Instead, I use them to
argue that both diversity in modern systems and diversity in landrace systems
matter for the future utilization of crop genetic resources by society. What are
the economic incentives for maintaining diversity in these two systems? The
next section presents hypotheses and references to case studies concerning the
private costs of diversity in (a) systems dominated by modern varieties today
(b) systems where both modern varieties and landraces, or landraces only, are
grown.

EVIDENCE ON THE COSTS OF CONSERVING CROP GENETIC DIVERSITY ON FARMS

Systems dominated by modern varieties

In systems of modern varieties the central economic questions involve the
direction of the relationships between genetic diversity and productivity, genetic diversity and stability, and genetic diversity and economic efficiency. The
positive role that diversity in genetic mechanisms *within* a variety can play in
enhancing the longevity of its resistance to some biotic stresses is now fairly
well accepted (Vanderplank, 1963; Johnson, 1984). A relationship between
genetic uniformity in disease resistance *across* the varieties or crop populations

grown in a producing region and vulnerability to potentially costly yield losses has also been generally accepted. Genetic uniformity occurs in this sense when many varieties share the same source of resistance, meaning that resistance is conferred by the same gene or gene complexes.

Applied economists have also recently sought to estimate the impact of genetic diversity on productivity and economic efficiency in modern production systems. Gollin and Evenson (1998) have investigated the economic value of yield enhancement and of traits incorporated through the utilization of specific types of genetic resources in rice breeding, including specialized search materials and landraces from ex situ collections. Widawsky and Rozelle (1998), Smale *et al.* (1998) and Meng *et al.* (1998) related indices of diversity in modern wheat varieties to productivity and economic efficiency through estimating production functions, cost functions and total factor productivity. While the more recent research in China is promising, there is still a need to overcome methodological problems and expand research to other crops and areas of the world. Preliminary results from Pakistan, China and Australia (Smale *et al.*, 1998) confirm the dampening effects of older variety age on productivity, demonstrating beneficial effects of genealogical diversity on productivity and yield stability, and suggesting that marginal costs may be associated with greater evenness in the spatial distribution among modern wheat types.

Though an inverse relationship between genetic uniformity in crop populations and crop yield stability has been generally postulated, the assertion that the spread of modern varieties increases yield instability has not borne statistical scrutiny. In 1989, on the basis of a comprehensive review of the evidence, Hazell concluded that the overwhelming sources of rising production variability in cereals over the 1960–82 period were increases in yield variance and simultaneous loss of offsetting variations. Contemporaneous covariance in crop yields were more likely to have resulted from synchronization of water, fertilizer, and other purchased inputs over large areas, than from greater sensitivity of new seed types and genetic changes.

In Hazell's analysis, production variability did not increase for all crops – in particular, it declined for wheat during the years of the Green Revolution. Later analyses conducted by either agronomists or economists confirmed this result for subsequent decades and different geographical scales (Pfeiffer and Braun, 1989; Sayre *et al.*, 1997; Singh and Byerlee, 1990; Smale *et al.*, 1998). Nor did crop yield instability appear to increase with the diffusion of modern varieties in the cradle areas of crop domestication and genetic diversity for rice and wheat (Brush, 1992) or for rice in Bangladesh (Alauddin and Tisdell, 1988).

Mixed and landrace systems

In mixed and landrace systems the essential question involves the costs to farmers from development opportunities forgone. The assumption has been made that modern varieties will inevitably replace traditional varieties. Brush (1995) and others have argued that the persistent cultivation of landraces in centres of crop origin and diversity such as Turkey for wheat and Mexico for maize, termed de facto conservation, attests to their continued private value to farmers or their competitive advantage relative to modern alternatives (Brush and Meng, 1998; Perales *et al.*, 1998).

To what extent do farmers forgo development opportunities when they grow landraces? The three factors hypothesized to determine the likelihood that farmers in a region will choose to cultivate landraces are population density, agroecology and commercialization. *The ratio of labour to land* explains much about where the transition from low-yield, land-extensive cultivation to land-intensive, double and triple crop systems has occurred (Boserup, 1965; Hayami and Ruttan, 1985; Pingali and Binswanger, 1987). The genetic changes embodied in seed constitute one type of intensification, which refers more broadly to the increase in output per unit of land used in production. Seed genetic change can lead to change in land productivity (yield) both directly and indirectly, in combination with other inputs. Predictably, the adoption of modern rice and wheat varieties in the developing world has been most complete in densely populated areas of their cultivation where traditional mechanisms for enhancing yields per unit area have been exhausted.

Intensification occurs in the less densely populated areas provided that soil conditions are suitable and markets are accessible, when (a) higher prices and elastic demand for output imply that the marginal utility of effort increases and/or (b) higher returns to labour encourage migration into well connected areas from neighbouring regions with higher transport costs (Pingali, 1997).[3]

Labour to land ratios interact with *agroecology* in predicting adoption of modern varieties. Since the initial adoption and rapid diffusion of the first semi-dwarf varieties in the high-potential, irrigated areas of the 1970s, more widely adapted descendants of these varieties have spread gradually into less favourable environments, including rainfed areas with relatively modest production potential. Today, the adoption of modern varieties of rice is virtually complete in irrigated areas and uneven in rainfed zones, while they are largely absent in the uplands and deepwater areas. Wheat landraces are cultivated extensively only in portions of the drier production zones of the West Asia–North Africa region and highlands of Ethiopia.

Maize is grown over a greater range of latitudes, altitudes, temperatures and moisture regimes than rice or wheat and, of the three crops, still has the greatest proportion of area planted to landraces. For many of these environments, suitable improved materials have not been developed by centralized breeding programmes (Byerlee, 1996; Perales *et al.*, 1998). The maize germ plasm that performs well in temperate climates of industrialized countries cannot be introduced directly into the non-temperate regions of developing countries without considerable additional breeding for adaptation (Morris, 1998). Nor are there economic incentives for a commercial seed industry since, even if adaptation problems could be overcome through breeding, farmer demand for improved seed may be small (ibid.). In maize, agroecology interacts with the development of commercial seed systems in determining where modern varieties will be grown.

Economic growth, urbanization and the withdrawal of labour from the agricultural sector lead to the *increasing commercialization of agricultural systems*

(Pingali, 1997). Agricultural commercialization implies that (a) production and consumption decisions of farm households are separated and mediated across markets, and (b) product choice and input use decisions are based on the principles of profit maximization. Farmers trade the output of specialized enterprises produced with purchased inputs for the attributes they demand on markets where transactions are impersonal. Agricultural production as a whole is reorganized from many units, each of which produces a similar set of crops and livestock products, into fewer, specialized units, each of which produces a single crop or livestock product. The opportunity costs of producing staple food, even in intensive systems, will rise with competing demands for farmers' time.

As the orientation of crop production shifts from subsistence towards commercial objectives, the locus of crop improvement and seed distribution moves from individual farmers towards an organized seed industry composed of specialized private and public organizations (Morris, 1998). Maize has moved substantially faster than rice and wheat in terms of increased reliance on commercially produced seed. In a stylized depiction of the maize seed industries in developing countries, subsistence production is characterized by open-pollinated varieties improved through farmer selection and on-farm seed production with local seed markets governed by custom. In a fully commercial system, the predominant seed type is a hybrid that is purchased annually. Seed is a globally traded product of specialized research that is both privately and publicly funded. The exchange of seed and the genetic resources used to improve it are enabled and protected by strict forms of intellectual property rights (Morris *et al.*, 1998).

In rice and wheat, which are self-pollinating crops, the incentives for privatization of research have not been as strong as for maize, although this depends on the institutional and economic context. In the industrialized countries, profound changes in science and in intellectual property protection over the past 20–30 years have been associated with a higher rate of investment in agriculture by the private sector than by the public sector and a shift in the composition of private investment from agricultural machinery and processing into chemical research and plant breeding (Alston *et al.*, 1998; Fuglie *et al.*, 1996). Privatization is greatest in the maize seed industry in developed countries and is increasing in the developing world, but has only occurred to a limited extent for wheat – in Europe. Almost all of the seed research for rice has been and continues to be conducted by the public sector, and most research has occurred in Asia (Pray, 1998).

Predictions

We can employ the three axes specified above to predict probabilities of landrace survival. Since rice and wheat are self-pollinated crops whose seed can be passed from farmer to farmer, the popularity of their modern varieties has depended more on agroecological factors and land to labour ratios than on commercialization. The high propensity of maize plants to cross-pollinate makes it difficult for farmers to maintain the genetic purity of maize seed saved from their own harvest. Maize growers who seek to commercialize their production are therefore dependent on reliable external sources of affordable seed in a way that growers of self-pollinated rice and wheat are not (Morris, 1998). It also explains the historical importance of hybrids, which are a self-enforcing form of intellectual property that generates strong incentives for privatization. Commercialization and the structure of the private seed industry will remain important for predicting where maize landraces will be grown.

We can also predict that, in the high-potential environments where commercialization occurs, landraces will be grown only when unique end-use characteristics for which specialized markets exist cannot be transferred efficiently through advanced breeding techniques (biotechnology) to modern types. In the worst growing environments, crop production may be abandoned entirely, as has already occurred in parts of Asia (Pingali, 1997). When there are limited opportunities for migration in these environments, farmers may remain on small landholdings growing landraces for subsistence.

Between these two extremes, the prospects for landrace cultivation are more interesting. In some of the more difficult growing environments for maize, landraces and rusticated modern types may remain the choice of farmers for some time, since germ plasm that better meets their needs may not be available. Even when an agroecological zone is suitable for the production of modern varieties, the development of commercial seed systems is not sufficient to ensure that modern types will replace landraces because of market imperfections (de Janvry *et al.*, 1991). Case studies demonstrate that, in many of the regions of the developing world where landraces are still grown, either markets for commercially produced seed or markets for the attributes demanded by farmers are incomplete (Brush and Meng, 1998; Brush *et al.*, 1992; Smale *et al.*, 2001). In some local communities, the traits demanded by farmers (grain quality, fodder, suitability for a certain soil type) cannot be obtained through the production of modern varieties or procured through impersonal market transactions, so that farmers must rely on their own or neighbours' production for their supply (Renkow and Traxler, 1994; Bellon and Taylor, 1993). The specialized uses of certain landrace varieties for medicinal purposes, rituals and festivals have been extensively documented by ethnobotanists and anthropologists.

Farmers often choose to grow both landraces and modern varieties. Small-scale farmers' choice to grow more than one variety simultaneously is likely to reflect their need to address numerous concerns that no single variety can satisfy (Bellon, 1996). Viewed in the conventional microeconomic literature as partial adoption, this observed pattern has been explained theoretically through attitudes towards risk and uncertainty, missing markets and differential soil quality or nutrient response combined with fixity or rationing (reviewed in Meng, 1997; Smale *et al.*, 1994).

Though treated as a transitional period to full adoption, the coexistence of modern varieties and landraces may represent an equilibrium if one or several of these aspects persist despite economic change. Zimmerer (1999) found that the capacity of farmers to grow diverse food plants (including maize) in Peru and Bolivia depends on whether they can cultivate them in combination with commercially developed, high-yielding varieties. Meng *et al.* (1998) concluded that multiple factors, including missing markets, yield risk, grain quality and agroclimatic constraints influence the probability that a Turkish household will grow a wheat landrace; a change in any single economic factor is unlikely to cause farmers to cease growing it.

Even when the pressures for commercialization are strong, the coexistence of modern varieties and landraces may persist with certain types of market-based incentives. The post-industrial agricultural economy is characterized by growth in demand for an array of increasingly specialized goods and services (Antle, 1999). Though the income elasticity of demand for staple grains may be low or even negative (Huang *et al.*, 1991), the income elasticity of demand for attributes of the grains is higher (Ben Senauer, personal communication; Pingali *et al.*, 1997). For example, high-income consumers spend more on rice by paying higher prices for varieties with preferred eating quality which they substitute for the lower-quality variety consumed when the income level was lower (Unnevehr *et al.*, 1992). In Asia, traditional varieties are generally of higher quality and fetch premium prices in the market (Pingali *et al.*, 1997). Thailand still grows low-yielding traditional rainfed varieties extensively for the export market. In South Korea, the modern 'tongil' variety was replaced by relatively low-yielding, traditional *japonica* rice as consumers expressed preference for *japonicas* by offering higher prices as incomes rose. Higher prices more than compensated for lower yields. As rice scientists have had limited success in developing high-yielding cultivars with better eating quality, the price difference between the standard and high-quality varieties has been growing in Asian markets.[4]

CONCLUSIONS

Crop genetic diversity is an impure public good, and as long as it is 'good', theory predicts that farmers will maintain a level of diversity in their fields that is lower than is socially optimal. There are intergenerational and political dilemmas associated with making decisions about whether or not to conserve it, and by how much. Estimating the quantitative value of the difference between the optima requires positing a social welfare function and private objective functions, imposing a rule of aggregation and assigning dollar values to abstract notions of benefits other than direct, current use value. Here, the discussion of this decision has been organized around a more intuitive criterion of least cost, minimum viable reserve.

Identifying the viable reserve relies to a large extent on the state of scientific knowledge concerning the location of on-farm genetic resources with the greatest expected use value to future producers and consumers, and the required size to allow for crop evolution. Depending on popular notions of centres of origin and diversity to locate reserves may be misguided. Nor is the belief that modern varieties categorically have a narrower genetic base than their predecessors entirely accurate or useful. Decisions over location and size in the three major cereal crops are limited by the fact that modern varieties now dominate global area. I have argued that conserving crop genetic diversity on farms involves both systems of modern varieties and systems dominated by landraces.

In modern systems, the major economic issue is the effect of genetic diversity on productivity, stability and economic efficiency. The evidence about productivity and efficiency in modern systems is as yet inconclusive; the hypothesis that the genetic structure of modern wheat and rice varieties has increased variability in crop output has been rejected.

In mixed and landrace systems, the economic question is the cost of growing landraces in terms of development opportunities forgone. Heuristically, three axes determine the probability that landraces will continue to be grown: population densities, the production potential of an area and commercialization. Predicted probabilities of landrace survival differ for rice, wheat and maize because of their biological properties. The propensity for maize to cross-pollinate and its capacity to withstand greater ranges in growing environment are of key importance.

The lower the predicted probability of landrace survival, the higher farmers' opportunity costs. As long as farmers find it in their own best interests to grow and manage these genetic resources, because of either market imperfections or market-based incentives, the public expense of mounting programmes to encourage them to do so is minimal since what is best for farmers and best for society at large, or the economic optima from both private and social standpoints, converges. Combining scientifically based assessments of location and size with economic analyses of costs can provide candidates for least-cost, minimum viable reserves of on-farm crop genetic diversity.

NOTES

[1] This divergence has both intergenerational and political aspects. The intergenerational aspect is that farmers today (and ironically some of the world's poorest) are asked to consider the needs of future generations in their decisions. The political aspect is that those who are encouraging them to do so for conservation purposes reside largely in other jurisdictions.

[2] These are speciality maizes or 'heirloom' varieties grown for fresh consumption, popcorns, or ornamental corns such as those marketed on holidays in the USA (M. Morris, personal communication).

[3] Examples of regions with low population density but intensive, market-oriented production are the central plains of Thailand and parts of Latin America's Southern Cone.

[4] The importance of Basmati rice in the irrigated production zones of India and Pakistan is another example of the way in which market demand for quality can influence the survival of traditional varieties and landraces even in the most favoured growing environments with dense populations.

BIBLIOGRAPHY

Alauddin, M. and Tisdell, C. (1988), 'Impact of new agricultural technology on the instability of foodgrain production and yield: data analysis for Bangladesh and its districts', *Journal of Development Economics*, **29**, 199–277.

Alston, J.M., Pardey, P.G. and Smith, V.H. (1998), 'Financing agricultural R&D in rich countries', *The Australian Journal of Agricultural and Resource Economics*, **42**, 51–82.

Antle, J.M. (1999), 'The new economics of agriculture' (Presidential Address), *American Journal of Agricultural Economics*, **81**, 993–1010.

Bellon, M.R. (1996), 'The dynamics of crop infra-specific diversity: A conceptual framework at the farmer level', *Economic Botany*, **50**, 26–39.

Bellon, M.R. and Taylor, J.E. (1993). '"Folk" soil taxonomy and the partial adoption of new seed varieties', *Economic Development and Cultural Change*, **41**, 763–86.

Bellon, M.R., Pham, J.-L. and Jackson, M.T. (1997), 'Genetic conservation: a role for rice farmers', in N. Maxted, B.V. Ford-Lloyd and J.G. Hawkes (eds), *Plant Genetic Conservation: The* In-Situ *Approach*, London: Chapman & Hall.

Boserup, E. (1965), *Conditions of Agricultural Growth*, Chicago: Aldine Publishing Company.

Brown, A.H.D. (2000), 'The genetic structure of crop "landraces" an' the challenge to conserve them in situ on farms', in S.B. Brush (ed.), *Genes in the Field: On Farm Conservation of Crop Diversity*, Ottawa: IPGRI, IDRC, Lewis Publishers.

Brown, G.M. (1990), 'Valuation of genetic resources', in G.H. Orians, G.M. Brown, Jr, W.E. Kunin and J.E. Swierbinski (eds), *The Preservation and Valuation of Biological Resources*, Seattle: University of Washington Press.

Brush, S.B. (1992), 'Reconsidering the green revolution: Diversity and stability in cradle areas of crop domestication', *Human Ecology*, **20**, 145–67.

Brush, S.B. (1995), '*In situ* conservation of landraces in centers of crop diversity', *Crop Science*, **35**, 346–54.

Brush, S.B. and Meng, E. (1998), 'Farmers' valuation and conservation of crop genetic resources', *Genetic Resources and Crop Evolution*, **45**, 139–50.

Brush, S.B., Taylor, J.E. and Bellon M.R. (1992), 'Biological diversity and technology adoption in Andean potato agriculture', *Journal of Development Economics*, **38**, 365–87.

Byerlee, D. (1996), 'Modern varieties, productivity, and sustainability: recent experience and emerging challenges', *World Development*, **24**, 697–718.

Cabanilla, V.L., Hossain, M. and Khush, G.S. (1999), 'Diffusion of breeding materials and genetic composition of improved rice in South and Southeast Asia 1965–98', paper presented at the IAEG Germplasm Research Impact Study Workshop in Nashville, Tennessee, 7–8 August.

Cox, T.S., Murphy, J.P. and Goodman, M.M. (1988), 'The contribution of exotic germplasm to American agriculture', in J.R. Kloppenburg, Jr (ed.), *Seeds and Sovereignty*, Durham, NC and London: Duke University Press.

de Janvry, A., Fafchamps, M. and Sadoulet, E. (1991), 'Peasant Household Behaviour with Missing Markets: Some Paradoxes Explained', *Economic Journal*, **101**, 1400–1417.

Evenson, R.E. and Gollin, D. (1997), 'Genetic resources, international organizations, and improvement in rice varieties', *Economic Development and Cultural Change*, **45**, 471–500.

Evenson, R.E., Gollin, D. and Santaniello, V. (eds) (1998), *Agricultural Values of Plant Genetic Resources*, Wallingford: CABI, FAO and Centre for International Studies on Economic Growth, Tor Vergata University, Rome.

Frankel, O.H. (1970) 'Genetic dangers of the Green Revolution', *World Agriculture*, **19**, 9–14.

Fuglie, K., Ballenger, N., Day, K., Klotz, C., Ollinger, M., Reilly, J., Vasavada, U. and Yee, J. (1996), *Agricultural Research and Development: Public and Private Investments Under Alternative Markets and Institutions*, Washington, DC:U.S. Department of Agriculture, Economic Research Service, AER no. 735.

Gollin, D. and Evenson, R.E. (1998), 'Breeding values of rice genetic resources', in R.E. Evenson, D. Gollin and V. Santaniello (eds), *Agricultural Values of Plant Genetic Resources*, Wallingford: CABI, FAO and Centre for International Studies on Economic Growth, Tor Vergata University, Rome.

Goodman, M.M. (1995), 'Maize', in J. Smartt and N.W. Simmonds (eds), *The Evolution of Crop Plants*, New York: Wiley.

Harlan, J.R. (1971), 'Agricultural origins: centers and noncenters', *Science*, **174**, 468–73.

Harlan, J.R. (1972), 'Genetics of disaster', *Journal of Environmental Quality*, **1**, 212–15.

Harlan, J.R. (1992), *Crops and Man*, Madison, WI: American Society of Agronomy, Inc. and Crop Science Society of America, Inc.

Harlan, J.R. and Zohary, D. (1966), 'Distribution of wild wheat and barley', *Science*, **153**, 1074–80.

Hawkes, J.G. (1983), *The Diversity of Crop Plants*, Cambridge, MA: Harvard University Press.

Hayami, Y. and Ruttan, V.W. (1985), *Agricultural Development: An International Perspective*, Baltimore, MD: Johns Hopkins University Press.

Hazell, P.B.R. (1989), 'Changing patterns of variability in world cereal production', in J.R. Anderson and P.B.R. Hazell (eds), *Variability in Grain Yields*, Washington, DC: Johns Hopkins University and the International Food Policy Research Institute.

Heisey, P.W., Lantican, M.A. and Dubin, H.J. (1999), 'An overview of the global wheat impacts study', in CIMMYT (ed.), *1998–9 World Wheat Facts and Trends*, Mexico, DF: CIMMYT.

Henry, J.P., Pontis, C., David, J. and Gouyon, P.H. (1991), 'An experiment on dynamic conservation of genetic resources with metapopulations', in A. Seitz and V. Loeschcke (eds), *Species Conservation: A Population-Biological Approach*, Basle: Birkhauser Verlag.

Huang, J., David, C.C. and Duff, B. (1991), 'Rice in Asia: Is it becoming an inferior good? Comment', *American Journal of Agricultural Economics*, **73**, 515–21.

Jarvis, D.I. and Hodgkin, T. (eds) (1998), *Strengthening the scientific basis of in situ conservation of agricultural biodiversity on-farm. Options for data collecting and analysis*, Rome: International Plant Genetic Resources Institute.

Johnson, R. (1984), 'A critical analysis of durable resistance', *Annual Review of Phytopathology*, **22**, 309–30.

Kloppenburg, J. and Kleinman, D.L. (1988), 'Seeds of controversy: National property versus common heritage', in J.R. Kloppenburg (ed.), *Seeds and Sovereignty: The Use and Control of Plant Genetic Resources*, Durham, NC: Duke University Press.

Krutilla, J.V. (1967), 'Conservation reconsidered', *American Economic Review*, **57**, 777–86.

Louette, D. (1994), 'Gestion traditionnelle de variétés de maïs dans la réserve de la Biosphère Sierra de Manantlán (RBSM, états de Jalisco et Colima, Mexique) et conservation in situ des ressources génétiques de plantes cultivées', PhD thesis, Ecole Nationale Supérieure Agronomique de Montpellier, France.

Maxted, N., Ford-Lloyd, B.V. and Hawkes, J.G. (eds) (1997), *Plant Genetic Conservation: The In-Situ Approach*, London: Chapman & Hall.

Meng, E.C.H. (1997), 'Land allocation decisions and in situ conservation of crop genetic resources: The case of wheat landraces in Turkey', PhD thesis, University of California, Davis.

Meng, E.C.H, Taylor, J.E. and Brush, S.B. (1998), 'Implications for the conservation of wheat landraces in Turkey from a household model of varietal choice', in M. Smale (ed.), *Farmers, Gene Banks and Crop Breeding: Economic Analyses of Diversity in Wheat, Maize and Rice*, Boston: Kluwer Academic Press and CIMMYT.

Meng, E.C.H., Smale, M., Rozelle, S., Ruifa, H. and Huang, J. (1999), 'The cost of wheat diversity in China', paper presented at the 1999 Meetings of the American Agricultural Economics Association, Nashville, Tennessee.

Morris, M.L. (ed.) (1998), *Maize Seed Industries in Developing Countries*, Boulder: Lynne Rienner and CIMMYT.

Morris, M.L. and Heisey, P.W. (1998), 'Achieving desirable levels of crop diversity in farmers' fields: Factors affecting the production and use of commercial seed', in M. Smale (ed.), *Farmers, Gene Banks and Crop Breeding: Economic Analyses of Diversity in Wheat, Maize and Rice*, Boston: Kluwer Academic Press and CIMMYT.

Morris, M.L. and López-Pereira, M.P. (1999), *Impacts of maize breeding research in Latin America, 1966–67*, Mexico, DF: CIMMYT.

Morris, M.L., Rusike, J. and Smale, M. (1998), 'Maize seed industries: a conceptual framework', in M. Morris (ed.), *Maize Seed Industries in Developing Countries*, Boulder: Lynne Rienner and CIMMYT.

Oka, H.I. (1988), *Origin of Cultivated Rice*, Tokyo: Japan Scientific Societies Press and Elsevier.

Pardey, P.G., Alston, J.M., Christian, LE. and Fan, S. (1996), *Summary of Productive Partnership: The Benefits of U.S. Participation in CGIAR*, EPDT Discussion Paper no. 18, Washington, DC: International Food Policy Research Institute and University of California, Davis.

Perales R.H., Brush, S.B. and Qualset, C.O. (1998), 'Agronomic and economic competitiveness of maize landraces and *in situ* conservation in Mexico', in M. Smale (ed.), *Farmers, Gene Banks and Crop Breeding: Economic Analyses of Diversity in Wheat, Maize and Rice*, Boston: Kluwer Academic Press and CIMMYT.

Pfeiffer, W.H. and Braun, H.J. (1989), 'Yield stability in bread wheat', in J.R. Anderson and

P.B.R. Hazell (eds), *Variability in Grain Yields*, Washington, DC: Johns Hopkins University and the International Food Policy Research Institute.

Pingali, P. (1997), 'From subsistence to commercial production systems', *American Journal of Agricultural Economics*, **79**,628–34.

Pingali, P.L. and Binswanger, H.P. (1987), 'Population density and agricultural intensification: a study of the evolution of technologies in tropical agriculture', in D.G. Johnson and R.D. Lee (eds), *Population Growth and Economic Development – Issues and Evidence*, Oxford: Clarendon Press.

Pingali, P., Bigot, Y. and Binswanger, H.P. (1987), *Agricultural Mechanization and the Evolution of Farming Systems in sub-Saharan Agriculture*, Baltimore, MD: Johns Hopkins University Press.

Pingali, P., Hossain, M. and Gerpacio, R.V. (1997), 'Asian Rice Market: Demand and Supply Prospects', in P. Pingali, M. Hossain and R.V. Gerpacio, *Asian Rice Bowls: the Returning Crisis?*, Wallingford: CABI and IRRI.

Porceddu, E., Ceoloni, C., Lafiandra, D., Tanzarella, O.A. and Scarascia Mugnozza, G.T. (1988), 'Genetic resources and plant breeding : Problems and prospects', Institute of Plant Science Research, *The Plant Breeding International Cambridge Special Lecture*, Cambridge, UK: Institute of Plant Science Research.

Pray, C.E. (1998), 'Impact of biotechnology on the demand for rice biodiversity', in R.E. Evenson, D. Gollin, and V. Santaniello (eds), *Agricultural Values of Plant Genetic Resources*, Wallingford: CABI, FAO and Centre for International Studies on Economic Growth, Tor Vergata University, Rome.

Renkow, M. and Traxler, G. (1994), 'Incomplete Adoption of Modern Cereal Varieties: The Role of Grain-Fodder Tradeoffs', selected paper presented at the annual meeting of the American Agricultural Economics Association, San Diego, 7–10 August.

Rozelle, S., Jin, E., Meng, E.C.H., Hu, R. and Huang, J. (2000), *Genetic diversity and total factor productivity: The case of wheat in China*, Economics Working Paper, Mexico, DF: CIMMYT.

Sayre, K.D., Rajaram, S. and Fischer, R.A. (1997), 'Yield potential progress in short bread wheats in northwest Mexico', *Crop Science*, **37**, 36–42.

Singh, A.J. and Byerlee, D. (1990), 'Relative variability in wheat yields across countries and over time', *Journal of Agricultural Economics*, **41**, 21–32.

Smale, M. (1997), 'The green revolution and wheat genetic diversity: some unfounded assumptions', *World Development*, **25**, 1257–69.

Smale, M. (1998), 'Indicators of variety diversity in bread wheat grown in developing countries', in R.E. Evenson, D. Gollin and V. Santaniello (eds), *Agricultural Values of Plant Genetic Resources*, Wallingford: CABI, FAO and Centre for International Studies on Economic Growth, Tor Vergata University, Rome.

Smale, M., Bellon, M. and Aguirre, A. (2001), 'Maize Diversity, Variety Attributes and Farmers' Choices in Southeastern Guanajuato, Mexico', *Economic Development and Cultural Change*, forthcoming.

Smale, M., Just, R.E. and Leathers, H.D. (1994), 'Land Allocation in HYV Adoption Models: An Investigation of Alternative Explanations', *American Journal of Agricultural Economics*, **76**, 535–46.

Smale, M., Hartell, J., Heisey, P.W. and Senauer, B. (1998), 'The contribution of genetic resources and diversity to wheat production in the Punjab of Pakistan', *American Journal of Agricultural Economics*, **80**, 482–93.

Traxler, G. and Byerlee, D. (1993), 'A joint-product analysis of the evolution and adoption of modern cereal varieties in developing countries', *American Journal of Agricultural Economics*, **75**, 981–9.

Unnevehr, L., Duff, B. and Juliano, B.O. (1992), *Consumer Demand for Rice Grain Quality*, Terminal Report of IDRC Projects, National Grain Quality (Asia) and International Grain Quality Economics (Asia), Ottowa: IDRC and Los Banos, Laguna, Philippines: IRRI.

Vanderplank, J.E. (1963), *Plant Diseases: Epidemics and Control*, New York: Academic Press.

Vaughan, D. and Chang, T.T. (1992), '*In situ* conservation of rice genetic resources', *Economic Botany*, **46**,369–83.

Vavilov, N.I. (1926), 'Centers of origin of cultivated plants', *Works of Applied Botany and Plant Breeding*, **16**, (2) (Leningrad).

Vavilov, N.I. (1951), 'The origin, variation, immunity and breeding of cultivated plants', *Chronica Botanica*, **13**, 139–248.

Widawsky, D. and Rozelle, S. (1998), 'Varietal diversity and yield variability in Chinese rice production', in M. Smale (ed.), *Farmers, Gene Banks and Crop Breeding: Economic Analyses of Diversity in Wheat, Maize and Rice*, Boston: Kluwer Academic Press and CIMMYT.

Witcombe, J.R. (1999), 'Does plant breeding lead to a loss of genetic diversity?', in D. Wood and J. Lenné (eds), *Agrobiodiversity: Characterization, Utilization and Measurement*, Wallingford: CAB International.

Wood, D. and Cox, T.S. (1999), 'The nature and role of crop biodiversity', in D. Wood and J. Lenné (eds), *Agrobiodiversity: Characterization, Utilization and Measurement*, Wallingford: CAB International.

Wood, D. and J. Lenné (1997), 'The conservation of agrobiodiversity on-farm: questioning the emerging paradigm', *Biodiversity and Conservation*, **6**, 109–29.

Zhukovsky, P.M. (1975), *World Gene Pool of Plants for Breeding: Mega-gene-centres and micro-gene-centres*, Leningrad: USSR Academy of Sciences.

Zimmerer, K.S. (1999), 'Overlapping patchworks of mountain agriculture in Peru and Bolivia: Toward a Regional–Global Landscape Model', *Human Ecology*, **27**, 135–65.

Zimmerer, K.S. (1996), *Changing Fortunes: Biodiversity and Peasant Livelihood in the Peruvian Andes*, Berkeley: University of California Press.

Zohary, D. (1970), 'Centres of diversity and centres of origin', in O.H. Frankel and E. Bennett (eds), *Genetic Resources in Plants: Their Exploration and Conservation*, Oxford: Blackwell.

KEIJIRO OTSUKA*

Population Pressure, Land Tenure and Natural Resource Management

INTRODUCTION

Massive degradation of natural resources, including forests, rangeland and irrigation water, has been taking place in the Third World. The growing population has increased demand for land, trees and water, which, coupled with tenure insecurity or the absence of clear property rights, has resulted in the overexploitation of these natural resources (Deacon, 1994). This in turn has threatened the sustainable development of agriculture, forestry and livestock sectors. The critical question is whether the current trend will continue and result in further degradation of natural resources and, ultimately, significant deterioration of human welfare.

Ester Boserup (1965) argues that population pressure does not necessarily result in disastrous consequences, as it will lead to the evolution of farming systems from land-using or natural resource-using systems, such as shifting cultivation, to land-saving and labour-intensive farming systems, such as annual cropping systems.[1] Her argument, however, is incomplete: while investment is required to establish intensive farming systems (for example, investment in the construction of irrigation facilities, terracing and tree planting), insufficient attention is paid to incentive systems which ensure that the appropriate investments are made. It is widely recognized that investment incentives are governed by the land tenure or property rights institution, as it affects the expected returns to investments accrued to those who actually undertake them (Besley, 1995). In sparsely populated areas of sub-Saharan Africa and islands in the South Pacific, land is often owned and controlled by the community, where individual land rights are severely restricted and benefits are shared widely among members of extended families (Johnson, 1972). If such communal ownership of land prevails and persists, investment incentives are likely to be weak and thus investments necessary for the intensification of farming systems may not be made (Besley, 1995; Johnson, 1972). Then the extensive and natural resource-using farming systems may continue to be practised, contrary to the Boserup hypothesis.

*International Food Policy Research Institute, Washington, DC, USA and Tokyo Metropolitan University, Japan. The author is indebted to Yujiro Hayami, Frank Place, Alain de Janvry, Elizabeth Sadoulet, Peter Hazell, Agnes Quisumbing and Jonna Estudillo for their useful comments on the earlier case studies on which this paper is based.

Hayami and Ruttan (1985) argue that not only technologies but also institutions are induced to change in response to the changing resource endowments in order to save increasingly scarce resources. This would imply in our context that land tenure institutions will change towards individual ownership so as to provide appropriate investment incentives to save the use of natural resources. Consistent with the induced innovation thesis, a theory of property rights institutions developed by Demsetz (1967) and Alchian and Demsetz (1973) asserts, on the basis of the historical experience of hunting communities in Canada, that property rights institutions evolve from open access to private ownership when natural resources become scarce. In many parts of sub-Saharan Africa, it is known that the system of communal property rights on cultivated agricultural fields has been considerably individualized (Bruce and Migot-Adholla, 1993). Yet no systematic research has been made as to the effect of population pressure on land tenure institutions and the effect of possible changes in land tenure institutions on the investment in land improvement towards the intensification of farming systems and the preservation of natural resources.

Based on the recently completed project on land tenure and the management of land and trees in Asia and Africa (Otsuka and Place, 2000), this article attempts to identify the process by which population pressure leads to the individualization of land rights and its consequences on the management of land and trees. A particular focus will be placed on the development of agroforestry systems growing commercial trees, such as cocoa, coffee, cinnamon and rubber, which are becoming important farming systems in agriculturally marginal areas, where people are particularly poor and natural forests have been degraded rapidly (Otsuka, 2000).[2]

The conceptual framework is discussed in the next section, which is followed by the examination of the results of case studies on the management of trees and cropland. Policy implications are discussed in the final section.

CONCEPTUAL FRAMEWORK

Communal ownership

In this study, the focus is on communal ownership,[3] as it is prevalent in our study sites, including south-western Ghana, the north and east of Uganda, all regions of Malawi, and western Sumatra. Under the communal ownership regime, uncultivated forest land, woodland and rangeland are owned communally and controlled by an authority such as a village chief, whereas exclusive use rights of cultivated land are assigned to individual households of the community and its ownership rights are held traditionally by the extended family.

The uncultivated portion of communally owned land can be regarded as common property, which is defined as the ownership and the joint use of property by a group of people, for example for hunting and extraction of trees and minor forest products.[4] From observation, however, this area is characterized by open-access for the community members almost without exception.

Thus uncultivated forests and woodlands have been rapidly cleared for cultivation with population growth in our study in our sites.

While the individual use rights on currently cultivated lands are established, the rights to transfer, including inheritance, sales and leasing, are often vested in the village community or the extended family. The ownership of cultivated land, however, has evolved towards more individualized ownership over time, for example, through a shift from the ownership of extended family to a single family (Ault and Rutman, 1979; Bruce and Migot-Adholla, 1993). This has led to the development of agroforestry systems in hilly and mountainous areas, where annual crop farming does not have a comparative advantage.[5]

An evolutionary view of land tenure institutions

Following Hayami and Ruttan (1985), a simplified version of our theoretical framework can be illustrated by assuming that there are only two factors of production: land and labour. Land represents natural resources and it could be cropland (with or without irrigation), rangeland, woodland or forest land. The central issue is how the stock of natural resources (both quantity and quality) changes with evolution of farming systems from extensive to intensive systems – or from natural resource-using to natural resource-saving systems. As a concrete example, consider the evolution from shifting cultivation to sedentary farming.

Under shifting cultivation, food crops are grown usually for a couple of years after clearing forest and a fallow period of varying length follows until next cultivation. As Boserup (1965) emphasizes, fallow land is not 'unused' land; fallowing is a labour-saving method of restoring soil fertility. If initially population is scarce and land is abundant with vast areas of virgin forests, people have little incentive to claim individual property rights in land and, hence, the use of forest areas is unrestricted except for the exclusion of outsiders.

Since land is abundant, it is cost-effective to practice shifting cultivation with sufficiently long fallow periods, which ensures complete restoration of soil fertility. Curve I_0I_0 in Figure 1 portrays the unit isoquant for an individual farmer to produce \$1.00 worth of food crops by using land and labour under shifting cultivation in period 0. Here land input is measured in terms of area 'used' for cultivation, including fallow land, some of which may be secondary forest or woodland, but excluding land which has never been cultivated. It is assumed for simplicity that the production function is subject to constant returns to scale, so that each technology or farming system is characterized by a single unit isoquant. The relative factor scarcity may be indicated by a relative factor price line, P_0.[6] Then the optimum production point is given by E_0, where the production is sustainable.

As population increases, however, land becomes scarce relative to labour. The growing population will require an increasing area for agricultural production and, hence, large areas of forest land are opened up. Eventually, however, the rate of area expansion falls short of the growth rate of population. As a result, the scarcity value of land increases relative to labour, which is reflected in changes in relative factor price ratio from P_0 to P_1 in period 1. Accordingly,

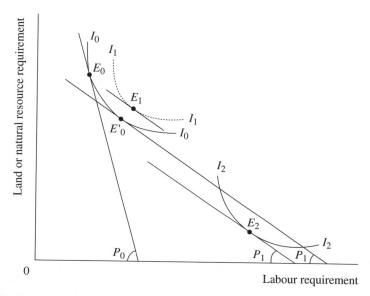

FIGURE 1   *A model of induced institutional innovation*

the optimum production point changes to E'_0, so long as shifting cultivation continues to be practised. Fallow period at E'_0 tends to be shorter than at E_0. Owing to the shorter fallow cycle, soil fertility declines and farming becomes unsustainable at E'_0, resulting in the shift of unit isoquant from I_0I_0 to I_1I_1. Thus the equilibrium point moves to E_1.

An alternative to unsustainable farming under shifting cultivation and continued deforestation is to improve land quality by investing in land and trees. To maintain soil fertility under continuous cultivation of annual crops, new farming systems may be adopted involving the application of compost made from grasses and leaf litter collected from the forest and woodland, as well as manure.[7] Relative to pure cropping systems, the productivity of tree farming systems can be sustainable for longer periods of time with lower application of organic or inorganic fertilizer primarily because of their deeper and denser rooting systems and perennial ground cover which make them less vulnerable to soil loss and nutrient leaching. Because of the increasing use of labour and continuous cropping, new farming systems are labour-using and land-saving. Thus the unit isoquant corresponding to this farming system is depicted by curve I_2I_2 in Figure 1.[8]

Given a relative factor price of P_1, the optimum is attained at E_2 in Figure 1 under the new farming system, at which production is assumed to be more profitable than at E_1, possibly E'_0 as well. The shift from E_1 to E_2, however, is not costless. As was mentioned earlier, physical investment, such as terracing and tree planting, is required to adopt the new farming system. Thus it does not pay to adopt the new farming system unless the difference in the short-run profitability between the old and new systems warrants the cost of long-term investment.

It must be emphasized that land tenure institutions must change in order to encourage investments. Since land use rights are not totally secure and transfer rights are restricted under traditional land tenure institutions, the expected returns to investment may be depressed: those who plant trees may not be able to reap the benefits owing to an inability to bequeath the property to desired heirs or to sell the land freely if the need arises (Fortmann and Bruce, 1988; Besley, 1995). This incentive issue is not considered in the Boserup model. I hypothesize that land rights institutions are induced to change towards greater individualization in order to provide appropriate incentives to invest in land and trees.

Possible pathways

Resource degradation may continue without accompanying intensification of farming systems, even if population pressure on increasingly limited land resources increases. Prohibitively high costs of investments in land improvements, poor returns from the investments, difficulties in reaching agreement on the communal rules of private ownership systems and legal restrictions on the choice of property rights institutions may all inhibit innovative institutional responses, resulting in the delay of rehabilitation efforts and continued resource degradation. Otherwise, in flat, non-arid areas where crop farming has a comparative advantage over agroforestry, privatization of property rights may occur, which would accompany investment in the improvement of land quality for continuous crop farming. In sloping areas where agroforestry has a comparative advantage, privatization of property rights may take place, which will induce investment in commercial trees. It is worth emphasizing that the individualization of land rights is a prerequisite for these desirable changes in farming systems.

The implication of these arguments for changes in the stock of natural resources can be explained by using Figure 2. Forest resources will be depleted over time with population growth following path I, so long as community members have free access to the forest areas. But increases in population may induce successful changes in land tenure institutions at period T^*, after which the stock of tree resources may increase following path II if agroforestry is developed. Timing of the turning point will depend not only on the cost of implementing the institutional innovation but also on the nature of the existing land tenure institutions. As Anderson and Hill (1990) demonstrate, if unexploited forest land is open-access and strong individual rights are granted on cleared land, socially excessive forest clearance takes place. This pattern prevails across the study sites from Asia and Africa.

If intensive annual crop farming systems are chosen, tree resources may continue to be depleted along path III, as secondary forest and bushland, which are fallow lands under shifting cultivation, will disappear. However, investment in land improvement will be conducive not only to the conservation of soil fertility of the cultivated land but also to the preservation of remaining

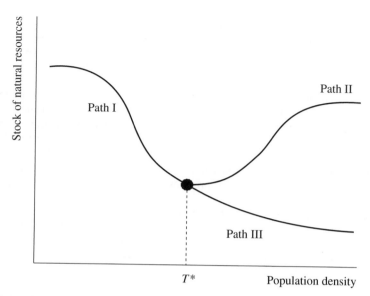

FIGURE 2   *Evolutionary changes in stock of natural resources*

uncultivated forest areas located elsewhere. This occurs because increased food production from the same unit of land will increase the supply of foods to the market and reduce food prices, thereby reducing incentives to clear uncultivated forest land for the production of food crops. In this way, the intensification of farming systems will contribute to the improvement of the natural resource base.

EMPIRICAL ANALYSIS

Characterization of study sites

There are similarities and dissimilarities among our four study sites (see Table 1). Both the Ghana and Sumatra sites have a comparative advantage in agroforestry over pure food production under shifting cultivation, owing to hilly or mountainous topography on which annual crops cannot be grown sustainably under increasing population pressure (Otsuka and Quisumbing, 2000). Usually, food crops are intercropped with young trees on agroforestry plots for a few years after tree planting. In Western Sumatra, large areas of primary forest still exist in the national park, even though some portions have been converted to irrigated paddy fields, crop fields under shifting cultivation system and fields of commercial trees such as rubber, coffee and cinnamon. In Western Ghana, primary forests have largely disappeared and been replaced either by crop fields under shifting cultivation or by cocoa fields.

TABLE 1   *Characterization of study sites*

Sites	Topography	Major products of agroforest/forest	Changes in land tenure
Ghana	Hilly	Cocoa	Emergence of gift under uterine matrilineal system
Sumatra	Mountainous	Rubber, cinnamon, coffee	Transition to single family ownership under matrilineal system
Malawi	Flat/hilly	None/minor forest products	Transition from matrilineal to patrilineal inheritance system
Uganda	Hilly/flat	Coffee/charcoal	Individualization of communal land (coexisted with private land)

While Malawi is also characterized by communal ownership, agroforestry systems are less profitable as compared to food cropping systems than in Ghana or Sumatra, as many areas are characterized by flat topography and dry climate. There are also communally owned forests on hilly portions of Malawi, but they are largely open-access (Place and Otsuka, 2001b). Most community woodlands have been converted to crop fields in this country (with the exception of the sparsely populated north). The Uganda sites consist of communal and privately owned areas, in which coffee is grown in hilly and humid areas nearer to Lake Victoria and charcoal is a major product of woodland in the other areas, which are generally flat and dry. As in Malawi, woodlands have been degraded and converted to crop fields in most areas (Place and Otsuka, 2001a).

In Ghana, the so-called 'uterine matrilineal inheritance system' is practised, in which land is bequeathed from a deceased man to his brother or, ultimately, to his nephew. The cultivated land is traditionally owned by the extended family, in which an individual household possesses no more than use rights. In this system, it is obvious that a wife and children have little incentive to help manage cocoa trees, even though weeding labour provided by the wife or children is critically important to grow trees successfully. According to Otsuka and Quisumbing (2000), profitability of cocoa agroforestry is much higher than that of shifting cultivation. In order to provide incentives to establish cocoa agroforestry, the new system called 'gift' has emerged, in which land is given to the wife and children while the man is still alive, provided that they have helped the establishment of cocoa fields. Although the transfer of land through gift must be approved by members of the extended family, once approved, strong individual rights are given to such land. In fact, there are cases in which even the right to sell land, which is the strongest right, is granted to gifted land (ibid.). This institutional rule is consistent with the common rule of communal societies that efforts to invest in land, including forest clearance and tree planting, are rewarded by strong individual land rights (Shepherd, 1991).

In Sumatra, a lineage ownership system, consisting typically of three generations, has been traditionally practised in which land use rights are transferred from a woman to her sisters, daughters and nieces. Exactly who receives land rights through inheritance is determined by the extended family in consideration of equity among family members. Therefore incentive problems akin to those in Ghana arise; there is no guarantee that those who invest in trees, or their desired heirs, will be able to reap returns to investment in future. Gradually over time, however, the lineage ownership system has been replaced by a joint family ownership system, in which two successive generations of family members jointly own the same piece of land, and further by a single family ownership system. In the case of the latter, rights to rent and pawn without the permission of any extended family members are given to land owners and even the right to sell may be granted, depending on the results of negotiation. As a matter of fact, private land transactions are relatively active in Sumatra. Such changes have been accompanied by efforts in planting and growing trees. As in Ghana, tree planting strengthens individual land rights (Otsuka and Quisumbing, 2000). Interestingly enough, although women tend to inherit paddy land in areas where it is primarily females who work in paddy production, men now tend to inherit rubber agroforest, in which they are the primary workers. If men and women work equally, such as on cinnamon fields, egalitarian inheritance by daughters and sons has become common. Thus the inheritance system seems to have evolved in such a manner as to provide appropriate work incentives to men and women.

Traditionally in southern and central Malawi, a matrilineal inheritance cum matrilocal residence system, in which land is transferred from a mother to her daughters and the husband resides in the wife's village, has been practised. Even under such a system, it is primarily men who make major farm management decisions, including decisions to invest in land improvement. If the wife dies or the couple are divorced, the husband has to leave his wife's village, which means that he may not be able to receive benefits from his past investments. Because of this tenure insecurity it is thought that men do not have enough investment incentives (Place and Otsuka, 2001b). In Malawi, the matrilineal/matrilocal system has given way to a patrilineal/patrilocal system, in which the wife moves to her husband's village. Since agroforestry systems do not have a comparative advantage in flat areas of Malawi, the incidence of commercial tree planting did not play a major role in the transition from matrilineal to patrilineal inheritance systems.

A patrilineal inheritance system is practised in Uganda, in which land is transferred from father to his sons. As in Malawi, men are the primary decision makers in farm management as well in inheritance. Thus a relatively small number of family members, usually a father and his sons, are involved in inheritance decisions. Under these conditions, the individualization of land rights seems to have taken place more rapidly than in a matrilineal society, where both men and women have interests in the same property. Another interesting feature of the land tenure system in Uganda is the coexistence of communal land and private ownership (*mailo*) created during colonial periods. Thus it is possible to make a comparison of management practice and efficiency of natural resource management under communal and private ownership systems. In relatively humid areas where coffee production is common, particularly strong land rights are conferred on those who establish coffee agroforest (Place and Otsuka, 2000a).

The case of trees

No strong evidence was found to support the validity of popular arguments that customary or communal land tenure systems hinder investment in Uganda, Ghana and Sumatra: commercial trees have been planted under communal ownership systems as widely and actively as under more individualized ownership systems, according to the results of the regression analyses of tree planting (Place and Otsuka, 2000a; Otsuka and Quisumbing, 2000). This is observed, in part, because land rights have become highly individualized as a result of investment in trees and continuous tree cultivation by farmers driven by high population pressure. Furthermore, given the positive and significant effect of tree planting on individual land rights, sufficiently strong incentives to plant commercial trees seem to exist under the communal ownership system. Indeed, once trees are planted, the land ownership system is often converted to de facto private ownership within a community. Thus, as verified by the estimation results of profit functions, the management efficiency of commercial tree fields under the communal system is generally comparable to other ownership systems (Otsuka and Quisumbing, 2000; Place and Otsuka, 2000a). In other words, communal systems evolve towards individualized systems and do not impede the development of agroforestry.

It is important to point out that the institutional rule to grant strong individual land rights on fields planted with trees has been established in communities where agroforestry is more profitable than other cropping systems. Since most areas of Malawi are characterized by flat topography, agroforestry has no inherent profit advantage compared with maize and tobacco production. In such a production environment, no institutional rule has emerged that grants strong individual land rights in return for tree planting. It is likely that the costs of reaching new communal agreements on property rights institutions and enforcing new community rules exceed the expected benefits. As a result, land tenure institutions affect the decision to plant trees in crop fields in Malawi, in which greater tenure security leads to more active planting of trees for poles, firewood and fruits (Place and Otsuka, 2000b).[9]

In sum, communal land tenure institutions in no way deter the development of agroforestry, irrespective of the levels of tenure security in these systems, because of the expected increase in land rights after tree planting. In other words, communal land tenure institutions have built-in rules to ensure the intensification of land use as predicted by Boserup (1965) in areas where agroforestry has a comparative advantage. Furthermore, it is important to realize that incentives for establishing and managing agroforestry systems are strong in more marginal areas and on fragile lands.

The case of cropland

Land tenure rules affect expected future benefits accruing to those who invest in land improvement, including tree planting. Therefore these rules affect long-term but not short-term management incentives. In support of this, I found that land tenure institutions did not have any impacts on production efficiency of food crop fields in Ghana and paddy fields in Sumatra, neither of which require much long-term investment (Otsuka and Quisumbing, 2000). The same point applies to farming of maize in Malawi, for which I again did not observe any difference in management efficiency between patrilineal and matrilineal inheritance systems, despite greater security of tenure under the former (Place and Otsuka, 2000b).

However, there are some differences in management efficiency of annual crop production under different land tenure institutions. In Malawi, farmers subject to patrilineal inheritance have introduced more profitable burley tobacco farming more quickly and more widely than those subject to matrilineal inheritance, after abolishment of the policy to prohibit burley tobacco production by small landholders in Malawi (ibid.). Being the new crop, investment in the acquisition of relevant new farming knowledge (for example on crop rotations), purchased inputs, such as chemical fertilizer, and in marketing relationships, was required for tobacco production. Unlike tree planting, however, the adoption of new technology does not confer strong individual land rights and, hence, those who are subject to tenure insecurity under matrilineal inheritance tend to adopt the new crop less actively.

Because of the increasing population pressure farmers in Malawi invested in terracing and water management to improve the quality of cropland, which required substantive work efforts. According to the analysis of the determinants of such investments by Place and Otsuka (2000b), there is no significant tenure effect. Although not directly confirmed from field research it is possible that, as with commercial tree planting in Ghana, Uganda and Sumatra, such a result might well have been obtained because of the tenure rules which confer strong individual rights on terraced land and land with better water management facilities.

According to the accumulated empirical evidence from sub-Sahara Africa, land tenure institutions do not seem to affect the productivity of sedentary farming significantly (Place and Hazell, 1993). A plausible hypothesis seems to be that, as in the case of tree planting, land investment, such as terracing and destumping, strengthens individual land rights whenever such investments are highly profitable. This hypothesis must be tested as carefully as possible, because unless and until this hypothesis is supported empirically, it is difficult to fully accept the Boserup hypothesis that population pressure by itself leads directly to the intensification of farming systems.

CONCLUDING REMARKS

Farmers engaged in shifting cultivation and management of agroforests generally belong to the poor segment of society, if not the poorest as in arid areas. Land is mostly sloping and, hence, often marginal for agriculture. Unless decent work opportunities are made available, it is practically impossible to relocate these farmers to restore forest conditions. Like forest, agroforestry provides positive environmental externalities such as carbon sequestration, increased flora biodiversity and the prevention of soil erosion (Gockowski *et al.*, 1998; Tomich *et al.*, 1998). Moreover, it is more sustainable and profitable than shifting cultivation in marginal areas because of the low yields of pure food crop enterprises on these lands. Therefore it is socially desirable to promote agroforestry systems.

It is widely believed, however, that because of weak individual land rights or tenure insecurity, trees are not planted and well managed under communal ownership in which the extended family has a strong influence over use rights in cultivated land (Johnson, 1972; Besley, 1995). If this is indeed the case, it will be difficult to disseminate agroforestry in marginal areas, even though agroforestry has a comparative advantage over food production under shifting cultivation. This paper clearly demonstrates that the communal tenure institutions do provide sufficient incentives to plant and manage trees, which enhance efficiency of land use and reduce the incidence of poverty in marginal areas.

Thus there are good economic and social reasons to support the development of agroforestry systems by means of public sector research and development, and publicly supported extension programmes. Nonetheless, to date, only a few isolated efforts have been made to develop agroforestry systems growing commercial trees.

While it is highly likely that increasing population pressure on land in marginal, sloping areas will induce the development of agroforestry systems in a manner consistent with the Boserup hypothesis, it is not clear whether and how land tenure institutions change in response to population pressure in high-potential agricultural areas where continuous crop farming has a comparative advantage. If land rights are strengthened by major investments in land improvement in such areas, serious efforts should be made to disseminate new technologies, which will enhance investment profitability. This development strategy will bring about the intensification of land use, which in turn will increase food production and contribute to the conservation of natural resources. On the other hand, if land rights in areas where they are insufficiently individualized are not strengthened by investment in land, entirely different development strategies must be sought for the sake of efficient management of land, trees and other natural resources in the Third World.

NOTES

[1]See Pingali *et al.* (1987) for the evidence on the intensification of farming systems associated with population pressure in sub-Saharan Africa.

[2]Note that such commercial tree crop systems in Africa are not found in what people would describe as the most marginal areas: they are in humid climate areas and higher elevations.

[3]Other important land rights institutions include private ownership, state ownership and common property. For the issues of common property forest management, see Kijima *et al.* (2000), Otsuka and Tachibana (2000) and Sakurai *et al.* (2000).

[4]There is much confusion in the terminology of land rights institutions in the land tenure literature. The distinction between communal ownership and common property is not made in many studies (for example, Johnson 1972). Demsetz (1967) and Alchian and Demsetz (1973) identify communal ownership with open-access; but open-access itself is considered to be a category of land tenure institutions by some researchers (for example, Feder and Feeny, 1993). I consider it more appropriate to regard open-access as an extreme outcome of land management rules, which can theoretically occur under any land tenure regime.

[5]I believe that the basis of comparative advantage of trees and tree crops on sloping land is the perennial cover that reduces soil erosion.

[6]While the straight factor price line indicates the existence of perfect factor markets, such an assumption is unnecessary for our arguments. A critical assumption is that the slope of the factor price curve becomes flatter as population pressure increases.

[7]Applications of commercial fertilizer can also be incorporated. To do this, however, requires an extension of the model to the case with more than two inputs, which is straightforward but cumbersome.

[8]Crops grown under the new farming system are likely to be different from crops grown under shifting cultivation. The efficiency of producing different crops in Figure 1 is directly compared, because the unit isoquant is defined in terms of the combination of inputs necessary to produce $1.00 worth of output, regardless of which crops are grown.

[9]Note that tobacco production relies on trees for drying and constructing drying sheds. Thus, as woodlands disappear, prices and profits of pole production should increase.

REFERENCES

Alchian, A.A. and Demsetz, H. (1973), 'The Property Right Paradigm', *Journal of Economic History*, **16**, 16–27.

Anderson, T.L. and Hill, P.J. (1990), 'The Race for Property Rights', *Journal of Law and Economics*, **33**, 177–97.

Ault, D.E. and Rutman, G.L. (1979), 'The Development of Individual Rights to Property in Tribal Africa', *Journal of Law and Economics*, **22**,163–82.

Besley, T. (1995), 'Property Rights and Investment Incentives', *Journal of Political Economy*, **103**, 913–37.

Boserup, E. (1965), *Conditions of Agricultural Change*, Chicago, IL: Aldine.

Bruce, J.W. and Migot-Adholla, S.E. (eds) (1993), *Searching for Land Tenure Security in Africa*, Dubuque, IA: Kendall/Hunt.

Deacon, R.T. (1994), 'Deforestation and the Rule of Law in a Cross-Section of Countries', *Land Economics*, **70**,414–30.

Demsetz, H. (1967), 'Toward a Theory of Property Rights', *American Economic Review*, **57**, 347–59.

Feder, G. and Feeny, D. (1993), 'The Theory of Land Tenure and Property Rights', in K. Hoff, A. Braverman and J.E. Stiglitz (eds), *The Economics of Rural Organization: Theory, Practice and Policy*, Oxford: Oxford University Press.

Fortmann. L. and Bruce, J. (1988), *Whose Trees? Proprietary Dimensions of Forestry*, Boulder: Westview Press.

Gockowski, J., Nkamleu, B. and Wendt, J. (1998), 'Implications of Resource Use Intensification for the Environment and Sustainable Technology Systems in the Central African Rainforest', paper presented at American Agricultural Economics Association, International Conference on Agricultural Intensification, Economic Development and the Environment, Salt Lake City, Utah.

Hayami, Y. and Ruttan, V.W. (1985), *Agricultural Development: An International Perspective*, Baltimore, MD: Johns Hopkins University Press.

Johnson, O.E.G. (1972), 'Economic Analysis, the Legal Framework and Land Tenure Systems', *Journal of Law and Economics*, **15**, 259–76.

Kijima, Y., Sakurai, T. and Otsuka, K. (2000), '*Iriaichi*: Collective vs. Individualized Management of Community Forests in Post-War Japan', *Economic Development and Cultural Change*, **48**, 867–86.

Otsuka, K. (2000), 'Role of Agricultural Research in Poverty Reduction: Lessons from Asian Experience', *Food Policy*, **25**, 447–62.

Otsuka, K. and Place, F. (2000), 'Land Tenure and Natural Resource Management: A Comparative Study of Agrarian Communities in Asia and Africa', mimeo, International Food Policy Research Institute, Washington, DC.

Otsuka, K. and Quisumbing, A.R. (2000), 'Land Rights and Natural Resource Management in the Transition to Individual Ownership: Case Studies from Ghana and Indonesia', in A. de Janvry, J.-P. Platteau and E. Sadoulet (eds), *Land Distribution and Rural Poverty*, Oxford: Clarendon Press.

Otsuka, K. and Tachibana, T. (2000), 'Evolution and Consequences of Community Forest Management in the Hill Region of Nepal', in Y. Hayami and A. Aoki (eds), *Community and Market in Economic Development*, Oxford: Clarendon Press.

Pingali, P., Bigot, Y. and Binswanger, H.P. (1987), *Agricultural Mechanization and the Evolution of Farming Systems in sub-Saharan Africa*, Baltimore, MD: Johns Hopkins University Press.

Place, F. and Hazell, P. (1993), 'Productivity Effects of Indigenous Land Tenure in sub-Saharan Africa', *American Journal of Agricultural Economics*, **75**, 10–19.

Place, F. and Otsuka, K. (2001a), 'Population Pressure, Land Tenure, and Tree Resource Management in Uganda', *Land Economics*, **76**, 233–51.

Place, F. and Otsuka, K. (2001b), 'Population, Land Tenure, and Natural Resource Management in Malawi', *Journal of Environmental Economics and Management*, **41**, 13–22.

Place, F. and Otsuka, K. (2000a), 'Population Pressure, Land Tenure, and Tree Resource Management in Uganda', mimeo, Tokyo Metropolitan University.

Place, F. and Otsuka, Keijiro (2000b), 'Tenure, Agricultural Investment, and Productivity in Customary Tenure Sector of Malawi', mimeo, Tokyo Metropolitan University.

Sakurai, T., Ryamajhi, S., Pokharel, R. and Otsuka, K. (2000), 'Private, Collective, and Centralized Community Management: A Comparative Study of Timber Forest and Plantation Management in Inner Tarai of Nepal', mimeo, Tokyo Metropolitan University.

Shepherd, G. (1991), 'The Communal Management of Forests in the Semi-Arid and Sub-Humid Regions of Africa: Past Practice and Prospects for the Future', *Development Policy Review*, **19**, 151–76.

Tomich, T.P., van Noordwijk, M., Budidarsono, S., Gillison, A., Kusumanto, T., Murdiyarso, D., Stolle, F. and Fagi, A.M. (1998), 'Agricultural Intensification, Deforestation, and the Environment: Assessing Tradeoffs in Sumatra, Indonesia', paper presented at American Agricultural Economics Association, International Conference on Agricultural Intensification, Economic Development and the Environment, Salt Lake City, Utah.

HANS BINSWANGER AND ERNST LUTZ*

*Agricultural Trade Barriers, Trade Negotiations and the Interests of
Developing Countries*

INTRODUCTION

More than two-thirds of the poor in the developing world live in rural areas.
The poverty there is not only wider spread, it is deeper, as measured by income
and by nutritional status. Ironically, hunger prevails in areas that grow food.

A poverty reduction strategy, in taking advantage of opportunities for rural–
urban migration, needs to address directly how to improve and sustain the
livelihoods of rural people – where they live. Rural growth is necessary for
rural poverty reduction. It is not enough, however, as Brazil dramatically
shows.[1] Growth must generate employment on farms and in the rural non-farm
sector and be widely shared. This outcome is more likely where family farms
dominate, rather than large, capital-intensive commercial farms.

This paper focuses on the demand-side conditions required to fuel the engine of rural growth – the agricultural sector – rather than achieving widely
shared rural growth, which is a matter investigated elsewhere (Stewart, 2000).
It is true that, with economic development, the share of agriculture in the rural
economy declines in favour of rural non-farm activities. But those activities
can only rarely be the driving force for rural growth. The reason? Most non-
farm activities in villages and rural towns are linked to agriculture through
forward, backward and consumer-demand linkages. The demand to fuel their
growth must thus come from agricultural growth.

Of particular importance in this are the consumer-demand linkages. Higher
agricultural profits and labour incomes stimulate the local production of labour-intensive consumer goods, services and construction activities. So, under
most circumstances, agricultural demand growth is a necessary condition for
rural non-farm growth and for rural growth in general.[2] But we all know that

*Hans Binswanger and Ernst Lutz, Rural Development and Environment Department for Africa,
World Bank, Washington, DC, USA. The views expressed are their own and do not necessarily
reflect those of the World Bank. The authors are grateful for assistance from members of the
Rural Sector Board, and also from Kym Anderson, Malcolm Bale, David Cieslikovski, Gershon
Feder, Bernard Hoekman, Don Larson, Will Martin, Milla McLachlan, Constantine Michalopoulos,
Don Mitchell, Frank Plessmann, William Prince, Sudhir Shetty, Anna Strutt, Bob Thompson,
Alberto Valdés and Patrick Verissimo. An earlier version was presented at the UNCTAD X Round
Table in Bangkok in February 2000. Klaus Deininger (World Bank) presented the conference
paper in the unavoidable absence of both authors.

the demand for basic staple food is inelastic with respect to income and to prices. That is why rural regions cannot generate sustained growth rates in agricultural demand unless they trade with cities, neighbouring countries and the rest of the world.

Two facts: world trade in agricultural and agri-industrial products has grown more slowly than general trade, and developing countries have not been able to capture as large a share of trade growth in agriculture as in industry. This has constrained agricultural growth and diversification in the developing world. The slower growth of agricultural trade, and the difficulties of developing countries in conquering a share of that growth, are not surprising. Both developed and developing countries have erected massive barriers to agricultural trade over the course of this century. Their joint negative impact on agricultural growth rates in the developing world is a major reason for the slow progress in rural development and rural poverty reduction over the last half-century. That is why the World Bank's rural development strategy states:

> Without improved demand for developing countries' agricultural products, the agricultural growth needed to generate employment and reduce poverty in rural areas will not come about. Therefore, the World Bank Group will actively promote greater access to OECD country markets for the agricultural and agro-industrial products of its client countries, and support actions in the WTO to achieve this objective. (World Bank, 1997, p.61)

Over the past 15 years or so, developing countries have significantly reduced the anti-agricultural barriers of their policy regimes. But the developed countries' agricultural policy reforms and the last round of the GATT negotiation made only a very modest start in dismantling barriers to agricultural and agro-industrial trade. That is why the constraints on agricultural trade continue to inflict enormous welfare losses on the developing world – losses that exceed those from restrictions in the textile trade. (They also continue to inflict equally large welfare losses on the developed countries.)

A key question is whether the agricultural growth rate in developing countries can rise fast enough for agriculture to be a major engine of rural development and poverty reduction. Can the barriers to international trade for agriculture and agro-industrial products be reduced far enough and fast enough for a poverty reduction strategy for rural areas of the developing world to be based primarily on agricultural growth and rural non-farm activities rather than social programmes and safety nets?

In looking at policy constraints on agricultural demand growth, much has been said about the counterproductive interventions and barriers put in place by developing countries themselves. A lot of progress has been made in dismantling these interventions. Many interventions remain, however, and second-generation agricultural policy reforms are needed. But the main focus here is on the constraints that developed countries impose on agricultural trade, and on the prospects of reducing them in the current round of WTO negotiations.

TRADE AS THE ENGINE FOR GROWTH AND POVERTY REDUCTION

The share of total developing country exports in world exports increased from 19 per cent in 1973 to 28 per cent in 1980 (partly owing to high oil prices) and remained stable at 22 to 23 per cent thereafter. From 1985 to 1995, the Asian shares increased from 10 per cent to 15 per cent, while the African dropped from about 4 per cent to about 2 per cent (WTO, 1996). The Middle Eastern countries also lost about half their market share, while Latin America largely held its ground.

Agricultural trade has been lagging significantly behind trade in manufactured products. World trade in all manufactured products expanded at 5.8 per cent from 1985 to 1994, but agricultural trade grew at only 1.8 per cent during the same period. One of the reasons for this difference is the high agricultural protection in industrial and developing countries.

The share of developing country (LDC) agricultural exports in total world agricultural exports has been decreasing steadily over time, from 40 per cent in 1961 to 27 per cent in 1990 (Table 1). It increased to 30 per cent in 1996 as a result of temporarily higher commodity prices. Of all the major developing country regions, only East Asia and the Pacific increased its market share, while all others regions lost shares. The loss of Africa is particularly striking, decreasing from 8.6 per cent in 1961 to 3.0 per cent in 1996 (Table 1).

During the same period, the terms of trade of agricultural exports have worsened. In fact, in 1999, prices in real terms (deflated by the manufactured unit value of exports from industrial to developing countries) reached a historical low for food and grains (Table 2). With the exception of 1992, the 1999 number was also a record low for all agricultural goods combined (Table 2). Thus, not only has the share of developing country agricultural exports decreased over time, but the purchasing power of the export revenues has also declined.

TABLE 1   *Market shares of agricultural exports in current US$ (in percentages)*

Region or Country Group	1961	1965	1973	1980	1990	1996
OECD high income	47.1	48.8	56.7	58.5	63.6	60.5
South, East & West Africa	8.6	8.0	6.3	5.1	3.2	3.0
North Africa & Middle East	3.6	3.4	2.7	1.6	1.7	1.5
East Asia & Pacific	9.1	9.0	7.5	8.7	9.9	13.3
South Asia	4.0	3.8	2.0	1.9	1.6	1.8
Latin America & Caribbean	14.6	14.4	12.7	13.3	10.5	10.1
LDC total	39.8	38.7	31.3	30.7	26.8	29.7
World	100.0	100.0	100.0	100.0	100.0	100.0

Source: FAO Trade, SIMA Data Base.

TABLE 2 Low and middle-income countries, commodity price indices, constant 1990 US dollar terms, 1960–99
(1990=100)

	Agriculture	Beverages	Energy	Fats & Oils	Fertilizers	Food	Grains	Metals & Minerals	Non-fuel	Raw Materials	Timber	Other Raw Materials	Other Food
1960	208.16	234.22	34.42	252.45	179.91	183.67	195.90	137.26	187.43	220.49	128.92	283.02	120.48
1961	197.12	213.67	32.60	272.00	174.61	189.20	203.47	131.21	177.96	195.11	129.34	240.03	113.39
1962	188.48	201.00	30.94	245.53	162.62	183.44	221.22	126.52	170.33	185.72	134.09	220.98	111.39
1963	203.88	206.43	31.12	260.94	168.01	219.24	224.93	127.91	181.52	182.17	134.60	214.66	181.89
1964	201.87	230.95	29.57	263.20	171.65	207.11	221.13	150.28	186.53	173.62	120.64	209.80	153.32
1965	193.20	213.54	28.75	291.19	178.91	196.67	211.68	172.84	187.08	173.67	130.38	203.23	110.84
1966	190.03	209.21	26.60	277.45	160.18	194.65	228.81	174.52	184.85	169.87	129.70	197.31	107.68
1967	186.26	204.61	25.71	255.27	143.70	196.21	255.64	149.03	174.63	159.86	133.21	178.06	114.50
1968	185.47	214.90	25.77	238.07	126.99	188.29	245.02	156.82	175.82	160.08	135.95	176.55	155.71
1969	183.99	217.50	23.52	225.94	123.06	184.44	223.35	168.64	178.01	158.62	126.81	180.34	128.64
1970	182.58	226.83	21.09	256.60	121.15	186.19	186.28	160.95	174.82	145.20	126.75	157.79	128.48
1971	167.71	190.90	27.94	245.44	117.12	178.90	174.25	137.85	157.93	136.13	120.46	146.83	127.02
1972	165.25	193.57	27.61	223.91	148.76	179.39	173.47	124.77	153.41	126.08	107.29	138.92	146.25
1973	226.72	218.18	36.77	399.60	180.62	274.32	301.78	147.56	203.19	171.64	124.27	203.98	156.31
1974	246.27	212.69	117.98	366.40	480.25	335.74	376.65	149.94	225.50	155.68	113.81	184.27	287.68
1975	178.86	179.68	100.86	227.73	349.69	223.35	257.63	116.60	165.96	120.85	91.61	140.82	200.53
1976	215.08	339.68	110.89	237.18	166.04	188.76	206.39	132.29	190.44	156.92	108.56	189.94	139.22
1977	251.87	529.44	109.07	266.91	148.58	177.80	171.69	130.08	214.78	142.24	99.38	171.50	108.25
1978	199.50	341.71	97.44	239.13	126.62	170.73	185.59	116.49	174.16	131.49	89.02	160.49	106.39
1979	196.70	314.89	206.24	240.19	152.61	171.53	172.70	128.14	176.21	141.81	110.03	163.50	114.65
1980	191.87	252.08	223.88	206.56	179.08	193.48	186.58	130.88	174.35	145.27	109.77	169.50	186.64
1981	162.72	201.00	214.60	196.10	169.26	170.06	198.33	113.93	149.16	124.95	94.60	145.67	132.88
1982	145.28	206.58	200.53	164.95	147.37	135.72	148.53	104.13	133.75	112.29	92.94	125.50	104.61
1983	160.86	223.73	186.41	194.93	141.12	151.50	157.67	116.35	147.79	126.46	91.54	150.30	112.46
1984	171.75	257.05	183.41	231.56	143.56	156.95	153.18	107.62	152.93	127.77	101.24	145.89	97.97
1985	145.89	238.65	173.17	164.71	129.76	125.79	130.05	101.02	132.82	103.25	86.08	114.97	91.53

Year													
1986	127.82	239.73	77.54	108.40	110.40	95.25	94.75	79.73	113.81	87.11	79.02	92.63	84.75
1987	111.10	152.07	89.28	113.96	106.24	95.08	87.20	87.84	104.42	101.49	90.40	109.07	84.02
1988	115.11	146.67	67.49	140.30	114.05	112.58	107.26	119.79	116.40	95.05	84.36	102.35	92.86
1989	111.74	120.10	82.38	126.21	112.16	114.18	118.38	117.55	113.39	102.43	98.45	105.14	101.96
1990	100.00	100.00	100.00	100.00	100.00	100.00	100.00	100.00	100.00	100.00	100.00	100.00	100.00
1991	95.43	90.62	82.82	102.21	100.20	96.98	99.47	86.77	93.12	96.99	101.95	93.60	91.31
1992	87.96	72.03	77.96	104.70	89.84	93.78	95.37	80.63	85.95	92.21	107.34	81.88	83.96
1993	92.80	78.25	69.24	104.88	78.68	92.70	88.08	69.21	85.78	103.69	143.30	76.65	85.32
1994	111.78	134.48	63.00	114.28	84.71	96.94	92.63	76.55	101.13	114.15	142.06	95.09	85.17
1995	110.10	126.60	62.97	114.55	86.90	98.06	100.98	85.21	102.46	113.43	117.06	110.95	82.92
1996	109.83	110.56	78.15	128.74	104.91	108.26	123.10	77.96	100.72	111.32	122.14	103.92	83.16
1997	118.78	157.54	77.32	136.32	110.47	107.30	103.44	83.09	108.51	104.94	116.10	97.31	85.69
1998	103.48	134.92	54.83	127.49	117.18	100.71	97.19	72.43	95.11	83.82	87.27	81.46	80.75
1999	89.57	103.97	76.27	101.43	110.15	84.53	83.39	71.17	84.95	85.44	107.94	70.07	71.32

Source: World Bank.

TABLE 3   *Growth of agricultural exports (average annual percentage growth rates in real terms)*

Region	1961–73	1973–80	1980–90	1990–96	1973–96
OECD high income	6.7	5.7	2.1	2.2	3.2
South, East & West Africa	1.9	–2.2	1.4	1.5	0.3
North Africa & Middle East	2.2	–5.8	1.5	5.5	0.2
East Asia & Pacific	4.8	6.2	4.9	0.9	4.2
South Asia	3.8	0.8	1.5	10.3	3.5
Latin America & Caribbean	2.9	3.2	3.1	3.1	3.1
All LDC	3.0	2.0	3.2	2.8	2.7

Source: FAO Trade, SIMA Data Base.

The change in shares of agricultural exports in world exports over time reflects different growth rates in volume terms as well as changes in the prices of the average basket of agricultural goods exported. For the period 1973–96, agricultural exports of OECD countries expanded at 3.2 per cent whereas developing countries' agricultural exports grew at 2.7 per cent. East Asia and Pacific countries achieved 4.2 per cent growth per annum, while African countries only reached 0.3 per cent (Table 3).

It is noteworthy that the growth rate of agricultural exports of the OECD countries increased by 6.7 per cent from 1961 to 1973 and by 5.7 per cent from 1973 to 1980. We believe that the protectionist policies and in particular export subsidies had much to do with this. Also note that GDP growth of the high-income OECD countries was 2.6 per cent on average from 1973 to 1996, compared to 3.5 per cent from low and middle-income developing countries (Table 4). The population growth rates for the same period for OECD countries was 0.63 per cent, and for developing countries 1.87 per cent (Table 5).

An income elasticity for food of say, 0.2 per cent in high-income OECD countries, would mean increases in food consumption of 0.6 per cent for the 1973–96 period. But agricultural GDP in high-income OECD countries, stimulated by protectionist incentives, increased by 1.5 per cent (Table 6), thus putting pressure on increases in exports. In comparison, with an assumed income elasticity for food of say, 0.6 per cent in developing countries, internal demand would have increased at around 2.1 per cent. Agricultural GDP for those countries increased at 2.8 per cent (Table 6), showing a smaller difference between agricultural GDP growth and expected food demand growth (0.7) than between the same variables for OECD countries (0.9 per cent).

Manufactured exports of developing countries did much better than agricultural exports, steadily increasing from 7 per cent of world manufactured exports in 1973 to 20 per cent in 1995. Those exports now account for more than 62 per cent of total developing country exports (WTO, 1996).

Why have developing countries failed to keep or increase their share in world agricultural exports? Aside from protectionism including export subsi-

TABLE 4   *Growth of GDP (average annual GDP growth rates in real terms, at constant 1995 US dollars)*

Region	61–73	73–80	80–90	90–96	73–96
East Asia & Pacific	7.4	6.7	8.0	9.1	7.7
Europe & Central Asia	—	—	—	–5.4	—
European Monetary Union	—	—	—	1.4	—
Heavily indebted poor countries	—	—	2.5	2.7	2.2
High income	5.3	3.0	3.1	1.9	2.7
High income: OECD	5.2	2.9	3.1	1.8	2.6
High income: non-OECD	8.5	7.5	5.6	6.0	6.1
Latin America & Caribbean	5.9	5.0	1.6	3.7	2.6
Least developed countries: UN classification	—	—	2.6	2.6	2.4
Low & middle income	6.2	5.1	3.5	3.0	3.5
Low income	5.3	4.7	6.6	7.6	6.1
Low income, excluding China & India	4.3	4.8	4.1	3.8	4.2
Lower middle income	—	—	—	–2.2	—
North Africa & Middle East	—	5.3	2.0	3.0	2.9
Middle income	6.6	5.2	2.6	1.5	2.7
South Asia	3.5	4.1	5.7	5.6	5.1
Sub-Saharan Africa	5.1	2.8	1.8	1.6	1.9
Upper middle income	7.0	5.5	2.7	4.0	3.3

Source: World Bank.

dies in industrial nations, there may have been a limited response in developing countries to trade opportunities. That is why the World Bank actively encourages policy and institutional reforms in developing countries to create a more favourable incentive framework so that developing countries can benefit more from international trading opportunities.

There are many good examples of developing countries that have succeeded in developing a strong market position in selected export products, particularly non-traditional ones. Brazil has done very well in sugar, soybeans and orange juice. Thailand, in addition to its traditionally strong position in rice, has developed other export products like sugar and cassava. Bangladesh developed shrimp exports from a very small base to a major export industry. Kenya's non-traditional exports (fresh fruits, vegetables and flowers) are doing well. And Tanzania has increased its cashew nut exports significantly during the last decade. A good example of a successful country is also Chile, where reliability in quality, timeliness of delivery and other contractual conditions have contributed to a strong market position. Chile may be somewhat exceptional because it has strong technical capacities to stay at the forefront and anticipate developments in the phytosanitary and other areas. It also can afford to support and

TABLE 5 *Population growth (average annual per cent)*

Region	61–73	73–80	80–90	90–96	73–96
East Asia & Pacific	2.43	1.71	1.60	1.33	1.56
Europe & Central Asia	1.21	0.99	0.91	1.20	0.75
European Monetary Union	0.74	0.41	0.26	0.39	0.34
Heavily indebted poor countries (HIPC)	2.47	2.71	2.68	2.49	2.64
High income	1.03	0.79	0.63	0.68	0.69
High income: OECD	0.96	0.71	0.58	0.63	0.63
High income: non-OECD	2.71	2.37	1.73	1.44	1.85
Latin America & Caribbean	2.61	2.34	1.97	1.70	2.01
Least developed countries: UN classification	2.45	2.60	2.62	2.32	2.54
Low & middle income	2.30	2.02	1.93	1.60	1.87
Low income	2.41	2.09	2.00	1.73	1.96
Low income, excluding China & India	2.50	2.62	2.52	2.29	2.49
Lower middle income	1.95	1.75	1.73	1.21	1.60
North Africa & Middle East	2.70	2.95	3.11	2.38	2.87
Middle income	2.06	1.87	1.77	1.30	1.68
South Asia	2.38	2.37	2.20	1.86	2.17
Sub-Saharan Africa	2.59	2.84	2.89	2.63	2.81
Upper middle income	2.23	2.07	1.83	1.45	1.80
World	2.04	1.79	1.71	1.46	1.67

Source: World Bank.

defend its position in trade disputes, whereas others may need technical assistance from the international community.

International trade has been one of the important engines of growth for industrial and developing countries. Agricultural trade can be equally important for growth of the agricultural sector, inducing non-farm employment and thus stimulating the whole rural economy. Aggregate agricultural exports are a robust explanatory variable for agricultural growth (Scandizzo, 1998).[3] In short, the agricultural sectors of countries with outward-looking policies and small distortions of their incentive frameworks benefited from international trade in agricultural commodities.

Adding value to locally grown agricultural products is one of the keys to an agriculture-led industrialization strategy. Hindering this potential today is tariff escalation in industrial countries; that is, increasing tariff rates with the degree of processing. This hurts the developing countries and must be reduced. In addition, developing countries need to pursue prudent development strategies conducive to efficient local processing.[4]

TABLE 6   *Growth of agricultural GDP (average annual growth rates in real terms, at constant 1995 US dollars)*

Region	61–73	73–80	80–90	90–96	73–96
East Asia & Pacific	4.9	2.5	4.4	3.6	3.8
Europe & Central Asia	—	—	—	–6.8	—
European Monetary Union	—	—	—	0.7	—
Heavily indebted poor countries (HIPC)	—	—	—	2.7	—
High income	—	—	—	0.3	—
High income: OECD	—	0.7	1.2	1.4	1.5
High income: non-OECD	—	—	—	—	—
Latin America & Caribbean	2.6	3.4	2.1	2.6	2.4
Least developed countries: UN classification	—	—	—	—	—
Low & middle income	3.0	2.7	3.4	1.5	2.8
Low income	3.1	2.1	4.1	3.6	3.6
Low income, excluding China & India	—	2.3	3.0	2.4	2.8
Lower middle income	—	—	—	–2.4	—
North Africa & Middle East	—	4.3	5.5	1.7	4.5
Middle income	—	3.2	2.6	–0.4	2.1
South Asia	3.1	2.0	3.2	3.5	3.1
Sub-Saharan Africa	—	1.5	2.5	2.1	1.9
Upper middle income	2.1	2.8	2.5	1.8	2.2
World	—	—	2.7	1.2	2.2

Source: World Bank.

LOSSES FROM AGRICULTURAL TRADE AND POLICY AND CORRESPONDING GAINS FROM LIBERALIZATION

OECD agricultural protection still harms developing countries. According to Anderson and others (2000), the farm policies of OECD countries – even after the reforms under the Uruguay Round have been taken into account – cause annual welfare losses of $11.6 billion for developing countries (Table 7). That is more than the losses that developing countries incur as a result of OECD countries' import restrictions on textiles and clothing ($9.0 billion).

The real income gains to households in poor countries from OECD agricultural policy reform would thus be sizeable. The average net gains would range from $1 per capita in South Asia to $4 in Southeast Asia, $6 in sub-Saharan Africa, and $30 in Latin America (Anderson *et al.*, 1999a). The average producer household in the major developing country regions would gain, while consumer households with a food deficit would lose. But the gains for producers would exceed any losses for consumers. They would also have dynamic multiplier effects for the rural areas and developing economies, so that consumers should also benefit in the longer run.

OECD countries themselves are incurring very large welfare losses from their own distortionary policies – $110.5 billion a year (Table 7). The main losers are large numbers of consumers, who pay higher prices for food products than they otherwise would for such commodities as milk, sugar and bananas. The main gainers are relatively small groups of producers, who will mount the strongest opposition to the needed liberalization. Because OECD consumers would gain more than producers would lose, consumers could, in principle, compensate producers for their losses and still be better off. It seems therefore that ways should be found in OECD countries to develop compensation mechanisms so that producers do not oppose liberalization.

TABLE 7   *Sectoral and regional contributions to the economic welfare gains from completely removing trade barriers globally, post-Uruguay Round, 2005*

Liberalizing Region	Benefiting region	Agriculture and food	Other textiles & primary clothing	Other manufactures	Total
(a) *In 1995 US$ billions*					
	High income	110.5	–0.0	–5.7	–8.1	96.6
High income	Low income	11.6	0.1	9.0	22.3	43.1
	Total	**122.1**	**0.0**	**3.3**	**14.2**	**139.7**
	High Income	11.2	0.2	10.5	27.7	49.6
Low income	Low income	31.4	2.5	3.6	27.6	65.1
	Total	**42.6**	**2.7**	**14.1**	**55.3**	**114.7**
	High income	121.7	0.1	4.8	19.6	146.2
All countries	Low income	43.0	2.7	12.6	49.9	108.1
	Total	**164.7**	**2.8**	**17.4**	**69.5**	**254.3**
(b) *As percentages of total global gains*					
	High income	43.4	0.0	–2.3	–3.2	38.0
High income	Low income	4.6	0.1	3.5	8.8	16.9
	Total	**48.0**	**0.0**	**1.3**	**5.6**	**54.9**
	High income	4.4	0.1	4.1	10.9	19.5
Low income	Low income	12.3	1.0	1.4	10.9	25.6
	Total	**16.7**	**1.1**	**5.5**	**21.7**	**45.1**
	High income	47.9	0.1	1.9	7.7	57.5
All countries	Low income	16.9	1.0	4.9	19.6	42.5
	Total	**64.8**	**1.1**	**6.8**	**27.3**	**100.0**

Notes: No account is taken in these calculations of the welfare effects of environmental changes associated with trade liberalization, which could be positive or negative depending in part on how environmental policies are adjusted following trade reforms.

Source: Provisional GTAP modeling results appear in final form in Anderson *et al.* (2000).

Agricultural trade reform would increase world food prices and would hurt low-income food-importing countries, especially their poorest consumers. That elicits much anxiety. But the expected price increases are not large, amounting to 4–6 per cent for wheat, rice and coarse grains (Valdés and Zietz, 1995) and many of these commodities show a downward trend in real prices over time. In addition, the terms of trade losses under the Uruguay Round tended to be relatively small – in only a few countries did the estimated welfare change constitute more than 1 per cent of GDP. And the least developed countries had the option to remove domestic barriers, allowing them to convert the small loss into a net gain (Ingco, 1997).

Concerns existed about the possible impact of the Uruguay Round on poor countries. These were recognized by the ministers at the Marrakech Meeting. They made a Ministerial Decision on 'Measures Concerning the Possible Negative Effects of the Reform Programme on Least-Developed and Net Food-Importing Developing Countries'. The intent of the Decision was to make sure that food aid could continue to meet the needs of developing countries. Rather than set quantitative targets, the Decision encouraged activities under the Food Aid Convention. But whether the Decision had any noticeable effect on the assistance to developing countries is unclear. Shipments amounted to 9.7 million tons a year from 1990/91 to 1994/95 and to 6.1 million tons a year from 1995/96 to 1997/98 (Tangermann and Josling, 1999). The new Food Aid Convention (effective 1 July 1999) reduced the minimum annual contributions of cereals to 4.9 million tons.[5]

Another chief worry was that agricultural trade liberalization would remove the ability of countries to deal with external price shocks. But the freer world trade is, the less volatile world food prices become, since surpluses and deficits can be evened out more easily when there are more trading partners with different climatic conditions for growing food crops (Bale and Lutz, 1979; Zwart and Blandford, 1989).[6] And aside from the scarcity of financial and other resources, there are hardly any constraints from the side of the WTO for least developed food-deficit countries to deal with the issue of national food supplies.

The policy positions by industrial countries on development and trade often conflict. Pronouncements are made on aiding the poorest and aid is given, but trade policies substantially negate the assistance provided. In 1998, official grant aid from industrial countries and multilateral agencies amounted to $5.4 billion, and export credits were $4.0 billion![7] Thus the costs of industrial country agricultural protectionism on developing countries are larger than the official grant aid and (net) export credits combined.

These issues are being discussed internally in the EU, particularly in the Directorate for Development (DG8). And they are debated in connection with the renewal of the Lomé Convention. Also of great importance is the future direction of the Common Agricultural Policy (CAP) on the expected expansion of the EU into Eastern Europe. Budget pressures will not permit extending an unrevised CAP to countries in Eastern Europe because this would mean a large expansion in subsidies. Even at lower internal EU prices, the central and eastern European nations joining the EU would be expected to expand their production so that the degree of self-sufficiency of the EU as a whole would not change much, if at all.

Put differently, developing countries can expect limited future opportunities for expanding their exports to the EU. They would, however, benefit from a reduction or outright ban on export subsidies. Without such subsidies, the EU would have to set internal prices somewhat lower so that it would be less likely to have surpluses: that is, it would have to achieve slightly less self-sufficiency. More important, the disruption of the international market from surplus disposal of the EU would be reduced, especially in periods of low world prices, as in the second half of the 1990s.

A new form of non-tariff protectionism is becoming more common: keeping out imports of a good produced with production processes not permitted in the country. Call it 'production process protectionism'. The motive for banning a production process is usually articulated on environmental or social grounds. Examples include attempts to keep out products produced using biotechnology ('genetically modified organisms'), certain pesticides, types of fishing nets, forest management practices, poultry or livestock production facilities that are judged not to protect the welfare of the animals, and labour practices (child and prison labour). We hope these issues will not hinder the current round of negotiations from making progress on the large unfinished agenda.

URUGUAY ROUND ACHIEVEMENTS FOR AGRICULTURAL TRADE

Agricultural trade has had a long history of exceptional treatment in GATT. Although non-tariff barriers have been prohibited for non-agricultural goods, quantitative restrictions were permitted by GATT for agriculture under certain circumstances. Over time, these circumstances were broadened, allowing the use of quotas, variable levies and other protective measures in almost every country. There was also protection by ordinary tariffs, but these were bound for only 55 per cent of the products in developed countries and only 18 per cent in developing countries (Hathaway and Ingco, 1996).

In export competition, agriculture also received special treatment under GATT rules. Whereas export subsidies are prohibited for industrial products, they were allowed in agriculture 'as long as the country using them did not gain more than an equitable share of the world market' (Article XVI:3). In practice, the equitable share concept proved useless, subverting GATT discipline over the use of export subsidies for agricultural products. So most countries in the OECD used (and continue to use) them, causing world market prices to be lower than otherwise, and harming producers in exporting countries with a true comparative advantage but without support from government subsidies. Export subsidies are also the key means for disposing of surpluses in industrial countries, produced inefficiently at high cost. They are thus a tool for rich countries to prop up their protectionist agricultural policies.

The Uruguay Round did bring agriculture under some multilateral discipline and agree to a partial, gradual liberalization. Behind this progress was the possibility of measuring agricultural protection and support much better (because of replacing quotas with tariffs) and thus of comparing countries' intervention policies and agreeing on verifiable cuts in interventions.[8] These measures revealed far greater barriers to trade in agricultural goods than in industrial goods.

Given agriculture's previous exclusion from the GATT, perhaps more was achieved than could have been expected at the beginning of the Uruguay Round. But the results and associated benefits for farmers in developing countries have been modest (International Agricultural Trade Research Consortium, 1997). Under the Agriculture Agreement in the Uruguay Round, tariffs are to be reduced by 36 per cent by 2001 in the industrial countries, and 24 per cent by 2005 for developing economies.[9] The parties also agreed to limit domestic and export subsidies. Developed countries must reduce by 36 per cent the value of direct export subsidies from their 1986–90 base and cut the quantity of subsidized exports by 21 per cent over six years. For developing countries, the required reductions are two-thirds of those applying to developed countries, and the implementation period is extended to ten years. No reductions in export subsidies (where they exist) are required for the least developed countries. One problem with this part of the agreement has been that unused export subsidies can be carried over from one year to the next and shifted between commodities.

On domestic subsidies, the Agreement acknowledged for the first time that domestic agricultural policies can, if income transfers are linked to the volume of production, distort trade. The Agreement categorized (in 'boxes') domestic agricultural policy measures by how much they distort trade. It bound the magnitude of trade-distorting subsidies, required reductions in this support relative to that in a base period, and encouraged their replacement with direct payments fully 'decoupled' from the volume of production.[10]

Unfortunately, the agreement to reduce trade-distorting agricultural support bound and cut only the aggregate support to the agricultural sector, rather than requiring uniform cuts in support afforded all commodities. As a result, the support to some politically powerful commodities rose relative to that for other commodities. There was almost no progress in reducing subsidies to sugar and dairy – two of the most politically powerful agricultural interests in high-income countries. These continuing barriers to production and trade ('peaks') need to be reduced more than proportionately in the next round.

Although the United States and the European Union did not make cuts in their internal support in the Uruguay Round, the negotiating process pushed both to reduce their subsidies and shift significant portions to direct payments decoupled from the volume of production ('blue box' exceptions).[11]

Under the Agreement, developed countries had to convert all non-tariff barriers into bound tariffs. The problem is that developed and developing countries often chose to bind their tariffs at rates higher than the actual tariff equivalents. This 'dirty' tariffication provides little, if any, reduction in protection – it only makes protection more transparent (Hoekman and Anderson, 1999).

Final bindings for the EU for 2000 are almost two-thirds higher than the actual tariff equivalents for 1989–93 (Anderson *et al.*, 1999b) and for the USA more than three-quarters higher (Ingco, 1995). Binding tariffs at such a high level allows countries to set the actual tariff below that level and to vary it to stabilize the domestic market in much the same way as the EU has done with its system of variable levies – even after 1995 (Tangermann, 1999). This implies little, if any, actual benefit from replacing non-tariff barriers with tariffs. It also implies little, if any, reduction in the price fluctuations in international food markets, which tariffication was expected to deliver.[12]

Until all countries' internal prices are relinked to world markets, world prices will continue to be much more volatile than is desirable. With the decoupling in US and EU agricultural price supports, neither is accumulating much in the way of public stocks of commodities, which previously stabilized world markets. The Uruguay Round Agreement provided for the first time a minimum of market access, another seemingly important objective. All countries were obliged to ensure that imports make up at least 5 per cent of a good's consumption by the end of the transition period. Minimum access is being provided under 'tariff quotas', considerably undermined, however, by state trading agencies with monopoly power and exclusive rights (Ingco and Ng, 1998).

The Agreement on Agriculture recognized that 'the long-term objective of substantial progressive reductions in support and protection resulting in fundamental reform is an *ongoing process*' (emphasis added). And it committed the signatories to reopen the negotiations by the end of 1999 to carry forward liberalization embarked on in the Uruguay Round (Croome, 1998). The Seattle meeting failed to start the process. It is now under way but not expected to make much progress until after the US presidential elections.

The Agreement on the Application of Sanitary and Phytosanitary Measures, linked with the Agreement on Agriculture, recognizes the right of governments to take measures to ensure food safety and to protect animal and plant health. It requires that such measures be applied only to the extent necessary to these ends and that they be based and maintained on scientific principles and scientific evidence. But, first, the SPS measures were not developed as part of the WTO process and left out the developing countries. Second, the measures are input-based (for example, one must have stainless steel up to a height of 2 metres on all walls) rather than based on the quality of the end product (for example, the level of *E. coli* bacteria must be less than some limit). Third, there is the issue that in some cases environmental concerns are used to serve protectionist ends. Fourth, even when the scientific basis of the restriction is sound, many developing countries have difficulties knowing what the applicable standards to their exports are and how to meet them. This causes problems for many countries, such as to Burkina-Faso for meats, Kenya for fresh fruits and vegetables, and Papua New Guinea for canned tuna (ibid.).[13] And finally, the cost of meeting legitimate SPS standards is large: Finger and Shuler (1999) estimated that meeting SPS requirements plus custom and intellectual property reform would cost a country some US$150 million, which is more than the development budget of many of the least developed countries.

Developing countries need help in this area. There is an important role here for UNCTAD, FAO, the World Bank and others, with technical assistance as well as with financial assistance for upgrading facilities to meet the require-ment (Krueger, 1999).[14]

The Uruguay Round introduced important differences in the obligation of developed and developing countries in agriculture, with special exemptions for the 48 least developed countries. The least developed countries can have bind-ings of tariffs rather than tariff equivalents. They are allowed lower rates of reductions in tariffs and domestic support. They have delayed tariffication for rice. They can use investment and input subsidies for low-income producers. They can subsidize low-income consumers. They can subsidize marketing and transport. And they can prohibit exports unless they are net exporters. The least developed countries are exempt from commitments to reduce tariffs. So, con-trary to popular assertions, the exemptions imply that there are almost no binding constraints in WTO rules on the ability of the least developed coun-tries to intervene in their agricultural trade – or to subsidize and otherwise promote their agricultural sectors.

THE AGRICULTURAL AGENDA FOR THE FORTHCOMING WTO NEGOTIATIONS

The Uruguay Round has been very important in putting agricultural trade on the agenda and starting the liberalization process, but a large unfinished agenda remains. For example, even if the Uruguay Round is fully implemented and China and Taiwan have joined the WTO by 2005, the agriculture and food processing sector will still have twice the average tariffs of textiles and cloth-ing – and nearly four times those for other manufactures (Anderson *et al.* 1999b). That makes it all the more important to adopt a bolder agenda for the current round, from which developing countries have much to gain.[15] One problem is that they have different perceived interests, and that could make it difficult to agree on a common agenda. Latin America, Chile, Argentina, Brazil and Uruguay belong to the Cairns Group, favouring deeper trade liberalization and strongly opposing export subsidies. Meanwhile, the English-speaking Car-ibbean countries, still pressing for trade preferences, are rather uncommitted to a more open trade regime for their economies.[16]

Although not homogeneous, the developing countries have a common inter-est in strengthening the system, given their limited bargaining power compared to the USA, the European Union or Japan. It is in their interest to participate in defining the agenda, and in the current round's substantive negotiations (Valdés, 1998; Tangermann and Josling, 1999).

Reform of domestic and trade policies in agriculture is the single most important agenda for developing countries in the forthcoming trade negotia-tions.[17] Negotiating agricultural trade demands trained policy analysts and negotiators. Given the limited capacity in developing countries, it is difficult for developing countries to face these challenges and to take advantage of opportunities. It is one of the important roles of international agencies to assist the developing countries in building local capacities. The new round of nego-tiations must seek to implement the following:

- *outlawing farm export subsidies.* Nothing less than a ban on farm export subsidies is needed to bring agriculture into line with non-farm products under the GATT. Credit subsidies need to be quantified and included in the export subsidies;
- *reducing domestic producer subsidies further.* This will involve binding aggregate support levels as well as support for individual commodities, outlawing carry-over of 'savings' from year to year, and cutting high peaks;
- *increasing access under tariff quotas* significantly from the current 5 per cent of consumption; and
- *getting the level and dispersion of bound tariffs on agricultural imports of high-income countries down substantially* – say, to the applied average tariff rates for manufactured goods. As in domestic support, the high 'peaks' should be cut more than proportionately. This is important since the process of tariffication under the Uruguay Round may have actually increased the dispersion of tariff levels.[18]

A reduction in the dispersion of tariffs would benefit agro-processing industries in developing countries now hindered by 'tariff escalation' in industrial nations. Raw materials face low tariffs, but the rates increase with the degree of processing. That provides high rates of effective protection to value-adding industries in importing countries and hinders exporting countries from generating more employment, value-added and export revenue through processing their raw materials prior to exporting them. Developing countries may not have a comparative advantage processing all their raw materials, but tariff escalation by industrial countries clearly hinders development in this high-potential area and gives processing firms in rich countries an unfair advantage.

Although OECD countries would themselves benefit greatly from reducing or abolishing their high agricultural protection, they may not be willing to do so without some reciprocal changes in developing countries – say, in liberalized investment and competition policies. So, to allow for 'give-and-take' in the current round (and to liberalize access of processed and unprocessed agricultural commodities from developing countries to industrial economies) the negotiations may need to include new trade issues of interest to the rich countries. That is why developing countries, in terms of their negotiating strategy, should agree to include such other agenda items as services, intellectual property rights and manufactured products.

One question for developing countries is whether to preserve or expand preferential treatment by individual industrial countries (or country blocs) or to concentrate on obtaining tariff reductions from industrial countries that are applicable to all economies. Under the Generalized System of Preferences, agricultural products have not been important elements. Temperate zone agricultural products have been largely excluded from preferential treatment or received it only within tight quotas, and for unprocessed tropical products (except sugar) the generally applicable developed-country tariffs are zero or relatively low anyway (Tangermann and Josling, 1999). But the developing countries should, if they can, keep what they got – for example, by having these preferences 'bound' in the current round.

Preferences under the Lomé Convention for the ACP countries have also been unimportant in the aggregate. They may have been significant for individual countries and for such commodities as sugar, bananas and beef, but it has been very inefficient to transfer aid in this form. For example, for bananas alone, it costs consumers in the EU about US$2 billion a year, while only US$150 million reaches its target (Borrell, 1999). One reason for the inefficiency is that, when the quota is fully utilized, a quota rent accrues, and so far the EU has given this rent to EU firms, thus limiting the potential benefit to ACP countries. There are also many uncertainties about the future benefits under the Convention.[19]

For sugar, the EU and the USA grant quota-restricted access to their highly protected markets. Producers in those countries as well as some exporting countries gain, while consumers in industrial countries and efficient producers lose. The overall losses of the highly distorted sugar policies amount to an estimated US$6.3 billion annually (Borrell and Pearce, 1999). The small net transfer in aid via the quotas should not be used as an excuse for not liberalizing the sugar markets during the current round.

If the new round can reduce agricultural tariffs by, say 40 or more per cent across the board, preferences will become less important and will cease to be relevant once trade is free. That is why developing countries should not rely on negotiations for special preferences, but should instead use their limited negotiating resources and limited leverage to focus on reducing most-favoured-nation tariffs (applicable to all countries) and removing industrial country export subsidies.

THE UNFINISHED AGENDA FOR AGRICULTURAL REFORM IN DEVELOPING COUNTRIES

Developing countries have to continue removing domestic policy distortions across the board. Benefits would amount to US$31.4 billion (Table 7). These reforms would counter the anti-agricultural and anti-rural bias in the trade regime. They would also open trade among developing countries, a good potential source of demand for their agricultural sectors. Distortions in need of reform have often included high protection of manufactured goods and services, overvalued exchange rates and direct taxation of agriculture (Schiff and Valdés, 1992, is dated but still relevant). Removing them would improve the allocation of resources and increase investment and profitability in agriculture. And removing them in all goods markets could bring gains to developing economies of $65.1 billion a year (Table 7).

Other desirable policy moves include the following:

- entry and arbitrage barriers, if significant, should be brought down to move towards regulatory regimes more supportive of growth and development;

- state trading entities should lose the exclusive right to import and export – and to control domestic supply and distribution of agricultural commodities;
- governments should be more proactive in promoting export diversification away from a limited set of unprocessed primary commodities (McCalla and Valdés, 1999). They could fund part of the cost of searching for new markets, because the private sector will underinvest in this, given the public good nature of this activity and the associated 'free-rider' situation; and
- opening trade would increase the number of processing technologies – and expand the productivity and value-added of agricultural products beyond the bounds of traditional agriculture. But success in this depends on good management to ensure time-coordinated sales contracts, temporary storage and quality controls in all phases of the product cycle.

The new round of trade negotiations might cover trade-impeding measures of domestic regulatory regimes, including subsidies, state trading, export controls, competition law, procurement practices and setting and enforcing product standards. But even if it does not, unilateral, domestic regulatory reform in agriculture would pay off in many countries.[20]

ASSISTING DEVELOPING COUNTRIES IN AGRICULTURAL TRADE

The IAAE, UNCTAD, FAO, the WTO and the World Bank can serve developing country interests by (a) building local capacity, (b) providing a discussion forum for them on trade and related issues, (c) maintaining trade-related databases and providing information, (d) undertaking high-quality analyses, (e) providing technical assistance in norms and standards and in dispute settlement, (f) advocating better market access in industrial countries, and (g) helping to build coalitions and achieve common developing country positions in multilateral trade negotiations.

For any assistance to produce lasting fruit, there must of course be developing country buy-in, local capacity must be built and international organizations must coordinate better.

NOTES

[1]Between 1950 and 1987, the Brazilian economy grew at an average annual rate of 6.7 per cent. Agricultural output grew less rapidly, at an annual rate of 4.4 per cent, while agricultural employment grew at only 0.9 per cent. (World Bank, 1990). The share of people living in urban areas rose from 68 per cent in 1980 to 75 per cent in 1991 (World Bank, 1995), but the massive rural–urban migration was unable to compensate for the absence of rural employment growth. While urban poverty (headcount index) in 1991 was 10.8 per cent for urban areas, it stood at 32.1 per cent for rural areas.

[2]Of course, rural development should exploit other sources of growth whenever possible.

Other sectors which sometimes fuel rural growth independent of agricultural growth are tourism, mining and handicrafts. They can be quite important for specific regions. However, for countries as a whole they are rarely sufficiently important in quantitative terms to make up for the absence of agricultural growth. Handicrafts in particular suffer from very serious demand-side constraints. There are also some notable exceptions where industrialization in sectors independent of agriculture has helped transform rural areas, such as the village and township industries of China, and rural industrialization in the province of Taiwan. These cases benefited from extremely high population densities in the rural areas affected. In China, moreover, the village and township industries are often near dynamic urban centres with adequate infrastructure, rather than in remote, marginal areas.

[3]The composition of the exports is also important: some primary commodities are under pressure from weak markets, and countries specializing in their production and exports may not gain as much, or even lose, in terms of demand-led growth as countries with more diversified products do (Scandizzo, 1998).

[4]This does not mean banning raw material exports (such as logs) altogether, which can increase smuggling and induces inefficient production (such as of furniture). It may mean some initial protection of local industry by giving it a cost advantage (such as by an export tax), but such protection should later be gradually reduced.

[5]One problem with food aid that should be noted is the tendency for shipments to increase when prices are low and to contract when prices are higher and when the needs in low-income developing countries may also be higher.

[6]Note also that different trade restrictions, or combinations thereof, have different levels of exporting domestically generated instability to the world market.

[7]Overall official development assistance from OECD/DAC members and the multilateral development agencies, which includes grants, export credits and loans, increased by $3.2 billion to a total of $51.5 billion (OECD, 1999). This represented 0.23 per cent of the combined GNP of the member countries. The crisis in confidence in emerging markets, which started in Asia in 1997, and later affected Russia and Latin America, led to a sharp fall in net private flows to developing countries and transition economies, from $242.5 billion in 1997 to $100.2 billion in 1998. Since the fall in total private flows was many times greater than the rise in official flows, the total net resource flows to these countries fell by over 40 per cent, from $325 billion to $181 billion (OECD, 1999).

[8]See also the paper by Winters (2000), which makes a passionate plea for further improvements in measurement.

[9]FAO has provided assistance to developing countries for implementing the Uruguay Round agreement, such as with the production of manuals and technical assistance. The World Bank has organized joint workshops with FAO, such as the one in Santiago, Chile, in November 1995 (FAO/World Bank, 1997) and in Katmandu, in May 1996 (World Bank/FAO, 1999).

[10]The Agreement acknowledged that there are many legitimate public goods functions of government in agriculture (listed in the 'green box') and suggested no restriction on them.

[11]The 'blue box' comprises US and EU direct payments to farmers who restrict their output or at least some inputs. These were granted exemption from challenge under the Blair House agreement to carry the Uruguay Round talks forward. In the next round, the 'blue box' should be eliminated.

[12]The reason is that, the more stable domestic prices are kept, the more domestic instability is exported on to the world market.

[13]At a workshop in San José, Costa Rica, 26–7 August 1999, which the World Bank helped organize, it was noted that most developing countries are working towards developing their own food safety strategies, particularly in response to opportunities and challenges presented by the SPS agreement. However, there is still a lack of priority setting in the sector with regard to investments, for example in export versus domestic products or niche market products versus staples. Most countries still have poor institutional arrangements for addressing agricultural health and food safety, with too many agencies and not enough coordination among them. There is also poor enforcement of existing regulations. In addition, most systems are still heavily biased towards the public sector.

[14]As one specific action, the World Bank will continue to assist with the organization of regional workshops to discuss these issues, as well as with consultations during the negotiations.

[15]Dynamic gains tend to be even larger than the calculated static gains.

[16]The World Bank, in collaboration with FAO, WTO and various regional organizations has been assisting developing countries by organizing seminars, such as a workshop in Chile, on 23–6 November 1998, or in Geneva 19–20 September 1999. The key objectives were to stimulate discussions on agricultural trade issues in the context of the WTO negotiations. Geneva material referred to below is in the process of publication, as M. Ingco and L.A. Winters (eds), *Agriculture and the New Trade Agenda in a New WTO Round from a Development Perspective*, by the World Bank and Cambridge University Press.

[17]For detailed discussions of the agricultural trade agenda from the viewpoint of developing countries, see Tangermann and Josling (1999) and Anderson, Erwidodo and Ingco (1999).

[18]This is because the Uruguay Round provided for a simple unweighted average reduction of 36 per cent, with a minimum cut of 15 per cent for each tariff. Thus many countries cut tariffs on important commodities by the minimum and make bigger percentage cuts on items of lesser domestic sensitivity.

[19]It has been ruled that the Lomé Convention is not in accordance with WTO rules. A waiver was granted, but it needs to be renewed annually, thus putting pressure on the EU to bring the Agreement or its successor into conformity with WTO rules. A WTO dispute settlement panel also ruled that quantitative restrictions by the EU for bananas were violating the rules.

[20]In addition to reforms, and for broad-based development to take place, there is of course also a need for improved financial intermediation, and infrastructure investments in transport, storage facilities and communications networks.

REFERENCES

Anderson, K., Erwidodo, and Ingco, M. (1999b), 'Integrating Agriculture into the WTO: The Next Phase', paper prepared for the World Bank's Conference on Developing Countries and the Millennium Round, WTO Secretariat, 19–20 September.

Anderson, K., Francois, J., Hertel, T., Hoekman, B. and Martin, W. (2000), *Benefits from Trade Reform in the new Millennium*, London: Centre for Economic Policy Research.

Anderson, K., Hoekman, B. and Strutt, A. (1999b), 'Agriculture and the WTO: Next Steps', paper presented at the Second Annual Conference on Global Economic Analysis, Avernaes Conference Centre, Helnaes, Denmark, 20–22 June.

Bale, M. and Lutz, E. (1979), 'The Effects of Trade Intervention on International Price Instability', *American Journal of Agricultural Economics*, **61**, 512–16.

Borrell, B. (1999), 'Bananas: Straightening Out Bent Ideas on Trade as Aid', paper presented at the World Bank Conference on 'Agriculture and the New Trade Agenda: Interests and Options in the WTO 2000 Negotiations', Geneva, Switzerland, 1–2 October.

Borrell, B. and Pearce, D. (1999), 'Sugar: The Taste of Trade Liberalization', paper presented at the World Bank Conference on 'Agriculture and the New Trade Agenda: Interests and Options in the WTO 2000 Negotiations', Geneva, Switzerland, 1–2 October.

Croome, J. (1998), *The Present Outlook for Trade Negotiations in the World Trade Organization*, Policy Research Working Paper no. 1992, Development Research Group, Washington, DC: World Bank.

FAO Regional Office for Latin America and the Caribbean and World Bank (1997), 'Implementing the Uruguay Agreement in Latin America: The Case of Agriculture', edited by J.L. Cordeu, A. Valdés and F Silva, Santiago: FAO.

Finger, J.M. and Shuler, P. (1999), 'Implementation of the Uruguay Round Commitments: The Development Challenge', paper presented at the World Bank Conference on Agriculture and the New Trade Agenda: Interests and Options in the WTO 2000 Negotiations, Geneva, Switzerland, 1–2 October.

Hathaway, D. and Ingco, M. (1996), 'Agricultural liberalization and the Uruguay Round', in W. Martin and L.A. Winters (eds), *The Uruguay Round and the developing countries*, Cambridge: Cambridge University Press for the World Bank.

Hoekman, B. and Anderson, K. (1999), *Developing Countries and the New Trade Agenda*, Policy Research Working Paper no. 2125, Development Research Group, Washington DC: World Bank.

Ingco, M. (1995), 'Agricultural Trade Liberalization in the Uruguay Round: One Step Forward, One Step Back?', Supplementary paper prepared for a World Bank Conference on the Uruguay Round and the Developing Countries, Washington, DC, 26–27 January.

Ingco, M. (1997), *Has Agricultural Trade Liberalization Improved Welfare in the Least-Developed Countries? Yes*, Policy Research Working Paper no. 1748, International Trade Division, International Economics Department, Washington, DC: World Bank.

Ingco, M. and Ng, F. (1998), *Distortionary Effects of State Trading in Agriculture: Issues for the Next Round of Multilateral Trade Negotiations*, Policy Research Working Paper No. 1915, Development Research Group, Washington, DC: World Bank.

International Agricultural Trade Research Consortium (1997), *Bringing Agriculture into GATT: Implementation of the Uruguay Round Agreement on Agriculture and Issues for the Next Round of Agricultural Negotiations*, London: IATRC.

Krueger, A.O. (1999), *Developing Countries and the Next Round of Multilateral Trade Negotiations*, Policy Research Paper no. 2118, Development Research Group, Washington, DC: World Bank.

McCalla, A. and Valdés, A. (1999), 'Diversification and International Trade', in G.H. Peters and Joachim von Braun, *Food Security, Diversification and Resource Management: Refocusing the Role of Agriculture?*, Proceedings of the 23rd International Conference of Agricultural Economists, Aldershot: Ashgate.

OECD (1999), 'Financial Flows to Developing Countries in 1998: Rise in Aid; Sharp Fall in Private Flows', News Release, 10 June, OECD, Paris.

Scandizzo, P.L. (1998), *Growth, trade, and agriculture: An investigative survey*, FAO Economic and Social Development Paper no. 143, Rome: FAO.

Schiff, M. and Valdés, A. (1992), 'The Political Economy of Agricultural Pricing', in *A Synthesis on the Economics of Developing Countries*, World Bank Comparative Study, vol. 4. Baltimore, MD: Johns Hopkins University Press.

Stewart, F. (2000), 'Income Distribution and Development', paper presented at a Round Table at the Tenth United Nations Conference on Trade and Development, Bangkok, February, available from the UNCTAD X website.

Tangermann, S. (1999), 'The European Union Perspective on Agricultural Trade Liberalization in the WTO', paper presented at the University of Guelph, February.

Tangermann, S. and Josling, T. (1999), 'The of Developing Countries in the Next Round of WTO Agricultural Negotiations', paper prepared for the UNCTAD Workshop on Developing a Proactive and Coherent Trade Agenda for African Countries, Pretoria, 29 June to 2 July.

Valdés, A. (1998), *Implementing the Uruguay Round on Agriculture and Issues for the Next Round: A Developing Country Perspective*, PSIO Occasional Paper, WTO Series no. 10, Geneva: The Graduate Institute of International Studies.

Valdés, A. and Zietz, J. (1995), 'Distortions in World Food Markets in the Wake of GATT: Evidence and Policy Implications', *World Development*, **23**, 913–26.

Winters, L.A. (2000), 'Trade Policy as Development Policy: Building on Fifty Years Experience', paper presented at a Round Table at the Tenth United Nations Conference on Trade and Development, Bangkok, February; available from the UNCTAD X website.

World Bank (1990), *Brazil: Agricultural Sector Review: Policies and Prospects*, Washington, DC: World Bank.

World Bank (1995), *Brazil: A Poverty Assessment*, Report no. 14323-BR, Washington, DC: World Bank.

World Bank (1997), *Rural Development: From Vision to Action; A Sector Strategy*, Environmentally and Socially Sustainable Development Studies and Monograph Series 12, Washington, DC: World Bank.

World Bank and FAO (1999), *Implications of the Uruguay Round Agreement for South Asia: The Case of Agriculture*, edited by B. Blarel, G. Pursell and A. Valdés, New Delhi: Allied Publishers.

World Trade Organization Secretariat (1996), *Participation of Developing Countries in World Trade: Overview of Major Trends and Underlying Factors*, Geneva: WTO.

Zwart, A. and Blandford, D. (1989), 'Market Intervention and International Price Stability', *American Journal of Agricultural Economics*, **71**, 379–86.

CONTRIBUTED PAPERS

Development and Research

GEORGE P. ZANIAS*

A New Approach to the Evolution of Primary Commodity Terms of Trade and
the Implications for Developing Countries

INTRODUCTION

On the basis of compilations by Nguyen (1981) and Diakosavas and Scandizzo (1991), it appears that about three-quarters of the voluminous empirical work that exists on the barter terms of trade between primary commodities and manu-factured goods indicates a long-term non-favourable movement for primary commodity prices. These results have been obtained from studies which aim at proving or disproving the existence of a time trend in the data, thus implying a gradually improving or worsening course in the relative prices along a determin-istic time trend path. In this case, economic forces are assumed to exist which 'push' the terms of trade to follow a continuously improving or worsening course, with deviations from this deterministic path being temporary in nature.

More recently, alternative ways of examining the long-term evolution of the terms of trade over time have been considered which include *other types of trends* as well as changes due to *regime shifts* (structural breaks). The most important studies in this vein include Cuddington and Urzua (1989), Powell (1991) and Zanias (1999), all of which use a data set developed at the World Bank by Grilli and Yang (1988) for empirical verification. Among these, Zanias extends the original data set, which covered the period 1900 to 1986, as far as 1997, thus creating the longest ever used barter terms of trade series. Using this data set and appropriate test techniques, it is found that the relative prices of primary commodities drop in 'instalments', when random shocks lead to structural breaks, and not in a gradual way as implied by a time trend. This difference has very different policy implications.

The findings of this new approach are extended here beyond the aggregate level by examining the evolution of the barter terms of trade for three groups of commodities (food, non-food agricultural products and metals). They are re-lated to the developing countries' barter terms of trade, the purchasing power of primary commodity exports and developing country income terms of trade. In this way, the total impact of trade on developing countries is evaluated. The econometric analysis of non-stationary series is used for most of this analysis. Policy implications are discussed.

*Athens University of Economics and Business and Centre of Planning and Economic Research. This is part of a larger study carried out by the author for the FAO.

TRENDS IN THE BARTER TERMS OF TRADE: METHODOLOGY

A statistical procedure is used which tests for the presence of different types of trends in the series (deterministic and stochastic) allowing for the possibility of structural breaks. Thus, assuming a structural break occurs at time $1 < T_b < t$, the relevant set of hypotheses to be tested is the following:

Null: $\qquad LCOMBTT_t = \mu + LCOMBTT_{t-1} + e_t$

Alternative: $\quad LCOMBTT_t = \mu + \beta TREND + (\mu_2 - \mu_1)DU_t + e_t$

where $LCOMBTT = \log_e (COM/MUV)$ with COM = the index of primary commodity prices, MUV = the index of prices of manufactured goods,[1] and $DU_t = 1$ if $t > T_b$ and 0 otherwise; $\mu_2 - \mu_1$ denotes the magnitude of the change in the intercept of the trend function occurring at time T_b. Rejection of the null hypothesis can tell us whether or not a deterministic trend (declining or otherwise) exists in the terms of trade. The statistical results for the dummy variable coefficient tell us whether a regime shift has taken place or not. Because the null hypothesis allows also for a *drift* in the unit root process (represented by μ in the above set of hypotheses), failure to reject it may also imply (if the estimator of μ turns statistically significant) a gradual movement in the terms of trade which differs from the gradual movement represented by a deterministic trend in allowing shocks to have a lasting influence on the series.

The above set of hypotheses can be tested using Perron's (1989) Augmented Dickey–Fuller (ADF) testing strategy which requires the estimation of the following augmented regression equations:

$$LCOMBTT_t = \hat{\mu} + \hat{\beta}TREND + \hat{\vartheta}DU_t\left(\hat{\lambda}\right) + \hat{a}LCOMBTT_{t-1} +$$

$$\sum_{j=1}^{k} \hat{c}_j \Delta(LCOMBTT)_{t-j} + \hat{e}_t \qquad (1)$$

where $\lambda = T_b/T$ (breakpoint). Selection of one structural breakpoint requires the estimation of the above equation for all possible breakpoints. This means estimation of (1) by ordinary least squares for the years $2/T$ through to $(T-1)/T$. For each value of λ the number of additional k regressors is selected by setting $k = k\max$ and working backwards until the t-statistic on c_k is greater than prespecified value. Additionally a Lagrange multiplier serial correlation test is applied to the residuals. With regard to the selection of the breakpoint, Zivot and Andrews (1992) as well as Perron and Vogelsang (1992) suggest the selection of the breakpoint which gives the least favourable result for the null hypothesis. This means selecting the minimum t-statistic for testing $a = 1$. The thus estimated t-statistic is then compared to the critical values which have been calculated by Zivot and Andrews.

If, when using testing equation (1), the trend coefficient turns statistically insignificant, a variant of the above test suggested by Perron and Vogelsang is also used. According to this, the testing procedure consists of regressing the terms of trade series on a constant term and the dummy variables accounting for the structural breaks, obtaining the residuals (*RES*) from this equation and using them in the following regression:

$$\Delta(RES)_t = \gamma RES_{t-1} + \sum_{j=0} \delta_j TB_{t-j} + \sum_{j=1} c_j \Delta(RES)_{t-j} + \xi_t \tag{2}$$

where $TB_t = 1$ when $t = T_b + 1$ and $TB_t = 0$ otherwise. The estimated *t*-value on γ is then used to test the unit root hypothesis.

TRENDS IN THE BARTER TERMS OF TRADE: STATISTICAL RESULTS

Estimation of testing equation (1) for the aggregate barter terms of trade case, and for all possible breakpoints, indicates the existence of two regime shifts in the 20th century, in 1920 and 1984. The first of these two breakpoints corresponds to the smallest $t_{\hat{a}}(\hat{\lambda})$ value this century and the second to the smallest $t_{\hat{a}}(\hat{\lambda})$ value this century after discounting the series for the first regime shift.

The test results for the trends in the barter terms of trade incorporating the two breakpoints appear in Table 1. For the aggregate case, the test results indicate a statistically insignificant time trend and statistically significant regime shifts. Discounting for the two regime shifts, the terms of trade series follow a stationary process. This result is also confirmed by testing equation (2), according to which the *t*-value of the estimator of γ is –5.56. When compared with the critical value, provided by Perron and Vogelsang, of –4.87 (1 per cent level of significance) this leads to the rejection of the null of a unit root in favour of a stationary series with two structural breaks in 1920 and 1984. The same conclusion is reached for the case of food products according to both the results of Table 1 and

TABLE 1   *Barter terms of trade testing results (1900–1997)*

Test	T_b	α	M	β	θ_1	θ_2	c_1	Critical value (for α)
Aggregate	1920,	–0.571	0.252	–0.0006	–0.194	–0.271	0.221	
	1984	(–6.90)	(5.95)	(–1.03)	(–4.63)	(–5.56)	(2.40)	–5.34 (1%)
Food	1920,	–0.486	0.143	0.0003	–0.147	–0.287	0.180	
products	1984	(–5.99)	(4.03)	(0.44)	(–3.11)	(–4.68)	(1.88)	–5.34 (1%)
Non-food agri.	1920,	–0.469	0.283	–0.0017	–0.161	–0.174	0.196	
products	1984	(–5.58)	(4.89)	(–2.11)	(–3.17)	(–3.39)	(2.00)	–5.34 (1%)
Metals	1920,	–0.335	0.177	–0.0006	–0.141	–0.020	0.347	
	1984	(–4.40)	(3.19)	(–0.73)	(–2.32)	(–0.41)	(3.35)	–4.15 (10%)
Metals	1920	–0.333	0.178	–0.0006	–0.134		0.348	
		(–4.40)	(3.23)	(–1.27)	(–2.31)		(3.37)	–4.15 (10%)

the *t*-value of the estimator of γ, which equals –4.92. The other two cases are somewhat different. Thus the non-food agricultural products combine the 'worst of both worlds' since they have 'suffered' two negative structural breaks and, in addition, they are following a negative deterministic trend. On the other hand, the terms of trade for metals have been affected only by the 1920 structural break and they do not show signs of following a deterministic trend (estimated *t*-value of γ equal to –4.22 with 5 per cent critical value at –4.25).

Therefore the null hypothesis of a unit root process, with or without a *drift*, is rejected in all cases in favour of the alternative of a stationary process with structural breaks (aggregate, food and metal cases) and in one case (non-food agricultural products) in favour of an alternative of two negative structural breaks and a negative deterministic trend. According to these results, the equations representing the evolution of the barter terms of trade series in the 20th century appear below (with graphical representations in Figures 1–4):

Aggregate: $LCOMBTT_t = 0.412 - 0.367DU1_t - 0.507DU2_t + \varepsilon_{t\alpha}$ (3)
                    (16.9) (–13.0)   (–14.9)

Food: $LCOMBTTF_t = 0.263 - 0.227DU1_t - 0.547DU2_t + \varepsilon_{1t}$ (4)
                    (8.02) (–5.99)   (–11.94)

Non-food: $LCOMBTTNF_t = 0.580 - 0.0034TREND - 0.330DU1_t - 0.355DU2_t + \varepsilon_{2t}$ (5)
                    (17.14) (–3.54)   (–5.94)   (–6.07)

Metals: $LCOMBTTM_t = 0.588 - 0.570DU1_t + \varepsilon_{3t}$ (6)
                    (13.27)(–12.03)

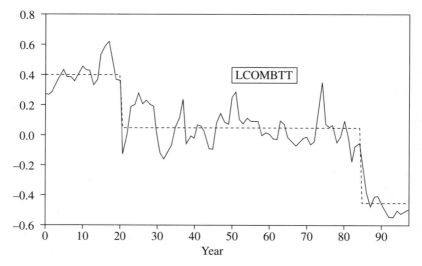

FIGURE 1   *Aggregate commodity terms of trade and structural breaks*

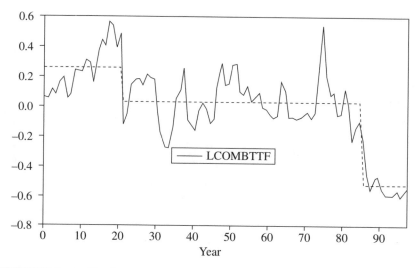

FIGURE 2   *Food commodities terms of trade and structural breaks*

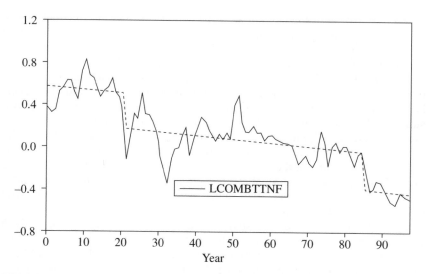

FIGURE 3   *Non-food agricultural commodities terms of trade and structural breaks*

According to the statistical results, the barter terms of trade for primary commodities declined considerably in the 20th century. This is true for the aggregate as well as for the groups of commodity terms of trade indexes. Thus the aggregate terms of trade declined at the end of the century to about one-

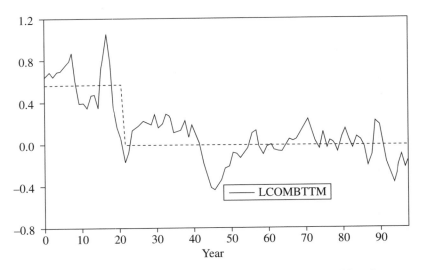

FIGURE 4   *Metal commodity terms of trade and structural breaks*

third of their level at the beginning of the century. According to equation (3), the barter terms of trade index declined by 36.7 per cent after the 1920 structural break and by 50.7 per cent after the 1984 break, leading to the above cumulative effect. The food products index dropped in 1920 by 22.7 per cent and in 1984 by 54.7 per cent of its post-first break level, leading to a cumulative drop of 65 per cent in the 20th century. The non-food agricultural products barter terms of trade index declined only by 56 per cent because of the two structural breaks (33 per cent after 1920 and 35.5 per cent after 1984). However, an additional gradual drop accumulating to 34 per cent in the 20th century led to a total reduction in the non-food index to about one-tenth of its level at the beginning of the century. On the other hand, the metals barter terms of trade have shown the smallest reduction over the century. Their index dropped by 57 per cent in 1920 and has remained stable since then, with deviations from stability being only temporary.

The statistical results of this study confirm the Prebisch (1950) thesis with regard to the *direction* of terms of trade long-term movement, but not with regard to the *way* this movement takes place. The decline in the terms of trade of primary commodities can be considered as dramatic, but things become even worse because structural breaks, unlike deterministic trends, cannot be predicted. Abstracting for a moment from the *way* the decline in the terms of trade takes place, it is clear that their behaviour has very important policy implications, calling upon primary commodity producers (mainly developing countries) to make efforts to increase their market share as well as diversify their exports to compensate for relative price reductions.

The policy implications of the *way* the decline takes place are related to the sources of the structural breaks. Searching for an explanation of breaks, one notices that both follow commodity price booms. The first is associated with the boost in commodity prices after the First World War and the second with the temporary rises in the prices of agricultural products around the time of the 1972–3 oil crisis and the 1972–4 world food crisis. It seems that the price booms led to productivity increases and therefore a build-up of excess production capacity not commensurate with the trend in demand. This proposition can more easily be substantiated with regard to the second structural break (Alexandratos, 1988, ch. 2, and especially pp.52–4). Thus production capacity in the 1970s expanded in order to meet the sharp increase in import demand for agricultural products, which was more than threefold in a very short period from the early 1970s to 1980. The surge in demand was halted since developing countries were facing a slowdown in income growth and had to service an enlarged external debt. Large countries like China and India managed to raise their domestic production and the European Community reduced its import requirements. The situation was exacerbated by the existence of agricultural protectionism which enhanced the impact of increased production on international prices of agricultural commodities. Their resulting collapse provided the impetus, for the first time, to bring the sector (with a minor exception in 1962) into the GATT talks for trade barrier reduction (Uruguay Round) which was concluded in the early 1990s. Since then, international primary commodity prices have been stabilized at a lower equilibrium level.

If this explanation is true, then the situation is one in which windfall revenues may lead to a post-boom situation which is worse than the pre-boom one. This view is supported by Varangis *et al.* (1995). Producers, especially in developing countries where they have few investment alternatives, tend to invest windfall revenues in booming commodity sectors. As a result, the diversification process is delayed and overcapacity is built up and may eventually lead to equilibrium situations of lower primary commodity prices.

Can governments do anything when such situations arise? A series of policy measures are available. Export taxes could be imposed, if they do not already exist. The impact of export taxes in such situations is to reduce overinvestment in booming sectors, thus limiting future overcapacity, at the same time providing incentives for diversification. The elimination or reduction of export taxes after the price boom ends can assist in stabilizing export revenues and expanding exports. However, export taxes should be set at levels that do not encourage tax evasion and smuggling. More important, if export taxes are going to have any effect on limiting the profitability of booming sectors, they have to be applied by all major producers of booming commodities, since individual country actions cannot have a sizeable effect on the market. Providing that this can be done (it has to be said that it could be difficult, judging from experience hitherto), the windfall government revenue should not be used to pursue a procyclical fiscal policy; that is, it should not be used to increase budgetary expenditure, at least by an equal amount. Instead, external debt reduction should be considered. In any case, governments should not commit themselves to long-term borrowing and not expand borrowing believing that windfall gains will be permanent. Finally, liberalization and development of financial and capital markets can help in providing investment alternatives, thus relieving the pressure to invest in the booming sectors.

TRADE IN PRIMARY COMMODITIES AND THE DEVELOPING COUNTRIES

The implications of secularly declining primary commodity prices tend to be associated mostly with the developing countries because of the important place of primary commodities in their exports. That impinges on their capacity to import and contract external debts, which is sometimes the principal means of financing the national budget and international investments. Some more information on the link between the commodity and developing country terms of trade is provided by the evolution of the barter terms of trade of the different commodity groups. Thus, with the developing countries being net exporters of agricultural raw materials, the near collapse of their relative prices in the 20th century is serious for them, especially after the 1950s, when the development of petroleum-based synthetic products had a devastating effect on the terms of trade which never recovered even after the oil shocks of the 1970s. On the other hand, the metals, of which they are major exporters, recorded a smaller drop in their terms of trade and stability during the last seven to eight decades, in contrast to the food products.

In an attempt to quantify the relationship between commodity and developing country barter terms of trade, the cointegrating equation between the two variables was estimated using the Johansen (1988) procedure:

$$LDGBTT_t = 0.160 + 0.281 LCOMBTT_t + \varepsilon_{4t}$$
$$(8.71) \quad (4.04)$$

where *LDGBTT* stands for the logarithm of the developing country terms of trade.[2] The above cointegrating equation indicates the existence of a long-run relationship between the two variables at a significance level around 10 per cent. A long-run elasticity of 0.28 cannot be considered as high (that is, owing to the diversification of trade of developing countries), but it is not negligible either. In addition the existence of cointegration shows that the developing country barter terms of trade follow the unfavourable structural breaks in the commodity barter terms of trade.

CONCLUSIONS

However, no conclusions should be reached on the impact of trade on primary commodity producers before examining the evolution of export quantities and total real income effects of trade. For this reason, in addition to the primary commodity barter terms of trade, the purchasing power index for primary commodity exports and the developing country income terms of trade have been calculated (see Figure 5). From this it becomes clear that the last two

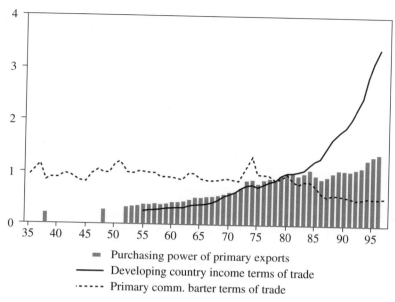

FIGURE 5   *Primary commodity, developing country and barter terms of trade*

indices are rising rather than falling (as the commodity barter terms of trade do), apparently because of the quantity effect of primary commodity exports and the diversification of exports from developing countries into non-primary commodity exports. Probably the most interesting conclusion drawn from this comparison is that the developing country income terms of trade and the purchasing power of primary commodity exports were moving almost together from 1938 to the late 1970s. Since then, the former has increased faster and the latter has nearly stagnated. This near stagnation of the purchasing power index is apparently related to the collapse in the primary commodity barter terms of trade, which appeared in our analysis as the second structural break in the series. The trade benefits for the developing countries must have improved since the 1980s because of the diversification of their exports towards much more exporting of manufactured goods.

NOTES

[1]COM and MUV data series for the aggregate case as well as for the three groups of commodities (MUV common for all) have been taken from Grilli and Yang for the period 1900–1986 and extended to 1997, using for the latter series the export unit value index of manufactured goods published in the *Monthly Bulletin of Statistics* of the UN and for the former the export price index of non-fuel primary commodities and non-ferrous base metals and its three components (food, non-food, metals) from the same source.

[2]Appropriate data to calculate the developing country terms of trade could not be found for the whole century. For this reason the analysis in this section is restricted to the period 1955–97 and it is based on data obtained from IMF sources.

BIBLIOGRAPHY

Alexandratos, N. (ed.) (1988), *Agriculture towards 2000, An FAO Study*, London and New York: Belhaven Press.

Cuddington, J.T. and Urzua, C.M. (1989), 'Trends and cycles in the net barter terms of trade: A new approach', *Economic Journal*, **99**, 426–42.

Diakosavas, D. and Scandizzo, P.L. (1991), 'Trends in the terms of trade of primary commodities, 1900–1982', *Economic Development and Cultural Change*, **39**, 231–64.

Grilli, E.R. and Yang, M.C. (1988), 'Primary commodity price manufactured goods prices, and terms of trade of developing countries: What does the long-run show?', *World Bank Review*, **2**, 1–48.

IMF (International Monetary Fund) (1982), *International Financial Statistics: Supplement on Trade Statistics*, Washington, DC: IMF.

IMF (International Monetary Fund) (1998), *Yearbook of Financial Statistics*, Washington, DC: IMF.

Johansen, S. (1988), 'Statistical Analysis of Co-integration Vectors', *Journal of Economic Dynamics and Control*, **12**, 231–54.

Nguyen, T. (1981), 'Trends in the terms of trade of LDCs', *Journal of Economic Studies*, **8**, 46–56.

Perron, P. (1989), 'The great crash, the oil price shock and the unit root hypothesis', *Econometrica*, **57**, 1361–401.

Perron, P. and Vogelsang, T.J. (1992), 'Nonstationarity and level shifts with an application to purchasing power parity', *Journal of Business and Economic Statistics*, **10**, 205–30.

Powell, A. (1991), 'Commodity and developing countries terms of trade: What does the long-run show?', *Economic Journal*, **101**, 1485–96.

Prebisch, R. (1950), *The economic development of Latin America and its principal problems*, New York: United Nations.

UNCTAD (United Nations Conference on Trade and Development) (1996), *Handbook of International Trade and Development*, Geneva: United Nations.

United Nations (various years), *Monthly Bulletin of Statistics*, New York: United Nations.

United Nations (various years), *Statistical Yearbook*, New York: United Nations.

Varangis, P.N., Akiyama, T. and Mitchel, D. (1995), *Managing commodity booms and busts*, Directions in Development Series, Washington, DC: World Bank.

Zanias, G.P. (1999), 'Testing for trends in the barter terms of trade between primary commodities and manufactured goods', paper presented at the Agricultural Economics Society Conference, Belfast, March.

Zivot, E. and Andrews, D.W.K. (1992), 'Further evidence on the great crash, the oil price shock and the unit root hypothesis', *Journal of Business and Economic Statistics*, **10**, 251–70.

JYRKI NIEMI*

Short-run and Long-run Elasticities for ASEAN Agricultural Exports to the
European Union: an Error-correction Mechanism Approach

INTRODUCTION

One of the characteristics often noted in the international trade literature has
been the tendency of world trade in agricultural commodities to lag behind
trade in manufactured goods. Moreover, it is noted that agricultural commodity
exports from the less developed countries have grown at a slower rate than
agricultural commodity exports from the industrialized countries. Several studies (see Singer, 1950; Prebisch, 1959; Lewis, 1980; Jepma, 1986) have suggested
that the comparatively slower expansion for less developed countries' agricultural commodity exports is explained by low income elasticities and price
elasticities of foreign demand. However, a number of authors have pointed to
the success of those less developed countries adopting outward-oriented development strategies as a proof of the irrelevance of this so called 'elasticity
pessimism' (see, for example, Balassa, 1971; Riedel, 1984; Bond, 1985;
Muscatelli et al., 1992).

Interest in income and price elasticities in agricultural commodity trade,
therefore, stems from concerns about the performance of less developed countries' agricultural exports in the existing international trade environment and
under conditions brought about by various policy initiatives (Lord, 1991).
Elasticity estimates of foreign demand are important, especially to policy
makers and exporters who want to expand agricultural exports and increase
export revenues. Estimates are commonly used to examine the effects of alternative trade policy options, which include exchange rate policies and export
promotion schemes.

For the purpose of policy planning and forecasting agricultural trade, long-
run elasticities of foreign demand are of particular interest. However, estimating
such relationships is likely to pose some problems because the variables used
in the analysis typically exhibit multicollinearity and non-stationarity. The
problems are often dealt with by taking first differences of all the variables
before any estimations are done. Nonetheless, taking first differences is a
major drawback because the low frequency (long-run) variation of the data is
removed. Consequently, only short-run effects are explained by the model
(Bentzen and Engsted, 1992).

*Agricultural Economics Research Institute, Helsinki, Finland.

It will be argued that, since time-series data used in trade analysis are often non-stationary unit root processes, econometric modelling of commodity demand should be based on methods which explicitly take this feature of the data into account, namely cointegration techniques and an error-correction model (ECM). There are several main advantages in using an ECM. First, it is possible to distinguish clearly between short-run and long-run effects, since both first differences and levels of the variables enter the ECM. Second, the speed of adjustment towards the long-run relationship can be directly estimated. Finally, the ECM has a sound statistical foundation in the theory of cointegration developed by Engle and Granger (1987).

The objective is to provide new estimates of short-run and long-run elasticities of import and export demand for commodities exported from ASEAN (the Association of Southeast Asian Nations) countries to the European Union (EU) by applying a theory-based, dynamic econometric modelling framework. Two separate issues will be considered here. The first is the long-term relationship in Europe between the rate of economic growth and that of commodity imports. The second issue relates to the capacity of the ASEAN countries to influence the level of their commodity exports to the EU.

THEORETICAL AND METHODOLOGICAL FRAMEWORK OF THE STUDY

Imperfect competition arising from product differentiation underlies the modelling framework of the study. According to the utility approach (Leontief, 1947), the importing decision is split into two stages. The solution to the utility maximization problem for the first level of decision yields the overall demand schedules for commodity imports M of importer j, given a commodity import price P and a level of constant dollar income Y, and is expressed as a logarithmic function:

$$\ln M_j^d = \ln k + \in_m^y \ln Y_j + \in_m^p \ln\left(P_j / D_j\right) \tag{1}$$

where k_1 is a constant with expected sign $k_1 > 0$; D is the deflator; and $\in_m^p$ is the price elasticity of import demand for good M. The income elasticity is equal to unity, a hypothesis that will be tested later.

Once the level of expenditures Y_j for the imported commodity M has been determined, the solution to the utility maximization problem of how much of the commodity to purchase from alternative suppliers – let us say an exporter of interest i and competitors k, which refer to each of the $n-1$ other foreign supplying countries, to market j whose corresponding export prices are P_{ij} and P_{kj} – may be expressed in the log-linear form as:

$$\ln X_{ij}^d = \ln k_2 + \ln M_j + \in_x^p \ln\left(P_{ij} / P_j\right) \tag{2}$$

where X_{ij}^d is the quantity of the good exported from country i to country j; k_2 is a constant; P_{ij} is the price of the good imported from country i to country j; P_j

is the average price of the good imported to country j; and $\in_x^p$ is the relative-price elasticity of export demand.

Empirical analysis of the study is based on econometric models that capture the dynamics underlying trade and price formation in commodity markets, and it is conducted by means of recently developed econometric concepts. Among these, the so-called 'general to specific' approach advocated by Hendry (1986) is applied in the context of data series whose (non-)stationary properties are investigated. Furthermore, the notion of cointegration (Engle and Granger, 1987) of a set of variables is analysed. The approach follows closely the modelling strategy developed in a series of papers by Davidson et al. (1978); Hendry (1986); Lord (1991) and Urbain (1992).

EMPIRICAL ANALYSIS OF ASEAN–EU AGRICULTURAL TRADE

Data, unit roots and cointegration

The empirical analysis of this study will be conducted with a sample of annual data that cover ASEAN's major commodity exports to the EU from 1961 to 1997. In 1997, these commodities together accounted for almost 60 per cent of ASEAN agricultural exports to the EU (Niemi, 1998). Volume and value data on trade flows over the period 1970–97 are obtained from UN Statistical Office. Volume data are compiled in metric tons, and value data in thousands of US dollars. The transaction value is that at which goods were sold by the exporter, and includes the cost of transport and insurance to the frontier of the exporting country (free-on-board (f.o.b) valuation). The unit prices of EU imports (P_{EU}) and unit prices of exports by an individual ASEAN country (P_i) are derived by dividing value by volume. The gross domestic product (GDP) index and the consumer price index (CPI) are used as a measure of economic activity (Y_{EU}) and price deflator (D_{EU}) of the EU, respectively. The source is the International Financial Statistics database of the International Monetary Fund (IMF).

Tests for unit roots are performed using the augmented Dickey–Fuller (1981) tests (Appendix A). Having established that certain series of the variables are integrated of order $I(I)$, tests for cointegration can be undertaken, and the nature of any cointegrating vectors explored. The augmented Dickey–Fuller (1981) and Phillips and Ouliaris (1990) cointegration test results are presented in Appendix B.

Modelling import demand functions

The first-order stochastic difference equation as a logarithmic function of the theoretical relationship in (1) is expressed in (3) as

$$\ln M_{jt} = \alpha_0 + \alpha_1 \ln Y_{jt} + \alpha_2 \ln Y_{j,t-1} + \alpha_3 \ln\left(P_j / D_j\right)_t + \alpha_4 \ln\left(P_j / D_j\right)_{t-1}$$
$$+ \alpha_5 \ln M_{j,t-1} + v_{1t} \quad (3)$$

where the expected signs are α_1, $\alpha_2 > 0$; α_3, $\alpha_4 < 0$; and $0 < \alpha_5 < 1$.

The results of the cointegrating regressions in Appendix B show that demand for commodity imports in the EU market ($\ln M_{EU}^d$) has a steady-state response to the domestic economic activity ($\ln Y_{EU}$) and a transient response to the constant dollar price of imports (P/D). Transformation of equation (3) to incorporate an ECM driven by economic activity, and with a 'differences' formulation of the constant dollar price term – nested in the levels form of the equation – results in the following import demand specification (equation 4):

$$\Delta \ln M_{jt} = \alpha_0 + \alpha_1 \Delta \ln Y_{jt} + \delta_2 \ln Y_{j,t-1} + \alpha_3 \Delta \ln \left(\frac{P_j}{D_j}\right)_t + \delta_4 \left(\frac{P_j}{D_j}\right)_{t-1}$$

$$+ \delta_5 \ln \left(\frac{M_j}{Y_j}\right)_{t-1} + v_{1t} \tag{4}$$

where $\delta_2 = (\alpha_1 + \alpha_2 + \alpha_5 - 1)$, $\delta_4 = (\alpha_3 + \alpha_4)$ and $\delta_5 = (\alpha_5 - 1)$. The expected signs of the coefficients are $\alpha_1 > 0$, $\delta_2 > \delta_5$, $-1 < \delta_5 < 0$, and α_3, $\delta_4 < 0$. The fifth term of the equation, $\delta_5 \ln (M_j / Y_j)_{t-1}$, is the mechanism for adjusting any disequilibrium in the previous period.

The long-run dynamic solution of a single-equation system generates a steady-state response in which growth occurs at a constant rate, say g, and all transient responses have disappeared (Currie, 1981; Lord, 1991). With growth rates of domestic economic activity and import demand, $\Delta \ln Y_{jt} = g_1$ and $\Delta \ln M_{jt} = g_2$, respectively, the long-run dynamic equilibrium solution of equation (4), in terms of the original (anti-logarithmic) values of the variable, is

$$M_j = k_1 Y_j^{1-(\delta_2/\delta_5)} \left(P_j / D_j\right)^{-\delta_4/\delta_5} \tag{5}$$

where $k_1 = \exp \{[-\alpha_0 + (1 - \alpha_1)g_1] / \delta_5\}$. Equation (5) encompasses the static equilibrium solution when $g_1 = 0$. The income elasticity of import demand is expressed as $\epsilon_m^y = 1 - (\delta_2 / \delta_5)$, while the price elasticity of import demand is $\epsilon_m^p = -\delta_4 / \delta_5$. The third response is stimulated by a change in the rate of growth of economic activity, and is expressed as

$$\epsilon^{YG} = \frac{\partial M_j}{\partial g_1} \frac{1}{M_j} = \frac{1 - \alpha_1}{\delta_5}$$

Modelling export demand functions

In terms of the general stochastic difference specification, the export demand relationship in (2) is expressed as

$$\ln X_{ijt}^d = \beta_0 + \beta_1 \ln M_{jt} + \beta_2 \ln M_{j,t-1} + \beta_3 \ln\left(P_{ij} / P_j\right)_t + \beta_4 \ln\left(P_{ij} / P_j\right)_{t-1}$$

$$+ \beta_5 \ln X_{ij,t-1}^d + v_{2t} \tag{6}$$

where the expected signs of the coefficients are β_1, $\beta_2 > 0$; β_3, $\beta_4 < 0$; and $0 < \beta_5 < 1$. Note that the dynamics for the export demand relationship can be assumed to be of relatively small order, and can therefore be restricted to cases where the lagged values of the variables are of one year. The Lagrange multiplier (LM) tests are again performed for omitted higher lagged variables.

The results of the cointegrating regressions suggest that the demand for exports of an ASEAN country $i(\ln X_i^d)$ has a steady-state response to the import demand of the EU $(\ln M_{EU}^d)$ and a transient response to the relative price of the EU market $(\ln P_i / \ln P_{EU})$. The following transformation of (6) incorporates an ECM driven by import demand M_j:

$$\Delta \ln X_{ijt}^d = \beta_0 + \beta_1 \Delta \ln M_{jt} + \gamma_2 \Delta \ln\left(P_{ij} / P_j\right)_t + \gamma_3 \ln\left(P_{ij} / P_j\right)_{t-1}$$
$$+ \gamma_4 \ln\left(X_i^d / M_j\right)_{t-1} + v_{2t} \tag{7}$$

where $\gamma_2 = b_3$, $\gamma_3 = (\beta_3 + \beta_4)$ and $\gamma_4 = (\beta_5 - 1)$. The expected signs of the coefficients are $\beta_1, \gamma_2 > 0$, $\gamma_3 < 0$, and $-1 < \gamma_4 < 0$. The relative price terms in the foregoing specification have been so transformed as to nest the 'differences' formulations of the variable in the levels form of the equation. The disequilibrium adjustment mechanism in the fourth term, $\gamma_4 \ln (X_{ij} / M_j)_{t-1}$, measures 'errors' (divergences) from the long-run equilibrium and corrects for previous non-proportional responses in the long-run dynamic growth of export demand.

Since in dynamic equilibrium $\Delta \ln M_{jt} = g_2$, $\Delta \ln X = g_3$ and $\Delta \ln (P_{ij} / P_j)_t = 0$, it follows that the solution of (7), in terms of the original values of the variable, is

$$X_{ij}^d = k_2 M \left(P_{ij} / P_j\right)^{-\gamma_3 / \gamma_4} \tag{8}$$

where $k_2 = \exp \{[-\beta_0 + (1 - \beta_1)g_2] / \gamma_4\}$. Therefore export demand is assumed to have a unitary elasticity with respect to the level of import demand in the geographic market. Where the long-run response between the export demand of a country i and imports of its trading partner j is not necessarily proportional, an additional term (explanatory variable for imports of a country j lagged by one period) is introduced into equation (8).

The price elasticity of export demand is expressed as $\epsilon_x^p = -\gamma_3 / \gamma_4$. The import growth elasticity, denoted ε^{MG}, is defined as a percentage change in export demand brought about by a 1 per cent change in the growth rate of import demand, and is expressed as

$$\varepsilon^{MG} = \frac{\partial X_{ij}^d}{\partial g_2} \frac{1}{X_{ij}^d} = \frac{1 - \beta_1}{\gamma_4}$$

REGRESSION RESULTS OF MODEL EQUATIONS

The import demand functions

The estimated equations of import demand and export demand are presented in Appendix C. As expected, income is found to be statistically significant in

explaining the level of demand for commodity imports in the EU. The estimated long-run income elasticities of import demand range from around 1.9
for cassava to significantly less than unity for palm oil and cocoa (Table 1).
The income elasticities for coconut oil and pepper are near unity. These large
differences have important implications for sales by exporters. Cassava exports
have a considerably stronger growth potential in the EU than other commodities, because of a strong response of EU buyers to improvements in their real
income. By the same token, cassava exports will also be susceptible to larger
swings of demand during business cycles. Overall, the results suggest a relatively weak growth potential for the selected commodities in the EU market.

TABLE 1　　*Short-run and long-run elasticities of import demand in the EU
for selected commodities*

| | Income elasticity | | Price elasticity | | |
Commodity	Short-run	Long-run	Short-run	Long-run	Income growth elasticity
Palm oil	—	0.35	−0.30	−0.61	−5.00
Coconut oil	—	0.81	−0.27	−0.16	−1.31
Rubber	0.53	0.24	—	−0.18	−3.39
Cassava	—	1.89	−0.93[a]	−1.27[a]	−1.60
Cocoa	0.64	0.31	−0.16	−0.21	−1.88
Pepper	0.85	0.87	−0.04	−0.05	−1.28
Tea	0.65	0.73	−0.07	−0.14	−1.33

Note:　　[a]In the case of cassava, the price elasticities are estimated using not the real
import price of cassava, but the relative price of cassava versus alternative
feed.

The price elasticities of import demand by the EU range from −0.04 to −0.30
in the short-run, and from −0.05 to −0.61 in the long run. The results confirm
the expectation that demand for commodity imports in the EU is relatively
inelastic. The policy implication of this fact is that exchange rate policies and
commercial policy intervention measures in the form of tariff and non-tariff
barriers to trade would not be very effective in changing the quantity of
imports demanded.

The coefficients of the error correction terms in the import demand relationships are, in general, close to unity in absolute terms. This reflects the relatively
quick response of EU importers to changes in income and prices. It does not
take a great deal of time for import demand to resume its long-term equilibrium growth path when a short-run disequilibrium arises between import demand
and income.

The export demand functions

As expected, relative price movements affect significantly the export demand of a country in nearly all commodities, implying that exporter's market share is influenced by price competitiveness (Table 2). In other words, ASEAN agricultural exporters confront a downward-sloping demand schedule in the EU markets. For the combined commodity exports of the region, the trade-weighted average price elasticity of export demand by the EU (which is equivalent to the elasticity of substitution for market share in the EU) is equal to –2.9 in the short run and –3.3 in the long run. These results can be contrasted with those for exports from the rest of the world to the EU, where the price elasticity is equal to –1.7 in the short run and –2.3 in the long run (Niemi, 2000). According to Lord (1991) exporters with high price elasticities have more developed

TABLE 2   *Dynamic equilibrium solutions of export demand functions for selected commodities from ASEAN into the EU*

Commodity Exporter	Relative price elasticity of export demand		Response to changes in the level of EU import		Import growth elasticity
	Short-run	Long-run	Short-run	Long-run	
Palm oil					
Indonesia	—	–1.22	1.06	1.00	0.08
Malaysia	–2.87	–6.67	0.74	1.45	–0.79
Coconut oil					
Philippines	–4.66	–2.39	1.05	1.00	0.23
Indonesia	–8.74	—	0.98	1.00	–0.12
Rubber					
Indonesia	—	—	0.62	1.00	–6.63
Malaysia	–3.98	–3.10	0.95	1.00	0.19
Thailand	–0.94	–3.52	0.73	1.00	–0.64
Cassava					
Indonesia	–1.66	–1.34	0.45	0.62	–0.74
Thailand	–2.89	—	0.99	1.00	0.23
Cocoa					
Indonesia	–1.02	–5.70	0.50	1.00	–1.85
Malaysia	–4.17	–7.32	0.75	1.00	–0.74
Pepper					
Indonesia	–1.73	–1.45	0.83	1.00	–0.20
Malaysia	–0.81	–0.65	0.54	0.89	–0.58
Tea					
Indonesia	–1.92	–2.09	0.85	1.00	–0.65
Vietnam	–0.65	–0.92	0.61	1.00	–0.12

marketing and trading practices than exporters with low elasticities. Hence one could conclude that the ASEAN exporters have been more flexible in their trading practices than the rest of world.

The results also suggest that export demands for commodities from ASEAN have a more or less proportional response to changes in the level of EU imports. Therefore any increase or decrease in commodity imports by the EU would be reflected in an almost equivalent percentage change in its demand for exports from ASEAN countries. The adjustment of export demand from one level of foreign import demand to another is determined by the error correction term. The coefficients of the error correction terms are close to unity in absolute terms. This fact reflects the relatively quick response of ASEAN commodity exports to changes in the level of EU imports and relative price.

Another influence on the export demand, or market share, of an exporter is the dynamic effect originating from changes in the rate of growth of imports. The estimated import growth elasticities of export demand range from –6.63 for Indonesian rubber to 0.23 for Philippines' coconut oil. Therefore, at given import quantity and relative-price levels, a 1 per cent increase in the rate of growth of EU rubber imports leads to a 6.6 per cent decrease in the average ratio of rubber exports from Indonesia.

CONCLUSIONS

This paper has attempted to apply a reasonably flexible data-determined, dynamic model to estimate the short-run and long-run effects of changes in income and prices on agricultural commodity trade between ASEAN and the EU. Therefore a modelling approach based on the error correction mechanism (ECM) was used in order to emphasize the importance of dynamics of trade functions. Application of a series of diagnostic tests supported this approach.

The overall results for the estimated import demand functions for the agricultural commodities covered by the study suggest that there is a relatively weak demand response to income changes in the EU. The results also demonstrate the inelastic nature of price responses in the EU demand for the imported commodities. The coefficient estimates of the export demand functions indicate that relative-price variations affect significantly the demand for ASEAN commodity exports by the EU. Therefore the findings support the theory of trade dealing with commodity differentiation and imperfect competition.

The estimated models of this study can be used to assess the results of trade policies on commodity trade between ASEAN and the EU. Hence a fruitful avenue for future research would be an analysis of the way different governments regulations affect the volume of trade and what kind of welfare effects such regulations might have.

REFERENCES

Balassa, B. (1971), *The Structure of Protection in Developing Countries*, Baltimore, MD: Johns Hopkins University Press.

Bentzen, J. and Engsted, T. (1992), *Short and Long Run Elasticities in Energy Demand*, Working Paper 18, Institute of Economics, Aarhus School of Business.

Bond, M. (1985), 'Export Demand and Supply for Groups of Non-oil Developing Countries', *IMF Staff Papers*, **32**, 56–77.

Currie, D. (1981), 'Some Long-Run Features of Dynamic Time Series Models', *Economic Journal*, **91**, 704–15.

Davidson, J.E.H., Hendry, D.F., Srba, F. and Yeo, S. (1978), 'Econometric Modelling of the Aggregate Time-Series Relationship Between Consumers' Expenditure and Income in the United Kingdom', *Economic Journal*, **88**, 661–92.

Dickey, D. and Fuller, W. (1981), 'Likelihood Ratio Tests for Autoregressive Time Series with a Unit Root', *Econometrica*, **49**, 1057–72.

Engle, R. and Granger, C. (1987), 'Co-integration and error correction: representation, estimation and testing', *Econometrica*, **55**, 251–76.

Hendry, D.F. (1986), 'Econometric Modelling with Cointegrated Variables: An Overview', *Oxford Bulletin of Economics and Statistics*, **48**, 201–12.

Jepma, C. (1986), *Extensions of Market Shares Analysis with an Application to Long Term Export Data of Developing Countries*, New Delhi: Indian Economic Association.

Leontief, W. (1947), 'Introduction to a Theory of the Internal Structure of Functional Relationships', *Econometrica*, **15**, 361–73.

Lewis, W. (1980), 'The slowing down of the Engine of Growth', *American Economic Review*, **70**, 555–64.

Lord, M. (1991), *Imperfect Competition and International Commodity Trade: Theory, Dynamics and Policy Modelling*, New York: Oxford University Press.

Muscatelli, V., Srinivasan T. and Vines, D. (1992), 'Demand and Supply Factors in the Determination of NIE-Exports: A Simultaneous Error-Correction Model for Hong Kong', *Economic Journal*, **102**, 1467–77.

Niemi, J. (1998), *Agricultural Trade Relations between ASEAN and the EU*, Research Reports 223, Helsinki: Agricultural Economics Research Institute.

Niemi, J. (2000), 'Modelling the EU Demand for Primary Commodity Imports Through Cointegration and Error Correction', Agricultural Economics Research Institute, Helsinki.

Phillips, P. and Ouliaris, S. (1990), 'Asymptotic Properties of Residual Based Tests for Cointegration', *Econometrica*, **58**, 165–93.

Prebisch, R. (195 9), 'Commercial Policy in the Underdeveloped Countries', *American Economic Review*, **49**, 251–73.

Riedel, J. (1984), 'Trade as the Engine of Growth in Developing Countries, revisited', *Economic Journal*, **98**, 138–48.

Singer, H. (1950), 'The Distribution of Gains between Investing and Borrowing Countries', *American Economic Review*, **40**, 473–85.

Urbain, J-P. (1992), 'Error Correction Models for Aggregate Imports: the case of two small and open economies', in M. Dagenais and P.-A. Muet (eds), *International Trade Modelling*, London: Chapman & Hall.

APPENDIX A

TABLE A.1   *The augmented Dickey–Fuller unit-root testing results for the variables*

Commodity	Levels			First differences		
Variable name	Model 1	Model 2		Model 1	Model 2	
Palm oil						
$\ln M_{EU}^d$	−2.901	−0.241	(0)	−4.025***	−4.025***	(2)
$\ln X_{IN}^d$	−2.029	−0.400	(3)	−3.377*	−3.507***	(2)
$\ln X_{MA}^d$	−1.846	−1.492	(0)	−3.222*	−3.260**	(1)
$\ln(P_{EU}/D_{EU})$	−2.775	−2.687*	(2)			
$\ln(P_{IN}/P_{EU})$	−3.303*	−3.357**	(3)			
$\ln(P_{MA}/P_{EU})$	−2.224	−1.881	(0)	−4.506***	−4.152***	(1)
Coconut oil						
$\ln M_{EU}^d$	−1.870	−0.574	(6)	−2.828	−2.903**	(5)
$\ln X_{IN}^d$	−2.021	−1.200	(0)	−3.407**	−3.386**	(2)
$\ln X_{PH}^d$	−1.434	−2.991	(0)	−4.801***	−4.805***	(3)
$\ln(P_{EU}/D_{EU})$	−4.239***	−3.770***	(1)			
$\ln(P_{IN}/P_{EU})$	−5.222***	−5.123***	(0)			
$\ln(P_{PH}/P_{EU})$	−2.826	−2.461	(0)	−3.943**	−3.844***	(4)
Rubber						
$\ln M_{EU}^d$	−2.586	−1.556	(3)	−3.496**	−3.568***	(3)
$\ln X_{IN}^d$	−2.127	−1.359	(0)	−3.838**	−3.988***	(1)
$\ln X_{MA}^d$	−1.847	−1.445	(0)	−3.449**	−3.267**	(1)
$\ln X_{TH}^d$	−0.000	−0.000	(4)	−0.000*	−0.000**	(3)
$\ln(P_{EU}/D_{EU})$	−3.321*	−3.295**	(1)			
$\ln(P_{IN}/P_{EU})$	−1.266	−0.779	(1)	−4.564***	−4.486***	(1)
$\ln(P_{MA}/P_{EU})$	−3.487**	−3.393**	(3)			
$\ln(P_{TH}/P_{EU})$	−0.000*	−0.000	(0)			
Cassava						
$\ln M_{EU}^d$	−1.283	−3.436***	(0)			
$\ln X_{IN}^d$	−2.682	−2.770*	(0)			
$\ln X_{TH}^d$	−1.590	−3.463***	(0)			
$\ln(P_{EU}/D_{EU})$	−0.489	−0.522	(2)			
$\ln(P_{IN}/P_{EU})$	−1.106	−0.817	(0)			
$\ln(P_{TH}/P_{EU})$	−1.992	−2.028	(0)			
Tea						
$\ln M_{EU}^d$	−1.958	−1.795	(2)	−3.736**	−3.566***	(3)
$\ln X_{IN}^d$	−1.629	−1.512	(3)	−3.674**	−3.700**	(2)
$\ln(P_{EU}/D_{EU})$	−2.496**	−2.582*	(0)			
$\ln(P_{IN}/P_{EU})$	−3.267*	−3.630	(0)			

TABLE A.1   *concluded*

Commodity Variable name	Levels Model 1	Model 2		First differences Model 1	Model 2	
Cocoa						
$\ln M_{EU}^d$	−0.460	−0.862	(1)	−5.435***	−4.419***	(1)
$\ln X_{IN}^d$	−1.445	−1.462	(0)	−4.214***	−4.062***	(1)
$\ln X_{MA}^d$	−1.165	−1.713	(0)	−3.601**	−3.198**	(2)
$\ln(P_{EU}/D_{EU})$	−2.123	−2.191	(1)	−3.399*	−3.327**	(2)
$\ln(P_{IN}/P_{EU})$	−2.127	−2.189	(0)	−3.471**	−3.502***	(1)
$\ln(P_{MA}/P_{EU})$	−1.933	−1.953	(0)	−3.283*	−3.318**	(1)
Pepper						
$\ln M_{EU}^d$	−3.053	−1.240	(0)	−4.027***	−4.081***	(2)
$\ln X_{IN}^d$	−2.294	−2.507	(0)	−2.758	−2.866**	(4)
$\ln X_{MA}^d$	−2.615	−2.091	(0)	−2.725	−3.639***	(2)
$\ln X_{SI}^d$	−1.348	−0.165	(2)	−3.007	−2.957**	(2)
$\ln(P_{EU}/D_{EU})$	−3.853**	−3.536***	(1)			
$\ln(P_{IN}/P_{EU})$	−4.276***	−4.633***	(0)			
$\ln(P_{MA}/P_{EU})$	−2.752	−2.773*	(0)			
$\ln(P_{SI}/P_{EU})$	−3.490**	−2.425	(0)			
All commodities						
$\ln Y_{EU}$	−2.109	−1.828	(1)	−4.243**	−3.658***	(2)

Notes: [a]The two forms of augmented Dickey–Fuller (ADF) regression equations for a time series Y_t are:

$$\text{Model 1} \quad \Delta Y_t = \delta_1 + \delta_2 t + \xi Y_{t-1} + \Sigma_1^m \Delta Y_{t-1} + e_t \quad \text{(with trend and drift)}$$
$$\text{Model 2} \quad \Delta Y_t = \delta_1 + \xi Y_{t-1} + \Sigma_1^m \Delta Y_{t-1} + e_t \quad \text{(with drift)}$$

where t is the time or trend variable.
[b]The next step is to divide the estimated ξ coefficient by its standard error to compute the Dickey–Fuller τ statistics and refer to Dickey–Fuller tables to see if the null hypotheses $\xi = 0$ (there is a unit root) is rejected. If the computed absolute value of the τ statistics (that is, $|\tau|$) is less than the absolute critical values, the time series is considered non-stationary.
[c]The number in parentheses denotes minimum value of m required to achieve white noise errors. These numbers are the same in both models.
*, ** and *** indicate statistical significance at the 10 per cent, 5 per cent and 1 per cent level, respectively. Critical values for model 1 are −3.13 (10 per cent), −3.41 (5 per cent) and −3.96 (1 per cent); and, for model 2, −2.57 (10 per cent), −2.86 (5 per cent) and −3.43 (1 per cent).

APPENDIX B

TABLE B.1　　*Cointegrating regressions, 1970–97*

Commodity	ADF-test			Phillips test	
Variable name	Model 1	Model 2		Model 1	Model 2
Palm oil					
$\ln M_{EU}^d - \ln Y_{EU}$	−3.138*	−3.590*	(0)	−3.170*	−3.608*
$\ln X_{IN}^d - \ln M_{EU}^d$	−2.816	−3.533*	(2)	−4.210***	−4.923***
$\ln X_{MA}^d - \ln M_{EU}^d - \ln P_{MA}$	−3.753**	−3.444	(0)	−3.757**	−3.417
Coconut oil					
$\ln M_{EU}^d - \ln Y_{EU}$	−2.654	−1.988	(6)	−2.694	−2.836
$\ln X_{IN}^d - \ln M_{EU}^d$	−3.487***	−6.904***	(3)	−3.368**	−6.891***
$\ln X_{PH}^d - \ln M_{EU}^d$	−3.259*	−3.270	(0)	−3.307*	−3.319
Rubber					
$\ln M_{EU}^d - \ln Y_{EU}$	−3.141*	−3.303*	(2)	−5.101***	−5.286***
$\ln X_{IN}^d - \ln M_{EU}^d$	−3.001	−3.523*	(3)	−4.781***	−4.907***
$\ln X_{MA}^d - \ln M_{EU}^d$	−3.521*	−3.663*	(0)	−3.607*	−3.732**
$\ln X_{TH}^d - \ln M_{EU}^d$	−1.213	−1.904	(2)	−4.003**	−3.756**
Cassava					
$\ln M_{EU}^d - \ln Y_{EU}$	−2.947	−3.302*	(3)	−4.001**	−4.307***
$\ln X_{IN}^d - \ln M_{EU}^d$	−1.921	−2.903	(3)	−4.221**	−3.907***
$\ln X_{TH}^d - \ln M_{EU}^d$	−3.317	−3.027*	(4)	−4.603***	−4.156***
Tea					
$\ln M_{EU}^d - \ln Y_{EU}$	−4.477***	−4.862***	(1)	−7.682***	−8.044***
$\ln X_{IN}^d - \ln M_{EU}^d$	−3.550**	−3.595*	(0)	−3.595**	−3.607*
Cocoa					
$\ln M_{EU}^d - \ln Y_{EU} - \ln P_{EU}$	−4.582**	−4.817***	(0)	−4.571*	−4.823***
$\ln X_{IN}^d - \ln M_{EU}^d - \ln P_{IN}$	−2.391	−3.878*	(0)	−4.493**	−3.874*
$\ln X_{MA}^d - \ln M_{EU}^d - \ln P_{MA}$	−3.834**	−5.550***	(0)	−4.485**	−3.417
Pepper					
$\ln M_{EU}^d - \ln Y_{EU}$	−4.210***	−4.291***	(0)	−4.232***	−4.295***
$\ln X_{IN}^d - \ln M_{EU}^d$	−7.601***	−7.582***	(0)	−6.896***	−6.838***
$\ln X_{MA}^d - \ln M_{EU}^d$	−3.148*	−3.231**	(0)	−3.232*	−3.314**

Notes:　Two models of the cointegrating regression equations (with m time series $Y_{t, \ldots}, Y_{tm}$) are:

$$(1)\ Y_{t1} = \zeta_0 + \sum_{j=2}^{m} \zeta_j Y_{tj} + u_t, \text{ and } (2)\ Y_{t1} = \zeta_0 + \zeta_1 t + \sum_{j=2}^{m} \zeta_j X_{tj} + u_t$$

A test for cointegration is given by a test for a unit root in the estimated residuals $\hat{u}_t$. The ADF regression equation is:

$$\Delta \hat{u}_t = h\hat{u}_{t-1} + \sum_{j=1}^{p} h_j \Delta \hat{u}_{t-j} + v_t$$

*, ** and *** indicate statistical significance at the 10 per cent, 5 per cent and 1 per cent level, respectively. Critical values with two variables are −3.04 (10 per cent), −3.34 (5 per cent) and −3.90 (1 per cent) for model 1; and −3.50 (10 per cent), −3.78 (5 per cent); and −4.32 (1 per cent) for model 2. Critical values with three variables are −3.45 (10 per cent), −3.74 (5 per cent) and −4.29 (1 per cent) for model 1; and −3.84 (10 per cent, −4.12 (5 per cent) and −4.66 (1 per cent) for model 2.

APPENDIX C

TABLE C.1 Regression results of import demand equation (5) of the EU for the selected commodities[a]

	$\ln Y_{EU,t}$	$\ln Y_{EU,t-1}$	$\ln\Delta\left(\dfrac{P_{EU}}{D_{EU}}\right)_t$	$\ln\left(\dfrac{P_{EU}}{D_{EU}}\right)_{t-1}$	$\ln\left(\dfrac{M_{EU}^d}{Y_{EU}}\right)_{t-1}$	$D(t)$	$D(t)$	const.	R^2	dw	d.o.f.	tests[b]
Palm oil		−0.15 (−1.9)	−0.30 (−5.2)	−0.14 (−2.7)	−0.23 (−2.1)	−0.28 (62) (−2.9)	0.25 (98) (3.1)	3.81 (2.8)	0.71	2.07	28	
Coconut oil		−0.17 (−1.0)	−0.27 (−3.5)	−0.14 (−1.8)	−0.89 (−7.6)	−0.65 (75) (−3.8)	0.68 (78) (5.6)	8.70 (5.2)	0.78	1.97	29	Aμ
Rubber	0.36 (1.0)	−0.29 (−2.8)		−0.08 (−1.9)	−0.31 (−3.8)	0.14 (78) (2.9)	−0.15 (98) (−3.0)	4.73 (3.2)	0.62	1.95	28	
Cassava		0.36 (2.5)	−0.93[a] (−6.0)	−0.51[a] (−3.3)	−0.40 (−5.4)	−0.63 (62) (−3.9)	−0.62 (95) (−4.1)	2.74 (−1.0)	0.85	1.89	28	
Cocoa	0.64 (2.4)	−0.58 (−8.8)	−0.16 (−5.0)	−1.10 (−8.9)	−0.84[b] (−9.5)	−0.14 (83) (−3.8)	0.33 (96) (7.5)	11.58 (9.0)	0.87	1.78	26	
Tea	0.64 (1.2)	−0.26 (−3.2)	−0.07 (−1.4)	−0.13 (−1.9)	−0.95 (−5.8)	0.17 (90) (2.9)		18.3 (3.1)	0.72	1.89	29	
Pepper	0.85 (3.1)	−0.11 (−3.3)	−0.04 (−1.2)	−0.04 (−1.9)	−0.87 (−5.7)	0.08 (78) (3.1)	0.10 (89) (2.6)	−0.15 (2.6)	0.89	2.05	27	

Notes:

[a] The price variable is not the real price of cassava, but the relative price of cassava compared with the average price of alternative feed.

[b] Here the ECM term is $\ln (M - Y - P)$.

365

APPENDIX D

TABLE D.1 Regression results of export demand equation $(9)^a$

	$\Delta\ln M_{EU,t}$	$\ln M_{EU,t-1}$	$\ln\Delta\left(\dfrac{P_i}{P_{EU}}\right)_t$	$\ln\left(\dfrac{P_i}{P_{EU}}\right)_{t-1}$	$\ln\left(\dfrac{X_i^d}{M_{EU}}\right)_{t-1}$	$D(t)$	const.	R^2	dw	d.o.f.	tests^b
Palm oil											
Indonesia	1.06 (4.2)			-0.94 (-1.2)	-0.77 (-5.5)	0.48 (79) (3.4); 0.73 (86) (4.8)	-1.39	0.72	2.21	30	
Malaysia	0.74 (4.3)	0.15 (2.0)	-2.87 (-4.0)	-2.20 (-3.1)	-0.33 (-3.4)	-0.32 (73) (-2.5); -0.52 (87) (-3.9)	-2.33 (-2.1)	0.79	2.03	28	
Coconut oil											
Philippines	1.05 (8.5)		-4.66 (-3.9)	-1.91 (-2.0)	-0.80 (-5.2)	0.45 (71) (4.1); 0.41 (81) (2.2)	-0.91 (-5.1)	0.84	2.11	30	
Indonesia	0.98 (1.6)		-8.74 (-6.7)		-0.17 (-1.8)	-1.31 (80) (-1.4)	-0.32 (-0.9)	0.81	2.05	22	
Rubber											
Indonesia	0.61 (4.3)				-0.05 (-3.3)	0.23 (82) (-1.4); -0.17 (95) (-3.3)	-0.74 (-2.0)	0.78	2.28	30	
Malaysia	0.81 (5.0)		-3.98 (-4.2)	-1.24 (-1.3)	-0.40 (-1.1)	0.13 (75) (2.0); -0.06 (80) (-2.3)	0.04 (1.4)	0.70	1.69	30	$A\mu$
Thailand	0.73 (1.1)		-0.94 (-1.2)	-1.48 (-2.2)	-0.43 (-4.6)	1.21 (71–84) (-4.8); 0.23 (94–98) (1.4)	-0.80 (-3.3)	0.63	1.89	20	$H\epsilon$
Cassava											
Indonesia	0.45 (2.9)	-0.28 (-6.0)	-1.66 (-4.6)	-0.997 (-3.1)	-0.74 (-7.2)	-0.92 (73) (-1.3); 0.85 (87) (5.8)	2.02	0.88	1.78	27	$A\mu$
Thailand	0.99 (33.1)		-2.89 (-4.9)		-0.18 (-2.1)	-0.08 (95) (1.9)	-0.05 (-1.8)	0.98	2.31	32	$A\mu$

Commodity / Country									R^2		d.o.f.	
Cocoa												
Indonesia			-1.58 (-3.8)	-1.31 (-1.7)	-0.27 (-2.5)	-0.36 (71–78) (-3.0)	-1.04 (98) (-5.4)	-1.01 (-2.1)	0.84	1.82	21	
Malaysia	0.75 (1.4)		-4.17 (-4.3)	-2.49 (-2.22)	-0.34 (-3.0)	0.71 (89) (2.5)	-0.86 (93–98) (-4.6)	-1.61 (-2.99)	0.75	2.18	20	Au
Pepper												
Indonesia	0.83 (1.7)		-1.73 (-4.0)	-1.22 (-2.3)	-0.84 (-6.6)	1.15 (75) (-6.1)		-0.17	0.91	1.48	20	
Malaysia	0.54 (2.9)	-0.09 (-2.9)	-0.81 (-5.6)	-0.52 (-3.2)	-0.80 (-8.4)	0.32 (75) (-5.5)	0.31 (87) (7.4)	0.33	0.90	1.52	18	
Tea												
Indonesia	0.85 (4.2)		-1.92 (-5.1)	-0.48 (-1.2)	-0.23 (-2.9)	0.39 (3.3)	0.29 (98) (2.2)	-0.17 (-2.9)	0.78	1.73	29	
Vietnam	0.61 (1.1)		-0.65 (-2.1)	-0.39 (-1.7)	-0.43 (-3.3)	1.02 (89) (2.1)	0.12 (95) (1.6)	-2.33 (-1.2)	0.67	1.43	19	Au

Notes:

[a] Tables A.3 and A.4 provide the coefficient estimates of the import and export demand equations. Each model is estimated by OLS. The sample covers the period 1970–96. Absolute t-values are given in brackets below the coefficient estimate. Other notations are R^2 for the adjusted square of the multiple correlation coefficient, and d.o.f. for the degrees of freedom.

[b] All the equations in Tables A.3 and A.4 were subject to diagnostic tests using 5 per cent critical values. The null hypothesis of parameter stability was never rejected by the Chow test. The RESET test provided no evidence of misspecification, and the Jarque-Bera tests indicated approximately normal distributions. H_e indicates that the null hypothesis of homoskedastic disturbances is rejected by the Breusch-Pagan-Godfrey test. A_u indicates that the null hypothesis of no serial correlation in the disturbances was rejected by Durbin's m-test.

CHRISTIAN FRIIS BACH AND ALAN MATTHEWS*

International Transfers and Food Security

INTRODUCTION

This paper uses RunAid, a global computable general equilibrium (CGE) model based on the GTAP modelling framework, to evaluate the effect of different development aid strategies in improving food security in developing countries. Food security is defined as a reduction in the numbers undernourished. The issue explored is whether the form of development aid has different impacts on food security. Three alternatives are examined: (a) untied programme aid (balance of payments support), (b) aid to promote agricultural investment in developing countries, and (c) food aid. To test the 'Food First' argument that, within the agricultural sector, promoting foodgrain production yields a bigger improvement in food security than encouraging cash or export crops, the nutrition impact of confining agricultural investment aid to foodgrains or to cash crops, respectively, is also examined. The CGE modelling framework captures both the price (food availability) and income (purchasing power) dimensions to undernutrition and thus can adjudicate on their relative importance given the particular economic structures in developing countries.

The CGE framework used is based on the GTAP applied general equilibrium model of the world economy (Hertel, 1997) and the GTAP database (version 4, with 1995 as the base year) (McDougall *et al.*, 1998). The model is solved using GEMPACK (Harrison and Pearson, 1996). The full version of the GTAP database covers 50 commodities and 45 regions. To keep the model within computational limits and focus on the issues of interest, the data are aggregated to nine regions and 15 commodities. The regions are the European Union (EU), Japan (JPN), the USA (US), sub-Saharan Africa (SSA), South Asia (SAS), East Asia (EAS), High Income Asia (HAS), Latin America (LTN) and the Rest of World (ROW). Commodities included are paddy rice, wheat, other grains, vegetables and fruit, other crops, unprocessed livestock and livestock products, natural resources, meat, vegetable oils and fats, dairy products, processed rice, sugar, other food products, manufactures and services.

To be able to capture the effects of international transfers, the standard global general equilibrium model (GTAP) has been modified in a number of ways. Development aid is introduced by simply adding a transfer variable to

*Christian Friis Bach, Royal Veterinary and Agricultural College, Denmark; Alan Matthews, Trinity College, Dublin, Ireland.

the income equations in each region. The restriction on the use of development aid to investment in agriculture is introduced as a separate equation that links the level of development aid to a capital subsidy in agriculture. Simplified, the equation becomes in the levels:

$$\sum_{cap}\sum_{agr}(pm_{cap,r} - pfe_{cap,agr,r}) \cdot qfe_{cap,agr,r} = AID_r,$$

where *pm* is the market price of capital, *pfe* the price of capital faced by the producer, *qfe* the quantity of capital endowment used in agriculture and *AID* the total aid level. The equation ensures that the total subsidy expenditure is equal to the amount of aid. The food aid experiment is modelled as an export subsidy which reduces the price of imported food to the recipient. This is intended to capture the characteristics of programme food aid in which food commodities are made available directly to recipient governments which then release them into normal marketing channels. The restriction is modelled by linking the amount of aid to the total expenditure on export subsidies on food from the donor country to the recipient:

$$\sum_{food}(pm_{food,r} - pfob_{food,r,s}) \cdot qxs_{food,r,s} = FOODAID_{r,s},$$

where *pm* is the market price of food in the donor, *pfob* is the f.o.b. price of food from donor to recipient, *qxs* the quantity exported and *FOODAID* the total amount of food aid.

The alternative development aid strategies are evaluated by their effects on nutritional status as well as by their effects on overall welfare. Nutritional status is measured by average per capita daily calorie intake. For this purpose FAO data on calories provided by different food groups have been mapped to GTAP (and subsequently RunAid) commodities. Using this mapping, average daily per capita calorie intakes are calculated using the food expenditure patterns generated in each RunAid experiment.

The advantage of the GTAP framework is that it allows simulations of alternative scenarios to be performed in an internally consistent way, and that interpretation of the results using the GTAP model can lead to a deeper understanding of the issues under investigation. A limitation of the GTAP model framework for food security analysis is that it works with a single representative household. If food-insecure households are disproportionately found among food purchasers rather than food sellers, then changes in food prices may have consequences for food security which are masked in the GTAP aggregation. Some attempt was made to account for distributional impacts, as follows.

Estimates of changes in the prevalence of malnutrition in different policy scenarios as measured by the proportion and number of people with inadequate access to food were generated using exogenous information on the distribution of food consumption. The estimates are made using the methodology devised by FAO for its *World Food Surveys*. The distribution of per capita calorie consumption within each country is assumed to be log-normal so that the levels of energy consumption throughout a population can be calculated simply from the mean and the standard deviation. Based on the average calorie intake in each country and on a value of the coefficient of variation (CV) derived from the FAO *World Food Survey*, the distribution of per capita calorie consumption for each country is generated. From this, the proportion and number of the population that consumes less than the minimum requirement is calculated. The distribution of calorie intake is assumed not to change between experiments. While this is an unsatisfactory assumption, it is the same as that used by FAO in tracking the numbers undernourished through time in successive *World Food Surveys*.

RUNAID EXPERIMENTS

Two sets of simulations are performed with the model, and within each set a number of experiments are run, as follows.

The first set investigates an approximately 20 per cent increase in EU aid to sub-Saharan Africa (SSA) amounting to $6 billion. The benchmark experiment (A1) is an unrestricted transfer of cash aid (equivalent to programme aid or pure balance-of-payments support). In other experiments, the effect of providing development aid for agricultural investment (A2) and as food aid (A3) are examined. As noted above, agricultural investment aid is modelled as providing a capital subsidy to agricultural production. In the foodgrain experiment (A2F), this subsidy is restricted to rice, wheat and other grain production, while in the cash crop experiment (A2C), it is restricted to fruit and vegetable production, other crops (including oilseeds and tropical beverages as well as pulses, roots and tubers) and livestock production. As an additional $6 billion of food aid to SSA alone would swamp existing flows (and, in modelling terms, lead to an infeasible solution), the experiment modelled is one where $1 billion of the additional aid is provided in the form of food aid and the remaining $5 billion is maintained as unrestricted aid. This relatively marginal change should be taken into account in comparing the results of this experiment with the baseline experiment of all restricted aid.

The second set of simulations distributes the increase in EU help proportionately across the four developing country regions in RunAid. This enables us to investigate the impact of economic structure in influencing the relationship between aid delivery and nutrition impact. The addition to regional income in each case amounts to 0.19 per cent of GNP. The same five experiments are performed as for the first set of simulations, with the one difference that on this occasion the food aid experiment allocates all of the additional aid to export subsidies on food from the EU.

RESULTS

The results of the experiments simulating different forms of EU assistance to SSA are shown in Table 1. Consider first the 'baseline' shock of an unrestricted

TABLE 1   *Food security impacts of EU aid on SSA*

Variable	Unrestricted aid	Agricultural investment	Food crop investment	Cash crop investment	Food aid
Experiment	A1	A2	A2F	A2C	A3
Equivalent variation ($m.)	7 707.9	7 917.4	5 938.4	7 749.6	6 948.4
Per capita utility (%)	2.75	2.83	2.12	2.77	2.48
Agric output (%)	−0.2	2.8	0.0	3.1	−0.2
Agric prices (%)	2.1	−1.3	0.3	−0.7	1.5
Food prices (%)	2.0	−1.0	−0.5	0.0	1.2
Daily calorie increase (cals)	44.2	64.6	57.0	58.3	43.5
Daily calorie increase (%)	2.0	3.0	2.6	2.7	2.0
Per cent undernourished (%)	33.4	32.4	32.8	32.7	33.4
Numbers undernourished (m.)	−12.5	−18.0	−16.0	−16.3	−12.2
Memo item EU changes:					
Equivalent variation ($m.)	−7 944.76	−7 400.85	−7 235.66	7 576.25	−8 293.93

aid transfer (experiment A1). The magnitude of the aid shock corresponds to 2.2 per cent of SSA GNP, and leads to an overall increase in per capita household utility of 2.8 per cent. Agricultural production falls slightly, despite a rise in agricultural prices of 2.1 per cent, as resources are shifted into non-agricultural production. Food prices overall rise by 2.0 per cent. However, because of higher overall incomes, there is an increase in daily calorie intake of 44 calories per head per day, or 2 per cent. This is sufficient to lift around 12.5 million people out of hunger, under the maintained assumption that the distribution of calorie intake is unchanged.

If the aid is tied to agricultural investment (experiment A2), then the overall increase in welfare and utility is slightly higher. Overall calorie intake increases by 65 calories or by 3.0 per cent and around 18 million people are moved out of hunger. From a food security perspective, tying aid to agricultural investment is a strategy preferable to allowing recipient governments to make unrestricted use of this aid. Does it make any difference if aid is directed to particular production sectors within SSA agriculture? Experiments A2F and A2C compare the consequences of restricting agricultural investment aid to food grain and cash crop production, respectively. It turns out that neither option outperforms the general investment aid experiment, this time confirming the view that restrictions reduce the value of aid to recipients.

The food aid experiment involves transferring one-sixth of the overall aid increase in the form of food aid and is thus hard to compare directly to the investment aid experiments. Compared to the baseline experiment, however, tying part of the additional aid to food aid reduces its overall welfare impact on the recipient and slightly lessens its food security impact. Domestic output of the food aid commodities declines, quite sharply in the case of wheat, which is a common criticism of programme food aid. Agricultural and food prices rise in a more restrained fashion compared with the baseline and the net impact (of a lower income increase but also of lower food price increases) is to reduce slightly the food security impact of the aid transfer.

The economic cost to the EU of making the same aid transfer in different ways also differs. In each case the cost of the transfer is greater than the transfer itself, but providing food aid turns out to be a particularly costly way for the EU to provide development assistance. This is because of the combination of the additional production distortions introduced by tying aid in this way, as opposed to making a straight transfer, together with the different general equilibrium effects of the way the different transfers are used in the recipient region.

We now turn to the second set of simulations which investigate the impact of regional economic structure on these results (Table 2). The ranking of different aid policies in terms of welfare measures is the same as in the first set of simulations. The only noteworthy feature is that, in this set, all additional aid is given as food aid and the welfare effects are very attenuated. The food security impacts are relatively slight on an annual basis. The aid shock applied is a 20 per cent increase in aid from the EU which currently accounts for about 40 per cent of all aid and is thus equivalent to an 8 per cent increase in total official development assistance (ODA). This increase leads to a maximum improvement in all developing country regions in calorie intake of about 0.35 per cent. Even if this was cumulative over a ten-year period, this amounts to an increase of just 3.5 per cent. In terms of the numbers malnourished, in some scenarios up to 9 million people could be removed from the hunger trap which again, if cumulative, would amount to 90 million people or just over 10 per cent of the estimated total malnourished in the world. Clearly, international assistance, however crucial, can only play a supporting role in meeting the World Food Summit target of a halving of the numbers malnourished by 2015. Spreading aid more widely has a smaller impact on hunger than concentrating it. The numbers removed from hunger in the second set of simulations vary between four and nine million, compared to 12–18 million if the aid increase were concentrated on SSA alone.

Given these generally minor impacts, it is important to know how the food security impact of additional aid transfers can be maximized. Unambiguously, the greatest food security impact in all regions occurs from foodgrain-focused investment aid (Latin America is an exception, where cash crop investment aid is slightly more powerful, though both are considerably more effective than other options). For SSA, this reverses the earlier conclusion that unrestricted investment aid dominates investment aid for either foodgrains or cash crops alone. This is a general equilibrium result and reflects the fact that the food security outcome is different where aid is being given to a number of competing regions simultaneously. We can hypothesize that the food security benefits

TABLE 2   *Impact of alternative EU aid strategies on four developing country regions*

Variable	Unrestricted aid	Agricultural investment	Food crop investment	Cash crop investment	Food aid
Equivalent variation (US$)					
SSA	707.19	818.47	733.55	829.46	332.32
EAS	2 313.45	2 555.46	2 513.05	2 544.85	253.13
SAS	954.30	1 101.86	1 064.04	1 110.74	139.96
LTN	3 813.10	4 154.74	4 179.88	4 127.15	480.37
Per capita utility (%)					
SSA	0.25	0.29	0.29	0.29	0.12
EAS	0.20	0.22	0.22	0.22	0.02
SAS	0.24	0.28	0.28	0.28	0.04
LTN	0.26	0.28	0.28	0.28	0.03
Daily calorie increase (cals)					
SSA	3.70	5.44	7.42	5.32	3.78
EAS	2.74	5.26	6.11	5.54	1.83
SAS	1.86	3.30	4.26	3.20	1.49
LTN	4.58	7.05	7.95	8.13	1.83
Daily calorie increase (%)					
SSA	0.17	0.25	0.34	0.24	0.17
EAS	0.11	0.22	0.25	0.23	0.07
SAS	0.08	0.14	0.18	0.14	0.06
LTN	0.17	0.26	0.29	0.30	0.07
Per cent undernourished (%)					
SSA	35.3	35.2	35.2	35.3	35.3
EAS	24.7	24.6	24.5	24.5	24.7
SAS	20.5	20.4	20.4	20.4	20.5
LTN	13.9	13.8	13.8	13.8	14.0
Nos undernourished (m.)					
SSA	−1.06	−1.56	−2.12	−1.52	−1.08
EAS	−1.86	−3.56	−4.13	−3.75	−1.24
SAS	−1.01	−1.79	−2.31	−1.74	−0.81
LTN	−0.56	−0.86	−0.97	−0.99	−0.22
Total	−4.49	−7.77	−9.53	−8.00	−3.35
Marginal increase in calorie intake per capita due to $100m. aid (cals)					
SSA	0.71	1.04	1.41	1.01	0.72
EAS	0.52	1.00	1.16	1.06	0.35
SAS	0.35	0.63	0.81	0.61	0.28
LTN	0.87	1.34	1.52	1.55	0.35
Marginal number of persons removed from hunger due to $100 m. aid (000s)					
SSA	−2.023	−2.974	−4.052	−2.907	−2.068
EAS	−3.545	−6.796	−7.879	−7.150	−2.361
SAS	−1.926	−3.412	−4.410	−3.310	−1.550
LTN	−1.063	−1.633	−1.840	−1.883	−0.425

of investing in cash crops are reduced if one's competitors are investing simultaneously, a variant of the well-known 'fallacy of composition' argument often made with respect to this kind of investment. In this set of simulations, where food aid transfers can be directly compared to all other options, food aid is clearly the worst performing option.

The results confirm that there are significant differences in food security impacts across regions. For all aid delivery options, the greatest impact on undernutrition is achieved in East Asia. This is not an obvious result. For example, it might be hypothesized that the greatest impact would be achieved by directing aid to the region with the lowest per capita calorie intake (SSA) or the region with the most equal distribution of food intake (SAS) but in neither case is this true. Exploring the reasons for the larger nutrition multipliers in East Asia is a fruitful avenue for further work.

CONCLUSIONS

This paper has examined the effectiveness of different aid strategies in combating hunger and malnutrition in developing countries. It uses the GTAP general equilibrium modelling framework and modifies it in a number of directions. First, methods are suggested to model different types of development assistance in the GTAP framework. Unrestricted development aid is introduced by adding a transfer variable to the income equations in each region. Investment aid is modelled as a capital subsidy to agriculture, and food aid is modelled as an export subsidy provided by the donor. Second, the GTAP database is extended to include a calorie database using FAO calorie intake statistics and a number of allocation rules to map these data on GTAP expenditure categories. Third, some attempt was made to overcome the drawback of the GTAP assumption of a single representative household in analysing food security, which is primarily a distributional issue, by making use of exogenous information on the distribution of food intake in each region, although the assumption had to be maintained that this initial distribution was unaffected by the changes in economic structure induced by each aid scenario.

While the inability to account fully for distributional changes is a weakness of the GTAP modelling framework in analysing food security issues, there are compensating advantages. Food security is a general equilibrium phenomenon; the net impact of a policy change on food security must take into account the impact on food availability (reflected in food prices) as well as on income. Furthermore, it would be hard to address the questions raised in this paper in an alternative framework. Some of the findings run counter to conventional wisdom, and at least provide grounds for thinking through the rationale for these findings to assess their possible relevance in real-world policy making.

An important finding is that, although international assistance may be crucial in supporting developing countries' efforts to alleviate hunger, its impact relative to the scale of the problem in the absence of structural changes in patterns of distribution can only be marginal. The results suggest that a 20 per cent increase in EU aid flows has the potential to decrease the number of hungry people by

4–9 million annually, although if this aid was concentrated on SSA alone the impact would be greater, with the numbers malnourished falling by 12–18 million. The paper estimates food security impact multipliers ranging from 1000 to 8000 persons removed from hunger (depending on region and the method of aid delivery) for every additional $100 million in aid. Taking a round figure of 800 million malnourished people in the world today, and assuming that aid impacts are cumulative over the period 1995–2015, this would necessitate an increase in aid flows by $250 billion annually – a quadrupling of aid – under the most optimistic multiplier estimate to reach the World Food Summit target of halving the numbers malnourished by the end of the period. The major effort to achieve this target, as the Summit's Rome Declaration recognized, must be made by the developing countries themselves. However, it is unlikely to be achieved without focused measures aimed at altering the distribution of food intake in favour of the poor and undernourished. In other words, investment strategies need to be geared towards resource-poor farmers or disadvantaged urban groups if alleviating malnutrition is a priority policy goal. This conclusion has been argued many times previously, most recently in the FAO's *Sixth World Food Survey*, which contains illustrative projections of the impact of different distributional assumptions on the hunger problem.

From a donor perspective, the most important finding is that nutrition impacts can be maximized by focusing development assistance on agricultural investment, and particularly investment in foodgrain production. Unfortunately, not only has development assistance in total been falling in recent years, but aid to support agricultural production has been falling even faster. The reasons for this include the poor performance of agricultural projects in the past, the rundown of agricultural expertise in major lending and donor institutions, crowding out by other sectoral uses of aid (including debt relief, the social sector and the environment) and limited political support for agricultural aid in both donor agencies and recipient governments (Matthews, 1999). This paper lends support to calls for the renewal of efforts to channel donor resources into agricultural production as the most cost-effective way of tackling hunger. The results also support the criticism of food aid in terms both of its value to recipients and of its greater cost to donors than other forms of aid transfer.

REFERENCES

FAO (1996), *Sixth World Food Survey*, Rome: FAO.

Harrison, W.J. and Pearson, K.R. (1996), 'Computing Solutions for Large General Equilibrium Models using GEMPACK', *Computational Economics*, **9**, 83–127.

Hertel, T. (ed.) (1997), *Global Trade Analysis: Modeling and Applications*, Cambridge: Cambridge University Press.

McDougall, R.A., Elbehri, A. and Truong, T.P. (1998), *Global Trade Assistance and Protection: The GTAP 4 Data Base*, Purdue University: Center for Global Trade Analysis.

Matthews, A. (1999), 'International development assistance and food security', in K. Gupta, (ed.), *Foreign Aid: New Perspectives*, London: Kluwer Academic Publishers.

KECUK SUHARIYANTO*

Agricultural Productivity Growth in Asian Countries

INTRODUCTION

The agricultural sector in Asian countries is being transformed from a traditional to a modern one. In order to increase production, more modern inputs such as high-yielding varieties, fertilizer and machinery have been applied. As a result, agricultural production has grown rapidly. However, the question of the role of agricultural total factor productivity (TFP) in output growth has not yet been answered. This study has been undertaken in order to answer the question. To measure agricultural TFP, the Malmquist productivity index is used because of its desirable properties. One of them is that the index decomposes productivity change into two components: technical efficiency change (TEC) and technical change (TC). This property is very useful, since the policies required to address a decline in productivity growth due to increased inefficiency are likely to be different from those required to address a decline stemming from a lack of technical change (Grosskopf, 1993).

A number of studies have examined agricultural productivity differences among countries using the Malmquist productivity index (see, for example, Thirtle *et al.*, 1995; Fulginiti and Perrin, 1997, 1998; Arnade, 1998). In this paper the Malmquist productivity index is constructed with respect to a *contemporaneous* frontier technology by applying a linear programming method known as data envelopment analysis (DEA). One of the critical issues not discussed in the previous studies is the dimensionality problem; that is, the dimensionality of the input/output space relative to the number of observations in the cross-section. The problem arises when the number of observations is relatively small compared with the number of factors (outputs plus inputs) used. The presence of the dimensionality problem may create two main difficulties. First, given enough inputs, all or most of the countries can be rated 'efficient' as a direct result of the dimensionality problem (Leibenstein and Maital, 1992). This causes the changes of technical efficiency to grow at zero rate and creates the situation where technical efficiency changes make no contribution to productivity growth. Second, production technologies move back and forth, producing a large number of intersections, making the results difficult to interpret. There is no exact rule on the relationship between the number of factors and the number of observations that should be used in the

*Centre Bureau of Statistics, Jakarta, Indonesia.

model. Charnes and Cooper (1990) stated that, for the DEA model to be discriminatory, the number of observations should exceed the number of factors by at least three times, while Fernandez-Cornejo (1994) argued that it should be larger than five. However, the simulation study done by Smith (1997) showed that, even though the number of observations exceeds the number of factors by more than 13 times, it still overestimates the true efficiency by 27.1 per cent.

Surprisingly, little attention has been paid to the problem of dimensionality in empirical studies, not only for the agricultural sector but also in general. Since the problem affects the results severely, this paper considers the issue further in empirical analysis. As a preliminary attempt, the Malmquist productivity index is constructed with respect to the contemporaneous frontier, following previous empirical studies. Further investigation shows that the results are unstable because of the dimensionality problem. For this reason, the Malmquist productivity index with respect to the contemporaneous frontier should not be used in a study involving only a small number of cross-section observations and a complicated technology. In order to solve the problem, this paper applies the Malmquist technique with respect to the *sequential* frontier, as the best alternative. It moves on to a description of sources and definitions of the data used before reaching the empirical results and conclusions.

MALMQUIST PRODUCTIVITY INDEX: SEQUENTIAL FRONTIERS

Tulkens and Vanden Eeckaut (1995) explained the basic difference between the contemporaneous and sequential frontiers. In the former approach, the frontier is constructed at *each period* using the observations at *that period only*; that is, the frontier is constructed for each year separately. It is assumed that the frontiers at each year are completely different from one another, without there being any *a priori* relation between them. The frontier may move inward, outward or intersect at any time, producing regress and progress in technology. This approach may be appropriate when the number of observations is large enough and the time period is short. When the number of observations is small, it can easily create the dimensionality problem. In the sequential approach, the frontier is constructed at *each year* on the basis of all observations from *the first year up to the year considered.* Using this approach, the frontier may move only by inward shift (in input orientation) producing only technological progress. No outward or intersect shift is possible, meaning that the possibility of technological decline is excluded. Technical knowledge is assumed to accumulate over time, that is, information is not lost as in econometric approaches. This can be appropriate when the number of observations is small and the time period is large. Furthermore, it will remove the dimensionality problem.

The Malmquist productivity index with respect to the sequential frontier can be described briefly as follows. Let country $j = 1, 2, ..., J$ use inputs $x^t \in R_+^N$ to produce outputs $y^t \in R_+^M$ during the period $t = 1, 2, ..., T$. The production technology set can be defined as

$$S^{(1,t)} = \{(x^s, y^s) : x^s \text{ can produce } y^s\}, s = 1 \text{ up to } s = t$$

Alternatively, the production technology may also be represented with an input requirement set $L^{(1,t)}(y^t) = \{x^t : (x^t, y^t) \in S^{(1,t)}\}$. The within-period input distance functions are defined as:

$$D_i^s(y^t, x^t) = \max\{\lambda : (x^t / \lambda) \in L^{(1,t)}(y^t)\}$$

and

$$D_i^{s+1}(y^{t+1}, x^{t+1}) = \max\{\lambda : (x^{t+1} / \lambda) \in L^{(1,t+1)}(y^{t+1})\}$$

The values of these distance functions are equal to or greater than one. Only if the values are equal to one are the countries efficient and therefore on the frontier. The adjacent-period input distance functions may also be defined as

$$D_i^s(y^{t+1}, x^{t+1}) = \max\{\lambda : (x^{t+1} / \lambda) \in L^{(1,t)}(y^{t+1})\}$$

and

$$D_i^{s+1}(y^t, x^t) = \max\{\lambda : (x^t / \lambda) \in L^{(1,t+1)}(y^t)\}$$

These four input distance functions can be used to construct the Malmquist productivity index. Following Fare *et al.* (1994a, 1994b), the Malmquist productivity index using input orientation for country i between period s and $s + 1$ is defined as

$$M_i^{s,s+1} = \left(\frac{D_i^s(y^t, x^t)}{D_i^{s+1}(y^{t+1}, x^{t+1})} \right) \left(\frac{D_i^{s+1}(y^{t+1}, x^{t+1})}{D_i^s(y^{t+1}, x^{t+1})} \frac{D_i^{s+1}(y^t, x^t)}{D_i^s(y^t, x^t)} \right)^{1/2}$$

The ratio in the first bracket captures technical efficiency change (TEC) and that in the second provides a measure of technical change (TC). TEC is greater than, equal to or less than unity as technical efficiency accordingly improves, remains unchanged or declines between periods s and $s + 1$. TC is greater than or equal to unity, and shows whether the frontier is improving or stagnant. *Notice that, using the sequential frontier, TC cannot decline.* The value of the Malmquist productivity index is greater than, equal to or less than unity. If the value of the index is greater than unity, it reveals improved productivity and, if the value is less than unity, a decrease in productivity occurs. For detailed explanation of the methodology and the calculation, see Grifell-Tatje and Lopez Sintas (1995) and Suhariyanto (1999). Note that the input-based Malmquist productivity in this study is expressed as the inverse of that in Fare *et al.* (1994a) for ease of interpretation.

SCOPE OF THE STUDY AND DATA SOURCES

The number of countries included in this study is 18 and the time period covered is 1961–96. Agricultural TFP is measured using one output–five input technology. The inputs are land, labour, livestock, fertilizer and machinery. The data on output are obtained from USDA, while the input information comes from FAO. In the analysis 'aggregate agricultural output' is the total value of agricultural production which is expressed in 1979–81 international dollars and includes food and non-food output (fibres, hides and skins, rubber and tobacco). 'Agricultural land' is the total area of arable and permanent cropland, measured in 1000 hectares, while 'agricultural labour' (in thousands) covers the economically active population in agriculture. 'Livestock' is the aggregate of the various kinds of animals in livestock units irrespective of their age and the place or purpose of their breeding. It includes cattle, sheep, goats, pigs, mules, horses, asses, buffaloes, camels, ducks, chicken and turkeys. The weights for aggregation are those used by Hayami and Ruttan (1985, p.450). 'Fertilizer' is the sum of the nitrogen (N), potassium (P_2O_5) and phosphate (K_2O) content of fertilizer used, measured in thousands of metric tonnes of nutrient units. The 'Machinery' variable covers the total number of wheeled and crawler tractors (excluding garden tractors) used in agriculture.

EMPIRICAL RESULTS AND CONCLUSIONS

The Malmquist productivity index is computed for 18 Asian countries over the period 1961–96 under the assumption of constant returns to scale using input orientation. In order to guarantee that the dimensionality problem does not exist at the beginning of the period of the study, it is assumed that technology in Asian agriculture was stagnant in 1961–65. This assumption is quite reasonable since the 'Green Revolution' did not occur in most Asian countries until the late 1960s. Using the assumption, the number of observations at the beginning of the period of the study is $18 \times 5 = 90$ observations. The ratio of the number of observations to the number of factors (1 output plus 5 inputs) is 15. Thus the condition that the ratio should exceed 13 in order to avoid the dimensionality problem, as shown in the simulation study done by Smith (1997), is satisfied.

Table 1 presents the annual growth rates of agricultural TFP, TEC, TC, output and inputs. The results show that only nine out of 18 Asian countries have positive productivity growth during the 1965–96 period. Four countries (China, Mongolia, Indonesia, Sri Lanka) have less than 1 per cent positive growth, two (Laos PDR and the Philippines) are between 1 and 2 per cent and only three countries (Malaysia, South Korea and Japan) grow at more than 2 per cent per annum. The productivity growth in these three countries is totally attributable to innovation, since their agricultural sectors are efficient for most of the period of study. Using the translog total cost function, Kuroda (1997) also found that, on average, 90 per cent of the TFP growth in Japanese agriculture is explained by the effect of technological change for the period 1960–90.

TABLE 1 *Percentage annual growth rates of productivity, output and inputs, 1965–96**

Countries	TEC	TC	TFP	Output	Land	Labour	Livestock	Fertilizer	Machinery
East Asia									
China	−0.41	0.88	0.47	4.34	0.14	1.77	2.45	10.64	8.85
Japan	0.00	2.70	2.70	1.15	−0.92	−4.06	1.66	−0.13	15.16
Korea, DPR	−0.70	0.40	−0.30	3.99	0.54	0.91	2.88	4.60	6.84
Korea, Rep.	0.00	3.30	3.30	3.78	−0.26	−1.71	3.46	3.05	31.77
Mongolia	−0.31	0.82	0.51	0.90	2.54	0.60	0.32	10.63	3.22
Southeast									
Cambodia	−3.02	1.19	−1.83	0.27	0.92	1.07	0.98	3.51	0.99
Indonesia	−0.45	0.63	0.18	4.04	0.60	1.65	1.42	11.37	7.60
Laos, PDR	−0.26	2.02	1.76	3.60	1.08	1.81	2.77	9.96	9.67
Malaysia	0.00	3.55	3.55	5.25	1.96	−0.01	1.05	8.77	9.58
Myanmar	−0.09	0.07	−0.02	2.78	−0.07	1.86	2.04	9.21	5.39
Philippines	0.07	1.26	1.33	2.74	1.29	1.66	−0.42	5.90	2.42
Thailand	−1.33	0.33	−1.00	3.89	1.87	1.84	0.37	12.32	11.10
Vietnam	−0.71	0.54	−0.17	3.67	0.33	1.78	1.51	7.66	12.24
South Asia									
Bangladesh	−0.77	0.35	−0.42	1.74	0.06	1.04	0.37	11.19	6.19
India	−1.05	0.55	−0.50	2.90	0.15	1.42	0.81	10.35	11.88
Nepal	−0.89	0.20	−0.70	2.73	1.17	1.96	2.13	16.48	10.35
Pakistan	−1.29	0.82	−0.47	3.72	0.54	2.11	2.27	11.85	13.54
Sri Lanka	−0.62	1.29	0.67	1.49	0.19	1.63	0.19	2.94	5.30

Note: *The data used cover 1961–96. However, the Asian data for 1961–65 have been pooled to ensure an adequate sample size at the beginning of the period of study.

For the other six countries which have positive growth, the agricultural productivity increases are mainly due to improvement in innovation (technical progress). All of them, except the Philippines, have experienced a fall in technical efficiency.

The other nine countries have experienced a productivity decline. They are North Korea, Cambodia, Myanmar, Thailand, Vietnam and all the South Asian countries, except Sri Lanka. Technical efficiency in all these cases has declined and at the same time there is no significant technological progress, except in Cambodia. In general, these results are in agreement with those obtained from the previous studies, even though the magnitude of growth rates differs slightly. Arnade (1998) found that these nine countries are among others whose agricultural productivity growth declined over the period 1961–93. Wong (1989) concluded that productivity had declined in Indian agriculture during 1964–83 at an annual rate of 1.63 per cent. The same results for Indian and Pakistan agriculture were also obtained by Frisvold and Lomax (1991), who estimated that agricultural productivity declined at annual rates of 1.15 per cent in India and 1.43 per cent in Pakistan during the period 1970–80.

Table 1 also presents the annual growth rates of output and inputs. It appears that Japan is the only Asian country which obtains growth in agricultural output due to growth in agricultural productivity. Notice that productivity growth in South Korea and Malaysia, even though high, is still lower than agricultural output growth. In South Korea, agricultural output growth stems from increased productivity and machinery use, while in Malaysia, it is caused by growth in productivity, fertiliser and machinery use. In the other Asian countries, agricultural growth has been due principally to increased input supplies. The growth of input use, especially fertilizer and machinery, in Asian countries is spectacular during the period 1965–96. This leads to a high growth rate of agricultural output, but not productivity. In Indonesia, for instance, the use of fertilizer and tractors, growing by almost 12 per cent and 8 per cent per year, respectively, result in an increase of agricultural output at an annual growth rate of 4.04 per cent. However, the productivity in this country increases only very slightly, at an average growth rate of 0.20 per cent per year. The same pattern also occurs in China. Countries in South Asia, except Sri Lanka, exhibit even more dramatic results. In Bangladesh, India, Nepal and Pakistan, both fertilizer and tractor use grow by more than 10 per cent annually, but productivity growth is negative. The evidence of declining productivity in many Asian countries shows that increased agricultural output has been achieved mainly by increasing the use of inputs. Thus agricultural output in most Asian countries is input-led rather than productivity-led.

A key finding from this study, therefore, is that, while agricultural output grows rapidly, agricultural productivity has declined in nine of the 18 Asian countries during the period 1965–96. This result confirms previous findings. Using the Malmquist productivity index with respect to a contemporaneous frontier, Fulginiti and Perrin (1997, 1998) and Arnade (1998) found that, on average, agricultural productivity seems to have declined in many developing countries. Using a different technique, Frisvold and Lomax (1991) also concluded that the developing countries experienced negative productivity growth between 1970 and 1980, with the notable exception of the Philippines. Note that, in the previous studies, a decline in productivity is mainly attributed to technological regression since the method they used allows a decline in technology. This study suggests a different explanation since the method used, which is a sequential frontier, excludes the possibility of technological decline. It can be concluded that agricultural productivity in Asian countries has dropped because many countries have experienced a loss in technical efficiency and stagnation in technological progress.

REFERENCES

Arnade, C. (1998), 'Using a Programming Approach to Measure International Agricultural Efficiency and Productivity', *Journal of Agricultural Economics*, **49**, 67–84.

Charnes, A. and Cooper, W.W. (1990), 'Data Envelopment Analysis', in H.E. Bradly (ed.), *Operational Research '90*, Oxford: Pergamon Press.

Fare, R., Grosskopf, S. and Lovell, C.A.K. (1994a), *Production Frontiers*, Cambridge: Cambridge University Press.

Fare, R, Grosskopf, S., Norris, M. and Zhang, Z. (1994b), 'Productivity Growth, Technical Progress, and Efficiency Change in Industrialised Countries', *American Economic Review*, **84**, 66–83.

Fernandez-Cornejo, J. (1994), 'Nonradial Technical Efficiency and Chemical Input Use in Agriculture', *Agricultural and Resource Economics Review*, **11**, 11–21.

Frisvold, G.B. and Lomax, E. (1991), *Differences in Agricultural Research and Productivity among 26 Countries*, Agricultural Economic Report no. 644, Washington DC: United States Department of Agriculture.

Fulginiti, L.E. and Perrin, R.K (1997), 'LDC Agriculture: Nonparametric Malmquist Productivity Index', *Journal of Development Economics*, **53**, 373–90.

Fulginiti, L.E. and Perrin, R.K. (1998), 'Agricultural Productivity in Developing Countries', *Agricultural Economics*, **19**, 45–51.

Grifell-Tatje, E., and Lopez Sintas, J. (1995), *Total Factor Productivity: Technical Efficiency, Bias and Technical Change in the European Textile-Clothing Industry, 1980-1989*, Management Report Series no.210, Rotterdam: Erasmus Universiteit Rotterdam.

Grosskopf, S. (1993), 'Efficiency and Productivity', in H.O. Fried, C.A.K. Lovell and S.S. Shelton (eds), *The Measurement of Productive Efficiency: Techniques and Applications*, New York: Oxford University Press.

Hayami, Y. and Ruttan, V.M. (1985), *Agricultural Development: An International Perspective*, Baltimore, MD: Johns Hopkins University Press.

Kuroda, Y. (1997), 'Research and Extension Expenditures and Productivity in Japanese Agriculture, 1960-1990', *Agricultural Economics*, **16**, 111–24.

Leibenstein, H. and Maital, S. (1992), 'Empirical Estimation and Partitioning of X-inefficiency: A Data Envelopment Approach', *American Economic Review*, **82**, 428–33.

Smith, P. (1997), 'Model Mis-specification in Data Envelopment Analysis', *Annals of Operations Research*, **73**, 233–52.

Suhariyanto, K. (1999), 'Productivity Growth, Efficiency and Technical Change in Asian Agriculture: A Malmquist Index Analysis', PhD dissertation, University of Reading, UK.

Thirtle, C., Hadley, D. and Townsend, R. (1995), 'A Multilateral Malmquist Productivity Index Approach to explaining Agricultural Growth in sub-Saharan Africa', *Development Policy Review*, **13**, 323–48.

Tulkens, H., and Vanden Eeckaut, P. (1995), 'Non-parametric Efficiency, Progress and Regress Measures for Panel Data: Methodological Aspects', *European Journal of Operational Research*, **80**, 474–99.

Wong, L.F. (1989), 'Agricultural Productivity in China and India: A Comparative Analysis', *Canadian Journal of Agricultural Economics*, **37**, 77–93.

JOHN DAVIS, LIMING WANG AND FU CHEN*

Land Reform Initiatives in China

INTRODUCTION

Various approaches to land reform are being pursued in most of the current and former command economies throughout the world. China has tended to emphasize reform of its systems of land-use rights whereas, in the Central and Eastern European countries, farmland privatization has generally been seen as a crucial component in economic transition. There is a fairly rich literature dealing with agrarian restructuring in these countries (Csaki, 1990; Csaki and Lerman, 1994, 1996; Brooks and Lerman, 1993, 1994, 1995; Swinnen, 1997; Lerman, 1999). Comparatively little, however, has been written about the reforms taking place in China, particularly in the last decade. Notable exceptions include Wenfang and Makeham (1992), Gaynor and Putterman (1993), Liu *et al.* (1996), Chen (1996) and Chen and Davis (1998). The main purpose of this paper, therefore, is to review some of the major land reform issues and developments in rural China since the mid-1980s and to examine four experimental reform models, which may be viewed as examples of induced institutional change.

Given the huge size of China and its diversity in natural endowments and economic development, it is not possible to be fully inclusive in a paper of this nature and so we restrict our coverage to what we see as the main issues and approaches. The paper is organized as follows. As institutional innovation is being driven by the weaknesses of the existing system, the next section provides an overview of the Household Responsibility System, focusing mainly on its institutional weaknesses. Bringing about further land reforms is bound to be a difficult and contentious process in China and the issues are being extensively debated internally. Therefore a review of some of the controversy and debate among Chinese economists about the nature and direction of reform is included after that. Later sections examine four reform models which illustrate the main approaches adopted since the mid-1980s. Finally, some conclusions are drawn about the experiences to date with land reform measures and some issues to be addressed in the possible deepening of the process are highlighted.

*John Davis and Liming Wang, The Queen's University of Belfast, UK; Fu Chen, South-China Agriculture University, Guangzhou, PR China.

LAND REFORMS AND THE HOUSEHOLD RESPONSIBILITY SYSTEM (HRS)

Since the founding of the People's Republic in 1949, China has experienced three major farmland reforms. First came a radical farmland revolution in the early 1950s. By expropriating landlords and distributing their land to landless peasants, China achieved the goal of 'tillers having their own land'. This had been the dream of Chinese farmers for thousands of years and created a stratum of private smallholders. Like other socialist countries, China shaped its policy around the Soviet Union model of collective ownership and unified collective operation. To achieve this goal, China carried out its second land reform, a campaign of collectivization in the mid-1950s, in which farmers were compelled to join collectives. The collectivization finally developed an institution called the 'People's Commune'. With centrally controlled property rights and a misapplied egalitarian principle of distribution, the communes destroyed farmers' operational freedom and their enthusiasm for production.

There is much literature illustrating the poor performance of the commune system: for example, Stavis (1982), Lin (1982), Lin (1987) and Chen (1994). At the end of the 1970s, China launched its economy-wide reforms, pioneered by rural reform. Breaking with Soviet doctrine, she introduced a family-based contract system, the so-called 'Household Responsibility System' (Perkins, 1988). Initially, this operated on an informal basis, with typical contract periods of only a few years. The system was formally adopted by the Central Committee in 1981 and in January 1984 the contract period was extended to 15 years (Central Committee, 1984). Since then, this has been the nationwide statutory pattern of agricultural land tenure. Honoured as the third land revolution in China, the Household Responsibility System was a great success. It provided farmers with incentives for production by giving them individual rights to residual income from agricultural land. They also had relative, though not absolute, freedom in land use and production decision making. As a result, China's agriculture was dramatically revived. Compared with the stagnation in the previous 30-year period, growth in agricultural output in the first half of the 1980s accelerated to a rate several times the previous long-term average. Output of the three main crops, grain, cotton and oil-bearing crops, increased at annual rates of 4.8, 7.7 and 13.8 per cent, respectively, between 1978 and 1984, compared with average annual rates of 2.4, 1.0 and 0.8 per cent from 1952 to 1978 (SSBC, 1985). Grain, the most important commodity, reached a peak of 407 million tonnes in 1984, a net increase of more than 100 million tonnes (40 per cent) in only six years.

The fundamental problem of feeding the giant population, a great pressure in China for several centuries, seemed to be solved. The subsequent performance, however, was less encouraging: a 6 per cent drop in grain output, followed by stagnation until the early 1990s (*China's Statistical Yearbook*, various issues). It appeared that the HRS had exhausted its benefits; although it should be said of course that grain price changes also played an important part in these trends.

The HRS was clearly a very important innovation but it could not address everything. Several years of practice exposed a number of inherent limitations and weaknesses. First, there was the emergence of tiny and fragmented farming units as farmland was distributed to individual households to farm independently. Land distribution derived directly from the principle that all farmland in a village was owned by all of its members collectively. As a result every member had an equal claim and the basis for distributing land, therefore, was size of peasant family. Given the high population density, the amount distributed to each household was very small. Moreover, as farmland differed from parcel to parcel owing to soil fertility, irrigation condition, location and so forth, a household had to obtain parcels from each of the grades. Thus the total was not only insufficient but also fragmented and scattered around villages. Large areas of cultivated land were wasted in the form of paths and boundaries separating individual holdings. A Ministry of Agriculture survey (MoA, 1993) showed that in 1986, among 7983 sample villages from 29 provinces, average cultivated area per household was 0.466 hectares (7*mu*), spread over 5.85 plots (Table 1). Although the number of plots per household declined, farming structure remained highly fragmented.

TABLE 1   *Structure of farming under the HRS*

	1986	1988	1990	1992
Cultivated area per household (ha.)	0.466	0.446	0.42	0.466
Number of plots per household	5.85	5.67	5.52	3.16
Average size per plot (ha.)	0.08	0.078	0.076	0.148

Source: Ministry of Agriculture (1993, p. 48).

Second, there was vagueness and uncertainty in property rights. As land eligibility was linked to a person's villager status, no matter when it was obtained, changes in village composition due to births, deaths, marriages and so on could trigger redistribution of land; when a member died his or her right would automatically disappear. An MoA survey showed that, by the early 1990s, 65 per cent of villages had found it necessary to redistribute land, about 30 per cent twice or more; the main reason given was population growth (Kong, 1993). Not only did this add to fragmentation, it also resulted inevitably in insecurity of tenure and short time horizons for farmers. There were, therefore, few incentives for them to invest in land improvement or infrastructure; indeed, the opposite was the case and there was considerable overexploitation of resources. The redistributions also incurred high transaction costs in terms of village and administrative manpower.

Third, the egalitarian basis of distribution (household size) meant that relatively little consideration was given to inter-family differences such as labour capacity, education and individual preference (Kong, 1993). As a result, some large households with limited available labour could have too much land to work. Smaller households, particularly those specialized in agriculture, could have insufficient land for full employment. This problem was much worse in areas experiencing rapid rural industrialization and urbanization. In these areas there was a general deterioration in the agricultural labour force as the higher-quality human capital tended to leave the villages. Adding to the problem was the fact that those finding off-farm work tended not to renounce their right to farm but to retain a part-time involvement. Many did not give priority to cultivation and at times even let their land lie idle. Thus the most scarce resource was underutilized and there was no effective institutional basis to facilitate land mobility. For example, MoA surveys (1991, 1993, 1996) showed that in the first half of the 1990s only 1 to 2 per cent of households were involved in subcontracting arrangements. These negative features of the HRS placed a constraint on agrarian development and China faced a challenge once again.

Internal debate on further land reform

By the mid-1980s, as problems with the HRS were emerging, China began to consider further institutional change under a call for 'the second stage of rural reform'. We now consider briefly some of the theoretical and ideological controversies surrounding that debate.

In the early stages, discussions mainly focused on whether or not collective ownership should be maintained and the form of property rights to be adopted. Two divergent ideas drew much academic attention. One group of economists advocated 'farmland nationalization', that is, state ownership of farmland with individual lifelong possession. They argued that collective ownership of farmland did not really exist in practice: rural collectives never had exclusive property rights on land under the collective system. During the commune era, collectives were prohibited from selling their 'owned' land (except to the state) or from buying land from other 'owners'. Moreover, the rigid state procurement and marketing system weakened farmers' land-use rights. Under the HRS, curtailment of their rights continued; for example, they did not have the right to transfer contract land. Thus it was argued that the state was the real landowner, 'the biggest landlord' in rural China. It would be better, therefore, to abandon the name 'collective' and institute state ownership instead. If farmland were nationalized, farmers should be granted permanent land-use rights; and they should be able to buy, sell, mortgage and inherit these rights. Although peasants would not be landowners, lifelong tenancy could in effect be as efficient as a system of owner–cultivators (Din and Cheng, 1994; Chen and Xiao, 1995).

Some economists bitterly criticized the idea of land nationalization, seeing it as intending a return to the commune system; others viewed it as a kind of quasi-private ownership. There were concerns about whether the state could manage farmland as well as collectives and whether it could afford the financial costs of such a massive purchase. These were persuasive internal arguments against the proposal.

A second group of economists took the more radical line of individual ownership as the only effective means of overcoming the deficiencies of collective ownership. As a means of avoiding criticism, they sought to 'reinter-pret' Marxist theory, arguing that socialism would rebuild society through 'socialized individual ownership'. The vital difference between socialism and capitalism is that, in the former, the main means of production are owned by all individuals but, in the latter, only by a small number. They argued for a break with the dogma that socialism requires state and collective ownership of land (Li and Li, 1989; Lin, 1989). These arguments rebelled against tradition and orthodoxy and did not find adequate internal support. The proposal was seen as capitalism by another name even though it was presented as a 'modern' inter-pretation of socialist ownership. There were fundamental concerns about whether privatization would be an effective solution to China's land problems. For example, there were fears that fragmentation would be further worsened. Re-creating the private sector would require very careful planning and would entail substantial economic, social and political risks. The problems encoun-tered in attempting rapid agrarian privatization in the CEE countries are well documented (Nikonov, 1992; Novoselov *et al.* 1993; Brooks and Lerman, 1995; Peters, 1995). There was also evidence that Chinese peasants did not show much enthusiasm for privatization. In a 1991 survey, almost 80 per cent expressed a negative attitude, a response which was fairly uniform across the various income strata at village level (Xian, 1992). There is, however, a need for a more up-to-date review of peasants' attitudes to this issue.

Gradually, the arguments of a third group of economists began to take hold. Their view was that the debate was trammelled by previous doctrine on owner-ship and, as Barzel (1989) points out, property rights should be seen as a package of rights; this includes rights to consume, to obtain income from and to alienate assets. The purpose of property rights should be to define clearly and unambiguously the interests and obligations among the various stakeholders. A more feasible and effective option for China would be to clarify land-use rights. The aim should be to give farmers full and exclusive use rights which would include the freedom to obtain income from and to alienate their use rights, thus greatly reducing the current uncertainties and ambiguities in the system and facilitating the introduction of market forces to land transactions.

Although differing in their approaches, all three groups seemed to agree about the need to clarify land property rights. Following the logic of the third group, this would be done within the framework of collective ownership but with reformed land-use rights. As a gesture in this direction, in the late 1980s, rural households engaged in non-farm businesses were allowed to sublease their land to other villagers in order to prevent land being left idle. In 1993, the Central Committee announced a policy initiative with a view to extending the contract to 30 years. This was followed by a detailed policy statement from the General Office in 1997 implementing the initiative, with the stated aim of stabilizing and improving the land contract system. According to the MoA, by mid-1999, about 77 per cent of all production teams had 30-year contracts issued (MoA, 1999). As part of this process the government also gave permis-sion for the initiation of experimental reform models which would seek to reflect the diversity of local conditions. We now examine four of these pilot projects.

MEITAN: FIXED RESPONSIBILITY FARMLAND CONTRACT

Meitan county is located in north Guizhou Province (see Figure 1) and has a rural economy typical of the province. About 93 per cent of its 400 000 population is engaged in agriculture. Meitan is rather poorly endowed with farmland. In 1987, the total 30 000 hectares of cultivated land occupied only 17 per cent of the territory: per capita cultivated land was a mere 0.087 hectares. In the process of implementing the HRS, land fragmentation emerged as a big problem owing to population growth and land redistribution. The level of fragmentation was very high. According to a survey, each household's cultivated land in the county was divided on average into 15 plots of land, with the largest, 0.13 hectares, and the smallest, 0.005 hectares. In one extreme case, Zhu Yuequan, a peasant householder with seven family members, had 128 plots of farmland (Li and Din, 1994). The boundaries and paths between plots occupied nearly 12 per cent of active land area in the county. The

Notes: 1, Meitan; 2, Pingdu; 3, Shunyi; 4, Nanhai.

FIGURE 1   *Location of experimental land reform districts*

fragmentation became intolerable to the extent that farmers themselves expressed a strong desire to stop land redistribution.

The local government response initially was to make another distribution and then to fix the structure for 20 years. Most peasants, however, disagreed with this proposal. An investigation among 510 peasant households showed that about 65 per cent wanted to stop redistribution at once. A local policy, therefore, of extending the tenure term from 15 to 20 years, and fixing contract land within this period irrespective of changes in household composition, was initiated in December 1987. After being carefully tested in two villages, the policy was extended to all rural areas of the county. Farmers were granted inheritance rights on their land, the ability to exchange land with one another, to subrent, pool and mortgage for credit. The local government encouraged households to farm wasteland, develop small family businesses such as processing and animal breeding, and to find off-farm employment (MRRDO, 1993).

After several years of operating the policy, some early effects were observed. According to Li and Din (1994), the policy was welcomed by most local farmers and only 10 per cent of households asked for land readjustment. Farmers had greater incentives for land investment and conservation. By 1993, there had been significant new land development, land fertility grades were advanced and farmers increased their purchases of fixed means of production. Land fragmentation was to a large extent brought under control. For example, the area occupied by paths and boundaries was stabilized. Land subdivision now took place mainly within a household as children matured instead of being redistributed among the households of a village.

In addition, farmers' attitudes towards increasing family size changed. Traditional Chinese culture equates more children with more happiness. However, under the new land system, as new babies are not able to get land during the contract term, 41.4 per cent of the sampled households showed a negative attitude to having more children (ibid.). In 1993, the policy of fixing contract land was formally legislated as the provincial land management law and applied in all rural areas of the province. In 1995, when the Chinese government issued the new land policy, in advance of the first 15 years tenure coming due, Meitan's experiment was included in the central government document. However, this document only suggested that appropriate villages should consider the policy. Nevertheless, this means that, after being experimented with for eight years in a small local county, the policy of fixing land was gradually becoming integrated into the nation's institutional arrangements; this was indeed a significant change.

PINGDU: TWO-LAND SYSTEM

China's strong desire for social equity in land matters was seen as limiting the national adoption of the fixed land system. An alternative which sought to promote economic efficiency while also addressing social equity was the so-called 'two-land system'. Pingdu is a county-level city in Shangdong Province and is the original location of the two-land system; we now examine the background to its adoption.

In Pingdu, cultivated land and collective economic infrastructure were relatively well developed in the people's commune era. After adopting the HRS, Pingdu was confronted with a growing number of issues which individual farm households found difficult to handle. These included how to encourage the use of advanced agricultural machinery and equipment and the further development of agricultural infrastructure. In 1984, Pingdu adopted the two-land system on a trial basis. In a relatively short period, the two-land system developed from a couple of village experiments to nationwide practice. By the early 1990s, it became a nationally accepted and popular form of agrarian institutional innovation. By 1990, 27 per cent of all villages in China accounting for 38 per cent of cultivated land under the HRS had adopted the system; and by 1994 these figures had increased to 32 per cent and almost 50 per cent, respectively (MoA 1991,1993, 1996).

Why did the two-land system achieve such apparent success in a relatively short time? A plausible explanation is that, by separating household land into two categories, the new system instituted a seemingly workable means of preserving social equity but at the same time allowing the pursuit of greater efficiency. Total cultivated land in a village is divided into food land (*kouliang tian*) and contract land (*chenbao tian*). Food land is for family consumption and contract land for commercial farming. All households have their own food land and can choose whether or not to take contract land. Usually, part-time farmers only take charge of food land for subsistence production; they also pay taxes including the state agricultural tax. Households who also take contract land have an obligation to fulfil government procurement quotas and pay taxes. They can, however, sell their surplus production in the free market, thus creating an incentive for production on contract land. The key feature of the two-land system is division according to usage. As food land is to guarantee subsistence requirements, it is distributed relatively evenly or equitably. In Pingdu, it was done using a formula based on human and animal consumption needs and on seed grain requirements. This usually translated into a food land requirement of at least 0.5 *mu* (0.07 ha.) per person, assuming a local grain yield of 650 to 700 kilograms per *mu*.

The main concern in allocating contract land is efficiency, and farmers bid competitively for this land. The bid price in Pingdu normally reflected obligations towards government procurement and the collective as well as land tax (approximately 4 *yuan* per *mu* of land). Bid prices reflected the grade of land. In 1988, the price range per *mu* per annum was 53–71 *yuan*, which typically represented 30 to 40 per cent of annual net income per *mu* of farmland. Allocation of contract land, however, was not decided solely on price. Owing to the relative scarcity of farmland and limited off-farm employment opportunities, some intervention was still judged to be necessary to prevent excessive competition between farmers. Usually a limit on cultivated area of between 5 and 15 *mu* per labour unit was imposed, depending on the land endowment of the locality. To encourage larger-scale operation, contract land was offered in relatively large parcels, usually between 20 and 30 *mu*, depending on locality and land quality. Group bidding by households was strongly encouraged in order to promote cooperative activity. Land was normally allocated for five years and the contract could not be changed within this term. However, during the period the relative amounts of food and contract land could be altered if household sizes changed. If they increased in size, the village would reduce a household's area of contract land or, alternatively, their procurement obligations, so as to increase the capacity for subsistence production; if a size reduction occurred the process operated in reverse. Despite the possibility of making these adjustments, the frequency of changes in the level of active contract land per household was reduced.

After only a relatively short period of operation, the two-land system seemed to have achieved some encouraging results. First and foremost, the previously even allocation of land among households was significantly altered. According to a survey of 120 households in 11 villages, 30 per cent of them increased land areas, with 50 per cent increasing by as much as 5 *mu* per household (Jiang *et al.*, 1994). Just over 9 per cent of households cultivated only food land using female labour: as a result, the male labour was able to concentrate on non-agricultural business. Agricultural performance also improved. Total grain output increased from 795 000 tons in 1987 to 1 041 000 tons in 1994 and grain yield per unit of land increased by 32.4 per cent. By the mid-1990s, Pingdu ranked tenth in grain output among 2200 counties and county-level cities in China. Per capita annual income of the rural population of Pingdu grew 2.3 fold in nominal terms, from 732 *yuan* in 1987 to 1658 *yuan* in 1994 (RIDA, 1995).

Towards the end of the 1990s, the two-land system has tended to fall from favour as a possible national model. The precise reasons are not clear but we believe that one factor has been administrative and bureaucratic 'difficulties' which have been the result, in part, of a lack of accountability at local level. We refer to these problems in the final section of the paper.

SHUNYI: COLLECTIVE FARMING

In the two models examined so far, individual farming, the core of the HRS, remains largely unchanged. However, as we have shown above, land fragmentation has been a big problem. Reconsolidation of farming land has, therefore, been seen as one of the further reform goals and is the subject of continuing debate. Perhaps surprisingly, collective farms began to reappear in some rural areas close to urban centres and in some coastal provinces in the late 1980s. This development attracted considerable international attention; see, for example, Reisch (1992). There was concern that it could signal a return to the people's commune system.

Shunyi, a suburb county located northwest of Beijing, is one location of such a collective farm. A very important factor in the successful establishment of this collective was the relatively high level of rural industrialization. About 60 per cent of the rural workforce had abandoned farming for work in township enterprises, and part-time farming became the norm: as the contribution of agriculture to household income declined, a lower priority was given to farming. Its location near the suburbs of a major consumption centre meant also that it had available to it well developed marketing channels, transport systems and advanced communication facilities.

Agriculture in the area, therefore, was experiencing major adjustment problems. For example, between 1978 and 1984, the annual growth rate of grain output was 6.4 per cent, but between 1984 and 1986 this fell to 1.2 per cent (Luo and Zhang, 1995). Most part-time farmers even wanted to return their entire land entitlement to the village cooperatives. In response to farmers' requests, collective farms were introduced in 1986 in order to achieve a more optimal-scale operation. According to a survey reported in the _Peasants' Daily_ (1994), by 1994 collective farms in Shunyi occupied about 63 per cent of cultivated land, equivalent to around ten hectares per employee.

The operation of these collective farms is significantly different from that in the peoples' commune era. Normally, the village provides agricultural machinery and is responsible for developing infrastructure. Collective farms are identified as the farming enterprises of the villages with which they have signed a contract and they operate independently. The employees of the farms earn wages rather than the working points of the old commune system. After completing the contract, which usually includes fulfilling state procurement quotas and a commitment to the cooperative, collective farms distribute part of their surplus as a bonus to employees according to their performance; the remainder, the farm's profit, is set aside as a common accumulation fund. Those who returned their land-use rights to the village are given the privilege of purchasing grain for their own consumption at special low prices. The collective farm operates under a system of collective responsibility rather than an individual household contract system. As the collective farm is registered as an enterprise of the village, it is possible for the village to transfer some profits from non-agricultural enterprises to the farm. The effects of this kind of operation are somewhat controversial. On the one hand, agricultural infrastructure is rapidly improved by the financial support from non-agricultural enterprises. On the other hand, there are concerns that the system may encourage free-rider behaviour, a common problem under the old commune system; this may depend on whether suitable incentive systems can be put in place.

Available evidence suggests that there have been some initial achievements by the collective farms in Shunyi. Although total grain output and yield per unit of land increased modestly between 1986 and 1994, grain output per agricultural worker grew dramatically, at an annual average rate of 30 per cent. Labour productivity was enhanced by rapid farm mechanization, from ploughing through to harvesting. As a result, employees of collective farms in the second half of the 1990s were earning higher incomes than part-time farmers employed by township enterprises. The internal accumulation by the collective farms reached 60 million _yuan_ in the five years from 1987 to 1992. Annual per capita nominal income of the rural population in the county grew from 600 _yuan_ in 1986 to 4000 _yuan_ in 1993 (RIDA, 1995).

NANHAI: FARMLAND SHAREHOLDING COOPERATIVE SYSTEM

This system has emerged as a completely different type of collective. So far, it has been confined to the Pearl River Delta area of Guangdong Province and has aroused considerable interest. It was initiated at the end of 1992 on an experimental basis in Xiabai, an administrative- level village in Nanhai county, one of the major growth centres in China over the last two decades. Nanhai became known as one of the so-called 'four tigers' in the area owing to its rapid industrialization and urbanization: in the period from 1978 to 1992, the annual average nominal GDP growth rate in the county was almost 22 per cent (*Guangdong Statistical Yearbook*, various issues). In the process of such rapid development, land reform emerged as an issue of great importance, for two main reasons, firstly to halt agricultural decline following the migration of farm labour, particularly by younger more educated workers, to the non-farm sector. These individuals usually retained their responsibility land owing to the perceived risk associated with losing land rights. In most villages farming had to be carried out by the residual labour force, mainly females, the elderly and even children. The view of the local administration was that economic and social modernization could not be sustained without agricultural development. Secondly, there was a need to develop a more integrated land-use planning system, taking account of the needs of agriculture, industry and urban development. The uncontrolled proliferation of small factories and towns had led to enormous waste of scarce land. This problem was worsened by the lack of clarity about who the responsible authority should be. Rural land was in the hands of natural villages, the basic unit in rural China, but these were too small to manage land planning effectively. The administrative village, a higher-level organization, had greater capacity but was not the landowner. In an attempt to resolve the conflicts the farmland shareholding cooperative system, a kind of land-as-stock system, was initiated.

Under this system the first step is to have a valuation of farmland and three bases have been used: (a) the prices paid by government for land conversion; (b) according to the net incomes of land after deducting input costs; and (c) a mixture of the first two methods (NRRDO, 1994). Although the methods were imprecise, this did not hinder the implementation of the system.

The key aspect of the system is the distribution of land shares to individual peasants. Membership of a cooperative serves as the main criterion for share entitlement. Age is an additional consideration. Normally, the principle of 'adult, full share and children, half share' is followed. Shares are paper entitlements and there are no financial transactions at distribution. When land shares are allocated there is no actual physical distribution of plots. Furthermore, the shares cannot normally be withdrawn or transferred. After receiving land shares, farmers return their land-use rights to the natural village to which they belong. The natural village then offers the land entitlement to the administrative village to which it belongs. The administrative village is now in charge of land use. Usually, an agricultural company subordinate to the administrative village is founded and this becomes responsible for agricultural land. The land is contracted to individual specialist farmers or farming teams based on a bidding process. In practice, most peasants did not bid to farm the land. However, as land shareholders, they are able to share dividends and also to promote their ideas at shareholder meetings; individual members also have incentives to monitor managers.

The system is an interesting and innovative institutional change which is still at quite an early experimental stage. Some positive effects have been observed. Within only three years, the system was introduced to almost all villages in Nanhai and other rural parts of the Pearl River Delta, and welcomed by local people. Agriculture was much improved, principally through the ability of the system to promote larger-scale farming. In 1993, cultivated area per labour unit in Nanhai increased to 7.6 hectares, a tenfold increase (RIDA, 1995). In Xiabai, the birthplace of the system, grain production was contracted to a group of 30 farmers. They manage the farm independently and provide the main source of grain for local consumption. Administrative villages have made comprehensive land-use plans and there is now at least a framework for more rational and efficient land utilization. It should be added, however, that there has been relatively little research on the progress or achievements of the system in recent years. Work by Chen (1999) suggests that it has not progressed much beyond its original areas in the Pearl River Delta and is not being seen as a suitable national model.

DISCUSSION AND CONCLUSIONS

Although China has been making some progress with the deepening of land reforms, the pace has been somewhat slower than expected and in some respects the process could be said to have stalled. The new approaches remain, at best, in the experimental stages and no mature national model has emerged. We now discuss four broad conclusions based on our review of experiences to date and our understanding of how the political economy of China may be influencing the process.

China's land reform process involves difficult political choices

These involve, for example, the classic trade-offs between egalitarianism and economic efficiency and the balancing of central and local government powers. The process since the mid-1980s has reflected these dilemmas. Where social equality or equity considerations predominate, economic efficiency has been held back. For example, the fixed responsibility land in Meitan could only be maintained for one contract term of 20 years; after that, redistribution of land could not be avoided. The equal distribution of land shares under the farmland shareholding system in Nanhai, effectively ignoring the relative contributions of workers to the collective, illustrates the priority given to the egalitarian principle. The implementation of the two-land system, arguably the most suitable for many rural areas as it is less restricted by local conditions, also illustrates some of the dilemmas. Although, as we outlined above, the system produced some initially encouraging results, the speed of its implementation has slowed in recent years; indeed, there are signs that it is falling from favour with government and farmers. In particular, the bidding process for contract land remains relatively minor and has not brought about the hoped-for consolidation towards larger-scale commercial farming. During the first half of the 1990s, only around 6 per cent of contract land nationally was leased on a bid basis. The remainder was allocated using standard HRS criteria of household size and labour availability (MoA, 1996). Thus the goals of equality or equity in land affairs still appear to be outstandingly important; and a workable reform strategy should reflect these priorities and recognize perhaps that greater efficiency can only be sought incrementally.

The clarification of land property rights is still at an early stage

Although the constitution states that land is owned by the collective, it is not at all clear at the local level who actually constitutes the collective: for example, whether it is the natural or administrative village, or some other body. The reform process so far has not provided farmers with sufficient clarity about their land property rights, in particular their individual rights vis-à-vis those of the collective and those of the state. For example, in the cases of the fixed responsibility contract and the two-land system, property rights are still unstable. As the contract term progresses to the due date there will be great uncertainty amongst farmers about whether they will lose productive capacity. This will tend to perpetuate the problem of underinvestment in land and fixed assets. In the case of the farmland shareholding cooperative system, the land shares are really just paper entitlements which lack the real attributes of shares in a joint-stock company. In particular, farmers cannot get compensation for their shares even when they move to a city and are no longer active in their village. It may be argued that the system is locked in a kind of path dependence (North, 1999) that currently hinders it from being developed further. Chen (1999) proposes that individual members should be able to purchase their shares, and have the right to alienate them for cash, effectively giving them full property rights. The current lack of incentives tends to make farmers reluctant to leave their village, and surplus agricultural labour continues to grow, slowing down the process of structural change. As the inadequacy of property rights will continue to hinder and frustrate the reform process, further clarification of farmers' land rights is undoubtedly an issue of prime importance. This area, however, remains very controversial. Further debate and research are urgently needed about the rationale and the scope for granting protected rights to farmers. In particular, as Liu *et al.* (1996) argue, it may be important to disaggregate land property rights into their multiple dimensions and to explore the productivity implications of different arrangements. The whole area of property rights also raises questions about the roles of central and local governments. To date the central government has tended to stand back and leave decisions to the local authorities. The latter, however, are calling for a clear general statement of policy on this issue of fundamental national importance. This goes wider than land rights and will extend to areas such as rural enterprise. The further deepening of property rights, of course, might be said to increase the perceived exposure and vulnerability of the state, the implications of which are difficult to predict.

Land reforms have reflected and will probably continue to reflect local conditions

In the early 1980s, the HRS emerged as the dominant national institution. Since then the deepening of the process has paid much more attention to regional diversity. On one level, this might simply be seen as a refinement of the HRS and the avoidance of fundamental changes to property rights which we point to above. At the same time there is sound logic in taking account of local conditions and in not being excessively dependent on an imposed imported model. Indeed, the more successful initiatives have been in those areas where there has been a clear understanding of local specificity. The tailoring of reforms, however, has had other unfortunate consequences which should be guarded against in the future. For example, administrative interference and rent-seeking behaviour are reported to have heavily distorted the two-land system in some areas. The levying of excessive charges for contract land meant that contracts were disrupted and some farmers lost half their original land. As a consequence, farmers' attitudes towards the system have become much less welcoming, even hostile in places (MoA, 1996). In some coastal areas farmers are reported (*People's Daily*, 25 September, 1996) to be abandoning their food land completely and the land is being tilled by village-organized farms: effectively, a move back to a one-land system.

A major challenge for the global agricultural economics profession

It may be a statement of the obvious, but the deepening of the rural reforms in China poses huge challenges for our research agenda, some of which have been identified above. Western economists can continue to make an important contribution in collaboration with Chinese colleagues. The limited availability and reliability of data are barriers to progress, but with greater openness these problems can probably be overcome. A more fundamental problem is the complexity of the issues. As North (1999) implies, the Chinese transition poses unique challenges to established economic paradigms; but that raises a set of questions which are beyond the scope of this paper.

REFERENCES

Barzel, Y. (1989), *Economic Analysis of Property Rights*, Cambridge: Cambridge University Press.
Brooks, K. and Lerman, Z. (1993), 'Land Reform and Farm Restructuring in Russia: 1992 Status', *American Journal of Agricultural Economics*, **75**, 1254–9.
Brooks, K. and Lerman, Z. (1994), *Land Reform and Farm Restructuring in Russia*, World Bank Discussion Paper 233, Washington, DC: World Bank.
Brooks, K. and Lerman, Z. (1995), 'Restructuring of Traditional Farms and New Land Relations in Russia', *Agricultural Economics*, **13**, 11–25.

Central Committee (1984), *The First Document of the Central Committee of the Communist Party of China*, Beijing: Central Committee.

Chen, F. (1996), 'Institutional Innovation of the Farmland Shareholding Co-operative System', *Economists*, **5**, 48–57.

Chen, F. (1999), 'A Study of the Shareholding Co-operative System of the Rural Community: An Institutional Economics Approach', doctoral thesis, College of Economics and Trade, South China Agricultural University.

Chen, F. and Davis, J. (1998), 'Land Reform in Rural China Since the Mid-1980s', *Land Reform (FAO)*, **2**,123–37.

Chen, J. (1994), 'On Property Institutions of the People's Commune', *Economic Research*, **7**, 47–73.

Chen, M. and Xiao, X. (1995), 'Nationalised Ownership and Individual Operation: The Direction of Land Reform in Rural China', *Contemporary Economic Science*, **6**, 18–23.

Csaki, C. (1990), 'Agricultural Changes in Eastern Europe at the Beginning of the 1990s', American Journal of Agricultural Economics, **72**, 1233–42.

Csaki, C. and Lerman, Z. (1994), 'Land Reform and Farm Sector Restructuring in the Former Socialist Countries in Europe', *European Review of Agricultural Economics*, **21**, 555–78.

Csaki, C. and Lerman, Z. (1996), 'Agricultural Transition Revised: Issues of Land Reform and Farm Sector Restructuring in East–Central Europe and the Former USSR', in *Plenary Papers, Redefining the Roles for European Agriculture*, VIIIth Congress, Edinburgh (UK): European Association of Agricultural Economists, pp. 61–96.

Din, J. and Cheng, G. (1994), 'Target Model of Farmland Property Institutional Reform in China', *Problems of Agricultural Economy*, **10**, 7–12.

Gaynor, M. and Putterman, L. (1993), 'Productivity Consequences of Alternative Land Division Methods in China's Decollectivisation: An Econometric Analysis', *Journal of Development Economics*, **42**, 357–86.

Jiang, Z., Chen, Z. and Jia, Y. (1994), 'Analyses of the Policy Effects of the Two-Land System in Pingdu', *Chinese Rural Economy*, **4**, 26–30.

Kong, J. (1993), 'Positive Analyses of Agrarian Institutional Innovations in Rural China', *Economic Research*, **2**, 65–72.

Lerman, Z. (1999), 'Land Reform and Farm Restructuring: What Has Been Accomplished to Date?', *American Economic Review*, **89**, 271–5.

Li, C. and Li, S. (1989), 'Obstacles to Rural Reform and Restructuring and Farmland Property Right', *Chinese Rural Economy*, **4**, 26–9.

Li, Q. and Din, Y. (1994), 'Adopting the Strategy of Permanently Fixed Farmers' Responsibility Land', *Chinese Rural Economy*, **2**, 52–5.

Lin, H. (1989), 'A Misunderstanding of Marxist Ownership Theory', *Problems of the Chinese Economy*, **2**,25–9.

Lin, J.Y. (1987), *Household Farm, Cooperative Farm, and Efficiency: Evidence from Rural Decollectivization in China*, Working Paper no. 553, Economic Growth Centre, Yale University: New Haven.

Lin, Z. (1982), *On The Household Responsibility System*, Beijing: Agricultural Publishing House.

Liu, S., Carter, M.R. and Yao, Y. (1996), *Dimensions and Diversity of Property Rights in Rural China: Dilemmas on the Road to Further Reform*, Staff Paper Series no. 395, University of Wisconsin-Madison: Madison.

Liu, Y. and Zhang, H. (1995), 'Agrarian Institutional Innovation Under the Household Responsibility System', *Economic Research*, **1**, 69–80.

Meitan Rural Reform District Office (MRRDO) (1993), 'The Experiment with Agrarian Institution in Meitan', *Chinese Rural Economy*, **2**, 61–5.

Ministry of Agriculture of China (1991, 1993, 1996), 'Survey of Agrarian Operations Under The Household Responsibility System in China', *Problems of Agricultural Economy*, **10**, 33–40; **11**, 45–52; **12**, 38–42.

Ministry of Agriculture of China (1999), 'Land Contract', *Management of Rural Co-operatives*, issue 12.

Nanhai Rural Reform District Office (NRRDO) (1994), 'Experiment with the Farmland Shareholding Cooperative System in Nanhai', *Rural South-China*, **1**, 10–16.

Nikonov, A.A. (1992), 'Agricultural Transition in Russia and the Other Former States of the USSR', *American Journal of Agricultural Economics*, **74**, 1157–62.

North, D. (1999), *Understanding the Process of Economic Change*, Wincott Memorial Lecture, London: Institute of Economic Affairs.

Novoselov, Y.A., Streletsky, A.Y., Lewis, C.E. and Greenberg, J.A. (1993), 'Agriculture and Economic Reform in Russia', *Agribusiness*, **9**, 623–30.

Peasants' Daily (1994), 19 January, quoted in Luo, Youshen and Zhang, Hognyu (1995), 'Agrarian Institutional Innovation Under the Household Responsibility System', *Economic Research*, **1**, 69–80.

Perkins, D.H. (1988), 'Reforming China's Economic System', *Journal of Economic Literature*, **26**, 601–45.

Peters, G.H. (1995), 'Agricultural Economics: An Educational and Research Agenda for Nations in Transition', *Agricultural Economics*, **12**, 193–240.

Reisch, E. (1992), 'Land Reform Policy in China: Political Guidelines', in E.B. Vermeer (ed.), *From Peasant to Entrepreneur: Growth and Change in Rural China*, Wageningen, Netherlands: Pudoc.

Research Institution of Development Assistance (RIDA) and The Overseas Economic Cooperation Fund (OECF) (1995), *Prospects for Grain Supply-Demand Balance and Agricultural Development Policy in China*, OECF Discussion Papers no. 6, 59–88.

State Statistical Bureau of China (various years), *China's Statistical Yearbooks*, Beijing: China Statistical Publishing House.

Stavis, B. (1982), 'Rural Institutions in China', in G. Barker (ed.), *The Chinese Agricultural Economy*, Boulder: Westview Press.

Swinnen, J.F.M. (ed.) (1997), *Political Economy of Agrarian Reform in Central and Eastern Europe*, Aldershot: Ashgate.

Wenfang, Z. and Makeham, J. (1992), 'Recent Developments in the Market for Rural Land Use in China, *Land Economics*, **68**(2), 139–62.

Xian, Z. (1992), 'Model and Choice of China's Agrarian System', *Rural Economy and Society*, **6**, 9–13.

K.N. NINAN*

Economic Liberalization and Rural Poverty Alleviation:
The Indian Experience

INTRODUCTION

The economic liberalization process, initiated by India in 1991 following a macroeconomic crisis, has evoked considerable debate and controversy, especially regarding its social implications. Will these reforms, consisting of a Stabilization and Structural Adjustment Programme (SAP), benefit the poor and other marginalized groups by reducing poverty, improving food entitlements and access to other basic needs, or will poverty and inequality be accentuated? These questions assume importance especially in the context of a widespread belief that the benefits of reforms have largely accrued to the rich and other better-off sections, with the costs having most often been borne by the poor. Evidence from some recent studies (Gupta, 1992, 1996; Ninan, 2000), suggesting an aggravation of poverty after the reforms, has provided critics with ammunition to point to adverse social effects.

There are several features of India's reforms which raise concern from the perspective of poverty reduction. In the absence of adequate safeguards, the low priority accorded to agriculture under India's SAP (unlike the case of Africa and Latin America), plus the emphasis on reducing public expenditures on the social sector, including food subsidies, as part of the government's deficit-curbing exercises, will hurt the poor and reverse the declining trends in poverty recorded after 1969. The initial endowments and favourable conditions, such as a more egalitarian distribution of land and other productive assets allied to human resource development, which facilitated the success of such reforms in East and Southeast Asia, are absent in India. That may well affect the quality and success of the reforms.

Keeping the above in view, the present study seeks to analyse the impact of the economic reforms in India from the perspective of the poor, and poverty reduction. The specific objectives are as follows:

(1) to analyse the trends in poverty in India in the post-reform period as compared with the pre-reform period, both at an all-India level and across states;

*Institute for Social and Economic Change, Bangalore, India.

(2)   to analyse the role of agricultural growth, food prices, access to subsi-
      dized food, and other factors of rural poverty, at the same levels;
(3)   to analyse the trends in (consumption) inequality in India in the pre- and
      post-reform period; and
(4)   to estimate the elasticities of rural poverty in India with respect to se-
      lected variables, as well as explore factors behind alterations in rural
      poverty levels in the post-reform period.

DATA AND APPROACH

The data for the analysis are drawn from a report by the World Bank (1997)
using its figures on 'Poverty and Growth in India' (Ozler *et al.*, 1996). These
have been supplemented by material from official publications of the Government of India such as the National Accounts Statistics, Estimates of State
Domestic Product, Bulletin of Food Statistics and Statistical Abstracts of India.
To cover the first objective, the analysis uses the estimates of poverty computed by Gaurav Datt (1997), and cited by the World Bank.

The estimates are based on the official poverty line determined by the
Planning Commission in 1993. It corresponds to a per capita monthly expenditure of 49 Rupees and 57 Rupees for rural and urban areas, respectively, at
October 1973–June 1974, measured at 'all-India' prices. These poverty lines
correspond to a total household per capita expenditure sufficient to provide, in
addition to clothing and transport, a daily intake of 2400 and 2100 calories per
person in rural and urban areas, respectively. The poverty line for rural areas
was adjusted for subsequent years using the Consumer Price Index for Agricultural Labourers (CPIAL) with 1960–61 = 100 and for urban areas, using the
Consumer Price Index for Industrial Workers (CPIIW) with 1960 = 100. The
poverty estimates by Datt and the World Bank have used a corrected CPIAL
series where upward adjustments were made to the nominal price of firewood,
which had been kept constant since 1960–61 in the official series. Owing to
variations in commodity prices and rates of inflation across states, the official
all-India poverty line at 1973–4 prices was adjusted using the state-specific
consumer price indices for rural and urban areas to derive the poverty lines by
state. These are inflated for subsequent years using the state-specific CPIAL.

There are three estimates of poverty based on the head count ratio (HCR),
the poverty gap index (PGI), and the squared poverty gap index (SPGI), which
belong to the general class of poverty measures commonly used (World Bank,
1997). They capture the extent, the depth and the severity of poverty. While the
HCR indicates the proportion of poor with reference to the specified poverty
line, the PGI measures the average distance below the poverty line in the
population (counting the non-poor as having a zero poverty gap), expressed as
a percentage of the poverty line. The SPGI is based on the individual poverty
gaps raised to a power of two; that is, it is the mean of the squared proportionate poverty gaps (Ravallion and Datt, 1996a, 1996b; World Bank, 1997).

Poverty estimates are available on an annual basis from the 1950s up to
1973–4 and thereafter, up to 1986–7, on a quinquennial basis. However, with a

view to rebuilding a time series, a decision was taken to revert to an annual basis from 1986–7, using a smaller sample. Despite the deficiencies of the material (such as the uneven spacing and length of the surveys), these are the only series available for such a long time span for any country, and hence have generated wide interest and research on temporal and spatial variations for India.

An earlier study noted that, while rural poverty trends at national and state levels registered a significant increase from 1957–8 to 1968–9, during the subsequent period from 1969–70 to 1986–7 they recorded a marked decline (Ninan, 1994, 1995–6). The rate of decline during the latter period was also higher than the rate of increase in rural poverty during the previous period, both for all India and most states. Hence 1969–70 has been taken as the starting point for analysis over the period up to 1993–4, the latest year for which poverty estimates are available. Although the analysis spans 25 years, we have only 14 observations at all-India level and 12 observations at state level, because of gaps in the data cited earlier. The pre- and post-reform periods are 1969–70 to 1990–91 and 1991–2 to 1993–4.

TRENDS IN POVERTY

For fitting trends the following model is used:

$$g_t = a_0 + a_1 t + a_2 d + a_3(d \cdot t) + u$$

where

g = head-count ratio or poverty gap index or squared poverty gap index,
d = dummy variable where $d = 0$ for the pre-reform period and $d = 1$ for the post-reform period,
t = time,
$d \cdot t$ = product of dummy and time variables,
u = error term.

From the estimated equations we can derive the equations for the pre- and post-reform periods (period I and period II) as follows:

$$\text{Period I } g_t = a_0 + a_1 t$$

$$\text{Period II } g_t = (a_0 + a_2 d) + (a_1 t + a_3 (d \cdot t))$$

This model offers advantages in terms of providing greater degrees of freedom for econometric analysis as inferences about the period-wise trends can be drawn from a single sample rather than two and, more important, it enables us to see whether the slope itself has undergone a change over the two periods. Ordinary least squares (OLS) has been used to estimate the trends in poverty. In the equations where autocorrelation was found to be serious the parameters were re-estimated using the Beach–Mackinnon method. The estimates for the pre- and post-reform periods presented in Tables 1 and 2 are derived from the estimated linear equations using the model for the three alternative measures of poverty.

Table 1 presents the trends in poverty and (consumption) inequality for India. During the pre-reform period from 1969–70 to 1990–91, rural poverty recorded a significant decline in terms of all three indicators, falling at a

TABLE 1   *Trends in poverty and inequality (consumption) in India during the pre- and post-reform period from 1969–70 to 1993–4*

Poverty indicator	Pre-reform period (1969–70 to 1990–91		Post-reform period (1991–2 to 1993–4)	
	Constant	Time	Constant	Time
Rural poverty				
HCR	59.16*	–1.02*	42.32	–0.10
PGI	18.79*	–0.46*	6.87	+0.10
SPGI	7.96*	–0.23*	1.47	+0.07
Urban poverty				
HCR	47.79*	–0.65*	66.49	–1.36
PGI	14.31*	–0.26*	18.65	–0.42
SPGI	5.68*	–0.12*	9.45	–0.26
Overall national poverty				
HCR	56.82*	–0.95*	48.99	–0.04
PGI	17.85*	–0.42*	9.20	–0.002
SPGI	7.49*	–0.20*	3.11	+0.001
Inequality (consumption)				
Rural Gini	29.91*	–0.03	30.26	–0.015
Urban Gini	34.07*	+0.05	67.21	–1.23
National Gini	31.06*	+0.001	38.56	–0.25

Notes: These equations are derived from the estimated equations using the model mentioned in the text. The trends computed here are linear trends.
In the tables in this paper, *,**, and *** indicate coefficients to be statistically significant at 1, 5 and 10 per cent levels of significance, respectively. In the equations for the post-reform period derived from the estimated equations, the significance of the constant term is inferred on the basis of the statistical significance of the dummy variable in the estimated equation, while that of the time trend variable is inferred on the basis of the statistical significance of the (*d.t*) variable.

Source: The basic data for the above analysis have been taken from World Bank (1997). The estimates of poverty using different indicators of poverty, and Gini ratios reported therein, have been computed by Gaurav Datt.

sharper rate than urban poverty. In contrast, the post-reform period from 1991–2 to 1993–4 recorded either a notable weakening of the negative trend in the head count ratio, or a reversal on the basis of PGI and SPGI, which measure the depth and severity of poverty. Urban poverty in terms of all indicators continued to record declining trends (though none were statistically significant). Trends in consumption inequality for rural India recorded a decline during both periods, whereas in respect of urban areas this trend was positive during the pre-reform period and negative in the latter period, but none were statistically significant.

Trends in rural poverty for 15 major states appear in Table 2. It is interesting to see that in the pre-reform period all 15 recorded a significant decline in poverty levels, in terms of all three indicators, but during the post-reform period there is a diversity of patterns. Eleven states continued to record negative trends in rural poverty for one or more poverty indicators, although these negative trends were not statistically significant in most cases. Only Gujarat and Karnataka continued to record significant declines in rural poverty levels across the three poverty indicators, and that, too, at a faster pace.

The intensification of rural diversification in Gujarat and Karnataka may explain the sharper decline in rural poverty levels in the post-reform period. Madhya Pradesh, Tamil Nadu and Assam recorded a significant decline in terms of HCR or SPGI. Four states report a reversal with the rural poverty trends changing from negative to positive, although these trends were not statistically significant. Of them, Orissa and West Bengal fall in the eastern belt of India where poverty appears endemic. But most surprising is that Punjab and Haryana, which had been in the forefront in ushering in the 'Green Revolution' in India, and where poverty levels recorded a significant decline earlier, report a positive trend (although not statistically significant) in terms of all three poverty indicators. The rate of increase in rural poverty levels for Haryana is also quite sharp. For instance, the HCR for Haryana which was 20.72 during 1990–91, rose to 21.73 in 1992 and 33.08 in 1993–4 during the post-reform period. Similarly, the PGI rose from 4.95 to 4.98 and 7.64 respectively; and the SPGI from 1.596 to 1.538 and 2.531, respectively. Sharp hikes in procurement and issue prices of food grains during the post-reform period in response to the pressures of the farmers' lobby appear to have worked to the detriment of the rural poor in the traditional green revolution belt of the country.

FACTORS AFFECTING RURAL POVERTY

Given that agriculture contributes more than a third of India's gross national product (GNP) and supports over two-thirds of the population, it is obvious that the fortunes of the rural poor are intrinsically linked to those of farming. Ahluwalia (1978, 1985) observed a close negative association between the incidence of rural poverty in India and agricultural performance. The impact occurs in several ways. Higher agricultural output helps reduce prices as well as improve food availability, both of which favour the poor. It will generate

TABLE 2   *Trends in rural poverty in India, statewise during the pre- and post-reform period from 1969–70 to 1993–4*

States	Period	Headcount ratio		Poverty gap index		Squared poverty gap index	
		Constant	Time	Constant	Time	Constant	Time
Andhra Pradesh	I	61.51*	-1.30**	19.68*	-0.58*	8.36*	-0.29*
	II	343.97	-12.12	113.22	-4.13	49.64	-1.85
Assam	I	56.67*	-0.60***	12.59*	-0.17	4.06*	-0.06
	II	248.78	-7.69	120.36	-4.26	55.25***	-2.02***
Bihar	I	69.91*	-0.49*	24.85*	-0.45*	11.45*	-0.28*
	II	175.31	4.30	79.91	-2.41	41.42	-1.35
Gujarat	I	64.59*	-1.17*	20.40*	-0.55*	8.44*	-0.26*
	II	404.88***	-14.24***	174.65***	-6.44***	83.85***	-3.13***
Haryana	I	37.38*	-0.76*	9.65*	-0.24*	3.47*	-0.10*
	II	-250.45	+10.90	-48.77	+2.16	-19.73	+0.85
Karnataka	I	61.14*	-0.72*	19.03*	-0.28*	7.95*	-0.13*
	II	439.39***	-15.32***	172.30***	-6.25***	79.26***	-2.92***
Kerala	I	75.01*	-1.86*	29.34*	-0.97*	14.25*	-0.54*
	II	101.70	-2.73	42.16	-1.37	14.77	-0.49
Madhya Pradesh	I	67.47*	-0.88*	23.54*	-0.50*	10.56*	-0.28*
	II	322.54***	-10.66***	76.69	-2.51	24.83	-0.80
Maharashtra	I	75.19*	-1.21*	24.83*	-0.54*	9.46*	-0.21
	II	320.90	-10.48	132.57	-4.59	55.31	-1.93
Orissa	I	70.14*	-1.40*	24.46*	-0.69*	11.26*	-0.38*
	II	-23.86	+2.47	-5.06	+0.53	-11.97	+0.57
Punjab	I	30.72*	-0.70*	7.52*	-0.24*	2.65*	-0.10*
	II	-30.80	+1.87	-17.48	+0.79	-6.74	+0.29

Rajasthan	I	67.40*	−1.16*	23.74*	−0.52*	10.88*	−0.27**
	II	143.32	−3.53	61.11	−1.90	31.17	−1.04
Tamil Nadu	I	67.54*	1.09*	22.28*	−0.48*	9.67*	−0.24*
	II	294.40***	−9.91***	119.56	−4.27	52.11	−1.89
Uttar Pradesh	I	54.62*	−0.84*	15.19*	−0.30*	5.72*	−0.13*
	II	196.49	−5.97	98.68	−3.42	55.17	−2.00
West Bengal	I	66.56*	−1.49*	21.42*	−0.62*	9.08*	−0.30*
	II	50.15	−0.88	10.34	−0.22	−0.27	+0.06

Notes: I, 1969–70 to 1990–91; II, 1991–2 to 1993–4.
See also notes to Table 1.

Source: As for Table 1.

employment opportunities on the land and spur growth in the non-agricultural sector, thereby creating income-earning opportunities. Agricultural growth on the whole will give a fillip to overall economic development. However, if it involves a shift from labour-intensive crops and technologies to labour-saving ones, this could work to the detriment of the rural poor, since agricultural wages constitute a major component of their incomes. Evidence from India, however, suggests that on balance the green revolution resulted in increased labour use and real wage rates (Dantwala, 1985).

Nevertheless, some argue that, in the context of the institutional and structural constraints characteristic of most low-income countries, the beneficial effects of growth can be mostly expropriated by the non-poor. The trickle-down effect implied by Ahluwalia's finding of a negative correlation between agricultural growth and the incidence of rural poverty was thus challenged by a number of researchers (Rajaraman, 1975: Griffin and Ghose, 1979). However, these observations are based on flimsy theoretical or empirical support. For instance, Rajaraman's findings implying a weak causal link between agricultural growth and rural poverty were based on just ten observations, of which only four were in the post-green revolution period. In specifying variables it was decided to use agricultural output expressed on a per capita basis, rather than on the per acre basis as in Datt and Ravallion (1998), who argued that, although output on a per person and per acre basis are highly correlated (the coefficient being 0.89 over 35 annual observations), for predictive purposes output expressed on a per acre basis is more appropriate for use in poverty equations. The reason is that, in a country like India, rapid population growth can negate the favourable impact of an improvement in crop yields on poverty levels.

Poverty is affected by inflation, which acts like a regressive tax on the poor, leading to a deterioration in their entitlements and real incomes (Sen, 1981). Since food constitutes the predominant portion of the consumption basket of the poor, rising food prices cause great anxiety. Even subsistence farmers who are net purchasers of foodgrains can be affected (Mellor and Desai, 1985; Ninan, 1994, 1995–6).

Population growth, poverty and the environment are closely interlinked. Rapid population growth affects poverty in many ways. It can offset the beneficial effects of economic growth on poverty as experienced by some South Asian countries. Moreover, poverty intertwined with rapid population growth exercises intense pressure on scarce environmental resources, resulting in environmental degradation through overexploitation of fragile resources.

Particularly since 1969, there have been a number of institutionalized welfare programmes aimed at poverty relief. Of these the provision of subsidized food through the public distribution system (PDS) has assumed great significance. However, except in some states in southern India, the programme is largely urban-oriented, although in the recent past improvements have been made to extend its reach to rural areas elsewhere and to improve selectivity. Time-series data are available only in the form of PDS offtake of foodgrains aggregated for rural and urban areas, as well as the number of fair price shops (available separately for rural and urban areas). These limitations have been kept in view while specifying the PDS variable. The role of other factors, such as inequality in rural consumption (which is a proxy for income inequality) and infrastructure development, are also examined.

It has been customary to include a time trend variable in poverty functions to serve as a cover-all variable for all other time-related factors influencing poverty not explicitly considered in a given model. This implicitly assumes that all time-related factors exercise unidirectional influences on poverty, which is questionable. The inclusion of a separate time trend variable in these circumstances is, therefore, questionable and could even affect the estimates of other explanatory variables.

Bearing these factors and data limitations in mind, the causal factors behind rural poverty in India between 1969–70 and 1993–4 can be examined. A time-series analysis at all-India level, and a cross-section analysis of inter-state data at two points of time, 1987–8 and 1993–4, which belong to the pre- and post-reform periods, respectively, are used. The variables are as a *dependent variable* (HCR, PGI or SPGI – all in percentages) and *independent variables*. To study the impact of agricultural growth (or performance), food prices, rural population pressure on environmental resources, access to subsidized food through the PDS, inequality in rural consumption levels, and infrastructure development on rural poverty levels, the following variables are considered.

(1) Agricultural output/performance variables (three specifications):
NDPAGRI – real net domestic product (NDP) from agriculture at 1960–61 prices per rural inhabitant,
NDPPRM – real NDP from the primary sector (excluding mining and quarrying) at 1960–61 prices per rural inhabitant,
SDPAGRI – state domestic product from agriculture per state rural inhabitant.

(2) Price variables (two specifications):
FDPR – consumer price index for agricultural labourers for food items (where 1960–61=100) for rural areas,
RELFDPR – relative food to general consumer price index for agricultural labourers (1960–61=100) for rural areas.

(3) Population pressure on environmental resources:
RPPAL – rural population pressure on agricultural land expressed in 100 000 people per ha. of gross cropped area (so as to take note of land-augmenting technologies which became prominent after the green revolution).

(4) Institutional intervention (PDS):
PDS – proportion of PDS offtake of foodgrains to total net availability of foodgrains, PDSFP – number of fair price shops per 100 000 people (for rural areas).

(5) Consumption inequality:
INEQUAL – inequality in rural consumption (Gini ratios).

(6) Infrastructure development:
INFRADEV – infrastructure development index as constructed by the Centre for Monitoring the Indian Economy, Bombay.

Not all these variables have been included in an equation because of the constraints of limited observations. Further, while some variables were common to both the time series and cross-section analyses, others were included in only one of them.

The agricultural, as well as price, variables were also used in their lagged forms. One could argue that the level of poverty in a given year is determined not only by that year's agricultural performance but also by that of the previous year. A good crop enables a poor household not only to repay past debts but also to build up reserves to meet unforeseen circumstances. Similarly, inflation has a lagged effect. For instance, given the low incomes of the poor, a steep rise in the prices of essential commodities may force them to borrow in order to arrest a deterioration in their consumption, the after-effects of which will be felt in subsequent years as well. To take note of these lagged effects, an alternative specification of the output and price variables is used which is computed at $\{t + (t - 1)\} / 2$.

Multiple linear regression using OLS was used to estimate the coefficients. In those equations where the Durbin–Watson statistic indicated serious problems of autocorrelation, the parameters were re-estimated using the Beach–Mackinnon method. The INFRADEV variable was found to be strongly correlated with the agricultural output variable in some equations, and hence dropped. Only those equations which gave meaningful results have been represented below.

Table 3, which presents the results time series analysis for all India, indicates that, while the agricultural output and PDS variables are negatively correlated with the incidence of rural poverty measured in terms of all the three indicators, the relative food price variable has a positive effect. The coefficients are statistically significant in most cases. The Gini variable which measures inequality in rural consumption (a proxy for income inequality) is also positively correlated with the incidence of rural poverty, although the coefficient is not statistically significant. These observations are also valid for the equations where we have used the lagged versions of the agricultural performance and relative food price variables. The R-squared values are very high. These variables are able to explain between 88 to 97 per cent of the variation in the incidence of Indian rural poverty.

Results of the cross-section analysis of the factors affecting the inter-state incidence of rural poverty for two points of time, 1987–8 and 1993–4 (pre- and post-reform, respectively), are presented in Table 4. Here again, while the agricultural performance and PDS variables are negatively correlated with the incidence of rural poverty across states, the food price, Gini and RPPAL variables are positively associated with poverty levels. The infrastructure development index variable is negatively correlated with incidence. The agricultural performance variable is statistically significant in most of the estimated equations. Although the other variables had the expected signs, none of them were statistically significant. In fact, the addition of the other variables even resulted in the agricultural performance coefficient becoming statistically not significant in some equations, which partly reflects the few degrees of freedom available for the analysis. An earlier study had estab-

TABLE 3 *Determinants of rural poverty in India 1969–70 to 1993–4*

Equation No.	Estimated linear equations	R^2	DW Statistic	Rho
	Dependent variable: head count ratio (per cent)			
1	−82.33−0.34 NDPAGRI* + 2.01 RELFDPR** − 2.13 PDS*	0.92	1.99	−0.74**
2	123.26* − 0.33 NDPAGRI* − 2.00 PDS* + 0.37 GINI	0.88	1.94	−0.58
3	−79.39 − 0.28 NDPPRM* + 1.89 RELFDPR** − 1.94 PDS*	0.94	1.80	0.77**
4	124.44* − 0.28 NDPPRM* − 1.72 PDS* + 0.01 GINI	0.90	1.91	0.53
5	−5.11 − 0.38 LNDPAGRI* + 1.21 LRELFDPR − 0.63 PDS	0.91	1.91	0.48
6	−105.85 − 0.31 LNDPPRM* + 2.08 LRELFDPR − 1.10 PDS**	0.89	1.59	—
	Dependent variable: poverty gap index			
7	−22.15 − 0.16 NDPAGRI* + 0.71 RELFDPR*** − 0.93 PDS*	0.94	2.12	−0.78**
8	53.34* − 0.16 NDPAGRI* − 0.87 PDS* + 0.03 GINI	0.91	2.05	−0.65**
9	−21.07 − 0.13 NDPPRM* + 0.65 RELFDPR** − 0.84 PDS*	0.97	1.96	−0.87*
10	−33.91 − 0.17 LNDPAGRI* + 0.79 LRELFDPR − 0.50 PDS**	0.91	1.72	—
11	−33.89 − 0.14 LNDPPRM* + 0.75 LRELFDPR + 0.47 PDS**	0.91	1.68	—
	Dependent variable: squared poverty gap index			
12	−7.03 − 0.08 NDPAGRI* + 0.30 RELFDPR* − 0.45 PDS*	0.95	2.13	−0.77**
13	−6.43 − 0.07 NDPPRM* + 0.27 RELFDPR** − 0.41 PDS*	0.97	1.94	−0.86*
14	−12.53 − 0.09 LNDPAGRI* + 0.34 LRELFDPR − 0.25 PDS**	0.91	1.67	—
15	−12.53 − 0.07 LNDPPRM* + 0.32 LRELFDPR − 0.23 PDS**	0.91	1.61	—

Notes: For a description of the independent variables refer to the text. Variables prefixed by the letter 'L' are lagged variables. Only the agricultural performance and price variables have been used in the lagged form in some equations. For *, ** and ***, refer to notes in Table 1.

Source: Table 1; also official documents such as the *Bulletin of Food Statistics, Statistical Abstracts of India*, Govt. of India.

409

TABLE 4 *Determinants of the inter-state incidence of rural poverty in India: a cross-section analysis for 1987–8 and 1993–4*

Equation No.	Estimated linear equations	R^2	DW statistic
	1987–8		
	Dependent variable: head count ratio (per cent)		
1	28.48 – 0.001 SDPA** + 0.03 FDPR – 2.91 PDSFP + 0.11 GINI	0.56	1.95
2	–49.34 – 0.01 SDPA** + 1.00 RELFDPR – 4.36 PDSFP + 0.13 GINI	0.57	2.09
3	–47.79 – 0.004 SDPA + 0.96 RELFDPR – 3.58 PDSFP + 0.46 GINI – 0.10 INFRADEV	0.62	1.92
	Dependent variable: poverty gap index		
4	–1.01 – 0.002 SDPA** + 0.01 FDPR – 1.97 PDSFP + 0.26 GINI	0.51	1.89
5	–32.62 – 0.002 SDPA** + 0.40 RELFDPR – 2.56 PDSFP + 0.27 GINI	0.52	2.04
6	–32.03 – 0.001 SDPA + 0.39 RELFDPR – 2.26 PDSFP + 0.39 GINI – 0.04 INFRADEV	0.58	1.79
	Dependent variable: squared poverty gap index		
7	–2.63 – 0.001 SDPA* + 0.005 FDPR – 1.04 PDSFP + 0.15 GINI	0.46	1.85
8	–17.99 – 0.001 SDPA** + 0.19 RELFDPR – 1.34 PDSFP + 0.16 GINI	0.49	2.00
9	–17.71 – 0.0004 SDPA + 0.18 RELFDPR – 1.19 PDSFP + 0.22 GINI – 0.02 INFRADEV	0.57	1.69
	1993–4		
	Dependent variable: head count ratio (per cent)		
10	–106.10 – 0.003 SDPA* + 1.54 RELFDPR – 3.69 PDSFP	0.46	2.38
11	–72.64 – 0.001 SDPA + 1.33 RELFDPR – 0.20 INFRADEV + 0.70 RPPAL	0.59	2.01
	Dependent variable: poverty gap index		
12	–33.57 – 0.001 SDPA** + 0.46 RELFDPR – 3.92 PDSFP	0.37	2.42
13	–30.21 – 0.001 SDPA** + 0.40 RELFDPR + 0.04 GINI	0.33	2.58
14	–23.43 – 0.0002 SDPA + 0.39 RELFDPR – 2.49 PDSFP – 0.05 INFRADEV + 0.17 RPPAL	0.47	2.18
	Dependent variable: squared poverty gap index		
15	–13.29 – 0.0003 SDPA*** + 0.17 RELFDPR – 1.93 PDSFP + 0.12 GINI	0.33	2.37
16	–16.16 – 0.00004 SDPA + 0.19 RELFDPR – 0.43 PDSFP + 0.14 GINI – 0.03 INFRADEV + 0.12 RPPAL	0.45	1.90

Notes: See Tables 1 and 3.

lished these variables as having a significant influence on the inter-state incidence of rural poverty in India (Ninan, 1994; 1995–6). The estimated equations are able to explain 33 to 62 per cent of the variations in the inter-state incidence of rural poverty.

ELASTICITIES OF RURAL POVERTY

The elasticities of rural poverty levels in India with respect to selected variables during the period under review show that a 1 per cent rise in the per capita real NDP from agriculture reduced rural poverty levels in India by over 1.4 per cent in terms of the HCR and still higher, by 2.5 to 3.4 per cent, in terms of the PGI and SPGI (Ninan, 2000). Similarly, a 1 per cent rise in the offtake of PDS foodgrains reduced rural poverty levels by 0.5 to 0.9 per cent across the three poverty indicators. A 1 per cent rise in the relative prices of food, however, led to a sharp rise in poverty levels, ranging from 5.3 to over 6.5 per cent across the three poverty indicators. The increase in poverty levels following a rise in relative food prices was sharper in the case of rural poverty as compared to urban poverty (ibid.). Similarly, an increase in the offtake of PDS foodgrains brought about a sharper reduction in rural poverty as compared with that in urban areas (ibid.).

The elasticities of inter-state incidence of rural poverty during 1987–8 (pre-reform) and 1993–4 (post-reform,) revealed that a 1 per cent rise in the per capita state domestic product (SDP) from agriculture and access to PDS reduced inter-state incidence by about 0.5 to 0.8 per cent and 0.03 to 0.3 per cent, respectively, during 1987–8 and 1993–4 across the three poverty indicators. The poverty-alleviating role of agricultural growth and access to PDS was sharper in terms of PGI and SPGI. A 1 per cent rise in relative food prices led to a more than proportionate rise in inter-state poverty incidence. But most interesting was that, while in 1987–8 this increase ranged between 1.04 to 1.4 per cent across the three poverty indicators, during 1993–4, after reform, this increase was sharper, ranging from over 2.6 to 3.2 per cent in terms of the three poverty indicators. The poverty-aggravating effect of a rise in relative food prices on rural poverty is more prominent in the post-reform period as compared with pre-reform years.

RESULTS OF STEPWISE REGRESSIONS

To find out the relative contribution of selected variables to variations in rural poverty levels in India during 1969–70 to 1993–4, stepwise regressions were computed. The R-squared values of these estimated equations, which shed light on the contribution of these variables to poverty, indicated that over 90 per cent of the variation in rural poverty levels in India was explained by NDPAGRI, RELFDPR and PDS (Ninan, 2000). The agricultural performance variable alone was able to explain about 79 to 86 per cent of the variation. The addition of a relative food price variable resulted in a 2 to 3 per cent improvement in the explanatory power of the estimated equations, while inclusion of the PDS variable further raised R-squared values by 5 to 9 per cent (ibid.).

The above, however, does not tell us what factors may have contributed to a worsening of poverty in India in the post-reform period. To investigate this, stepwise regressions were run to examine the contribution of selected variables to variations in the inter-state incidence of rural poverty. Although 1990–91, as the year on the eve of the reforms, would have been ideal to compare the situations, the poverty estimates for that year are based on a thin sample, unlike those for 1987–8 and 1993–4. The variables considered were SDPAGRI (per capita state domestic product from agriculture), RELFDPR (relative food price) and PDSFP (number of fair price shops per 100 000 population for state rural areas). The results indicated that, during 1987–8, 30 to 52 per cent of the variations in the inter-state incidence of rural poverty are accounted for by SDPAGRI alone (ibid.). These proportions were lower during 1993–4, ranging from 21 to 33 per cent. Most noteworthy, however, was that, when the RELFDPR variable was also included, the explanatory power of the estimated equations which recorded only a marginal improvement of 2 to 3 per cent during the pre-reform year, 1987–8, rose substantially, by 5 to 12 per cent, during the post-reform year, 1993–4. The role of food prices in affecting the inter-state incidence of rural poverty appears to be greater in the post-reform year as compared to the pre-reform year. The addition of PDSFP led to only a slight improvement in the R-squared values of the estimated equation for rural poverty in respect of two poverty indicators, HCR and PGI. But in respect of SPGI the value rose further, by 8 and 9 per cent, in 1987–8 and 1993–4, respectively (ibid.). While acknowledging a deterioration of rural poverty in India in the immediate year or two after the reforms, some have argued that a poor crop harvest was responsible for this. A close examination of the data, however, reveals that the per capita real NDP from agriculture during the post-reform period was conspicuously higher than during most years from 1969–70 to 1987–8 in the pre-reform period, as stated earlier (ibid.). Other factors may, therefore, account for the deterioration in rural poverty levels in the post-reform period.

RURAL POVERTY TRENDS UNDER WITH AND WITHOUT REFORM SCENARIOS

A general criticism of most studies that have assessed the social implications of such reforms in India, and elsewhere, is that they fail to provide a counter-factual analysis. In other words, what would the trends in poverty have been in the absence of the reforms? However, data inadequacies preclude us from attempting such a rigorous analysis except in the cases of Punjab and Haryana, under a with and without reform scenario. Using the model spelt out earlier, it was noted that, while rural poverty trends in both states recorded significant declines across the three poverty indicators in the pre-reform period, during the post-reform period these trends reported a reversal, though not to a statistically significant extent (Table 5). In the alternative case, under a without reform

TABLE 5   *Rural poverty trends in Haryana and Punjab under with and without reform scenarios during 1969–70 to 1993–4*

| State and poverty indicators | With reform scenario | | Without reform scenario |
	Pre-reform period	Post-reform period	Overall period
Haryana			
Head count ratio	−0.76*	+10.90	−0.55*
Poverty gap index	−0.24*	+2.16	−0.18*
Squared poverty gap index	−0.10*	+0.85	−0.07*
Punjab			
Head count ratio	−0.70*	+1.87	−0.62*
Poverty gap index	−0.24*	+0.79	−0.22*
Squared poverty gap index	−0.10*	+0.29	−0.09*

Notes: 1. Pre- and post-reform periods, 1969–70 to 1990–91 and 1991–2 to 1993–4, respectively; overall period, 1969–70 to 1993–4.
2. Trends computed here are linear trends.
3. * Statistically significant at 1 per cent level of significance.
4. In the equations for the with reform scenario, trends have been computed using the model explained in the text wherein a dummy variable is included to account for the pre- and post-reform period as indicated in the text. In the without reform scenario, trends have been computed for the period from 1969–70 to 1993–4, omitting the dummy variable; in other word, the trends are computed assuming a without reform scenario. Under this alternative case we have only one equation for the whole period.

scenario, trends have been fitted by omitting the dummy variable for the period 1969–70 to 1993–4. As is evident, under that scenario, rural poverty trends recorded a significant decline in terms of all three poverty indicators. Thus, as stated earlier, rural poverty in Punjab and Haryana seems to have been aggravated in the post-reform period.

CONCLUSIONS

Evidence presented here suggests that, while rural, urban and overall national poverty levels in India recorded a significant decline during the pre-reform period from 1969–70 to 1990–91, during the post-reform period from 1991–2 to 1993–4 these negative trends have weakened or even become reversed in terms of one or more of the three poverty indicators. While rural poverty levels in terms of HCR continued to record negative trends in the post-reform period, in terms of PGI and SPGI a reversal is reported, with the trends changing from negative to positive, although these are not statistically significant. Across states there is a diversity of trends and patterns. While during the pre-reform period all the 15 states recorded significant reductions in rural poverty levels in terms of all the three poverty indicators, during the post-reform period the scenario has changed. Only Gujarat and Karnataka continued to record significant declines in rural poverty – indeed, at a faster rate. Four states reported a reversal of fortunes with the negative trends turning positive during the post-reform period in terms of one or more poverty indicators. These include Orissa and West Bengal (in SPGI only) which fall within the eastern belt of the country known for its endemic poverty. But most surprising is that Punjab and Haryana, the two states which ushered in the green revolution in India and where rural poverty levels had recorded significant reductions earlier, have reported a reversal of fortunes.

The study also confirmed the strong negative association between agricultural growth, access to PDS and rural poverty levels in India, whereas relative food prices and inequality in rural consumption were positively associated with rural poverty levels. These were valid for all three poverty indicators. The infrastructure development index was negatively associated with the inter-state incidence of rural poverty in India, whereas rural population pressure on agricultural lands was positively associated.

The increase in poverty levels following a rise in food prices is sharper in the case of rural poverty, while the poverty-aggravating effect appears to be greater during the post-reform period. Whether the reforms per se are to be blamed for this, as opposed to the choice of inappropriate policies during the reform period (for example, the government's policy in effecting sharp hikes in procurement prices, and issue prices of PDS foodgrains) is a matter to be debated.

There is no doubt that rapid economic growth is essential for bringing about a significant reduction in poverty levels in India. But it is not only growth per se but also the pattern of growth that matters. Policies to promote agricultural growth, improve access to the PDS and infrastructure development, along with measures to control inflation, population growth and reducing inequalities, hold the key to making a dent in poverty in India and need to be taken note of in implementing reforms.

BIBLIOGRAPHY

Ahluwalia, M.S. (1978), 'Rural Poverty and Agricultural Performance in India', *Journal of Development Studies*, **14**, 298–323.

Ahluwalia, M.S. (1985), 'Rural Poverty, Agricultural Production and Prices: A Re-Examination', in J.W. Mellor and G.M. Desai (eds), *Agricultural Growth and Rural Poverty – Variations on a Theme by Dharm Narian*, Baltimore, MD: Johns Hopkins University Press.

Dantwala, M.L. (1985), 'Technology, Growth and Equity in Agriculture', in J.W. Mellor and G.M. Desai (eds), *Agricultural Growth and Rural Poverty – Variations on a Theme by Dharm Narian*, Baltimore, MD: Johns Hopkins University Press.

Datt, G. (1997), 'Poverty in India 1951–1994 – Trends and Decomposition', IFPRI, Washington, DC (mimeo).

Datt, G. and Ravallion, M. (1997), 'Macroeconomic Crisis and Poverty Monitoring: A Case Study for India', *Review of Development Economics*, **1**, 135–52.

Datt, G. and Ravallion, M. (1998), 'Farm Productivity and Rural Poverty in India', *Journal of Development Studies*, **34**, 62–85.

Griffin, K.B. and Ghose, A.K. (1979), 'Growth and Impoverishment in the Rural Areas of Asia', *World Development*, **7**, 361–83.

Gupta, S.P. (1992), 'Economic Reform and Its Impact on the Poor', *Economic and Political Weekly*, **30**, 1295–313.

Gupta, S.P. (1996), 'Recent Economic Reforms in India and Their Impact on the Poor and Vulnerable Sections of Society', in C.H.H. Rao and H. Linnemann (eds), *Economic Reforms and Poverty Alleviation in India*, Indo-Dutch Studies in Development Alternatives Series no 17, New Delhi: Sage.

Lipton, M. and Ravallion, M. (1995), 'Poverty and Policy', in J. Behrman and T.N. Srinivasan (eds), *Handbook of Development Economics*, vol. III, Amsterdam: Elsevier.

Mellor, J.W. and Desai, G.M. (eds) (1985), *Agricultural Growth and Rural Poverty – Variations on a Theme by Dharm Narian*, Baltimore, MD: Johns Hopkins University Press.

Ninan, K.N. (1994), 'Poverty and Income Distribution in India', *Economic and Political Weekly*, **24**, 1544–51.

Ninan, K.N. (1995–6), 'Agricultural Growth, Institutional Intervention and Rural Poverty Trends – Their Linkages in the Context of Structural Adjustment and Economic Liberalisation in India', *Regional Development Studies*, Winter, vol. II, United Nations Centre for Regional Development, Nagoya, Japan.

Ninan, K.N. (2000), *Economic Reforms in India – Impact on the Poor and Poverty Reduction*, IDS Working Paper no. 102, Brighton: Institute of Development Studies.

Ozler, B., Datt, G. and Ravallion, M. (1996), *A Data Base on Poverty and Growth in India*, Washington, DC: World Bank, Policy Research Department.

Rajaraman, I. (1975), 'Poverty, Inequality and Economic Growth: Rural Punjab – 1960–61 to 1970–71', *Journal of Development Studies*, **11**, 278–90.

Ravallion, M. and Datt, G. (1996a), *India's Chequered History in the Fight Against Poverty: Are There Lessons for the Future?*, Washington, DC: World Bank, Policy Research Department.

Ravallion, M. and Datt, G. (1996b), *Growth, Wages and Poverty – Time Series Evidence for Rural India*, Washington, DC: World Bank, Policy Research Department.

Sen, A. (1981), *Poverty and Famines: An Essay on Entitlements and Deprivation*, New Delhi: Oxford University Press.

Tendulkar, S.D. and Jain, L.R. (1995), 'Economic Reforms and Poverty', *Economic and Political Weekly*, **30**, 1373–8.

World Bank (1997), *India: Achievements and Challenges in Reducing Poverty*, report no. 16483-IN, Washington, DC: World Bank.

STEVEN FRANZEL*

Use of an Indigenous Board Game, 'Bao', for Assessing Farmers' Preferences among Alternative Agricultural Technologies

INTRODUCTION

Researchers in the tropics are increasingly recognizing the farmer as a partner, not just a client or a customer, in developing new agricultural technologies. The farming systems approach in the 1980s helped researchers to focus on smallholder farmers' needs and circumstances (Byerlee and Collinson, 1980; Caldwell, 1987). In the 1990s, the participatory research paradigm has helped scientists to understand how farmers experiment on their own and to seek partnerships with them in developing technology (Chambers *et al.*, 1989).

But a major weakness of participatory research is that few practical tools exist that both scientists and farmers can use together for diagnosing problems and developing new technologies (Okali *et al.*, 1994). In fact, economists often view participatory research approaches, such as informal surveys, as inimical to quantitative data analysis. On the other hand, participatory researchers often view accepted scientific research tools, such as trial replication or question-naire surveys, as incompatible with farmers' investigative processes. Conflicts are apparent in the way the two sides examine farmers' evaluations of technol-ogy. Participatory researchers view questionnaires that ask farmers to rate alternative technologies across selected criteria as 'top-down', Western cul-tural constructs that are not translatable to rural, third-world situations. In contrast, scientists view participatory approaches as subjective, lacking in detail, and, being qualitative, incapable of being subjected to tests of statistical significance. In fact, economists tend to shy away from investigating farmers' evaluations of technology altogether, preferring to calculate financial and eco-nomic returns or assess factors that influence adoption. The neglect of farmer evaluations is indeed misplaced, as knowledge of values, non-monetary as well as monetary, is a key element of agricultural economics research (Johnson, 1986).

The objective of this paper is to present a method for obtaining data on farmers' preferences that is of use and is user-friendly to both farmers and researchers. The method involves the use of 'bao', a traditional board game found throughout Africa, Indonesia and the Caribbean. The method permits the collection of quantitative data in a manner that allows the farmer to participate

*International Centre for Research in Agro-forestry (ICRAF), Nairobi, Kenya.

actively and benefit. First the method is described. Second, three case studies, two from Kenya and one from Burundi, are presented in which farmers use bao to evaluate technologies. Finally, bao's advantages and disadvantages for evaluating technology are compared with conventional scoring exercises using questionnaires and with a common participatory research tool, matrix ranking.

TOOLS FOR OBTAINING FARMERS' EVALUATIONS

In developed countries, tools for obtaining quantitative data on consumer evaluations are common and often involve asking respondents to score from poor to excellent, or 1 to 10, across selected criteria. A few examples exist in the literature of researchers in the tropics using such methods to ask farmers to rate or rank technologies (Franzel, 1983; Negassa *et al.*, 1991; Polson and Spencer, 1991). Even though they generate quantitative data, these methods are generally unsatisfactory, for three reasons. First, asking farmers to rate alternatives on a 1 to x basis (1 being a poor grade and x being an excellent grade) was generally problematic, because such verbal scoring exercises were not easily understood by farmers. Second, where terms such as 'excellent', 'good', 'fair' and 'poor' were substituted for numerical scores, farmers were better able to understand the scoring process. However, there were often considerable problems translating such terms into other languages and the data obtained could only be considered as ordinal, rather than interval, data (Clark and Schkade, 1974). Third, because the farmers' involvement was passive, that is, they merely answered questions, they quickly became bored with the process.

Participatory researchers, on the other hand, use visual, rather than verbal or written, tools for obtaining farmers' evaluation. These methods are more suited to farmers' conditions. For example, in matrix ranking, farmers draw a matrix on the ground and place alternative technologies (for example, crop varieties) along the left-hand side of each row, and symbols to denote criteria (for example, taste or drought resistance) across the top of each column. Farmers then rank the technologies on each criterion, using one stone to designate first place, two for second place, and so on (Ashby, 1990). Farmers control the ranking process and, along with researchers, observe the results of their ratings. In a review of 15 articles on preference ranking, Maxwell and Bart (1995) found three examples in which researchers used the tool to score rather than rank alternatives. However, none of the articles tabulated data from a sample of farmers and used statistical methods to describe the results. In fact, participatory research emphasizes working with groups of farmers and achieving consensus rather than collecting data from individual farmers.

THE BAO GAME

Bao players move seeds among carved-out pockets of the board, which are laid out in a matrix. The numbers of rows and columns vary, depending on the area. To use the game in evaluating different technological alternatives, such as tree species or crop varieties, researchers and farmers first need to find out the criteria farmers use in assessing alternatives. This is best done by touring the farm, viewing the different alternatives in question (for example, tree species) and discussing their performance, uses, advantages and disadvantages. During the discussions, researchers note the different criteria that farmers use in evaluating and comparing the species. For example, farmers may compare tree properties in relation to different end uses (straightness for timber or heat production for fuelwood) or different growth characteristics (speed of growth, compatibility with crops, or resistance to pests). Next, researchers and farmers find a comfortable place and, in the case of trees, put a twig of each important tree species next to each row of the game. Then, for each criterion the farmer mentioned during the tour, he or she rates each species from one seed to a pocket (performing poorly) to five seeds (performing well). Farmers are asked to add further criteria if they wish and researchers may also suggest criteria. The exercise often ends with farmers being asked to give overall scores for the species, taking into account all of the criteria. Scores are preferable to ranks because they provide interval data, whereas ranks give only ordinal data. Since 1992, ICRAF staff and partners have used the bao game to assess farmers' preferences among tree species in 13 exercises in six countries. Franzel (2000) provides detailed guidelines on how the game is used to obtain evaluations.

CASE STUDIES OF THE BAO GAME

In the three case studies presented here, farmers used the bao game to score alternative tree species and benefits obtained from using a new practice. In the first example, a sample of 25 farmers in central Burundi who expressed interest in trees at farmer meetings used the bao game to evaluate the different tree species on their farms (Franzel *et al.*, 1995). The objective of the exercise was to involve farmers in species selection; by finding out the criteria they used in evaluating trees and how trees they knew performed on the criteria, researchers could identify trees for testing that could meet farmers' needs and circumstances. In the second case study, 37 members of farmers' groups in western Kenya who were testing newly introduced tree species in an on-farm experiment used the bao game to score the species across criteria important to them (Franzel *et al.*, 1999). The objective was to find out which of the trees in the trial they wished to plant, and their reasons. In the third study, 67 farmers planting improved tree fallows (the planting of fast-growing trees and shrubs on fallow land to improve soil fertility) in western Kenya were asked to score the different types of benefits they obtained from the practice (Pisanelli *et al.*, 2000). The percentage of female farmers was 32 per cent in the Burundi sample, 51 per cent in the sample of farmers in western Kenya testing new trees, and 74 per cent for the improved fallow users.

In the Burundi case study, farmers rated eight wood-producing trees across seven criteria focusing on management, growth and uses for timber and firewood (Table 1). Overall, there were intriguing discrepancies between farmers' ratings and the prevalence of different tree species on farms. *Eucalyptus* and

TABLE 1   *Farmers' mean ratings, using the bao game, of selected tree species that grow on their farms, central Burundi*

Species	Management & growth			Use for timber		Use for firewood	
	Compatibility with crops	Speed of growth	Resistance to insects	Wood appearance	Straightness	Quick in drying	Durability of fire
Maesopsis eminii	3.8 (0.5)	4.7 (0.4)	4.2 (1.0)	4.8 (0.4)	4.2 (0.6)	3.1 (0.8)	3.5 (0.9)
Cedrela serrata	4.6 (0.5)	4.3 (0.7)	4.5 (0.8)	5.0 (0)	5.0 (0)	—	—
Grevillea robusta	4.9 (0.3)	4.6 (0.5)	2.5 (0.7)	2.6 (0.9)	4.1 (0.8)	3.2 (1.0)	2.8 (1.2)
Casuarina cunning hamiana	1.0 (0.0)	2.2 (0.8)	4.2 (1.0)	4.1 (1.1)	3.9 (0.9)	3.0 (0.6)	3.8 (0.7)
Markhamia lutea	3.7 (1.0)	1.9 (0.9)	4.5 (0.8)	4.3 (0.6)	1.8 (0.8)	2.3 (1.1)	4.2 (0.7)
Eucalyptus spp.	1.1 (0.3)	4.3 (0.8)	4.0 (1.2)	2.5 (0.5)	3.6 (1.0)	4.7 (0.5)	5.0 (0.0)
Cupressus lusitanica	1.0 (0.0)	3.2 (0.8)	4.5 (0.8)	4.6 (0.5)	3.9 (0.8)	4.6 (0.5)	3.5 (1.0)
Albizia chinensis	4.0 (1.2)	3.5 (1.3)	1.3 (0.7)	—	1.3 (0.4)	2.3 (0.8)	3.3 (0.7)

Notes: Twenty-five persons were interviewed; the number rating a specific species on a particular criterion varies from five to 20. The rating of 1 to 5 refers to the score in number of seeds the farmers gave to a species on a particular criteria. A rating of 5 was considered excellent, a rating of 1, poor (mean rating and standard deviation in parentheses). For some species certain criteria are irrelevant; for example, *C. serrata* is never used for firewood and *A. chinesis* is never used for timber.

Source: Franzel *et al.* (1995).

419

Grevillea robusta were the most common species found on farms and they were highly rated by farmers: *eucalyptus* for fast growth and firewood and *grevillea* for fast growth and compatibility with crops. But two other species, *Maesopsis eminii* and *Cedrela serrata*, were also highly rated but were not commonly grown. They were relatively new in the area and lack of information and planting material were the biggest constraints to their adoption. On-farm trials testing these species will help confirm their usefulness to farmers and should promote their diffusion.

The game was also useful in revealing other criteria that farmers use for rating trees. For example, males and females appeared to have similar interests in the various species, with one important exception. Women rated *Markhamia lutea* much more highly than men, because they use its leaves for preparing a medicine to treat diarrhoea in children.

In the case of new tree species in western Kenya, farmers rated five trees across six criteria including growth characteristics and use for fodder and firewood (Table 2). Standard deviations were highest for farmers' ratings in relation to compatibility with crops, reflecting farmers' uncertainty about how trees performed. Farmers were also asked to use the game to indicate which trees in the experiment they wished to plant on their farms. The influence of selected farm and household characteristics on farmers' ratings of their interest in planting different species was assessed using a linear logistic model for ordered category response data (Collett, 1991). The variables considered included wealth level, farm size, off-farm income, ethnic group, age, gender, district and livestock ownership. Only 'district' emerged as a significant variable, reflecting differences in biophysical circumstances, such as soil type, which affected tree growth. The small number of farmers who could be monitored in this experiment, 37, limited the degree to which factors affecting adoption potential could be rigorously examined.

As in the Burundi case, researchers learned about new criteria that farmers used in evaluating species. *Casuarina junghuhniana* was introduced into the trial as a wood species but grew poorly. Nevertheless, farmers rated it second on preference for planting because they appreciated it as an ornamental.

In the third case study, farmers' scores reflecting the importance of benefits that they obtained from improved fallows in western Kenya indicated that improved soils and crop yields were the most important. Improved soils and crop yields received mean ratings of 4.5 (SD = 0.78) and 4.4 (SD = 0.82) out of 5, respectively (Table 3). Fuelwood received a mean rating of 3.9 (SD = 1.19) and reduced weeds (mainly *Striga hermonthica*), 3.6 (SD = 1.26). These benefits were each mentioned by over 90 per cent of the farmers; other benefits, mentioned by fewer than half, included seed production and pest reduction. Females rated improved fallows significantly higher than males on improving soils (p = 0.04) and on reducing weeds (p = 0.06). Women's higher scores reflect the finding of Ohlsson *et al.* (1998) that women spend much more time in cropping activities than men and are thus more able to ascertain and appreciate the effects of improved fallows on soils and weeds. The higher standard deviations of men's estimates suggest that they have less knowledge about the fallows and are more uncertain about their performance.

TABLE 2 *Farmers' mean ratings of species in an on-farm trial using the 'bao' game, 30 months after planting, western Kenya*

Species	Growth	Biomass production	Compatibility with crops	Fodder	Firewood	% farmers preferring for future planting
Grevillea robusta	4.4 (0.9)	—	4.0 (1.3)	—	4.1 (1.0)	73
Casuarina junghuhniana	3.2 (1.1)	—	4.5 (0.7)	—	—	46
Leucaena leucocephala	—	3.4 (0.8)	3.8 (1.8)	4.0 (1.4)	3.8 (1.0)	29
Leucaena diversifolia	—	3.7 (0.9)	3.6 (1.6)	3.4 (1.5)	3.8 (0.7)	24
Calliandra calothyrsus	—	4.9 (0.2)	3.3 (1.8)	4.1 (1.3)	4.1 (1.1)	41
Eucalyptus spp.	4.3 (1.0)	—	1.4 (0.9)	—	3.6 (1.2)	27

Notes: Data from 37 farmers. The rating of 1 to 5 refers to the score in number of seeds the farmers gave to a tree on a particular criterion. A rating of 5 was excellent, a rating of 1, poor (mean rating and standard deviation in parenthesis).

TABLE 3 *Farmers' mean scores on the importance of different benefits of improved fallows using the bao game, western Kenya*

Benefit	Overall score		Males		Females		Difference in means (females–males)	Standard error of the differences	Significance of difference (p-value)	95% confidence interval for the difference
	No. of Farmers	Mean score	No. of farmers	Mean score	No. of farmers	Mean score				
Improved crop yields	63	4.4 (0.82)	16	4.2 (0.98)	45	4.5 (0.73)	0.3	0.23	0.169	(−0.14; 0.78)
Improved soils	63	4.5 (0.78)	17	4.1 (0.99)	45	4.6 (0.66)	0.5	0.22	0.037	(0.02; 0.90)
Reduced weeds	62	3.6 (1.26)	16	3.1 (1.29)	44	3.7 (1.20)	0.7	0.36	0.059	(−0.03; 1.14)
Fuelwood production	67	3.9 (1.19)	17	3.6 (1.23)	48	3.9 (1.18)	0.3	0.34	0.333	(−0.35; 1.01)
Seed production	31	3.7 (1.05)	13	4.0 (0.86)	17	3.4 (1.12)	−0.5	0.37	0.183	(−1.27; 0.25)
Pest reduction	10	3.3 (1.25)	4	3.8 (1.50)	6	3.0 (1.10)	−0.7	0.82	0.384	(−2.64; 1.14)

Notes: Sixty-seven farmers were involved in the evaluation. 'No. of farmers' refers to numbers mentioning a particular benefit. Numbers of males and females do not sum to totals because, in some cases, males and females preferred to score benefits together. Standard deviations in parentheses.

CONCLUSIONS

The bao game combines the strengths of conventional tools for scoring, such as questionnaires, with those of participatory research techniques, such as matrix ranking. Like questionnaires in consumer evaluations, the bao game is useful for generating quantitative data useful for testing hypotheses and statistical analysis. At the same time, bao is a participatory tool that the farmer finds engaging. Moreover, because farmers control the scoring process, they take the exercise more seriously than in responding to questionnaires. Finally, because the bao game is a visual tool, respondents can check their data and members of a group can discuss differences in scores among themselves. Obtaining farmers' evaluations of agricultural technology is a neglected subject among agricultural economists in developing countries. The bao game can be used for conducting such evaluations in an accurate, entertaining, yet statistically rigorous manner.

REFERENCES

Ashby, J.A. (1990), *Evaluating technology with farmers: A handbook*, publication no. 187, Cali, Columbia: International Centre for Tropical Agriculture (CIAT).

Byerlee, D. and Collinson, M. (1980), *Planning technologies appropriate to farmers*, Mexico, DF: CIMMYT.

Caldwell, J.S. (1987), 'An overview of farming systems research and development', in J.P. Gittinger, J. Leslie and C. Hoisington (eds), *Food policy: Integrating supply, distribution, and consumption*, Baltimore, MD: Johns Hopkins University Press.

Chambers, R., Pacey, A. and Thrupp, L.A. (1989), *Farmer first: farmer innovation and agricultural research*, London: Intermediate Technology Publications.

Clark, C.T. and Schkade, L.L. (1974), *Statistical analysis for administrative decisions*, Cincinnatti, OH: Southwestern Publ. Co.

Collett, D. (1991), *Modelling binary data*, London: Chapman & Hall.

Franzel, S. (1983), 'Planning an Adaptive Production Research Program for Small Farmers: A Case Study of Farming Systems Research in Kirinyaga District, Kenya', unpublished PhD thesis, Department of Agricultural Economics, Michigan State University, East Lansing, MI.

Franzel, S. (2000), *Use of an indigenous board game, 'bao', for assessing farmers' preferences among alternative agroforestry technologies*, working paper, Nairobi: International Centre for Research in Agro-forestry (ICRAF).

Franzel, S., Hitimana, L. and Akyeampong, E. (1995), 'Farmer participation in on-station tree species selection for agroforestry: a case study from Burundi', *Experimental Agriculture*, **31**, 27–38.

Franzel, S., Ndufa, J.K. and Obonyo, C. (1999), *Farmer-designed agroforestry tree trials: Farmers' experiences with newly introduced tree species in Western Kenya*, Nairobi: AFRENA Report 131, ICRAF.

Johnson, G.L. (1986), *Research methodology for economists: Philosophy and practice*, New York: Macmillan.

Maxwell, S. and Bart, C. (1995), *Beyond ranking: Exploring relative preferences in P/RRA*, PLA Notes no. 22, London: International Institute for Environment and Development.

Negassa, A., Tolessa, B., Franzel, S., Gedeno, G. and Dadi, L. (1991), 'The introduction of an early maturing maize variety to a mid-altitude farming system in Ethiopia', *Experimental Agriculture*, **27**, 375–83.

Ohlsson, E., Shepherd, K.O. and David, S. (1998), *A study of farmers' soil fertility management practices on small-scale mixed farms in western Kenya*, Interna Publikationer 25, Sveriges Lantbruks Universitet, Uppsala, Sweden.

Okali, C., Sumberg, J. and Farrington, J. (1994), *Farmer Participatory Research: Rhetoric and reality*, London: Intermediate Technology.

Pisanelli, A., Franzel, S., DeWolf, J., Rommelse, R. and Poole, J. (2000), *The adoption of improved tree fallows in western Kenya: farmer practices, knowledge, and perception*, Nairobi: ICRAF.

Polson, R.A. and Spencer, D.S.C. (1991), 'The technology adoption process in subsistence agriculture: the case of cassava in Southwestern Nigeria', *Agricultural Systems*, **36**, 65–78.

ELLEN HANAK FREUD*

Making Better Sense of the Numbers on Developing Country Agriculture

INTRODUCTION

The dilemma facing analysts of agricultural sectors in developing countries is time-worn and seemingly intractable. To inform policy choices and orient agricultural research, one needs to be able to follow trends on strategic variables: output, land use, on-farm and post-harvest productivity, internal and external trade, consumption. Yet getting accurate read-outs of the basic numbers is fraught with difficulties. The official aggregate series, such as those furnished by ministries of agriculture and the FAO, are often unreliable; statistical services frequently lack the resources to do proper surveys and the data are sometimes subject to revision by the authorities for non-technical reasons. Independent surveys tend to be too limited in sample size, geographical coverage and frequency to serve as an adequate substitute.

Analysts tend to cope with the problem in one of two ways: either by using the official series 'for want of something better', or else by extrapolating, at least implicitly, from survey data or more qualitative field observations. Studies rarely go back and forth between survey and aggregate data, and they rarely make use of alternative indicators. As a result, contradictions and inconsistencies among the sources go unnoticed and unassessed. Each study tells a part of the story, but there is no sense of collective responsibility for getting the whole story straight.

This paper argues that we can do much better, as a profession, in making sense of the numbers, if we develop the reflex to navigate across data sources rather than staying boxed into a particular approach at a particular level of analysis. This means applying some simple principles of circumspection and cross-checking to the data we do have, on the one hand, and making a judicious use of surveys to fill in knowledge gaps, on the other.

Following a presentation of these data handling principles, the paper illustrates their application with an example from the groundnut subsector in Senegal. The conclusion discusses possible ways of improving data analysis capacity.

*Ellen Hanak Freud, CIRAD, Nogent s/Marne, France. The author thanks David Rohrbach and John Sanders for helpful comments on an earlier version.

PRINCIPLES OF ECLECTIC DATA HANDLING

Two principles need to guide data handling methods. First, the inherent quality of data is variable and needs to be assessed. Second, doubtful numbers need to be subjected to a rigorous cross-examination. The following checklist enumerates some simple methods for applying these principles.

How reliable are official data series?

At the minimum, annual series are available for crop area, yield and output, and for imports and exports. For agro-industries, other series like factory purchases and sales will also exist. These data are not equally accurate. Is the series an estimate or an accounting value? If it is an estimate, how good was the collection method? If accounting values were used, were there strong incentives to over-report or under-report?

Generally, the greatest level of uncertainty surrounds output estimates for crops consumed on the farm or sold through the informal sector, and yield estimates for smallholder crops. Food consumption and land-use data derived from these numbers are just as questionable. Trade data are usually more reliable, unless there are reporting biases or large quantities of unofficial trade. So are factory data for industrial crops, agricultural inputs and industrially processed foods. Output series for industrial crops are, as a consequence, reasonably accurate. Series on the apparent consumption of imported foodstuffs are more reliable than those for locally produced foods. Yield data will tend to be more accurate for estate crops, which can be obtained with a minimal amount of survey work, and for crops managed by project authorities if they have their own survey teams.

Having access to at least some reliable series concerning the problem to be analysed is invaluable for cross-checking the accuracy of more doubtful numbers.

What are the limits of occasional survey data?

For certain variables, statistical services only collect data at much longer intervals. These may include food intake, agricultural revenues, input use or stocks. Independent surveys are crucial tools for filling in knowledge gaps on these variables and on the annual series. Yet these types of surveys have their own problems. Cost considerations tend to severely restrict either sample sizes or the precision of the data-gathering methods, and frequently both. The resulting limits of the data need to be made explicit to avoid misinterpretation and extrapolation errors.

How accurate are the data-gathering methods? In most cases, surveys rely on respondent recall, which leaves more or less room for error, depending on the nature of the question. For example, consumption today is easier to recall than that of several years ago, farming practices are remembered better than labour requirements, output of crops sold can be checked, unlike amounts kept for home consumption. What are the likely biases in the responses caused by the tendency to forget small transactions or to overstate consumption of certain items? Are there characteristics of the survey which could introduce biases, for instance strong seasonal effects or an unusual year? Is the sample size adequate to permit direct extrapolation?

Do alternative sources and indicators tell the same story?

It is almost always possible to find different types of data for the same phenomenon. If the story told by independent sources and methods is consistent, it is easier to place confidence in the numbers, especially if one of the sources is a relatively reliable aggregate series.

The most direct type of cross-checking is among different sources for the same variables, for instance independent field surveys and aggregate series on yields or output per farm household. Sometimes it is also possible to compare different types of indicators; for example, do household consumption data coincide with data on sales by the food industry? An extremely useful virtual indicator is obtained by putting the data into a less abstract form, to assess more directly whether the numbers make sense. For instance, translate the consumption data from per capita annual values into the number of weekly meals it implies, using local recipes and serving portions. Or calculate how many truckloads would be needed to move an estimated amount of informal trade. This type of 'reality check' helps reject estimates that are way off the mark.

Comparisons are often complicated by the use of different units of measurement: are the data expressed in net or gross yields, before or after processing? What are the loss rates or conversion rates used? Consistency checks obviously need to use a common base, and it sometimes takes digging to find out what the units are.

When there is inconsistency between uncertain aggregate data and independent survey results, the temptation may be to accept the latter as more reliable. One must first establish that the discrepancy does not stem from a sampling bias, especially given the small sample sizes of most surveys. Cross-checking can be a useful tool for verifying whether a sample is representative, especially when reliable aggregate series correspond to some of the survey questions.

Do the numbers add up?

Some fundamental relationships must hold among the basic aggregates of the agricultural economy. Production by definition equals the sum of its uses: local consumption, net exports and net stocks. The sum of area cultivated to different crops and fallows must equal the quantity of available agricultural land. Yields are generally a positive function of agricultural inputs and improved management practices. Consistency is not reassuring if some of the variables under consideration have been derived from these relationships. But it becomes a powerful analytical device when alternative sources can be exploited, particularly if some are known to be reliable.

AN APPLICATION TO THE SENEGALESE GROUNDNUT SECTOR

Groundnuts were the motor of the Senegalese economy throughout the colonial period and well into the 1970s, accounting for large shares of export earnings, rural employment and industrial output. Since the 1970s, their contribution to the formal sector has diminished radically, as sales to the oil industry have plummeted. The more modest decline in the official output series implies that the major change is the growth of an informal market for groundnut products (Figure 1). This widely held interpretation was bolstered by the fact that the parallel market became legal in the late 1980s, as a part of the liberalization programme begun earlier in the decade with the end of input credit programmes and cuts in seed distribution (Gaye, 1997).

Wishing to revive the subsector, the government and a major donor agency commissioned a study to verify the nature of the problem (CIRAD, 1997). By exploiting some basic accounting relationships in the oilseeds sector and a range of alternative data sources, including a light survey of groundnut farmers, the team was able, not only to raise doubts about the size of the parallel market, but to estimate its trajectory over the past 30 years. It also revised the series on production, re-estimated groundnut area and yields and, by extension, raised questions about the official trends in output of pearl millet, the other major crop in the farming system.

The principal accounting equation used was the requirement that output equal the sum of end-uses:

$$Q_G = S_R + S_{FS} + U_{FS} + U_{IS} + ST \tag{1}$$

where Q_G is groundnut output, S_R is farmer-held seed for the next season, S_{FS} is groundnut purchases by the oil industry for distribution as seed the next season, U_{FS} is groundnut purchases by the oil industry for processing, U_{IS} is

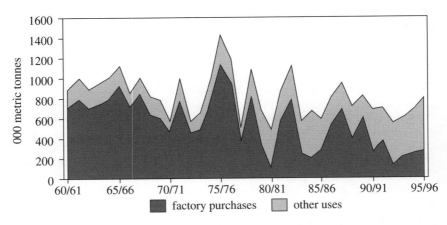

FIGURE 1   *Groundnut output estimates and factory purchases in Senegal*

groundnuts passing through the informal sector (market plus home consumption), and ST is farmer-held stocks other than seed, assumed negligible.

Both U_{FS} and S_{FS} are known values. A first approximation of S_R was made by assessing the additional quantities needed to cover the estimated area planted in year $t + 1$, using the coefficient given by the extension service (120kg/ha.). U_{IS}, the residual value on the right-hand side of equation (1), is hence the official estimate of informal uses. This level leapt from 100 000 tonnes in the 1970s to over 300 000 tonnes in the early 1990s.

To determine whether this amount was reasonable, it was then necessary to get a reading on the three components of U_{IS}:

$$U_{IS} = O_A / 0.28 + C_G / 0.7 + X_{IS} \qquad (2)$$

where O_A is artisanal groundnut oil, C_G is groundnut for human consumption (in whole nut or paste form), X_{IS} is net informal groundnut exports to neighbouring countries, and the denominators indicate average conversion ratios to unshelled groundnut.

Although there was much talk of informal exports in Senegal, oil industry surveys of informal trade and customs data on edible oil imports of neighbouring countries made it possible to estimate actual flows of X_{IS} at only 5000 tonnes per year, the level of sales to Mauritania. So the explanation for the growth in U_{IS} had to be an increase in local consumption. For groundnut consumed in whole or paste form, the informal market and farmer reserves are the only sources, so total consumption corresponds to C_G in equation (2). But for edible oils (C_O), other sources exist besides O_A, particularly sales of refined vegetable oil by the oil industry (O_{FS}):

$$C_O = O_{FS} + O_A \qquad (3)$$

Since O_{FS} is a known value, O_A can be calculated as a residual of equation (3) once one obtains a good estimate of total oil consumption.

The consumption estimates were based on two surveys. The first, by a nutrition research institute, measured household intake over a five-day period in a number of regions in the late 1970s and early 1990s. The second, by the study team, was based on rural household recall of oil use patterns at different points in the 1995/96 agricultural year and calculations of groundnut quantities remaining for home consumption after sales and seed use. The results of these studies converged. To obtain the final estimates, the data were also subjected to a 'reality check' in terms of numbers of typical oil and groundnut-based meals that they permitted consumers to eat each week. These estimates generously allowed for a per capita consumption of oil and oil equivalents of 16kg per year, a third higher than levels in neighbouring countries. It is worth noting that a third source, a household expenditure survey done for the World Bank in 1994, had to be rejected, because its estimates of spending on edible oils came out lower than industry sales of refined oil.

Even so, the resulting estimates of C_O and C_G suggest that there has not been a substantial growth in the local market for either groundnuts or artisanal

TABLE 1   *Area, output and yield estimates for groundnuts in Senegal*

	1960–69	1970–79	1980–89	1990–95
Official area (ha.)	1 087 000	1 111 000	1 033 000	875 000
Official output (t.)	932 000	862 000	761 000	667 000
Official yields (kg/ha.)	858	776	736	762
Revised output (t.)	932 000	837 000	652 000	464 000
Implied yields* (kg/ha.)	858	754	630	530

Note: *Calculated with revised output and official area.

groundnut oil. Although consumption has increased with population growth, so too have sales of (mainly imported) refined edible oil. The estimated value of U_{IS} comes out at only 120 000 tonnes in the early 1990s. By extension, this means that total output has been in the range of 450 000 to 500 000 tonnes, some 40 per cent below the official estimates (Table 1).

This revision also implied problems in the two components used to construct the official output estimate, area and yields. Recent official yields were of the order of 800kg/ha. – as high as 940kg/ha. in 1995/96 – as much or more than average levels of the 1970s. There were good reasons to believe that yields had fallen over this period. Although climatic conditions had not further deteriorated, demographic trends implied a decline in fallows. Fertilizer use on groundnuts (available from the input industry) had almost completely ended with the reforms in the early 1980s, and the quality of the seed stock had declined with cutbacks in the seed distribution programme soon afterwards. But had yields fallen as low as the revised output data implied (530 kg/ha.), or were area estimates also overstated?

To get a reading on this, the study used data provided by surveyed farmers on three variables: quantities of seed used (S), output (Q_G) and plot size (A_G) Although plot size estimates tend to be imprecise in these farming systems, the first two variables are well known by farmers. As such, one key element of yields, the seed multiplication coefficient (Q_G/S), could be fairly reliably assessed. This figure came out at 5 to 1, down from 7 to 1 in the years when seed quality was higher and general input supply conditions better. Before translating this into yields (Q_G/A_G), the ratio for the seed density (S/A_G) was verified, as field work from the late 1980s had indicated this was increasing (Kelly *et al.*, 1996). The survey results found average densities of 140kg/ha., a slight increase over the extension norms of 120 kg/ha. This result was consistent with farmers' responses to qualitative questions on this practice. *In summary*, the survey's yield estimate of 700kg/ha. for the 1995/96 crop year also implied that there were 130 000 fewer hectares planted to groundnuts that year than shown in the official series. In some years, the area overestimate is probably even larger.

Such major revisions in the numbers also raise questions about what is happening to pearl millet, the other principal food crop in these systems. Pearl millet accounts for roughly two-thirds of all cereal production in Senegal, and a far greater proportion of cereals in the groundnut basin, since rice, maize and sorghum are mainly grown in other regions. The official series show a long-term decline in millet output per rural inhabitant – moving from 170kg in the 1960s to just over 120kg in the 1990s – and implying a decline in on-farm consumption, marketed surpluses, or both. The data show no progression in either area or yields since the mid-1980s.

Yet various indicators suggest that the millet sector is far from moribund. For instance, per capita imports of rice and wheat have levelled off since the mid-1980s, there has been a rapid spread of millet-processing facilities in urban areas and of mechanical threshing equipment in the countryside, and there is a well established community of grain traders in major production and consumption areas. By the accounts of all observers (including the market information service which collects price and quantity information) the heart of the grain-belt is the Sine-Saloum region. This is the very region where ground-nut output was grossly overestimated. It is thus likely that the 'missing' groundnut area is actually being farmed with millet, a positive 'flip side' to the downward trends in the groundnut sector.

UNFINISHED BUSINESS

Clearly, the identification of data problems such as those illustrated under-scores the need to improve the quality of collection methods for the basic series. But this is easier said than done; at the time of the study in Senegal, the statistical services of the Ministry of Agriculture were in a third phase of a donor-funded project to improve crop estimates.

Until things improve, it is imperative to develop a planned effort to cross-check key variables. This means overcoming institutional barriers to making a better use of existing information. The compartmentalization of various statisti-cal services and research programmes limits the reflex to cross-examine data of different types and the scope for data exchange. People need to know who is doing what, and to have the possibility to share information and debate its interpretation. One solution, being tried in several African countries, is to estab-lish 'observatories' of strategic subsectors – small teams of analysts responsible for pooling information from different sources and making sense of it all.

More survey work is also necessary for understanding the trends. But what kind of surveys? When is informant recall adequate, and when must one take direct measurements? How big do samples need to be, and what kinds of sampling and extrapolation techniques are appropriate? To be sure, a theory base exists on these questions, but there is an unresolved tension, in practice, between statistical rigour and the available means. Time and cost considera-tions both imply opting for light surveys whenever possible, but in this activity there is still a lot of 'muddling through'. Statisticians, economists and farming systems specialists need to work together to establish pragmatic guidelines for raising the value-added in reliable data supply – one of the scarcest agricultural commodities that there is!

REFERENCES

CIRAD (1997), *L'arachide au Sénégal: Un moteur en panne*, Paris: Karthala-Cirad.

Gaye, M. (1997), 'Le phénomène du marché informel de l'arachide du Sénégal', *Arachide Infos*, **7**, 3–8.

Kelly, V., Diagana, B., Reardon, T., Gaye, M. and Crawford, E. (1996), *Cash Crop and Food Grain Productivity in Senegal*, International Development Paper no. 20, Michigan State University, East Lansing.

CARL E. PRAY AND KEITH FUGLIE*

Policies for Private Agricultural Research in Asian Developing Countries

INTRODUCTION

Public research in developing countries in Asia continues to grow, but in many countries the rate of change has slowed and it is lower than growth in agriculture. In Asia, private sector research grew twice as fast as public research (see Table 1). Using a new set of data on private research, this paper identifies the policies that encouraged growth in private agricultural research in the developing countries of Asia from 1985 to the late 1990s and suggests a few others which might have helped. This can provide guidance to policy makers in other developing countries who must develop agricultural science and technology policies in the shadows of globalization and the emergence of 'Life Science' corporations.

TABLE 1   *Growth of public and private research in Asia (millions of 1995 US$)*

	Public 85	Public 95	Growth (%)	Private 85	Private 95	Growth (%)
India	206	348	69	26	56	116
China	403	485	20	0	16	infinite
Indonesia	62	81	31	3	6	118
Malaysia	44	64	44	14	17	18
Philippines	17	38	113	6	11	69
Thailand	67	127	89	11	17	64
Pakistan	n.a.	n.a.	n.a.	2	6	138
Total	800	1 142	43	62	128	99

Sources: Case studies.

*Carl Pray, Rutgers University, New Jersey, USA. Keith Fuglie, International Potato Centre (CIP), Indonesia.

RESEARCH METHODS AND SOURCES OF DATA

To identify the key policies we conducted interviews with scientists and officials of private firms and governments, sent out mail surveys in some of the
larger countries, and collected published statistics in seven countries in South
and East Asia: India, Pakistan, Thailand, Indonesia, Malaysia, the Philippines
and the People's Republic of China. The first six were chosen because they had
been the subject of an earlier study conducted by Pray in the mid-1980s. China
was added because of its size and importance. The authors visited each country, except for Pakistan, for several weeks over the period 1996 to 1998,
conducting personal interviews with 70 to 80 in total. In Pakistan, consultants
were commissioned to conduct the survey. Because the number of countries is
so small, use is made of tabular and graphical analysis rather than econometric
methods.

STYLIZED FACTS ABOUT PRIVATE AGRICULTURAL RESEARCH IN ASIA

Between 1985–7 and 1995–8, private sector R&D grew in real terms in all of
the countries in our sample (Table 2). In four cases – India, Pakistan, Indonesia
and China – research more than doubled in size in ten years. The largest
amount of private research is in India, where investment was about $55 million
a year in the mid-1990s. The next largest amounts of private research expenditure are in Thailand, Malaysia and China. For the entire region, the agricultural
chemical industry conducted the most private research ($47 million), followed
by the agricultural processing and plantation industries ($41 million) and the
seed industry ($16 million) (Pray and Fuglie, 1999). Relative to the size of
China's agricultural economy, the investment in private research is particularly
small there – less than one-hundredth of 1 per cent of agricultural GDP on
private research (last column of Table 2). In contrast, in Thailand and Malaysia, firms spent about one-tenth of 1 per cent.

GLOBAL FORCES AFFECTING PRIVATE AGRICULTURAL RESEARCH IN ASIA

To identify the impact of policies on private research it is important first to
examine the importance of factors largely beyond the control of ministries of
agriculture or of science and technology ministries. These factors are the
changes in aggregate demand for food and fibre and the changes in the global
input supply industry.

Growth in consumer demand for food

The economic models of R&D expenditure by firms indicate that large markets
induce more private research (Griliches, 1957). Increased demand for agricul-

TABLE 2   *Private agricultural R&D expenditure, growth and research intensity*

Country	Private R&D expenditure* (million 1995 US$)		Increase in R&D (%)	Private research intensity (private R&D as % of ag. value added)	
	1985–7	1995–8		1985–7	1995–8
China	0.0	11–16.0	infinite	0.000	0.009
India	25.7	55.5	116	0.026	0.059
Malaysia	14.1	16.6	19	0.173	0.150
Thailand	10.6	17.4	64	0.124	0.095
Indonesia	2.8	6.1	118	0.010	0.018
Philippines	6.2	10.5	69	0.059	0.064
Pakistan	2.4	5.7	138	0.019	0.036
Total	61.8	123–8	99–107		

Note: *Adjusted to 1995 prices using US implicit GDP deflator.

Sources: Expenditure from 1985 Asian countries from Pray and Echeverría (1991); 1995–7 authors' survey. Research intensity calculated using Agricultural GDP data from World Bank (1987, 1997), *World Development Report*, Washington, DC: World Bank.

tural production in Asia at a time when investments in traditional sources of growth (land expansion, irrigation, additional agricultural labour and public research) were slowing down or declining led to an increase in demand for private research. In addition, demand for higher-value agricultural commodities – meat, fruits and vegetables – was growing particularly fast. Demand for more agricultural goods leads to demand for more modern inputs. As sales of modern inputs grow, private input firms and plantations raise their expectations about the future returns to research.

There is a closer relationship between growth of private agricultural research and growth in agricultural gross domestic product (GDP). Research intensity (research expenditure as a percentage of agricultural GDP) remained roughly constant from the mid-1980s to the mid-1990s in Thailand, Malaysia and the Philippines (Table 2). Thus research and production were growing at roughly the same rate, which suggests that the growth in value of agricultural production could account for most of the growth in private research in these cases. In the other four countries, research grew more rapidly than production. Thus increases in demand (as measured by value of production) can account for only part of the increase in research. In these countries we have to find other explanations for growth in private agricultural research.

Growth in the international supply of agricultural technology

The supply of science and technology from outside Asia has increased since 1995 for three reasons. First, the promise of agricultural biotechnology has turned into large sales of commercial products in the Americas. Second, there has been considerable consolidation of the biotech firms, seed firms, agricultural chemical firms and food and feed firms into large multinational 'Life Science' firms. Third, declining or stagnant demand for agricultural inputs in the USA and Europe have made the growing markets oᶠ countries of Asia look very attractive relative to US firms' traditional markets. Asia, in particular, appears promising because of the rapid growth in demand for modern inputs, especially for labour-saving items such as herbicides and machinery.

Two prominent examples of these trends are provided by Monsanto and DuPont. Representatives of both firms reported that, since 1985, their firms have made major policy decisions to expand into Asia and other developing countries. Monsanto's US investments in biotechnology, chemical and seed companies and research have led to more investments in Asian markets. In 1985, they did not sell seed in Asia and were not among the market leaders in Asian pesticide sales. Now they have bought into the seed industry in all seven countries, have expanded their herbicide sales greatly, and are making major investments in research in India. DuPont was not in the Asian seed industry until its recent purchase of Pioneer Hi-Bred which has a presence in all of these countries. DuPont is also investing in a major research facility in India.

These multinationals provide new technological opportunities, increasing the efficiency of research of Asian firms and Asian affiliates of the multinationals, and they provide new sources of money to finance research and technology transfer. Two types of evidence show the multinationals' importance for Asian research. First, foreign firms make up about half of the research that is conducted in the seven countries included in this study (Pray and Fuglie, 1999). They perform the majority of the private research in all countries except India, Pakistan and Malaysia. Second, foreign firms are concentrated in the industries where private agricultural R&D has been growing fastest – chemicals, livestock and seed – and play a small role in private plantation and machinery research, where R&D growth has been slower.

A small but growing trend in industry structure is the purchase of technology-based companies in industrial countries by emerging multinational corporations (MNCs) from developing countries. A pioneer in this area was the Thai firm Charoen Pokphand, which has extensive business interests in Southeast Asia, China and the USA. It has a long history of joint ventures in Asian countries, with DeKalb for seed and Arbor Acres for poultry genetics. It then decided to purchase the US broiler breeding company Avian Farms to give it another source of poultry genetics.

COUNTRY POLICIES AND PRIVATE AGRICULTURAL RESEARCH IN ASIA

In addition to the global forces described above, policies undertaken in individual Asian countries have also influenced incentives for private agricultural research and technology transfer.

Market liberalization and competition policy

The major policy change that stimulated more private research in Asia was input market liberalization, which eliminated public sector monopolies, reduced regulations, allowed imports, reduced restrictions on foreign direct investment and reduced subsidies for public sector input firms. The countries in which private research intensity grew fastest – China, India, Pakistan and Indonesia – all had major liberalization programmes during this period. China allowed foreign firms into the seed, pesticide, feed and agricultural machinery industries with Chinese joint-venture partners starting in the late 1980s. Before then, a few poultry genetics firms had been the only foreign ones allowed to sell technology in China. In India, the government gradually reduced restrictions on the foreign input firms, particularly in the seed industry but also in pesticides and agricultural machinery where foreign firms had been restricted to being minority partners in joint ventures. In the 1980s, both Pakistan and Indonesia reduced the role of the public sector in supplying subsidized inputs to farmers. In addition, Pakistan had a strong policy of privatization and liberalization after 1988. None of these countries eliminated, or even substantially reduced the size of, the government corporations in the agricultural input industries, but they did 'level the playing field' by reducing subsidies and eliminating monopoly powers of state-owned enterprises.

Intellectual property rights

Firms do not conduct research unless there is a way to capture some of the resulting benefits and turn them into profits. In Asia, input firms have primarily used technical means of protecting their intellectual property. Seed companies protect new plant varieties by only producing hybrids. Chemical companies protect new pesticides or pharmaceuticals by keeping the process of production secret and by making chemicals that are difficult to reproduce.

Almost all the research by private seed firms in Asia is on hybrid corn, hybrid sunflowers and hybrid vegetables which farmers and other seed firms cannot easily copy. Recent investments in research on normally self-pollinated crops – cotton, soybeans, rapeseed and rice – are due to new methods for capturing some of the benefits from research. Hybrids of rice and rapeseed have been developed. Some 'Life Science' firms can capture benefits from genetically engineered soybean and rice varieties because they will increase sales of their herbicides. China is the one place where *Bt* cotton has been commercialized. This is due in part to the fact that the Chinese joint venture partner is the government owned company which has the provincial monopoly on cotton seed.

In the countries in our survey, growth of private research was not closely associated with stronger legal protection for intellectual property rights (IPRs). China, Malaysia and Thailand made improvements to their patent laws. Research intensity grew in China but declined in Malaysia and Thailand. India and Pakistan, which had very limited changes in IPRs during this period, had the fastest growth in research intensity.

Appropriability of enough of the benefits from research to pay for further research is clearly important for firms. However, in Asia, the passing of stronger patent laws has not stimulated much research as yet. Anecdotal evidence suggests that the main problem now is enforcement of the patent laws.

Investments in public agricultural research

Public and private research can be either substitutes or complements. If public research institutions develop and disseminate technologies similar to those developed by private companies, public research could discourage the private sector from investing in new technology. However, public research can serve to provide important 'upstream' science and technology for private firms to adapt into product innovations. Public research institutions and universities also reduce the cost of research inputs for private companies by expanding the available pool of scientific and technical personnel or by providing contract research and field testing services for private firms.

Public research appears to have been an important force in stimulating private R&D in Asia. It certainly provided basic technology such as downy mildew-resistant corn in Southeast Asia and downy mildew-resistant pearl millet in India. These breakthroughs then facilitated the development of local hybrid seed industries. A survey of Indian private plant breeders found that the Indian public research system has been a major source of breeding material for cotton and sorghum, while the International Centre for Research in the Semi-Arid Tropics (ICRISAT) has been a major source of germ plasm for pearl millet (Pray *et al.*, 1998). In China, the two best known emerging local private plant breeding firms are evolving out of provincial hybrid rice and hybrid corn research programmes (Pray and Fuglie, 1999).

In addition, public research is providing technology to improve benefit appropriability by seed companies. Hybrid rice is now the focus of much private research in India and some private research in the Philippines, Pakistan and Thailand. This has been stimulated by the work of the International Rice Research Institute (IRRI) and of national government programmes, which developed hybrid rice technology for the tropics. In addition, hybrid rapeseeds were developed by an Indian university and a European firm.

Public research has also been very important as a source of scientists for private research. Almost all Asian private sector plant breeders first worked in government research institutes and/or international agricultural research centres. This is not surprising because there is virtually no other source from which to hire trained scientists. The important point is that firms are likely to invest more in research in countries where there are many well-trained agricultural scientists.

Public and private research expenditures and research intensities are positively related in the Asian countries in our sample. In addition, Table 1 shows that in all countries both the public and the private sector grew. However, the countries with the most rapid growth in public research – the Philippines and Thailand – had lower than average growth of private research and countries with slow growth in public research (China and Indonesia) had high growth of private research.

Other policies

In recent years Asian research systems have started to offer special subsidies and tax benefits to encourage private research. Our interviews with private companies did not find any evidence that either the tax policies or the research parks have had an important impact on private research. Most of these policies have just been established. Thailand has had R&D tax credits for a number of years, but none of the firms we interviewed were aware of them or took them into account in their research investment decisions. However, in the 1980s, the Thailand Board of Investments introduced incentives for the seed industry, including a ten-year tax holiday for new seed companies, a waiver of import duties on research equipment and materials, and permission for foreign companies to own agricultural land for research purposes. Some firms acknowledged that this was an important incentive for them to invest in seed processing and research in Thailand.

To protect farmers and consumers from health and environmental hazards, from fraud due to information asymmetries and from potentially harmful plant and animal diseases, governments have developed an extensive set of regulations on new plant varieties, seed and animal imports, pesticides, agricultural machinery and food. Some of these regulations can have an important impact on R&D.

Establishing a clear and consistent regulatory regime for agricultural inputs can encourage private companies to undertake research. For example, few international companies are willing to do research on transgenic plants unless a country has some system for government regulation of testing, because the adverse publicity of such activity in the absence of an approved regulatory framework would be too great. However, there can be a problem of balance since excessive regulation reduces the amount of private research by adding years of work and tens of thousands of dollars of research. Differences in regulations for testing genetically engineered plants in the field have meant that private agricultural biotechnology research is being conducted in Thailand, China and India, not in the Philippines. International chemical firms have also reported that, in the past, differences in regulations led companies to test and market chemicals more rapidly in Thailand than in India, even though it was a smaller market. However, recent changes in the way the Indian regulatory system works have increased firms' interest in doing research in India.

CONCLUSIONS

This new set of data on private research in seven Asian developing countries indicates that changes in the demand for inputs, the breakthroughs in biotechnology and the expansion of multinational life science companies are stimulating more private research in Asia. Analysis of the country case studies also indicates that policies have had an important impact on the amount and growth of private research. In Asia, liberalization, public research and, under certain circumstances, intellectual property rights and regulations can stimulate private R&D. However, these policies will have little impact on private research unless a country meets certain prior conditions, has passed through some minimum stages of development and has some key policies in place.

The first requirement for private research is a large and growing demand for agricultural products so that farmers demand modern, improved, inputs. Traditional agriculture or agriculture which does not have effective demand for modern inputs because infrastructure is inadequate or because policies discriminate against the farm sector will not attract private research. In countries where land rather than labour is the key constraint and adapted, modern technology is not readily available, public investments in research and some means of supplying inputs may be required. In small countries or niche markets private research may not develop or supply the needed technology; hence public research will continue to be important.

The second requirement is that private firms be allowed to supply agricultural inputs and operate plantations in a competitive market. Obviously, if there is a state monopoly of input supply, private investment will not grow. If public monopolies of input supply are turned into private monopolies, welfare losses are likely to increase. Allowing foreign investment and trade in the input industry is an important way of increasing competition and increasing a country's access to technology that has been developed and commercialized elsewhere in the world. Other policies that are needed are competition regulations to ensure that no local or foreign firm has too much market power.

When these conditions are in place, intellectual property rights and regulatory frameworks can be an important stimulus to private research. With rights protection, firms will have the ability to capture some of the benefits from research even in competitive markets. Firms will then choose to invest in developing improved inputs or management practices for which there is both potential demand and technological opportunity based on local public and private research or research done elsewhere. Finally, with intellectual property rights in place, tax subsidies for research or research parks may be important stimuli to further research. There was little evidence of the benefits of the latter types of policy in the seven countries studied here, but their effectiveness should be tested.

REFERENCES

Griliches, Z. (1957), 'Hybrid Corn: An Exploration in the Economics of Technical Change', *Econometrica*, **25**, 501–22.

Pray, C.E. and Echeverría, R. (1991), 'Private Sector Agricultural Research in Less Developed Countries', in P. Pardey, J. Roseboom and J. Anderson (eds), *Agricultural Research Policy: International Quantitative Perspectives*, Cambridge: Cambridge University Press.

Pray, C.E. and Fuglie, K. (1999), *The Private Sector and International Agricultural Technology Transfer in Developing Countries: Case Studies of China, India, Indonesia, Malaysia, Pakistan, the Philippines and Thailand*, Washington, DC: Economic Research Service, USDA.

Pray, C.E., Ramaswami, B. and Kelley, T. (1998), 'Liberalization, Private Plant Breeding and Farmers' Yields in the Semi-Arid Tropics of India', unpublished research paper, World Bank, Washington, DC.

RUBEN G. ECHEVERRÍA AND HOWARD ELLIOTT*

Competitive Funds for Agricultural Research:
Are They Achieving What We Want?

INTRODUCTION

Sustainable rural and agricultural development are essential in any strategy to reduce urban and rural poverty, increase food security and promote general economic growth while preserving the productive environment. Several factors are shaping the evolution of agriculture and development strategies towards a more knowledge-based approach. These include the persistence of poverty, the need for better understanding of the agriculture–environmental nexus, and the increase in global trade and changes in food demands. Conditioning this evolution are changes in science and technology, a revolution in information and communication technologies and major institutional changes including new roles for the public sector and civil society.

Agricultural technology generated by public and private investments in agricultural research in the more developed countries, in the international agricultural research centres and in the national agricultural research systems of less developed countries has contributed to the extraordinary success in worldwide agricultural production. However, agricultural innovation systems must now respond not only to the factors affecting productivity but also to growing demands for relevant, long-term, public-good research addressing other goals. Such research has traditionally fallen to the public sector both to fund and execute. It includes work in applied crop management, yield improvement of basic food crops, natural resource management, conservation of biodiversity and research achieved at alleviating poverty in areas of low potential.

As a result of profound economic and fiscal reforms, worldwide funding for public agricultural research grew at a slower rate in the 1990s than it did in the 1970s and 1980s, and in some countries it has even decreased. Its composition is changing: unrestricted budgetary support to public research institutions is declining while an increasingly large portion of public support is taking on new forms such a project-based or contract research. As a result, competition among institutions for available public funds has grown. This has led to increased efforts of research organizations to find alternative sources of research

*Ruben G. Echeverría, Sustainable Development Department, Inter-American Development Bank, Washington, DC, USA. Howard Elliott, International Service for National Agricultural Research (ISNAR), The Hague, Netherlands.

funds and of funding agencies to find new mechanisms to allocate these funds effectively.

In recent years, public research organizations have been faced by greater demands on their research capacity, but at the same time they are confronted by a vicious circle of increasingly tight budgets and lower research performance. That is, with fewer resources, research organizations may become less effective and efficient and, in turn, attract less funding. In Latin America, where the decline in funding first became apparent, new approaches for funding and organizing research (such as joint public/private-sector ventures, commercialization of research results, competitive schemes and farmer-managed levies on agricultural production) have developed over the past two decades. There is a growing feeling that the traditional public block grant funding to centralized suppliers of technology should be used more efficiently. As a consequence, future national research systems may exhibit considerable diversity in both funding sources and institutional plurality in conducting research (Echeverría *et al.*, 1996).

In addition to the factors internal to the research system that contribute to the decline in support, two overarching structural elements help explain the stagnation of public sector funding for agricultural research: (a) the perceived new, reduced role of the state, which increasingly uses market mechanisms (such as financing) instead of getting involved in producing goods and providing services, and (b) the movement of the agricultural sector itself towards a commercial agribusiness sector linked to global markets. The first factor has led to budget cuts, recommendations for more demand-driven mechanisms for allocating research funds, increased use of contracts, and pressure on public research organizations to obtain a larger share of funds by competitive means. The modernization of agriculture, liberalized markets and trade regimes, as well as strengthened intellectual property rights have created expectations that private companies will become increasingly active in developing countries, mainly through the sale of agricultural inputs and marketing of commodities. Trade liberalization has also promoted the transfer of technology embodied in inputs, decreasing the need for local research in some cases.

There is evidence that private sector agricultural production and research activities are increasing in developing countries (Pray and Umali, 1998). However, private sector activities are concentrated primarily in a few large economies (Brazil, India, China) and they are developing more slowly than in the more industrialized countries. Significantly, the increased participation of the private sector in agricultural research in most cases complements rather than substitutes for public sector activities. This may explain its concentration in countries with already strong research systems. This paper distinguishes between the roles of the public and private sectors in financing and executing agricultural research.[1] While the private sector may expand its role in *developing* agricultural technology, the public sector is still the main source of *funding* for agricultural research in developing countries.

However, the more traditional form of direct appropriations for research institutes is changing, and other instruments for funding research are being created. This paper focuses on one such mechanism: *competitive grant pro-*

grammes (CGPs). It assumes that the trend to allocate research resources competitively will continue and that research organizations will have to acquire a greater share of their funding through competition in the foreseeable future. Therefore a discussion of the preconditions for successful CGPs and of the criteria to evaluate their performance is timely.

Policy makers and donors may see CGPs as an effective tool to redirect priorities, increase accountability to funding sources and strengthen the participation of universities, foundations and other non-public research organizations in national research activities. Research managers, in turn, may see competitive grants as an additional source of resources – particularly of scarce operating funds – and as a device to develop joint ventures with other public and private sector research organizations. The growing attention given to CGPs (in particular by multilateral and bilateral development agencies) has focused mainly on the development of such schemes. Less importance has been given to the circumstances under which the use of CGPs can be most appropriate, the complementarity of CGPs to other funding instruments, and their sustainability. However, because they are 'in fashion', CGPs are at risk of being recommended as the panacea for several funding and institutional problems of national systems, diverting attention from the more crucial topics of lack of research resources and of national priorities to use them effectively.

In the United States and Australia, the trend towards CGPs has been a matter of concern to many authors. Huffman and Just (1994) argue that the growing proportion of public funds to agricultural R&D allocated competitively in the USA lowers economic efficiency because CGPs have high transaction costs. Similarly, Tisdell (1995, 1996), drawing on Australian experience, has pointed out how competitive bidding for research funds can lead to economic inefficiencies by involving short-term processes 'of a relatively destructive nature', and that competitive grants need to be supplemented by mechanisms for funding new researchers and institutions. In both cases, it has been argued that traditional institutional grants not only preserve the short-term stability of funding, but also allow for reallocation of funds in the longer term.

This paper examines the characteristics of successful CGPs in the overall context of financing agricultural research. Competitive funding is just one of several instruments to generate and allocate research funds; as such, institutional and competitive funding should not be viewed as substitutes but rather as complements. The question (still before us) concerns the appropriate mix of competitive and institutional funding for optimal research performance (Ruttan, 1982). To answer we need to look at, among other things, the full range of funding mechanisms, depending on the type of research, its purpose and the structure of distribution of research benefits (spillovers) in each particular case (Schweikhardt and Bonnen, 1997).

A PLURALITY OF FUNDING MECHANISMS

Traditional block grant funding is giving way to new mechanisms through which research is becoming more pluralistic in its financing and execution. In developing countries, several public and private sector organizations conduct research. They include public sector research institutes, agricultural universities, commodity institutes linked with producers' associations, foundations and public–private corporations, non-governmental organizations and private entities (plantations, input companies and the agribusiness and food sector). Many of them are directly linked to particular sources of funding not open to others. In addition, international research centres play a key role by conducting strategic research with wide distribution of benefits across countries.

During the past two decades, the somewhat reduced role of the state in the economies of many developing countries and a need for greater fiscal austerity have called into question the role of the public sector in supporting agricultural development in general, and agricultural research in particular. Despite the renewed interest in the private sector and a relative decline in the role of governments, there are areas of research that must be paid for (and probably also conducted) by the public sector. Otherwise, because of market failure, it is likely that crucial research activities will not be carried out. This so-called 'public good' research area is dynamic and, in many cases, shrinking as new products and processes (where intellectual property rights can be appropriated) are being developed by the private sector.

Because of such multiple and complementary roles for public and private sector funding of research, all the components of a national system may be active to varying degrees in any given country. Nevertheless, agricultural research in developing countries remains largely in the public sector, while most private sector effort is concentrated in the food industry, plantation crops, mechanical farm implements and chemicals, pharmaceuticals and seeds. And most of this research is not done by local companies alone, but also by multinationals on a worldwide basis.[2]

National agricultural research in developing countries relies on direct support from public sources (national and international), own resource mobilization and revenues from commercial operations. *Direct-block grants* and *earmarked transfers* have been the traditional public sector funding mechanisms to national research institutes and public universities, respectively. Increasingly, public funds are being channelled through contracts and competitive mechanisms.

In spite of this shift, CGPs still remain a small portion of the total. In the USA, competitive grants under the National Research Initiative accounted for about 12 per cent of the total research portfolio in 1999. In a recent submission, the National Science Council, the Committee for the National Institute for the Environment, recommended that the competitive share rise to 35 per cent. The Agricultural Research Council of South Africa, while struggling to take on the new challenges of emerging farmers while generating revenue from commercial farmers, argued that core funding from public sources (parliamentary grant) should not drop below 50 per cent. In New Zealand, block core funding of the Crown Research Institutes is now approximately 10 per cent; the rest is all competitive funding (Dunbier, 2000).

Mobilizing own resources is a second, increasingly important, source of funding for research organizations. *Grants from donors, income from endow-*

ments, charges for services and *check-offs* are used by research foundations and farmers' associations to fund their own programmes, or to contract other public and/or private sector providers. This is the case with grants to research foundations and levies on output to fund commodity institutes or other organizations by specific contracts. For instance, the Foundation for Agricultural Development of Ecuador (FUNDAGRO) was established as an endowment in 1986 to cover agricultural research, education and extension. With a strong preponderance of donor (that is, public) money behind it, FUNDAGRO was subjected to many of the same implicit constraints as the national institute had been (Sarles, 1990).

Retained earnings are, in turn, the most common source of research funding by the private sector, such as agricultural input companies or agribusiness and food sector organizations. Tax concessions are proving effective in increasing investment in research. Other significant sources for the public sector are joint-venture contracts as well as proceeds from user charges. Projects supported by research foundations are also becoming significant within the private sector.

Funding mechanisms vary widely across countries and within countries over time. For instance, in Latin America in the early 1990s, direct government transfers ranged from approximately 80 per cent in Brazil and Mexico to 40 per cent in Chile, where 26 per cent of funding came from sales of products and services (Cremers and Roseboom, 1997).[3] Financing in the more developed countries has also changed. In the Netherlands, where the public sector pays for 40 to 50 per cent of research, most work is now done through supplier contracts. The principal supplier is a recently created organization formed by merging the Agricultural Research Department of the Ministry of Agriculture and Fisheries and Wageningen Agricultural University. Roseboom and Rutten (1998) identify three trends in selected developed countries: an increase in public funds that match farmer levies through rural industry corporations (Australia); a switch from input to output financing and increasing reliance on private funding (the Netherlands and New Zealand); and a decrease in institutional funding with an increase in CGPs (USA).

Table 1 illustrates the relative effectiveness of alternative funding mechanisms as they relate to different programme objectives. The table reminds us that a portfolio of mechanisms is needed to ensure that the multiple objectives are addressed. The weights shown are subjective, but plausibly represent the usefulness of each mechanism in addressing the stated objective.

Competitive grants are often proposed as a way of introducing new priorities. However, their appropriateness relative to other funding mechanisms in a balanced portfolio of goals and mechanisms should be examined. It is often argued that a CGP pursuing scientific excellence or seeking to push yield ceilings upwards will favour wealthier regions and institutions while formula funding and special allocations better ensure that local equity concerns are taken care of. Where government contracts substitute for direct block grants as sources of funds, they may still have a positive effect on institutional development if allocated to new areas or used for training and research assistance. Conversely, they may divert resources to ad hoc projects and draw down both human and institutional capital. Certainly, every mechanism can be managed

TABLE 1   *Funding mechanisms and objectives*

Objective	Formula funding	Competitive grant programme	Special allocations	Government contracts	Private sector funding
Productivity	++	++	+	+	+++
Scientific innovation	++	+++	+	+	++
Scientific quality	++	+++	+	++	++
Client-driven research	+	++	+++	+++	+++
Equity by region or target group	++	+	+++	++	—
Institutional development	+++	+	++	+	+
Institutional collaboration	+	+++	+	++	+
Sustainability	+++	++	+	++	++

better: competitive grants may become more client-oriented by allocating resources to mission-oriented rather than fundamental research and special allocations may improve their quality by introducing both scientific peer review and 'merit review' procedures.

As mentioned earlier, CGPs funded from public sources are increasingly common in developing countries. The size of the competitive share in total research funding should be related to the capacity of the research system. Competitive funds are good for mobilizing and focusing existing resources. If the main priority is to develop research capacity rather than mobilize it, institutional block funding will be preferable to competitive grants. Clearly, the issue is one of the appropriate mix of competitive and institutional funding for optimal research performance or attainment of non-research goals.

ATTRIBUTES OF SUCCESSFUL COMPETITIVE GRANT PROGRAMMES

A recent review of the USDA 'National Research Initiative Competitive Grants Programme' (Board on Agriculture, 2000) highlights four key attributes of a successful CGP: (a) *quality* (the research is novel, valuable, feasible and technically sound); (b) *fairness* (proposals are evaluated seriously by a well-qualified group of reviewers with strict adherence to a set of criteria relating to quality and relevance); (c) *relevance* (the research will effectively meet national needs); and (d) *flexibility* (capacity to shift in response to emerging fields of research and to support the intrinsic flexibility in the research enterprise itself).[4]

TABLE 2 *A typology of competitive grants systems*

Type	Nature and objectives	Governance and *funding*	Example
National Multisectoral	Development of science, academic research, including unspecified themes based on scientific merit and contracts for specific research topics	Science & technology council *National budget*	CONICYT: Venezuela FONDECYT: Chile
	Strengthening research links between universities and other organizations	Science & technology council *Public grants*	FONDEF: Chile
	General technology development, open to all sectors of the economy	Development corporation *Loans, donor grants*	FONTEC: Chile
Agricultural sector	Agricultural technology development	Ministry of agriculture *USDA-USA*	FIA: Chile, NARF: Tanzania
	Applied research, transfer and training, small producers	Ministry of Agriculture *World Bank loan, Government*	PRONATTA: Columbia
	Agricultural technology development	National Institute–Research Council *World Bank Loan, grants*	PRODETAB Brazil, ARF: Kenya
	Specific commodity research, funded by Producers and public sector budget	Agricultural Development Corporation *Government/industry*	GRDC: Australia

448

Regional Multisectoral	Regional strategic agricultural technology development, funds from member countries	Scientific council *Multi-year plan*	INCO-DEV (European Union)
Agricultural Sector	Regional technology programmes, funds from member countries invested in endowment	Board of directors *Endowment fund administered by IDB*	Latin American Regional Fund for Agric. Research (FONTAGRO)
	Regional transfer of technology for small-holders	Steering committee *USAID funds*	East/Central Africa Fund (ASARECA)
International Foundations	Strategic socioeconomic development research	Non-profit foundation *Endowment*	Ford, Rockefeller
Development Research	Strategic economic development research	International council *Annual parliamentary grant*	IDRC: Canada
Agricultural research methodology	Support to ecoregional activities	Scientific Advisory Committee *Multi-year depleting fund*	Ecoregional Fund Dutch-Swiss grants (ISNAR administered)

Competitive schemes can be classified according to three characteristics: (a) their national, regional, or international reach, (b) their stated objectives and governance and (c) whether they are from endowed trusts or one-time depleting funds. The nature of support to research may be influenced by whether or not the funds are from annual grants or from stable investment income. Table 2 provides examples of CGP schemes with objectives that span the range from broad human welfare to specific methodology development. Before establishing a CGP scheme, it is essential to assess the merits of using such a mechanism for the objective to be pursued and the type of research to promote. Important structural considerations are the size of the system (the 'research market'), the scope of research eligible for submission to the competition, the creation of a sound and credible governance mechanism, and the potential sustainability of the system.

By widening the eligibility for grants, CGPs can also mobilize capacity in agricultural universities and research foundations, as well as provide opportunities to strengthen links among national and international research organizations. CGPs can generate a wider set of research ideas, among which the most promising could be actually funded. In this situation, CGP schemes may solve an information problem, focusing the competition on research topics (output) and not necessarily on research institutions (input). This may be of particular importance in more basic research areas, where funding agencies depend more on their interaction with scientists to develop a research portfolio. At the more applied end of the research spectrum, a CGP scheme may have a better defined set of research outputs to fund and the mechanism can be used in order to find the lowest-cost provider.

One of the major *disadvantages* of current CGPs (see Table 3) is lack of funding for human and physical capital. In order to be able to conduct research (and compete for grants), organizations must have a minimum budget to cover the costs of a critical mass of staff and for the maintenance and upgrading of physical and human resources. Given the nature of agricultural sciences, both elements depreciate quite rapidly. Moreover, a medium-term agenda requires continuity of funding over several years (for example, animal and plant breeding, natural resource management) and CGPs with a short-run bias may not be advantageous. Unless longer-term projects are funded, more basic research may be neglected in favour of short-term applied research.

Before launching CGPs, there is a need to analyse the *costs* of establishing and operating such mechanisms. Overhead costs of administration of a national CGP can be substantial if one fully costs activities such as (a) identifying priorities, (b) developing procedures (manuals of operation), (c) evaluating proposals, and (d) contracting and monitoring project execution. In addition, there are significant costs associated with preparing project proposals, panel and peer reviews for screening proposals, meetings of boards of directors, and publishing calls for proposals, results, annual reports and medium-term plans.

In spite of the fact that CGPs could provide better accountability, they are not immune to lack of transparency in the identification of priorities, conservatism in the allocation of resources and inflexibility in the use of funds. Managers of CGPs could bias priorities towards less productive research activities and, if

TABLE 3 *Potential advantages and disadvantages of having competitive grants programmes*

Advantages	Disadvantages
Increases research *effectiveness* by directing resources to the most productive scientists, by merit (improves costs quality and accountability of research)	Limited nature of funding (funds only operation costs; lack of support to core budget salaries and maintenance of research facilities)
Increases research *efficiency* by reducing direct costs via competition and cofinancing schemes, duplication of efforts, lack of accountability of research resources, underutilization of infrastructure by providing operating resources	Short-term funding, lack of support for medium- to long-term research agenda
	Low institutionalization, lack of support to human capital development and to new research infrastructure
Promotes the identification of and consensus on national research *priorities*	Higher funding uncertainty could affect long-term projects and reduce confidence of research staff
Increases *flexibility* to focus on newly emerging national/regional priority issues	High transaction costs from grant seeking, proposal writing and implementation reports; less time for research
Promotes a *goal-oriented* and demand-driven national research system	Reduces research flexibility to focus on additional (not open for competition) issues when researchers discover new research opportunities
Strengthens *vertical links* between research and extension organizations, agricultural production and agricultural policies	Higher risks involved when research consortia involve less well-known organizations
Strengthens *horizontal links* among national, regional and international public and private research organizations; promotes 'spill-ins'	Low sustainability of funding when national constituency is weak and external funding sources dry up (unless it is an endowment)
More *diversification of funding* by involving scientists from outside traditional organizations; promotes 'system'	Needs a *minimum market size*, a research system with a minimum number of competitors (larger countries probable best suited)
Induces *institutional change* in the national innovation system, separating research policy, funding and implementation	Legal, financial, administrative and technical *costs of setting up and administrating*
May mobilize *additional funding*	May be biased to strong research organizations, increasing 'equity issue' due to lack of competitive capacity of poorer/smaller organizations
Merit review process provides expert feedback to researchers' proposals and objectivity of the competitive process, *improving research quality*	Possibility of 'rent seeking' in the process of allocating resources to research

451

funding priorities are too rigid, a scientist's initiative to pursue promising new research activities can be hampered. In this sense, CGPs could become less client-driven than traditional institutional funding, and they could quickly redirect scarce funds to research priorities defined by technology funds managers. In addition, Huffman and Just (1995) examine the possibility that, given the high transaction costs of CGPs in the USA, they could increase rent-seeking activities by scientists relative to block grants or formula allocations. That could reduce both the real funding available to research and the productivity of research resource use.

KEY ELEMENTS FOR ESTABLISHING COMPETITIVE GRANTS

Given the particular national conditions facing agriculture and science and technology, each country would need a somewhat different competitive system. The following issues are minimum requirements (not rigorous recommendations) to be considered when establishing CGPs.

Research capacity

In a competitive research market, a substantial number of competitors are needed for CGPs to work. That is, a minimum research capacity and a level playing field are required for competition to operate, assuring a wide supply of high-quality competing research proposals. Research capacity relates to the relative number of scientists in any given discipline and the pool of potential reviewers of proposals, which in smaller systems may be limited. Moreover, if interinstitutional collaboration is required by the grant, the alliance may include all potential competitors. Therefore CGPs are more appropriate for the larger national agricultural research systems than for the smaller ones with few research organizations and a small number of scientists in relevant disciplines.[5] National research capacity could be expanded by open competition to providers from outside the country, and/or by setting up regional competitive funds.

Focus

A competitive fund should focus on a subset of the total priorities of the science and technology system best pursued by this mechanism. It need not take on all political objectives of the national system where other objectives are best pursued by other instruments. The identified priorities should be technically sound, feasible and attainable in the short-to-medium term. A limited number of priorities (which can gradually increase over time) will assure the consolidation of a CGP. Research priorities on a competitive programme should be defined in a participatory manner in order to build national consensus on strategic goals. Moreover, CGPs can be an effective instrument to promote research collaboration in new priority research areas that require multidisciplinary efforts. Maintaining a medium-term research focus will also help to avoid politically based allocations. Short-lived CGP schemes are less appropriate when the real need is to strengthen research infrastructure and when the desired results require research of a long-term nature.[6]

Governance

A CGP may be best located in an independent institution which does not itself bid for grants. The governing body should be high-profile and pluralistic, and set priorities in line with national priorities. A transparent management system is critical. It should be explained how priorities are identified, and how proposals are evaluated. Priorities and procedures should be publicized well in advance and not subject to unexpected annual changes. The call for proposals needs to be precise, must be public and widely distributed, accessible to all potential applicants and given sufficient time for quality proposals to be prepared. Clear statements on size of grant, nature of activities funded and specific conditions need to be published. Also, establishing an efficient system of awarding contracts could minimize conflicts of interest.

The expected value of a grant

The average size of award and the probability of success in achieving funding must be such that top-quality scientists are encouraged to submit proposals. From the scientist's point of view, the expected return on the costs of preparing a serious proposal must be adequate and the integrity of the review process must reduce the risk and uncertainty involved. From the society's point of view, transaction costs of the programme must be realistic both in terms of administration and review costs and in the costs of preparing proposals.

Quality of review

The process must be transparent, professional, anonymous and subject to external evaluation. A sound evaluation system based on merit should include at least the following criteria: technical quality, institutional capacity, expected socioeconomic impact (including efficiency and equity considerations) and environmental impact.

Sustainability

All the key elements discussed before influence the financial and institutional sustainability of CGPs. Because the costs of setting up and consolidating them high, and their impact in redirecting priorities and allocating resources can also be strong, it is essential that the life expectancy of a CGP be long, and that it becomes a stable mechanism for funding. Unless this stability is accomplished, depleting funds are usually at risk of non-replenishment.[7] Above all, the impact of agricultural research funded via CGPs will assure its sustainability; hence the importance of defining criteria to measure such performance.

CRITERIA FOR MEASURING PERFORMANCE

The performance of agricultural research is defined by its effectiveness in meeting goals and efficiency of execution. Relevance and quality of research affect effectiveness, while resource costs and management of research affect efficiency. Two other key factors influence performance: sustainability of relevant funding and the institutional setting in which research takes place. Table 4 identifies four criteria for measuring the performance of a CGP: increased effectiveness, increased efficiency, the promotion of favourable institutional change and observance of accepted public finance criteria.

Although all criteria are related (additional resources and institutional change may have a positive effect on research efficiency and effectiveness, and vice versa), performance must be judged first and foremost by its impact on the goals of the programme. This is why clear goals are essential at the outset. Where those are scientific, we need to look for indicators of research effectiveness (impact on factor productivity, rate of return to research, adoption of results, poverty) and research efficiency. The task becomes complex when there are multiple goals that are different in nature, for example, scientific, economic, political or institutional. It then becomes necessary to define indicators for the political and institutional objectives and some way of weighting these objectives against the efficiency and effectiveness objectives. Finally, the CGP can be judged in the same way we would judge any other public finance mechanism, that is by its revenue implications (additionality), allocative efficiency (distortion of expenditure) and administrative burden (costs of collection and disbursement).

ASSESSING THE PERFORMANCE OF AGRICULTURAL RESEARCH COMPETITIVE FUNDS IN CHILE

For more than two decades Chile has been a laboratory for successful market and institutional reforms. Chile is one of the few developing country cases where several national competitive grants systems for agricultural research have been in place for more than a decade. Examples of multisectoral CGPs are FONDECYT and FONDEF, both at the National Science and Technology Council level (CONYCIT), as well as two specific agricultural technology funds (FIA and PTT from INDAP) (Echeverría *et al.*, 1996).

As shown in Table 5, Chile demonstrates a generally positive trend in both total and agricultural R&D investment over the period 1979–97. Universities account for approximately half of the national research expenditure throughout the period, while the share of competitive funds has increased from less than 1 per cent at the end of the 1970s to about 25 per cent of the total national research expenditure by the end of the 1990s.

Public funds allocated competitively to agricultural research in Chile have increased significantly during the past 10 years: from less than US$2 million in 1988 to almost US$60 million in 1998 (MEFR, 1998). Block grants to the national research institute, INIA, increased over the same period from about

TABLE 4   *Criteria and indicators for measuring performance of competitive grants*

Criterion	Indicator (benchmark)
Increased effectiveness (impact of research results attributed to research projects financed by competitive grants)	Factor productivity (crop yields, labour productivity) Trend in natural resource degradation (soil erosion rates) Social rate of return to research (percentage) Rate of adoption of research results (shape of adoption curve) Absolute and relative poverty rates (percentage) Scientific quality and spillover benefits (publications, citations, peer evaluation)
Increased efficiency (costs of doing research attributed to research projects financed by competitive grants)	Outsourcing: share of contracted research within project activities (% of total) Delivery: number of projects completed within a year after the planned date Success rate: number of projects that have achieved the planned results Punctuality: ratio of realized and planned time for project execution (%) Length of project cycle (number of months)
Promotion of favourable institutional change	Partnerships: national, regional and international research joint ventures in a given year (number) Importance: trend of national research budget allocated to CGPs and to direct institutional funding (% over time) Confidence: share of private sector funding in total research expenditure (%) and number of joint ventures Ownership: stakeholder participation in governance, priority setting and planning events (numbers, share in total, level of responsibility) Institutional capacity: staff qualification index, annual turnover rate
Public finance	Additionality of resources attracted by CGP: from clients, government, private sector, partners (annual growth rate of national agricultural research budget) Allocative efficiency of resources and impact on research priorities in relation to national goals (change in resource allocation to new goals) Administrative costs of collection and disbursement of funds (relative to total grant activity) Transaction costs and preparation costs for applicants, reviewers, panel

TABLE 5   *Chile: National and agriculture R&D expenditures (1979–97)*

Year	Total national (US$m)	Universities (%)	Comp. funds (%)	Agriculture (% of total)
1979	82.56	44.3	0.47	
1980	107.59	45.3	1.12	
1981	123.86	52.9	2.29	
1982	108.91	57.1	3.32	
1983	96.21	54.5	1.48	
1984	99.63	51.2	4.82	7.28
1985	80.43	50.3	7.12	12.32
1986	81.19	50.6	9.16	15.53
1987	105.80	46.0	8.35	11.92
1988	109.33	49.1	12.75	13.72
1989	129.73	57.8	15.14	14.54
1990	154.93	54.7	13.37	19.84
1991	183.56	55.0	13.56	22.69
1992	248.90	26.3	22.63	19.49
1993	287.20	46.3	25.02	24.33
1994	338.59	48.9	22.16	27.24
1995	422.25	48.5	20.98	25.10
1996	461.77	46.1	23.89	26.08
1997	497.51	47.1	24.90	17.16

Source: CONICYT, *Indicadores Científicos y Tecnológicos*. An agriculture share is not available prior to 1984.

US$27 million to US$46 million. The Agricultural Investment Fund of the Ministry of Agriculture, with a current annual budget close to US$6 million, funds research projects of private companies (40 per cent), universities (30 per cent) and public institutes (30 per cent).

The National S&T Fund (FONDECYT) is the largest and oldest CGP in the country. It also provides the largest absolute amount of funding for agricultural research, although a significantly decreasing trend brought its support to agriculture to less than 5 per cent of its investment in 1998. FONDEF, on the contrary, has had an increasing trend in agricultural research investments since its creation in 1993, now reaching levels close to 50 per cent of its total. It is now the second most important CGP for agriculture in the country, followed by FONTEC, which is open to all sectors and is managed by a development corporation (CORFO) and FIA, managed by the Ministry of Agriculture.

Figure 1 shows the relative importance of each funding source, and the fact that CGPs have, in general, added resources to those of the national public research institute. INIA had the largest agricultural research budget in Chile, followed by the INDAP expenditure in transfer of technology. A large share (40 per cent) of INIA's budget still comes from government block grants.

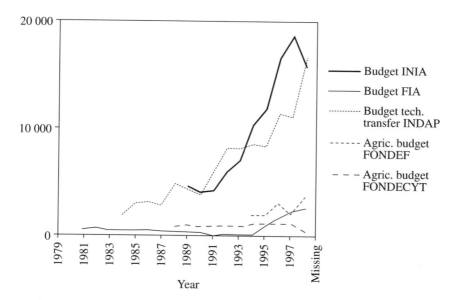

FIGURE 1   *Chile: National Agriculture Research Institute (INIA) and competitive agriculture funds investment trends (in constant 1997 Chilean pesos)*

Competitive funds from FONDEF, FONDECYT and FIA accounted for less than 2 per cent of the institute budget during the 1990s.

According to a recent study of CGPs in Chile by Escobar and Berdegué for ODI (reported in Gill and Carney, 1999), most funds related to agriculture have not promoted their stated objectives of participation, decentralization, networking and feedback to proponents of research projects. On the other hand, the CGPs have had an agile administration and transparency of operations.

When assessing the performance of competitive grants, we need to be precise about whose performance is being looked at. Is it (a) the impact of research on national goals partially funded by the CGP, (b) the increased allocative efficiency in research gained through the competitive grant mechanism, or (c) the efficiency and effectiveness of the competitive grant scheme as a fiscal mechanism? We need to set up and collect information relating to each of these.

Indicators must have a number of characteristics. They must be relevant, independent, precise and realistic, and verifiable at reasonable cost (TAC, 1998). To be relevant, the indicator must capture the essential achievement of the project from the point of view of the target group or funding agency. To be independent, the indicator must logically be at the same level as the corresponding objective, neither the cause nor the effect of achieving the objective. To be precise and realistic, the indicator might specify the target group, quantity and quality of the target achieved, the time frame and the location where

TABLE 6 *Chile: Criteria for assessing performance of competitive funds*

Criteria	Level of impact	Comments on indicators
Effectiveness		
Factor productivity	Macro	Yield data (at field level) on five commodities benefiting from investment in research
	Project	Data not disaggregated by commodity and source of funding
Trend in natural resource degradation	Macro	Data not available
Social rate of return to research	Project	Not included in analysis
Rate of adoption of research results	Project	An indicator of potential gains in factor productivity at field level coming from research (i.e. lower level than productivity indicator)
Absolute and relative poverty rates	Macro	Aggregate national poverty and rural poverty data an indicator of higher-order goals
	Project	If project addresses poverty directly, could be direct indicator
Increased efficiency of research		
Outsourcing: share of contracted research within project activities	Project	Intended indicator that research is being outsourced to most efficient supplier of services
Delivery: number of projects completed within 1 year of planned date	Project	Direct indicator of efficiency of design, selection and execution of projects. Data potentially available
	CGP	Aggregate data of percentage of such projects could be indicator of programme effectiveness
Success: number of projects that have achieved planned results	CGP	Indicator of effectiveness of the selection process
Efficiency of execution: ratio of actual to planned time required to complete project	Project	Direct indicator of efficiency of design, selection and execution of projects. Data potentially available
	CGP	Aggregate data of percentage of such projects could be indicator of programme effectiveness

458

Item	Level	Description
Length of project cycle (months)	CGP	Indicator of efficiency of management of CGP
Transactions costs of CGP as percentage of grants	CGP	Ratio of successful applications to total submissions. Indicator of efficiency of management of CGP
	Project	Preparation costs in relation to funding received
Institutional change		
Partnerships: national, regional, international joint ventures	Project	Indicator of change in mode of doing research at both the project and institutional levels; more pluralistic system
Importance of CGPs: trend in share of national research budget passing through CGP mechanisms	Macro	Indicator may have a double interpretation: in systems where total funding is rising it may indicate confidence; in shrinking systems it may indicate a lack of confidence and withdrawal of commitment
Public finance		
Additionality: new resources attracted by CGP	Project / Research system	Earmarked resources for new priorities and well-defined projects may attract funding
Allocative efficiency: improved resource allocation to new goals and priorities	Project / Research system	Allocation of competitive funds clearly different from allocation of traditional budget in the way that new priorities are effectively addressed
Administrative costs of collection and disbursement of funds	CGP	Effective check-off and earmarking system in place and record of expenditures
	Research system	Number of funds serving identified clients
	CGP	Common funding in place
Transaction costs: preparation costs for applicants, cost of reviewers and panels	Research system	Administrative, travel, honoraria, meeting costs
		Social costs of unsuccessful proposals

TABLE 7 *Chile: characteristics of the performance indicators utilized for each criterion*

Criteria and Indicators	Level of Impact	Relevant and Substantial	Independent	Verifiable	Target	Precise and Realistic			
						Quality	Quantity	Time	Location
Effectiveness									
Factor productivity	Macro, Project	Yield 5 crops	Yes	Yes	National	Yes	Yes	Yes	National
Trend in natural resource degradation	Macro	None	Yes	Yes, high cost	Subregion	Possible	Possible	Periodic	Subregion
Social rate of return to research	Project	Commodity rate of return	Yes	Case study	Crop programme	Costly cases	Case by case	Periodic	National, subregion
Rate of adoption of research results	Project	Technology or commodity	Prerequisite for impact	Case study	Single case	Costly cases	Case by case	One-off	Recommendation domain
Absolute and relative poverty rates	Macro or Project			Poverty survey	National or target group	Aggregate or project-related	National survey / Case study	Annual or periodic	National / Cases
Increased efficiency of research									
Outsourcing: share of contracted research within project activities	Project	Proxy for low-cost provider	Leads to efficiency, does not measure it	Yes	Project	Project document specifies	Project document specifies	Project-related	n.a.
Delivery: number of projects completed within 1 year of planned date	CGP	Measures achievement in design and execution	Yes	Yes	Project, CGP	CGP records	CGP records	Project related	
Success: number of projects that have achieved planned results	CGP	Measures achievement in design and execution	Yes	Yes	Project CGP	CGP records	CGP records		

460

Indicator	Level	Comment		Measurable	Source			Frequency	Coverage
Punctuality: ratio of actual to planned time required to complete project	CGP	Measures achievement in design and execution	Yes	Yes	Project, CGP	CGP records	CGP records		
Length of project cycle (months)	CGP	Measures efficiency of CGP itself	Measures CGP efficiency, proxy for research efficiency	Yes	CGP	CGP records	CGP records		
Transactions costs of CGP as percentage of grants	CGP, Project	Measures efficiency of CGP itself	Measures CGP efficiency, proxy for research efficiency	Yes	CGP, Donors	CGP records	CGP records		
Institutional change									
Partnerships: national, regional, international joint ventures	Project, Research system	A goal or a means to an efficiency goal	proxy for efficient research, independent goal	Yes	Research institutes	Data on organizations	n.a.	Periodic	National
Importance: trend in share of national research budget passing through CGP	Macro	A presumed means to efficient allocation	Lower-level indicator	yes	Research system donors	Funding data	Reports from CG Funds	Annual reports	National
Client confidence: share of private sector funding in joint total research and number of joint ventures	Macro, Project	Proxy for complementarity	Measures extent of collaboration	Yes					

461

TABLE 7 *concluded*

Criteria and Indicators	Level of Impact	Relevant and Substantial	Independent	Verifiable	Target	Precise and Realistic			
						Quality	Quantity	Time	Location
Ownership: stakeholder participation in governance, priority setting and planning	Project, Research system	Participation a means to efficiency and effectiveness	May be an objective as well as a means	Yes	Project and Institute	Reports of planning meetings	Continuous	Continuous	Institute, programme
Institutional capacity: staff qualification index, turnover	Institute, Project	Resource quality and stability	Prerequisite for efficiency and effective research	Yes	Institute or programme	Staffing statistics	Available	On record	Institute or programme
Public finance									
Additionality: new resources attracted by CGP	System, Project	Direct measure of new support	Yes	Yes	CGP, Project, System	Good	Available	Annual	CGP
Allocative efficiency: improved resource allocation to new goals and priorities	Project Research system	Identify increased flows to new priorities	Yes	Yes	Programme	Good	Good	Annual	CGP National
Administrative costs of collection and disbursement	CGP, System	Identify full cost of programme	Yes	Yes	CGP	CGP records	Good	Annual	CGP
Transactions costs: preparation costs for applicants, cost of reviewers and panels	CGP, System	Identify full cost	Yes, measure of input	CGP records	CGP, Donors	Good	Good	Annual	National CGP

the objective is realized. To be verifiable, we need to specify the information, source and responsibility for and frequency of collection of it.[8]

We draw on available information to assess the performance of the competitive grant system in Chile. We speak of a 'system' because research is funded from a wide range of science and technology funds, development funds and institutions using their own block grants. The varied nature of funding in Chile provides a good case study that brings out the complementarity between institutional block funding and competitive grant funds and their interaction as part of an overall system for funding agricultural research.

In Table 6 we look at the criteria for assessing the performance of CGPs, indicate the level (project, institutional, research system) at which the performance is measured and provide some initial evidence of the impact using secondary data from Chile that were collected for other purposes. The main lesson is that performance indicators need to be built into the programmes from the start for monitoring purposes. In Table 7, we specified the characteristics of the indicators for each given criterion.

CONCLUSIONS

This concluding section summarizes the foregoing discussions by making a number of points about CGPs that seem to be corroborated by the Chilean material.

- The competitive grant mechanism is capable of improving resource allocation within research but is not a solution for the problem created by general decreases in resources invested in research. Competitive grants may improve the productivity of existing research staff and infrastructure through provision of operating funds. In this respect they have a qualitative impact on research output that may be disproportionate to their share in total funding. They may represent an improvement in the mechanism by which research resources are allocated to national priorities. In the case of Chile, the philosophy of the market has created so many competing funds that there is danger of fragmentation of the system. Fortunately, institutional support has increased at the same time, so that an integrated programme can be maintained.
- If, by improving the image of research, they can lead to a resurgence of support to research of all kinds they contribute to the sustainability of research. The shift to competitive funding may provide increased accountability to funding sources and lead to sustained institutional support.
- Competitive funds need an institutional base on which to build. For a competitive grant system to work there must be competitors. The system must be sufficiently large and diverse for a market in research services to exist. Furthermore, there is a need to maintain a critical research capacity (infrastructure and human capital) through public institutional funding.

- CGPs are not designed for institution building, although provisions can be built into them that help sustain research capacity. First, they may systematically provide funds for training of junior researchers and incentives for established researchers to remain in the system. Second, they may bring new actors into the research market through requiring interinstitutional collaboration and providing for outsourcing of services. In the case of Chile, universities have taken up a large share of resources.

- CGPs are not especially well designed to support long-term research but procedures for development uptake and technology transfer can be built into the scheme if the CGP itself has a long-term life and sufficient vision.

- There is a need to identify the balance between institutional and project support that is optimal for the goals that are sought. Funding mechanisms are often linked to particular interests and specialized in the way they can be tapped and used. A portfolio approach to funding is needed. Strong institutional support exists in most of the advanced and market-oriented systems and, even there, the role of special non-competitive grants to less favoured regions and institutions is accepted. In the case of Chile, the constancy of institutional support has gone hand-in-hand with growing funding from competitive sources.

- Competitive grants for basic research can bring out the most innovative ideas; for applied research they can bring out the most efficient service provider.

- Competitive grant programmes become part of the science and technology policy of the country. They must be designed to fit into the policy and governance structures of the country in which they are located. This may entail concern with broader science and technology issues rather than agricultural research alone. The philosophy and politics of a country will have an influence on the operation of competitive funds, just as they have on traditional forms of support to research, unless the goals of the fund are very specific and the procedures for allocation to those goals very transparent.

- It is necessary to establish and defend the integrity of the goals of the fund. They must be clearly set out and high standards must be maintained from the start of operations. For this, indicators of performance must be set up at the time of creation of the fund. A system of direct and indirect indicators must provide fund managers with the information needed to take timely action to correct divergences from research goals, programme strategy and fund efficiency.

- In the case of Chile, of the four criteria for measuring the performance of CGPs, increased efficiency and public finance seem to have had a much larger effect than increased effectiveness and the promotion of institutional change.

NOTES

[1]The paper draws on an overview paper by Elliott and Echeverría (2000) presented at a conference on competitive funding organized by EMBRAPA in Brazil; a series of case studies on competitive funds in India, Chile, Colombia, Kenya, Tanzania, Mali and Senegal conducted by the Overseas Development Institute (ODI) of the UK (Gill and Carney, 1999); World Bank guidelines documenting the steps in the process of setting up and operating a CGP and lessons and challenges of competitive funding of agricultural research (George, 2000; Byerlee, 2000); and an ISNAR discussion paper on competitive funding (Echeverría, 1998). The interpretations and conclusions of the paper are those of the authors and should not be attributed to any agency mentioned in the paper. The collaboration of Germán Escobar and Julio Berdegué (RIMISP) with data from Chile is greatly appreciated.

[2]In Latin America in the mid-1990s, public sector research represented close to 70 per cent of the total agricultural research expenditure, while the shares of universities, private companies and farmers' funding averaged about 10 per cent each, with wide variation across countries (Echeverría, 1998b). By comparison, the private sector share of agricultural R&D in the USA and the UK was close to 60 per cent, with shares between 15 and 35 per cent for public institutes and 25 and 5 per cent for universities (Pray and Umali, 1998). See Alston *et al.* (1998) for worldwide trends in public investments in agricultural research and private sector research expenditure in OECD countries.

[3]The Brazilian cocoa research institute (CEPLAC) provides an example of funding variation over time: stable for over three decades, farmers' financing from a levy on production stopped after commodity prices plummeted and a serious disease affected production.

[4]See Echeverría (1998b) for a full description and examples of use of national, regional and international funds.

[5]Competition is effectively limited in countries with only one relatively large research organization (only one provider in the market). In fact, a competitive system may lead to decreased competition and increased inequality because of the lack of the capacity of smaller institutions to compete. This has occurred in countries where research institutions in relatively poor states compete with stronger institutions in the wealthy states and 'scientific quality' is the sole criterion for evaluating proposals.

[6]On the other hand, outside developing-country agriculture, CGPs are quite common within the long-term research establishment. Whether or not CGPs have a long time horizon and promote more basic research depends more on the mandate of the funding agency and sustainability of its funding than on the competitive mechanism as such.

[7]Endowments, on the other hand, have the advantage of financial sustainability. There are intermediate models between perpetual endowments and depleting funds, where for instance a combination of the investment income and the fund itself is used to support research activities over a specified period of time, say 10 to 15 years ('sinking fund').

[8]Where possible, we look for direct indicators that can be a precise and operational restatement of the objective. Such indicators are easier to formulate at the output level. Indirect or proxy indicators may be used where the objective is not directly observable (or the cost of collecting indicators is too high or the indicator only becomes verifiable after the end of the project).

BIBLIOGRAPHY

Alston, J., Pardey, P.G. and Roseboom, J. (1998), 'Financing agricultural research: International investment patterns and policy perspectives', *World Development*, **26**, 1057–71.
Beatie, A. (1997), 'From core grants to contracts for performance: Lessons from the UK experience', paper presented at a Department for International Development (DFID)-sponsored workshop on financing agricultural research, London, September.
Board on Agriculture (2000), *National Research Initiative: A Vital Competitive Grants Program in Food, Fiber, and Natural-Resources Research*, Washington, DC: National Academy Press.
Byerlee, D. (2000), *Competitive funding of agricultural research in the World Bank: lessons and challenges*, Washington, DC: World Bank.

Byerlee, D. and Alex, G. (1998), *Strengthening national agricultural research systems: Policy issues and good practice*, Washington, DC: World Bank, Rural Development Department.

Cremers, M.W.J. and Roseboom, J. (1997), *Agricultural research government agencies in Latin America: A preliminary assessment of investment funds*, ISNAR Discussion Paper no. 97–7, The Hague.

Dunbier, M. (2000), personal communication.

Echeverría, R.G. (1998a), *Will competitive funding improve the performance of agricultural research?*, ISNAR Discussion Paper no. 98–16, The Hague.

Echeverría, R.G. (1998b), 'Agricultural research policy issues in Latin America: An overview', *World Development*, **26**, 1103–11.

Echeverría, R.G., Trigo, E. and Byerlee, D. (1996), *Institutional change and effective financing of agricultural research in Latin America*, World Bank Technical Paper no. 330, Washington, DC: World Bank.

Elliott, H. and Echeverría, R.G. (2000), 'Characteristics of successful agricultural research competitive grants programs', paper presented at 'Competitive Grants in the New Millennium, a Global Workshop for Designers and Practitioners', organized by EMBRAPA, Brasilia, Brazil, 16–18 May.

George, P. (2000), *A guide to assist in designing and implementing a competitive agricultural technology fund: an implementation handbook*, Washington, DC: Agricultural Knowledge and Information Systems Thematic Group, The World Bank.

Gill, G. and Carney, D. (1999), *Competitive agricultural technology funds in developing countries*, London: Overseas Development Institute.

Huffman, W.E. and Just, R.E. (1994), 'Funding, structure and management of public agricultural research in the United States', *American Journal of Agricultural Economics*, **76**, 744–9.

Huffman, W.E. and Just, R.E. (1995), *Transaction costs, fads, and politically motivated misdirection in agricultural research*, Iowa State University Staff Paper no. 277, Ames.

Janssen, W. (1998), 'Alternative funding mechanisms: How changes in the public sector affect agricultural research', in S. Tabor, W. Janssen and H. Bruneau (eds), *Financing agricultural research: A sourcebook*, The Hague, ISNAR.

Kelman, A. and Cook, R.J. (1996), 'The role of a competitive research grants program for agriculture, food and natural resources', *BioScience*, **46**, 533–40.

MEFR (1998), *Secretaría Ejecutiva del Programa de Innovación Tecnológica*, Santiago, Chile: Ministerio de Economía, Fomento y Reconstrucción.

Pray, C.E. and Umali, D. (1998), 'Private agricultural research: Will it fill the gap?', *World Development*, **26**, 1127–48.

Roseboom, J. and Rutten, H. (1998), 'The transformation of the Dutch agricultural research system: An unfinished agenda', *World Development*, **26**, 1113–26.

Ruttan, V.W. (1982), *Agricultural research policy*, Minneapolis: University of Minnesota Press.

Sarles, M. (1990), 'USAID's experiment with the private sector in agricultural research in Latin America and the Caribbean', in R.G. Echeverría (ed.), *Methods for Diagnosing Research Systems Constraints and Assessing the Impact of Agricultural Research*, The Hague, ISNAR.

Schweikhardt, D.B. and Bonnen, J.T. (1997), 'The nature, governance and financing of agricultural research', paper submitted to the Committee on Agriculture, Nutrition, and Forestry of the U.S. Senate, Department of Agricultural Economics, East Lansing: Michigan State University.

Tabor, S., Janssen, W. and H. Bruneau, H. (eds), *Financing agricultural research: A sourcebook*, The Hague: ISNAR.

TAC (1998), 'Hints for the elaboration of indicators for the CGIAR Logical Framework', Annex 3 of Efficient Research Planning for the CGIAR, Workshop Report, Feldafing, Germany.

Tisdell, C.A. (1995), 'Transaction costs, and markets for science, technology and know-how', *Australian Economic Papers*, **34**, 136–51.

Tisdell, C.A. (1996), 'Public mechanisms: Block grants, competitive versus non-competitive research funding', in Secretariat of the Conference (ed.), *Proceedings of the Global Agricultural Science Policy for the Twenty-first Century Conference*, Melbourne, Australia.

CONTRIBUTED PAPERS

Trade, European Union and Methodology

ISABELLE SCHLUEP AND HARRY DE GORTER*

The Definition of Export Subsidies and the Agreement on Agriculture

INTRODUCTION

The Agreement on Agriculture (AoA), familiar from the Uruguay Round of the General Agreement on Tariffs and Trade (GATT) is being renegotiated in the context of the World Trade Organization (WTO). Reductions in support for agriculture will be tabled, which will affect amounts spent on export subsidies. This paper focuses on the definition of export subsidies used in the Uruguay Round (WTO, 1994). It suggests that the language in the AoA omits an important implicit subsidy in the form of price discrimination and revenue pooling (termed a 'consumer only-financed' export subsidy) and poorly defines 'producer-financed' export subsidies. 'Consumer only' and 'producer'-financed payments require government regulation to allow marketing orders, marketing boards or state trading enterprises (STEs) to operate (Alston and Gray, 1998; Annand and Buckingham, 1998; Dixit and Josling, 1997; Schluep, 1999). We show that domestic price discrimination alone is equivalent to a consumption tax (it is like policy for peanuts in the United States) while price discrimination in international markets alone is a production subsidy (as in the case of the New Zealand Dairy Board).

Several countries have called for the prohibition of export subsides in the forthcoming negotiations. The AoA in the Uruguay Round placed limits on both export volumes and expenditures. We show that the current definition of an export subsidy in the AoA and the Agreement on Subsidies and Countervailing Measures (ASCM) is inadequate in addressing taxpayer, consumer only and producer-financed export subsidies. In addition, the code on State Trading Enterprises is not well suited to capture practices of such implicit export subsidies. We use examples of dairy policies worldwide to illustrate the different types of export subsidies and the practices of state trading exporters. Finally, we discuss how the WTO could deal with export subsidies in the future.

*Isabelle Schluep, Centre for Agricultural and Rural Development, Iowa State University, USA. Harry De Gorter, Cornell University, USA.

THREE TYPES OF EXPORT SUBSIDIES

Taxpayer-financed export subsidies are well known, involving direct payments by governments and accounting for over 90 per cent of the export subsidies notified to the WTO in 1997. The European Union and the United States employ them for dairy products. A taxpayer-financed export subsidy includes transfers not only from taxpayers, but also from consumers to producers. This is shown in Figure 1 for a small country exporter. The intersection of the excess supply curve ES_1 (the horizontal difference between the domestic supply and demand curves S and D, respectively) and the horizontal excess demand curves given by P^w generates free trade exports of the distance $X_{fr.trade}$. The introduction of a taxpayer-financed export subsidy represented by the vertical distance XS_{tax} results in a wedge between the domestic price to consumers and producers (denoted by $P^{tax} = P^{pool}$) and the world price P^w. The domestic price increase causes production to increase to Q^{s1} and consumption to fall to Q^{d1}. Transfers from taxpayers to producers are the area $(Q^{s1} - Q^{d1}) * XS_{tax}$ and from consumers to producers of the area $(P^{tax} - P^w) * Q^{d1}$.

Exports under a taxpayer-financed export subsidy are X_{tax} where the wedge between the excess supply ES_1 and the excess demands curve equals XS_{tax}. Trade distortion is the distance ① plus ②.

A *consumer only-financed* export subsidy involves transfers to producers directly from consumers. Such an export subsidy has been identified for the export of Canadian dairy products in 1997 (WTO, 1999). Classified pricing in US marketing orders for milk and the policy of California having lower prices for exports conform to this definition of a consumer only-financed export subsidy as well. Neither the AoA nor the ASCM recognize this type of export

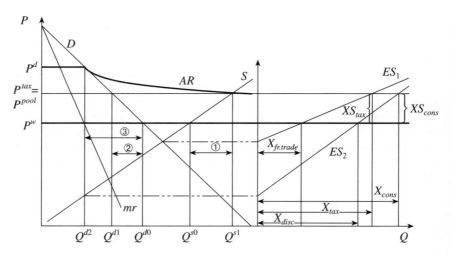

FIGURE 1   *Taxpayer versus consumer only-financed export subsidy (single product, small exporter)*

subsidy.[1] Therefore it is not part of the members' export subsidy reduction commitments. Indeed, no country has notified the WTO of this type of arrangement.

The prerequisites for a consumer only-financed export subsidy are both border protection that allows for price discrimination (across domestic and foreign markets for one product and/or across products in international markets) and pooling of revenues to producers. This type of implicit export subsidy is not contingent upon export performance as required by the GATT. The case of price discrimination for one product between domestic and foreign markets for a small country exporter is also depicted in Figure 1. Two situations are considered: price discrimination with and without revenue pooling.

Price discrimination is administered either directly by government regulation or through market power of a government-sanctioned marketing board. Consider the case where the domestic market price is set at P^d where the marginal revenue (*mr*) equals marginal cost (P^w). With price discrimination, but no revenue pooling, production stays at the free trade level Q^{s0}. However, price discrimination causes domestic consumption to contract to Q^{d2}.

The horizontal difference between the domestic supply curve S and domestic demand Q^{d2} results in the excess supply curve ES_2. Exports are X_{disc} where the excess supply curve ES_2 intersects the world price P^w. There is no wedge between the domestic supply and the world price under price discrimination only. This scheme is a consumption tax and the horizontal distance ③ represents the trade distortion. US peanut policy is an example.

Price discrimination in combination with revenue pooling does represent a consumer only-financed export subsidy. The average revenue or pool price is depicted where the average revenue curve AR equals the marginal cost S. Revenues from domestic sales of the amount ($P^d * Q^{d2}$) are pooled with revenues from sales in the world market of the amount ($Q^{s1} - Q^{d2}) * P^w$. The weighted average or pool price P^{pool} which the producer receives is calculated as

$$\{(Q^{d2} * P^d) + [(Q^{s1} - Q^{d2}) * P^2]\} / Q^{s1}$$

Output under the pool price P^{pool} expands to Q^{s1}, while domestic demand remains at Q^{d2} as under price discrimination only. The horizontal difference between the domestic supply curve S and domestic demand Q^{d2} generates the excess supply curve ES_2. Due to the higher producer price P^{pool}, exports increase from X_{disc} under price discrimination only to X_{cons}. Price discrimination in combination with revenue pooling therefore distorts international trade by the sum of the distances ① plus ③ which is more than under price discrimination alone (distance ③). The per unit export subsidy is depicted as the vertical distance XS_{cons} which also illustrates the wedge between the domestic and the world price and therefore confirms that a scheme that involves price discrimination and revenue pooling provides for an implicit export subsidy. Note that this implicit export subsidy is not contingent on export performance but rather is a by-product effect of price discrimination and revenue pooling.

With price discrimination only and the production at the level Q^{s0}, the revenue to farmers is ($Q^{s0} * Pw$)+ \{($Pd - Pw$) * Q^{d2}\}. A policy that combines price discrimination with revenue pooling results in revenue to farmers of the amount ($P^{pool} * Q^{s1}$) which must be equal to the revenue under price discrimination only. This is because the pool price is a weighted average of revenues from the domestic and export market. The pool price does not represent a marginal cost price. This implies that farmers overproduce under a scheme that involves price discrimination and revenue pooling by the amount ($Q^{s1} - Q^{s0}$) to receive the same revenue as under price discrimination alone. The deadweight cost of overproduction is represented by the triangle [$0.5 * (P^{pool} - P^{w}) * (Q^{s1} - Q^{s0})$]. Therefore farmers would be better off not to pool. We also want to emphasize that trade distortion of this type is larger (distances ① plus ③) than under the taxpayer-financed export subsidy (distances ① plus ②). The intuition for this result is that the consumer price for a consumer-financed export subsidy has to be higher than that in the taxpayer-financed case (and greater than the producer price). This means there is less domestic consumption with a consumer-financed export subsidy for the same producer price, and so trade distortion is greater than that with a taxpayer-financed export subsidy.

It is possible that a consumer only-financed export subsidy exists when a non-traded good like fluid milk faces price discrimination but a dairy product is traded at world prices (Sumner, 1996). Consumption of fluid milk is reduced and revenues are pooled to farmers, thereby increasing production. This acts as an export subsidy. ES_2 in Figure 1 would shift left as the price of the traded good declined towards the world price. Trade distortion would decline and perhaps be less than the taxpayer-financed equivalent export subsidy. The decline in consumption with the consumer-financed export subsidy would be greater than that for the taxpayer-financed export subsidy. However, the taxpayer-financed export subsidy also involves a decline in the consumption of the traded product. It can be shown that the extent of the trade distortion would depend on the relative demand elasticities,[2] the proportion of total production of the traded good consumed domestically,[3] the elasticity of supply, the level of farm price desired and the price gap between the export and non-traded good.

Mandatory or government regulated *producer-financed* export subsidies are also subject to reduction commitments in the AoA. A producer-financed export subsidy is contingent on exports and can only coexist with a taxpayer and/or a consumer only-financed export subsidy. However, the effects of a producer-financed export subsidy differ, depending on the initial export subsidy scheme. Introducing a producer levy with a taxpayer-financed export subsidy already in place increases the price to both farmers and consumers. If the levy maintains the net price (and producer welfare), the price to consumers increases and so increases the tax costs of the programme because the world price declines for a given level of exports. The only way a producer levy to finance part of the costs of a taxpayer-financed export subsidy programme can reduce tax costs is when producer welfare declines. Figure 2 shows how a producer levy of t shifts the domestic supply (S_1 to S_2) and excess supply (ES_1 to ES_2) curves left, generating tax revenue and reducing taxpayer costs. Trade distortion is less as production declines, and exports can even become less than free trade levels.

The situation differs for a producer levy to partially or fully finance exports under a consumer only-financed export subsidy scheme. A levy imposed on a

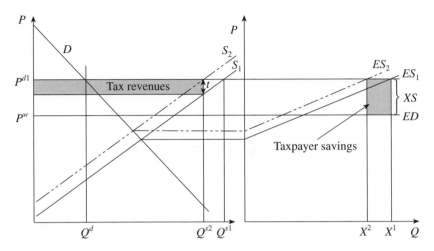

FIGURE 2   *Producer levy with a taxpayer-financed export subsidy (single product)*

consumer only-financed export subsidy results in the same average revenue (pooled domestic and export sales) curve because exports are not pooled at the world price anymore but at some higher price to justify the use of producer levies in the first place. Therefore a producer levy to finance part of the costs of a consumer only-financed export subsidy is identical to a consumer only-financed export subsidy alone, holding producer welfare constant. Note that two products are required for a levy to operate with a consumer-financed export subsidy. Otherwise, there is nothing to tax.

Figure 3 shows the situation of a levy t on a consumer only-financed export subsidy. The consumer only-financed export subsidy is depicted where consumption is at the level Qd owing to price discrimination and the pool price P^{pool} occurs where the average revenue AR (Pd, P^w) intersects the supply curve S and production is of Q^{s1}. Note that revenue is pooled from domestic sales at P^d and export sales at P^w. A levy t is imposed on a consumer only-financed export subsidy, where the average revenue AR (P^d, P^p) generates the pool price P^{pool*}. The difference here is that exports are not pooled at the world price but at a higher level, P^p. Therefore, an export subsidy of the amount B would be necessary to finance exports. Instead, a levy is imposed on the production that reduces output to Q^{s1} and provides the funds for the export subsidy $[Q^{s1} * (P^{pool*} - P^{pool})]$ equivalent to area B. Therefore a producer levy on a consumer only-financed export subsidy is identical to a consumer only-financed export subsidy alone, because one either pools P^d and P^w or P^d and P^p. In the latter pool, one is taxing it back from producers to sell at the world price, so a producer levy in this case is like taking money from one pocket and putting it in another.[4]

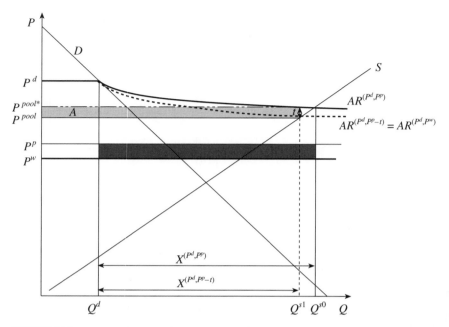

FIGURE 3   *Producer levy with a consumer only-financed export subsidy (two products)*

THE WTO DISPUTE SETTLEMENT PANEL RULING ON
CANADIAN DAIRY POLICY

The problem with the consumer only-financed export subsidy can be illustrated by the recent WTO Dispute Settlement Panel on Canadian dairy policy. The Panel concurred with the USA and New Zealand that milk sold at the world price below domestic prices was receiving a 'preferential' price because it required farmers to 'share the cost' of selling milk at a lower price than the pooled price from domestic sales. The WTO ruled that such a scheme is a producer-financed export subsidy because farmers have to 'forgo revenue' to provide the subsidy and is 'contingent on exports'. The Panel concluded that part of Canada's dairy export scheme is inconsistent with provisions on export subsidies in the AoA and provides export subsidies in excess of quantity ceilings committed to in Canada's Schedule (WTO, 1999).

We argue that the legal definitions of export subsidies in the AoA, the ASCM and Article XVI in the GATT 1994 are inadequate. The Canadian dairy export policy in question is only partly a producer-financed (equivalent to a consumer only-financed) export subsidy. The most important class of milk sold at world prices (below the domestic price) is in fact not receiving an export subsidy at all. The Panel's decision also has implications for other countries' dairy and other commodity policies.

Three milk class prices are contested: Class Vabc and Vd export sales that are from in-quota production and whose revenues are pooled with domestic sales; and Class Ve from over-quota production that is not pooled with domestic price sales and so is exported where the marginal cost of production equals the world price. Consequently, the economic definition of a consumer only (or producer-financed) export subsidy has Classes Vabc and Vd as export subsidies (although potentially less distorting than if no production quota exists). However, the Panel determines Class Vd and Class Ve as export subsidies but not Class Vabc, because access to the latter could also be gained by processors for the domestic market and are not 'contingent upon the export performance' (Table 1)[5] Class Vd and Ve provide a lower price to exporters than could be obtained from other sources and supplied through a government-sanctioned system. Pooling, and whether or not milk originates from in-quota or over-quota production, is not an issue in the WTO Panel findings.

TABLE 1   *The WTO Dispute Settlement Panel ruling on Canadian dairy policy*

Class	Economics	WTO Ruling
Vabc	Domestic *and* export sales Price pooling	Exports not 'preferential' Not contingent on exports because sold on domestic and world markets
Ve	Price pooling Exports only	Export subsidy because of 'preferential' ('share' cost at lower world price) and
Vd	No pooling Over-quota production Get world price only	'contingent on exports'

The Panel fails to take into account that over-quota sales of Class Ve sold at the world market price is produced where marginal costs equal the world price with price discrimination but no revenue pooling. Consumption declines but production remains unchanged compared with the free trade situation and hence no export subsidy can be inferred. The identification of an export subsidy by means of payment, benefit or revenue forgone is somewhat misleading.

Class Vd is an export subsidy because of price discrimination *and* pooling and so should be subject to the reduction commitments. However, the arguments of the USA, New Zealand and the Panel differ from ours. They allege that Class Vd is a producer-financed export subsidy (Article 9.1(*c*) of AoA) because producers forgo revenue owing to the government involvement in the administration of this export milk class. The Panel does not recognize the

TABLE 2   Total rents of New Zealand's dairy policy

Year	Downstream profits* Actual in US$m.	% of total rents	Tariff-rate-quota (TRQ) rents** Actual in US$m.	% of total rents	Domestic price premia*** Actual in US$m.	% of total rents	Total rents in US$m.	Total production value in US$m.	Percentage of production value from: Downstream profits	TRQ	Domestic price premia	Total rents
1990	410.25	73.75	114.87	20.65	31.179	5.60	556.30	1 641	25.00	7.00	1.90	33.90
1991	550.75	73.75	154.21	20.65	41.857	5.60	746.82	2 203	25.00	7.00	1.90	33.90
1992	620.25	73.75	173.67	20.65	47.139	5.60	841.06	2 481	25.00	7.00	1.90	33.90
1993	641.5	73.75	179.62	20.65	48.754	5.60	869.87	2 566	25.00	7.00	1.90	33.90
1994	644.75	73.75	180.53	20.65	49.001	5.60	874.28	2 579	25.00	7.00	1.90	33.90
1995	801.50	73.75	224.42	20.65	60.914	5.60	1 086.83	3 206	25.00	7.00	1.90	33.90
1996	831.25	73.75	232.75	20.65	63.175	5.60	1 127.18	3 325	25.00	7.00	1.90	33.90
1997	812.50	71.38	230.17	20.22	61.719	5.42	1 138.21	3 250	25.00	7.08	1.90	33.98

Notes: *Downstream profits have been calculated to be approx. 25% of total production value (New Zealand Business Roundtable, 1996).
**TRQ rents have been calculated for 1997 and are projected back. They are assumed to be 7% of total production value.
***Domestic price premia have been calculated to be approx. 1.9% of total production value (New Zealand Business Roundtable, 1998).

Source: OECD, New Zealand Business Roundtable (1996 and 1998) Schluep (1999).

difference between price discrimination with pooling and revenue raised by a levy on an existing export subsidy (taxpayer or consumer only-financed).

The Panel concludes that Class Vd confers a subsidy to processors because it is contingent on export performance (Article 1(*e*) of AoA) because lower prices can only be obtained for export sales. But this is not the case for Class Vabc because products from Class Vabc can be sold in either the domestic or the export market. Because of pooling, Class Vabc is an export subsidy but is not recognized as such by the WTO.

This ruling would allow STEs with price discrimination and pooling to continue the practices such as those of the New Zealand Dairy Board. The Board price discriminates among products in international markets and pools revenues, which provides for a production subsidy. Orders of magnitude are briefly summarized in Table 2. This is in addition to pooling the rents from tariff quotas, domestic price premia and downstream profits. But other schemes that are less trade distorting (like the US peanut programme that has no pooling but a high price for domestic consumption) are analogous to Canada's Class Ve and hence would be deemed an export subsidy on the basis of the Panel ruling. Table 3 summarizes the position. The WTO declares Class Vabc not to be an export subsidy when it is, Ve as an export subsidy when it is not, and Vd as an export subsidy when it is, but for the wrong reason (hence the latter is deemed a type III error).

TABLE 3   *WTO ruling versus economic definition on Canadian dairy pricing*

Class	WTO ruling	Economic definition	WTO error
Vabc	No	Yes ($16.6 m.)	Type I
Ve	Yes	No ($225.1 m.)	Type II
Vd	Yes	Yes ($32.8 m.)	Type III*

Note: *Type III error is defined here as correctly accepting the null hypothesis, but with an incorrect assumption.

The WTO's definition of an export subsidy is incomplete because (a) it ignores consumer only-financed export subsidies; (b) it does not properly identify the nature of producer-financed export subsidies and their relationship to consumer only and taxpayer-financed export subsidies; and (c) it has an excessive reliance on the notion of 'contingent on exports' rather than on the underlying characteristics of an export subsidy that has production expanding and consumption contracting simultaneously. The definitions of an export subsidy in the GATT 1994 leaves room for loopholes, circumvention and misinterpretation of what an export subsidy is. It should be more specific on those policies that have the dual effect of contracting domestic consumption and escalating domestic production. This definition would provide a more solid basis from which to recognize different types of export subsidies not now explicitly listed, including a consumer only-financed export subsidy.

CONCLUSIONS

This paper identifies three types of assistance: taxpayer, consumer only and producer-financed export subsidies. The GATT text does not fully account for all of them. Consumer-only financed export subsidies are not identified because they are not contingent on export performance, as required by the GATT. Producer-financed export subsidies are only partially identified but they can only exist with either a taxpayer or a consumer-only financed export subsidy. With a definition of an export subsidy accounting for the dual effect of contracting domestic consumption and escalating domestic production, the WTO could better recognize these more subtle forms of export subsidies.

NOTES

[1]Producer support derived from fluid milk premia is not documented in the AoA.

[2]For example, the more elastic the traded good, the greater the trade distortion with the taxpayer-financed export subsidy.

[3]The higher the proportion of production consumed domestically of the traded good, the less likely is that the consumer-financed export subsidy is more trade distorting.

[4]Producer levies are politically popular with farmers for either the taxpayer or consumer-financed export subsidy scheme. They guarantee extra transfers to farmers from consumers, with the consumer price greater than the net producer price.

[5]Article 1(*e*) of the Agreement on Agriculture defines an export subsidy as a subsidy contingent on export performance.

REFERENCES

Alston, J.M. and Gray, R. (1998), 'Export Subsidies and State Trading: Theory and Application to Canadian Wheat', in T. Yildirim, A. Schmitz and W. Hartley Furtan (eds), *World Agricultural Trade*, Boulder: Westview Press.

Annand, M. and Buckingham, D.E. (1998), 'State Trading Exporters and the World Trade Organization: What are the Rules?', in T. Yildirim, A. Schmitz and W. Hartley Furtan (eds), *World Agricultural Trade*, Boulder: Westview Press.

Dixit, P.M. and Josling, T. (1997), 'State Trading in Agriculture: An Analytical Framework', working paper 97–4, *International Agricultural Trade Research Consortium*.

Schluep, I. (1999), '*The Law and Economics of Consumer Only Financed Export Subsidies: A Context for the WTO Panel on Canadian Dairy Pricing Policy*', unpublished MS thesis, Cornell University, Ithaca, NY.

Sumner, D. (1996), 'The Role of Domestic Market Price Regulations in International Trade: the Case of Dairy Policy in the United States', paper presented to the American Agricultural Economics Association, San Francisco, January.

World Trade Organization (WTO) (1994), *The Results of the Uruguay Round of Multilateral Trade Organizations: The Legal Text*, Geneva, World Trade Organization.

World Trade Organization (WTO) (1999), *Final Report on Canada–Measures Affecting the Importation of Milk and the Exportation of Dairy Products*, Geneva: World Trade Organization, WT/DS103/R, WT/DS113/R, 17 March.

ALEXANDRE GOHIN AND HERVÉ GUYOMARD*

*The Agenda 2000 CAP Reform in the WTO Context: Distortion Effects of
Compensatory Payments and Area Set-aside Requirements*

INTRODUCTION

Although the immediate consequences of the Uruguay Round Agreement on
Agriculture (URAA) on world agriculture should only be modest, its significance should not be underestimated. It places agriculture on the agenda of the
next multilateral negotiations of the World Trade Organization (WTO) and it
defines a negotiation framework in the form of three main areas: export competition, market access and internal support (Vanzetti, 1996). Recognizing that
the long-term objective of substantial progressive reductions in support and
protection resulting in fundamental reform is a continuing process, Article 20
of the URAA includes a commitment to engage in a new round of multilateral
agricultural negotiations before the end of 1999. The so-called Millennium
Round (MR) will use the negotiation framework of the Uruguay Round (UR)
and the proponents of reform, that is the Cairns group and the United States
(USA), are likely push for further commitments in terms of export subsidy
cuts, market access improvement and internal support reductions.

The URAA commitments to reduce domestic support by 20 per cent will
impose no adjustment needs on the Common Agricultural Policy (CAP) because of the accommodating treatment of Aggregate Measure of Support (AMS)
reduction, in particular the exclusion of 1992 CAP reform compensatory payments from AMS computation and their inclusion in the so-called 'blue box'.[1]
But it is likely that the MR will expose these blue box payments to close
scrutiny; firstly, because the US FAIR Act of 1996 now leaves the European
Union (EU) alone in sheltering its direct payments from challenge by means of
the blue box (Josling and Tangermann, 1999) and, secondly, because most
countries have been able to reduce their amber support levels much more than
required under the URAA, suggesting that further internal support reductions
are economically and politically feasible (USDA, 1998).

The Agenda 2000 CAP reform adopted in Berlin in March 1999 will deepen
(cereals and beef) and extend (dairy products) the 1992 MacSharry reform

*INRA-ESR, Rennes, France. For this research, the authors have benefited from financial support
from the European Commission under the FAIR5-CT97-3481 project, which is gratefully acknowledged. However, the opinions expressed are those of the authors and are not intended to
reflect those of the European Commission.

through further shifts from price support to direct payments. Even if the EU does not assign weights to the various factors which have motivated this new reform of the CAP, it appears that it is mainly designed to cope with the constraints of the URAA, the preparation of the next WTO round and the EU enlargement to Central and Eastern European countries (Desquilbet *et al.*, 1999). The EU, however, makes no proposals to change existing world trade commitments and this suggests that what is proposed is as far as the EU is prepared to go in negotiation (Marsh, 1998).[2] In particular, in a WTO context, the Agenda 2000 reform appears to be based on the premise that blue box exemptions will be extended (Tielu and Roberts, 1998).

According to Article 1 of Annex 2 of the URAA, domestic support policies for which exemption from the reduction commitments is claimed 'shall meet the fundamental requirement that they have no, or at most minimal, trade distortion effects or effects on production' (Point 1 of Annex 2 of the URAA). However, this fundamental requirement has not really been used to determine whether specific policy instruments should be in the green box. In practice, policy measures have been considered as amber, blue or green according to Point 5 of Article 6 (which defines blue box direct payments under production-limiting programmes) and Points 2 to 13 of Annex 2 (which define green box 'government service programmes'). In particular, Point 6 of Annex 2 defines five criteria that direct payments to producers shall meet to be classified as decoupled income support measures. This box eligibility process has been criticized. For instance, the USDA (1998) notes that a problem of interpretation arises in implementing the URAA because of the undefined fundamental criteria for the green box that the reported programmes be no more than minimally distorting of production and trade. Consequently, 'some programmes reported in the green box could satisfy the policy-specific criteria for being green and yet also could have significant production effects with great enough financing and programme participation'. In the same vein, Tielu and Roberts (1998) state that, 'although the green box measures are supposed to be minimally production distorting, there could be substantial scope for reorienting support towards the measures in ways that could markedly increase production'. The purpose of this paper, then, is to analyse to what extent the Agenda 2000 CAP (with emphasis on cereals, oilseeds and protein crops) represents a further step in the direction of a more decoupled and less distorting internal support policy, firstly in terms of URAA green box criterion eligibility and secondly, in terms of distortion effects on production.

URAA GREEN BOX ELIGIBILITY OF AGENDA 2000 COMPENSATORY PAYMENTS

In this section, we only discuss the green box eligibility of compensatory payments granted in the arable crops sector (cereals, oilseeds and protein crops) and in the beef sector. As they are defined in the Berlin agreement, these compensatory payments satisfy the two basic criteria that domestic support policies shall meet to be included in the green box; namely, (a) they do not involve transfers from consumers and they are publicly funded, and (b) they do not have the effect of providing price support to producers.

Let us now analyse the characteristics of these compensatory payments in the light of the five criteria of Point 6 of Annex 2 of the URAA, which defines decoupled income support. They clearly satisfy the first criterion that eligibility is determined by clearly-defined criteria, here the status as a producer. However, they do not fully conform to the four other criteria. Criterion 2, which states that 'the amount of payments shall not be related to, or based on, the type or volume of production undertaken by the producer in any year after the base period', is clearly not fulfilled because area and headage payments differ. Criterion 3, which lays down that 'the amount of payments shall not be related to, or based on, the prices, domestic or international, applying to any production undertaken in any year after the base period', might not be respected if the possibility, introduced in the Agenda 2000 CAP reform, to alter direct aid payments in the light of production, productivity and market conditions is effectively applied. Criterion 4 stipulates that 'the amount of payments shall not be related to, or based on, the factors of production employed in any year after the base period'. It is clearly not satisfied because the amount of direct aids received by a producer depends on cultivated area and/or the number of bovine animals. Criterion 5 requires that 'no production shall be required in order to receive payments'. It also is not satisfied because the aids remain tied to the obligation of producing certain crops and/or bovine animals.

The cross-compliance requirements included in the Berlin agreement are not sufficient to switch compensatory payments for price support cuts from the blue box to the green box by considering them as payments under environmental programmes, in accordance with Point 12 of Annex 2. As they are currently defined, direct aids do not fulfil conditions (i) and (ii) of this point because, firstly, they are not part of a clearly defined government environmental or conservation programme and, secondly, the amount of payment is not limited to the extra costs or loss of income involved in complying with the government environmental or conservation programme. In addition, it is unlikely that many EU member states will introduce cross-compliance.

The mechanism of Agenda 2000 compensatory payments will probably be contested in the MR (Swinbank, 1999). However, the EU could rightfully argue that they achieve a (slightly) greater degree of decoupling relative to the 1992 CAP area compensatory payments. Firstly, compensatory payments for arable crops are now non-crop specific (with the 'minor' exceptions of protein crops and durum wheat). Secondly, the set-aside is remunerated at the same rate for land in cereals and oilseeds, so that a farmer may decide to set aside and to draw the common subsidy if this option is more profitable than production. This implies that the fifth criterion of Article 6 is now respected, at least as far as COP (cereals, oil and protein) crops and producers are concerned. Thirdly, the amount of direct aids available to producers is constrained by the historical base area in the arable crops sector and by the density factor and various ceilings in the beef sector. These ceilings have been reduced in Berlin, making them more restricting than in the past. As a result, the fourth criterion of Article 6 is now 'more' satisfied since the amount of direct aids for beef producers is less dependent on current livestock units and more dependent on the ceilings.

Finally, it is worth mentioning that the URAA definition of decoupled income support is somewhat fluid. Let us consider, for example, criterion 3 of Article 6 of Annex 2. The Agenda 2000 reform reserves the right to alter direct aid payments in the light of production, productivity and market conditions. This possibility is clearly introduced to avoid the repetition of the overcompensation which occurred following the 1992 reform. The EU could rightfully argue that the mechanism of reducing the level of compensatory payments if market prices are better than expected is a (second-best) way to reduce the distortionary effects of compensatory payments. Of course, the reasoning holds only if these compensatory payments are not increased when market prices are lower than expected.

PRODUCTION IMPACTS OF AGENDA 2000 COMPENSATORY PAYMENTS AND SET-ASIDE REQUIREMENTS

Several studies have already analysed the likely consequences of the Agenda 2000 CAP reform on market equilibria, agricultural incomes and budgetary costs (for example, FAPRI-UMC, 1999; Stolwijk and Merbis, 1999; USDA, 1999). Not all studies agree that the new policy is more decoupled and less distorting than the 1992 CAP. Differences arise because different choices are made concerning the base year/reference scenario against which the Agenda 2000 experiment is compared, alternative world price data are used, some studies have explicit as against implicit modelling of policy instruments, and there is dispute about whether or not changes in support prices are assumed to be fully transmitted to market prices.

A decomposition of effects on production and consumption is necessary to assess the degree of decoupling/distortion of the whole Agenda 2000 package and of each instrument. Cahill (1997) has performed this decomposition for the 1992 CAP. His results suggest that the 1992 compensatory payments are effectively fully decoupled for some crops (wheat, rapeseed and soybeans), but only partially decoupled from production in the case of coarse grains and sunflower. Moro and Sckokai (1998) have used the Cahill methodology to evaluate the degree of decoupling of the 1992 CAP in Italy. Their results suggest that the degree of decoupling of the whole package varies as a function of market price changes and that for some combinations of prices the whole can even be considered as fully decoupled. Of course this does not mean that the 1992 compensatory payments are decoupled per se. In the case of France, Guyomard *et al.* (1996) have shown that the 1992 compensatory payments have only small effects on production and that the package is to a large extent 'neutral' in so far as the effects of 'own crop' compensatory payments are offset by cross-compensatory payments on substitutable crops. Their results are conditional on the fact that the total area in COP crops is constrained to be equal to the historical base area.

This section follows Guyomard *et al.* (1996) in developing an analytical framework allowing estimation of the effects of the new instrumentation of the

CAP (price cuts, compensatory payments and land set-aside schemes) on crop area allocation, supply and yields. The model distinguishes seven crops (soft wheat, barley, maize, other coarse grains, rapeseed, sunflower seed and field peas). It is applied to France using the Maximum Entropy (ME) approach with parameter calibration to reproduce the situation of the reference year (1997). The model is briefly described in the Annexe.

Experiment design

Three experiments are performed. In the first (no area compensatory payments and no mandatory set-aside), crop market prices are assumed unchanged at 1997 levels, area compensatory payments are suppressed and the mandatory set-aside is set to zero. Experiment I allows us to measure the effects on production of the package of 1992 area direct payments, including the provision that professional producers of COP crops (that is, those having an area sufficient to grow 92 tonnes of cereals, which would be about 20 hectares, depending on region) receive these arable area payments only if they set aside part of their arable land. In the second experiment (Agenda 2000), policy measures adopted in Berlin in March 1999 are implemented. Market price reductions for cereals are assumed lower than corresponding support price cuts. They are thus decreased by 5 per cent for wheat and 7 per cent for barley, maize and other coarse grains (FAPRI-UMC, 1999). Market prices of oilseeds and protein crops are assumed unchanged at their 1997 levels. Compensatory payments are increased by 16 per cent for all the cereals, while they are decreased by 32 per cent for oilseeds and by 7 per cent for protein crops. The set-aside requirement corresponds to an increase of 2.2 per cent in land in COP crops. In the third experiment (Agenda 2000 without area compensatory payments and no mandatory set-aside) market price changes of the second experiment are applied. Comparing experiments II and III allows us to evaluate the degree of decoupling of the package of Agenda 2000 compensatory payments and set-aside requirements. Experiment results are shown in Table 1 (land area allocation) and Table 2 (output supply).

Experiment results

Let us first consider experiment 1. Although the compulsory set-aside rate is fixed to zero, total cultivated area in COP crops is lower than the total base area (12.458 million hectares compared with 12.536 million). There is still land left in fallow on a voluntary basis (78 000 hectares). This suggests that the total base area is not binding or, in other words, that it is not profitable to devote all the predetermined area corresponding to the base area to the seven COP crops. This first experiment leads to an increase by 6.9 per cent in cultivated land relative to 1997 (Table 1). The area increase is unequally distributed among the various crops, the area under cereals increasing by much larger percentages than the area under oilseeds. This outcome is directly linked to the fact that compensatory payments per hectare were initially much higher for oilseeds than for cereals. The first experiment leads to different supply

TABLE 1   *Experiment results: impacts on land allocation (1000 hectares, changes in percentages in parentheses)*

	Base levels	Current decoupling (I)	Agenda 2000 (II)	Agenda 2000 decoupling (III)	(III) – (I)	(III) – (II)
Wheat	4 844	5 237 (+8.12)	4 992 (+3.07)	5 156 (+6.45)	−81 (−1.55)	+164 (+3.28)
Barley	1 690	1797 (+6.34)	1 735 (+2.67)	1 780 (+5.30)	−17 (−0.95)	+45 (+2.59)
Maize	1 857	1 928 (+3.83)	1 887 (+1.58)	1 893 (+1.90)	−35 (−1.82)	+6 (+0.32)
Other cereals	794	976 (+22.95)	858 (+8.12)	934 (+17.67)	−42 (−4.30)	+76 (+8.86)
Rapeseed	988	995 (+0.75)	965 (−2.36)	994 (+0.60)	−1 (−0.10)	+29 (+3.01)
Sunflower seed	875	884 (+1.08)	847 (−3.17)	884 (+1.12)	0 (0)	+37 (+4.37)
Field peas	607	641 (+5.17)	627 (+3.27)	642 (+5.72)	+1 (+0.16)	+15 (+2.39)
Cultivated land	11 655	12 458 (+6.89)	11 911 (+2.20)	12 283 (+5.39)	−175 (−1.40)	+372 (+3.12)
Set-aside land	881	78 (−91.15)	625 (−29.00)	253 (−71.28)	+175 (+224.35)	−372 (−59.52)
Total land	12 536	12 536	12 536	12 536	0	0

TABLE 2   *Experiment results: impacts on production (1000 tonnes, changes in percentages in parentheses)*

	Base levels	Current decoupling (I)	Agenda 2000 (II)	Agenda 2000 decoupling (III)	(III) – (I)	(III) – (II)
Wheat	32 970	35 641 (+8.10)	33 703 (+2.22)	34 815 (+5.60)	−826 (−2.32)	+1112 (+3.30)
Barley	10 126	10 552 (+4.21)	10 204 (+0.77)	10 381 (+2.52)	−171 (−1.62)	+177 (+1.73)
Maize	16 832	17 567 (+4.36)	16 997 (+0.98)	17 058 (+1.34)	−509 (−2.90)	+61 (+0.36)
Other cereals	2 618	3 303 (+26.15)	2 783 (+6.31)	3 068 (+17.20)	−235 (−7.11)	+285 (+10.24)
Rapeseed	3 495	3 523 (+0.81)	3 404 (−2.61)	3 516 (+0.60)	−7 (−0.20)	+112 (+3.29)
Sunflower seed	1 995	2 031 (+1.80)	1 890 (−5.27)	2 033 (+1.88)	+2 (+0.10)	+143 (+7.57)
Field peas	3 055	3 187 (+4.32)	3 131 (+2.48)	3 187 (+4.32)	0 (0)	+56 (+1.79)

increases across crops (Table 2). The supply of other coarse grains rises by the most (26.6 per cent) while that of rapeseed rises least (0.8 per cent). From the tables it can be deduced that yields are not very sensitive to the removal of area compensatory payments and compulsory set-aside requirements.

Experiment I shows that the whole package of 1992 CAP compensatory payments, including the provision that these direct aids are contingent upon idling a certain proportion of land area for professional producers, leads to production decrease for the seven COP crops considered here relative to a regime where both area compensatory payments and compulsory set-aside requirements were removed. Of course this result is conditional on the mandatory set-aside rate applied in the 1997 reference year.

To a large extent, experiment II results are consistent with those of the FAPRI-UMC (1999). Total area under COP crops increases by 2.2 per cent relative to the 1997 base (11.911 and 11.655 hectares, respectively). However, the whole Agenda 2000 has differential impacts for the seven crops considered here. The four cereals and field peas are favoured (increased area and supplies) while the two oilseeds are at a disadvantage (area and supplies drop). For the four cereals and field peas the increase, in percentage terms, in planted area is higher than that in supply, indicating that yields decrease relative to 1997.

In experiment III, market price reductions are applied but there are neither area compensatory payments nor compulsory set-aside rate requirements. In this case land left in fallow is still positive (253 000 hectares). Total land under COP crops increases by 5.4 per cent relative to the 1997 base (12.283 million hectares and 11.655 million, respectively). This change is unequally distributed among the seven crops, the area under other coarse grains increasing the most (17.7 per cent) with the rapeseed change being smallest (0.6 per cent). This experiment also has differential impacts on production by favouring the supply of cereals and field peas to a much greater extent than oilseeds.

In the context of the decoupling/distortion issue surrounding the Agenda 2000 reform, it is interesting to compare experiments II and III (last column of Tables 1 and 2). Relative to experiment II, the third experiment leads to (a) an increase in total cultivated COP land by 3.1 per cent (b) an increase in area allocated to each crop (from 0.3 per cent in the case of maize to 8.9 per cent for other coarse grains) and (c) a production increase for each of the seven crops (from 0.4 per cent for maize to 10.2 per cent for other coarse grains). It can be concluded that the whole Agenda 2000 package has less distortionary effects than a scenario with price cuts not being compensated by area direct payments and without compulsory set-aside requirements. Of course this conclusion is conditional on the fact that land left in fallow on both a mandatory and voluntary basis decreases in experiment III relative to the 1997 base year.

CONCLUSIONS

Strengthening internal support disciplines is very likely to be a key component of the multilateral agricultural negotiations of the Millennium Round. The Cairns group considers that insufficient progress was made during the Uruguay

Round, while the blue box exemption is now less useful than in 1994 from a US perspective. The Agenda 2000 reform does not go far enough for the modified area compensation payments to be included in the green box. However, the EU can justifiably argue that the whole Agenda 2000 package (at least for COP crops) is less production and trade distorting than the 1992 CAP. This is due to the fact that area compensatory payments are granted in conjunction with compulsory set-aside requirements. Since professional producers must set aside a percentage of their planted area, the ultimate impact on production and trade will crucially depend on the amount of land going into set-aside. At this stage it is important to remember that the Agenda 2000 requirement has a base level of 10 per cent. However, the Council of Ministers can vary the level to be applied annually.

More generally, the analysis shows that the decoupling/distortion issue should not be addressed by considering each instrument independently from other policy measures. A policy is a package of measures. Millennium Round discussions of the internal support dossier will begin sensibly only if each country recognizes that the rules should be defined in relation to the effects on trade of the whole package, rather than by picking off separate policy provisions. That would be an improvement on the way in which the Uruguay Round negotiators operated when defining the items for inclusion in the various boxes.

NOTES

[1]Domestic policies considered to have no or minimal trade distortion effects are not subject to reduction commitments. In addition to these green box policies, production-limiting direct payments are also exempt from inclusion in the AMS. Examples of blue box instruments are 1992 CAP reform compensatory payments in the EU and 1990 FACT Act deficiency payments in the USA.

[2]Strictly speaking, the comments apply to the European Commission (EC) proposals of 1997 and 1998, but they seem equally applicable to the reform finally adopted in Berlin in 1999.

REFERENCES

Cahill, S.E. (1997), 'Calculating the Rate of Decoupling for Crops under CAP/Oilseeds Reform', *Journal of Agricultural Economics*, **48**, 349–78.

Desquilbet, M., Gohin, A. and Guyomard, H. (1999), *La réforme Agenda 2000 de la politique agricole commune : une perspective internationale*, working paper, Paris: INRA-ESR.

FAPRI-UMC (1999), *Implications of the Berlin Accord for EU Agriculture*, report 07-99, FAPRI-UMC.

Gohin, A., Chantreuil, F. and Levert, F. (1999), *Modélisation du secteur européen des grandes cultures, céréales, oleagineux et protéagineux*, working paper (in French), Paris: INRA-ESR.

Guyomard, H., Baudry, M. and Carpentier A. (1996), 'Estimating crop supply response in the presence of farm programmes: application to the CAP', *European Review of Agricultural Economics*, **23**, 401–20.

Josling, T. and Tangermann, S. (1999), 'The WTO Agreement on Agriculture and developments for the next round of negotiations', *European Review of Agricultural Economics*, **26**, 371-88.

Marsh, J. (1998), 'Redesigning the CAP for the 21st century', in M.R. Redclift, J.N. Lekakis and G.P. Zanias (eds), *Agriculture and World Trade Liberalisation: Socio-Environmental Perspectives on the Common Agricultural Policy*, Wallingford: CAP International.

Moro, D. and Sckokai, P. (1998), 'Modelling the 1992 CAP Reform: Degree of Decoupling and Future Scenarios', paper presented at the AAEA Annual Meeting, Salt Lake City, Utah, 2–5 August.

Stolwijk, H. and Merbis, M. (1999), *The Berlin compromise of Agenda 2000*, The Hague: CPB Report, 1999/3.

Swinbank, A. (1999), 'CAP reform and the WTO: compatibility and developments', *European Review of Agricultural Economics*, **26**, 389–407.

Tielu, A. and Roberts, I. (1998), 'Farm income support: Implications for gains from trade of changes in methods of support overseas', *ABARE Current Issues*, **98**(4), ABARE, Canberra.

USDA (1998), *Agriculture in the WTO: Situation and Outlook Series*, United States Department of Agriculture, Economic Research Service, International Agriculture and Trade Reports, WRS-98-4, Washington, DC.

USDA (1999), *The European Union – Agenda 2000*, United States Department of Agriculture, Economic Research Service (on Internet at *http://www.econ.ag.gov/briefing/region/europe/issagenda.htm*).

Vanzetti, D. (1996), 'The Next Round: Game-Theory and Public Choice Perspectives', *Food Policy*, **21**, 461–77.

ANNEXE: MAIN CHARACTERISTICS OF THE MODEL

The complete structure of the model is detailed in Gohin *et al.* (1999). The main characteristics that must be underlined in the context of this paper are as follows. The model is a static non-linear programming model which describes the behaviour of French producers of COP (cereals, oilseeds and protein) crops. It is benchmarked to data for 1997. Producers choose area allocation, output supply and yields per hectare by maximizing their profit subject to market and technical constraints. These two types of constraints are easily handled by the use of a programming model. In particular, the main instruments of the Common Market organization for arable crops, that is, intervention prices, direct aids to cultivated land, direct aids to land left in fallow, set-aside commitments, base areas and so on are explicitly taken into account. As a result, the model is particularly well suited to simulate the effects of reforms in the arable crops sector. One original feature of the model is the calibration process of behavioural parameters on the basis of the Maximum Entropy (ME) approach. The ME approach is increasingly used in agricultural economics because it makes it possible to solve ill-posed problems like ours when the number of parameters is greater than the number of observations.

Seven COP crops are considered: soft wheat, barley, maize, an aggregate for other cereals, rapeseed, sunflower seed and field peas. The model calibrated with ME duplicates the 1997 reference year.

MARTIN BANSE, WOLFGANG MÜNCH
AND STEFAN TANGERMANN*

Eastern Enlargement of the European Union:
General and Partial Equilibrium Analysis

INTRODUCTION

With their accession to the European Union (EU), agricultural policies in the countries of Central Europe (CECs) will change more or less dramatically as they are aligned with the Common Agricultural Policy (CAP). These policy adjustments clearly have significant implications for farmers and food consumers in Central Europe, for market balance and trade in agriculture, for budget expenditure and for macroeconomic conditions. A quantitative analysis of the implications is a demanding task for economic analysis. For example, capital flows between the CECs and Brussels change fundamentally as 'financial solidarity' under the CAP as well as other EU budget mechanisms come into play. This may well affect exchange rates, which then at the micro level of agricultural markets have an impact on price formation, which at the same time is also greatly affected by the introduction of the CAP. Such micro-level changes in the agro-food sector can then – considering the economic importance of this sector in the CECs – again produce significant repercussions at the macroeconomic level.

A number of studies have made estimates of the quantitative implications of eastern enlargement in the area of agriculture. Anderson and Tyers (1993) and Frohberg *et al.* (1998) used a partial equilibrium model. Other studies have used agricultural general equilibrium models (Jensen *et al.*, 1998; Liapis and Tsigas, 1998; Hertel *et al.* 1997). While partial equilibrium models are richer in policy and commodity detail, agriculture in the general equilibrium models interacts with other sectors of the economy. Both aspects are of importance when analysing CEC–EU accession effects.

We suggest that an appropriate analytical approach to studying the effects of such sweeping policy changes at both the macroeconomic level and the level of individual agricultural markets is a combination of computable general equilibrium models and partial equilibrium models. This approach was outlined in general form by Banse and Münch (1998). The current paper summarizes

*University of Göttingen, Germany. The quantitative analysis presented in this paper is based on research pursued in the project on 'Agricultural Implications of CEEC Accession to the EU', funded by the European Commission (project FAIR1-CT95-0029).

the results of applying the method to studying the impact of CEC in the sector of food and agriculture.

We start with an overview of the model structures used and the scenarios studied, then turn to some major results achieved in the analysis, and finally draw some conclusions.

PARTIAL AND GENERAL EQUILIBRIUM ANALYSIS

The partial equilibrium model used here, named the European Simulation Model (ESIM), was originally developed by USDA/ERS in cooperation with Josling and Tangermann (Josling *et al.*, 1998). It was first used in Tangermann and Josling (1994), and further developed in Tangermann and Münch (1995) and Münch (1995). More recently, the model structure was further adapted to simulate CEC accession to the EU.

ESIM is a price and policy-driven comparative static, multi-commodity agricultural world model with rich cross-commodity relations and the possibility to model price and trade policy instruments in great detail. The model includes EU-15 and ten CECs. Of these there are five, the Czech Republic, Estonia, Hungary, Poland and Slovenia, which are in the first wave of accession negotiations. Later references to CEC-4 exclude Estonia, for which a CGE model is not yet operational. The other five countries are Bulgaria, Latvia, Lithuania, Romania and Slovakia. All other countries are aggregated into the rest of the world (ROW). The agricultural sector comprises 27 products, which include three dairy and six oilseed products. Trade is modelled as the residual of supply and domestic use.

The policy instruments in ESIM (minimum price, variable or fixed export subsidies/import tariffs, productions quota, set-aside, direct payments and so on) are modelled to closely match actual EU regulations as well as those proposed for the future CAP. For reasons of simplification, it is assumed that these instruments are applied in the CECs. When simulating EU accession, the levels at which the instruments are employed in the individual countries approach those of the EU. In a second step the integration of the CECs into the Single European Market is simulated by applying the instruments to the extended EU, that is, including supply and demand of all member countries.

Three alternative policy scenarios merit particular attention and will be analysed: (i) CEC accession to EU without adopting the CAP and continuation of the current agricultural policies in Central Europe can serve as a reference base (MEMBER/NO CAP). Two scenarios analyse accession under a reformed CAP as outlined in Agenda 2000: (ii) One takes the recent discussion into account which argues for *not* extending the compensatory payments for area and livestock to CEC farmers (AGENDA). The main argument for this option is that these payments compensate EU farmers for price declines resulting from CAP reforms from 1992 (Buckwell and Tangermann, 1999). Since CEC farmers generally face price increases during accession, it is argued that there is no need to 'compensate' them. The opposite point of view is that these payments are in part coupled to production and are not of a temporary nature, so that they are an integral part of CAP support to agriculture. Following this line of argument, (iii) an Agenda 2000 version is evaluated which grants the unified area payments and payments for beef cattle and dairy cows to the new members (AGENDA+DIR).

The CGE models developed for Central Europe take in the Czech Republic, Hungary, Poland and Slovenia. They are based on a model structure originally developed by Adelman and Robinson (1978) and further extended by Banse (1997) for Hungary. The models have a recursive–dynamic structure with a one-period time lag for the instalment of new capital, which is then assumed to be sector-specific within each period. They include two types of labour (low and high-skill workers) which are perfectly mobile across all sectors. Land is modelled as a specific primary factor in agricultural production. The models specify the behaviour of optimizing consumers in two different types of households (an urban and a rural household). Aggregate domestic demand in the model has four components: private consumption, intermediate demand, government and investment. The CGE models include the major macro balances: savings, investment, government deficit and the balance of trade. In the trade balance equation, the value of imports must equal the value of exports (both at world prices) plus exogenously set foreign savings and net foreign borrowing by the country governments. Hence the real exchange rate adjusts to achieve equilibrium.

The partial and general equilibrium models are combined in this analysis to exploit their respective comparative advantages. In a first round of analysis, nominal rates of protection (NPRs) resulting from ESIM simulations of the alternative detailed policy scenarios are implemented in the CGE models for the CEC. The resulting developments of macroeconomic variables in the CGE models (for example, real income, factor prices, prices for agricultural intermediates and real exchange rates) are reported as part of the analytical results. At the same time they are fed back into ESIM, which then generates information on detailed market developments. Details of the project can be found in various publications of the authors of this paper which are cited in the references.

SELECTED RESULTS

ESIM results show that the average level of agricultural protection increases in most of the CECs when the CAP is adopted, which is assumed to be 2002 (Figure 1). The specific change of average protection in each CEC depends on pre-EU national policies and country-specific production structures. Hungary exhibits the largest increase in production, by more than three times, for two reasons. First, the initial level of protection at farmgate level (domestic policies) is almost zero and, second, highly protected commodities under the CAP have a large share in Hungary's production structure. The other extreme is Slovenia, where the crucial products almost match CAP protection at farmgate level, but exceed it at wholesale and processing level (Bojnec and Münch, 1999). As a result, the integration of Slovenia into the Common Market in

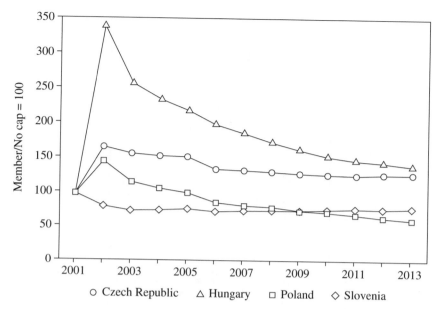

Source: Münch (2000a).

FIGURE 1 *Ratio between NPRs in the AGENDA scenario and the MEMBER/NO CAP scenario*

2002 leads to a decrease of protection by more than 25 per cent. Poland and the Czech Republic face an increase of protection by 50 per cent and 30 per cent, respectively. However, in 2005, Poland's agricultural sector enjoys a protection level which is similar to the MEMBER/NO CAP scenario. After 2005, agricultural protection is even lower than in the reference scenario. Note that the change between scenarios in NPRs is also affected by exchange rate developments in the NO CAP scenario, which is one reason for the declining relative NPRs after 2002, as shown in Figure 1.

As a result of these developments in protection, aggregate production in the CEC-4 grows more rapidly than domestic use, which means that there is an increase in net exports of most products over time (see Table 1). There are, however, country differences. Hungary, the only country which is currently a net exporter of agricultural and food products, increases exports. Other countries like Slovenia continue to import major products. In markets for highly protected commodities under the CAP, such as some coarse grains, sugar and dairying, production expands significantly, which leads to mounting surpluses during accession, unless quotas severely restrict production (Münch 2000a; Banze, 2000).

As far as budget implications are concerned, ESIM generates projections only for net expenditure on trade measures, that is, export subsidies minus

TABLE 1   Development of CEC-4 net exports under alternative policy scenarios (million tons)

	1990–91	Base	2006 MEMBER/ NO CAP	2006 AGENDA	2006 AGENDA + DIR	2013 MEMBER/ NO CAP	2013 AGENDA	2013 AGENDA + DIR
Cereals	1.38	0.32	11.3	13.4	13.3	18.0	17.7	17.6
of which:								
Wheat	0.65	1.02	5.13	3.30	2.87	8.15	4.91	4.23
Coarse grains	0.73	-0.70	6.20	10.1	10.4	9.86	12.8	13.4
Oilseeds	0.44	0.18	0.56	0.05	0.08	0.71	0.35	0.37
Sugar	0.52	0.16	0.77	0.39	0.38	1.38	0.46	0.45
Butter	0.02	0.04	0.04	0.06	0.06	0.05	0.05	0.05
Beef	0.15	0.21	0.41	0.28	0.34	0.63	0.21	0.25
Pork	0.19	0.01	-1.38	-1.28	-1.55	-2.06	-1.87	-2.03

Source: Münch (2000a).

tariff revenues, as well as compensation and headage payments. To make the model results comparable with EU guarantee spending, conversion factors have been applied to include expenditure on administration and storage. These conversion factors are based on results for the EU-15 for the base period and the actual budgetary outlays for the products in the model.

Government spending for agricultural policies in the CEC-4 under their national policies (MEMBER/NO CAP scenario) gradually rises to EURO2.5 billion in 2013 as a result of growing net exports and increasing protection due to appreciating real exchange rates. Note that support prices are assumed to be set in national currencies so that exchange rate revaluation raises the level of protection. Integration into the CAP under the AGENDA scenario (that is, without direct payments), would result only in a limited expenditure increase, to EURO3.5 billion. Owing to real appreciation of the CEC-4 currencies against the EURO and the resulting market effects, public expenditure under AGENDA grows less then if the CAP is not introduced. As a matter of fact, after the Agenda 2000 cut in the milk price in 2006, market expenditure under AGENDA ends up less than under national policies in the CEC (Figure 2).

Complete introduction of the Agenda 2000 including direct payments (AGENDA+DIR) greatly raises expenditures, to close to EURO10 billion. The

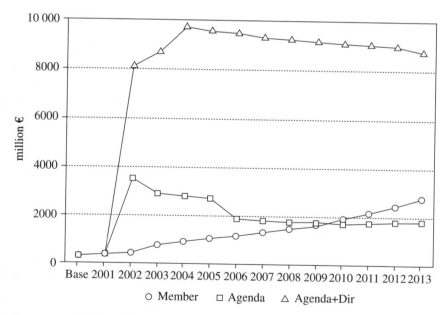

Source: Model results and data from EU Commission (1997).

FIGURE 2 *Development of budgetary expenditure on market guarantee (inclusive of direct payments) in the CEC-4 under alternative scenarios, 2001 to 2013*

largest part of the extra expenditure is for direct payments for arable crops. Total expenditure on the CAP in the CEC-4 under this scenario is slightly less than what the introduction of the pre-Agenda CAP in the CECs would cost.

In the CGE analysis it turns out that the net trade position in agriculture of the individual CECs is an important factor determining most of the macroeconomic consequences of introducing the CAP. For agricultural net importers, the mechanism of 'financial solidarity' under the CAP leads to an outflow of financial resources (visible or invisible in the form of higher price paid on imports from other EU countries) to Brussels (or a reduction in net inflow of money transferred from Brussels). Therefore Poland and Slovenia, remaining net importers, exhibit a small decline in GDP after introduction of the CAP (Table 2). Hungary and the Czech Republic, as agricultural net exporters, enjoy an increase in net transfers from the EU budget and, as a consequence, both countries' GDP increases as a result of CAP introduction, in 2006 by 0.4 per cent in Hungary and by 0.2 per cent in the Czech Republic.

The changes in GDP beyond 2002 are caused by changes in the NPR of the agro-food sector, which differ from country to country (see above). The effects of 'financial solidarity' are also mirrored in the development of real exchange rates. In Hungary and the Czech Republic, the inflow of financial resources under the CAP makes the real exchange rate appreciate in 2002, and vice versa in Poland and Slovenia (Table 2). Later developments of the real exchange rate are partly conditioned by changes in agricultural protection.

The adoption of the CAP (without direct payments) in the AGENDA scenario has a negative impact on non-agricultural value added in those countries where agricultural support is expected to increase: Poland, Hungary and the Czech Republic (see Table 3). On the other hand, Slovene non-agricultural value added increases by almost 1 per cent owing to a reduction in agricultural protection. Because of differences in the relative increase of agricultural NPR (see Figure 1), there is a high increase in value added in Hungarian and Czech agriculture, a small increase in Polish agriculture and a strong decline in Slovene agriculture.

The inclusion of direct payments modelled in the AGENDA+DIR scenario reduces the decline in Slovene agricultural value added. In the other three countries the direct payments magnify the increase of agricultural value added. Non-agricultural value added begins to increase in the AGENDA+DIR scenario, which is due to an increase in available income in rural households.

The changes in Polish agricultural and non-agricultural value added are mirrored in the change in rural and urban household welfare (Table 3). Rural welfare in Poland improves very little after introduction of the CAP, though direct payments would increase household welfare by more than 21 per cent. However, in Hungary and Slovenia, the relative change in agricultural value added is much higher than the change in rural household welfare. This discrepancy is due to different shares of agricultural income in rural household income. While in Poland most rural income stems from agriculture, similar households in Hungary and Slovenia gain most of their income from non-agricultural activities. Therefore rural household welfare in Hungary rises only by 1.5 per cent in the AGENDA scenario and by 6.9 per cent in the AGENDA+DIR

TABLE 2   *Impact of CAP adoption (agenda scenario) on GDP and on real exchange rates, percentage changes relative to MEMBER/NO CAP scenario*

	GDP				Exchange Rate			
	AGENDA		AGENDA + DIR		AGENDA		AGENDA + DIR	
	2006	2013	2006	2013	2006	2013	2006	2013
Czech Republic	0.2	0.2	0.7	0.8	−1.1	−0.8	−3.5	−1.2
Hungary	0.4	0.1	1.3	0.9	−1.6	−0.4	−5.4	−2.9
Poland	−0.2	−0.1	1.1	0.2	1.0	1.3	−2.3	0.4
Slovenia	−0.3	−0.3	−0.2	0.1	1.0	0.5	0.6	0.2

Source: Authors' calculations. Under the definition used a negative change in the exchange rate represents an appreciation.

TABLE 3   *Impact of CAP adoption on sectoral value added in 2005, percentage changes relative to MEMBER/NO CAP scenario*

Value added	AGENDA	AGENDA + DIR	Welfare	AGENDA	AGENDA + DIR
Poland			*Poland*		
Agriculture	0.3	2.6	Rural households	0.2	21.1
Non-agricultural sectors	−0.3	1.1	Urban households	−0.3	1.0
Hungary			*Hungary*		
Agriculture	12.6	13.4	Rural households	1.5	6.9
Non-agricultural sectors	−0.2	0.9	Urban households	−0.3	0.5
Slovenia			*Slovenia*		
Agriculture	−13.2	−11.4	Rural households	−1.3	1.8
Non-agricultural sectors	0.9	1.0	Urban households	1.1	1.3
Czech Republic			*Czech Republic*		
Agriculture	14.8	17.8	Private households	0.3	5.3
Non-agricultural sectors	−0.5	−0.1			

Source: Banse (2000).

scenario. Because of direct payments and an increase in non-agricultural income, welfare in Slovene rural households actually increases in the DIR scenario compared with the level in the MEMBER/NO CAP scenario.

CONCLUSIONS

The results of our quantitative analysis using a combination of partial and general equilibrium models show, among other things, that CEC accession to the EU leads to an increase in agricultural production and growing exports in the region. This is likely to have a noticeable impact on total expenditure under the CAP, even if direct payments are not made to farmers in the CECs. However, if national policies in the CECs were to remain in place, their national expenditure on agricultural market policies might grow over time by even more than introduction of the CAP, as reformed under Agenda 2000, is likely to bring about.

The picture changes drastically, though, if direct payments under the CAP are extended to the CEC, adding another EURO6.5 billion to agricultural expenditure in the CEC-4. Eastern enlargement would then make overall CAP expenditure increase by around a third. At the same time, farm incomes in the CECs would also increase noticeably. This clearly shows the incentives in the political bargaining that is likely to take place during the accession negotiations where one side hopes to avoid extending the direct payments to CEC farmers, while the other side wants to obtain them.

Our results also show that inclusion in the CAP may have major macroeconomic implications and noticeable effects on non-agricultural sectors in all acceding countries. As a result of introducing the CAP, most CEC currencies may exhibit a tendency towards appreciation, and total savings and investment may fall. In CECs with a net agricultural export position, inclusion in the CAP and in 'financial solidarity' is likely to have a positive impact on GDP, while GDP is reduced in net importing CECs. However, consumers and non-agricultural sectors in three out of the four CECs included in the analysis are likely to suffer economic losses from extending the CAP to the CECs. Slovenia is the exception. However, such negative effects could be reduced if the CAP were further reformed before eastern enlargement of the community.

BIBLIOGRAPHY

Adelman, I. And Robinson, S. (1978), *Income Distribution Policy in Developing Countries – A Case Study of Korea*, Stanford: Stanford University Press.

Anderson, K., and Tyers, R. (1993), *Implications of EU expansion for European agricultural policies, trade and welfare*, Discussion Paper no. 829, London: Centre for Economic Policy Research.

Banse, M. (1997), *Die Analyse der Transformation der ungarischen Volkswirtschaft – Eine Empirische Allgemeine Gleichgewichtsanalyse unter besonderer Berücksichtigung des Agrarsektors und der Ernährungsindustrie*, Berlin: Duncker und Humblot.

Banse, M. (2000), 'Macro-economic Implications of EU-Accession', in S. Tangermann and M. Banse (eds), *Central and Eastern European Agriculture in an Expanding European Union*, Wallingford: CAB International.

Banse, M. and Münch, W. (1998), 'Die Einführung einer GAP auf den Märkten in den Beitrittsländern Mitteleuropas: Effekte der gegenwärtigen GAP und der Agenda 2000', Sonderheft *Agrarwirtschaft*, **3/4**, 180–90.

Banse, M., Guba, W. and Münch, W. (1998), '*Eastern Enlargement of the EU: How competitive is the Agri-Food Sector in Central Europe under EU conditions? The Example of Hungary and Poland*', paper prepared for the EAAE/ISHS Conference, 'Understanding Competitiveness', Apeldoorn, 22–4 April.

Banse, M., Münch, W. and Tangermann, S. (1999), 'Accession of the Central European Countries to the EU: Implications for Agricultural Markets, Trade, Government Budgets and the Macro-Economy in Central Europe', in J.F.M. (Swinnen (ed.), *Agriculture and East–West European Integration*, Aldershot: Ashgate.

Bojnec, S. and Münch, W. (1999), 'Implications of Agricultural Accession to the European Union: The Case of Slovenia', in J.F.M. Swinnen (ed.), *Agriculture and East–West European Integration*, Aldershot: Ashgate.

Buckwell, A. and Tangermann, S. (1999), 'Agricultural Policy Issues of European Integration: The Future of Direct Payments in the Context of Eastern Enlargement and the WTO', *MOCT-MOST, Economic Policy in Transitional Economies*, special issue on 'Agricultural Transition and European Integration', **9**, 229–54.

European Commission (1997), *Twenty-Fifth Financial Report concerning the European Agricultural Guidance and Guarantee Fund E.A.G.G.F. Guarantee Section*, Brussels: European Commission.

Frohberg, K., Hartmann, M., Weingarten, P., Wahl, O. and Fock, A. (1998), 'Development of CEEC Agriculture under Three Scenarios – Current CEEC Policies, CAP 1995/96 and Agenda 2000', in M. Brockmeier, J. Francois, T. Hertel and P. Schmitz (eds), *Economic Transition and the Greening of Policies: Modelling the Challenges for Agriculture and Agribusiness in Europe*, Proceedings of the 50th European Seminar of the EAAE October 1996, Kiel: Wissenschaftsverlag Vauk KG.

Hertel, T., Brockmeier, M. and Swaminathan, P. (1997), 'Sectoral and Economywide Analysis of Integrating Central and Eastern Europe (CEE) Countries into the European Union (EU): Implications of Alternative Strategies', *European Review of Agricultural Economics*, **24**, 359–86.

Jensen, H., Frandsen, S. and Bach, C. (1998), *Agricultural and Economy-Wide Effects of European Enlargement: Modelling the Common Agricultural Policy*, Working Paper no. 11/1998, Copenhagen: Danish Institute of Agricultural and Fisheries Economics (SJFI).

Josling, T., Kelch, D., Liapis, P. and Tangermann, S. (1998), *Agriculture and European Union Enlargement. Markets and Trade*, Economics Division, Economic Research Service, Technical Bulletin no. 1865, Washington DC: U.S. Department of Agriculture.

Liapis, P. and Tsigas, M.E. (1998), 'CEEC Accession to the EU: A General Equilibrium Analysis', in M. Burfisher and E. Jones (eds), *Regional Trade Agreements and US Agriculture*, Economic Research Service, Agricultural Economics Report No. 771, Washington, DC: U.S. Department of Agriculture.

Münch, W. (1995), '*Possible Implications of an Accession of the Visegrad-Countries to the EU. Can the CAP do without Reform?*', Paper presented at the Agricultural Economics Society One-Day Conference, London.

Münch, W. (2000a), 'Effects of CEEC–EU Accession on Agricultural Markets in the CEEC and on Government Expenditure', in S. Tangermann and M. Banse (eds), *Central and Eastern European Agriculture in an Expanding European Union*, Wallingford: CAB International.

Münch, W. (2000b), 'Market and Budgetary Implications of Central European Accession to the Common Agricultural Policy: A Partial Equilibrium Analysis', Dissertation, University of Göttingen.

Münch, W., Bojnec, S. and Swinnen, J. (1998), *Exchange Rates and the Measurement of Agricultural Price Distortions in the CEECs and of CEEC–EU Accession Costs*, Working Paper 1/3, Joint Research Project, 'Agricultural Implications of CEEC Accession to the EU', University of Göttingen.

OECD (1998), *Agricultural Policies in Emerging and Transition Economies, Monitoring and Evaluation 1998*, Paris: OECD.

Tangermann, S. and Josling, T. (1994), *Pre-accession Agricultural Policies for Central Europe and the European Union*, study commissioned by GD I of the European Commission, Göttingen: University of Göttingen.

Tangermann, S. and Münch, W. (1995), *Agriculture in Poland, the Czech and Slovak Republics and Hungary and Possible Evolutions in the Medium Term – Using the ESIM Sector Model*, Final Report to the European Commission (DGVI), Göttingen: University of Göttingen.

GERALD WEBER*

The CAP's Impact on Agriculture and Food Demand in Central European Countries after EU Accession: Who Will Lose and Who Will Gain?

INTRODUCTION

The population of Central European countries (CECs) is becoming less enthusiastic about European Union (EU) accession than was the case immediately after the fall of the Iron Curtain. It is feared that consumers will have to pay higher food prices. National agricultural policies of most CECs are less protective than the Common Agricultural Policy (CAP). Its implementation is therefore expected to lead to adjustments in farm production, farm incomes and consumer welfare. Farmers in CECs are concerned about growing competition from Western Europe.

The 'Central and Eastern European Countries Agricultural Simulation Model' (CEEC-ASIM) (Frohberg *et al.*, 1997) is used to assess these impacts for Poland, the Czech Republic, Hungary, Estonia and Slovenia (CEC-I), the potential first-wave accession countries. In this paper a scenario of EU accession under full application of the EU market regulations is compared with one of unchanged national agricultural policies.

BRIEF DESCRIPTION OF THE MODEL

CEEC-ASIM is a partial equilibrium model with rational and perfectly informed economic agents and perfect markets. The supply and input demand equations are derived from a symmetric generalized McFadden profit function (Diewert and Wales, 1987), which fulfils all theoretical conditions implied by the assumption of profit-maximizing producers using multi-input and multi-output technologies. The demand equations are based on a normalized quadratic expenditure function (Diewert and Wales, 1988) assuming utility-maximizing consumers. The appropriate curvature conditions are imposed on these systems.

Price transmission equations establish links between the various price definitions at the different levels of the market chain. Policy variables like nominal protection rates, minimum prices and subsidies are part of the price transmission equations. Retail prices are linked to farmgate prices by exogenous retail

*Institute for Agricultural Development in Central and Eastern Europe, Halle (Saale), Germany.

margins. By assumption, domestic production and demand have no influence on international prices (small, open-economy, hypothesis). Quantity control policies like quotas and set-aside, which result in divergences between shadow prices and financial prices, are also implemented in the model.

For each of the accession candidates, one country model has been specified. It covers the supply of 12 primary agricultural commodities, the use of five intermediate inputs and agricultural labour input. The parameters of the supply and demand equations are calibrated so as to reproduce the base year (1997). The data sources are from FAO, OECD and national statistical services.

SCENARIO ASSUMPTIONS

A so-called *base-run* reflects a scenario of unchanged national agricultural policies (the situation of 1997). It serves as a reference for comparison with various policy scenarios. In the *EU accession scenario*, policies in the CEC-I are changed in order to apply the CAP market regulations as reformed by the Agenda 2000 decisions of the European Council of March 1999. It is assumed that, by the year 2007, the CEC-I will have fully implemented the CAP and that economic adjustments to these policy changes will be completed.

Base run: unchanged national agricultural policies

The changes in border prices between 1997 and 2007 are exogenous and are based on world market price projections of FAPRI (1999). The *nominal rate of protection* is defined as the percentage gap between farmgate and border prices. For the base run these rates are assumed to be those observed for 1997. The assumptions on autonomous *technical progress* are derived from the European Commission (1998) and reflect per hectare yield changes and per animal output changes, respectively. The annual rates of technical progress are mainly in the range of 1 to 3 per cent. Population and income growth are based on FAPRI (1999) projections.

EU accession scenario: Agenda 2000

For *farmgate prices* of cereals, sugar, beef and milk, it is assumed that policy-induced gaps between the joining countries and the EU are abolished. The price cuts of the Agenda 2000 of 15 per cent for cereals and milk and 20 per cent for beef are taken into account. If the farmgate prices calculated according to these assumptions are lower than the border prices, the latter are used as farmgate prices. This implies that negative protection is not allowed. For all other products, no border protection is in effect after EU accession (zero nominal protection rates).

The *area payments* for cereals amount to EURO 63/t. The reference yields used to calculate the payment per hectare are the average expected yields for wheat and coarse grains in 2001. For oilseeds and set-aside the same premium is received. Farmers are obliged to set aside 10 per cent of the area for 'grandes cultures' (cereals and oilseeds, though protein crops are not explicitly covered by the model). This rate is modified to a lower effective one to reflect the small producer regulation exempting non-professional producers from the obliga-tion. The *premium in the beef sector* is EURO290 per slaughtered male adult beast (special premium plus slaughter premium). The upper limit for the number of eligible animals is assumed to correspond to the base year's number of animals. For *milk*, a premium of EURO17.24 per ton is paid.

For the accession scenario, *production quotas* are implemented. Sugar and milk production are not allowed to exceed the 1997 levels augmented by the expected rises up to 2001 of per hectare yields and per cow yields, respec-tively. For milk, an additional 1.5 per cent increase in the quota reflecting the Agenda 2000 decisions is taken into account.

RESULTS

Prices

Adjusting support provided to CECs' farmers to that which the EU offers its agricultural producers changes the level and pattern of price support. Farmgate prices for many products fall to border price levels or come close to them. This is the case for wheat, potatoes, oilseeds, vegetables, pork, eggs and poultry. Sugar, milk and beef, however, become heavily protected. These changes in protection patterns lead to new relative incentive prices which turn less favour-able for potatoes, vegetables, pork, eggs and poultry, whereas they become more favourable for coarse grains, oilseeds, sugar beet, milk and beef (Table 1). The 'incentive prices', in this context, take into account farmgate prices plus some fractions of subsidies (direct payments, compensatory payments, input subsidies) which are assumed to influence producers' decisions.

Production, input use and demand

For crops the production adjustments due to EU accession are small (see Table 2). Total grain production and oilseed production decrease slightly as com-pared with the base run because of the set-aside obligation, the effect of which, however, is weakened by the small producer regulation. Within grains wheat is substituted for by coarse grains because their relative price is higher. This also reflects the reference situation of unchanged national agricultural policies in which wheat in CEC-I is more heavily protected than coarse grains. The relative incentive prices for sugar production rise strongly owing to high EU price support. But sugar output is restricted by the EU quota system.

In the livestock sector the marked changes in relative prices as well as the milk quota lead to significant adjustments in production structures. Compared with the base run, output of pork, poultry and eggs falls strongly (see Table 2) reflecting the fading out of price support for these products under the CAP. On the other hand, with relatively high border protection and direct subsidies for beef and milk, there are strong incentives for producers to increase output of

TABLE 1   *Relative producer incentive prices, CEC-I*

	1997	Base run 2007	Agenda 2000 2007	
	Wheat = 1	Wheat = 1	Wheat = 1	Deviation from base run (%)
Wheat	1.00	1.00	1.00	0
Coarse grains	0.79	0.69	0.83	21
Potatoes	0.36	0.36	0.31	−13
Oilseeds	1.64	1.35	1.58	17
Sugarbeet	1.58	1.37	1.91	40
Vegetables	0.83	0.82	0.75	−9
Milk	1.40	1.27	1.74	37
Beef	12.68	14.84	21.01	41
Pork	10.15	12.01	9.05	−25
Eggs	9.04	9.16	5.46	−40
Poultry	9.61	9.74	5.39	−45
Rest of agricultural output	7.79	7.73	7.05	−9
Fodder wheat	0.88	0.88	0.70	−20
Fodder coarse grains	0.71	0.61	0.57	−8
Fodder potatoes	0.25	0.24	0.21	−13
Fertilizer	2.04	1.69	1.54	−9
Rest of intermediate input	7.79	9.47	8.63	−9
Labour	1.99	3.54	3.23	−9

Sources: OECD, national statistics, own calculations carried out with CEEC-ASIM.

these two products. However, the milk quota has a dampening impact on milk output. The effect of the milk quota on beef depends on how strongly the two products are combined in production. The assumption in the model simulation is that farmers would react to milk quotas by setting up more independent beef production methods.

Use of cereals and potatoes for fodder declines because of lower livestock output after EU accession (Table 3). Wheat gains more importance within the feed mix since its price ratio vis-à-vis coarse grains is reduced. Input use of fertilizer and other intermediate inputs falls slightly. This is also the case for labour. The rather small reduction of labour input might be surprising in view of the relatively strong decline in production quantities. Owing to the fact that small-scale farming plays an important role in CEC farm sectors (in particular in Poland), this can, however, be explained by a relatively low intersectoral mobility of agricultural labour.

The impact of EU accession on non-agricultural demand for crop products is modest. Only for sugar is a significant drop in consumption expected as a result of the increase in sugar prices (Table 4). Stronger effects with opposite

TABLE 2   *Production quantities,[1] CEC-I*

	1997	Base run 2007	Agenda 2000 2007	
	1000t	1000t	1000t	Deviation from base run (%)
Wheat	15 480	19 102	17 547	−8
Coarse grains	27 807	33 301	32 952	−1
Potatoes	17 249	20 325	19 982	−2
Oilseeds	1 657	2 398	2 327	−3
Sugar	3 160	3 477	3 336	−4
Vegetables	6 780	7 887	7 898	0
Milk	16 490	17 995	17 778	−1
Beef	720	727	949	31
Pork	3 086	3 364	3 066	−9
Eggs	745	795	733	−8
Poultry	1 098	1 150	968	−16
Rest of agricultural output[2]	7 169	7 545	7 512	−0

Notes: 1 Production is net of waste and seed; for milk, net of waste and feed use.
2 EURO thousands at 1999 prices.

Sources: FAO, national statistics, own calculations carried out with CEEC-ASIM.

TABLE 3   *Agricultural input use, CEC-I*

	1997	Base run 2007	Agenda 2000 2007	
	1000t	1000t	1000t	Deviation from base run (%)
Fodder wheat	6 991	6 940	7 329	6
Fodder coarse grains	22 755	25 115	24 624	−2
Fodder potatoes	9 726	10 351	9 292	−12
Fertilizer	2 256	2 255	2 214	−2
Rest of intermediate input[1]	10 351	10 140	10 045	−1
Labour[2]	4 955	4 841	4 764	−2

Notes: 1 EURO thousands at 1999 prices.
2 Employees, thousands.

Sources: FAO, OECD, national statistics, own calculations carried out with CEEC-ASIM.

TABLE 4   *Demand for agricultural products, CEC-I[1]*

	1997	Base run 2007	Agenda 2000 2007	
	1000t	1000t	1000t	Deviation from base run (%)
Wheat	6 899	7 110	7 190	1
Coarse grains	3 962	4 120	4 136	0
Potatoes	7 672	7 897	8 068	2
Oilseeds	2 217	2 381	2 411	1
Sugar	2 332	2 481	2 311	−7
Vegetables	6 613	7 420	7 559	2
Milk	16 319	18 070	15 962	−12
Beef	685	693	462	−33
Pork	2 753	2 800	3 055	9
Eggs	739	913	1 106	21
Poultry	1 003	1 260	1 665	32
Rest of food expenditure[2]	12 190	16 726	16 941	1

Notes: 1 Human consumption, processing and industrial use.
          2 EURO thousands at 1999 prices.

Sources: FAO, national statistics, own calculations carried out with CEEC-ASIM.

sign are expected for livestock products. The price cuts for pork, poultry and eggs lead to higher consumption levels compared to the base run. Milk and beef consumption, on the other hand, strongly declines because of higher retail prices after EU accession.

Welfare effects

As a result of EU price support and direct subsidies, income from agricultural activity in CEC-I rises by 45 per cent (Figure 1). Slovenia's farms, however, are worse off since protection is lower after accession. Estonia's agriculture, being the least protected in the reference projection, profits the most from high income support by the CAP. Negative impacts of the CAP on consumers in CEC-I resulting from price increases for sugar, milk and beef are balanced by falls in prices for pork, poultry and eggs. The total impact on consumer welfare (measured by the equivalent variation) is small compared to producer welfare (Figure 1). This is also due to the low value share of agricultural products in food retail prices and the reorientation of the CAP from price support towards direct subsidies. The gains in producer incomes mainly result from transfers financed by the EU. The model estimates these additional budgetary costs at EURO4.3 billion at 1999 prices.

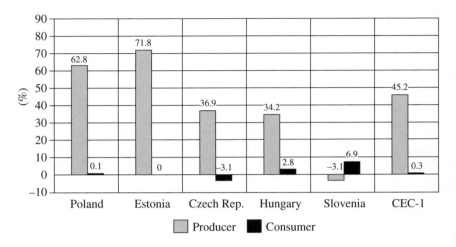

FIGURE 1   *Welfare changes in CEC-I: EU accession under Agenda 2000 conditions versus base run (%)*

CONCLUSIONS

Implementing the EU market regulations in the potential first wave accession countries (CEC-I) changes their levels and patterns of agricultural protection. In most of CEC-I higher protection would raise farm incomes. A low value share of agricultural products in retail prices, plus the further reorientation of the CAP from market price towards direct income support, reduce harmful effects on consumer welfare. The main source of gains in producer welfare is the direct subsidies financed by the EU budget. Total welfare in CEC-I increases provided that by far the greater share of the budgetary burden is paid by the old member states. Justifiable reasons to fear EU accession in countries like Poland, Estonia, the Czech Republic and Hungary can thus only be found (if at all) in areas beyond the scope of this partial analysis.

The estimated impact of accession on product balances is small. Price support will increase surpluses of sugar, milk and beef in the enlarged EU, but this effect is limited by the quota systems. For pork, poultry and eggs, a greater import potential in CEC-I could result in opening up additional export opportunities for farmers in the old member states.

REFERENCES

Diewert, W.E. and Wales, T.J. (1987), 'Flexible functional forms and global curvature conditions', *Econometrica*, 55, 43–68.
Diewert, W.E. and Wales, T.J. (1988), 'Normalised Quadratic Systems of Consumer Demand Functions', *Journal of Business and Economic Statistics*, **6**, 302–12.

European Commission (1998), *Agricultural Situation and Prospects in the Central and Eastern European Countries*, Working Documents, Brussels: European Commission.

FAPRI (1999), *World Agricultural Outlook* (http:\\www.fapri.iastate.edu).

Frohberg, K., Hartmann, M., Weingarten, P., Fock, A., Wahl, O. (1997), 'The Central European Agricultural Simulation Model (CEASIM) – An Overview', unpublished research report, Halle/Saale, IAMO.

CEMAL ATICI AND P. LYNN KENNEDY*

A Game Theoretic Analysis of Turkey's Integration into the European Union

INTRODUCTION

Turkey's quest for membership of the European Union (EU) has a long history, dating originally from the first application in 1959. The resulting negotiations led to the Ankara Agreement, creating an association between Turkey and the EC. The aim was to promote continuous commercial and economic relations between the two economies. To achieve this objective, the agreement established three stages: preparatory, transitional and final. The first stage, which included the provision of concessions from the EC to Turkey, began in 1964 and ended in 1969. From 1970, the second stage covered a 12-year transitional period, during which reciprocal concessions were made. Although the final stage was planned to start in 1995, the outcome of this process is still problematic (GATT, 1994).

While the political and economic conditions necessary for Turkey's accession have not yet been satisfied, the Luxembourg summit reaffirmed Turkey's eligibility to join the EU on the same basis as the other applicant states (Eurecom, 1998). To this end, the European Council has specified three areas it considers necessary for Turkish admittance to the Union: (a) intensification of the EU–Turkey Customs Union, (b) implementation of financial cooperation, and (c) approximation of Turkish laws to those of the EU (ibid.). The EU–Turkey Customs Union, which came into effect in January of 1996, guarantees the free circulation of industrial goods and *processed* agricultural products. Although basic agricultural products are excluded from the treaty, Turkey is progressively adopting many aspects of the Common Agricultural Policy (Republic of Turkey, 1994). The future inclusion of agriculture would increase the intensity of the EU–Turkey Customs Union and contribute towards Turkey's meeting the necessary conditions for EU admittance.

International agricultural trade negotiations, such as those between the EU and Turkey, reflect the linkages between domestic farm policies and agricultural protection. The recent agricultural negotiations conducted within the Uruguay Round of GATT highlighted several interdependencies. As Turkey and various other countries lobbied to form agreements with the EU, the potential trade effects were seen to influence the decisions of agricultural

*C. Atici, Andres Menderes University, Turkey. P.L. Kennedy, Louisiana State University Agricultural Centre, Baton Rouge, USA.

policy makers around the world. EU officials had to consider increased possibilities for production, shifts in consumer demand and preferences, and the potential interest group coalitions that might result from Turkish accession.

Scenarios of this type are examples of the problems that exist in analysing agricultural trade negotiations as the result of trade policy interdependence (Kennedy *et al.*, 1996). Countries considering the ratification of both bilateral and multilateral trade agreements must consider the results of their choices with respect to the policies of other countries. In addition, countries weighing the prospects of regional trade agreements must consider the reaction of cooperating countries and the rest of the world as they negotiate with prospective partners.

The impact of these interrelationships between countries raises questions as to how agricultural policies are formulated, given the reactions of other countries. Policy makers often have some knowledge of the response their new policies will induce among other nations. Rational countries will formulate agricultural policy based on the expected reactions of other relevant countries. As a result, game theory can provide a useful framework for analysing agricultural policy decisions, given the interdependence of agricultural policy.

In an interdependent world, agricultural policies affect both domestic and international markets. As a result, it is beneficial to know both the desired goal and potential consequences of various policy stances. The objective of the research presented here is to examine the effects of liberalized trade combined with Turkish accession to the European Union. Particular emphasis is placed on the impact of these policy changes on trade in agricultural products. The empirical analysis will involve ten agricultural products which play a significant role in Turkey and the European Union in terms of production or consumption. They are corn, cotton, oilseeds, rice, sugar, tobacco, wheat, dairy milk, lamb and poultry.

To accomplish these objectives use is made of a partial equilibrium trade simulation model, Modèle International Simplifié de Simulation (MISS) (Mahé *et al.*, 1988). MISS is a partial equilibrium trade model that simulates, in a comparative static framework, the effects of various policy decisions. In order to initialize the MISS model, data, composed of prices, protections, quantities and elasticities, were gathered from a number of sources, including the European Commission (1995), FAO (1996a, 1996b), OECD (1999), Turkish Ministry of Agriculture (1999) and USDA (1989, 1996).

Once the model is initialized, simulations are conducted that mirror the effects of the Uruguay Round agricultural agreement, Agenda 2000, and alternative levels of Turkish integration into the European Union. To mirror the policy decisions of the respective governments, consumer, producer and government budget weights, as components of a political preference function (PPF), are estimated, based on 1995 producer and consumer subsidy equivalents. These weights, when combined with the net gains or losses to producers, consumers and government, reflect the net gains or losses to the economies as perceived by policy makers. The PPFs resulting from the various scenarios are then evaluated in a game theoretic framework to determine a Nash equilibrium solution.

THEORETICAL FRAMEWORK

This analysis is based on a multi-commodity model of agriculture first developed by Mahé *et al.* (1988). Subsequently, a political economic submodel was added (Johnson *et al.*, 1993) and other modifications were made (Kennedy *et al.*, 1996). In the model, N commodities are produced, consumed and traded by two main countries, Turkey and the European Union, and the rest of the world. Governments intervene in domestic markets either through the use of price (π) or supply/demand shift (θ) instruments. Price instruments, denoted as $A_{ik}^{\pi S}$ for producers and $A_{ik}^{\pi Q}$ for consumers of commodity i in country k, affect the prices observed by the supply and final demand sectors. With the world price of commodity i represented as P_i^W, the domestic price functions for country k are:

$$P_{ik}^S = P_{ik}^S\left(A_{ik}^{\pi S}, P_i^W\right) \text{ and } P_{ik}^Q = P_{ik}^Q(A_{ik}^{\pi Q}, P_i^W), \text{ for } i = 1, 2, \ldots, N \qquad (1)$$

Supply/demand shift instruments, denoted as $A_{ik}^{\theta S}$ for producers and $A_{ik}^{\theta Q}$ for consumers of commodity i in country k, are implicit elements of exogenous variable vectors X_k^S and X_k^Q.

Throughout the process of agricultural policy formulation the welfare effects of various actions are taken into account by the government. Policy makers behave as though they are using a weighting system to compare the gains of certain groups versus the losses of others. In order to model this behaviour, a political preference function (PPF) is used. The PPF, a weighted, additive function of producer quasi-rents, consumer utility and budget costs, is the objective function which, through their policy choices, policy makers behave as though they seek to maximize. The weights are based on observed policies.

Several studies have estimated PPF weights for game theoretic analyses of this type. Rausser and Freebairn (1974) apply the PPF method to the case of US beef imports. Johnson *et al.* (1993) conduct an empirical analysis using the PPF, measuring the role of special interests in the USA and the EU. Similarly, Kennedy *et al.* (1996) modelled agricultural trade policy interdependence using a game theoretical framework and PPF. Their model distinguishes between the EU, the USA and a politically passive rest of the world. More recently, Abler and Sukhatme (1998) modelled the determinants of Indian wheat and rice policy using the PPF. They then examined policies towards international trade, grain procurement, public grain distribution and production inputs.

However, for this game to be well defined in extensive form, a number of conditions must hold (Bullock, 1994; von Cramon-Taubadel, 1992). These include knowledge of the welfare functions which map instruments to well-being, that the observed strategies be Pareto optimal for the given weights, and that the set of feasible welfare outcomes be compact and convex over the domain of policy instruments. To minimize these problems, the current analysis uses PPF weights based on the producer and consumer subsidy equivalents observed in the base period, 1995. Interest group weights for producers and consumers are calculated as percentage PSEs and an aggregate weighted CSE, respectively.

Let $-k$ denote the other main country while the actions of country k are represented by $A_k = \{A_k^{\pi S}, A_k^{\pi Q}, A_k^{\theta S}, A_k^{\theta Q}\}$. Producers are grouped according to commodities with their welfare defined as the profit obtained through the production and marketing of that commodity. Producer quasi-rents, consumer utility and the budget of country k are expressed as functions of government policies in the following equations:

$$-k(A_k, A_{-k}) = \Pi_k\{P_k^S[A_k^{\pi S}, P^W(A_k, A_{-k})], A_k^{\theta S}\} \tag{2}$$

$$U_k(A_k, A_{-k}) = U_k\{P_k^Q[A_k^{\pi Q}, P^W(A_k, A_{-k})], A_k^{\theta Q}\} \tag{3}$$

$$B_k(A_k, A_{-k}) = B_k\{P_k^S[A_k^{\pi S}, P^W(A_k, A_{-k})], P_k^Q[A_k^{\pi Q}, P^W(A_k, A_{-k})] \tag{4}$$

$$P^W(A_k, A_{-k}), A_k^{\theta S}, A_k^{\theta Q}\}$$

The budget weight is normalized to one and the PPF, expressed as a function of government policies, is shown as

$$V_k(A_k, A_{-k}) = -k(A_k, A_{-k}) \cdot \lambda_{Sk} + U_k(A_k, A_{-k}) \cdot \lambda_{Qk} + B_k(A_k, A_{-k}) \tag{5}$$

where λ_{Sk} is a strictly positive, $N \times 1$ vector that represents the relative political weights of the producer groups in country k, and λ_{Qk} is a strictly positive scalar representing the relative political weight of the consumer group in country k.

If the policy decision process of interdependent countries is to be modelled, a Nash equilibrium occurs where each country chooses its policy which maximizes its PPF, given the policy choice of the other. This equilibrium is defined using a *best response correspondence*. For a given A_{-k}, government k chooses A_k^*, one possible best response to A_{-k}, such that

$$V_k(A_k^*, A_{-k}) \geq V_k(A_k, A_{-k}), \text{ for all } A_k \in \mathbf{A}_k \tag{6}$$

where $\mathbf{A}_k$ is the set of all possible actions which can be employed by government k. Every A_{-k} element of $\mathbf{A}_{-k}$ has at least one A_k^* element of $\mathbf{A}_k$ which is a best response for country k. A Nash equilibrium is defined as the set of actions (A_k^*, A_{-k}^*) where A_k^* is a best response to A_{-k}^* for country k, and A_{-k}^* is a best response to A_k^* for country $-k$.

In this two-player, normal-form, non-cooperative game, defined by $G = \{\mathbf{A}_{TUR}, \mathbf{A}_{EU}; \mathbf{P}_{TUR}, \mathbf{P}_{EU}\}$, each country k chooses some action $A_k \in \mathbf{A}_k$ in order to maximize its PPF, given the action choices of the other country. The policy strategies analysed here are several different degrees of trade liberalization. The action space is defined by $\mathbf{A}_{TUR} = \{SQ_{TUR}, WTO_{TUR}, INT_{TUR}\}$ for Turkey and $\mathbf{A}_{TUR} = \{A2K_{EU}, WTO_{EU}, FT_{EU}\}$. Actions of Turkey are 'status quo' (SQ_{TUR}), protection reductions agreed to in the Uruguay Round of GATT (WTO_{TUR}) and integration into the European Union (INT_{TUR}). Actions of the European Union

TABLE 1　　*Political pay-off function weights and their ranking by interest group for Turkey and the European Union, 1995*

	Turkey		European Union	
	Rank	Weight	Rank	Weight
Lamb	7	1.28	1	1.77
Milk	1	1.46	3	1.53
Corn	8	1.18	8	1.46
Wheat	10	1.04	5	1.49
Rice	6	1.30	7	1.47
Oilseeds	5	1.33	2	1.54
Cotton	9	1.08	6	1.48
Sugar	4	1.34	4	1.50
Tobacco	2	1.39	10	1.20
Poultry	3	1.36	9	1.29
Consumers	11	0.98	11	0.71

Source:　　OECD (1999).

are adoption of its Agenda 2000 policies ($A2K_{EU}$), protection reductions agreed to in the Uruguay Round of GATT (WTO_{EU}), and free trade (FT_{EU}). Two sets of game simulations are conducted, with the difference being the PPF weights used. The first utilizes PPF weights all equal to one, while the second uses PPF weights based on 1995 producer and consumer support levels (see Table 1).

The base solution for 1995 using PPF weights all equal to one is presented in Table 2. Within this bimatrix, each pair of numbers represents the pay-off for Turkey and the European Union, respectively, corresponding to a specific action. For example, the pay-off associated with both countries adopting their

TABLE 2　　*PPF values for Turkey and European Union protection reductions using PPF weights of one, 1995*

	Turkey actions		
EU Actions	SQ_{TUR}	WTO_{TUR}	INT_{TUR}
$A2K_{EU}$	−5,386	55,398	−159,332
WTO_{EU}	−10,1066	49,1075	−24,1036
FT_{EU}	−42,1182	7,1171	85,1149*

Notes:　　The pair (P_{TUR}, P_{EU}) are the PPF for Turkey and the EU, respectively, measured in million \$US. *The unique Nash equilibrium occurs at (INT_{TUR}, FT_{EU}).

WTO commitments for Turkey and the European Union (WTO_{TUR}, WTO_{EU}) are 49 and 1075, respectively. Within this game the European Union's action choice results in its choosing the row, while Turkey chooses the column through its actions. In determining the equilibrium solution to this game the concept of *iterative elimination of strictly dominated strategies* is utilized. Regardless of the action chosen by Turkey, through choosing the Agenda 2000 ($A2K_{EU}$) strategy the EU receives pay-offs that are strictly greater than what it could acquire by choosing an alternative strategy. Thus the dominated strategies, WTO_{EU} and $A2K_{EU}$, can be eliminated from consideration. This simplifies the selection process for Turkey. It now maximizes its pay-off given the remaining alternatives and will choose INT_{TUR}. Thus the unique Nash equilibrium solution to this game is found at the point (INT_{TUR}, FT_{EU}).

The second game simulation is similar to the first, with the exception that the PPF weights are no longer equal to one; they are based on 1995 producer and consumer subsidy equivalents. In this case, the European Union, once again, has a strictly dominant strategy (Table 3). However, in this case $A2K_{EU}$ is the strictly dominant scenario. Based on this, Turkey evaluates the pay-offs of 9, −36 and 117, choosing 117 which corresponds with the Integration (INT_{TUR}) scenario. Thus, in this case, the unique Nash equilibrium solution is found at the point (INT_{TUR}, $A2K_{EU}$).

TABLE 3   *PPF values for Turkey and European Union protection reductions using PPF weights derived from producer and consumer support levels, 1995*

EU Actions	Turkey actions		
	SQ_{TUR}	WTO_{TUR}	INT_{TUR}
$A2K_{EU}$	9, 972	−36, −958	117, −1049*
WTO_{EU}	30, −3741	−17, −3730	148, −3782
FT_{EU}	148, −16108	81, −16091	−410, −15951

Notes: The pair (P_{TUR}, P_{EU}) are the PPF for Turkey and the EU, respectively, measured in million \$US. *The unique Nash equilibrium occurs at (INT_{TUR}, $A2K_{EU}$).

CONCLUSIONS

Through their actions, policy makers reveal their preferences with respect to various interest groups. This study utilizes these revealed preferences, in the form of producer and consumer subsidy equivalents, and uses them in weighting producer and consumer welfare as part of a political preference function. Since Turkey may join the EU, the economic integration of Turkey into the EU is modelled to measure the agricultural welfare change. Given this, the results of this analysis are consistent with trade theory, which suggests that the benefits from trade will be maximized with free trade, provided that all sectors are weighted equally. The real world, however, appears to be more consistent with the second game, in which interest groups possess differing weights from the perspective of the polity, revealed through the amount of protection interest groups are able to garner through the political process. The resulting choice of Agenda 2000 ($A2K_{EU}$) as the optimal strategy of the EU lends credence to this choice of weights, given the recent ratification of Agenda 2000 by the EU.

The results have several welfare implications for producers, consumers, the government and Turkey–EU relations. It is clear that the WTO and further trade liberalization will have unfavourable impacts on several producer groups in Turkey. However, producer welfare increases when Turkey joins the EU. The reason for this increase is most likely the higher level of producer protection in the EU. This is reinforced given that, with integration, if the EU chooses free trade, Turkish producer welfare will decrease, owing to lower protection. With integration, however, the welfare of several producers, such as those growing wheat, increases significantly. But Turkish consumers will experience a dual impact. Since they depend heavily on wheat, increased support for the producer group assures an adequate supply of a strategic commodity. At the same time, if the increase in protection in the sector is transmitted to consumers, their real income will decrease.

A noticeable welfare increase in a traditional crop such as cotton may increase production and assure an adequate supply for the textile industry, which is a significant contributor to the Turkish economy and export market. On the other hand, another traditional product, tobacco, loses with integration because protection in the EU is lower than that of Turkey. This change in protection will have a negative effect on the welfare of producers, influence export markets and decrease export earnings.

Turkish consumers gain from trade liberalization. Since they spend a great deal of their income on food, liberalization increases their real income. However, with integration, consumers experience a loss in welfare due to the higher level of agricultural protection in the EU. This loss is eliminated only if the EU implements free trade. The optimal agricultural policy should account for the needs of low-income consumers as well as influential producer groups. In order to compensate consumers for the harm of increased food prices and other income-distorting policies, a welfare system could be introduced that is aimed at low-income consumers and subsidizes their food expenditures.

Turkish budgetary costs will increase as it joins the EU owing to the high level of budget expenses for producers, but decrease with the EU's free trade action. Turkey's high level of budget expenditures could result in further inflation. However, if Turkey is compensated by the EUs fund for agriculture for these expenses, the pressure can be lightened.

In designing agricultural policies, the welfare of both producer and consumer must be considered. In addition to seeking policies that are Pareto optimal between countries, policies can be designed that are optimal within them. Since agricultural policies often have multiple goals, multiple measures are also needed. The overall consistency of various measures must be monitored to ensure they work as intended. In determining the domestic support levels, international markets must be considered. Changing world trade conditions and liberalization due to globalization put pressure on agricultural support and trade barriers. In the determination of policies, producer and consumer interests are critical. Subsidized food could be provided for low-income consumers. The selectivity of food subsidies is essential for both budgetary and equity considerations.

It is interesting to note that the Turkish choice of integration (INT_{TUR}) is not dependent on the weights used. In order to determine the dominance of this strategy, future simulations could be conducted over a broader range of weights and EU scenarios. It is also important to note that the EU does have a say regarding whether or not Turkey joins. Given the scenarios analysed here, the EU would improve its welfare if Turkey could be excluded. Thus future analyses should attempt to develop scenarios that would allow for this behaviour.

In considering multilateral trade agreements and integration with the EU, Turkey's policy decisions will affect manufacturing and services sectors in addition to agriculture. Future studies should consider other sectors in addition to agriculture in order to evaluate more completely Turkey's various policy actions. In addition, income distribution effects should be evaluated in these types of analyses, given that trade policies affect the distribution of welfare within an economy as it affects the welfare of various interest groups.

This study utilized a static partial equilibrium trade model to research the impacts of various agricultural trade policy actions of Turkey on producer and consumer welfare. However, it has limitations that must be considered in interpreting the results. One is that this analysis uses a partial equilibrium model, which considers the effects of various policy actions only in a specific sector. The interaction between sectors, such as agriculture, manufacturing and services, does not appear. General equilibrium studies consider the interaction between the sectors of an economy, such as factor mobilization, multisectoral input and output use and the overall welfare of an economy. Future studies can employ general equilibrium analyses to better understand these interactions.

An additional factor to be considered involves the theory of the model. This study uses a neoclassical approach in modelling. Recent advances involving new trade, new growth and economic geography theories offer many advantages over the neoclassical view, such as the benefit of free trade for developing countries and the role of trade restrictions on development. One of the most striking implications of new trade theory is that free trade can actually be damaging for developing countries because of the non-competitive nature of the international market. The implication of new trade theory shows itself in the determination of producer and consumer surpluses and choice of optimal trade policies in a game theoretical framework. On this basis, we could expect that, as Turkey chooses freer trade, its welfare could actually decrease.

Krugman's (1987) new theory of economic geography has interesting implications for Turkish agriculture. According to Krugman's assertions, we can expect that, in Turkey, traditional crops which have specific geographic and climatic requirements, such as cotton, tobacco and fruits, will have higher production when Turkey joins the EU. This would occur because producers of these products in other European countries will give up production and producers in Turkey will supply most of the needs for the EU. On the other hand, it could be expected that, in animal products, such as beef, lamb and dairy, other EU countries that are more efficient in the production of these products will replace Turkish production. Therefore, from a geographic perspective, it is implied that production of cotton, tobacco and fruits in the new EU would be concentrated in Turkey. At the same time Turkey's animal production would migrate to other EU countries. It could also be the case that Turkey will be a significant centre for textile production in the new EU. The incomes of traditional crops, therefore, will increase relative to animal production. These changes would shift income among producer groups in Turkish agriculture.

When making political decisions, economic studies can help policy makers to review and choose various policy actions. However, it must be kept in mind that empirical analyses are not the only criteria that are considered in the policy-making process. That is increasingly more complex and includes demands by various interest groups. In making decisions, political, social and environmental factors must be considered in addition to economic factors. Future studies can address these issues and provide various perspectives that can be used in the policy process.

REFERENCES

Abler, D. and V. Sukhatme (1998), 'The Determinants of Wheat and Rice Policies: A Political Economy Model for India', *Journal of Economic Development*, **23**, 195–215.

Bullock, D.S. (1994), 'In Search of a Rational Government: What Political Preference Function Studies Measure and Assume', *American Journal of Agricultural Economics*, **76**, 347–61.

Eurecom (1998), 'Luxembourg Sets Stage for EU Enlargement', *The Monthly Bulletin of European Union Economic and Financial News*, The European Commission, Luxembourg (at *http://www.eurunion.org/cgi-bin/frames.cgi?news/eurecom/1998/ecom0998.htm, 1998*).

European Commission (1995), *The Agricultural Situation in the European Union: 1994 Report*, Luxembourg: European Commission.

Food and Agriculture Organisation of the United Nations (1996a), *FAO Production Yearbook, 1995*, Rome: FAO.

Food and Agriculture Organisation of the United Nations (1996b), *FAO Trade Yearbook, 1995*, Rome: FAO.

General Agreement on Tariffs and Trade (1994), *Trade Policy Review: Republic of Turkey*, Geneva: GATT.

Johnson, M.A., Mahé, L. and Roe, T.L. (1993), 'Trade Compromises between the European Community and the United States: An Interest Group–Game Theory Approach', *Journal of Policy Modeling*, **15**, 199–222.

Kennedy, P.L., von Witzke, H. and Roe, T.L. (1996), 'Strategic Agricultural Trade Policy, Interdependence and Exchange Rate: A Game Theoretic Analysis', *Public Choice*, **88**, 43–56.

Krugman, P.R. (1987), 'Is Free Trade Passé?', *Economic Perspectives*, **1**, 131–44.

Mahé, L., Tavèra, C. and Trochet, T. (1988), 'An Analysis of Interaction Between EC and US Policies with a Simplified World Trade Model: MISS', background paper for the 'Report to the Commission of the European Communities on Disharmonies in EC and US Agricultural Policies', European Community, Brussels.

Organisation for Economic Cooperation and Development (1999), *Producer and Consumer Support Estimates – OECD Database, 1999 Edition*, Paris: OECD (database on CD-ROM).

Rausser, G.C. and Freebairn, J.W. (1974), 'Estimation of Policy Preference Functions: An Application to US Beef Import Quotas', *Review of Economics and Statistics*, **56**, 437–49.

Republic of Turkey (1994), *Ekonomik Rapor 1994*, Ankara: TOBB.

Turkish Ministry of Agriculture (1999), *Turkish Producer Prices – Electronic Data* (*www.tarim.gov.tr1999*).

United States Department of Agriculture (1989), *Elasticities in the Trade Liberalization Database*, Washington, DC: USDA, Economic Research Service.

United States Department of Agriculture (1996), *World Situation and Outlook* (various issues), Washington, DC: USDA, Economic Research Service.

von Cramon-Taubadel, S. (1992), 'A Critical Assessment of the Political Preference Function Approach in Agricultural Economics', *Agricultural Economics*, **7**, 371–94.

ANTONIO M.D. NUCIFORA*

Land Use in the European Union by 2020

INTRODUCTION

Recent revolutionary changes in European agricultural policies imply dramatic shifts in future land use needs. Even a superficial examination of recent trends would suggest that large parts of current agricultural land will not be needed in the future, and the idea of a land surplus in the European Union has been repeated more insistently in recent literature (Edwards, 1986; Lee, 1987; North, 1988; *inter alia*). However, some authors argue that, with declining profitability, the removal of inputs and resources will result in a less intensive production process and significant areas of land are unlikely to leave agricultural production (Bowers, 1988; Harvey and Whitby, 1988; Harvey, 1991; Swinbank, 1992).

The importance of assessing the degree of pressure placed on agricultural land in the medium term must not be underestimated. Land is a non-renewable resource and, as a result, land use planning is long-term in nature. In addition, land use demand changes incrementally because of rigidities and inertia. There is consequently a lag between the setting and implementation of a policy and its effect. As a result, accurate predictions of land use trends have an immediate and immense value to setting good policy.

This paper presents the results of forecasts for land use change in the EU-9[1] to the year 2020. The study addresses the need of policy makers to acquire information about the future implications of current land use trends, by developing an econometric model to forecast future land use. Because of the more appropriate methodology adopted, the forecasts of land use change estimated in this study constitute a marked improvement on previously available estimates.

THE MODELLING FRAMEWORK

A dynamic simultaneous land allocation model has been developed to explore future land use scenarios in the EU by 2020. Ideally, a simultaneous model of

*Antonio M.D. Nucifora, DISEAE Università di Catania, Italy. The author is indebted to George Peters for his many useful comments. Helpful suggestions by Chris Adam, Francesco Bellia, David Colman, Rosemary Fennell, Susan Leetmaa, Tim Lloyd, Tony Rayner and Iain Southall are also gratefully acknowledged.

the whole EU agricultural sector would have to be built in order to account fully for the relationship between prices, land use and production by endogenizing all prices. Building such a model was too demanding a task for this study and for the available data, however, and here cereal prices alone have been endogenized, with agricultural prices set to change proportionally to the change in the price of cereals after 1996.[2] Such an analysis falls short of the accuracy required for a precise investigation of future land use, but is expected to give sufficiently reliable forecasts for policy formulation.

The five land use categories considered in the model are cereal crops, oilseed crops, other arable crops (mainly fodder and root crops), permanent grassland and a residual other land uses category (mainly forest and urban uses).[3] The model has two components. In the first component, each individual land use is modelled as a function of the returns on the major agricultural products (namely cereals, oilseeds, root crops, milk and beef)[4] and income (in real per capita terms).[5] Input-deflated output prices have been used to approximate the expected returns (or profitability) in agriculture. Expectations have been modelled as an ARMA (3, 0) process, implying that price expectations depend on prices in the previous three years.

The second component is a price determination model. It is based on the premise that administered prices are not fully exogenous and cannot be set indefinitely without any reference to the current levels of domestic market imbalance and the situation in the international market(s). Ultimately, expenditure considerations would make it necessary either to reduce the market surplus or to reduce the spread between domestic and international market prices, or both. The price determination model for cereals comprises two equations, cereal price and cereal yield, and one identity. The identity defines production as the product of land and yield. Production enters the price determination equation where it contributes to setting the level of prices. The price level in turn plays a role in determining the desired yield and land use levels, in two respective equations. The land equation, of course, is also part of the first component of the model.

Crop yields have been modelled as depending on output prices deflated by the cost of inputs, on the area of land and on technological progress.[6] The price determination has been modelled as depending on the demand and production of cereals, on the price of close substitutes (notably oilseeds) and on the world price of cereals.[7]

To keep the model as simple as possible, no separate trade component has been estimated. Imports have been assumed to be constant over the forecast period. Excess supply is assumed to be subsidized and dumped on the world market. Exports are therefore assumed equal to excess supply and no stocks are assumed. World prices are assumed to be exogenous. In addition, a constraint has been introduced in the model such that domestic prices cannot fall below international prices.

All the equations have been estimated in first differences format in light of the results of unit root tests which indicate the presence of non-stationarity in the data series (not shown).[8] The equations have been estimated as log linear autoregressive distributed lag (ADL) equations.[9] The five log linear equations

TABLE 1   *Solved static long-run equation for individual land uses*

DLcerlan = +0.204 DLprxcer − 0.163 DLprxrap − 0.146 DLprxbef + 0.294 s0DLprxmlk − 0.201 DLgdp85c
(SE)   (0.080)   (0.096)   (0.042)   (0.089)   (0.082)

Dloillan = −1.756 DLprxcer + 2.691 DLprxrap − 1.303 DLprxrot
(SE)   (2.502)   (4.413)   (1.501)

DLncrlan = −0.733 DLprxcer + 0.427 DLprxrap + 0.247 DLprxbef − 0.573 DLgdp85c + 0.164 DLprxrot
(SE)   (0.357)   (0.246)   (0.204)   (0.314)   (0.053)

DLpgrlan = −0.131 DLprxcer + 0.217 S0DLprxmlk − 0.562 DLgdp85c + 0.014 DLprxrot − 0.185 s1DLmlkpro + 0.12 DLprxbef
(SE)   (0.061)   (0.065)   (0.167)   (0.021)   (0.307)   (0.040)

DLnaglan = −0.051 DLprxcer − 0.062 DLprxrap − 0.053 s0DLprxmlk − 0.017 DLprxrot + 0.175 DLgdp85c + 0.043 DLprxbef
(SE)   (0.011)   (0.013)   (0.011)   (0.004)   (0.018)   (0.008)

DLceryld = +0.029 + 0.661 DLcerlan + 0.058 DLprxcer
(SE)   (0.007) (0.721)   (0.168)

DLprxcer = +0.636 − DLprxrap − 0.891 DLcerpro + 1.269 DLcerdem − 0.102 DLprw85c
(SE)   (0.183)   (0.249)   (0.484)   (0.053)

Notes: DLcerlan = (change in log of) land in cereal crops, share,
DLoillan = (change in log of) land in oilseed crops, share,
DLncrlan = (change in log of) land in other arable crops, share,
DLpgrlan = (change in log of) land in permanent grassland, share,
DLnaglan = (change in log of) land in non-agricultural uses, share,
DLprxcer = (change in log of) price of cereal crops divided by price of arable inputs (index 1985 = 100),

518

DLprxrap = (change in log of) price of oilseed crops divided by price of arable inputs (index 1985 = 100),

DLprxrot = (change in log of) price of roots-fodder crops divided by price of arable inputs (index 1985 = 100),

DLprxmlk = (change of log of) price of milk divided by price of milk inputs (index 1985 = 100),

DLprxbef = (change in log of) price of beef crops divided by price of milk inputs (index 1985 = 100),

DLgdp85c = (change in log of) per capita real income (in ECU thousands at 1985 prices),

DLceryld = (change in log of) cereals yield (1000 kg/ha),

DLcerpro = (change in log of) cereals production (million tonnes),

DLcerdem = (change in log of) cereals demand (million tonnes),

DLprw85c = (change in log of) world price of cereals (real index 1985 = 100),

DLmlkpro = (change in log of) milk production (million litres),

s0 = dummy for: <1986 = 0; >1986 = 1,

s1 = dummy for: <1986 = 1;>1986 = 0,

s0DLprxmlk = s0 * DLprxmlk,

s1DLmlkpro = s1 * DImlkprod.

representing the land use model have been estimated individually[10] by ordinary least squares (OLS) for the period 1969–92.[11] Subsequently, the cereal land equation has been (re-) estimated simultaneously with the cereal yield and cereal price equations by FIML for the period 1961-92. All of the estimation work has been carried out using the econometric softwares PcGive 8.0 and PcFiml 8.0. For the sake of brevity, only the results of the long-run solutions of the individual equation are reported in Table 1.

For the five land use equations, all of the direct price elasticities in Table 1 have the expected positive sign. Note that cross-price elasticities in such a system do not have a definite expected sign. Complementarity among crops may arise from particular rotation features or from particular patterns of use of the different fixed factors (Sadoulet and De Janvry, 1995). In addition, complementarity may arise between crops and livestock production, since the former can be used as inputs in the production of the latter. The results displayed in Table 1 are therefore in line with economic theory.[12]

THE FORECAST SCENARIOS

The model is used to produce forecasts of land use in the EU by 2020. The forecast scenario accounts for the introduction of the MacSharry reforms, the GATT Uruguay Round agreement and the Berlin reforms of 1999 (MGB scenario). In brief, the MacSharry and the Berlin reforms introduced a reduction in the level of price support and a compulsory set-aside of arable land. Farmers were compensated both for the price reduction and for the area set-aside. The GATT agreement introduced a reduction in aggregate agricultural support (which in the case of the EU is mostly satisfied by the reductions carried out under MacSharry) and, more importantly, a reduction in the level of subsidized exports. Under the MGB scenario, the model has been modified to introduce the MacSharry and Berlin price reductions, the set-aside constraint and the relevant compensations. The agreed GATT limit on subsidized exports has also been incorporated into the model.

In order to produce the forecasts it is necessary to make assumptions about the future path of the exogenous variables. These are the world price of cereals, the demand for cereals and income per capita. (As discussed above, cereals imports and milk production have been assumed to stay constant after 1996). The world price of cereals has been projected to follow a logarithmic trend from 1997 onwards. This appears to fit well with the historical data, and gives plausible projections to 2020 (approximately a 60 per cent reduction in real terms over the 25-year period). The demand for cereals in the EU has been virtually stable up to 1992, before increasing substantially in the last few years because of the high world market prices for cereal substitutes. The price competitiveness of cereals vis-à-vis oilseeds, however, can be expected to remain relatively stable in the future since the two regimes have been unified under the Berlin reform. The domestic demand for cereals has therefore been assumed to remain constant over the forecast period. Finally, income per capita has been projected to follow a linear trend after 1996. This gives plausible projections to 2020 (about 1.7 per cent per annum).

The sensitivity of the results to the assumptions about the level of world prices, cereals demand and income per capita needs to be thoroughly investigated. Alternative scenarios for these variables have therefore been explored. The alternative scenario for world prices is based on the IFPRI world price forecasts generated by the IMPACT model (approximately a 15 per cent reduction in real terms by 2020 – see Rosengrant et al., 1995). The alternative scenario for cereal demand assumes an increase of 1 per cent per annum after 1996, to account for the increase in the use of cereals as livestock feed.[13] Finally, the scenario for income per capita displays a faster increase in the level of income (about 3 per cent per capita per annum).

The results of the forecasts under the MacSharry–GATT–Berlin (MGB) scenario are presented in Table 2. Baseline results (that is, without the MGB policy changes) are also presented in Table 2 and Figure 1. The agricultural area in EU-9 by 2020 is expected to decrease by 18 per cent (this is about 16 million hectares, an area equivalent to slightly less than three-quarters of the UK, or larger than Ireland, Denmark, the Netherlands and Luxembourg together). Most of this reduction in agricultural land occurs from permanent grassland (about 8 million ha.) and the area devoted to fodder and root crops (about 4 million ha.). Oilseeds land also appears to decrease significantly. Cereal land remains about constant. It is worth noting that these changes in land use occur in spite of an increase of almost 100 per cent in cereals production by 2020 (cereal yields are forecast to nearly double over the period).[14]

The introduction of the MacSharry reform accelerates the exit of land from agriculture by almost 15 per cent compared to the baseline scenario. The GATT agreement has no effect on the transfer of agricultural land, since it does not itself change the set of incentives affecting land use. However, the GATT limitation on the use of export subsidies effectively imposes a constraint on production which translates into a rate of set-aside of arable land above 50 per cent by 2020. The Berlin reform lowers domestic cereal prices to the level of the international prices (by 2005) and, therefore, makes set-aside redundant. The Berlin reduction in prices, however, further accelerates the exit of land from agriculture.

Overall, the reforms of the 1990s have substantially increased (by about 30 per cent) the area of land surplus to agriculture by 2020. In fact, most of the acceleration in the transfer of land is concentrated in the years immediately following the reforms, with the series going back to their normal trends by about 2005–10. Given this initial set of results, it is important to determine the sensitivity of the forecasts with respect to the assumptions made about world prices, cereal demand and income per capita. Three modified MGB scenarios have been run, varying one of the assumptions on each occasion. The results are presented in Table 2 as MGB-World price, MGB-Demand and MGB-Income scenarios.

The change in the assumption about cereals demand has very little impact on the results of the forecasts. This is probably because its impact on raising

TABLE 2   *Projections for agricultural land in EU-9 to 2020 and policy simulations (million hectares)*

		Agricultural land[1]	of which: Set-aside	Cereal land	Oilseeds land	Root and fodder land	Permanent grassland	Non-agricultural land
1960	EUROSTAT	98.830		26.213	0.311	23.882	41.760	51.403
1990	EUROSTAT	89.259		23.939	4.125	17.188	38.078	60.065
Basic scenarios								
2020	Baseline	77.778	0.0	20.916	3.231	16.678	30.463	72.706
2020	MacSharry	76.446	6.2	22.216	2.719	15.943	30.068	74.049
2020	GATT	76.446	18.8	22.216	2.719	15.943	30.068	74.049
2020	Berlin (MGB scenario)	73.461	0.0	23.555	1.076	13.322	30.008	77.034
Sensitivity analysis								
2020	Berlin (MGB-Demand)	74.156	16.2	24.752	1.215	12.588	30.101	76.339
2020	Berlin (MGB-Income)	69.653	0.0	23.711	1.099	12.045	27.298	80.841
2020	Berlin (MGB-World price)	74.590	0.0	24.988	1.407	12.488	30.207	75.904

Note: 1. The forecasts include 5.5 million hectares to account for permanent crops and some residual agricultural land.

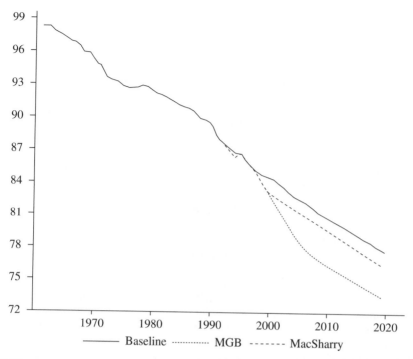

FIGURE 1   *Agricultural land in EU-9, 1961–2020: baseline, MacSharry–GATT and MGB scenarios (million hectares)*

the price level is not expected to be too large, as prices are more significantly affected by the impact of the reforms. Similarly, assuming a moderate rate of decrease in world prices also appears to have very little effect on the results. The assumption about income, on the other hand, has a strong impact on the land use forecasts. Assuming a faster increase in income per capita substantially raises the area of land moving out of agriculture and into other uses. This is because a higher level of income corresponds to a higher demand for non-agricultural land uses.

In any case, even under these alternative scenarios, the forecasts indicate that a sizeable area of land will leave agricultural use. Most of this land is coming out of permanent grassland, and is, therefore, marginal land which is leaving agriculture because of the reduction in its profitability. It seems plausible that a very substantial part of this land will actually be abandoned.

A number of limitations in the model have been indicated. Notably, the assumptions about relative prices in agriculture, and about the exogeneity of cereals demand and the level of the world prices, represent a source of weakness of the forecasts. In addition, there are a number of instances in which it would be desirable to distinguish between the short- and long-run relationships between the variables. For instance, in the yield equation, one would expect to find a relationship binding the yield level to the area of land, such that, in the long run, the level of yield is positively related to the area of land by an equilibrium relationship, while in the short run the two behave as substitutes. Cointegrating vectors, however, have not been estimated owing to the small sample size, and remain as a desirable extension for future studies.

CONCLUSIONS

The forecasts of land use in the European Union by 2020 presented in this study indicate that a very significant amount of land will leave agriculture in the next 20 years. Assumptions about the level of world prices and income per capita influence the forecasts; nevertheless, it appears that no fewer than 14 million hectares will leave agriculture by 2020 (15 per cent of EU-9 agricultural land in 1990).

The results of the forecasts indicate that the profitability of agriculture vis-à-vis alternative land uses plays an important role in determining the amount of land leaving agriculture, while it has little effect in influencing the level of yields. In fact, the decrease in the intensity of production resulting from price reductions is not very large compared with the effect of technological improvements on yield. Even reforms of the order of those carried out during the 1990s only slow down the rate of growth in yields temporarily. As real prices in agriculture continue to fall, therefore, there will be no significant extensification of agriculture. The intensity of agricultural production may be reduced a little, but this will not be sufficient to prevent very large areas of land from leaving agriculture.

An acceleration in the exit of land from agriculture is currently occurring as a result of the agricultural policy reforms of the 1990s. A large part of this 'surplus' land is set to be left abandoned. Clearly, adequate policies need to be implemented to prevent serious environmental effects. The value of continuing to limit urban expansion or, on the other hand, the encouragement of high-quality low-intensity organic agricultural production, or the creation of more recreational and/or environmentally protected areas, needs to be carefully (re)assessed.

NOTES

[1] Owing to the importance of using time series of a sufficient length, the study is limited to the nine countries which already belonged to the European Union before 1982, therefore excluding Greece, Portugal, Spain, Austria, Finland and Sweden.

[2] Specifically, it has been assumed that, within agriculture, relative prices will continue to change in line with historical patterns since the institution of the CAP.

[3] In line with historical experience, permanent crops have been assumed to remain constant over the forecast period.

[4] The prices of milk and beef have been included in the analysis as proxies for the profitability of livestock products, whose production has an impact on land use. The relationship between the milk and beef prices and the demand for fodder land and grassland is by no means a direct one, and ought to be better specified. This simple specification has been adopted here because a

careful model of livestock production, and its land use requirements, is beyond the resources available for this study. The difficulty in dealing with the livestock sector within the model is further complicated by the introduction of the milk quotas regime in 1984, which profoundly changed the nature of the market for milk. With the introduction of quotas in 1984, milk production is no longer dependent on the price of milk but it is determined by input prices and the level of quota, such that overshooting the quota is negatively related to production in the following years because of the heavy fines. To account for the effects of the milk quotas, the impact of milk price in the land use equations is limited to the period before 1986 (the year when the reform effectively became enforced) and milk production is introduced as an explanatory variable in the permanent grassland equation from 1986 onwards. Milk production is assumed to remain constant over the forecast period.

[5]Income is introduced in the equations to act as a proxy for the (increasing) value of both forest and other non-agricultural land uses.

[6]Owing to the absence of real data about weather, the weather effect has been simply omitted, on the assumption that its effects are randomly distributed.

[7]Demand for cereals has been assumed to be exogenous. This is because the demand for cereals is heavily determined by its feed use (approximately 65 per cent) and hence by developments in the livestock sector (see note 4 above).

[8]It should be obvious that all land (share) series must be stationary in the very long run by definition. However, although the series are stationary in the very long run, it is not reasonable to conduct inference on the series in levels. For inference to be valid, the data used in the analysis have to be stationary.

[9]For the five land use equations, the choice of the log linear functional form ensures that the estimated land shares are non-negative, but it does not ensure additivity. Additivity has therefore been imposed via an ad hoc restriction. In addition, the set of double log land demand equations cannot be derived as the result of profit maximization. This functional form, however, represents a first order approximation to any more complex functional form (by Taylor's expansion) and a set of log linear equations can therefore be taken as a good approximation to the true system of demand equations derived from profit maximization. Note that this format also imposes the restriction that elasticities are constant.

[10]Joint estimation was not feasible because of the limited number of degrees of freedom.

[11]The period 1993–6 has been used to test the forecasting performance of the model (not shown).

[12]Tests for homogeneity of the land use equations have been carried out (not shown). The null hypothesis of homogeneity is not rejected in any of the land equations at the 1 per cent level and is rejected only in the permanent grassland equation at the 5 per cent level. The results of these tests therefore appear to be consistent with profit maximization behaviour. A formal test for the symmetry of cross-price effects in the system of equations is not feasible because simultaneous estimation of the land use equations has not been carried out (because of the lack of degrees of freedom) and hence it is impossible to impose/test for cross-equation restrictions.

[13]This may seem small in comparison to recent increases since 1992, but is extremely large in relation to past experience. Recent changes are seen as a one-off adjustment to the reforms.

[14]A doubling of cereal yields by 2020 may appear striking. However, such high levels of yield are already achieved in laboratory trials and are close to yields achieved in the most productive areas of the Community.

REFERENCES

Bowers, J.K. (1988), 'Farm Incomes and the Benefit of Environmental Protection', in D. Collard, D. Pearce and D. Ulph (eds), *Economics, Growth and Sustainable Environments*, London: Macmillan.

Edwards, A. (1986), *An agricultural land budget for the United Kingdom*, Wye College, University of London, Ashford, working paper no. 2, Department of environmental studies end countryside planning.

Harvey, D.R. (1991), ''Agriculture and the environment: The way ahead?', in N. Hanley (ed.), *Farming and the countryside: an economic analysis of external cost and benefits*, Wallingford: CAB International.

Harvey, D.R. and Whitby, M. (1988), 'Issues and policies', in M. Whitby and J. Ollerenshaw (eds), *Land Use and the European Environment*, London: Belhaven Press.

Lee, J. (1987), 'European land use and resources: an analysis of future EEC demands', *Land Use Policy*, Special Issue on European land use alternatives (July), 179–99.

North, J. (1988), 'Future Land Use in the UK, Department of Land Economy, Cambridge University.

Rosengrant, M.W., Agcacoili-Sombilla, M.A. and Perez, N.D. (1995), *Global food projections to 2020*, Food, Agriculture and the Environment Discussion Paper 5, Washington DC: IFPRI.

Sadoulet, E. and de Janvry, A. (1995), *Quantitative development policy analysis*, Baltimore, MD: Johns Hopkins University Press.

Swinbank, A. (1992), 'A surplus of farm land?', *Land Use Policy*, **9**, 3–7.

ANDREA KNIERIM AND UWE JENS NAGEL*

Challenges and Constraints for Cooperative Conflict Management among Land Use Stakeholders

LAND USE CONFLICTS IN PROTECTED AREAS

Throughout the world land use conflicts are steadily increasing. Awareness of the need to preserve nature is confronted by the fact that virtually all natural resources serve, at the same time, as a base for food production and income generation. The establishment of protected areas through public agencies is one important instrument to ensure nature conservation (Reid and Miller, 1989). Biodiversity specifically is a good that needs protection on a fairly large scale (Kächele, 1999). The global concern for biodiversity and nature maintenance was expressed in the Agenda 21 declaration of the Rio Conference in 1992 (BMU, 1997). In practice, the number of protected areas increased dramatically during the last two decades, from some 2000 to nearly 8500 in 169 countries, with a total surface of 5.2 per cent of the world's land area, or 7.7 million km^2 (Pretty and Pimbert, 1995). Many environmentalists and conservationists feel that 'the less use, the better for nature' and, consequently, restrictions on both traditional and modern forms of productive use are favoured. Often plans for the resettlement of local residents are formulated (ibid.). Resistance of different people to these restrictions leads to land use conflicts in various forms.

In several industrialized and developing countries participatory and cooperative conflict management strategies are actively pursued (Nagel, 1993; Curtis *et al.*, 1995; DePhelps, 1996; Lawrence *et al.*, 1997). Empirical evidence shows that participatory and cooperative approaches lead to better results than classical methods of conflict resolution, at least in terms of sustainability and social acceptance. In Europe, attempts to integrate different interest groups in rural areas as equal partners in the management of land use conflict have started only recently.[1] Until now, these methods have not been systematically used when establishing protected areas and the application of institutionalized administrative procedures is still largely the norm. Analysts doubt whether cooperative methods will be quickly integrated into German administrative procedures as they demand effective participation and the willingness to compromise (Hoffmann-Riem, 1990).

This paper shows how concepts of social psychology relating to cooperative conflict management can be integrated into a model of interaction and commu-

*Humboldt University, Berlin, Germany.

nication. Experience and results of an action-oriented research project on cooperative conflict management in one protected area of the state of Brandenburg, Germany are analysed. Consequences, challenges and constraints for a potential transfer and wider application in Brandenburg's protected areas are discussed. On a more theoretical level, the insights gained will add to the relevant body of knowledge as well as generating questions for future research.

COOPERATIVE CONFLICT MANAGEMENT IN THEORY

Sociological, psychological and economics literature is abundant with conflict definitions (Glasl, 1994). None of them was found to be sufficiently clear and unequivocal to guide research and action of the present project, focusing on a practical land use conflict. The following definition has been developed with reference to Glasl (ibid.) and work by R.W. Mack and R.C. Snyder in the 1950s (cited by Grunwald, 1981):

> Land use conflicts are situations in which different stakeholders or actors claim on one and the same conflict issue, such as a piece of land, a river bank, trees and woods, animals etc. with different use or protection goals in mind. Conflict situations become real conflicts when one actor begins to act in favour of his interests and this is seen as a threatening or aggressive act by the other actor(s).

Conflicts have two dimensions: an object sphere (that is, the conflict issue with its legal, economic and social aspects) and a subject sphere (that is, the perception which people develop of each other as well as their communication and interaction based on these perceptions). Glasl states that, when dealing with conflicts, these two spheres have to be analysed and treated together within a holistic approach because those involved in conflicts also will not separate them (Glasl, 1994). The underlying paradigm of human behaviour is that of humanistic psychology and makes reference to new institutional and political economics. Human beings have different and varying needs, both physical and psychological, and human behaviour is related to actual interests and goals which, in turn, are also related to the perceived environment (Fisher, 1990; Gough, 1994; Söderbaum, 1999). In this context it is assumed that people no longer have the exclusive goal of maximizing individual gains, but that they have to find a balance between their immediate and long-term, their individual and social, interests and goals. Achieving this balance is a continuous process, both individually and socially determined (Gough, 1994).

The implication for conflict management and resolution is that it is not enough to find a one-and-forever optimal solution on the conflict *issue*, as often suggested in neoclassical economic approaches. It is equally important to develop an adequate solution to the *subject* sphere, which corresponds to the complex and dynamic situation of human beings in their environment.

SOCIAL AND PSYCHOLOGICAL CONCEPTS IN CONFLICT MANAGEMENT

Research in social and organizational psychology as well as in game theory shows that in most conflict situations cooperative behaviour leads to satisfying results for all persons involved (Deutsch, 1976; Hofstadter, 1998; Rapoport, 1981). Cooperative conflict management is determined by five important factors.

(1) Cooperative behaviour at the individual level is an attitude that can be characterized by personal openness, the willingness to exchange information, the search for common interests ('linking' rather than 'separating') and response to external demands (Deutsch, 1976).

(2) People must have common objectives; that is, different persons must be able and willing to identify one or more objectives which everybody wants to reach (ibid.). Usually, these objectives are located at a rather abstract level and the root issue of the conflict is not directly mentioned. Through common objectives at a given level a joint point of reference can be created.

(3) The focus on interests rather than on positions (Fisher and Ury, 1987) is important for several reasons. It means that at a general level interests of all participants are seen as relevant and serious. People who feel that they are being taken seriously can more easily accept diverging interests and look for similarities. Positions, on the other hand, are not perceived as negotiable. To hold on to positions means blocking the cooperative process.

(4) Procedural justice means that the decision-making procedures are clear to everyone and are accepted by everybody. In other words, the question of how the controlling or influencing power among participants in a decision-making process is distributed has been solved satisfactorily. Transparency of interaction and of the decision-making process can be achieved either through the use of already established and recognized standards and structures, or through procedures and criteria that have been jointly developed (Thibaut and Walker, 1975).

(5) Major preconditions for the structure of a cooperative conflict management process are the autonomy of the actors, their voluntary participation, development and coordination of labour division, and the delegation of tasks to single actors or subgroups (Grunwald, 1981).

These factors are important for the process as a whole but do not necessarily apply to everyone initially involved. The lead role may be taken by an individual who is convinced of the importance of cooperative conflict management, and who has relevant experience of it, sufficient to influence other participants (cf. Fisher and Ury, 1987; AGILNP, 1995). The elements can also be introduced and supported by an external actor, a so-called 'third party' (Glasl, 1994). The role of such a third party is, first, to analyse and to understand the conflict situation and, second, to be an advisor on methodological and procedural questions.[2]

THE FRAMEWORK MODEL OF ORGANIZED EXTENSION

Analysis and action in complex conflict situations such as land use conflicts in rural areas can be facilitated by a model that has been developed for agricultural extension (Albrecht, 1989). The original model which shows the interrelationship between the advisory and the target group systems has been expanded to include all relevant groups in a land use conflict (Figure 1). It shows interactions between the third-party (advisory) system, the project system representing the environmental actor who intervenes with a project dealing with conservation measures, and the stakeholder system, which stands for one or several different interest groups involved.

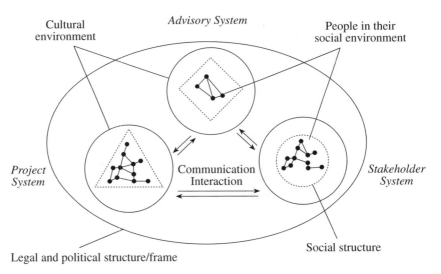

Source: Albrecht (1989), our adaptation.

FIGURE 1   *Framework model of organized extension*

In extension research where questions of transfer and exchange of knowledge between scientists and practitioners are investigated, the model helps to take into account all necessary factors for a meaningful problem analysis. For our case it illustrates that the analysis and management of conflict situations does not deal only with conflict issues and communication and interaction problems but also with social, cultural, legal and political structures. The latter may differ from actor to actor and thus be the base of misunderstandings and further conflict escalation.

THE CASE STUDY: PROCESS OF THE RESEARCH PROJECT

The research area is a biosphere reserve in the north-west of Brandenburg, located along the river Elbe. The conservation area covers about 53 000 ha., of which about 13 000 ha. are arable land and 17 000 ha. grassland. It is a rather remote and sparsely populated region with tourist attractions due to its natural beauty. The area contains many valuable biotopes with rare floral and faunal species (LAGS, 1999, p.19).

The process of cooperative conflict management was preceded by a pre-analysis of the conflict situation, including a stakeholder or interest group analysis.[3] This analysis revealed the main actors and their respective interests, identified in Table 1. A phase of informal talks on possible subjects and procedures with a group of agricultural land users preceded the actual process of cooperative conflict management. The final decision for starting such a process came from this group. They also decided on the topic to be dealt with, namely the extensive use of grassland. This relates clearly to the local agricultural situation, with an important number of grassland-dominated livestock farms.

Several problems and conflicts were listed:

(1) the consequences of the European Union Common Agricultural Policy/ CAP ('Agenda 2000'),

TABLE 1   *Main actors and their interests*

Main actors	Their interests (as expressed in interviews and publications)
Biosphere Reserve Administration (locally based) Board of Environment (district level)	To achieve an acceptable degree of protection for the whole area and differentiated protection according to the specific nature resources and their protection needs
Farmers Board of Agriculture (district level)	To reduce land use regulations as much as possible To minimize regulation of grassland use To minimize the damage by birds and other protected animals or to obtain adequate compensation
Community representatives (mayors and so on)	To minimize communal planning and implementation regulations in the area of construction and infrastructure
Other land users, such as foresters, hunters, anglers and tourists	To maintain protection of the environmental resources but also to get free access to the resources they intend to use (river banks, forests and so on)

Source: Knierim (1999).

(2)   the uncertainty of the state (Brandenburg) programme to support extensification of grasslands,
(3)   the (regional) programme of land care on a contract basis,
(4)   different planning horizons between official environmentalists and farmers,
(5)   the competition for land resources,
(6)   the uncertain legal and ecological consequences of extensive grassland use,
(7)   the dissatisfaction with the implementation of land care on contract basis.

These issues were mainly presented by the farmers. Only the last point was suggested by the biosphere reserve (BR) administration. The group as a whole formulated the following objectives for the common process.

(1)   People within the nature conservation area would jointly communicate their interests to external agencies such as the ministries of agriculture or environment.
(2)   The agricultural land users and the Brandenburg administration would regard each other as partners.
(3)   The contract basis for land care should be efficiently arranged for everyone.
(4)   All farms in the nature conservation area would be maintained.
(5)   All information on the subject of 'extensification' of grasslands (especially on supporting governmental programmes) would be exchanged.
(6)   Additionally, the farmers claimed that, in order to build up confidence, the administration had to put its plans on the table and to pass on information at its disposal.

The process of cooperative conflict management took place in the form of 15 group meetings (facilitated by one of the researchers) during a one and a half year time span. There were generally eight to 12 participants, including three to six farmers, two or three members of the Brandenburg administration and two to four members of the district administration. Table 2 shows the topics treated within three distinct phases of the process.

RESULTS OF THE PROJECT

Conceptually, results were to be reached both at the objective and at the subjective level. As for the first point, no pressing land use conflict has been resolved within the timeframe of the research project. But group members are satisfied with their achievement and have decided to continue to work on the conflict over ploughing up grassland.

On the subjective level, by contrast, a number of results were realized:[4]

● common objectives have been elaborated at a general level for the whole process as well as for specific issues;
● according to group members, exchange of information was the most important result. It was highly appreciated because of the directness and

TABLE 2 *Phases, topics and instruments*

Phase/no of meetings	Contents	Means
Situation analysis Meetings 1–4	Analysis of the local land use and land care Situation and of the political framework conditions in view of the agricultural policies at EU and federal state level	Information presentation by the Dept of Agriculture and by the BR administration
Identification and representation of interests Meetings 5–10	Identification of common and separate interests regarding the agricultural subsidy programme for extensive use of grasslands Elaboration and presentation of joint proposals to promote the extensive use of grasslands to the Minister of Agriculture Retrospective clearing up of a conflict situation over competition for land resources	Facilitated group discussion Preparation of documents in small groups Individual execution of organizational tasks Information presented, facilitated group discussion
Conflict management and joint planning Meetings 11–15	Conflict issue to be treated: whether and, if so, under what conditions, grassland can be ploughed up. At present, there are two contradictory agreements which are both valid A joint planning process is started on the categorization of grasslands on the basis of different use and protection criteria	Facilitated group discussion Use of external expertise Proposals to the ministries Facilitated group discussion, preparation of maps by stakeholders

the topicality of the material, as well as for the possibility of being able to clarify misunderstandings and open questions;

- supportive activities were voluntarily offered by individuals and small groups in the form of data seeking and supply, preparation of drafts for common documents, the organization of a visit by the Minister of Agriculture, and the elaboration of a joint proposal on the promotion of extensive use of grassland;
- the participants began to appreciate and accept their mutual interests to a growing extent in a process which was characterized by respect and understanding;
- transparency of the process was reached through open discussions supported by visual aids, decision making by consensus, explanations about the procedures by the facilitator, and through minutes which were controlled by the group;
- the structure that evolved is that of an open group with a fairly constant participation. Its composition was heterogeneous. As there is no farmers' organization operating at the state level, participating farmers do not have an institutional mandate. The Brandenburg administration is part of a larger administrative body, as are the representatives of the district administration.

CHALLENGES AND CONSTRAINTS FOR COOPERATIVE CONFLICT MANAGEMENT

The case study shows that it is possible to adapt and introduce methods for cooperative conflict management among land use stakeholders. Chances of a transfer of these methods to other conservation areas in Brandenburg and in Germany are good. However, some impediments to diffusing or scaling up this approach must be taken into account.

The general topic of the process was proposed by the agricultural land users; nearly all problems and conflicts mentioned reflected the questions and fears of farmers. While the facilitator suggested that it would be useful to distinguish between local conflicts and problems at higher levels (for example, CAP), this distinction could not be maintained in the group discussions. It became obvious that for farmers local, regional and international questions are intermingled and that they preferred not to restrict their discussions to local matters. This was not the case for the other participants. This can probably be explained by their different socioeconomic and cultural situation.

Farmers act as individual entrepreneurs. Many are responsible for a large number of employees and thus their objectives are profit generation, security against undue risks and long-term planning perspectives. They see themselves as part of the regional, social and cultural structure, and they feel a heavy dependence on external policies as well as on measures of the Brandenburg administration. The other participants were mainly members of administrative organizations. They had prescribed goals, but with some room for interpretation and fulfilment according to personal priorities. As they were members of a hierarchy, their room for manoeuvre could sometimes be quite clear, sometimes less easily predictable. As civil servants, they had no personal economic risk in the given situation.

For these different participants, getting together is a challenge in terms of communication and mutual understanding. Their socioeconomic background can be interpreted as involving two different cultures (the private business, locally integrated; the administrative bureaucracy, coming from outside) with different values and different styles of behaviour and ways of dealing with difficulties. The fact that it took ten meetings for an actual conflict to be openly addressed shows that there was a need to develop a common style of communication. One important feature was the fact that environmentalists involved were open to propositions and demands of the agricultural land users and that they also accepted the slow pace. This can be generalized. The challenge for using and scaling up the cooperative approach lies in the development of a mutually acceptable style of communication. This can only be achieved through conscious efforts and will take time, demand restraint and patience, and will require considerable flexibility in implementation.

During the process, the group approached the ministries of agriculture and environment several times with proposals, questions and demands for support. The agency directly superior to the Brandenburg administration was sometimes involved as an observer. On occasions when the group had questions or proposals, it turned out that there was no clear way, and certainly no fast way, for hierarchical organizations to respond to such 'basic' initiatives. This can produce frustrating effects on participants willing to cooperate and to look for compromise solutions. In addition, horizontal linkages within the region were not clearly defined, as exemplified by the non-official mandate of participating farmers.

This point needs to be addressed very early in the process. Once the group has managed internally to come to solutions, the question of how to integrate other land users may be difficult to solve. At present, there is no institutionalized model for stakeholder cooperation that could help to overcome the practical problems of vertical and horizontal communication.

CONCLUSIONS

Land use stakeholders in the protected area did not try to resolve an identified conflict directly and right away. Rather, creating a cooperative atmosphere and establishing a common basis were given first priority. Open information exchange was the most important instrument for reaching trust and cooperation. When the group finally started to resolve a pressing conflict, this happened in a very constructive and goal-oriented manner.

The process has been judged positively by the direct participants (and by the researchers). A transfer, or generalization, of experience seems possible, at least in principle. In order to institutionalize the approach, however, a number of practical as well as theoretical questions have to be solved. Two items seem to be crucial. First, the demand on participants to recognize and understand other people's interests is essential to cooperative conflict resolution. How can this understanding be developed for group settings, especially in conflict situation? This question has been widely neglected within social psychology and research on group dynamics (Scholl, 1997).

Second, how should such groups be organized? How can they be integrated into a larger context? Some experience has been gained in other parts of the world (for Australia, see Curtis *et al.*, 1995) but solutions must be location-specific and for Germany these are largely lacking. Joint efforts and the development of an interdisciplinary approach will be fruitful. Recent contributions have been made by new institutional economics and political economy, with their concepts of 'political economic organizations' (Söderbaum, 1999) and of the economic significance of discourse and communicative action.

NOTES

[1]Examples are stakeholder platforms and farmer cooperatives in the Netherlands (van Woerkum and Aarts, 1998; Wagemans and Boerma, 1998), the cooperation between private or semi-private enterprises and farmers in France (Gafsi and Brossier, 1999) and Germany (Mantau, 1992) and cooperation among scientists and rural stakeholders to promote sustainable land use forms (for example, the GRANO-Project, *www.zalf.de/grano/* and the Projektgruppe Kulturlandschaft Hohenlohe, *www.uni-hohenheim.de/%7ekulaholo*).

[2]The inherent ambivalence of such advisory work is discussed in detail by Glasl (1994).

[3]Data for this analysis were collected with the help of semi-structured interviews of regional stakeholders.

[4]Results have been documented in the form of written evaluations by participants as well as through minutes and records kept by the researchers.

REFERENCES

Albrecht, H. (1989), *Agricultural Extension. Basic Concepts and Methods*, Rural Development Series, Vol. 1, Eschborn.

Arbeitsgemeinschaft Integrierte Landnutzungsplanung (AGILNP) (1995), *Landnutzungsplanung. Strategien, Instrumente, Methoden*, Eschborn.

Bundesministerium für Umwelt, Naturschutz und Reaktorsicherheit (BMU) (1997), *Umweltpolitik, Agenda 21*, Konferenz der Vereinten Nationen für Umwelt und Entwicklung – Dokumente, Bonn.

Curtis, A., Birckhead, J. and de Lacy, T. (1995), 'Community Participation in Landcare Policy in Australia: The Victorian Experience with Regional Landcare Plans', *Society and Natural Resources*, **8**, 415–30.

DePhelps, C. (1996), 'Partnerships for preserving and enhancing the Padilla Bay agriculture/ esturiane ecosystem', *Journal of Soil and Water Conservation*, **July–August**, 274–9.

Deutsch, M. (1976), *Konfliktregelung: Konstruktive und destructive Prozesse*, Munich and Basle.

Fisher, R. and Ury, W. (1987), *Getting to Yes. Negotiating agreement without giving in*, London: Auflage.

Fisher, R.J. (1990), 'Needs Theory, Social Identity and an Eclectic Model of Conflict', in J. Burton (ed.), *Conflict: Human Needs Theory*, Macmillan: Basingstoke.

Gafsi, M. and Brossier, J. (1999), 'Collective dimensions and learning processes coping with change of farming practices to preserve water quality', paper presented at the 64th EAAE Seminar on Co-operative Strategies to Cope with Agri-Environmental Problems, Berlin, October.

Glasl, F. (1994), *Konfliktmanagement. Ein Handbuch für Führungskräfte und Berater*, Berne and Stuttgart: Auflage.

Gough, I. (1994), 'Economic Institutions and the Satisfaction of Human Needs', *Journal of Economic Issues*, **28**, 25–66.

Grunwald, W. (1981), 'Konflikt–Konkurrenz-Kooperation: Eine theoretisch–empirische Konzeptanalyse', in W. Grunwald and H.-G. Lilge (eds), *Kooperation und Konkurrenz in Organisationen*, Berne and Stuttgart: Haupt. utb.

Hoffmann-Riem, W. (1990), 'Verhandlungslösungen und Mittlereinsatz im Bereich der Verwaltung. Eine vergleichende Einführung', in W. Hoffman-Riem and E. Schmidt-Aßmann, *Konfliktbewältigung durch Verhandlungen.*

Hofstadter, D.R. (1998), 'Tit for Tat – Kann sich in einer Welt voller Egoisten kooperatives Verhalten entwickeln?' *Spektrum der Wissenschaft, Sondernummer, Kooperation und Konkurrenz*, **1/98**, 60–66.

Kächele, H. (1999), 'Auswirkungen großflächiger Naturschutzprojekte auf die Landwirtschaft', *Agrarwirtschaft, Sonderband 163*, Frankfurt: Agrimedia.

Knierim, A. (1999), 'Co-operative conflict resolution in a nature conservation area in Brandenburg, Germany – a case study', paper presented at the 64th EAAE Seminar on Co-operative Strategies to Cope with Agri-Environmental Problems, Berlin, October.

Landesanstalt für Großschutzgebiete Brandenburg (LAGS) (1999), *Die Großschutzgebiete in Brandenburg*, Eberswalde, July.

Lawrence, R.L., Daniels, S.E. and Stankey, G.H. (1997), 'Procedural Justice and Public Involvement in Natural Resource Decision Making', *Society and Natural Resources*, **10**, 577–89.

Mantau, R. (1992), 'Konfliktmanagement als Aufgabe der Beratung – dargestellt am Zielkonflikt, Landwirtschaft/Wasserwirtschaft – Berichte über Landwirtschaft*, **70**, 30–39.

Nagel, U.J. (1993), 'Developing a Participatory Extension Approach', *Schriftenreihe des Agrarbereiches*, no. 149, 2, Berlin: Auflage.

Pretty, J.N. and Pimbert, M.P. (1995), 'Beyond conservation ideology and the wilderness myth', *Natural Resources Forum*, **19**, 5–14.

Rapoport, A. (1981), 'Konflikt und Kooperation im Lichte der Entscheidungstheorie', in W. Grunwald and H.-G Lilge (eds), *Kooperation und Konkurrenz in Organisationen*, Berne and Stuttgart: Haupt. utb.

Reid, W.V. and Miller, K.R. (1989), *Keeping Options Alive: The Scientific Basis for Conserving Biodiversity*, Washington, DC:

Scholl, W. (1997), 'Gruppenarbeit die Kluft zwischen sozialpsychologischer Theoriebildung und organisationspsychologischer Anwendung', *Gruppendynamik*, **28**, 381–403.

Söderbaum, P. (1999), 'Values, ideology and politics in ecological economics', *Ecological Economics*, **28**, 161–70.

Thibaut, J.W. and Walker, L. (1975), *Procedural Justice. A Psychological Analysis*, Hillsdale, NJ: Lawrence Erlbaum Associates.

Wagemans, M. and Boerma, J. (1998), 'The implementation of nature policy in the Netherlands: platforms designed to fail', in N.G. Röling and M.A.E. Wagemakers (eds), *Facilitating Sustainable Agriculture*, Cambridge: Cambridge University Press.

Woerkum, C. van and Aarts, N. (1998), 'Communication between farmers and government over nature: a new approach to policy development', in N.G. Röling and M.A.E. Wagemakers eds), *Facilitating Sustainable Agriculture*, Cambridge: Cambridge University Press.

JUSSI LANKOSKI AND MARKKU OLLIKAINEN*

Targeting Farm Income and Nutrient Runoffs through Agrienvironmental Policy Mixes: Experience from Finland

INTRODUCTION

Recent agricultural policy and trade reforms are expected to improve the environmental performance of the agricultural sector as a result of the reinstrumentation of domestic agricultural policies from market price supports to decoupled direct payments. However, directed agrienvironmental policies must still play an important role in internalizing environment-related agricultural externalities.

Agricultural pollution is a typical example of non-point source pollution, which makes control and monitoring very difficult. Hence traditional direct instruments, such as effluent standards and effluent taxes, are inapplicable in agriculture. When effluents cannot be dealt with directly, the regulator has to use indirect instruments, for example input and ambient taxes and standards on farming practices (see, for example, Segerson, 1988; Braden and Segerson, 1993, for theoretical analysis and Vatn *et al.*, 1997, for applied research and interdisciplinary modelling of agricultural non-point pollution).

One of the major objectives of the Finnish application of European Union agrienvironmental regulation EEC 2078/92 is the reduction of nutrient runoffs. In what follows we assume that the government issues decision-in-principle water protection targets for the reduction and prevention of eutrophication, with the main goal of reducing nutrient runoffs from agriculture. From this starting point we consider how this kind of agrienvironmental policy should be executed by focusing on those policy instruments that are appropriate for achieving this goal (area-based subsidy, price support, fertilizer tax and buffer zone subsidy). Specifically, we assume that the government adjusts the relative rates of taxes and subsidies so that farmers' profits are kept constant (see Ollikainen, 1999). Consequently, however, the relative prices of inputs change so that the environmentally friendlier input use becomes more profitable and the farmer reoptimizes input use. We characterize alternative tax/subsidy mixes first qualitatively and then quantitatively by using a parametric simulation model, into which agrienvironmental measures can be introduced. The analysis is based on a standard profit maximization model of a representative farmer.

*J. Lankoski, Agricultural Economics Research Institute, Helsinki, Finland; M. Ollikainen, Department of Economics, University of Helsinki, Finland.

THE MODEL OF AGRICULTURAL PRODUCTION

Consider a competitive farm producing cereals using fertilizer l and capital k as inputs in the production. The total amount of arable land q is fixed, and the farmer can allocate it to cereal production $\hat{q}$ and to a buffer zone m (m is a share of total arable land) so that the acreage under cereal cultivation is $\hat{q} = (1 - m)q$. By a buffer zone we mean a managed, uncultivated area covered by perennial vegetation between arable land and watercourses. The aim is to reduce surface water pollution from nutrient runoffs.

The production function is given by:

$$Q = f(l, \hat{q}, k) \tag{1}$$

where Q denotes the cereal produced. That obviously depends on the use of fertilizer and capital, and on the area under cultivation. We assume that the quality of land is diminishing so that the production function is concave in its arguments; that is, each factor of production exhibits diminishing marginal productivity and the production function is linear homogeneous. Thus we have

$$f_l, f_k, f_q > 0; f_{ll}, f_{kk}, f_{qq} < 0 \tag{2}$$

For the buffer zone it holds that $f_m = -qf_q < 0; f_{mm} = q^2 f_{qq} < 0$.

We make the following assumptions concerning the cross-derivatives. Fertilizer and capital are assumed to be independent of each other; that is, their cross-derivative is zero. The same assumption holds for capital and soil. This can be justified on the grounds that technological improvements (like precision farming) are not feasible in the short run and thus an increase in capital does not increase the marginal product of soil. The cross-derivative of fertilizer and soil is positive, implying that these inputs are complements to each other. Thus an increase in fertilizer use increases the marginal product of soil. The sign of the cross-derivative between fertilizer use and land allocated to the buffer zone depends on the quality of land (especially in the field edges). If agricultural land is homogenous then allocating part of it to a buffer zone does not affect the marginal productivity of fertilizer. But if the land in the edge of the field is of lower (higher) quality, then allocating a part of it to the buffer zone will increase (decrease) the marginal productivity of fertilizers. In this paper we assume that the latter case is relevant for the analysis. Summing up, we impose the conditions that

$$f_{ql} > 0, f_{lk} = 0 = f_{qk} \text{ and } f_{lm} = -qf_{lq} < 0$$

The representative farmer, by assumption, is a price taker. Hence the prices of fertilizer c, capital r and cereal p are exogenous. The government pays a price support a so that the unit price of cereal is $p^* = p(1 + a)$. Moreover, a fertilizer tax t is levied on fertilizer use so that the after-tax price of fertilizer is $c^* = c(1 + t)$. For buffer zones the government pays a subsidy *b.* The cultivated arable land is entitled to a unit acreage subsidy *s*. The farmer's problem is to choose the input use of *l*, *k* and *m* to maximize the farm's profit; that is,

$$\underset{\{l,k,m\}}{Max}\,\Pi = p^* f(\hat{q},l,k) - c^*l - rk + bmq + s\hat{q} \tag{3}$$

The first-order conditions for the optimal choice of inputs are the following:

$$\begin{aligned}
\Pi_l &= p^* f_l - c^* = 0 \\
\Pi_k &= p^* f_k - r = 0 \\
\Pi_m &= -p^* q f_q + (b-s)q = 0
\end{aligned} \tag{4}$$

These first-order conditions require that the value of the marginal product of fertilizer and capital use equal the fertilizer price and the price of capital, respectively. Moreover, the land allocated to the buffer zone will be increased to the point where the reduction of the value of the marginal product of cultivating cereal equals the difference between the buffer zone subsidy and acreage subsidy. Note that the buffer zone subsidy must be greater than the acreage subsidy for an interior solution.

Comparative statics of input use

Given that the second-order conditions hold, we can derive the comparative-static analysis by perturbing the first-order conditions with respect to exogenous variables to obtain the following (see Appendix 1 for details):

$$l = l(\underset{+\ -\ 0\ -\ +\ -\ +}{p,c,r,b,s,t,a})$$

$$k = k(\underset{+\ 0\ -\ 0\ 0\ 0\ +}{p,c,r,b,s,t,a}) \tag{5}$$

$$m = m(\underset{-\ +\ 0\ +\ -\ +\ -}{p,c,r,b,s,t,a})$$

Equation (5) shows that input demand depends on exogenous parameters in the usual way; that is, the own-price effects are negative. More specifically, the use of fertilizer and capital depends positively on the output price, while the size of the buffer zone is negatively related to it. Increasing the buffer zone subsidy results in reduced fertilizer use and a larger buffer zone. An increase of acreage subsidy boosts the use of fertilizer and decreases the buffer zone area, whereas a fertilizer tax has the opposite effects. Higher producer price support, *a*, increases the use of fertilizer and capital and decreases the land area allocated to the buffer zone. Thus the area subsidy and producer price support tend to re-enforce environmental distortions, since they encourage the use of fertilization and discourage the allocation of arable land to the buffer zone.

Comparative statics of output supply

The comparative-static analysis of output supply is derived in Appendix 2, equation [A2.3]. It shows that the output supply depends on exogenous parameters in the conventional way. Increases in factor prices, fertilizer tax and buffer zone subsidy will decrease supply, while increases in output price, producer price support and acreage subsidy will increase output supply.

ENVIRONMENTAL EFFECTIVENESS OF ALTERNATIVE AGRIENVIRONMENTAL POLICY MIXES

Assume now that the government issues decision-in-principle water protection targets for the reduction and prevention of eutrophication and wishes to design an agrienvironmental policy so that it keeps the profits of the farmer constant. This latter goal can be achieved by changing one instrument and compensating it by a change in another. Before going into a detailed analysis of the policy, we must clarify first how to model the nitrogen runoff from the fields.

Runoff function of nutrients

Consider the following runoff function for nutrients:

$$z = g(l, \alpha, m) \tag{6}$$

This formulation, based on an economic interpretation of empirical runoff studies, was first proposed in Ollikainen (1995). According to (6), the runoff, z, depends on three factors: fertilizer use l, the gradient of fields near watercourses α and the size of the buffer zone m. The runoff depends positively on fertilizer use and on the gradient coefficient, and negatively on the size of the buffer zone. The coefficient can be regarded as a function of the size of the buffer zone; the larger the area allocated to it, the smaller the impact of the gradient coefficient on runoff, so we have $\alpha = \alpha(m)$. Thus the runoff from fields can be described as a function of fertilizer use l and $\alpha(m)$. The runoff function is assumed to be convex in l and concave in $\alpha(m)$:

$$z = \alpha(m)g(l) \tag{7}$$

where $g'(l) > 0; g''(l) > 0$ and $\alpha'(m) < 0; \alpha''(m) > 0$.

According to Gilliam *et al.* (1997), buffer zones are very effective in the removal of sediment-associated nitrogen from surface runoff and nitrate from subsurface flows, with removals of 50–90 per cent being common. However, the effectiveness of buffer zones in removing nutrients from surface and groundwater is highly dependent on hydrology. For example, surface flows should occur as sheet flow rather than focused flows, and groundwater should move at a slow speed through the buffer in order to remove nitrates effectively

(Correll, 1997). According to Hill (1996), vegetation uptake and microbial denitrification are two major mechanisms in buffer zones for removing nitrates from subsurface water, though the relative importance of these two processes is uncertain. Moreover, as pointed out by Gilliam *et al.* (1997), the increased denitrification in buffer zone areas may trade water pollution for atmospheric pollution due to increased generation of NO_2.

Environmental and supply effects of alternative policy mixes

The principle of changing the relative tax and subsidy rates so that the farmer's profits remain constant implies that, when one instrument entering into the profit function is increased, another instrument is decreased, so that profits remain constant. This kind of switch in the tax/subsidy rates changes the relative prices of inputs in favour of environmentally friendlier production, leading the farmer to reoptimize input use. Hence, after reoptimization, the farmer's profits may be higher or lower than before policy implementation, even though the government's net impact on the profit function remains unchanged. Notice that the government budget revenue constraint is not binding. This means that, after the farmer has reoptimized input use, the required overall net support may be higher or lower than before the policy. Hence this policy can be interpreted as reflecting a situation where the government finds the size of environmentally adjusted agriculture to be optimal and allows the overall net support to adjust as necessary. The basic features of this are outlined in equations (8)–(10).

Differentiating the profit function (3) with respect to t, b, s and a, while keeping the profits constant, gives the following differential equation to guide the instrument switches

$$0 = pf(\cdot)da - cldt + mqdb + \hat{q}ds \tag{8}$$

The resulting change in the agricultural runoff of nutrients is given through changes in fertilizer use and buffer zone area

$$dz = \underbrace{\alpha'(m)g(l)dm}_{(-)} + \underbrace{\alpha(m)g'(l)dl}_{(+)} \tag{9}$$

where the adjustment in the farmer's use of fertilizer (dl) and the buffer zone (dm) is given by the following differential equations, in which i and j denote the policy instruments that the government is adjusting:

$$\begin{aligned} dl &= l_i di + l_j dj \\ dm &= m_i di + m_j dj \end{aligned} \tag{10}$$

In what follows we study the qualitative effects of four alternative agrienvironmental policy mixes. First, the producer price support or acreage subsidy is reduced, and the environmentally motivated buffer zone subsidy is increased to compensate for this reduction. This derivation is followed by the analysis of fertilizer tax increase, which is compensated by an increase in acreage subsidy and buffer zone subsidy, respectively.

Policy mix 1 This involves a decrease in the producer price support and an increase in the buffer zone subsidy. As a result of intensification effects and related nutrient runoff, the government wishes to switch from producer price support towards buffer zone subsidy while keeping profits constant. From $mqdb + pf(\cdot)da = 0$ we obtain the required compensation to keep the profits constant:

$$da = -\frac{mq}{pf(\cdot)}db \qquad (11)$$

Using (11) in (10) and applying comparative static results from input use (equation (5)) produces

$$\frac{dl}{db} = \left[-\frac{mq}{pf(\cdot)} \underset{(+)}{l_a} + \underset{(-)}{l_b} \right] < 0 \quad \text{and} \qquad (12a)$$

$$\frac{dm}{db} = \left[-\frac{mq}{pf(\cdot)} \underset{(-)}{m_a} + \underset{(+)}{m_b} \right] > 0 \qquad (12b)$$

Applying these results to equation (9) yields the following effect on agricultural nutrient runoff:

$$dz = \underbrace{\alpha'(m)g(l)}_{(-)} \underbrace{\frac{dm}{db}}_{(+)} + \underbrace{\alpha(m)g'(l)}_{(+)} \underbrace{\frac{dl}{db}}_{(-)} < 0 \qquad (13)$$

Thus a switch from a producer price support towards a buffer zone subsidy decreases the use of fertilizers and increases the buffer zone area, resulting in unambiguously reduced nutrient runoffs. The shift also reduces output supply (see Appendix 2).

Policy mix 2 Here we have a decrease in the acreage subsidy and an increase in the buffer zone subsidy. Because of the production-stimulating and negative environmental side-effects of area subsidy, the government switches from that to a buffer zone subsidy. Applying the same procedure given in the previous policy mix, one obtains:

$$\frac{dl}{db} = \left[-\frac{m}{(1-m)} \underset{(+)}{l_s} + \underset{(-)}{l_b} \right] < 0 \quad \text{and} \qquad (14a)$$

$$\frac{dm}{db} = \left[-\frac{m}{(1-m)} \underset{(-)}{m_s} + \underset{(+)}{m_b} \right] > 0 \qquad (14b)$$

Using these results in equation (9) shows that the runoff decreases unambiguously. This policy mix also results in reduced output (see Appendix 2).

Policy mix 3   This policy mix includes an increase in the fertilizer tax and a rise in the acreage subsidy. Assume that the government increases the fertilizer tax and compensates this by increasing the acreage subsidy. From equations (15a) and (15b) it can be seen that the effects are ambiguous, at first, but by using comparative static results (see Appendix 3 for details of proving the sign) the signs of the effects are as follows:

$$\frac{dl}{ds} = \left[\frac{1}{cl} \underset{(-)}{l_t} + \underset{(+)}{l_s} \right] < 0 \qquad \text{and} \qquad (15a)$$

$$\frac{dm}{ds} = \left[\frac{1}{cl} \underset{(+)}{m_t} + \underset{(-)}{m_s} \right] > 0 \qquad\qquad (15b)$$

Hence this switch also results in unambiguously reduced nutrient runoffs according to (9). However, the effect may now be weaker than in the previous cases since the increase in the acreage subsidy reduces the impact of the fertilizer tax. The output supply decreases as well, but this reductive effect may be weaker than in the previous cases owing to production-stimulating effects of the acreage subsidy (see Appendix 2).

Policy mix 4   Finally, we have an increase in the fertilizer tax and an increase in the buffer zone subsidy. In this alternative, the government establishes its agrienvironmental policy by increasing the fertilizer tax and compensating this by increasing the buffer zone subsidy in order to have a substantial reduction in nutrient runoff. This leads to

$$\frac{dl}{db} = \left[\frac{mq}{cl} \underset{(-)}{l_t} + \underset{(-)}{l_b} \right] < 0 \qquad \text{and} \qquad (16a)$$

$$\frac{dm}{db} = \left[\frac{mq}{cl} \underset{(+)}{m_t} + \underset{(+)}{m_b} \right] > 0 \qquad\qquad (16b)$$

As in the previous cases, applying these results in equation (9) results in unambiguously reduced nutrient runoff. However, in this case the reductive effect on nutrient runoff is stronger, since the fertilizer tax and buffer zone subsidy reinforce each other. Naturally, the output supply decreases as well, and the effect is stronger than in the previous cases (see Appendix 2).

On the basis of the qualitative analysis, we can conclude that a policy mix of equation (16a) and (16b) is superior in terms of achieving the environmental goals, but it reduces output more than other mixes. As we cannot rank the other mixes qualitatively, it is useful to conduct a quantitative analysis.

PARAMETRIC MODEL AND SIMULATIONS

In this section we illustrate and compare numerically the environmental and economic effects of alternative agrienvironmental policy mixes developed in the previous section. For this purpose we build a parametric model of agricultural production with exogenous crop price, and execute the instrument mixes 1–4. Then we briefly rank the instrument mixes. As all switches will have the property of keeping the profits constant and achieving the environmental target (10 per cent reduction in nitrogen runoffs), these cannot be the yardsticks of ranking. Therefore we adopt the following properties as means of comparison. First we calculate the increase in the government net support per hectare required to keep the farmer's profits constant when nitrogen runoffs are reduced by 10 per cent. Then we calculate net support per output when profits are kept constant, and, finally, we compare the policy mixes in terms of the output produced per runoff to highlight the 'eco-efficiency' aspects of policy mixes.

Parametric model

Following the theoretical model, we start with agricultural production function and apply a quadratic nitrogen response function (with parameters estimated for barley) and augment it with buffer strips as follows:

$$y = a(1 - \phi m^2) + \alpha l + \beta l^2 \qquad (17)$$

where
a = production of unfertilized land,
l = fertilizer applied,
ϕm^2 = the share of output lost from unfertilized land if a share m of land is allocated to buffer strip.

We use the nitrogen leakage function estimated by Simmelsgaard (1991) on the basis of Danish leakage research:

$$y(N) = y_n \exp(b_0 + bN) \qquad (18)$$

where $y(N)$ = nitrogen leakage at fertilizer intensity level N, kg/ha., y_n = nitrogen leakage at average nitrogen use, b_0 = a constant (<0), b = a parameter (>0) and N = relative nitrogen fertilization in relation to normal fertilizer intensity for the crop, $0.5 \leq N \leq 1.5$.

This leakage function measures changes in nitrogen leakages solely as a function of the fertilization intensity level. Information on average fertilizer intensity and nitrogen leakages from average nitrogen use y_n is needed when applying this function to Finnish conditions. In the Finnish experimental studies on nitrogen leaching, the average nitrogen fertilization level for cereals has usually been 100kg/ha. Combined surface and drainage nitrogen leakages (y_n) at this level have been in the order of 10–20kg N/ha. (Sumelius, 1994).

We modify the leakage function to incorporate the reductive effect of buffer zone on nitrogen runoff Z as follows

$$Z = (1 - jr)y(N) \qquad (19)$$

where Z = nitrogen runoff, $y(N)$ = nitrogen leakage at fertilizer intensity level N, kg/ha., j = share of the surface runoff from combined surface and drainage runoff, and r = nitrogen removal effectiveness of buffer zone.

In Finland, Uusi-Kämppä and Yläranta (1992, 1996) have analysed the reductive effects of a grass buffer zone 10 metres wide on sediment and nutrient losses. Barley and oats were cultivated on experimental fields during the experimental period with fertilization levels of 90kg of nitrogen per hectare and 18kg of phosphorus per hectare. A grass buffer zone reduced surface runoff of total nitrogen and nitrates by 50 per cent. Note, however, that buffer zones reduce surface runoff of nutrients, but not runoff through drainage pipes. For example, in Finnish experiments measuring total nitrogen runoff from cultivated fields, over 50 per cent ran through drainage pipes (Turtola and Jaakkola, 1985; Turtola and Puustinen, 1998).

On the basis of these Finnish experimental studies on grass buffer zones and on the leaching of nitrogen, we make the following assumptions. In the policy simulations we assume that 50 per cent of the total nitrogen load is surface runoff (that is, parameter value j is 0.5) and a grass buffer zone, 10 metres wide, is able to reduce 50 per cent of the total nitrogen of this surface runoff. Thus parameter value r is set at 0.5. Moreover, since in Finnish experimental studies combined surface and drainage nitrogen leakages (y_n) at fertilization level 100kg N/ha. have been in the order of 10–20 kg N/ha., parameter value y_n is set at 15 in simulations.

Policy simulations

Parameter values used for the policy simulations are reported in Table 1. A quadratic nitrogen response function for barley has been estimated by Bäckman *et al.* (1997) on the basis of the long-term field trials (1973–93).

The base simulation of our parametric model is chosen to represent the policy regime for cereals (barley) in Finland in 1999. We execute the policy mixes 1–4 so as to reduce nitrogen runoffs by 10 per cent (from 18.6kg N/ha. in base simulation to 16.8kg N/ha. in policy mixes) while keeping the farmer's profits constant. Then we compare the effects of policy mixes 1–4 with each other and with the base simulation in terms of government net support per hectare and per output produced, as well as in terms of output per runoffs.

Simulation results

The simulation results for the policy mixes are given in Table 2 in terms of production, government net support per hectare, net support per kilogram of barley produced, and kilogram of barley produced per kilogram of nitrogen runoff.

All policy mixes achieved the required 10 per cent reduction target in nitrogen runoff. If we focus on the net support per hectare, then policy mixes 1, 2 and 4 achieve runoff reduction of 10 per cent even with lower government net support per hectare than in the base scenario. Hence these policy mixes give a more efficient instrument base than the current one, because with less

TABLE 1   *Simulation parameters*

---

p = price of barley, FIM 0.73/kg,
c = price of nitrogen fertilizer, FIM 5.95/kg,
a = constant parameter of response function, 1010 for barley,
α = parameter of quadratic nitrogen response function, 52.9 for barley,
β = parameter of quadratic nitrogen response function, –0.173 for barley,
y_n = nitrogen leakage at average nitrogen use, 10–20kg/ha.,
b = the value of b and $b0$ is 0.7, based on Danish leakage experiments,
N = relative nitrogen fertilization level, that is, optimal rate from economic
       model in relation to normal intensity for the crop,
j = share of surface runoff from combined surface and drainage runoff,
r = nitrogen removal effectiveness of buffer strip,
s = area support, FIM 2402 per hectare,
B = buffer zone support, FIM 3200–3600 per hectare.

Notes: Prices and support figures are from 1999. Price of nitrogen is calculated
            from compound fertilizer N–P–K. Area support is calculated for the
            support area A and it includes Common Agricultural Policy (CAP)
            compensation payments, environmental aid, and national support for crop
            production.

Sources: Bäckman *et al.* (1997), Ministry of Agriculture and Forestry, Association
            of Rural Advisory Centres.

TABLE 2   *Per hectare effects of alternative agrienvironmental policy
mixes: 10 per cent of nitrogen runoffs are reduced and farmer's profits are
kept constant*

Policy mix[1]	Production (kg/ha.)	Net support, (FIM/ha.)	Net support/ production (FIM/kg)	Production/ runoffs
Base	4 620	2 407	0.52	248
Policy mix 1	4 270	2 385	0.56	254
Policy mix 2	4 248	2 390	0.56	252
Policy mix 3	4 581	2 479	0.54	272
Policy mix 4	4 274	2 395	0.56	254

Notes: [1]Policy mix 1 = price support ↓ buffer zone subsidy ↑; policy mix 2 =
            acreage subsidy ↓ buffer zone subsidy ↑; policy mix 3 = fertilizer tax ↑
            acreage subsidy ↑; policy mix 4 = fertilizer tax ↑ buffer zone subsidy ↑.

support we have better environmental quality and still the profits remain unchanged. Note, however, that in terms of output produced the required net
support will increase.

If our yardstick is the net support per output produced, notice first that agricultural production decreases in all policy mixes, mainly because of a higher share of buffer zone in policy mixes 1, 2 and 4 and to reduced fertilizer use in policy mix 3. Policy mix 3, which compensates for the fertilizer tax with higher acreage subsidy, is second to none with respect to level of production. Therefore, policy mix 3 is the best one if our yardstick is the net support per unit of output produced. Moreover, owing to the higher level of production, policy mix 3 is second to none also with respect to the criterion of weight of barley produced per kilogram of nitrogen runoff. Hence we can conclude that, if either net support per output produced or output per runoff is used as the yardstick, policy mix 3 performs best. If net support per hectare is the yardstick, mix 1 is optimal.

CONCLUSIONS

We have analysed agrienvironmental policy in a simple model of agricultural production, where the farmer chooses the use of inputs so as to maximize profits. The input choice was affected by price support, fertilizer tax, buffer zone subsidy and area subsidy. Having determined the comparative static effects of these instruments, we studied both theoretically and empirically an agrienvironmental policy where the government searches for the best combination of instruments so as to promote environmental goals, while keeping the farmer's profits constant.

We demonstrated that an area subsidy and a producer price support create environmental distortions, since they encourage the use of fertilizer and discourage the allocation of arable land to the buffer zone. Thus, when land allocation is endogenized through the choice of a buffer zone, an area subsidy becomes a distortionary instrument. This clearly contradicts the conventional wisdom, which regards it as neutral. When alternative agrienvironmental policy mixes were theoretically evaluated from the viewpoint of environmental effectiveness, all policy options resulted in an unambiguously reduced nutrient runoff from agriculture. However, a policy mix which compensated for the increase in the fertilizer tax with higher buffer zone subsidy had the strongest reducing effect on nutrient runoff, since the instruments reinforced each other.

Policy simulations showed that all policy mixes achieve the target of 10 per cent reduction of nitrogen runoff. Moreover, policy mixes 1, 2 and 4 achieve runoff reduction with lower government net support per hectare than in the base scenario. Policy mix 3, which compensates for the fertilizer tax with higher acreage subsidy, was second to none with respect to level of production but performed poorly with respect to net support per hectare criterion. However, because of the higher level of production than in other policy options, policy mix 3 performed best with respect to the criteria of net support per unit of output produced and output produced against runoff.

To conclude, through selecting the correct instrument combination and adjusting the level of instruments, government is able to keep farmers' profits constant and to reduce nitrogen runoffs while keeping the required net support at its minimum. The selection of the policy mix depends on the weight given for production effects.

REFERENCES

Bäckman, S.T., Vermeulen, S. and Taavitsainen, V.-M. (1997), 'Long-term fertilizer field trials: comparison of three mathematical response models', *Agricultural and Food Science in Finland*, **6**, 151–60.

Braden, J.B. and Segerson, K. (1993), 'Information problems in the design of nonpoint source pollution policy', in C.S. Russell and J.F. Shogren (eds), *Theory, modeling and experience in the management of nonpoint source pollution*, Boston: Kluwer Academic Publishers.

Correll, D.L. (1997), 'Buffer zones and water quality protection: general principles', in N.E. Haycock (ed.), *Buffer zones: Their processes and potential in water protection*, Harpenden, UK: Quest Environmental.

Gilliam, J.W, Parsons, J.E. and Mikkelsen, R.L. (1997), 'Nitrogen dynamics and buffer zones', in N.E. Haycock (ed.), *Buffer zones: Their processes and potential in water protection*, Harpenden, UK: Quest Environmental.

Hill, A.R. (1996), 'Nitrate removal in stream riparian zones', *Journal of Environmental Quality*, **25**, 743–55.

Ollikainen, M. (1995), 'Cost-efficient control of agricultural water pollution', in L. Albisu and C. Romero (eds), *Environmental and land use issues – an economic perspective*, Proceedings of the 34th EAAE Seminar, Kiel: Wissenschaftsverlag Vauk.

Ollikainen, M. (1999), 'On optimal agri-environmental policy: a public finance view', *Kansantaloustieteen laitoksen keskustelualoitteita*, no. 457, Department of Economics, University of Helsinki.

Segerson, K. (1988), 'Uncertainty and incentives for nonpoint pollution control', *Journal of Environmental Economics and Management*, **15**, 87–98.

Simmelsgaard, S. (1991), 'Estimation of nitrogen leakage functions – Nitrogen leakage as a function of nitrogen applications for different crops on sand and clay soils' (in Danish: 'Estimering af funktioner for kvaelstofudvaskning. Kvaelstofudvaskning som funktion af kvaelstoftilförsel for forskellige afgröder dyrket på sandjord og ledord'), in S. Rude (ed.), *Nitrogen fertilizers in Danish Agriculture – present and future application and leaching*, Report 62, Copenhagen: Institute of Agricultural Economics (in Danish: Kvaelstofgödning i landbruget – behov og udvasking nu og i fremtiden).

Sumelius, J. (1994), *Controlling nonpoint source pollution of nitrogen from agriculture through economic instruments in Finland*, Helsinki: Agricultural Economics Research Institute Publications, no. 74.

Turtola, E. and Jaakkola, A. (1985), *Viljelykasvin ja lannoitustason vaikutus typen ja fosforin huuhtoutumiseen savimaasta* (in Finnish), Maatalouden tutkimuskeskus, Tiedote 6/85, Jokioinen.

Turtola, E. and Puustinen, M. (1998), 'Kasvipeitteisyys ravinnehuuhtoutumien vähentäjänä', *Vesitalous*, **1/1998**, 6–11.

Uusi-Kämppä, J. and Yläranta, T. (1992), 'Reduction of sediment, phosphorus and nitrogen transport on vegetated buffer strips', *Agricultural Science in Finland*, **1**, 569–75.

Uusi-Kämppä, J. and Yläranta, T. (1996), 'Effect of buffer strip on controlling erosion and nutrient losses in Southern Finland', in G. Mulamoottil, B.G. Warner and E.A. McBean (eds), *Wetlands: environmental gradients, boundaries and buffers*, Boca Raton: CRC Press/Lewis Publishers.

Vatn, A., Bakken, L.R., Botterweg, P., Lundeby, R.E., Rörstad, P.K. and Vold, A. (1997), 'Regulating Nonpoint Source Pollution from Agriculture: An Integrated Modelling Analysis', *European Review of Agricultural Economics*, **24**, 207–29.

APPENDIX 1: COMPARATIVE STATICS OF INPUT USE

The profit function of the representative farmer is

$$\Pi = p^* f(\hat{q}, l, k) - c^* l - rk + bmq + s\hat{q} \tag{A1.1}$$

where $\hat{q} = (1-m)q$.

The first-order conditions for profit maximization are

$$
\begin{aligned}
\Pi_l &= p^* f_l - c^* = 0 \\
\Pi_k &= p^* f_k - r = 0 \\
\Pi_m &= -p^* q f_q + (b-s)q = 0
\end{aligned} \tag{A1.2}
$$

Sufficient conditions for profit maximization require that the second partial derivatives are negative:

$$
\begin{aligned}
\Pi_{ll} &= p^* f_{ll} < 0 \\
\Pi_{mm} &= p^* q^2 f_{qq} < 0 \\
\Pi_{kk} &= p^* f_{kk} < 0
\end{aligned} \tag{A1.3}
$$

The cross-partial derivatives are imposed as

$$
\begin{aligned}
\Pi_{lk} &= 0 = \Pi_{kl} \\
\Pi_{km} &= 0 = \Pi_{mk} \\
\Pi_{lm} &= -p^* q f_{lq} < 0
\end{aligned} \tag{A1.4}
$$

Moreover, profit maximization requires that the determinant of the Hessian matrix is negative definite:

$$
H = \begin{bmatrix}
p^* f_{ll} & 0 & \Pi_{lm} \\
0 & p^* f_{kk} & 0 \\
\Pi_{lm} & 0 & p^* q^2 f_{qq}
\end{bmatrix} \tag{A1.5}
$$

$$\Delta = p^* f_{kk} [p^{*2} f_{ll} f_{qq} - \Pi_{lm}^2] < 0$$

In order to solve comparative statics, the first-order conditions are differentiated with respect to parameters, and then Cramer's Rule is applied to sign the effects.

APPENDIX 2: OUTPUT SUPPLY AND ALTERNATIVE AGRIENVIRONMENTAL POLICY MIXES

A Output supply

The supply function can be derived from the profit function by differentiating the profit function (3) with respect to output price (Hotelling's lemma), to give

$$\frac{\partial \Pi}{\partial p} = f(\hat{q}, l, k) \tag{A2.1}$$

so that we obtain the production function of this farm. Next we substitute the optimal input use into the production function and we get the profit maximizing level of output:

$$Y^* = f(m^*, l^*, k^*) \tag{A2.2}$$

Thus the supply function of this farm is

$$Y^* = Y^*(\underset{+}{p}, \underset{-}{c}, \underset{-}{r}, \underset{-}{b}, \underset{+}{s}, \underset{-}{t}, \underset{+}{a}) \tag{A2.3}$$

B The effects of alternative agrienvironmental reforms on output supply

A decrease in the producer price support and an increase in buffer zone subsidy:

$$dY = \underset{(+)}{f_k} \underset{(-)}{\frac{\partial k}{\partial b}} + \underset{(+)}{f_l} \underset{(-)}{\frac{\partial l}{\partial b}} + \underset{(-)}{f_m} \underset{(+)}{\frac{\partial m}{\partial b}} < 0 \tag{A2.4}$$

A decrease in acreage subsidy and an increase in buffer zone subsidy:

$$dY = \underset{(+)}{f_k} \underset{(0)}{\frac{\partial k}{\partial b}} + \underset{(+)}{f_l} \underset{(-)}{\frac{\partial l}{\partial b}} + \underset{(-)}{f_m} \underset{(+)}{\frac{\partial m}{\partial b}} < 0 \tag{A2.5}$$

An increase in fertilizer tax and a rise in acreage subsidy:

$$dY = \underset{(+)}{f_k} \underset{(0)}{\frac{\partial k}{\partial s}} + \underset{(+)}{f_l} \underset{(-)}{\frac{\partial l}{\partial s}} + \underset{(-)}{f_m} \underset{(+)}{\frac{\partial m}{\partial s}} < 0 \tag{A2.6}$$

An increase in fertilizer tax and an increase in buffer zone subsidy:

$$dY = \underset{(+)}{f_k} \underset{(0)}{\frac{\partial k}{\partial b}} + \underset{(+)}{f_l} \underset{(-)}{\frac{\partial l}{\partial b}} + \underset{(-)}{f_m} \underset{(+)}{\frac{\partial m}{\partial b}} < 0 \tag{A2.7}$$

APPENDIX 3: A PROOF FOR THE SIGNS OF (15A) AND (15B)

The government increases fertilizer tax and compensates for this with an increase in the acreage subsidy. One has for the fertilizer use

$$\frac{dl}{ds} = \left[\frac{1}{cl}\underset{(-)}{l_t} + \underset{(+)}{l_s}\right] \tag{A3.1}$$

Using the comparative statics effects yields

$$\underset{(-)}{\Delta^{-1}}\left[(\Pi_{lm}pf_{kk}q) + (cpf_{kk}pq^2 f_{qq}) + (clpf_{kk}\Pi_{lm})\right]$$

$$= \underset{(-)}{\Delta^{-1}}\left[\underbrace{\Pi_{lm}(pf_{kk}q + clpf_{kk})}_{(+)} + \underbrace{(cpf_{kk}pq^2 f_{qq})}_{(+)}\right] < 0$$

The change in the buffer zone is given by

$$\frac{dm}{ds} = \left[\frac{1}{cl}\underset{(+)}{m_t} + \underset{(-)}{m_s}\right] \tag{A3.2}$$

The relevant comparative statics effects are

$$m_s = \underset{(-)}{\Delta^{-1}}\left[qp^2 f_{ll}f_{kk}\right]$$

$$m_t = \underset{(-)}{\Delta^{-1}}\left[clp^2 f_{ll}f_{kk}\right] \underbrace{- \underset{(-)}{\Delta^{-1}}\left[c\Pi_{lm}pf_{kk}\right]}_{(+)}$$

Using these in (A3.2) yields

$$\underset{(-)}{\Delta^{-1}}\left[-qp^2 f_{ll}f_{kk} - \frac{1}{l}\Pi_{lm}pf_{kk} + qp^2 f_{ll}f_{kk}\right] > 0$$

ALFONS BALMANN, BRITTA CZASCH AND MARTIN ODENING*

Employment and Efficiency of Farms in Transition: an Empirical Analysis for Brandenburg

INTRODUCTION

Changes in the political, economic and legal framework after reunification led to major structural changes in East German agriculture. Altered factor and product price relations, abolition of traditional channels of distribution and problems with liquidity forced existing farms to adjust their organization and factor input, to increase productivity and to seek technical progress. Although the number of agricultural enterprises has grown continually as a result of the appearance of new and re-established farms, the number of people engaged in agriculture has fallen dramatically. In Brandenburg – the federal state surrounding Berlin – 31 per cent of those employed in agriculture in 1990 were forced into early retirement, and another 20 per cent took part in further education, retraining or employment creation schemes (MELF, 1997). Many of those workers who had been engaged in employment creation schemes became unemployed after completion. Even from 1992 to 1997, the workforce in agriculture decreased from 39 055 to 25 991 working units (WU).

The paper attempts to study the factors that have determined the employment decisions of farm operators and how they adjusted employment over time with particular regard to legal forms and production structures. This is achieved by applying a data envelopment analysis to a sample of 89 farms, existing over the period 1992/93 to 1995/96. The article is structured as follows. After presenting the theoretical background of labour deployment in enterprises undergoing transition, some hypotheses are developed as a guideline for the empirical investigation. The next section describes the method and the data which are utilized and that is followed by presentation and discussion of the empirical results.

THEORETICAL BACKGROUND

The annual Agricultural Report of the German Federal Government (*Agrarbericht*) draws attention to two interesting phenomena relating to the successors of the former agricultural production cooperatives (LPGs). Firstly,

*Humboldt University of Berlin, Germany.

those farms which are organized as legal entities operate at a significantly higher labour intensity than the new and re-established East German family farms and partnerships. Secondly, on average, profits are slightly negative for most financial years and regions. On the one hand, this may be understood to be a symptom of the general inefficiency of what are usually large farms mainly operating with hired labour. Proponents of transaction cost theory argue that the employment of hired non-family labour causes agency and monitoring costs which diminish existing economies of scale; moreover, cooperatives in particular are confronted by a 'free-rider' problem (Peter and Weikard, 1993; Beckmann, 1997; Schmitz and Noeth, 1999). Both aspects are regarded as being of considerable relevance for agriculture where production is based on natural processes that include seasonality and randomness (Allen and Lueck, 1999).

On the other hand, Balmann *et al.* (1996) provide two alternative explanations. Firstly, these successors are affected by significant sunk costs resulting from investments prior to the transition period. Dairy and pig farms, in particular, started transition with buildings whose opportunity costs were usually low. If an asset's costs are truly 'sunk', it is more than the use of the asset itself that can be affected. According to Johnson (1972), sunk costs of one factor also affect the use of other complementary factors (such as labour), which may be employed to a greater extent than when there is perfect mobility of all factors. Figure 1 depicts this effect. Considering productivity P and labour input L, sunk costs for assets lead to a change in the relevant marginal productivity curve of labour input from $\partial P / \partial L$ to $\partial P' / \partial L$.[1] If the optimality condition for labour input for a wage w is $\partial P' / \partial L = w$ and $\partial P' / \partial L > \partial P / \partial L$, then sunk costs cause the optimal employment to rise from L^* to L'. According to Figure 1, that shift implies that a farm operating at L' is very likely to show decreasing returns to scale, particularly since for L' the average and the marginal productivity differ more than for L^*.

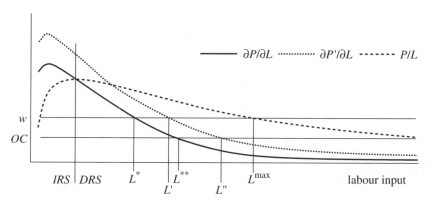

FIGURE 1   *Optimal deployment of labour, as dependent on sunk costs and labour costs*

Secondly, Balmann *et al.* (1996) hypothesize that cooperatively organized enterprises do not necessarily aim at profit maximization. For example, an enterprise where capital owners and employees are largely one and the same group may strive for an employment level that is not oriented to the wage w but rather to the employees' opportunity costs OC. The implication would be an increase of labour input from L^* to L^{**} and L' to L'', respectively. At that point the marginal labour productivity is equal to the workers' opportunity costs. A cooperative's strategy based on the opportunity costs of its members may, of course, be rational from the perspective of the whole group of members if it allows for internalizing pecuniary externalities caused by labour market distortions.[2] In the end, such a strategy has similar effects to those which Schmitt (1997), for example, considers to be relevant for family enterprises and which explain some interesting phenomena of family farm-dominated agriculture, notably persistent income disparities (Balmann, 1999). Moreover, whenever cooperative members and workers are an identical group, it does not appear implausible that cooperatives should aim for job maximization, as a result of their decision-making structures, since every member's vote has the same weight in the general meeting. This deviates from comparative – static approaches of analysing cooperative behaviour.

For example, Ward (1958) concludes that cooperatives maximize average productivity and thus show underemployment (cf. Weikard, 1996). If one assumes that capital depletion should not take place, the whole farm's capacity to pay for equity capital and labour input P may be used to pay wages. From the given wage rate w, the maximum level of employment L^{max} is reached where the average productivity P/L is equal to w.[3] Because there are no profits, this solution implies that capital provided by the members is not paid for.[4] Thus this solution only appears feasible in cases where the majority of members in a cooperative support the goal of job maximization, perhaps because job security is desired, or because of solidarity within the membership. In principle, if workers and shareholders are nearly identical and if shares are rather equally distributed, such goals could also be set by other legal forms of corporate farming (for example, limited liability enterprises). In fact, this is usually not the case; membership and employment structure differ depending on legal form (*Agrarbericht*, various years).

With regard to LPG successors burdened with so-called 'old debts', profit avoidance appears particularly plausible, because this simultaneously postpones the repayment of old debts. According to Forstner and Isermeyer (1997), legal entities without old debts performed much better and showed a lower labour intensity. These considerations suggest that empirical analysis might show that:

- efficiency in general and labour productivity in particular should, ceteris paribus, be lower for LPG successors than for newly and re-established farms;
- within the group of LPG successors efficiency should be lower (a) for farms with animal production than for cash crop farms, (b) for cooperatives than for other corporate farms, and (c) for farms with old debts;

- because the relevance of sunk costs decreases over time, the efficiency of successors should increase – particularly in animal production.

MODEL AND DATA

In order to shed some light on these aspects of the adjustment process, a data envelopment analysis (DEA) was applied to a sample of farms from Brandenburg (Germany). DEA is a non-parametric method of estimating a production frontier by means of linear programming.[5] It measures the relative performance of farms on the basis of Farrell's definition of efficiency, with a score between zero and one being attached to every farm appearing in the analysis. An advantage of this technique, exploited in the application, is that it easily accommodates multi-input/multi-output technologies. In particular, input-oriented models with constant and variable returns to scale are used. This approach allows us to distinguish between technical efficiency and scale efficiency and indicates whether a farm shows increasing or decreasing returns to scale. Furthermore, input slacks, that is, excess factor inputs, are reported for farms, which are located or projected on the vertical or horizontal axis of the production frontier.

The material for the empirical analysis is based on the farm accountancy network (FADN) of Brandenburg. A sample of 210 financial statements was drawn for the years from 1992/93 to 1995/96. Table 1 classifies the sample with respect to legal status, main production and financial year. Because of the low number of cases in some groups, general conclusions must be drawn carefully.

In DEA, all financial statements are analysed simultaneously in order to facilitate a comparison of different farm types, legal forms and financial years. This procedure can be justified by the fact that there were only moderate changes in prices and agricultural policies during the time period under consideration. Table 2 specifies the input and output variables which enter the DEA model.

Though capital, as a factor, can be expected to influence the efficiency results, this variable has not been included in the model at the present stage of analysis. Problems arise from a rather arbitrary evaluation of real assets used in the opening balances as well as from widely differing depreciation practices. Both facts cause serious distortions in the measurement of farm capital input.[6] The exclusion of the factor may underestimate economies of scale of large farms because of the cost-decreasing impact of large buildings and machines.

RESULTS AND INTERPRETATION

Efficiency results

Table 3 exhibits the average total efficiency values for the various farm types, legal forms and time periods under investigation.[7] According to Table 3,

TABLE 1   *The farm sample*

LF	1992/93				1993/94				1994/95				1995/96			
	All	CP	LF	MP	All	CP	LF	MP	All	CP	LF	MP	All	CP	LF	MP
NP	5	5			9	6	3		14	9	5		15	9	6	
LE	15	3	10		26	8	15	3	52	17	29	6	74	21	43	10
Coop	11	1	8	2	16	2	11	3	33	7	22	4	47	7	33	7
Other	4	2	2	2	10	6	4		19	10	7	2	27	14	10	3
Total	20	8	10	2	35	14	18	3	66	26	34	6	89	30	49	10

Notes: Legal form: NP – natural persons (family farms, partnerships); LE – legal entities; Coop – cooperatives. Farm type: CP – cash crop farm; LF – livestock farm; MP – mixed farms and pig farms. Cash crop (livestock) farms receive more than 50 per cent of standard farm income from cash crops (livestock).

TABLE 2 *Input and output variables of the DEA model*

Output variable	Unit	Definition	Input variable	Definition	Unit
y_1 Crop production	DM	Revenue from: – cash crops – change in stocks	x_1 Labour	Sum of working units per enterprise	WU
y_2 Animal production	DM	Revenue from: – animal products – increase/decrease in stock	x_2 Land	Worked land area in ha. weighted with the enterprise's average soil quality index	ha. * EMZ
y_3 Other	DM	Revenue from: – special business proceeds – subsidies	x_3 Variable inputs	Material costs for: – livestock – crop production – trade, services	DM

TABLE 3 *Evolution of average efficiency values (percentages)*

	Total efficiency: cash crop farms		Total efficiency: livestock farms		Scale efficiency		Relation IRS/DRS	
	Natural persons	Legal entities	Natural persons	Legal entities	Natural persons	Legal entities	Natural persons	Legal entities
1992/93	82	75	—	58	90	77	60 / 20	0 / 100
1993/94	85	75	93	62	93	78	56 / 11	8 / 92
1994/95	83	80	78	69	90	84	50 / 14	12 / 83
1995/96	85	77	85	71	93	83	40 / 13	9 / 88

Notes: IRS – increasing returns to scale; DRS – decreasing returns to scale.

'natural persons', that is, family farms and partnerships, reached an efficiency level of about 85 per cent irrespective of the farm type. In contrast, legal entities showed an efficiency level of 75 to 80 per cent for cash crop farming, while the level for animal farms rose gradually from 58 to 71 per cent.

Obviously, livestock farms that succeeded former LPGs required a much longer time to adjust to a more efficient resource use and technical productivity. This observation gives evidence for our initial thesis that sunk costs – which are particularly relevant for animal farming – have a strong impact on adjustment speed. An additional explanation for the delay in the catch-up-process, which holds for dairy farms, is the necessary, but time-consuming, replacement of traditional breeds by more productive types.[8] The higher efficiency of family farms and partnerships is plausible, since they normally started off with adequate production techniques. The same applies to corporate cash crop farms, which have better opportunities to incorporate technical progress as a result of rationalization investments and shorter investment cycles. As far as the evolution of efficiency of different legal forms is concerned, Mathijs and Swinnen (1997) arrive at a similar conclusion for all East German states. The only difference from our result is that they suggest there is a convergence of technical efficiency for all farm types, whereas our results indicate that in livestock production the technical efficiency of 'legal entities' is still lower than that of 'natural persons'.[9]

It is also interesting that the discrepancy in total efficiency between natural persons and legal entities is the result of a lower scale efficiency of the latter. Although decreasing returns to scale do not necessarily imply allocative inefficiency, they may indicate that these farms operate beyond the profit-maximizing level that would be relevant for the case of perfect factor mobility. With Figure 1 in mind, this can be seen as a further sign that the LPG successors either consider a significant part of their capital costs to be sunk, or they emphasize the employment interests of their members. Both would imply diseconomies of scale. However, although nearly all legal entities show decreasing returns to scale, it should be mentioned that the largest efficient crop farm operates with 61 employees, with the number being 71 for the largest efficient livestock farm. These numbers are far beyond average employment levels for the legal entities group as a whole.

As already mentioned, DEA allows for the calculation of input and output 'slacks'. According to Table 4, labour slacks appear in 'legal entities' particularly if they specialized in animal farming, but not when they produce cash crops, while for natural persons labour slacks occur for crop farms only. In principle, the labour slacks of legal entities again support the thesis of a slower adjustment in LPG successors with livestock and pig production. They could stem from the existence of sunk costs or from a more general tendency for employment to be higher than necessary for profit maximization. The latter, however, should imply labour slacks for corporate cash crop farms, too, but this is not the case. Furthermore, the slacks for cooperatives and other corporate farms within the groups of cash crop farms and livestock farms turn out to be similar despite differences in the relation of members, employees and

TABLE 4   *Input slacks in relation to absolute input and efficiency (%)*

	n	Labour	Land	Variable inputs	Total efficiency	Technical efficiency
Cash crop farms						
Natural persons	29	4	3	1	87	91
Cooperatives	17	1	4	0	78	93
Other corporate farms	22	0	10	0	77	91
Livestock farms						
Natural persons	14	0	17	0	84	90
Cooperatives	90	4	7	0	65	83
Other corporate farms	38	3	12	0	76	86
All						
Natural persons	43	2	8	1	86	90
Cooperatives	107	3	6	0	67	85
with old debts	53	2	7	0	66	83
Other corporate farms	60	1	10	0	77	88
with old debts	18	1	4	0	72	89

shareholders. These two observations lead to the conclusion that the inefficiency of legal entities could be a result of sunk costs rather than of members' employment interests.

However, when we consider all farms, differences between cooperatives and limited liability companies become obvious. Cooperatives show lower technical efficiency, lower scale efficiency and higher labour slacks. Moreover, the analysis shows that, for 15 of the 210 farms having considerable labour slacks of more than five working units, 13 are cooperatives. This supports the thesis that the legal form has an impact on a farm's employment strategy.

The explanation of this discrepancy is probably rather simple. Most corporate cash crop farms of the sample are limited liability companies (65 per cent) while most animal farms are cooperatives (76 per cent). Obviously, production structure and legal form are not independent. Cash crop farms seem to prefer limited liability while livestock and mixed farms preferred to become cooperatives, with stronger incentives to concentrate on the much more labour-intensive and, in general, less profitable animal production. This is supported by Beckmann (1997) who finds that the decision in favour of a particular legal form mainly depends on the number of persons involved (the number of shareholders) and their interest in employment. Accordingly, the choice of a particular legal form has to be understood as a strategic decision. Former LPGs with high employment potential (that is, animal farms) tended towards the cooperative form in order to serve employment interests. A similar effect resulted probably from the existence of old debts. Although Table 4 shows a rather small efficiency impact of old debts, 50 per cent of the cooperatives have old debts falling to 30 per cent for other legal entities. Obviously, the existence of debt had some effect on choice of legal form.

The slacks for labour in family farms and those for land in cash crop farms are difficult to interpret. The first may be a result of indivisibilities of labour units or simply overestimation of family labour input. The high land slack for livestock farms is likely to be caused by farms with suckler cow herds on marginal locations which receive considerable subsidies for 'extensification'. It is interesting that there are hardly any slacks for variable inputs. This provides evidence of rational behaviour independent of the legal form.

SUMMARY AND CONCLUSIONS

The empirical results suggest that the successors of the earlier East German production cooperatives (LPGs) made strenuous efforts to raise efficiency. On the one hand, this meant a marked reduction of the workforce, particularly affecting older and less-qualified workers (Czasch *et al.*, 1999). On the other hand, in doing so, they have probably helped to secure an important number of jobs because they adjusted slowly and still operate on a higher employment level. According to the results, during the first years after the beginning of transition, a strong positive employment effect emanated from sunk costs, resulting from a lack of alternatives for utilizing machinery and building capital that belonged to the legal successors of the non-liquidated LPGs. Moreover, the results suggest that there are positive employment effects resulting from the frequent identity of farm shareholders and farm workers. This identity has influenced the choice of legal form in order to serve the employment interests of the shareholders – particularly by choosing cooperative structures. Unfortunately, the results do not yet allow for a stricter measurement of the specific impacts of sunk costs, on the one side, and the legal form on the other. The reason is that these decisive variables are positively correlated. Further research will be necessary.

Although the 'legal entity' profits were still low in more recent periods, their technical productivity has sharply increased and has already surpassed the average West German family farm in several types of production (*Agrarbericht der Bundesregierung*, 1999; Balmann, 1999). In accordance with Mathijs and Swinnen (1997), the results indicate that the question of an optimal farm organization and farm size is much more complex than comparative–static transaction cost arguments suggest. This means that empirical results from comparative–static studies which ignore the historical background of transition should be interpreted cautiously. Ignoring sunk costs and the employment interests of the shareholders may be as misleading as ignoring them in the analysis of the family farming which dominates agriculture in most western countries. With regard to the future evolution of East German agriculture, two meaningful questions have to be answered. The first concerns the nature of organizational types (or type) which foster efficient management to serve the long-term interests of stakeholders. The second is the question of how a farm's organizational form might evolve if there were conflicting interests and asymmetric information among the shareholders.

NOTES

[1]Productivity is here understood as the residual factor income of labour, measured after all other variable factors are paid. If sunk costs for complementary factors exist, these are not relevant and therefore not considered. This implies that the marginal labour productivity reflects the shadow prices of labour input.

[2]For example, individual opportunity costs may deviate from wages if there is a danger of unemployment.

[3]Note that L^{max} is not necessarily larger than L' to L''. Rather, L^{max} has to be understood as an upper limit.

[4]Balmann *et al.* (1996) model a farm that can be seen as a representative legal entity with mixed production. The assumption of job maximization leads to the same number of employees as might be found for the average of the legal entities with mixed farming. Profit was in both cases slightly negative.

[5]There is an introduction to DEA in Charnes *et al.* (1994).

[6]Thiele and Brodersen (1999), for example, consider the balance, without the value of miscellaneous inputs and land, as a measure of capital input. However, this discriminates systematically against farms which operate with new buildings (for example, re-established dairy farms) and overestimates the efficiency of those with highly depreciated assets (LPG successors with buildings where there has been little effort to modernize equipment).

[7]Differences in standard deviations of the efficiency values are rather small and are not considered here.

[8]The replacement of the traditional 'Schwarzbuntes Milchrind' by Holstein-Friesian cows explains the enormous increases in milk yield, from a yearly average of 4439kg per cow in 1992/93 to 6107kg per cow in 1997/98 (*Agrarbericht der Bundesregierung*, various years).

[9]Considering the average corporate farm for Brandenburg leads to an increase in technical efficiency from 78 per cent in 1995/96 to 85 per cent in 1997/98, while the technical efficiency for an average family farm remains at the level of 66 per cent (that is far below our farm sample result for 'natural entities').

REFERENCES

Allen, D.W. and Lueck, D. (1999), 'The Nature of the Farm', *Journal of Land & Economics*, **XII**, 343–86.

Balmann, A. (1999), 'Path Dependence and the Structural Development of Family Farm Dominated Regions', *Organized Session Papers, IX European Congress of Agricultural Economists*, Warsaw, Poland, 24–8 August.

Balmann, A., Moosburger, A. and Odening, M. (1996), *Beschäftigungswirkungen der Umstrukturierung der ostdeutschen Landwirtschaft*, Working Paper 23, Wirtschafts-und Sozialwissenschaften an der Landwirtschaftlich-Gärtnerischen, Fakultät der Humboldt-Universität zu Berlin.

Beckmann, V. (1997), 'Transaktionskosten und institutionelle Wahl in der Landwirtschaft – Eine theoretische und empirische Untersuchung des Beitrages der Transaktionskostentheorie zur Erklärung der Organisation landwirtschaftlicher Produktion', dissertation, Georg-August-Universität, Göttingen.

Bundesministerium für Ernährung, Landwirtschaft und Forsten (annual), *Agrarbericht der Bundesregierung*, Bonn: Bundesministerium.

Charnes, A., Cooper, W., Lewin, A. and Seiford, L. (1994), *Data Envelopment Analysis: Theory, Methodology and Applications*, Boston: Kluwer Academic Publishers.

Czasch, B., Balmann, A. and Odening, M. (1999), 'Organisation and Efficiency of Agricultural Enterprises During the Transition Process, with Particular Reference to Labour. An Empirical Analysis for Brandenburg', Humboldt University, Berlin (mimeo).

Forstner, B. and Isermeyer, F. (1997), 'Zwischenergebnisse zur Umstrukturierung der Landwirtschaft in den neuen Ländern', Humboldt University, Berlin (mimeo).

Johnson, G.L. (1972), 'Introduction', in G.L. Johnson and C. Quance (eds), *The Overproduction Trap in U.S. Agrculture*, Baltimore, MD: Johns Hopkins University Press.

Mathijs, E. and Swinnen, F.M. (1997), *Efficiency During Transition: An Empirical Analysis of East German Agriculture,* Working Paper no. 7, Policy Research Group, Department of Agricultural Economics, Katholieke Universiteit, Louvain, Belgium.

Ministerium für Ernährung, Landwirtschaft und Forsten (MELF) (1997), *Brandenburg, Verschiedene Jahrgänge,* Bericht zur Lage der Land- Ernährungs- und Forstwirtschaft des Landes Brandenburg.

Peter, G. and Weikard, H.P. (1993), 'Betriebsgröße und Organisation für die landwirtschaftliche Produktion', *Agrarwirtschaft*, **42**, 313–23.

Schmitt, G. (1997), 'Unvollkommene Arbeitsmärkte, Opportunitätskɔsten der Familienarbeit und Betriebsgröße', *Berichte über Landwirtschaft*, **75**, 35–65.

Schmitz, P.M. and Noeth, C. (1999), 'Institutional and Organizational Forces Shaping the Agricultural Transformation Process: Experiences, Causes and Implications', in G.H. Peters and J. von Braun (eds), *Food Security, Diversification and Resource Management: Refocusing the Role of Agriculture?* (Proceedings of the Twenty-Third International Conference of Agricultural Economists), Aldershot: Ashgate.

Thiele, H. and Brodersen, C. (1999), 'Differences in Farm Efficiency in Market and Transition Economies: Empirical Evidence from West and East Germany', *European Review of Agricultural Economics*, **23**, 331–47.

Ward, B. (1958), 'The Farm in Illyria: Market Syndicalism', *American Economic Review*, **48**, 566–89.

Weikard, H.P. (1996), 'Beschäftigungseffekte genossenschaftlicher Unternehmensorganisation', *Schriften der Gesellschaft für Wirtschafts- und Sozialwissenschaften des Landbaues e.V.*, **32**, 93–102.

DAVID R. HARVEY*

Academic Rigour or Policy Relevance: Towards a Reconciliation

INTRODUCTION: THE PROBLEM AND THE POSSIBLE SOLUTION

Commenting on and summarizing the proceedings of the 23rd IAAE Conference, Michel Petit noted that, 'in the economics of policy and institutional change, there is a widening gap between academic excellence and social relevance'. The 24th Conference in Berlin in 2000 is particularly apposite for reconsideration of this critical problem.

The 'world common model' of liberal free-trading economies, coupled with universal suffrage and democracy, and with its associated common law, might now seem incontestable: the end of history (Fukuyama, 1992, 1995a)? The profession largely subscribes to this model, yet the policies and policy recommendations of the common model are frequently judged unacceptable by the political machinery of democratic control. Still less are they thought acceptable by the fragmented politics of many special interests or socioenvironmental concerns. Examples include virtually all of the live policy issues: farm policy reform; food, health and safety regulation; trade restrictions and competition regulation; environmental protection; rural development; climate change amelioration. Policy relevance is thus required to be different from and more inclusive than typical academic excellence. In simple terms, our capacity for excellent rigour seems mostly inapplicable to our requirements for policy realism.

Furthermore, it has never been true that agricultural or applied economics has had a monopoly of policy analysis and advice, or of the associated training and research fora. But it is now the case that neoclassical economics faces a very considerable challenge from a variety of companion or competitive disciplines, both in training and in research, and in policy analysis and advice. Neither our students nor our social science and humanitarian colleagues are necessarily convinced of the supremacy and natural authority of the scientific method or neoclassical logic, and hence of the theoretical underpinnings of the common model. Postmodernism is rife, whatever else it is.

*University of Newcastle-upon-Tyne, United Kingdom. I am profoundly indebted to John McInerney for extremely helpful discussion of earlier drafts of this and related papers. Daniel Bromley was also kind enough to make some useful and constructive suggestions on the argument as presented in Berlin, while Douglas Hedley raised the key question of the role and place of diplomacy during the discussion, which I have tried to deal with here. So far as I yet know, I remain solely responsible for errors of all types.

As Tweeten and Zulauf (1999) remark: 'postmodernism is the antithesis of the Anglo-American analytical thesis'. At the risk of both annoying committed post-modernists and of attempting the impossible, a brief caricature of the postmodern position is that *all* so-called realities or truths are necessarily social constructs. As such, these constructs are inevitably and continually debated, contested, deconstructed and reconstructed. The common model itself, from this perspective, is nothing more than a social construct – to be contested and debated. Furthermore, the rules and conventions according to which the contests are to be judged and the debates governed are also social constructs. In the end, we have rhetoric and persuasion (or coercion and oppression), not analysis and conviction.

Policy, though, can generally be described as seeking to generate a consensus for and pattern of social authority. Policy, therefore, is the outcome of debate, discourse and conceptual contests, and is thus aimed at generating consensual opinion. So long as the common model does not command universal assent, any successful policy must also be based on a synthesis between the postmodern antithesis and the common model thesis. As Tweeten and Zulauf (1999) go on: 'Out of the dialectical synthesis, however, an enriched new philosophy of science could, and we believe, will emerge.' Quite so. This paper seeks to outline the nature of a possible synthesis.

The foundations of synthesis: the nature of social truth

Any consensus or synthesis must necessarily imply a story of the way the world works – a 'metanarrative', to borrow the term for the thing whose objective existence postmodernism denies (see, for example, Midmore, 1996). It is this metanarrative which provides policy with its coherence and legitimacy (or not). Any sustainable story is necessarily founded on these basic ideas and acceptances of our 'social truths'. These truths are North's institutions (North, 1990): the codes, disciplines and understandings which we and our societies accept as the arbiters of our behaviours and actions.

Reference to the philosophical literature on the reasonable grounds for truth strongly suggests that there are only four fundamental foundations or axes to these social truths (see, for example, Edwards, 1967; de Bono, 1995): first, what will sell to constituents, either through market places or governing councils and executives, which establish the accepted *rules* of societies (correspondence theory); second, what can be established beyond reasonable doubt through logic, reason and science as being near enough for farm work, which establish the *reason* accepted by societies (coherence theory); third, what are taken as articles of faith, as self-evident truths, the current social *dogma* (performative theory); fourth, the village, urban, or street *myth* – the habits, conventions and conveniences inherited from the past and neighbours (pragmatic theory), without direct or explicit reference to the trinity of fundamental foundations: rules, reason, faith.

It is apparent that the present common model has not yet achieved consensus on any of the three fundamental axes, and perhaps cannot (for example, McClosky, 1983; Randall, 1993; Bromley, 1997). Its rules are contested as being inherently unfair, ineffective or unsustainable; its reason is contested as being partial, incomplete or fundamentally flawed; its dogma is often dismissed as a thinly veiled camouflage for selfish and acquisitive exploitation of the poor and disadvantaged by the rich and powerful. In short, it can only aspire to myth, the very point of the postmodernists.

Any synthesis of postmodern and neoclassical approaches must begin with a synthesis of the basis for social truths – out institutions. The three grounds of rules, reason and faith (or validity, veracity and value) are the only sustainable foundations for our continual reconstruction of our myths and current vernaculars. It is on our myths that we found our policies. In this sense, the postmodernists are right: our myths are being continually deconstructed and reconstructed.

The question then is: where do we get our myths – our social truths – and how do we contrive their perpetuation? Building on earlier conceptual developments (Harvey, 1995, 1997, 1998a, 1998b) this paper outlines the possible nature of such an alternative conjecture, and draws some implications.

THE EVOLUTION OF SOCIAL TRUTHS AND ASSOCIATED INSTITUTIONS: A CONJECTURE

The conjecture rests on four essential premises: first, that human institutions evolve (following, *inter alia*, North, 1990); second, that there exists an identifiable progression in this institutional evolution; third, that the major steps in this progression can be elicited from the broad patterns of human history; fourth, that this essential progression repeats itself and manifests itself in the exhibition of policies and market or social behaviours even at the local or specific span of generations as opposed to the aeons of natural evolutionary time. Thus, in the same way that the developmental stages of an embryo echo or mimic the evolutionary progress of the life form, so too might the developmental stages of policies echo or mimic the evolution of the institutions themselves.

Institutional evolution happens through conceptual 'memes' (Dawkins, 1989; Blackmore, 1998), as the major genus of North's institutions, rather than through biochemical genes. Social beliefs and institutions evolve as memotypes (as in genotype). And they spawn (as phenotypes): constituencies, market segments, social communities, political parties, pressure groups, nation states, and thus the associated policies and strategies which typify the behaviour patterns of these social communities. Memotypes are capable of taxonomy as phyla, genus and species, sterile hybrids and mutants, and are related to their ancestry and environments in similar fashion to their natural analogues. Institutional evolution, as the evolution of ideas, occurs very much more rapidly than through natural selection. Memes are also, in contrast to their natural ancestors, self-selected. In contrast to natural selection, which involves submission to the laws of biophysics, and the simple survivability test imposed by the surrounding and largely exogenous environment, we construct and reconstruct our own institutions. These, in turn, act as the selection criteria against which best-fitted actions, behaviours and organizations are judged to be competitive or not. This, in the end, is what our policies and strategies are intended to do. In that, too, postmodernists are clearly right.

Following the developing Capra (1996) (see also Deutsch, 1997) evolution happens in phases. Each phase consists of a set of principles or motive forces underlying the observable structures and patterns of the community or ecosystem – the society types and associated transaction systems (communism, capitalism, tribal or feudal systems and so on) as the phyla of institutional forms – with an evolutionary process operating to explain the progress from one phase to the next. Some now believe we are at such a cusp of institutional evolution (as argued, for example, by Fukuyama, 1992, 1995a). But substantiation of this claim requires a conjecture as to the natural progression of institutional phases. We begin at the beginning of human life as we now know it, to identify the evolutionary taxonomy of *principles* and the phyla of *institutional forms* as we trace our apparent history. The methodology employed is reverse engineering, deducing the principal elements and linkages from what we observe as the successful (and thus surviving) institutional forms.

Living systems and human systems

Capra (1996) differentiates living systems from inanimate systems by observing that the individuals which comprise living systems *mind* what happens to them and *respond* to what happens to them, whereas non-living things simply exist and react with their environments. Living systems thus adjust and adapt to their surroundings and generate an evolutionary system as a consequence. The principles through which evolution happens are survival (persistence) and replication. The structures are the species and genus which emerge as being best fitted to the changing environment and habitats. Human life is, according to this fundamental description, no different from other forms of life.

But human life not only minds and responds to what happens to it; it *cares* and *replies*: Max Weber's position in a nutshell (for example, Gerth and Mills 1998; Swedberg, 1998). Caring implies at least a primitive love for fellows (and its natural antonym – hate) and some corresponding if rudimentary belief or value systems, a proactive rather than simply responsive process, stemming from a perception of 'self' as distinct from 'other', and a corresponding recognition of others' existence, rights and responses. Roles become established amongst members of a tribe and relationships are formed, with rights, responsibilities and duties assigned and habitualized at each social level in the tribe. Social values thus emerge and become codified in the emergent phenomenon of the myths of early religions and tribal customs.

The innate and autonomic rules of biological survival and reproduction thus become augmented by conceptual codes and conducts, founded on belief. Our early ancestors simply could not have survived and prospered (as they obviously did) in a fundamentally capricious and frequently antagonistic environment without both self-belief and, as a necessary consequence, social (and environmental) belief and trust. We humans are naturally and irrevocably dogmatic – that is how we began. We may label this early stage of institutional evolution as a *tribe* for convenience, which can be imagined as our ancestral hunter–gatherer villages and communes. It is, therefore, our most primitive and deeply ingrained institution, largely based on belief, and is one to which societies are likely to revert, if and when more advanced institutions fail.

However, caring and replying is not sufficient to distinguish human life from higher forms of animal life. Higher animals are also sentient in that they are able to distinguish between 'self' and 'other' in at least a rudimentary way. Dogmatic dogs are commonplace. Clearly, human and intelligent life has moved beyond simply caring and replying, to develop cognition – conscious knowledge and understanding, and associated communication and interrogation. Cognition involves *recognizing* social and natural environments and *relating* to and with this recognition through the development of inferential beliefs about ourselves, our societies and our environments. We humans are therefore also naturally reasonable and reasoning; that is how we began to grow up.

The conscious inference and cognition necessary for this recognition are more obviously special human characteristics, reflected in human brain to brawn ratios. From such conscious thought and its application to the local environment emerged the early cultivator *community*, as opposed to their predecessors, the hunter–gatherer tribes. With cultivation apparently comes a near-necessary development of specialization of function and trade between members of the community. The intuitive but conscious acceptance of Adam Smith's 'invisible hand' becomes embodied in community relationships and tolerance of distinctions, roles and hierarchies, and commitment to the associated responsibilities and sociopsychological contracts: barter, in short. The economics of the self-sufficient peasant families and villages has long been recognized as a natural embodiment of our general equilibrium theory (see, for example, Sadoulet and de Janvry, 1995, ch.6). In effect, inferential reason is used to develop new rules, which may then become enshrined in dogma for the purposes of training, taming and civilizing the emerging human population.

Human institutional evolution

Recognizably human institutions thus emerge. Re-cognition (*sic.*) of the processes of human system development requires that the participants at least submit to the implicit or intuitive rationale of these systems, consciously adapting and adjusting their behavioural relations to best fit this apparent (but not yet articulate) rationale. Recognition and relation thus leads to charity in these community relations and specializations, as the conscious and cognitive acceptance of the capacity of the community and its practices to be benign and welfare-improving (or the exact opposite, malevolent and welfare-threatening, thus requiring substantive and cognitive opposition).

Thus civility emerges as the glue binding (or fracturing) communities into societies, in which each knows their place and understands their roles, rights, responsibilities and duties towards the other members of the society, with charity (or its antonym – intolerance or bigotry) as the fundamental motivation of this phase. The second rung of the invisible hand mechanism is now in place: acceptance through mutual respect for the activities of others as being in the community as well as personal interest (see, for example, Bromley, 1997; Bonnen *et al.*, 1997). Thus, by adolescence, the human race has become charitable, social and civilized, as well as dogmatic and reasonable.

Without some pressure of relative scarcity of resource (or of some social ambition plus faith in capacity to expand) recognition and relationships seem likely to be a dominant institutional form: our early ancestral tribal cultivators. Our apparently innate curiosity might be the only drive to further development. Indulgence in curiosity, though, is risky and requires some considerable security and relative prosperity. However, scarce resources will augment this natural or paternal curiosity, and mate it with maternal necessity, to produce invention. There is a curious anomaly in our human evolutionary history. Our genotypic diversity is inconsistently narrow relative to the span of our palaeontoligical record. The only sensible explanation of this anomaly is that there was at least one, and possibly several, natural catastrophes during our early development, which eliminated those tribes and communities which were less well adapted to coping with adversity and resource scarcity. Our current concise genotype reflects the survivors of adversity, and is preconditioned to adopt the inventive phase of institutional evolution capable of resolving resource scarcities.

Invention is necessarily associated with *rationalization* of the way things are and with the emergence of conjectural *reason* that things could be different. Consequently, our ancestors begin to make things different, inventing and reconstructing their tools, institutions, organizations, habitats and environments. We now have a recognizably different sort of community, which we might label a *society*, reflecting the particular character of this stage in institutional evolution as embodying more organized and conscious association than the parental forms: the tribes and communities. Human history provides ample evidence of this phase of institutional evolution, strongly suggesting that rationalization and reason can only take root and thrive in well-established (mature) and relatively secure communities, requiring sustained self-belief as a precondition. Otherwise, societies collapse into communities and tribes – the 'Dark Ages'.

The birth and development of the common model

Once rationalization and reason emerge to provide for control over the human condition and circumstance, societies naturally develop strong hopes and expectations for their future development and operation. Invention is now additionally spurred by ambitions for further growth. These expectations embrace not only likely futures, given current conditions and community actions, but also include an increasing number of possible or virtual alternatives. The natural consequence is for such societies to become fragmented and specialized as groups begin to develop their own comparative advantages and pursue their own ambitions or virtual realities. Or, in the event that they cannot realize their ambitions here, they exit from their parent societies and start again somewhere else: colonies are born. And they learn, perhaps too slowly, to trade with, rather than fight, one another. Our society has now evolved to a recognizable market *economy*, *expecting* and *relying on* outcomes as a consequence of contracts and formal exchange; specializing and trading (again echoing Adam Smith and Weber; see Swedberg, 1998).

But the long arm of the law is necessarily attached to the invisible hand: to enforce contracts, protect property rights and outlaw theft. Economies need and breed government, at the very least to provide for and enforce common law. Furthermore, when measured against the criteria of the earlier institutional forms, market redistributions of income, wealth and social power are frequently judged unjust, especially by those whose previous power base is being eroded by the growth of the market economy. Expectations of the powerful turn out to be ill-judged and reliance misplaced according to the previous institutional habits. As Bromley remarks (1997, p.1386): 'The necessary institutional arrangements underlying a viable market economy reminds us that shared values and norms of a particular society are the necessary precursors to such institutional arrangements.' *The evolutionary progression now becomes more or less consciously self-selected*, since the power to decide *in the public interest* is now explicitly conceded to the *state*. The law, on which our economy is co-founded, will be required to extend its ambit both to include politically determined redistributions and to manage the economy to correct for market failures and malfunctioning in the public interest.

Here we need to be careful about the meanings of the words 'state' and 'government' (Bromley, private correspondence). The previous institutional forms of tribe, community and society all manifest some form of government or governance, and frequently exhibit forms of collective power which can be labelled as states. However, until an economy develops to generate a 'self-made' power base, the legitimacy of previous states rests on some faith in God, lineage or natural authority, including historical accumulation of brute power. The emergence of substantial economic power, however, forces societies to judge between this self-made power and the ancestral and apparently exogenous sources of leadership and social control. The term 'state' is used here to encapsulate this emergent phenomenon of explicit and conscious collective judgment of the public interest (for example, Dunn, 1999). This is in contrast to the term 'government', which we can interpret to represent the more easily observable implementation apparatus of this collective judgment.

The inevitable tension between the market and the state spawns 'ocracies

The process of collective decision making breeds a new institutional form – the 'ocracy: autocracy, plutocracy, bureaucracy and perhaps, finally, democracy, when all the previous efforts have been tried and found wanting. Necessary failure to win control over market conditions (enforced by the conditions of competition) for suppliers will inevitably lead to these ambitions for control being pursued through the political machinery of the state. Here the marginal net returns to political action for suppliers are necessarily more concentrated than for consumers, because of specialization in production. Consumer dominion over the market place is thus necessarily overridden by producer (or factor ownership) domination of public intervention in the name of fair and just distribution or of prudent economic management. Developed country agricultural policies are the archetypal examples, typically resting on arguments about just farm incomes or contributions to economic activity and trade balances.

It follows that income distribution under any political economy general equilibrium, even under ideal competitive conditions, will be determined by political influence and authority, typically manifested as an uneasy balance between the owners of capital and of labour. Right and left are thus natural manifestations of state politics. The former is predisposed to believe in the supremacy of the market, which apparently generates the factor incomes. Paid labour (and atomistic sectors), on the other hand, find themselves governed by the apparently capricious markets and avaricious capitalists and seek remedy through the political system. Arrow's impossibility theorem demonstrates that such systems, even if defined as perfectly as possible, will frequently generate inconsistent public preferences, and will thus cycle, depending on rhythms of conviction amongst (especially) the labour constituency of the social desirability of unrestrained markets, and on the political control over the negotiating agenda.

The supremacy of the governed market system over other forms of institutional arrangement requires that political constituencies remain convinced of that supremacy. If the market fails to perform according to commonly held opinions of justice, fairness and equity, it will not be politically legitimized, and political action and intervention will necessarily undermine the social optimality of the market mechanism. The result, then, is an inevitable and concrete mixture of economy, (re-)enforced by state and bound together with the glue of 'ocracy.

Thus there are two conceptually distinct institutional forms bound together in a complex we typically label 'government'. First, as Dunn (1999) observes: 'coercion is the core of states'. And, for the coercion to be acceptable to the governed, and thus be sustainable and persistent enough to spawn offspring, the coercion must be responsive to the collective *demands* of the population. It is these motives which underpin the 'ocracies under which we choose to live. Democracy apparently becomes inevitable, albeit serviced (or abused) by bureaucracies, plutocracies and autocracies pretending to be democratic or to service popular or special interests (see Kuran, 1995). But, equal first, populations must also agree to *concede* superior power to the state and *respect* this power above all others. Human conventions are invented to command respect for this concession, to replace the earlier authorities of lineage, gods and nature itself. Our common model is thus founded on contract, coercion and convention.

The present condition of the common model

Much of the frustration with our modern mixed economies stems from the realization, conscious or not, that nothing serious can be changed in this complex without bringing into question major adjacent and related parts. Institutional change and progress tends to ossify for fear of the genuine uncertainty of real change. Consequently, public relations and presentation take over from public participation and substance. As Arrow predicts, we go round in circles, while bemoaning the logic of the vortex. We revert, naturally, to earlier forms of social institutions, the tribes, communities and societies of our ancestry, but re-dressed and re-formed to fit the state–democracy triad.

This, it seems, is as neat and concise an explanation as yet exists in the exploding literature of the twin features of our global common model – globalization of market/state/law systems and fragmentation of societies and communities into tribes. We either submit meekly to the ruling hegemony, or demand that it takes better care of our own cherished aspirations and necessarily special interests. Meanwhile, we claim the right to our individualities and peculiarities as enshrined in both democratic and consumer sovereignty principles. This is the apparent present evolutionary status of the common model.

Consider the fundamental lesson of our general equilibrium view of the world. There is a system through which scarce resources can be optimally allocated among near infinite possibilities such that the greatest good happens to the greatest number, given their initial endowments. This is nothing more nor less than an elegant restatement and formalization of the process of natural selection, as is increasingly being recognized by quantitative ecologists and biologists (see, for example, Jones, 1999).

But there is a critical difference between institutional (or meme) evolution and natural evolution – the selection process. There are, of course, other differences. Two are that we use specie (money) and they use food as the fluid of evolution; and that we evolve ideas, institutions and cultures while they evolve and adapt biological life-forms – genomes – and behavioural characters – phenomes. These distinctions are also critical, in every sense of the word. Firstly, we collect and accumulate rents, which is effectively impossible in the natural world. Secondly, the fluid or energy of institutional evolution is information (and its material form, understanding). The consequences of restrictions on the flow of this fluid, as is inevitable in its private or national or disciplinary appropriation, are intuitively momentous, compared with the free flow of food in the natural world. Either character of institutional evolution is fatal to the optimality of the common model's general equilibrium, quite aside from the impossible problems of (a) definition of optimal returns to factors independently of the optimal state (crucial to the marginal returns theorem) and hence of deciding on acceptable distributions, and (b) correcting for so-called market failures or non-existence, both of which are seen in the common model as the fundamental role of governments. But both bring us back to the fundamental difference – self-selection rather than natural selection. This, at root, is where we exercise our free will.

There is an escalating debate about the nature of free will. For instance, Susan Blakemore (1998, p.237) concludes on free will: 'there is no truth in the idea of an inner self inside my body that controls the body and is conscious. Since this is false, so is the idea of my conscious self having free will'. But such arguments miss the essential point. Our choice is of the social systems we choose to invent and then live within; our choice is necessarily collective and not individualistic. Our free will is an emergent phenomenon, not deducible or explainable simply with reference to its component parts.

A CONJECTURE ON NECESSARY AND SUFFICIENT CONDITIONS
FOR INSTITUTIONAL SUSTAINABILITY

The brief parables of the previous paragraphs can be seen as an outline of the necessary conditions for successful human civilizations. They seem to contain the essence of much of what we currently observe and of the events and debates (including wars and empires) of our history. In essence, they repeat Fukuyama's (1992, 1995a) argument of 'the end of history?' However, the 'motor of historical change' as outlined here is clearly incomplete. It leaves much out from what we observe. Nor can it be regarded as sufficient for sustainable success, as any intelligent, informed and rational contemplation of our current condition testifies. To identify the sufficient conditions, it is necessary to pursue the evolutionary parable of institutional and social development beyond these necessary (or historically observed) stages. What might our possible futures look like?

More sensibly, since evolution (as a chaotic system) is inherently unpredictable, what would we like our future to look like? It is possible to conceive, in principle, of governing institutions and practices which could convert the community population to *reverence* rather than mere respect for their government, and thus to their practically unanimous assent to governmental control over their lives and futures. This must be the goal of those who espouse and champion the common model. Otherwise, such systems will generate retaliation and conflict both within and between communities, well evidenced in our current condition. The search for a unique and unambiguous common model against which all human behaviours can be judged and governed thus becomes the social grail. When found, it might provide the foundation for a genuine meritocracy. Furthermore, having found it, our meritocracy would need to develop into an *empire* to be sustainable, as rightly feared by many postmodernists and their fellow travellers.

But consider the world which we seek, the one in which there *is* universal assent to our more common model. What would it look like? Such unanimity, even if achievable, will not be stable. As people devote time and energy to contemplation rather than the mundane issues of survival and prosperity, so the community's institutions and practices will be *questioned* and intelligent thought and *research* will be undertaken, in the *hope* of discovery of more generally beneficial, acceptable and sustainable rules and procedures which is, presumably, what we are all more or less trying to do already. Unless, that is, you are persuaded by the supposed postmodern logic that such systematic and scientific (reasonable) ambition is simply silly. In which case, without hope, we can only despair at the endless chatter and hopeless question of all attempt at reason.

Such research and question is now directed towards social institutions rather than physical and biological support systems, resources or tools. As such, it necessarily undermines the conventions of the revered government, market and legal systems. The evolutionary process has made our institutions ever more massive, thus requiring ever more effort and trauma to shift or change. In turn, these present systems can only be sustained through the imposition of particular ideologies and principles on the associated constituencies by current leaders and rulers. These people and their congregations will necessarily defend and protect their local power-bases to ensure their own continuation. Institutional research or thought which does not fit with existing ideologies will tend to be resisted, underfunded and ridiculed – the fate of postmodernism from the positivist common model perspective.

However, it is possible to suppose an ideal, though dynamic, outcome in which the population can become convinced that all is for the best in this best of all possible worlds. In such an idealized state, one can imagine a fully *committed* population, willingly and enthusiastically merging their own self-interests with those of the community in near unanimous harmony: the communist ideal in a nutshell. Obviously, this condition is extremely difficult, if not impossible, to achieve.

A penultimate phase of institutional evolution then becomes possible, in which a significant fraction of the population engages in creative *imagination* of how things might be even better and more harmonious, and is engaged in continual *re-creation* of the community and its environments, with the full support and commitment of the whole community in these endeavours – which might be the goal that postmodernists seek, if that is not a contradiction in terms. Such societies could reasonably be described as being driven by the pursuit of *fun*, where imagination and re-creation appear as scholarship or as play. A genuine *civilization* would then be born. The conversion of an empire to a civilization is clearly not easy.

The end result might be one in which the whole community is convinced and assured of the benevolence of their world – *not* as the best of all possible, but as capable of building and growing the best of all possible – secure in the knowledge and understanding of the ways in which their worlds work compared with all the possible ways in which they could work, and completely self-assured that they and their community can continue to develop and improve their lives indefinitely. In short, such societies can be characterized as having a common *faith* in the ultimate benevolence of their communities and in the 'fitness' of their world views, and an associated freedom to doubt (and hence question and seek to change) the rules, rulers and power bases, in the common belief and trust that such activity will be regarded as perfectly legitimate and respectable.

Not that there will be unanimous consent that the ultimate has yet been achieved, but unanimous consent that the principles and practices of the community systems in conjunction with all its associated environments is both capable of moving towards this state of perfect harmony, and that the whole population is committed to this pursuit above all others – in short, *careful charity*. We could, perhaps, label such an institution as a *culture*.

SUMMARY CONJECTURE ON THE PROCESSES OF
INSTITUTIONAL EVOLUTION

A more common model

Table 1 recapitulates and summarizes the 'natural' progression of social evolution proposed here, a taxonomy of the essential mechanisms of conscious institutional design – the more common model. The central proposition is that our history, and thus also our future, is explainable as an evolutionary process. There is an identifiable pattern to the flow of our evolutionary history. The structures generated by these flows are identified as the archetypal institutional form of each phase. The principles governing its operation are the major characters, responses and motives of people and their communities in each phase, which govern our social choices. The local process of each phase is identified as the result, which generates the archetypal negotiation or transaction system as the pattern of each phase. In the final column of the table, each phase is associated with its 'natural' social science discipline.

Three major disciplines are missing from this table: philosophy, theology and science. Philosophy is the study of rationality of cognition, inference and concept, and thus is the all-embracing discipline. If philosophy departments are shut, the lights go out and the heat of enquiry dissipates to entropy. Both science and theology are the social implementation of philosophy. If science is shut down, the motors of human (as opposed to animal) life support systems die, unless theology takes its place.

The rows of Table 1 should be interpreted as 'meme complexes' – as primary institutional types or phyla. Each can be thought of as a 'conceptual organism', consisting of interactive and mutually supporting systems of motivations, transactions, characteristics and responses. As such, each is capable, within limits, of independent recognition and taxonomy. However, like individual organisms of any one phylum, all will exhibit local variation, while none is actually capable of independent existence. Each relies on the other for its continued sustenance and reproductive capacity, and is modified according to its local circumstance and context: its local culture. The prototypical institutional evolutionary cycle is exhibited as a full circle. The careful charity of the 'last' phase underpins the 'foundation' phase of human cognitive and institutional evolution: the love, care and reply phase of the early tribes, generating the necessary consent to community. There is no beginning or end to this cycle; there is no first or last step to human happiness. The end of history is necessarily also the end of future. There is only a meta-process offering progress towards more complete lives and worlds, threatening to malfunction or dissipate into chaos when the tolerances of each phase are exceeded without the necessary foundations and counter-balances of the parental and successive phases being in place. A wheel, as the classic analogue of momentum, cannot perform unless it moves, and cannot continue to move unless all of the spokes are properly connected to the rim, and cannot move usefully unless connected to an axle. Table 1 illustrates the fundamental problem with our present common model. Its wheel of progress is triangular. Furthermore, it has no axle – it

TABLE 1   A conjecture on the natural taxonomy of institutional evolution

Institution type	Character	Response	Result	Transaction system	Motives	Discipline
Natural	Mind Neglect	Respond React	Adapt & adjust	Food & gene chains	Life (death)	Ecology
Tribe	Care Fight	Reply Retaliate	Hunt & gather	Consent (sentient)	Love (hate)	Anthropology
Community	Recognize Ignore	Relate Tolerate	Cultivate & tame	Cognition (investigative)	Inference (instinct)	Psychology
Society	Rationalize Reject	Reason Refute	Invent & reconstruct	Care (social)	Charity (bigotry)	Sociology
Economy	Expect Exit	Rely Reinvent	Specialize & trade	Contract (enterprising)	Barter (autarchy)	Economics
'Ocracy	Coerce Submit	Demand Revere	Institute & regulate	Coercion (conventional)	Fear (security)	Law
State	Concede Lead	Respect Reign	Govern & preach	Convention (realistic)	Habit (anarchy)	Politics
Empire	Question Accept	Research Test	Exhort & display	Commitment (curious)	Hope (despair)	Humanities
Civilization	Imagine Play	Re-create Teach	School & train	Curiosity (artistic)	Fun (spite)	Education
Culture	Believe Doubt	Trust Legitimize	Commune & cohere	Charity (aesthetic)	Faith (distrust)	Aesthetics

has no meaning. It has no connections with either our primary and primative motivations or our higher aspirations.

The real world

Of course, this is a fairy story. However, it seems more than possible to trace the history of successful civilizations according to this prototypical evolutionary process of phase changes and developments, and also to identify collapse and revolution of civilizations in these terms. The end of the cold war has transferred the critical conflicts over private versus public decisions of justice, equity and harmony from the primitive battle over geographical territory to the much more important struggle over the hearts and minds of people. This, at last, is the fundamental lesson of the collapse of the Union of Soviet Socialist Republics. Belief in the system is necessary for its operation, never mind its promise of optimality.

But such belief cannot now be generated simply through appeals to economic reason, since the reason on which market optimality and democracy are based is partial and thus flawed. In short, if communities do not follow this progressive cycle, and are not capable of sustaining the momentum of the evolutionary progression, they will collapse in some form or other to previous phases, just as a Mandelbrot fractal collapses when it exceeds its tolerance limits (for example, Capra, 1996).

Here, at last, is the supramodern role of diplomacy, statesmanship and leadership (Hedley, conference discussion): to reconcile and fit together the various spokes into a sustainable and enduring social system. This is the purpose of policy, the objective of all our business and public strategies. The essential problem with our analysis and understanding of these policies and strategies is that our aims (what we try to do to seek and pursue our objectives) are fundamentally disconnected from and incommensurate with these objectives. It is the meanings which provide the links.

The meanings: evidence and supporting argument

There is an apparent consensus within the current literatures on the principle motives for human behaviour (Boulding, 1973; Strange, 1994; de la Mothe and Paquet, 1996) as being love, barter (or exchange) and fear. It is logical to add habit (as the accumulated understandings and acceptances of past 'best practice'), to this triumvirate. Table 1 identifies these four key motives, but adds a further four (over and above the human preconditions of life and conscious inference). Of these, fun is probably uncontroversial as a fundamental motive for human behaviour. Pervin (1993), for example, identifies the prime axes of personality in terms of how individuals react to unfamiliar circumstances, which correspond very closely to this taxonomy. It is also of interest that the archetypal transaction systems identified in Table 1 correspond closely with Holland's (1973, 1985) characterization of peoples' attributes in relation to appropriate 'job fits'. Holland's archetypes have proved remarkably robust in providing useful recruitment service (see, for example, Furnham, 1992, especially, pp.104ff). The taxonomy suggested here indicates that there are two missing archetypes, curious and aesthetic. Inclusion of these two would improve the Holland characterization of 'occupation space'.

However, there may well be more quarrel over the final three motives: faith, hope and charity, at least amongst those not convinced of St Paul's recipe for human happiness. To echo and reflect the foundations of our social truths with which I began this conjecture, we need charity in our rules, lest we be mistaken; hope in our reason, that it is both veracious and valid; and faith in our beliefs about the way the world works. On this basis, the underpinning predispositions to form societies (expressed as personality traits) might indeed be 'hard-wired' in our genes rather than continually learned in our memes. And our various religions are still trying to teach us to be human, to subscribe to faith, hope and charity.

It is widely commented that lack of trust is an important problem for modern institutions, which generally substantially increases transaction costs and the probability of transaction failures (for example, Fukuyama, 1995b). Yet trust seems an extremely elusive concept. In Table 1, trust appears as an emergent phenomenon or response only at the climax of the evolutionary progression, itself only sustainable given the continuation of the supporting phases of evolutionary development, encapsulated in the present operations and patterns of social behaviour. Its elusiveness is inherent in its character as an emergent phenomenon – not deducible from its constituent parts. Its essential character is fundamentally dependent on both its breeding and its nurture.

No doubt there will be considerable dispute about the particular words (and associated concepts) chosen here to outline the nature of human institutional evolution. Such semantic debate is clearly fundamental to developing this outline into a serious discipline (psychohistory? – see Asimov, 1951–87), so as to establish its consistency. In addition, further refinement and closer definition of the terms used here will be necessary to confront the outline proposed here with the evidence from the development of human societies and institutions, to establish the coherence of the theory or story. Furthermore, much more work needs to be done on understanding the essential mechanisms and processes through which institutions translate information into knowledge, and cooperate (perhaps too infrequently) to breed and grow understanding and wisdom.

But the semantics themselves can only make sense when clearly and unequivocally linked through an appropriate grammar, which establishes the rules through which the concepts and constructs are connected so as to make sense, which is here taken as the logic of evolution. Even then, the consequent sentences and paragraphs can only make serious sense if they seem to tell a credible story. The story itself is the emergent phenomenon. It cannot be deduced from the parts, neither from the semantics nor from the grammar. It emerges only as the words unfold in a sensible and comprehensible order. Evolution cannot predict, it can only 'retrodict', and even then without chance of falsification. It is science, but not as we normally know it.

Ralph Dahrendorf (1995), makes a very similar argument, from a respected status as past Director of the London School of Economics. He concludes that

'There remains a common theme for a science of human society, and that while much progress has been made in developing its various facets and aspects, it is still important to try and tie the parts together – not in search of a "world formula" but to make sense of the social habitat in which we live, have lived and are likely to live.' Exactly so.

The fundamental problem facing our attempts to reconcile policy relevance with academic excellence is that our social sciences are fragmented and isolated from one another. We cannot trade ideas and concepts because we operate in increasingly self-contained disciplinary islands. When we attempt to trade, we tend to resort to barter or war. Our common models lack common understanding of the processes which generate what we see, so we argue about our observations and interpretations. Postmodernism merely pursues this obvious condition to its limits. And we have been here before. Tarnas (1991, especially pp.27ff) observes that the Sophists of ancient Greece mediated the transition from an age of myth to an age of practical reason. However, 'In such critical circumstances, the philosophical denial of absolute values and sophistical condemnation of stark opportunism seemed both to reflect and to exacerbate the problematic spirit of the times' (ibid., p.29). Postmodernism is an echo of these former philosophers: a potential mediator between the age of theoretical reason and a forthcoming age of genuinely practical rationality?

CONCLUSIONS AND IMPLICATIONS

The current common model is central to this proposed reconstruction: how could it be otherwise? The role and place of economics have already been illustrated in this account, as a useful analytical tool for understanding at least a part of the behaviour and proclivities of, particularly, the law/economy/state (LES) hegemony or hybrid. The extension to include political economy clearly captures major elements of the common model story as told here. We need not and should not chuck this out, which is a substantial relief.

However, if approximately legitimate, this process of institutional evolution implies that the apparent hegemony of the present common model is *unsustainable*. Barter, habit and fear are insufficient grounds for progressive human development. Yet, to a very large extent, our national and international institutions rely only on these fundamentals. Education or other forms of persuasion of the truth of our present common model is quite simply incapable of reaching the goals which we seek. Some version of our common model might be a necessary condition for the pursuit of sensible and sensitive development and human contentment, but it is clearly not sufficient.

More importantly, the more educated and informed the world becomes, the less likely is it that we will be able to get away with the pretence that it is sufficient. If we persist in believing that bribery, coercion, training or education is all we need to do to secure universal acceptance, we condemn ourselves to extinction. This, at last, is a counter-traditional if not counter-intuitive result, which strongly suggests that this logic and evidence is worthy of serious consideration and examination. Can we afford the risk that it is not?

So what?

While evolution does not allow prediction, it does allow cultivation. We are now in a position deliberately to cultivate our institutional evolution, which is what policy seeks to do. To practise effective and efficient cultivation requires an understanding of the effects of nature and nurture. To be selective in our selection processes, we need to distinguish the inherited features from those which are phenotypical. This conjecture is an attempt to identify the memotypes and distinguish them from the phenotypes.

At present, it is apparent that many communities and societies are not willing to grant that our rulers (rich governments, mighty multinational companies and powerful international organizations) are genuinely committed to general social progress, or ready to be openly and transparently curious, or sufficiently careful of our human (and thus planetary) inheritance. To many, these trust failures are the obvious consequence of primitive understandings; they reflect either more or less deliberate ignorance or self-seeking exploitation of love, thought and charity. In short, the traditional bureaucrats' creed that the devil is in the detail is exactly wrong. According to this account, life is in the detail; the devil is in the conception. But we have been told that before. The apple that Eve ate was of the tree of knowledge, not understanding.

Space does not permit elaboration and application of these ideas here. However, the framework appears sufficiently coherent, consistent and approximately legitimate to enable and encourage profitable and progressive debate. In economic terms, the nature of the problem addressed by this paper is that the production possibility frontier of our current academic excellence is disconnected from our social preference map of policy relevance. We have no basis or foundation for trade. I have presented a conjecture about the nature of the essential connections, and of the ways in which we might profitably trade.

In conclusion, if you do not accept the essential logic of this story, what is your alternative? Without one, I suggest your reservations are of detail and not of principle. We can argue about the price, and then dispute the quality.

REFERENCES

Asimov, I. (1951–87), *The Foundation Saga* (5 vols), London and New York: Panther Science Fiction.

Blakemore, S. (1998), *The Meme Machine*, Oxford: Oxford University Press.

Bonnen, J.T., Hedley, D.D. and Schweikhardt, D.B. (1997), 'Agricultural and the Changing Nation-State: Implications for Policy and Political Economy', *American Journal of Agricultural Economics*, **79**, 1419–28.

Boulding, K.E. (1973), *The Economy of Love and Fear: A Preface to Grants Economics*, Belmont, CA: Wadsworth.

Bromley, D.W. (1997), 'Rethinking markets', *American Journal of Agricultural Economics*, **79**, 1383–93.

Capra, F. (1996), *The Web of Life: A New Synthesis of Mind and Matter*, London: Harper Collins.

Dahrendorf, R. (1995), 'Whither Social Sciences?', *6th ESRC Annual Lecture*, Swindon, UK: Economic and Social Research Council.

Dawkins, R. (1989), *The Selfish Gene*, new edn, Oxford: Oxford University Press.

de Bono, E. (1995), *Parallel Thinking*, London and New York: Penguin

de la Mothe, J. and Paquet, G. (eds) (1996), *Evolutionary Economics and the New International Political Economy*, New York: Pinter.

Deutsch, D. (1997), *The Fabric of Reality*, London and New York: Penguin.

Dunn, J. (1999), *The Cunning of Unreason: Making Sense of Politics*, London: Harper Collins.

Edwards, P. (ed.) (1967), *The Encyclopaedia of Philosophy*, New York and London: Macmillan.

Fukuyama, F. (1992), *The end of history and the last man*, London: Hamish Hamilton.

Fukuyama, F. (1995a), 'The end of history, five years later', *History and Theory*, **34**, 27–43.

Fukuyama, F. (1995b), *Trust: the social virtues and the creation of prosperity*, London: Hamish Hamilton.

Furnham, J. (1992), *Personality at Work*, London: Routledge.

Gerth, H.H. and Mills, C.W. (trans.) (1998), *From Max Weber: Essays in Sociology*, London: Routledge.

Harvey, D.R. (1995), 'European Union Cereals Policy: an Evolutionary Interpretation', *Australian Journal of Agricultural Economics*, **35**, 193–217.

Harvey, D.R. (1997), 'The Role of Government in Agriculture in the next Decade', *Journal of the German Agricultural Economics Association*, **16**, 409–34.

Harvey, D.R. (1998a), 'The US Farm Act: Fair or Foul? An Evolutionary Perspective from East of the Atlantic', *Food Policy*, **23**, 111–21.

Harvey, D.R. (1998b), 'A Social Science Fiction: Future Directions of European Agricultural Policy', in T. Yildirim, A. Schmitz and W.H. Furtan (eds), *World Agricultural Trade*, Boulder: Westview Press.

Holland, J. (1973), *Making Vocational Choices: A Theory of Career*, Englewood Cliffs, NJ: Prentice-Hall.

Holland, J. (1985), *The Self-Directed Search – Professional Manual*, Florida: P.A.R.

Jones, S. (1999), *Almost like a whale: the Origin of Species updated*, London and New York: Doubleday.

Kuran, T. (1995), *Private Truths, Public Lies. The Social Consequences of Preference Falsification*, Cambridge, MA and London: Harvard University Press.

McClosky, D.N. (1983), 'The Rhetoric of Economics', *Journal of Economic Literature*, **21**, 481–517.

Midmore, P. (1996), 'Towards a Postmodern Agriculture', *Journal of Agricultural Economics*, **47**, 1–17.

North, D.C. (1990), *Institutions, Institutional Change and Economic Performance*, Cambridge: Cambridge University Press.

Pervin, L.A. (1993), *Personality: Theory and Research*, 6th edn, Chichester: Wiley.

Randall, A. (1993), 'What practising agricultural economists really need to know about methodology', *American Journal of Agricultural Economics*, **75**, 48–59.

Sadoulet, E. and de Janvry, A. (1995), *Quantitative Development Policy Analysis*, Baltimore, MD: Johns Hopkins University Press.

Strange, S. (1994), *States and Markets*, 2nd edn, London and New York: Pinter.

Swedberg, R. (1998), *Max Weber and the idea of Economic Sociology*, Princeton, NJ: Princeton University Press.

Tarnas, R. (1991), *The Passion of the Western Mind*, London: Random House.

Tweeten, L. and Zulauf, C. (1999), 'The challenge of Postmodernism to applied economics', *American Journal of Agricultural Economics*, **81**, 1166–72.

PANEL DISCUSSION REPORTS

ORGANIZER, CHAIRPERSON AND RAPPORTEUR

Bina Agarwal (Institute of Economic Growth, University of Delhi, India)

PANEL DISCUSSANTS

Exploring the Relationships between Gendered Land Rights, Intra-household Allocations and Productivity in Africa   *Cheryl Doss (Yale University, New Haven, USA)*

Gender Inequality in the Land Tenure System of Rural China   *Zhu Ling (Chinese Academy of Social Sciences, Beijing, China) and Jiang Zhongyi (Ministry of Agriculture, Beijing, China)*

Who Owns the Land? Gender and Land Titling Programmes in Latin America *Carmen Diana Deere and Magdelena Leon (National University, Bogota, Colombia)*

Economists have long emphasized the importance of secure land rights for promoting incentives and efficiency in agriculture. It is also well recognized that for millions of rural households in developing countries the ownership and control of agricultural land is crucially linked to viable livelihoods, a lower risk of poverty, a greater ability to bargain for higher wages, and better access to credit and improved agricultural technology. In other words, command over land is found to add both to welfare and to efficiency within agriculture (for references, see Agarwal, 1994).

However, although these linkages are well recognized at the household level, they have been relatively little examined at the intra-household level from a gender perspective. For instance, what is women's access to land within farming households? How does a gender gap in land ownership and control affect family welfare and farm productivity? What are the gender biases in the three main sources for land acquisition: inheritance, land markets and government schemes for land titling and distribution? Much of mainstream agricultural economics has failed even to raise these questions, much less answer them. Moreover, few agricultural censuses or other large surveys gather gender-disaggregated data on the ownership and use of land that would help us

585

monitor the implications of various land-related laws and land distribution programmes. This panel sought to address some of these questions on the basis of recent work on Africa, China and Latin America, while also building on earlier work on South Asia (for example, Agarwal, 1994).

The panellists focused on the gender gap in command over arable land and its implications for intra-household resource allocation, gender relations and agricultural productivity. Implicitly or explicitly, this and related work (for example, Udry *et al.*, 1995; Quisumbing, 1996; Agarwal, 1994) also call into question the assumptions underlying a unitary concept of the household, and show how gender differences in incentives, preferences and interests within households could have notable effects on household expenditures and on agricultural production decisions and outcomes.

Three papers were presented in this panel, focusing respectively on Africa, Asia and Latin America. The first paper, by Cheryl Doss, outlined several reasons why it is important to examine the issue of land rights in Africa from a gender perspective. One, it argued that such analysis is essential for understanding the gendered effects of prevailing and newly formulated land rights. Formal law, customary law and social norms all affect access to land. In many places there is also a continuing trend towards titling and registration of land. Definitions of ownership, and the rights that ownership confers, may themselves vary, in some cases giving the owner only rights of use and not of sale and so on. Rights may also be allocated among several people, and through different channels such as the village head or kinship networks. Gender can impinge on all these issues. For instance, men and women may be granted different land rights by law, or their access may be differently affected by laws and norms.

Two, women's land rights can affect agricultural productivity. It is often noted that productivity gains in African agriculture will depend, at least in part, on increasing the productivity of women farmers; and productivity-enhancing investments are in turn affected by security of land rights. Doss's research in Ghana, for instance, showed that gender differences in constraints, especially differential access to land, rather than different preferences, explained the gendered pattern of technology adoption among Ghanaian maize farmers. Gender was significant in explaining both land ownership and cultivation patterns. Women owned and cultivated smaller plots than men and were also much less likely than male farmers to use improved maize varieties or fertilizers. However, after controlling for land ownership, extension, education and household size, gender was not a significant determinant of improved technology adoption. Rather, headship mattered: women farmers in female-headed households were less likely to adopt improved technologies, while women in male-headed households made adoption decisions similar to men's in such households. Headship affected access to both land and other inputs.

Three, gender inequality in farmland distribution within households can affect household expenditure patterns. In Ghana, for instance, Doss found that budget shares for food increased, while those for alcohol, tobacco and recreation decreased, when women owned greater shares of the household's farmland. This suggests that land ownership enhances women's voice in household decisions.

Basically, Doss emphasized that gender differences in land ownership can affect both agricultural technology adoption decisions and household economic decisions. There is also notable evidence (reviewed in Doss, 1999) that many development projects have failed owing to lack of attention to gender issues. At the same time, Doss cautioned that Africa is a heterogeneous continent within which the relationships between land rights, intra-household allocation and productivity can vary widely. Also the relationships are complex and their effects on women are not always easy to predict. For example, land value rises through productivity-enhancing measures, such as improvements in irrigation and soil fertility, in production technology (through the use of modern seed varieties and fertilizers) and in marketing channels with infrastructural development or urbanization. At the same time, these changes may also reduce women's access to land, since existing literature on women farmers and technology adoption suggests that women are more likely to own land when it is less valuable, and may lose access to land as its value rises. Similarly, giving women land titles may reduce the investments that others are willing to make in their particular plots. Also intra-household economic relationships are dynamic and households may renegotiate many decisions (including decisions about labour allocations and expenditures) when circumstances change. These hypotheses need to be tested explicitly, but there is some supportive evidence from Africa suggesting that they are important.

The paper thus concluded that, while it is clear that land rights are important for women, more analysis is needed to identify the best ways of guaranteeing women's ownership and control of land so as to ensure that women actually realize the intended gains.

The paper by Zhu Ling and Jiang Zhongyi focused on the factors underlying gender inequalities in access to agricultural land and the welfare implications of this unequal access. The paper examined the nature of Chinese women's land rights in terms of both the current legal framework and the institutional arrangements that mediate such rights in practice. On the basis of a sample survey of 947 households undertaken in Shanxi Province in 1996, the authors outlined the current state of land distribution, identified the causes of insecurity in land rights that women face and the impact of this insecurity on their socioeconomic status, and spelled out policy implications.

In the absence of private land ownership in rural China, access to land is through state land distribution practices, rather than via inheritance. Each member of the village community is entitled to a share of village land, eligibility being based on permanent resident records. The study defines land rights as rights of use and management in which the farmers can take all decisions regarding input use, output disposal and so on. It finds that, while the existing institutions are meant to be gender-neutral, in practice loopholes in arrangements and women's social position undermine land access in significant ways, leading to substantial insecurities. For a start, women are seriously disadvantaged in their land claims owing to marriage relocation from their parental to their marital villages. While communities are expected to redistribute land every few years to take account of relocations, in practice many do so only at long intervals: between 1980 and 1990, one-third of China's villages did not redistribute land. Hence a newcomer to the village joins a 'waiting list' and gets a share only when someone dies or migrates out. A woman entering a village on marriage may thus have a long wait before she gets a plot, rendering her landless in the interim. Meanwhile, her marital family accommodates her and her children on the pre-distributed plot, rendering the whole family vulnerable to poverty.

Divorce introduces an even greater source of vulnerability which affects even the women who have a share of village land. More than 45 per cent of the women interviewed in the study reported that they would be unable to retain their land in the event of divorce. A divorced woman is socially pressured to move out of her ex-husband's village (and so forfeit her land claim). At the same time, she can seldom live for long periods with her parents or brothers if she returns to her natal village. Quick remarriage is often her only option, and again one which provides no guarantee of a land share in the new husband's village. Both marriage relocation and marital break-up thus make for insecure and unequal land rights for Chinese women, and render them much more vulnerable to poverty than men.

The study also finds that 60 per cent of women farmers did not participate in farm decisions on land use, agricultural credit and investment and product disposal. And the majority received no technical support from extension services. In agricultural wage employment, again, women were able to find work for fewer days and received lower daily wages than men; and men again were the ones better able to migrate to non-farm urban jobs, leaving women behind in agriculture, without the same security of land rights or the same livelihood options.

On the basis of their analysis, the authors emphasize the need to revise China's land laws in order to define more clearly women's land rights, and to reformulate government regulations on farmland tenure, land distribution and agricultural extension, so as to make them gender equal and women inclusive.

In contrast to the African and Chinese context, however, Latin America presents a somewhat more positive picture in relation to women's land claims. Carmen Diana Deere and Magdelena Leon's paper is on the gender impact of the state's land titling interventions in the 1990s, designed to promote security of tenure and enliven land markets. They review the titling programmes of seven Latin American countries. On the negative side, the authors find that the schemes were often designed without sufficient attention to civil codes and marital regimes which protect women's property rights. By assuming that the family farm is owned by the male household head, these interventions undermined women's ownership rights. They ignored the possibility that a household's total land endowment may belong partly to the wife, partly to the husband, and partly to both jointly. Nonetheless, on the positive side, the share of female beneficiaries in land titling in the 1990s has been much higher than the land share that women adjudicated under the agrarian reforms of previous decades. This is partly because the primary way that women acquire land is through inheritance, and inheritance in Latin American countries is more gender-equitable than other methods of acquiring land. Moreover, the implementation of the 1990s agrarian legislation was more gender-equal, especially where rural women's organizations were strong. Colombia and Nicaragua, for instance, which mandated joint titling to couples irrespective of marital status, and gave priority to female household heads, had strong rural women's organizations which both lobbied for and ensured the implementation of gender-progressive legislation. Here women constituted 44 per cent and 33.5 per cent, respectively, of the beneficiaries. Hondurus and Mexico, by contrast, lacked a strong national rural women's movement: here only 25 per cent and 21 per cent, respectively, of the beneficiaries were women. The authors stress the need to strengthen rural women's organizations and for them to give priority to women's property rights issues to ensure more gender equality in the land titling programmes which are continuing.

In conclusion, the evidence presented by the panel demonstrated that the issue of women's land rights, long neglected, is a critical one for analysis and policy. Existing research on it (including that presented by the panellists) is both illuminating and a pointer to notable gaps in our knowledge and data availability, both of which warrant urgent attention.

REFERENCES

Agarwal, B. (1994), *A Field of One's Own: Gender and Land Rights in South Asia*, Cambridge: Cambridge University Press.

Doss, C.R. (1991), *Twenty-Five Years of Research on Women Farmers in Africa: Lessons and Implications for Agricultural Research Institutions*, Economics Program Paper 99–02, Mexico, DF:CIMMYT.

Quisumbing, A. (1996), 'Male–Female Differences in Agricultural Productivity: Methodological Issues and Empirical Evidence', *World Development*, **24**, 1579–95.

Udry, C., Hoddinott, J., Alderman, H. and Haddad, L. (1995), 'Gender Differentials in Farm Productivity: Implications for Household Efficiency and Agricultural Policy', *Food Policy*, **20**, 407–23.

PANEL REPORT: TRANSFORMATION OF THE FARM SECTOR IN TRANSITION ECONOMIES IN THE FIRST DECADE

ORGANIZERS AND CHAIRPERSONS

Csaba Csaki (Hungary/World Bank) and Gershon Feder (Israel/World Bank)

PANEL DISCUSSANTS

Tomas Doucha (Research Institute of Agricultural Economics, Prague, Czech Republic), Klaus Frohberg (Martin Luther University, Halle, Germany), Zvi Lerman (Hebrew University of Jerusalem, Israel) and Johan Swinnen (University of Louvain, Belgium)

RAPPORTEUR

Gershon Feder (Israel/World Bank)

Each of the panellists made a brief introductory presentation. Tomas Doucha, speaking on the changes in the Czech Republic in the past decade, highlighted the fact that three-quarters of agricultural land is farmed by large collectives that are expected to evolve to capital-intensive corporate farms. Klaus Frohberg, from a more general perspective, described the lags in farm productivity resulting from differing farm structures in transition countries. Zvi Lerman and Johan Swinnen both gave broad overviews of the differing pace of farm transformation across the transition region. The spectrum includes some where privatization and individualization of land holdings is complete; others still maintain a large share of their agriculture in inefficient collectives, or in reconfigured joint stock farm entities functioning in essentially the same manner, and with the same performance, as in the socialist era.

Following the introductions, debate centred on the role of government policies in speeding up transformation. It was pointed out that policies recognizing private property rights in land, and a liberal approach to the land market, seem to be conducive to the evolution of a farm structure that responds to market forces. Such a structure includes a varied mixture of family farms, corporate farms and efficient smaller cooperatives in specialized branches of agriculture. Avoidance of preferential support to old-style large cooperatives and conglomerates (through directed credit subsidies, debt forgiveness and tax benefits) could help the emergence of a viable farming structure. The need to resolve the social functions (education, medical services, care for the old) traditionally provided by collectives was a hindrance to the willing transformation of the former socialist structure.

PANEL REPORT: INNOVATIVE APPROACHES TO POVERTY
ALLEVIATION IN ASIA

CHAIRPERSON

Ganesh Thapa (International Fund for Agricultural Development)

PANEL DISCUSSANTS

Rural Enterprise Development and Poverty Alleviation in China   *Jikun Huang (Centre for Chinese Agricultural Policy, Beijing, China) (with Scott Rozelle, University of California, USA)*

Are Rural Public Works Effective in Alleviating Rural Poverty in the Long Run? Evidence from India   *Katsushi Imai (University of Oxford, UK)*

Land Tenure, Land Reform and Rural Poverty in Asia   *Keijiro Otsuka (Tokyo Metropolitan University, Japan)*

Poverty Alleviation through Microfinance in Bangladesh: Success Stories and Emerging Concerns   *Rushidan Rahman (Bangladesh Institute for Development Studies, Bangladesh)*

RAPPORTEUR

Katsushi Imai (University of Oxford, UK)

Ganesh Thapa explained the background of the panel session. IFAD has undertaken a study entitled 'Regional Poverty Assessment for Asia and the Pacific 2000', which attempts to identify major issues in rural poverty. Each of the panel members helped with the work and this meeting provides an opportunity to discuss some of the key issues in poverty alleviation.

Jikun Huang, in considering rural industries in China, noted that average farm size declined in the period 1980–95 (from 0.56 hectares per farm to 0.41 hectares), though real per capita income was still increasing following a sharp improvement in labour productivity. Nevertheless, rural–urban migration had also risen while the *share* of income and employment earned in the agricultural sector declined. The importance of the non-agricultural sector also became greater with the share of township and village enterprises (TVEs) in the economy (GDP) increasing dramatically (10 per cent in 1985 to 27 per cent in 1998). The employment share of TVEs was also larger. Given all of these changes, poverty in rural areas decreased dramatically (absolute poverty was affecting 260 million persons in 1978, the number falling to 42 million in 1998). Strengthening the non-urban economy, as a whole, through rural enterprise development will be important as a means of reducing poverty still further.

While rural enterprise growth has been concentrated in the eastern coastal region, both rich and poor areas have greatly benefited from the rural industrialization in the rich coastal region through labour migration. Releasing the constraints on movement is therefore important in fostering change of this type, though there are also prospects for spreading the scope for TVEs to more regions, particularly if linkages between poor areas and the rest of China can be strengthened. For that to happen, and for it to be effective, improvements in rural infrastructure, human capital development and aid to entrepreneurship are of great importance.

Katsushi Imai also spoke about non-farm development in rural areas, though in that case in the context of India's rural public works and the Employment Guarantee Scheme (EGS). The main objectives have been to stabilize income fluctuations and to help correct regional wage disparities. Both the aims have been partially met and there have also been indirect transfer benefits in the form of upward pressure on agricultural wages. Unfortunately the targeting performance of the EGS was not good. It also had few dynamic effects. The *protective effect*, preventing the vulnerable from slipping into poverty, is more marked than the *promotional effect*, enabling the poor to escape persistent poverty. The latter is unlikely without larger outlay on the schemes and in the absence of other measures in agriculture (land reforms) and in health and education services.

Keijiro Otsuka, reverting to a more directly agricultural theme, attempted to clarify important issues in the debate on land tenure, land reform and rural poverty in Asia. Common features of land reform include tenancy changes (regulation of leasehold rent, prevention of arbitrary eviction of tenants and possibly the encouragement of share tenancy, even though this is often regarded as undesirable) and redistribution (transfer of land to actual tenant cultivators). The justifications for land reform are that tenants belong to the poorest segment of rural society, that smaller operators are more efficient than larger ones and that, on balance, leasehold tenancy and owner cultivation scores over share tenancy.

These presumptions, however, are empirically incorrect. In fact, the poorest of the rural poor are landless labourers, not tenants. Share tenancy is generally not very inefficient compared with leasehold tenancy and owner cultivation, unless tenancy contracts are distorted by land reform laws themselves. Furthermore, land reform tends to block the agricultural ladder for landless labourers to ascend by prohibiting or suppressing tenancy transactions, thereby perpetuating rural poverty. One key aim, therefore, should be to provide opportunities for landless labourers and marginal farmers to manage farms, even if that involves share tenancy. In addition, to promote 'market-assisted land reform', removal of all policies which favour large farmers would promote transfer of land to the landless and near landless.

Rushidan Islam Rahman observed that a positive effect of microcredit on income has been reported by a number of past studies in Bangladesh. Schemes are regarded as 'success stories'. The emerging concerns, though, are that household expenditure is almost the same irrespective of the duration of membership of the Bangladesh Rural Advancement Committee (BRAC) scheme. Assessment of targeting performance also shows that 48 per cent of the total participants were households above the poverty line and that the extreme poor were underrepresented among BRAC members. There is some merit in current target selection since the financial sustainability of microcredit institutions (MCIs) is a major concern for aid donors. Clearly, there is a need to maintain the good repayment practice already achieved by most of the non-governmental organisations (NGOs) involved.

The great challenge is to find ways of enabling more of the poorest households to become members of microfinance institutions. Often they need larger loans, at lower interest rates, than MCIs are prepared to offer. The dilemma is obvious. As long as aggregate repayment performance is satisfactory and most borrowers are paying realistic interest rates, there appears to be a need for some low cost funds to be channelled to specially selected groups. MCIs should, in effect, have a commitment to improve targeting and translate that commitment into action at the field level.

PANEL REPORT: THE NEXT WTO ROUND ON AGRICULTURE: TRADE LIBERALIZATION VERSUS FOOD SECURITY?

ORGANIZER, CHAIRPERSON AND RAPPORTEUR

Stefan Tangermann (Institute of Agricultural Economics, University of Göttingen, Germany)

PANEL DISCUSSANTS

A Perspective from an Asian Developing Country   *Ashok Gulati (Institute of Economic Growth, University of Delhi, India)*

The Importing Developed Countries   *Masayoshi Honma (Economics Department, Seikei University, Tokyo, Japan)*

A Latin American View   *Alberto Valdés (The World Bank, Washington DC, USA)*

Exporting Developed Countries   *Dan Sumner (Department of Agricultural Economics, University of California, Davis, USA)*

The background to this panel was the fact that food security is one of the most fundamental objectives of governments in all parts of the world. The extent to which the objective has been reached, though, differs very much between developed and developing countries, across different groups of developing countries, and among different groups of the population within individual countries. Overall, nearly 800 million people in the developing world are undernourished, according to FAO estimates. The improvement of food security in those places which suffer from chronic undernourishment should, therefore, be among the prime aims of international action in those policy fields that can make a contribution to securing enough food for everybody. It is then absolutely natural, and essential beyond any doubt, that efforts to liberalize international trade in agriculture, as pursued in the framework of the World Trade Organization (WTO), should be pursued with this criterion in mind. At the same time, domestic policies in countries engaged in international negotiations on agricultural trade liberalization must be designed to improve food security, not to threaten it.

However, as the presentations and the subsequent discussion showed, when it comes to understanding the relationship between agricultural trade liberalization and food security, and to finding agreement on the proper policy design, at both the domestic and the international level, there are widely diverging views. Among both analysts and policy makers, views differ strongly on how trade liberalization affects food security. Waters are even more muddy when the political economy of international trade negotiations is fully exposed in the arguments advanced by governments. In their negotiating statements, some governments argue that further agricultural trade liberalization threatens food security in their countries, while others hold that free trade in agriculture can make an important contribution to improving the situation. These different views came out clearly at the panel.

On both sides of the argument there are genuine concerns about the links between agricultural trade and food security. However, at the same time, the food security argument is also, again on both sides, often used as a pretext for pursuing special sectoral interests, typically of a producer-oriented nature. Governments of some countries without food security problems, and unlikely to have them even under completely free trade, play the food security card in international negotiations, to argue for continued protection of their domestic farmers, and oppose trade liberalization on those grounds. The argument typically is that only domestic food production is reliable in crisis times, and that domestic market instability, supposedly resulting from the opening up of domestic markets to international trade, can well threaten food security. Governments of some other countries, interested in finding better export markets for their farmers, strongly make the point that free international trade is the optimal way to enhance economic growth, improve living standards of the poor and hence create the economic conditions under which hunger can be eradicated. Moreover, they argue, free trade improves market stability and hence the continuous achievement of safe food supplies.

With such opposing views on the relationships between food security and agricultural trade liberalization it is not necessarily useful that the WTO Agreement on Agriculture names food security as one of the so-called *non-trade* concerns to be considered in implementing the reform programme agreed in the Uruguay Round. Non-trade concerns (presumably including food security) are also supposed to be taken into account in the negotiations on the continuation of the reform process, begun in early 2000. These clauses were obviously squeezed into the text of the Agreement by those countries wanting to retard the process of further trade liberalization in agriculture.

However, with the arguments outlined above, the protagonists of free trade can base their pleas for more determined progress towards trade liberalization on the same clauses. In short, the relationship between food security and agricultural trade liberalization is both an analytical puzzle and a highly politicized issue. As such it is likely to remain hotly debated for quite some time, and certainly throughout the new round of agricultural trade negotiations in the WTO that will be held over the coming few years.

Though none of the four panellists is anything like an official representative of his country, all of them have intimate insights into the characteristics of the economic and political situation of the region they are from. Among them, the four presentations therefore reflected different perspectives that to some extent are characteristic of the issues considered particularly important in the four regions of South Asia, Japan, Latin America and North America. Far from the political rhetoric prevalent in trade negotiations, even the profound academic analyses presented served to demonstrate that the links between food security and trade can be discussed from different vantage points. However, one common thread running through all the four presentations was the perception that food security is first and foremost an economic phenomenon, closely related to the purchasing power of the individual families concerned, rather than a matter of the physical availability of food at the country level. Starting from that common base, the issue then is how trade liberalization affects the economic ability of individual people to acquire food, in continuously sufficient quantities, considering both individual income levels and the price of food.

However, even this commonly accepted analytical starting point leaves much room for considering the various ways in which trade can affect the relevant variables. Trade liberalization can contribute to overall economic growth, but can also negatively affect income levels, and hence purchasing power for food, among groups of people exposed to more international competition. Farmers engaged in export production are influenced in a different way from farmers competing with imported products. Whether countries can fully utilize the opportunities of international trade depends, among other things, on their macroeconomic conditions, including the availability of foreign exchange. Short-run food insecurity requires other responses than long-run undernourishment. Governments have a choice of different options as to how to cope with either type of problem. Food price variability is an important aspect of short-run food security concerns, and alternative trade policies have different implications for domestic price variability.

All these aspects, and many more, were discussed in the four presentations, which jointly provided an excellent overview of the various elements in the complex web that connects trade and food security.*

---

*The panellists were kind enough to write up their presentations for publication as a Special Issue of the *Quarterly Journal of International Agriculture*, **39** (4), (2000).

PANEL REPORT: LATIN AMERICAN AGRICULTURE DURING THE
1990s

ORGANIZER, CHAIRPERSON AND RAPPORTEUR

C. Jaramillo (Colombia)

PANEL DISCUSSANTS

A Longer-term View of the Agricultural Effects of Economy and Sector Reforms
in Chile, 1965–2000   *Lovell Jarvis (University of California, Davis, USA)*

Brazilian Agriculture in the 1990s: Impact of the Policy Reforms   *Steven
M. Helfand (University of California, Riverside, USA) and Gervásio Castro de
Rezende (Universidade Federal Fluminense, Brazil)*

Mexico: Economic Reforms and Evolution of Mexico's Basic Crops' Subsector during the 1990s   *Antonio Yúnez-Naude and Rosa Martha Guerrero
(Centre of Economic Studies, El Colegio de México)*

Lovell Jarvis showed how Chilean agriculture has experienced major land and
economic reforms in the last four decades. Land reform took place from
approximately 1965 to 1979, including both expropriation and redistribution,
and major economic reforms occurred between 1974 and 1986, with important
fine-tuning afterwards. Land reform was intended to improve land management and increase economic and political equity, while trade and price reforms
were intended to reduce the implicit tax on agriculture imposed by an import-
substituting industrialization strategy and remove other price distortions, thereby
improving incentives for agricultural development.

Under land reform, 4 per cent of Chile's agricultural land was expropriated.
Eventually, part was returned to the original owners, part was auctioned and
part was redistributed to former workers on the expropriated farms. Economic
reforms were broad in scale, affecting trade, finance, labour, taxation and
expenditure, including the privatization of many government enterprises. These
reforms sought to end inflation, achieve fiscal and trade balance, and improve
economic efficiency throughout the economy. Little emphasis was placed on
equity, at least prior to the 1990s.

The reforms, seen today, were highly successful in many aspects, though
this was not clear during the first ten years following their initiation. During

1975–85, agricultural output grew slowly, the economy suffered two major recessions and unemployment was high. Real agricultural wages fell. Although Chile devalued sharply in 1974, efforts to control inflation led to steady appreciation of the peso. A rising exchange rate, the removal of protection for the principal agricultural products, and declining domestic demand led to a decline in the prices of Chile's principal traditional crops. The fruit sector began to grow rapidly in response to rising international demand, but it was initially a small sector and its rapid growth could not offset the decline in cereals, oilseeds, sugar beet, legumes and livestock products. Forestry plantings were heavily subsidized and area forested grew rapidly.

Policy discriminated against land reform beneficiaries. This discrimination, coupled with their relatively poor levels of education and managerial experience, and also with the very high prices for land that others could pay to initiate fruit production, led most beneficiaries to sell their land by the mid-1980s. Simultaneously, many larger farms were subdivided and sold, at least in part. Thus, largely as a result of land reform, Chile developed a dynamic land market that facilitated the entrance of new entrepreneurs and the development of new crops. Major shifts also occurred in the agricultural labour force. Most permanent farm workers lost their jobs, with employment becoming seasonal instead of permanent. Many workers began to work on a contract or piece rate basis and, in response, labour productivity rose rapidly. Females entered the labour force in growing numbers, particularly during the harvest.

After 1985, macroeconomic stability was achieved. Fruit output, quality and exports continued to grow rapidly and, as the fruit sector was highly labour-intensive, employment rose. Real agricultural wages began to increase in the early 1990s. Access to new technologies led to rising yields for cereals, oilseeds and sugar beet. As these are produced only for the domestic market, rising yields were associated with lower prices and declining acreage. Livestock technology also improved dramatically and, as domestic incomes and demand grew, livestock output increased rapidly. Wine production became highly profitable in the 1990s.

Chile has a fairly narrow comparative advantage in Mediterranean-type products such as fruits and vegetables, almonds, walnuts and wine, and also in forestry (wood and wood pulp). It produces grains, oilseeds and livestock products for the domestic market. As Chile becomes increasingly integrated with MERCOSUR, its agricultural sector will probably shrink and the growth rate is likely to slow. Nonetheless, broad-based land and economic reforms will have had many positive effects. The principal goal of reform was increased efficiency, not a particularly output-oriented goal. The agricultural sector today is significantly more technologically advanced than in the past. Management and workers are more skilled and motivated. Resources are allocated more efficiently, both in terms of factor use and output mix. Productivity has increased.

There is widespread support in Chile today for maintaining a market-oriented economy with an emphasis on individual initiative. There is a strong attitudinal shift towards political and economic moderation. There is confidence in the benefits of international trade, even if individual farm groups still lobby for policies that would benefit their special interests. Exporting is seen as a potential source of significant profit. Cheaper imports are seen as attractive because they lower production costs and provide higher-quality, cheaper consumer goods. A continued emphasis is needed on assisting with the transition of many, poorer farmers and agricultural workers towards employment in other sectors of the economy. The reform process has had greater success in increasing output and incomes than in increasing income equality. Nonetheless, the benefits of reform have been considerable.

The discussion centred on two contrasting issues: (a) the possibility of Chile's high agricultural rates of growth dropping in the near future, not because of liberalization but because of a threshold beyond which growth possibilities will be lower, and (b) the need to consider the harmful effects of liberalization on small farmers and farm workers (that is, on the poorer segment of Chile's agricultural sector).

As in other Latin American countries, Mexico's import substitution model has been abandoned. Since the 1990s (especially so since the beginning of the North American Free Trade Agreement implementation in 1994), the reforms have included the agricultural sector. Antonio Yúnez-Naude and Rosa Martha Guerrero pointed to the dualistic character of Mexico's agricultural sector and noted that the sub-sector of basic crops (beans, barley, maize, rice, sorghum, soy beans and wheat) was formerly the most protected. Producer prices were settled by the government and imports controlled by CONASUPO (Mexico's major state trading enterprise). However, on the basis of statistical time series covering 1970 to 1998, it seems that producer prices did not diverge greatly from international levels; but the market share going to local farmers was protected by CONASUPO, acting as the sole importer of basic crops. There has now been little effect on domestic production, but imports have increased. This conclusion is especially marked for maize, the most important staple in Mexico. In addition, maize production has not decreased since small farmers have not been directly affected by price reforms as they face high transaction costs and produce for their own consumption.

The paper ended with the following argument. Since liberalization is promoting efficiency in the entrepreneurial portion of Mexico's agriculture, the agricultural development policy challenge lies among small-scale producers. This is particularly so when it is remembered that it is in the rural sector that extreme poverty prevails and that its farmers are still controlling a high proportion of Mexico's natural resources.

Discussion was centred on three questions: (a) the effects of PROCAMPO (the decoupled agricultural support policy designed by the government to help farmers to face liberalization), (b) the changes in Mexico's agrarian structure provoked by the liberalization of land rights of the ejidal sector, and (c) the future of small-scale farming.

The Brazilian economy began a process of significant restructuring in the 1990s as a result of dramatic changes in economic policy. The import substitution industrialization (ISI) model was abandoned and the country began to shape a new path of development. Trade was liberalized, state-owned enterprises were privatized, domestic markets were deregulated, and a South

American Common Market (MERCOSUL) was formed. Agriculture was no exception to the economy-wide redefinition of the role of the state.

Steven M. Helfand and Gervásio Castro de Rezende discussed the impact of the policy reforms, and of the changing macroeconomic conditions, on Brazilian agriculture. Four aspects of the process that were either unexpected or not emphasized by writers in the period prior to the reforms were stressed.

(1) Events outside the agriculture affect its performance but also influence the timing and sequence of policy reform. In the ISI period it was clear that *indirect* policies, such as overvalued currencies and industrial protection, played a critical role in shaping the situation in farming, and it was expected that the reform of these policies would have a positive impact on the sector. What was unexpected – and this is especially true in the case of Brazil – was the difficulty and length of time that would be necessary to stabilize the economy. The numerous stabilization plans that were adopted in the 1980s and 1990s joined the more traditional indirect policies as a key force that shaped the performance of the sector. In this context, the reform of agricultural policies was almost entirely subordinated to the reform of ISI policies and the painful quest for price stability.

(2) Policy reform involved far more than trade liberalization. Deregulation and the reform of credit and support price policy have been central as well. In fact, the most dramatic transformations in the agricultural sector have taken place with those products that were most heavily regulated, such as wheat, milk, sugar and coffee. The products that lost import protection or gained a reduction in export taxation as a result of trade liberalization have also been affected, but to a lesser degree. For this group, the evolution of credit and support price policy has been extremely important.

(3) The impact of policy reform on input markets and productivity has been one of the key components of the adjustment process. Liberalization has altered relative input prices and increased access to high-quality imported inputs. It has also exposed domestic production to greater competition. Both of these factors have led to productivity gains and falling costs. Increases in productivity and efficiency, in addition to lower consumer prices, are among the most important measures of the success of the reforms.

(4) Reform was neither uniformly beneficial nor entirely prejudicial. Thus the authors' analysis seeks to distinguish between different groups of products, such as importables and exportables, geographic regions, farm sizes, and subperiods. The authors argued further that, since not all reforms were introduced simultaneously, the 1990s should be treated as a decade of transition in which the old model was replaced, but not all of the features of the new model were firmly established.

The discussion focused on three issues: (a) the relationship between macro–economic cycles and cycles of boom and bust within agriculture, (b) the impact on small and large farms of rural credit policy reform, and (c) the importance, difficulties, and challenges of designing a viable land reform programme in Brazil.

PANEL REPORT: FOOD SAFETY IN THE CHANGING WORLD FOOD SYSTEM

ORGANIZER, CHAIRPERSON AND RAPPORTEUR

Laurian J. Unnevehr (University of Illinois, USA)

PANEL DISCUSSANTS

Laurian J. Unnevehr (University of Illinois, USA), Jill Hobbs (University of Saskatchewan, Canada), Jutta Roosen (Catholic University of Louvain, Belgium), Istvan Feher (Gödöllö University, Hungary), Helen H. Jensen (Iowa State University, USA)

The panel considered how practices and policies are changing as food product trade grows and how different countries are responding to the challenge of controlling safety hazards. Some themes from the presentations include the similarity of policy issues in developed country markets, the interaction of food safety with structural changes in markets, the importance of a 'systems' or 'supply chain' approach to safety management and the importance of food safety in international trade.

Laurian J. Unnevehr (USA) opened with an overview of the structural changes in food markets that make food safety an issue of growing importance. These changes include better identification of food-borne hazards; changes in the way consumers obtain food, which alters risk responsibility; new management and regulatory paradigms for controlling hazards; and increased food product trade, particularly of fresh products. The challenges for economists are to measure the degree of market failure in food safety, the impact of policies, and the costs and benefits associated with control measures.

Jill Hobbs (Canada) discussed the division between public and private sector activities to improve food safety by addressing the information asymmetry in markets. Legal liability, private certification and public regulation are all creating incentives for supply chain coordination to improve food safety, including traceability of food products to their farm origins. Research is needed to understand the cost-effectiveness of 'trace-back' systems for food safety improvement.

Jutta Roosen (Belgium) presented a systems approach to the provision of food safety. Most processed foods are mixtures of products, having undergone substantial processing and preparation. Therefore the most severe food quality failures are systemic, arising in part as a consequence of the complexity and interconnectedness of the paths taken from source to table. Improvements in food safety must take into account the complementary interactions among system components.

Istvan Feher (Hungary) discussed the implications for Hungary of accession to the European Union. This will be a challenge for Hungarian food producers facing the competition of imported food products of high quality. A comprehensive system of quality policy measures has been elaborated and introduced in the Hungarian agri-food sector during the last ten years. Adequate operation of this system will result in a general quality improvement, which is essential for Hungary to be competitive, both in the single market of the EU and also in the domestic market.

Helen H. Jensen (USA) summarized the panel discussion. She highlighted the theme of incentives that runs throughout the statements. How and whether incentives are transmitted in markets, through international trade, or created by public policy is important in understanding how food safety can be improved.

The audience discussion was lively and raised several controversial issues not directly addressed by the panel. Some questioned whether food safety is really an important public health issue in light of general improvements in nutrition and life expectancy in developed countries. Responses from the panel and others in the audience highlighted the changing nature of food-borne pathogens and the better understanding of chronic effects of food hazards in longer-lived populations. Others questioned whether a concern with food safety is applicable in less developed countries, and whether they should or should not adopt higher standards. Responses to this issue highlighted the need for less developed countries to expand exports, on the one hand, and the need to address differing food safety and public health hazards for their own populations, on the other. Another concern raised was the extent to which agricultural economists can know what the costs and benefits would be of improving food safety. Such research is still relatively new and its findings are not widely appreciated in the profession.

PANEL REPORT: FOOD SECURITY IN THE CONTEXT OF CHANGING THE COURSE OF ECONOMIC REFORM IN THE WANA COUNTRIES

ORGANIZER, CHAIRPERSON AND RAPPORTEUR

Mamdouh Nasr (Ain-Shams University, Cairo, Egypt and Centre for Development Research (ZEF), Bonn University, Germany)

PANEL DISCUSSANTS

Ahmed Goueli (Cairo University, Egypt), Mohamed A. Sherif Omran (USAID/ Cairo, Egypt), Mohamed Jaouad (Agricultural Economist, Ministry of Agriculture, Morocco), Mohammad Rafiq Hamadan (University of Jordan, Amman, Jordan)

The discussants made brief presentations covering the North Africa and Middle Eastern region as a whole (Ahmed Goueli) followed respectively by comments on Egypt, Morocco and Jordan by the other discussants. The general view was that food security in the whole region is confronted by several threats and challenges in the 21st century. Agricultural and forest land is often fragile, hence there is a prime requirement for it to be protected. Dependence of production in the region on rainfed areas creates severe instability in food availability. There is an obvious need for irrigation and water conservation. Closely associated with that is the need to prevent conflict among countries over available supply in the region by negotiation and agreement. That is very much bound up with the need for enhancement of the welfare of the people and improvement of the quality of life, which, in turn, requires political stability. A just and comprehensive peace in the Middle East will contribute greatly to the prosperity and development of all.

Poverty alleviation has to be attacked in two dimensions. The first involves fairly standard prescriptions. Improvement in poor societies comes through education for work and for more general increases in knowledge on health, food and nutrition. Small and micro enterprises need to be promoted as a source of employment and income generation, and they need to be sustained by increasing resources devoted to local R&D. The dominance of young people in the population of the region, though it is an obvious advantage, requires large-scale creation of jobs. Agriculture would benefit directly from more exposure to international agricultural research and technology. Low-quality rural and trade infrastructure limits progress in increasing competitiveness of exportable products, which is a necessary condition in order to gain foreign exchange. Intraregional cooperation and integration would help with that.

The second dimension involves a change in the attitude of the government and of richer people towards the poor. Encouraging rich people to fulfil their social responsibilities towards satisfying the social expectations of the poor could do this. The gender gap in economic activities is large, which is a closely associated issue. At the practical level two measures are needed. The first is to decentralize the civil service structures and make social provision available in the poor areas with the same level of quality as in the rich. Second, if a government engages in any kind of subsidy, it ought to be aimed at relieving the insecurity of the poor.

At the international level the WTO has an indirect role in food security policies in developing countries. On one side, the distortion of international food markets is encouraging the developing countries to continue implementing their self-sufficiency policies through import substitution practices. Markets are thus lost to the developing world. On the other, the availability of relatively cheap food on international markets is a benefit, but one which is potentially short term, carrying with it the danger of reducing domestic food production capacities in more vulnerable regions.

PANEL REPORT: RURAL INFRASTRUCTURE: INVESTMENT, DELIVERY AND FINANCE

ORGANIZER, CHAIRPERSON AND RAPPORTEUR

Peter Hazell (International Food Policy Research Institute, Washington, DC, USA)

PANEL DISCUSSANTS

Shenggen Fan (International Food Policy Research Institute, Washington, DC, USA), Walter Huppert (Deutsche Gesellschaft für Technische Zusammenarbeit (GTZ), Germany), Ashok Gulati (Institute of Economic Growth, University of Delhi, India)

Peter Hazell introduced the topic, pointing out the critical importance of public investments in rural areas for achieving agricultural and rural economic growth and poverty reduction. He said that levels of public investment had stagnated or fallen in many developing countries, partly in response to financial retrenchments associated with macroeconomic policy reforms, but also because agricultural development has become a low priority for most donors and multilateral lending agencies. Countries will have to learn to do 'more with less' with their rural investments. Hazell identified three key issues for the panel discussion: (a) how to set priorities more efficiently for public investments to achieve growth and poverty reduction goals; (b) how to get better and more efficient service out of the institutions that provide public goods and services; and (c) how to pay for public goods and services on a financially sustainable basis. He was pleased to be able to introduce three distinguished panellists who would address each of these issues.

Shenggen Fan (IFPRI) gave a summary of some of his recent work on estimating the returns to public investments in rural India and China. On the basis of econometric analysis of time-series data available by subregions, he had been able to calculate and rank the additional amount of agricultural output and the number of poor people raised above the poverty line for additional units of expenditure on different types of public investment. He reported that, in India, additional government expenditure on rural roads has the largest impact on rural poverty reduction, as well as the second-largest impact on agricultural productivity growth. Investments in agricultural R&D have the second-largest impact on poverty reduction, but contribute the most to agricultural productivity growth. Education investments also score well for growth and poverty reduction, while the marginal returns to further rural electrification and irrigation are now quite low. Investments in soil and water conservation and rural development have useful poverty impacts but contribute virtually nothing to agricultural productivity growth.

In China, education investments have the largest impact on rural poverty reduction and the second-largest impact on agricultural productivity growth. As in India, agricultural R&D ranks the highest in terms of its growth impact, but ranks third for poverty impact. Additional investments in roads, electrification and rural telephones also give favourable returns in terms of agricultural growth and poverty reduction. As with India, additional expenditures on irrigation now contribute relatively little to growth or poverty reduction.

Fan also reported that a disaggregated analysis by different types of agricultural regions in India showed that the marginal returns to public investments are now higher in many rainfed zones than in the irrigated areas. Moreover, investments in some of the lower-potential areas are also becoming more attractive on the margin. He is also obtaining similar results in China. Fan's work is indicative of the kinds of policy research that can usefully guide policy makers in setting investment priorities to achieve growth and poverty alleviation goals more efficiently.

Walter Huppert (GTZ) discussed the importance of transparency and accountability in the provision of infrastructure services. Provision takes place in the context of a network of involved actors – different organizations, groups and individuals – and the nature and context of their interactions are crucial in determining whether the users' needs are met, and how efficiently and sustainably the service is provided. Understanding the mechanisms and incentive structures that condition these multi-actor relationships is crucial for improving service provision. Externally set and enforced laws and regulations are often an important conditioning factor, but so are the basic norms, values and understandings between actors, access to key information and the negotiating power of different groups. Good service provision requires accountability to the clients.

The new institutional economics draws attention to particular circumstances that tend to jeopardize accountability at different linkage points in the systems and create perverse incentives. The presentation and discussion focused on the presence of such 'principal–agent' phenomena in the context of water delivery services by large irrigation agencies. With case examples from Jordan and India, the causes of the emergence of principal–agent problems were discussed and practical approaches for possible solutions were highlighted

Ashok Gulati (India) discussed some of the key incentive issues related to financing rural infrastructure, drawing on experience with pricing irrigation water and rural electricity in India. The government recovers less than 10 per cent of the costs of providing irrigation water and rural electricity through direct user charges, hence nearly all the costs have to be recovered through indirect taxes. This leads to three important problems. First, because it delinks incentives for water and power use from their true costs, farmers have every incentive to overuse these inputs, with resulting economic and environmental costs. Second, because the institutions that supply water and electricity do not collect much revenue from their users, they are dependent on financial transfers from the government. This severely reduces their incentive or ability to operate on a financially sustainable basis. Third, since farmers do not pay for these services, they have little leverage over the quality of service they receive, which leads to poor service provision and corruption. Gulati said that India was in the process of trying to reform these service systems, but that it is politically very difficult because of powerful vested interests. The government would like (a) to increase water and power user charges to recover directly much higher shares of the supply costs, (b) to have the supplying institutions collect these user fees themselves and to reform their charters so that they are financially responsible for their own affairs and are fully accountable to their users, and (c) to open up the water and electricity sectors for private capital investment, with the government playing an appropriate regulatory role.

A lively discussion ensued that highlighted the widespread nature of incentive and financial problems in the provision of rural infrastructure services around the world, and the difficulties of reform because of vested interests and political intransigence. There is urgent need for further reform of the institutions that provide public services, including a greater role for the private and civil sectors where appropriate. But there is also danger in holding future rural investments hostage to such reforms, because of their critical importance for agricultural growth and rural poverty reduction.

PANEL REPORT: THE LIVESTOCK REVOLUTION IN DEVELOPING
COUNTRIES

ORGANIZER, CHAIRPERSON AND RAPPORTEUR

Simeon Ehui (Ethiopia) with Chris Delgado (USA)

PANEL DISCUSSANTS

Impact of the Livestock Revolution on Food Security and Poverty Alleviation
in Developing Countries   *Chris Delgado (International Food Policy Research Institute, Washington, DC, USA)*

Productivity Growth and International Trade in Livestock Products   *Thomas
Hertel with Alexandero Nin (Purdue University, West Lafayette, Indiana, USA)*

The Rise of Livestock Product Consumption and Human Nutrition   *Charlotte
Neumann (University of California at Los Angeles, California, USA)*

Livestock and Natural Resource Management in the Developing World
*Henning Steinfeld (Food and Agriculture Organization of the United Nations,
Rome, Italy)*

The panel focused on the implications of the livestock revolution in developing
countries for a number of key issues. It began with Chris Delgado, who
reported that, from the beginning of the 1970s to the mid-1990s, consumption
of meat and milk in developing countries increased by 175 million metric tons,
more than double the increase in developed countries. The market value of that
increase was approximately $155 billion (1990 US$), more than twice the
market value of increased cereals consumption during the 'Green Revolution'.
In the early 1990s, the share of the world's meat consumed in developing
countries was 47 per cent, and their share of the world's milk was 41 per cent,
up sharply from the early 1980s. IFPRI projections to 2020 place the developing countries' meat production share at 60 per cent, and that for milk at 52 per
cent, a veritable 'Livestock Revolution'. The population growth, urbanization
and income growth that fuelled the recent increases are expected to continue.
Farm income in those countries could rise dramatically, but whether this will
be shared by the rural poor who need it most is still undetermined. Furthermore, current rapid increases in pollution, land degradation and the incidence

of zoonotic disease from increasing concentration of animals near major cities are expected to continue and even accelerate.

Delgado also noted that structural changes and policies in three large countries – China, India and Brazil – are especially important in influencing the likely course of world real prices for meat and milk over the next two decades. However, the best estimate under a wide variety of scenarios is that inflation-adjusted world prices for livestock products will be within 20 per cent up or down from average real prices in the early 1990s, and thus will remain very substantially below the high prices of the early 1980s. While trade in livestock products is likely to expand rapidly, including North-to-South and South-to-South trade, it will be small relative to a projected huge increase in feedgrains exports from the more developed to the less developed countries. Though the shares of cereals and livestock in the total agricultural output of the OECD countries has remained fairly constant since the 1960s, the share of livestock in total agricultural output in the South is rising rapidly. Protection of the livestock sector in most rapidly growing East Asia economies – which account for 30 per cent of world meat trade – remains high. It is up to 70 to 80 per cent in the case of dairying, although it is unlikely that this will be maintained as countries in the region assess their overall interests with respect to forthcoming WTO negotiations.

Against this background, Hertel and Nin examined the evolving trends in global livestock productivity, as well as meat demand and trade, and made projections to the year 2010 using a global general equilibrium model. While their analysis of historical rates of productivity growth showed that developing countries have lagged behind high-income producers in the past three decades, they anticipate that this will be reversed in the coming decade. This change will be fuelled by productivity 'catch-up' in the developing countries. However, this acceleration in supply appears to be insufficient to satisfy the emerging demand for meats in the developing world. Therefore imports are expected to rise and developing countries are projected to absorb one-third of global meat trade by the end of the 1990s. The study (illustrated by the case of China) also suggested that the developing countries' net trade position is very sensitive to changes in either the livestock or the non-livestock economies. If livestock growth is at the high end of possible outcomes, and if there is a slow-down in the rest of the economy, developing countries such as China (where productivity growth is already high) could become a fierce competitor in export markets by 2010. However, slower than expected diffusion and adoption of livestock technology, coupled with a rapidly growing macro-economy, could make developing countries major importers of livestock products.

Charlotte Neumann argued that the implications of the livestock revolution for human nutrition are especially critical. As many as 1.3 billion people currently suffer from anaemia and hundreds of millions more from other forms of micronutrient malnutrition – the great 'silent hunger'. Deficiencies in intake of iron, iodine, vitamin A, zinc and other micronutrients are needlessly condemning masses of poor people in developing countries to disease and decreased ability to live a full and productive life. It is possible to deliver the needed nutrients through daily pills or a highly varied vegan diet. However, there is an increasing consensus that in rural areas in most developing countries only intake of at least a small amount of meat and milk can supply the necessary nutrients on a widespread sustainable daily basis in bio-available form. Fifty grams of meat daily for a young child could greatly improve nutritional status, including the utilization of ingested foods of vegetable origin. However, many developing countries are still far from reaching this level of consumption even on a national average basis, much less in the diets of the children of the poor.

Henning Steinfeld posed a problem: the implications of the livestock revolution for environmental sustainability are worrying, in both the North and the South. Livestock currently use just under half the world's arable area (26 per cent directly, 21 per cent indirectly for feedgrain). Much of East Asia, in particular, has seen increases in the density of annual carcass-equivalent meat production of at least 6 tons/km^2 over the last 25 years. Other 'hot spots' for nutrient loading are being observed in the southeastern seaboard of the USA, Northern Europe, Central America and Southeast and South Asia. Of the anticipated increase in world meat production up to 2020, 70 per cent is projected to come from non-ruminant sources. The primary associated pollution problems are nutrient loading and greenhouse gases from manure handling. These, as in the case of ruminants, can be successfully addressed by a combination of policy changes and technology development, but greater attention needs to be devoted to the interaction of the two instruments. Improved policy can capture the externalities inherent in point-source pollution, for example through the creation of markets for tradeable property rights for carbon sequestration and improved enforcement of regulatory control. Technologies can both lower the amount of waste and improve its utilization for purposes such as biogas.

The increasing concentrations of veterinary pharmaceuticals in both edible livestock products and residues are another major issue. In the North, such drugs account for roughly half of chemical input costs of livestock production. Food safety issues have also become more prominent with the rise in trade of meat and milk, and it will be critical to distinguish between vital food safety concerns and non-transparent use of health regulations for protectionist purposes. Evidence also suggests that the resolution of food safety and protection issues in developing countries can also have a major impact on the scale of livestock production units, and thus on how the growth of production affects poor rural people in developing countries.

PANEL REPORT: AGRICULTURAL ECONOMICS CURRICULA – DIRECTIONS AND STRATEGIES FOR CHANGE

ORGANIZER, CHAIRPERSON AND RAPPORTEUR

John P. Nichols (Texas A&M University, USA)

PANEL DISCUSSANTS

Agricultural Education in Institutions of Higher Agricultural Education in India: Needs and Strategies for Change   *Vasant P. Gandhi (Indian Institute of Management, Delhi, India)*

Training Agribusiness Managers for the Future: A Challenge for Agricultural Economics in South Africa   *C.J. van Rooyen, O.T. Doyer, J. van Zyl and J.F. Kirsten (University of Pretoria, South Africa)*

Agricultural Economics Curriculum Reform in Germany and Europe   *Ernst Berg (University of Bonn, Germany)*

Agricultural Economics Undergraduate Education in the United States: Issues and Strategies   *John P. Nichols and Kerry Litzenberg (Texas A&M University, USA)*

Economic systems are changing rapidly. The liberalization of both domestic and global relationships continues to advance. Business decision processes and policy arrangements are being dramatically altered. Increasingly, concerns about harmful effects of production agriculture, and its practices, on the environment and safety of food are given more weight in public debates. The challenge to agricultural higher education is to redesign programmes and curricula to address the new issues and decision problems facing farmers, agribusiness managers, government regulators and policy makers, and others involved in the global agricultural and food sector. Much of this agenda falls directly on faculties of agricultural economics in universities around the world. This challenge was taken as the starting point for panel presentations and discussions based on several country and regional perspectives.

The goals for the reform of curricula, departments and faculties include strengthening areas of theory and quantitative decision sciences relevant to the emerging private sector and new public policy issues, each tied increasingly to global forces. But especially important, and more challenging for traditional programmes, is to increase emphasis on the following:

- active learning methods,
- knowledge acquisition methods and skills,
- critical thinking and problem-solving skills,
- importance of lifelong learning to manage career evolution,
- integration of knowledge about our global economic and cultural environment, and
- communications skills in both written and oral formats.

Evolving business and policy environment

The degree of accommodation or resistance varies from place to place, but the forces of globalization are well known throughout the world. Each of the presentations summarized these drivers of change in different ways and from different perspectives. Some of the pressures on curricula and higher education in general are derived from these global forces. In some cases major institutional changes are linked to specific issues of national or regional societal change. Some generalizations are derived below which set the stage for understanding the strategies being adopted in different university settings.

Liberalization of domestic economies and integration global of markets

Evolving policies in Europe and the United States aim at reducing direct intervention in agriculture and encouraging more market-driven decisions by farmers and agribusinesses. In India, the economy is slowly opening to external investment and competition. Privatization of formerly state-owned enterprises in agricultural production, input supply and food processing is proceeding throughout the world. The completion of the Uruguay Round and establishment of the World Trade Organization have set the stage for much more integration of global markets. These changes are increasing the premium which can be derived from the analysis of market conditions and the behaviour of competitors. No longer is it enough to react to government policy and assume that success for the firm will follow.

In Europe, the integration of markets over the past decade has given rise to major opportunities for firms to engage in massive reorganization in pursuit of new economies of scale. New concerns relating to the environmental impacts of agriculture in the relatively densely populated rural areas of Europe are directing greater emphasis on sustainability and production management consistent with these new expectations.

In South Africa, an entire upheaval of social and political structures is sweeping aside old institutions and commanding others to alter programmes, services and the allocation of resources. New models for the delivery of education, training and outreach are being sought. Agricultural higher education institutions are expected to lead the way because of their traditional strengths in addressing problems of rural areas. This mirrors concerns and expectations facing university leaders throughout the world where agriculture and rural life is tied more directly to changes and societal expectations at the national and international level.

Changing consumer demand and technology

As the organization and openness of economies has changed, so too has the nature of consumer demand and the technologies available to agriculture and agribusinesses. Increasing incomes, and the accompanying increase in demand for products and services with more convenience and consumer choice, creates a business decision environment unlike anything seen before.

Likewise, increasing incomes allow for consumers to express their demand for environmental amenities and food qualities which previously were of lower priority. At the same time, choices among technologies facing producers are greater than ever. Managing the assets of farms and agribusinesses requires a capability of accessing and analysing an increasingly complex set of data and information. With the rapidly increasing power of new communication and information technologies, the educational requirements for managers have expanded to include new subject areas and new methodologies. Emerging supply-chain business models present new choices for farmers which require sophisticated analysis of investment and risk management options. Many of our traditional principles of economic analysis are finding their way into new managerial settings, but these applications must be studied, modelled, and taught in the classroom.

Technology for teaching and learning

On the research side, increasing computing power provides the capability of studying and modelling ever more complex systems. A meaningful translation of this power to teaching, training and outreach objectives poses challenges to the traditional curricula and educational methods. As information processing and management capabilities increase, so do the expectations of students and employers. Faculty retraining and increased expenditures on computer software and hardware are straining higher education budgets.

Computer and Internet usage in teaching is expanding, affecting the style and quality of classroom teaching. Computer and web-based, asynchronous learning methods provide the opportunity to reach ever greater numbers of students. The challenge of offering meaningful distance education is being met in many different ways, requiring new models of institutional organization to capture the potential economies of scale and still provide educational results that meet user expectations.

New student expectations and growing enrolment

Another factor affecting the higher education system is increasing demand by growing populations and the effect on that demand from growing numbers of students realizing the importance of a university degree. Students in many countries, being faced with a job market dominated by a new entrepreneurial vision, are more interested in learning how to 'manage' than they are in the fundamental principles and theories of economics. They are aware of the opportunity costs of their educational investment, even if they do not want to study the concept as a part of economic principles. In short, 'they want a good job' and expect the university to deliver it to them at the end of the prescribed degree programmes.

Whether we agree with them or not, these expectations affect both what is offered and how it is offered. Does the traditional resident student experience at a university fit into the needs of these students? Increasing numbers are returning to universities to complete a degree after being employed. Others desire to take courses and continue employment while doing so. Competing models of education through 'virtual' web-based universities may provide attractive alternatives which agricultural universities cannot ignore. In the agribusiness field, a straight business degree provides an alternative which has high status and which may better meet the requirements of many employers when compared to the more focused applied economics curricula offered by agricultural economics faculties. At the same time, career opportunities in other areas such as agricultural and rural development, resource and environmental management, and policy and international trade are growing as well. Evaluation of these employment markets can lead to other types of curricula changes.

Competition for public resources

In many countries, higher education in the public sector was heavily subsidized for the select few who qualified for entrance to university. With public pressure to offer greater access to a substantially higher share of aspiring students, limited public funds are stretched further than ever before. Public resources for higher education are not increasing fast enough to keep up with increasing demand. In developing and transition economies, where the demand for change in agricultural economics and agribusiness education is the greatest, public resources have not even kept up with inflation. In nearly all countries, public universities are now encouraged to find ways to generate more of their income through private sources, including student tuition and fees. Public/ private partnerships are sought to help fund a variety of programmess through endowments, scholarships and other direct support. This increased emphasis on resource acquisition and reallocation should be a motivation for experimentation and redesign, not only for curricula, but for reforming the entire institution of higher education in agriculture, including agricultural economics.

Strategies for change

A significant convergence of ideas was achieved among the presenters regarding how departments, universities and faculties could respond to the challenges posed by economic, social and industrial change in the global agro-food system. These strategies reflect both current institutional responses and those that were identified as yet to be achieved, but which are crucial if departments and faculties are to remain relevant as providers of educated managers and leaders for agriculture, agribusiness and society.

Increased emphasis on experiential or active learning opportunities

The lecture and exam method has been a benchmark of teaching throughout the world. In nearly every case discussed, it was agreed that a rapid transition of teaching methods to incorporate more opportunities for student-centred learning is needed. The use of interactive teaching methods which encourage greater student involvement in the learning process will better prepare students for employment in business and government positions. Analysis, synthesis and development of problem-solving skills can be encouraged through the use of projects, case studies, increased class discussion, internships and visiting lecturers. Teaching of theory, fundamental principles and methods of analysis is crucial to preparing students to enter productive employment. However, methods of instruction and curricula must change if we are to address the challenges implied by societal change or put forward more directly in the market place for our students.

This was not seen as an easy transition. Many members of faculty are not in a position to make the wholesale changes required in courses and teaching methods. Incentives and resources to encourage change are simply not available in many agricultural universities. Finding and mobilizing resources to allow faculty to reorganize and retrain is a huge task everywhere, but especially in developing and transition economies.

Active engagement with industry

Certainly the first order of business is to assess the needs of the market. Most departments of agricultural economics understand that economic liberalization and globalization of food and agriculture are dramatically shifting the requirements of employers. An active involvement of agribusiness leaders and other employers in assessing programmes and curricula and in advising and developing institutional strategies is an important part of reform. Surveys of employers in the USA, South Africa and Europe have provided key ideas regarding the skills and knowledge areas most valued in entry-level employees. Faculty development leaves spent with agribusinesses provide experiences that can be brought back to the classroom.

Consultancies could be actively encouraged, not just as a source of income to supplement salaries which often are too low, but as an active way to gain knowledge of important private sector decision problems. In addition, the problem-solving methods of executives and entrepreneurs can be observed and lessons brought back to the academic environment, improving both teaching and academic research endeavours. Centres for agribusiness management have been established at a number of universities to advance this interaction. The offices of the Agribusiness Chamber of Commerce of South Africa are co-located with the centre, giving even more direct engagement between academics and industry.

Other strategies for increasing involvement include engaging food industry and agribusiness managers, executives and leaders from the public sector in classroom presentations and faculty seminars. Development and offering of postgraduate programmes and short courses aimed at executive development offers another avenue for faculties and institutions to reach out to the business and public sectors where their students will be employed. The process of planning and marketing successful programmes of this type will enhance understanding and help in the transformation of faculty thinking and priorities. The ideas generated in this way can then be incorporated into curricula designed for degree-seeking students as well.

Institutional reorganization and design

Perhaps the most dramatic of strategies involve the restructuring of entire universities. In the case of South Africa, a total reform was undertaken in response to the political and economic imperatives of the last decade. Declining enrolments and high overheads associated with traditional agricultural colleges and departments have also contributed to a sense of urgency in testing new structures, to the point where existing departments were abolished and a smaller number of new ones put in place. At the University of Pretoria, the concept of a new 'strong school' was adopted in 1999, with an enlarged Faculty of Natural and Agricultural Sciences including a few semi-autonomous schools, each with fewer departments and the flexibility to establish more involvement with its many constituencies among students, industry and society at large. A holistic, supply chain approach is encouraged across the entire faculty.

In India, where the liberalization of the domestic economy is now gaining momentum, the evolution of the many traditional agricultural economics programmes is less dramatic. Involvement of leaders of the increasingly free private sector food and agribusinesses will be a force towards change. Other institutes and universities offering business management degrees provide alternatives for employers looking for educated entry-level employees. As with the wide availability of general business education in the USA, business schools or institutes in India may play a role in forcing change in agricultural economics curricula and departments. The Indian Institute of Management, Ahmedabad (IIMA) uses case study teaching methods and organizes short courses for updating knowledge and skills of managers and food and agribusiness executives. The existence of alternative sources of education and training in business management, even where not explicitly a part of an agricultural university, provides an alternative for the private sector. Competitors can be powerful models for institutional reform.

In the USA many departments of agricultural economics are located in large universities where general business education is strongly established. Many agribusiness firms, especially those at the consumer packaged food end of the supply chain, look to business schools as their primary source of entry-level managers. In recognition of this, several agricultural economics departments have sought ways to develop formal joint degrees. At Texas A&M University,

university-level degrees in agribusiness, at both the baccalaureate and masters levels, are jointly offered through the cooperation of the College of Agriculture and Life Sciences and the College of Business Administration. These degree programmes, directed by an intercollegiate faculty of agribusiness, are designed to meet international business school accreditation standards. Most departments of agricultural economics in the USA have created specific agribusiness options in their degree programmes or entirely new programmes. This evolution follows clearly from the analysis of competitive degree programmes and seeks in various ways to combine the traditional strengths of applied economics found in the agricultural economics traditions with the specific business management, marketing and finance education offered in business schools.

In Europe, yet another set of choices is being addressed. The tradition of 'binary differentiation' exists in most European Union countries, where there are both university and applied sectors in higher education. In Germany, university-level degrees in agriculture have been heavily science-oriented and comprise a single stage leading to qualification for a PhD programme. More emphasis is being given to reorganization of higher education. Continuous analysis of relevant job markets is called for. Some German universities are introducing a 'two-stage scheme' leading to a shorter completion time for an undergraduate BSc degree, followed by a two-year graduate programme leading to an MSc degree. This is being strongly promoted by policy makers as an effort to make German higher education more internationally compatible and attractive. This trend is in line with the forces of integration within the EU which encourage the mobility of students so that they may be educated in a way that will provide a strong basis for employment in firms which are looking across all of Europe, and beyond, for markets and business opportunities. In such transitions of degree programmes, concerns still exist that emphasis on strong theoretical education not be lost as time in residence is reduced and new business subjects are introduced. Clearly this is a difficult balancing act, but the market for graduates and public funding for higher education will be forces that cannot be ignored.

Another approach is development of multi-institutional coordination so that students can move more efficiently among institutions to get broader educational experience. This is one of the purposes of looking at standardized BSc degrees in Europe. In the USA, similar discussions have developed as a means of maintaining viable programmes in the face of declining enrolment in some regions. This approach deserves more attention. The development and adaptation of distance learning technologies should enhance the possibility of success.

Improved information and analysis of employment markets

In contrast to the agricultural and food markets that economists analyse in the normal course of their work, little effort has been spent on analysis of the markets for graduates. One of the primary limitations found in all countries is the lack of consistent market data on current and potential fields of employment. In the USA, a tracking system of students enrolled in agricultural disciplines provides data on supply-side trends. Periodic estimates are made of demand for graduates from primary disciplines. However, the redesign of curricula in every country could benefit from much greater effort to track market changes. Market demand is changing rapidly, as revealed by periodic surveys of employers, but curricula are slow to change. A better estimate of supply and demand on a regular basis would provide guidance for altering programmes and should give some stimulus to proactive reallocation of teaching resources.

More flexibility in faculty development and structure

Most of the strategies discussed above need to be initiated by faculties. One of the major challenges over the next decade is to retrain current faculty members extensively and to replace a large cohort of senior faculty nearing retirement age. This aging faculty population is observed in nearly all countries. For those who are eligible, greater emphasis should be given to sabbatical programmes and other opportunities to gain knowledge in new subjects relevant to the emerging privatized, entrepreneurial economies. Techniques which incorporate more interactive approaches to the teaching environment must be learned, often through study and observation of successful faculties, programmes and institutions. Experience of work in an agribusiness firm can provide invaluable lessons for faculty to bring back to the classroom. Another trend may be towards the employment of more part-time faculty staff in non-tenured positions. For other disciplines this is a trend that is already well under way. Such flexibility would allow the institution to adapt more quickly to changing market demands. Combining appointments with industry consultancies could also enhance interactive relationships between industry and academia. Such approaches need to be carefully designed and managed to avoid losing the core academic focus of university programmes. Nonetheless, in order to make the transition to new teaching models, and respond to new employment opportunities, flexibility in faculty recruiting will be a necessity.

Challenges for the profession

While the goal is clear and strategies are understood, the will to change and the availability of resources remain as crucial limiting factors. There is a need for more leadership in the global professional organizations to cope with changing requirements of society for market-ready graduates.

- *More emphasis on education–employment partnerships*: better links through our professional organizations with industry leaders are needed to develop industry executive education and to bring ideas back to the degree curricula. Emphasis should be given to application of the tools of economic analysis to the emerging strategic business decision problems facing agriculture and food businesses.
- *A need to expand our interdisciplinary vision*: we need to focus more on the subject content of other social and behavioural sciences which are required to understand how information links to decision making.

- *Expansion of international dialogue on teaching and curricula*: a broader comparative discussion of agricultural economics education and training across national boundaries is imperative if we are to stay in tune with employers. Our graduates will be challenged to develop their career in a business environment that is truly global in terms of markets, production technologies and societal expectations.

A forum to address these needs exists within the international professional organizations to which agricultural economists belong. But these organizations should be challenged to go beyond passive support for such efforts, taking the lead in addressing them as well. Economic structures in agriculture are being driven by changing consumer demand, technologies of production, processing and distribution. Employers of our graduates know this. While universities play a primary role, disciplinary societies and professional associations must actively seek to guide and direct these changes if they, and their members, are to play a significant and long-lasting role in the institutions that survive and thrive in the 21st century.

PANEL REPORT: SUB-SAHARAN AFRICA: SAME OLD CHALLENGES
IN THE NEW MILLENNIUM – WIDESPREAD POVERTY,
ENVIRONMENTAL DEGRADATION AND SHRINKING
OPPORTUNITIES IN A GLOBALIZED MARKET

ORGANIZER AND CHAIRPERSON

Chris Ackello-Ogutu (ARCC, Nairobi, Kenya)

PANEL DISCUSSANTS

Brian D'Silva (USAID, REDSO/ESA, Nairobi, Kenya), Anthony Ikpi (Department of Agricultural Economics, University of Ibadan, Nigeria), Akinwumi Adesina (Rockefeller Foundation, Zimbabwe), Isaac Minde (ECAPAPE, Entebbe, Uganda), Willis Oluoch-Kosura (Department of Agricultural Economics, University of Nairobi, Kenya – moderator)

RAPPORTEUR

Protase N. Echessah (ARCC, Nairobi, Kenya)

The organizer began by highlighting the myriad problems experienced in sub-Saharan Africa, among them cross-border wars and civil conflicts, droughts, famine, widespread poverty, environmental degradation and floods. The following questions were posed to the participants: will the past misfortunes that have bedevilled the region continue in the new millennium and what are the opportunities for sub-Saharan Africa in the new millennium? A panel of four distinguished scholars led the discussions by sharing their experiences and lessons learnt from different parts of sub-Saharan Africa, with the moderator leading the discussion.

Conflict and food security in the Greater Horn of Africa (GHA): lessons from Southern Sudan

Donors' experience with the issues of conflict and food security in GHA were presented by Brian D'Silva who observed that the crisis in GHA is a result of instability arising from economic, political, agricultural and climatic conditions that merge into a 'confluence of instabilities'. A combination of political weaknesses and instability, stunted economic progress, and unreliable agricultural production in some areas, creates conditions that are conducive for conflict. He argues that conflict, in turn, aggravates these instabilities and feeds into the cycle of crises witnessed in the region. Using US Agency for International Development (USAID)'s experiences in the West Bank of Southern Sudan, he noted specific trouble areas that have been sources of conflict in the region. These have included the Nile waters, Sudanese oil and cross-border livestock movements exacerbated by increased variability in rainfall, access to modern weapons and issues of traditional access to grazing lands. These conflicts have threatened food security in terms of physical availability (through production and importation), stability of supplies (through storage), economic access to food (incomes) and food utilization (nutrition and health status).

As a result of these crises and conflicts, USAID and other donor agencies have spent billions of dollars in humanitarian aid (emergency food aid and disaster assistance – health, water and sanitation, food security and agricultural rehabilitation) and development assistance. Millions of people in the region are affected by conflict and hence are in need of humanitarian assistance, yet there is little hope that the civil strife and the ensuing crises will subside in the near future. Since the current levels of humanitarian assistance are unsustainable, it is imperative that the international community devises innovative approaches for responding to the region's needs.

USAID has used selective humanitarian interventions in areas where there is a likelihood of greater and long-term benefits to the population. This helps to reduce relief costs and buttress the coping mechanisms of the Sudanese as a means of averting famines or minimizing their severity. The strategy aimed at undertaking rehabilitation-oriented activities that do not fall under the conventional definition of emergency assistance.

The rehabilitation activities implemented since 1994 have included road rehabilitation and maintenance, agricultural rehabilitation, local grain purchase (to stimulate markets and encourage transition from relief dependence to market orientation), local production of seeds and tools (to substitute for imports), improving traditional grain storage methods and having farmers adopt them, use of indigenous knowledge (wild plants and the indigenous knowledge system surrounding their use, as a means of promoting both food security and health), support for local rehabilitation initiatives, and promotion of trade. Development assistance under the Sudan Transition and Rehabilitation (STAR) programme is being used to strengthen grassroots organizations working to solve rehabilitation problems and to provide training for the nascent civil administration in transparency, accountability, public finance and respect for human rights. These interventions have proved very effective.

The USAID experience in southern Sudan demonstrates not only the ability but also the value in implementing transition activities in stable and secure areas prior to the peace agreement. This approach should be considered when designing assistance strategies for other conflict-torn countries of sub-Saharan Africa.

Civil strife and conflict resolution: lessons from West Africa

Anthony Ikpi led the discussion focusing on the causes of civil strife and conflict resolution with examples from West African states. Four broad categories of the causes of civil strife are recognized: political disputes (power struggle), between or within nations, social/religious conflicts, economic problems (due to resource endowment) and natural disaster (drought, famine and floods). Examples of conflicts arising from exploitation of natural resources can be found in Nigeria (the Niger Delta), Sierra Leone, Liberia and the Democratic Republic of Congo, while those due to political or power struggle can be found in Liberia. Other causes of civil strife such as religious/social considerations include Sharia law as experienced in Nigeria and the 'Bakassi Boy Syndrome', whereby individuals assume the role of police because of the ineffectiveness of the police force. Related to the latter is a state of anarchy, symptomatic of unjust judicial systems. The cost of all types of civil strife includes loss of human lives, destruction of farmland and food, and waste of government resources.

In Nigeria, efforts towards resolution of civil strife have included military suppression, organizing stakeholder conferences and constituting inter-community peace committees. Another attempt has been made through the restoration of civil government and democratization efforts, which have made Nigeria safer today than one year ago. It is also important that the judiciary be granted the autonomy to execute its duties. With regard to the Niger Delta problem, a formula has been developed for a proportion of proceeds arising from exploitation of resources to be ploughed back into the area. Infrastructural issues, including pollution and the settlement of the displaced people, are also being addressed. Overall, it was observed that civil strife is best addressed using home-grown solutions.

Africa's food crisis: old questions, new challenges and opportunities

According to Akinwumi Adesina, the challenges facing agricultural research, extension and policy for the promotion of agricultural transformation in Africa are varied, as are the options for resolving them. Research and development investments are needed to sharpen the pace of food production, given the population growth rate. This has not been the case for a number of reasons, among them poor economic performance, general lack of appreciation for research, weak demand constituencies for research and decline in overseas development assistance. The other reasons are poor management and weak performance of many research institutions.

The way forward is to strengthen farmer organization for demand-driven research and, more importantly, stronger political leadership supportive of agricultural research. Owing to the lack of political vision, dedication and commitment to agricultural transformation, Africa has lost to the donors the central position on issues that affect agriculture. The future of agricultural research will also need to be pluralistic, encompassing the public sector, private sector, universities and non-governmental organizations (NGOs). The private sector will be the key as experience the world over indicates that the biotechnology revolution is largely in the private sector, unlike the 'Green Revolution' that was driven by the public sector. In addition, research institutions need to improve accountability to stakeholders and their evaluation should be on the extent to which they have developed technical innovations that can help farmers to achieve their production targets in different agroecological zones. Other measures would include improvement in research coordination for greater effectiveness and in avoidance of undue duplication of efforts; strengthening CGIAR centres in Africa, including an improvement of their links with the national research institutions; and strengthening human and institutional capacities. Last, but by no means least, is the development of flexible technologies for easier adaptation by farmers, making them agroecological zone-specific.

But these efforts alone cannot guarantee success: infrastructural issues have to be addressed and governments have to encourage increased investments in agriculture, growth of non-farm income sources and better access to complementary inputs like credit and extension systems. Integrated input, output and credit markets are important for assuring investments in productivity-enhancing technologies. Continued market reforms and market expansion (through regional initiatives) are also prerequisites. Finally, agricultural services have to be demand-driven, flexible, participatory and sustainable.

Regional trade issues in eastern and southern Africa

On trade issues in eastern and southern Africa, Isaac Minde made reference to the Regional Trade Analytical Agenda (RTAA) which covers the two subregions and which was initiated in 1994 with funding from USAID/Regional Economic Development Services Office for East and Southern Africa (REDSO/ ESA). The agenda estimated informal cross-border trade (ICBT) and how that form of trade contributes to regional food security. It also analysed agricultural comparative advantage for seven countries in southern Africa as well as costs of transport along the major transit routes in the region. Results and lessons learnt from the regional trade component of the RTAA are summarized below. The ICBT border surveys revealed the following:

- this form of trade, at over US$600 million annually, with the bulk of it involving agricultural commodities, was significant, thus dispelling the view that the countries in the region have little potential to trade with each other;
- informal trade channels were used, even in cases where official tariffs were low or non-existent, implying existence of non-tariff barriers that consumed valuable time but did not necessarily lead to any significant cost increases for traders;
- traded commodities (such as unprocessed fish and grains) were of low value-added quality;
- informal trade contributed to food security (especially for border communities) and unofficial transactions were maintained even in cases of

official market failure caused, for example, by droughts, civil strife and legislated border closure or import/export bans;

- the direction of informal trade flows did not always reflect the underlying comparative advantage in production but, rather, supply availability and other factors such as information, capital, storage and infrastructure that influenced competitive advantage (for example, agricultural commodity flows between Mozambique and South Africa);
- all forms of cross-border trade were depressed in cases where road networks did not exist or were underdeveloped (as in the case of Tanzania and Uganda or Mozambique and Tanzania);
- there were serious weaknesses in institutional capacity, especially with regard to policy analysis and implementation of market reforms. These weaknesses have far-reaching consequences for the region's ability to take advantage of globalization and capacity to bargain/lobby effectively with industrialized countries (or their trading blocs such as the EU) and at the WTO platforms.

The ICBT follow-up work that aimed principally at in-depth analysis of the institutional and fiscal implications of regional integration (for example, who loses and who gains from trade liberalization as well as the question of safety nets) revealed extremely important points that should be taken into account when one is contemplating external intervention aimed at influencing trade policies in the sub-Saharan region.

- Losses from trade liberalization are quite significant for countries with a narrow tax base and do constitute a major obstacle to implementation of zero tariffs advocated under Free Trade Areas (FTAs).
- Sub-Sahara is characterized by frequent market failure that typically originates from natural resource use conflicts that often lead to full-blown wars. Market failure also arises from natural disasters (for example, the ravages of *El Niño* and, recently, the devastating floods in Mozambique), inappropriate policies and poor governance.
- If markets do not function, it would be reckless on the part of policy analysis to recommend unbridled trade liberalization unequivocally. Uganda for example argues, rather convincingly, that opening of its borders will open the flood gates for Kenya's manufactured products and thus kill the country's infant industries, lead to job losses, jeopardize food security and even fuel civil disobedience. As much as this argument may be one-sided (only considering the immediate costs of industrial adjustment that in any case have to be paid), trade policy intervention has to be cognizant of the serious political innuendoes it reveals.
- Preoccupation with national food security (taken literally to mean food self-sufficiency) was seriously hampering regional integration efforts. The issue of food security has to be tackled jointly with that of widespread poverty that generally has an adverse impact on agricultural productivity, household incomes and purchasing power, but also more

specifically on access to food. National parochialism and protectionist trade policies have been the consequence of these concerns and many stakeholders are worried that the many regional trade blocs being created in the sub-Sahara region may have a bleak future.

Concluding remarks

The mini-symposium was concluded with calls for political commitment to develop effective institutions, policies and infrastructure that will spur technological change in sub-Saharan Africa. Selective interventions in conflict-prone pockets of the region have been shown to yield encouraging results, and solutions to the conflicts must be home-grown. The mini-symposium called for the appreciation of the complexity of the agricultural and rural development process. The importance of involving the participation of all legitimate stakeholder groups in the process of implementing and sustaining market, institutional and political reforms was emphasized.

PANEL REPORT: POLITICAL ECONOMY OF AGRICULTURAL
REFORMS IN CENTRAL AND EASTERN EUROPE

ORGANIZER, CHAIRPERSON AND RAPPORTEUR

Klaus Frohberg (Institute of Agricultural Development in Central and Eastern Europe (IAMO), Halle/S, Germany)

PANEL DISCUSSANTS

Johann Swinnen (Catholic University of Louvain, Belgium), Eugenia Serova (Institute of Economy in Transition, Analytical Centre AFE, Moscow, Russia), Tibor Ferenczi (Budapest University of Economics Sciences, Hungary), Ewa Rabinowicz (Swedish Institute for Food and Agricultural Economics, Lund, Sweden), Stefan Tangermann (Georg-August-Universität Göttingen, Germany).

The panel discussion began by looking at aspects of transition (Swinnen, Serova and Ferenczi) before moving on to the particular problems of enlargement of the European Union as it will affect some of the countries of central and eastern Europe (Rabinowicz and Tangermann).

Johann Swinnen compared agricultural reforms in the acceding countries and member states of the Commonwealth of Independent States. He explained that initial conditions, the way land and the agricultural capital stock were privatized, agricultural policies and macroeconomic conditions explain a large part of the differences found in the performance of agriculture in transition countries. There is a fuller report of this material in a conference plenary paper (see above).

In similar vein, Eugenia Serova, also the author of a plenary paper, provided further insights into the evolution of Russia's reforms in agriculture and the food industry. She emphasized that Russia moves slowly forward on the path of agrarian reform but with its own special trajectory. Important historical factors include the fact that Russian peasant households almost never owned much land. When serfdom was abolished in 1861, ownership was transferred from landlords to the communes. In the first decade of the 20th century, Prime Minister Stolypin tried to implement an ambitious land reform, introducing individual property rights, but it was halted by the revolution. In the 1920s, during the New Economic Policy, there was a brief period when peasants enjoyed the full user rights for lands but this period was confined to five or six years. Lack of a landholding tradition was reinforced by the collectivization implemented in the 1930s. Since that time, three or four generations have lived in the *kolkhoz* system. This affected the mental make-up of rural populations as well as making land restitution in the countryside impossible.

In addition to the resistance to change, there are also geographical barriers. Owing to the huge area of the country, a very specific hierarchical system of administration evolved. As a result of this, the impact of any reform process decided on in the centre of power is reduced when it has to pass from one administrative level down to another one. At the lowest end, the impact is hardly felt. In addition, Russia consists of a huge number of nationalities with their own traditions, customs, attitudes towards land tenure and ways of farming. That explains the diversity of approaches in agrarian reforms in various parts of the country. It is also aggravated by the federal structure of the country. In accordance with Russia's constitution, land tenure is regulated by both federal and regional legislation. Since the various legislative bodies quite often pass laws which contradict each other, the process of agrarian reforms leads to much frustration.

It was never going to be easy to alter a sector with so complex a legacy, and so it is proving. However, to reinforce Swinnen's point about initial conditions, attention then turned to the political economy of agricultural reforms in Hungary, explained by Tibor Ferenczi. For decades Hungarian agriculture was considered to be efficient by comparison with other communist countries. This general view made it difficult to understand the policy objectives of transformation. Why should the sector be transformed and how should it be done?

Emerging political parties before the democratic elections in 1990 proposed two completely different approaches on farm restructuring. The Independent Smallholder Party wanted to accomplish two main objectives: first, to 'restitute' the land according to the ownership structure of 1947, the year before collectivization attempts started; second, to eliminate all collective and most state farms. All the other parties recognized the right for individuals to farm on their own account, but did not want to institutionalize the demolishing of the structures found then. The Independent Smallholder Party joined the governing coalition, which nominally accepted its policy but actually pursued a compromise in which nobody was satisfied. The main controversial issues for debate were land fragmentation and separation of land ownership from agricultural production. Land was distributed in three main parts: in a compensation process to individuals, to members of collective farms on their land titles, and to landless members and employees of collective farms and state farms. Following the compensation process and land restructuring, about 90 per cent of land is owned by individuals, with the rest remaining in the possession of the state. Joint stock companies and production cooperatives can only lease land from individuals (and from the state). The end result was that, by 1995, the area of individual holdings expanded, approaching half of the total, and later went above that figure. Other 'owners' still farm as cooperatives (though the area involved is now down to about 17 per cent of the total) or company shareholders.

The restructured sector now faces the challenge of accession to the European Union and the threat of competition in the enlarged market, with very uncertain rules of the game. This is a matter both of how price levels will be affected and of whether the principle of financial solidarity will apply to new member countries. It is very largely a debate about eligibility for 'direct payments', of the type introduced in the European Union in its 1992 'reform'. These were designed to compensate farmers (particularly grain producers) for reductions in supported selling prices. Farmers in the new member countries fear discrimination if they join a single market. They lack capital in the emerging structures, and such discrimination would weaken their ability to compete even for their domestic markets.

At this stage the panel turned to adjustments to be made in the Common Agricultural Policy (CAP) arising from the eastern enlargement. Ewa Rabinowicz stated that everyone is very well aware of the unfortunate consequences which the application of the CAP, as it is now, would have for the CEECs. One of the most central issues here is the eligibility of the CEECs for direct payments. All of them have demanded full participation in the CAP from day one. However, there is no money. In the financial perspective (budget) agreed in Berlin in 2000, provisions are not made for (compensatory) direct payments (DP) to the CEECs. The EU budget is annual. Hence possible savings arising from postponement of the accession cannot be rolled over.

One solution could be for the acceding countries to join, without their farmers receiving direct payments, in the belief that there would be general benefits from enlargement. But this is extremely unlikely. Taking Poland as a case in point, the large rural constituency (40 per cent of the population), being aware of the existence of direct payments, would never vote 'yes' in a referendum if farmers were denied equal treatment. It would also be difficult simply to add more money to the budget. The willingness of EU member states to contribute to common financing is low and even more pronounced in agriculture, where the legitimacy of the CAP is fading.

If any sort of compromise is possible it might lie in reduction and/or renationalization of compensation payments, while increasing funds available for rural development and environmental support. There are some signs that the CAP could move in this direction. The unequal distribution of direct payments is striking, while large farmers who are the main beneficiaries are not a politically strong group, especially in a Europe dominated by left-of centre governments. Environmental and rural groups are gaining momentum and might well form an alliance with small and middle-size farmers (who receive less from direct payments) to back a redirection of support mechanisms. In effect, the problem of dealing with the financing of enlargement could lie 'outside' the CEECs and within the existing EU.

The discussion turned finally to the potential contributions of Western countries in supporting the transition process. Stefan Tangermann elaborated on this topic. He began by asserting that Western countries wanted, and still want, to support the transition process in the countries in Central and Eastern Europe for clear-cut foreign policy reasons, but also for ideological reasons. The EU responded quickly, originally with Co-operation Agreements, but then with Europe Agreements (EAs), opening up the way towards membership of the EU for some countries. The first EAs, with Hungary and Poland, were signed as early as December 1991, soon after the process of transformation had started. These agreements provided for a gradual movement towards free trade in most sectors (it was 'asymmetric', in that CEECs could delay liberalization of their imports); for free movement of services, investment and, to some extent, of workers; and for a political dialogue (through association councils, association committees and joint parliamentary committees). Most importantly, the EAs explicitly opened up the possibility for the CEECs to become members of the EU at some stage. Accession negotiations are now proceeding.

Other Western countries also made efforts to integrate the CEECs fully into the Western world, thereby also supporting the process of political transformation. The steps taken included the offer of membership in NATO, preparations for WTO membership and support provided by the IMF. Support for transformation also came in very practical form, through instruments such as technical and financial assistance, for example provided by the EU through the PHARE programme. Some assistance may have been wasted because of a lack of experience in how best to foster the unprecedented process of transformation. Overall, however, it is probably fair to say that support provided by the Western countries was successful.

When it came to agriculture, the EU (on which these comments will concentrate) was in two minds. It was happy and quick to provide support for institutional development and structural improvement. The SAPARD programme has the potential of becoming an important element of that type of help. When it came to fostering the development of agricultural markets in the CEECs, though, the EU response can best be described as equivocal. Some preferential access to EU agricultural markets was provided, though it was mostly constrained to limited quantities. At the same time, however, the EU continued to ship agricultural exports, with heavy export subsidies, both to domestic markets in the CEECs and to third country markets in which there was EU/CEEC competition (including markets in the region of the former Soviet Union). Continued export subsidization by the EU was deplored by the CEECs.

Partly in response to such criticism, the EU has started to negotiate 'double zero' agreements under which the CEECs promise to allow for duty-free treatment of certain agricultural imports from the EU, while in exchange the EU promises not to grant export subsidies on its corresponding exports to the CEECs. These 'double zero' agreements are an interesting example of the strange economic consequences that response to political economy factors can have. The political attractiveness of this type of arrangement for the CEEC governments is that their farmers can no longer complain about their domestic markets being eroded by EU export subsidies. However, in economic terms, the elimination of EU export subsidies, in exchange for tariff elimination, means that the CEECs as nations now pay higher prices for agricultural imports that they continue to buy anyhow from the EU. This type of arrangement is analogous to a food consumer who goes to his food store and suggests that the shopkeeper should sell him food at double the normal price, because otherwise he tends to eat too much! For the shopkeeper, this arrangement would certainly be attractive – as it is to the EU, which now no longer needs to pay export subsidies on some exports to the CEECs. However, they suffer a terms of trade loss, and CEEC governments forgo tariff revenue. Indeed, it is possible that the losses will be as great as the financial assistance under SAPARD.

Such can be the undesirable economic consequences of arrangements that look attractive, to both sides involved, from a political economy perspective. Under the heading of 'preparations for EU membership', agreements are concluded that result in economic losses for the CEECs. If EU membership were to come soon, this would probably not be too disastrous. However, unfortunately it is still not clear when the first round of accession will take place. If the EU really wanted to support political and economic transformation in the CEECs to the maximum extent possible, it would make sure that accession happens soon.

DISCUSSION GROUP AND MINI-SYMPOSIUM REPORTS

INTRODUCTION*

The 2000 Berlin Conference continued the long tradition of having organized discussion groups as part of the programme, in fact for the 15th occasion. Typically each group had an organizer and rapporteur, while in some cases consultants served as catalysts for the discussion or made short formal presentations. Following the precedent set in Tokyo in 1991, mini-symposia also appeared. In that increasingly popular format, short papers are presented around which discussion can be structured. Symposia have become increasingly prominent in comparison with groups in recent conferences and were dominant in Berlin.

Meetings were for three sessions for a total of four hours. Conference participants were encouraged to stay with the same topic for all of the sessions to facilitate depth and continuity in the proceedings. Interest was widespread, many of the papers were of high quality and discussion was often spirited. A conservative estimate put the number of participants at 530. The final list includes 28 sessions for which short summaries are presented. A report of the meetings to honour the work of Professor Carl Eicher, originally intended as a mini-symposium, is included even though they occupied a rather longer time span. Titles used for each group are listed first, according to subject matter, under the four themes defining the Conference plenary sessions. The detailed reports then follow.

MOVING TOWARDS A GLOBAL AGRICULTURAL ECONOMY

Discussion group

GMOs and NTBs: trade and biosafety policy after the Cartagena protocol.

Mini-symposia

Food and agricultural sectors in developing countries: what do they have to gain or lose in trade negotiations?

The MERCOSUR, agribusiness and the new millennium.

Structural adjustments in the European Union and United States dairy industries: farm management implications.

*Herbert H. Stoevener (USA) was programme organizer for the discussion groups and mini-symposia and collated the reports. Judith Peters contributed to the editorial work.

635

Cotton and textile production in the global trading system: where does Africa stand?

IMPROVED MARKET INCENTIVES AND INSTITUTIONS

Discussion group

Analysing policy delivery systems.

Mini-symposia

Impact of policy reform on the well-being of vulnerable groups: evidence from the USA, Zimbabwe and Kenya.

New investment theory in agricultural economics: its implications for farm management, environmental policy and development.

Institution sequencing and timing in transition economies.

Building financial markets in developing countries for tomorrow's agriculture: status, reforms and innovations.

Reform and future of national agricultural statistics systems.

Improving land access and asset ownership by the poor through land reform: empirical evidence and policy implications.

Strengthening human and institutional capital to support rural development in Africa: what have we learned and what are the challenges? A symposium in honour of Professor Carl K. Eicher.

Performance of the non-viable farm sector in rural economies of agro-based developing countries.

Risk and agricultural input use: analysis and mitigation.

New and innovative instruments to manage rural risks.

How do farmers find their way in the new food system in transition economies?

AGRICULTURAL RESEARCH AND DEVELOPMENT POLICY

Discussion group

Genetically modified crops: the food industry, producers, consumers and environmentalists.

Mini-symposia

Biotechnology innovation and the private sector.

Crop genetic diversity in modern production systems: efficiency and policy implications.

Current and emerging issues in agricultural and rural development.

Agricultural research policy in an era of privatization.

MAKING AGRICULTURE ENVIRONMENTALLY SAFE

Mini-symposia

Dynamism of agricultural systems and rural communities in South Asia: from vulnerability to sustainability.

Integrating approaches for natural resource management and policy analysis: bioeconomic models, multi-agent systems and cellular automata.

Agriculture's provision of positive amenities: supply, demand and the role for government.

The economics and policy of organic farming: what can be learned from the European experience?

Economics of food safety.

Effects of health information on the demand for food: EU and US experiences.

GMOS AND NTBS: TRADE AND BIOSAFETY POLICY AFTER THE CARTAGENA PROTOCOL

ORGANIZERS   JIMMYE HILLMAN AND GEORGE FRISVOLD (USA)

RAPPORTEUR   KEVIN INGRAM (USA)

The group addressed policy issues concerning the management and trade of genetically modified organisms (GMOs) since the signing of the Biosafety Protocol. Their rapid development and adoption in agriculture has increased demands for regulation and oversight. However, problems exist in developing effective, efficient and acceptable regulations. The technology is novel, hence uncertainties exist about risks to consumers, the agricultural sector and the environment. The inability of current regulatory mechanisms in international trade and environmental agreements (for example, WTO and the Biosafety Protocol) to address concerns about GMOs has led to an impasse in the trade of grains, foods and fibre products in which they are contained. The principal difficulties in reaching an agreement include (a) inherent problems in harmonizing regulatory standards across countries, (b) political economy constraints arising from the potential impact of GMO products on comparative advantages in trade, (c) issues related to intellectual property rights (IPR) (that is, technology ownership and control) and the distribution of benefits resulting from GMO products, and (d) competing priorities between international agreements governing trade competition and environmental, consumer and agronomic protection.

Jimmye Hillman, as chairman, described the similarities between today's GMO debates and earlier discussions of trade. He noted that 40 years ago, at IAAE meetings, trade debates focused on the newly coined phrase 'non-tariff trade barriers' (NTBs). Hillman also distributed and briefly outlined a paper co-authored with George Frisvold entitled 'Genetically Modified Organisms and Non-Tariff Trade Barriers: Trade and Biosafety Policy after the Cartagena Protocol'. It described the evolution of the GMO debate and examined how the regulatory impasse has emerged. They considered the role played by the countervailing influences of the WTO Agreements, viz. the new Sanitary and Phytosanitary (SPS) Agreement and revised Technical Barriers to Trade (TBT) Agreement, and the Cartagena Protocol on Biosafety. The paper also discussed other key aspects of the GMO trade controversy, including IPR, the increasing private sector role in plant breeding and seed distribution, and the potential impact of GMOs on crop genetic diversity.

Donna Roberts (USA) next offered a detailed description, with reference to the Frisvold and Hillman paper, of the evolution of GMO debates in Geneva over the past five years. She agreed with the authors' identification of two major themes, namely NTB issues about the extent to which regulatory measures are intended to manage risk and protect against economic competition, and concerns about the control and ownership of GMOs, including the distribution of benefits from the new technology. According to Roberts, the initial debates, after the signing of the Uruguay Round of the WTO in 1995, were informal as governments reviewed their existing regulatory regimes for compatibility with the agreement. Formal discussion began in 1998 after the EU notified the TBT committee of a proposal for mandatory labelling of GM products and other countries gave their responses. These and subsequent events led to an impasse in public policy debates and in GMO-related trade. The limited capacity of the WTO Agreements and the Cartagena Protocol on Biosafety to deal effectively with both environmental and trade-related aspects of GMOs, as well as the competing nature of the agreements, were responsible. She also suggested that an overreliance on jargon in the GMO trade debates continues to stifle the inclusion of trade-off concepts. She noted how 'sound bites' (for example, 'sound-science', 'precautionary') flavour the discussion and stressed the difficulty of handling risk assessment against such a background. Other points made during this session related to the difficulty of sustaining an economic argument against labelling and to the importance of the labelling regime (that is, voluntary versus involuntary) for designing policy.

In the second session Timothy Josling (USA) commented on the implications of the Trade Related Aspects of Intellectual Property Rights (TRIPS) agreement as a framework obliging WTO members to establish certain standards for protecting property rights. He suggested that such agreements, coupled with litigation protecting IPR, might have the unintentional impact of creating barriers against entry to agricultural biotechnology development. This could shift responsibility for development from the public to the private sector, leading to the development of technology that might not be socially optimal. Josling described how the results have been very different industrial structures for 'red' (human/medical) and 'green' (agricultural) biotechnology. Numerous small firms, engaged in strategic alliances with major firms who supply capital, are found in 'red' biotechnology. In contrast, fewer, larger, firms dominate the 'green' sector and a higher degree of vertical integration has occurred. Josling's discussion then focused on how industrial structure influences technological development (for example, the crops selected), the distribution of innovations and benefits on a global scale, market concentration and power, and comparative advantage.

In the final session, David Harvey (UK) weighed the difficulties confronting economists interested in designing GMO trade and regulatory policy, noting that GMO technology could shift production functions and consumer preferences simultaneously, thus substantially complicating conventional welfare analysis. He also stressed the importance of full information for markets to work effectively; without it they could 'fail'.

Harvey further explained that imperfect information affects the GMO issue in two conceptually separate ways. Firstly, consumer and producer information is filtered through 'context, circumstance, character and culture' and the same material can be interpreted in quite different ways. The traditional economic recipe – increased competition – does not necessarily overcome this information failure. Secondly, the appearance of the GMO itself is 'new information'. Restriction of access to its use (entailed in private firms claiming property rights) amounts to a market failure, supposedly justified as a second-best way of dealing with the problem of generation and provision of the information in the first place. Harvey suggested that much of the popular opposition to GM stems from concern over private monopolization of the technology, and perceptions of the distribution of the benefits and costs. Rights to 'rent collection' need to be balanced with responsibilities for the socially desirable use of scarce resources.

FOOD AND AGRICULTURAL SECTORS IN DEVELOPING
COUNTRIES: WHAT DO THEY HAVE TO GAIN OR LOSE IN TRADE
NEGOTIATIONS?

ORGANIZER   JOHN G. STOVALL (USA)

RAPPORTEUR   JOHAN SWINNEN (BELGIUM)

Historically, developing countries have played a passive or reactive role in
multilateral trade negotiations. Rich countries, mainly the USA, Japan and the
EU, set the agenda and agreed terms, and the smaller and developing countries
followed their lead. As the recent Seattle WTO ministerial meeting made clear,
the system no longer works in that way. The dynamics of trade negotiations
have clearly changed in favour of developing countries and smaller economies.

The mini-symposium examined these issues more fully to bring about a
better understanding of the legitimate interests of developing countries and to
enlighten the policy-making process. It was organized around two themes. The
first, on the current status of international efforts to liberalize trade in agricultural products, was led by Tim Josling (Stanford University). The second,
centred on strategies for developing countries in trade negotiations, drew on
presentations by Kym Anderson (University of Adelaide) and Ashok Gulati
(Institute of Economic Growth, New Delhi).

Status and prospects for trade negotiations

Josling explained that the talks on agriculture were delayed but not directly
affected by the failure to reach agreement in Seattle. Several position papers
have now been submitted and much information is available. The key question
has changed from whether agriculture should be treated the same way as other
sectors, as it was prior to the Uruguay Round Agreement on Agriculture
(URAA), to whether agricultural reform should be implemented at the same
rate in all countries. The core issues of market access, aggregate support and
export subsidies remain important, though several additional ones are under
consideration. Developing countries (DCs) have expressed interest in 'special
differential treatment', although definition of the concept is unclear. Dealing
with food security in the WTO also raises problems. One other suggestion is
the launch of a 'development box' which such countries could use without
being challenged. However, 'developing countries' are a very heterogeneous
group both in terms of comparative advantage for exports and in relation to
current access to rich country markets through preferential agreements. This
affects their position and preferences on a variety of WTO issues.

The question of the advantages accruing to developing countries from the URAA was raised in discussion since it often appears that the balance lies with the developed world. Tim Josling argued for the establishment of favourable legislation to counteract the general view that DCs were disadvantaged by weak institutions and lack of skills in negotiation and analysis. Various ways forward were discussed, though it became clear that there is no miracle solution. The best that can be done is to proceed with negotiations but to back up the process by supporting stronger institutional backing both 'in Geneva and at home'. It might also be advantageous for developing countries (and especially the smaller ones) to negotiate collectively. This is happening to some extent, through joint tabling of papers and as a result of some countries integrating with the Cairns group. However, diversity remains as a continuing obstacle to collective action.

Strategies for developing countries

Kym Anderson emphasized that traditional issues in the WTO remain very important and that agriculture is now the most trade-distorted of all sectors, with very significant costs. On the basis of modelling analysis, he argued that developing countries would experience huge gains from further liberalization, though most of them had applied for, and received, very high bound tariff rates in the WTO. Banning export subsidies and tariff rate quotas (TRQs) should be a key objective. In his view the least developed would make a grave error in accepting the current proposal for free access, because it would undermine the bargaining position of the whole group without giving any substantial gains. But he did not want them to follow a protectionist path; it was something which should be avoided, particularly in some notable cases including that of China.

Ashok Gulati argued that most models underestimated the gains from trade for developing countries, but he also stressed that there are strong political and economic constraints in removing trade barriers within them. Food importers would need compensation, while transparency and a 'level playing field' would be required for lower trade barriers to be acceptable anywhere. He also warned of a proliferation of WTO boxes, such as a new 'development box' or a 'multifunctionality box'. This would merely further complicate negotiations and trade itself and have an undesirable effect. Instead he proposed that everything (including the existing 'green box') should be put into a single category and be made subject to a simple 'cap' on total support.

THE MERCOSUR, AGRIBUSINESS AND THE NEW MILLENNIUM

ORGANIZER　　LÉO DA ROCHA FERREIRA (BRAZIL)

RAPPORTEUR　　YONY SAMPAIO (BRAZIL)

MERCOSUR is an ambitious project of social, economic and cultural integration among six Latin American countries (Argentina, Brazil, Paraguay, Uruguay and, more recently, Bolivia and Chile). Established in 1991, it succeeds previous attempts at integration, such as ALALC (Latin American Free Trade Association) and ALADI (Latin American Association for Integration) and has shown some promising results in promoting regional trade and development.

International trade between member countries and between MERCOSUR and the rest of the world is limited to a relatively small group of commodities. There are also differences in size, population, market structure and stage of development among the members, suggesting that Argentina, Brazil and probably Chile will tend to play a leading role in the integration process, while Uruguay, Paraguay and Bolivia will lag behind. In this context, the search for adjustment and for equivalent and consistent macroeconomic policies is crucial for the eventual consolidation of MERCOSUR.

A paper from Paulo Araujo (written with G.E. Schuh and Alexandre C. Nicolella) provided macroeconomic data to illustrate the diversity of the economies in the region and considered some general characteristics of agriculture, with emphasis on Argentina and Brazil, which had the largest sectors. A major underlying theme of the paper is that agriculture may be a strategic sector for the consolidation and success of the MERCOSUR agreement. But stress was caused two years ago by the sudden devaluation of the Brazilian currency (the 'real'). Argentina has had an overvalued currency for a number of years owing to the linkage of the peso to the United States dollar and the attempt to 'dollarize' its economy. Fear of inflation has led to the continued use of this mechanism to force efficiency into the domestic economy, leading to political difficulties and painful adjustment problems for the labour force. The problems were exacerbated when Brazil devalued its currency by approximately 50 per cent, thus making the economy much more competitive relative to that of Argentina. The car industry became the centre of controversy, but Brazil's growing competitive edge in the international market for beef can be cited as another area of tension.

On the surface there appears to be ample room for a division of labour and specialization among the member countries of MERCOSUR. It is interesting to guess what trade patterns there would be if the members were pursuing flexible exchange rates. Argentina, for example, could become a substantial exporter of maize to Brazil. But Brazil should have a competitive edge in tropical crops, and possibly soybeans and livestock, while Argentina and Uruguay should have an advantage in temperate zone crops such as wheat, fruits and vegetables, and livestock. In fact, the emerging trade flows are consistent with these relative comparative advantages. Externally, there will be competition for third country markets for beef. All in all, the agricultural sectors of the member countries will have an important role to play in fostering the success of MERCOSUR. There should be widespread gains since all of them have some comparative advantage in the various primary crops, in livestock production and in processing. This remains the case despite the structural and institutional problems of the individual sectors.

Argentina has on several occasions suggested the dollarization of all the countries in the agreement, or the creation of an independent common currency. Although that might alleviate some of Argentina's adjustment problems in the short term, it is not likely to be a successful policy in the longer run. There are huge regional disparities in per capita incomes and in level of development within the countries of the region. Without flexible currencies to facilitate the adjustment process, internal political problems can hardly be avoided. The management of currencies is a hotly debated subject, evidenced by the lively exchanges in the symposium meetings.

The other factor that shapes competitiveness in the international agricultural economy, investment in research, is difficult to analyse without more primary data. Both Argentina and Brazil have vital agricultural research systems, and although support for both has declined in recent years, both are still very productive. Brazil, unlike Argentina, Paraguay, Bolivia and Uruguay, has the advantage of having vital PhD programmes to train its own agricultural scientists. That could eventually give Brazil a sustainable competitive edge, unless there is extensive investment in agricultural research by the private sector or a flow of new technology into the other countries from abroad.

Erly Cardoso Teixeira briefly described the results of a general equilibrium model for Argentina, Brazil and Chile. Lack of data resulted in the exclusion of Bolivia, Paraguay and Uruguay. The major conclusions of the study were that Brazil would experience a moderate rate of economic growth and might face a deficit in agricultural commodities markets such as wheat and maize.

STRUCTURAL ADJUSTMENTS IN THE EUROPEAN UNION AND UNITED STATES DAIRY INDUSTRIES: FARM MANAGEMENT IMPLICATIONS

ORGANIZER   STEPHEN HARSH (USA)

RAPPORTEUR   RUUD HUIRNE (THE NETHERLANDS)

The dairy industry in industrialized countries is rapidly undergoing a transformation. In both the United States (USA) and the European Union (EU), the number of farms is declining. Others are facing tighter profit margins and a consolidation of marketing channels. The structural change is due to new developments in production technologies (including biotechnology and computer-based control systems) and the increasing influence of world markets (leading to greater price instability and problems in market access).

Against this background, presentations were given by F. Kuhlmann (Germany) and S. Harsh (USA) on the cost structure and appropriate efficiency measures for German and US producers. Kuhlmann presented trends on production, costs and returns from a modest-sized dairy enterprise on a research farm at Marienborn. Production has increased, while prices received have steadily declined, the overall effect being a reduction in the production cost of a kilogram of milk. Nevertheless, current return over variable costs is positive, but when also accounting for fixed costs the returns are slightly negative. Kuhlmann also presented financial results from 13 corporate farms, located in the former East Germany, that were large by European standards. The farms had cost structures that were very similar to those at Marienborn and, on average, also incurred negative returns over total cost. Expanding on the discussion, colleagues from the National Dairy Research Institute at Braunschweig (Germany) presented results based on international comparisons, using different assumptions regarding the size of business and technology employed.

Harsh presented profitability and efficiency information on US farms. He contrasted the cost and return figures for large integrated cropping with dairy farms in Michigan with dairy enterprises of modest size, finding that expenses varied by category between the two groups although the overall profitability was very similar when adjusted for operator supplied capital and labour. Harsh had also prepared a comparison of farms involved in a detailed cost accounting project. This suggested that well-managed farms can cover all costs, despite the difficulties caused by a recent drop in milk prices, but poorer management inevitably results in losses.

Identifying the type of operation that will be able to survive in this changing environment for both areas formed the basis of the subsequent discussion.

Considering growth as a means used to enhance competitiveness, G. Hadley (USA) reported on his examination of large commercial dairy farms in Michigan and Wisconsin, where herd size had often doubled with farms becoming more specialized. The changes had enabled farms to maintain production and reduce the per kilogram cost of labour. The drawbacks were personnel management problems and public relations difficulties connected with waste disposal and contagious herd diseases. Farm profitability (measured by the percentage return on assets and the return on equity) for the first two years following expansion increased slightly over previous periods. Expansion appears to improve dairy farm viability and increase competitiveness. Expansion as a means to remain competitive in the EU was also discussed. However, the quota system has a tendency to limit growth opportunities. The problems related to expansion in the EU are very similar to those experienced in the USA, particularly those related to human resources management.

In the final presentation, C. Wolf (USA) dealt with risk and uncertainty associated with the recent structural changes. He indicated that American dairy farms have been growing and becoming more specialized for many years, though the past decade has witnessed an acceleration of the trend. Factors behind the change are prices (milk and feed), economies of size, demand changes, and cooperative and processor consolidation. Milk prices have been volatile in the 1990s as the government support price has been below market equilibrium. At the same time, feed prices have been low, allowing farmers to specialize in milk with little risk on the input side. Technology at the farm and processor level has allowed much larger firms to take advantage of spreading fixed costs across many units. A dramatic increase in per capita consumption of cheese has seen processor growth, with consolidation in a few large firms. Producer cooperatives have often merged to offset processor market power. Futures markets have sprung up as a potential method to offset milk price risk. Vertical coordination through contracting and outsourcing are also increasingly common risk management strategies. R. Huirne (The Netherlands) noted that EU producers are also experiencing more volatility in prices. However, they have had less experience in dealing with risk and uncertainty issues and are seeking advice and guidance.

COTTON AND TEXTILE PRODUCTION IN THE GLOBAL TRADING SYSTEM: WHERE DOES AFRICA STAND?

ORGANIZER AND RAPPORTEUR   MADELEINE GAUTHIER (USA)

In the current era of globalization a healthy, export-oriented textile and clothing sector can be a powerful engine of growth and development for poor countries, who should have a comparative advantage in labour-intensive manufacturing industries. While several African countries are significant cotton producers, most of their exports are in the form of raw fibre and the textile industry has remained relatively small. This is a puzzling outcome given (a) the availability of the raw material, (b) preferential access to the lucrative European Union market through the Lomé convention, and (c) a global relocation of textile mills from industrialized to developing (lower-wage) countries. It suggests that factors other than trade barriers have constrained expansion. The symposium sought to explore the role played by domestic policies (or lack thereof), market imperfections, relative factor endowment and institutions on cotton exports and the development of the textile and clothing industry. The participants were Philip Abbott (USA), John Baffes (USA), Madeleine Gauthier (USA), William Masters (USA), Joshua Nyoni (Zimbabwe), Eckhard Siggel (USA), Christopher L. Delgado (USA), Simeon Ehui (Ethiopia) and Shahla Shapouri (USA).

Cotton is interesting from the point of view of trade, economic development and policy analysis. It is one of the few crops that is economically significant in both developing and developed countries. It is also an important cash crop for millions of small farmers throughout the world, with government intervention being prominent, to meet various objectives, in almost every producing country. Cotton policies take in a range of price or border interventions to support producers' income, or of taxes to raise government revenue or support domestic textile industries.

Cotton is extremely important in Africa, particularly in Francophone West Africa. Intervention has mostly been through the monopoly power granted to marketing parastatals and export agencies. Most countries, however, have now implemented reforms as result of structural adjustment programmes, although with varying success.

There is a close linkage between cotton production and downstream processing activities. The quality and quantity of production directly affects the performance of the ginning sector, though state intervention to support the textile and clothing industry tends to be detrimental to the performance of cotton production. Support should only take the form of a direct transfer, supply-neutral policy. Because of the particular requirements of cotton production, with new varieties and production techniques appearing regularly, and the high vulnerability of the crop to pest and disease, market reformers must consider who, if not the government, ought to ensure the provision of research, extension and quality control services. The issue of credit availability to small farmers also needs to be addressed.

The Multifibre Arrangement (MFA), with its complex system of bilateral quotas, was said to have created trading patterns that have little to do with comparative advantage. Interestingly, trade has increased tremendously in the last 25 years, despite the apparent restrictiveness of the MFA. A close look at EU imports of textiles and clothing shows that the value of trade with Asian countries, who face both quotas and tariff, has increased rapidly. At the same time, Africa has remained an insignificant source of supply despite the fact that the Lomé convention grants free access to some countries. This is evidence that Asian producers have found ways to circumvent the quota constraints and that external, institutional and domestic resource factors have impeded African development of a manufacturing base to take advantage of Lomé preferences.

The argument of revealed comparative advantage is substantiated in a general equilibrium modelling exercise. Simulation of the impact of the Uruguay Round agreement to 2005, when the MFA phase-out is to be completed, shows Africa increasingly specializing in non-grain crop production (including cotton) and mining, while losing ground in light manufacturing, including textiles and clothing. These results stem to a large extent from initial endowments, where Africa has a relative abundance of land, natural resource and labour but a slow rate of capital accumulation from a low initial level. One key question here is whether foreign direct investment can modify these trends. Central to these issues is the long-debated question of the growth and development path to be pursued and of the real or perceived conflict between industrialization and an 'agriculture and natural resources'-based economy.

Detailed studies have exposed some of the challenges faced by Africa. In Kenya and Uganda, for instance, high interest rates, exchange rate distortions, high transport costs and corruption have clear detrimental impacts on the competitiveness of manufacturing firms, despite recent market liberalization. Even if indicators of competitiveness show that Kenya has some comparative advantage in textile and clothing manufacture, increasing cost distortions since the mid-1980s have led to a loss in export competitiveness. Hence trade reforms are insufficient to enhance competitiveness. Domestic policies must also be geared to the creation of an enabling business environment. In particular, the question of capital constraints was again debated in the light of firm-level evidence showing that capital costs and weak financial sectors are constraining manufacturing development in Uganda and Kenya. It is obvious that there is a huge unmet demand in East Africa, in particular, since there is so much reliance on imports of second-hand clothing from Asia and elsewhere.

In trying to explain poor performance in Africa, despite there being local cotton production and preferential access to the EU market, many of the factors can be traced to the institutional and policy environment. Clearly, the argument about whether Africa can compete in textiles and clothing is a critical one. The case of Morocco, however, brings some counterbalance to the argument. In recent years, Morocco has successfully developed an export-led clothing industry despite having no apparent comparative advantage. This is due in large part to foreign investment and contractual production with firms in importing countries, fostering a positive climate for progress. There is an urgent need to pinpoint the issues which constrain growth elsewhere.

ANALYSING POLICY DELIVERY SYSTEMS

ORGANIZER   ED ROSSMILLER (USA)

RAPPORTEUR   FRANCES SANDIFORD-ROSSMILLER (UK)

The group objectives included establishing the policy delivery system (PDS) as an important component of the policy process, and therefore a subject of critical analysis in its own right, and suggesting a structured way of thinking about the PDS as a basis for analysis. The PDS is the total modality of implementing a given policy, that is, the unique set of institutions, individuals, processes and rules that together deliver the benefits of a policy to a target group and enable control to be exercised to ensure adherence to the rules of access.

Robin Johnson (NZ) set the context for the ensuing discussion. To bring the methodology of economics to the analysis of PDS, the suggested framework is derived from public choice economics, agency theory and transaction cost economics, with some borrowing from organization theory. Government decision makers (politicians), policy advisors (bureaucrats) and the people representing pressure groups (interest groups) are the principal actors, and are generally assumed to be motivated by self-interest. For example, politicians seek re-election, bureaucrats protect their budgets and interest groups seek advantage (rents) from the political process. A general move towards market orientation with a changing role for governments, public and private institutions, a tendency to separate policy formulation from policy implementation, and the assumption of self-interest have increased the importance of policy delivery systems in the realization of policy objectives.

Frances Sandiford-Rossmiller sketched a structure–conduct–performance approach to studying policy delivery systems. The analytical framework consists of, first, defining the agreed policy objective, second, describing the structure of the PDS (institutions, instruments, processes) and analysing the functions that are apparently intended to be performed, that is, *the system as designed*, third, analysing the conduct or behaviour of the system as it actually works – how it deviates from the original design and intentions, that is, *the system as it operates*, and, finally, assessing the performance of the system in terms of achieving the original policy objective.

The top-level criterion for performance assessment is *effectiveness*, or 'doing the right thing': is the system operating so as to produce the desired outcome? Given effectiveness, there are three subsidiary criteria: (a) *efficiency*, doing the thing right, which concerns the cost of delivering the policy (in this context, efficiency has no meaning if effectiveness is not fulfilled); (b) *enforce-*

ability, whereby benefits reach the target group whilst others are excluded; and (c) *equity*, assurance of equal opportunity of access to the benefits under the rules.

Assessing PDS performance is a complicated process producing a wealth of information that must be assimilated purposefully, so the reason for studying a particular PDS should be clearly understood. For agricultural policies, probable reasons are the following:

- an existing PDS is believed to be inadequate and options are needed for improving its working or establishing an alternative;
- the government wishes to change the PDS for reasons unconnected with its performance, for example, to comply with GATT/WTO commitments or to reduce the policy costs, and needs to identify and examine alternatives;
- for ideological or budgetary reasons, changes to an existing PDS are under consideration, for example, the privatization of a parastatal marketing organization or a reduction in the number of public sector extension personnel; and
- a new policy is being introduced and a PDS must be designed to accommodate it, perhaps requiring substantial institutional change.

The structure–conduct–performance paradigm is just one way of structuring our thinking about policy delivery systems to enable a formal analysis of implementation options to be carried out.

Helmut Albert (Germany) articulated the German technical cooperation agency (GTZ) view of the relationship between the delivery of agricultural policy and agricultural services for rural development within the broader framework of international cooperation. Economic and social pressures are everywhere driving public sector reform. Governments cannot afford to finance and deliver the range of public services demanded; public institutions are not always benevolent in intent; highly centralized provision of public services tends to favour the urban middle classes; and centralization excludes local policy makers and users from the decision process. Policy reforms aim to increase reliance on the private sector, to decentralize control of a reduced public budget, to improve the selection of services for rural development, and to move from universal to more selective service provision. The consequential privatization and public management reforms radically shift political power, interest and authority to include civil society, with far-reaching implications for policy and service delivery systems, and hence technical cooperation. GTZ's support of partner governments and organizations is oriented towards sustained and sustainable capacity development, of individuals and institutions, so that people are able to take responsibility for improving their living conditions by their own efforts. This type of capacity building requires a long-term donor commitment, which has happened in Asia but has not yet been forthcoming in Africa.

Numerous policy implementation problems, analyses and solutions emerged during the discussions. Douglas Hedley (Canada) contributed an excellent example illustrating the initial unworkability and unintended consequences of the farm support PDS in Canada before it was revised and connected to the national income tax collection system. Additional problems have yet to be solved, showing that PDS analysis needs to be viewed as a process.

The discussions showed that many of the policy review and monitoring procedures established within, or by, governments focus on the budgetary accounting and regulatory aspects. By neglecting policy implementation (PDS) as an area of study, economists have failed to ensure that a broader range of socioeconomic factors are included in the assessment criteria. Economists have much to contribute through the development of tools such as the structure–conduct–performance approach. Unless they take this role seriously and ensure that their voices are heard, they, and civil society as a whole, will lose out to the fiscal bureaucrats, regulators, lawyers, accountants and auditors. This would be an unfortunate state of affairs for all concerned (except, of course, for fiscal bureaucrats, regulators and the rest).

IMPACT OF POLICY REFORM ON THE WELL-BEING OF
VULNERABLE GROUPS: EVIDENCE FROM THE USA, ZIMBABWE
AND KENYA

**ORGANIZERS   JEFFREY ALWANG AND BRADFORD MILLS
(USA), WERE OMAMO (KENYA)**

RAPPORTEUR   JOACHIM SCHLEICH (GERMANY)

New techniques for estimating welfare changes following different exogenous
shocks, such as policy changes or adverse weather conditions, formed the
subject of the mini-symposium.

Welfare policy in the United States underwent a major change in 1996. The
'Personal Responsibility and Work Opportunity Reconcilement Act' replaced
the 'Aid to Families with Dependent Children' programme for public cash-
assistance payments with state specific cash assistance schemes funded by the
federal 'Temporary Assistance to Needy Families' block grants. This welfare
reform has been praised for its success in improving the economic well-being
of the most vulnerable, in particular of single female-headed households with
children (SFHwC) in non-metropolitan areas. But there are other factors, which
may have contributed to those economic gains, such as changes in human
capital, family characteristics or regional economic conditions. Thus simply
comparing the means of per capita receipts for SFHwC provides little information on the underlying causes of shifts in the distribution.

Mills showed how new non-parametric kernel density estimation is a powerful tool to visualize the distributions and identify where shifts occur, without
imposing rigid assumptions associated with parametric specifications. Density
reweighting methods can then decompose the impact of factors that have
contributed to the observed shifts in the distribution of per capita receipts.
Using the 1993 and 1999 Annual Demographic Files of Current Population
Survey, Mills applied the techniques to explore the causes of the positive
changes in real per capita total receipts of single female-headed households
with children in non-metropolitan areas of the United States. The discussion
centred on the findings from this research and their significant implications for
the long-term efficacy of welfare reforms.

First, a portion of the economic gains for SFHwC can be explained by
welfare-to-work transitions, that is, by movement from being 'not in the workforce and on welfare' and into the generally more remunerative state of 'in the
workforce and not on welfare'. Second, and most important, changes in the
propensity of heads of SFHFwC in non-metropolitan areas to leave welfare
and enter the workforce are mainly due to changes in the characteristics of

family heads, such as increases in education levels, and changes in the area economic conditions, rather than welfare reform initiatives. Third, since changes in the unemployment rate explained only a minor portion of the influence of changes in workforce and welfare programme participation on per capita receipts, future economic downturns are not expected to reverse the observed shifts from welfare to work and the associated economic gains. Finally, the significance of increased education levels for movements off welfare and into the workforce highlights the importance of promoting further investment in human capital among heads of non-metropolitan SFHFv/C, in particular among those whose education was interrupted by the birth of a child.

After independence in the early 1980s, Zimbabwe's economic policy was characterized by central control and a heavy emphasis on social spending, in particular on education, health care, housing and agriculture. The resulting unsustainable fiscal situation and trade imbalances led to a major reform. The Economic Structural Adjustment Programme of 1990 liberalized many sectors of the economy, reduced public sector employment, and freed trade and finance. It was hoped that reforms would place the economy on a path of broad-based sustainable growth. In addition, Zimbabwe suffered from two severe droughts in 1991/1992 and in 1994/1995. By 1996, poverty was higher than at the beginning of the 1990s.

Alwang applied the semi-parametric techniques referred to above, on comparable national survey data for 1990 and 1996, to examine the sources of the observed increase in poverty. The aim was to identify the relative importance of structural adjustment (that is, sector employment shifts in urban areas), of rainfall variability in rural areas, of migration from rural to urban areas, and of households' human capital investments. In addition to the semi-parametric techniques, Alwang applied standard decompositions of the Foster–Greer–Thorbecke poverty indices, and consumption regression methods. The findings indicate that rainfall explained only a minor fraction of the overall change in well-being. Further, rural poverty is more prevalent and more severe than that in urban areas, but urban poverty has grown dramatically between 1990 and 1995/1996. Much of the growth is associated with economic restructuring and the failure of the urban economy to produce high-quality jobs. While educational attainment of the urban population grew during the 1990s, secondary and higher levels of education were no longer a guarantee of escape from poverty in 1995/96. In rural areas, all land use types exhibited an increase in poverty. Thus returns to both the levels of human capital and physical assets (land holding, livestock and so on) decreased.

Omamo presented an analysis of agricultural market reform in Kenya. While liberalization appears to have expanded trading opportunities in key segments of agriculture, it has not led to the anticipated mutually reinforcing combinations of technical change, intensification and on-farm specialization, particularly among smallholders, who continue to dominate the agricultural landscape. The analysis used numerical simulation techniques to investigate these outcomes, focusing on the potential role of high farm-to-market transaction costs in explaining key aspects of smallholder production and trading decisions. The discussion focused on applications of the modelling approach, highlighting its flexibility and likely usefulness in adding insights into interactions among key constraints, many of which are open to influence by policy. In addition, contrasts and complementarities with both parametric and non-parametric statistical approaches were discussed.

NEW INVESTMENT THEORY IN AGRICULTURAL ECONOMICS: ITS IMPLICATIONS FOR FARM MANAGEMENT, ENVIRONMENTAL POLICY AND DEVELOPMENT

ORGANIZERS AND RAPPORTEURS   MARTIN ODENING (GERMANY), JUSTUS WESSELER AND HANS-PETER WEIKARD (THE NETHERLANDS)

The motivation for this mini-symposium was the impression that 'new investment theory' – also named 'real option theory' – seems to be a research area within agricultural economics which offers numerous potential applications. Real option theory exploits the analogy between a financial option and a physical investment, facilitating the transfer of methodology and the main findings of option pricing to generic investments. Three preconditions have to be fulfilled to make the approach meaningful and non-trivial: firstly, the decision maker has the flexibility to defer the investment decision, secondly, the initial investment outlay is at least partially sunk; and thirdly, the investment returns are uncertain. Under these (realistic) assumptions it can be demonstrated that 'waiting' has a positive value. An immediate investment kills the option and hence the expected investment returns should cover the direct investment costs as well as the opportunity cost of the alternative 'wait and see' decision. Accordingly, real option theory yields investment triggers which are significantly higher than traditional investment criteria suggest.

On this basis a broad class of investment problems appears in another light. The objective of the meetings was to highlight the main ideas and the implications of real options, explore potential applications and identify problems and needs for further research. The discussion was structured around eight papers focusing on farm management, environmental issues and policy making.

Farm management

Oude Lansink and R. Huirne (Wageningen University, Netherlands) provided an overview of modelling investments in agriculture. They distinguished between positive (empirical) and normative approaches and showed how the concept of real options can be incorporated in traditional models. With a focus on adjustment cost models and stochastic dynamic programming, M. Odening and O. Mußhoff (Humboldt University, Germany) calculated critical values for the returns on investments in hog feeding under German market conditions. Option prices and investment triggers were determined using stochastic simulation. It turns out that the results depend heavily on the stochastic processes assumed for the investment cash flows. The investment trigger largely exceeds the investment costs for a geometric Brownian motion, but is close to it when a moving average model is used. T. Richards and G. Green (Arizona State University and Western Washington University, USA) investigated the investment behaviour of California wine grape producers. An econometric model was used to test whether option values for adopting a new variety cause economic hysteresis. The empirical results show a significant effect, its extent depending on the variability of crop revenues. It is concluded that the speed of adoption of new varieties can be increased by means of revenue insurance or contract production arrangements.

Environment and natural resources

Two papers dealt with natural resources. Ellen Burnes (Oregon State University, USA) analysed the value of a contract for harvesting a natural resource. To get prices right resource managers must consider an arbitrage free contract price. The speaker showed how such prices are constructed when harvest costs are included. The second presentation, by Hans-Peter Weikard (Wageningen University, Netherlands), dealt with the option value of biodiversity and conservation. Limited information about the value of ecosystems and species leads to a positive option value. The design of a conservation policy 'today' must take into account the possibility that more information about the attributes of ecosystems and species might be revealed 'in the future'. It was suggested that the possibility of learning leads to higher initial conservation efforts, even if that is at the expense of long-term measures.

Policy

Discussion of the relevance of new investment theory for efficient economic policies began with Gerald Shively (Purdue University, USA) considering the impact of product price uncertainty on the hurdle rate, and its implication for investments in soil conservation and policies promoting conservation. The main conclusion was that price uncertainty, in itself, can discourage farmers from adopting soil conservation methods. It provides an additional explanation of why their adoption rate is low despite the fact that traditional cost–benefit analysis shows a positive rate of return.

Gerd Nicodemus (FERI GmbH, Germany) presented a discussion of optimal resource allocation applied to climate change policies, under irreversibility and uncertainty in a decentralized economy. The paper showed that policies can improve the efficiency of the market outcome in the case of forest carbon sequestration. Justus Wesseler (Wageningen University, Netherlands) spoke on the application of new investment theory to the assessment of benefits and costs of biotechnology and discussed the optimal timing of releasing transgenic crops into the environment against the background of highly uncertain risks. One major empirical problem is the identification of the stochastic processes underlying the net benefit stream. All three speakers argued that economic policies will result in inefficient resource allocation if irreversibility and uncertainty are not incorporated.

INSTITUTION SEQUENCING AND TIMING IN TRANSITION
ECONOMIES

**ORGANIZER AND RAPPORTEUR   GERTRUD BUCHENRIEDER
(GERMANY)**

There is general consensus about the objective of transformation of the economic system in transition countries, namely the creation of an effective
market-oriented economy. The objective of institutional reform can be defined
as the quickest and largest possible reduction of transaction costs (TCs), which
are the total costs of doing business. They are inversely related to (a) the
efficiency of the institutional framework in terms of defining clear property
rights (PRs) and protecting them, and (b) the efficiency of the enforcement and
organizational arrangement. By focusing on areas where TCs can be reduced
rapidly (and visibly), institutional reform can make an important contribution
to economic recovery, thus increasing the political and social sustainability of
transformation itself.

The vital question, however, stems from the fact that everything cannot be
done at once, so what should be the sequence of measures? There is a related
problem with timing. While sequencing describes when one reform, among a
bundle of intended reforms, should begin, it does not look at the time required
for completion. Good timing is crucial to social acceptance and to the ultimate
success of the transformation process because it affects the social costs of
transformation.

Theorists and policy makers argue about the optimal order of sequencing
and timing in transition economies. In the literature on the appropriate timing
of reforms, two diametrically opposite approaches are always distinguished,
the shock strategy (also known as the 'big bang') and the gradual approach
(also known as 'piecemeal' change). Nevertheless, there is an air of unreality
in the debate between the two approaches. The difficulty is that stretching the
premises underlying the two approaches to their logical extremes leads to
caricature and untenable prescriptions. Thus the fundamentalist interpretation
of shock therapy is tantamount to advocating reform of everything at once, and
the fundamentalist interpretation of gradualism becomes a prescription for
total immobility. To the question of what is the 'optimal pace of reform' a
gradualist can only say 'it depends', which is also not a great help.

The central issues affecting the rural economy of several transition countries
were explored using a manuscript on 'Institution Sequencing and Timing in
Transition Economies' prepared by Gertrud Buchenrieder. The objective was
to ask whether there are specific components of the reform process which are
best implemented at specific stages of rural transformation. The manuscript

was organized in three sections covering institution sequencing and timing in the wider rural economy, in the agricultural sector and in the rural finance sector.

Institutional issues in reforming the rural economy were addressed using case studies from countries of Central and Eastern Europe, the former Soviet Union and China. A discussion of the applicability of theoretical ideas to the transition process of the rural economy (agricultural sector, non-farm sector and rural financial sector) began the proceedings. This was followed by two contributions, one dealing with general changes in the rural development policy framework in Russia and the other with water infrastructure in the Republic of Macedonia.

After a more general look at institutions in the rural economy, closer consideration of institutional changes in the agricultural sector followed. In three different contributions, the transformation of agricultural policy was analysed for Russia, the Ukraine and China. Common issues, objectives and different approaches in adapting agricultural policy were deduced from these contributions. There was then a contribution on sequencing and timing for the rural financial sector, which provided a detailed report on the institutional development in Romania.

The overwhelming opinion from the discussion was that the shock approach is the more promising method of transforming rural institutions because it creates the fewest market distortions and because it is virtually impossible to sequence and time reforms properly if a gradualist stance is adopted. However, detailed research suggests that, in reality, the shock approach is hardly ever followed, owing to the difficult political situation which often surrounds reform. Implementation seems to be driven more by opportunities, such as the availability of funding, or urgency of crisis management, and not by strategic choices. More strategy formulation could, nevertheless, improve the situation without going so far as rigidly to prescribe the sequencing and timing of reforms.

BUILDING FINANCIAL MARKETS IN DEVELOPING COUNTRIES FOR TOMORROW'S AGRICULTURE: STATUS, REFORMS AND INNOVATIONS

ORGANIZER   RICHARD L. MEYER (USA)

RAPPORTEUR   DOUGLAS H. GRAHAM (USA)

Nine presentations were made during this mini-symposium on three subjects: (a) the status of rural financial market reforms and access to financial services, (b) innovations to improve performance, and (c) methods to measure performance.

Claudio Gonzalez-Vega (USA) began by presenting a framework for reviewing the state of rural finance in Latin America. He emphasized its role in revitalizing agriculture and alleviating poverty by expanding the financial frontier through new lending technology. Though he acknowledged that opportunities exist for innovative breakthroughs, there are also dangers from exaggerated expectations of what finance can accomplish. Even the most successful lending techniques have important exclusionary features and efficiency effects. He described the policies, methods and organizations that have shaped rural finance in recent decades. The discussion focused on how the problems of seasonality of demand and covariant risk affect rural finance.

In the second presentation, Yoichi Izumida (Japan) described the key rural finance reforms implemented in Vietnam. The Agricultural Bank of Vietnam (ABV) reaches a large proportion of rural farmers with apparently unusually low costs and arrears. Subsidization of interest charges, however, still characterizes loan pricing. He argued that market liberalization has generated high rates of economic and agricultural growth and facilitated the emergence of healthy rural financial markets. The participants questioned the 'frozen debts' and rescheduled loans, which may artificially reduce the reported arrears rate. Questions were also raised about the credibility of the reported administrative costs, which seem low by international standards.

The third presentation, by Richard L. Meyer (USA), reported on a regional survey of Asian rural financial markets. The general conclusion was that most Asian countries have weak rural financial institutions in spite of huge amounts of funds having been spent by governments and donors in the past three decades in a supply-leading approach to rural finance. However, three flagship institutions in the region demonstrate the large outreach and sustainability that can be accomplished when appropriate policies and institutions are used. They are the Unit Desas of Bank Rakyat Indonesia, the Bank for Agriculture and Agriculture (BAAC) in Thailand and the Grameen

Bank in Bangladesh. These three institutions provide financial services to millions of rural clients.

In the second session, Douglas H. Graham (USA) identified the determinants of increased outreach and sustainability for the Centenary Rural Development Bank in Uganda. Technical assistance from International Projekt Consult (IPC) in Frankfurt from 1993 onwards transformed the bank through improved institutional and organizational design, governance structure and lending technology. An econometric model demonstrated the strategic role of IPC lending technology in lowering arrears and lending costs. The discussion focused on different model specifications to measure the impact of technology on bank performance.

Lucila A. Lapar (Philippines) reported on research to measure the effects of credit on output for a sample of rural non-farm enterprises in the Philippines. A switching regression model was used to correct for selectivity bias and endogeneity of credit status found in credit impact studies. The results showed a significant impact of largely informal finance on enterprise expansion, with a high marginal rate of return on capital. She concluded that credit does not require interest subsidies because the return on capital is substantially above market rates of interest. Participants raised questions about model specification and research design issues.

Michael Lyne (South Africa) discussed the recent evolution of land reform initiatives in South Africa, comparing direct allocation of commercial farmland through government grants to large groups of beneficiaries with market allocations through financial intermediaries. In the latter, newly constituted farm companies are created in which farm workers become co-owners with the original farmers or freehold buyers through mortgage bond loans. The cash flow problems encountered in the early years of these initiatives are reduced through interest subsidies provided by a land reform credit facility. The discussion focused on clarifying the details of the credit facility and how non-financial constraints faced by the new farmers are overcome.

In the third session, Geetha Nagarajan (USA) discussed the construction of poverty indicators for use by microfinance organizations (MFOs) concentrating on the poor. She presented the results of an attempt to develop reasonably efficient proxies that are consistent with national poverty benchmarks for Lima, Peru. The three measures of per capita household income, a housing index and household size offered some promise in matching the national poverty benchmark. However, they are sensitive to threshold levels and leakage, hence undercoverage can occur when they are used. They are also subject to site and time period effects. The ensuing discussion concentrated on the strengths and weaknesses of the three proxies.

Manfred Zeller (USA) and Manohar Sharma (USA) reported the results of four case studies conducted in South Asia and Africa using 15–20 indicators to measure different dimensions of the depth of poverty outreach for MFO and non-MFO poverty populations. The indicators showed that the MFO clients fairly well reflected the poverty profile found in the sampled areas. Principal component analysis was used to consolidate a weighting group of indicators into the composite index used in the study. The participants raised questions about the choice of indicators and why distance of clients from markets was not used as an indicator. The possible bias in using highly volatile variables like income per family was debated.

In the final presentation, Sergio Navajas (El Salvador) summarized an El Salvador study that explored the degree to which different lending techniques might exclude certain segments of the poor. Formal lenders reach only about 8 per cent of the rural population, while semi-formal NGOs and cooperatives serve an additional 12 per cent, with informal lenders reaching 22 per cent. A study of the clients of Calpia indicated that it is among the most successful lenders reaching the credit-worthy rural poor. The discussion revealed that Calpia's credit-worthiness indicators reflect capacity to repay; hence its clients reflect a slightly higher incidence of economic diversity, assets, proximity to markets and human capital than the non-borrowing rural poor.

REFORM AND FUTURE OF NATIONAL AGRICULTURAL STATISTICS SYSTEMS

ORGANIZER AND RAPPORTEUR   GLENN ROGERS (USA)

The organizer's background paper structured the mini-symposium around the broad themes of new information technology, public and private roles and future priorities. Recent experiences and future visions in the United States, Canada, Germany, the United Kingdom, Egypt and sub-Saharan Africa were discussed. Larry Sivers (USA) and Ross Vani (Canada) outlined current practices and plans in their countries. Ahmed Gueilli (Egypt) and Mohamed Omran (U.S. Agency for International Development), presented an Egyptian view and David Bigman (ISNAR) spoke on the needs of developing countries.

Discussion of the implications of new technology began with the theoretical proposition that, as the costs of information fall, it becomes difficult to put a 'price' on it, given weak enforcement of intellectual property rights and high fixed costs of preparation compared with low dissemination costs. Information must increasingly be customized for sale or for public co-financing with special interest groups. The value of information is rising for consumers, policy makers and producers, while government budgets have stagnated. Network effects, leading to demand-side economies of scale, are resulting in a more concentrated industrial structure and inequitable access to information among developed and developing countries. When combined with rapid change in information technology, and a tendency for technology 'lock-in', there is a need to accelerate sequential adoption of information technologies in developing countries.

The roles of local, national and multinational governments and private organizations were then highlighted. Statistical activities are centralized in one ministry in Canada. In the USA, state and federal partnerships are critical for implementation, co-financing (states provide 10 per cent of funding) and interaction with private sector associations. In both countries a formal advisory committee of data users provides advice on needs, respondents' ability to supply data, collection methods, content and form of reports, and publicity programmes to support the census. The Canadian committee includes members from Mexico and the USA. These committees are critically important in building consensus for private sector funding to complement public funding. The European Union administration is also pushing increased data collection and standardization by national governments, but this may squeeze out local priorities, given budget constraints. In Egypt, agricultural statistics work is a centralized activity under the Ministry of Agriculture. The Egyptian private sector is willing to pay to increase data collection, but this is not allowed under current regulations. Participants suggested the Egyptian government increase data collection using either public or private funding. In lower-income developing countries the paucity of data available to governments is striking. NGOs partially fill the gap with limited but useful surveys, though unfortunately this independent work is rarely combined for broader or multiple uses. ISNAR is assembling important data to facilitate comparisons over time and between countries.

Public and private sector conflict over information quality may grow as the importance of refined information in public policy decisions and good governance increases. Examples include debates over major irrigation projects in the USA and Egypt, current information campaigns regarding globalization, and allocation of public expenditures affecting rural or agricultural areas. In numerous countries policy and investment decisions are increasingly based on data that are not publicly available, so the needed public debate between government, civil society and the private sector is poorly informed.

The discussion of future priorities concluded that faster processing and dissemination of publicly available material is needed to improve decision-making systems for current social needs in both developed and developing countries. Data validation after collection was identified as the key blockage to more timely release of public statistics. In 2001, Canada will use intelligent character recognition for data input and is testing Internet use. The USA has initiated a 'Project to Reengineer and Integrate Statistical Methods' by 2002. The EU project 'Monitoring Agriculture with Remote Sensing' has so far concluded that sufficient accuracy has yet to be attained. Egypt is improving seasonal crop forecasts and shortening processing time to improve timeliness. Canada and the USA now have a combined data release for cattle and feed statistics. A better institutional framework is needed to provide incentives for private sector dissemination of information, especially in developing countries.

Another priority is balance between farm and non-farm public data, given budget constraints and an increasing private role. Genetically modified crop area data began to be collected in the USA in 2000. In geographic or sectoral areas of rapid national growth and change, such as horticulture, environment and trade-related needs, the data are often totally missing in low income countries. There is a huge private demand for trade data, especially international trade data. In developed countries, several examples were given of public sector regulations leading to private data provision (food safety and pesticide use provide examples).

It would also be useful to achieve better combination in the use of census, remote sensing and small survey data collected independently by public and private organizations. The balance between speed, cost and relevance of information means that pressure for cheaper data collection efforts will increase. Independent data are critical for checking results. This is a problem in many lower-income countries where only one national agency is responsible for all surveys, some of which may misinform decades of research. A set of small independent datasets linked to a GIS (geographic information system) may be more efficient for decision makers to use than more census data, which could mainly be used to validate and extrapolate data from other sources. Many countries are also trying to balance investment in survey and census data collection.

IMPROVING LAND ACCESS AND ASSET OWNERSHIP BY THE POOR
THROUGH LAND REFORM: EMPIRICAL EVIDENCE AND POLICY
IMPLICATIONS

ORGANIZER AND RAPPORTEUR   KLAUS DEININGER (USA)

The symposium dealt with five papers on land markets and land reform. It opened with analysis of the impact of a recent land-titling programme on land-attached investment, profits and land values in Nicaragua (Juan Sebastian Chamorro). This reported a surprisingly significant impact of possession of registered title on the dependent variables. To study the functioning of land markets in the Dominican Republic, Karen Macours and Alain de Janvry used community-level surveys to identify determinants of farmers' factor market participation. A third paper on the impact of land reform in the Philippines (Miet Maertens and Klaus Deininger) found a significant impact of the programme on investment and accumulation of human capital, but at the same time a deleterious effect on land access of the legislation accompanying the land reform.

An analysis of the Zimbabwean land reform (Bill Kinsey) used panel data specifically collected for the purpose. It indicated that land reform improved asset accumulation by beneficiaries. However, the impact on per capita income was less pronounced because, as a result of the economic crisis, relatively well-to-do land reform households faced considerable in-migration from family members coming from urban areas.

Finally, a recent analysis of the land reform programme in South Africa (K. Deininger and J. May) indicated that shortcomings in design reduced the speed with which the programme could be implemented. Nevertheless, poor people, especially those who made a contribution to managing the subproject in which they participated, were able to use the land reform programme to increase production. Participants discussed implications for government intervention aiming to improve the efficiency with which land markets function and with which property rights are defined. The conditions under which programmes of redistributive land reform might be desirable, as well as their design features, were also considered.

STRENGTHENING HUMAN AND INSTITUTIONAL CAPITAL TO SUPPORT RURAL DEVELOPMENT IN AFRICA: WHAT HAVE WE LEARNED AND WHAT ARE THE CHALLENGES? A SYMPOSIUM IN HONOUR OF PROFESSOR CARL K. EICHER

ORGANIZERS   ERIC CRAWFORD, JOHN STRAUSS, JOHN STAATZ (USA)

RAPPORTEUR   JULIE HOWARD (USA)

Carl K. Eicher, University Distinguished Professor at Michigan State University, recently retired after a 39-year career devoted to African agricultural development, training African students and strengthening universities and research institutions. To honour Professor Eicher, former students and colleagues gathered to discuss the three themes summarized below, which reflect his work.

The role of the African university in supporting agricultural transformation and economic development

Presenter   Eric Tollens, Catholic University of Louvain

African universities face several dilemmas. Demand for university education is expanding at a time of donor fatigue and diminishing funding. New university campuses are being created, but the quality of education, from low-paid faculty with few operational resources, is deteriorating. Governance is a problem since university leaders are often political appointees with short-term planning horizons. Universities not conforming with government views face reduced budgets. Donors have promoted the land-grant university model, but have not succeeded in helping African universities to build local constituencies that would give them political support.

University training of agricultural economists has not resulted in interventions that directly benefit the poor, which is a consequence of inappropriate curricula and inadequate institutional incentives for graduates to apply their training. Nonetheless, most participants disagreed with the current donor emphasis on primary education. While studies often show higher returns from primary than from university education, these calculations usually count only private benefits. Economists have failed to document the social benefits generated by universities, including creation of agricultural research capacity.

Others noted that the proliferation of public and private universities may be a normal part of economic development. The Philippines, as one case, had more than 1400 degree-granting universities responding to private sector needs as early as the 1970s. Some universities are changing to make themselves more relevant. For example, Makerere University in Uganda is experimenting with new programmes to improve local governance capacity, as political and fiscal authority is decentralized. African universities are partnering with Northern universities to create high-quality joint degree schemes. Regional centres of excellence are emerging; for instance the University of Pretoria is attracting agricultural economics students from across Africa because of its reputation for low-cost, locally relevant teaching. The foundations (Ford, Rockefeller and MacArthur) are also showing renewed interest in university capacity building.

Strengthening agricultural research, extension and policy analysis

Presenters   *Akin Adesina (Rockefeller Foundation) and Isaac Minde*
(ECAPAPA)
Discussant   *Doyle Baker (FAO)*

African agricultural research institutions have exhibited a steep decline in agricultural research expenditures; instability in research organization, leadership and staff; declining research output during the 1990s; and slow adaptation to the changes brought about by economic liberalization, the spread of AIDS and globalization.

Many problems also afflict agricultural extension in Africa: weak links between research, extension and farmers; lower status, respect and remuneration for extension agents than for researchers; expansion of extension agent numbers without expansion of operational budgets; irrelevant extension messages based on technology that does not fit farmer circumstances; weak agricultural extension curricula in higher education institutions; numerous alternative extension models, but little rigorous research on their cost-effectiveness; and little adoption yet of new information technologies.

Participants questioned whether governments should support research institutions as currently constituted. For two decades, donors and governments have focused on building technical agricultural research capacity, without imparting research management skills. Most countries are too small to afford programmes that cover all commodities and enterprises. Resolving these problems will require (a) setting hard priorities and improving the integration of different scientific disciplines, and (b) strengthening regional research organizations.

Research and extension services are increasingly under pressure to focus on commercial crops in high-potential areas. Subsistence farmers who are not well integrated into the market may be left out, unable to gain access to new technology. The emphasis on commercialization is also unlikely to stimulate development of technologies that help preserve the environment.

The role of cooperation from the North in strengthening human and institutional capital to support rural development in Africa

Presenters   *Derek Byerlee (World Bank), Lane Holdcroft (AEAI)*
Discussant   *Edouard Tapsoba (FAO)*

During the 1970s–90s, donors hoped that support of agricultural research and extension would bring a 'Green Revolution' to Africa. From 1981 to 2000, they invested about $1 million per scientist, or $200 per farmer. However, technology development and diffusion have been only modestly and narrowly successful. Unable to convince government leaders of the potential contribution of agricultural research and extension to economic development, despite impressive impacts for some discoveries, managers of these services have generally not won significant increases in government funding.

Donor aid to African agricultural improvement has been characterized by inadequate attention to building linkages with farmers and other local constituents who might provide financial and political support for research and extension services. More recently, donors have emphasized decentralization as a way to make agricultural services more responsive to users. Many participants saw this as positive, but were not convinced that it has yet resulted in broadly diffused technical change. Because participation is costly, there is urgent need to know at what level it is most useful. Also demand-driven governance systems may be difficult to establish if they are not valued by public institutions. Only in a few countries, such as Uganda, does political decentralization seem to enjoy substantial government backing and resources.

More generally, agricultural development programmes must increasingly compete for funds with special interest groups focused on AIDS, child health and the environment. While all these are important, donors need to recommit themselves to providing long-term support for the prime movers of agricultural development by investing in people, in universities and in agricultural research and extension.

PERFORMANCE OF THE NON-VIABLE FARM SECTOR IN RURAL ECONOMIES OF AGRO-BASED DEVELOPING COUNTRIES

ORGANIZER   T. SATYANARAYANA (INDIA)

RAPPORTEUR   TOMMY FENYES (SOUTH AFRICA)

In most agro-based developing countries it is evident that much of the farming is dominated by non-viable land holdings. For example, in India, 93 per cent of farm households hold fewer than four hectares of land. It is clearly important, therefore, that agricultural development policy should be directly concerned with the performance of weaker farming sectors. Policies and planning for the economic empowerment of the smallholding farming class is essential for agricultural change. Economic empowerment might possibly be achieved through the following approaches: (a) assured markets to provide remunerative prices for farm products, (b) assured supply of inputs at affordable prices, and (c) continuous upgrading of low-cost pre- and post-harvest technology.

Sustained returns from farm production enable smallholders to adopt improved technology to produce more. This, in turn, would stimulate rural industries, rural employment and overall rural development. Problems of rural health, education and poverty can be solved through the improved rural economy. The issues were discussed in six papers and by the participants.

In the first session, Ismail Sharif (USA) opened by reviewing the salient features of agriculture in developing countries and of its importance in economic growth. The scope of discussion extended to cover globalization and structural adjustment. He underlined the need to expand low-cost production techniques through land reforms, irrigation and drainage projects, and supply of proper and timely inputs supported by an efficient market network.

Philippe Burny (Belgium) described the growth path of the rice economy in South Vietnam. Five years of growth occurred in research in rice production, processing, marketing and exports in several different agroecological regions of the Mekong Delta. The impact of economic reforms in Vietnam in 1986 aimed at utilization of resources, with low-cost technology within the reach of smallholding rice farmers enabling the Mekong Delta region to use cheap manpower to raise production. This contributed to food security and assured rice exports.

In the second session, E.C. Teixeira (Brazil), in his presentation on income transfer from commercial and family farms, explained how the tax structure in the agriculture sector created an adverse growth environment in Brazil. The performance of family and commercial farms was compared in the context of subsidies provided to them and taxes paid. Until the 1980s, family farms growing rice and beans were not well treated, while family dairy farmers were on average taxed more heavily than commercial dairies during the 25 years in the study. During the late 1980s, their situation worsened. Subsidized credit helped commercial farmers more than the family farms. As a result, productivity and economic activity, particularly in the rice belt, were reduced. Secondly, the overvalued rate of exchange depressed rice, bean and milk prices, favouring imports over domestic produce. As domestic prices decreased to meet foreign competition, incomes decreased. The adverse influence of the exchange rate distorted agricultural production, mainly in the weaker sectors of farming.

Tom Fenyes (South Africa) examined the distortions in agricultural development stemming from government policies. Extra protection was given to export-oriented industries in the Northern Province of South Africa, a semi-arid agro-based region. The paper advocated the adoption of free markets for all commodities in place of the present controlled marketing system. Further, the trade-offs between domestic production incentives and food affordability could be relieved by various measures to increase farm income. In the long run, this requires sustained support for input and credit delivery systems, agricultural research and extension to generate and disseminate new technology and efficient product distribution and processing systems among the smallholding non-viable farming communities.

In the third session, E.M. Koffi-Tessio (Togo) considered the role of rural finance in the process of development. He gave a critical account of various institutional sources of credit in Togo, suggesting that the rural credit system has not contributed significantly to the promotion of food crop production. This is mainly due to lack of organized markets, leading to failure of incentives to invest in food sectors. With assured market support, producers venture to take higher risks to invest in agriculture and produce more. Therefore policy makers should understand the strong linkage between rural credit and the related performance of the food sector.

J.C. Umeh (Nigeria) examined the path of agricultural growth during pre- and post-independence periods in Nigeria and the role of the non-viable farming sector. Sources of empowering the rural farming sector have been identified as (a) suitable technology support, (b) adequate infrastructure, (c) subsidy support and low taxation and (d) remunerative prices for farm produce. The author suggested that the dwindling agro-based economy can be revived to yield improved agricultural development and more efficiently produced food supplies.

B. Najafi (Iran) highlighted the problems of water supply and output fluctuations in wheat production faced by small farmers who constitute 65 per cent of Iran's farming community. The country is importing around 65 million tonnes of wheat every year and the prices of wheat fluctuate violently. There is a great shortage of bread for the people even if they are prepared to pay more. Agricultural policy makers are now giving importance to better incentives for farmers to produce more. Improved extension services, pre-and post-harvest technology support for quality output of wheat, better procurement operations and market networks are being made available.

After a thorough discussion, the group concluded that measures to improve agriculture among small farmers provide the best way to trigger economic activity in rural areas and form the basis for rural employment, growth in rural industries and eradication of rural poverty. For agriculture that means:

(1) there should be a strong policy support for higher production among the non-viable farming groups;
(2) efficient market networks to absorb the produce and provide remunerative prices should be developed;
(3) active extension services to educate small farmers about technology should be fostered.

RISK AND AGRICULTURAL INPUT USE: ANALYSIS AND MITIGATION

ORGANIZERS   ERIC CRAWFORD, VALERIE KELLY, JULIE HOWARD, KAREN BROOKS (USA)

RAPPORTEURS   JULIE HOWARD, VALERIE KELLY (USA)

Risk and uncertainty remain major constraints on the adoption of improved production technologies. Risks are faced by farmers (who must specialize and rely on input and output markets) and by marketing and processing agents. Farmers in industrialized countries have many options for dealing with risks: for example, market and weather information, price supports, insurance, financial services, futures markets and production contracts. These options are generally unavailable to farmers in developing countries.

The objective of the symposium was to explore promising analytical tools and institutional innovations to reduce or mitigate agricultural risk in developing countries. The organizers acted as presenters, along with Sushil Pandey, Kees van der Meer, Vijay Kalavakonda, Ron Phillips, Mulat Demeke, Dismas Okello and Paul Seward. The four sub-topics were: (1) links between risk, technology adoption and poverty; (2) improving methods/institutions to decrease production risk; (3) designing cost-effective institutions to reduce marketing risk and uncertainty; and (4) field perspectives on methods/institutions currently used.

Risk, technology adoption and poverty

Participants first discussed the theoretical and empirical evidence linking risk to agricultural technology adoption and poverty. Coping mechanisms used by the rural poor result in the erosion of assets (for example, livestock sold at low prices, children kept out of school). As the poor grow poorer they become less willing to adopt technology.

The group reflected on the most appropriate approaches to risk mitigation in different situations. Might some risk management tools be better suited to poverty reduction objectives and others to promoting agricultural transformation? Are some more appropriate at different stages of development? In sub-Saharan Africa, could basic interventions (links to markets, better infrastructure, access to savings, and improved research and extension) provide more cost-effective risk reduction in the short run than price stabilization schemes and crop insurance?

Reducing production risk

Suggestions for dealing with production risk included research and extension programmes that offer farmers a menu of choices to help address particular risk problems, rather than a fixed technology package; use of simple budgets and biophysical models to predict technology performance and profitability; and rainfall-based insurance. Recent work in Asia has shown that research and extension is more effective when (a) risk mitigation occurs at the household rather than crop level; (b) researchers are rewarded for technology adoption; (c) extension addresses risk perceptions by providing farmers with more information; and (d) decentralized, adaptive research is carried out in collaboration with farmer associations and NGOs. Training extension agents to help farmers with simple budgets is critical for increasing knowledge about technology profitability. The key for improving biophysical–socioeconomic modelling is to build databases (soil, temperature, rain, solar radiation), to make them available to researchers and to develop modelling skills.

By relying on objective measurements (level and distribution of rainfall, monitoring of catastrophic weather events), rainfall-based insurance could avoid the moral hazard problems that plague crop insurance programmes. Participants expressed concerns about the cost of implementation and monitoring, and of developing crop- and region-specific models that would indicate suitable rainfall patterns.

Reducing marketing risk and uncertainty

Discussion focused on the use of commodity markets and hedging, and the role of regulatory reform and contract enforcement, in reducing input and output market risks. Price risk is important for both export crops (such as cotton, coffee, tea or cocoa) and non-tradeable cereal crops (such as millet and sorghum). In the post-liberalization period the former, still sold through marketing boards, are more likely to benefit from price stabilization schemes and hedging on commodity futures markets than the latter, usually sold by individual farmers or farmer associations. Greater price stability for export crops can result in farmers using inputs such as fertilizer on export crops rather than on food crops.

Risks posed by weak, unstable or missing input markets have become a serious constraint on technology adoption. This has been particularly true in sub-Saharan Africa (SSA) following the dissolution of parastatals, and the reluctance of the private sector to step into this environment of fluctuating prices, low profitability and uncertainty about government intervention.

Government policies and programmes can create risks that discourage private sector investment and participation with insufficient supply of public goods (for example, infrastructure, regulations, access to certifications, licences and permits, loan guarantees, law enforcement); undesirable interventions, such as disruption of production or reduced competition in trade of private goods; and sudden changes in policies related to input subsidies, export/import taxes or subsidies, and food safety regulations.

Field experiences with programmes to reduce agricultural risk and uncertainty

The public and private sectors should work in unison to reduce the risks that discourage technology adoption and private sector participation in new markets. Several innovative efforts were discussed: the MOA/SG2000 scheme in Ethiopia, the CLUSA programme in Zambia, the SCODP mini-fertilizer pack distribution in Kenya, and an input voucher effort designed for Zambia. These emphasize reducing risks by identifying technologies that increase farmer yields and profits and emphasize active farmer participation in technology development; giving farmers information about a variety of technologies rather than fixed packages; and reducing the transactions costs for the private sector in exchange for commitments to serve poorer or more remote farmers.

The discussion showed that risks are affected by such factors as climate (drought in Ethiopia, late rains in Zambia), marketing conditions (shortage of improved seed in Ethiopia, a bidding war for paprika that increased side-marketing and reduced loan repayment in Zambia), and programme conditions (lack of extension agents to support rapid expansion of the Ethiopia SG2000 programme). Programmes that encouraged local decision making, offered technology/commodity options and provided continuing education to farmers on business and agricultural practices seemed most promising.

NEW AND INNOVATIVE INSTRUMENTS TO MANAGE RURAL RISK

ORGANIZER   PAUL SIEGEL (ISRAEL)

RAPPORTEUR   VIJAY KALAVAKONDA (USA)

Risk and uncertainty are pervasive in rural areas. Some risky events are household-related and specific (for example, idiosyncratic risks such as family illness or death, injury or disability, life cycle events) and others spread across households and areas (for example, covariate risks such as drought and flood, commodity price fluctuations or macroeconomic shocks). These events cause losses of natural, physical, human and financial assets, declines in asset values and losses in revenues and incomes in the short and/or longer term. Also inefficient risk management (RM) strategies can incur costs (actual, opportunity and external) to households and communities, and result in losses in social welfare. The aim of the symposium was to look at the latest thinking on risk management and expose it to scrutiny. Some of the relevant material is now available on the Internet (see, for example, <www.zef.de> for D. Wiesmann and J. Juetting, *www.worldbank.org/sp* for P.B. Siegel and J. Alwang, and *www.cgiar.org/ifrpi* for J.R. Skees, P. Hazell and M. Miranda).

To some extent, self-insurance (crop and variety diversification, resistant crops, field fragmentation and staggered plantings, precautionary savings with livestock and food stocks, and so on) and informal risk arrangements (for example, social networks, moneylenders) can help poor households manage some idiosyncratic risks. However, for covariate risks (often manifested through fluctuations in commodity prices and/or yields), self-insurance might be insufficient and informal RM arrangements based on social networks tend to break down. Absent or poorly functioning finance and insurance markets, limited asset and risk pools, and poor integration into labour and product markets exacerbate the impacts of risks for many poor households, especially in remote rural communities.

There are several new and innovative RM instruments available for micro (individual, household), meso (community, financial institution, local government) and macro (national) levels. In many cases these instruments have been restructured (as opposed to merely resurrected) to deal better with efficiency and equity issues associated with moral hazard, adverse selection and transactions costs, and to provide coverage for broader segments of the rural population (rather than specific subgroups such as farmers/landowners).

There is a new focus on proactive management such as risk reduction (to prevent risky events) and mitigation (to provide compensation for losses), and in-place rather than ad hoc coping mechanisms (such as work or food programmes that can be scaled up or down as needed). Many of the instruments are 'hybrids' based on public–private sector partnerships, and formal–informal finance and insurance mechanisms.

The various instruments should be considered individually and together in order to identify links, overlaps, gaps (for example, information needs, institutions and delivery mechanisms, and coverage). It is also important to evaluate RM instruments not only for their ability to smooth income and consumption variability, but also for their ability to help households increase their assets and expected income and consumption over time. The types of instrument are listed below.

Commodity price insurance

Use of international commodity markets can provide floor prices for producers and ceiling prices for consumers. There can be delivery to macro, meso and possibly micro levels.

Natural disaster and hazards insurance

Catastrophe bonds and international reinsurance markets are available at the macro level (with indemnities, in turn, used by government to assist affected households). Weather and 'area yield-based index' insurance can replace some traditional crop insurance against yield risk. Delivery can be to meso levels (for example, financial institutions, farmer associations) and micro levels (to farmers and the broader rural population).

Rural financial institutions and micro-finance institutions

Credit–savings–insurance linkages can be provided by finance institutions. These can deal with both idiosyncratic and covariate risk using savings for self-insurance, risk-pooling insurance products and credit for consumption smoothing. Also various types of insurance can be linked to credit to insure a loan or the borrower/saver.

Formal insurance markets (including micro-insurance)

Life, health, disability or property insurance can be linked or unlinked to credit. Potential exists for delivery through rural finance and micro-finance institutions and/or through other meso-level institutions (for example, producer associations).

Interlinked contracts

Contract farming, outsourcing and vertical integration provide means for farm households and/or farmer associations to share risks with others in the marketing/distribution chain. All require contractual arrangements.

Safety nets and community projects

Safety nets take the form of social funds, work programmes, food subsidies and programmes to help the poorest and most vulnerable individuals and households (elderly, disabled, children and so on). There is potential to achieve both consumption smoothing and asset building for longer-term RM.

Off-farm employment and small enterprises

Finding another, or a supplementary, occupation is, in practice, the major means of household self-insurance, allowing for diversification of economic activities to spread risks and/or increase expected income. Policy reforms such as liberalization and privatization, investments in transport and communication infrastructure, legal rights and provision of labour market information can widen opportunities.

Agricultural research and extension

Work is needed on farming systems, resistant varieties, improved water management and better post-harvest technologies. One of the advantages of improved agricultural research and extension is the potential to both raise expected incomes and lower their variability. There is an important role for extension agents to provide information on risks and various RM instruments.

Attention was focused on natural disaster and hazard insurance, notably rainfall-based index contracts, and on health insurance. Both types of insurance can be linked or unlinked to credit – potentially lowering transaction costs. Also the new insurance instruments are designed to diminish moral hazard and adverse selection problems. In both cases the credit institution is only an intermediary for local insurance companies, which, in turn, depend on international reinsurance companies and/or other institutions (such as donors) for reinsurance services.

Notwithstanding the intuitive appeal of these insurance products, they have not achieved widespread popularity. That is due to problems associated with the design of contracts and delivery mechanisms (including 'trigger events' for indemnity payment), basis risk when using index contracts, and limited demand from rural households (owing to the lack of resources to invest in such instruments and/or the lack of appreciation of their potential contribution to household welfare). It was also pointed out that the lack of an insurance 'culture' in many countries is a constraint, as is the lack of trust in institutions to provide future compensation for losses while paying premiums in the present.

An important issue requiring more attention is how public and private sector partnerships can be established and strengthened to provide an enabling environment – with minimal distortions and subsidies – to achieve efficient and equitable management of risk by poor households. The public sector has a critical role to play through policies, regulations, enforcement of contracts and provision of information.

Despite increased interest in providing improved RM instruments for rural households, there are important hurdles to overcome. Not only is there no single 'silver bullet' instrument, but also there seems to be a need for location-specific RM packages. This is due to differences in risks faced by different households, and different economic, political, social and cultural conditions.

HOW DO FARMERS FIND THEIR WAY IN THE NEW FOOD SYSTEM IN TRANSITION ECONOMIES?

ORGANIZER   CSABA FORGACS (HUNGARY)

RAPPORTEUR   IRINA KHRAMOVA (RUSSIA)

This mini-symposium offered an opportunity for comparison of experiences of the countries where transition is under way. In some areas, including Russia and Bulgaria, progress is slow, but elsewhere, notably Eastern Germany, the adjustment process proved to be relatively short and successful. In this comparison an effort was made to answer questions about the extent to which small-scale farms have become characteristic of transition economies and about their future.

Eugenia Serova (Russia) raised a definitional question. What is a family farm and what is its place in the production structure of agriculture? In Russia any legally registered (new) farm, outside the pre-existing system, is considered to be a family farm. As such, the term 'family farm' combines different types of producers varying from large-scale commercial enterprises to subsistence household plots oriented only to self-sufficiency. The share of family farms, as defined, is still small in agricultural production and marketing. Each type has its own range of problems.

The basic difficulty is lack of market infrastructure. Small farms can hardly compete with large farms in access to markets. Processing plants and other intermediaries prefer to deal with large units to gain economies in purchasing raw materials and to reduce transaction costs. To become competitive, small farms need to grow sharply. Cooperatives for marketing, credit and input supplies could increase the bargaining power of individual producers and thus solve the problem of their inefficiency. However, cooperatives are poorly developed in Russia, the motivation for cooperation is weak, and there has been some loss in tax concessions.

The talk about re-established farms in the New German Länder (NGL), by Volker Mothes and Peter Tillack, analysed the special way in which this development has proceeded. The East German experience is an example of a successful and relatively painless adjustment to the market economy. It was brought about by massive state intervention aimed at levelling regional disparities through economic reforms following the country's reunification. The process of adjustment of the farm sector was analysed step by step. The present agricultural structure is characterized by the existence of three main groups of producers: private farms, partnerships and successor companies of former collective farms.

The first period of transformation was accompanied by drastic reduction of agricultural employees (as in other transition countries) and an increase in the number of unprofitable farms immediately after the ending of state subsidies. This resulted in significant changes in product specialization. However, several factors guaranteed the relatively successful and painless process of adjustment.

(1) Contrary to what is happening in the agriculture of other countries in transition, the national agricultural structures could be considered to be roughly homogeneous. Hence the profound and inefficient fragmentation of land holdings did not exist. The average size of 'small' private farms is now rarely less than 150 hectares.

(2) All types of producers have equal access to the market infrastructure.

(3) Massive and diversified state support exists for agriculture. The state-financed support for the transformation process was provided for all types of producers.

(4) There was also a positive psychological factor: the agricultural producers of Eastern Germany were ready to accept profound and rapid changes, notably because they were joining the European Union and becoming beneficiaries of the Common Agricultural Policy. This experience could hardly be repeated in the CEEC countries.

The presentation on survival of small farmers in the marketing chain by Plamen Mishev (Bulgaria) showed that economic reform in agriculture started at the beginning of the 1990s and led to a sharp growth in the duality of Bulgaria's farm structure and in the nature of product specialization. There are now huge numbers of small and very small farms producing vegetables and livestock, on the one side, and fewer large-scale effective agricultural enterprises oriented to crop production, on the other. The majority of farms (78 per cent) concentrate on self-sufficiency and either do not produce for the market or use only primitive forms of marketing. The main problems for this group of farms are (a) the lack of sufficient infrastructure for small-scale marketing, (b) the failure of cooperative or processor structures to emerge to serve them, (c) high production costs which can hardly be covered by selling prices, and (d) minimal state support. Two main efforts could improve the situation: (1) a state programme to amalgamate small farms to bring them up to medium size, backed by education of young farmers to enable them to understand modern agriculture; and (2) support to improve food marketing, notably by state promotion of producer associations and cooperatives to assemble and process and thereby to increase the bargaining power of small producers.

The following conclusions resulted from the discussion.

• Insufficient bargaining power of small-scale farms and low willingness to cooperate is a general problem in many transition countries. The growth in bargaining power can significantly increase small farm efficiency. However, cooperatives can face high transaction costs and they also require big investments, especially at the initial stage.

- It is rational for small farmers to want to sell some of their products for cash. But this raises the problem of social security for them: since they do not pay taxes from their cash revenues, they do not get pensions. The emergence of some new small-scale marketing channels is probably useful, but informality does not fit in easily with more general improvement in welfare standards.
- Farmers find finance to buy inputs hard to obtain in a situation of low access to input and credits markets. The use of land, which can sometimes be obtained via land leasing, and the use of family labour are still the main inputs in many cases.
- The future survival of small farms in a changing economy mainly depends on the policy and strategy of the national government. State intervention is considered to be of particular importance, as the market does not solve all problems. The diversified structure of agriculture in all transition countries requires different approaches for each type of producer. Large-scale full-time farms could be aided by general state agricultural support schemes. Small-scale, often part-time, farms need to have more legal protection.

GENETICALLY MODIFIED CROPS: THE FOOD INDUSTRY, PRODUCERS, CONSUMERS AND ENVIRONMENTALISTS

ORGANIZERS   VOLKER BEUSMANN (GERMANY), NICHOLAS G. KALAITZANDONAKES (USA), JOS BIJMAN (NETHERLANDS), PETER W.B. PHILLIPS (CANADA)

RAPPORTEUR   PETER W.B. PHILLIPS (CANADA)

Genetically modified crops have already induced major changes in agriculture. Nevertheless, controversies remain, within the scientific community and among the public, about the impact of biotechnology on farming, consumers, the environment, industry and society.

The future of biotechnology

Kalaitzandonakes asked whether biotechnology would transform the 40 per cent of the world's economy based on biological resources or whether it would simply wither and die. The current debate involves discussion about six 'Ps' – 'perversion, poisons, promiscuity, profit, power and proof – which by their presence or absence have raised serious public concerns. This is partly because the science is not yet equal to expectations. Single-gene transformations (for example, herbicide tolerance and insect resistance) are perceived to have delivered only limited public or consumer benefits. Output or quality trait transformation requires greater understanding of ways of coordinating multiple genes. Ultimately, genomics and bioinformatics may break the codes and enable technologies and products to develop sharply.

A major obstacle, however, is that fragmented, incomplete institutions are incapable of managing the attendant issues, with the result that private regulation remains in control. Bijman agreed with Kalaitzandonakes that institutions were very slow to change, noting a variety of different local and international experiences, distinct cultures and divergent power structures in the USA and EU which have led to different choices. Sylvie Bonny argued that a breakdown of trust in science, biotechnology, industry and governments has contributed to the divergent approaches. According to Beusmann, biotechnology has created an 'institutional vacuum', into which a number of agents have moved. In the EU, public interest groups, such as Greenpeace, have attempted to broaden the public choice debate, proposing that biotechnology is only one of the many technologies that could contribute to a future for agriculture that meets multifunctional needs. Jacques Loyat agreed, noting that the European Parliament, in particular, has used this issue as a means to increase its power generally. Peter Feindt suggested that new models of public involvement, such as citizen juries, might be appropriate.

Phillips stated that Canada, as a major exporter but lacking any national champions in the biotechnology industry, provides some alternative approaches to the US/EU focus. The debate centres on the risks associated with novel traits, rather than those of technology as such, and is associated with efforts to build international consensus about regulatory standards and broaden public dialogue. Traditionally, this was done through such groups as Greenpeace, more recently through a major effort to develop a voluntary labelling system. The Canadian Advisory Committee has also broadened public dialogue. Bijman observed that in Europe 'people' believe that they can and should control the new technology, though greater acceptance of private management and regulation prevails in the United States.

Public–private partnerships

Phillips observed that extended intellectual property rights, while providing incentives for private research, have generated concerns about the freedom to operate among many public and private researchers. While monopolistic exploitation is possible, the greatest impediment to R&D and new partnerships may be the attendant costs of protecting and transferring proprietary technologies and information. Kalaitzandonakes presented evidence that the practices of public–private partnerships in the USA and EU vary markedly. US relationships tend to be bilateral, while EU-based partnerships are denser, with more multiple partners, often extending offshore. Recently, there has been some convergence between these models.

Concern that the public sector role may not be well defined in many partnerships was expressed by Bijman, leading to debate about possible 'public' activities that have been pushed out. Bonny pointed out that public sector scientists, connected with private programmes through contracts, may lose their objectivity, or at least be perceived to have done so by the public. As a result, there may be nobody who can act as an honest broker in public discussions. John Miranowski raised the question of the cost and availability of reliable information, which is effectively a 'public good' problem. Furthermore, a number of participants suggested that efforts may shift away from basic research in search of patents and profits. Phillips noted that the structure of the partnerships may matter most. Bilateral, fee-for-service partnerships can reduce the public good while pre-commercial, non-competitive research into platform technologies may enhance public benefits. Miranowski noted that some public institutions might be more effective than others. He suggested that the CGIAR system had significant potential to act as a partner/agent to transfer new technologies into developing countries. Beusmann concluded by stressing the need to use different models and approaches as a source of learning.

Industrial structure

Discussion of intellectual property rights inevitably extends into debate about industrial structure. Miranowski argued that strong patents are a type of insurance which can foster consolidation between companies (for example, Delta and Pine Land and Monsanto). Kalaitzandonakes, however, countered with the view that weak patents can actually be a spur to consolidation in the input sector. Nevertheless, he argued that, because the input industry represents only about 6 per cent of value added in the American agri-food industry, it is being driven by the increasingly oligopolistic retail sector. Bijman concurred, noting that, in the EU, four or five companies already control 50–60 per cent of the market. The rise in private labels, consumer concerns about product quality, output trait products and industrial protocols will continue to be the driving force with the prospect of there being only three global retailers in a few years (Ahold, Carrefour and Walmart).

The retail chains and the food processors will, therefore, determine the fate of GM crops. For instance, the Dutch dairy industry has signalled that it will reject GM feeds if there is consumer opposition. While Shiva Makki felt that this would not necessarily be a problem, Phillips argued that producers, especially those smaller operators outside the new chains, could lose. Bill Kerr noted that it is an already established trend. Kalaitzandonakes countered by suggesting that some farmers might win as a result of bilateral dependency in the chains. Miranowski also noted that chains are likely to be unstable, with few switching costs, which should provide more power to producers; he suggested that we should use game theory to determine which situation is likely to occur. Vinus Zachariasse argued that switching costs could rise if labelling for production and processing methods is implemented (for example, setting up and using audit systems has significant sunk costs).

Conclusions

Beusmann expressed the desire for better communications to build a new base for credibility. Bijman agreed, though he viewed the basic problem as one in which the new, global, biotechnology market has not been matched by effective global institutions. Kalaitzandonakes also agreed, but offered the observation that effective institutions will not be forthcoming quickly, with the result that market-based management will continue to organize the introduction and adoption of new technology.

BIOTECHNOLOGY INNOVATION AND THE PRIVATE SECTOR

ORGANIZERS   **MARY BOHMAN, CARL PRAY AND DAVID SCHIMMELPFENNIG (USA)**

RAPPORTEUR   **CASSANDRA KLOTZ-INGRAM (USA)**

Several factors shape private sector research and development (R&D) in agricultural biotechnology and determine the distribution of benefits. The industry has evolved over the last decade through a cycle of mergers and acquisitions followed by spin-offs. Furthermore, public–private and cross-country research collaborations have become a significant means of developing new technology. Intellectual property rights (IPR) have also played a role in promoting R&D investments, enabling the private sector to appropriate more of the gains from biotechnology innovation. Finally, to gain access to critical protected technology (such as research tools) and facilitate R&D, researchers are finding it increasingly necessary to enter into licensing agreements.

The mini-symposium highlighted key aspects for understanding the economics of biotechnology research investments by private industry. Three papers were presented in each meeting, with at least one dealing with developing country experience. The first session focused on industry structure and concentration, including some discussion of private–public sector collaboration. The second and third dealt with the importance of property rights in R&D efforts and the distribution of benefits from innovation.

Jim Oehmke (USA) opened with a theoretical model of endogenous R&D and provided empirical evidence that concentration in the biotechnology industry is cyclical. The underlying theory is that firms invest in R&D races, with the first firm to invent reaping initial benefits. Rents are affected as other firms enter the race. He concluded that high concentration did not lower R&D activity. Next, Johann Kirsten (South Africa) described the structure and performance of the agricultural input industry in South Africa, which has changed dramatically since democratic reforms in 1994. He noted that there is an increasing presence of multinationals and, as in the USA, there has been considerable merger and acquisition activity. Additionally, farmers have readily adopted many new biotechnology inputs, mostly in maize and cotton. In the final presentation, Michael Morris (Mexico) described CIMMYT's experience in building research partnerships with private industry. These collaborative research efforts had many benefits and drawbacks, and solutions were developed to overcome diverging interests. To face the challenges ahead, Morris anticipates that public organizations will need to ensure freedom to operate, obtain legal and negotiating skills, build the capacity to manage intellectual property issues and change corporate culture.

The second session was begun by Cassandra Klotz-Ingram (USA) speaking on the development and marketing of a genetically modified (GM) high-pectin tomato. The tomato was developed jointly by Zeneca, the University of Nottingham and Petoseed. She indicated that, while patents were important in protecting property rights, plant variety protection certificates were not. The ability to license critical technological processes also fostered research. One of the most significant factors for protecting rights during product marketing was Zeneca's effective partnering and supply-chain management strategy. C.R. Srinivasan (UK) then discussed the potential impact of terminator technology, or the technology protection system (TPS), on research investments. TPS produces sterile seeds, thereby creating a natural form of IP protection. Srinivasan argued that TPS could be a response to existing weaknesses in arrangements for safeguarding rights. The TPS alone conveys no agronomic benefits to farmers. However, private companies can use the technology to switch useful traits on and off, or combine seeds with other inputs. He concluded that this form of safeguarding could be important for increasing seed developers' benefits and promoting R&D investments.

Carl Pray (USA) spoke at the end of the session about the development and adoption of *Bt* cotton in China and its release in Hebei province. Monsanto collaborated with the Chinese Academy of Agricultural Sciences to develop *Bt* varieties. Because IPR enforcement in China is weak, farmers sold *Bt* seed and use spread to other provinces. Adoption mostly benefited farmers and not consumers. Monsanto only received modest financial benefits, but they established an important presence in China.

Session three was opened by Nicholas Kalaitzandonakes (USA). He provided econometric results about the significant factors affecting GM crop adoption, including complementarities and substitutions among biotechnologies, labour and equipment savings, programme flexibility, weed and insect control effectiveness, and cross-technology impacts. He concluded that there are dynamic elements in adoption and benefits to farmers are probably substantially larger than previously estimated. Matin Qaim (Germany) then provided an *ex ante* analysis of welfare changes for producers and consumers from the introduction of virus-resistant sweet potatoes in Kenya and potatoes in Mexico. The technology transfer agreements between Monsanto and Kenyan and Mexican research organizations differed, as did the distribution of benefits. Kenya was granted a royalty-free licence to transfer the technology throughout Africa, whereas Mexico was granted limited use for certain varieties by specific companies. Qaim estimated that the welfare gains from these technologies would primarily benefit farmers, with modest consumer gains. He concluded that technology donations are possible and can be beneficial for developing countries. He also proposed assisting the poor through increased research on orphan crops.

George Norton (USA) concluded the mini-symposium by discussing the potential benefits of biotechnology in rice and vegetable systems in Asia. He maintained that health and environmental risk factors associated with current production practices can be reduced, particularly if research is directed towards specific features (for example, pest management, micronutrients, abiotic stress and nitrogen fixation). The distribution of benefits would be affected by several factors, including geography, income level, tenure status, biotechnology product, agricultural markets, institutional environment and efficiency of the research system. Low-income consumers are likely be the major beneficiaries, with producer effects being more difficult to predict without detailed empirical analysis.

CROP GENETIC DIVERSITY IN MODERN PRODUCTION SYSTEMS: EFFICIENCY AND POLICY IMPLICATIONS

ORGANIZER   ERIKA MENG (GERMANY)

RAPPORTEUR   MELINDA SMALE (USA)

The mini-symposium dealt with the economic policy implications of recent research in crop genetic diversity. A general belief exists that crop genetic resources are an important source of raw materials for crop improvement. However, at a broader policy level, governments and scientists may wonder why they should concern themselves with achieving genetic diversity, given potential trade-offs between its level and the goals of productivity and food security.

A rigorous framework for incorporating diversity issues into economic analysis has only recently begun to evolve. The mini-symposium focused on the utilization and productivity of diversity with specific emphasis on wheat production systems in China and Australia. There were presentations on the policy background for China by Jikun Huang (Chinese Academy of Agricultural Sciences) and for Australia by John Brennan (New South Wales Department of Agriculture). They examined past and current decisions in research priorities, funding for research and extension, market development and other government policies in the context of possible effects on diversity outcomes for wheat growing. The policy information provided the setting for presentation of applied work.

The selection of diversity measures was not specifically addressed, although the range of options and the importance of appropriate measures were recognized. In the applied work diversity indices adapted from ecological literature and representing various ways of measuring spatial diversity (for example, abundance, dominance and evenness of distribution) were calculated for China and Australia. Data used consisted of wheat variety pedigrees and morphological characteristics, as well as named varieties. The first application, presented by Melinda Smale (CIMMYT), estimated a system of reduced form equations for three concepts of spatial diversity – richness, abundance and evenness – at the shire level in New South Wales and at the province level in China. Explanatory variables included factors related to the supply of and demand for varieties, given physical features of the production environment.

The next two presentations examined the impact of diversity on total factor productivity (TFP) and production costs in seven major wheat-producing provinces in China during the period 1982–95. Diversity in both these studies was modelled as an endogenously determined variable. The study, presented by

Songqing Jin (University of California at Davis), also used diversity measures representing various spatial concepts in estimating a simultaneous, three-stage least squares (3SLS) system for the effect of diversity, technology and other explanatory variables (for example, infrastructure, institutional change and environmental factors) on productivity. Diversity was found to affect aggregate TFP positively in almost all of the specifications used. Although it is difficult to discern the exact nature of the link, the pattern of results suggests that diversity in terms both of named varieties and of morphological characteristics will contribute to an increase in TFP. This result implies that support for the use of diverse materials in breeding research will probably have positive effects on future productivity.

The cost function study used the Shannon-evenness measure of diversity based on morphological characteristic data. A five-equation system of spatial diversity, cost of production and cost share equations for fertilizer, pesticide and labour was estimated. Diversity was found to reduce significantly the cost shares for pesticide and labour, although its effect on total costs of production was positive.

The final session focused on policy implications from the empirical studies and addressed linkages between national level diversity outcomes and factors influencing diversity at less aggregated levels of analysis.

CURRENT AND EMERGING ISSUES IN AGRICULTURAL AND RURAL DEVELOPMENT

ORGANIZER   **WILLIAM H. MEYERS (ITALY)**

RAPPORTEUR   **KOSTAS STAMOULIS (ITALY)**

The mini-symposium discussed the results and implications of papers commissioned by FAO on contemporary agricultural and rural development, poverty and policy issues. The purpose of the project was to call attention to policy research needs that any government, academic or research institution dealing with food and agriculture (including FAO) could be interested in pursuing. The general format of the papers includes a review of the state of knowledge on each topic under study and the identification of issues for further research. The topics and authors of papers discussed were as follows:

Simon Maxwell and Robin Heber Percy, 'New Trends in Development Thinking and Implications for Agriculture' (discussed by Kostas Stamoulis in the absence of the authors);

Assefa Admassie and Joachim von Braun, 'Market Oriented Reforms, Poverty and Income Distribution : A Review with Special Reference to Agriculture and the Rural Sector';

Alberto Valdés and Johan Mistiaen, 'Rural Poverty in Latin America: Recent Trends and New Challenges';

Pranab Bardhan, 'Institutions, Reforms and Agricultural Performance' (discussed by Kostas Stamoulis in the absence of the authors).

Maxwell and Percy reviewed the current consensus (or conventional wisdom) with respect to 'food agriculture and rural development' (FARD) among major contributors in the policy debate (FAO, World Bank, IFPRI), looking at the relationship with more general themes in current thinking about overall development. Future research on FARD should emphasize (a) the non-material dimensions of (rural) poverty and social vulnerability, (b) the role of informal social protection systems and the more effective use of 'rights' approaches, (c) the impact of globalization on rural dwellers and on global public goods, (d) the pace and sequencing of liberalization (market and institutional reforms) and (e) the identification of successes and failures in applying the new 'instruments' or 'technologies' of aid and donor–recipient partnerships.

Admassie and von Braun dealt with the rationale, origin and major typologies of market-oriented reforms affecting agriculture and the rural sectors in different contexts (that is, in 'traditional' developing countries and those of 'transition economies'). The topics suggested for further investigation are (a) the role of institutions governing input and output markets, (b) the functioning of rural capital and labour markets for determining the pace of reforms, (c) identifying the new risks introduced by market reforms and the appropriate risk instruments to deal with them, (d) the new partnership arrangements between the state and the private sector in a more liberalized economic system, (e) the role of a more effective participation of the practitioners of policy in the poverty reduction debate, and (f) the renewed importance of good governance, participation and empowerment and necessary reforms in governance structures.

Valdés and Mistiaen reviewed poverty and inequality measures and discussed the patterns characteristic of the rural poor, pointing out their extreme variability with respect to location, occupation and income sources, demographic and other household characteristics. Proposed elements of a future research agenda are (a) who the poor are and why they are kept in poverty, (b) the role of non-farm rural activities and how to promote them in areas where the poor live, (c) the special conditions of women and indigenous groups, (d) the poverty–resource degradation nexus, (e) getting a rural rather than agricultural focus on the analysis of poverty, (f) implications of decentralization, and (g) the role and functioning of rural factor markets.

Bardhan examined the general issue of institutional development in developing countries in facilitating or impeding development. The research agenda includes (a) comparative–historical studies identifying which institutional arrangements can account for the differences in country performance, (b) the gender dimensions of agricultural reform, (c) the role of intellectual property rights in affecting agricultural growth, (d) the importance of redistributive conflicts and their impact on growth and productivity enhancement, and (e) the importance of institutional mechanisms for water distribution and pricing.

On the 'development' issue, additional research topics were the multifunctionality of agriculture, ways by which international public goods should be funded, and government decentralization and what it implies for rural poverty alleviation. On globalization, one should not only concentrate on the potential dangers to the poor of increasing integration but also look at the potential benefits deriving from the fall of information barriers, the possibility for greater technological transfers through foreign direct investment, and potential benefits associated with migration. The public–private sector debate highlighted ways in which cooperation could be used to channel benefits of biotechnology to the developing countries, especially to poorer farmers. On the question of aid, participants noted that it now represents a declining share of total transfers to developing countries. Regarding poverty and environmental/resource degradation, the identification of the 'correct discount rate' is essential, since the market interest rate is a distorted proxy of the discount rate.

There was a lively debate on poverty, revealing an urgent need to concentrate efforts on the 'food insecure' segment of the poor and to translate poverty alleviation into relief of food insecurity. Should anti-poverty measures be incorporated into adjustment packages or should they be taken as 'parallel measures' to reform programmes in order to buffer their potentially adverse effects on the poor? Poverty and income distribution issues should not be confused, as relationships between them are complex and need to be separated. The capacity of individual governments to design poverty reduction schemes should be carefully examined. Complex programmes can fail owing to institutional weaknesses on the part of the implementing governments. The issue of the efficiency of public services in reaching the poor was also raised. The rate of return to investment in education, for example, is said to be very low in agriculture, implying that education may increase returns to labour only for those who migrate from rural areas.

There was also a substantial debate on the 'processes of poverty', which, some feel, is the real issue in poverty research. For instance, what creates a poverty trap? Are labour and land market rigidities important? To what extent is lack of education an issue? What makes for differences among farmers in terms of their resilience to shocks, especially when returns on assets are often low in the first place? What are the effects of risk and fluctuations on poverty? There is a lack of research on most of these issues and an urgent need exists for more knowledge.

AGRICULTURAL RESEARCH POLICY IN AN ERA OF PRIVATIZATION

ORGANIZER   RUBEN ECHEVERRÍA (USA)

RAPPORTEUR   DEREK BYERLEE (USA)

The objective of this mini-symposium was to review contemporary experience on public and private sector roles in funding and executing agricultural research in developing countries in an era of general privatization. Two of the sessions assessed public–private collaboration in financing research through commodity levies and public–private collaboration in provision of research services through joint ventures and other types of partnerships. The final session focused on public sector responses to privatization. In each part, case studies were used to draw out major lessons for agricultural research policy. While the studies were largely drawn from the developing world, one from industrialized countries was included in each part to provide a comparative perspective.

The first meeting focused on public–private collaboration in funding of research, using the example of farmer financing through commodity levies. The three case studies critically examined how levies, combined with farmer empowerment over research priorities, have affected the efficiency and effectiveness of research. John Brennan and John Mullen ('Producers' and government joint funding of agricultural research in Australia') described producer funding through commodity levies combined with matching grants from government. This long-established system has undergone a number of changes resulting in the formation of commodity-based research and development corporations in which farmers have a major stakeholder interest. Ruben Diario, Rafael Posada and Federico Holmann ('Producers' funding for agricultural research in Colombia') showed how commodity associations for a range of cash crops have used levies to fund research in a variety of institutional settings, some in which work is conducted in-house and some in which it is contracted out. Finally, Mario Allegri ('Producers' and government joint funding of agricultural research in Uruguay') stated that a levy system on all agricultural products was established in 1990 to co-finance a national research institute. A clear lesson emerging from all of the studies is that strong producer organizations are needed to ensure successful implementation of levies.

Three studies of public and private sector collaboration in carrying out research were presented in the second session. The Netherlands initiated efforts to strengthen such partnerships more than a decade ago. As shown by Kees van der Meer ('Public–private cooperation in the Netherlands'), they are now part of the culture of the research system. Javier Ekboir and Gabriel

Parellada ('Public–private interactions in developing zero tillage innovations in Argentina') showed how producers, local agribusiness, multinational companies and national and international public research organizations interacted in the development, adaptation and transfer of technology. Finally, work by Andy Hall, R. Sulaiman, N. Clark, M.V.K. Sivamohan and B. Yoganand ('Public–private partnerships in Indian agricultural research') reveals the cultural gap between the public and private sector in developing viable partnerships. Together the case studies illustrate the adjustments that both public and private sectors must undergo for effective collaboration.

In the final session, public sector responses to growing privatization of research were presented. Paul Heisey (USA), S. Chittur and C. Thirtle (UK) ('Privatization of plant breeding in industrialized countries') provided an overview of public sector responses to privatization of plant breeding, with emphasis on major food crops. Public breeding programmes are redefining their roles and clients, and applied breeding work is rapidly shifting to the private sector. The next paper, by J. Huang and R. Hu (China), C. Pray and Scott Rozelle (USA) ('Public sector agricultural research reforms in China'), reviewed public sector agricultural research reforms in a period of market liberalization, culminating in a major effort to privatize many R&D activities and restructure those remaining in the public sector. A final paper, by Ken Fischer (Philippines) and Derek Byerlee (USA) ('Intellectual property rights; implications for public research organizations'), considered the growing use of intellectual property rights to protect new technologies, especially in biotechnology, using examples from Brazil, the Philippines and other developing countries. Together the papers in this session illustrated a wide range of public sector responses, which have been implemented with varying levels of success.

DYNAMISM OF AGRICULTURAL SYSTEMS AND RURAL COMMUNITIES IN SOUTH ASIA: FROM VULNERABILITY TO SUSTAINABILITY

ORGANIZER   KESHAV L. MAHARJAN (JAPAN)

RAPPORTEUR   TAKASHI TAKAHATAKE (JAPAN)

This mini-symposium dealt with the issues of incentives, institutions, infrastructure and innovations (the 4Is) in South Asia by looking at the dynamism of agricultural systems and rural communities. It dealt with some of the main constraints of the region (inaccessibility, fragility, marginality and vulnerability) and their consequences for resource management, the sustenance of communities and the betterment of the environment. There were eight brief presentations.

The first came from Pradeep Tulachan (India) who considered trends in three integral components of mountain farming in South Asia (production of food-grain crops, horticulture and livestock) using official time-series data. It was suggested that productivity of resource use has declined in spite of increases in production. The latter is obviously welcome but there must be concern about productivity effects, which clearly need further examinations at the micro level. An interesting view was then advanced by Ganesh Rauniyar (New Zealand), who examined social, economic and biophysical indicators of community sustainability. Indicators from development agencies and NGOs were reviewed and their relevance was analysed. Case studies were taken from rural community development projects, mainly in Nepal and Bangladesh. It was suggested that action-oriented plans that are designed 'with the people' and not 'for the people' are more effective in terms of sustainability and effectiveness.

The third speaker, Punya P. Regmi (Thailand), looked at an eco-restructuring approach to reconcile mountain farming systems, using evidence from the mid-west region of Nepal. The opinion expressed was that neither technological change nor improvement in infrastructure would be able to overcome the problems of inequality between the vast number of subsistence farmers, unable to meet their calorie requirements, and the few large farmers with huge surpluses. Thus access to resources to earn sufficient income, at least to fulfil basic minimum needs, is an important issue of mountain agriculture in Nepal.

Takashi Takahatake (Japan) also looked at Nepal, describing developments in the Ilam District, in the east of the country, currently undergoing a transformation from subsistence to cash crop farming. Cash crops, which enhance vegetation coverage, were said to be useful since they can provide farm income while stemming the tide of environmental degradation in the hill regions. This paper supplemented the findings of the previous one, suggesting the need for (and the possibility of) cash generation from farming, simultaneously using marginal and vulnerable lands in an environmentally friendly way. The main questions centred on the difficulties in replicating what has been happening in the Ilam District in other areas.

As the fifth presenter, Keshav L. Maharjan (Japan) described various local institutions for resource management and food procurement in rural communities of Nepal. The speaker stressed the geographical difficulties of the country, noting that its subsistence farming also faces population pressure. Some spontaneously formed local institutions, the so-called 'civil society organizations', which rest on traditional values and social norms, and are based on joint ownership and joint accountability, are developing versatile programmes to suit the needs of the people. Their performance in poverty alleviation seemed more effective than that of institutions formed exogenously for the sake of development intervention alone.

Following on, Yuba Raj Bhusal (Nepal) and Keshav L. Maharjan (Japan), assessed the institutional mechanism for rural poverty reduction in Nepal. The focus of the discussion was concerned with the funding of development projects by the central government in line with the recent commencement of the Local Self-Governance Act. The paper considered the design of a 'common basket', to enable the scattered and sometimes very nominal resources (public, private and civil societal) to be accumulated to allow poverty alleviation projects to be executed according to the needs and preferences of local people.

In the seventh contribution, Akinobu Kawai (Japan) turned to Bangladesh, specifically to the pattern of settlements in the deltaic plains. It discussed development efforts that never actually reach the people owing to the wide gap between the development administration centres and the village community. The final presentation, from Rie Ono (Japan), examined 'credit for the poor' in the rural development of Bangladesh and highlighted its limitations. Evidence was provided of how micro-credit programmes, generally regarded as one of the most effective tools for poverty alleviation, may not attain their objectives in the long run when they fail to consider the totality of needs of the people and bypass local social networks.

INTEGRATING APPROACHES FOR NATURAL RESOURCE
MANAGEMENT AND POLICY ANALYSIS: BIOECONOMIC MODELS,
MULTI-AGENT SYSTEMS AND CELLULAR AUTOMATA

**ORGANIZERS   THOMAS BERGER AND ALFONS BALMANN
(GERMANY)**

RAPPORTEUR   KATHRIN HAPPE (GERMANY)

Over the past decade a number of new simulation approaches geared towards
the understanding and management of spatial, economic and ecological changes
of agricultural systems have emerged. This is desirable because previous models appear to have taken a rather simplistic view of these issues, albeit because
of limited computing power. There are two main approaches. The so-called
'bioeconomic models' (BEM) explicitly take into account interrelated socioeconomic and biophysical processes. Second, there are models based on the
view that agricultural reality rests on individual actions and interactions. These
draw their inspiration from concepts of 'artificial intelligence' like cellular
automata (CA) and multi-agent systems (MAS). The aim was to bring these
different approaches together and to explore opportunities for integrating them.

Bioeconomic models and genetic algorithms

The paper by B. Barbier (Honduras), with Chantal Carpentier, gave examples
of BEM for tropical countries, aimed at studying land use dynamics and
farmers' reactions to changing external conditions such as population growth
and price changes. Geographic information systems (GIS) maps were the basis
for spatial representation and the methodology followed a top-down approach.
Recursive linear programmes were built on a regional level to optimize land
use patterns. Explaining the model results to farmers and officials in the
countries studied was also a key objective.

H. Jansen (Netherlands) provided an overview of a toolbox for land use
analysis on different scales as developed and applied by REPOSA (Research
Programme on Sustainability in Agriculture, Costa Rica) in a long-term interdisciplinary setting. In particular, the SOLUS regional system was discussed.
It follows a top-down approach combining the biophysical and socioeconomic
aspects of land use on the basis of linear programming and GIS. The central
objective of the research is policy analysis support.

The presentation from O.J. Cacho (Australia) addressed the application of
optimal control problems in natural resource economics. These problems are
conventionally solved using dynamic or non-linear programming techniques,

though some difficulties arise as the solutions obtained often only represent local optima. Genetic algorithms, alternatively, provide a mechanism for exploring the solution surface without sticking to local optima, even though they may converge to a global optimum very slowly.

Genetic algorithms were also the topic of the presentation by S. Geisendorf (Germany). She discussed their potential to depict bounded rationality in bioeconomic models. Her work interprets genetic algorithms as an adaptive learning process in which economic agents learn their behaviour in an environment. The simulation runs also show that the system's behaviour differs greatly if the agents are given different cognitive capacities. Therefore, she concluded, bounded rationality should not be neglected in resource use models.

Cellular automata and multi-agent systems

Alfons Balmann (Germany) presented a model of a fictitious agricultural region where farms are located on the grid of a cellular automaton. These farms are interpreted as agents interacting indirectly in the land market. Each agent's behaviour is determined on the basis of recursive linear programming. The model can be used to study structural change and the effects of different policy measures (transfer policy, price policy) on the system. The simulations used showed the impact of policies on endogenous structural change and hence on the evolution of farm sizes, efficiency and farmers' income.

Thomas Berger (Germany) extended the previous approach in several respects. Agents in his model follow heterogeneous decision rules, they communicate in information networks and they interact bilaterally over the land market. Furthermore, the model integrates the regional water resource system and considers tradeable water rights. Berger applied his model to a selected agricultural region in Chile to study the dynamic impacts of free trade-oriented policy options. The simulation runs help to predict the diffusion of specific innovations and the resultant resource use change under different scenarios.

The paper by E. Chattoe (UK) addressed general difficulties of building multi-agent models, and in particular the representation of social interactions. He identified three major difficulties. The absence of a sound data base for dynamic analysis, weak explanatory theories of social behaviour and lack of a general will to enhance the predictive power of social science.

Conclusions

The final discussion, opened by R.A.E. Mueller (Germany), dealt especially with the advantages of top-down and bottom-up approaches in the context of practical policy advice. Over the years, the more aggregate BEMs have become established as a good means of policy support. However, they fail to address certain research questions such as the role of externalities, the effects of interactions, self-organization and emergence, which are the strengths of MAS. Hence the participants of the mini-symposium agreed that bottom-up approaches can significantly extend the scope of economic analysis and should be seen as complements to the standard tools. This gives rise to further need to explore their particular strengths and to integrate them with existing bioeconomic models in order better to serve the primary objective of managing tomorrow's agriculture in a sustainable way.

AGRICULTURE'S PROVISION OF POSITIVE AMENITIES: SUPPLY, DEMAND AND THE ROLE OF GOVERNMENT

ORGANIZER   **DAVID R. OGLETHORPE (UK)**

RAPPORTEUR   **LAILA RACEVSKIS (USA)**

This mini-symposium was designed to provide a holistic appreciation of the provision of positive amenity from agriculture. The first step was to examine the *supply* of landscape and amenity goods and services through management of land use in agriculture. In the second session, an appreciation was developed of how best to place values on those goods and services to measure *demand*. The third session sought to bring supply and demand together in a complex and dynamic policy environment. Ultimately, the sessions helped to highlight key research questions and to identify the role of governmental intervention in the light of WTO and shifting global priorities. Figure 1 illustrates the dynamic or cyclical process the sessions were trying to mirror.

Agriculture is seen as a supplier of amenity for which society has demands. In order to meet those demands, given a non-market policy, signals need to be provided by governmental institutions, hence the 'role of government'. How-

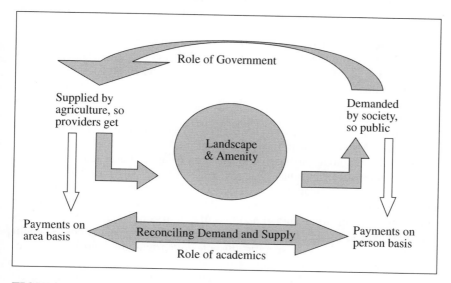

FIGURE 1   *Overview of the symposium*

ever, for that to be effective, there is a role for academics to reconcile area-based supply costs with person (or household)-based demand estimates.

The first presenter, Brian Jacobsen (Denmark), noted the increasing interest in nature amenities in Danish policy recommendations. Both mandatory and voluntary policies had been used to influence farmers and to shape natural landscapes to provide recreational areas, wildlife habitat and aesthetic quality. However, the reluctance of farmers to participate in voluntary programmes has led to attempts to identify the optimal means of achieving environmental amenities through policy signals. Developing this, Julian Smith (UK) and David Oglethorpe (UK) provided an innovative approach to modelling environmental amenity by linking ecological and economic systems in Scotland. The economic model used predicts how farmers will change management practices in response to a policy change. It has to be linked with a geographic information systems (GIS)-based model to simulate the response of vegetation cover to farmers' management changes. This dynamic system provides the opportunity for policy makers to examine the combined economic and ecological effects of agricultural and environmental policies.

A major challenge to reconciling supply models with demand models is to move to a situation where both demand estimates and supply costs can be made at the same (spatial) resolution and transferred across regions. Within the environmental economics literature, 'choice experiments' are providing a means to this end. The second session concentrated on these techniques. Nick Hanley (UK) (who had worked with Alistair McVittie and David Oglethorpe) showed that, through choices, survey respondents can reveal values for different attributes set at different levels. This method can be helpful to policy makers to determine priority levels for the protection of different landscapes. Olvar Bergland (Norway) also focused on choice experiments, but within a Scandinavian context. He stated that the literature on the perception of landscape is extensive and ranges across various fields. Factors found to be important in the appreciation of landscapes are variation, comprehensibility and degree of mysticism. From the discussion it emerged that choice models could allow reconciliation of supply and demand since policies taken up by farmers combine premiums for providing specific features (hay meadows, heather moorland, stone walls and so on) and choice surveys could reveal demand estimates for those specific features.

The first paper in the session on the role of government was presented by Laila Racevskis (USA) who recognized that the United States federal government has been somewhat passive in the area of agricultural land use policy. The structure of farming has changed markedly over the past 50 years and small farmers, now unable to compete with large corporate operations, are under pressure to sell land for commercial or residential development. This has led to problems of urban sprawl and loss of countryside amenity. Public interest in policies to protect open land is increasing. Policy makers could benefit from information about the specific attributes of agricultural land as a provider of open space that the public finds desirable.

The last speaker, Wilfrid Legg (OECD), dealt with the role of policy in contributing to the improvement of environmental performance and rural viability while meeting food demands. There is a need for a balanced approach so that farmers pay for the pollution they create but are also themselves paid for the amenities they provide. The policy mix is becoming more complex because of the need to achieve a variety of goals. Some countries fear that trade liberalization will constrain the provision of amenities demanded by the public, while others fear that supporting agriculture for its provision of amenities is disguised protectionism. The primary challenge to policy makers is to develop good policies to complement market approaches. The session ended with a discussion of the need to reconcile policy planning at local levels with national frameworks and international conventions. This was becoming increasingly important in the light of WTO negotiations and the importance of 'green box' payments. It was felt that research methods and techniques were moving in the right direction and the need to harmonize the science of supply simulation with the social science of demand estimation was becoming increasingly important.

THE ECONOMICS AND POLICY OF ORGANIC FARMING: WHAT CAN BE LEARNED FROM THE EUROPEAN EXPERIENCE?

ORGANIZER   STEPHAN DABBERT (USA)

RAPPORTEUR   PAUL WEBSTER (UK)

As a background to the discussion, Stephan Dabbert pointed out that organic farming represented selective use of particular technologies, including the choice *not* to use some types. This decision not to use technology may be made in order to achieve objectives which can be economic or non-economic. Across Europe there were, in 1999, around 3 million hectares (2.5 per cent of the cropped area) under organic agriculture. There were major differences across regions, with some having negligible amounts and others with up to 10 per cent. There were a number of reasons for recent growth, but the most important included increased demand and hence price premia for organic products, plus the influence of agricultural policy measures. Such measures included the introduction of EU-wide certification schemes as well as the various agrienvironmental programmes, which had been developed following the 1992 CAP reforms.

During the first session, Hiltrud Nieberg and Frank Offermann (Germany) gave a brief summary of a study of organic farming across 18 EU countries. Results showed crop yield reductions of between 10 and 50 per cent, depending on crop, and milk yield levels varying between 80 and 105 per cent of those from conventional herds. While there was some reduction in variable costs, the key to profitability lay in price premia obtained for organic products which varied across crops (wheat, 20 to 200 per cent; potatoes, 80 to 500 per cent; milk, 8 to 37 per cent) and also across countries. Simultaneous differences in price across countries could not be easily explained. Discussants pointed out the lack of 'transparency' in many of the markets for organic products. Organic farm profitability varied between plus or minus 20 per cent of the conventional systems and showed inter-year movements very much in line with those seen in conventional systems.

Discussions centred upon the objectives of organic farmers. Were they very different from those of conventional farmers? It was suggested that the early adopters were largely motivated by non-economic factors but, since then, and as many conventional systems had come into crisis, economic motives had underlain the decisions of later converters.

During the second session, discussion turned to questions relating to the future of organic farming in Europe. Danilo Gambelli (Italy) presented an approach to these questions using 'scenario analysis' and a 'fuzzy expert system'. His project team had acted as experts to define a series of 26 variables. These were classified either as external (eight, such as food scares, farmers' altruistic concerns, CAP reforms) or internal (18, classified as 'micro', including domestic demand for organic products, and so on; 'meso', notably availability of organic products, and 'macro', including, for example, the political climate with respect to agriculture). The experts next constructed a series of 200 rules linking the external and internal variables. Each variable could be designated 'high', 'medium' or 'low'. Five scenarios were defined by setting the external variables to specified levels and designated by a title ('Gloomy Liberalization', 'Organic Paradise' and so on). The fuzzy expert system was used to find values of the internal variables consequent upon the levels of the external variables as specified by the scenario. Rules could have timings specified before the variables took effect, which resulted in a time trajectory for the scenario to be played out. The five scenarios were analysed and the key results showed that the progress of organic agriculture in Europe would probably be most sensitive to three factors. These were the implementation of the agrienvironmental policies relating to Agenda 2000, the progress or otherwise of the WTO negotiations, and countries' attitudes towards food safety and genetic modification.

Discussion centred on the probable impacts of the WTO negotiations, which the group thought might be quite positive or somewhat negative, depending on the detailed outcome. It was also pointed out that organic farming was subject to the same vagaries of policy as conventional agriculture. The impact of policy on the sector depended very much on the commodities being considered (whether supported, like cereals, or unsupported, like vegetables) and also on methods of implementation within individual member states.

During the third session, Nic Lampkin (UK) led a discussion relating to the changing policy framework for organic farming in Europe. It was recognized that policy support through, firstly, the definition of organic food (regulation 2092/91) and, secondly, direct support in some countries using agrienvironmental programmes (regulations 2078/92) had also contributed in a major way. There would probably be further support for organic agriculture in EU policy circles because it could represent a set of ethical considerations (for example, environmental protection, animal welfare, sustainability) with which policy makers could identify. Other arguments for organics, based on 'infant industries' and 'public goods', were also used in different countries. The potential impact of Agenda 2000 was not yet clear, since many countries had not yet finalized their implementation plans. Progressive 'decoupling' was likely to be beneficial where yields per hectare were lower than in conventional systems.

The implementation of the EU's Rural Development Regulation was seen as an important issue for organic production. But the principle of 'subsidiarity' brought the possibility of very different levels of support for organic systems across countries and hence the further possibility of conflicts relating to the 'level playing field' for intra-EC trade. There was also consideration of the WTO negotiations where organic standards were not seen as trade restricting. But the future of direct payments for organic systems was uncertain; were they 'green box' or' blue box'? Were payments for environmental benefits to be regarded as trade distorting? If there were such environmental benefits, they needed to be identified and quantified. Were consumers already paying for environmental benefits in the premia obtained?

But a central question still remained about whether, and if so how, organic systems should be supported. Any payments from the public purse needed to be justified by the value of the public environmental benefits achieved. The identification and valuation of these benefits represented a considerable challenge for researchers in organic agriculture.

ECONOMICS OF FOOD SAFETY

ORGANIZER   T. ROBERTS (USA)

RAPPORTEUR   C. NARROD (USA)

This mini-symposium addressed the economics of human health risks associated with pathogens in the world's food supply: parasites and bacteria in meat, fungi producing mycotoxins in corn, and antibiotic use in animal feeds contributing to drug-resistance of bacteria causing human illness.

Public and private economic incentives for food safety

J. Hobbs (Canada), A. Fearne (UK) and J. Spriggs (Australia) began by looking at incentive structures for food safety and quality assurance. The forces escalating food safety actions in the United Kingdom have been better crisis management and restoration of consumer confidence, whereas in Canada and Australia risk management and prevention of trade-threatening food safety issues are more central. In Britain and Australia, food companies are increasing vertical alliances, partly in response to the UK 1990 Food Safety Act that requires 'due diligence' and increases legal liability for contaminated incoming products.

J. Skees, A. Botts and K. Zeuli (USA) dealt with recall insurance to improve food safety. It is possible to obtain insurance to protect businesses against losses due to food-borne pathogens from product recalls, disease outbreaks, sales losses or other business disruptions. To receive low insurance premiums, firms have an incentive to disclose their *maximum* food safety efforts. In contrast, under official regulations, firms have an incentive to identify the *minimum* number of critical control points for monitoring by regulators. There appears to be a case for institutional change.

T. Riggs, E. Elbasha and M. Messonnier (USA), looking at the effects of information on producer and consumer incentives to undertake food safety efforts, drew attention to a double moral hazard problem. It arises since neither consumers nor producers can accurately detect the other's efforts and both share the losses if illness occurs. Given this suboptimal outcome, government regulation could increase social welfare, especially if it increases information and causes changes in behaviour.

Private sector food safety incentives

E. Salay and A. Mercadante (Brazil) described how Brazilian feed companies attempt to control mycotoxins in corn, especially aflatoxin. Eighty per cent of

Brazilian corn goes into animal feed and mycotoxins can affect both animal and human health. The incentives for such private sector control come from client demands and competition with other companies, as well as a desire to improve process control and product quality.

R. Laxminarayan (USA) dealt with the complex economics of bacterial resistance in looking at optimal patent breadth for antibiotics used in animal feed and in human treatment. The incentives in the US patent system are designed to induce innovation and do not address the role of patents in protecting open-access resources like antibiotic effectiveness. When development of resistance occurs from antibiotic use it may be suboptimal, from society's perspective, to permit sales in two markets with different demand elasticities.

M. Gómez (USA) and J. Torres (Colombia), in looking at the Colombian poultry industry, suggested that the primary incentive for producers to become more efficient and to be able to ensure meat product safety is international competition. The WTO is causing traditional trade barriers to fall and Colombia is implementing new food safety regulations. The private sector is responding with its own food safety initiatives.

Food safety risk and its effect on technology choices

T. Roberts, C. Narrod and S. Malcolm (USA) began the third session by considering the control of *E. coli*. Many scientists investigating new control procedures for pathogens only report mean risk reductions. However, pathogen effects do not have a normal distribution and mean results can be misleading. Using control procedures in the beef slaughterhouse, examples are given of estimated generic *E. coli* risks in the mean model versus a probabilistic risk assessment model using the distribution of generic *E. coli*. Implications for policy making were discussed.

H. Jensen, D. Hayes, L. Backstrom and 1. Fabiosa (USA) examined the economic effects of a ban on the use of over-the-counter antibiotics in pig rations. Swedish producer responses to changes caused by the ban on antibiotics in pig feeds were analysed. If a similar ban were imposed in the USA, pork prices were estimated to increase by 5 cents per pound at the retail level. However, America may ban fewer antibiotics, while use of other substitutes in production may reduce the economic impact and lower the estimated increase in pork prices.

T. Wang, V. Diderrick, J. Kliebenstein, S. Patton, J. Zimmerman, A. Hallam, C. Faulkner and R. McCord (USA) dealt with *Toxoplasma gondii* levels in pig production. Ingestion of *Toxoplasma gondii* by pregnant women can cause abortions or mental retardation in foetuses. Producers can control *Toxoplasma gondii* levels in market hogs by using bait and/or traps for rodents and total confinement facilities. Producer costs for control of the parasite are minimal, notably because there are significant economies of scale associated with swine confinement operations which most US producers have.

Discussant Richard Williams (USA) pointed out that there does not seem to be a general theory relating to the minimum requirements necessary to make effective market changes. To spark debate, he presented four minimum conditions: some sort of desire for change, means to monitor change, financial ability to make change, and technical ability to make changes.

EFFECTS OF HEALTH INFORMATION ON THE DEMAND FOR FOOD: EU AND US EXPERIENCES

ORGANIZERS   WEN S. CHERN (USA) AND KYRRE RICKERTSEN (NORWAY)

RAPPORTEUR   JAYACHANDRAN N. VARIYAM (USA)

Increasing concerns about health risks related to diets have had significant effects on food consumption patterns in the United States and the European Union. The measurement of 'health information' parameters and the quantification of likely impacts on food and nutrient intake are important subjects of inquiry. The objective of this mini-symposium was to provide a forum for analysts to report and discuss 'state-of-the-art' developments in this area.

The programme began with an introduction by Wen Chern (USA) about the purpose and the focus of each session. Chern then presented his findings on the impact of a fat and cholesterol information index on American demand for ten food items with high to low fat content. The index was computed as a weighted average of the number of medical journal articles related to fats and cholesterol, with the weights declining over time. This eliminated the problem of the index proxying for the time trend. Health risk information, as measured by the index, increased the consumption of fresh fruit, vegetables and dairy products, but decreased the consumption of meats, eggs, and fats and oils.

In a similar vein, Rudy Nayga (USA) presented a cross-section study to assess the effect of nutrition label use on the intake of key nutrients as well as the overall diet quality of American adults. It used data from the 1994–6 *Continuing Survey of Food Intakes by Individuals* (CSFII) and the *Diet and Health Knowledge Survey* (DHKS). Nayga's results suggested that nutrition labels improved diet quality by as much as 4–6 points on a 100 point Healthy Eating Index scale.

The key variable mediating the effect of health information on food and dietary choices is educational attainment. Using quantile regression estimates, Jay Variyam (USA) showed that, for total fat, saturated fat and cholesterol intake of American men, the effect of education and nutrition information is much greater at the upper end of the intake distributions. Therefore the 'beneficial' effect of education on dietary behaviour may have been underestimated owing to the previous focus on conditional mean estimates. Justo Manrique (Spain) and Helen Jensen (USA) used Becker's household production model to show how nutrition knowledge affected total fat and cholesterol intakes of low-income American people. Greater self-assessed importance of avoiding too much fat translated into lower total fat intakes. Also better awareness of cholesterol-related health problems reduced cholesterol intakes.

The second day's session began with an introduction by Kyrre Rickertsen (Norway) concerning a European project to assess the impact of health information on food demand. The project involved the development of a common model as well as country-specific models using an 'Adjusted Global Index' as the health information measure. Stephan von Cramon-Taubadel (Germany) presented the results from the common model. While health information affected demand for the meat and fish group, this effect was significant only for Scotland. Combined with other unexpected findings, this suggested that a common model is too restrictive, and country-specific models would be more desirable. The spread of diet–health information has made consumers think more in terms of food nutrients than in terms of food products. This motivated A.M. Angulo, J.M. Gil and A. Garcia (Spain) to analyse food demand incorporating income, prices and nutrient intakes as its main determinants. Nutrient elasticities provide guidance for changes that would take place if nutritionists' recommendations were taken into account.

Susanne Wildner (Germany) and Stephan von Cramon-Taubadel's study compared the evolution of the demand for meat and fish and the response to health information in East and West Germany since reunification. A comparison of the effects of the Global Information Index and two German-specific indexes suggested that only the former produced plausible results. Health information effects were stronger in the West than in the East.

The third session focused on producer response to health information and methodology of incorporating information in microeconometric models. John Santarossa and David Mainland (Scotland) noted that attempts at altering the diet of the Scottish population by advertising campaigns have been unsuccessful. Therefore they considered the effects of a fiscal policy approach to reducing dietary fat intake. Simulations using an estimated demand model suggested that a tax policy could lower total fat intake as a percentage of energy to 30 per cent from the existing 38 per cent.

Since consumers have been shown to respond disproportionately to negative information, advertising campaigns financed by beef and pork producers may be relatively ineffective at countering negative publicity stemming from medical research that links dietary cholesterol to heart disease. Using an equilibrium-displacement model of the US meat sector, Henry Kinnucan (USA) and Oystein Myrland (Norway) estimated that the 7 per cent increase in the Health Information Index during 1993 generated losses to beef and pork producers equal to 8.1 and 3.9 per cent of farm revenue, respectively. Thus, to counter the adverse effects of health information, beef and pork producers should probably focus on product redesign, as advertising is likely to be ineffectual.

Diffusion of information about cholesterol–health linkage has been found to be a major reason for the decline of American egg consumption. Since individuals differ in exposure to media sources and in skills to process health information, aggregate time-series measures of health information may not fully capture consumers' specific health concerns. Kamhon Kan (Taiwan) and

Steven Yen (USA) used CSFII-DHKS micro data to estimate the effects of cholesterol information on egg consumption. Information, decisions to consume and the level of consumption were correlated, suggesting the importance of joint estimation of these equations.

Wen Chern concluded the symposium by stressing the need for quantifying the information about food products so that the estimates could become useful for policy makers. At present, micro studies use a variety of health information measures and there is need for standardization to ensure comparability. Validation of the measures is also essential. Studies need to report more descriptive statistics to aid interpretation of results.

POSTER PAPER ABSTRACTS*

*The sorting of papers is by *continent of residence of authors*, with first author names in alphabetical order.

POSTER PAPER ABSTRACTS

AFRICA

Determinants of adoption of dairy cattle technology in the Kenyan highlands: a spatial and dynamic approach – **I. Baltenweck and S.J. Staal**

Adoption of high-grade cows by smallholders is driven by the objective of increased milk production, for both home consumption and sale. Smallholders are believed to have a comparative advantage in rearing grade cows, but constraints to adoption are numerous: the cost of a grade cow is relatively high and dairying is risky. Risks include animal diseases and lack of reliable marketing outlets. Marketing risk is a common preoccupation for smallholders but it is particularly relevant for milk, which is bulky, highly perishable and sold daily. Using a dynamic and spatial framework, this study tests the hypothesis that access to credit facilitates adoption. Distances derived from GIS information are computed and introduced in a duration model in order to control for market access. Time is expected to play a key role in adoption and two time dimensions are introduced: an idiosyncratic time describing the conditions faced by the household at the beginning of the spell, and historical time accounting for the changes in the external conditions. Results show that access to credit cannot be excluded as a reason for delaying adoption of grade cows. Policy changes over time are also found to play a role in the adoption process, as the reduced availability of reliable market channels and veterinary services after liberalization in 1992 are shown to have shifted down the adoption function.

Contact: I. Baltenweck, International Livestock Research Institute, P.O. Box 30709, Nairobi, Kenya; *i.baltenweck@cgiar.org*

Factors affecting urban demand for live sheep in Addis Ababa, Ethiopia – **Samuel E. Benin and Simeon K. Ehui**

In most of sub-Saharan Africa household consumption of 'small ruminant' meat is undertaken by first purchasing the live animal and then slaughtering at home. Thus, as the share of small ruminant meat, especially sheep, in the demand and consumption of meat in general grows, information about consumer expenditure behaviour and demand parameters for live sheep will be valuable for several interest groups. A survey conducted in Addis Ababa in 1992/93 shows that the share of expenditure on live animals in total sheep meat expenditure is about 87 per cent. Using the Heckman two-stage approach, the

715

study shows that price and household income as well as sociodemographic factors, including household size and composition, significantly affect the likelihood of purchasing live sheep and spending on them. Projections of demand in 2010 and 2020 show that live sheep demand will reach about 0.5 and 0.6 million animals, respectively. Assuming that live purchases will continue to dominate total sheep meat purchases, will current sheep production trends in Addis Ababa be able to meet the increasing demand? Sheep supply projections (offtake of private holdings for sale) show that producers in Addis Ababa alone will be able to meet only 5 to 27 per cent of the total demand in 2010 and 2020, respectively.

Contact: Samuel E. Benin, International Livestock Research Institute, Addis Ababa, Ethiopia; *s.benin@cgiar.org*

Agricultural policy evaluation at the local level through a regional social accounting matrix: an example from Morocco – **Michel Benoit-Cattin**

In less developed countries policy evaluation methodology has to be reconsidered as the context has dramatically changed. For example, in Morocco, the main objective used to be self-sufficiency in basic commodities such as flour, sugar or milk. These objectives have justified heavy investments in large irrigation schemes. Nowadays, the problem is to evaluate the impacts of development alternatives on different kinds of economic agent: households, enterprises, public institutions and so on. For that, at national and local levels, the idea of using social accounting matrices is spreading. The methodology at the local/provincial level is illustrated by an example from Morocco where investments in irrigation are continuing but where there is also concern with poverty reduction in rainfed agriculture. During a research project on regional development, with a focus on agriculture and its upstream and downstream linkages, an SAM has been built for the province of El Djedida (on the Atlantic plain 90 km south-west of Casablanca) for the year 1997. This SAM, and the derived multipliers, is used to contribute to one aspect of the policy debate, namely whether it is better to invest in irrigated agriculture than in rainfed alternatives.

Contact: Michel Benoit-Cattin, Rachid Doukkali Institut Agronomique et Vétérinaire Hassan Il Rabat Morocco; *benoitca@cirad.fr*

Achieving greater impact from integrated nutrient management technologies: strategies for intensification of inorganic fertilizer on smallholder farms in semi-arid areas of Kenya – **H. Ade Freeman and John M. Omiti**

Application of inorganic fertilizer is a key component of integrated nutrient management (INM) strategies to address soil fertility maintenance and replenishment problems in Africa. Yet current levels of inorganic fertilizer applied on smallholder farms are lower than extension recommendations and there is a lack of empirical studies that articulate clear strategies for achieving greater use. Using household data from eastern Kenya, this study uses Tobit analysis to explore the determinants of inorganic fertilizer use and predicts probabilities of adoption and use intensities for specific farm types. The results suggest that appropriate targets, experimentation that improves efficiency of use, diversification into cash crops and a shift in soil fertility research from production to a sub-system focus will enhance the probability of achieving impact from INM technologies.

Contact: H. Ade Freeman, International Crops Research Institute for the Semi-Arid Tropics, P.O. Box 39063, Nairobi, Kenya; *h.a.freeman@cgiar.org*

Decentralized agricultural research priority setting (DARPS) under multiple objectives: an empirical experience of the Indian Punjab – **D.K. Grover**

In view of growing scarcity of research resources and expanding needs, the present study on priorities deals with the undulating plain zone of the Indian Punjab. The main objectives were identification of researchable problems; formulation of agricultural research agenda/projects; suggesting research priorities based on multiple goals; resource-gap assessment for projects; and institutionalization of the DARPS process. The identification of problems was based on secondary data, discussion with scientists, interactions with farmers, feedback from extension workers and rapid rural appraisals (RRAs). These problems were then short-listed on the basis of relative profitability and sustainability. The Simple Variant Economic Surplus and Scoring Model was attempted for ranking the priorities. The impact on value of production (VOP) due to each research project was estimated on the basis of expected impact of research (EIR) and conditioned by expected probability of research success, spread of researchable problem, expected ceiling rate of adoption, adoption lag and adoption pattern. Using the information on costs/benefits, net present value was estimated and used to rank the projects. They were then separately ranked on sustainability, equity/employment, export orientation and spill-in possibility. These ranks were combined using the weights derived from the expert panel. The intended priorities were matched with available resources and gaps identified. The institutionalization of the DARPS exercise helped in redeployment of resources to address the needs of the farming community.

Contact: D.K Grover, Department of Agricultural Economics, Alemaya University of Agriculture, Alemaya, Ethiopia; *alemaya. univ@telecom. net. et*

Smallholder irrigation in transformation: a case study from South Africa – **Bettina Hedden-Dunkhorst and Tlou Magdeline Mathonzi**

Smallholder irrigation farming in South Africa and elsewhere is in a stage of transformation. With government withdrawal from irrigation, new challenges and risks evolve. This study discusses the applicability of two 'modern' economic theories ('induced innovation' and 'new institutional economics') to smallholder irrigation. It then offers a theoretically based conceptual framework indicating determinants of smallholder irrigation performance, related to policy, institutions and infrastructure. Finally, the study describes these determinants in the South African context and assesses their impact on smallholder irrigation performance. The assessment points to a number of critical issues, which are primarily related to institutional arrangements. In particular, lack of appropriate extension, access to financial markets, scheme management and farmer organization limit performance. A simultaneous equation model supports the assessment of limited impact of the existing institutional set-up, but also indicates the potential of irrigation to contribute to smallholder welfare. To realize this potential, it is now important to get the institutional framework right. In this context new interventions are required. They could be based on a well-designed system of incentives, but, most of all, farmers' involvement, particularly that of women farmers, is essential to attain equity, employment and income generation through irrigation farming.

Contact: Bettina Hedden-Dunkhorst, University of the North, Department of Agricultural Economics, P.B. X1106, Sovenga, 0727, South Africa; *dunkhorst @unin.unorth.ac.za*

A methodology for the economic valuation of communal savannas: a study in the Eastern Cape Province of South Africa – **L. Mabusela, G.C.G. Fraser and G. Antrobus**

This presentation outlines a proposed methodology to be used in the economic evaluation of communal savannas in the Eastern Cape Province. It is hoped to expose the proposal to constructive discussions that will help to refine it prior to commencement of the study. This type of approach has not been attempted in the communally owned grazing areas of the province and it is anticipated that the local situation may result in unique analytic problems. The main objective is to estimate the annual direct use values of an average hectare of communal savannas in the area. Use and non-use resource values will be considered using both the demand and non-demand approaches. The demand approach will include the contingency valuation technique to estimate non-use values and the travel cost method. A non-demand curve approach will include the substitution cost method to estimate the use values. Non-use values considered are option values and community integrity benefits. The use values will include the current uses, namely livestock production, plant gathering and hunting. The survey results will be used to determine the impact of changes to the average use value using sensitivity analysis. Other variables of interest include total land productivity, composition of use values, trade-offs between value components, differences between private and social use values and their spatial variation.

Contact: G.C.G. Fraser, University of Fort Hare, Fort Hare, South Africa; *fraser@ufh.ac.za*

Seasonal food insecurity and household coping strategies in rural Tanzania –
Ntengua Mdoe, Abdul Mhinte and Gasper Ashimogo

The study was carried out to investigate seasonal food insecurity and coping strategies used by rural households in semi-arid areas in central Tanzania. A total of 270 randomly selected households were interviewed using a structured questionnaire, seeking information on household food supply, existence of seasonal food shortages and strategies employed to cope with the shortages. Descriptive statistics were obtained and a multiple regression model was used to determine factors influencing food available for household consumption. The results show that rural households in central Tanzania experience seasonal shortages. Own farm food production was generally inadequate and was readily available only for a short period after harvest. Post-harvest seasons are normally characterized by food insecurity. Most households consumed less than 80 per cent of the minimum of 2780 kcal per adult equivalent, per day. Poor households formed the most vulnerable group. Strategies used to cope with food insecurity include, in the following order, food buying, borrowing, and exchange of food for livestock or labour. The use of these strategies differs between poor and well-off households. Labour selling appears to be a common strategy among the poor. The results suggest that diversification of sources of rural livelihood rather than being entirely dependent on rain-fed agriculture would enable rural households to cope with food insecurity.

Contact: Ntengua Mdoe, Department of Agricultural Economics and Agribusiness, Sokoine University of Agriculture, Morogoro, Tanzania; *nmdoe@suanet.ac.tz*

Gender and transaction cost: a conjoint analysis of choice of livestock health service among smallholder dairy farmers in Kenya – **Leah Ndung'u and Thomas F. Randolph**

Poor adoption of livestock disease control technologies in developing countries is often attributed to the high transaction costs faced by livestock keepers in gaining access to livestock health services. These costs, though often described qualitatively, have rarely been analysed quantitatively. We report an approach for evaluation as reflected in the attributes that farmers consider when choosing a service provider. This technique is used to address the question of whether decision making about livestock disease control in Kenyan smallholder dairy farms is influenced by gender-based differences in perceptions of transaction costs. In addition to price, we identify five attributes of livestock health service provision that represent various aspects of search, negotiation and enforcement-related transaction costs: distance to service provider, degree of professionalism, familiarity with reputation, timeliness of service and availability of interlocked services. A conjoint analysis experiment was administered to 297 farmers in which they were asked to rank 20 different combinations of selected levels for these attributes based on a fractional factorial design with four holdouts. Farms within the sample were categorized by gender of the respondent and gender roles in managing the farm and their dairy animal health. Average part-worths of the levels for each attribute of service provision, as well as the relative importance of each of the six attributes, were compared across the various subgroups. The results highlight the minor importance of price relative to the other attributes, representing non-pecuniary transaction costs, in farmer decision making and potential opportunities for improving women's access to livestock health services.

Contact: Thomas F. Randolph, International Livestock Research Institute, Nairobi, Kenya; *t.randolph@cgiar.org*

Improving resource allocation for sustainable development through participatory farming systems analysis – **Arshford Njenga, Manfred Van Eckert and Justus Wesseler**

Information asymmetries between researcher and farmer create incentives not to disclose or to disclose biased information, thus resulting in inefficient design of development projects and government policies. The problem has long been recognized and several participatory approaches have been developed to overcome it by creating incentives for the disclosure of unbiased information. One approach, of Participatory Farming Systems Analysis (PFSA), which has been applied on many occasions, is presented here. The basic step is to organize a workshop where farmers and extension workers are trained in simple methods of farming systems analysis. Part of the workshop is the application of standard tools, including the analysis of the collected information. At the end of the workshop, information about the farming system is available, entered into the computer, and participants are trained in farming system analysis. Depending on the information needs, additional farms can be added to the data set. The approach does not make use of questionnaires or other forms of survey materials, so it requires a well-trained interviewing team. Another constraint is the relatively high amount of time needed per farm, with visits usually taking half a day or longer. Nevertheless, the approach has been successfully applied to provide information about farming systems for project planning, project pre-feasibility studies, monitoring and evaluation of project activities, and land use planning in countries such as India, Kenya, Malawi, Tanzania and the Philippines.

Contact: Arshford Njenga, Integration of Tree Crops into Farming Systems Project, ICRAF-House, Gigiri, Nairobi, Kenya; *m.eckert@cgiar.org*

Institutions and delivery of services to smallholder coffee farmers in Kenya under liberalized market policies – **Hezron Omare Nyangito**

A major challenge to agricultural development is how to ensure competitive provision of production and marketing services to farmers. Delivery of services was previously monopolized by public institutions, but, with liberalized market policies, farmers have perceived the reduced role of governments as a failure on the part of the government rather than a step in the right direction. This is because of poor delivery of services by the emerging former-controlled institutions and the private sector, and the accompanying low returns from agricultural output. An analysis of the delivery of services to coffee farmers in Kenya indicates that liberalized market policy reforms have yet to benefit smallholder farmers. Coffee production has declined since implementation of the policies. A major reason is that private organizations to take over functions previously undertaken by public institutions have yet to develop adequately. Instead, the public organizations, which were transformed to be brought under the control of farmers, are associated with poor management. They also play dual roles as regulators and providers of services leading to conflicts of interests. All these developments have led to poor coordination and control of service delivery, resulting in high transaction costs, which reduce returns to farmers. It is apparent that effective delivery of services in a liberalized market policy environment requires clear definition of roles among the various stakeholders and well functioning government institutions to enforce rules that govern transactions among various groups in the system.

Contact: Hezron Omare Nyangito, Kenya Institute for Public Policy Research and Analysis (KIPPRA), P.O. Box 56445 Nairobi, Kenya; *hnyangito@kippra.or.ke*

Assessment of increasing cattle prices on crop/livestock integration among Sahelian livestock farmers – **Amadou Sidibe**

In view of land scarcity and demographic pressure, agricultural intensification through crop and livestock integration could overcome low productivity, natural resource degradation and social conflict between farmers and herders in Sahelian countries. This paper examines how a rise in farm cattle prices can reinforce crop and livestock integration through forage production. A linear programming model is used to show the effects. Data were collected before currency devaluation, with prices after devaluation being used to represent the increase in the model. Two groups of livestock farmers were identified. Group II produce more cereals and have higher family labour than Group I. The optimal solution of the model indicates that the groups have the same strategy in selling animals, based on the sale of male cattle and old cows. Both groups produce insufficient quantities of forage and use it mainly to feed calves. Solving the model shows that land is not the constraint, hence cropping a large area seems to be less profitable. The increase of cattle prices would allow farmers to sell more cattle (from 10 to 21 per cent of the herd for Group I and from 15 to 21 per cent for Group II). The analysis of land and labour use shows that land is still available but not labour, with the latter now being insufficient to produce enough forage for all productive cattle.

Contact: Amadou Sidibe, Univ. Polytechn. de Bobo-Dioulasso, Burkina Faso; *asidibe@esi.univ-ouaga.bf*

Crop–livestock production paths: an economic analysis of alternative futures in semi-arid West Africa – **T.J. Wyatt and T.O. Williams**

In semi-arid West Africa, livestock and crop production are closely linked. Animals rely on crop residues as a major feed resource in the dry season, while draught power supplied by animals and nutrients deposited in the form of manure on croplands are indispensable to soil fertility maintenance and crop yields. The climatic, demographic and economic changes that have taken place in the region over the last three decades have, however, put enormous pressure on the complementary interactions between the two activities. These changes are occurring at a time when demand for livestock products is increasing and more effective measures are needed to maintain soil fertility. Improvement of livestock and crop production under this situation demands, amongst other things, new management practices and productivity-enhancing technologies that are biologically effective and economically viable. The data used come from studies conducted by the International Livestock Research Institute (ILRI) and the International Crop Research Institute for the Semi-Arid Tropics (ICRISAT) based in Niger. A bioeconomic, non-linear programming model of the whole farm is developed and used to consider potential development pathways for crop–livestock systems in the Sahel in the face of social, economic and policy changes. Various scenarios depicting improvements in crop and livestock productivity and economic incentives were analysed to determine the likely impact of potential technical and policy interventions on the livelihoods of smallholder farmers and the sustainability of crop–livestock production in semi-arid West Africa. Model results suggest that improvements in whole farm productivity and rural livelihoods can be achieved through better packaging of existing technologies and implementation of appropriate economic incentives and policies.

Contact: T.J. Wyatt, ICRISAT/ILRI, ICRISAT Sahelian Centre, BP 12404, Niamey, Niger; *t.o.williams@cgiar.org*

ASIA

Challenges of agricultural economy in Kyrgyzstan – **Jamin Akimaliew**

Agriculture is the leading sector of the Kyrgyz economy, contributing 50 per cent of GDP, with about 65 per cent of the population living in the rural areas. Almost three-quarters of them live below the poverty level. The republic faces a number of tasks. The principal ones are speeding up agricultural production and combating poverty. Shortages and high prices of fuel, fertilizers, pesticides, herbicides and machinery and spares are restraining agricultural growth. Prices of agricultural products are low in relation to those of industrial goods. The result of implementing agricultural reform should be to bring about drastic change in the management of agricultural markets in a transition economy. Successful functioning of the market requires independence and economic responsibility of commodity producers, flexible pricing, competition, financial institutions and structural balancing of the economy. In the transition to market relations a broad-based programme of privatization of state property is being carried out.

Contact: Jamin Akimaliew; *kaa@imfiko@bishkek.su*

Comparative economic analysis of conventional and organic hazelnut farming in Turkey – **Mehmet Bülbül and Harun Tanrivermiş**

Hazelnut is cultivated on 420 000 hectares land and engages 362 405 producers on small family farms in the Black Sea region. Turkey has a share of 62–77 per cent in world hazelnut production, and the largest volume of output. As the increases in production exceed demand growth, the amount of stock had increased to 220 000 tonnes by 1998. In these circumstances, there is need for new regulations to govern hazelnut production and marketing. One of the great advantages of growing hazelnuts is that cultivation can be organic, which has marketing advantages overseas. In the study, organic hazelnut production was shown to be more profitable than conventional methods. Organic farming could be increased and would succeed if demand could be stimulated.

Contact: Mehmet Bülbül, Ankara Univ., Turkey; *mehmet.bulbul@agri.ankara. edu.tr*

Are expenditures on a government food distribution system justified in developing countries? Perspectives from a comparative study of India and China – **Vasant P. Gandhi and Zhang-Yue Zhou**

Government food distribution systems are commonly found in developing countries but are frequently challenged because of the costs. A comparison of the systems in India and China reveals many similarities, differences and lessons. Both systems evolved out of repeated experiences of severe food price fluctuations and threats to food security when there was exclusive dependence on private markets. The Chinese system sought government control of the whole market and was much bigger, whereas that of India covered less than 10 per cent of grain output and let the market function with the rest. Pressures against the subsidy expenditure led to the reduction and near dismantling of the Chinese system, but immediate subsequent experience of sharp price instability forced the government to revive the system in a different form. The Indian system has withstood these pressures and the Chinese experience provides some lessons. Analysis also reveals that, as a percentage of total government expenditure, the food security subsidy in both countries is much lower (3–4 per cent) than the comparable social security expenditure in developed countries (22–34 per cent). It appears to be a small enough figure to be justifiable in both cases.

Contact: Vasant P. Gandhi, Centre for Management in Agriculture, Indian Institute of Management, Ahmedabad – 380 015, India; *gandhi@iimahd.ernet.in*

A partial equilibrium analysis on the effects of trade liberalization in the APEC food sector – **Shih-Hsun Hsu and Ching-Cheng Chang**

This paper considers the implications of trade liberalization for expanded trade in agriculture and food between the APEC group in Asia and the Pacific and non-APEC economies. The Global Trade Analysis Project (GTAP) Database Version 4 is used to calculate the revealed comparative advantage to explore the nature of agricultural and food trade. Using a Verdoorn-type partial equilibrium approach, the ex ante trade creation effects of an across-the-board tariff reduction are examined. Our results suggest that the exports within the APEC region are mostly complementary and a free trade scheme could make APEC an expanding market for cereal crops, with the best prospects in Japan, NIEs and ASEAN. It would also expand the markets for meat, dairy and other consumer-ready products, with additional prospects in China and Russia. The overall effects from free trade would amount to one-quarter of the current import level for agricultural and food products. The possibility of expanded imports from non-APEC economies is also strong for dairy, beverages, tobacco and processed products.

Contact: Shih-Hsun Hsu, Department of Agricultural Economics, National Taiwan University, No. 1, Roosevelt Road, Section 4, Taipei, 106-17, Taiwan; *hsu@taigem.agec.ntu.edu.tw*

A study of new Japanese farmers: their development and future perspectives – **Hiroki Inaizumi**

Last year Japan's Basic Law on Agriculture was revised. The law has encouraged the establishment of new farming enterprises (the New Farmers), not only by traditional farm successors but also by those outside farm communities. Some 15 years ago, Japan enjoyed a record-breaking economic boom, associated with extremely high levels of real estate pricing, partly including farmland. This situation caused pressure on Japanese agriculture, especially in terms of labour. However, following the economic crash around 1990, Japanese opinion has been gradually changing, particularly in regard to agriculture. There has been a marked increase in interest in farming and environmental issues. This demand has resulted in the re-establishment of educational institutions in agriculture and the opening of new ones such as the Agricultural Pre-Academy. This is designed for New Farmers from outside farming communities, to provide basic knowledge of general agriculture and specific subjects, focusing on individual needs. It works at weekends and during holidays. The students include civil servants, engineers, retired persons, and so on. The results show that New Farmers obviously have less skill with farming techniques, but there is great potential for development because some of them already have modern management skills, which has been one of the weakest points among traditional farmers in Japan.

Contact: Hiroki Inaizumi, Laboratory of International Agricultural Education, Department of Bio-Business, Tokyo University of Agriculture, Tokyo, Japan; *inaizumi@nodai.ac.jp*

Development of Japanese Black calf production by use of embryo transfer: situations and a regional case study in Japan – **Hirotake Miyaji**

Following the deregulation of Japanese beef imports, pressure from imported beef has affected dairy farmers who sell Holstein steers as by-products of milk production. As a result, the steer price declined from more than $1000/head in 1989 to about $160/head in 1998. On the other hand, the price of the Japanese Black calf, known to provide high-grade beef, has been relatively high. Thus, almost all dairy farms started to produce crossbred calves of Japanese Black/ Holstein for fattening to produce higher-grade beef, which is difficult with the pure Holstein. However, the price of crossbred calves has also declined. Given this economic situation, the recent advances in techniques of embryo transfer (ET) have attracted attention. Japanese Black calf production using ET has benefited dairy farms by enabling them to produce animals from famous bloodlines, which command a higher price. ET is not yet extensively used in Japan but it is evident that it could trigger changes at the farm level.

Contact: Hirotake Miyaji, Department of Grassland Management, National Grassland Research Institute, 768 Senbonmatu, Nishinasuno, Tochigi, 329-2793, Japan; *hirotake@ngri.affrc.go.jp*

Impact of rural small and medium enterprises on agriculture: a sectoral approach – **Anit N. Mukherjee and Yoshimi Kuroda**

In the light of the recent debate on decentralization of industries away from urban areas, the benefits of the development of rural small and medium enterprises (SMEs) have come under scrutiny. Apart from generating employment, which helps to generate income for rural households, our hypothesis is that SMEs also contribute either directly or indirectly to increasing productivity in agriculture through backward linkages. We analyse the rural sector of a developing economy comprising agriculture, traditional industries and modern SMEs. The latter supply goods, as well as services, which are local and non-substitutable by the urban sector. In a typical developing economy, such SME goods and services are constrained owing to various factors such as the government policy environment, poor quality of the infrastructure or low levels of education. We show theoretically, by means of a simple demand–supply model of the rural sector, that an increase in the availability of SME goods and services in the rural sector would positively affect the output in agriculture. Thereafter, we estimate a Cobb–Douglas type of production function in agriculture using time series data for India between 1980 and 1995 to confirm that the effect of SMEs on agricultural productivity is positive and statistically significant.

Contact: Anit N. Mukherjee, Tennodai 1-1-1, Tsukuba Science City, Ibaraki 305-8573, Japan; *anit@shako.sk.tsukuba.ac.jp*

Analysis of agricultural commodity systems in developing countries through econometric simulation models: the case of Indian cotton – **Gopal Naik and Sudhir Kumar Jain**

Though market structure analysis models can provide a sound base for econometric forecasts and policy analysis, their use in developing countries has been limited due to complexities involved in specification as well as difficulties in obtaining data. However, growing inter-linkages and complexities of agricultural commodity markets require use of econometric models for clearer understanding of their structure and economic behaviour. An econometric simulation model consisting of 24 equations has been developed to explain inter-linkages among major variables of the Indian cotton farming, spinning and weaving sectors considering various qualities of cotton, yarn and fabrics. The model has been estimated through three stage least squares. Forecasts have been made for the period 1995–96 to 2000–01. The results indicate that cotton farming and spinning sectors will have reasonable growth. However, there will be pressure on the weaving sector from increasing yarn prices and near stagnant fabric prices. This study shows that an econometric model can provide a sound base for understanding the structure of commodity markets and therefore help in addressing various policy related questions.

Contact: Gopal Naik, CMA, IIM, Vastrapur, Ahmedabad – 380 015; *gnaik@iimahd.ernet.in*

Estimation of stochastic frontier production functions using panel data from villages of Iran – **Bahaeddin Najafi and Mansour Zibaei**

A stochastic frontier production function with time-varying technical efficiencies is estimated using panel data from eight Iranian villages. A sample of 40 wheat producers was selected for study, over four years. The results revealed that technical efficiency of farms increased from 68.6 to 79.7 per cent during the period of study. It is suggested that improvement programmes, such as positive price policy and integrated extension services, have helped farmers' technical efficiency to increase considerably. It is also concluded that the gap between pioneer and lagging groups of farmers has been declining, but there is still a considerable difference between them. This implies that, by increasing the efficiency of extension, the present level of wheat production could be increased by around 20 per cent.

Contact: Bahaeddin Najafi, Department of Agricultural Economics, Shiraz University, Iran.

Irrigation efficiency in small-scale irrigation systems: a GIS approach in Nepal – **Takumi Kondo, Fumio Osanami, Anita Manandahr and Tokihisa Doi**

Irrigation investment is necessary to increase food production, especially in the dry season, in South Asia. Efficient use of irrigation water has the highest priority and more analysis is needed to solve allocation problems. The difficulty comes not only from various institutional structures, but also from the many geographical locations of irrigation systems. General views become impossible. This paper demonstrates how to utilize GIS information combined with farm surveys. The field survey used was conducted in the Sali Nadi natural gravity irrigation system in Sankhu village, Nepal. Net income per hectare in the head and middle canals is five to seven times higher than that in the tail because there is Pareto-inefficiency of water allocation during the dry season.

Contact: Fumio Osanami, Hokkaido University, Japan; *osanami@agecon.agr. hokudai.ac.jp*

A new approach to estimating consumer needs for farmers' markets in Japan: a choice-based conjoint analysis – **Yuji Oura, Kazunori Sato, Katsuya Takahashi and Izumi Yamada**

The paper examines the validity of a new approach, using conjoint analysis, to understand consumer needs for farmers' markets in Japan. Data came from a survey of 3000 persons in Ueda City, Nagano Prefecture. The questionnaire forms were sent by mail in the summer of 1998, and 1052 valid answers were obtained. Five attributes (parking lot, assortment, local products, culture, sales prices) were studied to determine their relative importance. It was concluded that a new approach using conjoint analysis is available as the way of understanding consumer needs.

Contact: Yuji Oura, National Agriculture Research Centre, Tokyo, Japan; *oura@narc.affrc.go.jp*

Agricultural commercialization and land use intensification: a microeconomic analysis of the northern uplands of Vietnam – **Sushil Pandey and Nguyen Tri Khiem**

Low food security, high rates of population growth and environmental degradation are some of the major problems of agricultural development in the uplands of Vietnam. Although Vietnam has now become a major rice exporter, food production in these remote upland environments is insufficient to meet the needs of the region's growing population. To increase farmers' incomes and their access to food, the government of Vietnam has encouraged production of cash crops in uplands through institutional reforms and investments in marketing infrastructures. Using survey data for 980 farmers in six upland provinces of northern Vietnam, this study examines the effect of improved access to markets and increase in the productivity of lowlands on land use intensity, labour productivity and food security in the uplands. Land and labour productivity was found to be substantially higher in areas with better access to markets, although the total rice production per household was similar. Intensity of land use in the uplands was found to be lower in communes which have a higher proportion of lowland fields. This indicates that further improvements in the productivity of lowland areas can be an important way of reducing the pressure for intensification of uplands for food production. Food security in communes that do not have access to lowland fields depends critically on the productivity of upland fields. As such areas are mostly remote, with very limited access to markets, market-based mechanisms for improving their food security are unlikely to be successful. Agricultural research in these areas should be focused on improving the in situ productivity of food grains.

Contact: Sushil Pandey, Social Sciences Division, International Rice Research Institute, Philippines; *spandey@irri.cgiar.org*

Analysis of the market integration of the corn futures market in Japan – **Jun Sasaki and Katsuhiko Demura**

The purpose of this study was to investigate price relationships in the corn futures markets in Japan and to examine the structure of price discovery. A cointegration analysis was performed using the corn futures prices and the exchange rate using daily data arranged for each contract month for the period from 1993 to 1997. The study shows that the various corn futures markets in Japan are integrated, with one leading market. The fact that the corn futures markets are integrated suggests that the price discovery process is dominated by the leading market.

Contact: Jun Sasaki, Research Fellow of the Japan Society for the Promotion of Science, Japan; *jsasaki@agecon.agr.hokudai.ac.jp*

Revealing Japanese consumers' preference for safety food: an empirical study of choice experiments – **Kazuo Sato, Hiroyuki Iwamoto and Katsuhiko Demura**

Recently, Japanese consumers have become very anxious about food safety, including that of rice, their staple food. There is a potential demand for rice produced with reduced amounts of chemical pesticides and fertilizers, though unfortunately supplies are scarce. In Hokkaido, the northernmost island of Japan, rice can be produced with fewer chemicals because insect pests are not as prevalent in the cooler temperatures. Rice producers are trying to make the name 'Hokkaido' a selling point. We conducted a 'choice experiment', using a multi-attribute preference-elicitation technique, to see whether this would be worthwhile. The main results are as follows: (1) Japanese consumers strongly preferred the rice produced with reduced chemicals or with no chemicals; (2) from the results of the simulation, 'Hokkaido rice' could be sold for higher prices, if produced with a smaller amount of chemicals or with no chemicals at all. All things being equal, the price of Hokkaido brand Kirara397 could be increased by 56.8 per cent if it were produced with a reduced amount of chemicals, and by 81.8 per cent if it were produced with no chemicals.

Contact: Kazuo Sato, Hokkaido University, Japan; *satokazu@agecon.agr. hokudai.ac.jp*

Vertical integration of agribusiness in China: a case study on Shangdong Province – **Minjun Shi**

This paper examines the policy concept, effects and prospects of vertical integration of agribusiness in China. Following the disintegration of the People's Communes, the shipping of agricultural products and the purchasing of raw materials is conducted by individual producers. To supplement the marketing efforts of individual producers, vertical integration of agribusiness has been extensively promoted. Two examples are provided from Shangdong Province. The first involves vertical integration of the production, processing and distribution of broilers on contract in Zhuchen County. The second involves vertical integration of the production, processing and distribution of vegetables on contract by the Heya vegetable production cooperative in Gaomi County. Vertical integration of agribusiness has the following four results in terms of the farm management: (1) by using agribusiness sales routes, producers can reduce transaction costs in shipment of produce; (2) the prices are consistent, alleviating market risk involved in farm management; (3) producers receive technical assistance from the agribusiness companies, removing technical entrance barriers; (4) the agribusiness company helps with credit sales of inputs, so reducing entrance barriers.

Contact: Minjun Shi; University of Tsukuba, Japan; *mjshi@farm.agbi.tsukuba.ac.jp*

Aquaculture and environment: an alternative approach to the measurement of the impact of technologies applied in India – **R.S.S. Shrivastava, A. Janaiah and A. Shrivastava**

This paper provides a conceptual framework to measure the impact of different technologies on sustainability by estimating a sustainable technology model. It defines the input–output relationships in a sustainable production system. The methodology could prove to be a superior alternative as it decomposes the overall economic efficiency loss into components of technical and allocative efficiency, between which there are trade-offs. The causes of the failure of intensive aquaculture because of the adverse impact on ecological environment of the pond ecosystem were examined. The demonstration of the application of the methodology was carried out by using panel data of progressive aquaculturists of the Punjab State of India. The extensive and semi-intensive systems were modelled. The estimated coefficients of the sustainable technology model are higher than in the other production systems. There were losses in technological and economic efficiency with the increasing intensification of aquaculture.

Contact: R.S.S. Shrivastava, IGIDR, India; *rss95@hotmail.com*

The behaviour of the cost and efficiency of transportation of vegetables distributed in the wholesale markets in Japan – **Taichi Takahashi**

In Japan, since vegetables are often eaten fresh and consumers attach importance to freshness, they have to be treated as highly perishable foodstuffs. The design of distribution systems in the wholesale markets has been one of the important subjects of policy making and research activities in this field. In this paper the cost and the efficiency of transportation in the wholesale markets in Japan were analysed using transportation data for 14 kinds of main vegetables in the period from 1978 to 1995. Linear programming for transportation problems was used. The findings are as follows: (1) the distances over which vegetables were transported had risen, (2) this expansion is attributable to the changes in product-gathering activities rather than to changes in the location of production, (3) the efficiency of the transportation of the vegetables distributed in the wholesale market has declined over the period.

Contact: Taichi Takahashi, National Agriculture Research Centre of MAFF of Japan, Tokyo, Japan; *taichi@narc.affrc.go.jp*

Agricultural trade liberalization and market integration: a study of Taiwan's livestock markets – **Rhung-Jeih Woo, Yung-Chi Chen and Pai-Lung Chou**

The main objective of this study was to explore the relevance of trade liberalization and market integration to the linkages between domestic and international livestock markets. We adopted unit roots tests and cointegration methods to analyse the long-run relationships between markets of Taiwan and the rest of the world. The empirical analysis revealed that, although all of the livestock markets showed short-run relationships between domestic and international markets (international prices led the domestic), a long-run cointegrating relationship existed only between the domestic and the international beef markets. Since the beef market is the only livestock market which has no non-tariff trade barriers in Taiwan, the results imply that trade liberalization could help in improving the degree of market integration.

Contact: Rhung-Jeih Woo, Department of Agricultural Economics, National Taiwan University, No. 1. Roosevelt Rd., Section 4, Taipei, Taiwan 106; *rjwoo@agec.ntu.edu.tw*

AUSTRALIA & OCEANIA

How well do microfinance institutions perform? Comparing the Philippines and the rest of the world – **Emmanuel F. Esguerra and Ma. Lucila A. Lapar**

This study is an inquiry into the effectiveness and efficiency of four types of microfinance institutions (MFIs): rural banks (RBs), cooperative rural banks (CRBs), credit cooperatives (COOPs), and credit-granting non-governmental organizations (NGOs) that operate in the Philippines. Effectiveness is measured in terms of an MFI's outreach and growth, while efficiency is measured in terms of a number of indicators of financial performance that include profitability, operational and financial self-sufficiency, financial productivity and leverage, and portfolio management performance, among others. The purpose is to identify the strengths and weaknesses of the different MFI types in relation to the policy objective of making microfinance services accessible to low-income households and small entrepreneurs in a manner that is cost-effective and financially sustainable. Analysis of available financial data and other related information indicates the following: formal MFIs (RBs and CRBs) have the potential to expand outreach, given their larger resource base and wider geographical network if only they can be induced to direct their activities increasingly towards low-income clients. Semi-formal MFIs (COOPs and NGOs), on the other hand, must reduce their costs and attain financial sustainability while continuing to serve their low-income clients.

Contact: Emmanuel F. Esguerra, School of Economics, University of the Philippines, Diliman, Quezon City, Philippines; *l.lapar@cgiar.org*

Hybrid rice for shifting the yield frontier in the tropics: an evaluation of farm-level experiences in irrigated systems in India – **A. Janaiah and Mahabub Hossain**

Policy makers and research managers considered hybrid rice, an innovative technology, in tropical Asia in the late 1980s as an available option to shift upwards the yield frontier under irrigated environments. However, certain quarters have raised the issue of whether hybrid rice would reverse the present declining yield trend in view of its slower adoption in the target environments. This paper aims to elucidate these issues, on the basis of empirical evidence obtained from sample farmers, seed growers, traders and millers of hybrid rice in irrigated rice systems in India during the 1997–8 crop year. On average, the yield gain of hybrid rice over that of popular inbred varieties was 16 per cent, with additional input cost of 19 per cent. But hybrid rice seed production was about 65 per cent more profitable than inbred rice production. The grain of hybrid rice was priced 11 per cent lower compared with inbred varieties because of lack of consumer demand for it, largely on account of inferior grain quality, poor cooking and eating quality and lower head rice recovery. Therefore the net return to hybrid rice production was 5 per cent lower than that of inbred rice. Higher seed cost, lower output price and inadequate yield gain (lower heterosis) brought about the lower profitability of hybrid rice production. Hybrid rice was also more cost-intensive and susceptible to major pests and diseases. For further development of hybrid rice, breeding for value addition, risk reduction and increase in farmer-realizable heterosis was identified as the top priority.

Contact: A. Janaiah, Social Sciences Division, International Rice Research Institute, Los Baños, Philippines; *a.janaiah@cgiar.org*

Effectiveness of border control strategies in minimising biosecurity risks to New Zealand agriculture – **Ganesh P. Rauniyar**

The study aimed to identify factors influencing behaviour of international passengers, assess the impact of current border strategies and identify additional border strategies for influencing passenger behaviour. A four-step procedure was employed and included a comprehensive review of current New Zealand literature, a behavioural study at the three major international airports, face-to-face interviews with 853 arriving passengers and interviews with key stakeholders. The study suggests that passenger profiling at the airport remains an effective tool for selecting the highest risk passengers for searches. While deterrence is difficult to quantify, detector dogs and x-ray machines both play a significant role in this endeavour. The first-time travellers from non-English-speaking countries, and people from continental areas (Europe, Asia) where quarantine is of relatively little importance are least likely to be aware of New Zealand's quarantine regulations. The most effective strategies in influencing passenger behaviour have been the x-ray machines, quarantine detection dogs and the Quarantine/Customs Declaration Forms. The impact of the in-flight quarantine video and loudspeaker announcements in the aircraft and at the airports, amnesty bins, display cabinets, multilingual signs and warnings posted in the baggage claim area have been relatively less effective. The requirement that every passenger arriving in New Zealand goes through the biosecurity area has no major discomfort for passengers. The biosecurity risk could be minimized further by adopting a combination of strategies directed at detection, deterrence and awareness. This will require a concerted effort from all stakeholders.

Contact: G.P. Rauniyar, Massey University, New Zealand; *g.p.rauniyar@ massey.ac.nz*

Ethnicity and gender roles in rural household decisions – **G.P. Rauniyar and D. Devkota**

Gender disparity in household decision making is common in developing countries. Ethnicity, culture and geographical location also influence decision-making processes in rural communities. Household decision-making processes in central rural Nepal were examined with a primary focus on gender roles and involvement of men and women in the context of three distinct ethnic communities: Brahmin/Chhetri, Gurung and Tharu. Three Village Development Committees (VDCs) of the Chitwan district of Nepal were purposively selected for the study. A combination of participatory rural appraisal ($n = 6$), gender analysis ($n = 6$), key informant interviews ($n = 14$) and household socioeconomic surveys ($n = 123$) was used to gather information and data for the study. At the household level, men and women were interviewed separately. The results indicated that both men and women consistently carried out certain crop production activities. Ethnic variation had an impact on gender roles and involvement of household members. Males dominated crop marketing in the Brahmin/Chhetri and Gurung communities, but this was a joint activity of the Tharus. Livestock-related work was primarily within the domain of women, but variation existed in gender roles across the ethnic groups. Women were more involved than men in household management in all three ethnic groups, with the highest level of participation amongst the Tharu women. Household decision making also depended on the level and source of income. The Gurung women exercised control over crop income. For all ethnic groups, men overwhelmingly dominated the access to agricultural and veterinary services, community activities and off-farm employment opportunities.

Contact: G.P. Rauniyar, Massey University, New Zealand; *g.p.rauniyar@ massey.ac.nz*

The role of off-farm income in sustaining rural households in Nepal – **G.P. Rauniyar and P. Kayastha**

Stagnant agricultural productivity and low returns in farming have led rural residents to look for opportunities to earn income from off-farm sources. This research dealt with eastern Nepal. Village Development Committee (VDC) areas were used from two ecologically distinct districts (Dhankuta in the Hill and Morang in the Terai). Six participatory rural appraisal (PRA) workshops, a household survey ($n = 150$) and six key informant interviews provided data for research. The average annual household income was Rs33 963 (approximately US$500 in 1999). The main sources of income were agriculture in the Hill households, and off-farm activities in the Terai households. Off-farm income, especially wages, was a major source of household income for the poor households in both zones. Income from business/enterprises in the Terai, and remittances in the Hill, were the primary sources of off-farm income for the non-poor households. Off-farm income also contributed nearly half of the household expenditure but it decreased as its area of landholding increased. Landholding, household size, ethnicity and the agroecological position of the households were the key determinants of household off-farm income. Characteristics of individuals such as gender, education level and ethnicity affected the type of employment taken up. The more educated males and those belonging to the Chhetri/Brahmin/Newar ethnic group dominated off-farm employment. Lack of adequate off-farm income opportunities was more prevalent in the Hill compared to Terai and reflected proximity to major market and employment centres.

Contact: G.P. Rauniyar, Massey University, New Zealand; *g.p.rauniyar@ massey.ac.nz*

Is the Green Revolution sustainable? Long-term productivity trends in a sample of Philippine rice farms – **Marites Tiongco and David Dawe**

The long-term sustainability and productivity of intensive rice production is a key issue affecting the future food security of Asia. We investigate long-term productivity trends in this important cropping system using periodic farm level survey data spanning more than 20 years of the Green Revolution in two rice bowls of the Philippines. Estimation of production functions with year dummy variables shows substantial declines in productivity from the early 1980s to the mid-1990s. However, examination of secondary data shows that the survey years were unrepresentative of long-term trends and were unduly influenced by exogenous yield shocks. Correction for these effects removes the productivity decline. Farmers in these areas are operating close to the technical efficiency frontier, implying that future increases in yield will need to come from new technologies that shift the function outward.

Contact: Marites Tiongco, International Rice Research Institute, Los Baños, Laguna, Philippines; *m.tiongco@cgiar.org*

East Asian approaches to food security and implications for the next WTO round – **Ray Trewin and Yiping Huang**

East Asia is made up of a diverse group of economies of various sizes and stages of development, yet food security is a policy priority in most countries because of their high population density. While some nations address the issue by applying an open trade and investment approach based on comparative advantage, many others follow a strong self-sufficiency approach. Some economies are self-sufficient in raw commodities whilst others import these but are net exporters of broader foods, building on their comparative advantage in labour-intensive food processing activities. The choices of food policy approaches by some East Asian countries have significant impacts on their own economies but also have implications for world markets. This paper first presents a broad picture of different approaches amongst East Asian economies and explores their determinants and implications. Alternative approaches to food security are analysed by comparing China and Japan, two large economies at different stages of development. Political economy perspectives are included in this analysis. Also included are applications of global trade modelling to quantify the implications of more open versus closed trade policies, as well as increased farm support. The possibility of regional arrangements on food security is also discussed in light of the forthcoming WTO round negotiations.

Contact: Ray Trewin, Asia Pacific School of Economics and Management, Australian National University, Australia; *ray.trewin@anu.edu.au*

Institutions and incentives for wetland conservation on private lands in Australia – **Stuart Whitten and Jeff Bennett**

Wetlands on private land generate both private and social values. The nature and extent of these values are dependent on the biophysical status of the wetlands. In turn, biophysical status is dependent on the land management strategies pursued. However, land management strategies are made primarily on the basis of the values received by wetland owners. Since these strategies also affect the wider community, via the social values of wetlands, the wider community may wish to influence the decisions of wetland owners. Altering the institutional and incentive framework within which wetland owners develop their land management strategies can alter the private and social values generated. In particular, altering the ownership balance of property rights can help society influence wetland management decisions via market mechanisms.

Contact: Stuart Whitten, University College, The University of New South Wales, Canberra ACT 2600, Australia; *sm.whitten@adfa.edu.au*

EUROPE

Price policies and agricultural supply: the responses of producers in Haryana (India) – **Véronique Alary and Daniel Deybe**

India is undertaking a process of liberalization of the agricultural sector as part of a structural adjustment programme. But several question arise. Can farmers react positively to a change in price policies which implies higher price fluctuations? Will these policies increase structural problems? Will they have a positive or negative impact on food security? A mathematical model is used to simulate farmers' reactions to some agricultural policy scenarios. Three objectives are pursued with the model: (1) to reproduce farmers' individual economic decision-making processes based on a seasonal and pluriannual optimization procedure subject to individual and regional constraints; (2) to mirror the exchanges between farmers (manure, draught power, land, labour); and (3) to consider different technologies or opportunities for crop and livestock systems in order to test various alternatives under different scenarios. Liberalizing the agricultural sector in the northern part of India could have a limited impact since farmers might have to face higher price risk. The rural population could also suffer lower nutritional damage, even if milk intake compensated for part of the adverse effect. The policy could also deepen the gap between better endowed regions where revenue could be increased (even if the internal distributive aspects might not be socially equitable) and the less endowed regions, which have greater agronomic difficulties.

Contact: Véronique Alary, Centre de Coopération Internationale en Recherche Agronomique pour le Développement, Department of Animal Production and Veterinary Medicine Department, Cirad-Emvt, Centre International de Baillarguet, BP 5035, 34032 Montpellier Cedex 1, France; *veronique.alary@ cirad.fr*

Food consumption assumptions and their implications in Romania – **Cecilia Alexandri**

In Romania, the prolonged transition has resulted in a significant decline in incomes. Food consumption has fallen for most products, except for dairy products, potatoes, cereals and alcoholic beverages. The present paper looks at the way food consumption might alter given four assumptions about future incomes compared with the 1998 level. The changes are 20 per cent decrease, 20 per cent increase, 50 per cent increase and 100 per cent increase. The results are based on regression equations, having total income per person as an independent variable. The information used comes from the Integrated Household Survey, which includes 36 000 dwellings located in urban and rural zones. The main results reveal that a drop in income would affect animal products (meat, cheese) and fruits. That would also apply, but as increases, for small and medium improvements in income. Under the hypothesis of income doubling, the food consumption level is expected to reach 3050 kcal. Comparisons between demand and domestic supply, at that level of income growth, reveal the potential occurrence of significant deficits for meat and meat-based products, sugar and fats (edible oils).

Contact: Cecilia Alexandri; Institute of Agricultural Economics, Bucharest, Romania; *alexandri@alcedoltd.ro*

Measuring the value of farm animal welfare legislation – **Johan Andersson and Peter Frykblom**

Non-market valuation has already been used to evaluate legislation dealing with farm animal welfare. This paper improves on the previous methods in several ways. First, by recognizing that markets already exist for many features associated with any suggested legislation, the market failures in modern animal welfare arrangements can be pinpointed. In those circumstances it is the marginal change which matters. Second, by using a methodology found in the experimental economics literature, it is possible to control for a number of biases that have been regarded as serious sources of error in the valuation literature. An applied contingent valuation survey suggests that there are no significant market failures in egg production.

Contact: Peter Frykblom, Department of Economics, The Swedish University of Agricultural Sciences P.O. 7013, SE-750 07 Uppsala, Sweden; *peter. frykblom@ekon.slu.se*

Animal welfare and profitability: a contradiction? – **Ruth Badertscher Fawaz and Stephan Pfefferli**

Animal-friendly housing usually causes higher investment costs, higher labour requirements and/or higher running expenses. Often these are not compensated by higher prices. Farmers, therefore, choose conventional housing systems. However, there is some evidence that animal health is better under animal-friendly conditions. Many studies show better udder health and better fertility of dairy cows in loose housing compared with stanchion barns. In our study we want to show the effect of including animal health, product quality, working conditions and environmental aspects in an economic comparison of conventional and animal-friendly housing systems. The interest is in two housing systems for dairy cows (stanchion barns/loose housing with litter and an outdoor run) and fattening pigs (slatted floors/systems with straw bedding and an outdoor run). We mainly use results of other studies in the case of dairy cows. There are very few data available relating to pigs, so a survey is being made of 90 farms to look at housing, management, animal health, performance and meat quality. The project started in 1998 and will be completed in 2003.

Contact: Ruth Badertscher Fawaz and Stephan Pfefferli, Swiss Federal Research Station for Agricultural Engineering, CH-8356 Taenikon, Switzerland; *ruth.badertscher@fat.admin.ch*

Parametric measurement of scale efficiency: evidence from Iranian dairy farming – **M. Bakhshoodeh and K.J. Thomson**

Many previous studies have applied a data envelopment approach to calculate farm-specific indices of scale efficiency. This paper focuses on a parametric measurement of such indices. The level of scale efficiency for individual farms is measured as the ratio of constant returns to scale technical efficiency (CRS TE) to variable returns to scale technical efficiency (VRS TE). Applying a transcendental frontier production function to 1995–6 data on 1626 Iranian dairy farms, the SE index was found to be about 0.80 on average, ranging from 0.25 to 0.95 and with more than one-third of the farms below the mean value. The index value was affected by farm size and by the proportion of pure-bred animals, but not by the use of modern farming techniques. In order to improve scale efficiency, expanding farms and increasing the number of pure-bred animals is recommended.

Contact: K.J. Thomson, Department of Agriculture, University of Aberdeen, 581 King Street, Aberdeen, AB24 5UA, Scotland, UK; *kj.thomson@abdn.ac.uk*

Methodological aspects of a linear programming model for evaluation of soil tillage technologies – **Maria De Belém Martins, Carlos Marques and Maria Raquel Ventura-Lucas**

The introduction of new methods of soil tillage, such as direct seeding and reduced cultivation, raises critical questions that should be taken into account in economic appraisal. These are: (1) the need to carry out cultivation operations during the precise number of days available, which depends on the different cultivation operations involved, precipitation and soil type; (2) the number of hours and horsepower necessary, in each of the technologies, for establishing the cereal crop. Analysis of the results demonstrates that a linear programming model can be developed which should be useful in further analysis of new techniques.

Contact: Maria de Belém Martins, Ministry of Agriculture, Lisbon, Portugal; *marbelem@draalg.min.agricultura.pt*

Approaching the level of losses caused by a lack of finance: the case of Russian farms – **Irina V. Bezlepkina and Nikolai M. Svetlov**

In Russia, weak financial discipline and an inefficient credit system result in insufficient financing of agricultural production. This study investigates whether a lack of finance causes losses for Russian agricultural producers. A modified Bayesian formulation allows us to employ scarce data to approximate losses. This formulation is incorporated in the objective function of an optimization model expressing the dependence of profit on cash flow and debts. Empirical application employs data from 60 quarterly reports of six agricultural enterprises from the Moscow Region in 1995–8. The losses are estimated at 42.6 per cent of total farm expenses.

Contact: Irina V. Bezlepkina, Wageningen University, The Netherlands; Moscow Agricultural Timiryazev Academy, Russia; *irina.bezlepkina@alg.aae.wau.nl*

On the efficient boundaries of the state: a transaction cost economics approach to the analysis of decentralization and devolution in natural resource management – **Regina Birner and Heidi Wittmer**

Decentralization of authority in natural resource management and the devolution of management functions to local user groups have gained increasing importance in developing countries. While there is an increasing number of empirical case studies, development of theoretical concepts for systematic analysis of the efficiency of the newly created institutional arrangements is remarkably scarce. Likewise, questions of institutional design, such as the optimal level of decentralization and devolution, have hardly been analysed from a theoretical perspective. The poster demonstrates how this gap can be filled by applying transaction cost economics, especially Williamson's recent approach on governance structures involving public bureaucracies. Use is made of the case of decentralization and devolution in biodiversity conservation to show (1) how to determine the relevant transactions and identify their key attributes, (2) how to derive the trade-offs among these transactions, and (3) how to assess alternative modes of governance on the basis of their structural attributes. The poster extends Williamson's framework in two ways: (1) by including additional types of transactions and attributes and (2) by enlarging the set of possible governance structures by including, in addition to Williamson's markets and hierarchies, cooperative governance. By analogy with Williamson's efficient boundaries of the firm, this approach makes possible the derivation of hypotheses about the efficient boundaries of the state. Thailand's community forestry bill is used to show how the theoretical framework can be applied empirically.

Contact: Regina Birner, Institute of Rural Development, University of Göttingen, Germany; *rbirner@gwdg.de*

Vertical and horizontal intra-industry trade: analysis of the agricultural and food trade for Slovenia – **Štefan Bojnec**

This paper analyses Slovenian agricultural trade structures. Following the literature on intra-industry trade (IIT) a distinction is made between IIT and inter-industry trade, and IIT is separated into vertical IIT and horizontal IIT. More than one-quarter of Slovenian agricultural and food exports is directed to the European Union (EU) and more than half to the traditional former Yugoslav markets, particularly to Croatia. More than half of Slovenian agricultural and food imports is from the EU, followed by the former Yugoslav republics and the Central European Free Trade Agreement (CEFTA) members (about 10 per cent from Hungary). The paper gives explanations for the trade patterns, the two components of IIT and their implications. The Slovenian trade in agricultural and food products with Hungary, Poland, the EU, Romania and Bulgaria is largely of the inter-industry type. Yet, for several products, there is no trade with certain countries, such as the CEFTA members. In trade with the EU there is a high percentage of one-way, import flows. The statistical analysis revealed that more than two-thirds of IIT is vertical IIT with either very high or very low export to import price ratios. The price, and hence the quality, differences in traded goods are important factors contributing to diversification of supply for consumers and creating pressures for restructuring and reallocation of production sectors.

Contact: Štefan Bojnec, KU Leuven, Belgium and University of Ljubljana, Slovenia; *stefan.bojnec@siol.net*

Age, entrepreneurship and commercialization in transition agriculture: evidence from Hungarian dairy farmers – **Štefan Bojnec, Erik Mathijs and Liesbet Vranken**

This paper uses survey data on Hungarian dairy farmers to investigate their enterpreneurial behaviour and identify its constraints. The analysis reveals that most producers are commercial and that both entrepreneurial ability and marketing constraints play a bigger role than capital constraints in the off-farm commercialization of dairy farm products. Successful dairy farmers are young, use external advice and live close to local consumption centres. In addition, they either use cooperatives or integrate with processors to market their products effectively. These results suggest that a prime role for policy support should be directed to improving human capital, extension services and marketing infrastructure, rather than to providing cheap credit.

Contact: Erik Mathijs, Department of Agricultural and Environmental Economics, Catholic University Louvain, W. de Croylaan 42, 3001 Louvain, Belgium; *erik.mathijs@agr.kuleuven.ac.be*

Why are most Europeans opposed to GMOs? Explanatory factors underlying the rejection movement – **Sylvie Bonny**

A strong opposition movement to GMOs (genetically modified organisms) arose in European countries at the end of the 1990s and spread to some other non-European countries. With many people considering biotechnology and genetic engineering as major sources of progress, one might ask what the origins of this opposition are. Some underlying explanatory factors motivating public concern about genetic engineering are presented. First, there are doubts about institutions and companies, which amounts to a loss of confidence in them. The contaminated blood and BSE affairs led to the belief that the goal of safeguarding economic interests had been allowed to override health concerns. The same fear surrounds GMOs. Second, there is now a general context of concern about the effects of highly industrialized agriculture. Biotechnology has been seen as an ultimate reinforcement of intensive farming. Third, the role of environmentalist associations and the media in dramatizing the potential risks of GMOs has been important since consumers often have more confidence in them as sources of information. There is a growing view that the expected benefits are assessed by the public as being very small, or non-existent. GMOs are seen as profitable only to some large companies.

Contact: Sylvie Bonny, INRA, Grignon, France; *bonny@grignon.inra.fr*

Reorganization of agriculture in the Czech Republic: the transaction cost problem in restructuring socialist large-scale agriculture – **Markus Brem**

Institutional change in transition countries has to face the problem of restructuring large-scale farm organizations by reorganizing farm boundaries and ownership structures. The new property rights structure affecting the assets of socialist large-scale farms provides incentives for the individual owner to redeploy assets in a more efficient way. The poster looks at four partial models which deal with (1) reinforcing a similar governance structure due to the existence of increasing returns; (2) the break-up of state farms caused by opportunistic behaviour of individuals among the farm's stakeholder group; (3) the trade-off between increased costs in oversized socialist farms versus leaving the organizations; and (4) the coexistence of cooperative and hired-labour farms caused by different levels of opportunity costs and moral hazards. Using data from a 1999 farm survey conducted in two Czech regions, it is suggested that (1) structural change in agricultural transition occurs slowly and is dependent on organizational history; (2) structural change also gives opportunities for stakeholders with informational advantages to grab large shares of the assets; (3) the level of exit costs from the socialist deployment of assets leads to there being various possible reorganization paths.

Contact: Markus Brem, Department of Agricultural Economics and Social Sciences, Humboldt University of Berlin, Germany; *markus.brem@gmx.de*

Consumer attitudes towards organic food in Germany 1984–99: an application of cohort analysis – **Maike Bruhn and Reimar von Alvensleben**

The poster presents the first results of the fourth phase of a long-term research project dealing with the change of consumer attitudes and behaviour in the organic food market in Germany. The data base is taken from the results of four consumer surveys ($n = 2000$) conducted in five-years intervals (1984, 1989, 1994, 1999) using the same questionnaire. This material is a unique data base for the application of cohort analysis to answer the following questions.

1 Are changes of attitudes and demand caused by:
   - a change of behaviour of the total consumer population (= period effect), or
   - a cohort succession, a replacement of old consumers by young consumers with different behaviour in a generational change (= cohort effect)?
2 Are differences of attitudes and demand between age groups caused by:
   - the ageing of consumers with age-specific attitude/behaviour patterns (= age or life cycle effect), or
   - by the specific conditions of socialization of the age groups (= cohort effects)?

The analysis based on the survey results of 1984, 1989 and 1994 showed that the changes of attitudes and behaviour are due to both period and cohort effects. However, declining cohort effects within the younger cohorts suggest that there will be declining growth rates of demand in the future.

Contact: Reimar von Alvensleben, Institute for Agricultural Economics, University of Kiel, Germany; *valvensleben@agric-econ.uni-kiel.de*

The horticultural sector in Romania: incentives necessary for recovery – **Gabriela Burghelea**

Because of its economic, social and ecological functions, the horticultural sector is of great importance to Romania. Almost 4.5 per cent of arable area is covered by vegetables, orchards and vineyards. Under new legislation, private ownership of land has become dominant, representing 71 per cent in tree growing, 76 per cent in viticulture and 94 per cent in vegetables. They each occupy an area in excess of 200 000 hectares. Romania is a traditional wine producer, with an average output close to that of Portugal and Germany. In 1998, the viticultural area was up by 20 per cent on 1989, with much of the growth being in hybrid plantings, the area of which doubled between 1989 and 1998. The main objective of the reform in this sector is that of obtaining additional quality production to meet the needs of the internal market and ensure the development of exports. The latter may require technical, financial and legal incentives.

Contact: Gabriela Burghelea, Institute of Agricultural Economics, Romanian Academy, Bucharest, Romania; *iea@ines.ro*

Economic impact of agenda 2000 on representative farms in Wallonia (southern Belgium) – **Ph. Burny**

Based on several hypotheses, including the reduction of selling prices of 15 per cent for cereals, 20 per cent for bovine meat and 15 per cent for milk, this paper illustrates the economic impact of Agenda 2000 on farms representative of Wallonian agriculture. It appears that Agenda 2000 will have an adverse impact on dairy farms, though it will have more favourable effects on the income of beef producers. It is expected that direct payments will play a significant role for all types of farm.

Contact: Ph. Burny, Unité d'Economie, Faculté universitaire des Sciences agronomiques, 5030 Gembloux, Belgium; *econgen@fsagx.ac.be*

A simulation of the effects of agricultural subsidies on irrigation water demand and nitrogen pollution in Spain – **Javier Calatrava and Alberto Garrido**

Irrigation water demand is largely dependent on the state of the market and on the income support mechanisms delivered by agricultural policies. Three processes of reform are currently going on in Spain that will have large effects in the pattern of water use in the agricultural sector. First, there is a change in market and income support which Agenda 2000 will bring about for the period 2000–2006. Second, the European Union Water Framework Directive, which is imminent, will change the whole philosophy about water charges for all European water users. Third, there is to be reform of the Spanish Water Law, which will liberalize allocation systems. To investigate the likely effects of these three major changes, a non-linear mathematical programming model has been developed and calibrated for a number of areas in Southern Spain. The results show that the combined effects are ambiguous from the point of view of water management but may be beneficial in reducing farmers' chemical pollution. There is some concern that initial water allowances are based on technical parameters, rather than on efficiency or equity grounds.

Contact: Javier Calatrava, Department of Agricultural Economics, Universidad Politécnica de Madrid, Spain; *javcal@arrakis.es*

Implications of EU enlargement for Slovak farms – **Pavel Ciaian, Zlata Sojkova, Ladislav Kabat and Artan Qineti**

The objective of the paper is to determine likely future implications of EU enlargement for farms in the Slovak Republic. The following policy scenarios were modelled for five farms, each situated in different regions for two distinct years, 2002 and 2007: (1) the continuation of existing policies in Slovakia, (2) reformed Common Agricultural Policy (Agenda 2000), (3) the complete liberalization of European agricultural policy. A linear programming technique was used to analyse effects on the financial indicators and production structure of the farms. The results show that the Agenda 2000 scenario led to increasing levels of farm profitability in both periods. The liberalization scenario led to a profitable structure only for farms situated in regions with better climatic conditions. From the results it is clear that current Slovak agricultural policy gives strong support to farms situated in regions with worse production conditions.

Contact: Pavel Ciaian, Catholic University Louvain, Belgium; *ciaian@yahoo.com*

Institutional configuration of agricultural extension in south-eastern Europe – **Lefter Daku, George W. Norton and George McDowell**

Effective extension is an important accelerator of development. It plays a key role as a support system, as a policy instrument and as a major component of the agricultural knowledge and information system helping farmers make informed decisions. Following economic reforms in the early 1990s, most of the south-eastern European (SEE) countries made efforts to establish extension services. However, a number of factors, including tight governmental budgets, lack of experience and the existence of vested interests, constrained the development. This poster examines the rationale for public funding of extension programmes and evaluates the incentive structure for private and public sector participation in providing a service. It sets out a medium- and long-term approach with a primary focus on institutional dimensions. Two groups of factors that affect the private sector supply of extension are analysed: (1) demand and supply-side factors that affect profitability, and (2) factors arising from the public good nature of extension output, externalities, moral hazards and economies of scale, that affect the appropriability of the returns from the service. The conclusion is that the SEE countries should try to achieve a public–private extension balance by following a more gradual approach towards privatization. However, there should be a phased withdrawal of the public sector from providing extension in areas best served by the private sector, while recognizing a continued important role for the public sector in correcting for undesirable effects of private extension.

Contact: Lefter Daku, Department of Agricultural Economics and Rural Development, Tirana Agricultural University, Albania; *ldaku@vt.edu*

Spatial and varietal aspects of agri-food prices – **Karine Daniel**

The paper investigates the contributions of spatial and variety dimensions to agri-food prices. It presents a stylized model of multiple producers, supplying differentiated products to consumers in different regions. Production is characterized by aspects that give rise to both increasing and decreasing returns. Marginal cost pricing is inappropriate in this context. The long-run equilibrium price received will reflect the premium paid by consumers who value variety. Differences between varieties can be due to differences in outputs (Appellation d'Origine Contrôlée). The open question is whether price premia could ever sustain the current farm structure without subsidies.

Contact: Karine Daniel, TEAM – University of Paris I Sorbonne and Institut National de la Recherche Agronomique, Nantes, France; *daniel@nantes.inra.fr*

Training for integrated pest management: rice farmers in Indonesia – **Daniel Deybe and Maurice Vaissayre**

In Indonesia, pest outbreaks affecting rice led to the implementation of the Integrated Pest Management Training Project (IPM/TP), with the technical assistance of FAO and funded by the World Bank. Farmers' Field Schools (FFS) were founded to train farmers in IPM practices and disseminate IPM principles in the community. The participatory process and the social dynamics involved enable farmers to develop collaborative efforts to ensure IPM implementation. At the request of the World Bank, Cirad carried out a pilot study in two provinces of Java to evaluate the qualitative and quantitative impacts on trained and untrained farmers. Through qualitative interviews and structured surveys it was possible to compare the practices and economic results. It appears that trained farmers are younger and better educated. They are better equipped, participate more in group activities, are more aware of environmental problems and employ safer techniques. Trained farmers' pesticide costs are lower with a higher gross margin/hectare.

Contact: Daniel Deybe, Centre de Coopération Internationale en Recherche Agronomique pour le Développement – Cirad, 45 bis Av. de la Belle Gabrielle, 94736 Nogent-sur-Marne Cedex, France; *deybe@cirad.fr*

An empirical study of the causes of agricultural labour adjustments during transition – **Liesbeth Dries, Karen Macours and Johan F.M. Swinnen**

Reforms have strongly affected agricultural employment in transition countries, but in remarkably different ways. In countries such as Hungary and Estonia, labour use in agriculture has declined dramatically. In others (such as Poland and Slovenia) it has decreased to a lesser extent and in some (for example, Romania and Russia) agricultural employment increased during transition. We show that the differences in labour adjustment during transition are due to a combination of variations in initial conditions and differences in reform policies and effects. Reform policies that had a strong influence on labour adjustment were price and trade liberalization, privatization of production factors, farm transformation policies and the set of general reform policies which liberalized factor markets and removed obstacles for improved allocation and mobility throughout the whole economy. Surplus labour outflow from agriculture is stimulated by liberalization and by the privatization of farm assets, since they improve incentives and remove constraints for optimal factor allocation and structural adjustment. The shift to individual farms, which was especially strong in labour-intensive production systems with low labour productivity, has reduced the outflow of labour from agriculture by improving farm governance and labour efficiency, although this effect was mitigated by losses in scale economies due to disruptions and market imperfections in transition. In general, labour outflow was considerably lower on individual farms than on corporate farms, owing to a combination of factors related to human capital, access to finance and physical capital, and social capital.

Contact: Liesbeth Dries, Policy Research Group, Department of Agricultural and Environmental Economics, Katholieke Universiteit Leuven, Belgium; *liesbeth.dries@agr.kuleuven.ac.be*

Thermometers for unhealthy Russian enterprises – **David Epstein**

The majority of Russian agricultural enterprises have been unprofitable since 1994, and have accumulated large liabilities. Reorganization and restructuring of debt are necessary. However, the differences in financial standing of enterprises should be identified and taken into consideration. A method is needed which enables relevant indices to be constructed as a basis for classifying enterprises into qualitatively different groups, depending upon their financial and economic standing. This is a complex and still unsolved task, since the reported accounting figures for unprofitable enterprises inaccurately reflect their costs (particularly in respect of depreciation deductions). Financial ratio analysis is a potential tool. Experimental checking of the scheme developed was performed with the figures of agricultural enterprises of the Leningrad region for 1997.

Contact: David Epstein, The North-West Research Institute of Agricultural Economics, Saint Petersburg, 189620, Saint Petersburg-Pushkin, Russia; *epstein@DE1150.spb.edu*

Rural policy and regional governance: a neural network approach – **Roberto Esposti and Franco Sotte**

The paper analyses the enforcement and effect of EU rural and agricultural policies at the local level. The different kinds of policy provide a complex system of incentives, constraints and opportunities interacting within the specific territorial context. The interaction between policies and the strategies of farmers and other local actors explains the spontaneous formation of emerging institutions, which provide the actual governance of the territory. An Artificial Neural Network model can well represent and simulate the functioning of this complex local system. It emphasizes the main features of the functioning of local rural systems. Heterogeneous agents strongly interact in a weakly hierarchic ordering, while remoteness and small scale imply a limited contextual knowledge with consequent bounded-rationality behaviour. However, the interaction between agents makes the local system capable of 'learning' to adapt to changing external conditions and policy provision. A simulation illustrates how such a modelled system can generate spontaneous local institutions.

Contact: Roberto Esposti, Dipartimento di Economia – Università di Ancona, Piazzale Martelli, 8, 60121 Ancona, Italy; *robertoe@deanovell.unian.it*

The impact of plant varieties rights on research: the case of Spain – **M. Carmen Fernández Díez**

The impact of plant variety rights on the public and private research sectors in Spain has been to provide positive incentives, especially for the private sector, which increased its market share as a result of higher appropriability conditions. The plant-breeding sector consists of both international and small domestic firms. Many foreign breeders focus their research efforts on hybrid varieties, which provide 'natural' property rights. Finally, as a result of an increase in the innovative activities of foreign breeders, Spain has expanded seed imports and reinforced technological dependence.

Contact: M. Carmen Fernández Díez, Department of Economics, University of Comillas, Madrid, C/Alberto Aguilera, 23, C.P.: 28.015 Madrid, Spain; *mcarmen@cee.upco*

Impact of market intervention on integration of Polish and world wheat prices – **Szczepan Figiel**

Market reforms implemented in Poland, especially greater openness to international trade, should result in increasing price integration between Polish and world markets for internationally traded commodities such as wheat. However, in a period of economic transformation, Polish agricultural prices have been very volatile and there has been resultant government intervention in the market. As a result, Polish monthly wheat prices were found, by regression and cointegration analysis, to be generally unrelated to selected world prices over the period of 1990/91 to 1996/97. The intervention also caused market distortions such as deviations from the normally expected seasonal pattern. The Polish experience provides two important lessons. First, inefficiencies caused by underdeveloped agricultural market infrastructure and insufficient market information resulted in strong political pressure under which the government of Poland decided to implement some market intervention programmes. Unfortunately, the established government agency became a dominant player in the grain and other agricultural markets. Such a situation hampers the broader participation of private businesses in procurement and larger-scale market transactions. Second, excessive market intervention programmes not only failed to help stabilize agricultural markets, but also led to serious distortions and a political temptation to urge the government to make even more intensive interventions. Therefore a successful market transformation requires establishing, as soon as possible, necessary market institutions and regulations. Otherwise, a lot of resources that could possibly be spent on further development of the market infrastructure could be wasted on costly and ineffective market intervention.

Contact: Szczepan Figiel, University of Warmia and Mazury, Olsztyn, Poland; *sfigiel@icbpm.uwm.edu.pl*

Combined and changing effects of market incentives, technical innovations and support on maize production in southern Mali – **Michel Fok, Mama Koné and Hamady Djouara**

The paper analyses the evolution of maize production during the last two decades in southern Mali, a region known mainly for its cotton. Maize production actually took off during the first half of the 1980s as a result of a voluntary programme bringing together technical support, effective input provision and a guaranteed price under compulsory state-controlled cereal trading. In 1986, while adoption of intensive maize cropping was in progress, the implementation of structural adjustment policy, through cereal market liberalization and abolition of input subsidies, at first led farmers to return to traditional intercropping with decreased fertilizer use. Maize has again been providing an increased contribution to food security, from the beginning of the 1990s and in particular after the 1994 currency devaluation. Farmers are adopting more intensive maize single cropping at the expense of millet and sorghum. Our case study emphasizes the need for long-term assessment of the impact of technical innovations, along with changes in market incentives. State market control has helped introduce technical innovations which farmers readopt after market liberalization, provided input provision remains effective.

Contact: Michel Fok, CIRAD-CA, BP 5035, 34032 Montpellier, France; *michel.fok@cirad.fr*

Primary demand for red meats in the UK – **Panos Fousekis and Brian J. Revell**

Flexible differential inverse systems are employed in this paper to analyse the farm-level demand for red meats (beef, pigmeat and lamb) in the UK for the period 1989:1 to 1998:12. A statistical selection process indicates that an inverse CBS model with variable scale effects but constant quantity effects (CBSIDS) performs better than the alternative systems of inverse Rotterdam (RIDS), the inverse Neves (NBRIDS) and the inverse AIDS (AIIDS). The CBSIDS is then used for hypothesis testing and computation of price flexibilities. The differential inverse demand models were specified in terms of weighted cost/revenue shares and did not display any significant effect due to BSE. The empirical results suggest that preferences over red meats are homothetic and separable in the partition ((pork, lamb), beef). They also suggest that beef and pork are closer substitutes, as compared with beef and lamb and pork and lamb. Finally, all own price uncompensated price flexibilities are less than unity in absolute values.

Contact: Panos Fousekis, Department of Agricultural Economics at the Agricultural University of Athens, Greece; *p.fousekis@aua.gr*

Economic rationality and farmers' adjustment strategies under the CAP's reforms: the case of Andalusia (Spain) – **Rosa Gallardo, Fernando Ramos and Eduardo Ramos**

The reforms brought about by the Common Agricultural Policy (CAP) aim to provide different support schemes for continental and Mediterranean crops. These different approaches have led to different adjustment strategies. However, there are farmers whose activities are located in areas sharing both continental and Mediterranean features. This, in fact, implies two opposing 'economic rationales' with which farmers have to deal. Work is focused on the study of the effects of CAP reforms on different farming systems: COP crops (cereal, oilseeds and proteins) in one of the main producing areas in Spain (Andalusia). Results obtained are from personal interviews with experts and from a survey carried out at the farm level in the study area. The observed adjustment strategy seems to indicate that most farmers do not follow a strict economic rationale.

Contact: Rosa Gallardo, Department of Agricultural Economics, Universidad de Córdoba, PBOX 3048, 14080 Córdoba, Spain; *es2gacor@uco.es*

The Romanian agri-food economy on the road towards globalization – **Dinu Gavrilescu and Camelia Serbanescu**

With an agricultural area of 14.8 million hectares, over 36 per cent agricultural employment, a share of 19 per cent in overall GDP and almost 60 per cent of the family budget spent on agri-food products, Romania is the second agricultural producer in Central and Eastern Europe, having excessive available labour and low productivity. The state of the transition is such that the first seven years of the process could be described as groping in a labyrinth, trying to solve severe short-term problems, rather then taking sequential steps in a longer-term approach. Over the last three years, the decision makers have enforced a more coherent reform programme including price and foreign trade liberalization, setting up a reasonable import tariff regime and joining CEFTA. Romania's presence at negotiations for joining the European Union raises more problems for the agri-food economy. There is still an urgent need to build appropriate market institutions and provide a much-needed legal framework.

Contact: Dinu Gavrilescu, Institute for Agricultural Economics, Bucharest, Romania; *iea@ines.ro*

The competitiveness of the Romanian agri-food sector in CEFTA – **Daniela Giurca and Camelia Serbanescu**

The major political orientation in Romania is directed towards making the necessary adjustments to the economy in order to be able to join the European Union as soon as possible. The CEFTA agreement can be considered as solid field training both for Romania and for other member states, to test their ability to evolve in a free trade framework, especially in relation to sensitive agri-food products. The initial objective of introducing complete free trade from the very beginning proved to be unrealistic and the member states have agreed to reach this objective by gradually reducing existing trade barriers. Just a few months after the initial enthusiasm, Romania realised that its agri-food sector faced strong competition. Until 1996, the trade balance with the five member states was positive; but immediately after Romania signed the agreement the balance reversed and the deficit increased even more in the next two years. The paper assesses the competitiveness of Romanian agri-food products in 1997–9, pointing out those having a comparative advantage.

Contact: Daniela Giurca; Institute for Agricultural Economics, Bucharest, Romania; *iea@ines.ro*

The application of agrienvironmental policies in Portugal – **Maria de Lurdes Ferro Godinho**

Recently, agricultural policies have been concerned with both the impact of intensive agricultural practices on environment and the problem of land abandonment in areas in which agriculture is no longer competitive. Major improving measures have been proposed and implemented. The so-called 'accompanying measures' of the 1992 Common Agricultural Policy reform (EC regulation 2078/92) are examples. Even though the overall objectives of these agrienvironmental measures are identical for every European Union country, different schemes have been defined and applied in each specific case. Farmers' acceptance of the measures and their effectiveness in changing farming systems and incomes are studied using multivariate analysis applied to regional data. The results show the major attributes that distinguish the non-participating farms from others and indicate the extent to which there have been reductions in the adverse effects of farming.

Contact: Maria de Lurdes Ferro Godinho, Universidade de Évora, Departamento de Gestão de Empresas, Portugal; *mgodinho@uevora.pt*

Identifying needs of tomorrow's agriculture: lessons from the use of a participatory approach in South Africa – **Marijke D'Haese, L. D'Haese, J. Van Rooyen, W. Anseeuw, H. Verschueren and A.M. De Winter**

During the last decade the logical framework approach (or one of many similar techniques) was often used in the project planning. The object is to provide an overview of field experience of the use of 'logframe' analysis as a participatory approach for identifying constraints and needs in three case studies in South Africa. Studies included are (1) analysis of on-farm problems related to restricted access to resources, support services and rights of progressive small-scale mango farmers; (2) analysis of the problems causing the low competitive power of the informal cut flower sellers of Pretoria; and (3) examination of the food security problems of women with small children in Soshanguve, a suburb of Pretoria. Through intensive group discussions with farmers and sellers and by prioritization of problems and constraints, the farming and marketing systems are described and analysed in a problem tree. The development of the problem tree is the first step of logframe analysis. The next step is to convert to an objective tree in order to identify alternative strategies to alleviate constraints and problems. These are then summarized in the logframe matrix. The methodology can be applied to a diversity of problems and target groups. The positive experience is mostly enhanced by the interactivity of the process and the involvement and concern of the target group and extension services.

Contact: Marijke D'Haese, Department of Agricultural Economics, Ghent University, Belgium; *marijke.dhaese@rug.ac.be*

Price adoption resulting from extending the CAP to the east: prospects of competitiveness – **Péter Halmai and Andrea Elekes**

Agriculture has a great macroeconomic significance in the economy of the CEECs as regards both their GDP contribution and their trade balance. Receiving higher prices will certainly have favourable effects on the income situation of producers, but it may threaten the (price) competitiveness of agriculture. There are two basic threats: first, higher producer prices can directly reduce competitiveness and, second, higher producer prices may increase consumer prices, causing problems on the demand side. The analysis concentrates mainly on Hungary. It is possible, because of the proposed reduction in institutional prices in the European Union and an expected rise in Hungarian real agricultural prices, that the difference between agricultural price levels may be reduced.

At the same time, obtaining direct payments (or at least part of them) and the special rural development grants will improve competitiveness and help the adoption process. It will be important to focus these additional resources on the restructuring of less effective enterprises and further improvement of export competitiveness.

Contact: Andrea Elekes, Gödöllõ University of Agricultural Sciences, Hungary; *andreaelekes@hotmail.com*

Explaining institutional change: agricultural land reforms in Bulgaria and Poland – **Markus Hanisch and Dominika Milczarek**

The poster presents a framework for the analysis of agricultural land reforms in Bulgaria and Poland as it emerges from contemporary theories of institutional change. It discusses to what extent the theories can contribute to an explanation of the policy design (formal rules) and the effective outcomes (formal plus informal rules) of land reform and agricultural privatization in both countries. The authors argue that the privatization processes took place without functioning markets in land, services, human and financial capital and physical agricultural assets. In this situation it is possible to model the process of land and asset reallocation as a bargaining game between managers, workers and land and asset owners. The recognition of differences between these actors in terms of specific resources crucial for bargaining success allows us to explain the pace of reforms in a different manner than pure public choice or transaction cost theories would suggest. The authors conclude that, in countries as different as Poland and Bulgaria, the analysis of the conflict about the potential gains from land and asset distribution, and the different ways in which the actors tried to influence the outcome of this conflict, can contribute much to the explanation of the whole process and its observable outcomes.

Contact: Markus Hanisch, Department of Agricultural Economics and Social Sciences, Humboldt University Berlin, Germany; *m.hanish@rz.hu-berlin.de*

How do the labour markets react to structural change in agriculture? – **Johannes Harsche**

Owing to general economic development, the agricultural transformation process in many European regions affects the farming household's decisions concerning on-farm and off-farm work. These decisions depend on various parameters, including specifically agricultural as well as general economic and sociodemographic variables. Using a panel data econometric model we establish in this study that several variables of this kind affect the agricultural labour markets. We use six years' panel data from 26 administrative districts (*Landkreise*) of the central German state of Hesse which has a very diverse agricultural structure and a long tradition of part-time farming. The econometric analysis produces significant results on the way various agricultural as well as non-agricultural parameters affect the labour market decisions of farmers. Variables concerning local economic structure indicate different influences on the magnitude of farming on the labour markets. Thus a growth in wages results in an increase in the proportion of part-time farms in relation to all farms and in a reduction in the number of all farms in comparison to all employees. Additionally, an increase in wages involves a decrease in the share of agricultural employees in relation to all employees. Consequently, attractive wages in other sectors may give an incentive to switch into them or to practise a combination of on-farm and off-farm work. In addition to this, the results show that agricultural labour markets are significantly influenced by natural conditions in the regions.

Contact: Johannes Harsche, Institute for Agricultural Policy and Market Research, Justus Liebig University Giessen, Senckenbergstraße 3, D-35390 Giessen, Germany; *johannes.harsche@agrar.uni-giessen.de*

Government intervention in central and eastern European agricultural markets: an empirical analysis – **Jason G. Hartell, Štefan Bojnec and Johan F.M. Swinnen**

The development of agricultural protection in central and eastern European countries (CEECs) has been closely watched because of the potentially substantial and costly adjustments that may be required at the time of accession to the EU and the adoption of the Common Agricultural Policy. Convergence, of both policy and protection level has therefore been considered a factor in reducing these costs. Using data for six CEECs from 1992 to 1998, we find, however, that despite some similarities in agricultural protection instruments, the actual level of aggregate protection (PSE per cent) does not convincingly demonstrate convergence either among the CEECs or with the EU. Subsequently, we empirically investigate the reasons for the variation in agricultural protection levels among CEECs within a political economy framework. To understand the distribution of costs and benefits of supplying agricultural protection, political economy models commonly focus on the relative size of groups and lobbying efficiency, the degree of entrenched vested interests, relative income developments and various structural characteristics of the economy. Pooled OLS regression analysis generally confirms that the determinants of agricultural protection found important in other countries are applicable to the CEECs and that differences in these factors across countries help to explain the lack of convergence. To further identify policy effects, future work will incorporate greater dynamic elements and interaction effects in the empirical model specification.

Contact: Jason G. Hartell, University of Kentucky, USA; PRG KU Louvain, Belgium; *jason.hartell@agr.kuleuven.ac.be*

Assessment of land use in marginal regions – **A. Heissenhuber, J. Kantelhardt and E. Osinski**

There is a conflict between the maintenance of land in use in less favoured areas in Germany and its abandonment. From the economist's point of view, any existing type of land use depends on natural and economic conditions. In a broader sense it is a matter of the capability of natural sites for agricultural purposes, the infrastructure, the agricultural market and the resulting farm perspective. Because of changing economic conditions, intensive agriculture, in the long term, will probably lose attractiveness and extensive agriculture and woodland (even fallow land) will gain in importance. This is especially likely in the less favoured areas, which are often characterized by high ecological and landscape values. In a country with high population density (Germany) both the economic and ecological/tourism aspects of land have to be remembered when policy attempts to influence land use are made. An example of a grassland area is used to show the relative merits of cattle farming against non-farming uses.

Contact: A. Heissenhuber, TU München – Weihenstephan, Lehrstuhl für Wirtschaftslehre des Landbaues, Alte Akademie 14, 85350 Freising, Germany; *heissenh@weihenstephan.de*

Strategies for survival: a modelling approach – **Ludger Hinners-Tobrägel**

In this study the question is whether strategies other than profit maximization can lead to a higher probability of farm survival. Monte-Carlo simulations were carried out with a very stylized model farm, producing plant and animal products with uncertain prices and polypolistic markets. The model is characterized by rolling planning with a horizon of one period, linear programming and rational expectations. The steps in business planning are forming expectations, actual planning, realization, surprise and new planning. Three strategies are compared. Unrestricted profit maximization is used as a reference. The diversification strategy is marked by the fact that investment in plant and animal production is fixed, although animal production is more profitable. A farmer following the risk discount strategy calculates optimal investment using lower prices than actually expected. In other simulation studies the success of a strategy depends on the activities of its competitors. To avoid this, each strategy is simulated in an identical environment. The results show that, in the special formulation of the model, the simple strategies such as diversification or risk discounts on both product prices reduce the risk of failure compared with unrestricted profit maximization.

Contact: Ludger Hinners-Tobrägel, IAMO, Theodor-Lieser-Str. 2, D-06120 Halle/Saale, Germany; *hinners@imao.uni-halle.de*

An integrated economic and environmental farm simulation model (FASSET) – **Brian H. Jacobsen, Jørgen E. Olesen, Bjørn M. Petersen and Jørgen Berntsen**

The model presented here – FASSET – can be used to assess the economic and environmental consequences of different policies at the farm level. The model is a result of interdisciplinary research aimed at making the concept of sustainability operational at the farm level. The current prototype consists of a planning module and a simulation module where climatic conditions also affect the result. FASSET gives a detailed description of the entire nitrogen flow in order to assess the nitrogen loss. The effect of different types of taxation of nitrogen inputs in one farm example is presented and the cost of reducing leaching is calculated.

Contact: Brian H. Jacobsen, Danish Institute of Agricultural and Fisheries Economics, Gl. Køge Landevej 1-3, 2500 Valby, Denmark; *brian@sjfi.dk*

Spatial equilibrium modelling for policy analysis: effects of WTO agreements on agriculture in Costa Rica – **Hans G.P. Jansen, Peter C. Roebeling, Aad Van Tilburg and Robert A. Schipper**

A spatial equilibrium model (SEM) is developed for the agricultural sector in Costa Rica to analyse spatial patterns of supply, demand, trade flows and prices for 17 major agricultural commodities in six planning regions and the rest of the world. Producer and consumer behaviour is modelled, while simultaneously taking transaction costs and government policies into account. The model is validated with 1995 data and used to assess the effects of a number of trade liberalization measures on spatial patterns of land use, trade flows and consumer and producer welfare. While raising aggregate welfare, especially for consumers and less so for producers, trade liberalization results in significant changes in patterns of agricultural production and trade. The main contributions of this research are (1) development of a well-established database on regional agricultural land use, production and prices for Costa Rica, (2) sound econometric estimates of regional demand and supply elasticities which were previously unavailable, and (3) an agricultural sector model that can be used by both policy makers and research institutions to evaluate alternative agricultural policy measures, also previously unavailable.

Contact: Hans G.P. Jansen, Agricultural Economics Research Institute (LEI-Wageningen UR), P.O. Box 29703, 2502 LS The Hague, The Netherlands; *h.g.p.jansen@lei.wag-ur.nl*

Motivations and influence of FDI in the Hungarian food sector – **Csaba Jansik**

Hungary has been a popular target for foreign investments since the beginning of political and economic reforms. The country has received one-quarter of the total FDI inflow into the Central and Eastern European region. Food processing was one of the first sectors to be privatized in Hungary. Foreign investors have participated very actively in the process since 1990. The share of foreign ownership in the Hungarian sector exceeded 60 per cent by 1997. The objective of this study is to analyse the major determinants that caused an uneven distribution of FDI among the 17 food processing subsectors. The factors that attracted large amounts of foreign investments into certain food industries are sought, using a regression model and cluster analysis. The study reviews the fears previously associated with foreign ownership in the food sector and weighs them against the results achieved up to 1999. The assessment provides the Hungarian agri-food sector, foreign investors and Central and Eastern European countries with valuable future reference material.

Contact: Csaba Jansik, Department of Agricultural Economics, Budapest University of Economic Sciences, 1093 Budapest, Hungary; *csabajansik@hotmail.com*

Viable insurance schemes for the rural poor in developing countries: lessons from a women's association in India – **Johannes Jutting**

The concept of mutual insurance is increasingly seen as a means of improving the access of poor people to efficient risk-sharing institutions. In this paper we analyse the mutual insurance scheme of an Indian self-help organization in order to identify criteria which help to explain why in some cases mutual insurance schemes are stable while in others they break down. The identified criteria for a viable scheme are (1) a careful selection of the risks covered, (2) experience in management and financial operations, (3) education and training of the staff and members, and (4) a low-cost incentive and enforcement structure which should contribute to the social capital stock of the community. As local mutual insurance schemes rarely insure against covariant risks, and participation is often biased against the poorer strata of the population, public institutions have to play a key role. In this respect, the case study of the Self Employed Women's Association (SEWA) in India shows that there are promising means of cooperation between state authorities and local self-help groups. In future this partnership should be enlarged to include private business, which could contribute to enlarging the risk pool and reducing unit transaction costs for contracts.

Contact: Johannes Jutting, University of Bonn, Germany; *j.jutting@uni-bonn.de*

Induced changes in land use and property rights under the influence of market access and demographic change: the Borana pastoralists in southern Ethiopia – **Abdul Kamara and Michael Kirk**

The study assesses the dynamics of land use and property rights in the Borana rangelands of southern Ethiopia, and evaluates their causes and consequences for livestock development. The driving forces are related to a complex set of endogenous and exogenous factors, among them rainfall variability, market variables and demographic forces. Theoretical considerations revolve around the theories of agricultural intensification and induced innovation, viewed from the perspective of collective action and interest group theories of institutional change. The dynamics of land use are an outcome of both exogenous processes related to changes in prices, technology, demographic and market variables, as well as endogenous processes initiated by the activities of interest groups. Local level responses may depend on endowments of natural resources, human capital and social capital. The study utilizes community-level data to test these hypotheses, using regression methods. The results indicate a general increase in crop cultivation and land allocation to private grazing. This process is largely related to rainfall variability, market variables, demographic change, and heterogeneity and social capital variables. The semi-arid nature of the area creates concern about its potential capacity to support a fully privatized system on a sustainable basis.

Contact: Abdul Kamara, Institute of Rural Development, University of Göttingen, Waldweg 26, D-37037 Göttingen, Germany; *akamara@gwdg.de*

Modelling the rural economy: an interregional general equilibrium approach in Latvia – **Artis Kancs**

A rural–urban interregional computable general equilibrium model (CGE) is constructed to simulate the effects of agricultural policies on household incomes, employment rates, farm and non-farm sectoral activity, allocation of factors across regions and sectors, regional costs of living and other economic indicators. Regions are characterized as open activity models with given endowments of natural resources and labour. Prices of differentiated commodities as well as of production factors are endogenous. The analysis is applied to Latvian economy using the 1996 input–output tables. The study provides a useful indication of conceptual and empirical issues that must be considered in further regional modelling efforts, issues which do not arise in static models. The application breaks new ground in interregional general equilibrium modelling of a transition economy and in disaggregating national economic data to the regional level.

Contact: Artis Kancs, Institute of Agricultural Development in Central and Eastern Europe, Theodor-Lieser-Str. 2, 06120 Halle/Saale, Germany; *kancs@ iamo.uni-halle.de*

Explaining EU-member states' positions towards Agenda 2000 and CAP reform – **Stelios D. Katranidis and Alexandra Vakrou**

Member states' positions towards the reform of the common agricultural policy (CAP), as they were presented during the discussions for the Agenda 2000 proposals, form the basis for this study. The work is underpinned by a New Political Economy framework in exploring the creation of inter-state groups and coalitions at EU supranational level. The empirical part is based on cluster analysis. The results indicate that the significance of pressure group activities and the importance of collective action as proposed by the lobbying model (interest group approach) cannot satisfactorily explain the discrepancy between national positions. The political importance of this conclusion is that, even in the presence of measures capable of relieving the pressures exerted by the lobbying groups, the impact of these measures on the final outcome would be marginal. The results obtained are more easily explained by using some elements of the politician–voter approach. Most of the countries, which are supporters of a protectionist agricultural policy, have been faced with a great agricultural adjustment problem. Measures supported by the Structural Funds, particularly those aimed at the lagging countries and regions of the European periphery, could contribute significantly to the adjustment, subsequently leading to an alignment of the political priorities of national governments. The main consequence of this process may well be a further advancement in liberalizing the CAP and international trade of agricultural products in general.

Contact: Stelios D. Katranidis, Department of Economic Science, University of Macedonia, Egnatia St. 156, 540 06 Thessaloniki, Greece; *katranid@uom.gr*

Multiple job holding: off-farm employment, labour demand and labour supply of Irish farm households – **Mary Keeney and Alan Matthews**

The supply of off-farm labour by farm families has received increased attention in recent years. Given the importance of off-farm income to Irish farm families, the attention is certainly justified. External employment by one or more family members is not only prevalent in Ireland but appears to be a permanent phenomenon. This study focuses on efforts to explain multiple job holding and its effect on the supply of agricultural labour. Contrary to assertions that it is essential to distinguish the firm from the household, it appears that such a distinction is not appropriate in the Irish context of predominantly family farming. Incomes earned elsewhere enable families to spread farm income risks, while capital tends to be directed into agriculture from external income sources. A number of factors hamper the adoption of off-farm employment as an adjustment strategy. The effects of these factors, some of which are market, and others institutionally, determined, may be accentuated for poorer farmers. For instance, the provision of subsidies serves to increase the off-farm reservation wage, thereby inhibiting participation in external labour markets. Also, when the labour market is depressed, some household members may not be able to obtain work. In regions with few off-farm jobs and a high proportion of the labour force in agriculture, the 'discouraged worker effect' is shown to be important.

Contact: Mary Keeney, Department of Economics, Trinity College Dublin, Ireland; *keeneym@tcd.ie*

Structural changes in the Russian food market: an institutional analysis –
Natalia Kireeva, Lyudmila Aleksandrova and Natalia Fisenko

The object is to investigate the structure of the Russian food market. The basis of the analysis is the study of institutional changes in the agri-food sector and their influence in defining the economic behaviour of producers. For estimation of market and non-market institutional efficiency, the use of transaction cost economics is suggested. The issues analysed, with reference to the grain market, are formal rules, the non-formal limitations and characteristics of various constraints, alternative models of behaviour and new perceptions of privileges and costs.

Contact: Natalia Fisenko, Institute of Agrarian Problems, Russian Academy of Sciences, Russia; *apk@mail.saratov.ru*

Spatial integration during transition? The Russian wheat flour market, 1994 to 1996 – **Michael Kopsidis and Guenter Peter**

According to the literature, agri-food markets in Russia are only poorly integrated. However, many important questions remain unanswered. In the case of spatial integration, different patterns in the relations between deficit and surplus regions have never been analysed for Russia. Our study closes this gap by analysing weekly wheat flour prices of seven Russian regional capitals, using cointegration analysis. We investigate whether integrated staple food markets have emerged during transition and which types of regions are part of a Russian domestic market and which are isolated from it. On the basis of our results, spatial integration of Russian wheat flour markets exists only to a very limited extent. Neither the two political and economic centres of Moscow and Saint Petersburg nor the poorly developed rural grain deficit regions at the southern border are integrated into a common Russian market. The only deficit regions which show a relatively high degree of domestic market integration are parts of the Russian hinterland, which earn large revenues from oil and gas and depend on domestic supplies owing to their location far away from any seaport.

Contact: Michael Kopsidis, Institute of Agricultural Development in Central and Eastern Europe, Theodor-Lieser-Str. 2, 06120 Halle, Germany; *kopsidis@ iamo.uni-halle.de*

Development trends in the Ukrainian agricultural market and its regulation –
Sergiy M. Kvasha

The transition to market relations in agriculture is one possible choice for
Ukraine. Analysis of the openness level by countries shows that Ukraine is a
country with high external trade activity, but also one which makes poor use of
its internal economic potential. There are three commodity groups in the Agro-
Industrial Complex (AIC) of Ukraine: (1) agricultural products produced by
farms, (2) processed food and (3) industrial (manufactured) goods for agricultural use. The gross grain output in 1999 was about 24.3 million tons, which is
the lowest since 1946. Only oilseeds output is still at the average level of the
1986–90 period. Main export agricultural products in 1998 were grain (20 per
cent), oil seeds (13 per cent) and meat and meat products (10 per cent).

Contact: Sergiy M. Kvasha, World agriculture and international agricultural
trade, Department of Agricultural Management, Kiev, Ukraine; *rectorat@nauu.*
kiev.au

Private incentives to invest in the agricultural firm during transition: with
illustrations from Sweden and Estonia – **Carl Johan Lagerkvist**

In restructuring the agricultural sector in Central and Eastern Europe, the
operation of asset markets and financial institutions, technology improvements
and increased competitiveness are in focus. This paper analyses the incentives
to invest, as reflected in the user cost of capital, in the agricultural firm in the
presence of adjustment costs, information asymmetries and financial constraints,
all typical characteristics of transition economies. It is shown that the user cost
of capital is dependent on which financial regime is active in the firm. It is also
found that, the more inefficient the technology used and the less efficient the
monitoring which financial institutions can provide, the higher is the user cost
of capital when used for new investments. In addition, if the farm operator
lacks collateral, owing, for example, to poorly functioning land markets, essential cost reductions are forgone. An empirical illustration is presented for
farms in Sweden and Estonia during 1986–97.

Contact: Carl Johan Lagerkvist, Department of Economics, Swedish University of Agricultural Sciences, P.O. Box 7013, S-750 07 Uppsala, Sweden;
carl-johan.lagerkvist@ekon.slu.se

Modelling income effects on long-term developments of agricultural world
markets: WATSIM simulation results – **Martin von Lampe**

Income growth is one of the major driving forces for the growing food demand
in developing countries. The recent Asian economic crisis has shown that
changes in income prospects significantly affect agricultural markets. Given

the increasing importance of international trade due to increased import reliance of many developing countries, and gradually reduced protection in many industrialized regions, market projections are becoming more relevant. The proper modelling of income developments is therefore considered to be crucial for both projections and impact analyses on changed income prospects. Using the WATSIM model developed at Bonn University, the use of constant income elasticities of food demand is replaced by log-quadratic demand functions with respect to real per capita income. This poster presents a cross-section analysis across the model regions used to estimate the impact of rising incomes on income elasticities. It is argued that this systematic adjustment of model parameters to economic growth can significantly improve both projection results and sensitivity of trade models. Comparing the baseline projections for the cereal and meat markets with a high-income scenario for three Asian regions, the results suggest that economic prospects have significant impacts on world market price development. The principal trend of decreasing real world market prices for agricultural commodities should slow down considerably in the future.

Contact: Martin von Lampe, Department of Agricultural Policy, University of Bonn, Nussallee 21, 53115 Bonn, Germany; *vlampe@agp.uni-bonn.de*

Opportunity costs and enforcement costs of groundwater protection under different institutional conditions – **Christian Lippert, Michael Köbler and Alois Heißenhuber**

Opportunity and enforcement costs of reducing the nitrate content of groundwater are estimated for the conditions prevailing in Southern Germany under four different assumptions concerning the necessary changes in farming practices. Starting from the assumption that the property rights related to groundwater attributes belong to farmers, two institutional arrangements are compared: (a) result related payments and (b) payments for defined actions (farming practices). Case (a) means that the state pays a bounty for the observance of a limiting nitrate content in soil, which entails costs of measuring, whereas case (b) is characterized by monitoring costs incurred when supervising the specific (nitrate-lowering) farming practices paid for. To make them comparable, 'monitoring costs' comprise not only the actual costs for monitoring measures but also the proportionate (lost) compensation payment for undetected contract breaches minus the proportionate fine from detected ones. They are calculated (minimized) using a small model including interdependent variables such as the probability of being caught in case of contract breach, the number of monitoring measures taken and the corresponding share of contract breaches. The results show that which of the two institutional arrangements is preferable from the budgetary point of view depends on the respective farming practice as well as on morality. Finally, some possible modifications of the model and some further characteristics of the two kinds of institutional arrangements are discussed.

Contact: Christian Lippert, Centre of Life Sciences Weihenstephan, Technical University of Munich, Alte Akademie 14, 85350 Freising-Weihenstephan, Germany; *lippert@weihenstephan.de*

Analysing financial health with artificial neural networks and fuzzy systems –
H. Loebbe

The assessment of financial health and the prediction of business failure are major problems of financial management. In this research an Artificial Neural Network (ANN) is used to analyse the financial health of farms in Germany. A multi-layer perceptron (MLP) is developed and applied to a data set of 10 012 farms in the years 1992 to 1997. The input variables originate from the financial statements. They can be subdivided into the areas of cash flow, risk, profitability and growth. This network classifies the farms in the two categories of healthy and unhealthy financial situations, respectively. Unfortunately, a classification criterion such as bankruptcy/non-bankruptcy exists only for a few German farms. An available event is 'financial distress'. But this event is subjective, not a fact and not directly available from the data analysis. Therefore the ANN is combined with fuzzy systems. In this research the event 'financial distress' is described by three ratios and these are merged by fuzzy logic. First, one ANN is developed for each of the three ratios. Then these three outputs are combined by fuzzy logic to form one event. The data sets of the output ratios are fuzzy sets. Thereby the ANN can 'learn' more accurately than traditional statistical instruments. The ANN is compared with a multiple discriminant analysis (MDA). The results show that the MLP performs better than the MDA.

Contact: H. Loebbe, Department of Agricultural Policy, University of Bonn, Nussallee 21, 53115 Bonn, Germany; *h.loebbe@uni-bonn.de*

Reshaping service provision in rural Russia: what role for private providers? –
Daniela Lohlein and Peter Wehrheim

Service provision in rural areas of the Russian Federation has been affected by two forces during the transition: agricultural reforms and decentralization of policy making. Large agricultural enterprises were the sole providers of rural services during the Soviet era. At the same time that these received the right to transfer their social assets to municipalities, the federal government shifted responsibility for service provision to the local level. The result in many regions has been a deterioration in both the quality and quantity of services. As some of the previously publicly provided goods are in fact merit and private goods, the potential role of the private sector is quite large. However, to this day there are few, if any, private service providers operating in rural Russia. Possible reasons for this are addressed. The discussion also covers the issue of why private providers should play a role in service provision. The poster concludes by giving policy recommendations for remedying this situation.

Contact: Peter Wehrheim, Centre of Development Research, University of Bonn, Nussallee 21, 53115 Bonn, Germany; *p.wehrheim@uni-bonn.de*

The impact of farm credit programmes on technical efficiency: a case study for northern Germany – **Jens-Peter Loy and Bernhard Brümmer**

The technical efficiency of dairy farms in Schleswig-Holstein included in the European Farm Credit Programme over the period 1987 to 1994 is analysed. The main objective of the programme is to increase the productivity of farms. Therefore participating farms should attain a higher level of technical efficiency, at least in the long run. However, several aspects of the implementation of the programme might obscure the realization of efficiency gains. This is the underlying hypothesis, which is tested by applying a stochastic frontier model. The approach is applied to explain differences in technical efficiency in terms of programme participation. Furthermore, the basic model is extended to allow for heteroscedasticity in the systematic error term. Statistical tests indicate the dominance of this model over alternative specifications. The results indicate a high average level of performance. However, participation in the programme appears to have resulted in a slight decrease of technical efficiency and the programme seems to have failed. This might stem from the institutional setting of the programme and the restrictions set by the Common Agricultural Policy. Both factors could explain the phenomenon that loans at a subsidized interest rate have not brought an increase in technical efficiency.

Contact: J.-P. Loy, Institute of Agricultural Economics, University of Kiel, Olshausenstr. 40, 24098 Kiel, Germany; *jploy@agric-econ.uni-kiel.de*

Market power of the German beer industry in export markets: an empirical study – **Jens-Peter Loy and Thomas Glauben**

The existence and magnitude of market power of the German beer industry on selected international markets (France, United Kingdom, Canada, United States) is estimated and tested. Two theoretical approaches to model imperfect (monopolistic) competition on export markets are employed, the 'pricing to market' (PTM) model and the 'residual demand elasticity' (RDE) approach. Both models allow testing for the existence of market power, but its extent can only be quantified by the RDE approach. Monthly data of German beer exports over the period from April 1991 to May 1998 are used. The number of observations allows analysis of the time series properties of the data-generating processes. While significant market power of German beer exporters on the US and Canadian markets is indicated by the PTM model, the RDE specification indicates that there is market power of German exporters only on the French market. Since the two approaches lead to different results, it is concluded that the underlying theoretical models have to be extended to match the observed situation. The explicit consideration of competitors' behaviour in international markets could enhance the understanding of pricing processes.

Contact: L-P. Loy, Institute of Agricultural Economics, University of Kiel, Olshausenstr. 40, 24098 Kiel; *jploy@agric-econ.uni-kiel.de*

Supply constraints, export opportunities and agriculture in the Western Cape of South Africa – **Scott McDonald and Cecilia Berning**

The benefits of trade and policy liberalization depend upon the ability of industries to respond to new opportunities. In the case of agriculture in the Western Cape, the availability of land imposes tight constraints on the ability of farming to respond to opportunities that may accompany trade and policy liberalization, and hence limit the benefits that may be realized. Recent years have seen a virtually complete liberalization of the agricultural policy environment in South Africa and this has led to a substantial increase in deciduous fruit and wine exports from the Western Cape. Results come from SAM-Leontief analyses, using a mixed multiplier model, of the impact of liberalization in the Western Cape when agriculture is supply-constrained. They indicate that increases in exports following liberalization should have benefited rural communities, especially farmworkers, but the benefits are supply-constrained. Relaxing the constraints, through raised productivity, would increase the benefits for agricultural and food processing industries. It was shown that higher levels of productivity in all agricultural sectors will greatly benefit farm households, and that there will be substantial benefits also to non-farm households, since limits on other activities consequent upon agricultural capacity constraints are relaxed.

Contact: Scott McDonald, University of Sheffield, United Kingdom and University of Pretoria, South Africa; *s.mcdonald@sheffield.ac.uk*

Modelling land use dynamics with special respect to farm interactions in typical Bavarian landscapes – **A. Meyer-Aurich, J. Kantelhardt, H. Schemm and A. Heißenhuber**

This study concentrates on the dynamics of land use in three typical Bavarian landscapes exhibiting different agricultural production conditions and farm structures. The selected regions (Feldkirchen, Haibach and Scheyern) represent favourable, marginal and medium production conditions. Owing to changes in prices and subsidies, a structural change is expected within the next decade. However, a high percentage of part-time farmers could have an influence on this process. The aim of the study is to analyse the driving and retarding forces of change in the selected regions with a modelling approach to predict future land use under different frame conditions with respect to the attitudes of the land users. Therefore a farm-based modelling approach, with a land market, was chosen to reflect the individual behaviour of different farmers. The model shows that the output of future land use is highly dependent on the economic frame conditions and specific farmers' attitudes. For example, it can be shown that in Haibach milk productions systems would almost disappear if the farmers laid a claim for a higher labour income for their on-farm activities. In that case land use systems with less labour input, such as suckle cow systems, would displace dairying. It can also be shown that this attitude has a marginal impact in other regions, such as Feldkirchen.

Contact: A. Meyer-Aurich, Department of Agricultural Economics and Farm Management, Technical University of Munich, Germany; *meyer@weihenstephan.de*

Tapping the potential of African universities for national agricultural research – **Heike Michelsen**

In order to improve the impact of agricultural research on development, it is important to evaluate the performance of those organizations conducting agricultural research. In the sub-Saharan African context, where national agricultural research systems (NARS) have been particularly criticized for lacking efficiency, effectiveness and sustainability, research performance evaluation is particularly important. This argument also applies to African universities more generally. Although considered part of the NARS, and having considerable human resources, they have often not contributed to development-oriented agricultural research. This paper describes the results from a comparative research performance evaluation study comparing universities and the public national agricultural research organizations (NAROs) in Benin, Burkina Faso, Côte d'Ivoire, Nigeria, Uganda and Zimbabwe. It shows that most university research is done independently of national priorities and plans and that, in many cases, universities have no specific budget for research. Universities are often not mandated to conduct research contributing to development. Thus they rarely systematically plan, coordinate, monitor and evaluate their work. The results also indicate that very limited collaboration exists between them and national research organizations. This is mainly due to the lack of specific policies to promote linkages of university research with other institutions. Contacts between universities and farmers, for example, are even less strong than those between NAROs and farmers. Finally, there is little information about research activities and resources available in nearly all research organizations, and there are no incentives to work jointly with other researchers. As an action research project, the study systematically provides several strategies to increase university contributions to national agricultural research.

Contact: Heike Michelsen, Policy and Management Development and Environment Programme, International Service for National Agricultural Research (ISNAR), The Hague, Netherlands; *h.michelsen@cgiar.org*

Prospects for international trade and marketing in Spain's olive oil sector –
Samir Mili and Manuel Rodriguez Zuñiga

The purpose of this study is to forecast main trends and likely developments affecting the Spanish olive oil export business over the next decade. A Delphi survey was conducted in 1999 with a qualified panel of experts in the olive oil sector who, over two rounds of mailings, have contributed their judgments about future export perspectives. Issues discussed include the expected evolution of world olive oil supply and demand, the likely implications of the major impending changes in the institutional setting, the competitive conditions of the Spanish olive oil export industry and the key international marketing variables for the future. In general, experts seem to draw a future scenario with increases in world supply above those in demand, lower requirements for regulation and intervention, and a greater focus on quality and marketing-mix functions as key factors of competitiveness.

Contact: Samir Mili, Instituto de Economía y Geografia (CSIC), c/ Pinar, 25, 28006 Madrid, Spain; *smili@ieg.csic.es*

Modelling regional trade offs using a true position land use prognosis approach: economic output versus landscape aesthetics versus groundwater recharge – **Detlev Möller, Bernd Weinmann, M. Kirschner and F. Kuhlmann**

Landscape functions are strongly connected to type and intensity of land use, forming a pattern which is a result of a complex network of economic, social, biotic and abiotic interactions. The main focus is to investigate the effects of variable field sizes on production costs and other regional key indicators, as well as looking at the trade-offs between economic, aesthetic and hydrological objectives. To investigate the potential allocation of land use systems, a GIS-based bioeconomic computer model of agricultural and forestry production named ProLand was employed. ProLand combines spatial explicit land use prognoses and the generation of key indicators representing a certain region considering a varying framework of land use decisions. The model uses the spatial distribution of achievable land rent as a decision criterion. Examining two example study areas, it was found that the spatial distribution of land use in the less favoured Aartal region of Germany shows a significant reaction to changing production cost due to a variation of field size from forestry to grassland systems. In the favoured region the effect is less significant; the arable farming area is quite stable. The less favoured region has advantages in providing groundwater and landscape aesthetics, while the favoured Amöneburg region has advantages in employing people and gaining income from agriculture and forestry.

Contact: Detlev Möller, University of Giessen, Germany; *detlev.moeller@ agrar.uni-giessen.de*

Strategy for integrated development of agriculture and rural areas in CEEC countries: the necessity for a comprehensive approach – **Tanja Möllmann and Kai Bauer**

The aim of the IDARA project (Strategy for Integrated Development of Agriculture and Rural Areas in CEE countries) is to identify key problems and discuss strategies for an integrated development of agriculture and rural areas in the first group of CEEC entering the EU. Such work must not restrict itself to a particular research field, however. At present, most countries lack integrated rural development policies and the supporting institutional structures. Most rural areas will undergo substantial agricultural adjustment and this will inevitably set labour free. Agricultural diversification can play a key role in stimulating local economic development. Finally, both the labour outflow and the income situation of households, central to a rural development strategy, will depend directly on agricultural production and price developments. In the light of these major interdependencies, the project has embraced a comprehensive approach to improve the understanding of three interdependent fields that have not yet been sufficiently addressed. These are the identification of adequate policy measures and institutional structures for the introduction of an integrated rural development policy in the CEEC, a thorough analysis of agricultural diversification patterns and their potential roles in rural development, and finally the development of a simulation model that allows a comprehensive estimation of the impact of different policy measures on agricultural production and income, on the EU budget and, in turn, its consequences for rural development strategies in the CEEC.

Contact: Tanja Möllmann, Institute for Agricultural Policy, Market Research and Economic Sociology, University of Bonn, Germany; *tanja.moellmann@ agp.uni-bonn.de*

Investigation of the production type and the size of private farms in the conditions of Bulgarian agricultural reform – **Nikolay Naydenov**

The results of a farm management investigation showed that 77 per cent of farmers prefer mixed farming with arable and livestock production, versus 20 per cent favouring arable specialization and 3 per cent opting for livestock farming. The findings can be explained by the trend towards diversification, as well as being an attempt to make better use of family labour. Most of the private farms are relatively small in size: 34.45 ha. on average for the mixed-type farms and 53.33 ha. for arable farms. However, the average size of a group of large rented farms is 391 ha. As private farmers own a relatively small amount of land (7 ha. on average), the proportion of rented land is very large. The preferred size of a sole private farm is 91.5 ha. on average, that is, two to three times larger than at present. The results obtained can help in designing the process of harmonization of farm businesses according to EU policy, as well as in restructuring and further development of the service units in agriculture.

Contact: Nikolay Naydenov, University of Rousse, BG - 7017 Rousse, Bulgaria; *nnaydenov@ecs.ru.acad.bg*

Contribution to climate stability via afforestation of marginal agricultural and waste lands in the Ukraine – **Maria Nijnik**

Afforestation of marginal agricultural lands and reforestation of previously wooded areas in the Ukraine are an attractive economic alternative to reducing carbon emissions. The paper explores the potential of afforestation of marginal agricultural waste, and unwooded lands within the State Forest Fund as an option for meeting the Kyoto commitments. The ultimate objective is to assess the Ukraine's potential to contribute to climate stability through the afforestation programme, to estimate costs of practical implementation of such a measure and to be able to compare the costs of various emission reduction options. The first step, a storage option presented in the paper, is to examine the impact of trees being grown for a period of 40 years. The option, in some cases, showed very poor returns because of the discounted opportunity costs of maintaining forests on agricultural land. The results also showed that it is important to define what use to make of trees after the 40-year time period. Considering the scarcity of oil in the Ukraine, the unreasonably high costs of coal extraction and all the problems connected with nuclear power plants, the energy option (wood burning to generate electricity) is likely to be the most attractive.

Contact: M. Nijnik, Department of Agricultural Economics and Rural Policy, Wageningen University, P.O. Box 8130 6700 EW Wageningen, The Netherlands; *maria.nijnik@alg.aae.wau.nl*

Trends in the development of agriculture in Yugoslavia – **Nebojsa Novkovic, Natalija Bogdanov, Slobodan Ceranic and Vesna Rodic**

Agriculture plays an important role in the Yugoslav economy since the country has substantial resources for agricultural development at its disposal. However, their qualitative attributes are known to be unfavourable, lagging behind the highly developed countries. Since the beginning of the 1990s, the production and economic indicators of Yugoslav agriculture have consistently been unfavourable. Production variability was high; labour productivity was poor; inputs were minimized; processing was monopolistic compared with farming; investment in agriculture was low; transition processes were slow; and the agricultural sector was used as a means of solving social problems, against its own interests. The reasons were partly outside the control of farm policy. There was war in the area and the sanctions imposed by the UN limited and hindered external trade; the disintegration of former Yugoslavia caused further trade problems; and the economic collapse decreased the purchasing power and the living standard of the population. But the lesson for the future is that there were other underlying problems which will have to be addressed. The state had shifted the social and economic aspects of the long-standing crisis to agriculture, maintaining social peace by insisting on low food prices. The disparity in agricultural product and intermediate goods prices had been at the expense of agriculture and there had been very inefficient distribution of agricultural products through 'grey' channels.

Contact: Nebojsa Novkovic, University of Novy Sad, Yugoslavia; *esan@polj. ns.ac.yu*

Impacts of agrienvironmental programmes in Germany – **Bernhard Osterburg and Hiltrud Nieberg**

Agrienvironmental schemes according to Regulation (EEC) 2078/92 were introduced with the 1992 reform of the European Union agricultural policy. The regional implementation of the regulation resulted in a diversity of measures, conditions and hectare payments in the EU member states. Because of the regional variations in Germany, an experimental case study is carried out in order to assess the impacts of this new policy on land use and environment, farm structures, factor markets, competition and farm incomes. Since 1996, about 30 per cent of Germany's agricultural area is managed under Regulation (EEC) 2078/92 measures. Very few EU member states have higher rates of participation. An analysis of regional and farm accounting data came to the following conclusions. Flat rate payments for agrienvironmental measures, calculated on the basis of average production conditions, lead to regional concentration of participation in areas with lower land use intensity. Thus only limited environmental benefits can be expected. Farms participating in agrienvironmental schemes reduced land use intensity, starting from a comparatively lower level. For example, they reduced fertilizer input and increased permanent grassland. Positive income effects could be shown, as well as a high competitiveness of programme participants in land and milk quota markets.

Contact: Bernhard Osterburg, Institute of Farm Economics and Rural Studies, Federal Agricultural Research Centre (FAL), Bundesallee 50, D - 38116 Braunschweig, Germany; *bernhard.osterburg@fal.de*

Moral hazard in agrienvironmental policy: risk aversion, monitoring costs and standard fixed payment contracts – **Adam Ozanne and Tim Hogan**

Principal–agent theory is used to analyse economic inefficiencies arising from moral hazard in agrienvironmental schemes employing compensation payments to farmers to secure environmental public goods. The model represents advances on the existing literature in three main respects; first, agrienvironmental policy is modelled as a social welfare maximization problem which recognizes both the importance of the social cost to taxpayers of implementing such public initiatives and the potential trade-off between increased environmental benefit and increased cost of monitoring compliance; second, farmer risk aversion is allowed for; and third, since it is an extension of an earlier adverse selection model, the theoretical framework developed covers both types of information asymmetry in agrienvironmental policy. It is shown that, if monitoring costs are negligible or fixed, or farmers are highly risk-averse, the moral hazard problem can be eliminated. However, if monitoring costs depend on monitoring effort and the degree of risk aversion is low, only a second-best solution can be obtained. Numerical simulations based on plausible representations of production technology, farmers' risk preferences and monitoring costs are used to further illustrate the results.

Contact: Adam Ozanne, School of Economic Studies, University of Manchester, UK; *adam.ozanne@man.ac.uk*

Ex-Soviet cropland expansion revisited: can Kazakh farms survive liberalization? Findings of a study on whole-farm risk – **Martin Petrick**

Against the background of increased risks due to liberalized markets, hard budget constraints and dwindling government protection of farms in northwestern Kazakhstan, the following questions are raised. How do these risks affect the performance of agricultural producers? Can the existing large-scale farms survive in spite of unfavourable natural conditions? To deal with these issues, use is made of the results of a quadratic risk programming model that depicts a typical farm in the Aktyubinsk region. Risk is considered as annual gross margin variation for the period 1993–8. The model solutions are (a) the ES frontier of a typical farm, and (b) a selection of efficient production programmes that reflect different return–risk combinations. Though the farm is profitable, the model exhibits a high profit variation which, in the presence of hard budget constraints, may well jeopardize its existence. Risk could be reduced by abandoning grain and shifting to lucerne and/or grassland hay production. To focus more on the cultivation of extensive fodder plants and the accompanying livestock is therefore regarded as a strategy to reduce risk and secure farm survival. The overall risk exposition of agriculture in north-western Kazakhstan is basically a result of the political decisions made during the Soviet era, which are briefly outlined. Nowadays, production structures inevitably have to adapt to natural and economic constraints. In most cases, a redundant labour force will then pose a major problem for government policy.

Contact: Martin Petrick, Institute of Agricultural Development in Central and Eastern Europe (IAMO), Theodor-Lieser-Str. 2, 06120 Halle (Saale), Germany; *petrick@iamo.uni-halle.de*

Impact of exchange rate policy on agriculture and food industry in CEECs –
Witold-Roger Poganietz

As a consequence of the breakdown of the socialist system at the beginning of the 1990s, the protection of agriculture and the food industry diminished. At the same time, when the economies 'opened', exchange rate policy grew in importance. In view of the characteristics of the agri-food sector and the situation in Central and Eastern European countries (CEECs) the question arose whether exchange rate policy is relevant for the sector. This question was considered in two studies. The objective of the first was to test the impact of exchange rate policy on agri-food trade. On the basis of data for five CEECs for the period 1992–96, a cross-country time-series OLS estimation was made. There was no significant influence of exchange rate policy on import and export in volume terms, but exchange rate policy had some impact on agri-food exports in value terms. In the second study, the effects of Russia's crisis in summer 1998 on the agri-food sector were analysed. Owing to a drastic devaluation of the rouble, demand for foreign foodstuff by Russian households dropped while they shifted to staple food. The change of consumption patterns should have provided the Russian food industry with a chance to expand production, though in fact it declined. Further analysis of this paradox is needed.

Contact: Witold-Roger Poganietz, Institute of Agricultural Development in Central and Eastern Europe (IAMO), Theodor-Lieser-Str. 2, 06120 Halle (Saale), Germany; *poganietz@iamo.uni-halle.de*

Farmers' clubs for preserving wildlife and landscape: the importance of institutional environment – **Nico B.P. Polman and Louis H.G. Slangen**

This paper analyses the influence of institutional environment on farmers organizing themselves with the aim of preserving wildlife and landscape. The organizations formed can be characterized as clubs producing activities and services for the members. The relevant theoretical background is club theory and the new institutional economics. The approach differs from the traditional approaches to clubs in the sense that it is assumed that any comparative advantage of a club is caused by its own 'internal institutions' or 'rules'. The (external) institutional environment of a club, together with other economic factors (for example, technology, rural amenities in an area, income and preferences), determines the development of clubs in the agricultural sector. A survey was conducted among farmers' clubs formed for the preservation of wildlife and landscape in The Netherlands. The survey is one of the first and most intensive to have been carried out among this kind of organization. One conclusion is that internal rules are important to clubs. The opportunities for shaping their internal organization in the way farmers wish and deciding on the activities they want to undertake are fundamental.

Contact: Nico B.P. Polman, Agricultural Economics and Rural Policy Group, Wageningen University, Hollandseweg 1, 6706 KN Wageningen, The Netherlands; *nico.polman@alg.aae.wau.nl*

Farm modelling for regional policy analysis in Costa Rica – **P.C. Roebeling, H.G.P. Jansen, R.A. Schipper and F. Sáenz**

Agricultural policy analysis can be performed at the regional level using agricultural sector models that maximize welfare, or at the farm level with models for representative farm types. While the former approach fails to model farm characteristics and behaviour, any aggregation of farm types to the regional level ignores their interaction in product and factor markets. Using data for Costa Rica, a regional equilibrium modelling approach is presented to incorporate farm types as well as product market equilibrium conditions. Compared with simple aggregation of partial results obtained with exogenous output prices, results of the regional model with endogenous product prices shows less specialization in production and lower incomes, profits and labour use. Therefore results obtained with a regional model including endogenous prices better reflect reality. Different policy scenarios are analysed, including a 20 per cent decrease in transaction costs, a 20 per cent increase in credit availability and a 40 per cent tax on chemical input prices. The former two lead to increased cash crop production and rising agricultural income, while taxing agrochemicals leads to less intensive production.

Contact: P.C. Roebeling, Development Economics Group, Department of Social Sciences, Wageningen University, The Netherlands; *peter.roebeling@alg.oe.wau.nl*

Technological innovation in agriculture: the contribution of agricultural input industries – **Johannes Roseboom**

This paper proposes a new analytical framework to measure and analyse the spill-ins of technology into primary agriculture and in particular those through purchased inputs. The paper first sketches a structural transformation path for primary agriculture in terms of its integration with the rest of the economy. In its transition from a low-income to a high-income economy, a country's primary agriculture moves from weak to strong forward and backward linkages. The intensity of input use by primary agriculture in Colombia, Brazil and The Netherlands roughly matches that of a low-, middle- and high-income country. However, their input use also differs in terms of composition, origin (local/ imported) and the technology embodied in the inputs. As a result, major differences were found in the amount and composition of acquired R&D through purchased inputs among the three countries. This reflects different levels and forms of technological interdependency between primary agriculture and the rest of the (world) economy. Colombia leans heavily on imported inputs and the (private) technology embodied in them. Its own capacity to produce high-tech agricultural inputs is very limited. Brazil's position in this regard is considerably better, although still notably weaker than that of The Netherlands. In addition, the Dutch agricultural sector imports substantial amounts of high-tech agricultural inputs. The technology intensity estimates also shed new light on the relative importance of private and public sources of technological innovation: agriculture in Colombia (and not The Netherlands) depends most heavily on privately generated technology.

Contact: Johannes Roseboom, ISNAR, The Hague; *h.roseboom@cgiar.org*

Rural households in Romania: between restructuring and resistance to change – **Marioara Rusu and Violeta Florian**

Structural changes at the microeconomic and macroeconomic level have drawn the attention of the Romanian scientific community to the rural household. There is a contrast, from the economic and social points of view, between the existence of an autarchic rural society and the metamorphosis of this rural world into a market economy. Transformation at the rather conservative rural household level, with many associated behavioural changes, takes place with difficulty as a response to external stimuli emerges. The problems of the transition period are so important that understanding rural processes is a key element in framing restructuring strategies.

Contact: Marioara Rusu, Institute of Agricultural Economics, Bucharest, Romania; *iea@ines.ro*

Valuing agrarian landscape: an application of conjoint analysis to sensitive mountain areas in south-eastern Spain – **S. Sayadi, M.C. Gonzalez Roa and J. Calatrava Requena**

Among the externalities produced by agriculture, one must consider its contribution to the shaping of the landscape, an aesthetic externality value of agrosystems. Recognizing and appraising this contribution is becoming more and more important. In this study, conjoint analysis is applied to the appraisal of the landscapes of Alpujarras (Granada, Spain) in order to estimate the level of preference of visitors for agrarian components, as opposed to other landscape features, coexisting in the area. Three main landscape components have been considered: type of vegetation, density of rural building and level of incline. Results show that the nature of the vegetation is the most relevant attribute in forming preferences for landscapes. Within this feature, the agrarian component is highly valued aesthetically, though irrigated lands rank above dry farming.

Contact: S. Sayadi, Departamento de Economía y Sociología Agrarias, Apartado 2027, 18080 Granada, Spain; *ssayadi@arrakis.es*

Crop residue management for erosion control: an optimal control approach –
Guenter Schamel and Daniel Mueller

An optimal control model of soil conservation is developed to analyse the optimal private and social path for erosion treatment over an infinite time horizon. To offset soil losses, crop residue management is used as an erosion control strategy and incorporated into the dynamic optimization model. Choice variables for the farmer are variable input use and the crop residue cover left on the soil surface to counteract topsoil loss. The universal soil loss equation (USLE) as an empirical measurement of water-induced soil losses is employed to model the change in the topsoil stock and to provide the possibility of an empirical application for different localities and conditions. The corresponding Hamiltonian is formulated to analyse the optimal private path of soil conservation. Integrating off-site costs leads to the socially optimal path of soil erosion. Including off-site damage increases the value of the soil resource (the shadow price) by the amount of damage per unit, thus making conservation efforts more attractive for farmers and inducing a higher surface residue cover. Because of the close correlation of on- and off-site damage, a mitigation of off-site effects resulting in a reduction of soil erosion can potentially yield on-farm benefits in the form of increased future production capacity. However, more active and widespread public intervention to counteract market failure and market imperfections is best justified by the existence of the adverse environmental impact resulting from the non-point source pollution of soil erosion.

Contact: Guenter Schamel, Institute of Agricultural Economics and Social Sciences of the Humboldt University, Berlin, Germany; *g.schamel@agrar.hu-berlin.de*

Macroeconomic shocks and trade responsiveness in Argentina: a 'VAR' analysis – **Michael Schmitz and Michaela Kuhl**

A vector autoregressive system including macroeconomic and trade variables for Argentina is estimated for the period 1976 to 1997 and analysed using impulse response functions and variance decomposition methods. The analysis shows marked reactions of the path of imports and exports to shocks in Argentine macroeconomic variables. Important differences exist in the reaction of trade flows to certain macroeconomic shocks when they are expressed in real pesos or in US dollars. While in both cases exports and imports increase in reaction to a monetary shock, imports in dollars do not react significantly to an inflationary shock, so no large quantitative changes can be expected to follow from the shock. While exports in real pesos increase after a real devaluation shock, the reaction in dollars also is not significant. For imports, a positive short-term reaction is changed to a negative one if imports are expressed in dollars instead of (real) pesos. Over time, imports decrease enough to more than compensate for the rise in their prices expressed in domestic currency.

The analysis shows less pronounced reactions of trade flows in dollars than in pesos. However, for profitability of exports and opportunity costs of import expenditures, the reactions in domestic currency might be better indicators. For investment decisions in the tradeables sectors, the relatively high influence of the real exchange rate, money growth and inflation shocks, which affect Argentina over the relevant time horizon, add to the uncertainty about general developments in world markets and in important partner countries.

Contact: Michael Schmitz, Department of Agricultural Policy and Market Research, University of Giessen, Diezstr. 15, 35390 Giessen, Germany; *michael.schmitz@agrar.uni-giessen.de*

Comparison of the development of land markets in European transition countries – **Eberhard Schulze and Peter Tillack**

The poster first discusses institutional requirements for the development of land and land lease markets and the impact of the economic environment. A further development of institutions must include a continuation of the privatization of land and the realization of land use rights. The ban on purchases of land by legal entities should be lifted in those countries where it currently applies. In addition, it would be appropriate to lift all restrictions on the sale and lease of land to non-nationals, provided they can present a convincing agricultural business plan. The agricultural sector in the transition countries would thus acquire foreign capital and expertise, which would ultimately benefit the entire economy. The second part aims to investigate what impact changes in the institutional and economic environments since the beginning of the transformation process have had. The recorded sales and lease prices for land are available for the various countries and are linked to performance criteria (agricultural GDP/ha.) and other income indicators. For nine of the ten EU associate countries, a correlation exists between sales prices for land and wheat prices, agricultural gross domestic product per hectare and monthly earnings per employee.

Contact: Eberhard Schulze, Institute of Agricultural Development in Central and Eastern Europe, Theodor-Lieser-Str. 2, 06120 Halle (Saale), Germany; *schulze @iamo.uni-halle.de*

Risk management on Hungarian farms – **Diána Sidlovits, András Bálint, Csaba Kovács and Katalin Szép**

To better understand the nature of agricultural risk, research was conducted into the behaviour of agricultural producers. We demonstrate the basic concept of risk perception and two potential types of risk management strategies. Farms in the transition period are characteristically undersized and insolvent; they are also exposed to financial leverage effects. To counter the relatively low income level and inflexible cost structure of agriculture, the launch of marketing initiatives and operations through price policies are possibly the most effective tools for limiting risk. The Commodity Exchange in Budapest enables producers to contract the sale of their output and avoid price fluctuations and counterpart risk with hedge transactions. Farmers participate very little on account of their small scale and because many of them do not even know of the opportunities provided by the Exchange. More marketing channels make farmers' lives easier. Direct marketing is an option which allows farmers to reduce marketing risks. The ability to adapt innovations is generally improved by close contact and direct exchange of information. Hazards are reduced by quick feedback.

Contact: Diána Sidlovits, Szent István University, Hungary; *sdia@omega.kee.hu*

A framework for analysing institutions of sustainable agriculture and rural areas – **Louis H.G. Slangen and Nico B.P. Polman**

Institutions are very important to the economic, environmental and social dimensions of sustainable agriculture and rural areas (SARA). This paper develops a conceptual framework for analysing the state of institutions and for designing new or better ones for realizing SARA. A distinction is made between formal and informal rules. The framework takes determinants or proxy variables into account on five different levels that may account for good performance in realizing SARA. The first level looks at government performance, the second at the agricultural sector and rural areas, the third at the formal rules of the institutional environment regarding SARA, and the fourth level at the informal rules of the institutional environment and of competencies (there is overlap between them and they can be taken together). The final level focuses on institutional arrangements. The question of what kind of institutional arrangements and design principles would be most suitable for realizing SARA is answered in relation to the level of competencies and the institutional environment performance.

Contact: Louis H.G. Slangen, Agricultural Economics and Rural Policy Group, Wageningen University, Hollandseweg 1, 6706 KN Wageningen, The Netherlands; *louis. slangen@alg.aae.wau.nl*

New approaches for the integration of consumer needs in the product innovation process – **Bernhard Stockmeyer**

Needs and requirements of today's consumers for food products are subject to continuous change. Food processors must be able to translate such changing requirements into new or improved products, otherwise their existence is at risk. Nevertheless, many new products do not meet these requirements and fail in the market place. In order to avoid the failure of new products, one key factor for new product development (NPD) is to be able to gather and to understand consumer requirements and to translate them into new food products. Traditionally, final consumers are not directly involved in NPD until market testing of new products. On the other hand, findings from various studies suggest that close interaction with consumers can be helpful in defining and developing new products and leads to more success in innovation. In the research project, approaches for involvement of customers in NPD have been developed. On the basis of findings from other industrial areas, two successful approaches for interaction have been analysed and adopted for the food industry. These are the lead user approach and quality function deployment. Both concepts have been tested in cooperation with food processors and proved to be a successful means for NPD. Development results have been improved and costs and time reduced.

Contact: Bernhard Stockmeyer, Forschungszentrum für Milch und Lebensmittel Weihenstephan (FML), TU München, Weihenstephaner Berg 1, D – 85354, Freising, Germany; *stockmeyer@bwl.blm.tu-muenchen.de*

Optimal identification and composition of investment projects in Russian agriculture – **Nikolai M. Svetlov**

The aim of the presentation is to discuss the agricultural application of a method that helps to identify and prepare investment projects. The general project cycle concentrates on project selection. In the case of Russian agriculture, most projects are usually rejected. Hence project identification and preparation processes need to be improved. To describe the problem of project composition, a formalization is suggested based on the following problem statement: given (a) the quantities of resources required for each goal, (b) opportunities to share resources between goals and to upgrade with superior resources, (c) effects of goals and costs of resources, (d) available financing and (e) incompatible goals, find the set of goals that maximizes the project's worth. The problem is an integer programming problem. A well-known ARIS project implemented in Russia is used for illustrative purposes. The project is spread over five territories and consists of four base components: marketing, consulting, seed processing and training, plus one supplementary component, the development of informational infrastructure. Different funding opportunities are considered. Even under complete financing, the best project worth is achieved if one rejects training, consulting and informational components in the South Urals, and seed processing plants in the northwest and Siberia.

Contact: Nikolai M. Svetlov, Moscow Agricultural Academy n.a. K.A. Timiryazev, Russia; *svetlov@mnts.msk.su*

Economic welfare effects of Romanian agricultural accession to the European Union – **Kenneth J. Thomson and Maria C. Firici**

The paper estimates the economic effects (costs and benefits) on Romanian farmers, food consumers and taxpayers which would occur as a result of the adoption of the EU's Common Agricultural Policy and Agenda 2000 proposals, in the assumed 'accession' year 2006. The results are based on the construction and use of a conceptually simple model (multi-market, partial-equilibrium, comparative-static), which covers 15 major Romanian agricultural products (65.2 per cent of total output in 1997). Assumptions are embodied within two scenarios for the year 2006: (a) non-accession and (b) accession, in particular trends after the base year of 1997, and longer-term supply and demand elasticities. Four model simulations (calculations for sets of accession assumptions) are reported. For each of these the effects of EU agricultural accession are estimated by comparing the market situation for each product, the public expenditure situation and the differences in the real income (economic welfare) positions of Romanian producers, consumers and taxpayers. Taken together, 'standard' economic and policy assumptions result in a small net welfare gain of about 0.5 per cent in 1997 Romanian GDP. This falls to about 0.4 per cent in the year 2006, given economic growth in the intervening period. Farm producers suffer net losses, and consumers are net gainers, especially in terms of livestock products. The budgetary implications (taxpayer effects) of agricultural accession under the standard assumptions are almost budget-neutral, given the current EU 15 budget pattern.

Contact: K.J. Thomson, Department of Agriculture, University of Aberdeen, 581 King Street, Aberdeen AB24 5UA, Scotland, UK; *k.j.thomson@abdn.ac.uk*

Profitability in Hungarian private agriculture – **József Tóth and Masahiko Gemma**

The study is a review of the performance of private farms in Hungary. Examination of the private sector could produce useful pointers for the future development of agricultural policy. In Hungary, many in the rural population own very small plots of agricultural land, typically of 0.1 to 2.0 ha. The analysis was carried out using survey data from 1580 agricultural producers. The determining factors of profitability in farming activities were identified using regression analysis. The study found that land area as well as quality, education, investment in machinery and buildings, certain factor endowments in vegetable and fruit production, and the share of own farm income in total income are the critical factors for the determination of profitability in individual farming. Policy should concentrate much more on the land issue than on that of income because that would provide more activity options without infringing upon the interests of certain groups of farmers.

Contact: József Tóth, Budapest University of Economic Sciences and Public Administration, Hungary; *jozsef.toth@gkd.bke.hu*

Agrarian production organization under transition to a market economy in Bulgaria – **Christian Tritten and Alexander Sarris**

The paper has two objectives. The first is to show that the Eswaran–Kotwal (1996) model provides an adequate description of the behaviour of agricultural producers in Bulgaria. In brief, the model shows that, in the presence of credit constraints, production behaviour is conditioned by asset holdings (in land and machinery), family size and availability of credit. Subsequently, this model is used to identify which markets work competitively and which do not. The observed behaviour of producers in Bulgaria is compatible with a version of the model where the land market is imperfect and the machinery market is competitive.

Contact: Alexander Sarris, Department of Economics, University of Athens, 8 Pesmazoglou Street, Athens, GR-10559, Greece; *asarris@hol.gr*

Agricultural policy in Ukraine and Poland: towards free agricultural trade in eastern and central Europe – **Olga V. Trofimtseva**

International marketing is one of the key elements for agricultural business. Agricultural policy and state regulation in agriculture need to take account of the potential feasibility of increasing trade relations between countries. The Ukraine and Poland, as adjacent countries, have comparative advantages for developing profitable trade relations in food products. Agricultural policy should provide some measure of protection for domestic producers but at the same time it should not discriminate heavily against either importing or exporting. The Ukraine could avoid many mistakes by learning from Polish experience. For instance, the practice of preferential credits for agriculture has resulted in a waste of funds, misallocation of resources and significant losses in efficiency.

Contact: Olga V. Trofimtseva, World agriculture and international agricultural trade project, Department of Agricultural Management, National Agricultural University, Kiev, Ukraine; *rectorat@nauu.kiev.ua*

Technical efficiency and competitiveness of Czech production in late transition – **Jarmila Ulmanová**

For the central and east European countries which applied trade and price liberalizations in the early 1990s, an important policy question is the impact of the newly established markets on the efficiency and competitiveness of agricultural production. The analysis presented in this poster seeks to address these issues in the case of the Czech Republic by (a) evaluating the level of technical and economic efficiency among agricultural enterprises, using parametric stochastic frontier production methods on panel data from the farm accounting data network operated by the Research Institute of Agricultural Economics, using a policy analysis matrix, and (b) providing a framework for measuring farm-level competitiveness. The poster compares the results of both techniques and explores the relationships between technical efficiency and indicators for competitiveness. Finally, the determinants of technical inefficiency and competitiveness of Czech agricultural enterprises are assessed.

Contact: Jarmila Ulmanová, Faculty of Agricultural Economics and Management, Czech University of Agriculture Prague, Kamýcká 959, 165 21 Prague 6, Czech Republic.

Factors influencing farmers' participation in agrienvironmental measures: a Belgian case study – **I. Vanslembrouck, G. Van Huylenbroeck and G. Verbeke**

The role of agriculture in providing environmental quality, or the farmer's role as a guardian of the countryside, is now generally acknowledged. The challenge is, however, to develop measures that reward farmers for the services they provide while meeting the expectations of society. This research explores farmers' willingness to accept (WTA) changes in their agricultural methods in order to preserve the agricultural landscape. The contingent valuation approach is used as the context in which to explore farmers' hypothetical decision making. In a questionnaire, two countryside stewardship policies have been proposed to farmers, who are asked to state their WTA for every single measure. A conceptual model, taking into account both decision subject and decision maker characteristics, is formulated to deal with the different factors influencing farmers' contingent behaviour. Empirical testing is based on the specification and estimation of a probit model. From the results, conclusions for agricultural policy are drawn concerning farmers' decision making in relation to countryside stewardship policies.

Contact: I. Vanslembrouck, Department of Agricultural Economics, Ghent University, Belgium; *isabel.vanslembrouck@rug.ac.be*

The effects of transaction costs on production decisions and land use patterns: evidence from large-scale agriculture in Spain – **Consuelo Varela-Ortega**

Diversity in cropping choice and production patterns has been explained by the fact that market failures and transaction costs play a major role in shaping agricultural production decisions. The objective of this paper is to analyse the causes of the different patterns of production decisions that farmers follow when transaction costs are considered (defined as an asymmetric access to input and product markets) in a region of large-scale commercial agriculture in

Spain. To analyse the farmers' behaviour, a mathematical programming model has been built incorporating transaction costs that characterize different forms of institutional arrangements (direct and indirect management and farming operations). Results of the model show that the type of institutional arrangement under which a farmer operates his farm is a determinant factor for explaining cropping choice, land use and farm income in different policy scenarios. Cropping patterns remain stable across farm sizes, and virtually no economies of scale are found. Institutional arrangements of lower transaction costs are perceived by the farmers as a surer environment and a more efficient risk shelter. Thus policy programmes can be expected to be more efficiently implemented when farmers engage in contractual agreements that will substantially reduce transaction costs.

Contact: Consuelo Varela-Ortega, Departamento de Economía Agraria, Universidad Politécnica, Ciudad Universitaria s/n, 28040 Madrid, Spain; *cvarela@eco. etsia.upm.es*

Integrating irrigation modernization programmes and water pricing policies: empirical evidence and water policy implications – **Consuelo Varela-Ortega, María Blanco and José M. Sumpsi**

As water becomes increasingly scarce worldwide, a preoccupation of public authorities is the enacting and implementation of water policies aimed at securing conservation and more efficient water management. An alternative to increasing costs and environmental damage of new public-funded irrigation networks will be to invest in the rehabilitation of existing systems that will enhance water conveyance efficiency. In Spain, irrigation agriculture is the largest consumer of water; hence the need to increase efficiency of allocation for irrigation is crucial for water policies. The objective is to investigate the combined effects of irrigation modernization policies and water pricing on conservation, farmer incomes and the government budget. An empirical dynamic model simulating farmers' behaviour has been developed and applied to different water districts in Spain. Results show that farmers' decisions are determined by technical, institutional and economic parameters, while the payments from irrigators to the water users' associations are insufficient to ensure network maintenance. In the absence of subsidies, irrigators will not invest in the modernization of their systems, even when water charges are high. No water conservation improvements are foreseen in the absence of price incentives, thus policies will attain their objectives only if subsidies for rehabilitation are granted in conjunction with the establishment of water prices. However, as the effects of these policies may vary across districts, supply-side and demand-side policies have to be carefully designed for attaining conservation objectives.

Contact: Consuelo Varela-Ortega, Departamento de Economía Agraria, Universidad Politécnica de Madrid, Ciudad Universitaria s/n, 28040 Madrid, Spain; *cvarela@eco.etsia.upm.es*

The Flemish greenhouse industry following increased pressure from competition and the environment – **Poi Verwilt, Erik Mathijs and Bart Minten**

The poster outlines the preliminary results of an attempt to formulate policy measures to enhance sustainable development in the Flemish greenhouse industry. The poster shows, first, how the industry could develop in the coming years with respect to firm size and location within the conditions of the market and the environment, when additional policy measures are absent. It is a reference scenario based on historical trends. The poster outlines the optimal structure (firm size and location) that is economically and ecologically optimal, calculated using programming techniques. Finally, the policy measures that best realize conditions for sustainable development of the sector are derived by comparing 'reference' and 'optimal' structures.

Contact: Poi Verwilt, Katholieke Universiteit Leuven, Belgium; *poi.verwilt@agr. kuleuven.ac.be*

Modelling agricultural policy impacts for EU accession candidates from central and eastern Europe – **Gerald Weber**

The partial equilibrium 'Central and Eastern European Countries Agricultural Simulation Model' (CEEC-ASIM) is designed for agricultural policy analysis. It fulfils all theoretical conditions implied by the assumptions that producers maximize profits using a multi-input–multi-output technology and consumers maximize utility. The supply and demand systems are derived from flexible functional forms of the producer profit and consumer expenditure functions. CEEC-ASIM depicts a wide range of agricultural policy instruments. One of the issues analysed with the model is EU accession. It is assumed that the Common Agricultural Policy's market regulations, as reformed by Agenda 2000, will be applied in ten Central and Eastern European countries (CEEC-10). This scenario is compared with a scenario of unchanged national agricultural policies as observed for 1997. The main results for the aggregate of the CEEC-10 with respect to the welfare effects are the following (all in prices of 1999). First, higher protection by the CAP raises revenues from agricultural activity (measured as net revenue minus labour costs) by Euro6.9 billion. The main sources for the producer welfare gains are area payments and the beef and milk premiums. Second, low value shares of agricultural products in retail prices and the further reorientation of the CAP from market price towards direct income support result in very small welfare impacts on the consumer side (measured as the equivalent variation). The financial burden for the EU budget in the form of area payments, animal premiums and export subsidies is estimated at Euro7.5 billion.

Contact: Gerald Weber, Institute of Agricultural Development in Central and Eastern Europe, Theodor-Lieser-Str. 2, 06120 Halle (Saale), Germany; *weber@ iamo.uni-halle.de*

Interregional and/or international integration of Russia's agri-food sector? An analysis based on two computable general equilibrium models – **Peter Wehrheim and Arnim Kuhn**

At present, various integration strategies for Russia's agri-food sector are matters of intensive domestic debate. First, Russia is applying for WTO membership. The expected effects of an international integration strategy on the sector are controversial, especially within Russia. Second, Vladimir Putin's reforms to counteract decentralization of policy making have again stimulated the debate on interregional integration strategies. Two stylized approaches towards economy-wide modelling are used to show the impact of various trade policies on the agri-food sector. The first model is a single-country CGE model; its strength is a fairly high disaggregation of the agri-food sector. It reveals that anti-liberal integration strategies would, overall, be detrimental for the Russian economy. In contrast, the second CGE model is designed to capture the effects of improved interregional integration of agri-food markets. In a stylized way, the influence of trade barriers is addressed, which are composed of transport and transaction costs plus external tariffs. The second model suggests that the decrease of transaction costs is superior in achieving internal and external trade integration and economic growth in contrast to lowered transport tariffs. The reason is that lower transaction costs set productive resources free. Their beneficial impact for the economy is comparable to an equivalent lowering of external tariffs. We conclude that, in order to fully materialize the benefits of interregional and international integration, not only a reduction of custom tariffs is necessary, but also the elimination of non-tariff barriers and institutional deficiencies.

Contact: Peter Wehrheim, Centre for Development Research, University of Bonn, Germany; *p.wehrheim@uni-bonn.de*

Demystifying women's participation: an analysis in rural Chad – **Katinka Weinberger**

Participation is understood as taking part in a process, which strengthens abilities and possibilities of poor people. It is considered as crucial for the success of development projects. But studies indicate that women's participation seems to be hampered by several factors. This research analyses the determinants of women's participation in local development organizations using data collected in a region in the south of Chad. A major result of the analysis is the identification of a 'middle class effect' of participation. Additionally it can be shown that an existing social network within communities is a precondition for participation. In terms of costs and benefits that arise from participation, it can be shown that a complex process is involved. Many factors, such as incomplete information, cultural, ethnic and economic restrictions, influence the decision-making process of women and costs and benefits vary according to specific community, group and household as well as individual characteristics. Factors that influence the creation of social capital are considered very important benefits of group membership. This suggests that interpersonal relations matter a great deal when physical and human capital is missing. Low transaction costs are important for members to join the group. The question remains, though, of how to reach the poorest and most disadvantaged of society, while at the same time not making transaction costs too high for wealthier participants. Certainly, no standard recipe can be applied when supporting rural women's groups. Instead, it is important to listen carefully when women talk about their needs and opportunities.

Contact: Katinka Weinberger, Centre for Development Research, University of Bonn, Germany, c/o AVRDC, P.B. 42, Shanhua, Tainan 741, Taiwan; *weinberg@netra.avrdc.org.tw*

Farm and off-farm income linkages at household level: the case of the Tigray region, northern Ethiopia – **Tassew Woldehanna**

A farm household model is developed that explicitly includes capital market imperfections so that farm households face binding liquidity (and borrowing) constraints. The model predicts that farm and off-farm income can be complementary, which is quite contrary to the predictions of a standard farm household model without liquidity constraints. Econometric models are developed and estimated to test the new formulation on Tigryan farm households (northern Ethiopia). The results reveal that the supply of labour for off-farm work (and hence off-farm income) is largely determined by farm characteristics, market wage rates and household composition. Farm households have an upward-sloping off-farm labour supply curve. External employment is complementary to farming activities in that off-farm income increases productivity and helps farmers to release liquidity constraints in the financing of agriculture. Farmers involved in better paying supplementary activities such as masonry and carpentry are in a better position to purchase farm capital inputs and hire farm labour. Therefore government policies simultaneously to increase agricultural productivity and provide alternative income-earning opportunities for the rural areas of the Tigray region seem complementary.

Contact: Tassew Woldehanna, Social Sciences Department, Wageningen University, Agricultural Economics and Rural Policy Group, Wageningen, The Netherlands; *mekelle.university@telecom.net.et*

Biodiversity and drinking water quality: an analysis of values and determinants of willingness to pay – **Tobias C. Wronka**

The danger posed to ecosystem services including biodiversity, drinking water quality and landscape aesthetics is that their scarcity is not reflected in prices and therefore not taken account of by the individual land user. This often results in a limited supply and an overconsumption of those services due to their public good features. The 'pricing' of services is seen as a possible solution to this market failure. In this study, the economic value of biodiversity and drinking water quality has been measured using a modern contingent valuation design. A multiple bound choice format was used and intensive measurement of environmental attitudes was done. Annual willingness to pay for biodiversity was Euro68 per household and Euro72 for safe drinking water quality as regards nitrogen pollution. These results have important policy implications for the development of sustainable agriculture in Europe: if these values of ecosystem services are not taken into consideration, the consequence may be an inefficient allocation of resources. Two regression models show that 34.4 per cent of the variation in WTP for biodiversity and 24.4 per cent for drinking water quality can be explained by the dependent variables. The newly constructed index of environmental attitude is significant in both models and the most important dependent variable after the income of the household. Most of the explanation variables are plausible and significant in both models. The contingent valuation method, therefore, seems to be able to place values on complex environmental goods. However, this study also shows that additional research is needed in the construction of scientific, sophisticated indicators of biodiversity and the refinement of the scenario for drinking water quality.

Contact: Tobias C. Wronka, Institut für Agrarpolitik und Marktforschung, Diezstrasse 15, 35390 Giessen, Germany; *tobias.c.wronka@agrar.uni-giessen.de*

NORTH AMERICA

The WTO and Indian agriculture – **David G. Abler, Latika Bharadwaj and Vasant A. Sukhatme**

Developing countries, among them India, are expected to play an increasingly proactive role in future world trade negotiations. This paper provides an overview of agricultural trade issues of probable importance to India in future WTO negotiations. We review recent policies in India toward agricultural trade, procurement, the public distribution system (PDS), stockholding and agricultural input subsidies. India's economic reforms since 1991 have reduced government intervention in the economy and promoted India's integration in world markets. The reforms in the trade and foreign exchange regime have eliminated a great deal of the bias against agricultural trade. Nonetheless, many elements of India's agricultural trade continue to be inward looking and high tariff and non-tariff barriers remain on many agricultural imports. Many agricultural products also continue to face numerous export restrictions. The paper then discusses opportunities and drawbacks from India's perspective of more liberalized agricultural trade. Further liberalization in developed country market access and domestic support could potentially necessitate major changes in Indian agricultural policy. There are several elements to India's food security policies, among them the system of domestic grain procurement and public distribution, agricultural input subsidies on fertilizer, water and electricity, and the need to maintain domestic agricultural output price stability. A future trade agreement that opened up agricultural markets in the developed countries could reduce world price instability and obviate the need for India to maintain policies to insulate domestic prices from the fluctuations in world prices. Evidence indicates that exports of rice, wheat, cotton, and even dairy products could increase rapidly as a consequence of a more liberal world trading environment.

Contact: David G. Abler, USA; *d-abler@psu.edu*

Technology adoption and agricultural sustainability: implications for groundwater conservation – **Talah S. Arabiyat and Eduardo Segarra**

The state of groundwater utilization in the Texas High Plains (THP) is a reflection of the combined result of current economic, social and political factors. The main reason why groundwater resources in the THP are being used at a rate higher than the natural rate of recharge is that the revenues stemming from their current use are greater than the associated cost of extraction. This study evaluates the trade-off between technology adoption (advanced irrigation technologies and anticipated biotechnological advances) and the sustainability of agricultural activities in the THP. Specifically, a county-wide dynamic optimization model is used to determine optimal groundwater use levels and cropping patterns, and evaluate the impacts of irrigation technology and biotechnology adoption on groundwater use under four scenarios. The results indicate that the current crop acreage allocation and levels of advanced irrigation technology adoption are not close to optimal. Approaching the issue of sustainability, the results show that the return trade-off to achieve groundwater conservation, in terms of what producers would have to give up in terms of net present value of returns to achieve groundwater supply stability, would be small.

Contact: Eduardo Segarra, Department of Agricultural and Applied Economics, Texas Tech University & Texas Agricultural Experiment Station, Texas A&M University, USA; *zgseg@ttu.edu*

The impacts of project-food aid on nutrition in rural Kenya – **Mesfin Bezuneh, Meheret Asfaw and Segu Zuhair**

As the total food aid available to distribution is declining, the role of effective targeting in selection, designing and implementing project-food aid programmes in recipient countries is becoming increasingly important. The purpose of this study is to assess 'directly' the impacts of project-food aid, Food For Work (FFW) in particular, on the nutritional status of children of FFW participant households. Since human capital formation, through improved nutrition, was one of the arguments for FFW projects, it is imperative that we assess its nutritional impacts on the most vulnerable group of the household, children. Anthropometric analysis is carried out on both FFW participant and non-FFW participant households in order to assess the changes in nutritional status arising from participation in FFW projects. It is based on primary data collected from 133 randomly selected farm households in Baringo District, Kenya. Results indicate that the nutritional status of children of the participant households is not significantly different from that of non-participants. The findings of this study are expected to contribute to designing more effective and well targeted food aid-supported projects (project-food aid).

Contact: Mesfin Bezuneh, Department of Economics, Clark Atlanta University, Atlanta, Georgia, USA; *mbezuneh@cau.edu.*

How many paths to the market? The organization of Polish hog transactions during transition – **Silke Boger, Jill E. Hobbs and William A. Kerr**

New institutional economics suggests that the evolution of market institutions and their influence on transaction costs can be of crucial importance for the speed and success of transition. The paper studies the development of hog marketing channels in Poland during transition, using data from a survey of farmers. A number of transaction cost-related variables were used to distinguish a producer's marketing behaviour. These include contractual arrangement, grading system, final weight, speed of payment, prices, bargaining power, investment and total sales. Cluster and discriminant analyses could identify groups of producers homogeneous in their marketing behaviour. Given the diversified structure of market transactions and hog production, different transition paths can be identified. Currently, there is a low level of cooperation between farmers and processors in the marketing chain and many farmers cannot safeguard their investments in production by contracting. Closer vertical relations, with formal contracting and advanced grading, have developed in only one group. Supply chain relationships, such as contracting, that encourage improved quality and stimulate further investment by providing sufficient security in the business relationship are likely to exhibit long-run transaction cost advantages.

Contact: Jill E. Hobbs, Department of Agricultural Economics, University of Saskatchewan, 51 Campus Drive, Saskatoon, Saskatchewan, S7N 5A8, Canada; *hobbs@duke.usask.ca*

Foreign direct investment and product characteristics of the processed food industry in a North-South framework – **Christine Bolling and Agapi Somwaru**

The importance of foreign direct investment (FDI) in the processed food industry is evidenced by its rapid growth during the late 1980s and 1990s. Most studies of US investment in the food trades concentrate on the characteristics which motivate FDI and trade in the host countries. FDI is more prevalent in some subsectors than others. A Tobit model relates countries' state of economic development to characteristics such as trade and tariff levels, industry size and concentration for evaluating the food processing industry in relation to foreign direct investment.

Contact: Agapi Somwaru, Economic Research Service, U.S. Department of Agriculture, USA; *agapi@econ.ag.gov*

The economic integration of Central European countries into world agricultural economies: the case of Poland and USA integration – **Milton Boyd and Raquel Christie**

For Central European countries, the transition from planned economies to more market-oriented systems has involved a number of price realignments for agriculture. This study focuses on price transmission and market integration in Poland in relation to price alignments to world levels. The USA is used as a benchmark with which price behaviour in Poland's agricultural sector for grain and livestock, both at the farm and retail levels, is compared. The transition process for grain and livestock in Poland appears to be under way. This is evidenced by commodity prices converging at the farm and at the retail levels across the two countries, and also for the farm to retail spread within Poland. Farm to retail price transmission was higher for Poland than for the USA, though this may be because Poland has a lower value added component making up retail price.

Contact: Milton Boyd, Department of Agricultural Economics, 357-66 Dafoe Rd., University of Manitoba, Winnipeg, R3T 2N2, Canada; *boyd@ms.umanitoba.ca*

Government v anarchy: modelling the evolution of institutions – **David S. Bullock and Klaus Mittenzwei**

In the economics literature, institutions are usually viewed as 'the rules of the game'. Little agreement exists, however, on the precise meaning of the term 'rules'. Contrary to most of the literature, we refuse to accept that institutions constrain choices. Instead, we argue that institutions determine the (expected) consequences of choices made by economic agents. Together with the imperfect enforcement of institutions, and their highly complex and hierarchical structure, this leads us to advocate that institutions should be formally modelled as 'correspondences'. We sketch a general formal framework for institutional analysis in which institutions are incorporated as correspondences that map elements of the combined information set and choice set into the outcome set. We illustrate the framework using a two-stage non-cooperative coordination game in which property rights over a natural resource emerge from an anarchy-like state of Nature. Two players have two strategies: to cooperate or to defect. Cooperation implies giving up some fraction of one's own personal resource to set up an enforcement mechanism that punishes a defecting player. A defecting player uses all of his/her personal resources to acquire the natural resource. We show that some institution will always emerge. Giving up own personal resources reduces the overall pay-off for the players, but can under certain conditions enable a Pareto improvement from anarchy (that is, unilateral defection) to government (that is, bilateral cooperation). One such condition is a sufficiently high enforcement technology. Another conclusion is that risk-averse behaviour makes the evolution of government more likely.

Contact: David S. Bullock, Department of Agricultural and Consumer Economics, University of Illinois at Urbana-Champaign, 305 Mumford Hall, 1301 W. Gregory Drive, Urbana, IL 61801, USA; *dsbulloc@uiuc.edu*

Hydroponic combines: site and technical choice under risk among Quebec shrimp fishermen – **Peter Calkins, Patrice Dionne, Robert Romain and Rémy Lambert**

A fishing captain seeking mobile shrimp is like a farmer who chooses to buy a combine and sell custom harvesting services to other, dispersed, farmers. Economic analysis of this situation must consider both the human ability to choose the correct site and the technical characteristics of the boat. A logit model of two sites in Quebec showed that shrimp fishermen are averse to risk, as measured by the variance in average individual yields observed the day before going out to sea. Therefore their choice of fishing site is not random. The number of boats having exploited a site the day before revealed that, at least in 1993, fishermen adopted a follow-the-leader strategy. The availability of quota also affected site choice. As to the choice of technical characteristics of the boat, only engine power significantly explained tonnage caught in four different sites under both transcendental and Cobb–Douglas forms. This result is important to shrimp captains desirous of optimizing the allocation of their investments in fishing vessels. The other consistently significant technical factor was hours spent fishing per day. Crew size is only significant when the capture process is represented by a Cobb–Douglas form.

Contact: Peter Calkins, Laval University, Quebec, Canada; *peter.calkins@eac. ulaval.ca*

How does gender affect the adoption of agricultural innovations? The case of improved maize technology in Ghana – **Cheryl R. Doss and Michael L. Morris**

Why do men and women adopt agricultural innovations at different rates? A national survey of maize farmers carried out in Ghana during 1997/98 revealed that improved maize production technologies promoted through the Ghana Grains Development Project have been adopted less extensively by women than by men. Only 39 per cent of female farmers reported planting modern varieties of maize, compared with 59 per cent of male farmers. Similarly, fewer female farmers (16 per cent) reported using chemical fertilizer than male farmers (23 per cent). When the adoption decision was modelled using a simultaneous probit approach, it was found, contrary to expectations, that gender per se is not significantly associated with adoption. Instead, the model results indicated that differences in adoption behaviour are associated with gender-linked differences in access to complementary production inputs, including land, male labour and extension services. This finding has important policy implications, not only in Ghana but also in other countries where women and men have been observed to adopt agricultural innovations at different rates. It suggests that ensuring more widespread and equitable adoption of improved technologies may not require changes in the research system. Rather, often what may be needed are policy measures to ensure that women farmers have better access to complementary inputs, especially land, labour and extension services.

Contact: Cheryl R. Doss, Yale Centre for International and Area Studies and Economics, Yale University, USA; *cheryl.doss@yale.edu*

'Separate spheres' agricultural household production within the humid forest benchmark – **Renata L. Elad, Jack E. Houston and Doyle Baker**

Resource allocation within households often constrains their ability to respond to new opportunities and incentives. We develop and evaluate a 'separate spheres' household production model incorporating the benchmark concept. Our model posits a gender-differentiated production system within Humid Forest Zone households of sub-Saharan Africa. This hypothesis of separate agricultural production processes is supported by the lack of significance of cross-prices in own output supply estimations. Imputed prices portray significant influences on female output, but less so on male output. Given the production technology of the benchmark zone, we find that the total outlay of female labour exacts a higher estimated shadow wage than does male labour. The benchmark hypothesis is verified in this analysis and provides useful information on farmer responses to their environment. Gender roles are found to be an integral part of the production systems and must be accounted for explicitly in national policies and programmes.

Contact: Jack E. Houston, Department of Agricultural & Applied Economics, University of Georgia, Athens, GA 30602, USA; *jhouston@agecon.uga.edu*

Forecasting global crop yields – **John N. (Jake) Ferris**

Important as forecasting crop yields from year to year has been for planning by farmers and agribusinesses, for developing farm policies and for administering food security programmes, analysts continue to assume normal weather and project yields as an extension of past trends. With improvements in long-range weather forecasting over the past decade, particularly with the information gleaned from El Niño/Southern Oscillation (ENSO), new approaches to crop yield forecasting are becoming feasible. In an analysis of global crop yields, ENSO variables were statistically significant in eight out of the 12 yield equations for coarse grain, wheat and oilseeds, and indirectly affected three of the other four. The incorporation of ENSO variables not only reduced the error terms but also converted the most highly skewed distributions to a more normal structure. Even so, yield equations with ENSO variables could not explain much more than 15 to 35 per cent of yield variation over the past 40 years. With or without ENSO considerations, analysts can provide more useful information by generating probability distributions of yields. This procedure was demonstrated by running AGMOD (econometric/simulation model of US agriculture) 500 times in forecasting distributions of yields and other agricultural variables for 2000 and 2001.

Contact: John N. (Jake) Ferris, Department of Agricultural Economics, Michigan State University, USA; *jakemax33@aol.com*

The market for spreads in an emerging market economy of Bulgaria – **W.J. Florkowski, W. Moon, L.R. Beuchat, M. Chinnan, P. Paraskova and J. Jordanov**

The objective of this paper is to identify socioeconomic and demographic factors influencing the consumption of selected spreads in Bulgaria. Knowledge from this study enables food manufacturers, distributors and retailers to improve marketing strategies and concentrate market development efforts on most promising products. Data for this study was collected in 1997 among members of the Bulgarian household panel. A total of 2133 respondents (85 per cent of the panel members) completed questionnaires providing insights into food consumption habits, economic and demographic background of the respondent and his or her household, and a measure of household income. Spread consumption information was recorded by respondents for four types of meals: breakfast, snack, dinner and supper. The choices of offered spreads included jam/jellies, mayonnaise, honey, processed cheese, margarine and butter. Because spreads were most likely to be eaten at breakfast or as a snack, the empirical model of the consumption decision was specified for these two cases. Household income and education of a consumer, which tend to be positively correlated, influenced the consumption of mayonnaise and processed cheese, two spreads consumed least frequently. With increasing incomes and improving education, the consumption of these spreads will probably increase. Currently, residents in southern and coastal regions are more likely to eat mayonnaise and processed cheese than are residents in the metropolitan area. Residents in northern Bulgaria are particularly unlikely to eat processed cheese. The regional differences occur after controlling for difference in income or educational attainment level and suggest distinct preferences for taste.

Contact: W.J. Florkowski, Department of Agricultural & Applied Economics, University of Georgia, College of Agricultural and Environmental Sciences Georgia Experiment Station, Griffin, Georgia, USA; *wflorko@gaes.griffin. peachnet.edu*

The household as a source of growth with increasing returns – **Beatriz Gaitan**

In the present work we explain how in the process of development countries move from household to market production and why some countries are unable to take advantages of economies of scale. Our model extends the neoclassical growth model by introducing household production and imperfect competition. We justify the simultaneous production of firms and households by the consumer's desire for variety. The proportion of household production to market production will depend on how cost-efficient the household is when compared to the market production, the level of technological change in each of them, and to the degree to which market and home-produced goods are good substitutes for each other. In addition, the larger the number of households a firm can sell to, the more the economy can take advantage of economies of scale, shifting household production to market production as population grows. Effectively, the economy becomes more competitive at producing a larger number of varieties relative to the household. We simulate the impact of alternative policies such as improving infrastructure or promoting investment and technological spillovers from abroad for some developing countries.

Contact: Beatriz Gaitan, University of Minnesota, USA; *gait0005@maroon.tc. umn.edu*

Ten institutionalist perspectives on agriculture and rural development: a conceptual framework for policy makers, managers and analysts – **Christopher D. Gerrard**

For developing and transition countries, macroeconomic stabilization, liberalizing foreign exchange markets and international trade, and removing price controls on agricultural commodities have not been sufficient. They must also address a set of 'second-generation' issues, which are primarily institutional, in order to achieve their desired rates of agricultural and rural development. Based upon work done at the World Bank Institute over the last five years, this paper presents ten institutionalist perspectives on the substance and the process of institutional reform which together comprise a conceptual framework and practical steps for addressing these second-generation issues in agricultural and rural development. Drawing heavily upon the new institutional economics, the paper clarifies terms like 'public' and 'private' goods in order to address in a logical fashion the roles of the central government, local governments, the private sector and civil society in agricultural and rural development. It also works through the complexity of agricultural and rural development in order to understand which institutional reform strategies are more likely to succeed in different subsectors, from agricultural marketing and agricultural extension on the one hand to rural infrastructure and natural resource management on the other. The paper concludes by stressing the importance of involving the participation of all legitimate stakeholder groups in the process of implementing and sustaining institutional reforms.

Contact: Christopher D. Gerrard, Operations Evaluation Department, The World Bank, 1818 H Street, N.W., Washington, DC, USA; *cgerrard1@worldbank.org*

Factors affecting obesity among school children in the United States – **Chung L. Huang, Jonq-Ying Lee, Biing-Hwan Lin and Nancy L. Canolty**

Despite increasing health consciousness and awareness, obesity has reached epidemic proportions in the United States, affecting demographic groups, with as many as 20 per cent to 25 per cent of the nation's youth being overweight or obese. The objectives of this study are to examine and determine the prevalence of obesity among school children, aged six to 17 years. Furthermore, the study will estimate and quantify the effects of selected socioeconomic factors, dietary patterns such as intakes of fat and cholesterol, and diet quality on body mass index (BMI) measures. The U.S. Department of Agriculture's 1994–6 Continuing Survey of Food Intakes by Individuals (CSFII) is the source of data. Regression results suggest that increases in BMI were associated with various socioeconomic and environmental factors. As expected, the study found a positive and significant relationship between fatness and the amount of time spent watching TV. A child's dietary quality, as measured by the healthy eating index, was also found to have a negative and significant effect on BMI. With respect to socioeconomic characteristics, results suggest that African-American and Hispanic school children are more likely to become obese than their counterparts. In addition, the result suggests that school children from higher income households were less likely to become overweight or obese than others.

Contact: Chung L. Huang, University of Georgia, Athens, GA 30602, USA; *chuang@agecon.uga.edu*

Marginal value of improved maize seeds and inorganic fertilizer under stochastic yield distribution – **Aloyce R.M. Kaliba, Wilfred Mwangi and David Norman**

This study's objectives were to determine the marginal value of adopting improved maize seeds and inorganic fertilizer by farmers in the intermediate altitude and lowland zones in Tanzania. Stochastic dominance analysis and Bayes' theorem were used to compare yields of local maize varieties and improved seeds with and without inorganic fertilizer application. Rainfall distribution was considered as the major source of production risk. The stochastic dominance results suggest that, in the intermediate zone, growing improved maize seeds with and without fertilizer application was equally superior. In the lowlands, growing improved maize seeds with fertilizer application dominated both growing local varieties and improved maize seeds without inorganic fertilizer application. The Bayes' theorem results, which take rainfall distribution into account, indicate that a farmer moving from growing local varieties to improved seeds without fertilizer application stands to gain about 7948 Tanzania shillings per acre in the intermediate zone and 3695 shillings per acre in the lowland zone. However, by moving from growing improved seeds alone to fertilizer application, the farmer potentially loses money (about 9305 and 1733 shillings per acre in the intermediate and lowlands zones, respectively). Promotion of inorganic fertilizer in both zones should go hand in hand with technologies that increase the efficient use of available moisture to minimize field loss.

Contact: Aloyce R.M. Kaliba (USA), Department of Agricultural Economics, Kansas State University, Waters Hall, Manhattan, Kansas 66506, USA; *akaliba@agecon.ksu.edu*

Efficiency and economies of scale and scope of Polish cooperative banks – **Tamar Khitarishvili**

Agriculture is an important sector of the Polish economy, employing about 28 per cent of the labour force and constituting 5.6 per cent of GDP in 1997. There is a serious problem of low productivity. With accession of Poland into the European Union, the pressures to improve the competitiveness of the sector will increase significantly. Rural financial institutions can assist the agricultural sector in this transition. However, these institutions are themselves undergoing changes, as they improve the efficiency of operations and economies of scale and scope. The current study analyses the efficiency of cooperative banks in Poland in 1997, using bank-level financial data. It identifies some of the determinants of profit inefficiencies and economies of scale and scope. Two approaches to measuring inefficiencies are employed: the stochastic frontier approach (SFA) and the thick frontier approach (TFA). The majority of studies that use the SFA assume the half-normal or the exponential distribution of the inefficiency term. These distributions imply that the density of the inefficiencies is concentrated near zero. In this study, that would mean that most cooperative banks are close to being fully efficient. This is not expected to be the case owing to the early stage of transformation attained among cooperative banks. To address this issue, the current study uses a more flexible gamma distribution of the inefficiency terms, and compares the results with those of the SFA half-normally distributed inefficiencies and with the TFA measures. Tests are conducted for the presence of the economies of scale and scope.

Contact: Tamar Khitarishvili, Department of Applied Economics, University of Minnesota, USA; *khit0001@tc.umn.edu*

Welfare impacts of economic reform: Poland in transition – **Sonya Kostova Huffman and Stanley R. Johnson**

This is a study of the welfare impacts of the economic reform in Poland. The costs of shortages/rationing are not captured by standard consumer price indices. Thus real GDP per capita is an overestimate of welfare losses of Poland and other transition economies. The analysis uses quarterly household expenditure data and a complete demand system. Virtual prices (at which consumers would voluntarily choose the rationed level of goods) provide a more precise and useful way to measure a welfare change if comparing periods in which there has been rationing of goods. Virtual prices are used to calculate the cost of living indices, making it possible to construct more accurate pre- and post-reform welfare comparisons. The cost of living index was increasing at a similar rate for all groups, but it increased the most for families with three children. The results for Poland show a roughly 75 per cent decline in welfare for households over the transition, with the most affected group being large families. Using virtual prices rather than actual prices for the rationed goods greatly reduces (by a factor of three) the estimated welfare loss during the transition. Specifically, incorporating the effects of consumer rationing can improve understanding of transition processes and provide an improved basis for targeting compensation packages that are a part of welfare policy formulation.

Contact: Sonya K. Huffman, 260 Heady Hall, Department of Economics, Iowa State University, Ames, IA 50011-1070, USA; *skostova@iastate.edu*

Food demand elasticities for the Hispanic community – **Bruno A. Lanfranco, Glenn W.C. Ames and Chung L. Huang**

Hispanics are the fastest growing ethnic community in the United States; by 2010, they will comprise 15.5 per cent of the population. Moreover, their buying power, estimated at $350 billion, grew at a compound annual rate of 7.5 per cent between 1990 and 1997. The primary reasons for the Hispanic market being the leading growth sector for food in the USA are income growth and high birth and immigration rates. Income and household size elasticities for nine main food groups – grains, vegetables, fruits, milk, meat, legumes, fats, sugars and beverages – were estimated from Engel curves for Hispanic households in the USA. Income demand elasticities were very low, with point elasticity estimates smaller than +0.5 in absolute value. Household size elasticities were higher. As the size of the household increased, the demand for meats – beef, pork and chicken – increased substantially. The educational level of the household head appeared to be one of the most important variables explaining the demand for food among Hispanic consumers, particularly for grains, fruits and legumes. Other socioeconomic characteristics such as home-tenure status, age and national origin, were also significant in explaining food demand. Consistent with programme goals, government income subsidies (Food Stamps or Women, Infants and Children (WIC) Certificates) received by low-income Hispanic households increased the demand for specific food groups, such as milk and fruits. Processors and retailers now perceive the emergent Hispanic communities as a primary sector of the food economy.

Contact: Glenn W.C. Ames, Department of Agricultural and Applied Economics, The University of Georgia, 315 Conner Hall, Athens, GA, 30602-7509, USA; *games@agecon.uga.edu*

Tomorrow's agriculture: an example of effects of proper diets on agriculture in Taiwan and China – **Kang E. Liu and Wen S. Chern**

Food consumption analysis is a mainstream of agricultural economics. Increasing concerns about proper diets not only affect food consumption patterns but also influence agricultural producers. A linear programming model of least cost minimization is applied to study the changes in food consumption needed to achieve the desired nutrient intakes in Taiwan and China. The results show that the desired dietary changes would have an impact on consumers and producers in the two countries domestically but also affect trade opportunities with other countries such as the United States. It will be a big challenge to world agriculture if all the people in the world achieve a proper diet. The resulting welfare changes among consumers and agricultural producers could be enormous.

Contact: Kang E. Liu, Ohio State University, Columbus, OH, USA; *liu.320@osu.edu*

Agribusiness as an engine of growth in developing countries – **Shirley Pryor and Tyler Holt**

The role of agriculture in the development process is often underemphasized. Simple, quantitative measures make it seem as if agriculture loses importance as economies grow, so most people conclude that the role of agriculture diminishes as development progresses. In most countries, however, the typical pattern is for agriculture to continue to grow in size and to modernize along with the entire economy, even as it declines as a share of total GNP. More importantly, as the entire economy develops, agriculture and related industries become more complex and increasingly integrated with the other sectors in the economy. In fact, a significant portion of the growth that occurs in other sectors of the economy can be attributed to concurrent development and modernization in agriculture. Agribusiness is the combination of all the inputs and outputs of agriculture. Combined, they represent much bigger shares of the economy than just agriculture alone. In the development process, both agriculture and agribusiness decline relative to other sectors of the economy, but, more importantly, the linkages between agribusiness and other sectors of the economy continue to grow and become increasingly complex. Based on the analysis of 11 input–output tables representing ten low- and middle-income countries, and the United States, this paper presents some important findings on the linkages between agriculture and other sectors of the economy that make up agribusiness.

Contact: Shirley Pryor, Europe, Africa, Middle East Branch, Market and Trade Economics Division, Economic Research Service, USDA; *spryor@mailbox. econ.ag.gov*

Testing, imperfect competition in agricultural markets: an alternative index measure – **Kwamena Quagrainie, James Unterschultz, Scott Jeffery and Michele Veeman**

Structural changes in the food processing industry arouse interest in the market power that may exist in the output markets associated with agriculture. A common approach to measuring such power involves the use of conjectural elasticity measures. Typically, this assumes that conjectural elasticities are identical across firms, represented by an index that, in essence, measures the wedge between the marginal value of a commodity and its price. This study presents an alternative index to measure market power. The procedure expresses the conjectural marginal input cost as a cost–output index and explicitly incorporates this into a translog profit function, building on the basic notion in modelling the production structure of the food industry that economic performance involves profitability and unit costs. If unit cost drops owing to technological or other factors, the associated increase in cost efficiency implies the use of fewer resources as well as potentially lower prices for consumers. If market power is exerted, 'mark-downs' of producer prices are expected. Industry conduct can be assessed over time with this approach and this may provide insights into pricing strategies in oligopsonistic market structures. The procedure is applied to assess 'price mark-down parameters' based on data for four food processing industries in Canada (meat and meat products excluding poultry, cereal grain flour, livestock feed, vegetable oil processing). The results do not suggest application of food industry market power in these Canadian markets.

Contact: James Unterschultz, Department of Rural Economy, University of Alberta, Edmonton, T6G 2H1, Canada; *jim.unterschultz@ualberta.ca*

Infrastructure investment, transactions costs and rural poverty alleviation – **Mitch Renkow and Daniel G. Hallstrom**

A conceptual framework for understanding the impact of publicly funded infrastructure investment on the welfare of semi-subsistence households is developed. It is suggested that such investments narrow the price bands facing households by lowering transaction costs associated with market exchange. If these are higher for poor households – as is commonly supposed – then public investments that lower unit transaction costs equally for all households are likely to increase the welfare of (richer) households (already participating in agricultural commodity and input markets) by more than they will benefit poorer households (many of whom will initially be autarkic). The success of infrastructure investment as a mechanism for enhancing the agricultural incomes of the poor therefore may well depend on the degree to which such investment can be aimed towards autarkic households (for whom transaction costs are highest). However, it is also argued that significant potential exists for infrastructure investment to reduce rural poverty via general equilibrium effects transmitted through both agricultural and non-agricultural sectors.

Contact: Mitch Renkow and Daniel G. Hallstrom, Department of Agricultural and Resource Economics, North Carolina State University, Raleigh, North Carolina, USA; *renkow-ma@are1.cals.ncsu.edu*

Foreign direct investment by US firms in processed foods: a comparison of developed and developing countries – **Agapi Somwaru, Chris Bolling, John Dunmore and Shiva Makki**

US firms' foreign direct investment (FDI) for processed foods totalled $33.8 billion in 1998. US FDI quadrupled to developing countries and more than doubled to developed countries in the years 1990–98. The increase in FDI sales of processed foods and the shift in trade shares from developed to developing countries has significant implications. We study sales for both US foreign affiliates and US exports in four developed and four developing countries and highlight the different results for both sets. Our study addresses the role of FDI as a complement to, or substitute for, US exports and hypothesizes that a nation's stage of development explains the differences in US FDI–trade relationships in food processing industries. We estimated a four-panel equation system separately for developed and developing countries using time-series, cross-section procedures for the two panel models. Our empirical results indicate that US exports of processed foods compete with US foreign affiliate sales in developed countries, but complement foreign affiliate sales in developing countries. Exports to developed countries are mostly consumer-ready products while those to developing countries are more likely to be intermediate inputs, which these countries are likely to process and then export. That is, developing countries often act as 'export platforms'. There is evidence that US firms' FDI in processed food industries varies according to the stage of economic development of host countries.

Contact: Agapi Somwaru, Economic Research Service, USDA, Washington, DC, USA; *agapi@econ.ag.gov*

Knowledge creation in tomorrow's agriculture – **S.T. Sonka and Donna Fisher**

This paper highlights key economic and strategic concepts that can serve as a framework for the evaluation of information technologies. These concepts are employed as a strategic lens to examine the future evolution of precision agriculture, with special attention directed to potential effects upon the broader agricultural and food sector. Managerial implications are identified.

Contact: Steve Sonka, National Soybean Research Laboratory, University of Illinois at Urbana-Champaign, 170 EASB, 1101 W. Peabody Drive, Urbana, Il 61801, USA; *s-sonka@uiuc.edu*

Income elasticity of rice demand in Japan and its implications: cross-sectional data analysis – **Kiyoshi Taniguchi and Wen S. Chern**

Researchers believe that in developed countries such as Japan rice became an inferior good a few decades ago. This study employs the flexible complete demand system for analysis of recent cross-sectional data. Contrary to other studies, the results clearly show that rice in Japan is a normal good. We use the monthly cross-sectional household data, *Annual Report on the Family Income and Expenditure Survey* (*FIES*) for 1997. Food items are non-glutinous rice, bread, noodles, fresh fish and shellfish, fresh meat, milk, eggs, fresh vegetables, fresh fruits, fats and oil, and food away from home. Single equation models used include the Working-Leser model estimated by OLS, Heckman's two-step estimator and the Tobit estimator. All coefficients have correct signs and are statistically significant. For the complete demand system analysis the technique was the linearly approximated almost ideal demand system (LA/AIDS). In order to overcome measurement error problems, the LA/AIDS model with the Stone index and the Laspeyres index are compared. Results from the model show that the expenditure elasticity of rice is positive and close to one. Marshallian and Hicksian own-price elasticities for rice are highly elastic for all models. Fresh meats and rice are mild complements in all models; however, fresh fish and rice show mixed results.

Contact: Kiyoshi Taniguchi, Department of Economics, Ohio State University, Columbus, OH, USA; *taniguchi.9@osu.edu*

CAP reform, wheat price instability and producer welfare – **Stanley R. Thompson and Wolfgang Gohout**

A simple nonlinear commodity market model was used to illustrate the impact of recent reform of the common agricultural policy (CAP) on the stability of European Union and world wheat prices. Second, within an expected utility framework estimates were made of the transfer and risk effects on producer welfare due to market-liberalizing reforms. It was found that wheat producers were overcompensated for losses due to lower prices following the 1992 reforms. The transfer effect clearly dominated while the risk component was effectively zero. Over the post-1992 reform period there was no significant increase in income instability, a major pre-reform fear.

Contact: Stanley R. Thompson, Environmental and Development Economics, Ohio State University, Columbus, OH, USA; *thompson.51@osu.edu*

Using food management and agribusiness education to understand the barriers to trade between the major trading blocs: the international food and agribusiness Masters experience – **Eric P. Thor, Jonathan Turner, Deevon Bailey, Olga Panteleeva and Tim Moruzzi**

The Phoenix Project, named after the Greek bird that arose from the ashes, is the symbolic character of student experiences gained from a new international degree scheme begun in 1997. It has evolved from the traditional Agricultural Economics curriculum in the early 1990s. This poster highlights the innovations, courses and curriculum. Students and faculty from 14 universities in nine countries have participated in the first three years. The events at the Seattle trade meetings highlighted the serious challenges in agribusiness trade and education issues. The International Food and Agribusiness Masters and the Phoenix Project have helped universities, countries, students and faculty to understand food management and trade 'wars', which cost hundreds of millions of dollars. A total of 23 disputes have been identified. The students from South America, nine European countries and three US universities have studied under the programme.

Contact: Eric P. Thor, Arizona State University, Tucson, Arizona, USA; *ethor@asu.edu*

Household motivations for in situ conservation of crop genetic resources: empirical results for the Mexican milpa agroecosystem – **M. Eric Van Dusen**

Results are presented from a new and unique household level data set to measure the motivations for in situ conservation of crop genetic resources in the Mexican milpa agroecosystem. Previous studies have focused on the conservation of varietal diversity within the principal crop. This study improves on previous work by explicitly incorporating the diversity of multiple varieties of multiple crops. A household–farm model is used to incorporate household characteristics concerning consumption, production and market integration. A nested model is used to test for the separability of the production and consumption decisions. Household participation in a given activity is controlled for in order to look at genetic erosion at the activity level, as well as to control for selection bias in the general model. Results from a single, aggregated Poisson regression and a system of three Poisson regressions by crop species are presented. Important findings are that ethnicity positively affects the level of household diversity, and the level of infrastructure negatively affects levels of household diversity. Policy implications are discussed for the targeting of in situ conservation programmes and for facing apparent contradictions between conservation and development.

Contact: M. Eric Van Dusen, Department of Agricultural and Resource Economics, UC Davis, CA, USA; *vandusen@primal.ucdavis.edu*

Market share analysis of the world wheat market – **Michelle Veeman, Terrence Veeman and Shiferaw Adilu**

Using two alternative models, the multinomial logit (MNL) model and the multiplicative competitive interaction (MCI) model, this study reports on an attempt to identify and evaluate the effects of market and non-market variables on time-series cross-sectional variation in market shares of major wheat-exporting countries of the world wheat market. The explanatory factors include FOB prices, distance from source to market, credit provisions, non-commercial shipments, long-term agreements (LTAs) and a measure of trade relations in other products. All variables but the FOB price and non-commercial shipments were significant in the MNL model, while all variables but the FOB price were significant in the MCI model at the 5 per cent level. Two major implications for policy of the results are (1) that non-market variables or export strategies, such as credit provisions and LTAs, are important determinants of international wheat market shares; and (2) that, although insignificant, the inverse relationship between prices (which were weighted by wheat types, thereby incorporating quality effects) and market shares suggests that prices are more important than quality in affecting market shares. Finally, although the MCI model gives slightly better statistical results, the principles of consumer choice underlying the MNL model provide this model with a stronger theoretical basis.

Contact: Michele Veeman, Department of Rural Economy, University of Alberta, Edmonton, Alberta T6G 2HI, Canada; *michele.veeman@ualberta.ca*

SOUTH AMERICA

Spatial determinants of labour productivity at the national level: the case of Honduras – **Bruno Barbier, Orlando Mejía and Grégoire Leclerc**

The study establishes the link between agricultural labour productivity and natural resources at the national level in Honduras. Using ordinary least square regression and GIS, we identified why some villages enjoy higher labour productivity than others. For every village in Honduras, we constructed 44 natural resources and socioeconomic variables that could have an impact on productivity. Soil variables were obtained by interpolating, within geological regions, the results of the analysis of 4000 soil samples. Climate variables were obtained by interpolating long-term averages of monthly data from 400 meteorological stations. The 25 socioeconomic variables, most of them derived from unit-level census data, were chosen to describe the main farm characteristics and their access to markets. We show that the impact of natural resource conditions on agricultural productivity is not as direct as could be imagined. Soil and terrain slope and altitude had little impact because the valuable coffee production, which is located in the hillsides, compensates for the supposed handicap of hillside areas. The length of the rainy season, however, showed the strongest correlation with labour productivity. Socioeconomic factors such as population density, adoption of new germ plasm, technical assistance and education were found to be strong determinants of labour productivity. The conclusion is that rainfall is the main factor. Thus migrations that are currently occurring from the dry, highly populated areas towards the rainy, less populated ones will improve the situation. There is also great scope to improve labour productivity through proper public investment.

Contact: Bruno Barbier, International Centre for Tropical Agriculture (CIAT), Tegucigalpa, Honduras; *b.barbier@cgiar.org*

Fostering agricultural development in Peru in the nineties, with special attention to innovation processes – **José Alfonso Heredia**

During the 1990s, attempts to foster sustainable innovation in the agricultural sector in developing countries took place against the background of significant tendencies towards deregulation and structural reform. In the case of Peru, the studies that have been done and the knowledge that has been gathered have produced data for assessment in order to modify the basic concepts of the actual reform process and to draw certain lessons from it. In this way, some information has been made available about concrete cases in the Peruvian agricultural sector and about the specific factors that brought about the start and influenced the development of those innovation processes.

Contact: José Alfonso Heredia, Pontificia Universidad Católica del Peru, Lima, Peru; *jheredi@pucp.edu.pe*

Identifying wheat germ plasm flows in Brazil: lessons for agricultural policies – **Daniela Horna and Javier Ekboir**

Brazil has strong public and private wheat breeding programmes, which have heavily relied on germ plasm developed locally and by CIMMYT. The aims of this paper are to identify germ plasm flows in Brazilian wheat-breeding programmes, and to estimate the impact of these flows. First, we recorded the origin of the parents of each variety and the institution responsible for crossing or selecting it. Then the contribution of each source of germ plasm to wheat production was estimated as a combination of the breeding work, the origin of the parents and the acceptability of each variety among farmers, expressed as a percentage of cultivated area occupied. The results showed that Brazilian institutions have been active in crossing, selecting and releasing new varieties for the two main production areas: Paraná (PA) and Rio Grande do Sul (RGdS). Brazilian contributions were concentrated in RGdS (an area with acid soil limitations) while CIMMYT contributions were concentrated in Paraná. The analysis of the contributions to wheat-breeding work in Brazil showed that (1) the impact of breeding programmes can be enhanced through active participation in international germ plasm exchange programmes, and (2) local work is important, especially in areas with particular ecologies. These two factors should be considered in the definition of agricultural research policies.

Contact: J. Daniela Horna, CIMMYT, Economics Programme, Lisboa No. 27, Aptdo. Postal 6-641, Col. Juarez, Deleg Cuauhtemoc 06600 Mexico DF, Mexico; *j.horna@cgiar.org*

Threats, risks and benefits of the commercial release of transgenic crops in Argentina – **Walter A. Pengue and J.E. Morello**

Argentina is the only country of South America that allowed the commercial release of transgenic crops. Indeed, it is the second in the world (following the United States) in transgenic crop planting and first in technology adoption. Transgenic crops used are soybean and maize, with traits such as tolerance to glyphosate or Lepidoptera. The rate of adoption of the new herbicide-resistant crop is higher than in the USA. But this fast adoption of biotechnology has not been a smooth one. In Europe, Japan and Brazil, consumers, environmentalists, policy makers, researchers, the popular press and other social groups have forced governments to review their regulatory systems. Concern of consumer groups about human health involves the problem of labelling the foods derived from transgenic crops. In a global context, while the USA is changing part of its position and segregating crops, and Brazil has not allowed transgenics, Argentina is alone in supporting their use. Given concerns about human health and environmental issues, where long-run studies are needed, Argentina is facing a market problem. This situation could affect the commercialization of soybean and maize in the near future. A change of policy and strategy is needed if Argentine production is to reach the high-income markets that the country could lose.

Contact: Walter A. Pengue; GEPAMA – Centre for Advanced Studies, University of Buenos Aires, Av. J. E. Uriburu 950 – Primer Piso, 1114 – Buenos Aires, Argentina; *wpengue@mail.agro.uba.ar*

Food consumption and income distribution in Argentina – **Elsa Rodríguez, Miriam Berges and Karina Casellas**

The debate over 'food security' has recently moved from concentration on production problems towards considering the entitlements to access to enough food to achieve a productive and healthy life. The gap in the income distribution worldwide indicates a growing inequality of access to nutrition levels which guarantee adequate individual welfare. Recent studies in Argentina reveal an increase in the concentration of wealth and in inequality between rich and poor. The aim of our research is to analyse food consumption behaviour for the country as a whole and for its regions. Income elasticities are calculated for different food groups by estimating Engel curves. Finally, through the application of Principal Components techniques, different classes of households with similar socioeconomic characteristics are studied. Preliminary results indicate a marked difference in the income and kinds of food consumed by households according to their geographical location.

Contact: Elsa Rodríguez, Economics and Social Science Faculty, National University of Mar del Plata, Mar del Plata, Argentina; *emrodri@mdp.edu.ar*

An integrated framework to analyse the impact of agricultural research – **Luis Romano**

The internal rate of return is the most frequently used indicator for economic efficiency in evaluation of the effects of agricultural research. While this indicator is useful in that context, it may be appropriate to find out more about distributional effects, technological consequences and overall economic effects (employment, household income, value added). The purpose of this paper is to work towards a more holistic framework for evaluating the impact of agricultural research.

Contact: Luis Romano, Programa Cooperativo de Innovación Tecnológica para la Región Andina, Prociandino, Colombia; *lromano@andinet.com*

Maize seed markets and institutional structure in Central America and the Caribbean – **Gustavo Sain and Greg Traxler**

Information is presented on the current structure of the maize improvement research and seed technology delivery system in CAC, using a general model of incentives for public–private cooperation in small markets. Research investments are meagre, with only 29 maize specialists being employed in national research systems of the whole region. There has been a high level of collaborative research between national efforts and CIMMYT. The contribution of regional collaboration is demonstrated by the fact that 90 per cent of the maize area cropped with improved varieties contained CIMMYT germ plasm. In 1996, only 21 per cent of the total maize area was sown with first-generation improved varieties. Nine private companies were active in Central America in 1997, but less than $500 000 was invested in private sector maize research. Weak economic incentives owing to the small market size and lack of infrastructure limit private sector interest. There has been a movement to improve the policy environment; most importantly, intellectual property rights legislation is being enacted in several countries, and discussion on harmonizing regional seed certification laws is under way. The low overall level of adoption of improved varieties remains an important concern.

Contact: Gustavo Sain, Regional Economist, CIMMYT, Apdo. 55-22000 San José, Costa Rica; *gsain@ilca.ac.cr*

Analysing the adoption of productivity-enhancing, resource-conserving (PERC) technologies in Central America using a logit and a structural equation model – **Monika Zurek, Gustavo Sain and Ernst-August Nuppenau**

Despite many efforts to foster the use of soil-conserving technologies by small farmers in Central America, overall adoption is low. This seems to result mainly from a technology and policy design process that does not account sufficiently for the differences between commercial and environmental innovations. Consequently, many promoted practices do not fit small farmers' circumstances in the region. A case study was conducted in the Polochic Valley in northeastern Guatemala on the adoption of the herbaceous legume Velvetbean (*Mucuna* spec.) as a cover crop in maize cropping systems. A logit model is used to identify factors that influence the adoption of this productivity-enhancing, resource-conserving (PERC) technology. A structural equation model (SEM) is also built to model links between food security needs of farmers, institutional factors, the intentions of farmers behind their choice of technologies and the adoption of soil conservation technologies. Results show that soil-conserving technologies that do not have additional substantial short-term effects in increasing productivity will always need strong external incentives for their adoption, while technologies combining both effects seem to be better suited for a rapid diffusion among small farmers in Central America.

Contact: Monika Zurek, IICA-CIMMYT, Apdo. Postal 55-2200 Coronado, Costa Rica; *mzurek@iica.ac.r*

COMPUTER DEMONSTRATIONS

AMERICAS

Measurement of technological change in the European Union – **Carlos Arnade, Susan E. Leetmaa and David Kelch**

This study calculates Malmquist productivity indices for all 15 EU countries from 1963 to 1997 and breaks them into efficiency and technical change components. It also demonstrates the performance of one country's technology variable, calculated using data envelopment analysis, when used as an explanatory variable in a country-specific supply response model. France is used for illustration. The commodities modelled were (1) wheat, barley, maize, rapeseed and other grains; (2) pulses and sugar beets; (3) aggregated vegetables and aggregated fruits; and (4) aggregated livestock products.

Contact: Susan E. Leetmaa, Economic Research Service, USDA; *sleetmaa@ econ.ag.gov*

Exploring the dynamics of future global protein consumption – **Donna Fisher, Steve Sonka and Randall Westgren**

Public policy decision making is particularly difficult in the case of research investments, where the uncertainty inherent in research and lengthy time lags require investments to be made long before outcomes are known. The Protein Consumption Dynamics (PCD) system is a tool created to assist managers to improve their perspective of future protein needs. This research effort was funded by the Illinois Soybean Checkoff Board to aid them in strategic allocation of research funds. The PCD system includes a system dynamics model, the output of which is displayed using a three-dimensional visualization tool, In3D. The system dynamics model component relates population and income growth to regional protein needs and malnutrition. The model tracks estimated consumption annually (for the years 2001 to 2025) of six agricultural commodities that serve as sources of protein for humans in eight regions that cover the world. The system dynamics model is designed so that alternative scenarios of the future can be examined using population and income projections of the World Bank and the UN's Food and Agriculture Organization. The visualization component was developed in collaboration with design experts from the National Center for Supercomputing Applications at the University of

Illinois. Through formal experiments with actual managers in the soybean sector, the effects of use of the PCD system are being formally evaluated. This evaluation documents the effects of scenario modelling and visualization on individual and group decision-making processes.

Contact: Donna Fisher, National Soybean Research Laboratory, University of Illinois at Urbana-Champaign, 170 EASB, 1101 W. Peabody Drive, Urbana, Il61801, USA; *dkfisher@uiuc.edu*

Communicating a vision of the future with optimization models and virtual landscapes: an application to community management of the Jalapa watershed in Honduras – **Grégoire Leclerc, Alexander Hernandez and Bruno Barbier**

The demonstration presents the results of exploratory work on the communication of possible scenario outcomes to the population of a small watershed. This is done by combining optimization models with computer-generated images of future landscapes. Five scenarios (rapid population increase, sustainable forest management, an increase in agricultural productivity, a new credit programme and a payment for environmental services) were introduced into a linear programming (LP) model which maximizes the total income of the watershed while finding the most profitable land use condition. The results of the model were fed into a virtual reality (VR) landscape rendering software that simulates the aspect of the watershed under given scenarios. The population were presented with realistic 'pictures' of the watershed based on the assumptions about the future. This included present and future roads, buildings, land use patterns and eroded hillsides. Animations were also generated which correspond to what an observer travelling through or flying over the landscape would see. Surprisingly, farmers have no problem grasping the profit maximization principle, and understand perfectly what would be the impact on the landscape. In fact, we found that VR helps to lower the level of abstraction typically associated with LP and GIS. VR animations reinforced the perceived realism of the simulated landscapes. This decision support tool will help communities forecast the impact of different collective actions such as new rules, new roads or adoption of new techniques on both their incomes and their landscapes.

Contact: Grégoire Leclerc, Centr. Internac. de Agricult. Principal (CIAT), Colombia; *g.leclerc@cgiar.org*

A computer program to evaluate competitive advantage in agricultural production – **Sinezio Fernandes Maia and Ricardo Chaves Lima**

This computer program evaluates the impact of the organization of economic blocks in the agricultural sector in each member nation, through the use of instruments of international market assessment. The method aims to identify market costs in agricultural production within and amongst each country in the region, to estimate opportunity cost and to determine comparative and competitive advantage amongst regions. The analytical model is based on the determination of effective production coefficients (EPC) and the cost of domestic resources (CDR). Both represent a way of using David Ricardo's classical approach of comparative advantage, adapted to modern situations. The program was developed in MS Excel spreadsheets, using Visual Basic. The spreadsheets are interlinked, requiring prices and technical coefficients from each region as input. The output identifies each country's (or each economic region's) competitive advantage in agricultural production. One of the spreadsheets refers to the total production cost, including fixed and variable costs. This spreadsheet is linked to another showing the break-even point for the economic activities, as well as the minimum competitive quantity and price.

Contact: Ricardo Chaves Lima, Department of Agricultural Economics, Federal University of Pernambuco, Pernambuco, Brazil; *rlima@npd.ufpe.br*

EUROPE

A decision support system for the economic–environmental assessment of crop production – **Guido Maria Bazzani, Paolo Caggiati and Carlo Pirazzoli**

The 'Crop Economic Analyzer Model' (CEAM) is a decision support system (DSS) for the economic–environmental assessment of agricultural crops, designed to answer both public and private needs. The software attempts to reconcile the demand for an eco-compatible agriculture with the farmers' need to obtain an adequate return on investment. CEAM operates at crop level, taking into account all the activities required by the production cycle; this permits it to quantify analytically the utilization of raw materials, labour and machinery and their cost. The program, which operates as a Windows application, consists of three main modules: problem definition, calculation and report generation. The user interface is user-friendly. The system supports the creation and storage of personalized archives pertaining to specific farm conditions and the scenario analysed. CEAM can be used at the farm level as a decision support tool for technicians and farmers, to estimate ex ante profitability and conformity to regulations, and to evaluate ex post compliance with standards, consumption of resources and economic return on the basis of real data. It should be emphasized that, for some practices, such as fertilization, it performs as an expert system, through the internal database on agricultural technologies and regulatory constraints, organized into a comprehensive evaluation process. At the public level, if adopted for the extension service, it permits the collection of homogeneous data on agricultural practices. Flexibility, coupled with simplicity of use, makes CEAM a powerful tool for guiding and monitoring agricultural activities.

Contact: Carlo Pirazzoli, Department of Agricultural Economics and Engineering, Faculty of Agriculture, University of Bologna, Italy; *cpirazzo@agrsci.unibo.it*

Agent-based modelling in agricultural economics – **Kathrin Happe**

With the rapid advance of computer technology, multi-agent system (MAS) approaches have become more and more suitable for modelling and understanding dynamic processes. They are computer models consisting of artificial entities, which can communicate with each other and act in an environment. In agricultural economics, MAS appears to be very suitable for studying endogenous structural change, intrasectoral distribution effects, possible adoption paths of new technologies and path dependence. The presentation consists of (a) a short introduction to multi-agent modelling in agricultural economics, to present the structure of an agent-based model for studying structural change and its implementation through computer simulation, and (b) an exemplary policy simulation, to give an idea about the simulation software and the way in which a simple policy measure effects the agents in the model. The simulation studies the impact of a simple direct income transfer policy on the system.

Contact: Kathrin Happe, Department of Farm Economics (410 B), University of Hohenheim, Stuttgart, Germany; *khappe@uni-hohenheim.de*

TRANS-FARM: a farm model to assess development strategies and predict effects of policy changes for agricultural enterprises, especially in Central and Eastern European countries – **Volker Mothes, Ludger Hinners-Tobraegel and Peter Tillack**

Farm reconstruction in Central and Eastern European countries (CEEC) has led to a great variety of farms and farm types. It can be assumed that these farms will follow very specific development paths. Farm models have to fulfil various demands to assess development strategies and to predict the effects of political instruments for agricultural enterprises. Firstly, they have to include the current situation on farms, such as factor availability, current use of factors and aims of farm managers. Secondly, they have to mirror the farm environment. Important factors for Central and Eastern Europe are high costs of capital, the availability of arable land, low labour cost and rapid changes of the terms of trade. Thirdly, they should consider the decision-making processes of farm managers. TRANS-FARM has been developed to plan growth and development strategies of agricultural enterprises. This LP model is able to show cost-saving effects of investments, the advantages of cooperation and the feasibility of growth strategies in relation to factor availability, the current use of factors and political programmes. TRANS-FARM is applied to assess farm growth strategies in Poland.

Contact: Volker Mothes, Institute of Agricultural Development in Central and Eastern Europe, IAMO, Halle, Germany; *mothes@iamo.uni-halle.de*

Is the CAP promoting viable technical change? The case of olive oil in Andalusia (Spain) – **Dionisio Ortiz, Felisa Ceña and Fernando Andrada**

The olive production system in Andalusia (Spain) has undergone a rapid and massive technical change, through irrigation, in the 1990s. The main reason has been the availability of incentives from CAP subsidies. The main aim of this paper is to analyse whether the strategy of introducing irrigation systems can guarantee farmers a lower dependence on subsidies in the future. A net income index has been built to measure the ability of olive farms to earn adequate returns on inputs. This 'competitiveness' index has been estimated for a group of standard farms (small = 5 hectares, medium = 30 hectares and large = 100 hectares), with and without irrigation, and with and without subsidies. The scenarios have been projected to the year 2002. According to the results, introduction of irrigation is not justified in all cases. This could be due to the high sensitivity of the index to yields. In any case, dependence on subsidies is widespread. Therefore the next reform of the regime should adopt mechanisms to guarantee the economic viability of the olive oil farming system, as its abandonment would have clear adverse effects on the region as a whole.

Contact: Felisa Ceña, Department of Agricultural Economics, University of Cordoba, Spain; *es1cedef@uco.es*

The experience of the Czech Republic with the implementation of its WTO commitments in agriculture and the assessment policy option for the pre-accession period – **Tomáš Ratinger and Jiřina Šlaisová**

It seemed at the time of signing the Agreement on Agriculture in Marrakesh that the relatively liberal Czech schedule would provide enough 'water' for supporting farming to the full extent that the economy would be able to bear during transition. This appeared to remain true (except for sugar) until 1999. However, the commitment may become a serious constraint for pre-accession policy and to some extent for accession itself. At the request of the Ministry of Agriculture, VÚZE has started to provide an assessment of policy options for gradually adopting the CAP, but if possible staying within the limits of the Czech WTO commitments. At the same time, VÚZE was asked to provide an analysis for a further specification of the Czech position for the new round of WTO/GATT negotiations. Since quick responses are needed, VÚZE has adopted a modular approach with an easily manageable computer solution. Two EXCEL templates (CSAD and AMS modules) were developed: (1) generating scenarios of price convergence in the pre-accession period (2000–2003); (2) showing bottlenecks of current commitments in the light of pre-accession processes; (3) showing the effect of some negotiation options; (4) illustrating the effect of adopting EU agricultural policy on the Czech commitment. The analysis to date has indicated that a gradual convergence of price levels is not feasible under the current Czech WTO commitments unless very restrictive production control is introduced.

Contact: Tomáš Ratinger, VÚZE Praha, Czech Republik; *ratinger@vuze.cz*

CLOSING SESSION

JOACHIM VON BRAUN*

A Synoptic View of the IAAE Conference, Berlin 2000

INTRODUCTION

With this session the formal part of the first conference in the new millennium of the IAAE is coming to an end. In my view it has been an extremely successful and stimulating meeting. Holding the 24th International Conference of Agricultural Economists in reunited Berlin guaranteed an especially exciting environment. Inasmuch as this city is forward looking, the topic of our conference was dedicated to the future: 'Tomorrow's Agriculture: Incentives, Institutions, Infrastructure and Innovations'. The fact that our conference was the biggest the IAAE has ever held, in terms of the number both of presented papers and of participants, emphasizes that we as a profession remain highly motivated to contribute to solving the increasingly complex tasks facing world agriculture, rural areas, producers, food industries, consumers, natural resource managers and related policy makers.

Acknowlededgments

Before attempting a synopsis let me immediately present some acknowledgements. The organization of the conference was terrific. The task of bringing together almost 1000 colleagues from around the world, with many spouses and companions, and providing them with an opportunity to meet, discuss and network was managed with excellence. Let me therefore take the opportunity to start with words of gratitude to all colleagues who contributed to the organization of this event. I want to thank the previous IAAE President, Douglas Hedley, for his guidance and leadership of the IAAE. During his presidency he masterminded important and timely change in management at a critical time for our profession. Having him as a colleague and friend serving as Past President in the executive committee for the next three years is reassuring for us. I also want to thank all other members of the executive committee for their service to our association.

The overall programme was designed by the Vice President Programme, Prabhu Pingali. He crafted a highly relevant agenda, intellectually sparkling events, a number of programme innovations, and a mixture of sessions and discussions addressing the major topics of the conference.

*University of Bonn, Germany

The contributed papers were organized by David Colman, who did a massive job in selecting stimulating papers that met high academic standards. He persuaded about 80 reviewers to screen the 419 papers that had been submitted. We are grateful to all of them. There were 135 selected contributed papers, giving an increase of 22 per cent in comparison with those presented three years ago in Sacramento. The number of poster papers and computer demonstrations was higher than ever before, and I acknowledge the excellent work by Monika Hartmann, and her team, in orchestrating the respective sessions, which were well placed within the programme.

The discussion groups and mini-symposia continue to be a vital and integral part of IAAE conferences; they probably represent the best option we have to discuss specialized topics with peers from all over the world. I would like to thank Herbert Stoevener for managing this part of the agenda so well.

All essentials for making this conference possible 'on the ground' were provided by the local organizing committee led by Harald von Witzke, aided by the superb management of Ulrike Marschinke. We very much enjoyed being your guests for a week here in Berlin, and we all owe the local organizing committee an immense debt. All of us enjoyed the field trips organized by Jens Uwe Nagel. The whole conference went very smoothly, unequivocally showing the signs of professional planning. Local fund raising, coordinated by Konrad Hagedorn, was of great importance.

I also acknowledge the contribution and cooperation of Stefan Tangermann and his colleagues in organizing the German agriculture session and the respective book. The book gives an up-to-date analysis of agricultural issues in Germany, and in so doing it indicates the growing complexity of 'Tomorrow's Agriculture' in the host country. In this respect I would also like to express our gratefulness to the German organizing committee led by Ulrich Köester and the German Association of Agricultural Economists (GEWISOLA) and its chair, Friedrich Kuhlmann.

Last, but not least, I want to thank all financial supporters of this conference. As you can see in the programme, the list of sponsors from both the public and private sectors is long. For me this is another sign of the relevance of our profession far beyond a narrowly defined farm production sector. I would like to mention in particular support provided by the German Federal Ministry of Food, Agriculture and Forestry in Bonn and the Humboldt University here in Berlin. Other major sponsors are the German Technical Cooperation Agency (GTZ), the International Maize and Wheat Improvement Centre (CIMMYT), the French Ministry of Foreign Affairs, the Rockefeller Foundation, the Landwirtschaftliche Rentenbank (Frankfurt) and the Agricultural Ministry of the State of Brandenburg. There was also a long list of smaller sponsors.

PARALLELS BETWEEN PAST AND FUTURE

The title 'Tomorrow's Agriculture' suggests that we ought to be looking into the future. As Peter Sellers, actor and comedian, put it: 'futurology is the art of scratching, before it itches'. There are certainly numerous food and agriculture issues which do not just itch, but rather seriously hurt: hunger, conflict over lands, governance and policy failures.

Prediction of what will happen in 'Tomorrow's Agriculture' cannot just be based on extrapolations. Agriculture continues to evolve from a sector with linear production–consumption chains into a complex system with many interdependent linkages. Douglas Hedley pointed this out in his stimulating Presidential Address. He stressed that we have to deal with a set of new participants who bring new rules of the game in agriculture policy. Douglas Hedley referred to 'citizen engagement', now demanded in policy formation and implementation at national and international levels. To analyse and model these changing systems, and their implications, poses a particular challenge for us. Douglas Hedley called upon us to serve society by providing information and analysis to governments as well as citizens generally. James Bonnen, in his visionary Elmhirst lecture, concluded that, as we are entering a fundamental transformation of the world economy, greater international collaboration of agricultural economists is required. Our profession must develop its human and institutional capacity and recognize that a broader education is necessary for agricultural economists. Obviously, we listened carefully to our distinguished Elmhirst lecturer and must find creative ways to respond to his calls under resource constraints.

When looking into the future we must also be looking into the past and asking ourselves: what can we learn from history? How to handle (and mishandle) globalization was also an issue early in the 20th century, and pathways to human welfare improvement out of food misery have also been travelled before. Indeed, some of the issues we are facing today may have parallels to those our profession faced 70 years ago. Let me refer to the last IAAE conference that took place in Germany, the third meeting of our association in 1934, which was moved from Berlin to the small town of Bad Eilsen to prevent exploitation of the international conference by the Nazi government. At that time the world was in a deep agricultural and overall economic crisis, and there were strong tendencies to block globalization in order to protect domestic farmers from exogenous price shocks and competition. We all know the terrible outcomes. The message of the Bad Eilsen conference, as stated in his concluding speech by then Vice President Max Sering, who was soon forced to emigrate to Canada, was that whatever separate nations might do is bound to fail without fair international cooperation. This message is at least as valid today as it was then.

PHILOSOPHICAL APPROACH AND PERSPECTIVES

The fall of the Berlin Wall ten years ago and the end of the cold war induced the start of economic transition in many former planned economies. This also set agricultural economics a task and indicated that our profession should assume a broader perspective in order to offer research results with strong explanatory power and advisory content. I am afraid we were rather unprepared, but we have been responding quickly with relevant research. The rise of institutional economics in the 1990s has been a response to this need. However, even though institutional economics was already well developed on the eve of transition, we were not always successful in explaining what really happened and effectively guiding the reform processes. I would like to ask why this is so. Might the philosophical approach which implicitly is driving our research need a fundamental rethink?

Although the two expressions *modernism* and *postmodernism* were not explicitly mentioned during this conference, many discussions implicitly centred on the topics, starting with the pre-conference panel and the opening session. Let me briefly sketch what is meant by the two terms. Modernism is associated with the tradition of the Anglo-American 'Enlightenment' thinkers, who endeavoured to develop an objective science with universal morality, embracing the idea of progress and hence linearity. Modernists envisioned that modern science would promote not only the control of natural forces but also our understanding of moral progress, the justice of institutions and even human happiness. Modernists, therefore, claimed that political decision making should be based exclusively on expert statements.

Postmodernism, on the other hand, must be seen as a response to the failures of modernism in the 20th century. Postmodernism basically started to become a forceful school of philosophical thought in Europe in the 1970s and 1980s. Postmodernists argue that *science* is more broadly based, democratic, and/or backed by a media-mediated discourse in which opinions are considered regardless of the empirical proofs demanded by the positivists of modernism. This brings the involvement of interest groups and the broader civil society onto the policy agenda, an issue which was openly raised by Douglas Hedley in his Presidential Address and by James Bonnen in his Elmhirst lecture. It is certainly true that the involvement of a broader set of groups and people in decision-making processes increases transaction costs. But the economic cost of not taking public opinion into account can be much higher, as the WTO-related 'Battle in Seattle', the dispute about the Bio-safety Protocol and other examples demonstrate. In general, we may have to take on the new trade issues related to property rights and standards more explicitly.

However, in my opinion our capacity to evaluate and analyse policy would suffer if we turned excessively postmodernistic. The core concepts of our profession should continue to consist of intelligent theorizing, logic, sound empirical research and rationality, aspects which are much closer to modernism. Nevertheless, I find it important that we as a profession broaden our perspective and learn to deal with changing public attitudes and decentralized decision-making processes. We should be creative enough to pick from both modernism and postmodernism for the benefit of research quality and policy to advance the best set of opportunities.

Modernism has been rather uncritical of technological innovations; postmodernity, on the other hand, is latently anti-technology. Neither of these two extremes really moves us forward. Clearly, in view of the food problems which *must be solved*, technological progress and its widespread acceptance will be essential for advancement of humankind. Agriculture is increasingly a science-based sector in most parts of the world. While our debates on biotechnology here were of excellent quality, we need to make 'communication' and 'risk perception' an integral part of the research agenda if we want to be relevant in the technology debates.

DISTRIBUTION OF PAPERS BY THEMATIC AREA

Before addressing the new and relevant facts that we have been exposed to during this conference that has focused on the four thematic 'Is' – institutions, incentives, infrastructure and innovation – let me present some statistics. Of course the definitions of these four thematic areas partly overlap, so that a clear-cut separation is difficult. Nevertheless, an attempt has been made to categorize the papers presented (that is, plenary, contributed and poster papers). About 13 per cent of papers had to be left aside, but the remainder fell into the following distribution:

- 27 per cent of the papers dealt primarily with incentives;
- 49 per cent fell into the category of institutions;
- 5 per cent referred to infrastructure; and
- 19 per cent of the papers dealt with innovations.

Evidently, institutional economics, including incentives, has become mainstream agricultural economics and has complemented the neoclassical paradigm which governed our profession for decades. No monolithic economic paradigm will be able to explain and analyse an increasingly complex and context-specific world. As we come to know more and more about 'the world', the reduction of reality to a few theoretical propositions becomes less and less convincing. Our fear of the pitfalls of generalization, however, must not turn us into story tellers. A theory-guided focus in our institutional research, including attention to the role of legal aspects and the judiciary for agricultural systems performance, could still be strengthened. The hot issues of land reform in Africa and in the transforming economies have been discussed here, but more in-depth policy research is called for.

In the remainder of my synoptic view I will briefly highlight some of the major propositions with respect to the four 'Is' which emerged from the meeting.

Incentives and institutions

The multitude of papers addressing incentives and institutions are intrinsically linked. Authors seem to agree that prices are the engine and institutions the grease. Incentives can always be conceptualized with the idea of 'prices' and it is today common to equate 'institutions' with both formal laws and rules and with the informal set of norms, traditions and cultural backgrounds which govern markets.

During the learning workshop on 'Food Security', D. Gale Johnson – a new honorary life member of the IAAE – was asked what importance he would attribute to the role of institutions for food security. He reported that, at the meetings of the IAAE in India in 1958, development perspectives for Africa were considered the brightest of the three major continents that were, at that time, regarded as the developing world. Latin America was next, but there was pessimism about Asia. Today we must acknowledge that this ranking has been reversed. D. Gale Johnson explained that the high expectations raised in the 1950s with respect to Africa were based on the much better person–land ratio of the continent at that time. We now know that resource endowments seem far less important, while institutions and policies have been more decisive in shaping the success of many countries in Asia.

Of course, this is a rough generalization and much more was said during the conference, for instance, on the timing and sequencing of institutional change. In fact, one of the mini-symposia organized by Gertrud Buchenrieder had more or less this title. Case studies presented in this mini-symposium highlighted the fact that the neglect of informal institutions by policy makers is often responsible for resistance to, and the unsuccessful implementation of, reforms. To identify and quantify the impact and effects of informal institutions will be an important task for our profession in the future in an attempt to provide policy conclusions which have the potential to be successful in a world that, using the words of Douglas Hedley, is becoming less coherent because of increasing complexity, horizontality and increased citizen engagement.

Looking at the catchword 'institutions', one could be tempted to assume that institutions are the only force driving our economies. This is clearly not the case, and the presenters at the conference highlighted the role of providing the proper incentives 'up front'. Alberto Valdés –another new honorary life member of the IAAE – for instance, stated that food security in Latin America has greatly improved during the last decade. The major force driving these developments was the reduction of macroeconomic distortions and, in particular, exchange rate distortions. The same phenomenon was mentioned by Ashok Gulati who, in his talk, 'Market Reforms in South Asian Agriculture: Will they deliver?', highlighted the overwhelming importance that macroeconomic reforms had and have with respect to India. Scott Rozelle and Jikun Huang argued in favour of gradualism, based on China's experience, a statement that remained controversial.

Infrastructure

As I have already mentioned in the grouping of papers, the thematic area of infrastructure appears to have been somewhat underrepresented, given its key role for rural growth. True, studies on rural infrastructure are not new to our profession. But still, the economic importance of basic infrastructure, such as road services, public transport and irrigation facilities, is evidenced by the high rates of return associated with related investments. Looking at roads, Shengen Fan pointed at 'win–win' outcomes with both productivity growth and poverty reduction. Apart from the more traditional public or quasi-public goods, we will also have to broaden our notion of infrastructure to include the provision of services that can improve the access of rural populations to new technologies. The existence and performance of national agricultural research and technology delivery systems as well as information and telecommunication services are good examples. Widening rural–urban disparities can only be avoided if we make sure that the countryside is connected to new technological developments through appropriate infrastructure. The poster by Mitch Renkow and Daniel Hallstrom also reminded us in a conceptual way of the important general equilibrium effects of infrastructure investments. The linkages of such effects are not yet sufficiently understood and require further research. Infrastructure remains an important area for agricultural economists. It is disturbing that investment in rural infrastructure is not only low but declining in many low income countries, as stated by Peter Hazell.

Our research seems to continue to have a strong land bias and underemphasizes water. This relates to taking water (not just irrigation) more explicitly into account in our research. We should have water policy issues more prominently on the agenda in South Africa.

Innovations

Let us come to the last of the four 'Is': innovations. In the resource-scarce situation faced on our increasingly crowded globe, technology and innovation are actually the keys to sustainable development. Julian Alston and Phil Pardey certainly challenged our notions of the very high internal rates of return to agricultural research investments, and I am sure that their paper will provoke discussion far beyond the confines of this conference. Ruben Echeverría, in his comment on the paper, called for a broader look at the issue of the role of research in agriculture. I think both are partly right and we ought to link profitability assessments with modelling endogenous growth in order to get on top of things in this area. Still, many of us find it worrying that public investment in international agricultural research and development is dwindling, despite allegedly very high returns on investment. Convincing policy makers and the public of the importance of spending on agricultural innovation will certainly be possible only from a strong research base.

There should be little doubt that sustained agricultural research is of crucial importance for a sufficient crop supply, stable world market prices and thus global food security. But what are the major research directions to be invested in? What are the technologies that will have major impacts on future developments? In general, information and communication technologies (ICTs) are considered to be one of the key technological areas in the early 21st century. Interestingly, however, only a comparatively small number of conference papers dealt with ICTs. Examples are the contributed paper of Abdul Bayes related to village telephone initiatives in Bangladesh, and the plenary paper by George Norton and Scott Swinton related to the use of ICTs in precision agriculture.

Another important area of innovation is certainly biotechnology. Most of you may have realized that during this year's conference there were many more papers and presentations relating to it than three years ago in Sacramento. Around one-third of all papers presented during this meeting in the innovation category explicitly tackled aspects of biotechnology, and many more papers dealt with the topic in a more implicit fashion. Biotechnology has many features that distinguish it from previous technologies, so that simple extrapolation based on past technological experience is probably inappropriate. As Walter Falcon pointed out, institutional innovation is definitely required at various levels to harness fully the potentials of biotechnological innovation. The importance of the private sector in research is huge and increasing, and public organizations have to adjust to this situation. Yet, as stressed in the invited panel session on agricultural research organized by Derek Byerlee, institutional adjustment in the private sector should not mean a reduction of public investment; there are many important technological areas which are not covered by the private sector. Instead, more public–private research partnerships are required, which have to be based on comparative advantage. A particular challenge in intersectoral partnerships certainly remains the identification of suitable frameworks for intellectual property rights that help to improve the access of poor farmers and consumers to proprietary technologies. Yet institutional innovation is also needed with respect to biosafety, food safety and biotechnology communication in the public arena. These institutional issues underline that we cannot assume a straightforward and linear relationship between research, technology and innovation.

We would manoeuvre ourselves into a reductionist corner of irrelevance if we viewed these trends and concerns, which also will affect trade, largely as new protectionism in disguise. Things are becoming more complex, and the importance of regulatory policies and other institutional issues is rising and needs to be reflected in our curricula. In particular, this is also a methodological challenge, which has not yet received sufficient attention from our profession. How can we model and explain increasingly complex interlinkages? Evidently, technological innovation requires not only institutional but also methodological innovation, so important to address properly the future of agriculture.

In that respect, as an aside, we ought to ask how many of the presented papers actually looked into the future. While many did discuss matters of long-run relevance, not more than 10 per cent of the presented papers explicitly dealt with prognoses or simulations of expected future developments. Systematic approaches to catch early trends in consumer behaviour, innovation pathways, and the emerging complex linkages and systems which replace the notion of the food chain, are needed.

CLOSING REMARKS

Let me conclude by stating that this conference has been a vibrant market place for new ideas and facts on how to shape agriculture's role in the future. I call upon you to address the future more explicitly. As a profession we must recognize the need to make use of a variety of theories and paradigms in order to explain better the role of 'Tomorrow's Agriculture' and play a role in shaping that future. Let us take a little dose of postmodernism home from Berlin: let us continue to look for 'the truth', while recognizing that there may sometimes be different perspectives on the truth, and its relevance, and linkages are often less linear than we may have thought for too long.

The IAAE Council yesterday again installed a highly diverse executive committee, with members standing for the multitude of research paradigms, which will serve the association as an effective team.

The sustainability of the success of this conference will depend on our individual ability to use this new knowledge constructively. After all, our constitution requests us (I quote), 'To foster the application of the science of agricultural economics in the improvement of the economic and social conditions of rural people and their associated communities; to advance knowledge of agricultural processes and the economic organization of agriculture; and to facilitate communication and exchange of information among those concerned with rural welfare throughout the world.' We can proudly state that this conference was much in line with our IAAE objectives.

NAME INDEX

Abbott, Philip 647
Abbott, Sarah xvi
Abdulai, Awudu xxi
Abler, David G. 508, 785–6
Acheampong, Yvonne xxx
Ackello-Ogutu, Chris 622
Acquaye, A.K.A. 228
Adelman, I. 490
Adesina, Akinwumi 622, 624, 668
Adilu, Shiferaw 801
Admassie, Assefa 691–2
Agarwal, Bina 585
Ahluwalia, M.S. 403, 406
Ajibefun, Igbekele xxv
Akimaliew, Jamin 722–3
Akso, Safak xxiv
Alary, Véronique 736
Albert, Helmut 651
Albrecht, H. 530
Alchian, A.A. 307
Aleksandrova, Lyudmila 759
Alexandri, Cecilia 736–7
Alfranca, Oscar xxi
Allcock, Sheila xvi
Allegri, Mario 694
Allen, Douglas W. xxiv
Alston, Julian xiii, 821
    on research returns 223–38
Alvensleben, Reimar von 742
Alwang, Jeffrey 653–4
Ames, Glenn W.C. 795–6
Amponsah, William xxiv
Anderson, Jock xiv
Anderson, Kym 327, 488, 641–2
    on genetically-modified organisms 61–82
Anderson, T.L. 310
Andersson, Johan 737
Andrada, Fernando 811

Andrews, D.W.K. 344
Angulo, A.M. xxi, 711
Anseeuw, W. 751
Antrobus, G. 718
Appel, Volker xv
Arabiyat, Talah S. 786
Araujo, Paulo 643
Armitage, R.M. xxvii
Arnade, Carlos 381, 807
Arriaza, Manuel xxvii
Asfaw, Meheret 786
Ashimogo, Gasper 719
Atici, Cemal xxi
    on Turkey's integration into the EU 506–14

Bach, Christian Friis xxxi
    on international transfers and food security 368–75
Backeberg, G.R. xxvii
Bäckman, S.T. 546
Backstrom, L. 708
Baffes, John 647
Bagwell, K. 81–2
Bailey, Deevon 800
Baker, Doyle 668, 790
Bakhshoodeh, M. 738
Bale, M. 252
Bálint, András 775
Ball, V.E. 215, 228–9
Balmann, Alfons xxiv, 698–9
    on employment and efficiency on farms in transition 553–62
Baltenweck, I. xxi, 715
Banse, Martin xiv, xxiii
    on eastern enlargement of the European Union 488–96
Barbier, Bruno 698, 802, 808
Bardhan, Pranab 691–2

825

Barichello, Richard xiii
Bart, C. 417
Barzel, Y. 387
Basu, Arnab K. xx
Batie, S.S. 282
Bauer, Kai 767
Baur, Priska T. xxv
Bayaner, Ahmet xxiv
Bayes, Abdul xxxi, 821
Bazzani, Guido Maria 809
Beckmann, V. 561
Beghin, John xxvii
Bell, Kathleen xiii
Benin, Samuel E. 715–16
Bennett, Jeff 735
Benoit-Cattin, Michel 716
Berg, Ernst 613
Berg, Marrit van der xxxi
Berger, Thomas xxi, 698–9
Berges, Miriam 804
Bergland, Olvar 702
Bermingham, Elizabeth xv
Berning, Cecilia 764
Berntsen, Jørgen 755
Beuchat, L.R. 791
Beusmann, Volker 683–5
Bezlepkina, Irina V. 739
Bezuneh, Mesfin 786–7
Bhalla, G.S. 181
Bharadwaj, Latika 785
Bhusal, Yuba Raj 697
Bigman, David xxi, 663
Bijman, Jos 683–5
Binswanger, Hans
    on agricultural trade barriers, negotia-
        tions and the interests of
        developing countries 319–36
Bipes, Laura xv
Birner, Regina 739
Black, J.R. xxx
Blakemore, Susan 573
Blanco, María 781
Blaug, M. 250
Bogdanov, Natalija 768
Boger, Silke 787
Bohman, Mary 686
Bojnec, Štefan xxiv, 740, 753
Bolling, Christine 787, 798
Bonnen, James T. 817–18
    on challenges for the governance of
        agriculture 12–33
Bonny, Sylvie 683–4, 741

Borlaug, Norman 52, 93, 120, 234, 290
Boserup, Ester 306, 308, 314
Botts, A. 707
Bouman, Bas A.M. xxvii
Boussard, Jean-Marc xxvi
Boyd, Milton 788
Braun, Joachim von xiii, xv, 691–2, 815–
        23
    on agricultural reform in China 123–
        42
Bravo-Ureta, Boris xxv
Brem, Markus xxiv, 741
Breneman, Vince xxiv
Brennan, John 689, 694
Brennan, Margaret xxiii
Brethour, Cher xxiii
Breu, Markus xv
Brink, Lars xxx
Britz, Wolfgang xx
Bromley, Daniel xxvii, 571
Brooks, Karen 673
Brown, Sorrell xvi
Bruhn, Maike 742
Brümmer, Bernhard 763
Brush, S.B. 296
Bruyn, J.N. de xxix
Bruyn, P. de xxix
Buchanan, J.M. 244, 246, 249
Buchenrieder, Gertrud 658, 820
Bülbül, Mehmet 723
Bullock, David S. 788–9
Bureau, J.-C. 6
Burghelea, Gabriela 742–3
Burnes, Ellen 657
Burny, Philippe 670, 743
Byerlee, Derek 669, 694–5, 822

Cacho, O.J. 698
Caggiati, Paolo 809
Cahill, S.E. 482
Calatrava, J. 743, 773
Calkins, Peter xxvii, xxxi, 789
Campbell, Keith 3
Canolty, Nancy L. 793
Capra, F. 568
Cardoso Teixeira, Erly 644
Carpentier, Chantal 698
Casellas, Karina 804
Casey, F. 281
Ceña, Felisa 811
Ceranic, Slobodan 768
Chakravorty, Ujjayant xxv, xxxi

Chambers, R.G. 137
Chamorro, Juan Sebastian 666
Chan-Kang, C. 224, 233
Chang, Ching-Cheng xxix, 724
Charnes, A. 377
Chattoe, E. 699
Chau, Nancy H. xx
Chavas, J.-P. 235
Chaves Lima, Ricardo 808–9
Chen, Chi-Chung xxix
Chen, Fu xxii
  on land reform initiatives in China
    383–96
Chen, Kevin Z. xxx
Chen, Yung-Chi 731
Chern, Wen S. 710, 712, 796, 799
Chinnan, M. 791
Chittur, S. 695
Cho, Guedae xxviii
Chomitz, Kenneth xiii
Chou, Pai-Lung 731
Christie, Raquel 788
Ciaian, Pavel 743–4
Clark, N. 695
Coelli, Tim xxv
Colman, David xiv, xvi, xxv, 816
Colman, Sue xiv, xvi
Conway, Gordon 93–4
Cooper, W.W. 377
Cox, T.L. 235
Cox, T.S. 290
Craig, B. 228, 235
Cramon Taubadel, Stephan von xvi, 711
Crawford, Eric 667, 673
Crawford, Sir John 258
Crawford, Roger xvi
Csaki, Csaba xxiii, 154, 590
Cuddington, J.T. 343
Cungu, Azeta xxvii
Cuyno, Leah C.M. xxix
Czasch, Britta xxiv
  on employment and efficiency of
    farms in transition 553–62

Dabbert, Stephan 704
Dahrendorf, Ralf 104, 579–80
Daku, Lefter 744
Dale, T. 252
Daniel, Karine 744–5
Daniell, M.H. 95
Datt, Gaurav 400, 406
Davis, Benjamin xxiii

Davis, John xxii
  on land reform initiatives in China
    383–96
Davis, L.E. 244
Dawe, David 734
De Belém Martins, Maria 738
De Bono, E. 566
de Brauw, Alan
  on agricultural reform in China 123–42
De Gorter, Harry xxv, xxx
  on the definition of export subsidies
    and the Agreement on Agriculture
    469–78
De Winter, A.M. 751
Deere, Carmen Diana 585, 587–9
Deininger, Klaus xxvi, xxxi, 666
del Ninno, Carlo xxvii
Delgado, Christopher xxi, 610–11, 647
Demeke, Mulat 673
Demsetz, H. 307
Demura, Katsuhiko 728–9
Devkota, D. 733
Deybe, Daniel xxviii, 736, 745
D'Haese, L. 751
D'Haese, Marijke 751
Dhehibi, B. xxvi
Diakosavas, D. 343
Diario, Ruben 694
Dickey, D. 355
Diderrick, V. 708
Diederen, Paul xxvii
d'Ieteren, Guy xxx
Din, Y. 389
Dionne, Patrice 789
Djouara, Hamady 748
Doi, Tokihisa 727
Dolekoglu, Turker xxiv
Dorosh, Paul xxvii
Doss, Cheryl 585–7, 790
Doucha, Tomas 590
Doyer, O.T. 613
Drescher, Klaus xxiii
Dries, Liesbeth 745–6
D'Silva, Brian 622
Dubgaard, A. 282
Dunmore, John 798
Dunn, J. 572

Echessah, Protase N. 622
Echeverría, Ruben xiv, 694, 821
  on competitive funds for agricultural
    research 442–64

Edwards, P. 566
Ehui, Simeon xxix, xxx, 610, 647, 715
Eicher, Carl K. 635, 667
Ekboir, Javier xxvii, 694, 803
Elad, Renata L. 790
Elbasha, E. 707
Elekes, Andrea xxviii, 751–2
Elliott, Howard
  on competitive funds for agricultural
    research 442–64
Emerson, R. 216
Engle, R. 354
Epperson, James E. xxx
Epstein, David 746
Ervin, D.E. 282
Esguerra, Emmanuel F. 731
Esposti, Roberto 746–7
Evans, L.T. 52
Evenson, R.E. 295–6

Fabiosa, I. 708
Falcon, Walter 22, 822
  on globalization of germ plasma 41–57
Falconi, Cesar Augusto xxx
Fan, S. 124–5, 135, 607, 820
Fang, Cheng xxvii
Faulkner, C. 708
Fawaz, Ruth Badertscher 737–8
Fearne, A. 707
Feder, Gershon 590
Feher, Istvan 603–4
Feindt, Peter 684
Feldman, M.P. 106
Fennell, Rosemary xvi
Fenyes, Tom xxix, 670–71
Ferenczi, Tibor xxx, 628–9
Fernandes Maia, Sinezio 808
Fernandez-Cornejo, J. 377
Fernández Diez, Carmen 747
Ferris, John N. 791
Figiel, Szczepan 747–8
Firici, Maria C. 778
Fischer, Joschka 31
Fischer, Ken 695
Fisenko, Natalia 759
Fisher, David 807–8
Fisher, Donna 799
Florax, Raymond xiii
Florian, Violeta 773
Florkowski, W.J. 791–2
Fok, Michel 748
Forgacs, Csaba 680

Forster, B. 555
Fousekis, Panos 748–9
Fox, G. 229
Frankel, O.H. 290, 294
Franzel, Steven xxviii
  use of 'bao' game for assessing
    farmers' preferences among
    technologies 416–23
Fraser, G.C.G. 718
Fratzscher, Günther xv
Freebairn, J.W. 508
Freeman, H. Ade 716–17
Freud, Ellen Hanak: on agricultural data
    425–31
Frisvold, George 381, 638
Fritzsching, Christina xv
Frohberg, Klaus xx, 488, 498, 590, 628
Frydman, R. 255
Frykblom, Peter 737
Fuglie, Keith xxi
  on private agricultural research 433–40
Fukuyama, F. 568, 574
Fulginiti, L.E. 381
Fuller, Frank xxiv
Fuller, W. 355

Gabre-Madhin, Eleni xxix
Gaiha, Raghav xxii
Gaitan, Beatriz 792
Galiba, Marcel xxviii
Gallardo, Rosa 749
Gambelli, Danilo 704
Gandhi, Vasant P. xxiv, 613, 723–4
Garcia, A. 711
Garrido, Alberto xxix, 743
Gauthier, Madeleine 647
Gavrilescu, Dinu 749–50
Gay, Stephan Hubertus xxiv
Geaun, Jerome xxvi
Gebremedhin, Berhanu xxxi
Geisendorf, S. 699
Gemma, Masahiko 778
Gerhards, R. 280
Gerrard, Christopher D. 792–3
Gil, Jose M. xxi, xxvi, 711
Gilliam, J.W. 541–2
Giurca, Daniela 750
Glasl, F. 528
Glauben, Thomas 763
Godinho, Ferro 750
Goetz, Renan-Ulrich xxix
Gohin, Alexandre xxi

on the Agenda 2000 reform of the
    CAP 479–86
Gohout, Wolfgang 800
Gollin, Douglas xxi, 295–6
Gómez, M. 708
Gomez-Limon, José A. xxvii
Gomez-Ramos, Almudena xxix
Gonzalez Roa, M.C. 773
Gonzalez-Vega, Claudio 660
Goodwin, H.L. xxvi
Goueli, Ahmed 605
Gow, H.R. 156
Graham, Douglas H. 660–61
Granger, C. 354
Green, G. 657
Griliches, Z. 215, 228
Grilli, E.R. 343
Grote, Ulrike xx
Grover, D.K. 717
Gueilli, Ahmed 663
Gulati, Ashok 185, 187, 595, 607–8,
    641–2, 820
    on market reforms in South Asia 178–
    88
Gunatilake, Herath M. xxxi
Gunter, Lewell F. xxx
Guyomard, Hervé xxi
    on the Agenda 2000 reform of the
    CAP 479–86

Hadley, G. 646
Haen, Hartwig de xiv
Hagedorn, Konrad xv, xxii, 816
Hailu, Atakelty xx
Hall, Andy 695
Hallam, A. 708
Hallstrom, Daniel G. 798, 821
Halmai, Peter xxviii, 751
Hamadan, Mohammad Rafiq 605
Hanf, Claus-Henning xxiii
Hanisch, Markus xxvii, 752
Hanley, Nick 702
Hannak-Freud, Ellen xxxi
Happe, Kathrin 698, 810
Hardaker, J.B. xxx
Harlan, J.R. 289–90, 294
Harsche, Johannes 752–3
Harsh, Stephen 645
Hartell, Jason G. 753
Hartmann, Monika xv–xvi, 816
Harvey, David R. xiv, xxxi, 639–40
    on academic rigour 565–81

Harwood, Joy xxiii
Hassen, Farah xx
Hassena, Mohammed xx
Hawkes, J.G. 290
Hayami, Y. 307–8
Hayes, D. 708
Hazell, Peter xxxi, 296, 607, 821
Heckelei, Thomas xx
Hedberg, Anna xxx
Hedden-Dunkhorst, Bettina 717–18
Hedley, Douglas D. ix–xii, 3–10, 13,
    651, 815, 817, 820
Heidhues, Franz xxviii
Heisel, T. 280
Heisey, Paul 695
Heißenhuber, Alois 754, 761, 764
Helfand, Steven M. 598, 601
Henf, Claus-Hennig xxix
Hengsdijk, Huib xxvii
Herdt, R.W. 41
Heredia, José Alfonso 802–3
Hernandez, Alexander 808
Herrmann, Roland xxiv
Hertel, Thomas xxiii, 610–11
Hightower, Amie xxviii
Hill, A.R. 542
Hill, P.J. 310
Hillman, Jimmye 638
Hinners-Tobrägel, Ludger 754, 810
Hobbs, Jill E. 603, 707, 787
Höffler, Heike xv
Hogan, Tim 769
Holcomb, Rodney xxvi
Holdcroft, Lane 669
Holden, Stein xxii
Holland, J. 578–9
Holmann, Federico 694
Holt, Tyler 796
Honma, Masayoshi 595
Hood, C. 251
Horn, M. 257
Horna, Daniela 803
Hoskinson, R.L. 280
Hossain, Mahabub xiv, xxiii, 732
Houston, Jack E. xxii, 790–91
Howard, Julie 667, 673
Hranaiova, Jana xxv
Hsu, Shih-Hsun 724
Hu, R. 695
Huang, Chung L. 793, 795–6
Huang, Jikun 592, 689, 695, 820
    on agricultural reform in China 123–42

Huang, Yiping 735
Hubbard, Lionel xxii
Huffman, Sonya Kostova 795
Huffman, Wallace E. xxi, xxviii, 452
    on human capital, education and
        agriculture 207–21
Huirne, Ruud xxx, 645–6, 656
Huppert, Walter 607–8

Iglesias, Eva xxix
Ikpi, Anthony 622, 624
Imai, Katsushi xxii, 592–3
Inaizumi, Hiroki 724–5
Ingram, Kevin 638
Irz, Xavier xxiv
Isermeyer, F. 555
Iwamoto, Hiroyuki 729
Izumida, Yoichi 660

Jackson, M. 291
Jacobsen, Brian 702, 755
Jaffe, A.B. 230
Jain, Sudhir Kumar 726
Janaiah, A. 730, 732
Jansen, Hans G.P. xxvii, 698, 755, 772
Jansik, Csaba 756
Janvry, Alain de xxiii, 666
Jaouad, Mohamed 605
Jaramillo, C. 598
Jarvis, Lovell 598
Jaster, Karl xv
Jeffery, Scott 797
Jensen, Helen H. xxiv, 603–4, 708, 710
Jin, Songqing 690
Johansen, S. 350
Johnson, D. Gale xiii, xvi, 819–20
Johnson, G. 3, 554
Johnson, M.A. 508
Johnson, Robin 650
    on the role of institutions in policy
        formulation and delivery 243–60
Johnson, Stanley R. 795
Jones, J. Owen xvi
Jones, W. 6
Jordanov, J. 791
Josling, Timothy 489, 639, 641–2
Jurschik, P. 280
Just, R.E. 452
Jutting, Johannes 756

Kaabia, Ben xxvi
Kabat, Ladislav 743

Kalaitzandonakes, Nicholas G. 683–5, 687
Kalavakonda, Vijay 673, 676
Kaliba, Aloyce R.M. 794
Kamara, Abdul 757
Kan, Kamhon 711
Kancs, Artis 757
Kantelhardt, J. 754, 764
Karagiannis, G. xx
Katranidis, Stelios D. 758
Kaushik, P.D. xxii
Kavcic, S. xxiii
Kawai, Akinobu 697
Kayastha, P. 734
Keeney, Mary 758–9
Kelch, David 807
Kelley, T. 187
Kelly, Valerie xxviii, 673
Kennedy, P. Lynn xxii
    on Turkey's integration into the EU
        506–14
Kerr, W. 685, 787
Keusch, Alois xxix
Khanna, M. 275–7, 281–2
Khiem, Nguyen Tri 728
Khitarishvili, Tamar 794–5
Khramova, Irina 680
Kim, Renee xxv
Kinnucan, Henry 711
Kinsey, Bill 666
Kireeva, Natalia 759
Kirk, Michael 757
Kirschke, Dieter xiv–xv
Kirschner, M. 766
Kirsten, J.F. xxix, 613, 686
Kliebenstein, J. 708
Klotz-Ingram, Cassandra 686–7
Knierim, Andrea xxvi
    on conflict management over land use
        527–36
Köbler, Michael 761
Koc, Ali xxiv
Koester, Ulrich xv, xxi, 816
Koffi-Tessio, E.M. 671
Komen, Marinus xxiii
Kondo, Takumi 727
Koné, Mama 748
Kopsidis, Michael 759
Kovács, Csaba 775
Krugman, P.R. 513
Kruska, R. xxi
Krutilla, J.V. 288
Kuhl, Michaela 774

Kuhlmann, Friedrich 645, 766, 816
Kuhn, Arnim 783
Kumar, P. 181
Kurkalova, Lyubov A. xxiv
Kuroda, Yoshimi 379, 725
Kvasha, Sergiy M. 760

Lagerkvist, Carl Johan 760
Lambert, Rémy 789
Lampe, Martin von 760–61
Lampkin, Nic 705
Lanfranco, Bruno A. 795
Langham, Max xv
Lankoski, Jussi xxv
    on agrienvironmental policy mixes
        538–49
Lansink, Oude 656
Lapar, Lucila A. 661, 731
Larivière, Sylvain xxxi
Larue, Bruno xxvii
Laxminarayan, R. 708
Leclerc, Grégoire 802, 808
Lee, Chinkook xxiii
Lee, David xxvii
Lee, Jonq-Ying 793
Leetman, Susan E. 807
Legg, Wilfrid 702
Leisinger, Klaus M.
    on the political economy of biotech-
        nology 86–109
Lei, Li–Fen xxvi
Leiva, F.R. 280
Lekprichakul, Thamana xxv
Leon, Magdelena 585, 588–9
Leontief, W. 354
Leos-Rodriguez, Juan xx
Lerman, Zvi 154, 590
Li, Q. 389
Lin, Biing-Hwan 793
Lin, J. xiv, 124, 128, 139, 153
Ling, Zhu 585
Lippert, Christian 761–2
Litzenberg, Kerry 613
Liu, Kang E. xxvi, 796
Liu, S. 395
Lloyd, Tim xx
Loebbe, H. 762
Lohlein, Daniela 762
Lohmar, Bryan xxii
Lomax, E. 381
Longworth, John xvi, 3
Lowenberg-DeBoer, J. 276

Loy, Jens-Peter xxix, 763–4
Loyat, Jacques 683
Lu, Y.-C. 280
Lurdes, Maria de 750–51
Lutz, Ernst: on agricultural trade barriers,
    negotiations and the interests of
    developing countries 319–36
Lyne, Michael 661

Mabusela, L. 718
McBride, W.D. 276
McCord, R. 708
McCorriston, Steve xx, xxviii
McDonald, Scott 764
McDowell, George 744
McErlean, Seamus xxx
McInerney, John xiv
Mack, R.W. 528
McMillan, John 124, 139
McMillan, Margaret xxviii
Macours, Karen 666, 745
    on productivity patterns 147–61
McVittie, Alistair 702
Maertens, Miet 666
Magdeline, Tlou 717
Maharjan, Keshav L. 696–7
Mahé, L. 508
Mainland, David 711
Makki, Shiva xxiii, 685, 798
Malcolm, Scott xxix, 708
Manandahr, Anita 727
Manrique, Justo 710
Mansfield, E. 230
Maredia, Mywish xxviii
Margai, Rinku xx
Marques, Carlos 738
Marra, M.C. 224, 233
Marschinke, Ulrike xv, 816
Marshall, Alfred 127
Martha, Rosa 598, 600
Martin, Frederic xxxi
Masters, William xxviii, 647
Mathijs, Erik 560, 562, 740, 782
Matthews, Alan xxviii, xxxi, 758
    on international transfers and food
        security 368–75
Maxwell, S. 417, 691
May, J. 666
Mdoe, Ntengua 719
Meer, Kees van der 673, 694
Meijerink, Gerdien xxi
Mejía, Orlando 802

Mendel, Gregor 109
Meng, E.C.H. 296, 299
Meng, Erika 689
Mercadante, A. 707
Mergos, George xxiii, xxvii
Messonnier, M. 707
Meuwissen, Miranda xxx
Meyer, Richard xv, 660
Meyer-Aurich, A. 764–5
Meyers, William H. 691
Mhinte, Abdul 719
Michelsen, Heike 765
Midmore, P. xx, 566
Mil, Samir 766
Milczarek, Dominika 752
Mills, Bradford 653
Minde, Isaac 622, 625
Minten, Bart xxxi, 782
Miranowski, John 684–5
Mishev, Plamen 681
Mistiaen, Johan 691–2
Mittenzwei, Klaus xxv, 788
Miyaji, Hirotake 725
Möller, Detlev 766
Möllmann, Tanja 767
Moon, W. 791
Morello, J.E. 803
Morgan, C.W. xx
Moro, D. 482
Morris, Michael xiv, 686, 790
Moruzzi, Tim 800
Mothes, Volker 680, 810–11
Mucavele, Firmino, G. xxix
Mueller, Daniel 774
Mueller, R.A.E. 699
Mukherjee, Anit N. 725–6
Mullen, John 694
Münch, Wolfgang xxiii
    on eastern enlargement of the Euro-
        pean Union 488–96
Murgai, Rinku xiv
Mußhoff, O. 656
Mwangi, Wilfred xx, 794
Myrdal, Gunnar 97
Myrland, Oystein 711

Nagarajan, Geetha 661
Nagel, Uwe Jens xv, xxvi, 816
    on conflict management over land use
        527–36
Naik, Gopal 726
Najafi, Bahaeddin 671, 726–7

Narrod, Clare xxiv, xxviii, 707–8
Naseem, Anwar xxviii
Nasr, Mamdouh 605
Naughton, Barry 124
Navajas, Sergio 662
Naydenov, Nikolay 767–8
Nayga, Rudy 710
Ndung'u, Leah 719
Nelson, Gerald C. xiii
Neumann, Charlotte 610–11
Nguyen, T. 343
Nichols, John P. 613
Nicodemus, Gerd 657
Nicolella, Alexandre C. 643
Nieberg, Hiltrud 704, 769
Nielsen, Chantal Pohl: on genetically-
        modified organisms 61–82
Niemi, Jyrki xxi
    on elasticities for ASEAN exports to
        the EU 353–60
Nieuwenhuye, Andre xxvii
Nieuwoudt, W. Lieb xvi, xxiv, xxvii
Nijnik, Maria 768
Nin, Alexandero 610–11
Ninan, K.N. xxii
    on economic liberalization and rural
        poverty alleviation 399–414
Njenga, Arshford 720
Noleppa, Steffen xv
Norman, David 794
North, D.C. 244, 246, 248, 395–6, 566–7
Norton, George xxix, 687, 744, 821
    on precision agriculture 269–83
Novkovic, Nebojsa 768–9
Nubukpo, Kako xxviii
Nucifora, Antonio xxvi
    on land use in the European Union by
        2020 516–24
Nuppenau, Ernst-August 805
Nyangito, Hezron Omare 721
Nyoni, Joshua 647

Odening, Martin xxiv, 656
    employment and efficiency on farms in
        transition 553–62
Oehmke, James xxviii, 686
Offermann, Frank 704
Oglethorpe, David 701–2
Oka, H.I. 291
Okello, Dismas 673
Olesen, Jørgen E. 755
Ollikainen, Markku xxv

on agrienvironmental policy mixes 538–49
Ollinger, Michael xxix
Oluoch-Kosura, Willis 622
Omamo, Were 653–4
Omiti, John M. 716–17
Omran, Mohamed 663
Ono, Rie 697
Ortiz, Dionisio 811
Osanami, Fumio 727
Osinksi, E. 754
Osterburg, Bernhard 769
Otsuka, Keijiro 592–3
    on population pressure, land tenure and natural resource management 306–16
Ouliaris, S. 355
Oura, Yuji 727–8
Ozanne, Adam xxv, 769–70

Paisner, Michael S.: on agricultural research, technology and the world food market 193–205
Palansami, K. xxvii
Pandey, Sushil 728
Panteleeva, Olga 800
Paraskova, P. 791
Pardey, Philip G. 56, 135, 821
    on research returns 223–38
Parellada, Gabriel 694–5
Park, Timothy A. xxx
Paroda, R.S. 181
Patel, N.T. xxiv
Patton, S. 708
Paulus, Iris xv
Pavel, Ferdinand xxvii
Peerlings, Jack H.M. xxiii
Pender, John xxxi
Pengue, Walter A. 803–4
Percy, Robin Heber 691
Perrin, R.K. 381
Perron, P. 344–5
Pervin, L.A. 578
Peter, Guenter xvi, 759
Peters, George xii, xiv
Peters, Judith xvi, 635
Petersen, Bjørn M. 755
Petit, Michel 565
Petrick, Martin 770
Pfefferli, Stephan 737
Philippidis, G. xxii
Phillips, Peter 355, 683–4

Phillips, Ron 673
Piesse, Jenifer xxiv
Piketty, Marie-Gabrielle xxvi
Pingali, Prabhu xii, 56, 153, 815
Pinstrup-Andersen, Per xiv
Pirazzoli, Carlo 809–10
Place, F. 315
Poganietz, Witold-Roger 771
Pohl, Barbar xv
Polman, Nico B.P. 771–2, 776
Poppe, Krijn xiv
Popper, Karl 106
Posada, Rafael 694
Powell, A. 343
Prante, Gerhard: on tomorrow's agriculture 113–20
Pray, Carl xxi, xxiii, xxviii, 686–7, 695
    on private agricultural research 433–40
Prebisch, R. 348
Pryor, Shirley 796–7
Pursell. G. 185

Qaim, Matin xxiii, 687
Qin, Xiang Dong xxiv
Qineti, Artan 743
Quagrainie, Kwamema 797
Quisumbing, A.R. 312

Rabinowicz, Ewa xxi, 628, 630
Racevskis, Laila 701–2
Rahman, Rushidan 592–3
Rahman, Sanzidur xxv
Rajaraman, I. 406
Rakotoarisa, Manitra xiv, xx
Ramos, Eduardo 749
Ramos, Fernando 749
Randall, A. 245–6
Randolph, Thomas F. 719–20
Rapacynski, A. 255
Raper, Kellier xxviii
Ratinger, Tomáš 811–12
Rauniyar, Ganesh P. 696, 732–4
Rausser, G.C. 508
Ravallion, M. 406
Rayner, T. xx
Regmi, Punya P. 696
Reinhard, Stijn xxii
Renkow, Mitch 798, 821
Revell, Brian xxiv, 748
Rezende, Gervásio Castro de 601
Ribas-ur, Joan xxix
Richards, T. 657

Rickertsen, Kyrre xxvi, 710–11
Riggs, T. 707
Ringler, Claudia: on agricultural research, technology and the world food market 193–205
Rivas, Teodoro E. xxv
Roberts, Donna 638–9
Roberts, I. 480
Roberts, Tanya xxix, 707–8
Robinson, S. 490
Rocha Ferreira, Léo da 643
Rodic, Vesna 768
Rodriguez, Elsa 804
Rodrik, Dani 16–20, 25, 30–31
Roebeling, Peter C. 755, 772
Rogers, Glenn 663
Roland, G. 155
Romain, Robert 789
Romano, Luis 804–5
Roosen, Jutta 603
Rooyen, C.J. van 613
Roseboom, Johannes 446, 772–3
Rosegrant, Mark W. xxviii, 181
   on agricultural research, technology and the world food market 193–205
Rossmiller, Ed 650
Rossmiller, G. 250
Roth, Thomas xv
Rozelle, Scott 155, 296, 592, 695, 820
   on agricultural reform in China 123–42
Ruben, Ruerd xxvii
Rusu, Marioara 773
Ruttan, V.W. 307–8
Rutten, H. 446

Sadoulet, Elisabeth xxiii
Saenz, Fernando xxvii, 772
Sain, Gustavo 805
Sakurai, Takeshi xxvii
Salay, E. 707
Sampaio, Yony 643
Sandiford, F. 250, 650
Santarossa, John 711
Sarris, Alexander xxx, 779
Sasaki, Jun 728–9
Sato, Kazunori 727
Sato, Kazuo 729
Sattar Mandal, M.A. xxi
Satyanarayana, T. 670
Sayadi, S. 773
Scandizzo, P.L. 343

Schamel, Guenter 774
Schemm, H. 764
Schiff, M. 185–6
Schimmelpfenig, David E. xxiii, 686
Schipper, Robert A. xxvii, 755, 772
Schleich, Joachim 653
Schluep, Isabelle xxx
   on the definition of export subsidies and the Agreement on Agriculture 469–78
Schlüter, Achim xxv
Schlüter, Gerald xxiii
Schmerler, J. 280
Schmitt, G. 555
Schmitz, P. Michael xv, 774–5
Schopen, Wilhelm xv
Schreiner, Mark xxxi
Schuh, G.E. 643
Schultz, Theodore W. 12–13, 31, 33, 228
Schulze, Eberhard 775
Sckokai, P. 482
Sears, Mark K. 96
Sedik, D.J. 154
Segarra, Eduardo 786
Senahoun, Jean xxviii
Sener, Ayut xxiv
Serbanescu, Camelia 749–50
Sering, Max 817
Serova, Eugenia 628, 680
   on land reform in Russia 163–76
Seward, Paul 673
Shapouri, Shala xiv, xx, xxvi, 647
Shariff, Ismail xxvi, 670
Sharma, Khem R. xxii
Sharma, Manohar 661
Sharma, R. 186
Sheldon, Ian M. xxviii
Sherif Omran, Mohamed A. 605
Shi, Minjun 729–30
Shipley, P.R. 279
Shiptsova, Rimma xxvi
Shively, Gerald 657
Short, Gill xvi
Shrivastava, A. 730
Shrivastava, R.S.S. 730
Sidibe, Amadou 721–2
Sidlovits, Diána 775–6
Siegel, Paul 676
Siggel, Eckhard 647
Simon, Herbert 19
Sivamohan, M.V.K. 695
Sivers, Larry 663

Skees, J.R. xxx, 707
Šlaisová, Jiřina 811
Slangen, Louis H.G. 771, 776
Smale, Melinda 689
  on economic incentives for conserving
    crop genetic diversity 287–301
Smith, Julian 702
Smith, P. 377
Snyder, R.C. 528
Sojkova, Zlata 743
Somwaru, Agapi xxiii, 787–8, 798–9
Sonka, S.T. 799, 807
Sotte, Franco 746
Soule, Meredith xxiv
Spriggs, J. 707
Srinivasan, C.S. xxviii, 687
Staal, S.J. xxi, 715
Staatz, John 667
Staiger, R.W. 81–2
Stamoulis, Kostas 691
Steiner, Bodo xxi
Steinfeld, Henning 610, 612
Stiglitz, J.E. 255
Stockmeyer, Bernhard 776–7
Stoevener, Herbert xv–xvi, 635
Stoforos, C. xxiii
Stovall, John G. 641
Strauss, John 667
Suhariyanto, Kecuk xxiv
  on agricultural productivity growth in
    Asian countries 376–82
Sukhatme, Vasant A. 508, 785
Sulaiman, R. 695
Sumner, Daniel A. xiii, xxv, 595
Sumpsi, José M. 781
Svetlov, Nikolai M. 739, 777
Swinnen, Johan F.M. 560, 562, 590,
    628–9, 641, 745, 753
  on productivity patterns 147–61
Swinton, Scott M. 276, 821
  on precision agriculture 269–83
Szép, Katalin 775

Takahashi, Katsuya 727
Takahashi, Taichi 730
Takahatake, Takashi 696
Tangermann, Stefan xiii, xv, xxiii, 595,
    628, 630, 816
  on eastern enlargement of the Euro-
    pean Union 488–96
Taniguchi, Kiyoshi 799–800
Tanrivermis, Harun 723

Tapsoba, Edouard 669
Tarnas, R. 580
Taylor, J. Edward xxvi
Teixeira, E.C. 670
Tesfaye, Girmay xxxi
Thapa, Ganesh 592
Thiam, Abdourahmane xxv
Thijssen, Geert xxii
Thirkawala, S. 277, 280
Thirtle, Colin xiv, xxxi, 695
Thompson, Robert xii, 3
Thompson, Stanley R. 800
Thomson, Kenneth J. xiv, xxv, 738, 778
Thor, Eric P. 800
Tielu, A. 480
Tillack, Peter 680, 775, 810
Tinbergen, Jan 15–16
Tiongeo, Marites 734
Tollens, Eric 667
Torres, J. 708
Tóth, József 778–9
Townsend, R.F. xxxi
Traxler, Greg 56, 805
Trewin, Ray 735
Tritten, Christian 779
Trofimtseva, Olga V. 779
Trueblood, Michael A. xxvi
Tsigas, Marinos xxx
Tulachan, Pradeep 696
Tulkens, H. 377
Tulloch, G. 246
Turner, Jonathan 800
Tweeten, L. 566
Tyers, R. 488
Tzouvelekas, V. xx

Ulmanová, Jarmila 779
Umali-Deininger, Dina xxvi
Umeh, J.C. 671
Umetsu, Chieko xxv
Unnevehr, Laurian J. 603
Unterschultz, James xxv, 797–8
Urff, Winfried von xv
Urzua, C.M. 343
Uusi-Kämppä, J. 546

Vaissayre, Maurice 745
Vakrou, Alexandra 758
Valdés, Alberto xvi, xxvi, 185–6, 595,
    691–2, 820
Van Dusen, M. Eric 801
Van Eckert, Manfred 720

Van Huylenbroeck, G. 780
Van Meijl, Hans xxvii
Van Rooyen, J. 751
Van Tilburg, Aad 755
Vanden Eeckaut, P. 377
Vani, Ross 663
Vanslembrouck, L. 780
Varangis, P.N. 349
Varela Ortega, Consuelo de xxvii, 780–81
Variyam, Jayachandran N. 710
Vasavada, U. 137
Vavilov, N.I. 289
Vavra, Pavel xxv
Veeman, Michele xxv, xxxi, 797, 801–2
Veeman, Terrence xx, 801
Ventura-Lucas, Maria Raquel 738
Verbeke, G. 780
Verbeke, Wim xxvi
Verdier, T. 155
Verschueren, H. 751
Verwilt, Poi 782
Vezina, Marc xxvii
Vianene, Jacques xxvi
Vink, Nick xxii, xxix
Vogelsang, T.J. 344–5
Voituriez, Tancrede xiv, xx
Vranken, Liesbet 740

Wang, Liming xxii
    on land reform initiatives in China
        383–96
Wang, T. 708
Ward, B. 555
Ward, Ronald W. xxvi
Warjiyo, P. 128, 130
Watkins, B. 280
Watt, Denise xvi
Weatherspoon, Dave xxviii
Weber, Gerald xxiii, 782
    on the impact of CAP on Central
        European countries 498–504
Weber, Max 568
Webster, Paul xxx, 704
Weersink, Alfons xxiii
Wefering, Frank M. xxix
Wehrheim, Peter 762–3, 783
Weibe, Keith xxiv
Weikard, Hans-Peter 656–7
Weinberger, Katinka 783–4
Weingarten, Peter xiv
Weinmann, Bernd 766
Weiss, M.D. 280

Weisz, R. 280
Welch, F. 214
Wen, J.G. 125
Were Omamo, Steven xxx
Wesseler, Justus 656–7, 720
Westgren, Randall 807
Whitten, Stuart 735
Wichern, Rainer xxix
Widawsky, D. 296
Wildner, Susanr.e 711
Williams, Timothy Olalekan xxii
Williams, R. 254, 260, 708
Williams, T.O. 722
Williamson, O.E. 244, 255
Wilson, Rebecca xvi
Wittmer, Heidi 739
Witzke, Harald von xv, 816
Wobst, Peter xxviii
Woldehanna, Tassew xxii, 784
Wolf, Christopher xxviii, 646
Wolters, Arjan xxvii
Wong, L.F. 381
Woo, Rhung-Jeih 731
Wood, D. 290
Wossink, Ada xxix
Wozniak, G. 214
Wright, B.D. 56
Wronka, Tobias C. 784–5
Wu, Pei-Ing xxvi
Wu, Ziping xxx
Wyatt, T.J. 722

Xuan, V.-T. 153

Yade, Mbaye xxviii
Yamada, Izumi 727
Yang, M.C. 343
Ye, Q. 124
Yen, Steven 712
Yläranta, T. 546
Yoganand, B. 695
Young, Dawn xvi
Yúnez-Naude, Antonio xxvi, 598, 600

Zachariasse, Vinus 685
Zanias, George P. xxx, 343
    on the evolution of primary commod-
        ity terms of trade 343–51
Zeller, Manfred 661
Zeuli, K. 707
Zhongyi, Jiang 585, 587–8
Zhou, Zhang-Yue 723

Zibaei, Mansour 726
Zilberman, D. 281
Zimmerer, K.S. 299
Zimmerman, J. 708
Zivot, E. 344

Zuhair, Segu 786
Zulauf, C. 566
Zuñiga, Manuel Rodriguez 766
Zurek, Monika 805–6
Zyl, Johann van xiv, 613

SUBJECT INDEX

Note: Page numbers in **bold** type refer to tables or figures.

academic rigour xxxi, 565–81
adjustment cost model of market
    flexibility 128–30
administrative models 256
Agenda 2000 479–93, 499, 507–12, 743,
    758
    incentive prices, production, inputs
        and demand **501–3**
agent-based modelling 810
agribusiness as an engine of growth 796–7
Agricultural Economics (journal) xvi
agricultural economics profession
    challenges for 31–3, 620–21
    educational curricula for 613–21
agrienvironmental policy mixes 538–49
animal welfare legislation 737
appropriability problem for research 223
aquaculture 730
arable land per farm worker **273–4**
attribution problem for research 223,
    229–38

'bao' game 416–23
    farmers' mean ratings and scores **419,
        421–2**
barter terms of trade **345, 351**
benefit-cost studies 224
biodiversity 784–5
bioeconomic models xxvii, 698–700
biosafety policy 638–40; *see also*
    Cartagena Protocol
biotechnology 20–25, 821–2
    achievements of 93–5
    as a catalyst for change **118–19**
    definition and key components of 91
    and disease resistance of livestock xxx
    expectations and objectives of 92–3

future impact of 116–17, 683–4
need for cooperation in 108
political economy of 86–109
political regulation of 100–101
potential risks of xxiii, 95–7
private sector domination of 97–9,
    686–8
public debate and dialogue on 99,
    102–8
public funding of research in 101–2
border control strategies 732

capital market in Russia 174–5
Cartagena Protocol on Biosafety 64–5,
    638–40, 818
CEEC-ASIM (Central and Eastern
    European Countries Agricultural
    Simulation) Model 498–9
cereals
    international prices for **199, 204**
    sources of growth in production of **196**
Charoen Pokphand (company) 436
CIMMYT (International Maize and
    Wheat Improvement Centre) 51,
    56–7, 98, 108, 233–5, 291, 294–5,
    686, 689
citizen engagement 8–10, 817
climate xxviii, 89, 768
collective farming 391–2
commercialization of agriculture xxii,
    728, 740
commodity price indices **322–3**
Common Agricultural Policy (CAP) xxii,
    xxiii, 488–96, 749, 800
    Agenda 2000 reform 479–86
    impact on Central European countries
        498–504

839

communal ownership of land 307–8
competition policy 437
competitive advantage 808–9
competitive grant programmes (CGPs) 443–64
  advantages and disadvantages of 451
  key elements for establishment of 452–3
  performance measurement for 447–63
  typology of systems 448–9
conflict management over land use 527–36
  phases, topics and instruments **533**
conjoint analysis 773
consolidation, industrial **119**
Consultative Group on International Agricultural Research (CGIAR) 57, 98, 233
contracts in agricultural markets 169–70
Convention on Biological Diversity (CBD) 49–50
cooperative banks 794–5
cost functions, estimation of xx
credit programmes xxxi, 763
curricula in agricultural economics 613–21

decision-making, models of 245–6
decision support systems 809–10
demand analysis xxi, xxvi
devaluation of currencies xxviii
drought management xxix
Dupont (company) 45, 436
dynamism of agricultural systems and rural communities 696–7

eclectic data handling 426–31
education 211–21
efficiency of markets xxix, 131–3, **140**
El Niño xxix
elasticities of import demand **358**
employment *see* labour market
entrepreneurship 740
environmental measures, participation in 780
erosion control 774
ESIM (European Simulation) Model 489–93
European Commission 66–7
European Union
  aid strategies **373**
  ASEAN exports to xxi, 353–60

enlargement of xxiii, xxviii, 488–96, 743–4, 782
integration of Turkey into xxii, 506–14, **510–11**
prospects for land use in 516–24, **522**
tariffs xxiv
see also Common Agricultural Policy
exchange rates xxviii
experiential learning in agricultural economics 617
export demand functions 356–7, 359–60
export subsidies xxx, 469–78
  definition of 477–8
  types of 470–4
exports, agricultural
  growth of **324**
  market shares of **321**
extension, agricultural 744
externalities, globalization of 29

family farms in post-socialist countries **166**
farm restructuring 152–3
farm simulation models 755
farmers' clubs 771
farmland, sale and leasing of **174**
financial health 762
financial markets 660–2
flexibility of markets 128–30, 136–41
food distribution systems 723–4
food safety xx, 61–82, 603–4, 707, 729
food security xxvi–xxvii, xxxi, 605–6, 719, 735, 819
  definition and characteristics of 89–90
  future of 86–9
  and good governance 89–91
  and international transfers 368–75
  versus trade liberalization 595–7
foreign direct investment (FDI) 756, 787–8, 798–9
forest management, economics of xxxi
forward contracts **170**
frontier production functions xx, xxv, 726–7
futurology 816–17
fuzzy systems 762

gender issues 585–9, 733, 790
General Agreement on Tariffs and Trade (GATT) 254–5, 478; *see also* World Trade Organization
general equilibrium modelling 757

genetic diversity of crops 287–301, 689–90
  costs of conservation of 295–300
  predictions on 298–300
genetic engineering *see* biotechnology
genetically-modified organisms (GMOs) 44, 48–9, 61–82, 116, 638–40, 683–5, 741
  effects of adoption of **70–71**, **74–5**, **78–9**
  effects of ban on imports of **74–5**
  effects of shift in preferences away from **78–9**
germ plasm flows 41–57, 803
Global Trade Analysis Project (GTAP) 68, 72, 368–9, 374
globalization xxx, 29–30, 749–50, 817
governance of agriculture 25–33
government decision-making, political economy of 245–50
Green Revolution xx, 52–4, 97, 734
gross domestic product (GDP), growth rates of **325**, **327**
groundwater protection 761, 766

'hate sites' 99–100
health information 710–12
health maintenance xxxi
hedging xxvi
hot spots in animal agriculture xxix
household model of agriculture 209–11
Household Responsibility System 384–7
  structure of farming **385**
housing quality xxii
human capital 667–9
  optimal production of **210**
hydroponic combines 789

IMPACT (International Model for Policy Analysis of Agricultural Commodities and Trade) 193–5, 198–205
imperfect competition 797–8
import demand functions 355–8
incentives 133, 181–5, 748, 819–20
income distribution 216–17, 804
income effects and elasticities 760–61, 799
individualistic model of government decision-making 245–6
information economy, the 18–20
information technologies 218–20, 270
infrastructure 607–9, 798, 820–21

innovation processes and systems xxvii, 802–3, 821
institution sequencing 658–9
institutional capital 667–9
institutional change xxv, 752
institutional environment 244, 253–5, 260
institutional evolution 569–70, 576–80, **577**, 788–9, 792–3
institutional roles in policy formulation 243–60
institutional sustainability 574–5
insurance xxix, 677–8, 756
integrated development 767
intellectual property rights xxi, 437–8
intensification, agricultural xxviii
International Association of Agricultural Economists International Conference (2000)
  contributed papers xx–xxxi
  discussion groups and mini-symposia 635–8
  distribution of papers by thematic area 819–22
  Elmhirst memorial lecture 12–33, 817–18
  organization of publications xvi–xviii
  presidential address 3–11
  programme xii–xv
  synoptic view of (closing session) 815–23
International Rice Research Institute (IRRI) 233, 291, 438
intra-industry trade 740
investment projects 760, 777
irrigation 717–18, 727, 743

knowledge creation and transfer 215–16, 799

labelling of food xx–xxi, 63–4, 67, 100, 282
labour market, agricultural xxii, 175, 212, 745–6
lag relationships 235–8
  and rates of return to research **237**
land markets 173–4
land reform xxii, 152, 163–76, 383–96, 666
  features of socialist countries prior to **164**
land tenure 306–16

land use xxv, 88–9, 754, 757, 764, 766, 780–81
  and conflict management xxvi, 527–36
  in the European Union 516–24, **522**
landscape, valuing of 773
liberalization, economic xxii, 125–7, 151–2, 614–15, 724, 731
  behavioural effects of 128–31
  and competition policy 437
  efficiency gains from 128–31
  impact on output and productivity 153–6
  and rural poverty alleviation 399–414
  versus food security 595–7
liberalization index 151, 153
licensing agreements 56–7
Limagrain (company) 56
livestock revolution, the 610–12

machinery, agricultural, output of **172**
macroeconomic shocks 774–5
MacSharry reform 520–21, **523**
Malmquist productivity analysis xxv, 377–82, 807
managerialism 251
market infrastructure 168–75
market intervention 747–8, 753
market power xxix, 28–9, 763
market reforms 178–88
market share analysis 801
market-sharing agreements 56–7
MERCOSUR 643–4
microfinance xxxi, 731
Millennium Round 479, 485
MISS (Modèle International Simplifié de Simulation) Model 507
modernism 818
modernization programmes 781
Monsanto (company) 44, 54, 57, 436, 687
moral hazard 769–70
multinational negotiations 27

neural networks 746–7, 762
new investment theory 656–7
new public management 251–3
nitrogen efficiency xxii
nitrogen runoffs **547**
Novartis (company) 44, 56
Novartis Foundation for Sustainable Development 98
nutrient management technology 538–49, 716–17

nutrition 786–7

obesity among school children 793
'ocracy as an institutional form 571–2
off-farm employment and incomes 734, 758–9, 784
official data, reliability of 426
optimization models 808
organic farming 704–6, 723, 742
output, agricultural
  causes of change in 155
  parametric decomposition of xx
  in transition economies **148, 150, 165**

patenting 55
pathogens xxix
payment in agricultural markets, forms of 170–72
pests and pest control xxiii, xxiv, xxix
philosophical approach and perspectives 817–19
Pioneer (company) 45, 56
plant genetics industry, changing structure of **46–7**
plant variety rights 747
policy formulation 3–10, 249
  role of institutions in 243–60
policy implementation 250–51, 650–2
political decision process 250
population growth rates and projections **87, 326**
positive amenities 701–3
postmodernism 818
poverty 28, 401–14
  alleviation of xxii, xxx, 399–414, 592–4, 798
  determinants of **409–10**
  trends in **402, 404–5**
precision agriculture 269–83
  benefits of **281**
  definition of 269–71
  environmental implications of 279–82
  prospects for 277–8
  reasons for adoption of 276–7
price policies 736
primary commodities, trade in 350–51
privatization 152, 154
processed food industry 787–8, 798–9
production paths 722
productivity, agricultural xx, xxiv, 147–61, 215, 802, 805

measurement of 227–9
trends in **149**, **228**, 376–82, **380**
productivity paradox xx
profitability 778–9
protein consumption 807–8
public interest model of government
    decision-making 245
public-private partnerships 684

rates of return **225–6**, **237**
rationality, economic 749
reform policies, agricultural 628–32
initial conditions for 147–51, 156–7
rent-seeking strategies xxvii, **476**
research, agricultural xxx–xxxi, 193–
    205, **433**, **456–7**
competitive funds for 442–64
funding mechanisms 444–7, **447**
impact of 804–5
overstatement of benefits 230–31
policy in an era of privatization 694–5
priority-setting for 717
public and private sector roles in xxi,
    433–40, **435**
returns to 223–38
understatement of costs 229–30
universities' potential for 765
responsiveness of markets 130–31, 139–
    41
restructuring of agriculture 219–20
risk aversion 769–70
risk management 673–9, 775–6
rules, importance of 247–8
RunAid 368–70
rural development 691–3

Sanitary and Phytosanitary Measures
    (SPS) agreement 65–7
self-sufficiency xxii, xxvii
'separate spheres' household production
    790–91
service delivery 721
site-specific technologies *see* precision
    agriculture
size of farms 767–8
small and medium enterprises 725–6
small-scale farms in transition economies
    167
social accounting matrix 716
social truths 567–73
spatial analysis xxi, 755
statistics systems, national 663–5

structural adjustments 645–6
structural change 752–3, 759
subsidies 743
survival strategies 754
sustainability 115–16, 720, 776, 786
institutional 574–5

Technical Barriers to Trade (TBT)
    agreement 65–7
technological change xxviii, 213
terms of trade
for food, non-food commodities and
    metals **346–8**
for primary commodities xxx, 343–51,
    351
textile production 647–9
tractors per farm worker **273**
trade agreements, regional xxiv
trade barriers xxiv, 319–36, 800
welfare gains from removal of **328**
see also Technical Barriers to Trade
    (TBT)
trade negotiations, gains and losses in
    641–2
transaction cost model of government
    decision-making 246–50, 256–60
transaction costs xxix, 719–20, 739, 741,
    780–81, 798
transgenic crops 48–9, 803–4
transition economies xxiv, xxviii, 147–
    51, 157–8
dynamics of 158–60
extreme patterns in 147–8
food systems in 680–82
transformation of farm sector in 553–
    62, 590–91
two-land system 389–91

uncertainty xxvi, xxix-xxx
United States Patent and Trademark
    Office (USPTO) 43–4
Uruguay Round 330–33, 485–6, 506–7,
    510
Agreement on Agriculture 469, 479–
    82, 641

vertical integration of agribusiness 729–
    30
virtual landscapes 808
vulnerable groups 653–5

water, markets for xxvi, 88, 781, 784–5

welfare analysis 778, 795
wetland conservation 735
wholesale markets 730
women's participation 783–4
World Trade Organization (WTO) xxviii,
	5–8, 27, 29, 254–5, 333–5, 469,
	479, 595–7, 785–6, 818
	Dispute Settlement Panel 474–8

and genetically-modified organisms
	64–7, 81–2

yield frontier 732
yield monitors **275**
yields 89, **115**, 195–9, **197**, 791

Zeneca (company) 687